Lecture Notes in Computer Science 3180

Commenced Publication in 1973
Founding and Former Series Editors:
Gerhard Goos, Juris Hartmanis, and Jan van Leeuwen

Editorial Board

David Hutchison
　Lancaster University, UK
Takeo Kanade
　Carnegie Mellon University, Pittsburgh, PA, USA
Josef Kittler
　University of Surrey, Guildford, UK
Jon M. Kleinberg
　Cornell University, Ithaca, NY, USA
Friedemann Mattern
　ETH Zurich, Switzerland
John C. Mitchell
　Stanford University, CA, USA
Moni Naor
　Weizmann Institute of Science, Rehovot, Israel
Oscar Nierstrasz
　University of Bern, Switzerland
C. Pandu Rangan
　Indian Institute of Technology, Madras, India
Bernhard Steffen
　University of Dortmund, Germany
Madhu Sudan
　Massachusetts Institute of Technology, MA, USA
Demetri Terzopoulos
　New York University, NY, USA
Doug Tygar
　University of California, Berkeley, CA, USA
Moshe Y. Vardi
　Rice University, Houston, TX, USA
Gerhard Weikum
　Max-Planck Institute of Computer Science, Saarbruecken, Germany

Fernando Galindo   Makoto Takizawa
Roland Traunmüller (Eds.)

Database and Expert Systems Applications

15th International Conference, DEXA 2004
Zaragoza, Spain, August 30 – September 3, 2004
Proceedings

 Springer

Volume Editors

Fernando Galindo
University of Zaragoza
Ciudad Universitaria, Plaza San Francisco, 50009 Zaragoza, Spain
E-mail: cfa@unizar.es

Makoto Takizawa
Tokyo Denki University
Ishizaka, Hatoyama-machi, Hiki-gun, 350-0394 Saitama, Japan
E-mail: taki@takilab.k.dendai.ac.jp

Roland Traunmüller
University of Linz, Institute of Informatics in Business and Government
Altenbergerstr. 69, 4040 Linz, Austria,
E-mail: traunm@ifs.uni-linz.ac.at

Library of Congress Control Number: 2004110971

CR Subject Classification (1998): H.2, H.4, H.3, H.5, I.2, J.1

ISSN 0302-9743
ISBN 3-540-22936-1 Springer Berlin Heidelberg New York

This work is subject to copyright. All rights are reserved, whether the whole or part of the material is concerned, specifically the rights of translation, reprinting, re-use of illustrations, recitation, broadcasting, reproduction on microfilms or in any other way, and storage in data banks. Duplication of this publication or parts thereof is permitted only under the provisions of the German Copyright Law of September 9, 1965, in its current version, and permission for use must always be obtained from Springer. Violations are liable to prosecution under the German Copyright Law.

Springer is a part of Springer Science+Business Media

springeronline.com

© Springer-Verlag Berlin Heidelberg 2004
Printed in Germany

Typesetting: Camera-ready by author, data conversion by Christian Grosche, Hamburg
Printed on acid-free paper   SPIN: 11310143   06/3142   5 4 3 2 1 0

Preface

DEXA 2004, the 15th International Conference on Database and Expert Systems Applications, was held August 30 – September 3, 2004, at the University of Zaragoza, Spain. The quickly growing spectrum of database applications has led to the establishment of more specialized discussion platforms (DaWaK Conference, EC-Web Conference, EGOVConference, Trustbus Conference and DEXA Workshop: Every DEXA event has its own conference proceedings), which were held in parallel with the DEXA Conference also in Zaragoza.

In your hands are the results of much effort. The work begins with the preparation of the submitted papers, which then go through the reviewing process. The accepted papers are revised to final versions by their authors and are then arranged within the conference program. All culminates in the conference itself. For this conference 304 papers were submitted, and I want to thank to all who contributed to it; they are the real base of the conference. The program committee and the supporting reviewers produced altogether 942 referee reports, in average 3,1 reports per paper, and selected 92 papers for presentation.

At this point we would like to say many thanks to all the institutions that actively supported this conference and made it possible. These were:
- University of Zaragoza
- FAW
- DEXA Association
- Austrian Computer Society

A conference like DEXA would not be possible without the enthusiastic employment of several people in the background. First we want to thank to the whole program committee for the thorough review process. Many thanks also to Maria Schweikert (Technical University, Vienna), Andreas Dreiling (FAW, University of Linz) and Monika Neubauer (FAW, University of Linz). Special thanks go to Gabriela Wagner. She is Scientific Event Manager in charge of the DEXA organization and has organized the whole DEXA event. The editors express their high appreciation of her outstanding dedication. The scientific community appreciates the way she helps authors and participants whenever necessary.

June 2004

Fernando Galindo
Makoto Takizawa
Roland Traunmüller

Program Committee

General Chairperson:
Fernando Galindo, University of Zaragoza, Spain

Conference Program Chairpersons:
Makoto Takizawa, Tokyo Denki University, Japan
Roland Traunmüller, University of Linz, Austria

Workshop Chairpersons:
A Min Tjoa, Technical University of Vienna, Austria
Roland R. Wagner, FAW, University of Linz, Austria

Program Committee Members:
Witold Abramowicz, The Poznan University of Economics, Poland
Michel Adiba, IMAG - Laboratoire LSR, France
Hamideh Afsarmanesh , University of Amsterdam, The Netherlands
Ala Al-Zobaidie, University of Greenwich, UK
Walid G. Aref, Purdue University, USA
Ramazan S. Aygun, University of Alabama in Huntsville, USA
Kurt Bauknecht, University of Zurich, Switzerland
Trevor Bench-Capon, University of Liverpool, UK
Elisa Bertino, University of Milan, Italy
Alfs Berztiss, University of Pittsburgh, USA
Bishwaranjan Bhattacharjee, IBM T.J. Watson Research Center, USA
Sourav S Bhowmick, Nanyang Technological University, Singapore
Christian Böhm, University of Munich, Germany
Alex Borgida, Rutgers University, USA
Omran Bukhres, Purdue University School of Science, USA
Luis Camarinah-Matos, New University of Lisbon, Portugal
Antonio Cammelli, CNR, Italy
Malu Castellanos, Hewlett-Packard Laboratories, USA
Tiziana Catarci, University of Rome "La Sapienza", Italy
Wojciech Cellary, University of Economics at Poznan, Poland
Elizabeth Chang, Curtin University, Australia
Sudarshan S. Chawathe, University of Maryland, USA
Ming-Syan Chen, National Taiwan University, Taiwan
Paolo Ciaccia, University of Bologna, Italy
Rosine Cicchetti, IUT, University of Marseille, France
Carlo Combi, University of Verona, Italy
Brian Frank Cooper, Georgia Institute of Technology, USA
Isabel Cruz, University of Illinois at Chicago, USA
John Debenham , University of Technology, Sydney, Australia
Misbah Deen, University of Keele, UK

Stefan Dessloch, University of Kaiserslauern, Germany
Elisabetta Di Nitto, Politecnico di Milano, Italy
Nina Edelweiss, Universidade Federal do Rio Grande do Sul, Brazil
Johann Eder, University of Klagenfurt, Austria
Gregor Engels, University of Paderborn, Germany
Peter Fankhauser, Fraunhofer IPSI, Germany
Ling Feng, University of Twente, The Netherlands
Eduardo Fernandez, Florida Atlantic University, USA
Simon Field, Matching Systems Ltd., Switzerland
Burkhard Freitag, University of Passau, Germany
Mariagrazia Fugini, Politecnico di Milano, Italy
Irini Fundulaki, Bell Laboratories, Lucent Technologies, USA
Antonio L. Furtado, Pontificia Universidade Catolica do R.J., Brazil
Manolo Garcia-Solaco, IS Consultant, USA
Georges Gardarin, University of Versailles, France
Alexander Gelbukh, CIC, Instituto Politecnico Nacional (IPN), Mexico
Parke Godfrey, The College of William and Mary, Canada
Paul Grefen, Eindhoven University of Technology, The Netherlands
William Grosky, University of Michigan, USA
Le Gruenwald, University of Oklahoma, USA
Abdelkader Hameurlain, University of Toulouse, France
Igor T. Hawryszkiewycz, University of Technology, Sydney, Australia
Wynne Hsu, National University of Singapore, Singapore
Mohamed Ibrahim, University of Greenwich, UK
H.-Arno Jacobsen, University of Toronto, Canada
Yahiko Kambayashi, Kyoto University, Japan
Gerti Kappel, Vienna University of Technology, Austria
Dimitris Karagiannis, University of Vienna, Austria
Randi Karlsen, University of Tromsö, Norway
Rudolf Keller, Zühlke Engineering AG, Switzerland
Latifur Khan, University of Texas at Dallas, USA
Myoung Ho Kim, KAIST, Korea
Masaru Kitsuregawa, Tokyo University, Japan
Gary J. Koehler, University of Florida, USA
Nick Koudas, AT&T Labs Research, USA
John Krogstie, SINTEF, Norway
Petr Kroha, Technical University Chemnitz-Zwickau, Germany
Josef Küng, FAW, University of Linz, Austria
Lotfi Lakhal, University of Marseille, France
Christian Lang, IBM T.J. Watson Research Center, USA
Jiri Lazansky, Czech Technical University, Czech Republic
Young-Koo Lee, University of Illinois, USA
Mong Li Lee, National University of Singapore, Singapore
Michel Leonard, University of Geneva, Switzerland
Tok Wang Ling, National University of Singapore, Singapore
Volker Linnemann, University of Luebeck, Germany
Mengchi Liu, Carleton University, Canada

Peri Loucopoulos, UMIST, UK
Sanjai Kumar Madria, University of Missouri-Rolla, USA
Akifumi Makinouchi, Kyushu University, Japan
Vladimir Marik, Czech Technical University, Czech Republic
Simone Marinai, University of Florence, Italy
Heinrich C. Mayr, University of Klagenfurt, Austria
Subhasish Mazumdar, New Mexico Tech, USA
Dennis McLeod, University of Southern California, USA
Elisabeth Metais, CNAM, France
Mukesh Mohania, IBM-IRL, India
Reagan Moore, San Diego Supercomputer Center, USA
Tadeusz Morzy, Poznan University of Technology, Poland
Noureddine Mouaddib, University of Nantes, France
Günter Müller, University of Freiburg, Germany
Felix Naumann, Humboldt-Universität zu Berlin, Germany
Erich J. Neuhold, GMD-IPSI, Germany
Wilfried Ng, University of Science and Technology, Hong Kong
Matthias Nicola, IBM Silicon Valley Lab, USA
Shojiro Nishio, Osaka University, Japan
Gultekin Ozsoyoglu, University Case Western Research, USA
Georgios Pangalos, University of Thessaloniki, Greece
Dimitris Papadias, University of Science and Technology, Hong Kong
Stott Parker, University of Los Angeles (UCLA), USA
Oscar Pastor, Universidad Politecnica de Valencia, Spain
Jignesh M. Patel, University of Michigan, USA
Glenn Paulley, iAnywhere Solutions (A Sybase Company), Canada
Verónika Peralta, Universidad de la Republica, Uruguay
Günter Pernul, University of Regensburg, Germany
Evaggelia Pitoura, University of Ioannina, Greece
Alexandra Poulovassilis, University of London, UK
Calton Pu, Georgia Institute of Technology, USA
Gerald Quirchmayr, University of Vienna, Austria,
and University of South Australia, Australia
Fausto Rabitti, CNUCE-CNR, Italy
Wenny Rahayu, La Trobe University, Australia
Isidro Ramos, Technical University of Valencia, Spain
P. Krishna Reddy, International Institute of Information Technology, India
Werner Retschitzegger, University of Linz, Austria
Norman Revell, Middlesex University, UK
Sally Rice, University of South Australia, Australia
Philippe Rigaux, University of Paris Sud, France
John Roddick, Flinders University of South Australia, Australia
Colette Rolland, University Paris I, Sorbonne, France
Armin Roth, DaimlerChrysler AG, Germany
Elke Rundensteiner, Worcester Polytechnic Institute, USA
Domenico Sacca, University of Calabria, Italy
Arnaud Sahuguet, Bell Laboratories, Lucent Technologies, USA

Simonas Saltenis, Aalborg University, Denmark
Marinette Savonnet, Université de Bourgogne, France
Erich Schweighofer, University of Vienna, Austria
Ming-Chien Shan, Hewlett-Packard Laboratories, USA
Keng Siau, University of Nebraska-Lincoln, USA
Michael H. Smith, University of Calgary, Canada, and University of California, USA
Giovanni Soda, University of Florence, Italy
Uma Srinivasan, CSIRO, Australia
Bala Srinivasan, Monash University, Australia
Olga Stepankova, Czech Technical University, Czech Republic
Zbigniew Struzik, The University of Tokyo, Japan
Katsumi Tanaka, Kyoto University, Japan
Zahir Tari, University of Melbourne, Australia
Stephanie Teufel, University of Fribourg, Switzerland
Jukka Teuhola, University of Turku, Finland
Bernd Thalheim, University of Kiel, Germany
J.M. Thevenin, University of Toulouse, France
Helmut Thoma, IBM Global Services Basel, Switzerland
A Min Tjoa, Technical University of Vienna, Austria
Aphrodite Tsalgatidou, University of Athens, Greece
Susan Urban, Arizona State University, USA
Genoveva Vargas-Solar, LSR-IMAG, France
Krishnamurthy Vidyasankar, Memorial University of Newfoundland, Canada
Pavel Vogel, Technical University Munich, Germany
Roland Wagner, FAW, University of Linz, Austria
Kyu-Young Whang, KAIST, Korea
Michael Wing, Middlesex University, UK
Vilas Wuwongse, Asian Institute of Technology, Thailand
Gian Piero Zarri, CNRS, France
Arkady Zaslavsky, Monash University, Australia

External Reviewers

Miguel R. Penabad
Manuel Montes-y-Gomez
Angeles Saavedra-Places
Hiram Calvo-Castro
Ma Luisa Carpente
Nieves R. Brisaboa
Fabrizio Angiulli
Eugenio Cesario
Massimo Cossentino
Alfredo Cuzzocrea
Sergio Flesca
Elio Masciari
Massimiliano Mazzeo
Luigi Pontieri
Andrea Tagarelli
Ioana Stanoi
George Mihaila
Min Wang
Qiankun Zhao
Ling Chen
Sandeep Prakash
Ersin Kaletas
Ozgul Unal
Ammar Benabdelkader
Victor Guevara Masis
Jens Bleiholder
Melanie Weis
Lars Rosenhainer
Sarita Bassil
Adriana Marotta
Regina Motz
Xiaohui Xue
Dimitre Kostadinov
Yufei Tao
Nikos Mamoulis
Xiang Lian
Kyriakos Mouratidis
Linas Bukauskas
Alminas Civilis
Vicente Pelechano
Juan Sanchez
Joan Fons
Manoli Albert

Silvia Abrahao
Abdelhamid Bouchachia
Christian Koncilia
Marek Lehmann
Horst Pichler
Domenico Lembo
Enrico Bertini
Stephen Kimani
Monica Scannapieco
Diego Milano
Claudio Gennaro
Giuseppe Amato
Pasquale Savino
Carlo Meghini
Albrecht Schmidt
Grzegorz Bartosiewicz
Krzysztof Wêcel
Roberto Tedesco
Matthias Beck
Gerhard Bloch
Claus Dziarstek
Tobias Geis
Michael Guppenberger
Thomas Nitsche
Petra Schwaiger
Wolfgang Völkl
Abheek Anand
Akhil Gupta
Feng Peng
Kapila Ponnamperums
Lothar Rostek
Holger Brocks
Andereas Wombacher
Bedik Mahleko
Didier Nakache
Nadira Lammari
Tatiana Aubonnet
Alain Couchot
Cyril Labbe
Claudia Roncancio
Barbara Oliboni
Björn Muschall
Torsten Priebe

Christian Schläger
André Costi Nacul
Carina Friedrich Dorneles
Fábio Zschornack
Mirella Moura Moro
Renata de Matos Galante
Vanessa de Paula Braganholo
Andreas Herzig
Franck Morvan
Yang Xiao
Alex Cheung
Vinod Muthusamy
Daisy Zhe Wang
Xu Zhengdao
Thomais Pilioura
Eleni Koutrouli
George Athanasopoulos
Anya Sotiropoulou
Tsutomu Terada
Jochen Kuester
Tim Schattkowsky
Marc Lohmann
Hendrik Voigt
Arne Ketil Eidsvik
Geir Egil Myhre
Mark Cameron
Surya Nepal
Laurent Lefort
Chaoyi Pang
K.S. Siddesh
Hanyu Li
Majed AbuSafiya
Ho Lam Lau
Qingzhao Tan
James Cheng
Jarogniew Rykowski

Huiyong Xiao
Lotfi Bouzguenda
Jim Stinger
Ren Wu
Khalid Belhajjame
Gennaro Bruno
Fabrice Jouanot
Thi Huong Giang Vu
Trinh Tuyet Vu
Yutaka Kidawara
Kazutoshi Sumiya
Satoshi Oyama
Shinsuke Nakajima
Koji Zettsu
Gopal Gupta
Campbell Wilson
Maria Indrawan
Agustinus Borgy Waluyo
Georgia Koloniari
Christian Kop
Robert Grascher
Volodymyr Sokol
Wook-Shin Han
Won-Young Kim
George A. Mihaila
Ioana R. Stanoi
Takeshi Sagara
Noriko Imafuji
Shingo Ohtsuka
Botao Wang
Masayoshi Aritsugi
Katsumi Takahashi
Anirban Mondal
Tadashi Ohmori
Kazuki Goda
Miyuki Nakano

Table of Contents

Workflow I

Supporting Contract Execution through Recommended Workflows 1
Roger Tagg, Zoran Milosevic, Sachin Kulkarni, and Simon Gibson

An Ontology-Driven Process Modeling Framework 13
Gianluigi Greco, Antonella Guzzo, Luigi Pontieri, and Domenico Saccà

Ensuring Task Dependencies During Workflow Recovery 24
Indrakshi Ray, Tai Xin, and Yajie Zhu

Web Service Based Architecture for Workflow Management Systems 34
Xiaohui Zhao, Chengfei Liu, and Yun Yang

Active and Deductive DB Aspects

Feasibility Conditions and Preference Criteria in Querying and Repairing
Inconsistent Databases 44
Sergio Greco, Cristina Sirangelo, Irina Trubitsyna, and Ester Zumpano

An Active Functional Intensional Database 56
Paul Swoboda and John Plaice

Optimal Deployment of Triggers for Detecting Events 66
Manish Bhide, Ajay Gupta, Mukul Joshi, and Mukesh Mohania

A New Approach for Checking Schema Validation Properties 77
Carles Farré, Ernest Teniente, and Toni Urpí

Workflow II

Autonomic Group Protocol for Peer-to-Peer (P2P) Systems 87
Tomoya Enokido and Makoto Takizawa

On Evolution of XML Workflow Schemata 98
Fábio Zschornack and Nina Edelweiss

A Framework for Selecting Workflow Tools in the Context of Composite
Information Systems 109
Juan P. Carvallo, Xavier Franch, Carme Quer, and Nuria Rodríguez

Queries I (Multidimensional Indexing)

Evaluation Strategies for Bitmap Indices with Binning... 120
Kurt Stockinger, Kesheng Wu, and Arie Shoshani

On the Automation of Similarity Information Maintenance in Flexible Query
Answering Systems.. 130
Balázs Csanád Csáji, Josef Küng, Jürgen Palkoska, and Roland Wagner

An Efficient Neighbor Searching Scheme of Distributed Collaborative Filtering
on P2P Overlay Network... 141
Bo Xie, Peng Han, Fan Yang, and Ruimin Shen

Applications

Partially Ordered Preferences Applied to the Site Location Problem in Urban
Planning.. 151
Sylvain Lagrue, Rodolphe Devillers, and Jean-Yves Besqueut

A Flexible Fuzzy Expert System for Fuzzy Duplicate Elimination in Data
Cleaning 161
Hamid Haidarian Shahri and Ahmad Abdolahzadeh Barforush

DBSitter: An Intelligent Tool for Database Administration 171
*Adriana Carneiro, Rômulo Passos, Rosalie Belian, Thiago Costa,
Patrícia Tedesco, and Ana Carolina Salgado*

Interacting with Electronic Institutions... 181
John Debenham

Queries II (Multidimensional Indexing)

Growing Node Policies of a Main Memory Index Structure for Moving Objects
Databases.. 191
Kyounghwan An and Bonghee Hong

Optimal Subspace Dimensionality for k-NN Search on Clustered Datasets 201
Yue Li, Alexander Thomasian, and Lijuan Zhang

PCR-Tree: An Enhanced Cache Conscious Multi-dimensional Index Structures.... 212
*Young Soo Min, Chang Yong Yang, Jae Soo Yoo, Jeong Min Shim,
and Seok Il Song*

Knowledge Processing und Information Retrieval

Classification Decision Combination for Text Categorization:
An Experimental Study 222
Yaxin Bi, David Bell, Hui Wang, Gongde Guo, and Werner Dubitzky

Information Extraction via Automatic Pattern Discovery in Identified Region 232
Liping Ma and John Shepherd

CRISOL: An Approach for Automatically Populating Semantic Web from
Unstructured Text Collections 243
Roxana Danger, Rafael Berlanga, and José Ruiz-Shulcloper

Text Categorization by a Machine-Learning-Based Term Selection 253
*Javier Fernández, Elena Montañés, Irene Díaz, José Ranilla,
and Elías F. Combarro*

Queries III (XML)

Update Conscious Inverted Indexes for XML Queries in Relational Databases 263
Dong-Kweon Hong and Kweon-Yang Kim

A Selective Key-Oriented XML Index for the Index Selection Problem in
XDBMS 273
Beda Christoph Hammerschmidt, Martin Kempa, and Volker Linnemann

SUCXENT: An Efficient Path-Based Approach to Store and Query XML
Documents 285
Sandeep Prakash, Sourav S. Bhowmick, and Sanjay Madria

Querying Distributed Data in a Super-Peer Based Architecture 296
Zohra Bellahsène and Mark Roantree

Digital Libraries and Information Retrieval I

Phrase Similarity through the Edit Distance 306
Manuel Vilares, Francisco J. Ribadas, and Jesús Vilares

A Document Model Based on Relevance Modeling Techniques for
Semi-structured Information Warehouses 318
Juan Manuel Pérez, Rafael Berlanga, and María José Aramburu

Retrieving Relevant Portions from Structured Digital Documents 328
Sujeet Pradhan and Katsumi Tanaka

Query IV (OLAP)

Parallel Hierarchical Data Cube for Range Sum Queries and Dynamic Updates..... 339
Jianzhong Li and Hong Gao

A Bitmap Index for Multidimensional Data Cubes 349
Yoonsun Lim and Myung Kim

Analytical Synopses for Approximate Query Answering in OLAP Environments.. 359
Alfredo Cuzzocrea and Ugo Matrangolo

Digital Libraries and Information Retrieval II

Morphological and Syntactic Processing for Text Retrieval 371
Jesús Vilares, Miguel A. Alonso, and Manuel Vilares

Efficient Top-k Query Processing in P2P Network 381
Yingjie He, Yanfeng Shu, Shan Wang, and Xiaoyong Du

Improved Data Retrieval Using Semantic Transformation 391
Barry G.T. Lowden and Jerome Robinson

A Structure-Based Filtering Method for XML Management Systems 401
Olli Luoma

Mobile Information Systems

Uncertainty Management for Network Constrained Moving Objects 411
Zhiming Ding and Ralf Hartmut Güting

Towards Context-Aware Data Management for Ambient Intelligence 422
Ling Feng, Peter M.G. Apers, and Willem Jonker

TriM: Tri-Modal Data Communication in Mobile Ad-Hoc Networks 432
Leslie D. Fife and Le Gruenwald

Knowledge Processing I

Efficient Rule Base Verification Using Binary Decision Diagrams 445
Christophe Mues and Jan Vanthienen

How to Model Visual Knowledge: A Study of Expertise in Oil-Reservoir
Evaluation 455
Mara Abel, Laura S. Mastella, Luís A. Lima Silva, John A. Campbell, and Luis Fernando De Ros

A New Approach of Eliminating Redundant Association Rules 465
Mafruz Zaman Ashrafi, David Taniar, and Kate Smith

An a Priori Approach for Automatic Integration of Heterogeneous and
Autonomous Databases 475
*Ladjel Bellatreche, Guy Pierra, Dung Nguyen Xuan, Dehainsala Hondjack,
and Yamine Ait Ameur*

Knowledge Processing II

PC-Filter: A Robust Filtering Technique for Duplicate Record Detection in
Large Databases 486
Ji Zhang, Tok Wang Ling, Robert M. Bruckner, and Han Liu

On Efficient and Effective Association Rule Mining from XML Data 497
Ji Zhang, Tok Wang Ling, Robert M. Bruckner, A Min Tjoa, and Han Liu

Support for Constructing Theories in Case Law Domains 508
Alison Chorley and Trevor Bench-Capon

Knowledge Processing III

Identifying Audience Preferences in Legal and Social Domains 518
Paul E. Dunne and Trevor Bench-Capon

Characterizing Database User's Access Patterns 528
Qingsong Yao and Aijun An

Using Case Based Retrieval Techniques for Handling Anomalous Situations
in Advisory Dialogues 539
Marcello L'Abbate, Ingo Frommholz, Ulrich Thiel, and Erich Neuhold

A Probabilistic Approach to Classify Incomplete Objects Using Decision Trees ... 549
Lamis Hawarah, Ana Simonet, and Michel Simonet

XML I

A Graph-Based Data Model to Represent Transaction Time in Semistructured
Data 559
Carlo Combi, Barbara Oliboni, and Elisa Quintarelli

Effective Clustering Schemes for XML Databases 569
William M. Shui, Damien K. Fisher, Franky Lam, and Raymond K. Wong

Detecting Content Changes on Ordered XML Documents Using Relational Databases 580
Erwin Leonardi, Sourav S. Bhowmick, T.S. Dharma, and Sanjay Madria

Timestamp-Based Protocols for Synchronizing Access on XML Documents 591
Sven Helmer, Carl-Christian Kanne, and Guido Moerkotte

Distributed and Parallel Data Bases I

On Improving the Performance Dependability of Unstructured P2P Systems via Replication 601
Anirban Mondal, Yi Lifu, and Masaru Kitsuregawa

Processing Ad-Hoc Joins on Mobile Devices 611
Eric Lo, Nikos Mamoulis, David W. Cheung, Wai Shing Ho, and Panos Kalnis

Preserving Consistency of Dynamic Data in Peer-Based Caching Systems 622
Song Gao, Wee Siong Ng, and Weining Qian

Efficient Processing of Distributed Iceberg Semi-joins 634
Mohammed Kasim Imthiyaz, Dong Xiaoan, and Panos Kalnis

Advanced Database Techniques I

Definition of Derived Classes in ODMG Databases 644
Eladio Garvi, José Samos, and Manuel Torres

Applying a Fuzzy Approach to Relaxing Cardinality Constraints 654
Harith T. Al-Jumaily, Dolores Cuadra, and Paloma Martínez

In Support of Mesodata in Database Management Systems 663
Denise de Vries, Sally Rice, and John F. Roddick

Distributed and Parallel Data Bases II

Moderate Concurrency Control in Distributed Object Systems 675
Yousuke Sugiyama, Tomoya Enokido, and Makoto Takizawa

Performance Evaluation of a Simple Update Model and a Basic Locking Mechanism for Broadcast Disks 684
Stephane Bressan and Guo Yuzhi

Adaptive Double Routing Indices: Combining Effectiveness and Efficiency in P2P Systems.. 694
Stephane Bressan, Achmad Nizar Hidayanto, Chu Yee Liau, and Zainal A. Hasibuan

Advanced DB Techniques II

Efficient Algorithms for Multi-file Caching 707
Ekow J. Otoo, Doron Rotem, and Sridhar Seshadri

A System for Processing Continuous Queries over Infinite Data Streams 720
Ehsan Vossough

Outer Join Elimination in the Teradata RDBMS.. 730
Ahmad Ghazal, Alain Crolotte, and Ramesh Bhashyam

Formalising Software Quality Using a Hierarchy of Quality Models 741
Xavier Burgués Illa and Xavier Franch

Bioinformatics

RgS-Miner: A Biological Data Warehousing, Analyzing and Mining System for Identifying Transcriptional Regulatory Sites in Human Genome 751
Yi-Ming Sun, Hsien-Da Huang, Jorng-Tzong Horng, Ann-Ping Tsou, and Shir-Ly Huang

Effective Filtering for Structural Similarity Search in Protein 3D Structure Databases.. 761
Sung Hee Park and Keun Ho Ryu

Fast Similarity Search for Protein 3D Structure Databases Using Spatial Topological Patterns... 771
Sung Hee Park and Keun Ho Ryu

Ontology-Driven Workflow Management for Biosequence Processing Systems 781
Melissa Lemos, Marco Antonio Casanova, Luiz Fernando Bessa Seibel, José Antonio Fernandes de Macedo, and Antonio Basílio de Miranda

XML II

Towards Integration of XML Document Access and Version Control.................... 791
Somchai Chatvichienchai, Chutiporn Anutariya, Mizuho Iwiahara, Vilas Wuwongse, and Yahiko Kambayashi

Prefix Path Streaming: A New Clustering Method for XML Twig Pattern Matching 801
Ting Chen, Tok Wang Ling, and Chee-Yong Chan

A Self-adaptive Scope Allocation Scheme for Labeling Dynamic XML Documents 811
Yun Shen, Ling Feng, Tao Shen, and Bing Wang

F2/XML: Navigating through Linked XML Documents 822
Lina Al-Jadir, Fatmé El-Moukaddem, and Khaled Diab

Temporal and Spatial Data Bases I

Declustering of Trajectories for Indexing of Moving Objects Databases 834
Youngduk Seo and Bonghee Hong

Computing the Topological Relationship of Complex Regions 844
Markus Schneider

A Framework for Representing Moving Objects 854
Ludger Becker, Henrik Blunck, Klaus Hinrichs, and Jan Vahrenhold

Temporal Functional Dependencies with Multiple Granularities: A Logic Based Approach 864
Carlo Combi and Rosalba Rossato

Web I

Device Cooperative Web Browsing and Retrieving Mechanism on Ubiquitous Networks 874
Yutaka Kidawara, Koji Zettsu, Tomoyuki Uchiyama, and Katsumi Tanaka

A Flexible Security System for Enterprise and e-Government Portals 884
Torsten Priebe, Björn Muschall, Wolfgang Dobmeier, Günther Pernul

Guiding Web Search by Third-Party Viewpoints: Browsing Retrieval Results by Referential Contexts in Web 894
Koji Zettsu, Yutaka Kidawara, and Katsumi Tanaka

Temporal and Spatial Data Bases II

Algebra-to-SQL Query Translation for Spatio-temporal Databases 904
Mohammed Minout and Esteban Zimányi

Visualization Process of Temporal Data.. 914
Chaouki Daassi, Laurence Nigay, and Marie-Christine Fauvet

XPQL: A Pictorial Language for Querying Geographical Data............................ 925
Fernando Ferri, Patrizia Grifoni, and Maurizio Rafanelli

Web II

HW-STALKER: A Machine Learning-Based Approach to Transform Hidden
Web Data to XML... 936
Vladimir Kovalev, Sourav S. Bhowmick, and Sanjay Madria

Putting Enhanced Hypermedia Personalization into Practice via Web Mining........ 947
Eugenio Cesario, Francesco Folino, and Riccardo Ortale

Extracting User Behavior by Web Communities Technology on Global Web
Logs.. 957
Shingo Otsuka, Masashi Toyoda, Jun Hirait, and Masaru Kitsuregawa

Author Index 969

Supporting Contract Execution through Recommended Workflows

Roger Tagg[1], Zoran Milosevic[2], Sachin Kulkarni[2], and Simon Gibson[2]

[1]University of South Australia, School of Computer and Information Science
Mawson Lakes, SA 5095, Australia
Roger.Tagg@unisa.edu.au
[2]CRC for Enterprise Distributed Systems Technology (DSTC)
Level 7, GP South, University of Queensland,
Brisbane, Q 4072, Australia
{zoran,sachink,sgibson}@dstc.edu.au

Abstract. This paper extends our previous research on e-contracts by investigating the problem of deriving business process specifications from business contracts. The aim here is to reduce the risk of behaviour leading to contract violations by encouraging the parties to a contract to follow execution paths that satisfy the policies in the contract. Our current contract monitoring prototype provides run-time checking of policies in contracts. If this system was linked to workflow systems that automate the associated business processes in the contract parties, a finer grain of control and early warning could be provided. We use an example contract to illustrate the different views and the problems of deriving business processes from contracts. We propose a set of heuristics that can be used to facilitate this derivation.

1 Introduction

Most business transactions are based on a contract of some form. However, in most of today's organizations, including their IT systems support, contracts are treated as isolated entities, far removed from their essential role as a governance mechanism for business transactions. This can lead to many problems, including the failures to detect in timely manner and react to business transaction events that could result in contract violations or regulatory non-compliance.

As a result, several vendors have begun offering self-standing enterprise contract management software [2][3][4][6]. These systems consist mostly of a number of pre-built software components and modules that can be deployed to specific contract requirements. However our earlier work [7][8] suggests that a more generic approach is needed that more closely reflects contract semantics, in particular in terms of the governance role. This means adopting higher level modelling concepts that directly reflect the business language of a contract and the policies that express constraints on the parties involved. Examples of these are obligations, permissions, prohibitions, authorisation etc. This implies a need for specialised languages to express these contract semantics.

In previous papers we presented our language-based solution for the expression of contract semantics in a way suitable for the automation of contract monitoring [7][8]. This language, Business Contract Language (BCL), is used to specify monitoring conditions that can be then interpreted by a contract engine. This paper investigates to what extent the semantics of contracts can be used to infer business processes which, if followed by the trading partners, would help reduce the risks associated with contract non-compliance. Such processes may be able to provide a finer grain of monitoring to complement that achievable through the BCL alone. We refer to these business processes as 'recommended' business processes - to reflect the fact that they can only be a guiding facility for managing activities related to contracts, and that the different parties' organisational policies and cultures may impose limitations on how far business processes can be structured or how strictly they should be mandated.

The paper begins with a motivating example of a water supply maintenance situation that could benefit from the automation of contract related activities. In the subsequent section we describe how BCL can be used to express monitoring conditions for this system. We then present a model of the same contract seen as a business process, following which we discuss the problems associated with the translation of contract conditions into a business process, referring to the lessons we learned in trying this. Next we present a proposed approach for derivation of business process from a contract, based on heuristics related to different types of contract and clause. This is followed with an overview of related work. The paper concludes with a summary of areas for future research and a brief conclusion.

2 Motivating Example

In this fictitious example, Outback Water (OW) is a utility organisation that provides water to agriculture, industry (primarily mining and oil/gas extraction) and small towns in certain central parts of Australia. It operates some storage lakes and both open irrigation canals and pipelines.

OW makes contracts with maintenance subcontractors for servicing and maintaining its assets (e.g. pumps, valves, etc) located in its facilities in various areas. The contracts are of a repetitive and potentially continuing nature. Contracts are for a year and cover a list of assets that have to be maintained.

From the point of view of OW's service to its customers, its Quality of Service (QoS) objective is to ensure that the average and worst loss of service to any customer is within a stated maximum number of days. OW uses MTBF (Mean Time Between Failures) and MTTR (Mean Time To Repair) as its main measures of asset availability.

The contract is summarised in the following table:

Table 1. Representation of the contract between Outback Water and a Maintenance Subcontractor

	Obligations: Subcontractor
s1	Make its best efforts to ensure that the following QoS conditions are met: - not exceed the maximum asset down time on any one asset - not exceed the call-out time limit on more than 5% of emergencies in a month - average above the specified MTBF and below the MTTR over a month The maximum or minimum values are provided in a schedule to the contract.
s2	Submit monthly reports on all preventative maintenance activities and emergency events, including full timing details and description of problems and action taken, broken down into labour, replacement parts and materials.
s3	Inform the asset operator within 24 hours of any event that might affect the ability to achieve the quality of service, e.g. resignation of subcontractor engineers, recurring problem with certain asset types
s4	Submit monthly invoices of money due to the subcontractor.
	Obligations: Asset Operator (OW)
ow1	Pay the subcontractor on monthly invoice within 30 days.
ow2	Provide list of assets to be maintained, with clear instructions of the maintenance cycles required (asset lists are in a schedule to the contract, maintenance manuals are in associated paper or on-line documents)
ow3	Provide clear MTBF and MTTR targets
ow4	Feed back to the subcontractor any information received about problems with the water supply, including emergencies reported by its customers within 24 hours
ow5	Give the subcontractor access to all the asset sites.
ow6	After each of the 1st and 2nd quarters, give guidance to the subcontractor on how any shortcomings in the service might be improved.
	Permissions: Asset Operator
ow7	May take on an additional subcontractor in the event that the appointed subcontractor is having difficulty in meeting the QoS targets.
ow8	After the 3rd quarter of the contract, may give the subcontractor notice to quit or to be asked to continue for another year
	Prohibitions: Subcontractor
s5	Not allowed to re-assign maintenance tasks to a sub-sub-contractor.

3 Expressing Contract Monitoring Conditions Using BCL

BCL is a language developed specifically for the purpose of monitoring behaviour of parties involved in business contracts. Key concepts of this language are [7]:
- Community – A container for roles and their relationships in a cross-enterprise arrangement. A Community may be instantiated from a Community Template.
- Policy – General constraints on behaviour for a community, expressed as permissions, prohibitions, obligations or authority. In combination these make up the terms of the contract.

- State – information containing the value of variables relevant to the community; may change in respect to events or time.
- Event – any significant occurrence generated by the parties to the contract, an external source, or a temporal condition.
- Event Pattern – an expression relating two or more events that can be detected and used in checking compliance with a policy (see [5] for similar concepts).

The BCL concepts introduced above can be used to express a model for a specific business contract, such as that between OW and a sub-contractor. These models are then interpreted by a contract engine, to enable evaluation of actual contract execution versus agreed contract terms. This evaluation requires access to the contract-related data, events and states as they change during the execution of business processes.

In the water supply example there are a number of clauses that are suitable for run time monitoring, but for brevity we choose only the clauses under s1 in Table 1. The contract should have a schedule describing each asset and the availability objectives associated with that asset. As part of the contract the sub-contractor must submit a monthly report outlining all tasks performed whether routine maintenance or emergency repairs. This report should contain basic details that will be used to calculate adherence to the QoS metrics. The report will need to identify the asset, and contain a description of the task, the start time and the finish time. In addition to this, for any emergency task the actual time of failure should be indicated.

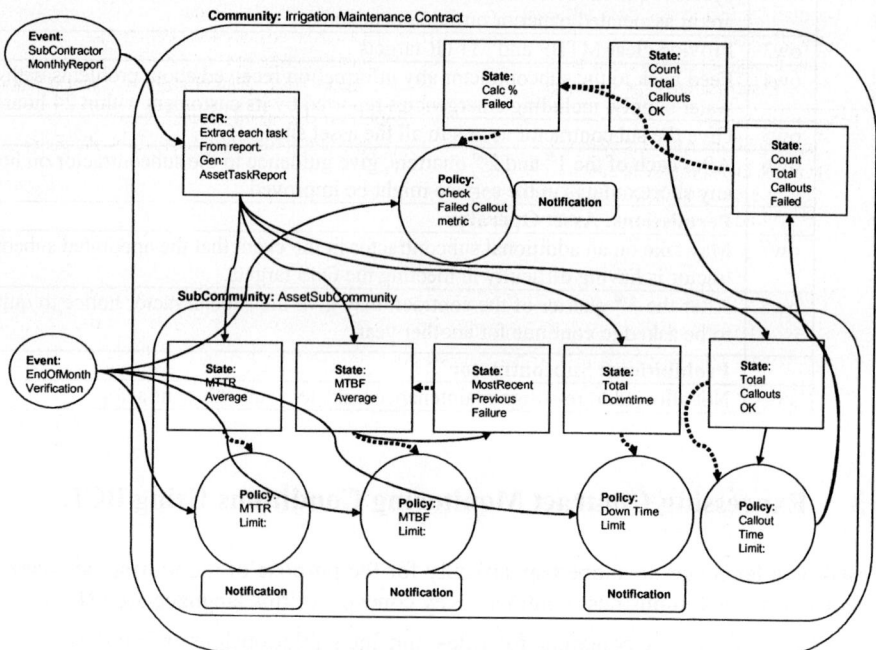

Fig. 1. BCL concepts for part of a water supply maintenance contract

To begin with, an overall community should be defined for the entire contract. In this example, each asset has some of its own monitoring behaviour and so each asset can be seen as being a sub-community of the overall community. Fig. 1 outlines some of the required constructs. The full lines indicate event flow and the broken lines indicate data flow.

The parent community template defines an event creation rule (ECR) that extracts each task from a SubContractorMonthlyReport event and passes the task as an event to the associated sub-community instance. There are a number of States that collect these events and perform an associated calculation. Policies can then use the value of these states as well as values defined in the contract schedule to determine whether constraints have been met or violated. The trigger for evaluating these Policies is when an event indicating the EndOfMonth is received. It should be noted that a Guard is placed on most of the Policies declaring that the SubContractorMonthlyReport must be received prior to the EndOfMonth event. Additional Policies could be used to enforce this behaviour but is not shown here for reasons of brevity. Notifications are used to notify human users that a violation has occurred. Table 2 provides BCL syntax for the specification of one fragment of the contract, namely asset downtime state, policies and notifications.

Table 2. BCL syntax examples for asset downtime specifications

EventCreationRule: AssetTaskReport
GenerateOn: SubContractorMonthlyReport
ContentToGenerate:
    Loop through report and create an
    AssetTaskReport for each task
	State: downtimeState
	On event: AssetTaskReport
	    If its an emergency task calculate the
	    total downtime and add it to total
	    total = Total + (FinishDateTime - TimeOfFailure)

Policy: downtimeLimit
Guard: SubContractorMonthlyReport
On event: EndOfMonthVerification
    Checks if downtimeState value is greater than
    the defined value of MaxAssetDowntime metric
	Notification: downtimeLimitNotification
	On event: downtimeLimitPolicyEvaluationEvent

Note that although we use an event-driven approach for the monitoring, these are infrequent events and this contract can be characterised as a system-state invariant contract. For more information about various characteristics of contract clauses, see their classification in section 6.

4 Deriving Business Processes from Contracts

A contract exists for a limited purpose – to express constraints on the behaviour of signatories with the aim of achieving their individual objectives in the presence of uncertainty. It does not attempt to prescribe the "how" of a business process; rather, it is limited to what conditions that need to be satisfied for the parties to comply with the contract. In practice, in order to ensure that a contract is satisfied, the parties – separately and together – must have processes (which may be in part informal) for meeting their obligations under the contract.

A formal workflow might be able to add the following to contract management:
- Guidance to the human participants in each contract party, particularly where the staff involved are not experienced in the pattern of collaboration – answering "what do we do next?"
- Auditing: answering "who actually performed the constituent activities?" in case of a breach in the contract
- Early warning: if activities in either party are behind schedule at a detailed level, it may be possible to re-assign resources to remedy this.

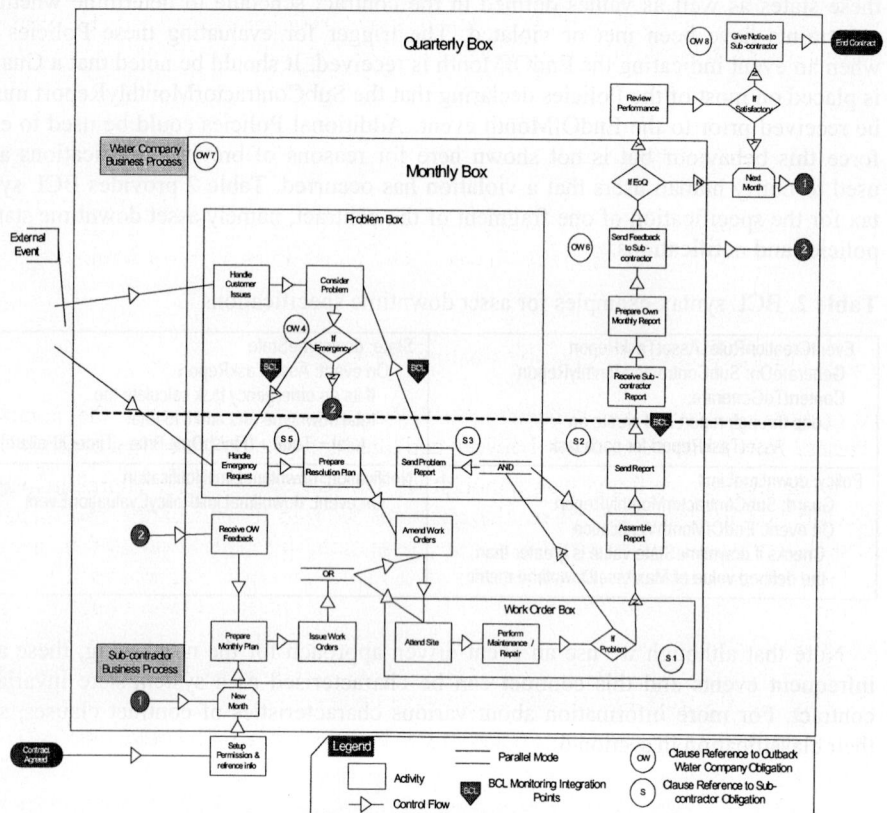

Fig. 2. A business process for the water supply maintenance example

A business process will generally be at a finer level of detail than the contract clauses. When trying to derive business processes for the water supply example (see Figure 2), we needed to introduce a number of assumptions which were not explicitly stated in the contract. Examples of such "introduced" behaviour are activities such as Issue Work Order, Amend Work Order and Prepare Resolution plan. Another example is the activity: "the sub-contractor can be given notice" which implies that the asset owner must review performance against the contract. This finding is in line with our previous experience reported in [1] and is a result of the fact that the contract only states a broad framework of possible executions and that many behaviour trajectories can satisfy the policies stated in the contract.

Therefore, the business process in Figure 2 is one possible way to satisfy the policies in this contract. The example also shows the separation of processes across OW and the sub-contractor; two levels of nesting for the month and quarter periods; and two repeating activities (problem and work order sub-processes). In addition it shows a need for supporting external events (not originating from within the workflow).

Once this process is in place, it would be then possible to use the events generated through the corresponding workflow system as input to a contract monitoring system, such as one that utilizes BCL and the underlying interpreter engine [7]. This figure highlights possible points where contract monitoring conditions can be applied (shown using the black BCL symbol).

5 Discussion Points

There are a number of considerations that we faced when working with this example. Some of the key questions and possible solutions are outlined in this section.

5.1 The Feasibility of Deducing Business Processes

How many activities are deducible by understanding the nature of the contract clauses? How much dependency between activities is explicitly stated in a contract?

In our analysis we found that, although we started from the same natural language specification as described above, the questions we had to ask for the two models, namely contract monitoring and workflow, were quite different. Several of the activities that the subcontractor should perform were not mentioned in the contract. We can deduce, for example, that the subcontractor must send a monthly report (and invoice) and inform OW immediately of any noteworthy problems. But it is not prescribed that the subcontractor must make a monthly plan and create work orders, or that they should revise the work orders following an emergency.

It is difficult to envisage any general rules that could be applied to all types of contracts and clauses.

5.2 Inter-organizational Workflow Versus Separate Workflows

Supposing we can deduce a recommended business process, how can it be usefully expressed?

One possibility is to propose a single inter-enterprise workflow. However this is not likely to be politically acceptable unless the parties to the contract have a very high level of mutual trust, and are not so concerned about their autonomy.

An alternative is to offer the workflow in two separate sections, one for each party, showing where they need to interact with the other, as in BPEL [10]. However highly autonomous parties may still object to too much detailed prescription, and may already have their own workflow patterns for performing services of this type. A water system maintenance subcontractor might have, for example, worked on maintenance for other clients. In this case, it would be better to leave the finer process detail as "black boxes" for each party's managers to decide themselves.

It is really a part of contract negotiation to agree what level of integration of process and data the parties to a contract will subject themselves to. If cooperation needs to be close however, too little control might not be adequate. Someone in one organisation may need to ask the other "where exactly are you on this?" In such cases it could be desirable for each company to allow some inspection of their own local workflow status by their collaborators.

5.3 Dependence on Data Capture

How do we verify that data relating to the contract clauses is reliably captured? For example, are there remotely readable real time meters on the pumps, or does OW have to rely on the subcontractor? How do we know that the subcontractor's engineer has properly serviced a pump, or that the required report contains at least the prescribed minimum details?

Verification of completion of activities is not necessarily assured by simply automating the workflow or the contract monitoring. Many workflow management systems (WfMS) allow a performer to simply click a link that says "Completed".

In obligations and prohibitions, and in the effectiveness of the granting of permissions, how do we monitor non-compliance? In our example, how does anyone find out if a sub-sub-contractor has been called in discreetly, or that a key to an installation has not been provided? There are cases where it may be against the interests of one party to reveal the data.

In general, if contract clauses rely critically on the values of captured data, then a loop to verify those data may be needed. This can be added as an additional element in the recommended process.

5.4 Overriding the Contract Due to Force Majeure

A further question is, what happens if the contract itself has to be altered? An example might be a drought that caused a systematic failure in many pumps due to impurities. Such overrides would need to be reflected in any running workflows as well as the contract. If the contract is subject to such alteration, it would imply the need for any software supporting a workflow implementation of the business processes to allow easy adaptation of the workflow template at run time.

6 Proposals

This section provides a number of proposals to assist in deriving recommended business processes based on the contract expressions. They represent our early ideas to this mapping problem and will need to be further elaborated in our future research.

6.1 Analysis of the Types of Contracts and Contract Clauses Involved

Contract clauses vary a lot in style - and the contracts as a whole in their balance of these. The following classification is suggested, based on previous examples in the e-commerce area and the example we are currently using.

- System state invariant – this means that certain measurements on the real world situation must not be allowed to go outside certain bounds at any time. In our example this measurement could be the MTBF, MTTR and total down time. A procedure must exist within the party responsible for the system state for achieving this. In our case there has to be a maintenance plan, scheduling when each pump is going to be maintained. If the subcontractor falls behind on its work, then the impact on the contract may not be immediate. The MTBF and MTTR figures will only show up when they are next re-calculated and reported. Depending on the data, it may be possible to provide early warning of likely failure to meet the requirement
- Deadline – this means that some event must occur by a certain date (usually relative to a starting point or a previous event). In our case study, examples are submission of a monthly report, and of additional events and feedback in both directions. Early warning may be possible if the activities can be broken down into smaller measurable stages
- Event-dependent – this implies that some activity must occur following some specified event. In our example, the event could be an emergency in which an irrigation pump for a critical crop failed. In an e-business contract, the event could be the placing of an order.
- Artefact quality – for the contract to succeed, this implies an inspection stage, which may be followed by an iterative re-work loop. The artefact may be physical (e.g. delivered goods) or informational (e.g. a report or design).
- Nested – some contracts are at a single level, e.g. the once-off supply of a number of a particular product. More often the contract has multiple instances, in possibly more than one dimension. In our case study, we have multiple assets. Many other contracts cover multiple business cases, repeated orders etc. This implies processes at both the individual level and at the overall contract level.
- Periodic – some contracts are for a single instance of some activity, others are subject to regular calendar-based repetition, including our own example. Therefore there are processes that repeat within each calendar period.
- Exception specification – this explicitly states a process that is to be followed if things go wrong. In our example, OW can terminate the contract after the 3rd

quarter. In other cases, there may be penalty clauses, procedures for agreeing extensions and so on. It often makes sense to provide prompting to parties to a contract that they should enforce their rights.

6.2 Heuristic Rules for Deriving Recommended Sub-workflows

While it is possible for contract architecture and business process model to be derived independently – as we have done – there does seem to be the opportunity for recommending a set of heuristic rules that may help to suggest the structure of the recommended workflow, based on clause characteristics.

The following table shows a summary of the heuristics that could be applied:

Table 3. Summary of suggested heuristics

Heuristic	Contract types	Deontic modality	Comments
Introduce escalation branches (penalties, extensions etc.)	Exception	Obligations, Permissions, Prohibitions	This is the easiest to derive, as the process is usually explicit in the contract
Introduce sub-processes for activities inside the nesting or periodicity	Nested, Periodic	All	Progress on the individual business cases, or periods, is the best early warning
Introduce loops for checking the deliverable and iterating to achieve quality	Quality	Obligations	The requestor may want to reserve the right not to accept the completion of the service.
Introduce planning activities corresponding to a required level of performance	Status	Obligations, Permissions	The party requesting the service may want to be confident that the subcontractor has adequate resources and procedures to meet the requirement
Introduce a renegotiation phase in case the contract needs changing	Nested, Periodic	All	If things don't go right in one period, or on one business case, the parties may want to allow adjustment of the contract process itself
Introduce related reporting and other information flow phases	All except exceptions	Obligations	If required performance is specified, but no reporting activity, then this should be added

6.3 Introduction of Additional "Accepted Practice" Sub-workflows

Some parts of widely-used business processes are available for re-use within some of the well-known workflow management systems, e.g. Action Works Metro [9]. Typical examples are getting feedback from a number of people on a draft document, or common business applications such as invoice/payment. Such business processes could be considered to be used as a potential solution for implementing certain processes that satisfy contract conditions.

6.4 Cross-Checking of Business Process Models

As discussed earlier, the parties to a contract may wish to tailor any recommended workflows to meet their internal organisation culture, or they may already have their own workflows. Another approach is to analyse the difference between the process models of the individual parties and the "recommended" model. As we found from our own experience, even deriving a recommended model can introduce the possibility of inconsistency with the BCL model, so cross checking is also needed here. In our own example, we can highlight the fact that there is no explicit measuring of the call-out time in the process model. We may allow this to be included by the subcontractor in "Perform Maintenance/Repair", or we may feel that this does not encourage the call-out time to be reliably captured.

7 Related Work

Very few researchers have addressed the relationship between contracts and workflow. In the paper of Van den Heuvel and Weigand [11] and in the European Cross-Flow project [12], contracts are introduced as a means of coordinating, at a higher level, the workflows of individual organisations in a B2B environment. In the commercial field Dralasoft, a vendor of component workflow software, has recently (23/02/04) announced a link with diCarta [13], but further details are not yet known. We believe our approach is currently unique in trying to re-use contract information to infer the workflows that should exist within and between the parties.

8 Future Work and Conclusions

To further this work a natural follow on is to analyse a larger number of contracts to examine whether there are some other clause/contract characteristics and come up with a more comprehensive classification of contracts. This would also help identify possible further patterns which would suggest heuristics for deriving business processes from natural language expression of contracts. Until this is done, we believe that it is premature to develop software approaches for this derivation, such as intelligent agents which could be used for building knowledge bases containing suitable derivation heuristics. Further, the development of tools for cross checking between the BCL and process models is also dependent on a greater understanding of the variety of contract clause types. Another problem is to what extent derived workflows can be feedback into the contract negotiation.

It is worth noting that our original hypothesis was that it may be possible to translate a business contract expressed in a language such as BCL into a business process language that could be used in a workflow management system, but this did not prove to be realistic. This research found that the types of contract, and the nature of the politics between and within the parties to a contract, were too variable. We have proposed a set of heuristics that can help guide the design of recommended workflows that could guide parties to implement contract-compliant behaviour.

Acknowledgements

The work reported in this paper has been funded in part by the Co-operative Research Centre for Enterprise Distributed Systems Technology (DSTC) through the Australian Federal Government's CRC Programme (Department of Industry, Science & Resources).

The authors would also like to thank to Dr Michael Lawley and Tony O'Hagan for their comments to an earlier version of this paper.

References

[1] Z. Milosevic, G. Dromey, *On Expressing and Monitoring Behaviour in Contracts*, EDOC2002 Conference, Lausanne, Switzerland
[2] iMany, http://www.imany.com
[3] DiCarta, http://www.dicarta.com
[4] UpsideContracts, http://www.upsidecontract.com
[5] D. Luckham, *The Power of Events*, Addison-Wesley, 2002
[6] Oracle Contracts, http://www.oracle.com/appsnet/products/ contracts/content.html
[7] P. Linington, Z. Milosevic, J. Cole, S. Gibson, S. Kulkarni, S. Neal, A unified behavioural model and a contract for extended enterprise, Data Knowledge and Engineering Journal, Elsevier Science, to appear.
[8] S. Neal, J. Cole, P.F. Linington, Z. Milosevic, S. Gibson, S. Kulkarni, *Identifying requirements for Business Contract Language: A Monitoring Perspective*, IEEE EDOC2003 Conference Proceedings, Sep 03.
[9] Action Technologies, Inc, http://www.actiontech.com
[10] http://www-106.ibm.com/developerworks/library/ws-bpel/
[11] van den Heuvel, W-J and Weigand, H "Cross-Organizational Workflow Integration using Contracts" http://jeffsutherland.org/oopsla2000/vandenheuvel/vandenheuvel.htm
[12] Damen, Z, Derks, W, Duitshof, M and Ensing, H "Business-to-Business E-commerce in a Logistics Domain" http://www.crossflow.org/ link to Publications
[13] Dralasoft Inc Press Release, http://www.dralasoft.com/news/dicarta.html

An Ontology-Driven Process Modeling Framework

Gianluigi Greco[1], Antonella Guzzo[1], Luigi Pontieri[2], and Domenico Saccà[1,2]

[1] DEIS, University of Calabria, Via Pietro Bucci 41C, 87036 Rende, Italy
[2] ICAR, CNR, Via Pietro Bucci 41C, 87036 Rende, Italy
{ggreco,guzzo}@si.deis.unical.it, {pontieri,sacca}@icar.cnr.it

Abstract. Designing, analyzing and managing complex processes are recently become crucial issues in most application contexts, such as e-commerce, business process (re-)engineering, Web/grid computing. In this paper, we propose a framework that supports the designer in the definition and in the analysis of complex processes by means of several facilities for reusing, customizing and generalizing existent process components. To this aim we tightly integrate process models with a domain ontology and an activity ontology, so providing a semantic vision of the application context and of the processes themselves. Moreover, the framework is equipped with a set of techniques providing for advanced functionalities, which can be very useful when building and analyzing process models, such as consistency checking, interactive ontology navigation, automatic (re)discovering of process models. A software architecture fully supporting our framework is also presented and discussed.
Keywords: Process Modeling, Mining, Inheritance, Workflows, Ontologies.

1 Introduction

Process modeling has been addressed for decades and a lot of frameworks were proposed in several research fields, like Workflow Systems and Business Processes. This topic is a subject of interest in novel and attractive areas (e.g., Web/grid computing, e-commerce and e-business [4,6]), where customization and reuse issues play a crucial role.

In this paper we devise a framework which supports designers in the definition, analysis and re-engineering of process models in complex and dynamic contexts. The main goal of our approach is to fully exploit the experience gained by designers over time, and somehow encoded in the process models defined so far. In order to support reuse, customization and semantic consolidation, process models are integrated into an ontological framework, which encompasses the description of the entities involved in the processes (e.g. activities and associated input/output parameters). Moreover, in order to make easier the exploitation of design knowledge, we use specialization/inheritance relationships to organize process models into taxonomies, which can sensibly reduce the efforts for reusing and customizing a model.

The exploitation of ontologies for describing process models and reasoning on them is not new. For example, domain and task ontologies are extensively used by Semantic Web Services approaches (see, e.g., [2]), which are mainly devoted to automatic execution issues, rather than to exploiting design knowledge. Conversely, Business Engineering approaches (see, e.g., [10]) focus on structuring design knowledge through process taxonomies, but typically give little attention to the specification of the execution flows. Execution flows can be effectively expressed, through, e.g., one of the formalisms adopted in Workflow Management Systems ($WFMS$). Interestingly, inheritance of workflow models was investigated in [11], but principally with respect to adaptiveness and dynamic change issues, involving, e.g., the migration of executions produced by several variants a given workflow. As a consequence, the approach relies on a formal notion of inheritance, focused on behavioral features and specifically defined for workflow models represented in terms of Petri nets.

By contrast, as we are mainly interested in structuring and exploiting design knowledge, in our approach the definition of specialization between process models is not necessarily bound to a rigid notion of behavioral inheritance, so leaving more freedom to the designer about the meaning of all the concepts and relationships in the knowledge base. In a sense, our framework tries to take advantage of ideas from all the above mentioned process modeling perspectives, in order to provide a complete and effective support to designers.

The formal framework for process modeling has been implemented in a prototype system that can assist the user in both design and analysis tasks, by providing a rich and integrated set of modeling, querying and reasoning facilities. In the paper, we discuss the system architecture and focus on some of its advanced functionalities, such as consistency checking and interactive ontology navigation. We devote particular emphasis to the description of a module for the automatic (re)discovering of process models. Actually, some *process mining* techniques[1, 5] were recently introduced to derive a model for a given process based on its execution logs. Here, we extend such approaches to extract hierarchical process models, to be profitably integrated into our ontological framework.

2 Process Modeling Framework

In this section, we present a modeling framework, where process models can be specified in terms of ontology concepts, and can be related among each others, to facilitate the reuse and consolidation of design knowledge.

2.1 Process Schemata

The basis for a semantic view of a process model is the ontological description of the activities and domain concepts which it involves.

Let A be a set of *activities*. An activity ontology O_A for A is a tuple $\langle \text{ISA}, \text{PARTOF} \rangle$ such that $\text{ISA} \subseteq A \times A$ and $\text{PARTOF} \subseteq 2^A \times A$, where 2^A denotes the set of all the subset of activities, such that for each $a \in A$, there exists no $A' \in 2^A$ such that $a \in A'$ and A' PARTOF A. Roughly speaking, the relation a ISA b, for two activities a and b indicates that a is a refinement of b, while A' PARTOF a for $A' \subset A$ specifies that a consists in the execution of all the "finer" activities in A'. Hence, we say that $a \in A$ is a *complex activity* if there exists $A' \subset A$ such that A' PARTOF a; otherwise, a is said *simple*.

Practically, the relation PARTOF describes how a process can be broken down (or "decomposed") into sub-activities. Moreover, the relation ISA allows the designer to specialize a given activity. Some major issues related to the specialization of complex activities are discussed in the next subsection.

Running Example. In order to make clear our approach, we shall use the following example throughout the paper. Assume that a process model has to be designed to handle customers' orders in a company. The first step is to define the activities that must be carried out in the business cases. To this aim the ontology O_A includes the *Order Management* activity, which, in turn, consists of the following ones: (a) receive an order, (b) authenticate the client, (c) check the product availability, (d) ship the product, (e) send an invoice. □

Let D be the domain of our application, and let O_D be a domain ontology. The *interface* of an activity a in D is a pair $\mathcal{I}^a = \langle \text{InPort}^a, \text{OutPort}^a \rangle$ of set of concepts in D, where OutPort^a specifies the result of the enactment of a, while InPort^a specifies what is required for enabling a.

In general, the input concepts required by a sub-activity either are produced by other activities in the process or are (external) inputs of the process itself. Similarly, the outputs of an activity can be delivered within or outside of the process. A more detailed description of the structure of a complex activity, including the input/output dependencies between the involved sub-activities, can be obtained by the following notion of *Process Schema*.

Definition 1 (Process Schema). Let O_A be an activity ontology, O_D be a domain ontology, and a be an activity in A. A *process schema* $\mathcal{PS}^a$ for a is a tuple $\langle I, T, a_0, F, \mathcal{CF}, \text{IN}, \text{OUT}_{min}, \text{OUT}_{max} \rangle$, such that:

- I is the interface of a (i.e., $I = \mathcal{I}^a = \langle \text{InPort}^a, \text{OutPort}^a \rangle$);
- T is a set of activities s.t. T PARTOF a is asserted in O_A;
- $a_0 \in A$ is the starting activity and $F \subseteq A$ is the set of final activities;
- $\mathcal{CF}$, referred to as *control flow graph* of $\mathcal{PS}^a$, is a relation of precedences among activities s.t. $\mathcal{CF} \subseteq (A - F) \times (A - \{a_0\})$ and $E \subseteq \mathcal{CF}^+$ is s.t.
  - $(x, y) \in E$ implies that $\text{InPort}^y \cap \text{OutPort}^x \neq \emptyset$, and
  - for each $y \in T$ and for each $c \in \text{InPort}^y$, either (i) $c \in \text{InPort}^a$ or (ii) there exists $(z, y) \in E$ s.t. $c \in \text{OutPort}^z$
  - for each $c \in \text{OutPort}^a$, there exists $x \in T$ s.t. $c \in \text{OutPort}^x$.
- $\text{IN}, \text{OUT}_{min}$, and OUT_{max} are three functions assigning to each activity in A^a a natural number such that (i) $\text{IN}(a_0) = 0$, $\forall a \in F$, (ii) $\text{OUT}_{min}(a) = \text{OUT}_{max}(a) = 0$, and (iii) $\forall x \in A^a$, $0 < \text{IN}(x) \le \text{InDegree}(x)$ and $0 < \text{OUT}_{min}(a) \le \text{OUT}_{max}(a) \le \text{OutDegree}(a)$

where $\mathcal{CF}^+$ denotes the transitive closure of $\mathcal{CF}$, $\text{InDegree}(x)$ is $|\{e = (y, x) \mid e \in \mathcal{CF}\}|$ and $\text{OutDegree}(x)$ is $|\{e = (x, z) \mid e \in \mathcal{CF}\}|$. □

Intuitively, for any activity having a significant level of complexity, a process schema allows us to define the involved sub-activities, with their mutual information flow. For instance, the process schema for the *Order Management* activity is shown in Figure 1. *Receive Order* is the starting activity while *Send Invoice* is a final one. The values for IN and OUT_{min} are also reported, while any OUT_{max} value is assumed to coincide with the out-degree of the associated activity.

The informal semantics of a process schema is as follows. An activity a can start as soon as at least $\text{IN}(a)$ of its predecessor activities are completed. Two typical cases are: (i) if $\text{IN}(a) = \textit{InDegree}(a)$ then a is an *and-join* activity, for it can be executed only after all of its predecessors are completed, and (ii) if $\text{IN}(a) = 1$ is called *or-join* activity, for it can be executed as soon as one predecessor is completed. As commonly assumed in the literature, we consider only *and-join* and *or-join* activities: Indeed, by means of these two elementary types of nodes, it is possible to simulate the behavior of any activity a such that $1 < \text{IN}(a) < \textit{InDegree}(a)$. Once finished, an activity a activates any non-empty subset of its outgoing arcs with cardinality between $\text{OUT}_{min}(a)$ and $\text{OUT}_{max}(a)$. If $\text{OUT}_{max}(a) = \textit{OutDegree}(a)$ then a is a *full fork* and if also $\text{OUT}_{min}(a) = \text{OUT}_{max}(a)$ then a is a *deterministic fork*, as it activates all of its successors. Finally, if $\text{OUT}_{max}(a) = 1$ then a is an *exclusive fork* (also called *XOR-fork*), for it activates exactly one of its outgoing arcs.

2.2 Process Schema Inheritance

Specialization/inheritance relationships are a mean for structuring process knowledge into different abstraction levels. Indeed, they allow for organizing a set of related process schemata into a taxonomy, i.e. an acyclic graph where each node corresponds to a concept more general than those associated with its children. Undoubtedly, such a structure can help in effectively exploiting the design knowledge encoded in the involved process models. A key point here is what is the meaning of specialization for process schemata. Diverse notions of specialization were defined in several contexts, e.g., OO-Design/Programming [9,4,16], Enterprise Modeling [10,14], and Workflow Modeling[12]. The question is particularly intriguing if one looks at the behavioral features expressed by a process schema, representing a finite set of legal executions.

A behavioral notion of inheritance, presented in [14], w.r.t. dataflow models, states that all the execution instances of a schema must also be instances of any schema generalizing it. A different meaning of inheritance is adopted in [3],

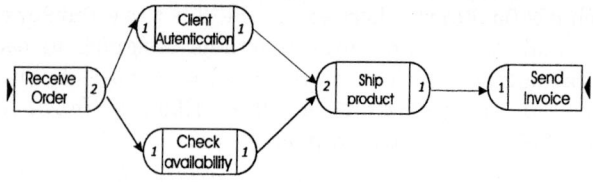

Fig. 1. Process schema for the *Order Management* activity

where two basic notions are defined w.r.t. a special kind of workflow models (a class of Petri Nets, called *WF-nets*). In particular, [3] states that the external behaviors exhibited by a schema and by any of its specializations must not be distinguished whenever: *(a)* only common activities are performed (*protocol inheritance*, a sort of "invocation consistency"[16]), or *(b)* one abstracts from activities which are not in the original schema (*projection inheritance*, a sort of "observation consistency"[16]).

We believe that any of these notions could be more or less suitable to the given application context, and there is not a best one among them. Therefore, we prefer to leave the designer free of specializing a process model in different ways. In general, a new model could be derived from one or more existing models, by specializing functional and/or behavioral features (e.g., input, output, activities, dependencies and constraints on activities).

Let WS be a schema. A schema WS^1 is said a specialization of WS if it is obtained by one of the following operations:

- *Specializing an activity* in the original schema. An activity A in WS is replaced with an activity A^1 representing a specialization of A in the ontology O_A. Note that the inverse derivation is not allowed, that is no activity of WS can be a specialization of some activity in WS^1.
- *Deleting an activity* A of WS. Removing an activity corresponds to exclude any process execution involving it, or, equivalently, to add further constraints to the process schema. Obviously, deletions are legal only if both the initial activity and at least one of the final activities are left.
- *Adding an activity* A to WS.
- *Specializing the execution flow* expressed WS, by either removing links (and/or weakening some constraints), or adding further links between the activities (and/or constraints over them).
- *Specializing the interface* of the complex activity modeled by WS.

Note that, as adding an activity to WS corresponds to deleting an activity from WS^1, we could rather consider WS as a specialization of WS^1, thus apparently getting a contradiction. But the contradiction is only apparent as two opposite abstractions cannot be asserted at the same time: the designer makes a choice between the two alternatives. Moreover, we observe that some of the above operations may lead to specializations which are "unsafe" w.r.t. some of the inheritance notions discussed above. For example, adding an activity is "unsafe" w.r.t. the inheritance notion in [14], as it admits executions which were not captured by the original schema. Such an inconsistence, however, could be temporarily allowed as an exception in a hierarchy of concepts (process models) which is unable to suitably fit the new concept (derived process model). So, later on, the hierarchy should be restructured in such a way that there is not need to include exceptions anymore. To this aim, our system is equipped with facilities for recognizing and recovering inconsistencies, w.r.t. the chosen notion of inheritance, while a taxonomy of process models is being built.

Different examples of specialization for the sample process *Order Management* are depicted in Figure 2, where: the process *Order without shipment* is obtained by deleting the "ship product" activity; the process *Order with credit card* is obtained by adding the "insert term of payment" activity at the more general process; and finally, the "client authentication" activity is replaced with a more specific one ("credit card authentication") in the *Order with credit card*.

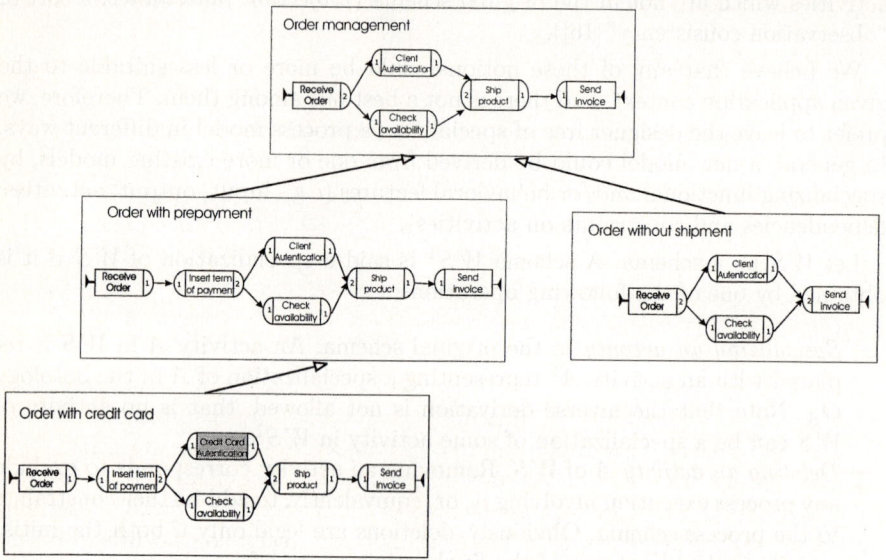

Fig. 2. An example of "temporary" specialization hierarchy

3 System Architecture

This section illustrates the main features of a software system (implemented in JAVA), supporting the design, analysis and usage of process models. From a conceptual point of view, the system architecture, sketched in the right side of Figure 3, is centered upon a rich knowledge base, which stores a semantic description of the processes, according to the framework presented above. Moreover, a set of modeling, querying and reasoning tools is provided, which allow to build and extend this knowledge base, as well as to exploit it in several tasks of a process model's life cycle, such as: *(i)* defining or re-engineering a process model and its components, *(ii)* specializing or generalizing existing models, *(iii)* checking the workflow schema of a process and *(iv)* analyzing its behavior. The main modules in the architecture are the followings:

The **XML repository** represents the core of the system knowledge base. It is a native XML database managing the representation of both process schemata and execution instances, encoded in an XML-based format. Notably, all the semantic relationships involving schemata, activities and other domain entities are explicitly stored in the repository.

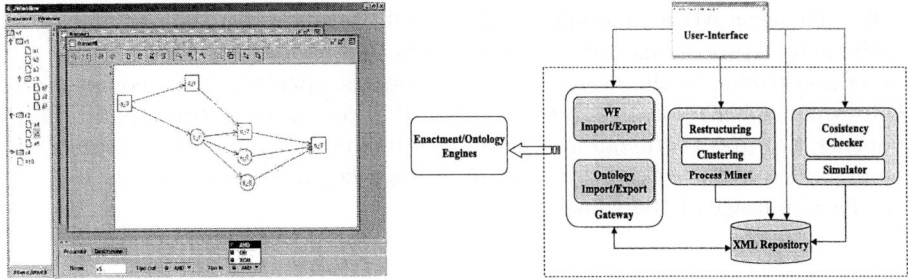

Fig. 3. System Architecture (*right*) and a screen-shot of the user interface (*left*)

The **Ontology I/O module** offers mechanisms for connecting to, browsing and importing parts of an external ontology, provided that this exposes itself in the Web Ontology Language (OWL) [15], a semantic markup language by the World Wide Web Consortium. In addition, the module allows to make available contents of the knowledge base to the outside of the system as an ontology, still adopting the standard OWL format.

The **WF I/O module** provides the ability of translating a given process schema into an executable specification to be enacted by a suitable engine. In the current implementation of the system, Business Process Execution Language (BPEL) [8] has been chosen as such a specification language, mainly because this XML-based language represents a widely accepted notation for describing processes, fully integrated with the Web Services technology, while run-time environments supporting it are become available.

The **Consistency Checker** is in an early stage of development, and is intended to provide a number of facilities for analyzing the defined process schemata. Currently, the module allows the user to assess the syntactic and semantic correctness of a designed process model, by providing automatic support to consistency check and schema validation analysis regarding both the static features of a model and its dynamic behavior. Further, we intend to give further support to the analysis of process behaviors, by developing a **Simulation engine** to simulate the execution of a given process in various situations. Some interesting applications of such a tool might be the investigation of the process model by means of "what if" scenarios and the comparison of alternative design choices. Details on the techniques we plan to exploit in the development of such an engine can be found in a previous work [7].

The **User Interface**, a screen-shot of which is shown on the left side of Figure 3, enables the system to be used in an easy and effective way. Notably, the whole content of the knowledge base can be accessed by users through a general-purpose query engine associated with the *XML repository*. Moreover, the exploration of such data is made easier by exploiting the taxonomical structures in which the various kinds of concepts are organized, according to the specialization and partonomy relationships which relate them (look at the tree-like structure on the left side of the screen-shot).

The **Process Miner** module is substantially devoted to enable the automatic derivation of process models, based on induction techniques. Therefore, it can be of great value to the design of process models, specially when complex and heterogenous behaviors are to be modeled. It is composed of two separate components, i.e., *Restructuring* and *Clustering* modules, whose functionalities will be described in the next section, since this is a key module paving the way for an effective usage of the whole approach.

3.1 Building and Using a Process Model Knowledge Base

This section describes the core techniques implemented in the *Process Miner* module, which can be profitably used in the re-design and analysis of process models. Notably, these tools can be very useful when modeling processes with complex and unexpected dynamics, which would require expensive and long analysis for a complete design. To this aim, a sample of executions is exploited to build a hierarchy of process schemata conforming to our framework, which model the behaviors of the underlying process at different refinement levels.

In order to better explain our approach, we first introduce some preliminary definitions and notation. Let A_P be the set of identifiers denoting the activities involved in a given process P. A *workflow trace* s over A_P is a string in A_P^*, representing a sequence of activities, while a *workflow log for* P, denoted by $\mathcal{L}_P$, is a bag of traces over A_P. Then, a set of traces produced by past enactments of the process P is examined to induce a hierarchy of process schemata representing the behavior of P at different levels of refinement.

The algorithm ProcessDiscover, shown in Figure 4, starts with a preliminary model $\mathcal{WS}_0^1$, which only accounts for the dependencies among the activities in P. Then it refines the current schema in an iterative and incremental way, by exploiting a suitable set of features, which allow to different behavioral patterns. The result of the algorithm is a taxonomy of schemata, that we actually represent as a set of schemata, where each schema $\mathcal{WS}_i^j$ is identified by its level i in the hierarchy (i.e., the number i of refinements required to produce the schema) and by the position j where it occurs inside that level.

The schema $\mathcal{WS}_0^1$ is computed by mining a control flow $\mathcal{CF}_\sigma$, according to a minimum support threshold σ, through the procedure *minePrecedences*, mainly exploiting techniques already presented in the literature (see, e.g., [1, 13]). $\mathcal{WS}_0^1$ is then inserted in T, and the algorithm starts partitioning it. After the initialization described above, the algorithm performs two separate phases.

In the first phase, the taxonomy of schemata is built through a top-down refinement of each schema, implemented by the recursive procedure *partition*. The procedure *partition* mainly relies on identifying different patterns of executions by means of an algorithm for clustering the process traces $\mathcal{L}(\mathcal{WS}_i^j)$ associated with each element WS_i^j in the hierarchy. It is based on projecting these traces onto a set of properly defined *features*. Thus, in order to reuse well know clustering methods (incidentally, *k-means* algorithm is adopted in our implementation), the procedure *refineWorkflow* translates the logs $\mathcal{L}(\mathcal{WS}_i^j)$ to relational data by

Input: A set of logs $\mathcal{L}_p$, a threshold σ, and a natural number m.
Output: Taxonomy of process schemata, $T = \{WS_i^j\}$.
Method: Perform the following steps:
1 $\mathcal{CF}_\sigma(\mathcal{WS}_0^1) := minePrecedences(\mathcal{L}_p)$;
2 let $\mathcal{WS}_0^1$ be a schema, with $\mathcal{L}(\mathcal{WS}_0^1) = \mathcal{L}_P$;
3 $mineLocalConstraints(\mathcal{WS}_0^1)$;
4 $T = \{WS_0^1\}$;
5 $partition(T, 0, 1)$;
6 return T;

Procedure $partition(T: $ schema taxonomy, $i: $ level, $j: $ schema$)$
1 if $|\mathcal{L}(\mathcal{WS}_i^j)| > m$ do
2   let C be a list of schemata,
3      $C := refineWorkflow(T, i, j)$;
4   for each $\mathcal{WS}_{i+1}^{j'} \in C$ do   //recursive processing
5          $partition(T, i+1, j')$;
6   end for
7      $\mathcal{WS}_i^j := generalizeSchemata(C)$;
8 end if;

Function $refineWorkflow(T: $ schema taxonomy, $i: $ level, $j: $ schema$)$: list of schemata
1 $\mathcal{F} := identifyRelevantFeatures(\mathcal{L}(\mathcal{WS}_i^j), \sigma, maxFeatures, \mathcal{CF}_\sigma)$;
2 $\mathcal{R}(\mathcal{WS}_i^j) := project(\mathcal{L}(\mathcal{WS}_i^j), \mathcal{F})$;
3 $k := |\mathcal{F}|$;
4 if $k > 1$ then
5      $j' := \max(\{j' \mid \mathcal{WS}_{i+1}^{j'} \in T\} \cup \{0\})$;
6      $\langle \mathcal{WS}_{i+1}^{j'+1}, ..., \mathcal{WS}_{i+1}^{j'+k}\rangle := k\text{-}means(\mathcal{R}(\mathcal{WS}_i^j))$;
7   for each $\mathcal{WS}_{i+1}^h$ do
8          $T = T \cup \{\mathcal{WS}_{i+1}^h\}$;
9          $\mathcal{CF}_\sigma(\mathcal{WS}_{i+1}^h) := minePrecedences(\mathcal{L}(\mathcal{WS}_{i+1}^h))$;
10         $mineLocalConstraints(\mathcal{WS}_{i+1}^h)$;
11   end for
12 end if
13 return $\langle \mathcal{WS}_{i+1}^{j'+1}, ..., \mathcal{WS}_{i+1}^{j'+k}\rangle$;

Fig. 4. Algorithm `ProcessDiscover`

using the procedures *identifyRelevantFeatures* and *project*. Then, if more than one features are identified, it computes the clusters $\mathcal{WS}_{i+1}^{j+1}, ..., \mathcal{WS}_{i+1}^{j+k}$, where j is the maximum index of the schemata already computed for the level $i+1$, by applying the *k-means* algorithm on the traces in $\mathcal{L}(\mathcal{WS}_i^j)$. Finally, the procedure *mineLocalConstraint* is applied to each schema in the taxonomy, in order to identify a suitable set of local constraints.

The second phase of the algorithm `ProcessDiscover` is instead a bottom-up one, where different schemata previously computed are merged and generalized by means of the procedure *generalizeSchemata*, which is implemented in the *Restructuring* module of the system. This latter procedure, which we do not fully explain for lack of space, allows to produce a generalized process schema from a given set of schemata, substantially by modeling only their common features, while abstracting from details. The resulting schema will then represent a more general process (possibly abstract, i.e., not executable) than the processes modeled by the input schemata.

4 Conclusions

We have proposed a formal framework that supports the designer in defining and analyzing complex and highly dynamic processes by several facilities for reusing, customizing and generalizing existent process components. The model can be used for specifying process at the desired level of details as well as to semantically characterize them by capturing both concepts of the business domain and relationships among them. The model is actually supported by means of a software architecture comprising several useful components that may be profitably exploited for designing complex processes. Among them, we have described in details the process miner module which implements an algorithm for automatically discovering an unknown process model for a given collection of log. As a further research, we plan to extend our system for also supporting advanced reasoning facilities useful for simulation purposes.

Acknowledgments

Part of this work was performed within the framework cooperation of ICAR and EXEURA srl with CM Sud for the project "G4B". This work was also partially supported by a grant of MIUR, within the FIRB project "Grid.it".

References

1. R. Agrawal, D. Gunopulos, and F. Leymann. Mining process models from workflow logs. In *Proc. 6th Int. Conf. on EDBT'98*, 469–483, 1998.
2. Anupriya Ankolekar and Mark Burstein et al. DAML-S: Semantic markup for web services. In *Proceedings of the International Semantic Web Workshop*, 2001.
3. T.Basten and W.van der Aalst.Inheritance of behavior. *JLAP*, 47(2):47–145, 2001.
4. E. Bertino, G. Guerrini, and I. Merlo. Trigger Inheritance and Overriding in an Active Object Database System. *IEEE Trans. Knowl. Data Eng*, 12(4): 588–608,2000.
5. J.E.Cook and A.L. Wolf. Automating process discovery through event-data analysis. In *Proc. 17th Int. Conf. on ICSE'95*, 73–82, 1995.
6. E. Di Nitto, L. Lavazza, M. Schiavoni, E. Tracanella, and M. Trombetta Deriving executable process descriptions from UML. In *Proc. 22th Int. Conf. on ICSE'02*, 155–165, 2002.
7. G. Greco, A. Guzzo, and D. Saccá. Reasoning on Workflow Executions. In *Proc. 7th Int. Conf. on ADBIS03*, 205–219, 2003.
8. IBM. Business process execution language for web services- bpel4ws. http://www-106.ibm.com/developerworks/webservices/library/ws-bpel/.
9. P. kueng, P. Kawalek, and P. Bichler. How to compose an object-oriented business process model, available by http://www.cs.man.ac.uk/ipg
10. Thomas W. Malone, Kevin Crowston, and Brian Pentland et al. Tools for inventing organizations: Toward a handbook of organizational processes. *Theoretical Computer Science*, 45(3):425–443, 1999.
11. W.M.P. van der Aalst. Inheritance of business processes: A journey visiting four notorious problems. In *Petri Net Technology for Communication-Based Systems*, 383–408, 2003.

12. W.M.P. van der Aalst and T. Basten. Inheritance of workflows: An approach to tackling problems related to change. *TCS*, 270(1–2):125–203, 2002.
13. W.M.P. van der Aalst, B.F. van Dongen, J. Herbst, L. Maruster, G. Schimm, and A. J. M. M. Weijters. Workflow mining: A survey of issues and approaches. *DKE*, 47(2):237–267, 2003.
14. G.M. Wyner. Defining specialization for process models.
available at http://citeseer.ist.psu.edu/467393.html
15. W3C. OWL web ontology language reference.
16. M. Stumptner, and M. Schrefl. Behavior Consistent Inheritance in UML. In Proc. 19th Int. Conf. on Conceptual Modeling (ER 2000), 527542, 2000.

Ensuring Task Dependencies During Workflow Recovery

Indrakshi Ray, Tai Xin, and Yajie Zhu

Department of Computer Science
Colorado State University
{iray,xin,zhuy}@cs.colostate.edu

Abstract. Workflow management systems (WFMS) coordinate execution of multiple tasks performed by different entities within an organization. In order to coordinate the execution of the various tasks in a workflow, task dependencies are specified among them. These task dependencies are enforced during the normal execution of the workflow. When a system crash occurs some tasks of the workflow may be committed, some may be partially executed and others unscheduled. In such a situation, the recovery mechanism must take appropriate actions to react to the failure. Although researchers have worked on the problem of workflow recovery, most of these work focus on restoring consistency by removing the effects of partially executed tasks. However, these work fail to address how to ensure task dependencies during workflow recovery. In this paper, we consider the workflow recovery problem and propose a recovery scheme that ensures the satisfaction of dependencies in a workflow and restores consistency as well.

1 Introduction

Workflow management systems (WFMS) are responsible for coordinating the execution of multiple tasks performed by different entities within an organization. A group of such tasks that form a logical unit of work constitutes a workflow. To ensure the proper coordination of these tasks, various kinds of dependencies are specified between the tasks of a workflow. The scheduler of a workflow is expected to enforce these dependencies during normal execution of a workflow. In addition, we must also ensure that these dependencies are enforced in the event of a failure. In this paper we focus on how to ensure dependencies when system crashes or failures occur.

A large body of research exists in the area of workflows [1, 5, 7, 9, 10]. Researchers [1, 2, 7] have focused on how to specify workflows, how to ensure the correctness of the specification, and how to control the execution of tasks in a workflow in order to satisfy the dependencies. Workflow recovery, however, has received very little attention. Most of the research [5, 10, 9] in workflow recovery focuses on how to restore a consistent state after a failure and they do not address the issue of enforcing task dependencies. In this paper we provide an automated approach to workflow recovery that not only restores consistency but also ensures the satisfaction of task dependencies.

Before describing our approach, let us illustrate the problem that occurs if task dependencies are not enforced during recovery. Consider a workflow W_k consisting of two tasks: reserving a room in a resort (t_{ki}) and renting a car (t_{kj}). These two tasks

F. Galindo et al. (Eds.): DEXA 2004, LNCS 3180, pp. 24–33, 2004.
© Springer-Verlag Berlin Heidelberg 2004

t_{ki} and t_{kj} have a dependency between them: if t_{ki} begins then t_{kj} should begin. This dependency can be enforced by starting t_{kj} after t_{ki} begins. Suppose t_{kj} gets completed before t_{ki} and a crash occurs before t_{ki} completes. Since t_{kj} is completed and t_{ki} is incomplete, the recovery algorithm to restore consistency undoes only t_{ki}. This results in an undesirable situation. Thus, restoring consistency by removing the effects of partially executed tasks is not enough for workflow recovery: the recovery algorithms must also take into account the effect of task dependencies.

In this paper we elaborate on the different kinds of task dependencies present in a workflow and show how these task dependencies impact the recovery process. We discuss what information is needed and how this information is stored to perform an effective recovery. Finally, we give a recovery algorithm that restores consistency and enforces task dependencies.

The rest of the paper is organized as follows. Section 2 discusses some related work in this area. Section 3 describes our workflow model and enumerates the different kinds of dependencies. Section 4 identifies the information necessary for workflow recovery. Section 5 presents our workflow recovery algorithm. Section 6 concludes the paper with some pointers to future directions.

2 Related Work

Although a lot of research appears in workflow, we focus our attention to those discussing workflow dependencies and workflow recovery. An approach for specifying and enforcing task dependencies have been proposed by Attie et al. [2]. Each task is described by a set of events, such as, start, commit and rollback. Dependencies between the tasks connect the events of various tasks and specify a temporal order among them. These dependencies are specified using Computation Tree Logic (CTL). With respect to recovery, the authors mention what data is needed to recover from failures but do not provide details. They also do not address how task dependencies can be enforced during recovery.

Eder and Liebhart [5] classify workflow as document-oriented workflow and process-oriented workflow, and identify potential different types of failure. This paper proposes different recovery concepts, such as forward recovery and backward recovery, and enumerates how the workflow recovery manager can support these concepts. But no detailed approach for workflow recovery process is provided.

Failure handling and coordinated execution of workflows was also proposed by Kamath and Ramamritham [9]. The approach describes how to specify different options that can be taken in the event of a failure. The workflow designer can then choose from these options and customize the recovery process to ensure correctness and performance. Thus, a workflow designer needs to have a comprehensive knowledge about both the business process and the workflow model in order to specify all possible recovery actions.

3 Model

We begin by extending the definition of a workflow given in the Workflow Reference Model [8].

Definition 1. [Workflow] *A workflow W_i is a set of tasks $\{ t_{i1}, t_{i2}, \ldots, t_{in} \}$ with dependencies specified among them that achieve some business objective.*

Next, we define what a task is. We assume that each task in a workflow is a transaction as per the standard transaction processing model [3].

Definition 2. [Task] *A task t_{ij} performs a logical unit of work. It consists of a set of data operations (read and write) and task primitives (begin, abort and commit). The read and write operations that task t_{ij} performs on data item x are denoted by $r_{ij}[x]$ and $w_{ij}[x]$ respectively. The begin, abort and commit operations of task t_{ij} are denoted by b_{ij}, a_{ij} and c_{ij} respectively.*

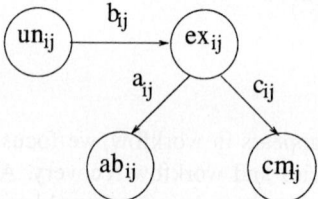

Fig. 1. States of Task t_{ij}

A task t_{ij} can be in any of the following states: *unschedule* (un_{ij}), *execute* (ex_{ij}), *commit* (cm_{ij}) and *abort* (ab_{ij}). Execution of task primitives causes a task to change its state. Executing the begin primitive (b_{ij}) causes a task to move from unschedule state (un_{ij}) to execute state (ex_{ij}). Executing commit primitive (c_{ij}) causes the task to move from execute state (ex_{ij}) to commit state (cm_{ij}). Executing abort primitive (a_{ij}) causes the task to move from execute state (ex_{ij}) to abort state (ab_{ij}). This is illustrated in Figure 1.

To properly coordinate the execution of tasks in a workflow, dependencies are specified between the task primitives of a workflow. Task dependencies are of different kinds. Some researchers classify the dependencies as *control flow dependencies*, *data flow dependencies* and *external dependencies*. In this paper, we focus only on control flow dependencies.

Definition 3. [Control Flow Dependency] *A control flow dependency specifies how the execution of primitives of task t_i causes the execution of the primitives of task t_j.*

The common types of control flow dependencies found in workflow are enumerated below. For a complete list of the different kinds of dependencies, we refer the interested reader to the work by Chrysanthis [4].

1. *Commit Dependency*: A transaction t_j must commit if t_i commits. We can represent it as $t_i \rightarrow_c t_j$.
2. *Abort Dependency*: A transaction t_j must abort if t_i aborts. We can represent it as $t_i \rightarrow_a t_j$.
3. *Begin Dependency*: A transaction t_j cannot begin until t_i has begun. We can represent it as $t_i \rightarrow_b t_j$.
4. *Begin-on-commit Dependency*: A transaction t_j cannot begin until t_i commits. We can represent it as $t_i \rightarrow_{bc} t_j$.
5. *Force Begin-on-commit Dependency*: A transaction t_j must begin if t_i commits. We can represent it as $t_i \rightarrow_{fbc} t_j$.
6. *Force Begin-on-begin Dependency*: A transaction t_j must begin if t_i begins. We can represent it as $t_i \rightarrow_{fbb} t_j$.
7. *Force Begin-on-abort Dependency*: A transaction t_j must begin if t_i aborts. We can represent it as $t_i \rightarrow_{fba} t_j$.
8. *Exclusion Dependency*: A transaction t_i must commit if t_j aborts, or vice versa. We can represent it as $t_i \rightarrow_e t_j$.

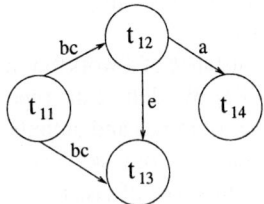

Fig. 2. Tasks and Dependencies in Example Workflow

Example 1. Consider a workflow W_1 consisting of the following set of tasks $\{t_{11}, t_{12}, t_{13}, t_{14}\}$ where each task is described below.

Task t_{11} Reserve a ticket on Airlines A
Task t_{12} Purchasing the Airlines A ticket
Task t_{13} Canceling the reservation
Task t_{14} Reserving a room in Resort C

The various kinds of dependencies that exists among the tasks are shown in Figure 2. There is a begin on commit dependency between t_{11} and t_{12} and also between t_{11} and t_{13}. This means that neither t_{12} or t_{13} can start before t_{11} has committed. There is an exclusion dependency between t_{12} and t_{13}. This means that either t_{12} can commit or t_{13} can commit but not both. Finally, there is an abort dependency between t_{14} and t_{12}. This means that if t_{12} aborts then t_{14} must abort.

4 Information Needed by the Recovery Algorithm

Workflow recovery is much more complex than the recovery in traditional transaction processing system. Consider Example 1. Suppose a crash occurs while t_{12} is executing and after t_{11} and t_{14} have committed. The traditional recovery mechanism will consult the log and undo t_{12}, but it will not have enough information to perform the recovery such that the dependency $t_{12} \rightarrow_a t_{14}$ is satisfied.

The recovery process will need to know the state of the workflow when it crashed and it will also need to know the actions needed to perform the recovery. In our algorithm, the log records store the information about the state of the workflow. The workflow schema stores the information about the actions needed for workflow recovery. We describe these below.

4.1 Workflow Schema

In any organization there are a finite number of types of workflow. We refer to these as workflow schemas. A *workflow schema* defines the type of a workflow. A workflow schema is specified by (1) the types of inputs and outputs needed by workflows instances satisfying this schema, (2) the specification of the types of tasks, and (3) the dependencies between these tasks.

Each workflow is actually an instance of a workflow schema. We denote the schema associated with workflow W_i as WS_i. We denote the type of task t_{ij} as $ty(t_{ij})$. Each type of task is specified by (1) the types of inputs and outputs, if any, needed by tasks of this type, (2) recovery attributes for this type of tasks, (3) compensation-flow for this type of tasks, and (4) alternate-flow for this type of tasks.

Each type of task is described by attributes. Those attributes that are needed by the recovery process are known as the recovery attributes. Recovery attributes can be *compensatable, re-executable* and *alternate executable*. Compensatable identifies whether tasks of this type can be compensated or not. Re-executable indicates whether the tasks of this type can be re-executed or not. Alternate executable signifies whether tasks of this type can be substituted by alternate tasks or not.

For any type of task $ty(t_{ij})$ that is compensatable, the *compensation-flow* includes the set of types of tasks $\{ty(t_{ik}), ty(t_{il}), \ldots, ty(t_{in})\}$ that can compensate $ty(t_{ij})$, the task dependencies between the tasks in this set, and the inputs to the compensation process. For any type of task $ty(t_{ij})$ that is alternate executable, the *alternate-flow* includes the set of types of tasks $\{ty(t_{ik}), ty(t_{il}), \ldots, ty(t_{in})\}$ that can substitute $ty(t_{ij})$, the task dependencies between the tasks in this set, and the inputs to the alternate execution process.

The information about all the workflow schemas is maintained in stable storage.

4.2 Workflow Log Records

In order to recover from a workflow system failure, the state information of a workflow need to be logged onto some stable storage. We propose that such information be stored in the system log. Execution of a workflow primitive, a task primitive, or a task operation results in the insertion of log a record. Moreover, the logs also contain records associated with checkpointing.

Execution of a begin primitive in a workflow results in the insertion of the following log record. $< START\ W_i, WS_i >$ where W_i indicates the workflow id and WS_i indicates the schema id that corresponds to the workflow W_i. The completion of the workflow is indicated by a log record $< COMPLETE\ W_i >$.

Execution of the primitive begin for task t_{ij} results in the following records being inserted in the log: $< START\ t_{ij} >$ where t_{ij} is the task id. Note that the task id includes information about the workflow id of which the task is a part. Similarly, execution of the primitives commit or abort result in the following log records for task t_{ij}: $< COMMIT\ t_{ij} >$ or $< ABORT\ t_{ij} >$. Execution of operations also cause log records to be inserted. A write operation causes the log record $< t_{ij}\ X, v, w >$ where X is the data item written by the workflow and v and w indicate the old value and the new value of the data item written by task t_{ij}. The inputs to the task and the outputs produced by the task are also recorded as log records.

Checkpointing. Our checkpointing technique, based on the non-quiescent checkpointing performed on an undo/redo log in the standard transactional model [6], involves the following steps.

1. Write a log record $< START\ CKPT(t_{wi}, t_{yj}, \ldots, t_{zk}) >$ and flush the log. The tasks $t_{wi}, t_{yj}, \ldots, t_{zk}$ denote all the tasks that have started but not yet committed or aborted when the checkpointing started.
2. Write to disk all dirty buffers, containing one or more changed data item.
3. Append an $< END\ CKPT >$ record to the log and flush the log.

5 Recovery Algorithm

We assume that a system crash can take place at any time. A crash may occur after a workflow is completed or during its execution. When a crash occurs, the task of a workflow may be in unschedule, commit, abort, or execute state (please refer to Figure 1). If a crash occurs when the task is in the execute state, then we say that the task has been *interrupted*.

Our recovery algorithm proceeds in three phases. The first phase is known as the *undo* phase. In this phase, the log is scanned backwards to identify tasks that have been committed, aborted or interrupted. The aborted and interrupted tasks are undone in this phase by restoring the before image values of updated data items. After an interrupted task t_{ij} has been undone, we write a $< RECOVERY\ ABORT\ t_{ij} >$ log record and flush this to the disk. The purpose of this log record is to indicate that this task t_{ij} has been undone, but the dependencies associated with the tasks have not been dealt with.

The second phase is the *redo* phase. In this phase the the data items updated by committed tasks are set to the modified values. The third phase is the *re-execution and dependency adjustment* phase. In this phase, we start from the very first workflow that was interrupted. From the schema, we identify all the tasks of the workflow that have been committed, aborted, interrupted and unscheduled. Starting from the first task that was interrupted, we try to re-execute this task. If the task can be re-executed, then we do not have to worry about the dependency implications of this task. Otherwise, we have to take care of the dependencies of this task. This, in turn, may require some other tasks to be aborted or re-scheduled. The dependencies of these tasks must now be considered. We continue this process until all the dependencies have been considered. The tasks to be scheduled are inserted into a list called *toschedule* that is submitted to the scheduler. Finally, we write an $<ABORT>$ log record for all the tasks that were aborted.

Algorithm 1. *Workflow Recovery Algorithm*
Input: *the log, file containing workflow schemas*
Output: *a consistent workflow state in which all the task dependencies are enforced*

Initialization:
/* lists keeping track of incomplete workflows and tasks in them */
$completeWF = \{\}$, $incompleteWF = \{\}$
$globalCommitted = \{\}$, $globalInterrupted = \{\}$, $globalAborted = \{\}$
/* lists keeping track of tasks in each workflow */
$committed = \{\}$, $interrupted = \{\}$, $unscheduled = \{\}$
$adjustSet = \{\}$, $tempAborted = \{\}$, $toschedule = \{\}$
/* the endCkptFlag set to false */ $endCkptFlag = 0$
Phase 1 *Undo Phase*
begin
    do /* Scan backwards until the $<START\ CKPT>$ */
        get last unscanned log record
        case *the log record is* $<COMMIT\ t_{wi}>$
            $globalCommitted = globalCommitted \cup \{t_{wi}\}$
        case *the log record is* $<ABORT\ t_{wi}>$
            $globalAborted = globalAborted \cup \{t_{wi}\}$
        case *the log record is* $<RECOVERY\ ABORT\ t_{wi}>$
            if $t_{wi} \notin globalCommitted \cup globalAborted$
                $globalInterrupted = globalInterrupted \cup \{t_{wi}\}$
        case *the log record is update record* $<t_{wi}, x, v, w>$
            if $t_{wi} \notin globalCommitted$
                change the value of x to v /* restores before image of x */
            if $t_{wi} \notin globalCommitted \cup globalAborted$
                $globalInterrupted = globalInterrupted \cup \{t_{wi}\}$
        case *the log record is* $<START\ t_{wi}>$
            if $t_{wi} \in globalInterrupted$
                write a $<RECOVERY\ ABORT\ t_{wi}>$ record and flush to the disk
        case *the log record is* $<COMPLETE\ W_k>$
            $completeWF = completeWF \cup \{W_k\}$
        case *the log record is* $<START\ W_k>$
            if $W_k \notin completeWF$
                $incompleteWF = incompleteWF \cup \{W_k\}$
        case *the log record is* $<END\ CKPT>$
            $endCkptFlag = true$ /* we have found an end ckpt record */
    until log record is $<START\ CKPT(..)>$ AND $endCkptFlag = true$
    /* Find the incomplete tasks in the $<START\ CKPT(...)>$ record */
    for each task t_{ij} in $<START\ CKPT(...)>$ record
        if $t_{ij} \notin globalCommitted \cup globalAborted \cup globalInterrupted$
            $globalInterrupted = globalInterrupted \cup t_{ij}$

```
        /* Scan backward to undo the aborted and incomplete tasks */
        do
            case the log record is update record < t_{wi}, x, v, w >
                if t_{wi} ∉ globalCommitted
                    change the value of x to v /* restores before image of x */
            case the log record is < START t_{wi} >
                if t_{wi} ∈ globalInterrupted
                    write a < RECOVERY ABORT t_{wi} > record and flush to the disk
        until all < START t_{kj} > is processed where,
        t_{kj} ∉ globalCommitted AND t_{kj} ∈< START CKPT(...) >
end
Phase 2 Redo Phase
begin
        do /* Scan forward from the < START CKPT(..) > found in Phase 1
            case the log record is update record < t_{wi}, x, v, w >
                if t_{wi} ∈ globalCommitted
                    change the value of x to w /* restores after image of x */
        until end of log is reached
end
Phase 3 Re-executing and Dependency Adjusting Phase
begin
        for each Workflow w ∈ incompleteWF
        begin
            Get the workflow schema WS_w
            for each task t_{wx} defined in workflow schema WS_w
                if task t_{wx} ∈ globalInterrupted
                    interrupted = interrupted ∪ {t_{wx}}
                else if task t_{wx} ∈ globalCommitted
                    committed = committed ∪ {t_{wx}}
                else if task t_{wx} ∉ globalAborted
                    unscheduled = unscheduled ∪ {t_{wx}}
            /* Processing the Interrupted Task, re-executing phase */
            for each t_{wi} ∈ interrupted /* start from the earliest task that was interrupted */
            begin
                interrupted = interrupted − {t_{wi}}
                if t_{wi} is re-executable AND all inputs in log
                begin
                    Re-execute t_{wi}
                    committed = committed ∪ {t_{wi}}
                end
                else /* t_{wi} is aborted and dependencies must be checked */
                begin
                    tempAborted = tempAborted ∪ {t_{wi}}
                    /* Find out all the affected tasks in committed_list */
                    for each task t_{wk} ∈ committed
                        if (t_{wi} →_a t_{wk} OR t_{wi} →_b t_{wk})
                            for each task t_{wj} in compensation-flow of t_{wk}
                            begin
                                toschedule = toschedule ∪ {t_{wj}} /* Compensate task t_{wk} */
                                adjustSet = adjustSet ∪ {t_{wk}}
```

end
/* Find out all the affected tasks in interrupted_list */
for each task $t_{wj} \in$ interrupted
   if $(t_{wi} \rightarrow_{fba} t_{wj})$
      toschedule = toschedule $\cup \{t_{wj}\}$
   if $(t_{wi} \rightarrow_a t_{wj}$ OR $t_{wi} \rightarrow_b t_{wj}$ OR $t_{wj} \rightarrow_c t_{wi})$
      interrupted = interrupted $- \{t_{wj}\}$
      adjustSet = adjustSet $\cup \{t_{wj}\}$
      tempAbort = tempAbort $\cup \{t_{wj}\}$
/* Find out all the tasks that need to be scheduled in unscheduled_list */
for each task $t_{wm} \in$ unscheduled
   if $t_{wi} \rightarrow_{fba} t_{wm}$ OR $t_{wi} \rightarrow_{ex} t_{wm}$
      toschedule = toschedule $\cup \{t_{wm}\}$
   if t_{wi} is alternate-executable
      for each t_{wj} in alternate flow of t_{wi}
         toschecule = toschecule $\cup \{t_{wj}\}$
end
/* Processing the tasks that got affected */
while adjustSet $\neq \{\}$
   if $t_{wt} \in$ adjustSet
      for each task $t_{wr} \in$ committed
         if $(t_{wt} \rightarrow_a t_{wr}$ OR $t_{wt} \rightarrow_b t_{wr}$ OR $t_{wr} \rightarrow_c t_{wt})$
            for each $t_{wx} \in$ compensation-flow of t_{wr}
               toschedule = toschedule $\cup \{t_{wx}\}$
            adjustSet = adjustSet $\cup \{t_{wr}\}$
      adjustSet = adjustSet $- \{t_{wt}\}$
end while
Submit toschedule to the scheduler
for each $t_{wi} \in$ tempAborted
   write log record $<$ ABORT $t_{wi} >$ and flush the log
/* Reset variables for the next workflow */
committed = $\{\}$, interrupted = $\{\}$, unscheduled = $\{\}$
toschedule = $\{\}$, tempAborted = $\{\}$
   end
end

6 Conclusion

In order to coordinate the execution of the various tasks in a workflow, task dependencies are specified among them. System crash or failures might occur during the execution of a workflow. When a failure occurs, some tasks may have been partially executed. This results in an inconsistent state. The recovery mechanism is responsible for restoring consistency by removing the effects of partially executed tasks. The task dependencies may be violated while consistency is being restored. In this paper, we study how the task dependencies impact the recovery process and propose an algorithm that restores consistency and also respects the dependencies.

In future, we plan to give more details about this recovery process. For instance, we plan to discuss the kinds of checkpointing that are possible in workfbw systems, and how to optimize the recovery process. Finally, we would also like to expand our work and address issues pertaining to survivability of workfbws. This will include how we can recover from attacks caused by malicious tasks on the workfbw, how we can confine such attacks, and prevent the damage from spreading.

References

1. V. Atluri, W. Huang, and Elisa Bertino. An Execution Model for Multilevel Secure Workflows. In *Database Securty XI: Status and Prospects, IFIP TC11 WG11.3 Eleventh International Conference on Database Security*, August 1997.
2. Paul C. Attie, Munindar P. Singh, Amit P. Sheth, and Marek Rusinkiewicz. Specifying and enforcing intertask dependencies. In *19th International Conference on Very Large Data Bases, August 24-27, 1993, Dublin, Ireland, Proceedings*, pages 134–145. Morgan Kaufmann, 1993.
3. P. A. Bernstein, V. Hadzilacos, and N. Goodman. *Concurrency Control and Recovery in Database Systems*. Addison-Wesley, Reading, MA, 1987.
4. P. Chrysanthis. *ACTA, A framework for modeling and reasoning aout extended transactions*. PhD thesis, University of Massachusetts, Amherst, Amherst, Massachusetts, 1991.
5. J. Eder and W. Liebhart. Workflow Recovery. In *Proceeding of Conference on Cooperative Information Systems*, pages 124–134, 1996.
6. H. Garcia-Molina, J.D. Ullman, and J. Widom. *Database Systems: The Complete Book*. Prentice-Hall, 2002.
7. D. Georgakopoulos, M. Hornick, and A. Sheth. An overview of workflow management: From process modeling to workflow automation infrastructure. *Distributed and parallel Databases*, 3:119–153, 1995.
8. D. Hollingsworth. Workflow Reference Model. Technical report, Workflow Management Coalition, Brussels, Belgium, 1994.
9. M. Kamath and K. Ramamritham. Failure Handling and Coordinated Execution of Concurrent Workflows. In *Proceeding of the Fourteenth International Conference on Data Engineering*, February 1998.
10. B. Kiepuszewski, R. Muhlberger, and M. Orlowska. Flowback: Providing backward recovery for workflow systems. In *Proceeding of the ACM SIGMOD International Conference on Management of Data*, pages 555–557, 1998.

Web Service Based Architecture for Workflow Management Systems

Xiaohui Zhao, Chengfei Liu, and Yun Yang

CICEC – Centre for Internet Computing and E-Commerce
School of Information Technology
Swinburne University of Technology
PO Box 218, Hawthorn, Melbourne, VIC 3122, Australia
{xzhao,cliu,yyang}@it.swin.edu.au

Abstract. With limitations in nature, current workflow management systems are insufficient to meet the arising requirements from the evolving e-Business applications such as global running, process migration, inter-organisational cooperation etc. For this reason, this paper proposes a new architecture for workflow management systems, with an emphasis on supporting inter-organisational interoperability, flexibility, reliability and scalability, based on the Web service technology. With provision of a novel agreement management service and an enhanced definition template library, this architecture offers full support to business process collaborations among participating organisations, including both the horizontal and vertical partitioning schemes.

1 Introduction

In an e-Business environment, a business process can be modelled as a set of steps that are executed following the control and data flow dependencies among them. This corresponds to a workflow process, where the coordination, control and communication of activities are automated, although activities themselves can be performed either automatically or manually [1-3]. New e-Business applications require more demanding features, such as inter-organisational collaboration, flexibility, reliability and scalability. Therefore, new technologies are required to support these features. Recently it has seen a considerable body of research on building special architectures for workflow management systems (WfMSs).

- WISE (Workflow-based Internet SErvices) enables the interaction among heterogeneous workflow applications on the Internet by providing a broker based platform [4]. WISE employs a simple coordination mechanism based on central control, which may not fit the large scale and complex interactions among organisations.
- The jointFlow specification is based on OMG's Workflow Management Facility RFP. This specification defines architecture, including interfaces that support runtime interaction among workflow components, and enables interoperability of workflow components across business domains [5]. However, its reliance on

CORBA technology limits its application in a loose and heterogeneous environment, such as the Internet.
- CrossFlow proposes a contract based inter-organisational workflow system to control the execution of business services offered by different organisations [6]. As these services are always routine ones, the extended workflow management system is tailored for supporting standard cooperation for a supply chain in a static virtual enterprise environment.
- RosettaNet is an industry-specific framework, with industry-specific vocabularies. It contributes to provide a comprehensive description of business processes in an information and communication technology industry [7]. As RosettaNet is initially designed for a particular industry, its application area is restricted.

The above projects attempt to enhance the scalability and interoperability of workflows by exchanging services and standardising interaction behaviours. However, due to the variety and incompatibility of the client-server solutions, they can hardly work well in a global environment. And this leads to the problems on data integrity and validity in the process of exchanging the models or instances among different organisations.

Driven by the widespread use of the Web and new ways organisations conducting their businesses, Service Oriented Computing (SOC) is emerging as a new computing paradigm for distributed computing and business integration. SOC builds on the notion of an Internet-accessible service to represent applications and business processes for integration [8-10]. The key success of SOC is the interoperability support for facilitating the development of distributed applications consisting of components that have been developed by different vendors using different tools provided, and the creation of corporate applications that put software modules from systems in diverse organisational departments or from different organisations together. In this way, business partners can collaborate based on matching and invoking each other's Web services to interact and perform transactions with a minimal programming effort.

Currently a set of standards is proposed by W3C on Web service orchestration, i.e., how to compose a set of Web services to automate a business process. The representing standards are BPEL4WS [11], WS-Transaction (WS-T) [12] and WS-Coordination (WS-C) [13]. BPEL4WS, based on IBM's Web Service Flow Language (WSFL) [14] and Microsoft's XLANG, is a workflow-like definition language that describes sophisticated business processes that can orchestrate Web services. WS-C and WS-T complement BPEL4WS to provide mechanisms for defining specific standard protocols for use by transaction processing systems, workflow systems, or other applications that wish to coordinate multiple Web services.

Apart from standardisation, researchers started to put effort on deploying the Web service technology on building e-Business applications [15, 16]. In this paper, we will address a different problem on deploying the Web service technology to implement WfMS. A novel workflow management system architecture will be proposed based on Web services with an emphasis on inter-organisational interoperability, flexibility, reliability and scalability. To the best of our knowledge, little work has been done along this line.

The rest of the paper is organised as follows. In Section 2, we analyse the requirements for WfMS in the present global business environment. Aiming at these requirements, a Web services based architecture for WfMS is presented in Section 3. Section 4 addresses the issue of inter-organisational support. Concluding remarks are given in Section 5, together with an indication of the future work.

2 Requirements Analysis

In meeting the ever-increasing requirements from evolving e-Business applications, we believe that a WfMS should support the following features:

- *Inter-organisational collaboration support.* In a virtual organisation environment, it is important and necessary for a WfMS to automate and manage the virtual workflows, whose activities or sub-processes might be mapped onto different workflows or part of workflows from different organisations. Figure 1 shows an example of this scenario.

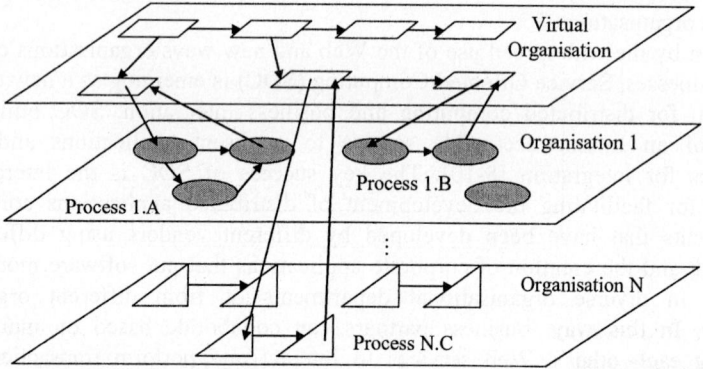

Fig. 1. An inter-organisational workflow

- *Interoperability and Migration support.* Business processes are ubiquitous. To achieve this, they should be able to run in environments with scarce resources, and they should also have an open architecture. Process migration is also important where it is inevitable to migrate a single or batch process instances from one workflow system to another in a virtual organisation. Without affecting the execution of other processes in the sender or the receiver system, this function shifts the workflow interoperability to the level of complete control on transferring batches of processes. Its application covers from simple dynamic load balancing and redundant backup, to business transfer among departments or organisations.
- *Adaptability and Flexibility.* Workflows should be adaptive to the changing requirements of the business processes [17]. As such, a workflow model may be specified as a template that can be dynamically enriched by adding new activities along with their control and data flows, or skipping some parts of the template. Also, each functional module should be changed according to the new business environment, and even at runtime.

- *Reliability.* Errors and invalidity of workflow data would cause fatal conflicts. Actually there are many such occasions in process migration and interactions among organisations [18]. Therefore, a data recovery mechanism is required.

3 System Architecture

We target at the requirements identified in the proceeding section by proposing a Web service based WfMS architecture. Before we introduce the architecture, we briefly describe a seven layer supporting functions and their corresponding protocols as shown in Figure 2. Except the top layer, each layer uses the current transfer or Web service protocols. Web services' interface and implementation are written in Web Service Description Language (WSDL) and WSFL respectively, and these services are invoked through HTTP/SOAP. The top layer, which is responsible for routing, reliability and transaction, will be addressed by our proposed architecture.

Routing & Reliability Transaction : WfMS		
Workflow : WSFL		
Services Discovery & Integration : UDDI	Management	Quality of Services / Security
Services Description : WSDL		
Messaging : SOAP		
Transport : HTTP, SMTP, FTP		
Internet : IPv4/6		

Fig. 2. Web service stack

Figure 3 shows our proposed WfMS architecture based on Web services, where WSFL is suggested as the specific workflow language. An end user can activate workflow activity services through the *workflow domain manager* over the network. Each activity service can be provided from anywhere over the Internet, and can be dynamically modified when needed. With the specific parser and communication mechanism, the *agreement management service* enables the interoperability across organisations. In the following, we introduce the main components of the architecture.

3.1 Workflow Domain Manager

A *workflow domain manager* plays a role of a classical workflow engine, responsible for process generation and execution coordination. In a Web service based WfMS, the workflow domain manager acts as a service requestor. The manager locates a workflow process instance by calling *wf def. library service*, and initiates it with necessary workflow data, which may come from the activity result of other organisations through the *agreement management service*. According to the control data in the WSFL style process description, the manager interprets the implementation sequence, and locates the corresponding service providers using

WSDL descriptors. When an activity is finished, the manager updates the status of the process and begins to handle the following activated activities, with the support of the *wf data service set*. On the other hand, the workflow domain manager is also responsible for the interactions with Web users including user input, work list display, process status listing and modification.

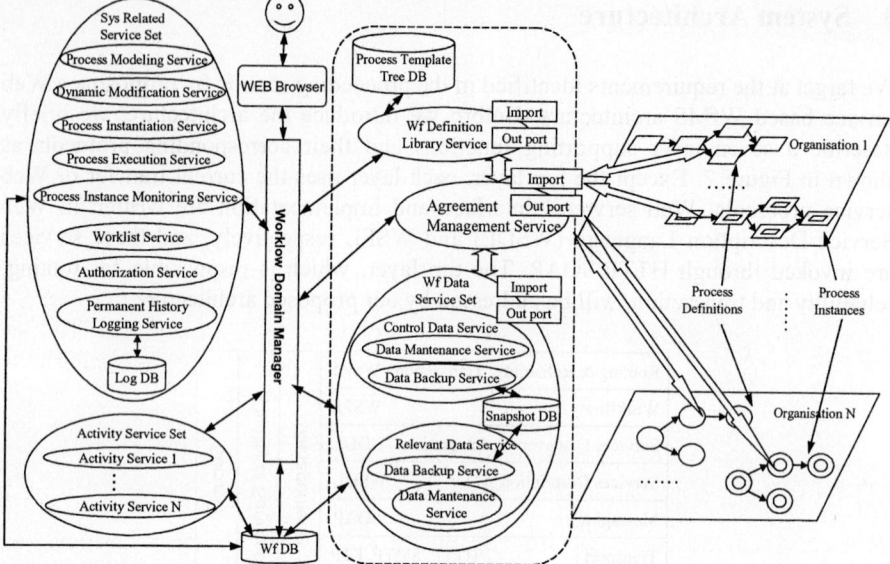

Fig. 3. An architecture for WfMS based on Web services

3.2 System Related Service Set

A *system related service set* provides the main functions of workflow management for the workflow domain manager. These include process modelling, monitoring, modification, user authorisation, work-list handling, process instantiation and execution, etc. All these services have a direct access to the *workflow database*, which stores workflow control and relevant data. Only the workflow domain manager owns the access to these services. In addition, a permanent history logging service is provided to record critical behaviours of these functions.

3.3 Activity Service Set

An *activity service set*, including various activity services, is responsible for actual business functions according to workflow definitions. Each activity service is invoked by, and receives user input data from the workflow domain manager. After finishing an activity, the new workflow relevant and control data generated by the activity are stored by the workflow domain manager in the *workflow database*. Each activity service can be modified and enriched at runtime, and the only requirement for doing this is a new service descriptor. This aspect enhances the flexibility and scalability of WfMS in function extension.

3.4 WF Definition Library Service

A *wf definition library service* is responsible for the storage of workflow definitions and templates. A process model can be defined by using a modelling service, migrating from other organisations through the *agreement management service*, or enriching an existing process template.

3.5 Workflow Data Service Set

A *workflow data service set* includes services for workflow control data and workflow relevant data management. One aim of these services is to guarantee the integrity and validity of data, especially in the course of process migration. This set also has corresponding backup services and a snapshot database for data replication, which enables backward recovery for the reliability purpose.

3.6 Agreement Management Service

Different from the above services which are responsible for local functions, an *agreement management service* is responsible for the inter-organisational communication, such as data conversion, version checking, partner verification etc. Specially, this service is able to directly communicate with agreement management services from other organisations. The use of this unit, in the support to inter-organisational collaboration, will be given in Section 4.

Apart from the features inherited from the Web service framework, the proposed architecture also has the following appealing features:
- Despite the central control on a process instance basis, the run-time system inherits all benefits of a highly distributed environment. The workflow process definitions and instances can be dynamically migrated for better balance, better performance and availability.
- Since no prior installation of any WfMS software is required on the client side, the system is highly dynamic and thus any activity service implementation may be upgraded at anytime anywhere.
- The services under such an open framework are easy to be merged into other systems. Moreover, it is able to interact with other workflow systems by exchanging workflow definitions, instances and necessary data. Therefore, this architecture provides an ideal platform for e-Business applications in an inter-organisational environment.

4 Inter-organisational Support

In an inter-organisational workflow process, several business partners are involved for performing one or more activities of the shared workflow process. van der Aalst [1] classifies workflows interoperability into types of capacity sharing, chained execution, subcontracting, case transfer, extended case transfer and loosely coupled. Except the capacity sharing, the other five types partition a workflow in two ways, i.e., vertical partitioning and horizontal partitioning, as shown in Figure 4. Vertical partitioning uses the case dimension to distribute the workflow, i.e., the cases are distributed over several business partners but the process is not cut into pieces. Horizontal partitioning is based on the process dimension, i.e. the process is cut into pieces and cases are not allocated to specific business partners. The subcontracting and loosely coupled types use a horizontal partitioning; the case transfer and extended case transfer types use a vertical partitioning; and the chained execution type uses a mixture of horizontal and vertical partitioning. Our proposed architecture provides full support to both vertical and horizontal partitioning schemes.

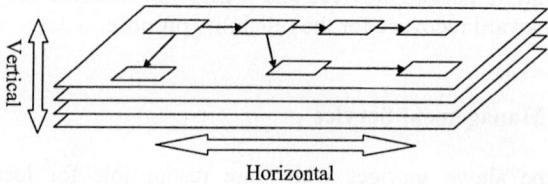

Fig. 4. Partitioning schemes

4.1 Vertical Partitioning

In the vertical partitioning scheme, each involved partner keeps a copy of the shared process definition from the chief organisation of its organisation union. Nevertheless, this does not mean that each partner has full control of the shared process. The process definition distribution is realised by a system-level workflow control activity, which is specified when the union is established.

As illustrated in Figure 5, let P be a shared process, which starts from activity $A1$ followed by activity $A2$ and then other activities. $A1$ and $A2$ belong to two different organisations $O1$ and $O2$, respectively. The definition of P, containing the control structure for collaboration and the normal workflow data (workflow control data, relevant data and application data), is stored in the workflow definition library of the involved partners, including $O1$ and $O2$. Firstly, $M1$ (the workflow domain manager of $O1$) initiates an instance, say $I1$ of P at $O1$, and then invokes proper activity services corresponding to $A1$, say $S11$ and $S14$ at $O1$. At the moment that $A1$ is finished, $A1$'s status turns to 'finished' and $A2$'s to 'ready'. Following the collaboration control structure defined in P, $M1$ knows that next activity $A2$ belongs to $O2$, and starts to transfer $I1$ to $O2$. This step involves the agreement management services (AS) of both partners as shown in Figure 5. $AS1$ at $O1$ is responsible for data wrapping, i.e. formatting the workflow data in WSFL. When $AS2$ at $O2$ receives $I1$ in the format of WSFL, $AS2$ first unwraps the workflow data out of $I1$, and then checks the version of $I1$ and P in the local workflow definition library. In case P is older, $AS2$ will inform $M2$ to contact the chief organisation for instruction on whether the process should continue with the old process definition or handover to follow a new version [17]. After that, $M2$ initiates an instance of P, $I2$, and fills $I2$ with the workflow data extracted from $I1$. $I2$ is executed by invoking activity services of $O2$, say $S25$, to complete $A2$. After that $I2$ will be transferred to the next partner following the collaboration control structure of P. During this course, dynamic change to the process definition of P is allowed. If this happens, the involved partner may first modify the process definition locally, and then send the updated version to the chief organisation, which will update the process definition of other partners upon request later. One limitation of the vertical scheme is that only one organisation is allowed to work on a process at a time.

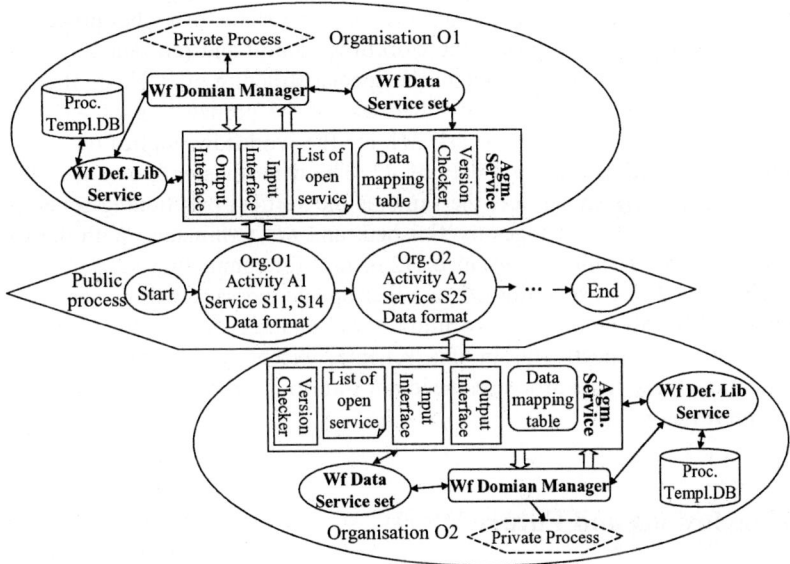

Fig. 5. Inter-organisational interaction

4.2 Horizontal Partitioning

In the horizontal scheme such as the loosely couple type, a global process is cut into disjoint pieces and each of the partners has its own 'local' workflow processes which are private. A business partner has full control over its local processes. However, these local processes need to communicate and be synchronised at certain points because they depend on each other for correct execution of the global process. In this scheme, a 'global' process will be distributed from the chief organisation of the union. The difference to a 'shared' process is that a global process mainly concerns the control structure for interaction and the workflow control data, instead of the inner structure of its activities, i.e., those local processes. The control structure includes navigation information, correspondence between activities or local processes, and synchronisation points. Partner organisations use this global process to maintain the interaction progress. At the same time, partner organisations can keep their internal work private by wrapping the certain details in local processes, since local processes work as black boxes to others.

Suppose we have a global process, P, which has a similar control flow as the shared process discussed above. In addition, local processes $LP1$ at $O1$ and $LP2$ at $O2$ are responsible for executing $A1$ and $A2$, respectively. In the horizontal scheme, each workflow domain manager keeps a definition of P, a well as a copy of instance $I1$ of P to trace its status. When $O1$ finishes $A1$ of $I1$ by executing instance $LI1$ of $LP1$, $M1$ sets $A1$'s status to 'finished'. Though $LI1$ is already finished at this moment, $LI1$ still exists in $O1$ with status 'semi-finished', which means that $LI1$ is waiting for transferring the result workflow application data to subsequent activities. Then $M1$ sends an update message through the agreement management service to other partners' workflow domain managers to update the status of global process instance $I1$. Note this step mainly updates the workflow control and relevant data, rather than the workflow application data, due to the special structure of P. Next, after updating, $M2$ finds that $A2$'s status is 'ready' because of the propagation of $A1$'s 'finished' status. In this case, $M2$ needs to ask $M1$ for the workflow application data of $LI1$, which will be used as the input data of $A2$. The data transfer is also handled by the agreement management service, the same as the vertical partitioning scheme. At the same time, $LI1$'s status changes to 'finished' and $LI1$ terminates. With the workflow application data, $M2$ initiates instance $LI2$ of $LP2$ for completing $A2$ of $LI1$. When $A2$ is finished by $M2$ by executing $LI2$, another update message will be sent out and the execution of $I1$ will go on. The execution of $LI1$ and $LI2$ may use the activity services of $O1$ and $O2$, respectively. In this scheme, except the change of the interface specification, these local processes need not inform or update others about their inner definition revision.

5 Conclusions and Future Work

In this paper, we have introduced the main ideas for building workflow management systems based on Web services technology. A novel architecture is proposed to meet the new-emerging requirements for workflow systems, such as inter-organisational collaboration support. This architecture enables the automatic execution of Web services for both workflow system management and workflow activity execution. With a special agreement management service and a template service, this architecture offers strong support to inter-organisational workflow processes in both the vertical and horizontal partitioning scenarios.

There are many issues that need to be investigated further with this architecture, including the support for transactional workflows, versioning of workflow processes, resource management security and communication. We will investigate these issues in the near future. Specially, as for the sophisticated cooperation and access control policies, we will enhance our work by referring the work done in this area.

Acknowledgements

This work is partly supported by Swinburne VC Strategic Research Initiative Fund 2002-4.

References

1. W.M.P. van der Aalst. Process-oriented Architecture for Electronic Commerce and Interoganizational Workflow. Information Systems (2000) 24(8).
2. Workflow Management Coalition. The Workflow Reference Model, [WfMC1003] WFMC TC00-1003 (1995).
3. X. Zhao. Workflow Simulation across Multiple Workflow Domains. In Proceedings of DEXA'02 (2002) 50-59.
4. A. Lazcano, H. Schuldt, G. Alonso and H. J. Schek. WISE: Process based E-Commerce. IEEE Data Eng. Bull. 24(1) (2001) 46-51.
5. Object Management Group, Workflow Management Facility, Joint Revised Submission, OMG Document bom/98-06-07 (1998).
6. CrossFlow. Http://www.crossflow.org/ .
7. RosettaNet. Http://www.rosettanet.org/rosettanet/ .
8. W3C. Web Services. http://www.w3.org/2002/ws/
9. M. E. Orlowska, S. Weerawarana, M. P. Papazoglou and J. Yang. Proceedings of ICSOC 2003, Trento, Italy, (2003).
10. M. P. Papazoglou, D. Georgakopoulos. Service-Oriented Computing, Communications of the ACM, 46(10) (2003) 24-28.
11. T. Andrews et al. Business Process Execution Language for Web Services (BPEL4WS) 1.1, http://www.ibm.com/developerworks/library/ws-bpel .
12. F. Cabrera et al. Web Services Transaction (WS-Transaction), http://www.ibm.com/developerworks/library/ws-transpec/ .
13. F. Cabrera et al. Web Services Coordination (WS-Coordination), http://www.ibm.com/developerworks/library/ws-coor/ .
14. W3C. Web Services Description Language (WSDL) 1.1, http://www.w3.org/TR/wsdl .
15. L. Zhang (Ed.). Proceedings of ICWS 2003, Las Vegas, USA. (2003).
16. M. Jeckle, L. Zhang (Eds.). Proceedings of ICWS-Europe'03, Erfurt, Germany. (2003).
17. C. Liu, M. Orlowska and H. Li. Automating Handover in a Dynamic Workflow Environment. In Proceedings of CAiSE'98 (1998) 158-171.
18. C. Liu, X. Lin, M. Orlowska and X. Zhou. Confirmation: Increasing Resource Availability in Transactional Workflows. Information Sciences 153 (2003) 37-53.

Feasibility Conditions and Preference Criteria in Querying and Repairing Inconsistent Databases*

Sergio Greco, Cristina Sirangelo, Irina Trubitsyna, and Ester Zumpano

DEIS, Univ. della Calabria, 87030 Rende, Italy
{greco,sirangelo,irina,zumpano}@si.deis.unical.it

Abstract. Recently there has been an increasing interest in integrity constraints associated with relational databases and in inconsistent databases, i.e. databases which do not satisfy integrity constraints. In the presence of inconsistencies two main techniques have been proposed: compute repairs, i.e. minimal set of insertion and deletion operations, called *database repairs*, and compute *consistent answers*, i.e. identify the sets of atoms which we can assume true, false and undefined without modifying the database. In this paper feasibility conditions and preference criteria are introduced which, associated with integrity constraints, allow to restrict the number of repairs and to increase the power of queries over inconsistent databases. Moreover, it is studied the complexity of computing repairs and the expressive power of relational queries over databases with integrity constraints, feasibility conditions and preference criteria.

1 Introduction

Obtaining consistent information from inconsistent databases, i.e. databases which do not satisfy integrity constraints, is a primary issue in database management systems. Typically, two main techniques have been proposed to manage the presence of inconsistent information: compute repairs, i.e. minimal set of insertion and deletion operations, called *database repairs*, and compute *consistent answers*, i.e. identify the sets of atoms which we can assume true, false and undefined without modifying the database.

In repairing an inconsistent database it could be desiderable to specify feasibility and preference conditions among the set of candidate repairs. Feasibility conditions express a set of basic principles regulating how the presence of conflicts has to be solved and must be satisfied by a repair in order to be feasible. In the presence of alternative repairs an update strategy could be expressed by defining preference criteria, i.e. desiderata on how to update the inconsistent database, satisfied, if possible, by a generic repair.

The paper introduces a simple mechanism which allows to easily express feasibility conditions and preference criteria and to use them to select feasible

---
* The first author is also supported by ICAR-CNR and Exeura Srl.

and preferred repairs. Thus, in the presence of inconsistent databases preference criteria are used to define an intended repairing strategy whose degree of satisfaction models a partial order among feasible repairs. The goodness of a repair is measured by estimating how much it violates the desiderata conditions, thus a repair is "preferred" if it minimizes the value of the function used to express the preference criteria. The use of integrity constraints represents a powerful tool for repairing input databases and expressing hard problems. Indeed, we will show that decision problems in the second level of the polynomial hierarchy can be expressed by universally quantified integrity constraints with feasibility conditions, whereas search and optimization problems in the first level can be expressed by a restricted form of universally quantified integrity constraints (called *monotonic*) with, respectively, feasibility conditions and preference criteria.

Related Work. The problem of reasoning in the presence of inconsistencies has recently received a renewed attention and many approaches have been proposed in the literature for managing inconsistent database.

Earlier approaches considered the problem of consistent querying over possibly inconsistent databases in the presence of restricted classes of integrity constraints (functional dependencies and key constraints) [2, 9]. Recent approaches consider both the problems of repairing and querying inconsistent databases in the presence of more general constraints.

In [6] a technique for integrating and querying inconsistent databases in the presence of key and foreign key constraints defined upon the global schema, is proposed, whereas in [24] a quite general and flexible technique which allows the computation of "trustable answer" for conjunctive queries and full dependencies, is presented.

In [3] it is introduces a logical characterization of the notion of consistent answer in a possibly inconsistent database. The technique, based on semantic query optimization, has been shown to be complete for universal binary integrity constraints and universal quantified queries.

A more general approach for obtaining consistent query answers, based on disjunctive extended logic programs with positive and negative exceptions, has been proposed in [4].

Independently, in [12] (see also [14]) it is proposed a technique based on the rewriting of integrity constraints into disjunctive rules with two different forms of negation (negation as failure and classical negation). The derived program can be used both to generate repairs for the database and to produce consistent answers. The technique, more general than techniques previously proposed, has been shown to be sound and complete as each stable model defines a repair and each repair is derived from a stable model. The technique has been further extended through the introduction of preference criteria, expressed by means of real (polynomial) functions, on the set of repairs [15] [1].

---

[1] The use of preference criteria has been deeply investigated in different contexts such as logic programming. [5, 8, 19, 21, 25].

Contribution. In this paper the framework presented in [15] is extended by introducing a more general form of constraints, called feasibility conditions. It is provided an in depth analysis of the complexity of computing (preferred) repairs and consistent answers to queries over inconsistent databases and of the expressive power of relational queries over inconsistent databases. We show that the problem of checking if there exists a repair satisfying the constraints is $\Sigma_2^P - complete$ in the general case and $\mathcal{NP} - complete$ for a significant restricted class of constraints, called monotonic constraints. Thus, the introduction of feasibility conditions does not increase the complexity of computing repairs. Considering the expressive power of relational queries, we show that that under the possible and certain reasoning, general constraints permit us to express all queries defining problem in the second level of the polynomial hierarchy, while monotonic constraints allow us to express all queries defining problem in the first level. We also show that preference criteria allow to express hard optimization problems.

2 Preliminaries

2.1 Relational Databases

The existence of alphabets of relation symbols and attribute symbols is assumed. Relation symbols have a fixed arity, whereas attribute symbols have associated finite domains. The domain of an attribute A_i is denoted by $dom(A_i)$ and all attribute domains are contained into the database domain Dom. Every relation R has an associated schema $Rs = r(A_1, ..., A_n)$, where r is a relation symbol with arity n and $A_1, ..., A_n$ are attribute symbols, and an instance of R is any subset of $dom(A_1) \times \cdots \times dom(A_n)$. A database schema $\mathcal{DS}$ is a finite set of relation schemas. A database (instance) over $\mathcal{DS} = \{Rs_1, ..., Rs_k\}$ is a set of finite relations $D = \{R_1, ..., R_k\}$ where each relation R_i is an instance over the relation schema Rs_i. The set of all possible tuples over a fixed database schema $\mathcal{DS}$ will be denoted by $\mathbf{DB}$, whereas $\mathbf{D}$ denotes the set of all the possible database instances over $\mathcal{DS}$ ($\mathbf{D}$ consists of all possible subsets of $\mathbf{DB}$). Given a set of relations D and a relation symbol r, $D[r]$ denotes the set of r-tuples in D, the instance of r. A (relational) query over a database defines a function from the database to a relation. Queries can be expressed by means of alternative equivalent languages such as relational algebra ($\mathcal{RA}$), 'safe' relational calculus ($\mathcal{S}\text{-}\mathcal{RC}$) or 'safe' non recursive Datalog ($\mathcal{SNR}\text{-}\mathcal{DAT}^\neg$) [23]. A *query* Q over a database D with schema $\mathcal{DS}$ is a pair $\langle p, \phi \rangle$ where p is a relation symbol (output relation) with schema $Ps = p(B_1, ..., B_m)$ and ϕ is an expression of one of the above mentioned languages. The application of a query $Q = \langle p, \phi \rangle$ to a database D over $\mathcal{DS}$, denoted as $Q(D)$, gives a relation P over Ps satisfying ϕ, i.e. $P \subseteq Dom(D)^m$, where m is the arity of p and $\phi(D, P)$ is true. Note that ϕ is an expression over $\mathcal{DS}$, p and universally and existentially quantified variables (denoted by $\forall X(\exists Y(\phi(\mathcal{DS}, p, X, Y))))$.

2.2 Search and Optimization Queries

Given a database schema $\mathcal{DS}$, an additional relation symbol p with arity m (the output relation) and a formula ψ over a fixed query language $\mathcal{L}$, a search query $Q = \langle p, \psi \rangle$ is a (possibly partial) multivalued recursive function[2] which maps every database D on $\mathcal{DS}$ to a finite, non-empty set of finite (possibly empty) relations $P \subseteq Dom(D)^m$. Thus, $Q(D) = \{P | \psi(D, P) \text{ is true }\}$ yields a set of relations on the goal, that are the *answers* of the query; the query has no answer if this set is empty or the function is not defined on D. Search queries generalize relational queries as no assumption about the formula ψ (and the underlying query language $\mathcal{L}$) has been made and the result is multivalued. Since queries are multivalued, the deterministic answer is given by considering the two classical forms of reasoning: brave and cautious.

Definition 1. The answer to a search query $Q = \langle p, \psi \rangle$ over a database D is $\cup_{P \in Q(D)} P$ under *brave reasoning*, and $\cap_{P \in Q(D)} P$ under *cautious reasoning*. □

Given a search query $Q = \langle p, \psi \rangle$, an *optimization query* $OQ = opt(Q)$, where opt is either max or min, is a search query refining Q such that for each database D on $\mathcal{DS}$ for which Q is defined, $OQ(D)$ consists of the answers in $Q(D)$ with the maximum or minimum (resp., if $opt = max$ or min) cardinality. For the sake of simplicity, we are, here, considering queries computing the maximum or minimum cardinality of the output relation, but we could consider any polynomial time computable function. Given a language $\mathcal{L}$ and a database schema $\mathcal{DS}$, the set of all queries over $\mathcal{DS}$ expressed in $\mathcal{L}$ will be denoted by $\mathbf{Q}_{\mathcal{L},\mathcal{DS}}$ or simply $\mathbf{Q}_{\mathcal{L}}$ whenever $\mathcal{DS}$ is understood. As for a given $\mathcal{DS}$ the language $\mathcal{L}$ determines $\mathbf{Q}_{\mathcal{L}}$, if there is no ambiguity, $\mathcal{L}$ will also be used to denote $\mathbf{Q}_{\mathcal{L}}$.

2.3 Query Complexity

In classifying query classes, the following complexity classes of languages will be referred: the class $\mathcal{P}$ (languages that are recognized by deterministic Turing machines in polynomial time), the class $\mathcal{NP}$ (languages that are recognized by nondeterministic Turing machines in polynomial time), and the class $co\mathcal{NP}$ (the class of problems whose complement is in $\mathcal{NP}$) — the reader can refer to [17, 20] for sources of information on this subject. In the following the complexity classes $\Sigma_2^p = \mathcal{NP}^{\mathcal{NP}}$ (languages that are recognized by nondeterministic Turing machines in polynomial time using an $\mathcal{NP}$ oracle), and the class $\Pi_2^p = co\mathcal{NP}^{\mathcal{NP}}$ (the complement of Σ_2^p) are also referred. Given a complexity class $\mathcal{C}$, $\mathcal{CMV}$ and $OPT\,\mathcal{CMV}$ denote, respectively, the class of search and optimization problems corresponding to $\mathcal{C}$. Thus, $\mathcal{NPMV}$ denotes the class of $\mathcal{NP}$ search problems and $OPT\,\mathcal{NPMV}$ denotes the class of $\mathcal{NP}$ optimization problems. Analogously, $\mathcal{QC}$, $\mathcal{QCMV}$ and $OPT\,\mathcal{QCMV}$ denote the classes of queries defining decision, search and optimization problems for the class $\mathcal{C}$.

---

[2] A multivalued function from A to B is a subset S of $A \times B$, such that for every $a \in A$ there is at least one $b \in B$ such that $(a, b) \in S$.

It is well known that a search query $Q = \langle p, \psi \rangle$ is in $\mathcal{QNPMV}$, iff there exists a sequence $\hat{s}$ of relation symbols $s_1, \ldots, s_k$, distinct from those in $\mathcal{DS} \cup \{p\}$ and a closed first order formula ϕ over $\mathcal{DS}, p$ and $\hat{s}$ such that for each database D on $\mathcal{DS}$, $Q(D) = \{ P : P \subseteq Dom(D)^{|p|}, S_i \subseteq Dom(D)^{|s_i|} (1 \leq i \leq k)$, and $\phi(D \cup S, P)$ is true $\}$. Thus, a search query $Q = \langle p, \psi \rangle$ is in $\mathcal{QNPMV}$, iff ψ is of the form $\exists \hat{s}(\forall X(\exists Y(\phi(\mathcal{DS}, p, \hat{s}, X, Y))))$. Analogously, $Q = \langle p, \psi \rangle$ is in $\mathcal{Q}\Sigma_2^p\mathcal{MV}$, iff ψ is of the form $\exists \hat{s}_1(\forall \hat{s}_2(\forall X(\exists Y(\phi(\mathcal{DS}, p, \hat{s}_1 \cup \hat{s}_2, X, Y)))))$. Observe that a query $Q = \langle p, \psi \rangle$ is in $\mathcal{QCMV}$ if, and only if, for each database D on $\mathcal{DS}$ and for each relation P on p, deciding whether P is in $Q(D)$ is in $\mathcal{C}$.

2.4 Integrity Constraints

Generally, a database D has an associated schema $\langle \mathcal{DS}, \mathcal{IC} \rangle$ defining the intentional properties of D: $\mathcal{DS}$ denotes the structure of the relations, while $\mathcal{IC}$ contains the set of integrity constraints expressing semantic information over data.

Definition 2. An *integrity constraint* is a first order logic formula of the form: $(\forall X) [\Phi(X) \supset (\exists Z)\Psi(Y)]$ where X, Y and Z are sets of variables with $Y \subseteq X \cup Z$, Φ and Ψ are two conjunctions of literals such that X and Y are the set of variables appearing in Φ and Ψ respectively, $Z = Y - X$ is the set of existentially quantified variables. □

In the definition above, the conjunction Φ is called the *body* and the conjunction Ψ the *head* of the integrity constraints. The semantics of the above constraint is that for every value of X which makes the formula $\Phi(X)$ true there must be an instance of Z which makes $\Psi(Y)$ true. The class of first order logic constraints will be denoted by $\mathcal{FOC}$.

In the following we consider universally quantified formulae of the form: [3] where $A_1, \ldots, A_m, B_1, \ldots, B_n$ are base positive literals, φ is a conjunction of built-in literals, A_0 is a base positive atom or a built-in atom and X denotes the list of all variables appearing in $B_1, \ldots, B_n$; variables appearing in $A_0, \ldots, A_m$, and φ also appear in $B_1, \ldots, B_n$. It is worth noting that in the above formula there is no restriction about the form of the head as a universally quantified constraint with conjunction of literals in the head can be rewritten into multiple constraints with only one literal in the head. First order logic constraints restricted to universally quantified formulae will be denoted by $\forall\text{-}\mathcal{FOC}$.

Given a language $\mathcal{L}$ and a database schema $\mathcal{DS}$, the set of all integrity constraints over $\mathcal{DS}$ expressed in $\mathcal{L}$ (called constraint language) will be denoted by $\mathbf{IC}_{\mathcal{L},\mathcal{DS}}$ or simply $\mathbf{IC}_{\mathcal{L}}$ whenever $\mathcal{DS}$ is understood. Moreover, as for a given $\mathcal{DS}$ the language $\mathcal{L}$ determines $\mathbf{IC}_{\mathcal{L}}$ $\mathcal{L}$ will be used to also denote $\mathbf{IC}_{\mathcal{L}}$. Therefore, $\forall\text{-}\mathcal{FOC}$ will be used to also define the class of constraints which can be defined by the language $\forall\text{-}\mathcal{FOC}$.

---

[3] Often we write this constraint as *denial* (a rule with empty head) which is satisfied only if the body is false.

3   Feasible Repairs and Preference Criteria

In this section the formal definition of consistent database and repair is first recalled and, then, a computational mechanism is presented that ensures selecting preferred repairs and preferred answers for inconsistent database.

Given a database D and a set of integrity constraints $\mathcal{IC}$ on D, D is *consistent* if $D \models \mathcal{IC}$, i.e. if all integrity constraints in $\mathcal{IC}$ are satisfied by D, otherwise it is *inconsistent*. Given a (possibly inconsistent) database D, a *repair* for D is a pair of sets of atoms (R^+, R^-) such that 1) $R^+ \cap R^- = \emptyset$, 2) $D \cup R^+ - R^- \models \mathcal{IC}$ and 3) there is no pair $(S^+, S^-) \neq (R^+, R^-)$ such that $S^+ \subseteq R^+$, $S^- \subseteq R^-$ and $D \cup S^+ - S^- \models \mathcal{IC}$. The database $D \cup R^+ - R^-$ will be called the *repaired database*. Thus, repaired databases are consistent databases which are derived from the source database by means of a minimal set of insertion and deletion of tuples. Given a repair R, R^+ denotes the set of tuples which will be added to the database, whereas R^- denotes the set of tuples of the database which will be deleted. In the following, for a given repair R and a database D, $R(D) = D \cup R^+ - R^-$ denotes the application of R to D. The set of all repairs for a database D and integrity constraints $\mathcal{IC}$ is denoted by $\mathbf{R}(D, \mathcal{IC})$.

Definition 3. Given a database D over a relational schema $\mathcal{DS}$ with integrity constraints $\mathcal{IC}$ and a relational query $Q = \langle p, \phi \rangle$, the consistent answer to Q, denoted $Q(D, \mathcal{IC})$ is given by the set $\{Q(R(D)) | R \in \mathbf{R}(D, \mathcal{IC})\}$.   □

Since in the presence of integrity constraints, there can be more than one repair, the deterministic semantics of queries is given by considering the set of repaired databases under brave and cautious reasoning.

Definition 4. Let $Q = \langle p, \phi \rangle$ be a relational query over a database D with integrity constraint $\mathcal{IC}$. The deterministic answer to Q over a database D is

- $\bigcup_{R \in \mathbf{R}(D, \mathcal{IC})} Q(R(D))$, under brave reasoning, and
- $\bigcap_{R \in \mathbf{R}(D, \mathcal{IC})} Q(R(D))$, under cautious reasoning.

□

The consistent answer consists of true and undefined atoms.

Definition 5. Let $Q = \langle p, \phi \rangle$ be a relational query over a database D with integrity constraint $\mathcal{IC}$. The (deterministic) consistent answer to the query Q over a database D is

- $Q^+(D, \mathcal{IC}) = \bigcap_{R \in \mathbf{R}(D, \mathcal{IC})} Q(R(D))$, denoting the set of *true* atoms, and
- $Q^u(D, \mathcal{IC}) = \bigcup_{R \in \mathbf{R}(D, \mathcal{IC})} Q(R(D)) - Q^+(D, \mathcal{IC})$, denoting the set of *undefined* atoms.

□

The set of false atoms consisting of all atoms which are neither true nor undefined is $Q^-(D, \mathcal{IC}) = \mathbf{D} - Q^+(D, \mathcal{IC}) - Q^u(D, \mathcal{IC}) = \mathbf{D} - \bigcup_{R \in \mathbf{R}(D, \mathcal{IC})} Q(R(D))$.

3.1 Feasible and Preferred Repairs

Polynomial time functions are now introduced expressing feasibility conditions and preference criteria. The feasibility functions introduce necessary conditions to be satisfied by repairs and (source) databases[4]. The function defining preference criteria is applied to (feasible) repairs and introduces a partial order among them. Moreover, preferred repairs are defined as repairs that are minimal w.r.t. the partial order.

Definition 6. *Feasible repair.* Given a (possibly inconsistent) database D over a fixed schema $\mathcal{DS}$ and a set $\mathcal{F}$ of polynomial time computable functions f_i : $(\mathbf{D},\mathbf{D}) \times \mathbf{D} \to \Re$ from the set of repairs and databases to the domain of real numbers, then a repair R is *feasible* (w.r.t. $\mathcal{F}$) if for all f_i in $\mathcal{F}$ is $f_i(R,D) \leq 0$. □

Above, $\mathbf{D}$ denotes the domain of all possible database instances, whereas $(\mathbf{D},\mathbf{D})$ denotes the domain of all possible database repairs as a repair consists of two sets of tuples. In the following the functions in $\mathcal{F}$ will be called *feasibility functions* or *feasibility bounds*. Every repair satisfying the bounds defined by the feasibility functions in $\mathcal{F}$ will be said $\mathcal{F}$-*feasible*. The class of all polynomial feasibility functions will be denoted by $\mathcal{FP}$, whereas $\forall\text{-}\mathcal{FOC}^{\mathcal{FP}} = \{(\mathcal{IC},\mathcal{F}) | \mathcal{IC} \in \forall\text{-}\mathcal{FOC}, \mathcal{F} \in \mathcal{FP}\}$ will denote the class of all pairs of sets of universally quantified constraints and sets of polynomial feasibility functions. $\forall\text{-}\mathcal{FOC}^{\mathcal{FP}}$ defines a language expressing integrity constraints and feasibility conditions.

Example 1. Consider the database $D = \{$ $Teaches(t_1,c_1)$, $Teaches(t_2,c_2)$, $Faculty(t_1,f_1)$, $Faculty(t_2,f_1)$, $Course(c_1,f_1)$, $Course(c_2,f_2)\}$ and the integrity constraint $\forall (P,C,F) \, [\, Teaches(P,C) \wedge Faculty(P,F) \supset Course(C,F) \,]$. There are three repairs for D: $R_1 = (\emptyset, \{Teaches(t_2,c_2)\})$, $R_2 = (\emptyset, \{Faculty(t_2, f_1)\})$ and $R_3 = (\{Course(c_2,f_1)\},\emptyset)$. Consider now the feasibility bound $|R^+[Course]| \leq 0$ stating that the number of atoms inserted into the relation $Course$ must be equal to zero. Therefore, under such a bound only the repairs R_1 and R_2 are feasible, whereas the repair R_3 is not feasible. □

Definition 7. *[15] Preferred repair.* Given a (possibly inconsistent) database D over a fixed schema $\mathcal{DS}$ and a polynomial time computable function g : $(\mathbf{D},\mathbf{D}) \times \mathbf{D} \to \Re^+$ from the set of repairs and databases to the domain of nonnegative real numbers, then a repair R_1 is *preferable* to a repair R_2, w.r.t. the function g, written $R_1 \ll_g R_2$, if $g(R_1,D) < g(R_2,D)$.

A repair R for D is said to be *preferred* w.r.t. the function g if there is no repair R' for D such that $R' \ll_g R$. A repaired database $D' = D \cup R^+ - R^-$ is said to be a *preferred repaired database* if $R = (R^+,R^-)$ is a preferred repair. □

The above function g will be called *(repair) evaluation function* as it is used to evaluate a repair R w.r.t. a database D. A preferred database minimizes the value of the evaluation function g applied to the source database and repairs. In the following, for the sake of simplicity, functions minimizing the cardinality of a set will be considered.

---

[4] Obviously, explicitly repaired databases need not to be explicitly considered as they can be derived from the application of repairs to the source database.

Example 2. Consider the database D and the integrity constraint of Example 1. Let R be a repair for the database D, possible evaluation functions are:

- $g_1(R,D) = |R^+|$ computing the number of inserted atoms,
- $g_2(R,D) = |R^-|$ computing the number of deleted atoms,
- $g_3(R,D) = |R^-|+|R^+|$ computing the number of deleted and inserted atoms.

The repairs of D: $R_1 = (\emptyset, \{Teaches(t_2,c_2)\})$, $R_2 = (\emptyset, \{Faculty(t_2,f_1)\})$ and $R_3 = (\{Course(c_2,f_1)\}, \emptyset)$ can be partially ordered with respect to the above evaluation functions producing the following relations: i) $R_1 \ll_{g_1} R_3$, $R_2 \ll_{g_1} R_3$ and ii) $R_3 \ll_{g_2} R_1$, $R_3 \ll_{g_2} R_2$. Thus, considering the minimization of the above evaluation functions it follows that i) under g_2, R_3 is the unique preferred repair, ii) under g_1, there are two preferred repairs: R_1 and R_2, and iii) under g_3 all repairs are preferred. □

Definition 8. Given a database D, a set of integrity constraints $\mathcal{IC}$, a set of feasibility functions $\mathcal{F}$ and an evaluation function g, we denote with $\mathbf{R}(D, \mathcal{IC}, \mathcal{F}, g)$ the set of feasible repairs for D which are preferred with respect to g. □

In the following a set of integrity constraints with feasibility and evaluation functions will be denoted $\mathcal{IC}^{\mathcal{F},g}$. Consequently, the set of feasible, preferred repairs for a database D will be also denoted as $\mathbf{R}(D, \mathcal{IC}^{\mathcal{F},g})$. Moreover, constant functions can be deleted as they are useless and the following notations will be used: i) $\mathbf{R}(D, \mathcal{IC}^{\mathcal{F}}) = \mathbf{R}(D, \mathcal{IC}, \mathcal{F})$ and ii) $\mathbf{R}(D, \mathcal{IC}^g) = \mathbf{R}(D, \mathcal{IC}, \{\}, g)$.

3.2 Feasible Preferred Answers

The computation of consistent answers in the presence of feasibility conditions and preference criteria is carried out by only considering repairs which satisfy integrity constraints and feasibility functions and minimize the value of the evaluation function.

Definition 9. Given a database schema $\mathcal{DS}$ and a set of integrity constraints $\mathcal{IC}^{\mathcal{F},g}$, a query over $(\mathcal{DS}, \mathcal{IC}^{\mathcal{F},g})$ is a tuple of the form $Q = \langle p, \phi \rangle$ where ϕ is a $\mathcal{SNR\text{-}DAT}^{\neg}$ program (or equivalently, a $\mathcal{S\text{-}RC}$ formula or a $\mathcal{RA}$ expression) over $\mathcal{DS}$ and p.
The result of the application of Q to a database D over $\mathcal{DS}$ is

$$Q(D, \mathcal{IC}^{\mathcal{F},g}) = \{ P \mid \exists R \in \mathbf{R}(D, \mathcal{IC}^{\mathcal{F},g}) \text{ and } \phi(R(D), P) \text{ is true } \} \qquad \square$$

Obviously, for any consistent relational database D, $Q(D)$ is unique as there is only one repair, namely the empty repair. Since in the presence of integrity constraints, the query is multi-valued, the semantics of queries is given by considering the set of repaired databases under brave and cautious reasoning.

Definition 10. Let $Q = \langle p, \phi \rangle$ be a $\mathcal{SNR\text{-}DAT}^{\neg}$ (or equivalently, a $\mathcal{S\text{-}RC}$ or a $\mathcal{RA}$) query over a database D with integrity constraints $\mathcal{IC}^{\mathcal{F},g}$. The deterministic answer to the query Q over D and $\mathcal{IC}^{\mathcal{F},g}$ is

- $\bigcup_{R \in \mathbf{R}(D,\mathcal{IC}^{\mathcal{F},g})} Q(R(D))$, under brave reasoning, and
- $\bigcap_{R \in \mathbf{R}(D,\mathcal{IC}^{\mathcal{F},g})} Q(R(D))$, under cautious reasoning.

whereas the (deterministic) consistent answer is

- $Q^+(D, \mathcal{IC}^{\mathcal{F},g}) = \bigcap_{R \in \mathbf{R}(D,\mathcal{IC}^{\mathcal{F},g})} Q(R(D))$, and
- $Q^u(D, \mathcal{IC}^{\mathcal{F},g}) = \bigcup_{R \in \mathbf{R}(D,\mathcal{IC}^{\mathcal{F},g})} Q(R(D)) - Q^+(D, \mathcal{IC}^{\mathcal{F},g})$. □

Thus, answers under brave and cautious reasoning and consistent answers are computed in the same way by only considering repairs which satisfy feasibility conditions and are preferred w.r.t. the evaluation function.

4 Complexity and Expressiveness

The introduction of feasibility and preference conditions reduces the number of repairs to be considered. In this section the expressive power and complexity of relational queries over databases with integrity constraints, feasibility and preference conditions is studied.

Definition 11. Let D be a database over $\mathcal{DS}$ with integrity constraints $\mathcal{IC}^F$, and $Q = \langle p, \psi \rangle$ a search query over $(D, \mathcal{IC}^F)$. Then the corresponding boolean query is $bool(Q) = \langle bool(p), \psi \rangle = \langle q, \psi \cup \{q \leftarrow p(X)\} \rangle$ over $(D, \mathcal{IC}^F)$, whereas the corresponding optimization query is $opt(Q)$ over $(D, \mathcal{IC}^F)$ with $opt \in \{min, max\}$. □

The following fact states that optimization queries over databases with integrity constraints and feasibility conditions can be expressed as search queries over databases with integrity constraints, feasibility and preference conditions and vice versa.

Fact 1 Let D be a database over $\mathcal{DS}$, then for every optimization query $min(Q) = \langle min(p), \psi \rangle$ (resp. $max(Q) = \langle max(p), \psi \rangle$) over $(D, \mathcal{IC}^F)$ there exists an equivalent search query $Q = \langle p, \psi \rangle$ over $D, \mathcal{IC}^{\mathcal{F},g}$ with $g = |R(D)[p]|$ (resp. $g = -|R(D)[p]|$) and vice versa. □

Thus $opt(Q)$ over $(D, \mathcal{IC}^{\mathcal{F}})$ can be expressed as a search query $\langle p, \psi \rangle$ over $(D, \mathcal{IC}^{\mathcal{F},g})$ where $g(R, D) = |\{x | p(x) \in R(D)\}|$ if $opt = min$ and $g(R, D) = -|\{x | p(x) \in R(D)\}|$ if $opt = max$. It is important to note that equivalence stated by the previous fact refers to queries, but it does not hold for repairs. Moreover, since we are here interested in queries, in the following we concentrate on boolean, search and optimization queries over databases with integrity constraints and feasibility conditions. Therefore, we study the (data) complexity and the expressive power of relational queries (expressed in $\mathcal{RA}$, $\mathcal{S}$-$\mathcal{RC}$ or $\mathcal{SNR}$-$\mathcal{DAT}^{\neg}$) over databases with universally quantified integrity constraints and polynomial feasibility conditions ($\forall$-$\mathcal{FOC}^{\mathcal{FP}}$). The expressive power of a query language $\mathcal{L}_1$ and a constraint language $\mathcal{L}_2$, denoted by $\mathcal{EXPR}(\mathcal{L}_1, \mathcal{L}_2)$, will be compared with a complexity class $\mathcal{C}$ through the collections of queries $\mathbf{Q}_{\mathcal{L}_1}$

over databases in $\mathbf{D}$ and constraints in $\mathbf{IC}_{\mathcal{L}_2}$ and the collection of queries $\mathbf{Q}_{\mathcal{C}}$ over databases in $\mathbf{D}$ defining problems in $\mathcal{C}$. It is worth noting that we concentrate on the study of the expressive power of queries and constraints as $\mathcal{EXPR}(\mathcal{L}_1, \mathcal{L}_2) \supseteq \mathcal{C}$ implies that the complexity of queries in $\mathcal{L}_1$ and constraints in $\mathcal{L}_2$ is, in the general case, no lesser than $\mathcal{C}$. While the class of (search) queries expressed by means of a language $\mathcal{L}$ will be compared with complexity classes expressing search problems, the classes of boolean and optimization queries expressed in a language $\mathcal{L}$, and denoted, respectively, by $bool(\mathcal{L})$ and $opt(\mathcal{L})$, will be compared with complexity classes defined for decision and optimization problems, respectively. Moreover, for boolean queries we consider the expressive power of queries under brave reasoning (denoted by $\mathcal{EXPR}^\exists$) and cautious reasoning (denoted by $\mathcal{EXPR}^\forall$), whereas for search and optimization queries we only consider brave reasoning. We first consider the general class of constraints and next a restricted class consisting of monotonic constraints.

4.1 $\forall$-$\mathcal{FOC}$ Integrity Constraints

Theorem 1. *Let D be a database, $\mathcal{IC}^\mathcal{F}$ a set of $\forall$-$\mathcal{FOC}^{\mathcal{FP}}$ integrity constraints, with feasibility functions $\mathcal{F}$ and A a ground atom. Then,*

1. *checking if there exists a $\mathcal{F}$-feasible repair R for D s. t. $A \in R(D)$ is Σ_2^p-complete;*
2. *checking if $A \in R(D)$ for all $\mathcal{F}$-feasible repairs R of D is Π_2^p-complete.* □

The expressive power of relational queries over database with feasible integrity constraints is now discussed.

Theorem 2.

1. $\mathcal{EXPR}^\exists(bool(\mathcal{S}\text{-}\mathcal{RC}), \forall\text{-}\mathcal{FOC}^{\mathcal{FP}}) = \Sigma_2^p$,
2. $\mathcal{EXPR}^\forall(bool(\mathcal{S}\text{-}\mathcal{RC}), \forall\text{-}\mathcal{FOC}^{\mathcal{FP}}) = \Pi_2^p$. □

Therefore, all Σ_2^p and Π_2^p decision problems can be expressed using relational queries over databases with feasible integrity constraints.

4.2 Monotonic Integrity Constraints

A subset of integrity constraints is now considered with a lesser expressive power and computational complexity. The characteristic of this class is that it is not possible to have two different repairs in which the same atom is inserted and deleted. Moreover, in the general case, checking if a set of integrity constraints satisfies such a condition is undecidable and, therefore, syntactic restrictions are introduced.

Definition 12. *Let D be a database over $\mathcal{DS}$ and $\mathcal{IC}^\mathcal{F}$ a set of feasible integrity constraints. $\mathcal{IC}^F$ is said to be strict monotonic if after rewriting $\mathcal{IC}$ as denials, for each predicate symbol p in $\mathcal{DS}$, appearing in $\mathcal{IC}$ as both positive and negated, there is in F a feasibility function of one of the following forms: i) $|R^-[p]| \leq 0$, or ii) $|R^+[p]| \leq 0$.* □

For instance, the integrity constraint of Example 1 is strict monotonic since all predicate symbols appear only once.

$\forall\text{-}\mathcal{FOC}^{\mathcal{FP}^+}$ will denote the subset of $\forall\text{-}\mathcal{FOC}^{\mathcal{FP}}$ whose integrity constraints are strict monotonic.

Theorem 3. *Let D be a database, $\mathcal{IC}^{\mathcal{F}}$ a set of strict monotonic, integrity constraints and A a ground atoms. Then,*
1. *checking if there exists a $\mathcal{F}$-feasible repair R for D s. t. $A \in R(D)$ is $\mathcal{NP}$-complete;*
2. *checking if $A \in R(D)$ for all $\mathcal{F}$-feasible repairs R for D is $co\mathcal{NP}$-complete.* □

The following theorem states that $\mathcal{NP}$ and $co\mathcal{NP}$ boolean queries can be expressed by means of boolean $\mathcal{S}\text{-}\mathcal{RC}$ queries over databases with strict monotonic integrity constraints.

Theorem 4.
1. $\mathcal{EXPR}^{\exists}(bool(\mathcal{S}\text{-}\mathcal{RC}), \forall\text{-}\mathcal{FOC}^{\mathcal{FP}^+}) = \mathcal{NP}$,
2. $\mathcal{EXPR}^{\forall}(bool(\mathcal{S}\text{-}\mathcal{RC}), \forall\text{-}\mathcal{FOC}^{\mathcal{FP}^+}) = co\mathcal{NP}$. □

The next corollary states that $\mathcal{NP}$ search and $\mathcal{NP}$ optimization queries can be expressed by means of search and optimization $\mathcal{S}\text{-}\mathcal{RC}$ queries over databases with monotonic integrity constraints.

Corollary 1.
1. $\mathcal{EXPR}^{\exists}(\mathcal{S}\text{-}\mathcal{RC}, \forall\text{-}\mathcal{FOC}^{\mathcal{FP}^+}) = \mathcal{NPMVQ}$,
2. $\mathcal{EXPR}^{\exists}(opt(\mathcal{S}\text{-}\mathcal{RC}), \forall\text{-}\mathcal{FOC}^{\mathcal{FP}^+}) = OPT\,\mathcal{NPMVQ}$. □

Moreover, from Fact 1 it follows that $\mathcal{NP}$ optimization queries can be expressed by means of $\mathcal{S}\text{-}\mathcal{RC}$ queries over monotonic integrity constraints with feasibility conditions and preference criteria. In the previous corollary used the existential quantifier have been used as the output is nondeterministic, i.e. i) for search queries the output is a relation satisfying the constraints and the feasibility conditions and ii) for optimization queries the output relation also minimizes the value of the evaluation function.

5 Conclusions

The main contribution of this paper consists in the proposal of an easy mechanism for expressing and managing feasibility conditions and preference criteria that, combined with the use of integrity constraints, represents a powerful tool for repairing input databases and for formulating powerful queries over inconsistent databases. The complexity and the expressive power of the proposed approach have been investigated which resulted suitable for expressing decision, search and optimization problems. Indeed, it has been proved that decision problems in the second level of the polynomial hierarchy can be expressed by means of relational calculus queries over database with integrity constraints and feasibility conditions.

References

1. Abiteboul, S., Hull, R., Vianu V. *Foundations of Databases.* Addison-Wesley, 1994.
2. Argaval, S., Keller, A. M., Wiederhold, G., and Saraswat, K., Flexible Relation: an Approach for Integrating Data from Multiple, Possibly Inconsistent Databases. *ICDE*, 1995.
3. Arenas, M., Bertossi, L., Chomicki, J., Consistent Query Answers in Inconsistent Databases. *PODS*, pp. 68–79, 1999.
4. Arenas, M., Bertossi, L., Chomicki, J., Specifying and Querying Database repairs using Logic Programs with Exceptions. *FQAS*, pp. 27-41, 2000.
5. Brewka, G., Eiter, T., Preferred Answer Sets for Extended Logic Programs. *AI*, 109(1-2): 297–356, 1999.
6. A. Cali, A.,Calvanese, D., De Giacomo, G., Lenzerini, M., Data Integration under Integrity Constraints, *CAiSE02*, pp. 262-279", 2002.
7. Cali, A., Lembo, D., Rosati, R., On the decidability and complexity of query answering over inconsistent and incomplete databases. *PODS*, pp. 260-271, 2003.
8. Chomicki, J., Querying with Intrinsic Preferences. *EDBT*, pp. 34-51, 2002.
9. Dung, P.M., Integrating Data from Possibly Inconsistent Databases. *CoopIS*, 1996.
10. Eiter, T., Gottlob, G., and Mannila, H., Disjunctive Datalog. *ACM Transactions on Database Systems*, 22(3), 364–418, 1997
11. Greco, S., Saccà, D., Search and Optimization Problems in Datalog. *Computational Logic: Logic Programming and Beyond*, pp. 61-82, 2002.
12. Greco, S., Zumpano E., Querying Inconsistent Database *LPAR Conf.*, pp. 308-325, 2000.
13. Greco, G., Greco, S., Zumpano E., A Logic Programming Approach to the Integration, Repairing and Querying of Inconsistent Databases. *ICLP Conf.*, pp. 348-364, 2001.
14. Greco, G., Greco, S., Zumpano E., A Logical Framework for Querying and Repairing Inconsistent Databases. *IEEE Trans. Knowl. Data Eng.* 15(6): 1389-1408, 2003.
15. Greco, S., Sirangelo, C., Trubitsyna, I., Zumpano, E., Preferred Repairs for Inconsistent Databases. *IDEAS Conf.*, pp. 202-211, 2003.
16. Grant, J., Subrahmanian, V.S., Reasoning in Inconsistent Knowledge Bases. *TKDE* 7(1): 177-189, 1995.
17. Johnson, D.S., A Catalog of Complexity Classes. In *Handbook of Theoretical Computer Science*, Vol. 1, J. van Leewen (ed.), North-Holland, 1990.
18. Lin, J., A Semantics for Reasoning Consistently in the Presence of Inconsistency. *Artificial Intelligence*, 86(1): 75-95, 1996.
19. Marek, V.W., Truszczynski, M. Revision Programming. *Theoretical Computer Science* 190(2), pp. 241-277, 1998.
20. Papadimitriou, C.H., *Computational Complexity.* Addison-Wesley, 1994.
21. Sakama, C., Tnoue, K., Priorized logic programming and its application to commonsense reasoning. *Artificial Intelligence*, No. 123, pp. 185-222, 2000.
22. Selman, A., A taxonomy of complexity classes of functions. *JCSS* 48:327-381, 1994.
23. Ullman, J. K., *Principles of Database and Knowledge-Base Systems*, Vol. 1, Computer Science Press, 1988.
24. Wijsen J., Condensed Representation of Database Repairs for Consistent Query Answering, *ICDT*, pp. 378-393, 5003.
25. Zang, Y., Foo, N., Answer sets for prioritized logic programs. *ILPS*, pp. 69-83, 1997.

An Active Functional Intensional Database

Paul Swoboda and John Plaice

School of Computer Science and Engineering
The University of New South Wales
UNSW SYDNEY NSW 2052, Australia
{pswoboda,plaice}@cse.unsw.edu.au

Abstract. We introduce a new kind of functional database that unifies concepts from the realms of publish-subscribe middleware, pervasive computing, and intensional programming. The AFID (Active Functional Intensional Database) Project allows the distribution of both pervasive context and related, versioned content, and offers the means of effecting a client's interaction with both. The AFID data model builds on existing infrastructure from the Intense project for the efficient manipulation and networked distribution of intensional context, adding the ability to encode multiple versions of any complex entity, where each version may vary in both content and structure, at any level of granularity. Further, the system ensures that clients may listen to structured, minimal changes in *specific logical versions* of encoded entities, as they occur, whenever any change is made to the total entity encoded in the database.

1 Introduction

This paper introduces a first attempt at the development of an active database that supports communities, as proposed by Buneman and Steedman [1]:

> Now is the time for a radical revision of the way we publish data on the Web. The traditional view of a database as an inert structure, only to be observed through the machinery of a query language or browser, is no longer tenable. In the future our databases and Web documents are going to become vehicles of communication between their communities of users. The challenge is to support and enable this development.

The AFID project is comprised of an *active, pervasive context server*, which doubles as a functional database, an intensional context (§2.1) and versioning library, and a client/server protocol and associated APIs for the distribution of context. This active database allows the storage and distribution of both pervasive context and contextually versioned entities, which can themselves have multiple, versioned components and arbitrary, versioned structure. Further, AFID allows both networked clients and the content on which they operate to be simultaneously versioned in a medium that blends the notions of distributed context and distributed intensional content. The client is versioned at all levels using the distributed context as a mechanism for pervasive runtime configuration management, whereas the versioned content on which the client operates can be stored in the context server itself.

The AFID system addresses another issue visited by Buneman and Steedman, that of the importance of communication via annotation:

> Our claim is that annotation is becoming a new form of communication, and that understanding and managing this new medium presents a major challenge.... Databases are rather rigid structures and typically do not provide *room* for annotations.

With AFID, distribution of both context and content uses *context operators*, a structured form of annotation, akin to the deltas of software configuration. AFID goes even further, allowing entities in the database to be *interpreted* according to an adjacent context, so that context operators applied to either the total entity or the context of interpretation result in *interpretive context operators* describing the *interpretive annotation* under interpretation.

2 Background

2.1 Intensional Programming

Intensional programming [2] refers to programs that are sensitive to a global multidimensional runtime context, which the program itself can modify. In the general case, an intensional program contains a number of versioned entities, each of which has a single valid instance under a particular global context. The set of (*versioned entity, current context*) pairs is termed an *intension*, whereas a specific, resolved version of the entity is termed an *extension*. As the program executes, intensional entities are resolved to single versions against the global context. With intensional languages, a versioned entity consists of a set of pairs of context-tagged extensional values (E_x, C_x), termed *versions*. The process of determining which of these versions should be used is termed a *best-fit*: a partial order called *refinement* [3] is defined over the set of all contexts; the context tags of an entity are compared to the global reference context C_r. The set of all tags in a versioned entity is termed a *context domain*.

The distinction between an intensional program and one that merely uses a context or pervasive data source as a polled reference for runtime configuration is that the semantics of an intensional program varies implicitly with the context, often with language-level support for versioned control flow. In the extreme case, anything with an identifier can exist in multiple versions, including all functions and data structures, as with the Perl-like language ISE [5].

2.2 Contexts and Context Operations

The Intense library [4, 6] was developed to provide a comprehensive set of generic tools for C++, Java, and Perl, to perform fast intensional versioning of arbitrary software entities with language-level constructs. In the C++ implementation, for example, templates are provided to version any existing typed entity, with support for a thread-safe pervasive runtime context. The context model used by Intense is tree-structured, with arbitrary depth and arity at each node. Each node in a context is indexed by a string *dimension*, unique to the parent node, and may optionally contain a *base value*, a scalar which can be used to reference any entity. A similarly-structured *context operator* is used to modify a context — each node in an operator may contain a new base value or a base value clearing flag ('-'), and a pruning flag ('--'). The latter prunes all subcontexts in the target context node which are not present at the corresponding node in the operator. An example application of an operator to a context is as follows:

```
<dim0:<"base0"+dim01:<"base01"+dim02:<"base02">>
["newbase"+dim0:[-+--+dim02:["newbase02"]+dim03:["newbase03"]]]
```

```
<"newbase"+dim0:<dim02:<"newbase02">+dim03:<"newbase03">>>
```

In the above, the operator (delimited, in canonical text format, by `[ ]`) inserted a new base value `"newbase"` at the root dimension of the context (delimited by `< >`), pruned and cleared the base value under dimension `dim0`, changed the base value for dimension `dim0:dim02` to `"newbase02"`, and inserted a new subcontext `dim0:dim03:<"newbase03">`. A key benefit of encoding context operators with the same structure as contexts is that we can apply them in a single recursive pass; another benefit is the fast serialization of operators for transmission in a networked environment. The context operators provided by Intense are fully associative, and can be applied efficiently to one another, to yield an operator whose effect is equivalent to applying its component operators to a context in succession.

2.3 The Æther

An *æther*, first introduced in the Intense project, is a context which *participants*, connected at any node, can use both as a contextual reference and as a structured medium for contextual discourse. The latter is achieved by sending and receiving context operators to and from the æther, modifying the æther in the process. A participant receives all operators that are applied to its own node, or to descendants of its own node. In the latter case, an operator appears to the participant as an operator relative to the participant's node. For example, if we treat the context above as an æther, participants registered at the following dimensions in the æther would see the following operators:

```
dim0:         [-+--+dim02:["newbase02"]+dim03:["newbase03"]]
dim0:dim03:   ["newbase03"]
dim0:dim02:   ["newbase02"]
dim0:dim01:   [-+--]              -- pruning
dim1:         []                  -- no change
```

Tree manipulation aside, the important innovation here is that, as a reference data structure for efficient intensional versioning, the æther and context may be used interchangeably. A typical use of an intensional participant is to recompute best-fit entities on each notification of an operator; the operator itself may be considered by the participant to see if recomputation is actually necessary. For example, a participant may consider a number of sub-æthers under its node to be intensional reference contexts. In this case, recomputation of a best-fit for an entity controlled by one of the reference contexts must only be performed if an operator affects the entity's particular context.

2.4 Æther Protocol

The Intense project includes a protocol (AEP, for Æther Protocol) and associated server and client APIs for the networked sharing of context between distributed participants. The æther server, aepd, exists in a threaded C++ implementation and is geared towards scalability in the number of networked æther participants, as well as in traffic volume, i.e., the number of context operators per second.

The latest version of AEP allows multiple participants to use the same connection, where a single connection corresponds to a single remote æther. A context operator may be optionally ignored by its originating participant, or by all participants in the same connection.

In a very large AEP-based system, context operator frequencies can occur in the range of hundreds to bursts of tens of thousands per second. In this case, it is often not feasible to rebroadcast all operators to listening participants. Instead, the æther server makes use of the full associativity of context operators, applying successive operators to one another between *associative fences*, prior to rebroadcast of the resultant operator to listeners. To this end, a participant is able to label a submitted operator as a fence, meaning it cannot be added to previous operators, or have successive operators added to it. The æther server employs a number of internal operator queuing mechanisms to handle the application of operators to one another.

To facilitate the processing of context operators on both the client and server sides of AEP, integer sequences are employed. The AEP client API generates a unique sequence for every client/participant connection, and the æther server maintains a sequence for all client-server operations. In this manner, a client is able to tell if a rebroadcast operator is or contains an operator which the client submitted, i.e., if the server sequence for the rebroadcast operator is equal to or greater than the server sequence number given to the client's operator.

The AEP design is abstract, in that it requires a concrete implementation in some host protocol. The concrete implementations supplied with Intense include a shared (threaded) implementation that simply passes protocol token objects between client and server threads. Also provided are a number of stream-based implementations; these include, in order of efficiency, implementations using direct binary serialization of protocol token objects, XDR (from Sun RPC, architecture-independent) serialization, and AETP, a textual, stream-parsing implementation for maximum client-server compatibility. With stream-based AEP connections, a mechanism is provided to negotiate the fastest of these modes. Where necessary, it will be possible to encapsulate AEP in OORPC transport layer such as CORBA.

3 AFID: Motivation and Intuition

To date, no-one has created a database that can be used both as an active context server *and* as an active storage mechanism for intensional entities, i.e., a service that can deliver updates to clients of changes in intensional entities, *as they occur*. Some networked directory services such as LDAP and various publish/subscribe middlewares do come close with respect to context distribution, although few provide active contextual updates to clients and almost none do so in the form of structured context operators or deltas. Certainly, no previously existing directory service has attempted to provide a concrete means for the interpretation of structured directory data itself as an intensional context. Tools such as XQuery do allow us to perform functional data extraction from trees, but the infrastructure on which they operate (i.e., XML "databases") is by no means suitable for efficient intensional computing.

The inability to use existing database infrastructure in implementation lends us a bit of freedom in design. The desired system should not only encapsulate the context used to version intensional clients, as well as the intensional content, but it should use the same medium of interaction to effect changes to both. Further, a client should be able to listen to a networked context either as an interpreted intensional entity, or as a pure context (an uninterpreted, atomic entity). Since the shared context is active, and both content and pure context are encoded in it, changes in either can be used to drive the execution of the participants. In the general case, an intensional participant should only have to deal with changes to the particular logical version of itself or the data on which it operates. The existing Æther Protocol and associated æther server have been modified to achieve these purposes.

The central intuition for AFID is that the set of (E_x, C_x) version pairs that comprise a context domain can be encoded in the Intense context structure, as subcontexts of a node representing the domain. Under a domain node are nodes for each version in the domain; each version node contains one or more nodes for its tag contexts, as well as a node for its versioned content.

Given a reference context, a domain node is *interpreted*, which means that one or more of the version nodes below it will be selected, and the content nodes below each of the selected versions will be used as the content. The interpretation process continues recursively on the content nodes, until uninterpretable (pure context) nodes are reached.

A second intuition is that we can aggregate the components of a compound intensional entity, simply by using further dimensions in or above the same context to define structure and ordering of various components, as is common practice in structured markup languages such as XML.

A straightforward means of aggregating ordered components using the same context node is through the concatenation of the interpretations of lexicographically ordered dimensions, termed a *join*. Figure 1 shows an entity composed of multiple intensional components, each of which is named by a single dimension, and is versioned with the dimensions `lang`, `size`, and `rev`.

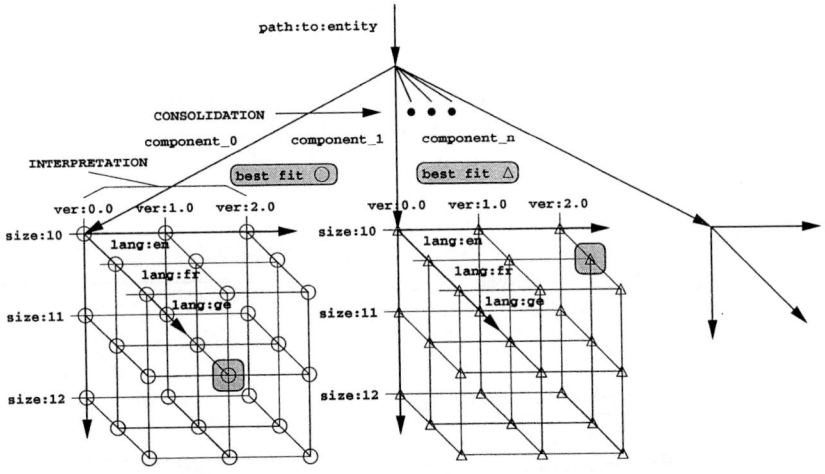

Fig. 1. Accessing sequenced components of an intensional entity under lexicographically ordered subdimensions

The final and most important intuition is that we can encode the structure of an entity in a hierarchical fashion, using nodes to denote the concatenation of ordered subcomponents, as well as to denote best-fits of intensional subcomponents. In this manner, we can easily encode entities whose content *and structure* can be simultaneously versioned by the same adjacent reference context. Under one logical version of an encoded document, a section might be omitted, added, or rearranged, and certain elements of content might appear in a different format or language. Significantly, due to the fact that a single logical version of an entity is represented by a portion of the context encoding the entity, the *difference* between two logical versions can be directly represented with a *context operator*. The resulting system can be used as an infrastructure for arbitrary intensional tools, with several key benefits — the abstraction of intensional content into a structured database, the networked distribution of the content with the possibility of contextual collaboration between interacting clients, and the simultaneous versioning of both the application and content with the same medium.

4 AFID: A Structural Overview

The AFID server is derived from the Intense æther server codebase, and adds one key abstraction to the æther server: the *context interpretation*. This is the mapping of a reference context to specific portions of an interpreted context or æther, as discussed in Section 3, where the æther has been encoded with a functional mapping at each interpreted node. An important feature of AFID's context interpretation is that the result of an interpretation is another context that *parallels* the context rooted at the interpreted node; i.e., the interpretation has its root at the same dimension in a parallel context. While the result of an interpretation is a context, the semantics of each interpretation is list-valued, where the elements of the list are references to descendent nodes in the interpreted context, as shown in Figure 2. This allows the result of an interpretation to be passed to a parent interpretation, while also allowing the result to denote a portion of the context rooted at the interpreted node.

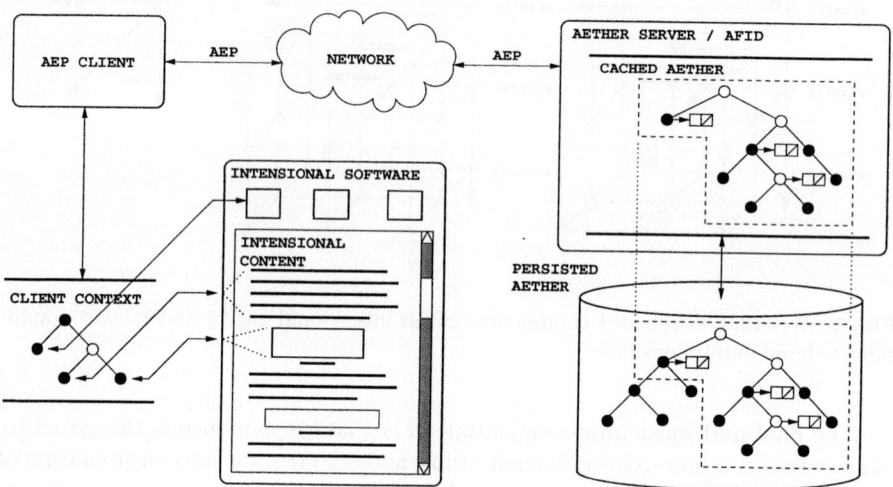

Fig. 2. The AFID architecture

The key interpretations in the first version of AFID are *literal*, *join*, and *best-fit*. A literal interpretation yields a single-element list comprised of a reference to the interpreted context node, and does not require any special encoding in the interpreted node. A join interpretation concatenates the lists resulting from the interpretation of its argument parts. A best-fit interpretation is a best-fit selection of a single value from the interpretations of all subcontexts of the dimension versions, where each version is comprised of an interpreted *value* branch and an interpreted list of *tag contexts*, comprising the context domain.

For the transmission of context operators to an interpreting client, the server should only send branches of the interpreted entity that correspond to actual content. Further, we stipulate that reinterpretation of the partial entity at the client end must produce the same results as the initial interpretation in the server. For example, in a best-fit interpretation, it is unnecessary to send the tag branches under each version, or to send any part of non-best-fit versions. If an

Table 1. AFID Interpretations

Function	Semantics
$I(C)$	identity — equal to a single-element list $\{C\}$
$J(C)$	a list of the joined interpretations of all subcontexts of C, in lexicographic order of their dimensions
$B(C_{ref}, C)$	an empty or single-element list $\{C_{best}\}$, where C_{best} is the interpretation of the `value` dimension under the best-fit subcontext of the `versions` dimension. The tags of the context domain are formed from the interpretation of each of `versions`:seq_i:`tag`, and the best-fit is performed with respect to C_{ref}.
$N(C_{ref}, C)$	a possibly-empty list of near-fit contexts $\{C_i\}$, where the context domain for the near-fit is formed as per $B(C_{ref}, C)$.
$F(C_{ref}, C)$	an empty or single-element list consisting of the first element returned by $N(C_{ref}, C)$.

interpretation changes structurally, we generate a context operator that prunes removed branches. In general, a reinterpretation creates a context operator that transforms the previous interpretation to the new one.

We can often avoid total recomputation of an encoded entity, when changes are made to a single portion of the entity in the database. There are two basic varieties of changes we must consider, (extensional) changes made to the total encoded entity, and changes in the reference context used for interpretation.

In the first case, where some portion of the encoded entity is modified, recomputation need only be propagated up the context until either the root node of the interpretation is reached, or until an interpretation node is reached, whose result remains unchanged. The difference between a previous interpretation and the result of this smaller recomputation may still be sent to a listening interpreter in the form of a minimal context operator.

In the second case, where changes are made to the intensional reference context, reinterpretation must of course be performed again from the root of the encoded entity; however, since only intensional interpretation nodes are affected by a change in context, we need only recompute those branches of the entity that contain intensional nodes. In each interpretation node, we use a count of all context-sensitive interpretations at or beneath the node; where subinterpretations are considered, only those branches containing a non-zero intensional node count are reinterpreted.

The first version of AFID supports the interpretations shown in Table 1. We add two new intensional interpretations, *near-fit* and *first-fit*.

5 Applications

5.1 Networked Intensional Desktop Environments

A clear application of the functional intensional database is in the simultaneous versioning of applications and content in a local-area setting. The corporate and classroom environments could both benefit tremendously from such infrastructure, with fine-grained runtime configuration management of applications. Because the Intense framework is based on intensional logic, desktop users can set personal preferences in local contexts, that may or may not be overridden by controlling applications on servers. A teacher might invoke changes in the context controlling a document being viewed by an entire class, for example advancing a presentation to the next section, with individual students following the document in another language, or without images, or in a certain font. Likewise, a document or database posted in AFID on a corporate intranet could support interpretations specific to the department or profession of the user who views it.

5.2 Collaborative Content Authoring

Using AFID, collaborative annotation, as suggested by Buneman and Steedman, is directly realisable for both concrete and abstract or programmatic content.

By *concrete content*, we mean content *processed* by applications, such as structured textual documents, database records, images, and multimedia content. Concrete content can be annotated in realtime by any number of authors, each of whom may listen to changes in either the raw content, or to changes in specific logical versions (contextual interpretations) of the content. The annotations of one or more authors, in the form of context operations, may or may not be perceived as deltas in the interpretations of any specific listener.

By *abstract content*, we mean content that, while encoded in the AFID mechanism with structure, requires further interpretation on the part of a listener, to be rendered to concrete content. As with the latter, annotations can be submitted collaboratively, but are perceived selectively under different interpretations.

By *programmatic content*, we mean manipulation of structured, AFID-encoded software constructs, which can be used by interpreting clients, and may or may not govern the execution of a client. A simple example would be the encoding in AFID of an algorithm as an object-oriented data structure. This is very simple to achieve, but has powerful applications — multiple clients can thus annotate the encoded algorithm, while differing interpreters are free to perceive and subsequently apply/use it, under differing contexts.

5.3 Versioned Software Repositories

An obvious use of AFID is as a repository for *entire* software projects, where each file in the project can be versioned with arbitrary dimensionality. Changes to individual files, components of files, and the additional, removal or reorganization of directory structure can all be effected with context operators; aspects such as (ordinary) revision control, branching, and release tagging *come for free*.

6 Future Directions

We leave open the possibility for interpretations that operate on arguments other than entire subcontexts (for example, programmatic case-statement functions, that depend either on the reference context or on specific base values in the interpreted context).

Although the primary use of context interpretation is the extraction from the encoded entity of a set of literal-interpretation "leaf" contexts, there exists the possibility of *higher-order context interpretation*, as is understood in the functional programming sense. Since the `interpret` dimension in an interpreted node can itself contain an arbitrarily complex subcontext, we can conceive of best-fit interpretations, or in the general case, interpretations encoding interpretations.

An abstraction currently being developed is the notion of a *disjunct interpretation*, essentially an adjacent function definition for context interpretations. With this scheme, the intensional qualities of an interpretation node can be specified by supplying arguments; the interpretation can be referenced by dimension from other interpretations with the equivalent of a function call.

A generic, server-side scripting API is also being developed to allow manipulations of interpretations, using `Perl` as the scripting framework. Such code fragments would be stored in the context directly, and are compiled on insertion into the æther, to be executed efficiently during interpretation.

References

1. Peter Buneman and Mark Steedman. Annotation – The new medium of communication. *Grand Challenges for Computing Research*, October 2002.
http://www.nesc.ac.uk/esi/events/Grand_Challenges/panelb/b2.pdf.
2. A.A. Faustini and W.W. Wadge. Intensional programming. In J.C. Boudreaux, B.W. Hamil and R. Jenigan, eds., *The Role of Languages in Problem Solving 2*, Elsevier North-Holland, 1987.
3. John Plaice and William W. Wadge. A new approach to version control. *IEEE Transactions on Software Engineering* 19(3):368–276, March 1993.
4. Paul Swoboda. *A Formalisation and Implementation of Distributed Intensional Programming*. Ph.D. Thesis, The University of New South Wales, Sydney, Australia, 2004.
5. Paul Swoboda and William W. Wadge. Vmake, ISE and IRCS: General tools for the intensionalization of software systems. In M. Gergatsoulis and P. Rondogiannis, eds., *Intensional Programming II*, World-Scientific, 2000.
6. Paul Swoboda and John Plaice. A new approach to distributed context-aware computing. In A. Ferscha, H. Hoertner and G. Kotsis, eds., *Advances in Pervasive Computing*. Austrian Computer Society, 2004. ISBN 3-85403-176-9.

Optimal Deployment of Triggers for Detecting Events

Manish Bhide, Ajay Gupta, Mukul Joshi, and Mukesh Mohania

IBM India Research Laboratory
Block-1 IIT Delhi, Hauz Khas, New Delhi-110016
{abmanish,agupta,mukuljos,mkmukesh}@in.ibm.com

Abstract: In active databases, rules are represented in the form of ECA (event-condition-action). Database events can be detected by defining triggers on the underlying application databases. Many-a-times, temporal conditions that limit the validity period of the event are associated with the ECA rule. The performance of the database can get adversely affected if such temporal constraints are checked (either at the application level or at database level) for every transaction (event) irrespective of whether that transaction (event) has occurred within the said time interval. This drawback can be avoided by optimizing the temporal constraints associated with the sub-events of a composite event based on the semantics of the composite event operators. This paper describes such an algorithm that optimizes the temporal constraints associated with (composite) events and improves the efficiency of the databases by creating and destroying triggers dynamically such that the semantics of the event is unchanged. The efficiency of the technique is validated by our experimental results.

1 Introduction

1.1 Motivation

In active databases [1,8], rules are represented in ECA (event-condition-action) format. Relational databases incorporate active functionality in the form of database triggers. These triggers also have an ECA format where the event can be any update, delete or insert transaction executed on the database. The condition and action part of the trigger can consist of SQL statements, which can be used to check conditions on the database state. The presence of a trigger changes the query plan [4] making it more complex resulting in increased execution time of queries. Conventional database can handle efficiently a maximum of 20 database triggers. Beyond that, the performance of the database deteriorates and it is not advisable to use such large number of triggers. If the ECA rules are to be represented in terms of database triggers then in any practical scenario, the number of database trigger are quite large making the use of such a mechanism unrealistic.

Many-a-times the ECA rules have temporal constraints associated with them, which limit the time period in which the rule is active or the time period in which an event can occur. These temporal constraints could be in the form of lifespan of the ECA rule or could be a lifespan of the event in the ECA rule. An example of such a rule is: "Notify the security manger if a critical error is reported on a weekend". In this rule the event (notification of an error) has a temporal constraint that it should occur only on a weekend. In conventional system, triggers reside on the database permanently irrespective of the presence of temporal constraints. To the best of our knowledge, none of the existing systems make use of these temporal constraints to restrict the number of triggers defined on the databases. In this paper we present a system that can optimize the lifespan of the events and can create and destroy such triggers dynamically such that the performance of the databases is not compromised. The composite events with temporal constraints can get quite complex which might lead to inefficient use of triggers. Such rules are widely used in Business Intelligence systems [1,9], Workflow systems [10] and other database applications. We provide an example of an employee evaluation process in a company. An evaluation process can have the following steps:

1. **Event E1**: Initial notification of evaluation sent by Manager to employees. This has to happen between the 15th and 20th of December each year.
2. **Event E2**: Suggestions/Feedback (if any) of employees to Manager. The employee can provide a feedback within 2 days of receiving the initial notification.
3. **Event E3**: Final Notification of evaluation sent by Manager to Employee. This has to happen between the 18th and 22nd of December each year.
4. **Event E4**: Final signed evaluation by employee and Manager. This should happen latest by the 28th of December and should happen within 7 days of receiving the final evaluation i.e., event E3.

This entire process happens online, and all these events are marked by an insert/update in a database. Hence these events can be detected using database triggers. When the final process is completed a mail is sent to the Director. This entire process is a composite event. In the above example, an employee may or may not provide the suggestion to the manager i.e., event E2 may not occur. Hence the final composite event is: AND(OR(SEQUENCE(E1,E2,E3), SEQUENCE(E1,E3)), E4). If the triggers are defined using the given lifespan, then it will lead to a sub-optimal definition of triggers.

1.2 Contributions of this Paper

In this paper we present an efficient system for detecting events defined in ECA rules. Specifically we address the following research problems:
1. How to optimally define the triggers on the databases so that the triggers are present on the database only when necessary.
2. How to optimize the temporal constraints defined on the triggers dynamically at run time based on the history of other events taking part in the composite events.
3. How to make use of these temporal constraints to create and destroy the triggers on the databases.

In Section 2 we outline the prior art and some of the terms used in this paper. Section 3 describes the architecture and the algorithm used in our optimization process. We present our performance results in Section 4 and Section 5 concludes the paper.

2 Preliminaries

2.1 Related Work

In active system, situations (events) are continuously monitored to initiate appropriate actions in response to their occurrences [12]. In commercial database systems (such as DB2 [7], Oracle [11]), the limited active functionality can be achieved by defining triggers on database tables. Current systems detect events with temporal constraints by defining a trigger and checking the time of occurrence of the event using a User Defined Function (UDF) or application code. These database systems do not support a mechanism to create and destroy triggers dynamically based on a temporal condition.

There are many research database prototypes where productions rules have been integrated in a database system that provides features like integrity constraints enforcement, triggers etc. In POSTGRES [13], Ariel [6] and Starburst systems, rules are explicitly triggered by events (insertions, deletions, or updates on a particular table). In Starburst, a rule may specify more than one triggering operation on the same table and the rule is triggered when any of the operations occur. None of these systems provide temporal conditions on events and rules i.e., rules and events that have lifespan. The HiPAC project [5] allows by far the most complex triggering events (including database, transaction and temporal) of any database rule language, but it has not been implemented fully in the database systems, particularly; it does not support temporal conditions and timing constraints on rules and events. Hence the current state of the art does not offer any mechanism to handle ECA rules with temporal constraints.

2.2 Definitions

We now outline some of the keywords that are used in the rest of the paper.

Primitive Event: An event that cannot be split into smaller events is called a primitive event.
Composite Event: When multiple events are combined using composition operators like AND, OR, NOT, SEQUENCE, TIMES etc. to form a single event the resultant event is called as a composite event.
Lifespan of an Event: If an event has temporal conditions that restrict the time interval in which the event can occur then such an event is said to have a lifespan. The lifespan of an event is expressed in terms of an interval of time.
Time Span of a Composite Event: Composite events can have an additional type of temporal constraint that restricts the time span within which its participating events can occur, so that the composite event is said to be true. For example consider the

composite event "If a login failure is reported thrice within a time span of one hour on a weekend". This is a composite event where the event "login failure is reported" is combined using the operator TIMES. This composite event has a lifespan [00:00 hours Saturday, 23:59 hours Sunday]. In addition to this there is an additional temporal constraint that the events should occur within one hour of each other. Such a temporal constraint is called as time span of the composite event.

3 Architecture of the System

The architecture of our system is shown in Figure 1. As explained earlier, commercial database cannot detect composite events. Such events are detected by an application that uses database triggers to detect the primitive events taking part in the composite event. Our system consists of a java application that optimizes the lifespan of the primitive events and uses these lifespan to create and destroy the triggers dynamically using a JDBC connection to the database. The ECA rule given by the user forms the input to our system. We now describe the various components of our system and its optimization algorithm.

1) **Temporal Condition Identifier**: This component takes the ECA representation of the rule and it identifies the presence of (a) a lifespan of an event and (b) the

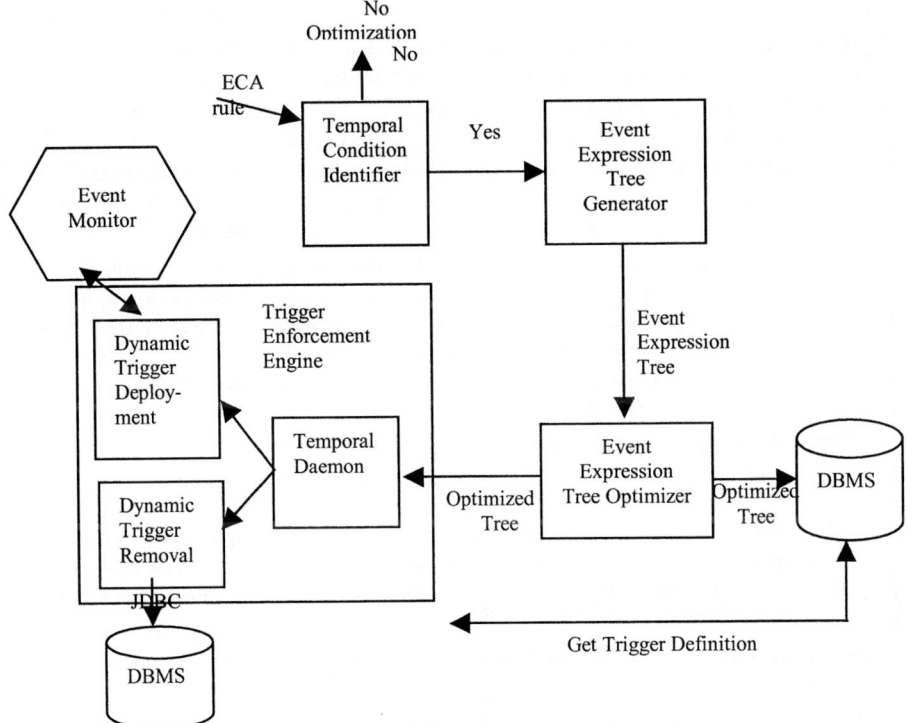

Fig. 1. Architecture of the system

time span of the composite event (and composition operator). If a rule has any of these temporal constraints, then it is a possible candidate for optimization.

2) **Event Expression Tree Generator**: This module generates an event expression tree that denotes the execution plan (for detection) of an event. In this tree, each leaf node denotes an event that may have a lifespan and each non-leaf node denotes an operator (like AND, OR, SEQUENCE, etc.) that may have a lifespan and a time span. For example the event expression tree for a composite event OR(E1,E2,E3) AND E4 is shown in Figure 2.

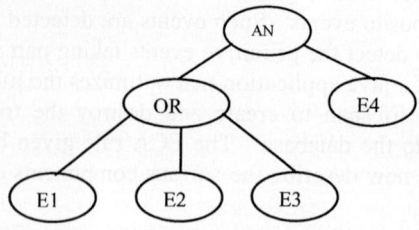

The lifespan of the events are: E_1: {13,16} E_2: {16,18} E_4: {18,21}. The event E_3 does not have a predefined lifespan. The lifespan of the AND node is {12,20} with time span 3 time units and the lifespan of the OR node is {11,17}.

Fig. 2. Event Expression Tree

1) For each child node i' of node i, check if node i' has its lifespan or not.
    a. If No, then assign the life span of node i to node i'.
    b. If yes, check if the lifespan of the child node is overlapping with the lifespan of the parent node. Then check if there is some intersection between the lifespan of the node i and i'.
        i. If Yes, then the new lifespan of node i' will be (Max(TS(B_i), TS($B_{i'}$)), Min(TS(E_i), TS($E_{i'}$))).
        ii. If No (that is both the parent lifespan and the child node lifespan do not overlap), then
            i. If the operator associated with node i is AND, SEQUENCE or TIMES, remove the sub-tree rooted at node i. Replace the node i by FALSE and re-evaluate the event-expression tree and start from step 1.
            ii. If the node is OR, remove the sub-tree rooted at node i' and also remove the edge connecting node i to i'.
2) If the node i has time span associate with it and its type is AND, then
    a. Find the maximum beginning lifespan from the set of beginning lifespan of all its child nodes. Let this be TS($B_{j'}$)
    b. Subtract the time span of node i from this timestamp TS($B_{j'}$). Let this value be $S_{i'}$. If $S_{i'}$ is negative set it to 0. An event occurring before $S_{i'}$ will not contribute to the occurrence of the event represented by node i. Hence there is no need to define the trigger of any of the child nodes of node i before this time.

Optimization Algorithm…Continues

- c. Replace the timestamp of beginning lifespan of each child node (say i') of node i by $S_{i'}$ if it is less than $S_{i'}$. If this new beginning lifespan is greater than $E_{i'}$ (i.e. the end of lifespan of node i'), then remove the sub-tree rooted at node i. Remove all the ancestors of node i (and their children) till you reach the child of an OR node or the root node. If the root node is reached (and it is not an OR node), the rule will never fire. If a child of an OR node is reached, remove its edge with its parent and execute step 1 for parent OR node.
- d. Find the minimum timestamp of ending lifetime from the set of ending lifespan of all child nodes. Let this be $TS(E_{i'})$
- e. Add the time span of node i into this timestamp $TS(E_{i'})$. Let this value be $S_{j'}$. An event occurring after $S_{j'}$ will not contribute to the occurrence of the event represented by node i. Hence there is no need to define the trigger of any of the child nodes of node i after S_i.
- f. Replace the timestamp of ending lifespan of each child node (say i') of node i by $S_{j'}$ if it is more than $S_{j'}$. If the new ending lifespan is less than $B_{i'}$ (i.e., the begin of the lifespan of node i'), then remove the sub-tree rooted at node i. Remove all the ancestors of node i (and their children) till you reach the child of an OR node or the root node. If the root node is reached (and it is not an OR node), the rule will never fire. If a child of an OR node is reached, remove that child and its edge with its parent and execute step 1 for the parent OR node. Thus the new lifespan of node $i' = (Max(B_{i'},S_{i'}), Min(E_{i'},S_{j'}))$

3) If the node i has time span associate with it and its type is SEQUENCE, then
- A. Optimise the lifespan of its child nodes (except the first node) based on the lifespan of the predecessor nodes in the sequence. Starting from the first node, for each consecutive pair of nodes i', i'' (with lifespan $(B_{i'},E_{i'})$ and $(B_{i''},E_{i''})$ respectively) in the sequence, where node i' appears earlier in the sequence, perform the following steps:
    - I. If $TS(B_{i'}) > TS(B_{i''})$, then set $TS(B_{i''}) = TS(B_{i'})$. If the event represented by node i'' happens between the time $TS(B_{i''})$ and $TS(B_{i'})$ then it won't contribute to the occurrence of the sequence. Hence the $TS(B_{i''})$ is changed to $TS(B_i)$.
    - II. If $TS(B_{i'}) > TS(B_{i''})$, then set $TS(B_{i''}) = TS(B_{i'})$. If the event represented by node i'' happens between the time $TS(B_{i''})$ and $TS(B_{i'})$ then it won't contribute to the occurrence of the sequence. Hence the $TS(B_{i''})$ is changed to $TS(B_i)$.
    - III. If $TS(B_{i''}) > TS(E_{i'})$, remove the sub-tree rooted at node i. Remove all the ancestors of node i (and their children) till you reach the child of an OR node or the root node. If the root node is reached (and it is not a OR node), the rule will never fire. If a child of an OR node is reached, remove that child and its edge with its parent and execute step 1 for the parent OR node.
    - IV. If $TS(E_{i'}) > TS(E_{i''})$, then $TS(E_{i'}) = TS(E_{i''})$,
    - V. If $TS(B_{i'}) > TS(E_{i'})$ remove the sub-tree rooted at node i. Remove all the ancestors of node i (and their children) till you reach the child of an OR node or the root node. If the root node is reached (and it is not a OR node), the rule will never fire. If a child of an OR node is reached, remove that child and its edge with its parent and execute step 1 for the parent OR node.
- B. Repeat steps of 2

4) Set the lifespan of the node i to $(Min(B_{j'}), Max(E_{k'}))$, where $B_{j'}$ and $E_{k'}$ are the minimum and maximum lifespan of all the child nodes of node i respectively. If the lifespan of node i gets changed, perform step 1 for the parent of node i.

5) Repeat steps 1 - 4 for each child of nde i till the entire tree is optimised.

Fig. 3. Optimization Algorithm

3) **Event Expression Tree Optimizer**: This module is responsible for optimizing the lifespan of each node in the tree, based on the lifespan and time span associated with its parent node. It also assigns the lifespan to all those nodes that do not have a lifespan. During optimization, the tree can be trimmed if the lifespan of a node falls outside the lifespan of its parent node. The optimization algorithm is described in Figure 3. Due to space constraints, the algorithm deals only with the AND, OR and SEQUENCE operators, but it can be easily extended to other kinds of operators. This algorithm is invoked for with the root node of the event expression tree. In this algorithm, node i' is the child node of node i. (B_i, E_i) and $(B_{i'}, E_{i'})$ are the lifespan of node i and i', respectively, where B_i is the beginning lifespan and E_i is the ending lifespan. $TS(B_i)$ and $TS(E_i)$ denotes the timestamp of beginning and ending lifespan of node i, respectively.

We now apply the optimization algorithm to the example shown in Figure 2.
Step 1: The lifespan of the E_4 node will be reduced to {18,20} as the initial lifespan {18,21} lies outside the lifespan of the parent node i.e. {12,20}. Similarly the lifespan of the OR node will be trimmed from {11,17} to {12,17}, the lifespan of event E_1 will be (15,16) that of event E_2 will be (16,17) and E_3 will be (15,17).
Step 2: AND node has a span of 3 time units.
    a. Higher timestamp of beginning lifetime will be 18 (from {12,19} and {18,19})
    b. S_i = 18-3=15. Replace the beginning lifetime of AND node by 15
    c. Lower timestamp of ending lifetime will be 17
    d. S_m= 17+3 =20. Ending lifetime of each OR and E_4 will not change
    e. New lifetime of AND node will be {15,17}
    f. Similarly, E_4 lifetime will be {18,19}

4) **Trigger Enforcement Engine**: The optimised event expression tree has a lifespan with each of the event nodes. This tree representation is fed to the temporal daemon and to the components of dynamic trigger deployment and dynamic trigger removal. The roles and responsibilities of these components are articulated below:
- **Temporal Daemon**: This is a daemon that provides facilities to register alarms and it sends notifications when an alarm fires. This daemon registers alarms for the start and the end of the lifespan for each of the events. When an alarm of the start of the lifespan fires, a notification is sent to the dynamic trigger deployment module and when an alarm for the end of the lifespan fires a notification is sent to the dynamic trigger removal module.
- **Dynamic Trigger Deployment**: When a notification is received from the temporal daemon, this module identifies the triggers that need to be activated at that time. This can be done by querying the meta-data, where the mapping between the event id and the trigger definition is stored. Once the module has the event id, it defines the trigger on the underlying application database. An exception to this is in case of the Sequence operator. Consider an event Sequence(E_1,E_2,E_3). In this composite event, if the event E_1 has not occurred then the Dynamic Trigger Deployment module will not deploy the trigger for event E_2 even if it receives a notification from the temporal daemon. The

trigger will be deployed only when the event E_1 occurs and if the lifespan of the event E_2 is active. In order to support this there is a need for an event monitor that will notify the Dynamic Trigger deployment module once the sub-events, taking part in a Sequence Composite event, fire.

- **Dynamic Trigger Removal**: If during the execution of the rule it becomes evident that a composite event can no longer be true, then the triggers defined for the events constituting the composite event can be removed provided these events are not being re-used in any other rule. The conditions under which a composite event can become false will depend on the semantics of the composite event operator. In our implementation prototype we have considered the operators AND, OR, NOT, TIMES and SEQUENCE. But the idea of identification of triggers that are no longer required based on the truth-value of the composite operator is very general and can be applied to all the composite event operators. The steps involved in the dynamic trigger removal are:

    1. This module receives a notification at the end of the lifespan of any event from the temporal daemon. When the notification is received the module removes the trigger for the expired event.

    2. It also checks the validity of the composite events in which the expired event participated. Depending on the semantics of the composite event it identifies whether the composite event can no longer be true. If the composite event can no longer fire, then the module removes the triggers that have been defined for this composite event and it also removes the alarms registered for this composite event with the temporal daemon.

Consider the example event expression given in Figure 2. The Trigger Enforcement Engine will get the optimised tree that has a lifespan for all the events in the event expression. The temporal daemon will define alarms for the start and end of the various events. Thus at time 15, the Dynamic Trigger Deployment module will receive an alarm to define trigger for event E_1 and E_3. This module will get the trigger definition from the meta-data and it will define the trigger on the application database. The Dynamic Trigger Removal component will be invoked at the expiry of a lifespan. If at time 17, the Dynamic Trigger Removal component finds that the event E_3 and the OR composite event has not occurred even once in its lifespan, then it will remove the temporal alarms for events E_4 and it will delete the trigger defined for E_3. This is done as in the given situation the composite event AND will never be true. The occurrence information of event E_1 and E_2 can be obtained by querying the event monitor.

4 Performance

In this section we outline some of our performance results to support our claims. In our experiments we defined different kinds of triggers on the IBM DB2 database, which was populated with the standard TPC-R [14] data. Transactions were run on this database and we evaluated the effect of the triggers on the transaction performance. The total size of the data populated in the database was approximately 100 MB. Our experiments were conducted on a P-4 1.70 GHz machine with 256 MB RAM. On an average a single transaction update resulted in update of 5 database records.

In our first experiment we evaluated the effect of the triggers on the performance of the transaction. In this experiment a fixed number of transactions were executed on the table. We varied the number of triggers that were defined on the table. Figure 4(a) shows the effect of the triggers on the time taken to execute the transactions. The figure clearly shows that the performance of the database degraded with an increase in the number of triggers defined on the table. Therefore, it is necessary to create and destroy these triggers dynamically if they have temporal constraints. In our next experiment we evaluated the performance of the database when the triggers are created and destroyed dynamically. In this experiment we measured the performance of the database by varying the percentage of time for which the trigger was present on the table for transactions of different batch sizes. In our approach if an event has temporal constraints, then the trigger for that event is defined on the table only during the lifetime of the event. Hence in our approach the trigger will be present for a smaller amount of time that the conventional case. Figure 4(b) shows the time taken to execute the transactions of different batch size. The legend denotes the batch size. The figure shows that the performance of the database falls when the trigger is present for a larger amount of time. This confirms that our technique will lead to an improvement in the performance of the database.

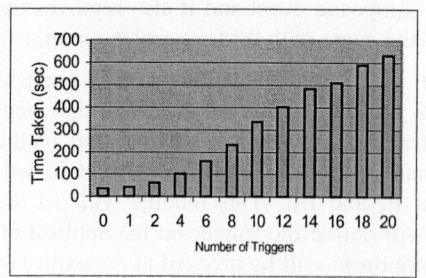
(a) Effect of Index

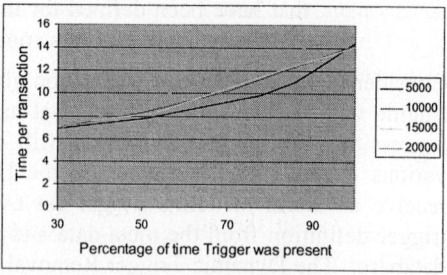
(b) Effect of Dynamism

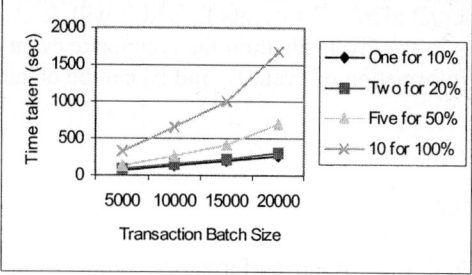
(c) Effect of Dynamism

Fig. 4: Performance Results

In a similar experiment, we installed 10 triggers on a database and measured the total time taken to perform a set of transactions of different batch sizes. In this experiment we measured the database performance by varying the total time for which each trigger was present on the table. Figure 4(c) shows the result of this experiment. Note that in this experiment, all 10 triggers were installed and removed dynamically, but all of them were sitting in the database only for a short duration. For example the graph corresponding to "One for 10%" indicates the time taken to execute a batch of transactions where each trigger was sitting for 10% of the total transaction batch size. Similarly the one corresponding to "Five for 50%" indicates the time for the case in which at any given point in time five triggers out of 10 were sitting. In other words 5 triggers were defined for the time when the first 50% of the transaction were executed and then they were removed. For the rest 50% of transactions, the other 5 triggers were defined. It can be noted that, for a given transaction batch size, as we go on increasing the "dynamic" nature of trigger installation and removal, there is an improvement in the performance. Also it is interesting to note that for a given dynamic nature of triggers the performance decreases as transaction batch size goes on increasing. This implies that our techniques will be more useful for large transaction sizes.

5 Conclusions

In this paper we have proposed a technique that makes the optimal use of triggers to detect events related to ECA rules. Our technique uses the temporal constraints associated with the policies and changes the lifespan of the events such that the correctness of the rule is not hampered. We detect dead events, i.e. events that can never be true and provide a mechanism to optimize the composite event expression. None of the existing techniques had exploited the temporal constraints to optimize the lifespan of the ECA rules. The existing techniques require the triggers to be present permanently on the application database, which limited the practicality of such a mechanism. Thus we provide a practical way to detect ECA rules using triggers, by decreasing the number of triggers that have to be defined on the databases. Our technique optimizes the lifespan of the triggers with respect to the lifespan and span of other events taking part in the composite events of a single policy.

References

[1] Aiken, A., Hellerstein,J.M., Widom,J., Static Analysis Techniques for Predicting Behavior of Active Database Rules, *ACM Transactions on Database Systems*, 20(1):3-41, 1995.
[2] Adaikkalavan, R., Chakravarthy S., Snoop, I.B.: Interval-Based Event Specification and Detection for Active Databases. *ADBIS* 2003. 190-204.
[3] Chakravarthy , S. and Mishra, D., Snoop: An Event Specification Language for Active Database, *DKE* 14(1): 1-26 (1994).
[4] Chamberlin, D., A Complete Guide to DB2 Universal Database.

[5] Dayal, U. et al., The HiPAC project: Combining active databases and timing constraints, *SIGMOD Record* 17(1):51-70, March 1988.
[6] Hanson, E.N., Rule condition testing and action execution in Ariel, In *Proceedings of the ACM SIGMOD International Conference on Management of Data*, June 1992.
[7] http://www-3.ibm.com/software/data/
[8] Kiernan, J., and Maindreville, C., Implementing high-level active rules on top of relational databases, *Proceedings of the 18th International Conference on Very Large Databases*, August 1992.
[9] Lehner, W., Modeling Large Scale OLAP Scenarios, *EDBT 1998* Valencia, Spain, 153-167, Springer LNCS 1377.
[10] Miller, J., Sheth, A., Kochut, K., Perspectives in Modeling: Simulation, Database, and Workflow, *Conceptual Modeling 1997*, 154-167.
[11] http://otn.oracle.com/products/designer/pdf/9i-1_migration-guide.pdf
[12] Paton, N.W., and Diaz, O., "Active Database Systems", *ACM Computing Surveys*, 31(1):63-103, March 1999.
[13] Stonebraker, M., and Kemnitz, G., The POSTGRES next-generation database management system, *Communications of the ACM*, 34(10):78-92, October 1991.
[14] Transaction Processing Performance Council, http://www.tpc.org/tpcr/

A New Approach for Checking Schema Validation Properties[*]

Carles Farré, Ernest Teniente, and Toni Urpí

Universitat Politècnica de Catalunya
08034 Barcelona, Catalonia (Spain)
{farre,teniente,urpi}@lsi.upc.es

Abstract. We propose a new approach to check whether a given database schema satisfies a set of desirable properties such as liveliness of a predicate, redundancy of integrity constraint specifications, schema satisfiability or reachability of partially specified states. Our approach is based on defining each schema validation property in terms of a constraint-satisfiability checking problem. Then, we propose to use the CQC Method (which was originally proposed for query containment checking) to verify whether these properties hold for a given database schema. Our aim is to define an effective and efficient method as the starting point to develop a practical tool for validating database schemas in commercial DBMSs.

1 Introduction

Database schema validation is related to check whether a database schema correctly and adequately describes the user intended needs and requirements. The correctness of the data managed by database management systems is vital to the more general aspect of quality of the data and thus their usage by different applications.

As an example, assume we have two tables containing information about departments and employees: *dept*(<u>Ndept</u>, *Budget, City*) and *emp*(<u>Nemp</u>, *Name, Ndept*). Underlined attributes correspond to primary keys and where ndept is a foreign key for the *emp* table. We could define views and assertions on those tables using standard SQL as follows:

```
CREATE VIEW niceDept AS
      SELECT ndept FROM dept WHERE budget > 50.000
CREATE VIEW happyEmp AS SELECT emp.nemp FROM emp, dept
      WHERE emp.ndept = dept.ndept AND budget>60.000 AND
      city='Barcelona'
CREATE VIEW empNiceDept AS
      SELECT emp.nemp FROM emp, niceDept
      WHERE emp.ndept = niceDept.ndept
CREATE ASSERTION happyEmpWorkInNiceDepts AS CHECK (NOT EXISTS
      (SELECT * FROM happyEmp WHERE nemp NOT IN (SELECT nemp
      FROM empNiceDept)))
```

---

[*] This work is partially supported by Microsoft Research Ltd. under grant 2003-192.

In principle, it may seem that this schema is perfectly right. The three views provide information about nice departments, happy employees and employees working in nice departments while the assertion restricts happy employees to work in nice departments. However, a deeper analysis of the schema allows determining that the assertion is redundant (and thus it should not be defined) since the view definitions alone already guarantee that happy employees work in nice departments.

Unfortunately, little research has been devoted to database schema validation in the past. This is probably the reason why no relational DBMS is currently able to deal satisfactorily with this important problem [TG01]. An exception is [DTU96] where a set of desirable properties that a database schema should satisfy was defined. However, to the best of our knowledge, there exists no effective or efficient method yet that is able to check all these properties. This is indeed the main goal of this paper.

Hence, the main contribution of our work is to propose an effective and efficient way to check desirable properties of a database schema. This is achieved by means of two different steps. First, we propose to define each property as a constraint-satisfiability checking test. Then, we show how to use the CQC Method [FTU03a] to effectively and efficiently perform those tests and, thus, to validate the properties. With this approach we are able to validate database schemas that may contain general integrity constraints (i.e. assertions), negated views and built-in predicates. To facilitate the comprehension of our examples, we assume that the database schemas are defined in logic although we could have defined them also in SQL.

The CQC Method performs constraint-satisfiability checking tests by trying to construct a database for which the tested property does not hold, i.e. a counterexample. The method uses different *Variable Instantiation Patterns (VIPs)* according to the syntactic properties of the views and the databases considered in each test. Such a customization only affects the way that the facts to be part of the counterexample are instantiated. The aim here is to prune the search of counterexamples by generating only the relevant facts and, thus, to address in an effective and efficient way the required tests.

We want also to remark that the proposal that we present in this paper is aimed at developing a practical tool for validating database schemas in commercial DBMSs. Indeed, our work is partially granted by Microsoft Research to develop such a tool for SQL Server. A first prototype is presented in [FTU+04].

This paper is organized as follows. Section 2 sets the base concepts used through the paper. Section 3 describes the general approach to use constraint-satisfiability checking for database schema validation. Section 4 proposes how to use the CQC method for checking these properties. Section 5 compares our method with related work. Section 6 presents a prototype for validating SQL database schemas. Finally, we present our conclusions and point out future work in Section 7.

2   Base Concepts

A *deductive rule* has the form:

$$p(\bar{X}) \leftarrow r_1(\bar{X}_1) \wedge \ldots \wedge r_n(\bar{X}_n) \wedge \neg r_{n+1}(\bar{Y}_1) \wedge \ldots \wedge \neg r_m(\bar{Y}_s) \wedge C_1 \wedge \ldots \wedge C_t$$

where p and $r_1, \ldots, r_m$ are *predicates* (also called *relation*) names. The atom $p(\bar{X})$ is called the *head* of the rule, and $r_1(\bar{X}_1), \ldots, r_n(\bar{X}_n), \neg r_{n+1}(\bar{Y}_1), \ldots, \neg r_m(\bar{Y}_s)$ are positive and negative *ordinary literals* in the body of the rule. The tuples $\bar{X}, \bar{X}_1, ..., \bar{X}_n, \bar{Y}_1, ..., \bar{Y}_s$ contain *terms*, which are either variables or constants. Each C_i is a *built-in literal* in the form of $A_1 \; \theta \; A_2$, where A_1 and A_2 are terms. Operator θ is $<, \leq, >, \geq, =$ or $\neq$. We require that every rule be *safe*, that is, every variable occurring in $\bar{X}, \bar{Y}_1, ..., \bar{Y}_s, C_1, ...$ or C_t must also appear in some $\bar{X}_i$.

The predicate names in a deductive rule range over the *extensional database* (EDB) predicates, which are the relations stored in the database, and the *intensional database* (IDB) predicates (like p above), which are the relations defined by the deductive rules. EDB predicates must not appear in the head of a deductive rule. A set of deductive rules P is *hierarchical* if it contains no recursively defined IDB relations.

A *constraint* has the denial form of:

$$\leftarrow r_1(\bar{X}_1) \wedge ... \wedge r_n(\bar{X}_n) \wedge \neg r_{n+1}(\bar{Y}_1) \wedge ... \wedge \neg r_m(\bar{Y}_s) \wedge C_1 \wedge ... \wedge C_t$$

where $r_1(\bar{X}_1), ..., r_n(\bar{X}_n), \neg r_{n+1}(\bar{Y}_1), ..., \neg r_m(\bar{Y}_s)$ are (positive and negative) ordinary literals; and $C_1, ..., C_t$ are built-in literals. We require also that every variable occurring in $\bar{Y}_1, ..., \bar{Y}_s, C_1, ...$ or C_t must also appear in some $\bar{X}_i$.

A *database schema* S is a tuple (DR, IC) where DR is a finite set of deductive rules and IC is a finite set of constraints.

For a database schema $S = (DR, IC)$, a *database state*, or just *database*, D is a tuple (E, S) where E is an EDB, that is, a set of ground facts about EDB predicates. $DR(E)$ denotes the whole set of ground facts about EDB and IDB predicates that are inferred from a database state $D = (E, S)$. $DR(E)$ corresponds to the fixpoint model of $DR \cup E$.

A database D *violates* a constraint $\leftarrow L_1 \wedge ... \wedge L_n$ if $(L_1 \wedge ... \wedge L_n)\theta$ is true on $DR(E)$ for some substitution θ. On the contrary, a database D is *consistent* when it violates no constraint in IC.

Example 2.1: The following database schema (an extension of the one shown in the introduction) will be used throughout the paper.

   niceDept(D) ← *dept(D,B,C)* ∧ *B>50.000*
   happyEmp(E) ← *emp(E,N,D)* ∧ *dept(D,B,barcelona)* ∧ *B>60.000*
   empNiceDept(E) ← *emp(E,N,D)* ∧ *niceDept(D)*
   badEmployee(E) ← *emp(E,N,D)* ∧ *dept(D,B,C)* ∧ *B<20.000* ∧ *niceDept(D)*
   ← *happyEmp(E)* ∧ ¬ *empNiceDept(E)*
   ← *emp(E,N,D)* ∧ *empNiceDept(E)* ∧ ¬ *happyEmp(E)*
   ← *empNiceDept(E)* ∧ ¬ *happyEmp(E)*

3 Schema Validation by Constraint-Satisfiability Checking

The goal of this section is to define the properties that were proposed in [DTU96] in terms of constraint-satisfiability checking problems. Let $S = (DR, IC)$ be a database schema, $G = \leftarrow M_1 \wedge ... \wedge M_n$ a goal. We say that $S \cup G$ is *constraint-satisfiable* if there is at least one consistent database $D = (E, S)$ such that $(M_1 \wedge ... \wedge M_n)\theta$ is true on $DR(E)$ for some substitution θ. That is, $DR(E)$ satisfies G and it does not violate any constraint in IC.

3.1 Liveliness

Predicates that are not lively correspond to relations that are empty in each consistent state of the database. This may be due to the presence of some integrity constraints, to the view definition itself (for derived predicates) or to a combination of both. Such predicates are clearly not useful and possibly ill specified.

Let $S = (DR, IC)$ be a database schema. A predicate p is *lively* in S if there is a consistent database $D = (E, S)$ in which at least one fact about p is true. That is, p is lively in S if $p(\bar{X})\theta \in DR(E)$ for some substitution θ.

To state this property in terms of a constraint-satisfiability checking problem we only have to define the goal G corresponding to the property we want to achieve. In this case, G is just the predicate p we want to check whether it has an empty extension. Then, we have that p is lively in S if and only if $S \cup G = \leftarrow p(\bar{X})$ is constraint-satisfiable.

As an example, we have that predicate *badEmployee* of Example 2.1 is not lively. Note that an employee may only be bad if he works in a nice department with a budget lower than 20.000. However, this is not possible since nice departments will always have a budget greater than 50.000. Then, it is impossible to have any instance of *badEmployee* in the previous database schema.

3.2 Integrity Constraint Redundancy

Roughly, an integrity constraint (or a subset of constraints) is redundant if database consistency does not depend on it. In other words, it is redundant when it is already guaranteed that the database instances that it wants to avoid will never occur. We distinguish two different types of redundancy. We say that a constraint is absolutely redundant if it may never be violated. On the other hand, we say that a constraint is relatively redundant wrt a set of constraints if it may never be violated when none of the constraints in the set is violated.

Formally, let $S = (DR, IC)$ be a schema and $C_i = \leftarrow L_1 \wedge \ldots \wedge L_n$ an integrity constraint in IC. Then:

- C_i is *absolutely redundant in S* if C_i is satisfied in each database state of S. That is, if there is exists no database $D = (E, S)$ such that $(L_1 \wedge \ldots \wedge L_n)\theta$ is true on $DR(E)$ for some substitution θ.
- C_i is *relatively redundant in S* if C_i is satisfied in each consistent database of S' $= (DR, IC\text{-}\{C_i\})$. That is, if there is exists no consistent database $D = (E, S')$ such that $(L_1 \wedge \ldots \wedge L_n)\theta$ is true on $DR(E)$ for some substitution θ.

Both kinds of redundancy can be expressed in terms of constraint-satisfiability:

- C_i is absolutely redundant in S if and only if $S' \cup G$, with $S' = (DR, \emptyset)$ and $G = C_i$, is not constraint-satisfiable.
- C_i is relatively redundant in S if and only if $S' \cup G$, with $S' = (DR, IC\text{-}\{C_i\})$ and $G = C_i$, is not constraint-satisfiable.

Note that integrity constraint redundancy is best stated in terms of constraint-satisfiability by verifying or falsifying the lack of redundancy. Then, according to the previous definitions, we will check this property by attempting to construct *one* state which would show that the constraint under investigation can be violated and, hence, cannot be discarded.

Regarding Example 2.1, we have that the first integrity constraint is absolutely redundant since the definition of views *happyEmp* and *niceDept* already entails that happy employees may only work in nice departments. Moreover, we also have that the second integrity constraint is relatively redundant. Clearly, *empNiceDept(e)* already requires *e* to be an employee. Then, it is not possible to violate the second constraint without violating also the third one. For these reasons, we have that the database schema of Example 2.1 would allow the same consistent states than the one containing just the third constraint.

3.3 State Satisfiability

A database schema $S = (DR, IC)$ is *state-satisfiable* if there is at least one database $D = (E, S)$ in which no integrity constraint in *IC* is violated. In other words, $S = (DR, IC)$ is state-satisfiable if and only if S is constraint-satisfiable. Note that in this particular case no additional goal G is needed to specify the property.

The database schema of Example 2.1 is satisfiable. For instance, we have that E = {*emp(1,john,sales)*, *dept(sales,70.000,barcelona)*} defines a model $DR(E)$ = { *emp(1,john,sales)*, *dept(sales,70.000,barcelona)*, *happyEmp(1)*, *niceDept(sales)*, *empNiceDept(1)* }. The empty EDB would also define a model (the empty one).

3.4 Reachability

A database designer may be interested also in more general properties like checking whether certain conceived goals may be satisfied according to the current schema. This is usually known as checking reachability of partially specified states.

Let $S = (DR, IC)$ be a database schema. A sentence (i.e. a conjunction of literals) H is *reachable* in S if there is a consistent database $D = (E, S)$ in which H is true. In other words, H is reachable in S if and only if $S \cup G = \leftarrow H$ is constraint-satisfiable.

For instance, the database designer could be interested to check whether the database schema of Example 2.1 allows having two different employees working at the same department being one of them happy and the other not. This property may be stated in terms of reachability by means of the sentence:

$emp(E,N,D) \land emp(E',N',D) \land E \neq E' \land happyEmp(E) \land \neg happyEmp(E')$

It is not difficult to see that it is impossible to reach a state where such a property holds. An employee to be happy requires him to work in a department with a budget greater than 60.000. Then, the department must be necessarily a *niceDept* which, at the same time, entails both employees to be *empNiceDept* (since they work in the same department). However, the third constraint requires that each *empNiceDept* must be a *happyEmp* and then it is not possible that only one of them is happy. If the designer knows that this situation may happen in the real world, it means that the database schema does not precisely define his requirements.

4 Schema Validation with the CQC Method

We show in this section how to use the CQC Method [FTU03a, Far03] to effectively and efficiently check desirable properties of database schemas once they have been specified in terms of constraint-satisfiability checking problems.

4.1 The CQC Method

The main goal of the CQC Method is to perform query containment tests. This problem is concerned with checking whether the answers that a query obtains are a subset of the answers obtained by another query for every database. This is done by trying to construct a database for which the tested containment relationship does not hold, i.e. a counterexample. If the method is able to find such a counterexample, then query containment does not hold. Otherwise, it holds.

The CQC Method allows checking query containment, in the absence/presence of integrity constraints in a rather rich setting that subsumes those that have been considered in other research works, in which both queries and integrity constraints may contain the following features:
- Negation on IDB and EDB subgoals.
- Equality/inequality comparisons ($=$, $\neq$).
- Order comparisons ($<, \leq, \geq, >$) on either a dense or discrete order domain.

Let $S = (DR, IC)$ be a database schema and Q_1 and Q_2 two queries defining the same n-ary query predicate q. The CQC Method requires two main (explicit) inputs. The first one is the definition of the *goal to attain*, which must be achieved on the database that the method will try to obtain by constructing its EDB. For query containment checking, this goal is $G_0 = \leftarrow q_1(X_1, ..., X_n) \land \neg q_2(X_1, ..., X_n)$, meaning that it is required to construct a database where $q_1(X_1,...,X_n)\theta$ is true and $q_2(X_1,...,X_n)\theta$ is false for some substitution θ.

The second main input for the CQC Method is the set of constraints to enforce, which must not be violated by the constructed database. This set is defined either $F_0 = IC$ or $F_0 = \emptyset$, depending on whether or not we want to restrict the search of the counterexample by considering only those EDB that satisfy the set IC that contains the integrity constraints of the schema.

The generality of the approach followed by the CQC Method does not restrict its application to query containment only since, in general, the initial goal to attain may be any conjunction of literals (subgoals) expressing a certain property. Consequently, the CQC Method can check any property that may be formulated in terms of a goal to attain (G_0) under a set of constraints to enforce (F_0). In particular, as we will see in section 4.2, it is suited to check the database schema validation properties we have defined in section 3 since all of them are aimed to prove that a certain goal is satisfied provided that it does not satisfy a set of integrity constraints.

The CQC Method has been proved to be sound and complete both for success and for failure. Then, the following properties are guaranteed:
- If the method builds a finite counterexample, when recursively-defined IDB relations are not considered, then the property being checked holds (*finite success soundness*).

- If there exists a finite counterexample that ensures that a certain property is satisfied, then the method finds it and terminates (*finite success completeness*) when the database is either hierarchical or stratified and strict [CL89].
- If the method terminates without building any counterexample, then the property being checked does not hold (*failure soundness*).
- If a certain property does not hold, then the method fails finitely (*failure completeness*) when recursively-defined IDB relations are not considered.

The CQC Method uses different *Variable Instantiation Patterns (VIPs)*, which define the strategy to follow when instantiating the EDB facts to be included in the EDB under construction. The application of a certain VIP depends on the syntactic properties of the queries and the databases considered in each concrete test. In this way, [FTUa03] defines four VIPs:

1. The *Simple VIP*: in the absence of negation and integrity constraints.
2. The *Negation VIP*: in the presence of negation and/or integrity constraints.
3. The *Dense Order VIP*: in the presence of order comparisons over a dense domain (e.g. real numbers).
4. The *Discrete Order VIP*: in the presence of order comparisons over a discrete domain (e.g. integer numbers).

It is worthy of note that such a customization does not undermine the generality and uniformity of the calculus defined by the CQC Method but instead only affects the exact way in which the EDB facts to be part of the counterexample are generated. The aim here is to limit the search of possible counterexamples by generating only the relevant ones but, at the same time, not diminishing the requirement of completeness

Constraint-satisfiability is undecidable for the general case. Therefore in some cases, e.g. in the presence of solutions with infinite elements, it may happen that the CQC Method does not terminate unless we do not impose some heuristic controls on the algorithm such as to limit the number of constants to be used, for instance. However, the previous completeness results guarantee that if either there exist one or more finite states for which the property does not hold or there is no state (finite or infinite) satisfying the property, the CQC Method terminates.

4.2 Checking Schema Validation Properties with the CQC Method

Once a validation property is formulated by means of constraint-satisfiability checking, we may use the CQC Method to check whether such a property holds. We have to express first such property in terms of the initial goal to attain (G_0) and the set of integrity constraints to enforce (F_0) and then apply the CQC Method to see whether it constructs an EDB that proves or refutes the property being checked.

Given a database schema $S = (DR, IC)$, and according to the particular property being validated, G_0 and F_0 should be defined as follows.
- **Liveliness of a predicate**. Let p an EDB or IDB n-ary predicate. If p is lively then the CQC Method will succeed in constructing and EDB E from the initial goal $G_0 = \leftarrow p(\bar{X})$ and the initial set of constraints to enforce $F_0 = IC$.
- **Absolute redundancy of an integrity constraint**. Let $Ic1 \in IC$ an integrity constraint. If $Ic1$ is absolute redundancy then the CQC Method will not be able to

construct any EDB from $G_0 = \leftarrow Ic1$ and $F_0 = \varnothing$. In other words, no EDB violates $Ic1$.
- **Relative redundancy of an integrity constraint.** Let $Ic1 \in IC$ an integrity constraint. If $Ic1$ is relative redundant then the CQC Method will not be able to construct any EDB from $G_0 = \leftarrow Ic1$ and $F_0 = IC - \{Ic1\}$. In other words, no EDB consistent with respect to $IC - \{Ic1\}$ violates $Ic1$.
- **State satisfiability of a schema.** If a database schema S is state-satisfiable then the CQC Method will succeed in constructing an EDB E from the initial goal $G_0 = \varnothing$ and $F_0 = IC$.
- **Reachability of a partially specified state.** Let H a partially specified state expressed in terms of a goal. If H is reachable then the CQC Method will succeed in constructing an EDB E from the initial goal $G_0 = H$ and $F_0 = IC$.

5 Related Work

As we said, [DTU96] proposed the set of desirable properties that a database schema should satisfy and that we have considered in this paper. Moreover, they proposed to validate these properties by means of a view updating method. An important advantage of this approach is its generality since a single method may be used to check all properties, in the same way we have proposed in this paper. However, current view updating methods present important drawbacks when dealing with existentially derived predicates [MT99] that do not allow them to be used in practical situations. Recently, we have sketched a view updating method [FTU03b] aimed at overcoming this limitation.

Other authors have dealt also with schema validation tasks separately. In this way, satisfiability was addressed in [BM86, BDM88, BEST98]. In particular, [BEST98] proposes to use the EP Tableaux [BT98] to check satisfiability of schemas whose integrity constraints are expressed in terms of fully quantified, closed, first order formulas, the so-called PRQ formulas. EP Tableaux extend PUHR Tableaux [MB88, BY00] and they are not only refutation complete but also complete for finite satisfiability. In addition to the fact that EP Tableaux do not deal with built-in predicates, it is not obvious that they could handle IDB predicates since IDB rules are considered as integrity constraints, assuming that there is no a 'strict separation between extensional and intensional database'.

Predicate liveliness has been addressed in [ZO97, HMSS01] under different designations. In this way, [ZO97] provided a method for checking predicate liveliness, named IRC refuting there, where predicates would express conjunctive queries, that is, they would be defined by deductive rules with no other IDB predicates occurring in their bodies. The integrity constraints can be expressed in terms of the so-called implication constraints and referential constraints. Both kinds of constraints are a subset of the kind of constraints that the CQC Method can handle.

In [HMSS01], predicate liveliness is addressed under the name of predicate satisfiability. However, in this latter case, integrity constraints are not considered. Therefore, according to this approach, a predicate could be made "satisfiable" by some EDB that does not satisfy one or more integrity constraints.

Finally, relative redundancy, referred to as *constraint subsumption*, can be handled as a particular case of Query Containment [GSUW94]. According to this proposal, integrity constraints must be rewritten in terms of *query constraints*. One of the positive aspects of the approach of [GSUW94] is its independency of the particular method used to check query containment. Therefore, we can take advantage of the CQC Method again, since it is the method for query-containment checking that covers more cases of queries and integrity constraints [Far03, FTU03a].

6 The SVT Prototype

Our aim is to develop a practical tool for validating database schemas in commercial DBMSs by implementing the ideas presented in the previous sections. In a first step pursuing such a goal, we have developed an initial prototype named Schema Validation Tool, SVT for short [FTU+04]. SVT allows a database designer to perform several tests to check desirable properties of database schemas defined in Microsoft SQL Server. This initial prototype accepts schemas defined by means of a subset of the SQL language provided by SQL Server. This subset includes:
 – Primary key, foreign key, boolean check constraints.
 – SPJ views, negation, subselects (exists, in), union.
 – Data types: integer, real, string.

SVT assumes a set semantics of views and queries and it does not allow null values neither aggregate nor arithmetic functions.

The whole SVT has been implemented in the C# language by using Visual .NET Studio as a development tool. Our implementation can be executed in any system that features the .NET framework and has access to a local or remote SQL Server system.

7 Conclusions and Further Work

We have proposed a new approach to check predicate liveliness, integrity constraints redundancy, schema satisfiability and reachability of partially specified states in a uniform, effective and efficient way. Our approach consists on formulating these properties in terms of a constraint-satisfiability checking problem and then using the CQC method to validate them.

An important advantage of our approach is its generality since it relies on a single method to check all schema validation properties. Moreover, it allows to validate schemas whose expressive power is greater than the one of the schemas that have been addressed by other research works since we admit queries and integrity constraints that contain negation on IDB and EDB subgoals, equality/inequality comparisons and order comparisons on either a dense or discrete order domain.

We may ensure also that the way we propose to check these properties is sound and complete both for soundness and for failure. In this way, we may guarantee that our method obtains a solution if and only if there exists one and that our method fails finitely if and only if there is no solution. Moreover, the use of the VIP patterns allows us to consider only relevant instantiations and not all possible ones when dealing with existential derived predicates.

We have also implemented the ideas proposed in this paper in a prototype of a practical tool to validate database schemas in relational DBMSs and, in particular, for SQL Server. When addressing schema validation in this setting we are faced with new problems that are not yet solved and thus worthy of a further work like, for instance, providing an appropriate treatment for null values. Moreover, we would like to extend the subset of the SQL supported by our current implementation.

References

[BDM88] F. Bry, H. Decker, R. Manthey. A Uniform Approach to Constraint Satisfaction and Constraint Satisfiability in Deductive Databases. In *EDBT'88*: 488-505, 1988.

[BEST98] F. Bry, N. Eisinger, H. Schütz, S. Torge. SIC: Satisfiability Checking for Integrity Constraints. In *Proceedings of DDLP'98*: 25-36, 1998.

[BM86] F. Bry, R. Manthey. Checking Consistency of Database Constraints: a Logical Basis. In *Proceedings of VLDB'86*: 13-20, 1986.

[BT98] F. Bry, S. Torge: A Deduction Method Complete for Refutation and Finite Satisfiability. In *Proceedings of JELIA'98*: 122-138, 1998.

[BY00] F. Bry, A. Yahya. Positive Unit Hyperresolution Tableaux an Their Application to Minimal Model Generation. *Journal of Automated Reasoning* 25: 35-82, 2000.

[CL89] L. Cavedon, J.W. Lloyd. A Completeness Theorem for SLDNF Resolution, *Journal of Logic Programming*, 7(3):177-191, 1989.

[DTU96] H. Decker, E. Teniente, T. Urpí. How to Tackle Schema Validation by View Updating. In *Proceedings of EDBT'96*: 535-549, 1996

[Far03] C. Farré. *A New Method for Query Containment Checking in Databases*. PhD. Thesis, Universitat Politècnica de Catalunya, 2003

[FTU03a] C. Farré, E. Teniente, T. Urpí. Query Containment With Negated IDB Predicates. *Proceedings of ADBIS 2003*: 411-429, 2003.

[FTU03b] C. Farré, E. Teniente, T. Urpí. Handling Existential Derived Relations in View Updating. *Proceedings of the ICLP 2003*: 148-162, 2003.

[FTU+04] C. Farré, E. Teniente, T. Urpí, C. Beltrán, D. Gañán. SVT: Schema Validation Tool for Microsoft SQL-Server. To appear in *Proceedings. of the VLDB 2004*.

[GSUW94] A. Gupta, Y. Sagiv, J.D. Ullman, J. Widom. Constraint Checking with Partial Information. In *Proceedings of PoDS'94*: 45-55, 1994.

[HMSS01] A.Y. Halevy, I.S. Mumick, Y. Sagiv, O. Shmueli. Static Analysis in Datalog Extensions. *Journal of the ACM*, 48(5): 971-1012, 2001.

[MB88] R. Manthey, F. Bry. SATCHMO: A Theorem Prover Implemented in Prolog. In *Proceedings of CADE'88*: 415-434, 1988.

[MT99] E. Mayol, E. Teniente. A Survey of Current Methods for Integrity Constraint Maintenance and View Updating. In *Proc. of the ER'99 Workshops*: 62-73, 1999.

[TG01] C. Türker, M. Gertz. Semantic Integrity Support in SQL-99 and Commercial (Object-)Relational Database Management Systems. *VLDB Journal* 10(4): 241-269, 2001.

[ZO97] X. Zhang, M.Z. Ozsoyoglu. Implication and Referential Constraints: A New Formal Reasoning. *IEEE TKDE*, 9(6): 894-910, 1997.

Autonomic Group Protocol for Peer-to-Peer (P2P) Systems

Tomoya Enokido and Makoto Takizawa

Department of Computers and Systems Engineering
Tokyo Denki University
{eno,taki}@takilab.k.dendai.ac.jp

Abstract. We discuss a group protocol which supports applications with group communication service in change of QoS supported by networks and required by applications. An autonomic group protocol is realized by cooperation of multiple autonomous agents. Each agent autonomously takes a class of each protocol function. Classes taken by an agent are required to be consistent with but might be different from the others. We make clear what combination of classes can be autonomously taken by agents. We also present how to change retransmission ways.

1 Introduction

Peer-to-Peer (P2P) systems [1] are getting widely available like autonomic computing [2]. Multiple peer processes first establish a *group* and then messages are exchanged among the processes [3–7]. Group communication protocol [3–7] supports basic communication mechanism like the causally ordered and atomic delivery of messages to realize cooperation of multiple peer processes. A group protocol is implemented in protocol modules which is composed of protocol functions; multicast/broadcast, receipt confirmation, detection and retransmission of messages lost, ordering of messages received, and membership management. There are various ways to realize each of these functions like selective go-back-n retransmissions of messages [8].

The complexity and efficiency of implementation of a group protocol depends on what type and quality of service (QoS) are supported by the underlying network. Since messages may be lost and unexpectedly delayed due to congestions and faults in the network, QoS parameters are dynamically changed. The higher level of communication function is supported, the larger computation and communication overheads are implied. Hence, the system has to take classes of functions necessary and sufficient to support service required by application.

The paper [3] discusses a communication architecture which satisfies application requirements in change of network service. However, a group protocol cannot be dynamically changed each time QoS supported by the underlying network is changed. In addition, each process has to use the same protocol functions. In ISIS [4], protocol modules which support service required can be constructed. However, a protocol module of each process cannot be changed and every process has to take the same module. It is not easy to change protocol functions in all the processes since a large number of processes are cooperating and some computers like personal computers and mobile computers are not always working well.

In this paper, we discuss an *autonomic* group protocol which can support QoS required by applications even if QoS supported by the underlying network is changed. Each protocol module is realized in an autonomous agent. An agent autonomously changes classes, i.e. implementations of each protocol function depending on network QoS monitored. Here, an agent might take different classes of protocol functions from other agents but *consistent* with the other agents. We discuss what combinations of protocol function classes are consistent. If a group is too large for each agent to perceive QoS supported by other agents and manage the membership, the group is decomposed into views. Each agent has a *view* which is a subset of agents to which the agent can directly send messages.

In section 2, we show a system model. In section 3, we discuss classes of protocol functions. In section 4, we present an agent-based group protocol. In section 5, we discuss how to change retransmission functions.

2 System Model

2.1 Autonomic Group Agent

A group of multiple *application processes* $A_1, ..., A_n$ ($n \geq 2$) are cooperating by taking usage of group communication service. The group communication service is supported by cooperation of multiple peer *autonomous group* (AG) agents $p_1, ..., p_n$ [Figure 1]. For simplicity, a term "*agent*" means an AG agent in this paper. The underlying network supports a pair of agents with basic communication service which is characterized by QoS parameters; delay time [msec], message loss ratio [%], and bandwidth [bps].

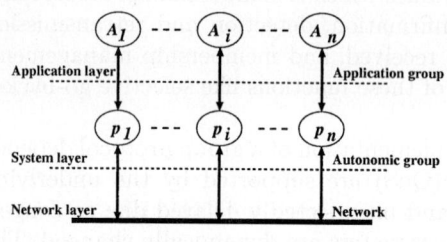

Fig. 1. System model

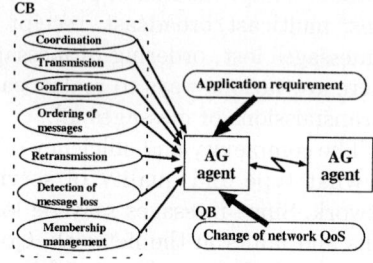

Fig. 2. Autonomic group protocol

A group protocol is realized in a collection of protocol functions; coordination, transmission, confirmation, retransmission, ordering of message, detection of message lost, and membership management. There are multiple ways to implement each protocol function. A *class* shows a way to implement a protocol function. The classes for each function are stored in a protocol class base (CB) of each agent. Each agent p_i autonomously takes one class for each protocol function from CB, which can support an application with necessary and sufficient QoS by taking usage of basic communication service with given QoS supported by the underlying network. Each agent p_i stores QoS information of the underlying network in a QoS base (QB) of p_i. If enough QoS cannot be supported or too much QoS is supported for the application, the agent p_i reconstructs a combination of protocol function classes by autonomously selecting a class for each protocol function in CB. Here, even if a pair of agents take classes different from one another, the agents can support group communication service if the classes are consistent. Each agent negotiates with other agents to make a consensus on which class to take for each protocol function if some pair of agents are inconsistent.

2.2 Views

A *group* G is composed of multiple autonomous group (AG) agents $p_1, ..., p_n$ ($n > 1$). In a group G including larger number of agents, it is not easy for each agent to maintain membership information of the group. Each agent p_i has a view $V(p_i)$ which is a subset of agents to which the agent p_i can deliver messages directly or indirectly via agents. Thus, a view is a subgroup of the group G. For every pair of agents p_i and p_j, p_i in $V(p_j)$ if p_j in $V(p_i)$. Each agent p_i maintains membership of its view $V(p_i)$. For example, a view can be a collection of agents interconnected in a local network. A pair of different views V_1 and V_2 may include a common *gateway* agent p_k. A collection of gateway agents which are interconnected in a trunk network is also a view V_3.

An agent p_i which belongs to only one view is a *leaf* agent. An agent p_i which takes a message m from an application process A_i and sends the message m is an original *sender* agent of the message m. If an agent p_j delivers a message m to an application process, the agent p_j is an original *destination* agent of the message m. If an agent p_k forwards a message m to another agent in a same view V, p_k is a *routing* agent. A *local* sender and destination of a message m are agents which send and receive m in a view, respectively.

3 Functions of Group Protocol

In this section, we discuss what classes exist for each protocol function. There are *centralized* and *distributed* classes to coordinate the cooperation of agents in a view. In the centralized control, there is one centralized controller in a view. In the distributed control, each agent makes a decision on correct receipt, delivery order of messages received, and group membership by itself.

There are *centralized*, *direct*, and *indirect* classes to multicast a message in a view [Figure 3]. In the *centralized* transmission, an agent first sends a message to a controller agent. Then, the controller agent forwards the message to all the destination agents in a view [Figure 3 (1)]. In the *direct* transmission, each agent directly sends a message to each destination agent in a view V [Figure 3 (2)]. In the *indirect* transmission, a message is first sent to some agent in a view V. The agent forwards the message to another agent and finally delivers the message to the destination agents in the view V [Figure 3 (3)].

There are *centralized*, *direct*, *indirect*, and *distributed* classes to confirm receipt of a message in a view V. In the centralized confirmation, every agent sends a receipt confirmation message to a controller agent in a view V. After receiving confirmation messages from all the destination agents, the controller agent sends a receipt confirmation to the local sender agent [Figure 3 (1)]. In the *direct* confirmation, each destination agent p_i in the view V sends a receipt confirmation of a message m to the local sender agent p_i which first sends the message m in the view V [Figure 3 (2)]. In the *indirect* confirmation, a receipt confirmation of a message m is sent back to a local sender agent p_i in a view V by each agent p_j which has received the message m from the local sender agent p_i [Figure 3 (3)]. In the *distributed* confirmation, each agent which has received a message m sends a receipt confirmation of the message m to all the other agents in the same view [7] [Figure 3 (4)].

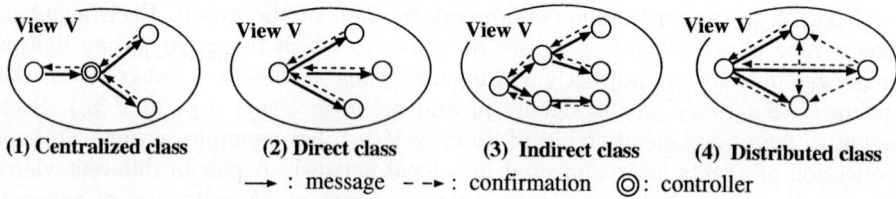

(1) Centralized class (2) Direct class (3) Indirect class (4) Distributed class

⟶ : message   --▸ : confirmation   ◎ : controller

Fig. 3. Transmission and confirmation classes

A message m_1 *causally precedes* another message m_2 ($m_1 \rightarrow m_2$) if and only if (iff) a sending event of m_1 *happens before* a sending event of m_2 [5–7]. A message m_1 is *causally concurrent* with another message m_2 ($m_1 \parallel m_2$) if neither $m_1 \rightarrow m_2$ nor $m_2 \rightarrow m_1$. In order to causally deliver messages, realtime clock with NTP (network time protocol), linear clock [5], and vector clock [6] are used.

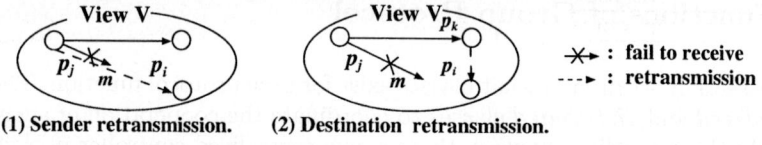

(1) Sender retransmission.   (2) Destination retransmission.

✗▸ : fail to receive
--▸ : retransmission

Fig. 4. Retransmission classes

There are *sender* and *destination* retransmission classes with respect to which agent retransmits a message m lost [Figure 4]. In the *sender* retransmission, the local sender agent p_j which has first sent a message m in the view V retransmits m to p_i which fails to receive m. In the *destination* retransmission, one or more than one destination agent in the view V which have safely received the message m forwards m to p_i which fails to receive m. In the *distributed* confirmation, each agent can know if every other destination agent safely receives a message m. If a destination agent p_j receives no confirmation from an agent p_i, p_j detects p_i to lose the message m. Then, the agent p_j can forward m to p_i.

There are *centralized* and *distributed* classes for managing the membership. In the centralized class, one membership manager communicates with all the member agents to obtain their states. In the distributed one, each agent obtains the states of the other agents by communicating with other agents.

A *centralized* system is a system which takes centralized classes for coordination, transmission, and confirmation. Most traditional distributed systems like Amoeba [9] take the centralized approach. A system with distributed coordination, transmission, and centralized confirmation system is classified to be *decentralized*. ISIS [4] takes the decentralized approach. Takizawa *et al.* [7] take the *distributed* approach which take distributed classes for coordination, transmission, and confirmation.

4 Autonomic Group Protocol

4.1 Local Protocol Instance

In this paper, we consider protocol functions, coordination, transmission, confirmation, and retransmission functions, which are the most significant to design and implement a group protocol. Let **F** be a set of the significant protocol functions $\{C(\text{coordination}), T(\text{transmission}), CF(\text{confirmation}), R(\text{retransmission})\}$. Let $Cl(F)$ be a set of classes to implement a protocol function F in the significant protocol function set **F**. Table 1 shows possible classes for the protocol functions, C, T, CF, and R.

Table 1. Protocol classes

Function F	Protocol classes $Cl(F)$
F_1	$\{C(centralized), D(distributed)\}$
F_2	$\{C(centralized), D(direct), I(indirect)\}$
F_3	$\{Cen(centralized), Dir(direct), Ind(indirect), Dis(distributed)\}$
F_4	$\{S(sender), D(destination)\}$

Table 2. Protocol profiles

Control	Transmission	Confirmation	Retransmission	Signature
Centralized	Centralized	Centralized	Sender	CCCenS
Distributed	Direct	Direct	Sender	DDDirS
		Distributed	Sender	DDDisS
			Destination	DDDisD
	Indirect	Indirect	Sender	DIIndS
		Distributed	Sender	DIDisS
			Destination	DIDisD

We rewrite **F** to be a set $\{F_1, F_2, F_3, F_4\}$ of protocol functions where each element F_i shows a protocol function, i.e. $\langle F_1, F_2, F_3, F_4 \rangle = \langle C, T, CF, R \rangle$. A tuple $\langle c_1, c_2, c_3, c_4 \rangle \in Cl(F_1) \times Cl(F_2) \times Cl(F_3) \times Cl(F_4)$ is referred to as *protocol instance*. Each agent takes a protocol instance $C = \langle c_1, c_2, c_3, c_4 \rangle$, i.e. a class c_i is taken for each protocol function F_i ($i = 1, 2, 3, 4$). Here, each agent cannot take every protocol instance. Some protocol instances out of possible 48 ones cannot work in an agent.

[**Definition**] A protocol instance $\langle c_1, c_2, c_3, c_4 \rangle$ is *consistent* iff an agent taking the protocol instance can work with other agents which take the same protocol instance to support group communication service.

An agent can take only a consistent protocol instance. A protocol *profile* is a consistent protocol instance. In Table 2, seven possible protocol profiles are summarized. A protocol profile *signature* "$c_1 c_2 c_3 c_4$" denotes a protocol profile $\langle c_1, c_2, c_3, c_4 \rangle$. For example, $DDDirS$ shows a protocol profile $\langle D, D, Dir, S \rangle$ which is composed of distributed control (D), direct transmission (D), direct confirmation (Dir), and sender retransmission (S) classes. Let $PF(1)$, $PF(2)$, $PF(3)$, $PF(4)$, $PF(5)$, $PF(6)$, and $PF(7)$ show the protocol profiles $CCCenS$, $DDDirS$, $DDDisS$, $DDDisD$, $DIIndS$, $DIDisS$, and $DIDisD$, respectively, which are shown in Table 2. Let **P** be a set $\{PF(i) \mid i = 1, ..., 7\}$ of all the protocol profiles. In $PF(i)$, i is referred to as the protocol profile number.

4.2 Global Protocol Instance

Let C_i be a consistent protocol instance $\langle c_{i1}, ..., c_{i4} \rangle \in \mathbf{P}$, i.e. protocol profile taken by an agent p_i ($i = 1, ..., n$). A *global* protocol instance C for a view $V = \{p_1, ..., p_n\}$ is a tuple $\langle C_1, ..., C_n \rangle$ where each element C_i is a protocol profile which an agent p_i takes. Here, each C_i is referred to as *local* protocol instance of an agent p_i. In traditional protocols, every agent has to take a same local consistent protocol instance. That is, every protocol module is a same program. A global protocol instance $C = \langle C_1, ..., C_n \rangle$ is *complete* if $C_1 = \cdots = C_n$. A global protocol instance $C = \langle C_1, ..., C_n \rangle$ is *incomplete* if $C_i \neq C_j$ for some pair of agents p_i and p_j. When some agent p_i changes a class c_{ik} of a protocol function F_k in a protocol profile C_i with another class c'_{ik} in a complete global protocol instance, all the agents have to be synchronized to make an agreement on a new global protocol instance $\langle C'_1, ..., C'_i, ..., C'_n \rangle$ where $C'_1 = \cdots = C'_i = \cdots = C'_n$. Thus, it takes time to change a protocol profile in every agent.

A global protocol instance C is *globally consistent* if a collection of agents where each agent p_i takes a protocol profile C_i ($i = 1, ..., n$) can cooperate. A *global protocol profile* is a consistent global protocol instance. In this paper, we discuss a group protocol where a view V of agents $p_1, ..., p_n$ can take an incomplete but consistent global protocol instance $C = \langle C_1, ..., C_n \rangle$. First, following types of protocol instances are globally inconsistent:

[**Property**] A global protocol instance $C = \langle C_1, ..., C_n \rangle$ of a view V is not consistent if V is composed of more than three agents and the global protocol instance C satisfies one of the following conditions:

1. At least one agent in V takes the protocol profile $CCCenS$ and the global protocol instance C is not complete.

2. At least one agent takes an *indirect* transmission class in V and at least one other agent takes a *direct* confirmation class in V.

We introduce a notation α_I where $I \in 2^{\{1,...,7\}}$ as follows:

1. α_i indicates a global protocol profile where all the agents take the same local protocol profile $PF(i)$ ($i = 1, ..., 7$).
2. Let I be a sequence of protocol profile numbers $i_1 \cdots i_l$ ($l \leq 7$), α_I shows a global protocol instance where each agent takes one of the local protocol profiles $PF(i_1), ..., PF(i_l)$ and each protocol profile $PF(i_k)$ is taken by at least one agent ($k = 1, ..., l$).

For example, α_{23} means a global protocol instance where every agent takes $PF(2) = DDDirS$ or $PF(3) = DDDisS$, at least one agent takes $DDDirS$, and at least one agent takes $DDDisS$.

[**Definition**] A global protocol instance α_I can be transited to another global protocol instance α_J ($\alpha_I \rightarrow \alpha_J$) iff
1. if $J = Ii$, the agents can support group communication service even if an agent taking $PF(k)$ where $k \in I$ autonomously takes $PF(i)$ ($i \neq k$).
2. if $I = Jj$, the agents can support group communication service even if an agent taking $PF(j)$ takes $PF(k)$ where $k \in I$.
3. For some global protocol instance α_K, $\alpha_I \rightarrow \alpha_K$ and $\alpha_K \rightarrow \alpha_J$.

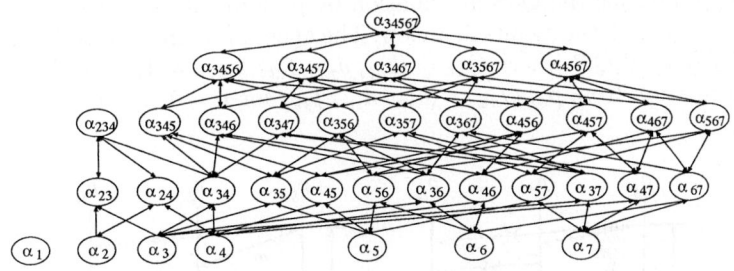

Fig. 5. Hasse diagram

According to the definition, the transition relation "$\rightarrow$" is symmetric and transitive. Figure 5 shows a Hasse diagram where a node shows a global protocol profile and a directed edge from α_I to α_J indicates a transition relation "$\alpha_I \rightarrow \alpha_J$". For example, $\alpha_2 \rightarrow \alpha_{24}$ since an agent can autonomously change a local protocol profile $PF(2) = DDDirS$ to $PF(4) = DDDisD$.

5 Retransmission

5.1 Cost Model

We discuss how an autonomous group (AG) agent can autonomously change the retransmission classes in a group as an example. Suppose there are three AG agents p_s, p_t, and p_u in a view V. An agent p_s sends a message m to a pair of agents p_t and p_u. Then, the agent p_t receives m while p_u fails to receive m. Let d_{st} be delay time between agents p_s and p_t [msec], f_{st} show probability that a message is lost, and b_{st} indicate bandwidth [bps].

First, let us consider the sender retransmission. Let $|m|$ show the size of a message m [bit]. It takes $(2d_{su}+ |m| / b_{su})$ [msec] to detect message loss after p_s sends a message m. Then, p_s retransmits m to p_u. Here, the message m may be lost again. The expected time ST_{su} and number SN_{su} of messages to deliver a message m to a faulty destination p_u are given as $ST_{su} = (2d_{su} + |m| / b_{su}) / (1 - f_{su})$ and $SN_{su} = 1 / (1 - f_{su})$.

In the destination retransmission, some destination agent p_t forwards the message m to p_u [Figure 6]. The expected time DT_{su} and number DN_{su} of messages to deliver a message m to p_u are given as follows:

1. $DT_{su} = (d_{su} + |m| / b_{su} + d_{ut}) + (2d_{ut} + |m| / b_{ut}) / (1 - f_{ut})$ if $d_{st} \le d_{su} + d_{ut}$, $(d_{st} + |m| / b_{st}) + (2d_{ut} + |m| / b_{ut}) / (1 - f_{ut})$ otherwise.
2. $DN_{su} = 1 + 1 / (1 - f_{ut})$.

If $ST_{su} > DT_{su}$, the destination agent p_t can forward the message m to the faulty agent p_u because the message m can be delivered earlier.

Each agent p_t monitors delay time d_{ut}, bandwidth b_{ut}, and message loss probability f_{ut} for each agent p_u which are received in the QoS base (QB). For example, p_t obtains the QoS information by periodically sending QoS information messages to all the agents in a view. The agent p_t maintains QoS information in a variable Q of QB where $Q_{ut} = \langle b_{ut}, d_{ut}, f_{ut} \rangle$ for $u = 1, ..., n$. If p_t receives QoS information from p_s, $Q_{su} = \langle b_{su}, d_{su}, f_{su} \rangle$ for $u = 1, ..., n$.

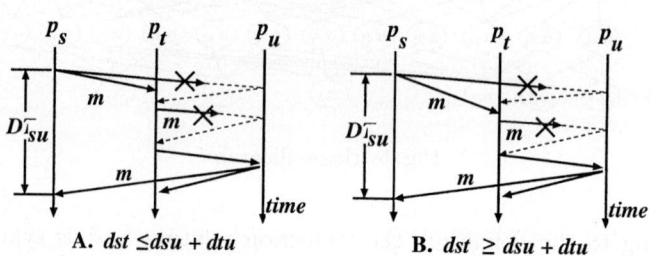

Fig. 6. Destination retransmission

5.2 Change of Retransmission Class

Suppose an agent p_s sends a message m and every agent p_t take the sender retransmission class, $C_t = \langle \cdots, S \rangle$. An agent p_u fails to receive m. According to the change of QoS supported by the underlying network, the sender agent p_s makes a decision to change the retransmission class with the destination one, say an agent p_t forwards m to p_u. However, p_t still takes the sender retransmission. Here, no agent forwards m to p_u.

Next, suppose all agents are taking the destination retransmission class. Here, QoS supported by the network is changed and an agent p_t decides to take the sender retransmission class. However, no agent forwards a message m to p_u since the sender p_s still takes the destination retransmission class. In order to prevent these silent situations, we take a following protocol:

1. A sender agent p_s sends a message m to all the destination agents. Every destination agent sends receipt confirmation not only to the sender agent p_s but also to the other destination agents.
2. If an agent p_t detects that a destination p_u has not received m, p_t selects a retransmission class which p_t considers to be optimal based on the QoS information Q.
   2.1 If p_t is a destination agent and changes a retransmission class, p_t forwards m to p_u and sends *Retx* message to the sender p_s.
   2.2 If p_t is a sender of a message m and takes the sender retransmission class, p_t retransmits m to p_u. If p_t takes a destination retransmission class, p_t waits for *Retx* message from a destination. If p_t does not receive *Retx*, p_t retransmits m to p_u.

[Theorem] At least one agent forwards a message m to an agent which fails to receive the message m.

5.3 Evaluation

We evaluate the autonomic group protocol (AGP) in terms of delivery time of a lost message. We make the following assumptions on this evaluation.

1. $d_{st} = d_{ts}$ for every pair of p_s and p_t.
2. The protocol processing time of every process is same.
3. No confirmation message is lost.

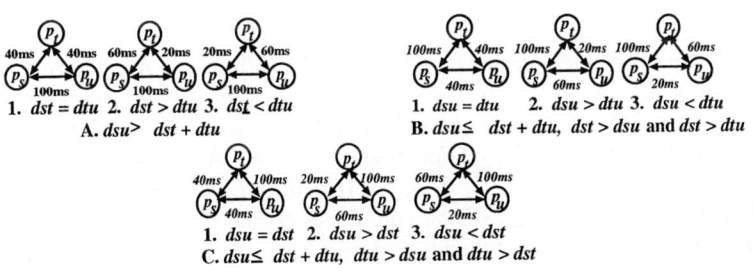

Fig. 7. AG agent graph

Let us consider a view $V = \{p_s, p_t, p_u\}$ where every agent takes a profile *DDDisS*. Here, suppose that an agent p_s sends a message m to a pair of agents

p_t and p_u in a view V. Then, the agent p_t receives m while another agent p_u fails to receive m. After the sender p_s and destination p_t detect the destination agent p_u fails to receive m, p_s and p_t autonomously select the retransmission class based on the QoS information. Here, we evaluate time to deliver a message m to a faulty agent p_u. In the view V, we assume that bandwidth between every pair of agents is same ($b_{st} = b_{su} = b_{ut} = 10$Mbps) and $f_{st} = f_{su}$ and $f_{ut} = 0$ %. Figure 7 shows an agent graph for V where each node denotes an agent and each edge shows a communication channel between agents. A label of the edge indicates delay time.

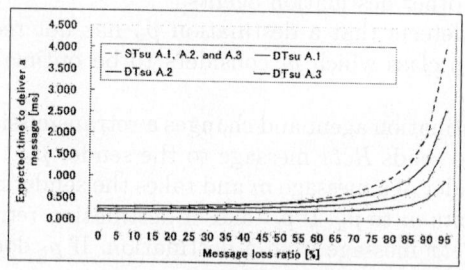

Fig. 8. $d_{su} \geq d_{st} + d_{ut}$

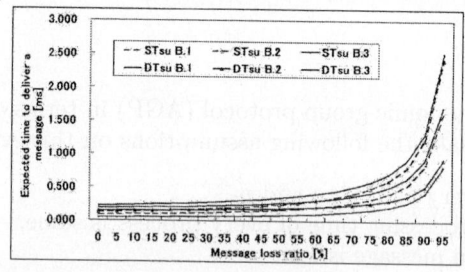

Fig. 9. $d_{su} \leq d_{st}+d_{ut}$, $d_{st}>d_{su}$, and $d_{st}>d_{ut}$

First, we consider a case $d_{su} \geq d_{st} + d_{ut}$ [Figure 7 A]. There are further cases: $d_{st} = d_{ut}$ [A.1], $d_{st} > d_{ut}$ [A.2], and $d_{st} < d_{ut}$ [A.3]. Figure 8 shows the expected time DT_{su} for three cases. In Figure 8, horizontal axis shows a message loss probability of f_{su} and f_{ut}. For case of Figure 7 A.2, $DT_{su} < ST_{su}$. For case of Figure 7 A.1, $DT_{su} < ST_{su}$ if $f_{su} > 15\%$ and $f_{ut} > 15\%$. For case of Figure 7 A.3, $DT_{su} < ST_{su}$ if $f_{su} > 50\%$ and $f_{ut} > 50\%$.

Next, there are further following cases for $d_{su} \leq d_{st} + d_{ut}$ [Figure 7]:

a. $d_{st} > d_{su}$ and $d_{st} > d_{ut}$: $d_{su} = d_{ut}$[B.1], $d_{su} > d_{ut}$[B.2], and $d_{su} < d_{ut}$[B.3].
b. $d_{ut} > d_{su}$ and $d_{ut} > d_{st}$: $d_{su} = d_{st}$[C.1], $d_{su} > d_{st}$[C.2], and $d_{su} < d_{st}$[C.3].

The expected time DT_{su} [Figure 7 B and 7 C] is shown for these six cases in Figures 9 and 10. For Figure 7 B.1 and B.3, $DT_{su} > ST_{su}$. For Figure 7 B.2, $DT_{su} < ST_{su}$ if $f_{su} > 20\%$ and $f_{ut} > 20\%$. For Figure 7 C, $DT_{su} > ST_{su}$.

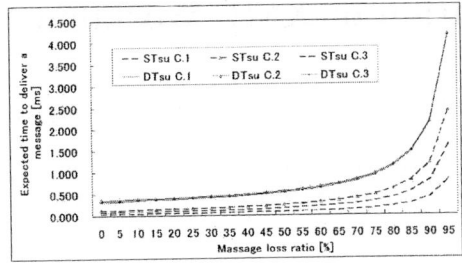

Fig. 10. $d_{su} \leq d_{st} + d_{ut}$, $d_{ut} > d_{su}$, and $d_{ut} > d_{st}$

6 Concluding Remarks

In this paper, we discussed an agent-based architecture to support distributed applications with autonomic group service in change of network and application QoS. We made clear what classes of functions to be realized in group communication protocols. Every AG agent autonomously changes a class of each protocol function which may not be the same as but are consistent with the other agents. We discussed how to support applications with the autonomic group service by changing retransmission classes as an example. We showed which retransmission class can be adopted for types of network configuration in the evaluation.

References

1. Agre, P.E.: P2P and the Promise of Internet Equality. Communication of the ACM **46** (2003) 39–42
2. IBM Corporation: Autonomic Computing Architecture : A Blueprint for Managing Complex Computing Environments. (2002) http://www-3.ibm.com/autonomic/pdfs/ACwhitepaper 1022.pdf.
3. van Renesse, R., Birman, K.P., Maffeis, S.: Horus: A Flexible Group Communication System. CACM **39** (1996) 76–83
4. Birman, K., Schiper, A., Stephenson, P.: Lightweight Causal and Atomic Group Multicast. ACM Trans. on Computer Systems **9** (1991) 272–290
5. Lamport, L.: Time, Clocks, and the Ordering of Events in a Distributed System. CACM **21** (1978) 558–565
6. Mattern, F.: Virtual Time and Global States of Distributed Systems. Parallel and Distributed Algorithms (1989) 215–226
7. Nakamura, A., Takizawa, M.: Reliable Broadcast Protocol for Selectively Ordering PDUs. Proc. of IEEE ICDCS-11 (1991) 239–246
8. Kaashoek, M.F., Tanenbaum, A.S.: An Evaluation of the Amoeba Group Communication System. Proc. of IEEE ICDCS-16 (1996) 436–447
9. Steketee, C., Zhu, W.P., Moseley, P.: Implementation of Process Migration in Amoeba. Proc. of IEEE ICDCS-14 (1994) 194–201

On Evolution of XML Workflow Schemata

Fábio Zschornack and Nina Edelweiss

Universidade Federal do Rio Grande do Sul – UFRGS
{fabiozs,nina}@inf.ufrgs.br

Abstract XML is arising as a new format to represent the enterprises' business processes, since it is a flexible and interchangeable language. In the workflow area, one of the most discussed questions is the evolution of the workflow representations, in order to meet new requirements. Despite the number of existing proposals, none of them deals with evolution of workflows that use the XML syntax. In this paper, we present a proposal for workflow evolution in which the workflow schema is represented in XML. The proposal is based on versioning concepts, that allow the storage and use of different versions of the same workflow schema. An evolution architecture is proposed, in order to separate the involved concepts in a set of managers. Two of these managers are discussed in this paper – Version Manager and Modification Manager.

1 Introduction

Enterprises are driven by business processes, and typically use workflow technology in order to achieve better results. According to [1], workflow is the automation of a business process, in whole or part, during which documents, information or tasks are passed from one participant to another for action, according to a set of procedural rules. A workflow management system (WFMS) completely defines, manages and executes workflows through the execution of software whose order of execution is driven by a computer representation of the workflow logic [1].

A workflow can be represented in different formats (e.g. Petri nets, graph models, etc.). Nowadays, XML is arising as an interesting way of workflow modeling [2,3,4], mainly due to features like flexibility and interchange facilities.

One of the most important questions in workflow management is the dynamic behaviour of business processes. This reflects in workflow construction, that in many cases cannot be defined completely in advance or must be modified when external or internal changes occur. Although there are some proposals that deal with workflow evolution issues (e.g. [5,6,7]), there is a lack of suitable mechanisms to model evolution when workflow is represented in XML, regarding specially the hierarchical arrangement of its elements.

In this paper, we propose an evolution architecture to manage modifications of XML workflows, based on versioning features. In summary, we make the following contributions: (*i*) We present a language that models workflow versions in XML in a hierarchical way. (*ii*) We propose a versioning approach in order

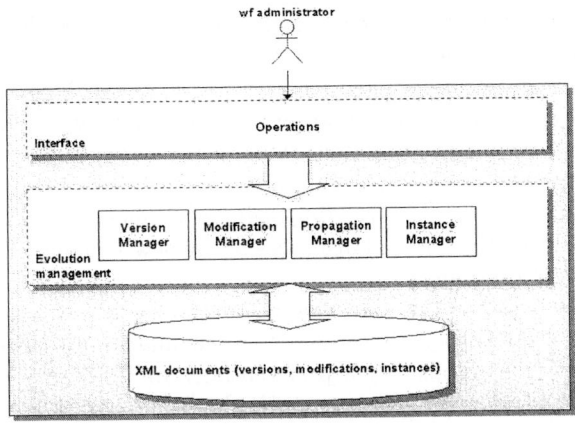

Figure 1. Overview of the proposed evolution architecture

to store many alternative versions for the same schema, thus preserving the whole history. (*iii*) We present a set of generic modification operations, which can be used to change a schema version. (*iv*) We show how generic operations are implemented in terms of an existing XML update language.

The remainder of this paper is organized as follows. Section 2 presents an overview of our evolution architecture, describing shortly its constituent parts. An example is shown in section 3. Section 4 describes the language used to represent XML workflow and the schema version management approach. In section 5 we present the modification strategy to change workflow schema versions. Section 6 presents some related work. We conclude the paper and point out some future work in section 7.

2 Evolution Architecture Overview

In order to allow the definition and management of workflow versions, an evolution architecture is proposed here. It deals with the pair *schema-instances*, in which the schema is the workflow representation that acts as a pattern, and the instances are the enactments (or executions) of a particular schema. In our approach, the schema can hold many versions, so that instances are, in fact, bound to schema versions.

The evolution architecture, presented in figure 1, is divided into three major parts:

- **Interface** – allows the workflow administrator to execute some high-level operations related to schema evolution and versioning as well as instances manipulation. These operations act on the respective modules in the underlying layer.
- **Evolution Management** – constitutes the core of the architecture. It contains a set of modules (managers) that effectively accomplish the operations

defined in the interface: (i) *Version Manager* – validates the schema specification passed by the administrator and controls the whole versions' lifecycle, from their creation to their deletion. (ii) *Modification Manager* – implements changes on a specific version and verifies the correctness of the version after the application of the modifications. (iii) *Instance Manager* – creates a new workflow instance based on a schema version specified by the respective operation on the interface. (iv) *Propagation Manager* – is responsible of migrating/adapting the affected instances to the new schema version, according to their execution points.
– **Repository** – all information handled by the Evolution Management layer is stored in a repository. Since workflow schemata are represented in XML (see section 4), the repository is preferentially an XML native database. The upper layer can also retrieve and modify the documents, whenever necessary.

This paper details the first two managers, addressing the creation and maintenance of schemata and versions (Version Manager), as well as changes that can be applied over versions (Modification Manager).

3 A Motivating Example

We illustrate the need of evolving workflow with an example, adapted from [4]. It is an on-demand computers assembly process, that is divided into two basic parts: the order reception from the customer and the computer assembly. In the first part of the process, some checks are performed in the incoming order, like budget and technical checks. The order must also be approved by a responsible person. After the successful conclusion of the first part, the ordered computers can be assembled. The organization must then request third-party components, since they do not have stocks. At the end of this process, the ordered computers are sent to the customer. The workflow describing this process we name $P1$.

Later the process must to be changed, in order to cope with new internal requirements. For instance, the manager, from that point on, approves all orders, while the vice-president is freed from this responsibility. Another change is that deliver and billing tasks must be done in parallel, saving time in the entire process. So, based on $P1$, we can create new workflow representations, e.g. $P2$, $P3$, and so on, that hold the process variants. The orders that have started under $P1$ can be concluded normally, with no modifications in their executions.

4 Version-Based Schema Representation

The architecture presented in section 2 is conceived to deal with any form of workflow representation. However, since we are considering evolution in an XML environment, our workflows are modeled in XML, as follows.
Workflow Representation in XML. The conceptual basis of our workflow schema modeling language is the *structured workflow* as defined in [8]. Briefly, a structured workflow consists of an activity S, that can be atomic or complex.

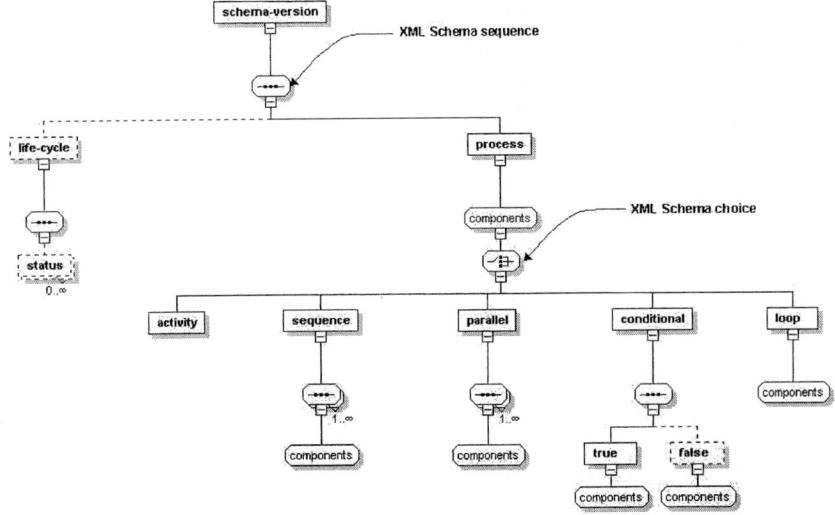

Figure 2. Structural hierarchy of the workflow modeling language

An atomic activity cannot be decomposed any further. On the other hand, a complex activity consists of a sequential, parallel, conditional, or loop structure, each of which is either atomic or complex.

All activities in structured workflows are properly nested, in other words, the structures cannot be overlapped. The nesting feature is inherent to well-formed XML documents [9], which impose the total "enclosure" of the respective elements. So, XML can be used to represent structured workflows.

A language to model workflows in XML, taking into account evolution questions, is presented in [10]. The language is based on proposals like XRL [3] and WQM [4]. Only the control flow is represented, disregarding other aspects like data flow and the organizational model. We adopt this strategy mainly because the most important changes on workflows are applied to their control flows, according to the number of existing proposals in the literature, e.g. [5,7,11,12].

Figure 2 depicts the hierarchical representation (XML Schema) of the elements defined in [10]. Elements are modeled by rectangles, dotted lines represent optional elements/relationships, and full lines represent required ones. Attributes are omitted in this figure. The process element embodies all the structures, being the unique starting and ending point of the control flow. Inside this element, one component is allowed, which can be a simple activity (activity element) or a complex structure (sequence, parallel, conditional, or loop element). A sequence element can hold one or more components, denoting that the various internal elements will be executed in a sequential way. A parallel element is sintatically similar to sequence, holding many components. However, the semantics is different, since a parallel structure can execute the internal elements at the same time. A conditional element can have only two internal elements: true and `false`. A condition is evaluated at the start of the structure execution and depending on the boolean result, the right path is chosen. The `loop` element executes a simple or complex activity repeatedly.

Figure 3 shows the workflow process $P1$ described in section 3 according to the language defined above.

```
<?xml version="1.0"?>
<schema-version>
  <process>
    <sequence>
      <loop until="order='ok'">
        <sequence>
          <conditional condition="new_order">
            <true>
              <activity name="Enter order"/>
            </true>
            <false>
              <activity name="Revise order"/>
            </false>
          </conditional>
          <parallel>
            <conditional condition="order&gt;50000">
              <true>
                <activity name="Vice-pres apprv."/>
              </true>
              <false>
                <activity name="Manager apprv."/>
              </false>
            </conditional>
            <activity name="Technical check"/>
            <activity name="Budget check"/>
          </parallel>
        </sequence>
      </loop>
      <parallel>
        <activity name="Order video"/>
        <activity name="Order card"/>
        <activity name="Order case"/>
      </parallel>
      <activity name="Receive parts"/>
      <activity name="Assemble"/>
      <activity name="Deliver"/>
      <activity name="Bill"/>
    </sequence>
  </process>
</schema-version>
```

Figure 3. Representation of $P1$ in XML

A document that follows the specification described in this section is named a *workflow schema version*. To create a new workflow schema, the administrator uses the *createSchema* operation available in the interface, passing a workflow specification document as a parameter to the Version Manager. In the following section, the versioning approach used by the architecture is better explained.

Schema Versioning Approach. The Version Manager implements versioning in order to allow the storage of multiple alternatives for the same workflow schema. This capability enables the maintenance of various active versions at the same time, each one holding many enacted instances. Moreover, it permits the storage of the whole schema derivation history, since our approach does not allow physical removal of (at least stable) versions.

The main attribution of the Version Manager is to control both schemata and versions in a suitable way. This is performed through the use of a structure named *Versioned Schema*. One versioned schema is defined for each created workflow schema. A versioned schema models the relationships among versions of the respective workflow schema in a tree-based fashion. In other words, a specific version may have many descendant versions, but only one ascendant (except the root version). This can be represented in XML format as depicted in figure 4, that shows a versioned schema structure of our workflow schema in section 3. According to this figure, the `versioned-schema` element contains two versions, $P1$ and $P2$, $P1$ being the ancestor of $P2$. If another version is derived from $P1$, it is represented as a $P2$ sibling.

A schema version can be created in two ways: (i) by the *createSchema* operation (previously described), or (ii) by a derivation. In the former case, the

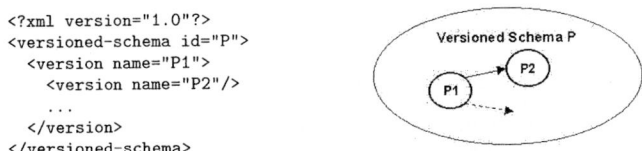

Figure 4. Versioned schema P represented in XML

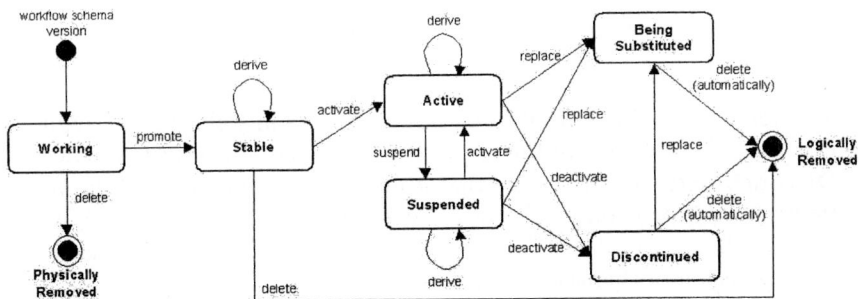

Figure 5. State diagram of a schema version

workflow specification passed to the Version Manager becomes the root version of the newly created versioned schema. This is the case of version $P1$, that was created by the administrator. In the latter case, the administrator uses a specific operation to derive a new version ($P2$ was created by a derivation on $P1$).

A schema version can assume a set of states, reflecting its evolution during lifetime, from creation to the (logical) removal. Figure 5 shows the state diagram for a schema version, together with the operations that perform the state transitions.

The states that a schema version can go through are described below:

- **Working** – each new schema version is created in this state. It is a transient state, in which modification operations can be applied over the version (see section 5). A version in the working state can be physically deleted if necessary.
- **Stable** – from this state on, all information about the version evolution is stored. This state is reached through a promote operation, from the working state. In this state, new versions may be derived, but no physical deletion is permitted, since the version may have derived some other versions. Only logical remove may be done.
- **Active** – in the active state, it is possible to create new instances according to the schema version representation (instances are beyond the scope of this paper), as well as to derive new versions. No removal is allowed, since there can be enacted instances.
- **Suspended** – this state is similar to active except that it cannot be used to create new instances. The enacted ones can run their executions normally.

```
<?xml version="1.0"?>
<schema-version>
  <life-cycle>
    <status name="working" itime="1" ftime="2"/>
    <status name="stable" itime="2" ftime="5"/>
    <status name="active" itime="5" ftime="15"/>
    <status name="discontinued" itime="15"/>
  </life-cycle>
  ...
</schema-version>
```

Figure 6. States of schema version $P1$

New versions can be derived from this version, as in stable and active states. It is possible to return to the active state, through an activate operation.

- **Discontinued** – this is a state that leads to a logical removal of the version. However, this will only take place when all the instances of this version finished their executions. The delete operation is done automatically after the conclusion of the last instance.
- **Being substituted** – as the discontinued state, this state leads the version to the logically removed phase. Nevertheless, enacted instances must migrate to another version in order to continue their executions. Instances adaptation is done by the Propagation Manager, not addressed in this paper.
- **Logically removed** – in this state a version cannot derive new versions nor hold or create instances, being stored for historical purposes only.

For each transition presented in figure 5, there is a correspondent operation (promote, derive, activate, deactivate, replace and delete).

In the approach proposed in this paper, the Version Manager also stores the version lifetime. This is done by the `life-cycle` and `status` elements, shown in figure 2. Each operation is passed to the Version Manager, that updates the version document accordingly. The `status` element has `itime` and (optionally) `ftime` attributes, that store the initial and final times when a state was the current one. In figure 6 the states for schema version $P1$ are shown, disregarding the control flow. The last `status` element does not have a `ftime` attribute, denoting this is the current state.

5 Modification of Workflow Schema Versions

Changes on schema versions are suitably handled by the Modification Manager, retrieving the right document and applying modifications on it. As described in section 4, a version can only be modified when it is in the working state. To assure this constraint, the Modification Manager checks the current state of the version and performs the changes only when allowed. In this section, we present a set of operations that can be applied over versions, while verifications performed by the Modification Manager are beyond the scope of this paper.

5.1 Generic Modification Operations

In general, a workflow can be modified in several ways. Activities may be inserted or deleted, new branches may be added to a total or partial fork, activities can change their positions, among others [5,11,7,12].

Concerning XML documents, modifications can be delete, rename, insert (after/before), and replace elements, attributes and/or PCDATA. These operations can be applied to any XML document, that must be further revalidated against a DTD or XML Schema, in order to guarantee correctness.

As our approach relies exclusively on XML documents to model workflow evolution, we take into consideration those operations that are useful or "make sense" when the document represents a workflow. We identify four operations in this case, that may be executed in conjunction or not. They are:

- **Insertion** – a new component is put into the workflow document, in a specific position.
- **Deletion** – this operation performs a removal of a component of the workflow document.
- **Movement** – the position of a component is changed to another place on the same workflow document.
- **Structure transformation** – a component is transformed to another component, thus changing its original semantics.

The operations above act only on elements, since we are interested in control flow changes and attributes have little influence on such part.

Analyzing the structures presented in section 4 and considering that a workflow document is valid and each operation is solely applied, we observe that the insertion operation can be normally performed into `sequence` and `parallel` elements, because these structures accept more than one direct sub-element. In `conditional` element, the operation can be done only if it inserts a `false` element, since it is optional. While a `loop` permits only one direct sub-element, insertions are not allowed into it. The deletion operation can be performed in a restricted way in case of `sequence`, `parallel` and `conditional` elements, and is denied for `loop`. For `sequence` and `parallel`, deletion operation cannot result in less than one sub-element. From the `conditional` element only the `false` sub-element can be removed, while no removal is allowed in `loop`. The movement operation may be considered a composite operation, as it combines an insertion and a deletion. So, effects in the structures must be evaluated in a whole, following the insertion and deletion rules. Finally, the structure transformation converts one complex structure to another, whenever possible. In this way, the operation can only result in a valid document if it transforms a `sequence` into a `parallel` or vice-versa, because these two structures are sintatically identical.

Obviously, these operations can be applied over a schema version in conjunction, modifying many parts of the same version. Although each operation separately may carry the version to a invalid document, the final result must be a valid workflow schema version, as transactions in a traditional DBMS.

5.2 Operations Implementation

The Modification Manager can perform the operations described above using a modification language, XUpdate. XUpdate is designed to change any XML document, and can hold many modification operations in it. This language was chosen because it describes the operations in XML syntax, so we have all the components (versions, versioned schemata, modifications) in a standard way of representation.

When a modification is needed, the administrator executes the *changeSchema* operation in the interface, specifying the version to be modified and the XUpdate document that contains the changes. The operation is passed to the Modification Manager, that retrieves the version and applies the changes over it, but only when the version is in the working state. The resulting document must be revalidated for correctness purposes.

Each generic modification operation defined in section 5.1 can be mapped to one or more XUpdate commands, in order to implement changes on workflow schema versions.

The insertion operation can be implemented in two ways: (i) `insert-before` (`insert-after`), that puts a new element before (after) a given element, and (ii) `append`, that inserts a new element as the latest child of another element. The deletion can be simply implemented by a `remove` command, that deletes an element from the document. For the movement operation, we must use `variable` and `value-of` commands in conjunction with one insertion and the deletion operations. The `variable` command binds an element to a defined variable, while the `value-of` command restores an element previously stored with a `variable` command. Finally the structure transformation can be implemented by a `rename` command, that changes the name of an element.

6 Related Work

Workflow Evolution and Versioning. On the evolution side, the most important proposals are [5] and [6]. The former provides a set of modification operations that allow to change a workflow schema and to migrate active instances to the modified schema. However, versioning concepts are not considered, so there is only one active schema at a moment. The same drawback is present in [6]. But differently from [5], that approach relies on an instance-based model, allowing *ad-hoc* changes on specific instances. Compared with these two proposals, our approach has versioning features, that offer the storage of the different version alternatives and allow many active schema versions, and is based on schemata rather than on instances.

The proposals described in [7], [11], and [12] deal with the versioning concept. In the model presented in [7], each schema is versioned. A set of operations is defined, as well as migration conditions, that rule new versions derivation and instances migration. The proposal developed by [12] is very similar to [7], providing an evolution strategy that is independent from the workflow representation, preserving internal migration algorithms. The proposal presented in [11], although based in versioning, has limitations in respect to instances migration and does not offer details of its modification operations. The three proposals allow versions removal, which is not permitted by our approach.

Workflow Representation in XML. There are a few workflow modeling languages in XML. We point out three proposals: [3], [4], and [2]. The first one, a language that enables document routing on the Internet, is composed by a set of basic building blocks, with semantics expressed in terms of Petri Nets. The approach presented in [4], whose main objective is to provide queries over workflows also works with building blocks, the language being described in terms of XML Query Algebra. The language presented in [2], a generic model for business processes interchange among different workflow modeling tools, is not based on structures, modeling transitions between activities in a explicit way. This feature helps in designing complex control flows, but workflow modifications are not intuitive to the user, since in most cases attributes values must be changed to reflect modifications. Moreover, to ensure correctness of resulting flows is sometimes a difficult task, in contrast to structured proposals, where this problem is almost trivial.

None of these proposals deal with questions like evolution or versioning of the workflow models. Our work has enriched the two first proposals, considering evolution aspects and versioning features.

7 Concluding Remarks and Future Work

This paper proposed an evolution architecture for workflow representations in XML, that regards versioning related to workflow schemata. The language that models workflows in XML is based on structures, which are easy to manipulate. The use of versions increases the power of the evolution strategy, because we can have many alternative versions at the same time, each active one with enacted instances. In addition, our approach does not allow versions removal, which is permited in other proposals, considering that the history maintenance enables queries over past versions and instances. We presented one specific manager of the architecture, Version Manager, that encapsulate all necessary functionality to control workflow versions (and schemata). One of the main characteristics of this work is that all components (versions and versioned schemata) are represented with the same syntax, XML. This is a desirable feature since we have a unique form to manage and handle the components of the architecture.

As future work we point out the definition of the other managers of the architecture (Instance Manager and Propagation Manager), in order to integrate all the proposed modules. Finally, the integrated architecture will be implemented and connected to a WFMS that deals with XML representations, in order to provide this system with evolution capabilities and check the feasibility of the proposed architecture.

References

1. Workflow Management Coalition: The Workflow Reference Model (1995) Available at: http://www.wfmc.org/standards/docs.htm.
2. Workflow Management Coalition: XML Process Definition Language, Version 1.0 (2002) Available at: http://www.wfmc.org/standards/docs.htm.
3. Aalst, W., Kumar, A.: XML Based Schema Definition for Support of Inter-organizational Workflow. Technical report, University of Colorado, Boulder (2000) Available at: http://spot.colorado.edu/~akhil/pubs.html.
4. Christophides, V., Hull, R., Kumar, A.: Querying and Splicing of XML Workflows. In: Proc. of the 9th International Conference on Cooperative Information Systems, CoopIS, Trento, Italy, Berlin, Springer-Verlag (2001) 386–402
5. Casati, F., Ceri, S., Pernici, B., Pozzi, G.: Workflow Evolution. Data & Knowledge Engineering **24** (1998) 211–238
6. Reichert, M., Dadam, P.: $ADEPT_{flex}$ – Supporting Dynamic Changes of Workflows Without Loosing Control. Journal of Intelligent Information Systems **10** (1998) 93–129
7. Kradolfer, M., Geppert, A.: Dynamic Workflow Schema Evolution Based on Workflow Type Versioning and Workflow Migration. In: Proc. of the 4th International Conference on Cooperative Information Systems, CoopIS, Edinburgh, Scotland, Los Alamitos, IEEE Computer Society Press (1999) 104–114
8. Kiepuszewski, B., Hofstede, A., Bussler, C.: On Structured Workflow Modelling. In: Proc. of the 12th Conference on Advanced Information Systems Engineering, CAiSE, Stockholm, Sweden, Berlin, Springer-Verlag (2000) 431–445
9. World Wide Web Consortium: Extensible Markup Language (XML) 1.0 (Second Edition) (2000) Available at: http://www.w3.org/TR/REC-xml.
10. Zschornack, F., Edelweiss, N.: Uma Linguagem para Representação de Workflow em XML com Suporte a Evolução e Versionamento de Esquemas. In: XXVIII Conferencia Latinoamericana de Informatica, Montevideo, Uruguay (2002) (in portuguese).
11. Joeris, G., Herzog, O.: Managing Evolving Workflow Specifications. In: Proc. of the 3rd International Conference on Cooperative Information Systems, CoopIS, New York, Los Alamitos, IEEE Computer Society Press (1998) 310–319
12. Dias, P., Vieira, P., Rito-Silva, A.: Dynamic Evolution in Workflow Management Systems. In: Proc. of the 3rd International Workshop on Web Based Colaboration, WBC, Prague, Czech Republic, Los Alamitos, IEEE Computer Society Press (2003) 254–260

A Framework for Selecting Workflow Tools in the Context of Composite Information Systems

Juan P. Carvallo, Xavier Franch, Carme Quer, and Nuria Rodríguez

Universitat Politècnica de Catalunya (UPC)
c/Jordi Girona 1-3, Campus Nord, mòdul C6, 08034 Barcelona
{carvallo,franch,cquer}@lsi.upc.es,
nuria.rodriguez-camara@upc.es

Abstract. When an organization faces the need of integrating some workflow-related activities in its information system, it becomes necessary to have at hand some well-defined informational model to be used as a framework for determining the selection criteria onto which the requirements of the organization can be mapped. Some proposals exist that provide such a framework, remarkably the WfMC reference model, but they are designed to be applicable when workflow tools are selected independently from other software, and departing from a set of well-known requirements. Often this is not the case: workflow facilities are needed as a part of the procurement of a larger, composite information system and therefore the general goals of the system have to be analyzed, assigned to its individual components and further detailed. We propose in this paper the MULTSEC method in charge of analyzing the initial goals of the system, determining the types of components that form the system architecture, building quality models for each type and then mapping the goals into detailed requirements which can be measured using quality criteria. We develop in some detail the quality model (compliant with the ISO/IEC 9126-1 quality standard) for the workflow type of tools; we show how the quality model can be used to refine and clarify the requirements in order to guarantee a highly reliable selection result; and we use it to evaluate two particular workflow solutions available in the market (kept anonymous in the paper). We develop our proposal using a particular selection experience we have recently been involved in, namely the procurement of a document management subsystem to be integrated in an academic data management information system for our university.

1. Introduction

The goal of workflow management systems is to provide automated support to the enactment and coordination of business process in an organizational context [1]. This type of systems is being used more and more not only in staff-intensive environments but also in all those contexts in which clearly defined circuits for types of data exist.

This increasing use of workflow technologies has mainly two consequences. On the one hand, it is necessary to improve the state of the art of the workflow solutions available in the market with new functionalities or improving their quality of service (e.g., [2, 3]). On the other hand, we need to bridge the gap among workflow producers and consumers to facilitate the adoption of the adequate solutions with respect the requirements of organizations. This paper focuses on this second aspect.

There are several proposals that identify relevant criteria for driving the selection of a workflow tool, issued both by academic parties [1, 4, 5] and professional firms (e.g., [6, 7]). These proposals are enough for those cases in which the requirements over the tool are clear and the tool is selected without considering its connections with other subsystems. However, the situation is often different. The usual case is that organizations establish some departing requirements that are very diverse in nature, including not only workflow-related services but also other type of functionalities such as customer relationship management, document management, and others. Therefore, it is necessary to identify the types of components that form composite information system that is being procured, and refine the departing requirements into more detailed ones, assigning them to the components.

In this paper we present MULTSEC (**MULT**iple **SE**le**C**tion), a method that can be applied in the selection of multiple components, and we explain its application in a concrete real case, the procurement of a subsystem for managing documents in an academic setting. MULTSEC consists of four activities (see fig. 1): determination of the goals of the system-to-be; identification of the types of components of the system and assignment of the goals to these types; development of an informational model for describing the selection criteria (i.e., the quality factors) for the types of components; and stepwise refinement of the departing goals into detailed requirements expressed in terms of the selection criteria. The last two activities are carried out tightly intertwined.

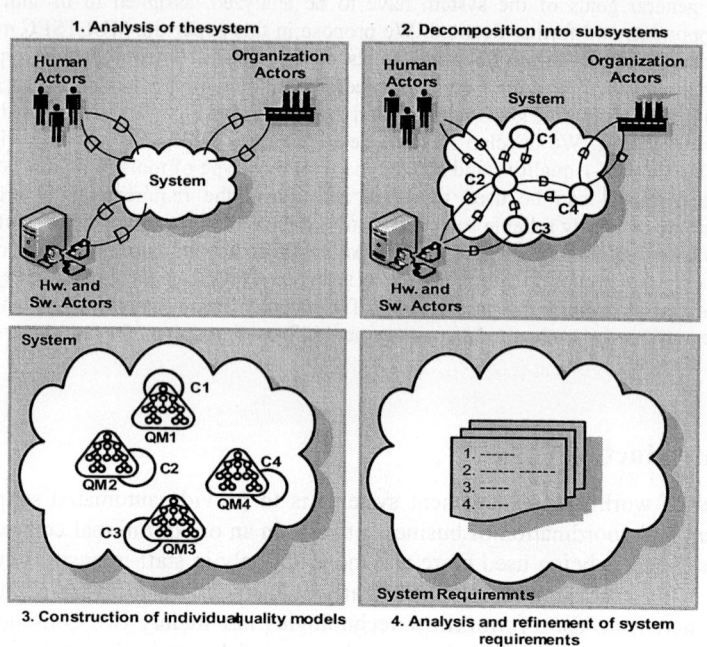

Fig. 1. Representation of the MULTSEC method

One of the key points of our MULTSEC is the convenience to have a uniform informational model for representing the selection criteria, in order to allow the simultaneous analysis of the components. We use the ISO/IEC 9126-1 quality standard [8] as such a framework. It proposes to structure the selection criteria as a quality model, defined as a hierarchy of quality factors, and fixes the higher levels of this hierarchy, whose factors must be subsequently refined. The quality models of all the types of components of the systems share these higher levels.

The rest of the paper is structured as follows. In section 2 we present the case study that drives the paper and determine a set of initial goals of the system, used in section 3 to identify the types of components of the system. Section 4 analyses the construction of quality models for the types of components, and in section 5 we develop in some depth the construction of an ISO/IEC 9126-1-compliant quality model for workflow tools. In section 6 we show how the quality factors can be used to refine and analyze the requirements. In section 7 we evaluate two real workflow tools using the quality model. Finally, section 8 provides the conclusions of the work.

2. PRISMA: A System for Academic Data Management

PRISMA is an ongoing software project carried out in the Universitat Politècnica de Catalunya (UPC) at Barcelona, Spain. The goal of the project is to provide the UPC with an integrated management of academic data such as students, courses, departments, etc., instead of the departing situation in which every school owns its particular management system. The PRISMA system has already been successfully used in several designated pilot schools and it is supposed to be fully delivered during 2004.

At the heart of such a system, we find the need of storing, manipulating, rendering and eventually removing (when obsolete or useless) a great deal of documents of several types, such as student application forms, school curricula, academic diplomas, official advertisements and so on. The authors of this paper were in charge of procuring a subsystem to be integrated into the PRISMA system in charge of these services. We applied the MULTSEC method with this aim.

As first step of MULTSEC, the PRISMA team determined a set of initial high-level goals addressing this part of the system functionality. Some relevant goals appear at table 1. We can distinguish among goals that are functional in nature, e.g. goals 1 and 2, and goals that are non-functional, e.g. goals 4 and 8.

3. An Architecture for the System

The second step in MULTSEC aims at decomposing the system into types of components and assigning the system goals to these types. Examples of type of components are document management and workflow management. Please note that a particular component may cover more than one type of component, e.g. there are a lot of document management tools that offer workflow capabilities. In our approach, it is crucial to keep these two concepts (type of component and component) separated because the types are the ones that determine the selection criteria.

The decomposition in MULTSEC is driven mainly by two different carriers:
– Since we use goals as the starting point of system decomposition, we follow a goal-oriented framework to guide this decomposition process and represent the

resulting architecture. Among different available options, we have opted by the *i** goal-oriented specification language [9] and in particular its SD models. In SD

Table 1: Some initial goals of the PRISMA system with respect to academic data management

Number	Goal
1	The system shall capture both paper documents and electronic documents in different formats
2	The system shall define and control automatically the flow of documents
3	The system shall visualize documents in the web when required
4	The system shall be easy to configure
5	The system shall present multi-language interfaces
6	The system shall define different types of users with their own access rights
7	The system shall provide version management
8	The system shall keep data privacy
9	The system shall react quickly to external stimuli

models, intentional actors depend on others to attain their goals. Actors and dependencies, which form together an intentional network, are determined from the initial goals of the system. Actors represent types of components and dependencies reflect how a type of component needs another for attaining goals, satisfying quality of service levels, performing tasks or consuming resources.
- To facilitate reuse and make the decomposition process more agile, types of components can be arranged in a taxonomy [10]. The taxonomy can be build from categorizations proposed by professional consultant companies, third-party organizations and knowledge accumulated from previous experiences. In [11] we have presented the rationale for building a taxonomy for business applications which includes some of the types of components that appear in our case study, remarkably the one of workflow tools. Fig. 2 shows an excerpt of this taxonomy. In order to make the taxonomy usable in our MULTSEC, the goals for each type of component should be clearly stated. For instance, the goal of the *Workflow* type may be formulated as "Facilitate or even automate business processes".

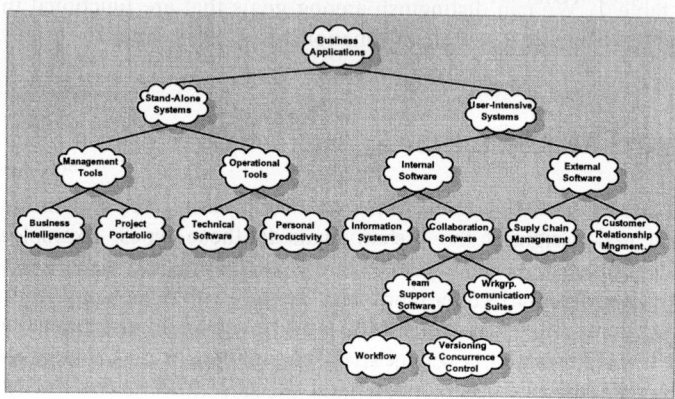

Fig. 2. An excerpt of a taxonomy for business applications

Fig. 3 shows an *i** SD model embracing the most representative type of components of the system and some of the relationships among them. The precise meaning of the

3 types of dependencies shown in the figure is out of the scope of the paper, see [9] for details. Table 2 reallocate the system goals into the types of components. We can check that functional-like goals are covered by a few, often just one, system components; on the contrary, non-functional-like goals are cross-cutting and therefore affect the majority, often all, of the system components.

Table 2: Relationships of the system goals and the system architectural components

Number	Components			
	DM	W	WCM	DI
1	x			x
2		x		
3			x	
4	x	x	x	x
5	x	x	x	x
6	x	x	x	
7	x			
8	x	x	x	x
9	x	x	x	x

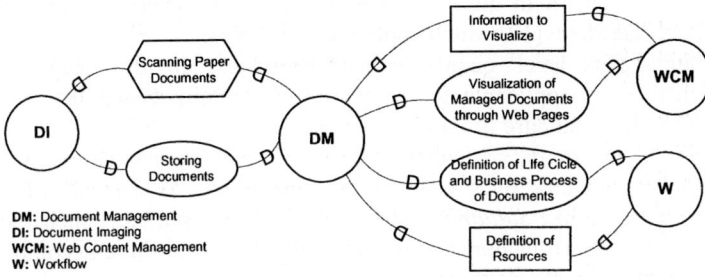

Fig. 3. Some types of components of the PRISMA document management subsystem and their relationships represented with an i^* SD model

4. Building Individual Quality Models for the System Components

In the third and fourth steps of MULTSEC the types of components are analysed in order to determine which are the relevant quality features that need to be assessed during system procurement. The starting point of the analysis of a type of component are the system goals that have been assigned to this component. These goals are to be decomposed using a quality framework for obtaining both more detailed system requirements, and measurement criteria for them in the form of quality attributes. In our method, we have chosen the ISO/IEC 9126-1 quality standard [8] as quality framework. It is one of the most, if not the most, widespread software quality standards available in the software engineering community. The fact of having the same quality framework for all the types of components of the system makes the resulting requirements more structured and easy to analyse, as shown in section 6.

An ISO/IEC-9126-1-compliant quality model is defined by means of general characteristics of software, which are further refined into subcharacteristics, which in turn are decomposed into attributes. Attributes collect the properties that software components belonging to the domain under analysis exhibit. Intermediate hierarchies of subcharacteristics and attributes may appear making thus the model highly structured.

The ISO/IEC 9126-1 standard fixes 6 top level characteristics: functionality, reliability, usability, efficiency, maintainability and portability. It also fixes their further refinement into 27 subcharacteristics but does not elaborate the quality model below this level, making thus the model flexible. The model is to be completed based in the exploration of the software domain under analysis; because of this, we may say that the standard is very versatile and may be tailored to domains of different nature, such as the one of workflow tools.

5. A Quality Model for Workflow Management Systems

In this section we give a more detailed presentation of the quality model that we built for the workflow domain in the context of the PRISMA project. We followed a method defined elsewhere [12] which applies several steps:

1. Determining first-level quality subcharacteristics. In this step we chose subcharacteristics applicable to the workflow domain among the 27 that the ISO/IEC 9126-1 standard provides.
2. Defining a hierarchy of subcharacteristics. Subcharacteristics are further decomposed into new ones yielding to a hierarchy. As a result we obtained subcharacteristics like *Suitability* which were decomposed into subcharacteristics specific to the workflow domain and others like *Security* whose decomposition is fairly common in different domains. Some subcharacteristics appear in more than one decomposition, like *Interface parameterization*. Table 3 shows some subcharacteristics of *Functionality*, *Usability* and *Efficiency* characteristics.
3. Decomposing subcharacteristics into attributes. We decomposed the abstract subcharacteristics into quality attributes. Some attributes were directly measurable but others required further decomposition. Table 3 shows some quality attributes for some of the subcharacteristics therein.
4. Assigning metrics for the attributes. Metrics either quantitative or qualitative are defined. Typical issues like scale of the metric, measurement protocol and others [13] must be taken into account.

6. Analysis of System Requirements Using the Quality Models

The resulting quality model can be used not only to describe quality requirements in a structured manner, but also as a framework to support requirements elicitation. On the one hand quality model construction can be driven towards the identification of the quality attributes which make operational the abstract goals of the system, in such way that quality requirements can be expressed as constraints over them. On the other hand attributes in the quality model can be used to discover new system requirements

which were not originally considered. When making abstract goals of table 1 operational in terms of quality attributes several situations arose:
- Some goals such as goal 5 were directly mapped into a single attribute in the model, the *Interface languages supported*. This attribute belongs to the *Interface Language Issues* subcharacteristic. Once located, we realized that this subcharacteristic has other attributes that could also contribute in a positive way to

Table 3: Quality model for the *Workflow* type of component: An excerpt

Characteristic	Subcharacteristics Level 1	Subcharacteristics Level 2	Attributes
Functionality	Suitability	Process Definition	
		Task Management	
		Organization and Notifications	Notification rules administration
			User notification types
			User notification mechanisms
			E-mail notification format
			Organizational model administration
			Substitution rules
			Support rules
			Directories importation
		Monitoring Processes and Activities	
		Reports	
	Security	Data Protection	Security provider
			Security transfer protocols
			Certification services
			Encryption algorithms
			Electronic signatures
		ACL Management	ACL support
			Access rights
			Group restrictions
			User restrictions
Usability	Understand-ability	Interface Parameterization	(see decomposition in *Operability* below)
		Interface Languages Issues	Interface languages supported
			Modification of text labels of the application
			Vendor support to provide the interface in a particular language
	Learnability	Documentation and Support	
	Operability	Interface Parameterization	Interface standards
			Interface parameterization offered
		Accounts Administration	Individual users and groups
			Private and public accounts
			Individual and shared directories
			LDAP
			Single sign-on
			Connection with other directories
Efficiency	Time Behavior	Response Time	Estimated work time for each activity
			Average time to complete the tasks from a workflow process instance

the attainment of the goal, namely *Modification of text labels of the application* and *Vendor support to provide the interface in a particular language*. Thus we proposed additional requirements of the system based on these attributes.
- In the case of goals 2 and 4 the situation was more complex, they implied a mixture of functionalities, supported by the selection of several attributes of the model. In the case of goal 4, it was made operational in terms of attributes of the *Operability* subcharacteristic, e.g. *Accounts Administration* and *Interface Parameterization* among others. In the case of goal 2 attributes related to some *Suitability* subcharacteristics such as *Process Definition, Task Management* and *Organization and Notifications,* were required. The attributes of these subcharacteristics define the core functionality of the workflow component, thus they are hardly reusable in other domains. However, they became the main source of requirements for the workflow component. Needless to say that this is due to the fact that individual attributes of the quality model help to identify and/or refine requirements related to them.
- The case of goal 6 was similar to goals 2 and 4, it was also made operational in terms of several attributes of the model, namely those belonging to the *Accounts Administration* and *ACL Management* subcharacteristics. However when considered the system as a whole we found two different situations. On the one hand we considered highly desirable that all the components of the system use the same *Directory Service*, so we identified a new actor in the system providing this functionality with its own quality model; as a consequence, quality attributes concerning users were defined once instead of several times. This case aligns with the iterative nature of the MULTSEC method in which additional components of the system (in this case a directory service) can be identified at any stage of the process. On the contrary, ACLs are not common to every application, e.g. document management tools will include permissions to add, edit, delete or publicise documents, whilst workflow systems may include the abort process, reassume, reassign or expedite permissions, among others.
- Several security-related quality attributes, e.g. *secure transfer protocols, certification services, encryption algorithms* and *electronic signatures,* were used to operationalize goal 8. As in the previous case it was considered desirable that all the components in the system share the same security mechanisms.

In general it can be said that cross-cutting goals let to the identification of system level requirements. This is one of the reasons why quality models of the different components of the system are build upon the same standard and with the same method. This easies the matching of quality attributes of the different models and the statement of system-level quality requirements common to all of them.

As a further example of the utility of this characteristic consider a requirement to measure the time required by the system to incorporate a document in the system, several throughput and response times have to be considered, including: the capturing rate of document imaging tool, the response time of the document management tool and its document processing rate, the time required by the content management tool to publish documents, and the response time overhead of the workflow process managing the different tasks. Although all of them belong to different quality models, they are categorised under the same subcharacteristics. Thus by navigating the same branch of the hierarchy in all the models at the same time they can be reconciled.

A final matter which is worth to remark is that some attributes identified in individual quality models may also lead to the identification of system-level requirements. This is the case of the *Single sign-on* quality attribute which was first identified when constructing the workflow quality model. Other components also require logging into the system (usually by supplying a username and a password), but it can be desirable to avoid this redundancy in order for the system to be perceived as a single unit.

7. Evaluation of Workflow Tools

Once the quality model for workflow and the rest of system types of components was completed, we evaluated several tools. As mentioned in section 3, some tools covered more than one type of component, in which case we evaluated altogether the criteria of the involved types. In the case of workflow tools, after a first screening process usual in COTS selection processes [14] we evaluated in detail two particular tools. Both are mainly workflow tools, aiming at simplifying the management of complex processes by providing an intuitive visual design environment and the ability to track workflow process events during process enactment. We observed that (see table 4):

- Some attributes had the same value in both tools. For instance, *User notification mechanisms*: both offer the possibility of receiving notifications via email or in the lists of things to do in the activities page, as well as a simple advice in the screen.
- In addition to those attributes that are evaluating the same in both tools, we sometimes found that one tool has more values in a quality attribute than the other but this difference was not important (e.g., *Interface languages offered*). In this cases the attributes were not impacting in the selection.
- In other quality attributes we detected that they can take more values than the ones that appear considering just the requirements. This is the case of *Security transfer protocols*: initially we just required S-HTTP, but then we observed that both were also offering SSL and then we added this as requirement.
- The real relevant attributes were those related to the selection goals with significant differences. This is the case of *Support rules*: although both tools support the organization rules *by role* and *by user,* Tool 1 adds the *by department* and *by group*.

Table 4: Matching requirements and tools information with the quality attributes

Attribute	Requirements	Tool 1	Tool 2
User notification mechanisms	As much as possible	e-mail, task page, message (screen)	e-mail, task page, message (screen)
Interface languages offered	Catalan, Spanish and English	English, Catalan, Spanish and other 13	English, Catalan, Spanish and other 27
Security transfer protocols	SHTTP	SHTTP, SSL	SHTTP, SSL
Support rules	As much as possible	By role, by group, by department, by user	By role, by user

8. Conclusions

Lots of work have been done in the context of improving workflow technologies with new facilities. Also, some approaches exist for the assessment of the quality of service of workflow tools considered isolated [1, 4, 5, 6, 7]. However, to the best of our knowledge, there is a lack of studies for assessing the quality of service of workflow tools when considering the procurement of a complex system in which workflow facilities are just a part of the entire functionalities, which turns out to be a very usual situation. The goal of this paper has been to provide a solution to this problem.

The most salient features of our approach are:
- We have considered workflow tools selection in the most usual context, i.e. as a part of a more comprehensive selection process. We have supported this by using the same informational quality model for all the types of components. Although it may be argued that for some types of components well-defined reference frameworks exist (e.g., the WfMC framework), we do believe that in the context of composite systems, uniformity can be more important. Also, it is worth to remark that a way to overcome this problem is to provide a mapping from the domain-specific reference frameworks to the common informational quality model.
- This informational quality model has been chosen to be one of the most, if not the most, widespread quality models in the software engineering field, the ISO/IEC 9126-1 standard. Using a widespread standard facilitates knowledge reuse, transfer of knowledge among different types of components (i.e., quality subcharacteristics and attributes that behave the same), and dissemination of results.
- The informational quality model is tightly bound to the requirements elicitation, analysis and operationalization activities.
- We use in the approach some artefacts such as i^* diagrams and taxonomies that provide a degree of formalism that makes our process more reliable. Also these elements support reusability (types of components appear in different projects; the quality models are inherited downwards the taxonomy) and understandability (relationships are made explicit).

References

1. Workflow Management Coalition. "The Workflow Reference Model". TC00-1003, 1995.
2. H. Schuschel, M. Weske. "Integrated Workflow Planning and Coordination". In *Proceedings of 14th International Conference on Database and Expert Systems Application* (DEXA'03), LNCS 2736, 2003.
3. M. Shen, D.-R. Liu. "Coordinating Interorganizational Workflows Based on Process-Views". In *Proceedings of 13rd International Conference on Database and Expert Systems Application* (DEXA'01), LNCS 2113, 2001.
4. C. Patel, K. Supekar, Y. Lee. "A QoS Oriented Framework for Adaptative Management of Web Service Based Workflows". In *Proceedings of 14th International Conference on Database and Expert Systems Application* (DEXA'03), LNCS 2736, 2003.
5. J. Cardoso, A. Sheth, J. Miller. "Workflow Quality of Service". *Procs. IFIP TC5/WG5.12 Intl' Conference on Enterprise Integration and Modeling Techniques* (ICEIMT'02), 2002.
6. http://www.document-management-software-system.net/rfp_template_db-gen.html. Last accessed March 2004.
7. http://www.wngs.com/wgs_e/wfsp4.htm . Last accessed March 2004.

8. *ISO/IEC Standard 9126-1 Software Engineering, Part 1: Quality Model, 2001.*
9. E. Yu. "Towards Modeling and Reasoning Support for Early-Phase Requirements Engineering". In *Procs. 3rd IEEE Intl' Symposium on Requirements Engineering* (ISRE), 1997.
10. R. Glass and I. Vessey, "Contemporary Application-Domain Taxonomies". *IEEE Software*, 12 (4), July 1995.
11. J.P. Carvallo, Xavier Franch, Carme Quer, Marco Torchiano. "Characterization of a Taxonomy for Business Applications and the Relationships among them". In *Proceedings of the 3rd International Conference on COTS-Based Software System* (ICCBSS), LNCS, 2004.
12. X. Franch, J.P. Carvallo. "Using Quality Models in Software Package Selection". *IEEE Software*, 20(1), January/February 2003, pp. 34-41.
13. N. Fenton, S. Pfleeger. *Software Metrics: A Rigorous and Practical Approach.* PWS, 1998.
14. N. Maiden, C. Ncube. "Acquiring Requirements for COTS Selection". *IEEE Software*, 15(2), 1998.

Evaluation Strategies for Bitmap Indices with Binning[*]

Kurt Stockinger, Kesheng Wu, and Arie Shoshani

Lawrence Berkeley National Laboratory
1 Cyclotron Road, Berkeley, CA 94720, USA
{KStockinger,KWu,AShoshani}@lbl.gov

Abstract. Bitmap indices are efficient data structures for querying read-only data with low attribute cardinalities. To improve the efficiency of the bitmap indices on attributes with high cardinalities, we present a new strategy to evaluate queries using bitmap indices. This work is motivated by a number of scientific data analysis applications where most attributes have cardinalities in the millions. On these attributes, binning is a common strategy to reduce the size of the bitmap index.

In this article we analyze how binning affects the number of pages accessed during query processing, and propose an optimal way of using the bitmap indices to reduce the number of pages accessed. Compared with two basic strategies the new algorithm reduces the query response time by up to a factor of two. On a set of 5-dimensional queries on real application data, the bitmap indices are on average 10 times faster than the projection index.

1 Introduction

Large scale, high-dimensional data analysis requires specialized data structures to efficiently query the search space. Both commercial data warehouses and scientific data are typically read-only, and index data structures do not require transactional support for update operations. Under these conditions bitmap indices are suitable for complex, multi-dimensional data analyses.

The basic idea of bitmap indices is to store one slice of bits per distinct attribute value (e.g. all integers from 0 to 140). Each bit of the slice is mapped to a record or a data object. The associated bit is set if and only if the record's value fulfills the property in focus (e.g. the respective value of the record is equal to, say, 87). One of their main strengths is that complex logical selection

---

[*] The authors thank Ekow Otoo, Doron Rotem, and Heinz Stockinger for their constructive comments during the writing of this article. This work was supported by the Director, Office of Science, Office of Laboratory Policy and Infrastructure Management, of the U.S. Department of Energy under Contract No. DE-AC03-76SF00098. This research used resources of the National Energy Research Scientific Computing Center, which is supported by the Office of Science of the U.S. Department of Energy.

operations can be performed very quickly by means of Boolean operators such as AND, OR, or XOR.

The contributions of this article are as follows. We summarize the current state of the art of bitmap index technologies and focus in particular on queries against scientific data. Next we introduce a novel bitmap evaluation technique and compare it with currently deployed methods. We provide both analyses and experimental measurements to show that the new strategy indeed minimizes the number of records scanned. In some cases we observe a factor two improvement in query response time using the new strategy.

2 Related Work

Bitmap indices are mostly used for On-Line Analytical Processing (OLAP) and data warehouse applications [1] for complex queries in read-only or append-only environments. The most commonly used bitmap encoding strategies are *equality*, *range* or *interval* encoding [2, 3]. Equality encoding is optimized for so-called exact match queries of the form $a = v$ where a is an attribute and v the value to be searched for. Range encoding, on the other hand, is optimized for one-sided range queries of the from $a\ op\ v$ where $op \in \{<, \leq, >, \geq\}$. Finally, interval encoding shows the best performance characteristics for two sided-range queries of the form $v_1\ op\ a\ op\ v_2$.

Traditional bitmap indices are typically used on integer and string values. However, scientific data is often based on floating point values which requires other kinds of bitmap indices based on binning [6, 7]. In this case, one bitmap does not represent one attribute value but one attribute range (see Figure 1).

Assume that we want to evaluate the query $x < 63$. The bitmap that holds these values is bitmap 4 (shaded in Figure 1). This bitmap represents floating point numbers in the range of 0 to 80. In order to evaluate the query $x < 63$, two additional steps are required in order to retrieve the values that match the query condition.

Note that bitmap 4 represents values in the range of 0 to 80, which is more than what we have specified as our query condition (63). We now combine bitmap 4 and bitmap 3 with the logical operator XOR and get those values that are in the range of 60 to 80. As depicted in Figure 1, two values are left that need to be read from disk and checked against the query constraint $x < 63$. We call this additional step the *candidate check*.

There are a number of approaches to reduce the index size and increase the performance of the bitmap index for high cardinality attributes. These approaches include multicomponent encoding [2, 3], binning the attribute values [6, 7] and compressing the bitmaps [4, 8].

3 Evaluation Strategies

The query example in Section 2 is a typical one-dimensional query since the query condition consists of only one attribute. For multi-dimensional queries that contain several attributes, for instance $x_1 < 63$ AND $x_2 > 72$ AND $x_3 \leq 5.2$, the

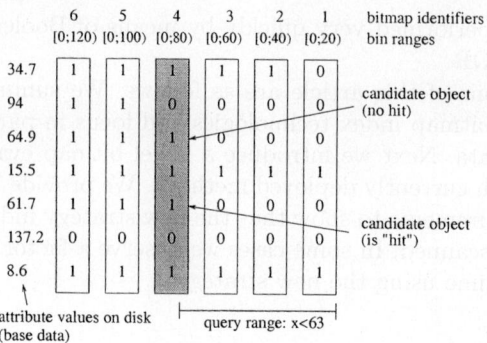

Fig. 1. One-sided range query $x < 63$ on a range encoded bitmap index

results of several bitmaps need to be combined. The goal is to calculate the intermediate result of each query dimension in such a way that the number of candidates and thus the number of disk scans is minimized. In this section we present three different techniques for evaluating bitmap indices with binning.

Assumptions and Definitions: The following analysis assumes all attributes have uniform distribution. This represents the worst case for the bitmap indices, which are usually more efficient on real application data as demonstrated in Section 5. Without loss of generality, we further assume the domain of each attribute is normalized to be [0, 1]. We limit all queries to be conjunctive with a one-sided range condition on each attribute $x_i < v_i$. The bin boundaries just below and above v_i are denoted by $\underline{v}_i$ and $\overline{v}_i$ respectively. For the attribute x in the domain of [0, 140], the query $x < 63$ shown in Figure 1 is normalized to be $x < 0.45$. The lower and upper ranges of the candidate bitmap are 60 and 80. After normalization, we yield $\underline{v}$=0.43 and $\overline{v}$= 0.57.

Strategy 1: Figures 2a) - g) show a graphical interpretation of the bitmap evaluation strategy on a 2-dimensional query. In the first phase, the bitmap index is scanned for both attributes. The result is an L-shape which represents the candidate records (see Figure 2) of both dimensions 1 and 2. We refer to these candidates as C_{tot}. Since the domains of the attributes are normalized, the number of records in C_{tot} is equal to the area of the L-shape times the total number of records N.

Let us assume the hit area for attribute i is denoted as H_i and the candidates for attribute i are denoted as C_i. We can calculate the candidate L-shape C_{tot} as follows: $C_{tot} = (H_1 \vee C_1) \wedge (H_2 \vee C_2) - H$, where $H = H_1 \wedge H_2$. This is equivalent to what is shown graphically in Figure 2.

In the next phase, the candidate check for attribute 1 is performed by reading the attribute values from disk and checking them against the range condition. All records represented by C_{tot} are checked (see Figure 3a)). The records satisfying

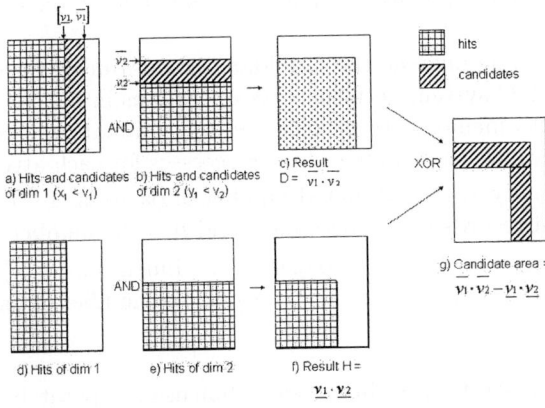

Fig. 2. Calculation of the candidate area for strategies 1 and 3

the range condition involving attribute 1 is recorded as r_1. Finally, the candidate check for dimension 2 is performed by reading all attributes represented by the area r_1 (see Figure 3b)). The results of the 2-dimensional query are shown in Figure 3c).

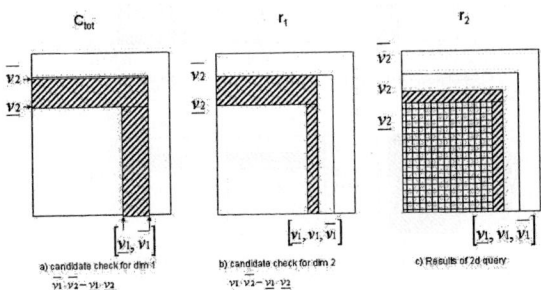

Fig. 3. Bitmap evaluation strategy 1

Let the candidate selectivity of ith dimension s_i be the fraction of records that need to be scanned, the candidate selectivity of the first dimension $s_1 = \overline{v}_1 \overline{v}_2 - \underline{v}_1 \underline{v}_2$, and the candidate selectivity of the second dimension $s_2 = v_1 \overline{v}_2 - \underline{v}_1 \underline{v}_2$. In general, the equation for the candidate selectivity is:

$$s_i = \left(\prod_{j=1}^{i-1} v_j \prod_{j=i}^{d} \overline{v}_j \right) - \prod_{j=1}^{d} \underline{v}_j \tag{1}$$

where d refers to dimension. The total number of records scanned $S = N \sum_{i=1}^{d} s_i$.

Ideally, we would only read the candidate records during the candidate checking. Since most I/O system performs disk operations in pages, more records are actually read into memory. To more accurately evaluate the cost of candidate checking, we compute the number of page accesses for each attribute. Given the candidate selectivity s, the estimated number of pages is $(1 - e^{-\frac{sN}{p}})p$, where N is the number of records of the base data and p is the number of pages for one attribute [5]. The total number of pages for all dimensions is $\sum_{i=1}^{d}(1 - e^{-\frac{s_i N}{p}})p$. For the next two bitmap evaluation strategies, the number of pages is estimated analogically.

Strategy 2: This strategy evaluates each dimension separately. Using the same 2D example as before, the bitmap index for the first attribute is evaluated first and the candidates of this attribute are checked immediately afterward (see Figure 4a)). After these operations the condition involving the first attribute is fully resolved. In Figure 4 the result is denoted as H_1. Similarly, dimension 2 is evaluated. Since the query conditions are conjunctive, the final answer must be from H_1. Therefore, the candidates to be checked must be both in H_1 and C_2. This reduces the area from $\overline{v}_2 - \underline{v}_2$ to $v_1(\overline{v}_2 - \underline{v}_2)$.

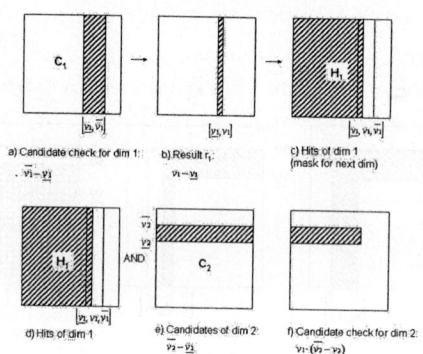

Fig. 4. Bitmap evaluation strategy 2

It is straightforward to extend this strategy to resolve more attributes. The candidate selectivity of attribute i is as follows:

$$s_i = \left(\prod_{j=1}^{i-1} v_j\right)(\overline{v}_i - \underline{v}_i) \qquad (2)$$

Strategy 3: This strategy is an optimal combination of Strategies 1 and 2. Given the values are binned, it checks the minimal number of candidates.

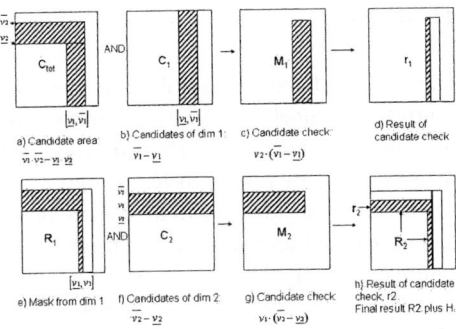

Fig. 5. Bitmap evaluation strategy 3

The first phase of this technique is identical to Strategy 1. Once the L-shaped area C_{tot} is computed, the candidate check for dimension 1 can begin. However, rather than scanning all attributes represented by C_{tot}, this area is reduced by "AND"ing together the candidate bitmap C_1 with C_{tot} (see Figure 5c)). In this case the candidate selectivity is $s_1 = (\overline{v}_1 - \underline{v}_1)\overline{v}_2$. The result of this candidate check r_1 is combined with C_{tot} and C_1 to produce a refined candidate set $R_1 = C_{tot} \wedge \neg(M_1 \wedge \neg r_1)$, where $M_1 = C_{tot} \wedge C_1$.

To determine the minimal candidate set for attribute 2, the refined candidate set R_1 and the candidate set C_2 are "AND"ed together, which produces M_2. The area representing M_2 is $v_1(\overline{v}_2 - \underline{v}_2)$. Let r_2 denote the result of this candidate check. The final result of the two dimensional query is $H \vee R_2$, where $R_2 = R_1 \wedge \neg(M_2 \wedge \neg r_2)$.

The whole process is depicted in Figure 5. In general, the candidate selectivity for attribute i is as follows:

$$s_i = \left(\prod_{j=1}^{i-1} v_j\right)(\overline{v}_i - \underline{v}_i)\left(\prod_{j=i+1}^{d} \overline{v}_j\right) \tag{3}$$

This strategy checks the minimal number of candidates. It achieves this with some extra operations on bitmaps. The first two strategies only need to access the bitmap indices once. However, this strategy has to access the bitmap indices twice: once to determine the initial candidate set C_{tot} and once to determine the candidates for the ith attribute to compute C_i. In addition, it needs more bitwise logical operations after each candidate checking to refine the candidate sets. These extra bitmap operations clearly require time. One question we seek to address is whether the savings in reduced candidate checking is enough to offset these extra operations on bitmaps.

4 Analytical Results

In this section we evaluate the three strategies discussed in Section 3 according to the number of candidates checked and the number of pages accessed. All evaluations are carried out on a data set of 25 million records with 10 attributes. All attributes are uniform random values in the range of [0, 1]. We have chosen 25 million records since our real data used in the next section also comprises of 25 million entries. For each dimension we assume a bitmap index with 300 bins as in the performance tests in the next section. The page size is 8KB. Each attribute value takes 4 bytes to store and all pages are packed as in a typical projection index [5]. In many data warehouse applications, the projection index is observed to have the best performance in answering complex queries. We use it as a reference for measuring the performance of the various bitmap schemes. To simplify the evaluation, we set all v_i to be the same. Furthermore, we assume the query boundaries are never exactly on the bin boundaries, i.e., $v \neq \overline{v} \neq \underline{v}$. Figure 6 shows the number of candidates expected (according to Equations 1, 2 and 3) and Figure 7 shows the number of page accesses expected.

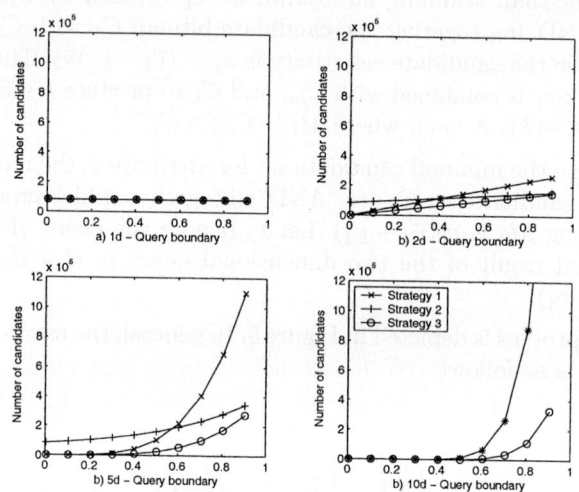

Fig. 6. Total number of candidates for multi-dimensional queries

For one-dimensional queries there is no performance difference among the strategies (see Figure 6a)). In all cases, the candidate selectivity is 0.3% (= 1/300) which corresponds to all entries of one candidate bitmap. Note that since each page contains 2048 records, selecting one out of every 300 records means all pages are accessed.

When more than one attribute is involved, there is a significant difference among the strategies. We observe that Strategy 1 performs better than Strategy 2 for queries with boundaries below 0.5. For query with boundaries above 0.5,

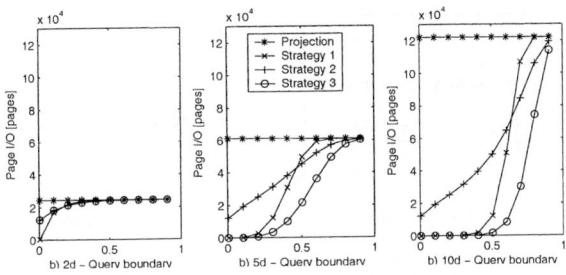

Fig. 7. Page I/O for multi-dimensional queries

Strategy 2 performs better than Strategy 1. However, in all cases Strategy 3 shows the best performance characteristics.

5 Bitmap Index Performance

Querying Synthetic Data: We first verify the performance model on uniform random attributes. As in the previous section, we generated a bitmap index for 25 million records and 10 attributes. The index consists of 300 range-encoded bins. The whole bitmap index is compressed with the WAH scheme [8]. The size of the base data is 1 GB. The size of the bitmap indices is about 10 times larger because range-encoded bitmap indices are hard to compress. The experiments are carried out on a 2.8 GHz Intel Pentium IV with 1 GB RAM. The I/O subsystem is a hardware RAID with two SCSI disks.

To verify the performance model, we ran the same benchmarks as reported in Section 4. The results for multi-dimensional queries with query boundaries in the range of [0, 1] are shown in Figure 8. We can see that in all cases strategy 3 results in the lowest number of candidates to be checked. The number of candidates checked is exactly as expected.

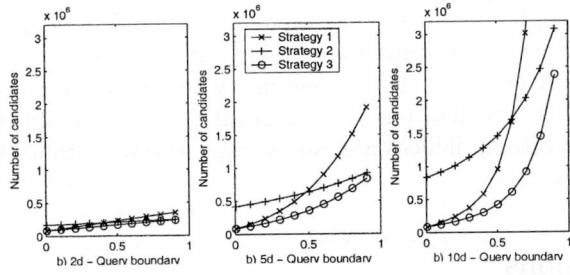

Fig. 8. Total number of candidates for multi-dimensional queries against uniformly distributed random data

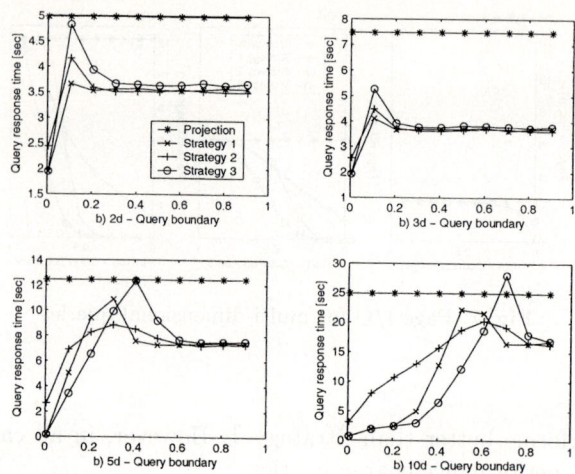

Fig. 9. Response times for multi-dimensional queries against uniformly distributed random data

Figure 9 shows the query response time. As we expected from our analytical results, strategy 3 performs best in most cases and has a performance gain of up to a factor of two. We also see that apart from one case, the bitmap index performs always better than the projection index.

Querying Scientific Data: We also tested our new bitmap evaluation strategies on a set of real data from combustion studies. The data was computed from a direct numerical simulation of hydrogen-oxygen autoignition processes. Our timing measurements use randomly generated conditions on 10 chemical species involving hydrogen and oxygen [9]. For each attribute we built a range-encoded bitmap index with 300 bins. In this case, the total index size is only 40% larger than the base data because the distribution of the real data is not uniform. The query performance results are presented in Figure 10. We observe that all bitmap schemes work significantly better than the projection index. The relative differences among the three bitmap based evaluation strategies are small because fewer candidates are scanned than on the uniform random data. In general, Strategy 1 uses more time than others, and Strategies 2 and 3 use about the same amount of time. The average query response time using compressed bitmap indices is less than one second in all tests. For 5-dimensional queries the compressed bitmap indices are, on average, about 13 times faster than the projection index.

6 Conclusions

We introduced a novel bitmap evaluation strategy for bitmap indices with bins. It minimizes the number of records scanned during the candidate checking, but

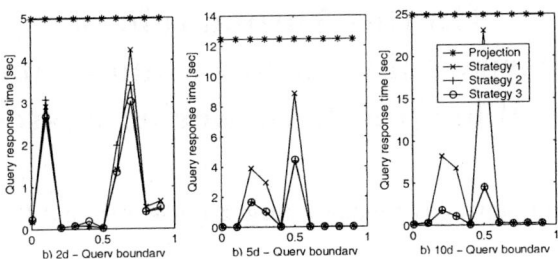

Fig. 10. Response times for multi-dimensional queries against real data

requires more operations on bitmaps. We provided detailed analyses and experimental measurements to verify that the new scheme is indeed efficient. In many cases the new strategy scans much fewer records than previous strategies, and in some cases, it can improve the query response time by a factor of two. All strategies are shown to outperform the projection index in the majority of the cases.

Since the new bitmap index evaluation strategy uses more bitmap operations, it occasionally uses more time than others. In the future, we plan to develop a way to optimally combine the three strategies.

References

1. S. Chaudhuri and U. Dayal, An Overview of Data Warehousing and OLAP Technology, *ACM SIGMOD Record 26(1)*, March 1997.
2. C. Chan and Y.E. Ioannidis, Bitmap Index Design and Evaluation, *In SIGMOD 1998*, Seattle, Washington, USA, June 1998, ACM Press.
3. C. Chan and Y.E. Ioannidis, An Efficient Bitmap Encoding Scheme for Selection Queries. In *SIGMOD 1999*, Philadelphia, Pennsylvania, USA, June 1999, ACM Press.
4. T. Johnson, Performance Measurements of Compressed Bitmap Indices, *In VLDB 1999*, Edinburgh, Scotland, UK, September 1999, Morgan Kaufmann.
5. P. O'Neil and D. Quass. Improved Query Performance With Variant Indices. In *SIGMOD 1997*, Tucson, Arizona, USA, May 1997, ACM Press.
6. A. Shoshani, L.M. Bernardo, H. Nordberg, D. Rotem, and A. Sim. In *SSDBM 1999*, July 1999, IEEE Computer Society Press.
7. K. Stockinger. Bitmap Indices for Speeding Up High-Dimensional Data Analysis, In*DEXA 2002*, Aix-en-Provence, France, September 2002, Springer-Verlag.
8. K. Stockinger, K. Wu, and A. Shoshani. Strategies for Processing ad-hoc Queries on Large Data Warehouses. In *(DOLAP 2002)*, McLean, VA, USA, November 2002. ACM Press.
9. K. Wu, W. Koegler, J. Chen, and A. Shoshani, Using Bitmap Index for Interactive Exploration of Large Datasets. In *SSDBM 2003*, July 2003, IEEE Computer Society Press.

On the Automation of Similarity Information Maintenance in Flexible Query Answering Systems

Balázs Csanád Csáji[1], Josef Küng[2], Jürgen Palkoska[2], and Roland Wagner[2]

[1] Computer and Automation Research Institute
Hungarian Academy of Sciences
Kende u. 13-17, H–1111, Budapest, Hungary
csaji@sztaki.hu

[2] Institute for Applied Knowledge Processing (FAW)
Johannes Kepler University, Altenberger Strasse 69, A–4040, Linz, Austria
jkueng@faw.uni-linz.ac.at

Abstract. This paper proposes a method for automatic maintaining the similarity information for a particular class of Flexible Query Answering Systems (FQAS). The paper describes the three main levels of this approach: the first one deals with learning the distance measure through interaction with the user. Machine-learning techniques, such as reinforcement learning, can be used to achieve this. The second level tries to build a good representation of the learned distance measure. This level uses distance geometry and multidimensional optimization methods. The last level of automation uses statistical optimization techniques to further decrease the dimension of the similarity data.

1 Introduction

Similarity search has emerged and become a fundamental requirement for a variety of application areas such as multimedia [19] [15], data mining [8], CAD database systems [5], time-series databases [9], information retrieval (IR) systems [4], geographical information system (GIS) and tourist information system [16], etc. In these contexts one of the most important tasks is to find the data object(s) that is most similar to a given query object. A particular challenge is to gain this similarity search functionality autonomously through the system without any similarity engineering which has to be done manually.

1.1 Flexible Query Answering Systems

Query processing in the conventional data base systems is not flexible enough to support similarity search capabilities directly. That means when the available data does not match a users query precisely, the system will only return an empty result set to the user. This limits their applicability to domains where only crisp answers are meaningful. In many other application domains, however, the users expect not only the crisp results returned but also some other results close to the query in a sense. Systems that can solve this problem are called flexible query answering systems (FQAS).

1.2 Vague Query Systems

One of these FQAS is a system called VQS (Vague Query System) [13], [14]. It is designed as an add-on module for still existing relational data bases. So similarity search functionality can be reached also for old data sets without reorganizing its data structure.

1.3 Numeric Coordinate Representation Tables

The basic idea of VQS is that values of non-numerical attributes are mapped to points in a multidimensional feature space. Each attribute domain can have its own feature space. So similarity of two database objects can be derived from the metric distances in these spaces. The data base tables which hold this mapping of attribute values to multidimensional points are called NCRT (Numeric Coordinate Representation Tables). They can be seen as a semantic background information pool that supports an application domain appropriate similarity search.

2 Learning the Distance Measure

The first step toward the automation of similarity information maintenance is to automate the similarity measure generation. We can use *machine-learning* techniques such as *reinforcement learning* (RL) to learn the distance measure from the interaction with the user. In the classical case, this is the work of a knowledge engineer or a domain expert. He designs the similarity measure between the possible values of the data type and later from this information an NCRT is built. The information of the similarity measure can be placed in a natural way in a matrix, however this similarity matrix must have special properties in order to be possible to build a representation from it. A matrix which has these properties is called *Euclidean Distance Matrix*.

Definition 1. *A matrix* $D \in \mathbb{R}^{n \times n}$, $D = (d_{ij})_{i,j=1}^{n}$ *is called Euclidean Distance Matrix (EDM) if and only if the following four properties are satisfied:*

1. $\forall i,j : d_{ij} \geq 0$ *(non-negative)*
2. $\forall i : d_{ii} = 0$ *(zero diagonal)*
3. $\forall i,j : d_{ij} = d_{ji}$ *(symmetric)*
4. $\forall i,j,k : d_{ij} + d_{jk} \geq d_{ik}$ *(triangular inequality)*

In a FQAS, if a user searches for a record and the system could not find that then it offers some other records which are *similar* to the searched one. Then the user chooses a record from the offered ones. We can refine our similarity measure with the aid of the user: we can treat his choice as a *reinforcement* that the chosen record is the closest one to the originally searched record in the offered list. Or, for a quicker convergence, we can even ask him to mark the offered records. It is known that we can speed up the convergence of our learning algorithm if we start from a good initial point. Because of this we first make an excursion in which we show that for some special cases we can extract a raw distance measure from the database by methods which are often used in *data mining* or *clustering* systems.

2.1 Similarity and Signatures

Our aim in this section is to get a raw similarity measure to start with. For numerical fields (like "price" or "duration") it is straightforward to define such a similarity. However, it is more difficult for fields which have a set of informal values. We can give a raw similarity measure even for these fields if we treat them as bitvectors of features. For example if we have records about hotels we can map a bitvector to the field describing whatever property amenities they have (e.g. room service, swimming pool, handicap accessible, internet, etc.). Or if we deal with web-pages, we can treat a link from one page to another as a feature that the source page has. If we have a (probably very large) vector of bits, which represents a set of features, we can define the similarity of two vectors in the following way: we can denote the number of indexes in which both vector has 1 by a and the number of indexes in which only one of them has 1 by b. Note that we skip the number of those indexes in which both vectors have 0. Then we can define the similarity of the two vectors by: $a/(a+b)$. For example, if we have $u = (0,1,1,0,1,0)$ and $v = (1,0,1,0,1,1)$ then their similarity will be: $sim(u,v) = 2/5 = 40\%$. However these feature vectors could be very large, in that case we can map (hash) each vector v to a small amount of data $sig(v)$, which is called the *signature* of v, such that $sig(v)$ is small enough that a signature for each vector can be fit in the main memory and additionally for each u and v: they are highly similar if and only if $sig(u)$ and $sig(v)$ are highly similar. A simple example of doing it could be if we map each vector v to $h(v)$ that is the number of the first index in which vector v has a 1. The probability that $h(v) = h(u)$ is the same as $sim(v,u)$. Then we can permute (virtually) the indexes of vectors a several times and approximate $sim(v,u)$ with the relative frequency of $h(v) = h(u)$. This basic method is called *min hashing*. A more sophisticated method for doing this is the *locality-sensitive hashing* (LSH) which is described in [11]. Even if we can define similarity in this way, it will be quite raw and does not contain the fine and hardy formalizable considerations of users. Now we get back to our original goal, to learn the similarity measure through interaction. In the next section, we will give a short overview on the technique of reinforcement learning.

2.2 Reinforcement Learning

Two main paradigms of machine-learning are known: learning with a teacher, which is called *supervised learning*, and *learning without a teacher*. The paradigm of learning without a teacher is subdivided into *self-organized (unsupervised)* and *reinforcement learning*. Supervised learning is a "cognitive" learning method performed under a tutelage of a teacher: this requires the availability of an adequate set of input-output examples. In contrary, reinforcement learning is a "behavioral" learning method, which is performed through *interactions* between the learning system and its environment. The operation of a reinforcement learning system can be characterized as follows [12]:

1. The environment stochastically occupies a finite set of discrete states.
2. For each state there is a finite set of possible actions that may be taken.
3. Every time the learning system takes an action, a certain reward is incurred.
4. States ($s_t \in S$) are observed, actions ($a_t \in A$) are taken, and rewards ($r_t \in \mathbb{R}$) are incurred at discrete time steps ($t \in \mathbb{N}$).

The goal of the learning system is to maximize its *cumulative reward*. This does not mean maximizing immediate gains, but the profit in the long run. In our automated FQAS the states of the reinforcement learning are the searched records (the queries of the users), the actions are the selection of similar records which will be offered to the user and the rewards are computed from the reaction of the user or from his marks.

Markov Property. An important assumption in reinforcement learning is the *Markov property*. A sequence of random variables $\{X_t\}$ where $t \in \mathbb{N}$ have the Markov property if they satisfy the following equality:

$$P(X_t = j \mid X_0 = i_0, X_1 = i_1, \ldots, X_{t-1} = i_{t-1}) = P(X_t = j \mid X_{t-1} = i_{t-1}) \quad (1)$$

Or in other words, the present is conditionally independent of the past. The environment satisfies this property if its state signal compactly summarizes the past without degrading the ability to predict the future. A reinforcement learning task is called a *Markov Decision Process* (MDP) if its environment satisfies the Markov property [20].

Markov states provide the best possible basis for choosing actions. Even if the state signal is non-Markov, it is appropriate to consider it as an approximation to a Markov state. During the paper we presuppose that our system satisfies this property (e.g. the queries are independent of each other).

Temporal Difference Learning. Reinforcement learning methods are based on a policy π for selecting actions in the problem space. The policy defines the actions to be performed in each state. Formally, a policy is $\pi : S \times A \to [0, 1]$ a partial function from state and actions to the probability $\pi(s, a)$ of taking action

a in state s. A *value* of a state s is the expected return (sum of rewards) when starting in s and following π thereafter:

$$V^{\pi}(s) = E_{\pi}\{R_t \mid s_t = s\} = E_{\pi}\{\sum_{k=0}^{\infty} \gamma^k r_{t+k+1} \mid s_t = s\}, \qquad (2)$$

where r_t is the reward at time t and γ is a parameter, $0 \leq \gamma \leq 1$, called *discount rate* (if $\gamma = 0$ then the system is "myopic", and as γ approaches 1, it becomes more and more "farsighted"). As in most reinforcement learning work, the aim of the system is to learn the value function of the optimal policy π^*, denoted by V^* rather then directly learning π^*. To learn the value function we can apply the method of *temporal difference learning* known as $TD(\lambda)$, developed by Sutton [20]. The value function $V^{\pi}(s)$ is represented by a function approximator[1] $f(s, w)$ where $w \in \mathbb{R}^d$ is a vector containing the parameters of the approximation (e.g. weights if we use artificial neural networks as approximators). If the polict π were fixed, $TD(\lambda)$ could be applied to learn the value function V^{π} as follows. At step $t + 1$, we can compute the temporal difference error at time t as:

$$\delta_t = r_{t+1} + \gamma f(s_{t+1}, w) - f(s_t, w), \qquad (3)$$

then we can compute the smoothed gradient:

$$e_t = \nabla_w f(s_t, w) + \lambda e_{t-1}, \qquad (4)$$

finally, we can update the parameters according to:

$$\Delta_w = \alpha \delta_t e_t, \qquad (5)$$

where λ is a smoothing parameter that combines the previous gradients with the current one (e_t), and α is the learning parameter. This way, $TD(\lambda)$ could learn the value function of a *fixed* policy. But we want to learn the value function of the *optimal* policy. Fortunately, we can do this by the method of *value iteration*. During the learning we continually choose an action that maximizes the predicted value of the resulting state (with one step lookahead). After applying this action, we get a reward, and update our value function estimation. This means that the policy continually changes during the learning process. $TD(\lambda)$ still converges under these conditions [20].

2.3 Dual Ways

One should be cautious when learning a similarity matrix, because when the matrix or its approximation is updated then one should check that the new matrix is still an EDM. Testing the first three properties after a cell has changed is straightforward, however verifying the triangular inequality could need a lot

---
[1] Using an approximator in our case means that we do not store the whole similarity matrix, only an approximation of it which requires a much lesser storage space.

of computation. We have another choice namely we do not learn the similarity matrix but we learn directly the NCRT instead (with the same reinforcement learning method which we have presented). In this way we do not need to check the EDM properties. However this approach has a major drawback, viz. in that case changing the dimensions of the representation is hard, or even realizing that we need a higher dimensional NCRT during the learning is non-trivial. Moreover, we need to have an advance estimation of the NCRT dimension, but if we learn the distance matrix then we do not need such an estimation. Both ways have their own advantages/disadvantages, we will continue with the case when we have learned the distance matrix and we need to build an NCRT from it. If we have learned directly the NCRT then we can only need a statistical optimization.

3   Building a Representation

If we have an Euclidean Distance Matrix (EDM), for example we have learned it from the interaction with the user or a knowledge engineer designed it, then we need to find a "good" representation of it. We have already mentioned that Numeric Coordinate Representation Tables (NCRT) provide an efficient way of representing similarity information. The problem of finding a representation is to build such an NCRT from, a possibly sparse, EDM which means that we have to find a mapping ϕ that projects our points to a sufficiently high dimensional Euclidean space $\mathbb{R}^r$ in a way that the distances of the points in that space equals to the desired distances in the given EDM. Naturally, our aim is to minimize the number of needed dimensions, as well. Formally: we need to find the smallest $r \in \mathbb{N}$ and $x_1, x_2, \ldots, x_n \in \mathbb{R}^r$ such that:

$$\forall i,j \in \{1,\ldots,n\} : d_{ij} = \|x_i - x_j\|_2 \qquad (6)$$

Question 1. At this point a few questions arise: do such an r and $x_1, x_2, \ldots, x_n$ always exist? What is the minimal dimension that we need? How can we find a good representation for our points?

Remark 1. If D is an EDM then such points always exist (in a sufficiently high dimensional space) and the number of needed dimensions is always $\leq n-1$.

Problems like this was first studied by Cayley in 1841. Later in 1928 the problem was systematically investigated by Menger. In 1935 Schönberg found an equivalent characterization of Euclidean distances and realized the connection with bilinear forms. The problem given above was stated as the fundamental problem of *distance geometry* and formulated by Blumenthal [6] in 1953. Distance geometry has received much attention in recent years because of its many application in fields such as chemistry, statistics, archaeology, genetics and geography. A detailed discussion on distance geometry can be found in [21]. We will discuss the representation problem in two steps. First, an easier case will be presented, when all the distances are exactly given. Then, we present a harder problem, when only a few distances are given (so the distance matrix is sparse).

3.1 Complete Distance Information

If all the distances are known then we can find the minimal dimension that we need with the help of the following theorem [7]:

Theorem 1. *If* $x_1, x_2, \ldots, x_n \in \mathbb{R}^r$ *and* $\forall i, j \in \{1, \ldots, n\} : d_{ij} = \|x_i - x_j\|_2$ *then the rank of the following matrix is at most* $r + 2$:

$$\begin{pmatrix} 0 & d_{12}^2 & \cdots & d_{1n}^2 \\ d_{21}^2 & 0 & \cdots & d_{2n}^2 \\ \vdots & \vdots & \ddots & \vdots \\ d_{n1}^2 & d_{n2}^2 & \cdots & 0 \end{pmatrix}$$

Remark 2. If $dim(Span\{x_1, \ldots, x_n\}) = r$ and $n \geq r+2$, which is true for almost all cases that have practical importance, the rank of the matrix is exactly r+2.

Thus, with this theorem we can compute exactly the minimal dimension of the target Euclidean space. We can use the eigenvectors of a specially designed matrix to find the coordinates of the points immediately [6]. Regarding the complexity, this problem is *tractable*, because both computing the rank of a matrix and finding the eigenvectors can be done in polynomial time, more precisely in $O(n^3)$ if the matrix is $n \times n$. However there is another approach which is much faster than building the representation by eigenvectors. This algorithm is called *fastmap* and it can place n points in a k dimensional space in $O(nk)$ time [10].

3.2 Incomplete Distance Information

When we have given only a sparse set of distances then the distance geometry problem become very hard to solve. Easy to see that this problem is equivalent to the *graph embedding* problem, which we present here:

Definition 2. *Let* $G = (V, E, \omega)$ *be an undirected edge-weighted graph with vertex set* $V = (v_1, v_2, \ldots, v_n)$, *edge set* $E \subseteq V \times V$ *and a non-negative* ω_{ij} *for each* $(v_i, v_j) \in E$. *G is said to be r-embeddable if there exists a mapping* $\phi : V \to \mathbb{R}^r$ *such that for every edge* $(v_i, v_j) \in E$, *the Euclidean distance* $\|(\phi(v_i) - \phi(v_j)\|_2 = \omega_{ij}$.

As we saw, the distance geometry problem is tractable if all the distances are exactly given. Unfortunately, the following theorem shows that if we have only a sparse set of distances then the problem becomes *intractable*:

Theorem 2. $\forall r \in \mathbb{N}$: *the r-embeddability problem of an integer-weighted graph* $G = (V, E, \omega)$ *is NP-Hard.*

Proof. Saxe showed that the one dimensional distance geometry problem with incomplete distance information is equivalent to a set-partition problem which is known to be NP-hard. He extended his proof to higher dimensions, as well. The complete proof can be found in [18]. □

Remark 3. The problem remains NP-hard even if the weights w_{ij} are restricted to 1 and 2, only.

We will solve the distance geometry problem with incomplete distance information as an optimization problem, but first we need some estimation about the dimensions that we need for such an embedding. Barvinok proved in [3] the following theorem on graph embeddings:

Theorem 3. *If $G = (V, E, w)$ is r-embeddable for an $r \in \mathbb{N}$, then it is r^*-embedddable, as well, where $r^* = \lfloor (\sqrt{8|E|+1} - 1)/2 \rfloor$.*

Remark 4. If the distances are given by a (possibly sparse) EDM then it is always $n-1$ embeddable, so the estimation can be used in all cases.

A constructive proof of this theorem and more information on graph embeddability can be found in [2]. Now, we can transform the distance geometry problem to a least-square optimization problem. If we had all the distance information given then we could define an error function, by which we could measure how good our estimation is, as follows:

$$f(x_1, \ldots, x_n) = \sum_{i=1}^{n-1} \sum_{j=i+1}^{n} (\|x_i - x_j\|_2 - d_{ij})^2 \tag{7}$$

Now we consider the case when we have only a few distances given: let $S \subset \{1, \ldots, n\} \times \{1, \ldots, n\}$ be the index set of the given distances. A little bit more sophisticated error function could be when we "forget" about the square roots in the norm definition (because the square root is a monotone function and therefore it does not effect the outcome of the minimization) and we count the relative error between the calculated and the given distances:

$$f(x_1, \ldots, x_n) = \sum_{(i,j) \in S} \left(\frac{\|x_i - x_j\|_2^2 - d_{ij}^2}{d_{ij}^2} \right)^2 \tag{8}$$

It is easy to see that $x_1, \ldots, x_n$ is a solution of the distance geometry problem if and only if it is the global minimizer of f with global minimum equal to zero. Thus the distance geometry problem is formulated as an optimization problem:

$$\min_{x_1, \ldots, x_n} f(x_1, \ldots, x_n) \tag{9}$$

Finding the global minimum of the function f is intractable in general. There are a lot of multidimensional minimization methods avaliable, however there is no "perfect" optimization algorithm. The choice of the method depends on a number of things. E.g. if we do not want (or we cannot) compute the derivates then we can use methods like the *downhill simplex method* or the *Powell's method*. However the storage requirement of these methods is $O(n^2)$ which could be a problem in practice. If we can also compute the first order derivates of our function (which is the current case) then we can use *conjugate gradient methods* with only $O(n)$ storage, like the *Polak-Ribiere algorithm* or the *Fletcher-Reeves algorithm*. More detail on optimization can be found in [17].

From this section we can conclude that we can build a representation (NCRT) in two steps. First we need to find the minimal dimension of our Euclidean space. We can compute this dimension immediately if we have all of the distances, otherwise we can estimate it with Barvinok's theorem. We can build an NCRT by finding eigenvalues or with the fastmap algorithm if we have all exact distances, otherwise we need to use a multidimensional optimization method.

4 Statistical Optimization

After we have built an NCRT, it is advised to do some statistical optimization to further decrease its dimension. If we have built our NCRT from incomplete distance information (or we have learned the NCRT directly) then we had only an upper estimation (for example with Barvinok's theorem) of the needed dimension but it may happen that we need a much lower dimension than our estimation was. Even if we had all exact distances and we have computed the exact minimal dimension of the target Euclidean space we should do a statistical dimension reduction (such as PCA or ICA) because with them we can further reduce the dimension of the data by leaving out those components which have a small variance only. Therefore, here we propose the usage of statistical dimension reduction (compression) methods after we have built an NCRT.

In a lot of cases we can assume that our points in the Euclidean Space have Gaussian distribution. In this case we can use second-order methods to reduce their dimension, because all the information of (zero-mean) Gaussian variables is contained in the covariance matrix. Another reason for second-order methods is that they are computationally simple, often requiring only classical matrix multiplications. To further simplify the discussion we can assume that our variables are centered, which means that they have already been transformed by $x = x_0 - E\{x_0\}$ where x_0 are the original non-centered variables. We will present a classical second order method here:

4.1 Principal Component Analysis

Principal Component Analysis (PCA) is widely used in signal processing, statistics and neural computing. In some application areas it is also called the (discrete) Karhunen-Loève transform, or the Hotelling transform. The basic goal of PCA is to reduce the dimension of the data. It can be proven that the representation given by PCA is an optimal linear dimension reduction technique in the mean-square sense [1].

The basic idea in PCA is to find the components $s_1, s_2, \ldots, s_n$ so that they explain the maximum amount of variance possible by n linearly transformed components. PCA can be defined in an intuitive way using a recursive formulation. Define the direction of the first principal component, w_1, by:

$$w_1 = \arg\max_{\|w\|=1} E\{(w^T x)^2\}, \qquad (10)$$

where w_1 is of the same dimension m as the random data x. Thus this principal component is the projection on the direction in which the variance of the projection is maximized. Having defined the first $k-1$ principal components, the direction of the k-th principal component is determined as follows:

$$w_k = \arg\max_{\|w\|=1} E\{[w^T(x - \sum_{i=1}^{k-1} w_i w_i^T x)]^2\} \qquad (11)$$

The principal components are then given by $s_i = w_i^T x$. In practice, the computation of the w_i can be simply accomplished using the (sample) covariance matrix $C = E\{xx^T\}$. The w_i are the eigenvectors of C that correspond to the n largest eigenvalues of C.

If our data is non-Gaussian or we do not need the reduction in the mean-square sense then we need higher-order methods like Independent Component Analysis (ICA). A detailed description of ICA and other higher-order methods can be found in [1].

5 Conclusion

In this paper we discussed a crucial open issue we have when similarity searches should be enabled through a mapping of objects to points in a multidimensional space. We investigated questions like: How can we obtain a similarity measure automaticly? What is the minimal number of dimensions we need and what methods can be used to let the mapping done autonomously by the system? We proposed that the system should use machine-learning techniques, such as reinforcement learning to learn the distance measure from the interaction with the user. We have shown a solution which builds a representation in polynomial time when all distances between the objects are known. However, this is mostly not the case in practice. Normally, it is not possible to gain all the distances. For that case only an upper bound of the minimal number of dimensions can be computed and the mapping can be handled as an optimization problem. Unfortunately, the problem with incomplete distance information is NP-hard. Only heuristic application domain specific methods can decrease that complexity. At the end we have shown a statistical optimization method to further decrease the number of dimensions that we need for such a multidimensional space.

Acknowledgments

During this work Balázs Csanád Csáji was supported by a CEEPUS grant of the H-81 network, which he greatly acknowledges.

References

1. H. Aapo: Survey on Independent Component Analysis. Neural Computing Surveys **2** (1999) 94–128
2. A.Y. Alfakih, H. Wolkowicz: On the Embeddability of Weighted Graphs in Euclidean Spaces. CORR98-12, Department of Combinatorics and Optimization, University of Waterloo, Canada (1998)
3. A.I. Barvinok: Problems of Distance Geometry and Convex Properties of Quadratic Maps. Discrete and Computational Geometry **13** (1988) 189–202
4. R. Baeza-Yates, B. Ribeiro-Neto: Modern Information Retrieval. ACM Press Books (1999)
5. S. Berchtold, H.P. Kriegel.: S3: Similarity Search in CAD Database Systems. ACM SIGMOD International Conference on Management of Data (1997)
6. L.M. Blumenthal: Theory and Application of Distance Geometry. Chelsea, Bronx, New York (1970)
7. C. Borcea, I. Streinu: On the Number of Embeddings in Minimally Rigid Graphs. SoCG'02, Barcelona, Spain (2002)
8. B. Braunmueller, M. Ester, H.P. Kriegel, J. Sander: Efficiently Supporting Multiple Similarity Queries for Mining in Metric Databases. ICDE'00 (2000)
9. C. Faloutsos, M. Ranganathan, Y. Manolopoulos: Fast subsequence matching in time-series databases. ACM SIGMOD International Conference on Management of Data (1994)
10. Ch. Faloutsos and King-Ip (David) Lin: FastMap - A Fast Algorithm for Indexing, Data-Mining and Visualization of Traditional and Multimedia Datasets. ACM SIGMOD, San Jose CA (1995) pp. 163–174
11. A. Gionis, P. Indyk, R. Motwani: Similarity Search in High Dimensions via Hashing. The VLDB Journal (1999)
12. S. Haykin: Neural Networks. A Comprehensive Foundation. 2nd edition, Prentice Hall (1999)
13. J. Küng, J. Palkoska: VQS-A Vague Query System Prototype. DEXA'97, IEEE Computer Society Press (1997)
14. J. Küng, J. Palkoska: Vague Joins-An Extension of the Vaque Query System VQS. DEXA98, IEEE Computer Society Press (1998)
15. M. Ortega, Y. Rui, K. Chakrabarti, S. Mehrotra, T.S. Huang. Supporting Similarity Queries in MARS. ACM International Conference on Multimedia (1997)
16. J. Palkoska, A. Dunzendorfer, J. Küng: Vague Queries in Tourism Information Systems. Information and Communication Technologies in Tourism, ENTER 2000, Spain (2000)
17. W.H. Press, S.A. Teukolsky, W.T. Vetterling, B.P. Flannery: Numerical Recipes in C, The Art of Scientific Computing. Second Edition. Cambridge University Press (1992)
18. J.B. Saxe: Embeddability of Weighted Graph in k-space is Strongly NP-hard. Proc. 17th Allerton Conf. in Communications, Control and Computing (1979) 480–489
19. T. Seidl, H.-P. Kriegel: Efficient User-Adaptable Similarity Search in Large Multimedia Databases, VLDB97, (1997)
20. R.S. Sutton, A.G. Barto: Reinforcement Learning. The MIT Press (1998)
21. J. Yoon, Y. Gad, Z. Wu: Mathematical Modeling of Protein Structure Using Distance Geometry. Technical Report TR00-24 for the Computational and Applied Mathematics Department of Rice University (2000)

An Efficient Neighbor Searching Scheme of Distributed Collaborative Filtering on P2P Overlay Network*

Bo Xie, Peng Han, Fan Yang, and Ruimin Shen

Department of Computer Science and Engineering
Shanghai Jiao Tong University
Shanghai 200030, China
{Bxie,phan,fyang,rmshen}@sjtu.edu.cn

Abstract. Distributed Collaborative Filtering (DCF) has gained more and more attention as an alternative implementation scheme of CF based recommender system, because of its advantage in scalability and privacy protection. However, as there is no central user database in DCF systems, the task of neighbor searching becomes much more difficult. In this paper, we first propose an efficient distributed user profile management scheme based on distributed hash table (DHT) method, which is one of the most popular and effective routing algorithm in Peer-to-Peer (P2P) overlay network. Then, we present a heuristic neighbor searching algorithm to locate potential neighbors of the active users in order to reduce the network traffic and executive cost. The experimental data show that our DCF algorithm with the neighbor searching scheme has much better scalability than traditional centralized ones with comparable prediction efficiency and accuracy.

1 Introduction

While the rapid development of network and information technology provides people with unprecedented abundant information resources, it also brings the problem of "information overload". So how to help people find their interested resources attracted much attention from both the researchers and the vendors. Among the technologies proposed, Collaborative Filtering (CF) has proved to be one of the most effective for its simplicity both in theory and implementation. Since Goldberg et al [1] published the first account of using it for information filtering, CF has achieved great success both in the research [2, 3] and application [4, 5, 6] area.

The key idea of CF is that users will prefer those items that people with similar interests prefer. Due to different techniques used to describe and calculate the similarities between users, CF algorithms have often been divided into two general classes [3]: memory-based algorithm and model-based algorithm. Memory-based algorithms directly calculate the similarities between the active users and other users, and then use the K most similar users (K nearest neighbors) to make prediction. In

---

* Supported by the National Natural Science Foundation of China under Grant No. 60372078.

contrast, model-based algorithms first construct a predictive model from the user database, and then use it to make prediction. As the calculation complexity of both the calculation of similarities and the construction of model increased quickly both in time and space as the record in the database increases, the two kinds of algorithms both suffered from their shortage in efficiency and scalability.

So recent years, Distributed CF (DCF) has gained more and more attention as an alternative implementation scheme of CF based recommender system [8, 9] because of its advantage in scalability. However, as there is no central user database in DCF systems, the task of neighbor searching becomes much more difficult. In [8], Tviet uses a routing algorithm similar to Gnutella [15] to forward the neighbor query information. As it is a broadcasting routing algorithm, when the user number is large it will cause unimaginable heavy traffic in the network. In [9], Olsson improves this by only exchanging information between neighbors, however it also reduces the efficiency of finding similar users. Still, as they all used a totally different mechanism to make prediction, their performance is hard to analyze and the existing improvement on CF algorithms cannot be used any more.

In this paper, we first propose an efficient distributed user profile management scheme based on distributed hash table (DHT) method, which is one of the most popular and effective routing algorithm in Peer-to-Peer (P2P) overlay network. Then, we present a heuristic neighbor searching algorithm to locate potential neighbors of the active users. The main advantages of our algorithm include:

1. Both the user database management and prediction computation task can be done in a decentralized way which increases the algorithm's scalability dramatically.
2. The implementation of our neighbor searching algorithm on a DHT-based P2P overlay network is quite straightforward which can obtain efficient retrieval time and excellent performance at the same time.
3. It keeps all the other features of traditional memory-based CF algorithm so that the system's performance can be analyzed both empirically and theoretically and the improvement on traditional memory-based algorithm can also be applied here.

The rest of this paper is organized as follows. In Section 2, several related works are presented and discussed. In Section 3, we give the architecture and key features of our algorithm, and describe the implementation of it on a DHT-based P2P overlay network in Section 4. In Section 5 the experimental results of our system are presented and analyzed. Finally we make a brief concluding remark in Section 6.

2 Related Works

2.1 Memory-Based CF Algorithm

Generally, the task of CF is to predict the votes of active users from the user database which consists of a set of votes corresponding to the vote of user i on item j. The memory-based CF algorithm calculates this prediction as a weighted average of other users' votes on that item through the following formula:

$$P_{a,j} = \overline{v_a} + \kappa \sum_{i=1}^{n} \varpi(a,j)(v_{i,j} - \overline{v_i}) \qquad (1)$$

Where $P_{a,j}$ denotes the prediction of the vote for active user a on item j and n is the number of users in user database. $\overline{v_i}$ is the mean vote for user i as:

$$\overline{v_i} = \frac{1}{|I_i|} \sum_{j \in I_i} v_{i,j} \qquad (2)$$

Where I_i is the set of items on which user i has voted. The weights $\varpi(a,j)$ reflect the similarity between active user and users in the user database. κ is a normalizing factor to make the absolute values of the weights sum to unity.

2.2 P2P System and DHT Routing Algorithm

The term "Peer-to-Peer" refers to a class of systems and applications that employ distributed resources to perform a critical function in a decentralized manner. With the pervasive deployment of computers, P2P is increasingly receiving attention in research and more and more P2P systems have been deployed on the Internet. Some of the benefits of a P2P approach include: improving scalability by avoiding dependency on centralized points; eliminating the need for costly infrastructure by enabling direct communication among clients; and enabling resource aggregation.

As the main purpose of P2P systems are to share resources among a group of computers called peers in a distributed way, efficient and robust routing algorithms for locating wanted resource is critical to the performance of P2P systems. Among these algorithms, distributed hash table (DHT) algorithm is one of the most popular and effective and supported by many P2P systems such as CAN [10], Chord [11], Pastry [12], and Tapestry [13].

A DHT overlay network is composed of several DHT nodes and each node keeps a set of resources (e.g., files, rating of items). Each resource is associated with a key (produced, for instance, by hashing the file name) and each node in the system is responsible for storing a certain range of keys. There are two basic operations: (1) put(key, value); (2)lookup(key), and two layers: (1)route(key, message); (2)key/value storage in the DHT overlay network. Peers in the DHT overlay network can announce what resource they have by issue a put(key, value) message, or locate their wanted resource by issue a lookup(key) request which returns the identity (e.g., the IP address) of the node that stores the resource with the certain key. The primary goals of DHT are to provide an efficient, scalable, and robust routing algorithm which aims at reducing the number of P2P hops, which are involved when we locate a certain resource, and to reduce the amount of routing state that should be preserved at each peer. In Chord [11], each peer keeps track information of logN other peers where N is the total number of peers in the community. When a peer joins and leaves the overlay network, this highly optimized version of DHT algorithm will only require notifying logN peers about that change.

3 Our Neighbor Searching Algorithm

3.1 Distributed User Profile Management Scheme

Distributed user profile management has two key points: *Division* and *Location*. In our scheme, we wish to divide the original centralized user database into fractions (For concision, we will call such fractions by the term *bucket* in the following of this paper) in such a manner that potential neighbors can be put into the same bucket. So later we can access only several buckets to fetch the useful user profiles for the active users since retrieve all the buckets will cause unimaginable traffic in the network and often unnecessary. Here, we solve the first problem by proposing a division strategy which makes each bucket hold a group of users' record who has a particular <ITEM_ID, VOTE> tuple. It means that users in the same bucket at least voted one item with the same rating. Figure1 illustrate our division strategy:

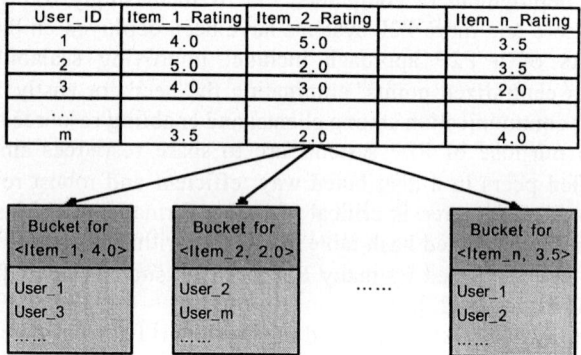

Fig. 1. User database division strategy

Later when we want to make prediction for a particular user, we only need to retrieve those buckets which the active user's record is in. This strategy is based on the heuristic that people with similar interests will at least rate one item with similar votes. As we can see in Figure 3 of section 5.3.1, this strategy has a very high hitting ratio. Still, we can see that through this strategy we reduce about 50% calculation than traditional CF algorithm and obtain comparable prediction as shown in Figure 4 in section 5.

After we make the proper division and choosing strategy of buckets, we still need an efficient way to locate and retrieve the needed buckets from the distributed network. As we mentioned in section 2.2, DHT has provided an efficient infrastructure to accomplish this task. We will discuss this in detail in section 4.

3.2 Neighbor Searching in DCF

3.2.1 Return All vs. Return K

In the buckets choosing strategy mentioned in section 3.1, we return all users which are in the at least one same bucket with the active user. As we can see in Figure 5 in section 5.3.2, this strategy has an O(N) fetched user number where N is the total user number. In fact, as Breese presented in [3] by the term inverse user frequency, universally liked items are not as useful as less common items in capturing similarity. So we introduce a new concept significance refinement (SR) which reduces the returned user number of the original strategy by limiting the number of returned users for each bucket. We term this strategy improved by SR as "Return K" which means "for every rated item, we return no more than K users for each bucket" and call the original strategy as "Return All". The experimental result in Figure 5 and 6 of Section 5.3.2 shows that this method reduces the returned user number dramatically and also improves the prediction accuracy.

3.2.2 Improved Return K Strategy

Although the Return K strategy proved to increase the scalability of our DCF algorithm, it has the shortage of unstable when the number of users in each bucket increases because the chosen of the K users is random. As we can see in Figure 7, when the total number of users is above 40,000, the average bucket size is more than 60. So the randomization of neighbor choosing will cause much uncertainty in prediction. There are two natural ways to solve this problem: increase the value of K or do some filtering at the node holding the bucket. However, the first method will increase the traffic dramatically while the second will cause much more calculation. In our method, we add a mergence procedure in our neighbor choosing strategy, which we called "Improved Return K" strategy. In this new strategy, before we retrieve the user record back, we first get the user ID list from each bucket which will cause little traffic. Then we merge the same user ID locally and generate a ranked list of user ID according to their occurrence. The user ID with the most occurrences, which mean those users who have the most same voting as the active user, will appear at the top of the list. After that, we only fetch the top K users' record in the ranked list and made prediction based on them. We can see from Figure 5 and 6 in Section 5, the improved return K strategy has a better scalability and prediction strategy.

4 Implementation of Our Neighbor Searching Algorithm on a DHT-Based P2P Overlay Network

4.1 System Architecture

Figure 2 gives the system architecture of our implementation of DCF on the DHT-based P2P overlay network. Here, we view the users' rating as resources and the system generate a unique key for each particular <ITEM_ID, VOTE> tuple through the hash algorithm, where the ITEM_ID denotes identity of the item user votes on and VOTE is the user's rating on that item. As different users may vote particular item with same rating, each key will correspond to a set of users who have the same <ITEM_ID, VOTE> tuple corresponding to the key in their rating vector. As we stated in section 3, we call such set of users' record as *bucket*. As we can see in Figure 2, each peer in the distributed CF system is responsible for storing one or several buckets using the distributed storage strategy described in Figure 1. Peers are connected through a DHT-based P2P overlay network. Peers can find their wanted buckets by their keys efficiently through the DHT-based routing algorithm which is the foundation of our implementation. As we can see from Figure 1 and Figure 2, the implementation of our PipeCF on DHT-based P2P overlay network is quite straightforward.

DHT has provided a basic infrastructure to do the following things:
1. Define IDs, Vote ID to Node ID assignment
2. Define per-node routing table contents
3. Lookup algorithm that uses routing tables
4. Join procedure to reflect new nodes in tables
5. Failure recovery

For our DHT-based CF scenario, IDs are 128-bit numbers. Vote IDs are chosen by MD5 hash of user's <ITEM_ID,VOTE> tuple, and Node IDs are chosen by MD5 hash of user's <IP address, MAC address>. Key is stored on node with numerically closest ID. If node and key IDs are uniform, we get reasonable load balance.

There are already two basic operations in DHT overlay network: put(key, value) and lookup(key). And for our special DHT-based CF scenario, we present two new operations: getUserID(VoteKey) and getUserValue(VoteKey,userKey). The first operation returns many userIDs which have the same <ITEM_ID,VOTE> tuple with the active user, and the second operation returns the candidate user's real rating vectors.

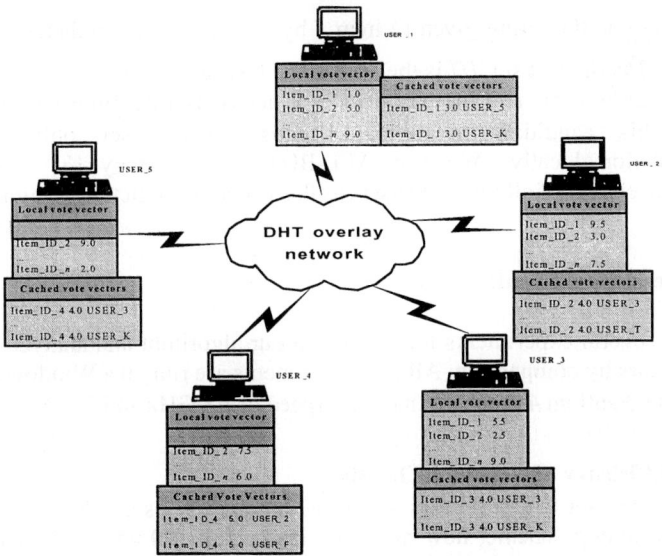

Fig. 2. System architecture of distributed CF recommender system

5 Experimental Results

5.1 Data Set

We use EachMovie data set [7] to evaluate the performance of improved algorithm. The EachMovie data set is provided by the Compaq System Research Center, which ran the EachMovie recommendation service for 18 months to experiment with a collaborative filtering algorithm. The information they gathered during that period consists of 72,916 users, 1,628 movies, and 2,811,983 numeric ratings ranging from 0 to 5.

5.2 Metrics and Methodology

The metrics for evaluating the accuracy of we used here is statistical accuracy metrics which evaluate the accuracy of a predictor by comparing predicted values with user-provided values. More specifically, we use Mean Absolute Error (MAE), a statistical accuracy metrics, to report prediction experiments for it is most commonly used and easy to understand:

$$MAE = \frac{\sum_{a \in T} |v_{a,j} - p_{a,j}|}{|T|} \quad (3)$$

Where $v_{a,j}$ is the rating given to item j by user a, is the predicted value of user a on item j, T is the test set, $|T|$ is the size of the test set.

We select 2000 users and choose one user as active user per time and the remainder users as his candidate neighbors, because every user only make self's recommendation locally. We use ALL-BUT-ONE strategy [3] and the mean prediction accuracy of all the 2000 users as the system's prediction accuracy.

5.3 Experimental Result

We design several experiments for evaluating our algorithm and analyze the effect of various factors by comparison. All our experiments are run on a Windows 2000 based PC with Intel Pentium 4 processor having a speed of 1.8 GHz and 512 MB of RAM.

5.3.1 The Efficiency of Neighbor Choosing

We used a data set of 2000 users and show among the users chosen by Return-All neighbor searching scheme, how many are in the top-100 users who have the most similarities with active users calculated by the traditional memory-based CF algorithms in Figure 3. We can see from the data that when the user number rises above 1000, more than 80 users who have the most similarities with the active users are chosen by our Neighbor choosing scheme.

5.3.2 Performance Comparison

We compare the prediction accuracy of traditional CF algorithm and our Return-All algorithm and the results are shown as Figure 4. We can see that our algorithm has better prediction accuracy than the traditional CF algorithm. This result looks surprising at the first sight as the traditional CF selecting similar users from the whole user database while we use only a fraction. However, as we look in depth into our strategy, we find that we may filter out those users who have high-correlations with the active users but no same ratings. We have found that these users are bad predictors in [16] which provide explanation to our result.

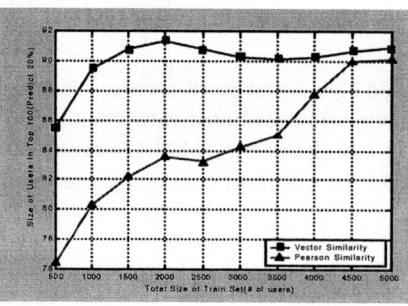

Fig. 3. How many users chosen by DHT-based CF fall in traditional CF's top 100

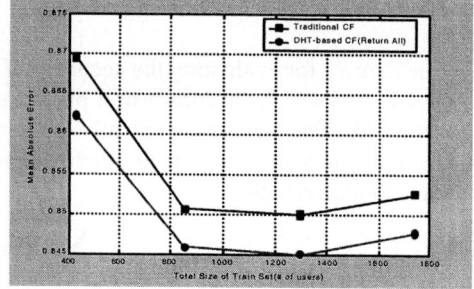

Fig. 4. DHT-based CF vs. traditional CF

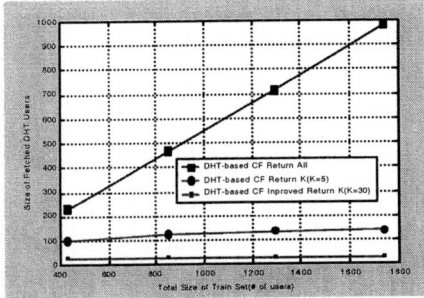 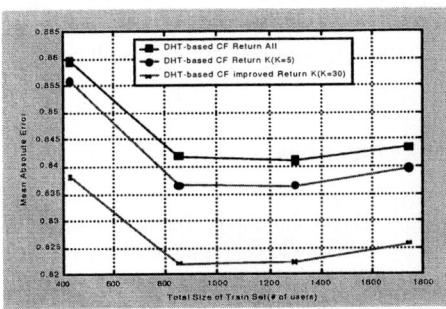

Fig. 5. The Effect on scalability of our neighbor searching strategy

Fig. 6. The effect on prediction accuracy of our neighbor searching strategy

We then compared the performance of Return K and Return All by setting the K as 5. From the result Figure 6 we can see that by eliminating those users who have same ratings on popular items, the prediction accuracy can be increased further.

DHT-based bucket distribution is illustrated in Figure 7, we can see that the more users, the larger bucket size, and when the total number of users is above 40,000, the average bucket size is more than 60.

At last, we compare the performance of Improved Return K strategy. We can see In Figure 6 that we can obtain better performance while retrieving only 30 user records.

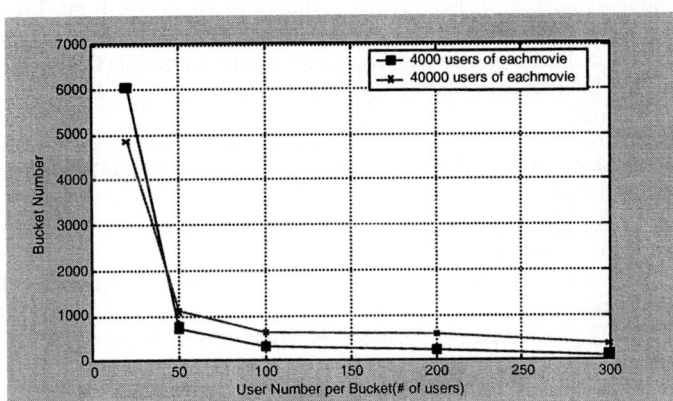

Fig. 7. The DHT buckets size distribution

6 Conclusion

In this paper, we first propose an efficient distributed user profile management scheme based on distributed hash table (DHT) method in order to solve the scalability problem of centralized KNN-based CF algorithm. Then, we present a heuristic neighbor searching algorithm to locate potential neighbors of the active users in order to reduce the network traffic and executive cost. The experimental data show that our DCF algorithm with the neighbor searching scheme has much better scalability than traditional centralized ones with comparable prediction efficiency and accuracy.

References

1. David Goldberg, David Nichols, Brian M. Oki, Douglas Terry.: Using collaborative filtering to weave an information tapestry, Communications of the ACM, v.35 n.12, p.61-70, Dec. 1992.
2. J. L. Herlocker, J. A. Konstan, A. Borchers, and J. Riedl.: An algorithmic framework for performing collaborative filtering. In Proceedings of the 22nd annual international ACM SIGIR conference on Research and development in information retrieval, pages 230-237, 1999.
3. Breese, J., Heckerman, D., and Kadie, C.: Empirical Analysis of Predictive Algorithms for Collaborative Filtering. Proceedings of the 14th Conference on Uncertainty in Artificial Intelligence, 1998 (43-52).
4. Paul Resnick, Neophytos Iacovou, Mitesh Suchak, Peter Bergstrom, John Riedl.: GroupLens: an open architecture for collaborative filtering of netnews, Proceedings of the 1994 ACM conference on Computer supported cooperative work, p.175-186, October 22-26, 1994, Chapel Hill, North Carolina, United States.
5. Upendra Shardanand, Pattie Maes.: Social information filtering: algorithms for automating "word of mouth", Proceedings of the SIGCHI conference on Human factors in computing systems, p.210-217, May 07-11, 1995, Denver, Colorado, United States.
6. G. Linden, B. Smith, and J. York, Amazon.com Recommendations Item-to-item collaborative filtering, IEEE Internet Computing, Vo. 7, No. 1, pp. 7680, Jan. 2003.
7. Eachmovie collaborative filtering data set.: http://research.compaq.com/SRC/eachmovie
8. Amund Tveit.: Peer-to-peer based Recommendations for Mobile Commerce. Proceedings of the First International Mobile Commerce Workshop, ACM Press, Rome, Italy, July 2001, pp. 26-29.
9. Tomas Olsson.: "Bootstrapping and Decentralizing Recommender Systems", Licentiate Thesis 2003-006, Department of Information Technology, Uppsala University and SICS, 2003
10. J. Canny.: Collaborative filtering with privacy. In Proceedings of the IEEE Symposium on Research in Security and Privacy, pages 45--57, Oakland, CA, May 2002. IEEE Computer Society, Technical Committee on Security and Privacy, IEEE Computer Society Press.
11. S. Ratnasamy, P. Francis, M. Handley, R. Karp, and S. Shenker.: A scalable content-addressable network. In SIGCOMM, Aug. 2001
12. Stocal I et al.: Chord: A scalable peer-to-peer lookup service for Internet applications (2001). In ACM SIGCOMM, San Diego, CA, USA, 2001, pp.149-160
13. Rowstron A. Druschel P.: Pastry: Scalable, distributed object location and routing for large scale peer-to-peer systems. In IFIP/ACM Middleware, Hedelberg,Germany,2001
14. Zhao B Y et al.: Tapestry: An infrastructure for fault-tolerant wide-area location and routing. Tech.Rep.UCB/CSB-0-114,UC Berkeley,EECS,2001
15. M.Ripeanu, "Peer-to-peer Architecture Case Study: Gnutella Network", Technical Report, University of Chicago, 2001.
16. Han Peng,Xie Bo,Yang Fan,Shen Ruimin, "A Scalable P2P Recommender System Based on Distributed Collaborative Filtering", Expert systems with applications,27(2) Elsevier Sep 2004 (To appear)

Partially Ordered Preferences Applied to the Site Location Problem in Urban Planning

Sylvain Lagrue[1], Rodolphe Devillers[2,3], and Jean-Yves Besqueut[4]

[1] CRIL, CNRS - Université d'Artois, Rue Jean Souvraz, SP 18, Lens 62307, France
  lagrue@cril.univ-artois.fr
[2] Centre de Recherche en Géomatique - Université Laval
  Québec (QC), G1K 7P4, Canada
[3] Institut Francilien des GéoSciences, Université de Marne-la-Vallée
  5 Bld Descartes, 77454 Marne la Vallée, France
  rodolphe.devillers.1@ulaval.ca
[4] SOMEI - 115 rue St Jacques, 13006 Marseille, France
  jean-yves.besqueut@somei.fr

Abstract This paper presents an application that aims at identifying optimal locations based on partially ordered constraints. It combines a tool developed in this project that allows the management of partially ordered constraints and a Geographical Information System (GIS) allowing spatial data mapping and analysis.
Experts in urban planning provides constraints, being in our application a combination of legal constraints and preferences expressed by the property developer. As these constraints can hardly be totally ordered because they are not comparable, constraints are partially ordered.
The experiment was performed using about 3800 cadastral parcels and 12 different constraints, each parcel being characterised for each constraint using GIS analysis operators. Data are then processed by the program mpropre (Managing PaRtially Ordered PREferences) that provides in output one or several optimal parcels. Results are finally validated by an expert and using ortho-images of the geographic area of interest.

1 Introduction

The geographic information field can be applied to a variety of application domains, using for instance Geographical Information Systems (GIS) for mapping or spatial analysis purposes. A typical problem in GIS applied to urban planning is the identification of locations, on a given territory, that best fits with several characteristics [1]. This can be for instance the identification of an optimal location to build a power plant, based on the field characteristics (e.g. field size, topography, slope), proximity of resources (e.g. rivers, electrical and sewer networks), and limiting visual sound pollution. Different works address the problem, generally using multi-criteria approaches that can be linked to GIS software ([2], [3] or [4]). These approaches often use a raster representation of data in order to produce matrices for each criterion of interest [4]. Matrices can then be combined, using certain weights on each criteria according to its importance.

However, such approaches have several limits. On one hand they use raster representations of data initially represented by vectors, introducing then error in the model and sometimes causing problems related to a wrong choice of matrices resolutions [5]. On the other hand, the weight of criteria does not allows the identification of some parameters seen as mandatory before considering other criteria. For instance, if the field size is too small, or is not available, it is not necessary to know if it is close enough to the sewer network, the field being directly excluded from the analysis.

Moreover, the different constraints, or preferences (these two terms being used in this paper in their wider definition) provided by the expert should often be comparable to be integrated in these methods. This is a limit, mostly if the constraints are not related to each other. Furthermore, considering these constraints as being equally preferred instead of considering them *incomparable*, often lead to false results because it is too risky.

This paper presents a method using partially ordered preferences for the selection of locations that best fit with certain constraints or preferences. Section 2 presents an application that aims at finding the optimal cadastral parcel for building a house in an urban area. Section 3 presents the method developed to manage partially ordered constraints. Finally, section 4 presents the results of the experimentation for the application and a discussion of these results, identifying advantages and limits of the approach.

2 Problem of the Selection of an Optimal Location for Building a House

The problem of selecting a location that best fits with a set of constraints is a real-life problem occurring frequently in the urban planning and development domain. The objective of this application is to help an expert to find the "best" possible location to build a house according to a set of constraints.

Constraints - Constraints examples are provided in the table1. In this application, constraints can be legal, such as "parcel has to be located at less than 150m from a fire hydrant" or structural, such as a minimal parcel size needed to build the house: "parcel size has to be more than $1000m^2$". These two constraints are strong and are mandatory for cadastral parcels selections.

Similarly, experts may want to express other constraints, like cost ones. It can be for instance the constraint "parcel should be available". Indeed, a parcel being available will avoid demolition fees. Expert may also ask for parcels having a minimum slope to limit excavation fees and increase building stability. Finally, the property developer could express constraints that will make the parcel more attractive to potential customers. It can be for instance "parcel should be located at less than 500m from commercial strip" or "parcel should be located at less than 250m from a river or lake, or be located at less than 500m from a park". These constraints are defined *a priori* and the expert cannot clearly evaluate

Table 1. Constraint examples

Strong constraints (legal & structural)
C_1 : parcel size has to be more than $1000 m^2$
C_2 : parcel should be located at less than 150m from a fire hydrant

Cost constraints
C_3 : parcel should be available
C_4 : parcel slope should be minimised

Property developer constraints
C_5 : parcel should be located at less than 500m from a commercial strip
C_6 : parcel should be located at less than 250m from a river or lake or less than 500m from a park

their impact. He only knows that certain constraints have more impact than others.

Constraints Ordering - If the expert provides several constraints, probability is high that no parcel will satisfy all of them. Then, an expert is asked to give preferences on the different constraints. For instance, strong constraints will be preferred to all the other ones. Similarly, property developer can evaluate, without providing a precise quantification, constraints that will have more impact than others. Cost constraints can also be ordered by the expert depending on the cost implied by demolition or excavation for instance. However, expert can't provide preferences between cost constraints and property developer constraints. Constraints can then only be *partially* ordered.

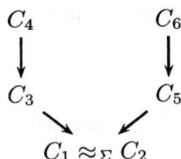

Figure 1. Partial pre-order on constraints

Figure 1 shows how the expert can order constraints. An arrow between two constraints means that the constraint identified by the arrow is preferred to the other one. For instance, constraint C_3 is preferred to constraint C_4. Strong constraints are preferred to all the other ones, cost constraint C_3 is preferred to the cost constraint C_4 and the property developer constraint C_5 is preferred to the property developer C_6. However, no preference can be identified between incomparable cost constraints and property developer constraints, without quantifying precisely the impacts of these constraints.

3 Management of Partially Ordered Constraints

This section presents a method for managing partially ordered constraints. Such method allows to select the best geographic locations, with respect to a partial order based on a set of constraints. This method is based on the concept of comparator which allows comparing subsets of constraints from a partial order of constraints. We first present some basic definitions.

3.1 Basic Definitions

Let $\Sigma = \{C_1, C_2, \ldots, C_n\}$ be a *finite* set of constraints. A partial pre-order $\preceq_\Sigma$ on Σ is a reflexive ($C_i \preceq_\Sigma C_j$) and transitive (if $C_i \preceq_\Sigma C_j$ and $C_j \preceq_\Sigma C_k$ then $C_i \preceq_\Sigma C_k$) binary relation. In this paper, $C_i \preceq_\Sigma C_j$ intuitively means that the constraint C_i is at least as preferred as C_j.

A strict partial order $\prec_\Sigma$ on the set of constraints Σ is an irreflexive ($C_i \prec C_i$ does not hold and transitive binary relation. $C_i \prec_\Sigma C_j$ means that C_i is strictly preferred to C_j. A strict partial order is generally defined from a partial pre-order as $C_i \prec_\Sigma C_j$ if $C_i \preceq_\Sigma C_j$ holds but $C_j \preceq_\Sigma C_i$ does not hold.

The equality is defined by $C_i \approx_\Sigma C_j$ if and only if $C_i \preceq_\Sigma C_j$ and $C_j \preceq_\Sigma C_i$. Intuitively, $C_i \approx_\Sigma C_j$ means that C_i and C_j are equally preferred. We finally define incomparability, denoted by $\sim_\Sigma$, as $C_i \sim_\Sigma C_j$ if and only if neither $C_i \preceq_\Sigma C_j$ nor $C_j \preceq_\Sigma C_i$ holds. $C_i \sim_\Sigma C_j$ means that neither C_i is preferred to C_j, nor the opposite.

In the following, $C_i \not\preceq_\Sigma C_j$ (resp. $C_i \not\prec_\Sigma C_j$, $a \not\approx b$) means that $C_i \preceq_\Sigma C_j$ (resp. $C_i \prec_\Sigma C_j$, $C_i \approx_\Sigma C_j$) does not hold.

A total pre-order $\leq_\Sigma$ is a partial pre-order such that $\forall C_i, C_j \in \Sigma : C_i \leq_\Sigma C_j$ or $C_j \leq_\Sigma C_i$.

Let $\prec_\Sigma$ be a strict partial order on a set Σ. The set of minimal elements of Σ, denoted by $Min(\Sigma, \preceq_\Sigma)$, is defined as follows: $Min(\Sigma, \preceq_\Sigma) = \{C_i \in \Sigma : \nexists C_j \in \Sigma, C_j \prec C_i\}$. Note that only the strict partial order is useful for determining minimal elements of Σ.

3.2 Comparing Subsets of Constraints

Let $L = \{l_1, l_2, \ldots, l_p\}$ be the set of possible locations. Roughly speaking, the location l_i is strictly preferred to the location l_j, denoted by $l_i \triangleleft_L l_j$, if the set of formulas falsified by l_j is preferred to the set of formulas falsified by l_i.

Therefore, we need to define a relation of preference on constraints subsets from a partial pre-order on a set of constraints. Such a relation is said to be a *comparator*. There are several ways to define a comparator (see [6], [7], [8] and [9] for more details on comparisons between subsets). We use the following one: a subset of constraints X is preferred to a subset of constraints Y if and only if for each element in Y, we can find a better element in X. More formally:

Definition 1. *Let $(\Sigma, \preceq_\Sigma)$ be a set of partially ordered constraints and $X, Y \subseteq \Sigma$ (we assume that neither X nor Y is empty), X is strictly preferred to Y,* denoted by $X \triangleleft Y$ iff: $\forall C_j \in Min(Y, \preceq_\Sigma), \exists C_i \in Min(X, \preceq_\Sigma)$ such that $C_i \prec_\Sigma C_j$.

If $X = Y = \emptyset$, we then consider that neither $X \triangleleft Y$ holds, nor $Y \triangleleft X$, and it can be demonstrated that $\triangleleft$ is a strict partial order. Example 1 illustrates this definition.

Example 1. We consider again the case presented on the Figure 1, which was such that
$$\Sigma = \{C_1, C_2, C_3, C_4, C_5, C_6\}$$
and $\preceq_\Sigma$ was such that :
$$\begin{cases} C_1 \approx_\Sigma C_2, \\ C_1 \prec_\Sigma C_3 \prec_\Sigma C_4, \\ C_1 \prec_\Sigma C_5 \prec_\Sigma C_6. \end{cases}$$

Let X be such that $X = \{C_3, C_4, C_5\}$ and Y be such that $Y = \{C_4, C_6\}$. We then have $X \triangleleft Y$, indeed C_3 is preferred to C_4 and C_5 is preferred to C_6.

We can now introduce our method for choosing the "best" locations for building a house.

3.3 Selecting the "Best" Locations

Let $(\Sigma, \preceq_\Sigma)$ be a partially ordered set of constraints and L the set of all possible locations. We suppose that for each location l, we dispose of all constraints that are falsified by l. This set of falsified constraints is denoted by $\lceil l, \Sigma \rceil$. Note that, in the context of our application, this set of falsified constraints is provided by the GIS. This section aims to show how to compare the different possible spatial locations, according to the partially ordered constraints they falsify.

To achieve this goal, we define a strict partial order $\triangleleft_L$ on the set of possible locations. Let $l1$ and l_2 be two elements of L, the location l_1 is preferred to the parcels l_2 (denoted by $l_1 \triangleleft_L l_2$) if and only if the set of constraints that are falsified by l_2 is preferred to the set of constraints falsified by l_1. For comparing these subsets of Σ, we use the comparator defined in the previous section.

Definition 2. *Let Σ be a set of constraints and $\preceq_\Sigma$ a partial pre-order on Σ. Let L be the set of possible locations and l_i and l_j two locations. Then:*
$$l_i \triangleleft_L l_j \quad \text{iff} \quad \lceil l_j, \Sigma \rceil \triangleleft \lceil l_i, \Sigma \rceil.$$

Note that $\triangleleft_L$ is a strict partial order. We illustrate this definition by the following example.

Example 2. Let us consider again the Example 1. We consider two locations l_1 and l_2. The set of constraints they falsify ($\lceil l_i, \Sigma \rceil$) and the set of constraints they satisfy ($\Sigma \setminus \lceil l_i, \Sigma \rceil$) is presented in the Table 2.
We have $l_1 \triangleleft_L l_2$. Indeed we have $\{C_3, C_4, C_5\} \triangleleft \{C_4, C_6\}$ and then $\lceil l_2, \Sigma \rceil \triangleleft \lceil l_1, \Sigma \rceil$.

punctual road intersections were derived from linear roads; parcel slopes were derived from linear elevation contour lines).

A subset of the available data for the area of Sherbrooke was produced, including urban and rural areas, with a total of 3782 cadastral parcels. Different metric (e.g. distance, buffer) and topologic operators (e.g. inclusion, intersection) allowed identifying how each individual parcel respects or not each constraint. For instance, the metric operator "is within the distance of" allowed to identify all parcels located at less than a certain distance from fire hydrants, commercial strips, parks, etc. These operations allowed to associate a binary value in a database indicating if each parcel respects or falsifies each constraint. This file is then exported to the program 'mpropre' in order to be processed according to the constraints partially ordered by the expert. Once data processing is performed in 'mpropre', the program provides in output a set of object instances ID identifying parcels that best respect constraints according to the partial order defined. It is then possible to identify the selected parcels and visualise them on aerial ortho-images in order to validate the selection.

This method provides results based on the general quality of the parcels. As geographic data qualities can be very heterogeneous, it can be interesting to only select reliable parcels. Based on different quality information issued for instance from metadata (i.e. data describing the different datasets), an average quality is associated to each cadastral parcel. This quality criterion can have three discrete values being "bad", "average" or "good". A first analysis is performed using 'mpropre' for the subset of parcels having a "good" quality. A second analysis relaxes quality by accepting both values "average" and "good". This second analysis allows to include in the parcel selection a larger number of parcels.

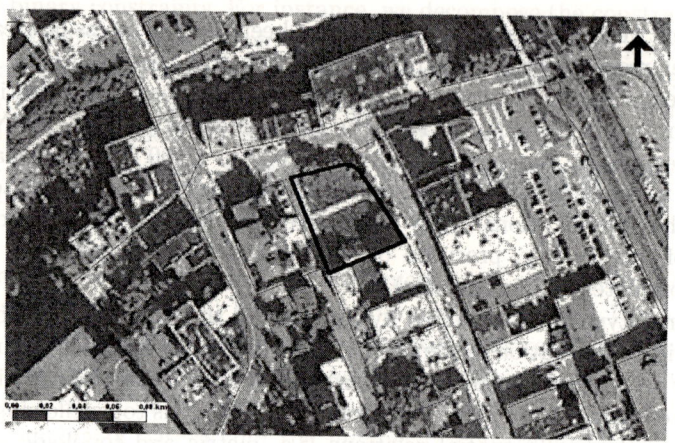

Figure 3. Selected parcel 1625

The program has been tested using different orders for the constraints, for the entire parcel dataset. Program execution time is almost instantaneous. Results provided by the program were validated by experts having a knowledge of the area and also by a visual validation using ortho-rectified aerial images. Different tests has also been performed in order to exclude a priori parcels that are not available for construction (e.g. roads - that are represented by polygonal objects similar to parcels - and other public spaces such as parks, parkings, squares, etc.). Figure 4 represents the first of the two parcels selected.

5 Conclusion

This paper presented an original approach of constraint-based reasoning applied to a common geographic information problem. This approach applies an algorithm allowing the management of partially ordered constraints to the problem of selection of an optimal cadastral parcel for building a house.

This innovative approach for the problem of optimal site selection avoid some drawbacks of traditional geographic multi-criteria approaches, being for instance the need to quantify each criterion. Weights are often hard to obtain from the experts and the results depend strongly of this quantification. On the contrary, our method allows an expert, which do not know the selection method, to qualitatively order the constraints. Moreover experts do not have to compare all constraints, which are not always linked between each other.

An application based on real constraints and data was developed in order to validate the approach. The algorithm, tested with 12 constraints and more than 3700 geographic objects showed an excellent performance and provided results validated by an expert.

Future developments could incorporate fuzziness in the constraints. Indeed, the break down into binary constraints is not realistic when the number of constraints increase: the graph of preference becomes no more readable. Another future development could take more into consideration the aspects related to geographic data quality in parcels selections. How to incorporate the quality of data sets in the choice of location when the constraints on this locations are partially ordered ?

Acknowledgments

This work was supported by the European Community through the REV!GIS project ♯ IST-1999-14189 (http://www.cmi.uni-mrs.fr/REVIGIS) and by the Ministère de la Recherche Science et Technologie (MRST) of Quebec government, Canada. GeoMedia Professional GIS software was kindly provided by Intergraph inc through SOMEI. Thanks are also due to the city of Sherbrooke, the government of Quebec (MRN) and the government of Canada (CTI-S) for providing the geographic datasets.

References

1. Church, R.L.: Location modelling and GIS. In Longley, P., Goodchild, M., Maguire, D., Rhind, D., eds.: Geographical information systems (2nd Ed.), New York, John Wiley (1999) 293–303
2. Schärlig, A.: Où construire l'usine? La localisation optimale d'une activité industrielle dans la pratique. Dunod (1973)
3. Pereira, J.M., Duckstein, L.: A multiple criteria decision-making approach to GIS-based land suitability evaluation. International Journal of Geographical Information Systems **7** (1993) 407–424
4. Joerin, F.: Méthode multicritère d'aide à la décision et SIG pour la recherche d'un site. Revue internationale de géomatique **1** (1995)
5. Monmonier, M.: A case study in the misuse of GIS: Siting a low-level radioactive waste disposal facility in new york state. In: Proceedings of the conference on Law and Information Policy for Spatial Databases, Tempe (USA) (1994)
6. Halpern, J.Y.: Defining relative likelihood in partially-ordered preferential structures. Journal of AI Research **7** (1997) 1–24
7. Cayrol, C., Royer, V., Saurel, C.: Management of preferences in assumption-based reasoning. In: Proceedings of Information Processing and the Management of Uncertainty in Knowledge based Systems (IPMU'92), Springer (1992) 13–22
8. Benferhat, S., Dubois, D., Lang, J., Prade, H., Saffiotti, A., Smets, P.: Reasoning under inconsistency based on implicitly-specified partial qualitative probability relations: a unified framework. In: Proceedings of the 15th National Conference on Artificial Intelligence (AAAI-98). (1998) 121–126
9. Benferhat, S., Lagrue, S., Papini, O.: Reasoning with partially ordered information in a possibilistic framework. Fuzzy Sets and Systems **144** (2004) 25–41

A Flexible Fuzzy Expert System for Fuzzy Duplicate Elimination in Data Cleaning

Hamid Haidarian Shahri and Ahmad Abdollahzadeh Barforush

Faculty of Computer Engineering and Information Technology
Amirkabir University of Technology (Tehran Polytechnic), Tehran, Iran
hhaidarian@aut.ac.ir, ahmad@ce.aut.ac.ir

Abstract. Data cleaning deals with the detection and removal of errors and inconsistencies in data, gathered from distributed sources. This process is essential for drawing correct conclusions from data in decision support systems. Eliminating fuzzy duplicate records is a fundamental part of the data cleaning process. The vagueness and uncertainty involved in detecting fuzzy duplicates make it a niche, for applying fuzzy reasoning. Although uncertainty algebras like fuzzy logic are known, their applicability to the problem of duplicate elimination has remained unexplored and unclear, until today. In this paper, a novel and flexible fuzzy expert system for detection and elimination of fuzzy duplicates in the process of data cleaning is devised, which circumvents the repetitive and inconvenient task of hard-coding. Some of the crucial advantages of this approach are its flexibility, ease of use, extendibility, fast development time and efficient run time, when used in various information systems.

1 Introduction

The problems of data quality and *data cleaning* are inevitable in data integration from distributed operational databases and OLTP systems [9]. That is due to the lack of a unified set of standards spanning over all the distributed sources. One of the most challenging and resource intensive phases of data cleaning is the removal of fuzzy duplicate records. The term "fuzzy duplicates" is used for tuples, which are somehow different, but describe the same real-world entity, i.e. different syntaxes but the same semantic. *Eliminating* fuzzy duplicates is applicable in any database, but critical in data integration and analytical processing domains, where accurate reports/statistics are required. Some of the application domains of fuzzy duplicate elimination include data warehouses especially in the dimension tables, OLAP and data mining applications, decision support systems, on-demand (lazy) web-based information integration systems, web search engines, meta-crawlers and numerous others. Consequently, a flexible approach to detect the duplicates can be utilized in many *database applications*.

In this paper, section 2 describes the design of a fuzzy expert system. Section 3 explains the characteristics of the system. Section 4 contains the experimental results and their evaluation. Section 5 gives an account of the related work in the field of duplicate elimination and section 6 summarizes with a conclusion.

2 Design of the Fuzzy Duplicate Elimination System

Detecting fuzzy duplicates using a human and by hand, requires assigning an expert, who is familiar with the table schema and semantic interpretation of attributes in a tuple, for comparing the tuples using his expertise and concluding, whether two tuples refer to the same entity or not. So, for comparing tuples and determining their similarity, internal knowledge about the nature of the tuples seems essential. Generally, an "equational theory" is utilized to compare two tuples and infer the probability of them being the same [5]. Considering the uncertainties involved, sometimes the decision making is indeed difficult, for a human as well. It is very practical and beneficial to automate this long and cumbersome task, by replacing the human with an expert system.

For finding fuzzy duplicates, Hernandez suggests the *sorted neighborhood method* (SNM) [5], in which a key is created for each tuple, such that the duplicates will have similar keys. The tuples are sorted using that key. The sort operation clusters the duplicates and brings them closer to each other. Finally, a window of size w slides over the sorted data and the tuple, entering the window, is compared with all the $w-1$ tuples in the window. Hence, performing $n(w-1)$ comparisons for a total of n tuples. In previous methods in the literature, the comparison is done using a set of static and predefined conditions or declarative rules that are hard-coded, which is different from this approach, and much more time consuming.

The principal procedure is as follows: to feed a pair of tuples (selected from all possible pairs) into a decision making system and determine, if they are fuzzy duplicates or not. A detailed workflow of the duplicate elimination system is demonstrated in Figure 1. Firstly, the data should be cleaned, before starting the duplicate elimination phase. That is essential for achieving good results. In a dumb approach, each record is selected and compared with all the rest of the tuples, one by one (i.e. a total of $n(n-1)$ comparisons for n records). To make the process more efficient, the cleaned tuples are *clustered* by some algorithm, in hope of gathering the tuples that are most likely to be duplicates, in one group. Then, all possible pairs from each cluster are selected, and the comparisons are only performed for records within each cluster. The user selects the *attributes* that are important in comparing two records, because some attributes do not have much effect in distinguishing a record uniquely. A fuzzy expert system, which uses attribute similarities for comparing a pair of records, is employed to detect the duplicates.

This novel duplicate elimination system allows the user to *flexibly* change different parts of the process. In Figure 1, by following the points, where the user can intervene, it is observed that the forthcoming items can be easily selected from a list or supplied by the user (from left to right): 1) clustering algorithm, 2) attributes to be used in the comparison of a pair of tuples, 3) corresponding similarity functions for measuring attribute similarity, 4) fuzzy rules to be used in the inference engine, 5) membership functions, 6) merging strategy. Most of these items are explained in this section. Fuzzy rules and membership functions will be explained further in the next sections.

In this system, the creation of a key, sorting based on that key, and sliding window phase of the SNM method, is considered as a clustering algorithm. The moving window is a structure, which is used for holding the clustered tuples and actually acts like a cluster. The comparisons are performed for tuples within the window. Any other existing *clustering algorithm* can be employed, and even a new hand coded one can be added to the bank of algorithms. For example, another option is to use a priority queue data structure for keeping the records instead of a window, which reduces the number of comparisons [8].

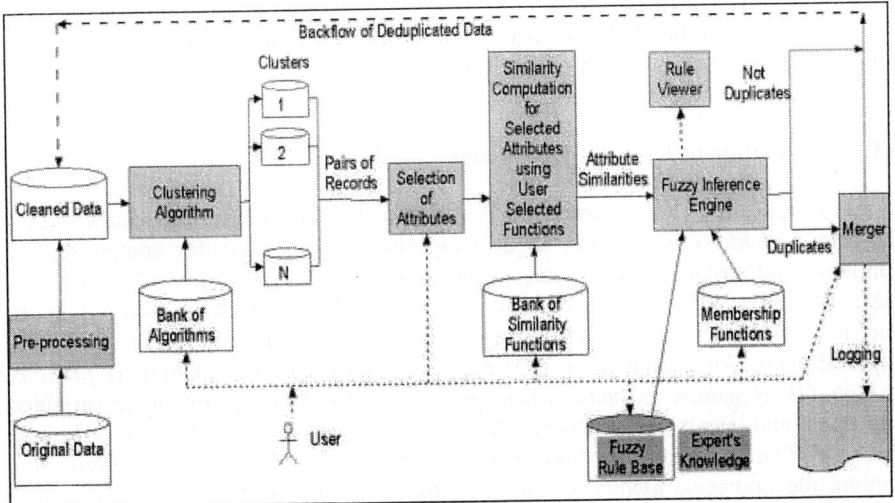

Fig. 1. A detailed workflow of the fuzzy duplicate elimination system

The *tuple attributes* that are to be used in the decision making are not fixed and can be determined by the user, at run-time. The expert (user) should select a set of attributes, which best identifies a tuple, uniquely. Hence, the number of attributes in the tuple is not very critical. Then, a specific *similarity function* for each selected attribute is chosen, from a library of hand coded ones, which is a straight-forward step. The similarity function should be chosen according to attribute data type and domain, e.g. numerical, string, or domain dependent functions for address, surname, etc. Each function is used for measuring the similarity of two corresponding attributes, in a pair of tuples. In this way, any original or appropriate similarity function can be easily *integrated* into the fuzzy duplicate elimination system.

At the end, the system has to eliminate the detected duplicates, by merging them. Different *merging strategies* can be utilized, as suggested in the literature [5], i.e. deciding on which tuple to use, as the prime representative of the duplicates. Some alternatives are using the tuple, which has the least number of empty attributes, the newest tuple, or prompting the user to make a decision, etc. All the merged tuples and their prime representatives are recorded in a *log*. The input-output of the fuzzy inference engine (FIE) for the detected duplicates is also saved. This information helps the user to review the changes in the duplicate elimination process and verify them. The *rule viewer* enables the expert to examine the input-output of the FIE and fine-tune the rules and membership functions in the system by hand. The rule viewer has been implemented and is described in [4].

3 Characteristics of the System

This design for the fuzzy duplicate elimination system, as described in the previous section, has several interesting features that are explained here in more detail. The decision making process is intrinsically difficult considering the ambiguity and uncertainty involved in the inference. It is also time consuming and quite impossible to assign humans to this task, especially when dealing with large amounts of data. The solution here is a flexible fuzzy expert system.

3.1 Acquisition of Expert's Knowledge

In this system, fuzzy rules specify the criteria for the detection of duplicates. In fact, the rules provide a simple way of utilizing any complex logic for computing text similarity and string manipulations, in terms of similarity functions selected by the user. The rules effectively *capture expert's knowledge*, which is required in the decision making process. The essence of reasoning based on fuzzy rules [7] is briefly explained here. An example of a fuzzy rule that describes a simple fact is: IF *pressure* is *high* THEN *volume* is *small*, where pressure and volume are linguistic variables, and high and small are linguistic terms that are characterized by *membership functions*. Due to the concise form of fuzzy if-then rules, they are often employed to capture the imprecise modes of reasoning that play an essential role in the human ability to make decisions in an environment of uncertainty and imprecision. The variables are partitioned in terms of natural language linguistic terms. This linguistic partitioning, an inherent feature of what Lotfi Zadeh calls *computing with words*, greatly simplifies model building. Linguistic terms represent fuzzy subsets over the corresponding variable's domain. These terms are what we actually use, in our every-day linguistic reasoning, as we speak.

In contrast to the fuzzy reasoning approach of this system, the previously suggested conditions and declarative rules for comparing tuples are particularly difficult and time consuming to code and the coding has to be repeated for each different table schema. The fuzzy reasoning approach provides a *fast* and *intuitive* way of defining the rules by the expert in *natural language*, with the aid of a simple GUI. This eliminates the repetitive process of *hard-coding* and reduces the development time. An example of a rule in this system is as follows: IF (LastNameSimilarity is *high*) ∧ (FirstNameSimilarity is *high*) ∧ (CodeSimilarity is *high*) ∧ (AddressSimilarity is *low*) THEN (Probability is *medium*). The antecedent part of each rule can include a *subset* (or *all*) of the attributes, which the user has selected in the previous stage. The consequence or output of the rule represents the probability of two tuples being duplicates.

In defining the membership function for each linguistic (input) variable, e.g. LastNameSimilarity, two linguistic terms (low, high) are used. When the similarity of attributes (as measured by the user-selected function) is not high, the actual similarity value and how much different the attributes are, are of no importance. Hence, there is no need for more than two terms. Having two linguistic terms also limits the number of possible rules. The shape of the membership function for each linguistic term is determined by the expert.

3.2 Handling Uncertainty

When the expert is entering the rules, he is in fact just adding his natural and instinctive form of reasoning, as if he was to perform this task by hand. However, in previous methods, there are much more problems, when thresholds and certainty factors for rules [6] and other parameters, have to be hard-coded. The previously proposed certainty factor represents the belief of the expert, who is coding the rules, in the effectiveness of a rule. By using fuzzy logic, *uncertainty* is handled differently in the *fuzzy inference* process and there is no need for a certainty factor. Fuzzy inference inherently handles the uncertainty involved in the decision making, because it measures the *degree* to which an instance fits a certain rule. Additionally, here, the problem of parameter tuning of the hard-coded program, which is quite time consuming and a matter of trial and error, is alleviated.

Generally, the fuzzy-system model determines the value of the consequent variable, for a given manifestation of the antecedent variables. In essence, a fuzzy-system model is a knowledge-based representation of the functional relationship, between the antecedent variables and the consequent variable. Such a model's inference mechanism is straight-forward, as formalized below. In Mamdani method of inference [7], the consequent variable is a fuzzy subset, for example, a rule ends with something like Probability = high, etc. If the final consequent of the fuzzy inference system is above a certain threshold, the tuples are classified as duplicates. The actual and appropriate value for the threshold should be determined, according to the consequence of the rules. [4] explains the inference with more details and an example.

Consider that there are n rules and the ith rule is: IF V_1 is A_{i1} & V_2 is A_{i2} & ... & V_p is A_{ip} THEN U is B_i, where V_i's are the antecedent variables and U is the consequent variable. A_{ij} and B_i are fuzzy subsets over the corresponding variable's domain. With this representation for a fuzzy rule, the output for a given input, $V_j = x_j^*$, is determined in the following process:

1. Calculate each rule's firing level as, $\lambda_i = \underset{j=1,...,p}{Min}\{A_{ij}(x_j^*)\}$. Here, $A_{ij}(x_j^*)$ is the membership grade of x_j^* in the fuzzy subset A_{ij}.
2. Calculate each rule's effective output by weighting its consequence by its firing level. This process produces the fuzzy subset F_i, where $F_i(y) = \lambda_i B_i(y)$.
3. Aggregate the effective outputs to obtain a fuzzy subset F corresponding to the overall system output, where $F(y) = \underset{j=1,...,n}{Max}[F_i(y)]$.
4. Calculate the crisp specific model output y^* from F, using a defuzzification step. This produces a unique value for the consequent variable.

3.3 Other Features

The user can change different parts of the process, as previously illustrated in Figure 1. Consequently, duplicate elimination is performed very freely and *flexibly*. Since, the expert determines the clustering algorithm, tuple attributes and corresponding similarity functions for measuring their similarity, many of the previously developed methods for duplicate elimination can be integrated into the system. For example, the user can employ complex learnable string similarity measures [1] or domain independent ones [8], etc. Hence, the system is quite *extendible* and serves as a *framework* for implementing various approaches.

Obviously, domain knowledge helps the duplicate elimination process. After all, what are considered duplicates or data anomalies in one case, might not be in another. Such domain-dependent knowledge is derived naturally from the business domain. The business analyst with subject matter expertise is able to fully understand the business logic governing the situation and can provide the appropriate knowledge to make a decision. Here, *domain knowledge* is represented in the form of fuzzy rules, which resemble human's way of reasoning under vagueness and uncertainty. These fuzzy if-then rules are simple, structured and *manipulative*.

An expert fuzzy inference engine applies the rules to the input and quickly performs the reasoning using basic arithmetic operations that require little computational power. The *computational efficiency* provided by this approach is arguably higher than the code developed in [5] and the expert system suggested in [6] using the Rete algorithm. The reason is that here the rules are all fired in parallel and the processing is a basic min or max operation, unlike previous methods. There is no need to run a code step by step. This is a crucial advantage, when comparing millions of tuples in a large database. The system also provides a rule viewer that enables the expert to see the exact effect of the fired rules for each input vector. This in turn, allows the manipulation and fine-tuning of problematic rules by hand. The rule viewer also provides the reasoning and explanation, behind the changes in the tuples and helps the expert to gain a better understanding of the process.

4 Experimental Results and Evaluation

For implementing the fuzzy duplicate elimination system, the Borland C++ Builder Enterprise Suite and Microsoft SQL Server 2000 are used. The data resides in relational database tables and is fetched through ActiveX Data Object (ADO) components. The Data Transformation Service (DTS) of MS SQL Server is employed to load the data into the OLE DB Provider. The hardware in these experiments is a Pentium 4 (1.5 GHz) with the Windows XP operating system. The dataset used in our experiments is made up of segmented census records originally gathered by Winkler [11] and also employed in some of the previous string matching projects [2]. The data is the result of integration of two different sources, and each source has duplicates, as well as other inconsistencies. The table consists of 580 records, of which 332 are unique and 248 are duplicates. The structure of records and some examples from the actual dataset are shown in Table 2 below.

As illustrated in the examples above, some attributes in a record can be null. The similarity function returns a code for those attributes and consequently those attributes are not used in the comparison of the two records. For the purpose of these experiments and investigating the effectiveness of the approach, a very simple similarity function is used in our implementation, which only matches the characters in the two fields and correspondingly returns a value between zero and one. However, by adding more sophisticated and smarter attribute similarity functions that are

A Flexible Fuzzy Expert System for Fuzzy Duplicate Elimination in Data Cleaning

domain dependant (handling abbreviations, address checking, etc.), the final results can only improve.

Table 1. Structure of records and examples from the actual dataset

Record Source	Last Name	First Name	Middle Initial	Code	Address
A	RUSSALL	MYRIAM	A	624	OCONEE
A	RUSSELL	MIRIAM	M	624	OCONEE
A	JIMENCZ	IRVIN	A	-	BANK
B	JIMENCZ	AUNDERE	I	214	BANK

Here, the process is explained for the first two records in the table above. Four of the attributes as selected by the user (last name, first name, code and address) are employed in the inference process. The basic SNM is exploited for the clustering of records. Two linguistic terms of high and low are used for the bell-shaped membership functions of the input variables in this example, as shown in Figure 2 (left), which allows for the definition of a total of 4^2 rules. The output variable consists of three linguistic terms (low, medium, high), as demonstrated in Figure 2 (right). The user adds eleven rules, similar to the following, in natural language, with the aid of a GUI:

- IF (LastNameSimilarity is *high*) ∧ (FirstNameSimilarity is *high*)
  ∧ (CodeSimilarity is *high*) ∧ (AddressSimilarity is *high*)
  THEN (Probability is high).
- IF (LastNameSimilarity is *low*) ∧ (FirstNameSimilarity is *low*)
  THEN (Probability is *low*).

The input vector of the fuzzy inference engine, as calculated by the simple attribute similarity function, is: (0.857, 0.958, 1, 1) and the unique output produced by the rules using the Mamdani method is 0.939, which is above the 0.8 threshold set by the user for this test and hence, the tuples are detected as duplicates, which is actually correct. Due to space constraints, the inference process is not explained any further and the reader can refer to [7] for more details. The user can efficiently *visualize* the effect of rules in the inference process with the aid of the logging mechanism and the rule viewer.

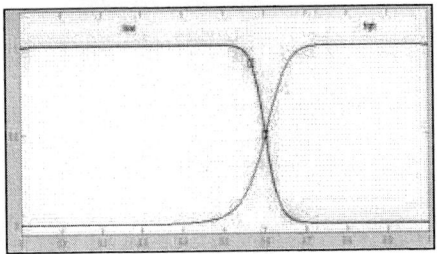 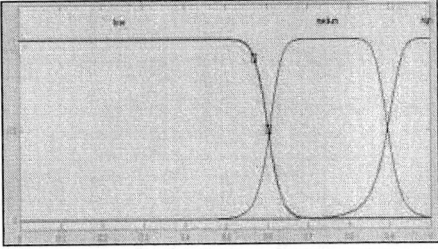

Fig. 2. Linguistic terms (low, medium, high) and their corresponding membership functions for the four input variables (on the left), and the output variable (on the right)

Figure 3 is showing the effect of window size, and different keys that are employed in sorting the data in the SNM method, in single-pass and multi-pass, with the eleven rules of the previous example. Using an unsuitable key, which is not able to group the duplicates together, has a deterring effect on the result, i.e. more false duplicates are detected than true ones, using the address key with a window size of 3. Hence, key creation is important in the SNM. Generally, as in the figure, the increase in window size enhances the results, but not much is achieved by using a very large window, which increases the execution time and number of comparisons. In multi-pass, when several runs of the process is repeated using a different key each time, only a small window suffices and with a window size of 3, the rules effectively identify 79% of the duplicates with a precision of 85%. The resultant data is of good quality, with considerably less duplicates, i.e. 195 of the 248 duplicates are eliminated.

Figure 4 demonstrates the precision-recall curve for the above rules with a window size of 6 using multi-pass, which describes the trade off between the critical parameters of precision and recall. By following the curve, it can be inferred that the system performed quite well on the dataset, effectively finding 175 of the 248 duplicates at one point, which is a recall rate of 70 percent, while sustaining a 90 percent precision. By employing other sets of simple rules, *worded* easily in natural language by the user, who is familiar with the records, similar results have been achieved. Overall, it is observed that the system is capable of handling the ambiguity and uncertainty involved, in the cumbersome task of fuzzy (approximate) duplicate elimination. In this approach, very little time is spent on phrasing the rules, which mitigates the burden of writing hard-code with complex conditions that has to be repeated for different database schemas. This is not a surprise, because it is the inherent feature of fuzzy logic. However, our design for the duplicate elimination system, exploits that feature to allow users to de-duplicate their integrated data, effortlessly. The system provides flexibility for the user to change or manipulate various parts of the process and implement many of the existing methods for this task.

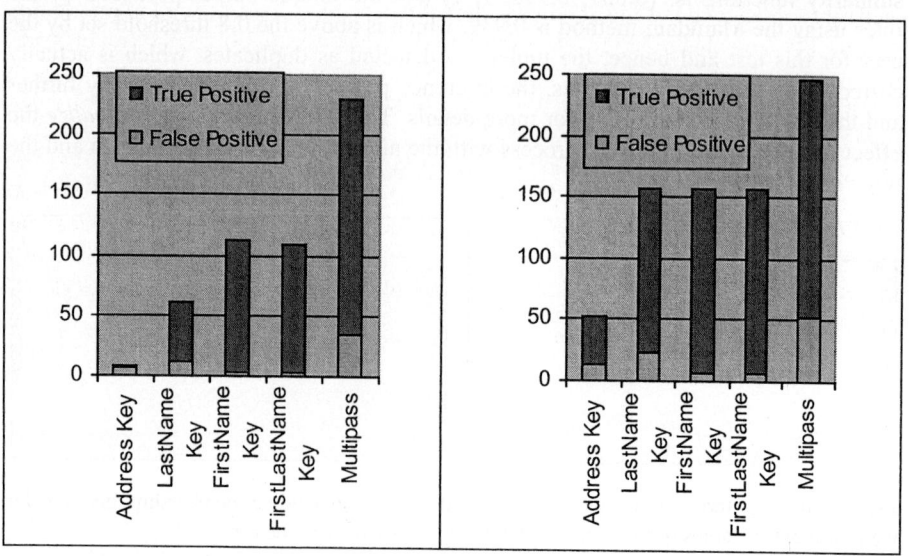

Fig. 3. The effect different keys in single-pass and multi-pass with window sizes of 3 on the left and 10 on the right hand side. 248 duplicates exist in the dataset of 580 records

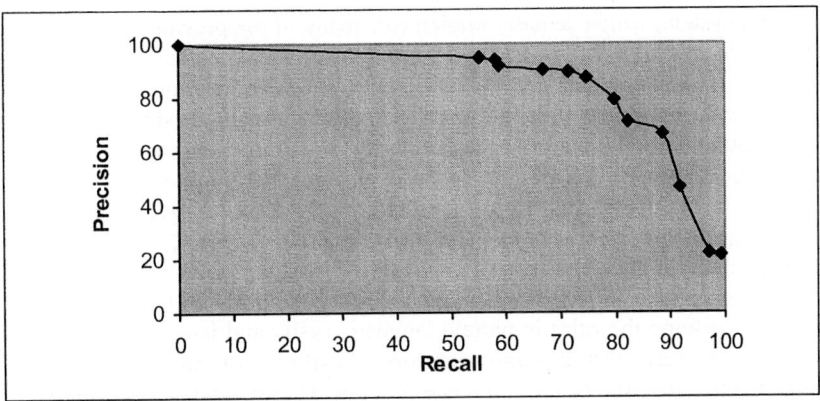

Fig. 4. The precision-recall curve for the eleven rules with a window size of 6 using multi-pass

5 Related Work

Generally data cleaning is a practical and important process in the database industry and different approaches have been suggested for this task. Some of the differences of our system, to the previous work done on approximate duplicate elimination, have been mentioned throughout the paper, especially in section three. This design can be used for integrating many of the previously suggested methods in the literature, like various clustering algorithms, similarity functions and mergers. Additionally, utilizing a fuzzy expert system introduces some new beneficial features. The seminal SNM method from [5] and the idea of an equational theory have been utilized in our de-dup system. The knowledge-based approach introduced by Lee [6] is similar to our work, in the sense of exploiting hand-coded rules to represent knowledge. [6] suggests using a certainty factor, for the rules and for computing the transitive closures, which is not required here.

[10] describes an interactive data cleaning system, that allows the user to see the changes in the data with the aid of a spreadsheet-like interface. It uses gradual construction of transformations through examples, to eliminate the need for programming. AJAX [3] presents an execution model, algorithms and a declarative language, similar to SQL commands, to express data cleaning specifications and perform the cleaning efficiently.

6 Conclusions and Future Work

This paper introduces the application of *fuzzy logic* for de-duplication for the first time. Essentially, it would not be possible to produce such a flexible inference mechanism, without the exploitation of fuzzy logic, which has the added benefit of removing programming from the production of an "equational theory." Utilizing this reasoning approach paves the way, for an easy to use and accommodative duplicate elimination system, which actually implements many of the previous methods. Hence, the development time for setting up a de-dup system is reduced considerably. Another advantage of the Mamdani method of inference is computational efficiency. The inference produces a unique value for the consequent, using a simple computation, and computational efficiency is important for providing the rapid response time needed in performing comparisons, when evaluating many tuples. The experiments reveal that, in multi-pass SNM, the rules effectively identify 79% of the duplicates with a precision of 85%, using a very small window size of 3, which significantly reduces the number of comparisons and run-time.

The advantages of utilizing fuzzy logic for fuzzy duplicate elimination include: the ability of specifying the rules in natural language easily and intuitively, removing the hard-coding process, fast development time, flexibility of rule manipulation, and computational efficiency of the inference process. These features make the approach very suitable and promising to be utilized, in the development of an *application-oriented* commercial tool for duplicate elimination, which is our main future plan. Discovering more about the rules that are required, based on the attributes selected by the user, and perhaps automating the rule production, is another avenue for further research. The possibility of adding learning mechanisms to the system looks very promising as well, and is going to be investigated.

References

1. Bilenko, M., Mooney, R.J.: Adaptive Duplicate Detection Using Learnable String Similarity Measures. Proceedings of the Ninth ACM SIGKDD International Conference on Knowledge Discovery and Data Mining (KDD'03), Washington, DC, August (2003)
2. Cohen, W., Ravikumar, P., Fienberg, S.: A Comparison of String Distance Metrics for Name-Matching Tasks. In IIWeb Workshop 2003 (2003)
3. Galhardas, H., Florescu, D., et al.: Declarative Data Cleaning: Language, Model, and Algorithms. In Proc. of the 27th VLDB Conference (2001)
4. Haidarian Shahri, H., Barforush, A.A.: Data Mining for Removing Fuzzy Duplicates Using Fuzzy Inference. 23rd International Conference of the North American Fuzzy Information Processing Society (NAFIPS 2004), Banff, Alberta, Canada, June 27-30 (2004)
5. Hernandez, M.A., Stolfo, S.J.: Real-world Data is Dirty: Data Cleansing and the Merge/Purge Problem. Data Mining and Knowledge Discovery 2 (1) (1998) 9–37
6. Low, W.L., Lee, M.L., Ling, T.W.: A Knowledge-based Approach for Duplicate Elimination in Data Cleaning. Information Systems 26 (2001) 585-606
7. Mamdani, E.H.: Advances in Linguistic Synthesis of Fuzzy Controllers. Int. J. Man Machine Studies, Vol. 8 (1976)
8. Monge, A.E., Elkan, P.C.: An Efficient Domain-independent Algorithm for Detecting Approximately Duplicate Database Records. Proceedings of the SIGMOD 1997 Workshop on Data Mining and Knowledge Discovery, May (1997)
9. Rahm, E., Do, H.H.: Data Cleaning: Problems and Current Approaches. Bulletin of the IEEE Computer Society Technical Committee on Data Engineering, Special Issue on Data Cleaning, 23(4) December (2000)
10. Raman, V., Hellerstein, J.M.: Potter's Wheel: An Interactive Data Cleaning System. In Proc. of the 27th VLDB Conference (2001)
11. Winkler, W.E.: The State of Record Linkage and Current Research Problems. Statistics of Income Division, Internal Revenue Service Publication R99/04 (1999)

DBSitter: An Intelligent Tool for Database Administration

Adriana Carneiro, Rômulo Passos, Rosalie Belian, Thiago Costa,
Patrícia Tedesco, and Ana Carolina Salgado

Universidade Federal de Pernambuco
Centro de Informática, Recife – PE Brasil
Phone: +55 8132718430
{apcc,ranop,rbb,tac,pcart,acs}@cin.ufpe.br

Abstract: Database administration routines involve manual or semi-automatic methods for monitoring the environment and solving problems that arise. In this work, we propose a novel alternative approach to this task, which unifies two Artificial Intelligence techniques: Case Based Reasoning and Intelligent Agents. Our prototype, DBSitter, consists of a Multi-agent system for automatic monitoring and fault correcting in a relational DBMS, where problems are represented as Cases. In searching for better solutions, the system can also interact with the Database Administrator. The main functionalities provided are failure prediction and adaptation of problem-solving capabilities through the chosen learning mechanism.

1 Introduction

By analyzing the Database Administrators' (DBAs) daily work, one can observe that various types of problems (e.g. performance, security, bad physical dimensioning) are found repeatedly. Moreover, professionals frequently forget the best solution last applied to a problem, especially when working under lots of pressure. Remembering the correct solution can take much longer than anticipated, irritating users and compromising the quality of service. Nowadays there are some alternatives that help DBAs in their work, such as specialized Help Desks [1] and Expert Systems [2].

Help Desk solutions, however, are limited to the fact they are only a repository for problems and their respective solutions. They cannot predict problems, act efficiently and learn new solutions. Furthermore, in this approach the problems repository must be filled manually, either by the expert or by operators. Expert Systems such as Oracle Expert [3] and Progress Fathom [4] have some functionalities that help the DBA's work. For example, they enable the definition of monitoring events together with scripts that can be executed to solve the failure that is being monitored. Furthermore, they can also capture alert messages, thus enabling the DBA to be pro-active.

The major drawback of these solutions is their inflexibility, together with the lack of a learning mechanism. They take actions or suggest solutions based in information previously stored in a Knowledge Base. Those systems are unable to, for example, solve unknown problems, combine previous solutions or even adapt catalogued ones. They also cannot automatically add new information to their knowledge base.

Our prototype, DBSitter, consists of a Multi-agent system for automatic monitoring and fault correcting in a relational Database Management System (DBMS). It helps the DBA in the decision-making process, suggesting the most adequate solution(s) to each situation, taking advantage of its library of previously solved problems. In order to do so, it combines two well-known Artificial Intelligence techniques: Case Based Reasoning (CBR) [5] and Intelligent Agents [6]. Our novel approach uses intelligent agents to monitor the DBMS and actuate on it, correcting faults or suggesting solutions to the DBA. By using CBR, we are able to adapt known solutions and enrich the knowledge base. DBSitter was implemented using open-source technologies: the prototype was implemented in Java [7]; we have used RMI [7] for communication between agents; and JEOPS [8] was chosen as a knowledge representation and inference mechanism.

This paper is organized as follows: section 2 describes the current state of art in database monitoring systems; section 3 discusses our approach; section 4 presents our prototype, DBSitter; section 5 details the experiments we have carried out; and section 6 presents our conclusions and suggestions for further work.

2 Intelligent Tools for Monitoring Databases

We have carried out a survey of the main market tools for database monitoring. The tools were chosen due to their completeness as well as their similarity to DBSitter. Thus in this section we present a comparative analysis of the following tools: IBM Tivoli Monitoring Databases [9], CA Unicenter Database Administration for Distributed RDBMS [10], HP-Openview Database PAK 2000 [11], BMC PATROL® - DB-Maintain [12], Quest Central ™ - Foglight [13], Progress Fathom [3] and Oracle Expert (from the Oracle Enterprise Manager Suite) [4]. These tools are used to monitor, diagnose and help correcting faults in DBMS such as Microsoft SQL Server, DB2, Informix, Sybase, Progress and Oracle, as shown in Table 1.

In our comparative study, the chosen evaluation criteria were: failure detection, automatic failure correction, failure prevention capability, learning ability, and solution suggestion (through case similarities) to the DBA.

Most analyzed tools presented functionalities for detection and automatic failure correction. With this purpose, Ca Unicenter tool has an event correlation feature. In particular, Oracle Expert has a mechanism known as "fix it job", which consists in a series of corrective scripts. These scripts are previously defined and are automatically executed when certain failures occur. The system then informs the DBA via email.

Concerning the capability of failure prediction, Progress Fathom, BMC PATROL, Quest Central (mainly for performance monitoring), Ca Unicenter and HP-Openview implement it. In Progress Fathom, this is done by capturing alert messages of imminent errors before they actually occur. BMC PATROL presents a mechanism called "what if" that performs a trend analysis based on historical data. The other tools have statistic-based tools with this objective.

Learning functionalities and case solution suggesting are not implemented by any of the tools described in Table 1. Oracle Expert has a similar feature that allows it to suggest configuration changes to improve the DBMS as a whole.

In this light, we propose DBSitter, a new intelligent monitoring tool that unifies two Artificial Intelligence techniques: Case Based Reasoning and Intelligent Agents. DBSitter is presented in detail in section 3.

Table 1. Comparative Study of Intelligent Monitoring Systems

Tool	Failure detection	Failure correction	Failure prevention	Learning ability	Case similarity	DBMS
Oracle Expert	Yes	"fix it job"	No	No	No	Oracle
Progress Fathom	Yes	Yes	Yes	No	No	Progress
BMC PATROL® - DB-Maintain	Yes	Yes	Yes	No	No	DB2, Oracle
Quest Central for Databases	Yes	Yes	Yes	No	No	Oracle, DB2, MS SQL Server
IBM Tivoli Monitoring Databases	Yes	Yes	No	No	No	DB2, Oracle, Informix and MS SQL Server
CA Unicenter Database Administration for Distributed RDBMS	Yes	Yes	Yes	No	No	DB2, Oracle, Sybase, Informix and MS SQL Server
HP-Openview Database PAK 2000	Yes	Not informed	Yes	No	No	Oracle, Informix and Sybase

3 DBSitter: An Intelligent Tool for Database Administration

DBSitter is a software tool capable of suggesting to the DBA more than one option to solve certain problem, even showing its success degree and implementation difficulties, based on solutions previously applied to similar cases. DBSitter has the differential of knowledge learning capability. When a new solution is created or adapted from others, it is stored in the case repository (that is the way of representing problems) enriching DBSitter and incorporating this knowledge to the system. This last feature is obtained by the use of CBR technology.

DBSitter was implemented using Java based technologies conferring to it platform independence. Its architecture is based on distributed intelligent agents, which allows the monitoring of distributed databases in a network environment. Besides, this feature gives our system scalability and flexibility to monitor any kind of DBMS.

DBSitter is a Multi-agent System [6], where a set of intelligent agents is dispersed in the environment collecting information for the system's decision-making. Agents use their sensors for capturing changes in the environment (and thus finding problems).

Processes

In this section, we describe the processes in DBSitter. The Similarity Identifier (SI) tries to establish a ratio of confidence between the data acquired from Sensor Agents and the cases in the Case Repository. That enables us to analyze also the cases that are similar to what the SAs provided.

The History Recorder stores in the HR the current and complete state of the system, represented by the values of the sensors. The Timer (also part of the Logger Agent) controls the frequency in which the HR is refreshed. It is based in a predefined reference time and in a real time analysis of the Sensor Agents states variation (done by the Environment Changing Manager Agent), to define the recording frequency.

The Coordinators are responsible for managing the registry that monitors the entrance or exit of agents in the system. Both SAs and AAs are remote and replicable processes and, thus, it is necessary that a registry stores and strictly identifies each reference to an agent instance. Once a new agent is created in the environment it has to be registered to be able to communicate. The Application Manager allows the communication between external client applications and DBSitter.

3.3 DBSitter Functionalities

DBSitter presents the following functionalities:
- **Failure Prevention:** In order to prevent a failure the system has to analyze the behavior of the values provided by SAs involved in a certain case. This analysis is based on the log values stored in the HR. DBSitter uses the linear least squares[2] method [15] with a grade two polynomial approximation in order to estimate the values read by the sensors along time. Once this is done, it is possible to predict the behavior of the DBMS being monitored. Fig. 2 shows an example of the values provided by the table fragmentation SA along time. Once the system has them, it is possible to estimate polynomial parameters and thus predict possible faults.

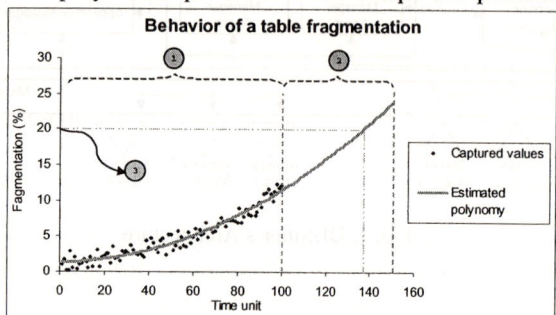

Fig. 2. Graph showing table fragmentation values along time. (1) Values approximation curve (2) Prediction (3) Threshold value indicating table fragmented

This functionality is realized by the Failure Predictor, via a macro analysis of the history of system states, algorithms of prediction, search in the Case Repository

---

[2] The least square method is widely used for one-dimensional estimative of parameters.

and the Similarity Identifier, which tries to find the most similar cases to the information collected by the Sensor Agents.

- **Failure Detection:** This is guaranteed by the interaction of the RA and the SAs, as the role of the RA is to monitor the various parameters captured by the SAs dispersed in the database environment. Logical expressions are built from those parameters, characterizing the problems to be detected. The Failure Detector then matches the current system state with a similar case (suggested by the Similarity Identifier process), as a way to assess the possibility of a system fault.
- **Failure Correction:** Corresponds to the action taken by the actuator agent when a solution for a problem is found in the Case Repository. After that, the failure is corrected, or a message is sent to notify the DBA.
- **Failure Cases Gathering**: Specialized users (DBAs) can feed the Case Repository, adding new cases manually when required or when they come across an unknown and not catalogued problem.
- **Failure Seeking**: Occurs when a DBA queries directly the Case Repository to search for information about a certain failure.
- **Suggestion of solutions to failures**: This happens when a certain problem has more than one solution, and it comes with a degree of success for each case. The DBA then chooses the most adequate solution.
- **Solution Adaptation/Learning:** Consists in the improvement of the Cases Repository when a new and unknown problem comes out. The solution can be an adaptation of previously known solutions catalogued in the repository. In order to enable learning from the examples collected in the HR, we have used Decision Trees [14], which are simple to implement and generate new rules. These can, in turn, be used to implement new cases.

In our prototype, only the functionalities of Prevention, Detection and Correction of failures were fully implemented. The functionality of solution adaptation is partially implemented.

4 The Prototype

Since DBSitter's conception, we were concerned with building a multi-platform system. Thus, we have used open source technologies in its development. Java was the chosen programming language. It provides object orientation, which is useful for modularity and essential for extensibility. Both characteristics were fundamental to us, as we adopted the proposal of creating a *framework* for Database solution developers.

For the communication middleware, we used Java's **Remote Method Invocation, RMI**. It is used either for the communication between the system and the actuator and sensor agents as for the communication between the application and the database administrator's interface.

For the case descriptions, we used the *framework* **Jeops** [8], with the aim of employing the logic programming paradigm integrated to system objects. Through Jeops it is possible to define rules that determine the conditions triggering events that indicate adverse situations in the database system. The system reasons about both run time information and history data. The descriptions enable the AAs to act either directly in the system or to provide information for the DBA to take over.

For the system's internal repositories, we have used: **MySql**, the internal database system, storing the sensor and actuator registry, and **XML Files**, to save or load configuration parameters when the system shut down or starts.

Target DBMS for the implementation of SAs and preliminary tests were Microsoft **SQL Server** and **Oracle**. A process call written in **Object Pascal** was used for the implementation of the SAs. These processes are used for monitoring environment states (for example, processor or memory states), as for direct database queries for analyzing database states. The learning functionality is still in implementation stages.

4.1 An Use Example of DBSitter

As a sample of the proposed solution we have built a Case Repository with some initial cases catalogued by DBA experts that used an Oracle DBMS for monitoring the problems during the rush hours at Serpro[3].

In this example, we will consider that the problem described in Table 2, which describes the situation when a table that has reached unacceptable fragmentation levels. This problem is perceived when a **Sensor Agent** detects that a specific table has reached a critical fragmentation level. This is done through the event of fragmentation monitoring, witch is basically a cyclic SQL query to the Oracle Data Dictionary looking for information of the table. The SA then sends a message to the **Environment Change Manager Agent**, which in turn interacts with the **Reasoning Agent**. After that, the RA searches the Case Repository for a case that best conforms to the problem.

When a similar case is found, the RA sends a message to the Coordinator, which notifies the corresponding AAt of the solution to be automatically done, sending later a message to the DBA, stating that an action was taken to correct the problem. After the action from the Actuator Agent, the table is defragmented, and the **Log Agent** is triggered to record the action in the HR. If the system cannot find a similar case, it tries to adapt the solutions described in the most similar cases. Alternatively, DBSitter can also ask the DBA about the actions to be carried out.

5 Evaluating DBSitter

We have carried out a series of tests to evaluate the efficiency of DBSitter. This section describes the main results, together with the scenario of the experiments.

The platform adopted for tests was a client-server environment using a Windows 2003 server with the SQL Server 2000 and Oracle Enterprise Edition 8.1.7.0.0 DBMS installed. The client side had Windows XP SP1 and Oracle and SQL Server software clients, both representing the DBMS we tested DBSitter with. They were connected via an Ethernet TCP/IP. Table 3 describes the case tests.

---

[3] Serpro stands for Brazilian Federal Data Processing Services.

Table 3. Cases Evaluated

Tested case	Simulated error	Action	Monitored DBMS
DBMS not available	The DBMS service was stopped.	Put the DBMS online	Oracle and SQL Server
Table's Fragmentation	A table partitioned in various small pieces was created. Then, various registers were inserted, until the table's fragmentation limit was reached (diagnosed by an SQL query).	Defragment the table	Oracle and SQL Server
Insufficient Memory	First, the SHARED_POOL_AREA was set to a small value. After that, a large procedure code that caused the memory hit ratio to be less then the acceptable 90% was invocated	Increase the SHARED_POOL_AREA parameter, which controls the memory area allocation.	Oracle
Tablespace overflow.	A tablespace with IM datafile was created. Then, a table with 100k extents was created. After that, an allocation of 10 extents was provoked on the same table, which caused the ORA-01653 error, indicating tablespace overflow.	Increase the datafile of the overflown tablespace.	Oracle
Preventing Tablespace overflow	Similar to the above, only that the actuator intervened before the amount of extents generated the error	Increase the datafile of the overflown tablespace.	Oracle

The last case was included in the tests in order to evaluate the prevention functionality. The results obtained were promising, indicating that the solution works as predicted. An experienced DBA observed the results, and concluded that the actuator's intervention was appropriate in all case tests above.

Also, the fact that the tests were done with two different platforms reinforces the argument that DBSitter is indeed a flexible tool,, needing only some platform-specific customisations in order to execute in different environments (DBMSs).

It should be noted that, due to the expertise of the authors, we were only able to carry out tests with two DBMSs, Oracle and SQL Server.

6 Conclusions and Further Work

The main goal of this work is to provide the DBA with a tool that helps him/her in the difficult decision-making process that has to happen rapidly when there are database problems. The idea was not only to automate known solutions, but also to record novel approaches to problems. Thus, this paper has presented DBSitter, a tool that combines two well-known AI techniques in a novel approach.

We emphasize that among the main differentials of DBSitter (relative to the Intelligent Monitoring Tools presented in section 2) is the fact it can be used in the monitoring of any DBMS. Moreover, the combination of the two AI techniques, Case Based Reasoning and Intelligent Agents, makes the implementation of characteristics of detection, problem prevention, learning and adaptation of solutions possible. Furthermore, our prototype was implemented with open-source technologies, which makes it that much easier to be spread and refined by different developers. Additionally, to the best of our knowledge there are no other monitoring systems that have achieved the same functionalities with the novel combination of techniques.

Another important contribution of this approach is the Case Repository (open to the DBA) that assists in the propagation of knowledge among DBAs, thus making their daily tasks simpler and enhancing of the level of service. The DBA's cooperation to add info is crucial to the enrichment of the Case repository.

The automatic detection of problems done by sensors and the prediction capability of the system help DBA to act proactively by being able to detect and act on the errors sooner. From our point of view, this is another important advantage of our approach, as discussed earlier in the paper.

The platform was tested with two different DBMS (SQL Server and Oracle 8i). This evaluation has yielded promising results, which not only indicates that the approach is an interesting one, but also reinforces the portability of the prototype.

The next steps of our research and development include enhancing the implementation of the learning functionality and adaptation of solutions. We have already started this process, laying the necessary architectural foundations.

References

1. M. Graves, M. Domsch, D. Kennedy: HelpDesk A Multi Agent System – CS 367 Spring 1998, Vanderbilt University.
2. 2.Expert Systems and Applied Artificial Intelligence, Turban, E. McMillan, 1992
3. Progress Software Corporation 1993-2004. Last Access: 16 feb. 2004: http://www.progress.com/products/documentation/startffm/index.ssp .
4. Oracle Corporation: Oracle Enterprise Manager Oracle Expert User's Guide - Release 1.4.0 - A53653_01
5. Aamodt A., Plaza E. (1994): Case-Based Reasoning: Foundational Issues, Methodological Variations, and System Approaches. AI Communications. IOS Press, Vol. 7: 1, pp. 39-59.
6. Russel, S. J.; Norvig, P. : Artificial Intelligence: A Modern Approach (2nd Edition). Prentice Hall; 2nd edition. December, 2002.
7. The Source for Java Technology http://java.sun.com . Last Access: 21 set. 2003.
8. Figueira Filho, C.; Ramalho G. JEOPS – Java Embedded Object Production System. Monard, M. C; Sichman, J. S (eds). Advances in Artificial Intelligence, International Joint conference, 7th Ibero-American Conference on AI, 15th Brazilian Symposium on AI, IBERAMIA-SBIA 2000, Proceedings. Lecture Notes in Computer Science 1952. Springer 2000, pp. 53-62.
9. IBM 2004. http://www.ibm.com/br/products/software/tivoli/products/monitor-db/ . Last Access: 16 feb. 2004
10. Computer Associates International 2004.
11. http://www3.ca.com/Solutions/Product.asp?ID=1357 . Last Access: 16 feb. 2004
12. Hewlett-Packard Company 1994-2003. Last Access: 16 feb. 2004: http://www.openview.hp.com/products/dbpak2k/prod_dbpak2k_0003.html .
13. BMC Software 2004. BMC Patrol DB_Maintain http://www.bmc.com . Last Access: 19 feb. 2004
14. Quest Software 1985-2004. Quest Central http://www.quest.com/foglight . Last Access: 19 feb. 2004
15. Machine Learning, T. Mitchell, 1997, McGraw-Hill.
16. Numerical Calculus: Theoretical and Computational Aspects . Márcia A. Gomes Ruggiero e Vera Lúcia da Rocha Lopes. Makron Books, 1997. (in Portuguese)

Interacting with Electronic Institutions

John Debenham

Faculty of Information Technology, University of Technology, Sydney
debenham@it.uts.edu.au

Abstract. A three-year research project is investigating the evolution of social (business) networks in an eMarket environment. To address this issue a complete, immersive, distributed virtual trading environment has been constructed. That environment is described here. Virtual worlds technology provides an immersive environment in which traders are represented as avatars that interact with each other, and have access to market data and general information that is delivered by data and text mining machinery. To enrich this essentially social market place, synthetic bots have also been constructed. They too are represented by avatars, and provide "informed idle chatter" so enriching the social fabric. They acquire their information with text and data mining machinery that continually scans market data and general financial news feeds. The middle-ware in this environment is based on powerful multiagent technology that manages all processes including the information delivery and data mining. The investigation of network evolution leads to the development of "network mining" techniques.

1 Introduction

Markets play a central role in economies, both real and virtual. One interesting feature of the development of electronic markets has been the depersonalisation of market environments. The majority of on-line trading today is conducted by "filling in pro formas" on computer screens, and by "clicking buttons". This has created a trading atmosphere that is far removed from the vital atmosphere of traditional trading floors. What used to be the trading floor of the Sydney Stock Exchange is now a restaurant, although the trading prices are still displayed on the original board. All of this sits uncomfortably with work in microeconomics that has demonstrated both theoretically and in practice, that a vital trading environment provides a positive influence on liquidity and so too on clearing prices. See, for example, the work of Paul Milgrom, from his seminal "linkage principle" to his recent work [1].

This issue is being addressed by this project in which, virtual worlds technology, based on Adobe Atmosphere is being used to construct a virtual trading environment that may be "hooked onto" real exchanges. That environment is immersive and complete. It is "immersive" in that: an avatar that may move freely through those virtual trading areas in which it is certified represents each real player. It is complete in that each real player has ready access to all the information that she requires, including general information extracted from newsfeeds. The environment also contains synthetic characters that can answer questions like "how is gold doing today?" with both facts and news items. The environment may be seen at: http://research.it.uts.edu.au/emarkets/ — first click on "virtual worlds" under "themes and technologies" and then click on "here". To run the demonstration you will need to install the Adobe Atmosphere plugin. Figure 1 shows a screenshot of a market scenario in a virtual world. The avatar with its "back to the camera" is the avatar representing the agent on the workstation from which the "photo" was taken.

Fig. 1. A screen shot of one of the eMarkets, including the "chatterbot" avatars

Other related projects include the design of trading agents that operate in these information-rich environments [2], and an electronic institution framework that "sits beneath" the virtual environment. The design of this framework is influenced by the Islander framework developed in Barcelona [3]. Unstructured data mining techniques are being developed to tap real-time information flows so as to deliver timely information, at the required granularity [4]. Network mining techniques are presently a major focus.

2 The Virtual Trading Environment as a Multi-agent Virtual 3D World

A marketplace is a real or virtual space populated by agents that represent the variety of human and software traders, intermediaries, and information and infrastructure providers. Market activities include: trade orders, negotiations and market information seeking. These activities are *intrinsically social* and *situated*. There is a number of ways to implement an electronic market [5]. The virtual trading environment is *a multi-agent virtual world* [6]. In this environment every activity is managed as a constrained business process by a multiagent process management system. Players can trade securely via the process management system, in addition "chat channels" support informal communication. The technology of 3D virtual worlds, initially developed for computer games and interactive multimedia applications, are increasingly appearing on Internet systems. "Virtual worlds" are constituted by *representations*, which may or may not be related to instances in the non-virtual world. Representation refers to all aspects of the appearance of objects, avatars, bots and other elements of the virtual world [7].

The conceptual framework is shown in Fig. 2. The virtual trading environment is a multi-agent virtual world (Fig. 1), which integrates a number of technologies: (i) an electronic market kernel (Java-based), which supports the actual market mechanisms; (ii) a virtual world, involving all aspects of the appearance and interactions between market players, bots and other objects in the e-market place (based on Adobe Atmosphere); (iii) a variety of information discovery bots (Java-based), and; (iv) a multi-agent system, which manages all market transactions and information seeking as industry processes (based on Australian JACK technology). This environment was originally designed to support investigation into the evolution of electronic markets through entrepreneurial action, supported by the timely delivery of market information. That former project addressed the problem of identifying timely information for e-markets with their rapid, pervasive and massive flows of data, distilling it from individual market and other signals in the unreliable, information-overloaded Internet.

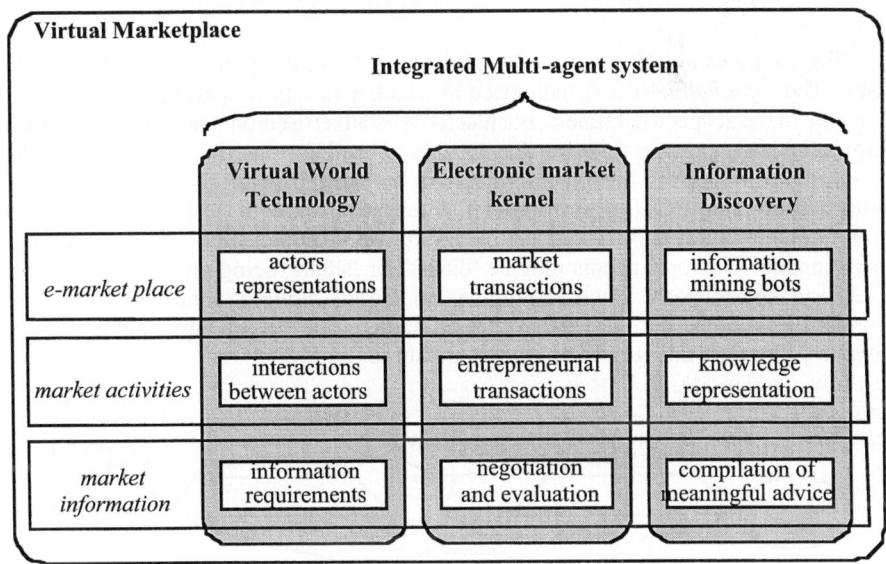

Fig. 2. Conceptual framework of the virtual marketplace

In the virtual trading environment, all transactions are managed as heavily constrained business processes using a multiagent system. Constraints include process-related (eg: time, value, cost) and player-related (eg: preferences derived from inter-player relationships). The latter are based on a model of 'friendship' development between pairs of actors [8]. Existing process-related constraints will be extended to include measures, (eg. costs) associated with developing and sustaining complex business networks. Research on the evolution of player strategies, with prior work focusing on highly stylised environments (eg. [9]). The way strategies develop in a virtual marketplace as a result of timely information provision is the subject of current work which will provide the basis for relating strategies to social networks.

Each player in the virtual trading environment, whether a human or a software agent, is represented by an avatar. Generated complex data about interactions between players in different market scenarios, the corresponding transactions and information seeking strategies, reflect all aspects of the market players' behaviour and the interactions between different players involved in electronic market scenarios.

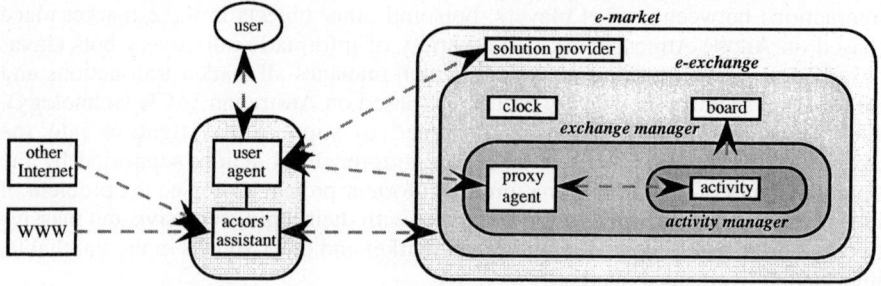

Fig. 3. High-level view of the environment and a user

Fig. 3 shows a high-level of the environment and its interaction with a single user. The *e-exchange* is a virtual space in which a variety of market-type *activities* can take place at specified times. Each activity is advertised on a notice *board* which shows the start and stop time for that activity as well as what the activity is and the *regulations* that apply to players who wish to participate in it. A human player works though a PC (or similar) by interacting with a *user agent* which communicates with a *proxy agent* or a solution provider situated in the trading environment. The user agents may be 'dumb', or 'smart' being programmed by the user to make decisions. Each activity has an *activity manager* that ensures that the regulations of that activity are complied with. The set of eight actor classes supported by the trading environment is illustrated in Fig 4.

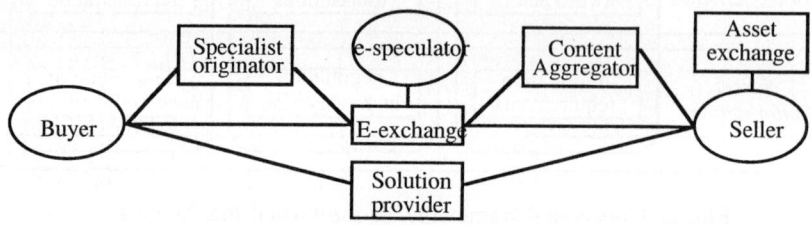

Fig. 4. The eight actor classes

The activities in the environment support opportunities to trade. In the exchanges trading is managed by *market mechanisms*. In line with the work in [3] the mechanisms are represented implicitly through the specification of dialogical frameworks that are issued to players by the trading environment. One important feature of a mechanism is the 'optimal' strategy that a player should use, and whether that strategy is "truth revealing". Mechanisms can be for single-unit (ie a single good) or multi-unit (ie a number of identical goods). Any single-unit mechanism may be trivially extended to a multi-unit mechanism by using it to establish a price for a good, permitting the 'winner' to take as many goods as required at that price (and maybe then permitting other buyers to take further goods at that price), then putting the remaining goods up for sale to determine another price, and so on, until the process terminates. The majority of mechanisms address single-issue negotiation, although much of the trading executed in eProcurement is multi-issue.

The following actor classes are supported. *E-speculators* take short term positions in the e-exchange. This introduces the possibility of negative commission charges for others using an e-exchange. Sell-side *asset exchanges* exchange or share assets between sellers. *Content aggregators*, who act as forward aggregators, coordinate and package goods and services from various sellers. *Specialist originators*, who act as reverse aggregators, coordinate and package orders for goods and services from various buyers. The specialist originators, content aggregators and e-speculators represent their presence in the trading environment as avatars that create activities.

There are valuable studies on the cognitive processes and factors driving alertness to opportunities. There is also a wealth of established work in economic theory, that provides a basis for work in e-markets [10], including: the theory of auctions, theory of bargaining, and theory of contracts. [11] presents mechanisms for negotiation between computational agents. That work describes tactics for the manipulation of the utility of deals, trade-off mechanisms that manipulate the value, rather than the overall utility, of an offer, and manipulation mechanisms that add and remove issues from the negotiation set. Much has to be done before this established body of work may form a practical basis for an investigation into electronic market evolution. Little is known on how entrepreneurs will operate in electronic market places, although the capacity of the vast amount of information that will reside in those market places, and on the Internet generally, to assist the market evolution process is self-evident.

3 Smart Information System

In 'real' problems, a decision to use an e-exchange or a solution provider will be made on the basis of general knowledge that is external to the e-market place. The negotiation strategy used will also depend on general knowledge. Such general knowledge will typically be broadly based and beyond the capacity of modern AI systems whilst remaining within reasonable cost bounds. Once this decision has been made, all non-trivial trading relies on the provision of current information. The *smart information system*, or "actors assistant", aims to deliver "the right information, at the right granularity, to the right person, at the right time".

E-markets reside on the Internet alongside the vast resources of the World Wide Web. The general knowledge available is restricted to that which can be gleaned from the e-markets themselves and that which can be extracted from the Internet in general—including the World Wide Web. The actors' assistant is a workbench that provides a suite of tools to *assist* a trader in the e-market. The actors' assistant does *not* attempt to replace buyers and sellers. For example, there is no attempt to automate 'speculation' in any sense. Web-mining tools assist the players in the market to make informed decisions. One of the issues in operating in an e-market place is coping with the rapidly-changing signals in it. These signals include: product and assortment attributes (if the site offers multiple products), promotions shown, visit attributes (sequences within the site, counts, click-streams) and business agent attributes. Combinations of these signals may be vital information to an actor. A new generation of data analysis and supporting techniques—collectively labelled as *data mining* methods—are now applied to stock market analysis, predictions and other financial and market analysis applications. The application of data mining methods in e-business to date has predominantly been within the B2C framework, where data is mined at an on-line business site, resulting in the derivation of various behavioural metrics of site visitors and customers.

The basic steps in providing assistance to actors are:

• identifying potentially relevant signals;
• evaluating the reliability of those signals;
• estimating the significance of those signals to the matter at hand;
• combining a (possibly large) number of signals into coherent advice, and
• providing digestible explanations for the advice given.

The estimation of the significance of a signal to a matter at hand is complicated by the fact that one person may place more faith in the relevance of a particular signal than others. So this estimation can only be performed on a personal basis. This work does *not*, for example, attempt to use a signal to predict whether the US dollar will rise against the UK pound. What it *does* attempt to do is to predict the value that an actor will place on a signal. So the feedback here is provided by the user in the form of a rating of the material used. A five point scale runs from 'totally useless' to 'very useful'. Having identified the signals that a user has faith in, "classical" data mining methods are then applied to combine these signals into succinct advice again using a five point scale. This feedback is used to 'tweak' the weights in Bayesian networks and as feedback to neural networks [12]. Bayesian networks are preferred when some confidence can be placed in a set of initial values for the weights. The system is able to raise an alarm automatically and quickly when a pre-specified compound event occurs such as: four members of the board of our principal supplier "Good Co" have resigned, the share price has dropped unexpectedly and there are rumours that our previous supplier "Bad Co" is taking over "Good Co".

4 Evolution of Business Networks

As noted above the virtual trading environment is being employed to investigate the evolution of business networks, and so that project is briefly described.

Markets are driven by knowledge and people. Knowledge leads to the recognition of opportunities to trade for mutual advantage. What gets organised in markets is not just economic exchange but human social relations [15]. Innovation and market evolution come from the discovery of new opportunities (new knowledge), which are seized and implemented by people. New links with potential among existing ideas are discovered in part by individual minds, but science and innovation are being increasingly recognised as social processes in which links are made between existing ideas across people and organisations, rather than with them. Thus science proceeds through building on the ideas of others.

Knowledge is in part embedded in networks of relations among people within and between organisations and the interaction of people is intimately involved with the interaction of ideas and knowledge development. Even so called creative techniques build on this social process of interaction among ideas and the need to suspend initial judgment as to the worth of some of these ideas and potential links for fear of dampening the creative process. What all this means is that innovation and opportunity discovery comes from networks of interacting people in firms or in the pub. Furthermore, the exploitation of these ideas is through networks of interacting people and firms employing money, resources and technologies [16].

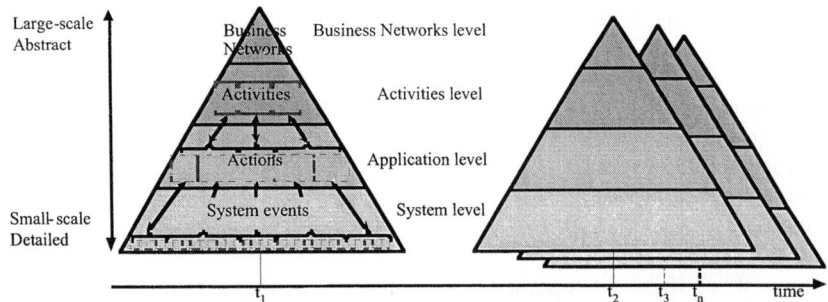

Fig. 5. Business networks dynamics in terms of the different levels of information abstraction and granularity in the virtual marketplace

This project brings forward the role of communication between individuals in electronic marketplaces, focusing on the social or people networks as central to the *recognition* of opportunities and productive links among existing ideas and to their *exploitation* and *implementation*. The important question is how business relationships/networks start and evolve as a result of a "sequence of *virtual interactions*", and of the changing beliefs the interactants form about them. Communication processes may cause changes in the contextual and structural characteristics of the relationship or the network. Hence, the relationships and networks, therefore, can be derived from the knowledge about the communication processes occurring within them. Fig. 5 illustrates the dynamics of business networks.

5 Synthetic Characters

If trading environments are to provide the rich social experience that is found in a real, live exchange then they should also contain other classes of actors in addition to essential classes described above. For example, anonymous agents that can provide intelligent casual conversation - such as one might have with a stranger in an elevator. To have a positive role in an eMarket environment, such anonymous agents should be informed of recent news, particularly the news related to the market where the agent is situated (eg. financial news, news from major stock exchanges, news about related companies). If so then they provide a dual social function. First, they are agents to whom one may "say anything", and, second, they are a source of information that is additional, and perhaps orthogonal, to that provided directly to each trading agent as it has specified.

Anonymous synthetic characters have been embedded in the virtual trading environment. Avatars represent these agents visually. They provide casual, but context-related conversation with anybody who chooses to engage with them. This feature markedly distinguishes this work from typical role-based chat agents in virtual worlds. The later usually are used as "helpers" in navigation, or for making simple announcements. They are well informed about recent events, and so "a quick chat" can prove valuable. A demonstration that contains one of these synthetic characters is available at: http://research.it.uts.edu.au/emarkets/. We describe the design of these agent-based characters, and the data mining techniques used to "inform" them.

The following issues have to be addressed in the design of any synthetic character:

- its appearance
- its mannerisms
- its sphere of knowledge
- its interaction modes
- its interaction sequences

and how all of these fit together. Appearance and mannerisms have yet to be addressed. At present the avatars that represent the synthetic characters simply "shuffle around".

An agent's sphere of knowledge is crucial to the value that may be derived by interacting with it. We have developed extensive machinery, based on unstructured data mining techniques, that provides our agent with a dynamic information base of current and breaking news across a wide range of financial issues. For example, background news is extracted from on-line editions of the Australian Financial Review. The agent uses this news to report facts and not to give advice. If it did so then it could be liable to legal action by the Australian Securities and Investment Commission ASIC!

Our agent's interaction modes are presently restricted to passive, one-to-one interaction. They are passive in that these agents do not initiate interaction. We have yet to deal effectively with the problem that occurs when a third party attempts to "barge in" on an interaction.

The interaction sequences are triggered by another agent's utterance. The machinery that manages this is designed to work convincingly for interactions of up to around five exchanges only. Our agents are designed to be "strangers" and no more - their role is simply to "toss in potentially valuable gossip".

The aspects of design discussed above cannot be treated in isolation. If the avatars are to be "believable" then their design must have a unifying conceptual basis. This is provided here by the agent's character. The first decision that is made when an agent is created is to select its character using a semi-random process that ensures that multiple instances of the agent in close virtual proximity have identifiably different characters.

The dimensions of character that we have selected are intended specifically for a finance-based environment. They are:

- Politesse
- Dynamism
- Optimism
- Self-confidence

The selection of the character of an agent determines: its appearance (ie: which avatar is chosen for it) and the style of its dialogue. Future plans will address the avatars mannerisms. The selection of agent's character provides an underlying unifying framework for how the agent appears and behaves, and ensures that multiple instances of the agent appear to be different.

The selection on an agent's character does not alone determine its behaviour. Each agent's behaviour is further determined by its moods that vary slowly but constantly. This is intended to ensure that repeated interactions with the same agent have some degree of novelty. The dimensions of moods are:

- Happiness
- Sympathy
- Angry

Text mining as opposed to classical data mining techniques is used here to extract knowledge from unstructured text streams.

The agents do not know in advance what will be "said" to them. So they need to be able to access a wide range of information concerning the world's and the market's situation, much of which may not be used. This large amount of information is extracted from different sources on the web, including news pages, financial data and all the exchanges that are part of the virtual environment. Within a particular interaction, the agent's response is driven only by keywords used by his chattermate - just as a human may have done. Despite this simple response mechanism, the agent's dialogue should not appear to be generated by a program. This has partly been achieved by using a semantic network of keywords extracted from the input streams. Words are given a relational weight calculated against others. By analysing which words are related to those used by the chattermate, the agent expresses himself and, to some extent, is able to follow the thread of the discussion. All of this takes place in real time.

In addition to the semantic network, the agent has a personal character and background history, which influences his appearance and the way in which he employs the keywords in his responses. The agent's knowledge is divided into two classes: general and specific. Specific information is contained in a particular data structure. Both classes of information are extracted on demand if they have not previously been pre-fetched.

To extract the general knowledge, a suite of extractors are activated that fetch predefined text streams from the web. After an extractor has retrieved its raw data (for example, all headlines from sportingnews.com in order to be able to speak about current results in a particular sport), the raw data is manipulated by an intermediate module that converts it into structured data ready for classical data mining techniques.

6 Conclusion

The virtual trading environment has emerged from the necessities defined by two research projects. First, an investigation of the evolutionary mechanisms in electronic markets, and second a current investigation of the evolution of business networks in electronic trading environments. Both of those projects rely on the availability of a complete, immersive trading environment so that experiments could be performed. The environment is interesting in its own right as it presents a richer view of the electronic trading experience than is generally available. It is information-rich in that players have access to current market data, and general data extracted from news feeds and reports. It is immersive in that the player can move through the virtual spaces and will find all that is required to trade represented there. It is social, even to the extent of having "friendly strangers" to chat to that are also well-informed.

References

[1] Milgrom, P. 2004. *Putting Auction Theory to Work.* Cambridge University Press.
[2] Debenham, J.K., 2003. *An eNegotiation Framework.* Proceedings International Conference AI'03. Cambridge, UK.
[3] Esteva, Marc; de la Cruz, David; Sierra, Carles, editor. *Proceedings of the First International Joint Conference on Autonomous Agents and Multiagent Systems,* Bologna, Italy.
[4] Simoff, S. J. (2002). *Informed traders in electronic markets - mining 'living' data to provide context information to a negotiation process.* In Proceedings of the 3rd International We-B Conference 2002, 28-29 November, Perth, Australia.
[5] Barbosa, G.P. and Silva, F.Q.B.: An electronic marketplace architecture based on technology of intelligent agents. *In: Liu, J. and Ye, Y. (eds): E-Commerce Agents.* Springer-Verlag, Heidelberg (2001)
[6] Debenham, J. and Simoff, S.: Investigating the evolution of electronic markets. *Proceedings 6th International Conference on Cooperative Information Systems, CoopIS 2001.* Trento, Italy (2001) 344-355
[7] Capin, T.K., Pandzic, I.S., Magnenat-Thalman, N. and Thalman, D.: *Avatars in Networked Virtual Environments. John Wiley and Sons, Chichester (1999)*
[8] Debenham, J.K.: Managing e-market negotiation in context with a multiagent system. *Proceedings 21-st International Conference on Knowledge Based Systems and Applied Artificial Intelligence, ES2002: Applications and Innovations in Expert Systems X.* Cambridge, UK (2002) 261-274
[9] Tesfatsion, L.: How economists can get alife. In: Arthur, W.B., Durlauf, S. and Lane, D.A. (eds): *The Economy as an Evolving Complex System II.* Addison-Wesley Publishing, Redwood City, CA (1997), 534-564
[10] Jeffrey S. Rosenschein and Gilad Zlotkin. *Rules of Encounter.* MIT Press, 1998.
[11] Peyman Faratin, Carles Sierra and Nick Jennings. Using Similarity Criteria to Make Issue Trade-Offs in Automated Negotiation. *Journal of Artificial Intelligence.* 142 (2) 205-237, 2003.
[12] Kersting, K. and De Raedt, L.: Adaptive Bayesian logic programs. In: Rouveirol, C. and Sebag, M. (eds): *Proceedings of the 11th International Conference on Inductive Logic Programming.* Springer-Verlag, Heidelberg (2001), 104-117.
[13] Müller, JP. *The Design of Intelligent Agents: A Layered Approach* (Lecture Notes in Computer Science, 1177). Springer Verlag (1997).
[14] Rao, A.S. and Georgeff, M.P. " BDI Agents: From Theory to Practice", in *proceedings First International Conference on Multi-Agent Systems (ICMAS-95),* San Francisco, USA, pp 312–319.
[15] Krikorian, D.H., Lee, J.-S., Chock, T.M. and Harms, C.: Isn' t That Spatial?: Distance and Communication in a 2-D Virtual Environment. *Journal of Computer Mediated Communication.* 5 (4) (2000).
[16] Simoff, S.J. and Maher, M.L.: Analysing participation in collaborative design environments. *Design studies.* 21 (2000) 119-144.

Growing Node Policies of a Main Memory Index Structure for Moving Objects Databases*

Kyounghwan An and Bonghee Hong

Department of Computer Engineering, Busan National University
30 Jangjeon-dong, Geumjeong-gu, Busan, 609-735, Republic of Korea
{khan,bhhong}@pusan.ac.kr

Abstract. Recent studies on main memory index structures focus mainly on cache-conscious structures to minimize L2 cache misses; for example, in one dimensional data, CSB+-tree eliminated pointers to pack more entries in a node, and in multi-dimensional data, CR-tree compressed MBRs in order to increase utilization of the L2 cache line. Previous studies used a fixed node size that is a multiple of the cache line size. If a node overflows, it splits, regardless of the search performance. Since the time of split is determined by only the node size, the split may increase a node's probability of being accessed. However, if the node size is not fixed, the previous case can be avoided. In this paper, we suggest a new cost model to determine whether to grow or split a node. In the cost model, we consider all relevant factors, such as cache misses, instruction counts, TLB misses, and the probability that nodes will be accessed. Use of our growing node policy has the following advantages: (i) it can have the effect of a delayed split that does not depend on the insertion order, and (ii) it can reduce the number of generated nodes and the height of the tree.

1 Introduction

Ubiquitous computing, enabled by the emergence of mobile computing devices (e.g. PDA, cellular phone and GPS) and technologies (e.g. RFID, wireless communications), is becoming a new paradigm of computing technology. In such an environment, there are enormous numbers of "moving objects" to be managed and queried. Since the moving objects should report their locations frequently, a database system should be able to handle a huge number of updates and queries quickly. In these environments, traditional disk-resident DBMSs (henceforth DRDBMSs) cannot be used because the number of updates required by a large number of moving objects and the frequencies of updating moving locations exceed the disk's capacity. However, main memory resident DBMSs (henceforth MMDBMSs) may provide a solution, in view of the increasing capacity of the memory chips.

Recent studies on index structures in MMDBMSs have focused mainly on cache conscious structures to minimize L2 cache misses. One of the earliest main memory indices is the T-tree [5], which is a binary tree that has many elements in a node. It has both a binary search and B+-tree characteristics. Other work that uses a one-

---

* This work was supported by Korea Research Foundation Grant (KRF-2003-002-D00278).

dimensional index is the CSB+-tree [7], which eliminates pointers in a node to increase utilization of the cache line. For multidimensional databases, the CR-tree [4] compresses keys (MBRs) to reduce L2 cache misses during search operations, because the size of the keys is much larger than that of the pointers in a node.

The primary design decision made with respect to those cache-conscious indices is to define and fix the node size as a multiple of the L2 data cache line. This is similar to defining the node size to be equal to, or a multiple of, the disk page size in traditional disk-based index structures. However, in MMDBMSs, a fixed node size does not always guarantee good search performance [2]. There are factors that affect the search performance other than cache misses. The size should be determined by considering all factors, such as cache misses, instruction counts, TLB misses, etc.

Using a fixed node size has the following problems. First, the time of the split depends on the maximum number of entries, regardless of the search performance. If the split results in a higher probability of a node to be accessed than not splitting the node, search performance may deteriorate. Second, the search performance of the R-tree depends greatly on the insertion order. The ordinary insertion algorithm of the R-tree may generate a poor structure, depending on the insertion order. Since moving objects report their location continuously, it may be more efficient to use a delayed split technique.

To solve the above-mentioned problems, we suggest a new cost model for main memory index structures and growing node policy. In contrast to the traditional cost model, which deals only with the number of disk accesses, our cost model considers several factors that affect search performance. It considers the probability of accessing a node, cache misses, the number of comparisons, and TLB misses. The cost of a node is calculated by the product of the probability of accessing a node by the cost of a node to be processed. The total cost of a main memory index can be obtained by the sum of all the nodes. The growing node policy is to use the cost model to determine whether a node will split or grow when it overflows. If the computed cost after splitting is greater than that of growing, the node grows.

Use of the proposed algorithm offers several advantages. If the capacity of the node increases dynamically, it can improve update performance by reducing the number of nodes to be generated. It also improves search performance by minimizing both the probability of accessing a node and the cost of a node to be processed. It also has an effect of delayed split, so the insertion order affects it less than it does the ordinary R-tree algorithm.

The remainder of this paper is organized as follows. In section 2, we define the problem regarding the main memory index for moving objects databases. Section 3 presents a new cost model for the growing node policy. Section 4 describes the algorithms of the proposed technique. Section 5 shows the experimental results of query and update performance. A summary of the paper is presented in section 6.

2 Problem Definition

Traditional disk-based indices have a fixed node size that is typically equal to the size of a disk page. R-tree variants considered in this paper also have a fixed node size. In main memory environments, however, this restriction can result in deterioration of the search performance of the index. For example, Fig. 1 shows a case in which the restriction is detrimental to performance. It assumes that the maximum number of entries (M) is four and the minimum number of entries (m) is two. When the node overflows after the fifth line segment is inserted, the node splits as shown in Fig. 1. We can see that the MBRs of two split nodes are highly overlapped. Since this overlapped region causes the search operation to follow multiple paths, it affects the search performance.

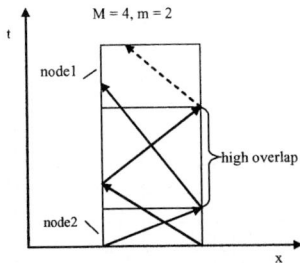

Fig. 1. Highly overlapped region after split

The solution to the above-mentioned problem is to avoid the split when the search performance degenerates, by increasing the capacity of the node dynamically. We call this technique a growing node policy. The growing node policy has the following advantages. First, it can solve the problem of highly overlapped regions. If the split results in high overlap, the node can become a growing node. Second, it has the effect of delayed split. If a node is grown, there is a greater probability that the related line segments are grouped together. Third, it can reduce the number of generated nodes and the height of the tree.

Splitting and growing are alternative methods, and each is superior in different cases. If splitting results in a good clustering of entries, the node should be split. If, on the other hand, splitting causes highly overlapped region, it is better to grow the node. To measure the efficiency of the methods when a node overflows, we propose a new cost model to determine whether to grow or to split.

3 Cost Model

In this section, we introduce a new cost model for a main memory index for moving objects databases. The cost model is used as a decision function in the growing node policy. By using the growing node policy, a node can grow or split when a node overflows.

3.1 Cost Model for Range Queries

We begin by explaining symbols used throughout the cost model. Let d be the dimension of the data space and $WS = [0, 1)^d$ be the n-dimensional unit work space. A data object is either a point p or an interval i. A point p is given by its coordinates, p =

($p.x_1$, $p.x_2$, ..., $p.x_d$), $p \subseteq WS$ and an interval is given by its coordinates, $i = [i.l_1, i.u_1] \times ... \times [i.l_d, i.u_d]$, $I \subseteq WS$. Let RS(G) be the R-tree structure for storing the set G of data objects. RS(G) is composed of nodes $n = \{n_1, n_2, ..., n_N\}$. For each node n_i in RS(G), a node region R_i is a d-dimensional interval enclosing all objects in n_i. A point query $pq \subseteq WS$ is a d-dimensional point and a window query $wq \subseteq WS$ is a d-dimensional interval. The symbols are summarized in Table 1.

Table 1. Symbols used in this paper

Symbol	Definition	Symbol	Definition
d	the # of dimensions	Ne_{ij}	the # of entries in a node n_{ij}
m	the minimum node capacity	R_{ij}	the node region of n_{ij}
M	the maximum node capacity	E	the # of entries fitting in a cache line
h	the height of the tree	T_{buff}	the latency of buffer miss
N	the # of tree nodes	T_{tlb}	the latency of TLB miss
N_i	the # of nodes at the ith level	T_{cache}	the latency of cache miss
n_{ij}	the jth node at the ith level	T_{comp}	the time for comparing cached keys
$n_{ij,k}$	the extent of n_{ij} in dimension k	T_{trav}	the time to visit a node

Previous studies on cost models measured only the expected number of node accesses, since disk access is a dominant factor regarding performance [3, 6]. If point queries are uniformly distributed, the expected number of accesses can be expressed by Eq. 1. In Eq 1, the first term means the probability of retrieving a root node and the other term is the probability of retrieving all nodes except the root. The probability of accessing a node can be obtained by the product of the extents for each dimension in the unit work space. The second term is the sum of the probabilities at each level of the tree.

$$EA(RS(G), pq) = \sum_{i=1}^{h}\sum_{j=1}^{Ni} Prob(a\ point\ query\ retrieves\ a\ node\ n_{ij}) = 1 + \sum_{i=2}^{h}\sum_{j=1}^{Ni}\prod_{k=1}^{d} n_{ij,k} \quad (1)$$

For window queries, the expected number of nodes that will be accessed by window queries wq is expressed by Eq 2. It is similar to Eq. 1, but the extents are inflated by the extents of the query window wq.

$$EA(RS(G), wq) = \sum_{i=1}^{h}\sum_{j=1}^{Ni} Prob(a\ window\ query\ retrieves\ a\ node\ n_{ij}) = 1 + \sum_{i=2}^{m}\sum_{j=1}^{Ni}\prod_{k=1}^{d}(n_{ij,k} + wq_k) \quad (2)$$

From Eqs. 1 and 2, it is possible to calculate the expected number of node accesses. To get the expected time for range queries, we can just multiply Eq. 2 by T_{buff}. T_{buff} is the time to transfer a disk page to memory.

$$ET(RS(G), wq) = T_{buff} \times EA(RS(G), wq) = T_{buff} + \sum_{i=2}^{m}\sum_{j=1}^{Ni}\prod_{k=1}^{d}(n_{ij,k} + wq_k) \times T_{buff} \quad (3)$$

In traditional disk-based indices, the dominant performance factor is disk I/O operations. However, in main memory indices, many factors can affect the performance of the indices. The factors considered in this paper are the time for caching the TLB(Translation Look-aside Buffer) entries, the time for caching data in the L2 cache, the time for key comparison time, and the time to visit a node (usually this is incurred by function call overhead). Since we assume that the node size is not larger than the size of a memory page, each access to a node incurs only one TLB miss. Cache misses can occur several times, depending on the node size. If the node size is larger than the size of the cache line, the number of cache misses can be computed by dividing the node size by the size of the cache line. After nodes are cached, it takes time to compare keys with the search value. Finally, to visit a node, we need to call a function. This should be also considered as a cost. For simplicity, we do not consider the effect of cache hit ratio and omit the effect of the instruction cache. By assuming that neither nodes nor TLB entries are cached, we can obtain the following equation.

An expected time of range queries in a main memory index is

$$ET(RS(G), wq) = (Time\ for\ processing\ a\ node) \times EA(RS(G), wq)$$

$$= (T_{tlb} + \left\lceil \frac{Ne}{E} \right\rceil \times T_{cache} + Ne \times T_{comp} + T_{trav}) \times EA(RS(G), wq)$$

$$= T_{tlb} + \left\lceil \frac{Ne_{root}}{E} \right\rceil \times T_{cache} + Ne_{root} \times T_{comp} + T_{trav} \qquad (4)$$

$$+ \sum_{i=2}^{h} \{ (\sum_{j=1}^{Ni} \prod_{k=1}^{d} (n_{ij,k} + wq_k)) \times (T_{tlb} + \left\lceil \frac{Ne_{ij}}{E} \right\rceil \times T_{cache} + Ne_{ij} \times T_{comp} + T_{trav}) \}$$

The expected time is calculated by the product of the expected number of accesses by the time for processing a node. As explained above, to process a node, four factors are summed together: TLB miss, cache misses, key comparisons, and function overhead. The expansion of the equation is shown in Eq. 4.

From Eq. 4, the following issues will be evident. First, we should find an optimal node size to minimize the cost. If the node size increases, both the cache miss and the key comparison time increase. By contrast, if the node size decreases, both TLB miss and the function overhead increase, due to the increased number of nodes. Second, we should reduce the probabilities accessing nodes. If the sum of the node region R_i is minimized, we can accomplish better search performance. In this paper, we do not use traditional compaction algorithms or clustering algorithms to solve the above problems. We use a dynamic node size technique, namely the growing node policy.

3.2 Decision Function for the Growing Node Policy

The insertion algorithm is an essential element of our approach. The insertion algorithm of the R-tree splits a node when it overflows, regardless of the search performance. Our algorithm, however, does not always split a node. We use the cost model (Eq. 4) as a decision function to determine whether to split or to grow a node when it overflows. The insertion algorithm computes the value of the decision function D (=C_s-C_g) after splitting (C_s = ET(RS(G), $wq)_{split}$) or growing (C_g = ET(RS(G), $wq)_{grow}$) and then makes a decision.

When making a decision, it is not necessary to compute the cost values of all the nodes, because only the nodes that are in the insertion path are affected. Fig. 2 shows the nodes of which the cost is to be changed. Split may occur only in the leaf node, or may occur in several non-leaf nodes, or may generate a new root node. In Fig. 2(a), s denotes the number of splits. Although all the nodes in the insertion path are affected, only the nodes of level (s+1) are checked, because the cost of nodes above that level will be the same.

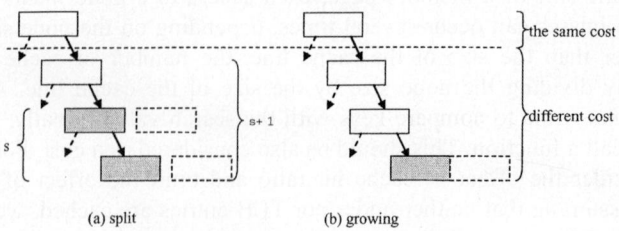

(a) split   (b) growing

Fig. 2. Nodes that changes their cost

The cost of splitting is shown in Eq. 5. The first term is the cost value of the tree before splitting. It is the same as the first term of Eq. 4. The second term is the cost of the affected nodes. In this case, the number of affected nodes is one more than the number of splits. The third and fourth terms are the cost values of the modified nodes after splitting. In the third term, Ne_m^1 and Ne_m^2 are the number of entries in the split nodes. The fifth term is the cost of the parent node of the split nodes.

$$C_s = ET(RS(G), wq) - \sum_{l=1}^{s+1} \{(\prod_{k=1}^{d}(n_{l,k} + wq_k)) \times (T_{tlb} + \left\lceil \frac{Ne_l}{E} \right\rceil \times T_{cache} + Ne_l \times T_{comp} + T_{trav})\}$$
$$+ \sum_{m=1}^{s} \{(\prod_{k=1}^{d}(n_{m,k}^1 + wq_k)) \times (T_{tlb} + \left\lceil \frac{Ne_m^1}{E} \right\rceil \times T_{cache} + Ne_m^1 \times T_{comp} + T_{trav}) +$$
$$(\prod_{k=1}^{d}(n_{m,k}^2 + wq_k)) \times (T_{tlb} + \left\lceil \frac{Ne_m^2}{E} \right\rceil \times T_{cache} + Ne_m^2 \times T_{comp} + T_{trav})\}$$
$$+ \prod_{k=1}^{d}(n_p + wq_k) \times (T_{tlb} + \left\lceil \frac{Ne_p}{E} \right\rceil \times T_{cache} + Ne_p \times T_{comp} + T_{trav}) \quad (5)$$

The cost of growing is shown in Eq. 6. The first term denotes the cost value of the tree before growing. The second term denotes the cost of the affected nodes. The third term is the cost of the changed nodes after growing.

$$C_g = ET(RS(G), wq) - \sum_{l=1}^{s+1} \{(\prod_{k=1}^{d}(n_{l,k} + wq_k)) \times (T_{tlb} + \left\lceil \frac{Ne_l}{E} \right\rceil \times T_{cache} + Ne_l \times T_{comp} + T_{trav})\}$$
$$+ \sum_{m=1}^{s+1} \{(\prod_{k=1}^{d}(n_{m,k} + wq_k)) \times (T_{tlb} + \left\lceil \frac{Ne_m}{E} \right\rceil \times T_{cache} + Ne_m \times T_{comp} + T_{trav})\} \quad (6)$$

To determine whether to grow or to split, we use the decision function D. Since the first term and the second term of Eq. 5 and Eq. 6 represent the same cost, they are removed in D. The decision function D consists of only the changed or split nodes. If the decision function value D is lower than or equal to 0, we split the leaf nodes. If D is greater than 0, we increase the capacity of the leaf node and insert the new data.

The decision to grow or split depends on the dataset and the insertion order. If the MBBs of objects in the dataset are highly overlapped, it is likely that more growing nodes exist. The optimal node size is not fixed in advance but adjusted dynamically, according to the properties of the dataset.

4 Updating and Searching

In this section, we explain the insertion and search algorithms for the growing node policy. For the update operations, we describe only the insertion algorithm. We assume that the delete operation is the same as with the ordinary R-tree algorithm. For the search operation, we give the algorithm for the range queries. Henceforth, we call the tree that uses the following algorithms the Growing 3DR-tree (or just G3DR-tree).

sIn the insertion algorithm, the central difference from the ordinary R-tree is the method of overflow handling [1]. When a node overflows, the algorithm computes the decision function, and then determines whether to split or to grow the node. If the decision is to grow, it simply increases the capacity of the node by the default node size and inserts the leaf entry. Splitting is similar to the original algorithm. Since moving objects databases need a high speed of insertion, it is better to use a linear split algorithm than to use complex algorithms such as quadratic, exhaustive or the R*-tree split algorithm. In the following pseudocode, the differences in the insertion algorithm from the ordinary R-tree algorithm are marked by underlined text.

```
Insert (e: LeafEntry)
begin
    node = root
    while (node is not a leaf) do
        node = ChooseSubtree(node, e)
    end while
    InsertInLeaf(node, e)
    // if the leaf overflows
    // check whether to split or to grow
    // else adjust the path
    if (node overflows) then
        // Compute the decision function
        decision = ComputeDecisionValue()
        if (decision is grow) then
            GrowAndAdjust(node)
        else
            SplitAndAdjust(node)
    else
        AdjustPath(node)
    end if
end
```

It is important to consider the time taken to compute the decision function. The computation can slow down the speed of the insertion. However, since a growing node delays the splits, it can reduce the number of the nodes and the height of the tree. It can compensate for the loss of time caused by the computation.

The search algorithm is almost the same as the original algorithm of the R-tree. The only difference is that the sizes of the nodes vary. The search algorithm should consider the difference in the size when comparing keys in a node. If a query window is small, a large size of growing node may be thought inefficient. The search performance, however, does not deteriorate, because the decision function considers the probability of retrieving a node and the other factors. If a query window is large, the growing node can be efficient because the number of accessed nodes is small. In

Fig. 4(b), (c) show the search performance when using 1% and 10% query windows, respectively. Overall, the performance for the G3DR-tree is better than that of the R-tree. When using 10% query windows, the performance gap increases. The G3DR-tree is more efficient when query regions are larger, because the number of visited nodes is smaller than for the original algorithm.

6   Conclusions

Studies on traditional disk-based indices focus on the split algorithm when a node overflows. In the case of main memory indices, most of the studies are concerned with the compaction of a node to reduce cache misses. However, neither kind of study considers the effect of fixed node size. In main memory environments, several factors affect the effective node size, such as TLB miss, cache misses, the number of key comparisons, and the function overhead of visiting nodes. We defined the cost model of the main memory R-tree considering all the related factors and used it to determine whether to split or to grow a node. By using the cost model, we can reduce the probability of a node's being selected and the cost of a node's being processed. By using the proposed policy, we achieved good search performance while maintaining insertion speed. Our experiments show that the improvements range from 5 to 15 percent over the original algorithm.

References

1. A. Guttman, "R-trees: A Dynamic Index Structure for Spatial Searching," Proceedings of ACM SIGMOD Conference, 1984, pp. 47-57.
2. R. A. Hankins and J. M. Patel, "Effect of Node Size on the Performance of Cache-Conscious B+-trees," SIGMETRICS 2003, 2003, pp. 283-294.
3. I. Kamel and C. Faloutsos, "On Packing R-trees," Proceedings of ACM CIKM Conference, 1993, pp. 490-499.
4. K. H. Kim, S. K. Cha, and K. J. Kwon, "Optimizing Multidimensional Index Trees for Main Memory Access," In Proc. of ACM SIGMOD Conf., 2001, pp. 139-150.
5. T.J. Lehman and M.J. Carey, "A Study of Index Structures for Main Memory Database Management Systems," Proceedings of VLDB Conference, 1986, pp. 294-303.
6. B.U. Pagel, H.W. Six, H. Toben, and P. Widmayer, "Towards an Analysis of Range Query Performance," In Proceedings of ACM PODS, 1993, pp. 214-221.
7. J. Rao and K.A. Ross, "Making B+-trees Cache Conscious in Main Memory," Proceedings of ACM SIGMOD Conference, 2000, pp. 475-486.
8. Y. Theodoridis and M. Nascimento, "Generating Spatiotemporal Datasets on the WWW," ACM SIGMOD Record, Vol. 29(3), 2000, pp. 39-43.

Optimal Subspace Dimensionality for k-NN Search on Clustered Datasets

Yue Li, Alexander Thomasian, and Lijuan Zhang

Computer Science Department
New Jersey Institute of Technology - NJIT
Newark, NJ 07102, USA
emails{yue,athomas,lijuan}@cs.njit.edu

Abstract. Content based retrieval is an important paradigm in multimedia applications. It heavily relies on *k-Nearest-Neighbor (k-NN)* queries applied to high dimensional feature vectors representing objects. *Dimensionality Reduction (DR)* of high-dimensional datasets via *Principal Component Analysis - PCA* is an effective method to reduce the cost of processing k-NN queries on multi-dimensional indices. The distance information loss is quantifiable by the *Normalized Mean Square Error (NMSE)*, which is determined by the number of retained dimensions (n). For smaller n the cost of accessing the index (an SR-tree is used in our study) for k-NN search is lower, but the postprocessing cost to achieve exact query processing is higher. The optimum value n_{opt} can be determined experimentally by considering cost as a function of n. We concern ourselves with a local DR method, which applies DR to clusters of the original dataset. Clusters are obtained via a PCA-friendly clustering method, which also determines the number of clusters. For a given NMSE we use an algorithm developed in conjunction with the *Clustered SVD - CSVD* method to determine the vector of the number of dimensions retained in all clusters ($\boldsymbol{n}$). The NMSE is varied to determine the optimum $\boldsymbol{n}$, which minimizes the number of accessed pages. To verify the robustness of our methodology we experimented with one synthetic and three real-world datasets. It is observed that the NMSE yielding the optimum $\boldsymbol{n}$ varies over a narrow range and that the optimal value is expected to be applicable to datasets with similar characteristics.

1 Introduction

k-Nearest-Neighbor - k-NN queries are used in a wide variety of applications, such as content-based retrieval from image and multimedia databases. Objects are represented by the (endpoints of) feature vectors in a high-dimensional space. The "similarity" of two objects is determined by the *distance metric*, such as the Euclidean distance. "Quadratic distance functions", which are expensive to compute, are also used in some applications [5].

Sequential processing of k-NN queries or sequential scans, can be quite slow on large high-dimensional datasets. Multi-dimensional indices can be used to reduce the number of points to be considered for k-NN search. However, as the dimensionality increases, the cost of accessing multi-dimensional indexing structures, measured by the number of accessed pages, increases rapidly, which is one manifestation of the "dimensionality curse" [10].

This problem can be solved by an appropriate *dimensionality reduction DR* method, which reduces the number of dimensions of a dataset (in a transformed coordinate system) without losing too much distance information. *Singular Value Decomposition* (SVD), *Principal Components Analysis* (PCA), and the *Karhunen-Loeve-Transform* (KLT) are three related methods for DR. KLT is optimal in the sense that it attains the minimum distance error for a given number of retained dimensions selected from the principal components [5].

We are given a dataset X with M points (rows) and N dimensions (columns), whose covariance matrix is $C = X^t X/M$. PCA decomposes C as follows: $C = V\Lambda V^t$, where Λ is a diagonal matrix holding the eigenvalues. Without loss of generality, we assume that the eigenvalues are ordered in non-increasing order: $\lambda_1 \geq \lambda_2, ..., \geq \lambda_N$. V is the corresponding matrix of eigenvectors $V = (v_1, v_2, ..., v_N)$, which are in fact the principal components of X [5]. Dataset X is transformed to $Y = XV$, so that the axes of Y are aligned with the principal components of X. KLT retains the first n dimensions, since they correspond to the eigenvalues with the highest energy, but the value of n remains to be determined.

SVD decomposes X directly: $X = USV^t$, where U is an $M \times N$ matrix, which is of little concern here, although it is utilized in [9], S is a diagonal matrix of singular values, which are related to eigenvalues according to $\lambda_i = s_i^2/M$, and V is the matrix of eigenvectors.

DR methods can be classified as global and local methods. Global methods rely on global information derived from the dataset, and are more effective when the dataset is *globally correlated*. In other words, they work well for a dataset whose distribution is well captured by the centroid and the covariance matrix. When the dataset is not globally correlated, which is often the case for real-world datasets, performing DR using SVD or PCA on the entire dataset may cause a significant loss of information, as illustrated by Figure 1(a). In this case subsets of the dataset may exhibit local correlation. Local methods partition the original dataset into clusters, before applying DR using SVD or PCA separately on each cluster, as shown in (Figure 1(b)).

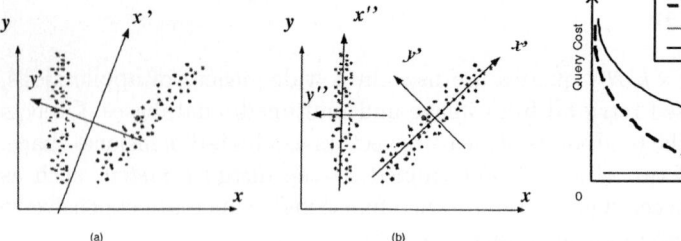
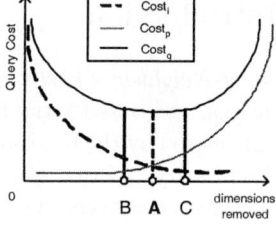
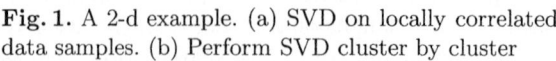

Fig. 1. A 2-d example. (a) SVD on locally correlated data samples. (b) Perform SVD cluster by cluster

Fig. 2. Optimal subspace dimensionality with respect to minimal query cost

The *Clustering and Singular Value Decomposition* (CSVD) method [16, 3] partitions a dataset into clusters using an off-the-shelf clustering method, such as the k-means method, and then performs DR on all clusters. The *Local Dimensionality Reduction* (LDR) method [4] starts from spatial clusters and rebuilds clusters by assigning each point to a cluster requiring minimum dimensionality to hold it with an error *ReconDist* $<$ *MaxReconDist*. The two methods are compared in [3, 17].

k-NN search methods can be divided into two categories: *exact* methods ([13, 7, 11, 14]) and *approximate* methods ([3]). Exact k-NN search returns the same k closest points as would have been obtained without DR, i.e., a *recall* value $R = 1$ [5], where *recall* is defined as the fraction of retrieved points which are relevant. A k-NN search on dimensionality reduced data is inherently approximate and may result in $R < 1$. Post-processing can be used to deal with this loss of accuracy [11, 14].

The number of dimensions to be retained is a critical issue, regardless of the k-NN search method being used. When the index is created on dimensionality reduced data, the query processing cost ($Cost_q$) is composed of two parts: the cost of querying the index ($Cost_i$) and the post-processing cost ($Cost_p$):

$$Cost_q = Cost_i + Cost_p \qquad (1)$$

$Cost_i$ decreases as more dimensions are removed, but at the same time, $Cost_p$ increases, because there is more distance information loss. We hypothesize, and verify by experimentation, that there is a point, or rather an interval, in which the minimum $Cost_q$ is reached, e.g., point A and interval [B, C] in Figure 2.

The problem of modeling query cost for multi-dimensional index structures has been studied extensively [6, 15, 10, 1, 2]. A model to analyze the cost of processing range queries in R-trees is given in [6], while [10] presents a cost model for k-NN search for two different distance metrics. Both studies consider the effect of correlation among dimensions by considering the *fractal dimension*, but the models are limited to low-dimensional data space. A cost model for high-dimensional indexing is proposed in [1], which takes into account the *boundary effects* of datasets for such spaces, but it assumes the index space to be overlap-free, which is not achievable in currently known high-dimensional indexing structures. We therefore decided not to analyze query cost by modeling.

The optimal number of dimensions for global methods with respect to k-NN search can be obtained experimentally by varying the number of retained dimensions (n). Local DR methods generate a number of clusters, denoted by H, each one of which may have different *Subspace Dimensionalities - SDs*, so that it is much more difficult to find the optimal SDs $\boldsymbol{n} = (n_1, n_2, \ldots, n_H)$. where n_h denotes the number of dimensions in cluster h.

We present a hybrid method which utilizes the SVD-friendly clustering algorithm specified in [4], but removes dimensions from each cluster according to a global metric, the *Normalized Mean Square Error - NMSE* (specified in Section 2), which is specified in conjunction with CSVD method [3]. Subspace dimensionalities determine the index size and the NMSE. The former affects the cost of accessing the index in processing k-NN queries and the NMSE affects the accuracy of the retrieval (quantified as recall). We use off-line experiments to determine the "optimum" SDs in minimizing query processing cost.

CSVD combines clustering and dimensionality reduction [3], but since it uses the k-means method for clustering, it is not able to identify locally correlated clusters. Some high-dimensional clustering methods can discover clusters embedded in subspaces, but cannot be used in conjunction with our method, since they can only find correlations along the dimensions in the original space. The LDR method [4] can identify locally correlated clusters, but fails to address the relationship between the NMSE and SDs.

The paper is organized as follows. The proposed method is described in detail in Section 2. Experimental results are given in Section 3, followed by the conclusion in Section 4.

2 The Hybrid Method for Clustered Datasets

Our method applies DR (data reduction) to clusters of the original dataset as shown in Figure 3. The following definitions are in order.

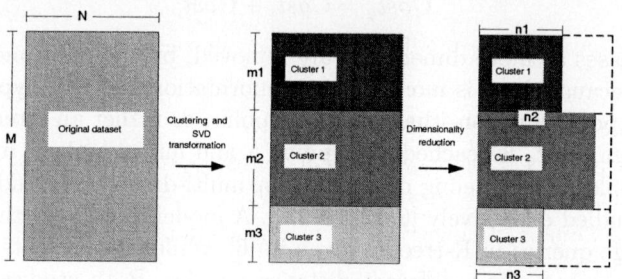

Fig. 3. Clustered dataset and dimensionality reduced clustered dataset

Definition 1. *A* **Clustered Dataset** $\mathcal{X}_C$ *is generated by a clustering method and is specified as* $\mathcal{X}_C = \{X_1, X_2, \ldots, X_H\}$, *where H is the number of clusters. The number of points in cluster* $\mathcal{X}_h$ *is* m_h *and* $\sum_{h=1}^{H} m_h = M$.

Definition 2. *A* **Dimensionality Reduced Clustered Dataset** $\mathcal{X}_{DRC}$ *differs from* $\mathcal{X}_C$ *in that the dimensionality of the cluster has been reduced:* X_h *is* n_h $(n_h \leq N)$. *The average dimensionality is* $\bar{n} = \sum_{h=1}^{H} n_h m_h / M$.

Distance Information Loss and Subspace Dimensionality: The problem at hand is to determine the optimum number of dimensions to be retained for the H clusters: $\boldsymbol{n} = (n_1, n_2, \ldots, n_H)$. The configuration which minimizes the cost of processing k-NN queries on a certain indexing structure is considered optimal. We solve this problem in steps by noting that the quality of k-NN search is related to the *Normalized Mean Square Error - NMSE*. Given that we retain $n \leq N$ dimensions of $Y = XV$, especially those with the largest eigenvalues $\lambda_j, 1 \leq j \leq n$, then the NMSE is minimized according to:

$$NMSE = \frac{\sum_{i=1}^{M} \sum_{j=n+1}^{N} y_{i,j}^2}{\sum_{i=1}^{M} \sum_{j=1}^{N} y_{i,j}^2} = \frac{\sum_{j=n+1}^{N} \lambda_j}{\sum_{j=1}^{N} \lambda_j}. \quad (2)$$

It follows that the NMSE is the ratio of the eigenvalues corresponding to the discarded dimensions and the trace of the covariance matrix. In the case of clustered datasets we have:

$$NMSE = \frac{\sum_{h=1}^{H} \sum_{i=1}^{m_h} \sum_{j=n_h+1}^{N} (y_{i,j}^{(h)})^2}{\sum_{h=1}^{H} \sum_{i=1}^{m_h} \sum_{j=1}^{N} (y_{i,j}^{(h)})^2} = \frac{\sum_{h=1}^{H} m_h \cdot \sum_{j=n_h+1}^{N} \lambda_j^{(h)}}{\sum_{h=1}^{H} m_h \cdot \sum_{j=1}^{N} \lambda_j^{(h)}}. \quad (3)$$

Eq.(3) expresses the relationship between the NMSE and the SD (subspace dimensionality) for each cluster: $NMSE = f(n_1, n_2, ..., n_H)$, given a *target NMSE (tNMSE)*, there are many ways for choosing $n_1 \sim n_H$.

The dimensionality reduction method in [3] uses a min-priority queue Q, implemented as a heap. Each entry in the heap has three fields: the eigenvalue (key), the cluster to which the eigenvalue pertains, and the associated dimension number in that cluster, The algorithm is shown in Table 1, named Algorithm 1. There are at most $K = H \times N$ items in the queue, so that the cost of Algorithm 1 is $O((KlogK)$.

Table 1. Selecting subspace dimensionalities

Algorithm 1: Selecting subspace dimensionalities.

Input: (1) The size m_h and eigenvalues in decreasing order: $\lambda_1^{(h)} \geq \lambda_2^{(h)} \geq ... \geq \lambda_N^{(h)}$ for all clusters C_h, $h = 1, ..., H$. (2)$tNMSE$.

Output: The number of dimensions to be retained in all clusters: $n_1, ..., n_H$.

1. Insert eigenvalues of all clusters into Q in increasing order.
2. Compute sum of eigenvalues as entries are being inserted:
   $sumBase \leftarrow \sum_{h=1}^{H} \sum_{j=1}^{N} m_h \lambda_j^{(h)}$.
3. $sumRemoved \leftarrow 0$.
4. For $h = 1$ to H initialize: $n_h \leftarrow N$.
5. If Q is empty goto step 7, otherwise remove smallest entry $\lambda_i^{(h)}$ from Q, h is the index of the cluster and i the column.
6. $sumRemoved \leftarrow sumRemoved + m_h \times \lambda_i^{(h)}$.
7. $currentNMSE \leftarrow sumRemoved/sumBase$.
8. If $currentNMSE < tNMSE$, $n_h \leftarrow n_h - 1$, goto step 5.

Once the clustered dataset is obtained we can vary the NMSE, by utilizing the above algorithm. We use the clustering method developed for the LDR method [4], since it carries out clustering based on local correlations. Our experimental results show that varying a key LDR control parameter (*MaxReconDist*) is not a good choice, since it just reflects the information loss of individual points, while the NMSE is a measure of total distance information loss.

The Hybrid Method: The hybrid method is specified in Table 2.

Table 2. Outline of our method

Algorithm 2: Outline of our method.
1. Perform the clustering algorithm of a local dimensionality reduction method (like LDR) to obtain clusters and the principal components. Ignore the subspace dimensionalities generated by the LDR method.
2. For $tNMSE = minNMSE$ to $maxNMSE$ step $incrNMSE$.
    (a) Perform Algorithm 1 for DR according to $tNMSE$ to determine the dimensionalities of all clusters: $\{n_1, n_2, ..., n_H\}$.
    (b) For each cluster $\mathcal{C}_h$ build an index using an existing multi-dimensional indexing structure.
    (c) Perform a sufficient number of k-NN searches with biased sample queries (query points selected from the dataset) to obtain a good estimate for the average I/O cost in term of number of accessed pages.
3. Plot the I/O cost versus the NMSE to obtain the optimum NMSE and the corresponding SDs.

Step 1 generates locally correlated clusters. Step 2 is a search for the optimum NMSE over a range of reasonable values of the tNMSE, e.g., $minNMSE = 0$, $maxNMSE = 0.3$ and $incrNMSE = (maxNMSE - minNMSE)/8$.

Optimal Dimensionality: Searching the index structure built on a dimensionality reduced dataset results in *false alarms*, which can be removed by accessing the original dataset to obtain the original distances. The distances between projected points with SVD lower bounds the distance between the original points, so that there are no *false dismissals* for range queries [5]. A technique to carry out exact k-NN queries is described in [11], which requires accessing the original dataset, which constitues the postprocessing step. In [12] we generalize this method to multiple clusters in the context of CSVD. In experimenting with SR-trees, we use the exact method given in [14] and also utilized in [4], since it minimizes the number of visited nodes.

Based on Eq. (1), $Cost_i$ drops with the number of dimensions removed, but $Cost_p$ increases with increased NMSE, because there are more *false alarms*. When many dimensions are removed, while $Cost_i$ becomes very low, $Cost_p$ may become very high, due to excessive information loss. We expect $Cost_q$ to be a convex function of the NMSE and verify this experimentally. Therefore there is an optimal SD at which the query cost is minimized. This optimal SD may be affected by indexing methods or DR methods, but for a given indexing and DR method, it is determined solely by the NMSE.

Besides query cost, the cost of storing the index also affects the overall cost, but this is a less of a problem with rapidly diminishing disk storage prices.

3 Experiments

We use the hybrid method to experiment with the three real-world and one synthetic dataset, as shown in Table 3. For each dataset, two clustered datasets are generated by varying the LDR parameters as shown in Table 4.

Table 3. Datasets

Name ($M \times N$)	Description
TXT55 ($79,814 \times 55$)	Gabor, spatial, and wavelet features, from 400 photos [3].
GABOR60 ($56,644 \times 60$)	Gabor features extracted from MMS images from different parts of the country. Obtained from Dr. V. Castelli
SYNT64 ($99,984 \times 64$)	Synthetic dataset from [4].
COLH64 ($68,014 \times 64$)	8×8 color histograms extracted from color images.

Table 4. Clustered datasets generated by LDR with different parameters. CD - clustered dataset, LT - *local_threshold*, FO - *FracOutliers*, MS - *MinSize*, MRD - *MaxReconDist*, H - Number of clusters

Datasets	CD	LT	FO	MS	MRD	H
SYNT64	1	1.0	0.15	800	0.7	9
	2	1.0	0.15	800	0.8	8
GABOR60	1	3.0	0.15	300	1.0	5
	2	3.0	0.15	300	2.0	4
TXT55	1	10.0	0.15	800	4.0	7
	2	10.0	0.15	800	6.0	6
COLH64	1	2.0	0.15	800	0.25	4
	2	2.0	0.15	800	0.35	3

We use SR-trees (with split-factor=0.4 and reinsert factor=0.3) as the indexing method [8], because it has been shown to be more efficient than R-trees at higher number of dimensions. We use an exact method for k-NN queries as discussed earlier. The query costs appearing in all figures are averaged over one thousand 20-NN queries, which are randomly selected from each dataset.

3.1 NMSE versus the Average Subspace Dimensionality

We use the LDR method for clustering, but ignore the subspace dimensionality obtained by LDR for the following reasons:

– The average SD is not always a monotonous function of *MaxReconDist* (see GABOR60 in Figure 4(a), even when all other parameters are fixed.
– For SYNT64 in Figure 4(a), the average SD is 18 at *MaxReconDist* = 1, while for GABOR60, LDR does not get such a level of dimensionality reduction until *ReconDist* $\geq$ 4. So that the choice of LDR parameters very much depends on the dataset, while with CSVD the effect of the NMSE on DR is very straightforward, as shown in Figure 4(b).

3.2 Query Costs and Subspace Dimensionality

We implement Algorithm 2 on the clustered datasets in Table 4, whose characteristics are given in Table 3. Results are summarized in Figure 5. The query cost is the sum of the number of 4 Kilobyte pages accessed from the index and from

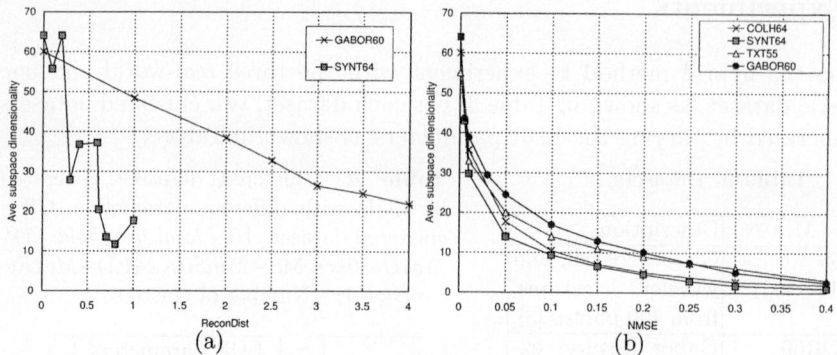

Fig. 4. (a) Average SD versus the LDR threshold $ReconDist$ for GABOR60 ($local\_threshold = 3, FracOutlier = 0.15, MinSize = 300$) and SYNT64 ($local\_threshold = 1.0, FracOutliers = 0.15, MinSize = 800$). (b) Average SD versus the NMSE using Algorithm 1

the original dataset for post-processing. As in [4], we store the reconstruction error in an extra dimension to obtain more accurate estimate of distances. The results of two clustering datasets generated with the LDR method are specified as Clustered Dataset 1 and 2 in the figures. The following conclusions can be drawn:

- The query cost versus average SD is convex and an optimal SD does exist. At the point where the cost is minimized, there is a significant data reduction, e.g., 2/3 dimensions for COLH64 (Figure 5 (f)).
- The optimal SDs for clustered datasets of the same original dataset are obtained at about the same NMSE.
- Different datasets have different optimal mean dimensionalities, since the correlation degrees are different. But they have almost the same NMSE values with respect to the minimum query costs. From Figure 5 we can see that the optimal subspace dimensionality is attained at around 20 for SYNT64, 23 for TXT55, 20 for COLH64 and 32 for GABOR60, but the minimum costs are attained at $NMSE \approx 0.03$. It means minimum query cost is strongly related to NMSE.

In conclusion, for the limited number of datasets considered in this study, the minimum k-NN query cost with SR-trees is obtained at $NMSE \approx 0.03$ for LDR generated clustered datasets, for both synthetic dataset or real-world image datasets.

4 Conclusion

We have presented a method to obtain an "optimal" index configuration, i.e., the set of subspace dimensionalities, which minimizes the cost of processing k-NN queries on a very efficient high-dimensional indexing structure, the SR-tree. Our

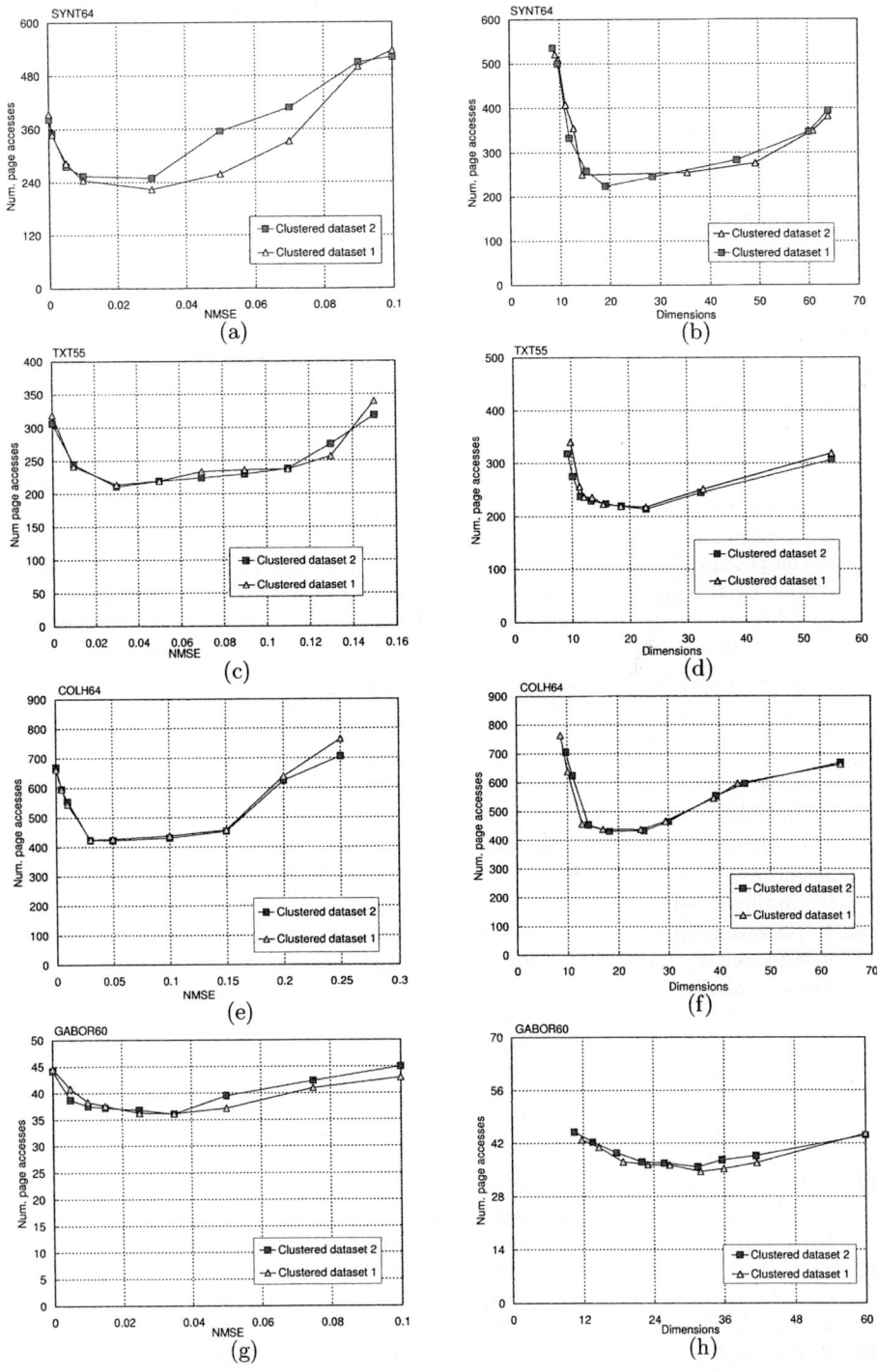

Fig. 5. I/O costs for 20-NN queries versus the NMSE ((a), (c), (e), (g)) and the I/O cost versus average subspace dimensions ((b), (d), (f), (h)) for the four datasets with SR-trees

method relies on the fact that the quality of k-NN search is determined by the ratio of information loss of the whole dataset and that by varying the NMSE we can find the point where the sum of the index accessing cost and postprocessing cost is minimized. It is observed that a significant reduction in the number of dimensions yields the optimal performance.

As part of future work we plan more experimentation to determine whether the optimal SDs obtained for various datasets are applicable to other datasets in the same category. Similarly, it needs to be determined, if the optimal SDs for the SR-tree apply to other indexing structures.

References

1. C. Böhm. A cost model for query processing in high-dimensional data space. *ACM Trans. Database Systems (TODS)* 25(2): 129–178 (2000).
2. A.K. Singh and C.A. Lang. Modeling high-dimensional index structures using sampling. In *Proc. ACM SIGMOD Int'l Conf. on Management of Data*, Santa Barbara, CA, pages 389–400, 2001.
3. V. Castelli, A. Thomasian, and C.S. Li. CSVD: clustering and singular value decomposition for approximate similarity search in high dimensional spaces. *IEEE Trans. on Knowledge and Data Engineering (TKDE)* 14(3): 671–685 (2003).
4. K. Chakrabarti and S. Mehrotra. Local dimensionality reduction: A new approach to indexing high dimensional space. In *Proc. Int'l Conf. on Very Large Data Bases (VLDB)*, pages Cairo, Egypt, pages 89–100, 2000.
5. C. Faloutsos. *Searching Multimedia Databases by Content*. Kluwer Academic Publishers, Boston, MA, 1996.
6. C. Faloutsos and I. Kamel. Beyond uniformity and independence: Analysis of the R-tree using the concept of fractal dimension. In *Proc. ACM Symp. on Principles of Database Systems (PODS)*, Minneapolis, MN, pages 4–13, 1994.
7. G.R. Hjaltason and H. Samet. Ranking in spatial databases. In *Proc. 4th Symp. Advances in Spatial Databases, Lecture Notes in Computer Science 951*, pages 83–95. Springer-Verlag, 1995.
8. N. Katayama and S. Satoh. The SR-tree: An index structure for high dimensional nearest neighbor queries. In *Proc. ACM SIGMOD Conf. on Management of Data*, Tucson, AZ, pages 369–380, 1997.
9. F. Korn, H.V. Jagadish, and C. Faloutsos. Efficiently supporting ad hoc queries in large datasets of time sequences. In *Proc. ACM SIGMOD Conf. on Management of Data*, Tucson, AZ, pages 289–300, May 1997.
10. F. Korn, B. Pagel, and C. Faloutsos. On the "dimensionality curse" and the "self-similarity blessing". In *IEEE Trans. on Knowledge and Data Engineering (TKDE)* 13(1):, 96–111 (2001).
11. F. Korn, N. Sidiropoulos, C. Faloutsos, E. Siegel, and Z. Protopapas. Fast nearest neighbor search in medical image databases. In *Proc. 22nd Int'l Conf. on Very Large Data Bases (VLDB)*, Mumbai, India, pages 215–226, 1996.
12. Y. Li, A. Thomasian, and L. Zhang. "An exact search algorithm for CSVD", *Technical Report ISL-2003-02*, Integrated Systems Lab, Computer Science Dept., New Jersey Institute of Technology, 2003.
13. N. Roussopoulos, S. Kelley, and F. Vincent. Nearest neighbor queries. In *Proc. Conf. ACM SIGMOD*, pages 71–79, 1995.

14. T. Seidl and H.P. Kriegel. Optimal multi-step k-nearest neighbor search. In *Proc. ACM SIGMOD Int'l Conf. on Management of Data*, Seattle, WA, pages 154–165, 1998.
15. Y. Theodoridis and T. Sellis. A model for the prediction of R-tree performance. In *Proc. ACM Symp. on Principles of Database Systems (PODS)*, Montreal, Canada, pages 161–171, 1996.
16. A. Thomasian, V. Castelli, and C.S. Li. RCSVD: Recursive clustering and singular value decomposition for approximate high-dimensionality indexing. In *Proc. Conf. on Information and Knowledge Management (CIKM)*, Baltimore, MD, pages 267–272, 1998.
17. A. Thomasian, Y. Li, and L. Zhang. "Performance comparison of local dimensionality reduction methods", *Technical Report ISL-2003-01*, Integrated Systems Lab, Computer Science Dept., New Jersey Institute of Technology, 2003.

PCR-Tree: An Enhanced Cache Conscious Multi-dimensional Index Structures

Young Soo Min[1], Chang Yong Yang[1], Jae Soo Yoo[1],
Jeong Min Shim[2], and Seok Il Song[3]

[1] Department of Computer and Communication Engineering, Chungbuk National University
48 Gaesin-dong, Cheongju Chungbuk, Korea
{minys,cyyang,yjs}@netdb.chungbuk.ac.kr
[2] Electronics and Telecommunications Research Institute
161 Gajeong-dong, Yuseong-gu, Daejeon, Korea
jmshim@etri.re.kr
[3] Department of Computer Engineering, Chungju National University
Iryu Meon Gumdan Lee, Chungju Chungbuk, Korea
sisong@chungju.ac.kr

Abstract. Recently, to relieve the performance degradation caused by the bottleneck between CPU and main memory, cache conscious multi-dimensional index structures have been proposed. The ultimate goal of them is to reduce the space for entries so as to widen index trees, and minimize the number of cache misses. They can be classified into two approaches according to their space reduction methods. One approach is to compress MBRs by quantizing coordinate values to the fixed number of bits. The other approach is to store only the sides of MBRs that are different from their parents. In this paper, we investigate the existing multi-dimensional index structures for main memory database systems through experiments under the various work loads. Then, we propose a new index structure that exploits the properties of the both techniques. We implement existing multi-dimensional index structures and the proposed index structure, and perform various experiments to show that our approach outperforms others.

1 Introduction

Recently, as the performance gap between CPU and main memory gets larger, it becomes increasingly important to consider cache behavior and to reduce L2 cache line misses for the performance improvement of MMDBMs [1], [2]. Subsequently, several researches to improve the performance of index structures for MMDBMSs by reducing L2 cache misses have been done actively in the database community [3], [4], [5], [6], [7], [8]. Since the end of 1990s, cache conscious index structures have been one of the primary concerns to improve the performance of MMDBMSs. Particularly, in the beginning of the 2000s, some cache conscious multi-dimensional index structures have been proposed to enhance the performance of modern applications such as GIS

(Geographical Information Systems) and LBS (Location Based Systems) based on MMDBMSs.

To our knowledge, most recent cache conscious multi-dimensional index structures are cache conscious R-tree (CR-tree)[7], partial R-tree (PR-tree)[8] and normal R-tree[9] with a small node size, a cache line size or its multiple. CR-trees compress MBRs by quantizing coordinate values to the fixed number of bits. PR-trees store only the sides of MBRs that are different from their parents. The ultimate goal of both index structures is to reduce the space for MBRs so as to widen index trees and minimize the number of cache misses.

In this paper, we investigate existing multi-dimensional index structures for MMDBMSs such as CR-trees, PR-trees and normal R-trees through some experiments. Then, we propose a new index structure that exploits the properties of CR-tree and PR-tree. Actually, the partial MBR method of PR-tree works well when the number of entries is small, generally 3~7. However, the number of entries of CR-tree that uses compression techniques is much more than that of normal R-tree. In that reason, partial MBR method seems to be inadequate for CR-tree. Through experiments, we investigate that integrating CR-tree with PR-tree is valuable. Finally, we perform extensive experiments to show that our proposed index structure outperforms CR-tree, PR-tree and R-tree in various environments.

This paper is organized as follows. In section 2, we describe existing cache conscious uni-dimensional and multi-dimensional index structure. In Section 3, we analyze PR-tree and CR-tree in detail, and propose PCR-tree in section 4. Section 5 presents experimental results that proposed algorithm outperforms existing index structures through various experiments. Finally, section 6 concludes this paper.

2 Related Works

In the end of 1990s, Rao and Ross proposed two index structures for MMDBMs that consider cache behavior. The index structures are Cache-Sensitive Search tree (CSS-tree)[3] and Cache-Sensitive B+-tree (CSB+-tree)[4]. CSS-tree designed for OLAP environments is a very compact and space-efficient B+-tree. It eliminates pointers of index trees completely, and stores keys in contiguous memory. CSB+-tree applies the idea of CSS-tree to an index structure for OLTP environments that should support efficient update. Partial key B+-tree (pkB+-tree) are proposed in [5]. The partial key approach of pkB+-tree uses fixed-size parts of keys and information about key differences to minimize the number of cache misses. [6] applies to prefetch techniques to B+-tree to eliminate the cache miss latency efficiently. The approach of pkB+/pB+-tree is orthogonal to that of CSS/CSB+-tree. Above methods are for uni-dimensional index structures such as B+-tree. Cache-conscious R-tree (CR-tree) and partial R-tree (PR-tree) are multi-dimensional index structures. We describe the features of the two index structures that form the basis of our proposed index structure.

In the PR-tree, usually the node size of R-trees in MMDBMSs is a cache line size (32 ~ 64 bytes) or the multiple of a cache line size. The authors of PR-trees performed an experiment to show how many MBRs in R-tree share their sides with their parents. According to the results of the experiment, on average about 1.75 sides of a MBR are shared with parent MBR.

In the CR-tree, the ultimate goal of partial key techniques is to widen index trees by eliminating redundant information from entries in a node. CR-trees also pursue the same goal as PR-tree but its approach is quite different. The basic idea of CR-tree is to widen index tree by compressing MBRs so as to make R-trees cache conscious.

3 Analysis of CR-Trees and PR-Trees

PR-trees work well when the number of entries of a node is small enough (about 3~7). As the number of entries in a node increases, the ratio of the number of shared sides to total number of sides in a node is reduced. For instance, when the maximum number of entries in a node is 3 in 2 dimensional data spaces, the minimum number of sides that are shared with their parent MBR is 4. If the data type of each side is 4 bytes, 48 bytes are required for 3 MBRs. However, if we do not store the shared sides, only 32 bytes are required. In this example, 33% space is saved.

PR-trees need additional information to indicate whether a side is stored or not. For a 2 dimensional MBR, 4 bits are used, so additional 12 bits are needed for 3 MBRs. Finally, total space for 3 MBRs is 33.5 bytes. However, when the number of maximum entries of a node is 40, the minimum number of shared sides is 4. Subsequently, the total space for them is (640-16) bytes + (4*40) bits = 644 bytes. That is, no space gain is produced.

The MBR compression technique of CR-tree increases the fanout of nodes. When the cache line size is 64 bytes, a pointer to a child node group is 4 bytes, the number of entries is 4 bytes and the flag to indicate the node is leaf or non leaf is 1 byte, the absolute MBR of the node is 16bytes, 39 bytes are used as the space for QRMBRs. Therefore when the coordinate values are quantized into 4 bits, the maximum number of entries of a node is about 19. As we mentioned in the previous paragraphs, applying the partial MBR technique to CR-tree would be meaningless since the number of entries becomes larger than normal R-trees. However, the compression technique of CR-tree enlarges MBRs to align MBR to quantized coordinate values. Consequently, the probability of sharing sides of MBRs in a node with the parent MBR of the node may increase.

We performed experiments to count how many discriminators in a CR-tree share sides with their parents when the number of bits used for compression is 4 and 8 bits. The results in Table 1 are for a CR-tree with 19 and 9 entries per node when the number of bits used for compression is 4 and 8 bits, respectively.

Table 1. Ratios of shared sides in CR-trees

	4 bits compression	8 bits compression
Uniform	43.75 %	28.125%
Real (TIGER)	50 %	34.375%

When 4 bits are used for compression, on average about 45% of space for a MBR is saved. When 8 bits are used, on average about 30% of space for a MBR is saved. Additional information (bit fields) is not considered in the results. Considering the additional information, the average saved space is 20% for 4 bits compression and 18% for 8 bits compression. From these facts, we conclude that the combination of the partial technique and the compression technique would be meaningful.

4 Proposed Partial CR-Tree (PCR-Tree)

The main idea of our proposed PCR-tree is the combination of the partial technique of PR-tree and the compression technique of CR-tree. Generally, it is well known that as MBRs become large, overall search performance is degraded in R-trees. However, CR-trees show that even though MBRs become large, fat index trees compensate the disadvantage and provide good search performance. Our approach is to widen CR-trees by applying the partial technique of PR-trees without any loss of accuracy of MBRs. The quantization levels are made the same for all nodes. The structure of our PCR-trees is shown in Fig 1. *NE* denotes the current number of entries in a node. *CP* denotes the child node group for non-leaf nodes and records for leaf nodes. *AMBR* is the absolute MBR of a node. The MBRs of the node is recalculated relatively to this absolute MBR. *BF* and *ENTRIES* denote bit fields of entries and entries, respectively. Each entry of *ENTRIES* includes a pointer to the record object.

Fig. 1. Node structure of PCR-tree

NE which denotes the number of entries in a node plays another important role. On every insertion and deletion in a node, insert procedure or delete procedure check if the partial technique is meaningful for the node, i.e., total size of the node with partial technique is greater than that of the node without partial technique. If the partial technique is meaningless, we convert the *NE* as negative values. Traversers must note *NE* to read entries in a node with the partial technique correctly since to access *ENTRIES* they need to know the size of *BF* which is determined by the *NE*. However, if the partial technique is not applied to the node, *BF* does not have any value. Therefore, actually, *BF* is not needed and the negative value of *NE* indicates that this node does not have *BF*. In the following, we describe the detailed algorithms of insert and search operations.

Insert operations proceed in two phases like other R-tree families. In the first phase, a leaf node where a new entry is placed is located. *locateleaf()* performs this operation. *locateleaf()* of our algorithm is similar to that of PR-tree and CR-tree. Therefore, we omit the detailed procedure of *locateleaf()* in the Fig. 2 for brevity. *locateleaf()* put visiting nodes into *ps* for backtrack operations. Once the leaf node is located, an inserter checks if the node is overflowed.

```
         Variables to be used in the following pseudo code
ps : path stack, global variable
newentry : a new entry to be inserted into a node
  a leaf entry includes the pointer to an object and its MBR
  a non-leaf entry only includes a MBR for its corresponding child
node
node : leaf or non-leaf node
leaf : leaf node
pnode : a node that has partial MBRs
qnode : a node that has QRMBRs
space : number of bytes required to store actual entries of a node

insert(newentry, root){
  node = locateleaf(newentry, root);
  overflow = putentry(node, newentry);
  if (overflow){
     splitnode(node, newentry);
     return;
  }
}
putentry(node, newentry){
  calculate space_pnode and space_qnode for entries of node and
newentry;
  if (space_pnode < space_qnode) space = space_pnode;
  if (space > maximum node size )return true;
  place newentry on node;
  reorganize node;
  if (node.AMBR dose not include newentry.MBR){
     update node.AMBR;
     updateMBR(node.AMBR);
  }
  return false;
}
splitnode(node, newentry){
  classify node.ENTRIES and newentry into two groups;
  decide node type(i.e., pnode or qnode) of two groups;
  create newnode;
  place entries of both groups into node and newnode;
  node = pop(ps);
  overflow = putentry(node, newnode.AMBR);
  if(overflow) splitnode(node, newnode.AMBR);
  return;
}
updateMBR(MBR){
  node = pop(ps);
  if(node.AMBR includes MBR) return;
  Calculate space_pnode and space_qnode;
  when enlarging node.AMBR to enclose MBR;
  if (space_pnode < space_qnode) space = space_pnode;
  if (space >= maximum node size){
     splitnode(node, null);
     return;
  }
  update node.AMBR to enclose MBR;
  reorganize node according to its node type(i.e., pnode or qnode);
  updateMBR(node.AMBR);
}
```

Fig. 2. Insert algorithm

If overflow occurs, the node is split by *splitnode()*. Otherwise, the inserter put the entry into the leaf node, and decides the node type of the leaf node, i.e., node type is *pnode* or *qnode*. *pnode* means that the node can partial MBRs and *qnode* means that we cannot apply partial technique to the node. After placing the new entry into the leaf node, the inserter checks if the AMBR of the node is changed. If the AMBR is changed, *updateMBR()* is called. *updateMBR()* enlarges the MBRs of ancestor nodes to enclose the new entry. Note that *updateMBR()* may call the *splitnode()*. The change of AMBR of a node may convert the node type of the node from *pnode* to *qnode*. This may increase the total space of entries of the node.

Overall search algorithm of the proposed method is the combination of PR-tree and CR-tree. However, when visiting a node, searchers must first check if the node type is *pnode* or *qnode*. If the node is *qnode*, i.e., the NE of the node is positive value, the search algorithm of CR-tree is applied. Otherwise, the both search algorithms of CR-tree and PR-tree are applied. Fig. 3 shows this procedure. Once searchers visit a node, they *searchnode()* like Fig. 3. The NE that denotes the number of entries in a node indicates that the node is *pnode* or *qnode*. The positive value of NE indicates that the node is *pnode*, so searchers must restore all sides of MBRs of ENTRIES in the node by referring to BF and AMBR of the node. After that, they perform the search procedure of CR-tree.

```
searchnode(node, range)
{
  if (node.NE >= 0){
    read node.BF;
    restore MBRs of ENTRIES;
  }
  remained procedures are same to that of CR-tree;
}
```

Fig. 3. Range search algorithm

5 Performance Evaluation

5.1 Description of Evaluation

Our experiments were performed on a Pentium 4 1GHz with 256 Mbytes main memory under Windows 2000. The size of a level 2 cache line is 64 bytes. We implemented CR-tree, PR-tree, R-tree and our PCR-tree. Commonly, we used the quadratic splitting algorithm for all trees. Also, the bulk loading technique was implemented. The used technique is sort tile recursive (STR)[10].

Two kinds of data set such as uniformly distributed synthetic data set and real data set (TIGER) were used in our experiments. We obtained the TIGER data set from website[11] and generated the synthetic data set as follows. First we generated integers between 0 and 100 by using random number generator and stored them to a 2-dimensional array sequentially. Then we recursively constructed MBRs by grouping 2 elements of the array from the beginning. We did not limit the side length of a MBR so the areas of MBRs were varied. We built trees with the STR bulk loading algorithm. Then, we measured search performance under various conditions. We measured search performance after inserting a certain number of entries one by one into bulk loaded trees. The number of entries inserted by one-by-one method was varied. Also, to measure insertion performance, we inserted 10,000 entries to bulk-loaded index trees. We generated 10,000 range queries and measured the number of node accesses, execution time and the number of cache misses with varying the size of range queries from 0.001 to 0.1. The values on Fig. 4 to 11 are average values of the results of the experiments.

5.2 Experimental Results

Fig. 4 to 6 show the node accesses, execution time and cache misses of range search operations executed with uniform distribution data set. CR-tree(2) and PCR-tree(2) mean that the size of a MBR key of index structures is 2 bytes, i.e., MBRs of index tree are compressed with 4 bits, while CR-tree(4) and PCR-tree(4) mean that the size of a MBR key of index structure is 4 bytes, i.e., MBRs are compressed with 8 bits. Fig. 4 shows the number of node accesses of search operations of each index structure. In Fig. 4, PCR-tree(4) outperforms the others. However, PCR-tree(2) is less efficient than CR-tree(4). As mentioned in [7], the number of compression bits affects the performance of CR-tree. In our experiments, 8 bits compression shows best performance. In Fig. 4 to 6, the performance of R-tree and PR-tree changes as the node size varies but our PCR-tree is not affected and particularly, PCR-tree(4) outperforms the others.

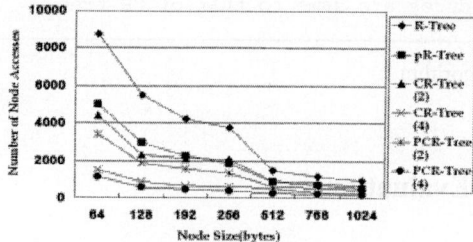

Fig. 4. Node accesses (uniform distribution, search)

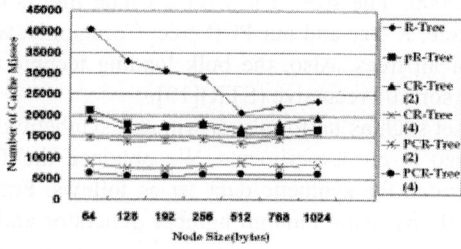

Fig. 5. Cache misses (uniform distribution, search)

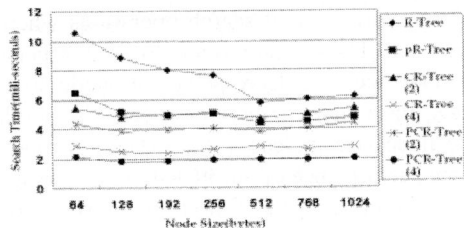

Fig. 6. Execution time (uniform distribution, search)

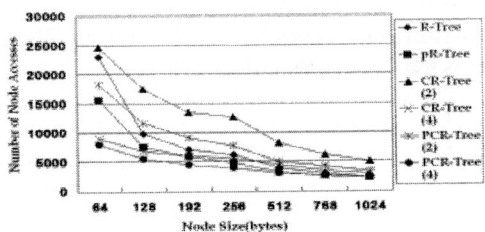

Fig. 7. Node accesses (real data, search)

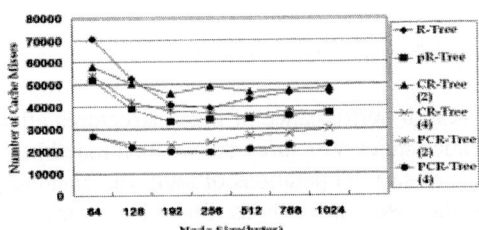

Fig. 8. Cache misses (real data, search)

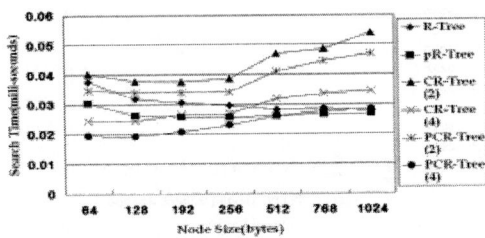

Fig. 9. Execution time (real data, range search)

Fig. 7 to 9 show the performance of search operations when the experiments are performed with real data set. Theses show some different aspects from Fig. 4 to 6. In Fig. 7, the number of node accesses decreases as the node size increases. When the node size is 1024 bytes, most index structures access the similar number of nodes. Also, in Fig. 9, as the node size increases, the execution time increases. When the node size is 64 bytes, the performance of our PCR-tree(4) is best.

Also, we measured the execution time of insert operations with inserting 10,000 entries in one-by-one fashion to bulk-loaded index structures. Our PCR-tree have rather complex insert algorithm than those of the other index structures. PCR-tree need to determine whether the compression technique is meaningful and calculate relative coordinates. As shown in Fig. 10, insert time of R-tree is fastest in all cases. However, when the node size is 64 or 128 bytes, the insert time of R-tree and PCR-tree is almost same and the search performance is best in 64 bytes nodes. Therefore, the insert performance of PCR-tree is the same to that of the others.

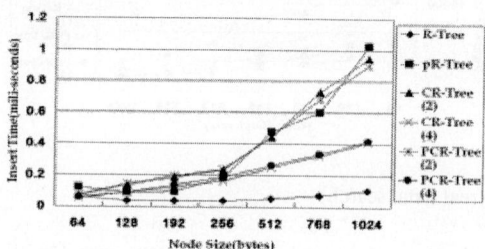

Fig. 10. Execution time (uniform distribution, insert)

Fig. 11 shows the search performance of index structures after inserting a number of entries into bulk-loaded index structures. As we mentioned in the beginning of Section 5, the performance of search operations of multi-dimensional index structures are different according to the insertion methods. Fig. 11 is to show that PCR-tree works well even in one-by-one insertion. As shown in Fig. 11, our PCR-tree(4) outperforms others in all cases. The number of node accesses of PCR-tree(4) increases moderately, while others increase steeply.

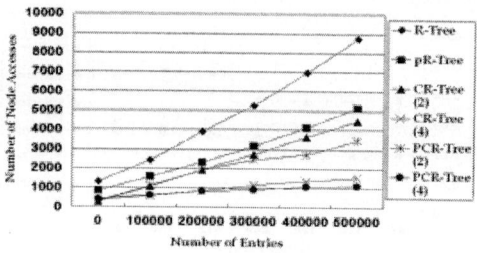

Fig. 11. Node accesses (uniform distribution, search, after dynamic insertion)

6 Conclusion

In this paper, we proposed a cache conscious multi-dimensional index structure that exploits the properties of existing methods. Through extensive performance comparisons under the various conditions, we show that the proposed PCR-tree outperforms the existing methods. Our contributions are summarized as follows. First, we investigated existing cache conscious multi-dimensional index structures. Second, we implemented existing multi-dimensional index structures and the proposed index structure, and performed various experiments to show that our approach outperforms others.

Acknowledgement

This work was supported by grant No. (R01-2003-000-10627-0) from the Basic Research Program of the Korea Science & Engineering Foundation and the bioinformatics program of the KISTEP.

References

1. A. Ailamaki, D.J. DeWitt, M.D. Hill and D.A. Wood: DBMSs on a Modern Processor: Where Does Time Go? In Proceedings of VLDB Conference (1999) 266-277
2. S. Manegold, P.A. Boncz and M.L. Kersten: Optimizing database architecture for the new bottleneck: Memory access. In VLDB Journal Vol. 9, No. 3 (2000) 231-246
3. J. Rao and K.A. Ross: Cache Conscious Indexing for Decision-Support in Main Memory. In Proceedings of VLDB Conference (1999) 78-79
4. J. Rao and K.A. Ross: Making B+-trees Cache Conscious in Main Memory. In Proceedings of ACM SIGMOD Conference (2000) 475-486
5. P. Bohannon, P. McIlroy and R. Rastogi: Main-Memory Index Structures with Fixed-Size Partial Keys. In Proceedings of ACM SIGMOD Conference (2001) 163-174
6. S. Chen, P.B. Gibbons and T.C. Mowry: Improving Index Performance through Prefetching. In Proceedings of ACM SIGMOD Conference (2001) 235-246
7. K.H. Kim, S.K. Cha and K.J. Kwon: Optimizing Multidimensional Index trees for Main Memory Access. In Proceeding of ACM SIGMOD Conference (2001) 139-150
8. I. Sitzmann and P.J. Stuckey: Compacting discriminator information for spatial trees. In Proceedings of the Thirteenth Australasian Database Conference (2002) 167-176
9. A. Guttman: R-trees: A Dynamic Index Structure for Spatial Searching. In Proceedings of ACM SIGMOD Conference (1984) 47-47
10. S.T. Leutenegger, J.M. Edgington and M.A. Lopez: STR: A Simple and Efficient Algorithm for R-tree Packing. In Proceedings of ICDE Conference (1997) 497-506
11. http://www.cs.du.edu/~leut/MultiDimData.html

Classification Decision Combination for Text Categorization: An Experimental Study

Yaxin Bi[1,2], David Bell[1], Hui Wang[3], Gongde Guo[3], and Werner Dubitzky[2]

[1]School of Computer Science
Queen's University of Belfast, Belfast, BT7 1NN, UK
[2]School of Biomedical Science
University of Ulster, Coleraine, Londonderry, BT52 1SA, UK
[3]School of Computing and Mathematics
University of Ulster, Newtownabbey, Co. Antrim, BT37 0QB, UK
{y.bi,da.bell}@qub.ac.uk
{h.wang,g.guo,krc.greer}@ulster.ac.uk

Abstract. This study investigates the combination of four different classification methods for text categorization through experimental comparisons. These methods include the Support Vector Machine, kNN (nearest neighbours), kNN model-based approach (kNNM), and Rocchio methods. We first review these learning methods and the method for combining the classifiers, and then present some experimental results on a benchmark data collection of 20-newsgroup with an emphasis of *average group performance* – looking at the effectiveness of combining multiple classifiers on each category. In an attempt to see why the combination of the best and the second best classifiers can achieve better performance, we propose an empirical measure called closeness as a basis of our experiments. Based on our empirical study, we verify the hypothesis that when a classifier has the high closeness to the best classifier, their combination can achieve the better performance.

1 Introduction

With huge amount of information in text natural being spread on the Internet the development of highly effective text categorization systems is attracting increased interest from researchers in the areas of information retrieval and machine learning. The ultimate goal of developing text categorization systems is to achieve the best possible classification performance for the automatic classification task. This objective conventionally leads to the development and application of different learning methods for the text categorization problem. The results of experimental assessment of the different methods is seen as a basis for choosing one of the classifiers as a solution to the problem. It has been recognized in such studies that although one of classifiers would yield the best individual performance, and different classifiers may only obtain different degrees of success, none of them is totally perfect [1]. The sets of documents misclassified using the different classifiers would not necessarily overlap. This potentially offers a source of complementary information about the different classifiers. Thus it is desirable to develop an effective methodology for combining them by taking advantage of the strengths of individual classifiers and avoiding their weakness, thereby improving the performance of classifiers.

The benefits of combining multiple classifiers based on different classification methods for text categorization have been studied in [2, 3, 4, 5]. In our work [4], we presented a method for combining text classifiers based on Dempster's rule of combination. We studied its distinguishing characteristics, and the partially experimental results on *average category performance*. In [5], we proposed a novel structure for representing outputs from different classifiers. It breaks down a output consisting of a number of classification decisions into three subsets based on the confidence values of labels, called *focal element triplet*, which is referred as a piece of evidence. The merit of this structure is that it is capable of distinguishing important elements from trivial ones. In this paper, we focus on examining the other experimental results in terms of *average groups performance*. Unlike the average category performance, it averages the performance of document categories; the average group performance provides a measure, which examines the effectiveness of combining multiple classifiers on each category. In an attempt to answer the question why the combination of the best and the second best classifiers can achieve better performance than the other combinations, we here propose an empirical measure called *closeness*. In our empirical study, we look at the situation where a classifier has highest closeness with the best classifier, and seek insight into whether their combination can enhance the performance.

2 Four Learning Algorithms for Text Categorization

The Rocchio method was originally developed for query expansion by means of relevance judgments in information retrieval. It has been applied to text categorization by Ittner et al. [6]. There are several versions of the Rocchio algorithm. In our work, we implement the version used by Ittner et al.

kNN, an instance-based classification method, has been effectively applied to text categorization in the past decade. In particular, it is one of the top-performing methods on the benchmark Reuters corpus [7]. Unlike most supervised learning algorithms that have an explicit training phase before dealing with any test document, kNN makes use of the *local contexts* derived from the training documents to each test document to make the classification decision on that document.

SVM (Support Vector Machine) is a high performance learning algorithm, which has been applied to text categorization by Joachims [8]. In our work, we integrate a version of the SVM algorithm implemented by Chang and Lin [9] in our prototype system for text categorization. There are two advantages of this algorithm: the first is that it has ability to cope with the multi-class classification problem; and the second is that the classified results can be expressed as posterior probabilities that are directly comparable between categories.

kNNModel is an integration of the conventional kNN and Rocchio algorithms [10]. It improves a kNN method by finding some representatives from the whole training data to build several local models for each category regardless of finding k. These local models are, in turn, treated as local centroids for the respective categories to overcome the deficiency of mis-clustering some data points when linearly clustering the space of data points. It combines the strengths of the kNN and Rocchio methods.

3 The Classification Decision Combination

Consider a document space D consisting of documents d_i, each of which is identified by one or more index terms; terms can either be weighted according to their importance or be represented as boolean values 0, 1 according to whether they are present. The task of text categorization is to assign each document into one or more predefined categories c_i. Formally, let $D = \{d_1, d_2, ..., d_{|D|}\}$ be a document space as a set of training documents, where d_i is represented by a weighted vector $\{w_{i1}, ..., w_{im}\}$, and $C = \{c_1, c_2, ..., c_{|C|}\}$ be a set of categories, then we regard a classifier generated by a learning method as a mapping function:

$$\varphi : D \rightarrow C \times [0,1] \quad (1)$$

where $C \times [0,1] = \{(c_i, s_i) \mid c_i \in C, 0 \leq s_i \leq 1\}$ and we also define a function ϖ, $\varpi(c_i) = s_i$ and $\varpi^\sigma(s_i) = c_i$. We now denote the output of φ by $\varphi(d) = [s_1, ..., s_{|C|}]$. The componenets $\{s_i\}$ can be regarded as the posterior probabilities for the categories, given a test document d, i.e. $s_{\langle c_i, d \rangle} = p(c_i \mid d)$. Alternatively, s_i can be viewed as belief, certainty, or other measurements. Based on the output information level of classifiers, Bezdek et al. proposed the three types of classifiers: crisp, fuzzy and possible classifiers [11], we adapt this notion in this work, and group classifiers into three categories as follows:

1. Boolean classifier: $\varpi(c_i) \in \{0,1\}$, $\sum_{i=1}^{|C|} \varpi(c_i) = 1$.
2. Probabilistic classifier: $\varpi(c_i) \in [0,1]$, $\sum_{i=1}^{|C|} \varpi(c_i) = 1$.
3. Similarity classifier: $\varpi(c_i) \in [0,1]$, $\sum_{i=1}^{|C|} \varpi(c_i) > 1$.

The output information given by the three types of classifiers can be viewed as intermediate results. At the final stage of classification the output information we only want to know is a decision made on which category a document comes from. This is typically done by the maximum membership rule:

$$\varphi(d) = \varpi^\sigma(s_k) \Leftrightarrow s_k = \max_{i=1,...,|C|}(\{\varpi(c_i)\}) \quad (2)$$

Notice that some categories of classifiers can be transformed to others in some way. For example, similarity classifiers of kNN, kNNM and Rocchio can be transformed to probabilistic classifiers using the following normalization formula:

$$\varpi(c_i) = \frac{\varpi(c_i)}{\sum_{j=1}^{|C|} \varpi(c_j)} \quad (3)$$

Likewise, a probabilistic or a similarity classifier can be transformed into a Boolean classifier. However, the reverse transforming process is difficult to perform, it is not easy to transform a Boolean classifier into either a probabilistic or a similarity classifier. Thus the similarity classifier is more general than the other two classifiers. The combination of classifiers can be carried out between classifiers with the same type or different types. In this work, we assume that classifiers to be combined are probabilistic classifiers since the similarity classifiers kNN, KNNM and Rocchio can be easily transformed into probabilistic classifiers using formula (3).

Given a set of classifiers $\varphi_1, \varphi_2, \ldots, \varphi_L$, the output of classifier φ_i is denoted by $\varphi_i(d)=\{s_{i1},\ldots, s_{i|C|}\}$, where s_{ij} is the degree of support given by classifier φ_i, to the proposition which document d comes from category c_j, and it can be normalized as basic probability assignments produced by classifier φ_i. Thus each output $\varphi_i(d)$ is regarded as a piece of evidence, and two or more pieces of evidence can be combined by using Dempster's rule of combination as follows:

$$m = m_1 \oplus m_2 \oplus \ldots \oplus m_L \qquad (4)$$

where m_i is a mass function derived from $\varphi_i(d)$. In order to improve the efficiency of computing Dempster's rule and the accuracy of final decisions, we have developed a new structure, called a *focal element triplet*, which partitions $\varphi_i(d)$ into three subsets in the form $Y = \langle A_1, A_2, A_3 \rangle$, where $A_1, A_2 \subseteq C$ are singletons and A_3 is the whole set C. More details can be found in [5].

4   Decision Making about Classification

By using Equation (4) to obtain a set of classifications to which documents should belong, we can use the decision rule of formula (2) to determine the final category in the general case [5]. However, this decision rule may not be most suitable for the three scenarios presented in Figure 1, where the first and second categories are different and the difference between their degrees of confidence is small, leading to a conflict situation. In this case, we devise three decision rules to resolve such conflict cases. For convenience of our discussion, we consider only decision rules based on the combined results of any two triplets. These rules can be directly applied to cases where the results are recursively yielded by combining more than two triplets.

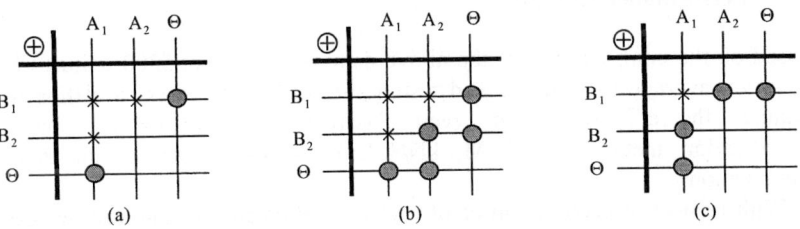

Fig. 1. Scenarios of decisions making in combining two triplets (●: intersection is nonempty; ×: intersection is empty)

Given two triplets $Y_1 = \langle m(A_1), m(A_2), \Theta \rangle$, $Y_2 = \langle m(B_1), m(B_2), \Theta \rangle$, three conflicting cases are shown in Figure 1 (a), (b) and (c), respectively. Figure 1 (a) presents the case where a decision made is based on the first elements of two triplets and $A_1 \cap B_1 = \phi$, $A_2 \cap B_2 = \phi$, and $|m(A_1 \cap \Theta) - m(B_1 \cap \Theta)| \le \alpha$ ($\alpha \le 0.00001$) In this situation, the final decision will be determined by the prior performance of the classifiers which yield these two triplets.

Figure 1 (b) demonstrates the case where $A_1 \cap B_1 = \phi$ and $A_2 \cap B_2 = C_i \ne \phi$. In this situation, the final decision is C_i, although $m(A_1 \cap \Theta)$ and $m(B_1 \cap \Theta)$ may be greater than $m(C_i)$. The reason for this is that the number of votes for decision C_i is larger than $m(A_1 \cap \Theta)$ and $m(B_1 \cap \Theta)$, respectively.

Figure 1 (c) demonstrates the case where $A_1 \cap B_1 = \phi$, $A_1 \cap B_2 = C_1$, $A_2 \cap B_1 = C_2$, and $|m(A_1 \cap B_2 \cap \Theta) - m(A_2 \cap B_1 \cap \Theta)| \le \alpha$. In this case, a decision can be made on the basis of neither the majority voting nor the degrees of belief committed to two categories since the measurements of both categories of A_1 and B_1 are almost the same, leading to a difficulty in determining which one should be regarded as the final decision. One possible way to resolve this contradiction could again be the use of prior knowledge, as for the case shown in Figure 1 (a). However a decision made in this way may still not be reliable. In this situation, we assume two categories should be presented as the final decision made since there is no reason to decide which one is better.

5 Evaluation

There are a number of methods to evaluate the performance of learning algorithms. Among these methods, one widely used in information retrieval and text categorization is the micro-averaged F_1 defined on a pair of measures, called Precision and Recall [12]. For our experiments we use 10 out of 20-newsgroup a benchmark dataset, i.e. 10 categories. Each category has 1,000 documents (Usenet articles), so that the dataset contains 20, 000 documents in total. The documents within each category are further randomly split into 5 groups based on the number of documents, i.e. 200 documents, 400, 600, 800, and 1000 documents.

5.1 Performance Analysis

Based on the configuration of the above data set, we select 5300 features from each group on average for training and testing, and use a ten cross-validation method to evaluate the effectiveness of each classifier generated by the four different classification methods of SVM, kNNM, kNN and Rocchio, and their various combinations.

With respect to each classifier of a classification method, its testing result is put into a contingency table. This table is then used to measure the performance of the classification method by micro-averaged F_1, i.e. *classification accuracy (CA)*. For the performance on each group of data, it is a mean value averaged over the 10 categories of documents, referred to as *average category performance (AC)*; whereas for the performance on each category, it is a mean value averaged over the five groups of data, referred to as *average group performance* (*AG*). Thus the performance of one classification method is the average of *AC* and *AG*.

Figure 2 demonstrates the comparison of *average group performance* between the best combined classifier and individual classifiers on each document category. As we see, the best combined classifier outperforms any individual classifiers on the average of five document groups with ten categories. In particular, there is a big performance margin between the best combined classifier and the others on the categories C2, C3, C4, C5, C6. This suggests that on the categories which the individual classifier predict poorly, our combination method could play a complementary role in crossing the validation of the results yielded from the different individual classifiers, resulting in a average 4.24% improvement of classification accuracy on these categories.

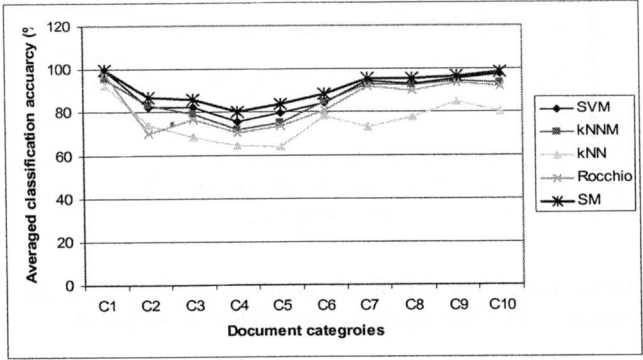

Fig. 2. The best combined classifier SM averaging the five groups of documents against the individual classifiers averaging the five groups of documents

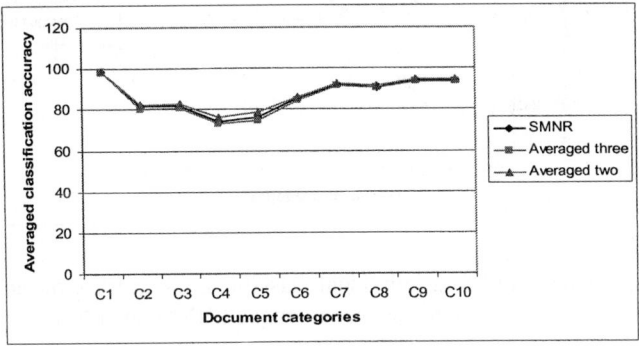

Fig. 3. The comparison of the combinations of four classifiers SMNR (SVM, kNNM, kNN and Rocchio), the average of all the combinations of three classifiers, and the average of all the combinations of two classifiers

Figure 4 presents a comparison of the combined classifier of four individuals SVM, kNNM, kNN and Rocchio, the average of the four combined classifiers of three individuals, such as SVM, kNNM, kNN, and SVM, kNNM, Rocchio, etc. (averaged three), as well as the average of the six combined classifiers of two individuals such as SVM, kNNM, and SVM, kNN, etc (averaged two). It can be observed that the performance of the combinations of the four classifiers is almost the same as that of the averaged three, and the performance of the averaged two is better by 2.63% than that of averaged three, and by 1.54% than that of the combined four classifiers on the categories C3, C4, C5, C6 on average. It can therefore be concluded that the combination of two classifiers would be the best combination in this particular setting.

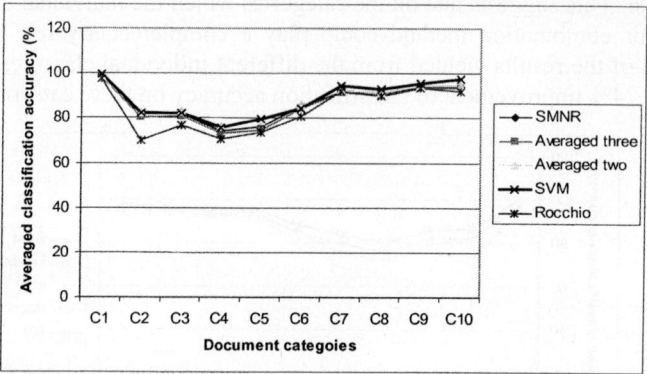

Fig. 4. The combination of four individual classifiers, the average of the combination of three classifiers, two classifiers against averaged SVM and Rocchio

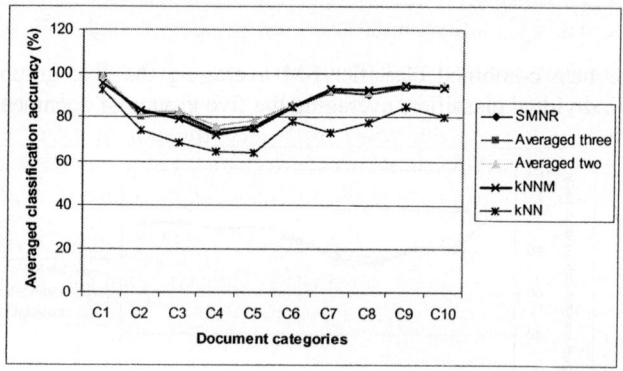

Fig. 5. The combination of four individual classifiers, the average of the combination of three classifiers, two classifiers against averaged kNNM and kNN

Figure 5 illustrates the comparison of the averaged two and three, and the combination of the four individual classifiers with the averaged SVM and Rocchio on *average group performance*. The averaged SVM outperforms any of the combined classifiers, but the performance of the averaged two and three is better than Rocchio's performance, in particular, on the categories C2, C3, C4, C6. The idea of Figure 6 is similar to that of Figure 6, it demonstrates the *average group performance* comparison of the combined classifiers on each category against the performance of kNNM and kNN, as illustrated that the performance of kNNM is slightly better than that of the combination of four classifiers and the averaged three on the categories C2 and C8. Its performance is lower than that of the averaged two on the categories C3, C4. C5, C6. The performance of kNN is lower than any of the combined classifiers.

5.2 Measuring Closeness between Classifiers

From the previous experimental results on as *average category performance* [5] and the present study for *average group performance*, we concluded that 1) the combination of the best and the second best classifiers can achieve the best performance; 2) the performance of combining two classifiers is better than that of combining three classifiers on average. Now we attempt to give an answer to the question why such results can be achieved, we propose a measure in terms of *closeness*. It is used to measure how pairs of classifiers close to a reference classifier on each point of classification accuracy.

Let $\varphi_1, \varphi_2, ..., \varphi_L$ be a group of classifiers, and let $C = \{c_1, c_2, ..., c_{|C|}\}$ be a set of categories. It is assumed that these classifiers have been sorted according to their classification accuracy - φ_1 has the highest performance and φ_L has the lowest performance. We also denote by π_φ the final decisions of classifier φ, called a decision performance profile as follows:

$$\pi_\varphi = [\pi_\varphi(c_1), \pi_\varphi(c_2), ..., \pi_\varphi(c_{|C|}), AV_\varphi] \tag{8}$$

where $\pi_\varphi(c_i)$ is a classification accuracy on category c_i and AV_φ is the mean value of the classification accuracy of |C| categories.

Suppose we are given two classifiers φ_i and φ_j, the closeness between the classifiers is based on the difference of the classification accuracy of two classifiers using two indicators: difference on each category point and the mean value. The measuring process based on the decision performance profile consists of three steps. The first is to take the best classifier φ_1 and then calculate $\pi_{\varphi_i} - \pi_{\varphi_1}$ and $\pi_{\varphi_j} - \pi_{\varphi_1}$, as a result, two new decision performance profiles are obtained. The second step is to count the numbers of categories on which the classification accuracy produced by classifier φ_i is greater than that produced by φ_j via formula (9). The third step is to incorporate the mean values of φ_i and φ_j classification accuracies into the differences of classification accuracies obtained step 2 above.

$$\hbar_{\varphi_i} = \{c \in C \mid \pi_{\varphi_i}(c) > \pi_{\varphi_j}(c), \text{ where } i \neq j\} \tag{9}$$

$$closeness\ (\varphi_i) = \varepsilon \times AV_{\varphi_i} + (1-\varepsilon) \times |\hbar_{\varphi_i}| \tag{10}$$

The closeness between pairs of classifiers is given by formula (11), where ε is a coefficient obtained by tuning. In the following setting, its value is 0.4. Having introduced the method for measuring the closeness between classifiers, we now examine the closeness between any pairs of classifiers. Table 1 summarizes the micro-averaged F_1 values of the four classifiers over the five groups of documents with the 10 categories, where the best classifier φ_1 is SVM, the second best φ_2 is kNNM, the third one φ_3 is Rocchio and the worst one φ_4 is kNN.

Table 1: The performance of the four classifiers

	C1	C2	C3	C4	C5	C6	C7	C8	C9	C10	AV
SVM	99.65	82.46	81.97	75.41	79.45	84.32	94.53	92.85	95.46	97.78	88.39
kNNM	95.45	83.01	79.29	72.21	74.82	84.62	93.09	92.57	94.23	93.44	86.27
kNN	92.33	74.27	68.51	64.36	63.63	77.92	72.80	77.74	84.84	80.40	75.68
Rocchio	97.43	69.76	76.34	70.59	73.65	80.53	91.94	89.75	93.41	91.80	83.52

Table 2: Accuracy difference between kNNM and kNN (2: π_{φ_2}, 3: π_{φ_3})

	C1	C2	C3	C4	C5	C6	C7	C8	C9	C10
2	4.20	-0.55	2.68	3.21	4.64	-0.30	1.44	0.27	1.23	4.35
3	7.32	8.20	13.46	11.06	15.82	6.40	21.73	15.11	10.62	17.38

Let us now look at how formulae (9) – (12) can be used to calculate the closeness between the classifiers. Table 2 gives the pair of classifiers φ_2 and φ_3. figure 8 gives their closeness to the best classifier φ_1..

$\hbar_{\varphi_2} = \{c1, c2, c3, c4, c5, c6, c7, c8, c9, c10\}$ and $\hbar_{\varphi_2} = \{\}$

closeness $(\varphi_2) = 0.4 \times 86.27 + 0.6 \times 10 = 40.508$

closeness $(\varphi_3) = 0.4 \times 75.68 + 0.6 \times 0 = 30.272$

Fig. 6. The closeness of classifiers φ_2 and φ_3

Similarly, we can obtain the closeness of the pairs of classifiers φ_2 and φ_4, φ_3 and φ_4 with the best classifiers below:

$\hbar_{\varphi_2} = \{c2, c3, c4, c5, c6, c7, c8, c9, c10\}$, and $\hbar_{\varphi_4} = \{c1\}$

closeness $(\varphi_2) = 0.4 \times 86.27 + 0.6 \times 9 = 39.008$

closeness $(\varphi_4) = 0.4 \times 83.52 + 0.6 \times 1 = 34.008$

$\hbar_{\varphi_3} = \{c2\}$, and $\hbar_{\varphi_4} = \{c1, c3, c4, c5, c6, c7, c8, c9, c10\}$

closeness $(\varphi_4) = 0.4 \times 86.27 + 0.6 \times 9 = 39.008$

closeness $(\varphi_3) = 0.4 \times 75.68 + 0.6 \times 1 = 30.872$

Fig. 7. The closeness of classifiers φ_2 and φ_3, φ_3 and φ_4

From Figures 6 and 7, we can see that classifier φ_2 has the highest closeness to the best classifier φ_2. Therefore the combination of the best classifier φ_1 with classifier φ_2 can achieve the best performance as described in [4].

6 Conclusion

Our experimental results show that the performance of the combined classifiers is directly affected by the performance of individual classifiers; the combination of the best and the second best classifiers outperforms anyone of the individual classifiers, and also outperforms the combination of the best and worst classifiers and the other combinations. Therefore, the performance of the combined classifiers is relative to that of individual classification methods implemented. In attempt to answer the question arisen why the combination of the best and the second best classifiers can achieve better performance than the other combinations, we propose an empirical measure of closeness. Based on our empirical study, we find that when a classifier has the highest closeness to the best classifier, their combination can achieve the best performance [4]. This finding provides an insight into the complementary characteristics used when combining classifiers.

References

1. Lei Xu, Adam Krzyzak and Ching Y. Suen, (1992). Several Methods for Combining Multiple Classifiers and Their Applications in Handwritten Character Recognition. IEEE Trans. on System, Man and Cybernetics, Vol. 22 (3), pp. 418-435.
2. Larkey, L.S. and Croft, W.B. (1996) Combining classifiers in text categorization. In Proceedings of SIGIR-96, 19th ACM International Conference on Research and Development in Information Retrieval, pp. 289-297.
3. Yang, Y., Thomas Ault, Thomas Pierce. (2000). Combining multiple learning strategies for effective cross validation. The Seventeenth International Conference on Machine Learning (ICML'00), pp. 1167-1182.
4. Bi, Y., Bell, D., Wang, H., Guo, G. and Greer, K. (2004). Combining Multiple Classifiers Using Dempster's Rule of Combination for Text Categorization. International Conference of Modelling Decision for Artificial Intelligence.
5. Bi, Y., Bell, D, Guan, J.W. (2004). Combining Evidence from Classifiers in Text Categorization. To appear in 8th International Conference on Knowledge-Based Intelligent Information & Engineering Systems.
6. Ittner, D.J. Lewis, D.D, and Ahn, D.D. (1995). Text categorization of low quality images. In Symposium on Document Analysis and Information Retrieval, pp. 301-315.
7. Yang, Y. (2001). A study on thresholding strategies for text categorization. Proceedings of ACM SIGIR Conference on Research and Development in Information Retrieval (SIGIR'01), pp. 137-145.
8. Joachims, T. (1997). A probabilistic analysis of the Rocchio algorithm with TFIDF for text categorization. The Fourteen International Conference on Machine Learning (ICML'97).
9. Chang, C.C., and Lin, C.J. (2001). LIBSVM: A library for support vector machines (http://www.csie.ntu.edu.tw/~cjlin/libsvm).
10. Guo, G., Wang, H., Bell, D., Bi, Y., and Kieran Greer, K.(2003). kNN model-based approach in classification. Cooperative Information Systems (CoopIS) International Conference. Lecture Notes in Computer Science, pp. 986-996.
11. Bezdek, J.C. Keller, J.M., Krishnapuram, R. and Pal, N.R. (1999). Fuzzy Models and Algorithms for Pattern Recognition and Image Processing. Kluwer Academic Publisher.
12. van Rijsbergen, C. J. (1979). Information Retrieval (second edition). Butterworths.

Information Extraction via Automatic Pattern Discovery in Identified Region

Liping Ma and John Shepherd

School of Computer Science and Engineering
The University of New South Wales
Sydney NSW 2052, Australia

Abstract. Pattern discovery has become a fundamental technique for modern information extraction tasks. This paper presents a new two-phase pattern (2PP) discovery technique for information extraction. 2PP consists of orthographic pattern discovery (OPD) and semantic pattern discovery (SPD). The OPD determines the structural features from an identified region of a document and the SPD discovers a dominant semantic pattern for the region via inference, apposition and analogy. 2PP applies discovered pattern back into the region to extract required data items through pattern matching. Experimental evaluation on a large number of identified regions indicates that our 2PP technique achieves effective results.

1 Introduction

A large amount of electronic information such as emails and web pages is primarily unstructured and comprised of natural language, but with some genre-based structuring conventions. We denote such documents as partially-structured, largely-natural-language (PSLNL) documents. Such information can only be retrieved via simple keyword-based search, unless the data is extracted and stored in a more structured form, such as XML or relational tuples. The aim of information extraction (IE) [2, 3] is to find individual data items in a document, relate these data items to a pre-defined schema and then integrate them into a structured information resource according to that schema. In conventional IE systems, data items are usually extracted by creating patterns to match the possible linguistic realizations of those items.

However, because of the complexity of natural language, it is not practical to describe all of these patterns, nor does it seem capable of improving significantly after reaching levels which were deemed interesting but not fully satisfactory. Therefore, a fundamental problem with information extraction applications oft he complex type is that a system is tailored to a predefined schema and cannot easily adapt to a different schema as would normally be required by a change of domain or the specific interests of the users. This gives rise to the issue of automatically discovering patterns in differing and new application domains.

The work presented in this paper is situated in the context of our previous work [9, 10], including a document classifier [10] which relates a document Joan appropriate user-defined schema, and a region recognizer [9] which identifies contiguous regions of the document. An important characteristic of a region is that the region is a contiguous subsection of a document which contains information of a particular type, such information is often structured as a sequence of records. For instance, the region of "program committee" in a conference announcement typically contains a list of members, mostly one per line, where each member is identified by a name, an affiliated organisation or country. Our pattern discovery techniques are applied after the document has been classified and regions have been identified; the information available is the text of the region, the region title, and the schema for the document class. In this work, we consider line-based patterns and generalised patterns are investigated in [8].

The remainder of the paper is organized as follows. Section 2 presents related work on information extraction and text mining (i.e. pattern discovery). Section 3 describes the problem space and our solution outline. Section 4 and 5 present the various granularities of pattern discoveries from orthographic to semantic, and briefly covers the process of data item extraction by pattern matching. After giving our experimental results in Section 6, we conclude our work in Section 7.

2 Related Work

Pattern discovery is useful, since it enables us to classify data items flexibly. Therefore, there have been a lot of researches in the database and machine learning communities on the problem of pattern discovery from text. Various methodologies have recently been developed for information extraction and representation to assist in managing web data. WIEN [6] automatically extracts data from web pages although it also works with plain text files. The advantage of the system is that little user interaction is required. However WIEN is only able to handle sources with a fixed ordering of items. STALKER [11] generates extraction rules that are expressed as landmark grammars based on training examples. While both systems use delimiter-based extraction patterns and do not use syntactic or semantic constraints, they both work well on relatively well-structured data.

The use of machine learning techniques to induce information extraction has received more and more attention. Techniques of early researches learned extraction patterns from collections of parsed documents that have been annotated to identify fragments of interest. These patterns are then reviewed and manually installed into a large information extraction system. SRV [5] is a top down relational algorithm for IE which tries to identify a "best" rule by matching all examples and describes how grammatical inference can improve the precision oft he data extracted. However, SRV does not solve any new fields outright and there is plenty of residual error when pieces of text with new formats occurs. NoDoSE [1] is a semiautomatic information extraction system where the user manually specifies a set of candidate rules for pattern extraction and introduces the parsing steps, and the system follows a simple generate and verify hypothesis model to find the best pattern.

Kushmeric [6] introduces wrapper induction technique, where the wrapper represents a rich logical framework structured by the limited tags of the HTML. Wrapper, such as ROADRUNNER[4], XWrap [7], Lixto [3], STALKER [11], and[2] are usually generated by taking uses of: (1) additional information, typically a set of labelled samples by the user or some other external tools (2) positive examples which infer the wrapper (3) some a priori knowledge about those pages to be parsed and (4) HTML pages with a regular syntax which are examined one by one. For example, ROADRUNNER generates wrappers automatically, and does not rely on any a priori knowledge about the target pages and their contents. However, users must name all of the fields manually after the dataset has been extracted. An important requirement of the input is that all the HTML pages must have a regular structure (e.g. book information on a given publisher's website, which is typically generated from a backend structured data source).

The solution presented in this paper is different from existing systems as follows: (1) application domain: PSLNL documents are more general than HTML files, we can view HTML tags as special instances of orthographic markers in our system; (2) feature space: we consider not only linguistic features but also semantic information to infer potential patterns; (3) dependency: our system learns patterns inside regions without reliance on previous orthographic and semantics analysis; and (4) new domain or format: the novelty of our solution is not to rely on pre-defined pattern, rather to discover pattern from a region and apply the discovered pattern back to the region.

3 Solution Outline

Outline One major difficulty in the IE task is the fact that data items may differ in format and properties even over a range of documents of the same type. Attempting to parse all of the data in an unstructured document may cause problems of misclassification and/or inefficiency. To tackle this problem, we have developed a topdown method to process input documents in three major steps, called **textclassification** [10], **region recognition** [9] and **data extraction**. This paper presents, in particular, the solution to the last step which is based on work done in the first two stages.

The information supplied by the user consists of a document class/type, its schema and a collection of keywords corresponding to the schema that maps to expected information items. Once a document is classified, a schema is determined, as shown in the right side of Figure 1. The schema gives the structure of the final information resource, and also provides important information about the types of data values that we expect to see in the documents and how these values might be related in the text. Typical data values would include names (of people, places and organisations), email addresses, URLs, dates/times, etc.

As illustrated in Figure 1, our system first attempts to discover patterns within regions, where pattern discovery is processed from orthographic patterns (see Section 4) to semantic patterns (see Section 5). It then relates these patterns to the schema and identifies data items inside each region. Finally it maps the data items that comprise instances of the patterns into the output document. The process of matching patterns to the schema relies on both the region title (to suggest overall placement in the schema) and the patterns of data types within the region (to relate to fields within the schema).

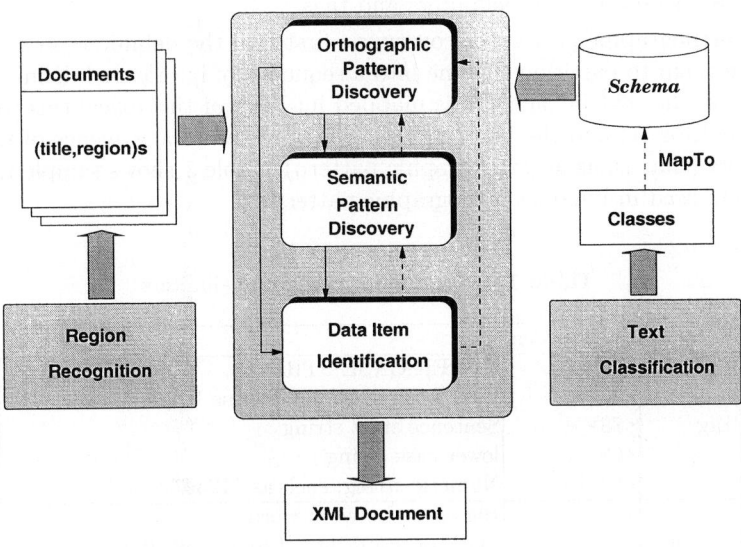

Fig. 1. IE via two-phase pattern discovery

The processes of pattern discovery and data item identification run recursively with communication among each component, expressed as solid and dash lines in Figure 1. The recursion provides a way of "finding" and "correcting" problems (i.e. it allows for one component to feed back information to assist the other component). Using this approach we can detect and deal with problems such as missing data, variations in orthographic patterns and unrecognisable data items. Details of this processing are given in the following sections.

4 Orthographic Pattern Discovery

The orthographic pattern discovery (OPD) uses robust orthographic features, and is able to handle a wide range of orthographic structures. Orthographically unresolvable ambiguities, such as undefined data items (i.e. an uncommon person name), are treated with a tag-based approach. Under this approach, undefined data items are inferred and identified by appositive comparison. An orthographic pattern consists of two types of information: orthographic delimiters and orthographic features. Orthographic delimiters are defined as characters other than alphabetic and digit characters (e.g. "," "*") and unusual typographic features (e.g. large amounts of white space). Line boundaries are the indices between delimiters. The beginning and end of a line are considered as two special delimiters. It is important to note that orthographic delimiters are domain-independent[1]. Orthographic features are style characteristics that are used to convey the role of text fragments, where text fragments can often be represented by orthographic tags. Table 1 details both delimiters and tags.

For orthographic pattern discovery, we first find the delimiters in a line and then use them to partition the line into a sequence of interleaved delimiters and text slots. The text in each slot is mapped into one of the lexical categories (or tags, see Table 1) and the line can then be expressed as a sequence of tags and delimiters (that is, as an orthographic pattern). Table 1 shows sample tags and delimiters used in building orthographic patterns.

Table 1. Orthographic tags and delimiters

	Notation	Descriptions
	<C>	UPPER CASE STRING
	<SC>	First Letters Of All Tokens Upper Case
Tag	<SS>	Sentence start string
	<L>	lower case string
	<N>	Numeric string, such as "1234"
	//	Big space between words
Delimter		(with position(int) of first char after the space)
	, ( )	Special char
	...	...

Orthographic discovery uses syntactic analysis to map each line into a tag sequence, identifies the most common tag sequence, and then treats that as the "orthographic pattern" for the region. PSLNL documents are structured in variety of ways, but the wide range of possible formatting strategies can be classified into a relatively small number of pattern classes: single-line patterns, multiple-line patterns, single-block patterns, multiple-block patterns and paragraph patterns. We use those five types of patterns to handle typical presentation styles for data in PSLNL documents. In brief, *line patterns* assume that an individual line contains a collection of data items related to a particular concept(from the schema), and that adjacent lines will contain similar collections of items. *Block patterns* assume that the items for as a particular concept may bespread over several lines, and thus relate a group of lines to a schema concept.

The complete algorithm for orthographic discovery is given in **step 1** of Figure 2. The goal is to find the pattern that best reflects the region. In this

---

[1] Orthographic delimiters depend on the representation of the document, not the kind of information that it contains. For example, the delimiters of HTML documents should be mainly based on HTML tags.

process, the first loop tries to identify all the possible general patterns[2] and replaces the found patterns with general tags (e.g. url, date). The second loop decomposes all of the lines in a region into a combination of text slots and delimiters (where general tags remain the same), then substitutes all the slots with orthographic tags. This gives a representation for each line in terms of a sequence of tags and delimiters. Finally, the most frequent orthographic pattern is discovered as the pattern with most frequency.

Table 2 describes the orthographic discovery process as follows: (1) identify names using dictionaries, dates and addresses via generic patterns; (2) identify boundaries by searching for delimiters; (3) partition into a sequence of interleaved delimiters and text slots; (4) map each text slot to its representative tag (lexical category); (5) reduce line tag pattern to $\{tags\} \cup \{delimiters\}+$; and (6) identify the most frequently-occurring pattern (P_m) in a region.

Table 2. Orthographic pattern discovery example

Processing	Result of processing
original text	Florence, Italy, August 30 - September 3, 2003
identify general pattern	Florence, Italy, <*Date*>
text slots and delimiters	s_1=Florence , s_2=Italy , s_3=<*Date*>
orthographic pattern	<SC>, <SC> , <*Date*>

5 Semantic Discovery

Discovery In the previous section, we identified the orthographic patterns for regions, where those patterns are combinations of tags and delimiters. These patterns provide a representation of the structure of data items in the region, but do not relate this to the final schema. Semantic discovery is the key step which relates the specific data to be extracted to the defined schema. Semantic discovery uses a collection of type-recognisers to identify the data types of individual data items (subconcept); these types are then matched against the schema to determine where data values should be placed.

A semantic pattern consists of data types and orthographic delimiters and describes its corresponding text. The pattern is derived according to user defined schema and the orthographic pattern discovered. For example, the semantic pattern "<*city*>, <*country*>, <*conferenceDate*>" describes the content of a textline better than its corresponding orthographic pattern "<SC>, <SC>, <Date>". The sample semantic pattern includes three types of data, namely city, country, and

---

[2] General patterns define classes of text phrases for different kinds of data. Examples of general patterns include date, URL, person (with title), address (mail or email), etc. The characteristics of general patterns are predictable by parsing the data orthographically and semantically.

conferenceDate, where those types come from the user defined schema of conference information.

The type recognisers include parsers to recognise well-structured text (i.e. general patterns) such as dates, email addresses and URLs, as well as dictionary based recognisers to deal with names of people, cities and countries. Recognition of proper names has been extensively studied and a number of schemes exist (e.g. [12]) that can be employed here. Note that we don't require tag patterns to match exactly, since we need to allow for the kinds of minor variation that occur in all "free form" text (e.g. a missing comma between a name and an address).If we find that a region has a mixture of tag patterns, we arbitrarily choose to examine only the sub-region with the most common tag pattern (P_m). Based on P_m and the dictionaries, we map each text slot to a sub-concept (sc) and derive concept/semantic pattern P_c. If we observe repeating concept patterns on each line in a sub-region, we assume that the sub-region is composed of multiple columns of a simple concept pattern.

A simplified algorithm for semantic pattern discovery is shown in Figure 2. We use an example of a "single line pattern" to describe the algorithm (which also forms the basis for other types of pattern discovery). In the initial stage of the semantic discovery process, there is no "meaningful" information available about the region. The information we require about the target semantic pattern P_c is contained in the user-provided schema and the dictionaries. Our goal is to infer and assign a concept to each slot (si). We decide between alternatives (if any) simply by choosing the one that occurs most frequently. Semantic pattern discovery is accomplished by a two-stage parsing process: horizontal and vertical stages.

In the horizontal stage, we match through all the temporary line patterns (P_k) with P_m. When P_k approximately[3] matches P_m, we parse all the corresponding text fragments of all the slots, and try to identify the text fragments via the dictionary. If we identify a certain slot s_i as concept c_i positively, we substitute the s_i with the c_i. For example, a region with title of "program committee" will expect data of person, organization, country and email. Also, P_m = <SC>//<SC>,<SC>23, and P_k = <SC>//<SC>,<C>23 (derived from data "T Y Lin San Jose State University, USA") approximately matches the P_m. After parsing the data, P_k is assigned as "<SC>//<$organization_¿$,<$country$>23" since "University" is a keyword of organization and "USA" is a country. In the end, "T Y Lin" is still ambiguous, and a <SC> still stands.

After the horizontal stage, each P_k that approximately matches with P_m now consists of orthographic tags, concepts and delimiters. As slots in the same orthographic position in the P_ks might have different concepts or orthographic tags, we parse a certain slot (i.e. $s_i|c_i$) through all the P_ks (vertically). Each slot is defined as follows: (1) the most frequent concept when some c_i exists; (2) the

---

[3] An approximate match is the state when P_m and P_k have same numbers of slots and delimiters, but differ only in the type of tags in some corresponding slots. For example, we consider "¡SC¿,¡SC¿" and "¡SC¿,¡C¿" to be an approximate match.

```
Input:    {t_i, r_i}, {tags}, {delimiters}, {general pattern}, {schema}, {dictionary}
Output:   the concept/semantic pattern P_c
begin
step 1:   foreach l ∈ r_i do
              if(exit general pattern(l))
                  identify and substitute them with corresponding tags;
              end;
          end;
          k := 1;
          foreach l ∈ r_i do
              decompose l into slots(s_i) and delimiters(d_i);
              S_k := s_1 d_1 s_2 d_2 ... d_{n_k-1} t_{n_k};
              k++;
          end;
          P_m := max_{freq}{P_1, P_2, ..., P_{|L|}} = t_1 d_1 t_2 d_2 ... d_{m-1} t_m;
step 2:   k = 1
          foreach l ∈ |L| do
              if(approx match(P_k, P_m))
                  match each slot s_i with the certain dictionary
                  substitute the identified slot s_i with concept c_i;
                  P_k := s_1|c_1 d_1 s_2|c_2 d_2 ... d_{m-1} s_m|c_m;
              end;
              k++;
          end;
          for i = 1 ... m do c'_i = max_{freq} s_i|c_i, l ∈ |L|; end;
          P_c := c'_1 d_1 c'_2 d_2 ... d_{m-1} c'_m;
end;
```

Fig. 2. Two-phase pattern discovery algorithm

most "likely" concept when no c_i exists[4]; and (3) "other information" when no other possible concept can be found.

After discovering pattern, P_c is defined as a sequence of concepts and delimiters. Therefore, each slot of a line can be identified by matching P_c and theine pattern. Generally, pattern matching is performed in textual order to locate more specific patterns before less specific ones. However, this is insufficient for data extraction because: (1) the purpose of pattern matching here is not just for the "matching", but for the "identification" of data items. One important task of text matching is the discovery of patterns that relate specific words and phrases. If a mismatch occurs, it will be necessary to analysis pattern and original text and perform a new match; (2) slots presented in the most common tag pattern P_m may be missing in a temporary line pattern P_k; (3) P_k may contains extras lots comparing to P_m; and (4) slots in P_k may not match slots in P_m,

---

[4] Suppose that s_j does not map to any concept and that the the semantic pattern (in Figure 2) P_c is expressed as $P_c = c'_1 d_1 c'_2 d_2 ... s_j ... d_{m-1} c'_m$. Let $C_{\lceil} = \bigcup_{\S=\infty}^{\updownarrow}\{J'_\S\}$ be the concepts defined currently, where $x \neq j$; and let C_∇ be the data types expected from the region, then s_j will be identified from " $C_\nabla - C_{\lceil}$".

such more or less specific (5) delimiters in P_k may not go with delimiters in P_m. Therefore, our approach is developed based on total and partial matching of P_m and P_k. Details refer to [8].

We have described a complete information extraction process so far through a simplified text case (i.e. single line pattern), however there are other more complex text formats to consider, namely multiple line pattern, single block pattern, multiple block pattern and paragraph pattern. Details refer to [8].

When no syntactic or semantic regularity can be identified, we must resort to using data-type recognisers to search for data items related to subconcepts of the schema. If no such data items can be identified or related meaningfully to the schema, we will simply store all of the data as the content of an ELEMENT in an XML document, or as a text field in a relational database.

6 Experiment

To measure the effectiveness of our 2PP approach, we have built a complete information extraction system and tested in on a sample of 178 PSLNL documents, containing around 800 regions. The system extracted 6500 data items on which our evaluation is carried out.

Evaluation consists of determining that the appropriate data items are extracted from regions. Standard precision, recall and F-measurement work well when a classifier can make a "clear decision" for all the cases to be classified. For example, in region decomposition, a line must be classified as one of 0, 1 or 2. Comparing with the "clear decision", data extraction is more complex. There are four cases to consider: (1) correct: data extracted and data expected are considered identical; (2) incorrect: data extracted and data expected are not identical; (3) partially correct: data extracted and data expected are not identical, but partial credit should still be given; and (4) missing: data that should have been extracted is missing. Let c, i, p and m denote the amounts of these four cases respectively. The precision ($\mathcal{P}_1$), recall ($\mathcal{R}_1$), error rate $\mathcal{E}\_rceil$ and F-measure ($\mathcal{F}_\beta$) for data extraction are then defined as:

$\mathcal{P}_1 = \frac{]+(\cdot \cdot \nabla \times \sqrt{)}}{]+)+\sqrt{}}$	$\mathcal{R}_1 = \frac{]+\sqrt{+)}}{]+)+\sqrt{+\mathfrak{x}}}$
$\mathcal{E}_1 = \frac{)+(\cdot \cdot \nabla \times \sqrt{)+\mathfrak{x}}}{]+)+\sqrt{+\mathfrak{x}}}$	$\mathcal{F}_\beta = \frac{(\beta^\in +\infty)\mathcal{PR}}{\beta^\in \mathcal{P}+\mathcal{R}} \sqsupseteq \langle]\nabla]\beta = \infty$

The data extraction experiment proceeded as follows: (1) according to our algorithms, we generate our output file called "Cfp.xml"; (2) we use regular expression to group data inside "Cfp.xml" by different types, such as conferencenames, start date, program committee, etc. Let $\times$ denote all the sets of data output, and Θ_i denote a set of data items of a type, thus $\times = \{\times_\infty, \times_\in \ldots \times_\backslash\}$; (3) we manually extract data items for the original document according to the same schema and group the extracted data by their types as well, denote as

$x' = \{x'_\infty, x'_\in \ldots x'_\{\}$; (4) we compared Θ_i and Θ'_i, and determined how many # correct, # incorrect, # parcorrect and # missing data items; and (5) we calculated ($\mathcal{P}_1$, $\mathcal{R}_1$, $\mathcal{E}_1$ and $\mathcal{F}_\beta$ using formulas defined above.

Table 3 provides a list of results related to several data types of different structure levels, such as conference name, dates about the conference, interesting topics, submission details for authors,etc. The table contains five tuples where each tuple refers to experiments we have conducted on the particular data items. The table indicates very promising results of the data extraction. (1) The system performs perfectly for general pattern representable information, such as date information. (2) The accuracy is fairly high for data which can not be described by general patterns but with certain well-defined orthographic features, such as "interesting topics". (3) The worst case is identifying information from plain text data, and the accuracy largely depends on region recognition, such as "submission details".

Table 3. Data extraction results

	Precision(%)	Recall(%)	F-measure(%)	Error Rate(%)
conference name	68.5	100	81.3	31.5
start date	100	100	100	0
end date	100	92.7	96.1	0
location	87.6	87.6	87.6	12.4
topics	84.3	100	94.5	15.7
submission details	72.1	80.8	76.2	34.5

7 Conclusion

This paper presented 2PP technique that extracts data without depending specific extraction rules. In particular, the core techniques of data extraction in our system are text pattern mining and text matching. In summary the system (1)collects orthographic, semantic and general pattern features; (2) learns all the possible regularities; (3) discovers orthographic patterns; (4) derives semantic patterns; and (5) utilizes the patterns back to the original region via pattern matching. Novelty of 2PP is that it does not rely on any pre-defined pattern, but rather discovers a pattern from a region and uses the discovered pattern in subsequent analysis of the region. This solution is independent from specific rules, and thus is flexible and adaptable. Experimental results indicate that the patterns produced lead to effective extraction of data items.

References

1. B. Adlberg. Nodose - A tool for semi-automatically extracting structured and semistructured data from text documents. In *SIGMOD'98, Proceedings ACM SIGMOD International Conference on Management of Data*, pages 283-294, Seattle, Washington, USA, June 1998. ACM.
2. A. Arasu and H. Garcia-Molina. Extracting structured data from web pages. In *Proceedings of the ACM SIGMOD, International Conference on Management of Data*, pages 337-348, San Diego, California, June 2003.
3. R. Baumgartner, S. Flesca, and G. Gottlob. Visual web information extraction with lixto. In *Proceedings of 27th International Conference on Very Large Data Bases*, pages 119-128, Roma, Italy, September 2001.
4. V. Crescenzi, G. Mecca, and P. Merialdo. Roadrunner: Towards automatic data extraction from large web sites. In *Proceedings of 27th International Conference on Very Large Data Bases*, pages 109-118, Roma, Italy, September 2001.
5. D. Freitag. Multistrategy learning for information extraction. In *Proceedings of 15th International Conference on Machine Learning*, pages 161-169, Madison, Wisconsin, USA, July 1998.
6. N. Kushmerick, D. S. Weld, and R. Doorenbos. Wrapper induction for information extraction. In *Proceedings of the Fifteenth International Joint Conference on Artificial Intelligence, IJCAI'97*, pages 729-737, Nagoya, Japan, August 1997.
7. L. Liu, C. Pu, and W. Han. Xwrap: An xml-enabled wrapper construction system for web information sources. In *ICDE 2000, In Proceedings of the 16th International conference on Data Engineering*, pages 611-621, San Diego, California, February 28-March 03 2000. IEEE Computer Society.
8. L. Ma. *Information Extraction from Unstructured Documents*. PhD thesis, School of Computer Science and Engineering, University of New South Wales, 2003.
9. L. Ma, J. Shepherd, and Y. Zhang. Extracting information from semistructured data. In *WAIM 2002, International Conference on Web-Age Information Management*, Beijing, China, August 2002.
10. L. Ma, J. Shepherd, and Y. Zhang. Enhancing text classification using synopses extraction. In *WISE 2003, 4th International Conference on Web Information Systems Engineering*, page 115 124, Roma, Italy, December 2003.
11. I. Muslea, S. Minton, and C. Knoblock. A hierarchical approach to wrapper induction. In O. Etzioni, J. P. Müller, and J. M. Bradshaw, editors, *Proceedings of the Third International Conference on Autonomous Agents (Agents'99)*, pages 190-197, Seattle, WA, USA, 1999.
12. 1N. Wacholder, Y. Ravin, and M. Choi. Disambiguation of proper names in text. In *Proceedings of Fifth Conference on Applied Natural Language Processing*, pages 202-208, Washington, DC, USA, 1997.

CRISOL: An Approach for Automatically Populating Semantic Web from Unstructured Text Collections

Roxana Danger[1], Rafael Berlanga[2], and José Ruíz-Shulcloper[3]

[1] Universidad de Oriente, Santiago de Cuba (Cuba)
[2] Universitat Jaume I, Castellón (España)
[3] Institute of Cybernetics, Mathematics and Physics, La Habana (Cuba)
roxana@csd.uo.edu.cu, berlanga@uji.es, recpat@icmf.inf.cu

Abstract. Currently, the main drawback for the development of the Semantic Web stems from the manual tagging of web pages according to a given ontology that conceptualizes its domain. This tasks is usually hard, even for experts, and it is prone to errors due to the different interpretations users can have about the same documents. In this paper we address the problem of automatically generating ontology instances starting from a collection of unstructured documents (e.g. plain texts, HTML pages, etc.). These instances will populate the Semantic Web that is described by the ontology. The proposed approach combines Information Extraction techniques, mainly entity recognition, information merging and Text Mining techniques. This approach has been successfully applied in the development of a Semantic Web for the Archaeology Research.

1. Introduction

The Semantic Web (SW) is intended to succeed the current web by creating knowledge objects that allow both users and programs to better exploit the web resources [1]. Usually, three components take part in the Semantic Web, namely: an ontology that conceptualizes the knowledge of the resources, a collection of documents annotated with the elements of the ontology, and software agents able to process the knowledge objects and to exchange results with other users or programs. As it can be notice, the usefulness of the SW depends on the availability of a large collection of semantically tagged resources that must be reliable and meaningful.

The main drawback in the current development of the SW arises from the manual annotation of resources, which makes difficult its scalability. This process is guided by the ontology of the domain, and it is usually performed by non expert users. In [2] it is shown how the ontology is of little help in classification tasks mainly because the ontology has been designed to facilitate automated reasoning.

As a consequence, automatic or even semi-automatic resource tagging will become a necessary and urgent task to scale up the contents of the SW.

In the literature we can find numerous techniques to automatically classifying documents according to a given taxonomy of topics. Some of these techniques have been successfully applied to integrating ontologies [3]. They could be also applied to

Definition 1. Let L be a logical language having a formal semantics in which inference rules can be expressed. An abstract ontology is a structure $O = (C, \leq_C, R, \sigma, \leq_R, IR)$ consisting of:
- two disjoint sets C and R whose elements are called concepts and relations, resp.,
- a partial order $\leq_C$ on C, called concept hierarchy or taxonomy,
- a function $\sigma: R \rightarrow C \times C$, called signature,
- a partial order $\leq_R$ on R where $r_1 \leq_R r_2$ implies $\sigma(r_1) \leq_{C \times C} \sigma(r_2)$, for $r_1, r_2 \in R$, called relation hierarchy,
- a set IR of inference rules expressed in the logical language L,
- the function $dom: R \rightarrow C$ with $dom(r) = \Pi_1(\sigma(r))$ gives the domain of r, whereas $range: R \rightarrow C$ with $range(r) = \Pi_2(\sigma(r))$ gives its range,
- and the function $dom_C: C \rightarrow 2^{|\gamma|}$ gives the domain of definition of each concept.

As an example, Figure 2 shows an ontology to describe the artifacts made by artists and where they are exhibited. Concepts are enclosed in both circles and boxes, depending on their domain (objects vs. values). Double line arrows represent the taxonomy relation $\leq_C$, single line arrows denote the different relationships between concepts, and finally doted line arrows represent the partial order $\leq_R$.

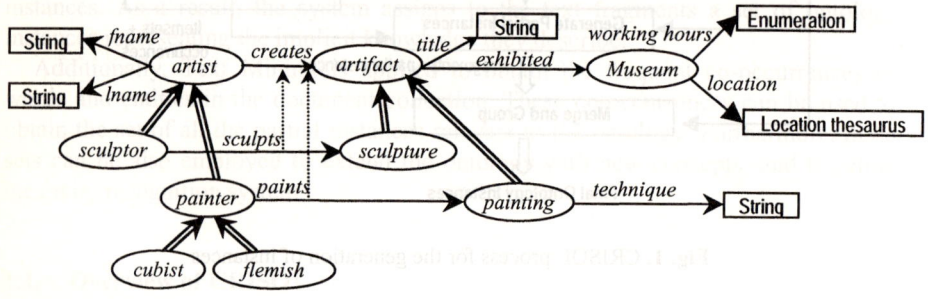

Fig. 2. Example of an ontology

Definition 2. We define an *instance related to the object o of the class c or simply an instance* to the set

$$I|_o^c = \{(o,r,o') / \exists r \in R, \sigma(r) = (c^*, c'),$$

$$o \in dom_c(c^*), o' \in dom_c(c'), c^* \leq_C c, \neg \exists r', c^* \leq_C dom(r') \leq_C c\}$$

In order to denote the instance associated with an instance o, we will use $I(o)$. Additionally, we will denote with $I|_o^c = \{(o,*,*)\}$ the empty instance of the class c.

Notice that an instance is a set of triples that represents the conceptual graph of the ontology similarly to RDF graphs. It can contain any relation inherited from the super-concepts of c whenever it does not override any relation of c.

Taking the previous example, the following sets are examples of instances:

$$I|_{o_1}^{cubist} = \{(o_1, artist.fname, "Pablo"), (o_1, artist.lname, "Picasso"),$$
$$(o_1, painter.paints, o_2), (o_1, painter.paints, o_3)\}$$
$$I|_{o_2}^{painting} = \{(o_2, painting.techniques, "Oil\ on\ canvas")\}$$
$$I|_{o_3}^{painting} = \{(o_3, painting.techniques, "Oil\ on\ canvas"), (o_3, artifact.exibited, o_4)\}$$
$$I|_{o_4}^{Museum} = \{(o_4, Museum.title, "Reina\ Sofia\ Museum"),$$
$$(o_4, Museum.workinghours, \{(9{:}00-14{:}00, 16{:}21{:}00)\})\}$$

Definition 3. We call a specialization of the instance $I|_o^c$ to the class c', $c \leq_C c'$, denoted by $I|_{o \to o'}^{c \to c'}$, to the instance

$$I|_{o'}^{c'} = \{(o', r, x) / (o, r, x) \in I|_o^c, \neg \exists r' \in R, r \leq_R r', dom(r) \leq_C c', range(r) = c_x,$$
$$x \in dom_C(c_x), o' \in dom_C(c')\} \cup \{(o', r', x') / (o, r, x) \in I|_o^c, r \leq_R r',$$
$$dom(r) \leq_C dom(r') \leq_C C', \neg \exists r'', r' \leq_R r'', dom(r') \leq_C dom(r'') \leq_C C,$$
$$range(r') = c_x, x \in dom(c_x)\}$$

Basically, this definition stays that an instance can be specialized by simply renaming the object with a name from the target class in all the instance's triples that can be used in the specialized class.

For example, the specialization of the instance

$$I|_o^{artist} = \{(o, artist.fname, "Pablo"), (o, artist.lname, "Picasso"),$$
$$(o, artist.creates, o_2), (o, artist.creates, o_3)\}$$

to the class *painter* is:

$$I|_{o'}^{painter} = I|_{o \to o'}^{artist \to painter} = \{(o', artist.fname, "Pablo"), (o', artist.lname, "Picasso"),$$
$$(o', painter.paints, o_2), (o', painter.paints, o_3)\}$$

Definition 4. We call an abstraction of the instance $I|_o^c$ to the class c', $c' \leq_C c$, denoted by $I|_{o \uparrow o'}^{c \uparrow c'}$, to the instance

$$I|_{o'}^{c'} = \{(o', r, x) / (o, r, x) \in I|_o^c, \exists r, c_x, dom(r) \leq_C c', range(r) = c_x, x \in dom(c_x)\} \cup$$
$$\{(o', r', x') / (o, r, x) \in I|_o^c, r' \leq_R r, C' \leq_C dom(r') \leq_C dom(r),$$
$$\neg \exists r'', r'' \leq_R r', C' \leq_C dom(r'') \leq_C dom(r'), range(r') = c_x, x' \in dom(c_x)\}$$

Similarly to the previous definition, we can obtain an abstract instance by selecting and renaming all the triples whose relation name can be abstracted to a relation of the target class c' and the instance's object.

For example, the abstraction of the instance $I|_{o_1}^{cubist}$ to the class painter is:

$$I|_{o'}^{painter} = I|_{o_1\uparrow o'}^{cubist \uparrow painter} = \{(o', artist.fname, "Pablo"),$$

$$(o', artist.lname, "Picasso"), (o', painter.paints, o_2),$$

$$(o', painter.paints, o_3)\}$$

Definition 5: We call union of the instances $I_1|_o^c$ and $I_2|_{o'}^{c'}$ and it is denoted by $I_1|_o^c \,\hat{\cup}\, I_2|_{o'}^{c'}$ to the set:

$$I_1|_o^c \,\hat{\cup}\, I_2|_{o'}^{c'} = \begin{cases} I_1|_o^c \cup I_2|_{o'}^{c'} & \text{if } I_1|_o^c \neq \{(o,*,*)\} \wedge I_2|_{o'}^{c'} \neq (o',*,*) \wedge (c \leq_c c' \vee c' \leq c) \\ I_1|_{o \to o'}^{c \to c'} & \text{if } I_2|_{o'}^{c'} = \{(o',*,*)\} \wedge c \leq_c c' \\ I_1|_o^c & \text{if } I_2|_{o'}^{c'} = \{(o',*,*)\} \wedge c' \leq_c c \\ I_2|_{o'}^{c'} & \text{if } I_1|_o^c = \{(o,*,*)\} \wedge c \leq_c c' \\ I_2|_{o' \to o}^{c' \to c} & \text{if } I_1|_o^c = \{(o',*,*)\} \wedge c' \leq_c c \\ \phi & \text{otherwise} \end{cases}$$

Definition 6: We call difference of the instances $I_1|_o^c$ and $I_2|_{o'}^{c'}$ and it is denoted by $I_1|_o^c \,\hat{-}\, I_2|_{o'}^{c'}$, to the set:

$$I_1|_o^c \,\hat{-}\, I_2|_{o'}^{c'} = \begin{cases} I_1|_o^c - I_2|_{o \uparrow o}^{c' \uparrow c} & \text{if } c \leq_c c' \\ I_1|_o^c - I_2|_{o' \to o}^{c' \to c} & \text{if } c' \leq_c c \\ \phi & \text{otherwise} \end{cases}$$

Definition 7: We call symmetric difference of the instances $I_1|_o^c$ and $I_2|_{o'}^{c'}$ and it is denoted by $I_1|_o^c \,\hat{\div}\, I_2|_{o'}^{c'}$ to the result of $I_1|_o^c \,\hat{-}\, I_2|_{o'}^{c'} \,\hat{\cup}\, I_2|_{o'}^{c'} \,\hat{-}\, I_1|_o^c$.

Definition 8: We say that two instances, $I_1|_o^c$ and $I_2|_{o'}^{c'}$ related with the objects o and o' of classes c and c', respectively, $c \leq_c c'$, are complementary if they satisfy at least one of the follow conditions:

1. $(\neg \exists (o', r, x), (o', r, x') \in I_1|_{o \to o'}^{c \to c'} \,\hat{\div}\, I_2|_{o'}^{c'}, x \neq x', r$ is biyective) and $(\neg \exists (o, r, x), (o', r', x') \in I_1|_o^c \,\hat{\cup}\, I_2|_{o'}^{c'}, r \leq_R r', r \neq r', (x \neq x'$ or $I(x)$ not complementary to $I(x')))$

2. at least one of the instances $I_1|_o^c$ or $I_2|_{o'}^{c'}$ is empty.

Two instances are complementary if they have not any contradiction between the values of his similar relations.

For example, the following instances are complementary:

$$I|_o^{artist} = \{(o, artist.fname, "Pablo"), (o, artist.lname, "Picasso")\}$$

$$I|_{o'}^{painter} = \{(o', painter.paints, o_2), (o', painter.paints, o_3)\}$$

However, $I|_o^{artist}$ is not complementary with $I|_{o'}^{sculptor} = \{(o', artist.lname, "Rodin")\}$. Notice that in this case the relation *artist.lname* is a biyective relations.

Definition 9: We say that two complementary instances $I_1|_o^c$ and $I_2|_{o'}^{c'}$ are unifiable in $I|_{o_u}^{c'} = I_1|_{o \to o_u}^{c \to c'} \hat{\cup} I_2|_{o' \to o_u}^{c' \to c'}$, $c \leq_C c'$.

For example, $I|_o^{artist}$ and $I|_{o'}^{painter}$ are unifiable, producing the following instance:

$$I|_{o_u}^{painter} = I_1|_{o \to o_u}^{artist \to painter} \hat{\cup} I_2|_{o' \to o_u}^{painter \to painter} = \{(o_u, artist.fname, "Pablo"),$$
$$(o_u, artist.lname, "Picasso"), (o_u, painter.paints, o_2), (o_u, painter.paints, o_3)\}$$

Definition 10: We say that two instances, $I_1|_o^c$ and $I_2|_{o'}^{c'}$ are aggregable in $I|_o^{c^*} = I_1|_{o \to o}^{c \to c^*} \cup \{(o, r, o'')\}$, if $\exists r \in R$, $\sigma(r) = (c^*, c'')$, $c \leq_C c^*$, $c'' \leq_C c'$, and o'' is the name of the instance $I|_{o''}^{c''} = I_2|_{o' \to o''}^{c' \to c''}$.

For example, $I|_o^{artist}$ and $I|_{o_2}^{painting}$ are aggregable in

$$I|_o^{painter} = I|_{o \to o}^{artist \to painter} \cup \{(o, painter.paints, o'')\} = \{(o, artist.fname, "Pablo"),$$
$$(o, artist.lname, "Picasso"), (o, painter.paints, o'')\}$$

where $I|_{o''}^{painting} = \{(o'', painting.techniques, "Oil on canvas")\}$

2.2 Extracting Instances from Texts

Although the previous concepts give the necessary base for the extraction of instances from a text, we need to add some constraints when merging instances to take into account their occurrences in the text.

Let T be a text fragment formed by the sequence of terms $(w_1, \ldots, w_n)$, which can be either words or extracted entities. We will denote with $I|_{o,[i,j]}^c$ to the instance described by the subsequence of terms between w_i and w_j ($j \geq i$).

In this context, two instances of the text T, $I_1|_{o,[i_1,j_1]}^c$ and $I_2|_{o',[i_2,j_2]}^{c'}$, with $c \leq_C c'$, are unifiable if they are complementary according to Definition 8, and there not exists any instance between them that can be a specialization, a generalization or an aggregation of any of them. In this case, the unification of both instances is the following one:

$$I\Big|_{o_u,[\min\{i_1,i_2\},\max\{j_1,j_2\}]}^{c'}, \text{ where } I\Big|_{o_u}^{c'} = I\Big|_o^c \stackrel{.}{\cup} I\Big|_{o'}^{c'}.$$

For example, given the following text:

> fname:Pablo lname:Picasso was a very famous painter, specifically he was an eminent cubist. In his paintings title:Woman and title:Guernica he used oil on canvas.

We extract the following instances:

$$I\Big|_{o_1,[1,7]}^{painter} = \{(o_1, artist.fname, "Pablo"), (o_1, artist.lname, "Picasso")\}$$

$$I\Big|_{o_2,[13,13]}^{cubist} = \{(o_2, *, *)\}$$

$$I\Big|_{o_3,[16,17]}^{painting} = \{(o_3, artifact.title, "Woman")\}$$

$$I\Big|_{o_4,[18,18]}^{atifact} = \{(o_4, artifact.title, "Guernica")\}$$

$$I\Big|_{o_5,[21,23]}^{painting} = \{(o_5, painting.techniques, "Oil on canvas")\}$$

According to the previous definition, the instances $I\Big|_{o_1,[1,7]}^{painter}$ and $I\Big|_{o_2,[13,13]}^{cubist}$ are complementary and they are unifiable in

$$I\Big|_{o_2,[1,7]}^{cubist} = \{(o_2, artist.fname, "Pablo"), (o_2, artist.lname, "Picasso")\}$$

Similarly, two instances are said to be aggregable in a text fragment T if there not exists any other instance that contains any attribute with the same type that the type of the aggregated object. Those instances are aggregable in the new instance

$$I\Big|_{o,[\min\{i_1,i_2\},\max\{j_1,j_2\}]}^{c^*}.$$

For example, the instance $I\Big|_{o_2,[1,13]}^{cubist}$ can aggregate $I\Big|_{o_3,[16,17]}^{painting}$ and $I\Big|_{o_4,[18,18]}^{atifact}$, being the result

$$I\Big|_{o_2,[1,23]}^{cubist} = \{(o_2, artist.fname, "Pablo"), (o_2, artist.lname, "Picasso"),$$

$$(o_2, painter.paints, o_3), (o_2, painter.paints, o_4)\}$$

Taking into account these definitions above, CRISOL generates the set of instances associated to each text fragment as follows. Firstly, it constructs all the possible partial instances with the concept, entity and relation names that appear in the text fragment. Then it tries to unify partial instances, substituting them by the unified ones. Finally, instances are aggregated to form complex instances.

2.3 Extracting Instances from Frequent Sets

As earlier mentioned, the sets of terms that frequently appear in a text collection can give us a better way to obtain the ontology instances since they represent sets of semantically related terms. To obtain the frequent sets of a text collection we have applied the text mining algorithm described in [7]. Basically, this algorithm computes the maximal frequent sets by recursively combining and extending the already computed sets (initially pairs of frequent sets), until a maximal set is formed. We have introduced a pruning strategy based on the ontology, so that frequent sets are valid only if the terms it contains are semantically related to each other according to the ontology. In this way, the algorithm only combines those frequent sets that can produce new valid frequent sets.

3. Experiments

In order to validate the proposed system, we have tested it over an ontology for the Archeological Research[1]. This ontology contains 164 concepts, 92 properties or relations, and 390 predefined literal values. We have selected 16 excavation reports from the *"Direcció General de Patrimoni Artistic de la Generalitat Valenciana"* [8].

The following table shows some examples of instances generated by the system. We have divided the results according to the three main parts of the ontology, namely: stratigraphy, artifacts and excavation methods referred to an archeological site.

Ontology Part	Maximal Frequent Set Examples	Instance Examples
Excavation	{@direction@, building} {@location@, @century@}	{(site1, is_of_type, "building"), (site1, have_direction, "east"), (site1, have_dating, "s. XI"), (site1, have_location, "Castellón")}
Artifacts	{ceramic, @century@} {ceramic, glaze, black}	{(ceramic1, have_dating, "s XV"), (ceramic1, have_glaze_color, "black")}
Stratigraphy	{stratum, @measure@, homogeneous, soil} {stratum, @direction@, rock} {stratum, @measure@, thickness}	{(stratum1, have_soil_structure, "homogeneous"), (stratum1, have_soil_type, "rock"), (stratum1, have_direction, "north"), (stratum1, have_thikness, "100m")}

As a result, generating instances directly from the texts has a poorer precision (number of correct instances versus the total number of generated instances) than getting them from the frequent sets. For the former we obtain a precision of 0.78 whereas for the latter is about 0.98. The former method mainly fails to build complex instances since some terms of the ontology are commonly used without actually referring to ontology concepts (e.g. quantifiers, colors, etc.), and therefore they interfere when aggregating partial instances. On the other hand, the main drawback of the second method is that the generated instances are usually small, and they do not take into account the infrequent information that refers to the ontology.

---

[1] http://tempus.dlsi.uji.es/TKBG/Arqueologia.rdfs

4. Conclusions

This work has presented a new approach to the automatic generation of ontology instances from a collection of unstructured documents named CRISOL. This approach is based on the combination of Information Extraction (IE) and Text Mining techniques. On the contrary to traditional IE systems, we do not define any grammar nor extraction rule to obtain the ontology instances. Instead, our system try to form correct partial instances by taking the words and entities appearing in the texts, and to combine them to form correct and complete instances.

Our experiments on a real-application ontology show that directly generating the instances from texts is very prone to errors. This is because some words have different meanings apart from those of the ontology, and therefore they produce lot of noise when merging partial instances. Much better results are obtained when using maximal frequent sets of words and entities. In this case, ontology instances can be directly generated from these frequent sets with very good precision.

As future work we plan to combine both approaches to incorporate infrequent information to the generated instances. Additionally, we will investigate how the automatic clustering of texts according to the ontology can improve the creation of very complex instances (for example a complete archeological site).

Acknowledgements

This work has been partially funded by the research project of the Spanish Program of Research CICYT TIC2002-04586-C03.

References

1. Berners-Lee, T., Hendler, J., Lassila, O. "The Semantic Web". Scientific American, 2001.
2. Forno, F., Farinetti, L., Mehan, S. "Can Data Mining Techniques Ease The Semantic Tagging Burden?", SWDB 2003, pp. 277-292, 2003.
3. Doan, A. et al. "Learning to match ontologies on the Semantic Web". VLDB Journal 12(4), pp. 303-319, 2003.
4. Appelt, D. "Introduction to Information Extraction", AI Communications 12, 1999.
5. Llidó, D.M., Berlanga, R., Aramburu, M.J. "Extracting Temporal References to Assign Document Event-Time Periods". DEXA 2001, pp. 62-71, 2001.
6. Maedche, A., Neumann, G. and Staab, S. "Bootstrapping an Ontology based Information Extraction System". Studies in Fuzziness and Soft Computing, Springer, 2001.
7. Danger, R.M., Berlanga, R., Ruiz-Shulcloper, J. "Text Mining using the Hierarchical Syntactical Structure of Documents". X Conferencia de la Asociación Española para la Inteligencia Artificial (CAEPIA 2003), pp. 139-14, 2003.
8. Dirección General del Patrimonio Artístico. http://www.cult.gva.es/dgpa/

Text Categorization by a Machine-Learning-Based Term Selection*

Javier Fernández, Elena Montañés, Irene Díaz,
José Ranilla, and Elías F. Combarro (University of Oviedo)

Artificial Intelligence Center - University of Oviedo (Spain)
ir@aic.uniovi.es

Abstract Term selection is one of the main tasks in Information Retrieval and Text Categorization. It has been traditionally carried out by statistical methods based on the frequency of appearance of the words in the documents. In this paper it is presented a method for extracting relevant words of a document by taking into account their linguistic information. These relevant words are obtained by a Machine Learning algorithm which takes manually selected words as training set. With the lexica obtained by this technique Text Categorization is performed by using Support Vector Machines. The results are compared with one of the most used method for term selection (based just on statistical information) and it is found the new method performs better and has the additional advantage of automatically selecting the filtering level.

1 Introduction

One of the main processes to be carried out in most Information Retrieval (IR) and Text Categorisation (TC) tasks is that of transforming documents into a form suitable for automatic processing. This chore can include the removal of tags, the elimination of non-informative words (like articles, conjunctions and other *stop-words*), the reduction of the remaining words to their common roots or stems and the final selection of the features which represent the documents [17].

The most widely used document representation consists of identifying each document with a numerical vector whose components measure the importance in the document of the different words. This representation is known as *bag of words* (see [13] or [7]).

However, it is infeasible the use of most algorithms if the documents are represented by a vector of all the words appearing in it. Even more, it is widely accepted among IR researchers [13], that only a small percentage of words are really useful for the classification. Additionally, a reduction of the vector size makes the computational time be decreased. Thus, it is interesting to study methods for the removal of non-informative features.

---
* The research reported in this paper has been supported in part under MCyT and Feder grant TIC2001-3579

This paper explores the hypothesis that incorporating linguistic knowledge into the representation task can lead to improvements in the overall performance of an IR task. Concretely it is studied the behavior of two Machine Learning (ML) systems when they are used to perform feature selection and the influence of taking into account different attributes (pos-tags, syntactical, statistical and term location data) for the examples used by the learning process. The different example characterizations and systems supplies the features (after applying the rules given by the classifier) with which TC is being performed.

TC is formally defined as the process of determining whether a document belongs or not to a category from a set of categories. Among the classifiers previously used for TC, we choose SVM, since they have been shown to offer better results [8] than other traditional text classifiers. The key of this performance is that they are good handlers of many features and they deal well with sparse example vectors.

The rest of the paper is organized as follows: Section 2 makes a brief survey of related work; in Section 3 the proposed system is described in detail; Sections 4 and 5 are respectively devoted to the description of the experiments and to the evaluation of the results; finally, in Section 6 some conclusions and further research are presented.

2 Related Work

An approach to feature reduction widely adopted in TC consists of ordering the words according to a measure of their relevance and selecting those with the highest score. For instance, one can count the total number of appearances (*tf*) of each word in the corpus and then keep only the most frequent ones. Information about the dispersion of the word in the corpus can also be considered with *tfidf* defined by $tfidf = tf \log(\frac{N}{df})$ where *tf* is, again, the frequency of the word, N is the number of documents in the corpus and *df* is the number of different documents in which the word appears.

If the corpus under study is a set of categorised documents (for example, in most TC problems) it can also be useful to take into account the distribution of a word over the different categories. This is the case of measures as *information gain* (IG) or *mutual information* [19]. Some authors have used these statistical measures together with some contextual information such as relative position and length of the words (see [2] and [16]). In addition, in [15], this kind of information is used to keyphrase extraction.

All these approaches have in common the use of mainly statistical information of the different words and their appearances in the documents. However, it seems clear that other factors, including (but not limited to) the syntactic categories for lemmas, the grammatical function of the words and the location in which they appear, may successfully determine the importance of the words in the documents. In fact, some of the authors cited above do use some lexical information, but usually only a quite restricted one.

There are some other related works. For example, pos-tagging information is used extensively in [14]. This work is focused on wordnet-hypernym-based representation. Other works use pos-tagging to distinguish between proper and common nouns [3]. Finally, linguistic generalization is is used for improving categorization in [6].

3 The System

The system proposed can be considered as a *supervised learning approach* to the task of feature reduction. The system is, in fact, a general inductive process which automatically builds a binary classifier to decide whether a word can be regarded as a descriptive term for a certain document or not. This inductive process starts from a set of attributes of a set of words that have been previously classified either as relevant or not by a domain expert. From these data the inductive process harvests the characteristics that a word should have in order to be classified as a descriptive term. Finally, text classification is made according to the lexica provides by the inductive process. The process is summed up in Figure 1

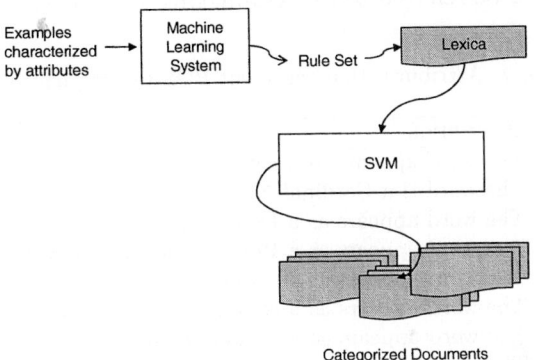

Figure 1. Scheme of the process of TC with the Machine-Learning-based Feature Selection

3.1 Term Selection Based on Machine Learning

The ML systems used are the last free version of C4.5-rules developed by J.R. Quinlan [10] and Arni-rules [11,12].

C4.5-rules is a well-known classifier which has been used before in TC and IR [1]. Arni-rules is a ML system based on a measure called *impurity level* [11] to estimate the quality of the rules. The process of building the decision tree is identical to that of C4.5 but using the *impurity level* instead of the uncertainty. However, to synthesize the final set of rules, Arni-rules takes from FAN [11] a set of heuristics as an alternative to the MDL (Minimum Description Length) of C4.5-rules. The result is a system which shows an accuracy higher than C4.5-rules in common ML problems and which produces less rules.

3.2 The Input

The training set consists of words manually classified as descriptive terms or not. Each word is represented by a set of attributes which provide linguistic information of such word in the context of each document under study. We will train each ML system with the same examples characterized by different combination of attributes to test the influence of each attribute group. Linguistic information is divided here into three different types:

- **P: POS-Tagging Information**: This group of attributes represents the lexical functions that a word can play in a document. This information is obtained by using Eric Brill's tagger [4]. It assigns one of the *part of speech* (POS) tags described in the *Penn Treebank* project [9] to each word appearing in a document.
  Once that all the text is tagged, we carry out a post-process in order to transform the tags in a series of attributes that can be represented with the habitual format of ML systems. Namely, POS-tagging information is represented by means of the 12 attributes shown in Table 1. This set of attributes will be referred to as POS-tagging attributes.

Table 1. Attributes that represent POS-tagging information

Name	Description
Conjunction	The word appears as a Coordinating Conjunction.
Number	The word is a Cardinal Number.
Determiner	The word appears as a Determiner.
Preposition	The word appears as a Preposition or a Subordinating Conjunction.
Adjective	The word appears as an Adjective.
Noun	The word appears as a Noun.
Predeterminer	The word appears as a Predeterminer.
Possessive	The word appears as a Possessive.
Pronoun	The word appears as a Pronoun.
Adverb	The word appears as an Adverb.
Verb	The word appears as a Verb.
Others	The word appears with no one of the previous tags.

For each of these attributes the value assigned to a certain word will be the number of times that the word has the corresponding tag in a document.
- **S: Syntactic Information**: It groups the attributes which represent the syntactic functions that a word can play in a document. This attributes are extracted from text with the AGFL tool ([18]). The AGFL system generates parsers from grammars and lexica. As for POS-tagging attributes, a postprocess to transform the *Syntactical Information* is carried out. In fact, *Syntactical Information* is represented by the five attributes showed in Table 2. This set of attributes is named *Syntactical Attributes*. These are also

Table 2. Attributes that codify the syntactical information

Name	Description
Subject	The word belongs to the Subject of a sentence of the document.
Object	The word belongs to the Object (Direct Complement) of a sentence of the document.
Object_i	The word belongs to the Indirect Object (Indirect Complement) of a sentence of the document.
Circumstantial	The word belongs to the Circumstantial Complement of a sentence of the document.
Predicate	The word belongs to the Predicate of a sentence of the document and doesn't carries out another syntactical function.

numerical attributes which store the number of times that a word carries out each one of that syntactical functions in a document.

- **T: Term location:** It includes information about the position of the word in the document (the word appears in the title, at the beginning of a phrase, at the end of a phrase, at the beginning of the document,...) The term location represents the position of a word within the phrase and the document in which it appears. It is clear that some words can be more informative than others because of their position in the text. For instance, a word appearing in the title tends to be more important than others that do not. Something similar happens to the words appearing at the beginning of the document (which is usually an outline of the rest) and at the end (which may represent a summary of what has been said).

In order to collect this information, we will say that a word is at the beginning of a document if it appears at least once in the first 30% of it and that a word is at the end of a document if it appears at least once in the last 30% of it. These thresholds have been empirically adjusted.

It is also taken into account the position of a word within the phrase to distinguish between the words at the beginning of such phrase and the rest. To this extent, it is considered that a word is at the beginning of a phrase if it appears at least once in the first 40% of it. It is additionaly important to differentiate the words appearing just before a verb and also those appearing in an inverted commas phrase, because the latter is a way to emphasize some text within a document.

The values of these attributes can be of two different types. Either we can assign to them a boolean value (true or false) or a numerical value (the number of times that the word appears in the corresponding location).

The document below belongs to Reuters collection. It is labelled by a domain expert. Italic words are considered as relevant for this document by the domain expert.

<DOCTRAIN> <TOPIC> <D> acq </D> </TOPIC>
<TITLE> LANDMARK *savings* LT; LSA COMPLETES OFFICE *sale* </TITLE>

<BODY> Landmark *Savings* Association said it completed the *sale* of its Whitehall, Pa., office, including *deposits* of about 31 mln *dlrs*, to Parkvale *savings* Association. Landmark said it realized a *gain* of about 1.1 mln *dlrs* on the *sale*. The *price* was not disclosed </BODY> </DOC>

From previous document a set of examples is extracted. Let us consider the vector associated to *savings*. The example is represented by the vector

$$< 0,0,0,0,0,2,0,0,0,0,0,0,0,2,0,0,0,0,1,2,2 >,$$

where the first component means the word appears 0 times as Conjunction in the document, the second one 0 times as Number, ..., the sixth means it appears 2 times as Noun and so on.

Each different word appearing in at least one document will constitute an example for the ML system. Consequently, the values of the attributes of a word in the different documents need to be aggregated. According to the results obtained in [5] we have aggregated the values by adding the values of the attributes if they have numerical values and by performing the "or" operation with them if they are boolean ones and then multiplying it (only if the attribute has a numerical value) by $\log(\frac{N}{df})$, where df is the number of documents in which the word appears and N is the total number of documents.

Hence, each word w is defined as $w = < w_1, w_2, ...w_n >$ when n is the number of aggregated attributes considered. Then each unit of text is represented by a set of POS tags, syntactical information and term location features from which the machine learning system will classify the term as relevant or not.

4 Description of the Experiments

The experiments have been conducted with documents of the Reuters-21578 and Ohsumed corpora[1].

There is no available example set of descriptive terms for these collections so that the training set has been extracted manually. As manually selecting the relevant words of a document is a complex task, we have not worked with all the documents neither of Reuters-21578 nor of Ohsumed.91. For this purpose, the experiments are performed with all the documents of the categories *Alum* and *Cocoa* of the Reuters-21578 corpus (selected because they are of intermediate size) and with a subset of the Ohsumed.91 collection formed by 60 documents of *C06* (one of the most representative categories of the collection).

As it was detailed above, the input to the ML systems is a set of training examples which has been generated from linguistic information of a set of documents. We have divided the linguistic information into three groups: POS-tagging (P), Syntactic (S) and Term-location (T) information. This last one at the same time has been treated either as a boolean or a numeric attribute.

---

[1] Reuters is located at:
http://www.daviddlewis.com/resources/estcollections/reuters21578/,
Ohsumed at http://trec.nist.gov/data/t9-filtering/.

The influence of word frequency in the extraction of informative words from a document is also taken into account as another attribute. We are interested in checking the influence of every set of attributes and in finding out which one offers the best results. Thus, each ML system (C4.5-rules or Arni-rules) is trained with each one of the 18 combinations of attributes of Table 3. Each experiment provides a set of rules whose application gives the lexica with which the collection is represented and then categorized. The performance of the term selection

Table 3. Different attribute combinations

Acronym	Combination of attributes
P-TNu-Tf	POS-tagging, Numerical Term Location, Tf
P-TNu	POS-tagging, Numerical Term Location
P-T-Tf	POS-tagging, Boolean Term Location, Tf
P-T	POS-tagging, Boolean Term Location
P-Tf	POS-tagging, Tf
P	POS-tagging
S-TNu-Tf	Syntactic, Numerical Term Location, Tf
S-TNu	Syntactic, Numerical Term Location
S-T-Tf	Syntactic, Boolean Term Location, Tf
S-T	Syntactic, Boolean Term Location
S-Tf	Syntactic, Tf
S	Syntactic
A-TNu-Tf	POS-tagging, Syntactic, Numerical Term Location, Tf
A-TNu	POS-tagging, Syntactic, Numerical Term Location
A-T-Tf	POS-tagging, Syntactic, Boolean Term Location, Tf
A-T	POS-tagging, Syntactic, Boolean Term Location
A-Tf	POS-tagging, Syntactic, Tf
A	POS-tagging, Syntactic

method itself with the different combinations are shown in [5] where in addition one can see that it is better to carry out stemming. Thus, here we perform text classification with the different sets of terms selected.

5 Results

The effectiveness of the classification is quantified with the F_1 measure, widely used in TC [19] and defined by

$$F_1 = \frac{1}{0.5\frac{1}{P} + 0.5\frac{1}{R}}$$

This measure gives equal significance to *precision* (P) and to *recall* (R). The former quantifies the percentage of documents that are correctly classified as belonging to the category while the latter quantifies the percentage of documents of the category that are correctly classified.

5.1 The Results

In this section we present the results obtained by SVM for the different vocabularies extracted with one of the two ML systems (C4.5-rules or Arni-rules) and with the examples characterized by one of the different combinations of attributes described above.

To compare our term selection method with the traditional ones we have classified Cocoa, Alum and C06 when the terms are selected according to the scoring measure. Table 4 shows the performance of this classification in terms of F_1 when $tfidf$ is used as scoring measure and the filtering level ranges from 20% to 98%. The best F_1 obtained for each collection is boldfaced.

Table 4. F_1 (in %) of SVM when $tfxidf$ is used as scoring measure for Alum, Cocoa and C06

Filtering Level	Alum	Cocoa	C06
20	48.28	88.89	61.95
40	51.85	88.89	61.87
60	50.00	88.89	61.22
80	55.17	88.89	61.28
85	55.17	88.89	61.51
90	**55.17**	88.89	61.63
95	53.33	**96.55**	59.63
98	48.28	88.89	**61.95**

In Table 5 we present the F_1 obtained in the experiment for the three studied categories with the different lexica.

If the proposed selection method is compared to the traditional one based on scoring the words with *tfidf* (which only consider statistical information) of Table 4, we can see that there exist at least one combination of attributes which provides a lexica improving the performance.

However, the system chose to perform feature selection has influence in the overall results mainly because of its stability with regard to the different collections. If the ML system is C4.5-rules, then the performance of our system is the best. For other choices of the parameters and classifying with Arni-rules the results are also better than those of the traditional measures for most filtering levels. Therefore, since the combination of attributes and the ML system which lead to the highest F_1 are sometimes different from one collection to another one, it is proposed an uniform choice of parameters which works well in all the collections. This choice consists of learning the features using $C4.5 - rules$ with the attribute combination $A - T - Tf$ characterizing the training examples.

Table 5. F_1 (in %) of the SVM when classifying with the lexica obtained with the different attribute sets. The values of F_1 higher than the one obtained with the best filtering level for $tf{\times}idf$ are boldfaced

	Arni-rules			C4.5-rules		
	Alum	Cocoa	C06	Alum	Cocoa	C06
P-TNu-Tf	50.00	88.89	61.67	**64.52**	**100.00**	60.63
P-TNu	50.00	88.89	**62.82**	**64.52**	**100.00**	60.09
P-T-Tf	**60.00**	88.89	**62.05**	60.00	**100.00**	61.96
P-T	**60.00**	88.89	61.78	60.00	**100.00**	61.10
P-Tf	**60.00**	88.89	61.62	60.00	60.00	**62.24**
P	50.00	88.89	61.53	60.00	60.00	61.77
S-TNu-Tf	50.00	**96.55**	**62.35**	60.00	**100.00**	**62.77**
S-TNu	**64.52**	**96.55**	**62.01**	60.00	**100.00**	**63.09**
S-T-Tf	50.00	88.89	**62.08**	**64.52**	63.15	61.48
S-T	**60.00**	**100.00**	**62.29**	**64.87**	**100.00**	61.92
S-Tf	55.17	88.89	61.56	**64.52**	**100.00**	61.84
S	50.00	**100.00**	61.20	**68.75**	50.00	**62.25**
A-TNu-Tf	**60.00**	88.89	**62.50**	60.00	**100.00**	**62.77**
A-TNu	**60.00**	**96.55**	61.64	60.00	**100.00**	**62.65**
A-T-Tf	**60.00**	88.89	**62.13**	60.00	**100.00**	**62.99**
A-T	**60.00**	**100.00**	61.92	60.00	**100.00**	**62.24**
A-Tf	55.17	88.89	61.76	60.00	60.00	61.70
A	55.17	88.89	**62.29**	60.00	60.00	61.60

6 Concluding Remarks

We have presented a system for the extraction of informative words from a document which takes into account POS-tags, syntactical, term location and statistical information. We have carried out experiments with 3 different categories of documents from 2 different collections with several sets of attributes and 2 different ML systems. Finally we have used the different obtained lexica to classify the collections with SVM.

If the parameters are properly chosen, the system proposed here reaches a performance higher than the obtained by the traditional filtering measure Additionally, with this system it is not necessary to select the filtering level since it is automatically obtained because the machine learning system automatically determines the terms representing the document set. This shows evidence in favor of the hypothesis that adding linguistic information to statistical data can help in the identification of informative words in a document.

However, some parameters must be study in depth to improve this methodology. For example, it is necessary to know which is the most appropriate number of examples to avoid overfitting and to explore the use of another systems to "learn" the rules used to select the lexica.

References

1. K. Aas and L. Eikvil. Text categorisation: A survey. Technical report, Norwegian Computing Center, 1999.
2. K. Barker and N. Cornacchia. Using noun phrase heads to extract document keyphrases. *Lecture Notes in Computer Science*, 1822:40–52, 2000.
3. R. Basili, A. Moschitti, and M.T. Pazienza. Language-sensitive text classification. In *Proceeding of RIAO-00, 6th International Conference "Recherche d'Information Assistee par Ordinateur"*, pages 331–343, Paris, FR, 2000.
4. E. Brill. *A Corpus-Based Approach to Language Learning*. PhD thesis, Philadelpha, PA, 1993.
5. J. Fernández, E. Montañés, I. Díaz, J. Ranilla, and E.F. Combarro. Extraction of document descriptive terms with a linguistic-based machine learning approach. In *To appear in LNCS (Proceedings of the ICCS 2004)*, Krakow, Poland, 2004.
6. A. Gelbukh, G. Sidorov, and A. Guzmán-Arenas. Use of a weighted topic hierarchy for document classification. *Lecture Notes in Artificial Intelligence*, 1692:130–135, 1999.
7. T. Joachims. Making large-scale support vector machine learning practical. In A. Smola, B. Scholkopf, C. Burges, editor, *Advances in Kernel Methods: Support Vector Machines*. MIT Press, Cambridge, MA, 1998.
8. T. Joachims. Text categorization with support vector machines: learning with many relevant features. In Claire Nédellec and Céline Rouveirol, editors, *Proceedings of ECML-98, 10th European Conference on Machine Learning*, number 1398, pages 137–142, Chemnitz, DE, 1998. Springer Verlag, Heidelberg, DE.
9. M.P. Marcus, B. Santorini, and M.A. Marcinkiewicz. Building a large annotated corpus of english: The penn treebank. *Computational Linguistics*, 19(2):313–330, 1994.
10. J.R. Quinlan. Constructing decision tree in c4.5. In *Programs of Machine Learning*, pages 17–26. Morgan Kaufman, 1993.
11. J. Ranilla and A. Bahamonde. Fan: Finding accurate inductions. *International Journal of Human Computer Studies*, 56(4):445–474, 2002.
12. J. Ranilla, O. Luaces, and A. Bahamonde. A heuristic for learning decision trees and pruning them into classification rules. *AICom (Artificial Intelligence Communication)*, 16(2):in press, 2003.
13. G. Salton and M.J. McGill. *An introduction to modern information retrieval*. McGraw-Hill, 1983.
14. S. Scott and S. Matwin. Text classification using WordNet hypernyms. In Sanda Harabagiu, editor, *Use of WordNet in Natural Language Processing Systems: Proceedings of the Conference*, pages 38–44. Association for Computational Linguistics, Somerset, New Jersey, 1998.
15. P. Turney. Coherent keyphrase extraction via web mining. In *IJCAI-03*, pages 434–439, 2003.
16. P.D. Turney. Learning algorithms for keyphrase extraction. *Information Retrieval*, 2(4):303–336, 2000.
17. C.J. Van-Rijsbergen, D.J. Harper, and M.F. Porter. The selection of good search terms. *Information Processing and Management*, 17:77–91, 1981.
18. E.J. Verbruggen, C.H.A Koster, C.F. Derksen, and J.I. Potjer. *Manual for the AGFL system version 2.0*. AGFL Grammar Work Lab, August 2001.
19. T. Yang and J.P. Pedersen. A comparative study on feature selection in text categorisation. In *Proceedings of ICML'97, 14th International Conference on Machine Learning*, pages 412–420, 1997.

Update Conscious Inverted Indexes for XML Queries in Relational Databases[*]

Dong-Kweon Hong[1] and Kweon-Yang Kim[2]

[1] Dept. of Computer Science, Keimyung University, South Korea
dkhong@kmu.ac.kr
[2] Dept. of Computer Engineering, Kyungil University, South Korea
kykim@kiu.ac.kr

Abstract. Recently, there have been some efforts to add XML full-text retrievals and XML updates into new standardization of XML queries. XML full-text retrievals play an important role in XML query languages. Unlike tables in the relational model, an XML document has a complex and unstructured nature. XML update is another core function that an XML query should have in order to be a full-fledged query language for XML documents. In this paper we propose an inverted index to support XML updates and XML full-text queries in relational environment. Performance comparisons exhibit that our approach maintains a comparable size of inverted indexes and it supports many full-text retrieval functions very well. Foremost our approach handles XML updates efficiently by removing cascading effects.

1 Introductions

With the wide spread of XML in internet applications several query languages including W3C XQuery have been proposed as a candidate standard XML query language [1]. Until now most specifications mention ways to retrieve information from XML documents. Recently, there have been some XML query standardization efforts to include XML full-text retrievals and XML updates [2, 3, 4, 5]. XML full-text retrievals play an important role in XML query languages. Unlike tables in the relational model, an XML document shows a complex and unstructured nature. To obtain information from unstructured XML documents, full-text retrieval queries are a much more convenient approach than regular structured queries. An XML update is another core function that an XML query should have to be a full-fledged query language for XML documents. In many applications an XML query should have the ability to update a part of XML document efficiently. A few XML native DBMS already announced their update capability of XML documents [6, 7]. The relational model has been used for more than 20 years and is still the most widely used one. There have been some active researches to store and retrieve XML documents in relational databases [8, 9, 10, 11, 12, 13]. Commercial products like Oracle, Microsoft SQL server

---

[*] This work was supported by grant number (R01-2003-000-10001-0) from the Basic Research Program of Korea Science & Engineering Foundations.

and IBM DB2 also support some form of XML data types for XML documents management. We believe that a relational model will evolve continuously in order to support many XML query functionalities [14]. In this paper we propose a relational schema for inverted indexes to support both of XML full-text retrievals and XML updates in the relation model. By using our table schema we can support diverse functions of XML full-text retrievals efficiently with minimal modifications of inverted indexes when updates of XML documents occur.

2 Related Work

Functions of XML queries continue to evolve. W3C XQuery also supports full-text retrievals as well as structural queries [2]. In some other XML queries they even include XML updates in their basic interfaces [5]. Much research on XML indexing for efficient XML search have been done actively and most can be classified as one of two approaches: a string-based approach such as Index Fabric [15] or a join-based one such as XISS [16]. XISS uses join operations to support tree traversals of the XML document and it uses a static numbering scheme to evaluate the parent-child relationships among elements in XML documents. Due to the static numbers of elements XISS incurs difficulties in maintaining indexing information when XML updates are occurring. Another join-based approach in the paper [10] uses binary table instead of a static numbering scheme. It has no limitations on XML updates, but is not a good one when the length of the search path is deep. In their approach the number of joins is proportional to the length of search path and join is the most time consuming operation when we deal with large XML documents.

Many of previously proposed indexing methods for structural queries on XML documents have also been applied to indexing methods for XML full-text retrievals [10]. Indexing methods of XML structural queries and inverted index methods of Information Retrievals have been combined to retrieve more precise results by supplying some forms of hierarchical path information [10, 11, 17]. When we use relational databases to manage XML documents many previous research results need to be presented as an efficient relation table schema. All of the hierarchical and structural information of an XML document should be expressed as a relation schema and XML queries need to be translated to SQL queries [10]. In this relational approach an efficient relational schema plays an important role to acquire high performances. Even though this relational approach might have some difficulties to express some functions XML queries it can utilize many full-bloomed existing capabilities of relation technologies [13, 19]. In the recent approach [17] path strings have maintained in relational table for containment operations and XPath operations. By adopting a string-based approach the approach [17] shows a very stable performance even when the depth of XML is very deep. But still it has used sequence numbers of keywords such as *start* and *end* attributes of the schema. This kind of static numbering scheme is a very serious impediment to XML updates because a little change of XML documents may incur changes of whole numbers of the XML documents.

3 Inverted Indexes for XML Update and Full-Text Retrievals

The inverted index that proposed in this paper accomplishes two main requirements of an XML query that are fast retrievals and efficient updates. Our approach efficiently supports XML structural and full-text retrieval queries and at the same time it immediately reflects frequent updates of XML documents into their inverted indexes.

3.1 Motivations

Based on our preliminary research results a string-based approach seems better than a join-based one when we manage an XML document with some depth. Static information such as a numbering scheme is not a proper choice when we consider XML updates. In addition a simple keyword search is not enough for XML queries. Functions of XML updates can handle addition, deletion and replacement of a part of XML documents. In this paper we assume that the interface of XML update functions are as in Table 1 based on XMLDB:initiative [5].

Table 1. Functions of XML updates in our approach

Functions	Meanings
insert(Element, ordno, XMLcontent)	Insert XMLcontent as *ordno*th child of Element
delete(Element)	Delete XML content that has *Element* as its root element
replace (old_element, new_element)	Replace *old_element* with *new_element*

3.2 XFTS

Our approach that is named as XFTS (XML Full-Text Search with update) maintains the following relational schema of a Table 2 to store inverted indexes to fulfill our goals. *XML_Document* table is a space for XML documents themselves. The other 3 tables are built to store inverted indexes for our XFTS. In the XFTS table *Location* is for storing structural information of XML document and *Element* is for storing information of elements and *Word* is for storing information for key words of XML documents. For simplicity we omit information on attributes of XML in our approach.

Table 2. Relational schema for XFTS inverted indexes

XML_Documents (<u>id</u>, docname, isidx, contents)
Location (<u>docid, pathid</u>, path, depth, path_cnt)
Element (<u>docid, eid</u>, name, sibord, pathid, key_count, value)
Word (word, position, depth, docid, eid, pathid)

Attribute *id* assigns a unique sequence number to each XML document in database and *docname* has the name of each XML document. In table *Location* attributes *do-*

cid, pathid are for identifying a path in an XML document. Attribute *path* is a string from a root element to a terminal element and *depth* represents the length of the path from root to terminal. For each path we maintain *path_cnt* to count the number of paths that have the same path string but are actually different paths. When we insert path strings into *Location* we use '~' as in the paper of [17].

In table *Element* attribute *sibord* is to support order related operations such as '//author/family[2]' of XQuery. In order to process '//author/family[2]' we are searching '~%/author~/family' from path column of *Location* and then are looking an element that has value 2 in *sibord* column in table *Element*. And attribute *value* saves the full context of an element. Attribute *key_count* stores a distinct number of keyword in the contents of an element. This column is very useful when we are looking for an element that contains only a specific key word. No other key word is allowed in it. For example, if we are looking for elements that contain only 'cs department' in them, then elements that contain 'The cs department', 'cs .. cs department' or 'cs department .. department' should be selected as search results. These contents contain 'cs' and 'department' and their *key_count* is 2.

Attribute *word* in table *Word* is for saving key words. When we extract key words from XML documents we remove all kinds of stop words. Attribute *position* represent a relative position of a key word in element contents. This information is very useful when we measure the distance among key words[18]. Attribute *depth* is useful for finding elements which have search key words in their direct children rather than in their descendants.

1. Exact key word containment operation (tight containment [2]) by using value and key_count.

```
//keyword='semistructured data'
SELECT E.DOCID, E.EID
FROM LOCATION L, ELEMENT E
WHERE L.PATH LIKE '~%/keyword'
AND E.VALUE LIKE '%semistructured data%' AND E.KEY_COUNT = 2
AND L.DOCID = E.DOCID AND L.PATHID = E.PATHID;
```

Fig. 1. Translation of tight containment query to SQL

Many other XML queries can be translated to SQL in similar ways. Due to space limitations many other translations can not be presented here.

3.3 Updates of XML Documents

Several inverted index approaches have been published but none have seriously considered XML updates. If a part of XML document is changed, the entire inverted index related to the XML document should be rebuilt in previous results [10 - 13]. In the research of XISS [16] they reserved some number intervals in their numbering scheme for a few possible addition or deletions of elements. However, their approach only can handle some limited number of XML updates operations.

In our XFTS, XML updates can be processed very efficiently. When a part of an XML document is changed we only need to change only a small part of inverted index.

3.3.1 Updates of Contents in an Element.

Adding a key word or deleting an existing one involves quite similar procedures. Hence we only take a look at the procedures of insertion here. Changing the contents of an element is the simplest one because it does not change the structure of the XML document.

3.3.2 Insertion of XML Content as a Child of an Existing XML Document.

Operation *insert(Element, ordno, XMLcontent)* inserts *XMLcontent as an ordno*th child of *Element*. Insertion of an XML contents into an existing XML document changes the structure of the XML document. The structural changes of XML make us to add new path strings to the inverted index. If the newly generated path string is already in *Location* table attribute *path_cnt* is just incremented by 1. In Fig. 2 we explain the procedure to add new path string that generated by inserting the XML contents, <FAMILY>Hong</FAMILY>, into existing books.xml as fifth child of the element <AUTHOR>.

```
/ 1. Check the existence of newly generated path string /
SELECT PATH_CNT INTO L_PATH_CNT
FROM LOCATION
WHERE PATH = '~/books~/book~/author~/family';
/ 2. in case there already exists the same string    /
UPDATE LOCATION(PATH_CNT) SET PATH_CNT = PATH_CNT + 1
WHERE PATH = '~/books~/book~/author~/family';
/ 3. updates elements order
UPDATE ELEMENT(SIBORD) SET SIBORD = SIBORD + 1
WHERE PATH LIKE '~%/books~/book~/author' AND SIBORD > 4;
/    Key word insert will be followed /
```

Fig. 2. Procedure to add XML contents to XML document

3.3.3 Deletion of a Part of XML.

Operation *delete(Element)* deletes an XML content rooted *Element*. When we delete a part of XML we specify the root element of contents to be deleted and the subtree rooted by supplied element is deleted. In our approach we use a trigger mechanism to delete all elements in the subtree. After deleting the subtree the related path string should be removed from the inverted index. And *path_cnt* and *sibord* need to be updated properly. The general procedure of deletion is similar to insertion. As shown by the procedures, we only need to update a small fraction of the inverted index to reflect XML updates.

4 Analysis and Performance Evaluations

In order to analyze the performance of our XFTS we compared its performance with previous approaches. In our comparison we used Oracle 9i, Java 1.4.2, and JDOM API to extract key word and structural information from XML documents and to save the extracted information. The system that runs the database server is a dual CPU system with Pentium3 1.2GHz and has 1.5GB main memory. In our experiments we have used 3 kinds of XML documents in Table 3.

Table 3. XML documents used in our experiments

document	type	no. of files	total size(MB)	avg. depth
Shakespeare's work	Real	37	7.53	5.95
DBLP	Real	1	50.3	4.00
Auction	Synthetic	1	115.5	7.02

4.1 XML Queries in Our Experiments

In our experiments we have used several XML queries to retrieve information from XML documents of Table 4. Those query syntax are basically based on W3C XQuery specifications [1, 2]. We tried to select some representative XML queries that can describe the characteristics of XML full-text queries [2]. In order to compare several approaches in the same conditions we set our experiments to return element identification number rather than document ID.

Table 4. XML queries in our experiments

	XML queries		XML queries
QS1	contains(text(), 'XML')	QS2	/PLAY/TITLE/'The Comedy of Errors'
QS3	/PLAY/ACT/SCENE/SPEECH/SPEAKER/'DUKE SOLINUS'		
QS4	//SPEAKER='AEGEON'	QS5	//TITLE/'ACT'
QS6	//ACT//SPEECH/SPEAKER= 'KING JOHN'	QS7	//SCENE/*/LINE/'love'
QD1	contains(text(), 'SQL')	QA1	contains(text(), 'pencil')
QD2	/DBLP/ARTICLE/TITLE/'SQL Reunion'	QA2	/SITE/REGIONS/ASI
QD3	//AUTHOR='Frank Manola'	QA3	//name='preventions'
QD4	//INPROCEEDINGS/TITLE/'Dynamite'	QA4	//item/payment/'Personal check'

We measured 3 kinds of performance metrics in order to analyze the performance of our approach.

1. Spaces of inverted index and index creation time
2. XML full-text query response time by using queries of Table 4

3. Portions of inverted indexes to be changed in order to reflect XML document updates. For convenience we named the one in the paper of D. Florescu [10] as I_INDEX approach, the one of C. Zhang [11] as C_INDEX approach.

4.2 Creation of Inverted Indexes

Table 5 shows the size of inverted indexes of 3 approaches.

Table 5. The size of inverted indexes (MB)

	I_INDEX	C_INDEX	XFTS_INDEX
Shakespeare's work	101	13	21
DBLP	429	78	110
Auction	3000	243	373

4.3 Response Times of XML Full-Text Queries

The average response times of queries in Table 4 has been measured. We have done the experiments 5 times and measured their average response times. In Fig. 3 we observe that the query performance of our XFTS is comparable to I_INDEX approaches.

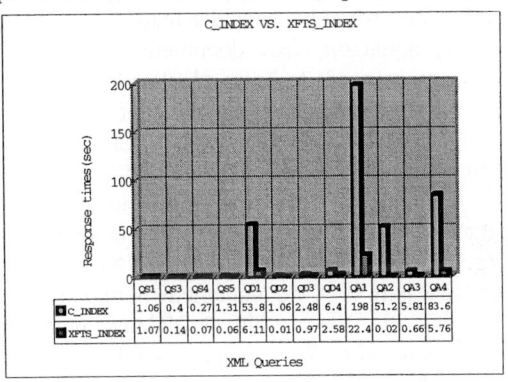

Fig. 3. Comparison of C_INDEX vs. XFTS

4.4 Relationships with the Depth of XML Documents

In Fig. 4 we have compared C_INDEX and XFTS_INDEX to see the effects of the depth of a XML documents. C_INDEX is a join-based approach so that its response time increases with the depth of the XML document. While XFTS_INDEX is a string-based approach it is insensitive to the length of XML document but a little sensitive to the number of results.

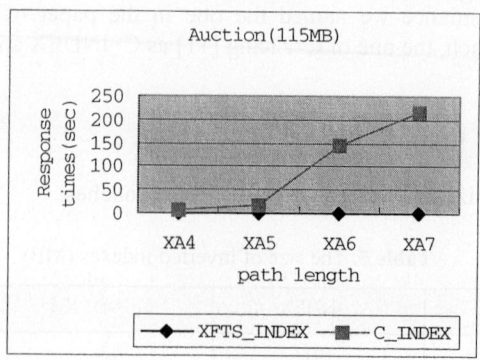

Fig. 4. Effects of path length for Auctions (large size)

4.5 Effects of XML Documents Update

As we observe from the previous experiments, the string-based approach shows more stable performance than the join-based one when we are dealing with large size of XML documents. However, many string-based approaches suffer from maintaining hierarchical information of XML by using a numbering scheme. A numbering scheme could be a good choice only when we consider read only XML documents. If we use a numbering scheme for updatable XML documents all of the information related to the updated XML document needs to be recalculated and all these new information should be updated to inverted indexes. If we consider incorporating XML update capability into our XML queries we have to devise a way to update inverted indexes at very low cost. If you adopt a numbering scheme and a deletion or insertion of XML contents happens all numbers after insertion or deletion point should be recalculated and properly propagated to the inverted index. That is a very critical problem, especially for very large size of XML documents. I_INDEX also uses a numbering scheme. In that case if a part of XML document is updated, all word numbers and element numbers locating after the insertion or deletion point should be recalculated and updated to the inverted index. We call it a cascading effect. Say that the number of records to be updated or inserted for new XML contents as N(T) and the total number of words and elements in an original XML document as N(O). Those numbers can be expresses as follows:

$N(T) = No\_of\_path + No\_of\_word + No\_of\_element + No\_of\_sibling$

$N(O) = total\_no\_of\_word + total\_no\_of\_element$, (In general $N(O) \gg N(T)$)

The average number of records to be updated or inserted to reflect an insertion of XML contents into the existing XML document is $N(T) + 1/2 N(O)$. Due to cascading effects, a 1/2 N(O) number of records need to be updated or inserted into the inverted index. In XFTS, however, there are no cascading effects. When we delete a part of XML contents from an XML document similar analysis results can be obtained.

5   Conclusions

Until now most XML query specifications mention the ways to retrieve information from XML documents. Recently, some efforts add XML full-text retrievals and XML updates into a new standardization for XML queries. XML full-text retrievals play an important role in XML query languages. Unlike tables in a relation model, an XML document shows a complex and unstructured nature. We believe that when we attempt to obtain some information from unstructured XML documents a full-text retrieval query is a more convenient approach than a regular structured query. XML update is another core function that an XML query requires. In many applications an XML query should have the ability to update a part of XML document efficiently. A few XML native DBMS already announce their update capability for XML documents. The XFTS inverted index that is proposed in this paper accomplishes two main requirements that seems to conflict with each other. First, our approach efficiently supports XML structural and full-text retrieval queries. Secondly, it can synchronize its inverted index with frequent updates of XML documents. Our approach is a string-based approach and it is better than a join-based one when we manage an XML document with some depth. And static information such as a numbering scheme is not used to support XML updates efficiently. Performance comparisons exhibit that XFTS maintains a comparable size of inverted indexes and it supports many full-text retrieval functions well. It also shows a stable retrieval performance, especially for a large size of XML documents. Most importantly, our XFTS handles XML updates efficiently by removing cascading effects.

References

1. XQuery 1.0: An XML Query Language W3C Working Draft 12 Nov 2003. http://www.w3.org/TR/Query.
2. XQuery and XPath Full-Text Requirements W3C Working Draft 02 May 2003. http://www.w3.org/TR/xquery-full-text-requirementsxQuery
3. I. Tatarinov, Z. Ives, A. Halevy, D. Weld, "Updating XML" in Proceedings of ACM SIGMOD May Santa Barbara, CA 2001.
4. Bluestream Database Software Corp.'s XStreamDB. http://www.bluestream.com/XStreamDB
5. XML:DB Andreas Laux and Lars Martin. XUpdate Working Draft-2000-0914. http://www.xmldb.org
6. Excelon from ODI: http://www.oid.com/excelon
7. Tamino from SoftwareAG: http://www.software.con/tamino
8. J. Shanmugasundaram, J. Kienan, E. Shekita, C. Fan, John Funderburk,"Querying XML views of Relational Data" in Proceedings of the 27th VLDB Conference 2001.
9. J. Shanmugasundaram, E. Shekita, R. Barr, M. Carey, B.Lindsay, H. Pirahesh, B. Reinwald, " Efficiently Publishing Relational Data as XML Documents" in Proceedings of the 26th VLDB conference 2000.
10. D. Florescu, D. Kossmann, and I. Manolescu, "Integrating keyword search into XML query processing"   WWW9/Computer Networks, 33(1-6) 2000.
11. C. Zhang, J. Naughton, D. DeWitt, Q. Luo, G. Lohman, "On supporting Containment Queries in Relational Database Management Systems" in Proceedings of ACM SIGMOD, May Santa Barbara, CA 2001.

12. I. Tatarinov, S. Viglas, K.Bayer, J. Shanmugasundaram, E. Shekita, C. Zhang, "Storing and Querying Ordered XML Using a Relational Database System" in Proceedings of ACM SIGMOD 2002.
13. J. Shanmugasundaram, K. Tufte, G. He, C. Zhang, D. DeWitt, and J. "Relational Databases for querying XML documents: Limitations and Opportunities" in Proceedings of the 25th VLDB Conferences, Edinburgh, Scotland, 1999.
14. International Organization for Standardization(ISO), "Information Technology - Database Languages - SQL - Part 14: XML Related Specification(SQL/XML). Standard No. ISO/IEC 9075-14, 2003.
15. B. Copper, N. Sample, M. Franklin, G. Hjaltason, and M. Shadmon, "A Fast index for Semistructured Data" in Proceedings of the 27th VLDB Conference, Roma, Italy,2001.
16. Q. Li and Bongki Moon, "Indexing and Querying XML Data for Regular Path Expression" in Proceedings of the 27th VLDB Conference, pp 361-370 Roma, Italy, 2001.
17. M. Yoshikawa, T. Amagasa, T. Shimura, and S. Uemura, "XRel: A Path-Based Approach to storage and retrieval of XML documents using Relational Databases" in ACM Transactions on Internet Technology, vol 1, No. 1, August 2001, pp 110-141.
18. Jan-Macro Bremer, Michael Gertz.: XQuery/IR: Integrating XML Document and Data Retrieval. Proceedings of the 5th International Workshop on the Web and Databases.(2002) 1-6
19. N.Fuhr, K.Grossjohann, "XIRQL: An extension of XQL for information Retrieval" in Proceedings of SIGIR 2001.

A Selective Key-Oriented XML Index for the Index Selection Problem in XDBMS

Beda Christoph Hammerschmidt, Martin Kempa[1], and Volker Linnemann

Institut für Informationssysteme
Universität zu Lübeck
Ratzeburger Allee 160, D-23538 Lübeck, Germany
{bchammer,kempa,linnemann}@ifis.uni-luebeck.de
http://www.ifis.uni-luebeck.de

Abstract. In relational database management systems indexes are used to accelerate specific queries. The selection of indexes is an important task when tuning a database which is performed by a database administrator or an index propagation tool which suggests a set of suitable indexes. In this paper we introduce a new index approach, called key-oriented XML index (KeyX), that uses specific XML element or attribute values as keys referencing arbitrary nodes in the XML data. KeyX is selective to specific queries avoiding efforts spent for elements which are never queried. This concept reduces memory consumption and unproductive index updates.
We transfer the Index Selection Problem (ISP) to XDBMS. Applying the ISP, a workload of database operations is analyzed and a set of selective indexes that minimizes the total execution time for the workload is suggested. Because the workload is analyzed periodically and suitable indexes are created or dropped automatically our implementation of KeyX guarantees high performance over the total life time of a database.

1 Introduction

The Extensible Markup Language (XML) is designed to become the standard data format for exchanging information in the Internet. The increasing usage of XML data by web applications in electronic commerce for instance demands the connection between XML technology and database management systems, because the latter provide a fast, robust, and application independent way of storing and accessing data.
In recent years the functionality of (object-)relational database management systems was extended by supporting XML data [12,19,16]. In contrast to these *XML enabled database systems* a new paradigm called *native XML database management systems* (XDBMS) [6,20] was introduced to manage XML data exclusively. Therefore an XML database system stores the XML data persistently in its native form, avoiding a costly transformation into relations and vice versa. Queries are usually expressed using an XML related query language like XQuery

---
[1] Current address: software design & management, Carl-Wery-Str. 42, D-81739 München, Germany.

[22] or XPath [24]. Most XML query languages use path expressions which describe a navigation path through the semistructured XML data. Therefore the efficient execution of path expressions is an important task in XDBMS.

In relational databases indexes are used to reduce the execution time of frequently occurring queries. In this case, an index is a data structure optimized for fast retrievals of a given key reducing the access to the physical layer of the database. An inevitable side effect of indexes is that they consume additional space and every modification (insert, update, delete) of an indexed column requires a costly update of the involved index structure. Thus not every column is worth to be indexed. In RDBMS indexes and index structures are well-understood and widely used.

Indexes and index structures for XDBMS or semistructured data are still an important and active research topic in recent years. Several structures have been proposed to speed up query execution on XML data. One common approach is to restrict the search to only relevant portions of the XML data by utilizing a *structural summary* [14, 15, 3]. A structural summary records all paths of the stored XML data from the root. These index structures in XDBMS differ significantly from indexes in RDBMS. Instead of accelerating specific queries very efficiently they try to improve the evaluation of path expressions in general. This leads to large memory consumption and exhaustive navigation for partial matching path queries. In contrast to indexes in RDBMS where indexes are selected by the database administrator, structural summaries are permanently enabled.

Our Contributions. In this paper we introduce a new selective index structure, called key oriented XML index (**KeyX**), which accelerates specific path and predicate queries very efficiently. In contrast to structural summaries KeyX indexes only relevant parts of the XML Data. Therefore not every modification of the XML data leads to a costly index update.

- **Query Support:** KeyX supports pure path queries (/book/author), queries with a predicate (/book/author[.='Dan']) , range queries (/book[.year <2003]) and queries with the self-or-descendant axis (//name). The indexes for all these queries use the same data structure, so we do not need different techniques to support the different query types.
- **Multi-key Indexes:** Queries with multiple keys ([author='Jim' AND year<2003]) are supported using a multi-key index (similar to multicolumn indexes in relational databases). This is an important feature which most XML index approaches ignore.
- **Key Value - Return Value Discrimination:** Our index is built upon specific element or attribute values which we call *keys*. The return value of the query is a reference to one ore more nodes in the XML data and may differ from the key. Thus KeyX avoids costly navigations in the XML data if the key of a predicate-query is not the returned element (e.g. /book/title[../author= 'Jim']).

- **Schemaless Data:** Our approach is capable to support XML data without known DTD or XML Schema which is an important demand for XDBMS. In schemaless XML data element types may appear or disappear during the lifetime of the database. This is the reason why it is impossible to define indexes in advance. This is a significant difference to schema based approaches like [9], *sidetables* in IBM's *XML-Extender* [12] or indexes in the native XDBMS *Tamino* [20].
- **Index Selection Problem:** Last but not least the KeyX approach supports the tuning of a database for specific queries by applying solutions of the well-known Index Selection Problem from the relational world to XDBMS.Up to our knowledge this is done for the first time. A solution of the Index Selection Problem tries to find an optimal index configuration for a database instance and a given workload of query and update operations. Our implementation analyzes the logged workload periodically and updates the optimal index configuration automatically. On this account the underlying native XDBMS becomes adaptive.

The remainder of this paper is organized as follows: in Section 2, we survey related work summarizing the state of the art in the field of XML database indexes. Our key-oriented XML index approach KeyX is introduced in Section 3. The Index Selection Problem in general and how it is transferred to XML data and KeyX is described in Section 4. In Section 5 we present details of the KeyX implementation. With an outlook on future work in Section 6 we conclude the paper.

2 Related Work

In this section we introduce recent approaches for indexing XML data. The survey begins with techniques which accelerate queries with a predicate, sometimes called *key queries* or *value queries*, and proceeds with concepts dealing with path expressions, named *pure path queries* or *navigational queries*.

Key-Oriented Index Techniques: Accelerating value queries for XML data by information retrieval techniques is one popular proposal. But adopting approaches like signatures, inverted lists or tries means a full text search over the whole document without paying attention to the given document structure.

A more sophisticated approach is presented by *SEQL (Search Engine Query Language)* [18], managing an additional inverted list for the element names. Nevertheless, because SEQL regards XML data as a text document as well and not as a tree of nodes, it returns text positions instead of nodes.

The *Index Fabric* [5] is a balanced tree structure storing the encoded paths from the root to each node and its values. The structure is tailored to answer queries starting from the document root. For replying to local path queries the selective *Refined Path* index is proposed, which has to be manually preselected by the database administrator. As described in [5] range queries cannot be executed upon multi-key indexes as all keys are concatenated to one atomic artificial key.

The *Value Index* of the *Lore* project [14] is a selective index for element values. As the path to the elements is ignored the value index cannot distinguish between elements with the same name but different paths (e.g. author of a book vs. author of an article).

Pure-Path-Oriented Index Techniques: *XASR (extended Access Support Relation)* [7] is a general index structure containing the parent-child relation and the preceding-following relation of the nodes in the database. The structure is originally designed for XML data stored in relational database systems. Because path expressions can express more complex queries than covered by the parent-child and preceding-following relations the evaluation of a path expression implies several join operations in general.

Strong DataGuides [14, 15] provide a general index structure to accelerate path expressions starting at the root by a structural summary. A DataGuide is a non-selective index covering all occurring paths in the XML data. A DataGuide can be larger than the original XML data if its structure is irregular. Queries with the self-or-descendant axis or wildcards cannot be performed efficiently as the whole DataGuide has to be evaluated.

Table 1. Comparison of different XML index approaches

	Sel	PPQ	SKQ	RQ	DQ	WQ	MKQ	K≠V	Nav
Raw Paths (Index Fabric)	⊖	⊕	⊕	⊖	⊖	⊖	⊖	⊖	–
Refined Paths (Index Fabric)	⊕	⊕	⊕	⊖[3]	⊕	⊖	⊕	⊕	–
Value Index (Lore)	⊕[2]	⊖	⊕[1]	⊖[1]	⊖[1]	⊕	⊖	⊖	–
Strong Data Guide (Lore)	⊖	⊕	⊖	⊖	⊖	⊖	⊖	⊖	$O(n)$
APEX	⊕	⊕	⊖	⊖	⊕	⊕	⊖	⊖	$O(n)$
XASR	⊖	⊕	⊕	⊕	⊕	⊕	⊖	⊖	$O(n)$
T-Index	⊕	⊕	⊖	⊖	⊕	⊕	⊖	⊖	–
KeyX	⊕	⊕	⊕	⊕	⊕	⊕	⊕	⊕	–

⊕: feature supported, ⊖: feature not directly supported
Sel: index is selective and optimizes frequent specific queries
PPQ: pure path query (e.g. /dblp/inproceedings/author)
SKQ: single-key query (e.g. /dblp/book/author[.='Suciu'])
MKQ: multi-key query (e.g. /dblp/book[author='Suciu' AND year=2004])
RQ: range query (e.g. /dblp/article/year[.<2004])
DQ: descendant query (e.g. //title)
WQ: wildcard query (e.g. /dblp/*/title)
K≠V: return value does not have to be the key value (reduces navigation)
Nav: navigation complexity in index structure (n is length of query)

The *Adaptive Path Index (APEX)* [3] is an extension of DataGuides consisting of two structures: a graph G_{APEX} (with the structural summary) and a tree of hashtables H_{APEX} representing the incoming path to nodes of G_{APEX}. H_{APEX} is a selective index optimized for frequent queries. Like Strong DataGuides APEX requires a navigation in the index structure when evaluating the query.

The *Template Index (T-index)* [17] can be regarded as another enhancement of DataGuides enabling the acceleration of local path expressions and path expressions with wildcards. T-indexes can grow polynomially in the size of the database.

We collect the characteristics of the surveyed index approaches in Table 1.

The comparison shows that most indexes do not support all query types, e.g. all structural summaries do not support a predicate in a query. The column *Sel* identifies if an index is selective to specific queries. If not, the Index Selection Problem cannot be applied. The column *Nav* states whether further navigation in the index structure is required when evaluating a query. $O(n)$ means linear complexity in the length of the query whereas '-' identifies that no additional navigation process is required. K$\neq$V identifies whether an index structure differentiates between the indexed keys and the return values (e.g. indexing of all books of given author).

3 KeyX: Key-Oriented XML Indexes

The example in Figure 1 introduces the XML data used in this paper. It is a semistructured representation of publications, consisting of books and articles. The left side provides a textual representation while the right side shows the corresponding DOM tree [23]. The text nodes of the elements are omitted to keep the DOM-tree readable.

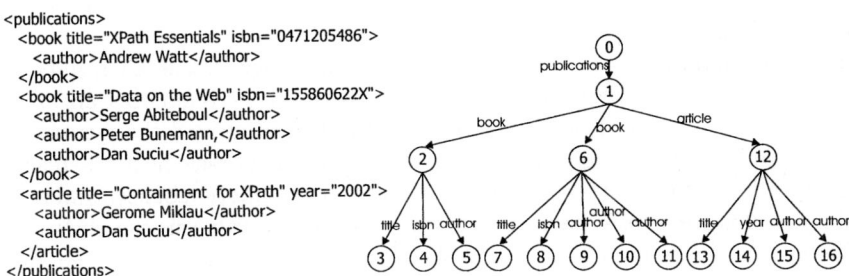

Fig. 1. Example of XML data and DOM representation

One of the fundamental concepts of XML query languages like XPath [24] and XQuery [22] are path expressions to access the tree-like structure of XML data. In our notion we define *simple path expressions* as path expressions without predicates containing the axes *self, parent, child, descendant, ancestor, attribute* and *wildcards*. Based on the definition of simple path expressions we define *general path expressions* which may include one or more predicates. Predicates are

---

[1] Provided if the path has exactly one step.
[2] Provided, but elements with same name but different paths are not distinguishable.
[3] Range queries are supported as single-key queries, but not as multi-key query.

used to compare the values of elements or attributes with a given constant value by the boolean operators $=, \neq, \leq$ or $\geq$. Predicates are enclosed in square brackets and may be combined by boolean operations. A path expression is *absolute* if it starts with /. The set of all absolute path expressions is denoted by P. A more formal definition of path expressions in KeyX can be found in [10].

For instance, the following absolute path expressions can be expressed upon the sample XML data. We denote our examples in the abbreviated syntax of XPath as specified in [24] to keep the presentation readable.

- $p_1 = /publications/article[year > X]$
  With expression p_1 we can find all articles published after X.
- $p_2 = /publications/book[author = "X"]$
  Path p_2 selects all book nodes of a given Author X.
- $p_3 = /publications/ * [author = "X"]$
  Path p_3 selects all book and article nodes of a given Author X.
- $p_4 = /publications/article[author = "X" and year > Y]$
  Path p_4 selects all article nodes by a given author X and year Y (two keys).
- $p_5 = /publications/article$
  With the pure path expression p_5 we select all articles without further predicate.

The Key-Oriented XML Index KeyX: Our approach uses the values of elements or attributes which are accessed by a specific path expression as *key values*. For query p_1 these are the values of all year elements of articles. The path expression may also contain axes like *descendant*(//) and *wildcards*(*); therefore it is possible to keep both the authors of books and articles in one index structure as example p_3 shows. The keys are extracted from the XML data by evaluating the *key paths* of a query. All keys are kept in a tree structure to gain logarithmic key retrieval time.

Each key references one ore more corresponding nodes in the XML data. For instance, the key '2004' in the index structure for p_1 references all articles which are written in 2004. In most queries the key value and the return value are different: in p_2 the keys are the values of the author-element whereas the return values are the corresponding books. The discrimination of keys and return values avoids the costly navigation from a key to the value in the XML data. This can easily be seen in Figure 2 showing the index structure i_{p_2} for query p_2. Note that this index is selective for queries p_2: the key 'Dan Suciu' in the index structure references the book he wrote but not his article. For queries containing more than one key our KeyX approach offers *multi-key indexes* for the best performance. Query p_4 contains the two keys author and year. A multi-key index in KeyX is constructed like in RDBMS: the index's tree structure is ordered by a first key (e.g. author), the values of this keys are indexes which are built upon the next key (year) and so on. In example p_4 we have a tree consisting of trees; the second tree's values reference the corresponding nodes in the XML data.

Pure path oriented queries are queries with a path expression but without any predicate. An example for this query type is p_5. Pure path oriented queries can easily be supported by KeyX if we interpret the whole path as a key and store it in an index dedicated to pure path oriented queries only. In p_5 the

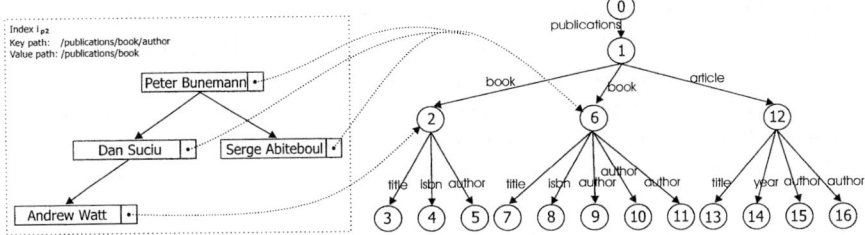

Fig. 2. Established index i_{p_2} for query p_2

path expression /publications/article is one key and returns references to all article nodes instantly.

When executing a query the query optimizer of our implementation looks for indexes which correspond to the query. This is done by comparing the key paths and the value path of the query and the index structure. If a suitable index is found the query can be executed without navigating the XML data: the key of the predicate is extracted and looked up in the index structure. The XML nodes which are referenced by the key are the return values of the query. If there is no suitable index the query has to be evaluated conventionally by the XPath engine of the underlying native XDBMS. Apart from the accelerated execution it makes no difference if the query is evaluated using an index or not as both approaches return the same result.

Definition: KeyX index specification
Formally a *key-oriented XML index specification* i is defined as a pair $i = (k, v)$ where k is a list of absolute simple path expressions, referring to the key nodes, and $v \in S$ is a simple path to the value nodes. The set of all index specifications is denoted by I.

For Instance, a suitable index for accelerating path expression p_3 is
$i_{p_3} = ([/publications/*/author], /publications/*)$.

4 Index Selection Problem Applied to KeyX Indexes

Relational ISP: In this section we introduce the *NP*-complete *Index Selection Problem* (ISP) which is well known in the relational world. The ISP selects a *set of indexes* (called *index configuration*) which is optimal for a given workload of database operations. A constraint is that the space of all realized indexes must not exceed a predefined limit. In this vein the ISP is comparable to the knapsack problem and inherently computationally difficult [4]. Details and formal definitions of the ISP can be found in [1][4] for instance.

We show that the ISP can be applied to XML data if the definition of the problem is adapted and a selective index structure like KeyX is used. Today, all important relational database manufacturers offer index tuning or index propagation tools, proving the relevance of the ISP. Examples include the *Microsoft Index Tuning Wizard* (a.k.a *Autoindex selection tool*) [2], IBMs *DB2 Advisor* [21] for the DB2 Universal Database and the *Index Tuning Wizard* for the Oracle database. But in contrast to all these systems that work in the design phase of the database requiring a database administrator we want our KeyX implementation to update indexes automatically depending on the typical load of the database. Thus we memorize all database operations that occur in a given time period in a bag called *workload W*. We distinguish between querying and modifying operations because the first propagate an index while the latter reduce the index's profit by requiring maintenance expenses.

The paths to the keys and the return value of each path expression of a database operation $o \in W$ define a set of *index candidates*. The *index candidates* are defined as a function $ican : P \to \mathcal{P}(I)$ returning a set including all possible indexes for a given path expression $p \in P$. This is done by combining and permuting all key nodes.

$$ican(p) = \{([k_1, k_2, \ldots, k_m], value(p)) \mid k_j \in key(p) \land$$
$$1 \le j \le m \land 1 \le m \le |key(p)|\}$$

The functions $value(p)$ and $key(p)$ extract the path to the value nodes respectively the paths to the key nodes from a path expression p. Index candidates may reduce the execution time of a querying database operation. To consider the whole workload W we need to regard the index candidates of all database operations $o \in W$. This is the union of all index candidates called the *total index candidate set TIC*.

$$TIC = \bigcup_{o \in W} ican(o) = \{i_1, i_2, \ldots, i_l\} \text{ with } i_j \in I \text{ and } 1 \le j \le l$$

TIC consists of all indexes which may be relevant for the workload W. As most of these indexes are dropped during ISP calculation, we call them candidates. Index candidates are virtual and not yet realized in the database.

Please notice that the number of index candidates grows exponentially with the number of keys of a path expression. Heuristics to decrease the computational expense have to start at this point by reducing the number of index candidates.

An *index configuration c* points out which indexes $\in TIC$ are activated when executing the workload W. The set of all possible index configurations is denoted by $CONF$. Because every combination of active indexes leads to a different index configuration it is obvious that $|CONF| = 2^{|TIC|}$ which reveals the inherent complexity of the ISP.

The *Index Selection Problem* looks for the best index configuration $c_{solution} \in CONF$. The workload is executed for each index configuration while the one with minimal costs (execution time for all $o \in W$) is memorized.

$$c_{solution} = \min_{c \in CONF} \left[\sum_{op \in W} cost_{time}(op, c) \right],$$
$$cost_{space}(c_{solution}) \le maxspace$$

Configurations which exceed a given space limit $maxspace$ are dropped. The evaluation of a given configuration is performed by the query optimizer and relies on the following cost function with o a database operation and c a configuration $\in CONF$:

$$cost_{time}(o,c) = \begin{cases} cost_{time}(path(o), best(path(o),c)) & \text{if } type(o) = query \\ \sum_{i \in \mathit{aff}(path(o),c)} cost_{time}(path(o), i_i) & \text{if } type(o) \in \{insert, \\ & update, delete\} \end{cases}$$

$path(o)$ denotes the path in o, $type(o) \in \{query, insert, update, delete\}$ is the type of o. A query operation is served by the best index $best(path(o),c))$ that is available in the current index configuration. Other indexes which may accelerate the query less than the best index can be ignored as it suffices to serve the query by one index. On the other hand, operations that modify the database lead to an update of all affected indexes in the configuration and therefore to a higher total execution time. Affected indexes are indentified by the function $\mathit{aff}(o,c)$.

As not all indexes of a configuration are established the query optimizer has to estimate their costs by determining the amount of relevant keys n in the XML data. As an index has logarithmic complexity we can use a simple cost model to determine the query execution time $cost_{time} = \alpha\ log(n) + \beta$, with α and β being system dependent constants which are determined automatically by test runs.

Queries without a suitable index in the configuration are executed conventionally and the real execution time of the underlying XDBMS is measured. Analog to the time costs we have a function in the query optimizer which estimates the storage costs of all selected indexes in an index configuration.

5 Implementation

In order to evaluate our approach we set up a testing environment with the general architecture illustrated in Figure 3. The system consists of two main components: the XML database management system extended by KeyX indexes and the index selection tool. Our KeyX index enabled XDBMS [8] contains the three subcomponents *data storage*, *index storage* and *query optimizer*. The

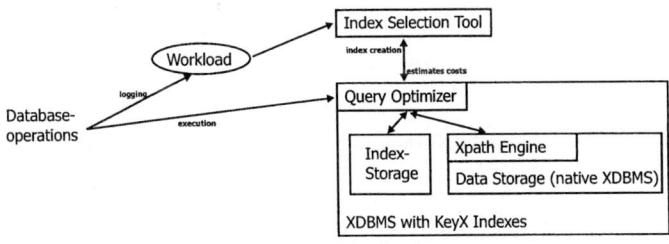

Fig. 3. Architecture of prototypical system

data storage, which stores the XML data persistently, is realized by the native XDBMS Infonyte DB [13] providing an embedded XPath query engine. The query optimizer examines the path expression to be evaluated and checks if a suitable index exists in the index storage.

The index selection tool is called periodically and finds a good index configuration for a given workload by using ranking heuristics. For the heuristic H_{rank} we calculate the profit of each index candidate and choose the most profitable ones until the space restriction is reached. The heuristic H_{div} ranks the indexes by the quotient $\frac{profit}{spacecosts}$.

The ISP tool communicates with the query optimizer to determine the evaluation costs of a given path expression and an assumed index configuration. After calculating an optimal index configuration the index selection tool triggers the creation of this index configuration passed to the index storage.

In order do determine the quality of our index selection tool we set up a scenario with 24 different database operations. The ratio of querying and modifying operation differs in 2 workloads: W_1 contains only queries whereas W_2 has 33% modifying operations requiring the index to be updated. The indexes and their profits for the workloads W_1 and W_2 are shown in Table 2. The optimal solution would suggest 8 indexes with a space consumption of 28.3MB. A space restriction of 10 MB prevents all indexes from being realized. We calculated an exact solution of the ISP with exponential complexity by analyzing all configurations. Because this scenario consists of only 8 index candidates and small workloads this can still be done in acceptable time.

Table 2. Characteristics of the index candidates (n: number of keys, k number of return values, d: space consumption in kilobytes, p_i profit of workload W_i)

	n	k	d	p_1	p_2	p_1/d	p_2/d
I_1	1,088	1,337	60.2	248.3	233.4	4.125	3.877
I_2	11,057	50,035	975.8	481.8	456.4	0.494	0.468
I_3	1,004	1,004	53.2	1,016.1	1,001.2	19.100	18.820
I_4	122,305	305,806	8,317.2	411.3	390.6	0.049	0.047
I_5	41	1,337	15.1	548.6	454.1	36.331	30.073
I_6	147,668	151,268	7,862.4	567.9	552.2	0.072	0.070
I_7	51	30,806	3,060.3	1,136.3	824.5	0.371	0.269
I_8	150,264	150,264	7,964.0	1,546.4	1,530.6	0.194	0.192
Σ			28,307.6				

A comparison between the gained profits of the exact solution and both heuristics H_{rank} and H_{div} is presented in Table 3.

Table 3. Comparison of exact solution and heuristics H_{rank} and H_{div} (p_Σ: total profit, d_Σ: total space consumption)

	Exact			H_{rank}			H_{div}		
	selected Indices	p_Σ	d_Σ	selected Indices	p_Σ	d_Σ	selected Indices	p_Σ	d_Σ
W_1	I_1,I_2,I_3,I_5,I_8	3,841.2	9,068.3	I_8,I_3,I_5,I_2,I_1	3,841.2	9,068.3	I_5,I_3,I_1,I_2,I_7	3,431.1	4,164.6
W_2	I_1,I_2,I_3,I_5,I_8	3,675.7	9,068.3	I_8,I_3,I_2,I_5,I_1	3,675.7	9,068.3	I_5,I_3,I_1,I_2,I_7	2,969.6	4,164.6

Exhaustive performance measurements comparing the query execution time of KeyX and implementations of the Strong DataGuide [14, 15], Index Fabrics Raw and Refined Path [5] and APEX [3] can be found in [11].

6 Concluding Remarks

In this paper, we proposed the – to our knowledge new – idea of facing the Index Selection Problem for XML database management systems with a new selective index structure called KeyX. Traditional XML index structures found in the literature define general structure summaries accelerating path expressions to a very limited extent only. In contrast our approach introduces a selective index improving a multitude of queries very efficiently. Our idea has been prototypically implemented on top of a native XDBMS including a new query optimizer and a separate index selection tool. The implementation has been successfully evaluated with some example data. Ongoing and future work extends our approach to more general path expressions integrating full text search (LIKE operator) and queries with regular expressions (MATCH operator).

Acknowledgments

The authors would like to thank Timm Gehrmann and Alexander Pfalzgraf for implementing wide parts of KeyX within the scope of their theses in computer science.

References

1. Alberto Caprara, Matteo Fischetti, and Dario Maio. Exact and approximate algorithms for the index selection problem in physical database design. *IEEE Transactions on Knowledge and Data Engineering*, 7(6):955–967, December 1995.
2. Surajit Chaudhuri and Vivek R. Narasayya. An efficient cost-driven index selection tool for microsoft sql server. In *VLDB'97, Proceedings of 23rd International Conference on Very Large Data Bases, August 25-29, 1997, Athens, Greece*. Morgan Kaufmann, 1997.
3. Chin-Wan Chung, Jun-Ki Min, and Kyuseok Shim. Apex: an adaptive path index for xml data. In *SIGMOD 2002, Proceedings of the 2002 ACM SIGMOD International Conference on Management of Data, Madison, Wisconsin, USA*, pages 121–132. ACM Press, 2002.
4. Douglas Comer. The difficulty of optimum index selection. *ACM Transactions on Database Systems*, 3(4):440–445, December 1978.
5. Brian F. Cooper, Neal Sample, Michael J. Franklin, Gísli R. Hjaltason, and Moshe Shadmon. A fast index for semistructured data. In *Proceedings of 27th International Conference on Very Large Data Bases*, Roma, Italy, September 11-14 2001. Morgan Kaufmann.
6. T. Fiebig, S. Helmer, C. Kanne, G. Moerkotte, J. Neumann, R. Schiele, and T. Westmann. Anatomy of a native xml base management system. In *The VLDB Journal*, volume 11, pages 292–314, 2002.

7. T. Fiebig and G. Moerkotte. Evaluating queries on structure with extended access support relations. In *Informal Proceedings WebDB*, pages 41–46, Dallas, Texas, 2000.
8. Timm Gehrmann and Alexander Pfalzgraf. Indizierung von schemalosen xml-dokumenten anhand von xpath-anfragen. Bachelor thesis, Institute for Information Systems, University of Lübeck, 2004.
9. Zhimao Guo, Zhengchuan Xu, Shuigeng Zhou, Aoying Zhou, and Ming Li. Index selection for efficient xml path expression processing. In *ER2003 Workshops, 22nd International Conference on Conceptual Modeling, Chicago, Illinois, USA, 13 October 2003*, 2003.
10. Beda C. Hammerschmidt, Martin Kempa, and Volker Linnemann. On the index selection problem applied to key oriented xml indexes. Technical report, A-04-09, Institute of Information Systems, University of Lübeck, 2004.
11. Beda C. Hammerschmidt, Martin Kempa, and Volker Linnemann. Keyx: a selective key-oriented xml index for native xml databases. submitted for publication.
12. IBM Corporation. IBM DB2 XML Extender. URL: http://www-3.ibm.com/software/data/db2/extenders/xmlext/.
13. Infonyte GmbH. Infonyte DB. URL: http://www.infonyte.com, 2003.
14. J. McHugh, S. Abiteboul, R. Goldman, D. Quass, and J. Widom. Lore: A database managment system for semistructured data. *SIGMOD Record*, 26(3), 1997.
15. J. McHugh, J. Widom, S. Abiteboul, Q. Luo, and A. Rajamaran. Indexing semistructured data. Technical report, Stanford University, 1998. Computer Science Department.
16. Microsoft Corporation. SQL Server 2000 Web Services Toolkit, 2002. URL: http://www.microsoft.com/sql/techinfo/xml/default.asp.
17. Tova Milo and Dan Suciu. Index structures for path expressions. In *Proceedings of Database Theory - ICDT '99, 7th International Conference*, volume 1540 of *Lecture Notes in Computer Science*, pages 277–295, Jerusalem, Israel, January 10-12 1999. Springer.
18. J. F. Naughton, D. J. DeWitt, D. Maier, A. Aboulnaga, J. Chen, L. Galanis, J. Kang, R. Krishnamurthy, Q. Luo, N.n Prakash, R. Ramamurthy, J. Shanmugasundaram, F. Tian, K. Tufte, S. Viglas, Y. Wang, C. Zhang, B. Jackson, A. Gupta, and R. Chen. The niagara internet query system. *IEEE Data Engineering Bulletin*, 24(2):27–33, June 2001.
19. Oracle XML DB. URL: http://otn.oracle.com/tech/xml/xmldb/index.html.
20. Harald Schöning. Tamino - a dbms designed for xml. In *Proceedings of the 17th International Conference on Data Engineering*, pages 149–154, Heidelberg, Germany, April 2-6 2001. IEEE Computer Society.
21. G. Valentin, M. Zuliani, and D. C. Zilio. Db2 advisor: An optimizer smart enough to recommend its own indexes. In *Proceedings of the 16th International Conference on Data Engineering, 28 Feb. - 3 Mar., 2000, San Diego, USA*. IEEE Computer Society, 2000.
22. W3C. An XML Query Language (XQuery). URL: http://www.w3.org/TR/xquery.
23. W3C. Document Object Model (DOM). URL: http://www.w3.org/DOM.
24. W3C. XML Path Language (XPath). URL: http://www.w3.org/TR/xpath.

SUCXENT: An Efficient Path-Based Approach to Store and Query XML Documents

Sandeep Prakash[1], Sourav S. Bhowmick[1], and Sanjay Madria[2]

[1] School of Computer Engineering Nanyang Technological University, Singapore
[2] Department of Computer Science, University of Missouri-Rolla
Rolla, MO 65409, USA
assourav@ntu.edu.sg, madrias@umr.edu

Abstract. This paper describes SUCXENT, a novel system for the storage and querying of XML data using a relational database system (RDBMS). The relational schema proposed under SUCXENT does not require the knowledge of the DTDs of the XML documents being stored. In this approach we store only the leaf nodes and their text values together with their ancestor list. Doing so will eliminate θ ($<$ or $>$)-joins to answer XPath-expression based queries. θ-joins account for a major performance bottleneck in current approaches for storing XML data in an RDBMS. We also compare the performance of our system to two existing approaches for relational storage of XML documents, XRel and XParent, to demonstrate the effectiveness of our approach. We show that our system performs significantly better than XRel and XParent in terms of insertion, extraction and querying of XML documents.

1 Introduction

The eXtensible Markup Language (XML) is quickly becoming popular for exchanging and representing data over the Internet. An important question is what is the best way of storing XML documents since the performance of the underlying storage representation has a significant impact on query processing efficiency. The relational storage approach has gained popularity due to the simplicity, stability, and expressiveness of relational databases. In this paper we present SUCXENT (**S**chema **U**nconcious **XML** **En**abled System - pronounced "succinct"), an efficient path-based approach for the storage and querying of XML documents using an RDBMS. Relational storage approaches for XML can be classified into two categories: *Structure-mapping* and *model-mapping* [3]. Examples of these approaches are enumerated in [2,1]. In this paper, we discuss SUCXENT which takes the model-mapping approach.

Several model-mapping relational approaches have been proposed that capture the tree structure of XML documents. The system proposed by Zhang et. al in [4] stores each node and uses a node numbering scheme that allows for the deduction of ancestor-child relationships. Zhang et al. use a numbering scheme in which each node is labelled with its preorder and postorder traversal numbers. Then, ancestor-descendant relationships can be resolved using the property $preorder(ancestor) < preorder(descendant)$ and $postorder(ancestor) >$

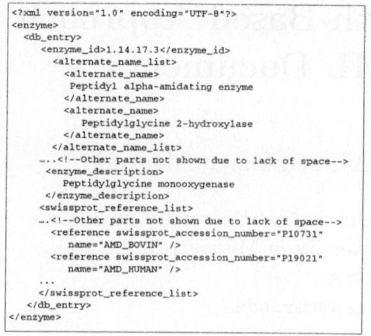

Fig. 1. Sample XML data

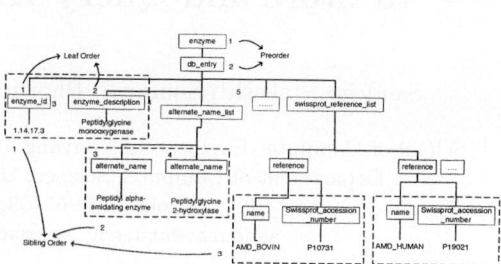

Fig. 2. Tree representation

postorder(descendant). However, these approaches generate as many joins as there are path separators.

To solve this problem of multiple joins, XRel [3] stores the path of each node in the document. Then, the resolution of path expressions only requires the paths to be matched using string matching operators. However, XRel still requires the use of $\theta(<\ or\ )$ joins to resolve ancestor-descendant relationships. These have been shown to be quite expensive due to the manner in which an RDBMS processes joins [4]. In fact, special algorithms such as the Multi-predicate merge sort join algorithm [4] have been proposed to optimize these operations. However, to the best of our knowledge there is no off-the-shelf RDBMS that implements these algorithms.

XParent [1] solves the problem of θ-joins by using an Ancestor table that stores all the ancestors of a particular node in a single table. It then replaces θ-joins with *equi*-joins over this set of ancestors. However, XParent still stores every node in the document and in addition every ancestor of a node is also stored. This leads to a substantially larger database size and at the same time leads to a considerable increase in insertion and extraction times.

SUCXENT solves the above problems by maintaining ancestor information only for the leaf nodes. We follow an approach where we store the paths and values of the leaf nodes together with a list of their ancestors. This will be elaborated on in Section 2. Our approach allows us to capture the tree structure of the XML document succinctly. Storage of ancestor information allows effective evaluation of queries without involving θ-joins.

The main contribution of this paper is a mechanism to efficiently store and query XML data in a relational database system by storing only the leaf nodes and their ancestors. SUCXENT performs up to three times better than XRel in terms of document insertion time and up to 10 to 15 times better in query performance. SUCXENT also significantly outperforms XParent in terms of insertion/extraction times, storage size (up to 20%) and query performance (up to 25%). A detailed performance evaluation can be found in Section 4.

SUCXENT: An Efficient Path-Based Approach

Document (DocId, Name)

Path (PathId, PathExp)

PathValue (DocId, PathId, LeafOrder, SiblingOrder, LeftSibIxnLevel, LeafValue)

TextContent (DocId, LinkId, Text)

AncestorInfo (DocId, SiblingOrder, AncestorOrder, AncestorLevel)

Fig. 3. SUCXENT schema

Document

DocId	Name
1	Enzyme1.14.17.3
2	

Path

PathId	PathExp
1	enzyme.db_entry.enzyme_id
2	enzyme.db_entry.enzyme_description
3	enzyme.db_entry.alternate_name_list.alternate_name
4	enzyme.db_entry.catalytic_activity
5	enzyme.db_entry.cofactor_list.cofactor
6	enzyme.db_entry.comment_list.comment
7	enzyme.db_entry.prosite_reference.prosite_accession_number
8	enzyme.db_entry.swissprot_reference.reference.@name
9	enzyme.db_entry.swissprot_reference.reference.swissprot_accession_number

TextContent

DocId	LinkId	Text
1	Link:comments	with neutral...
2	...	...

PathValue

DocId	PathId	LeafOrder	SiblingOrder	LeftSibIxnLevel	LeafValue
1	1	1	1	-1	1.14.17.3
1	2	2	1	2	Peptidylglycine monooxygenase
1	3	3	2	2	Peptidyl alpha-amidating enzyme
1	...	...	...	...	...
1	8	11	7	2	AMD_BOVIN
1	9	12	7	2	P10731
1	...	...	...	...	...

AncestorInfo

DocId	SiblingOrder	AncestorOrder	AncestorLevel
1	1	1	1
1	1	2	2
1	2	1	1
1	2	5	3
..	..	..	..
1	7	1	1
1	..	..	..

Fig. 4. SUCXENT: XML data in RDBMS

2 Storing XML Documents in SUCXENT

This sections presents the database schema for storing XML documents. Then, the algorithm for lossless extraction of XML documents from the relational database is presented. The XML document in Figure 1 and Figure 2 is used as an example.

2.1 Relational Schema

The relational schema for SUCXENT is shown in Figure 3. The shredded document is shown in Figure 4. The semantics of the schema are as follows. The table Document is used for storing the names of the documents in the database. Each document has unique id recorded in DocID. Path is used to record the path of all the leaf nodes. For example, the path of the leaf node "enzyme_id" in Figure 2 is enzyme/db_entry/enzyme_id. This table maintains path_ids and relative path expressions recorded as instances of PathID and PathExp respectively. This is to reduce the storage size so that we only need to store path_id in PathValue.

PathValue stores the leaf nodes. The DocID attribute indicates which XML document a particular leaf node belongs to. The PathID attribute maintains the id of the path of a particular leaf node as stored in the Path table. LeafOrder is used to record the node order of leaf nodes in an XML tree. For example, when we parse the XML document, we will find leaf node *enzyme_id* with value "1.14.17.3" as the first leaf node in the document. Therefore, we assign a LeafOrder value of "1" to this leaf node. The next leaf node we find is the node *enzyme_description* with value "Peptidylglycine monooxygenase". Therefore, the LeafOrder of this node is "2". Two leaf nodes have the same SiblingOrder if they share the same parent. For example, leaf nodes with LeafOrder equal to "3" and "4" have the same SiblingOrder equal to "2" since they share the same parent node (node *alternate_name_list*). The dotted boxes in Figure 2 indicate the leaf nodes which have the same SiblingOrder. LeftSibIxnLevel (Left Sibling Intersection Level) is the level at which the leaf nodes belonging to a particular sibling order intersect the leaf nodes belonging to the sibling order that comes immediately before i.e., it is the level of the highest common ancestor of of the

```
Input: ℒ = {n₁,···,nₖ}, a list of leaf nodes arranged in order of LeafOrder values
Output: 𝒟 is the document to be returned.
 1: c is an XML node.
 2: c ← φ
 3: C ← list of XML nodes.
 4: for all nᵢ in ℒ do
 5:    /* /book/authors/author would give p = [book,authors,author]*/
 6:    p is the array of nodes in a path.
 7:    p = nᵢ.Path.GetNodes()
 8:    /*s is a counter*/
 9:    s ← 0
10:    if c = φ then
11:       c ← new XmlDocumentNode( p[0] )
12:       /* Make c the root. This happens only once. */
13:       𝒟.AddNode( c )
14:       C.Add( c )
15:       s ← 1
16:    else if
       then
17:       s ← nᵢ.BranchOrder()
18:    end if
19:    /* Keep only those nodes in C that are common between nᵢ₋₁ and nᵢ. */
20:    C.ClearFromIndex( s )
21:    q is an XML node
22:    /*Need to keep it as the starting node for processing nᵢ₊₁ */
23:    q ← c
24:    while s < p.Length() do
25:       m ← new XmlDocumentNode(p[s])
26:       q.AppendChild( m )
27:       C.Add( m )
28:       q ← m
29:       s + +
30:    end while
31: end for
```

Fig. 5. Extraction algorithm

Fig. 6. XQuery and translation

leaf nodes in question. Consider the leaf nodes with `SiblingOrder` equal to "2" in the XML tree depicted in Figure 2. These leaf nodes will intersect with leaf nodes with `SiblingOrder` equal to "1" at the node *db_entry* which is at level 2. So, the `LeftSibIxnLevel` value for these nodes is "2". Similarly, the node name with value AMD_HUMAN has a `LeftSibIxnLevel` value of "3" (intersecting at *swissprot_reference_list*). `PathValue` stores the textual content of the leaf nodes in the column `LeafValue`. For example, the textual content for the leaf node with `LeafOrder` "1" would be "1.14.17.3". However, for large textual data (eg. DNA sequences, mixed content etc.) a separate table `TextContent` is maintained and only a link is stored in `LeafValue`. The attribute `LeftSibIxnLevel` in this table is useful mainly for constructing the XML documents from relational database. This attribute enables us to "stitch" the XML document together from the individual leaf nodes given their paths (`PathId` together with `PathExp`) and values (`LeafValue`). Note that we can reconstruct the document by maintaining the `RightSibIxnLevel` as well. However, doing so would require a backtrack as standard XML parsers would traverse the document in a left to right order.

The table `AncestorInfo` stores the ancestor information for each leaf node. As we know that nodes with the same parent have the same `SiblingOrder` we only need to maintain this information for distinct `SiblingOrder` values. For example, in Figure 3 we do not need to store the ancestor information for both leaf nodes *enzyme_id* (`LeafOrder` = 1) and *enzyme_description* (`LeafOrder` = 2). We only need to maintain the ancestor information for `SiblingOrder` = 1. The `DocID` attribute indicates which XML document a particular ancestor node belongs to. `AncestorOrder` stores the unique ID, which is the preorder traversal value, of the ancestor node in question.

The `AncestorInfo` table is used when answering queries. For example, consider the XPath expression //db_entry[enzyme_id="1.14.17.3"]. The leaf

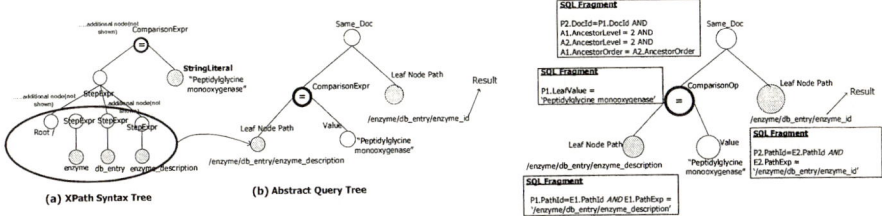

Fig. 7. XPath parse tree and corresponding AQT

Fig. 8. AQT Annotated with SQL Fragments

node *enzyme_id* with value "1.14.17.3" can be obtained from `PathValue`. However, in order to retrieve the *db_entry* node we need to obtain all its other descendants (e.g. *enzyme_description*, *alternate_name_list*, *alternate_name*, *swissprot_reference_list*, *reference* etc.) as well. In order to do this we need to retrieve those leaf nodes whose path starts with *db_entry* and this *db_entry* node should be the same as that for the *enzyme_id* with value "1.14.17.3". So, we need to retrieve those leaf nodes that have the same ancestor as the *enzyme_id* node at level "2". This information is provided by `AncestorInfo`.

2.2 Document Extraction

The algorithm for reconstruction is presented in Figure 5. A list of leaf nodes arranged in ascending `LeafOrder` is given. Each leaf node path is first split into its constituent nodes (lines 5 to 7). If the document construction has not yet started (line 10) then the first node obtained by splitting the first leaf node path is made the root (lines 11 to 15). When the next leaf node is processed we only need to look at the nodes starting after `LeafLeafIxnLevel` of that node as the nodes till this level have already been added to the document (lines 20 to 22). The nodes starting after this level are now added to the document (lines 27 to 32). Document extraction is completed once all the leaf nodes have been processed. This algorithm can be used to construct the whole document if all leaf nodes in the document are used or a fragment of the document given a partial list of consecutive leaf nodes. Query results are returned as such a list of leaf nodes and the result XML fragment(s) are constructed from them using the above approach.

3 Query Translation

Consider the XQuery query of Figure 6(a). and its corresponding SQL translation in Figure 6(b). The translation can be explained as follows: (1) Lines 4 to 6 of Figure 6(b) resolve the part of the query that seeks an entry with `enzyme_description="`*Peptidylglycine monooxygenase*`"`. Remember that we store only the leaf nodes (and their textual content and `path_id`) in the `PathValue`

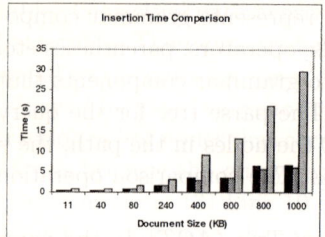
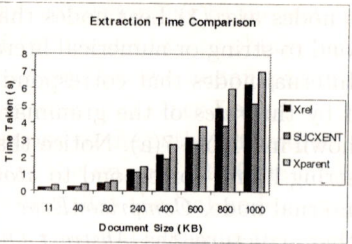

Fig. 10. Storage

Fig. 9. Storage and extraction performance comparison

terms of insertion times as shown by the results in Figure 9. However, XParent is outperformed by up to six times. Insertion time is directly related to the number of tuples being inserted in the database. XRel inserts every node in the document as a tuple. It adds information such as the path of the node etc. too. In addition to this, it inserts *Element, Attribute* and *Text* nodes in different tables. XParent stores an even greater amount of information in the form of parent-child edges and ancestor list of every node. So, it is expected that XParent would perform the worst when it comes to insertion times. SUCXENT, on the other had, inserts only the leaf nodes of a document and their ancestor lists. This would definitely take more time than XRel. However, in SUCXENT only two tables are involved in storage and this reduces the difference between XRel and SUCXENT.

In our experiments we calculate extraction time as the sum of the time taken to retrieve the tuples from the database and the time taken to reconstruct the XML document. This test is also necessary to validate our approach (that is, to ensure that decomposition using our approach is lossless). So, extraction performance would depend both on the time it takes to retrieve the tuples and reconstruct the document in memory.

The extraction performance of SUCXENT is only slightly better than XRel or XParent as shown by the results in Figure 9. Even though, we have to deal with a smaller data set (only leaf nodes and their paths) when reconstructing an XML document, we still have to perform *substring* operations to determine the nodes in a path in order to create the document tree. In Step 7 of Figure 5 the process of obtaining the node array from the path is accomplished by the *substring* operation. This means that retrieval time from the database is better in our approach but the time taken for reconstruction is more. In fact, for smaller documents, when the number of tuples stored in the database is not very significant, SUCXENT performs worse than XRel or XParent.

4.2 Storage Size

Figure 10 summarizes the storage requirements of the three approaches for the Shakespeare data set [1]. We see that SUCXENT takes up significantly more storage space than XRel. This is because the storage of the ancestor list of every leaf node leads to more database entries than the total number of nodes in the

```
Q1: /PLAY/ACT
Q2: /PLAY/ACT/SCENE/SPEECH/LINE/STAGEDIR
Q3: //SCENE/TITLE
Q4: //ACT//TITLE
Q5: /PLAY/ACT[2]
Q6: /PLAY/ACT/SCENE/SPEECH[SPEAKER='CURIO']
Q7: /PLAY/ACT/SCENE[//SPEAKER = 'Steward']/
    TITLE
```

```
DQ1: Select conference papers published in the year 2000 on
     XML.
DQ2: Select papers written by Michael Stonebraker.
DQ3: Select papers written by Michael Stonebraker or Jim
     Gray.
DQ4: Select papers published between 1990 and 1994 with title
     starting with ``database''.
DQ5: Select journal papers that have a cite entry CARE84.
DQ6: Select papers by Michael Stonebraker quoted by papers
     published in the year 1994.
DQ7: Select papers by Jim Gray that are quoted by Michael
     Stonebraker.
```

Fig. 11. Queries: Shakespeare data set   **Fig. 12.** Queries: DBLP data set

document. Several non-leaf nodes are stored more than once as they can be ancestors of more than one leaf node. However, this is needed to avoid θ-joins when executing queries. However, SUCXENT uses far less storage space than XParent. This is to be expected as XParent stores every node in the document, every parent-child edge, and the ancestor list of each node.

4.3 Query Performance

We use two data sets for comparison - the Shakespeare data set and a 20.2 MB segment of the DBLP data set [1]. The DBLP data set is used to demonstrate the performance of more complex queries. The queries used with the Shakespeare data set are shown in Table 11. This set of queries was also used in [1]. Figure 13 shows the query performance comparison. There are some observations regarding the performance of these queries. 1) Queries Q1 to Q5 perform worse than Q6 and Q7 in all three approaches. This is because, these are simple path expression queries and the number of tuples returned would be large in all approaches. 2) SUCXENT outperforms XRel for Queries Q1 to Q5 by up to 4 times. This is because the number of tuple returned in the case of SUCXENT would be far less. Only the leaf nodes are returned (as these are what is stored) and the document sections are reconstructed from these. In the case of XRel all the nodes that satisfy these path expressions are returned. XParent performs comparably to SUCXENT as it stores the leaf nodes separately in the *Data* table. (3) SUCXENT outperforms XRel for Queries Q6 and Q7 more substantially than it does for Q1-Q5. The SQL translation using SUCXENT generates no θ-joins for either Q6 or Q7. However, XRel's translation leads to quite a few θ-joins. SUCXENT performs better than XParent too - though the difference is not as substantial as XRel. This is because XParent avoids θ-joins as well.

The data shown here is for the Shakespeare data set which does not have a complex structure and therefore, the number of leaf nodes is not much less than the total number of nodes as shown in Table 6. We expected our approach to show even better performance when this difference increases as well as when more complex queries (not just simple path expressions) are executed. So, we decided to compare the performance of these three approaches for a larger data set with queries that are more complex than simple path expressions. Figure 14 compares the query elapsed times for the DBLP data set of size 20.2MB. The queries used are listed in Figure 12. These queries were also used in [1].

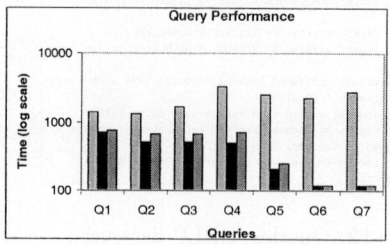

Fig. 13. Query performance comparison for the Shakespeare data set

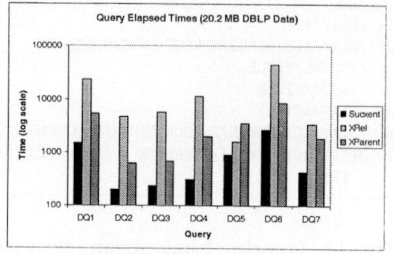

Fig. 14. Query performance comparison (DBLP data set 20.2MB)

SUCXENT is up to 30 times faster. The difference is much more substantial than for the Shakespeare data set as the DBLP data set used is larger and the queries are more complex. These queries lead to several θ-joins in the XRel approach. SUCXENT, on the other hand, completely avoids θ-joins in the SQL translation. XParent also performs better than XRel. However, it is significantly outperformed by SUCXENT (up to 4 times faster). This can be attributed to the fact that the ancestor list of every node is stored in the XParent. SUCXENT stores the ancestor list for only the leaf nodes. This leads to a substantial difference in the number of tuples that are stored. Therefore, a query needs to be executed over a smaller number of tuples in SUCXENT. This leads to a substantially lower I/O-cost. We believe that this difference will increase as the size of the XML data being queried increases.

4.4 Scalability

Three samples of the DBLP data set - 5.1MB, 10.2MB and 20.2MB were used to compare the variation of query execution times with increasing data size. The 5.1MB data set is taken as the baseline for comparison. The increase in query execution time when the data set size is increased is measured as a **ratio** against the time taken for the baseline data set.

The results for XRel are not presented as it is outperformed by XPARENT [1]. XParent is outperformed by SUCXENT in terms of scalability. This is especially true for the more complex queries DQ6 and DQ7. Again, this can be attributed to the lower storage space and therefore lower I/O-cost involved in evaluating queries in SUCXENT. Another interesting observation is that the difference in query times for DQ 6 is substantially more than that for other queries as the data size increases from 5.1MB to 10.2MB. We investigated this further and found that the number of results returned by the second part of the query (i.e., papers written by 'Jim Gray') increases substantially when the data size is increased and therefore there is a greater jump in query processing time. However, when the data size is doubled again (to 20.2MB) the query performance change is comparable to that of the other queries.

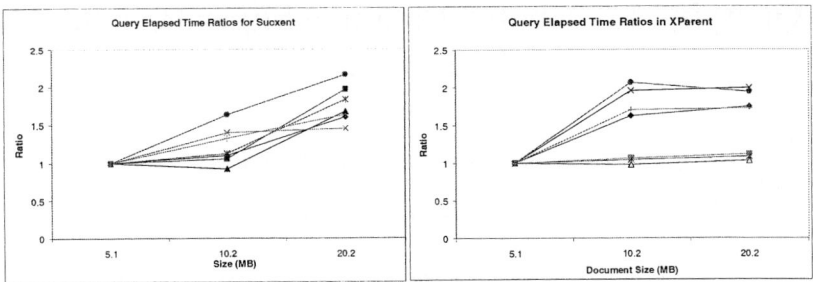

Fig. 15. Scalability Comparison (SUCXENT vs XParent)

5 Conclusions

In this paper, we have described SUCXENT, a novel approach for the storage of XML documents in an RDBMS. We follow an approach where we store only the paths and values of the leaf nodes. In addition, we store the ancestors of leaf nodes in order to answer queries efficiently. SUCXENT completely avoids θ-joins by utilizing this approach. XParent follows a similar approach but stores the ancestor list of each node in the document. This leads to a substantially larger storage space requirement and therefore larger I/O-cost when evaluating queries. Though XParent performs significantly better than XRel by avoiding θ-joins it is outperformed by SUCXENT. Our results also show that the insertion/extraction times for SUCXENT are substantially less than XParent and comparable to XRel. Though storage requirements for SUCXENT are more than that for XRel, they are less than that for XParent.

References

1. H. Jiang, H. Lu, W. Wang and J. Xu Yu. Path Materialization Revisited: An Efficient Storage Model for XML Data. *2nd Australian Institute of Computer Ethics Conference (AICE2000)*.
2. F. Tian, D. DeWitt, J. Chen and C. Zhang. The design and performance evaluation of alternative XML storage strategies. *ACM Sigmod Record, Vol. 31(1), 2002*.
3. M. Yoshikawa, T. Amagasa, T. Shimura, and S. Uemura. XRel: a path-based approach to storage and retrieval of xml documents using relational databases. *ACM Transactions on Internet Technology (TOIT)* 1(1):110-141, 2001.
4. C. Zhang, J. Naughton, D. Dewitt, Q. Luo and G. Lohmann. On Supporting Containment Queries in Relational Database Systems. *Proceedings of the 2001 ACM-SIGMOD Conference*, Santa Barbara, CA, May 2001.
5. Sandeep Prakash and Sourav S. Bhowmick. Sucxent: An Efficient Path-Based Approach to Store and Query XML Documents, 2003. http://www.cais.ntu.edu.sg/~v431194/docs/dexa_full.ps.

Querying Distributed Data in a Super-Peer Based Architecture*

Zohra Bellahsène[1] and Mark Roantree[2]

[1] LIRMM, UMR 5506 CNRS/Université Montpellier II, France
bella@lirmm.fr
[2] Interoperable Systems Group, Dublin City University, Ireland
mark@computing.dcu.ie

Abstract. Data integration is a significant challenge: relevant data objects are split across multiple information sources, and often owned by different organizations. The sources represent, maintain, and export the information using a variety of formats, interfaces and semantics. This paper addresses the issue of querying distributed data in a large scale context. We present a p2p information mediation framework based on the notion of super-peers, providing a *super-peer* network. This makes it possible for a super-peer to reach every other peer (data source) in the system, thus realizing the concept of a integrated schema formed from all possible information sources. This is achieved by classifying data sources into domains and creating user profiles for query optimization purposes.

1 Introduction

The area of information integration has been moved towards flexible architectures [18], and more recently the integration of purely semi-structured sources [7], and both structured and semi-structured data in the same system. Some of this research has focused on large scale integration where the number of information sources numbers thousands [2]. Here, we are interested in providing a logical architecture where the number of information sources has no set limit. The assumption is that data is spread over a wide area and includes database systems, legacy systems and unstructured and semi-structured sources such as web servers. In order to provide such an architecture, it is necessary to use research and technology more associated with wide area networking than information management. This is due to the fact that conventional integration architectures cannot scale to the numbers envisaged in these systems.

Motivation. Before the emergence of internet-based data, information was generally stored in database systems or proprietary file systems. There have been many solutions offered to the integration of these systems, and although this is still an on-going problem, the issues involved are well-understood. In fact, the problems have (more or less) moved from structural integration issues to semantic integration issues [8], and sometimes focuses on the integration of behavior [24], metadata modeling [20], or integrity constraints [5]. What is generally accepted is that no solution is complete without addressing the more recent topic of semantic integration. As is shown in [8], the

---

* Supported by Ulysses Research Grant FR/2004/032.

integration of data sources from homogeneous domains generally assists the process of semantic integration.

However, the focus point in data integration has shifted for many researchers with the proliferation of web-based data sources. In many applications, it is no longer sufficient to integrate traditional database systems, as often there is equally important information located in newer unstructured or semi-structured sources. Furthermore, web servers are many and thus, the additional problem of large-scale integration must be addressed. The motivation for this work is two-fold: to provide an architecture which can address the large-scale issue; and also to provide a smarter integration strategy assuming that the concept of a single global schema is infeasible due to the large scale and heterogeneity of data sources. In this respect, the support services (query and metadata) are vital in the provision of scale, quality (in terms of data accessed), and dependability.

Contribution of this Paper. Our contribution to this problem is to employ networking technology in the form of peer to peer networks, while modifying the traditional approach to suit the integration of information systems. This usage of P2P is not new as it has been used in the Piazza project [9] but this work is extended by using the *super-peer* concept [17] to assist in the management of global servers, where a super-peer acts as a mediator to a cluster of information sources. Additionally, we adopt a flexible approach to integration in mediated schemas, as this is best suited to a super-peer network approach. This paper primarily focuses on architectural issues, but also includes an overview of Query Service pragmatics.

Outline. This paper is organized as follows. The large scale context of data integration is described in §2; the logical architecture of our system is presented in §3; We then move to describe our Query Service in §4 while §5 reviews different solutions currently available both in the industry and in the literature; concluding remarks and current research are described in §6.

2 The Peer to Peer Context

The limitation of a traditional client-server architecture is clear in a large scale distributed environment as resources are concentrated into a small number of nodes and features such as replication and caching must be introduced in advance. Peer to Peer systems appear to offer an alternative to the client/server architecture in a large scale network because they distribute the main costs of sharing data (i.e. disk space and bandwidth for transferring them). Each node participating in a peer to peer system acts as both client and server, and as a result each peer allows other peers access to some of its resources. There are several types of file exchange in peer to peer with different degrees of centralization. In pure peer to peer systems like Gnutella, peers all play the same roles (client and server) and have the same responsibilities, as there is no centralization policy. A query is addressed to a peer which then forwards this to its neighbors and so on, until an answer is found or the lifetime of the message has exceeded. The advantages of the pure peer to peer approach are a better load balance of communication and processing, and a natural robustness. The main drawback of this approach is the large number of messages that are generated in the network. In peer to peer systems like Napster, there is a centralized directory of all sites. A query is sent to the site housing the directory which finds the appropriate sources. As a result, the hybrid approach provides an improved query performance. However, the storage of the directory is costly: the single node may entail a performance and scalability bottleneck. Furthermore, this approach is oriented towards a client-server rather than peer to peer architecture.

More recently, the *super-peer* approach has been designed for the Morpheus system [17]. This approach presents a cross between pure peer to peer and hybrid systems. A super-peer is a node in the peer to peer network that acts as a centralized server to a subset of nodes representing clients. Super-peers are connected to other super-peers in the network. Queries are submitted by clients to the super-peer which then finds the appropriate sources and returns the results to the clients. Super-peers combine the pure and the centralized distributed approaches and therefore represent a hybrid approach. More precisely, it combines the efficiency of a centralized client-server architecture with the autonomy, load balancing and robustness of distributed search. The behavior of the super-peer system has been studied in [26], where a set of basic rules that capture the main tradeoffs in super-peer networks have been proposed.

However, queries are executed "blindly" with no requirement for specifying data sources or prior knowledge of database schemas. This is acceptable where the architecture is aimed at a general purpose solution. However in the context of this research, we are dealing with the integration of information systems where it is assumed that some form of traditional query processing is supported. Thus, solutions such as the Time to Live (TTL) protocol use by Gnutella are not sufficient here. With this method, a query is broadcast in all directions, and continues to move past each super-peer until the required information is found or its TTL expires (typically by decrementing some counter after each super-peer is visited). This solution is insufficient as no exploitation of schema knowledge takes place.

3 The XPeer Logical Architecture

In this section, we present the logical architecture of our current project named *Xpeer*. The goal of Xpeer is defining and implementing a mediation system that allows querying a large scale P2P Database Management System by hiding the distribution, localization and heterogeneity of data sources and providing acceptable query response times. The architecture for our system is based on the *super-peer* concept. We recall that the only assumption needed regarding the topology of a peer to peer network is that it contains a strongly connected graph to provide all required functionality. Thus, the network topology shown in this section is provided for reasons of consistency only. Furthermore, we assume that both data and metadata flows are XML-based.

In order to exploit the *data web* one of the main issues is to describe data in semantic terms in order to facilitate its correct usage by software systems and improve understanding for the human reader. There are currently two main approaches to this problem. The first approach is adopted by the A.I. community: it uses knowledge representation languages to specify concept senses or reasoning techniques on the data which follows the RDF format. However, most of these approaches exploit neither the structures of data items nor the fact that there is an increasing volume of XML data on the web.

The strong interest of the database community for the semantic web can be seen as a continuation of data integration research. The second approach is adopted by projects such as Piazza [9] where mediation is based on semantic descriptions not only from data sources but also from the links between those sources (or peers). Scalability is performed in a simple incremental manner: adding a new peer (or source) requires that this peer describes its data, and adding new links to its closest neighbors (on a semantic level). However computing all result sets for conjunctive queries in the case where the network is non-acyclic is too expensive. To reduce this complexity, the authors of [11] propose to use an ontology based on an atomic class and to describe the mapping as query containment. Queries are then a combination of atomic classes. However query expressiveness is unsatisfactory and query performance is not considered.

To extend these approaches, we propose a "semantic" representation of both sources and data in order to improve query performance. Data sources are modeled through a hierarchy (ontology) of concepts associated with a super-peer architecture.

3.1 Cluster Level

In the XPeer architecture, an information system plays the role of a *peer*. We group together a set of peers sharing the same schema into a cluster where the mediated schema for the set is managed by a *cluster-peer* node. This is illustrated in Fig.*1* where the *cluster-peer* is connected to each of its *peers*. One can see that a *cluster-peer* plays the same role as a *super-peer* in the present literature [26]. We also retain the term *cluster* to group together a *cluster-peer* with its *peers*.

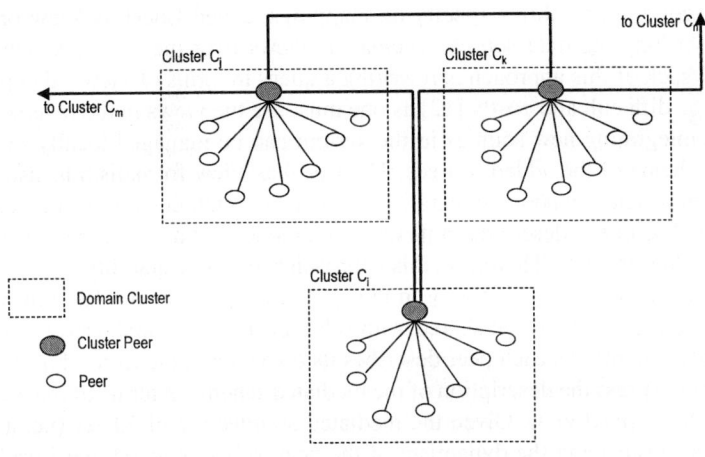

Fig. 1. Clusters in the XPeer Architecture

3.2 Domain Level

While a cluster-peer provides an integration of a set of peers within its cluster, this alone is insufficient in providing a large scale information system. For example, if we want to construct an information system for healthcare we need to group together information from physicians, clinics, medicine industries as well as government resources. These different resources do not share the same schema and even the same resource may have different schemas and data access. To facilitate these heterogeneities, we introduced two further layers in our peer hierarchy: domain-peers which a single domain-peer manages a set of cluster-peers, and a global-peer which manages the entire set of domain-peers. We define a *domain* as a set of clusters sharing the same category of information (physicians for instance). We also define a special node called a *domain peer* for each domain, and this acts as the entry point for this domain. We next describe the different functionalities for each of the system components.

4 Query Services

4.1 Schema Mediation

In data integration systems [16], queries are performed through a mediated schema. The system translates the user query into appropriate queries over related data sources according to semantic mappings. There are two main ways to specify mappings between the mediated schema and the data sources, and both are based on view mechanisms. The first approach relies on defining the mediated schema as a set of views over the schema of the data sources. This is the so-called Global as View approach or GAV [18]. The main advantage of this approach lies in the fact that the process of rewriting queries on the mediated schema is more straightforward. However the integration of new data sources is hard since the mediated schema must be updated accordingly.

The second approach for specifying mappings, called Local as View or LAV requires describing the data source schemas as views over the mediated schema. The main drawback of this approach is rewriting a query in terms of views: this problem is known to be difficult and costly [12] as one must use the views in the reverse direction. However, integrating new sources in the system can be managed locally by updating the view schema of the added sources. The Local as View formalism is also more appropriate in a heterogeneous integration system that includes many sources, since a newly added source is described in its own data model and need not be translated (to a common model format). Therefore, this approach supports scalability.

In our architecture a peer may join the system in one of two roles: posing queries and providing a schema to be shared with other peers (client and server); and posing queries only (client). As each peer describes its own data in the form of a schema, it is necessary to express the description of the mediated schema in terms of the peers which comprise the unified view. Given the mediated architecture of XPeer (i.e. a mediated schema per cluster) and the dynamism of the peer to peer context, the Local as View is the more appropriate approach. However, since each peer may also act as a client, XPeer differs from the original research as it employs a mixed approach for describing the connection between the schemas of peers and the mediated schema of the cluster-peer schema within each cluster.

More precisely, within a cluster peers must conform to a unique schema (i.e. XML Schema). This means that each peer should export its data according to this DTD, and is used in services as WAP. Concerning the view on which a peer acts as a client, a simple process filters the cluster schema according to the needs of each peer, thus a peer is provided with a view over the cluster DTD. To summarize, schema mappings between peers and their cluster peer are defined following the Local as View approach where the cluster schema is a fixed DTD. The main advantage of our approach is that a peer may be added or dropped without affecting other peers and more importantly, without affecting the mediated schema. The sole requirement is to update the list of available peers. Furthermore, when a client wishes to query the entire information system, the peer is provided with a mediated schema over pertinent cluster schemas. This process is done with respect to the Global as View approach.

4.2 The Peer View

When a peer (as client) joins the system, it specifies its requirements by accessing the complete list of domains (D_1 to D_n). Those are specified as label descriptions (visible to clients), and managed by the Metadata Service in order to filter clusters of interest, and to optimize queries by removing lookup steps. In this way, each client will have their own customized Schema. This interface is actually a set of domain schemas, called the Peer View. Each domain schema is an integrated view of different exported clusters schemas on a specific domain. The main issue is to define the mappings between the view schema and the exported cluster schema. Indeed, for building such a view it is necessary to perform a semantic integration of the exported cluster schemas. Schema matching is not the main focus of this paper as it is covered in [23] where the semantic integration and the mapping generation are addressed.

Consider a healthcare application in the European Union. Suppose one is interested in studying some diseases and their treatment used in different countries across the E.U. This is illustrated in Fig. 2 where a *cluster* represents the prescriptions for one hospital, a *peer* a hospital department and a *domain* the prescriptions for a country.

Example 1. Assume that a doctor working in a French hospital has a requirement to perform statistics on prescriptions concerning asthma disease in Ireland. For this purpose, he defines the following view using XQuery:

For $d in domains
Where $d/name = "Ireland" AND d/clusters/keyword = "asthma"
Return
<cluster_desc>
{$o/name/clusters/desc}
</cluster_desc>

The returned clusters are integrated to form a single Domain Schema on which the peer will formulate its queries.

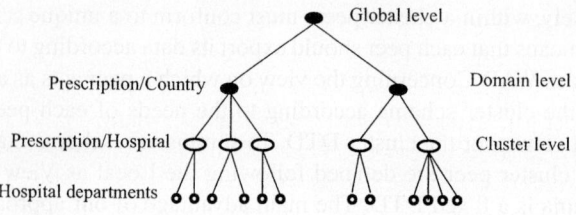

Fig. 2. Hospital Sample Schema

4.3 Query Processing

In the XPeer system, a peer (i.e. the user) formulates its query Q using the mediated schema corresponding to its (peer) view. Next, this query is sent to the cluster peer, which will process the query as follows:

The query Q formulated by the peer on its Peer View schema is rewritten into a set of queries $\{Q_1, Q_2, ..., Q_k\}$, where k is the number of cluster schemas that have been integrated. Each query Q_1 is related to one cluster schema. Each cluster may now process the related query as follows:

Inside each cluster, the sub query Q_i ($i=1, k$) is translated to a set of local peer queries $\{Q_{i1}, Q_{i2}, ..., Q_{im}\}$, on the real peer schemas according to mapping rules, where m is the number of peer schemas that have been referenced in the related cluster. Finally, the results sent by the local peers are integrated by the domain peer, via the cluster peers, into one result that will be returned to the peer that initiated the query.

Example 2. Consider a query Q that retrieves the drugs prescripted for the asthma disease.

    For $h in hospitals
    Return
    <name>
    {$o/hospitals/prescriptions/drugs/name}
    </name>

Let us briefly explain how this query will be processed. Suppose a doctor formulates this query via the peer P. At first, Q is rewritten into a query Q' with respect to the mappings in the cluster where P is located. Next, the system uses the mappings between the P View Schema and the related cluster schema to expand Q. Then, inside each related cluster peer C_k, Q will be rewritten into query Q_k ($k=1, M$) according the mappings between C_k schema and its peers schemas, where M is the number of cluster schemas that have been returned in the view schema previously computed from peer P. Finally, each cluster will return one result to the cluster peer which has initiated the query Q. The union of all the results provided by the cluster peers and those of Q' is computed. Then, this cluster peer returns the final result after eliminating redundancies to P.

5 Related Work

The first attempt to design a database based on a peer to peer network was done in the Piazza project [9]. Their architecture focused on dynamic data placement and was organized on spheres of cooperation. A data origin is modeled as a distinct entity from the other peers. Larger spheres of cooperation may be built by nesting existing ones.

A solution to data mediation in peer to peer database management systems has been presented in [13]. That paper focused on a peer programming language for mediating peer schemas. More precisely, this language allows users to specify mappings between a pair or small set of peers using peer descriptions instead of a mediated schema. This language also enables the storage description of each peer. Given these descriptions, a query formulation algorithm has been proposed. There are many differences between our approach and those of Piazza:

1. Our architecture is based on the super-peer network whereas Piazza is based on a pure peer to peer network. Therefore, our approach combines the efficiency of centralized information retrieval by providing a mediated schema per cluster with those of pure peer to peer (reliability, distribution of the load, etc.)
2. Piazza does not provide a mediated schema but mappings between a small set of peers. In our approach, a single mediated schema per cluster is provided.
3. A user is provided by a set of mono-domain mediated schemas. In Piazza, a peer is connected into a small set of peers, and by iteration, it can reach many peers. However, this solution is prone to degradation of query performance.

A distributed caching system for OLAP queries based on a peer to peer network has been proposed in [15]. This architecture is called PeerOLAP and was described as a set of peers that access data warehouses and pose OLAP queries. Each peer has a local cache and implements a mechanism for sharing its cache contents and computational capabilities with other peers. Queries are addressed to a peer that may either process them locally if it has the required data or propagate the queries to its neighbors. The network architecture is based on classical peer to peer. Therefore the efficiency of query processing is compromised. Moreover, data at sources may change at different speeds and intervals, making it difficult to maintain both the fragments stored at the peers, and at the different data warehouses.

The main difference with our approach relies in the fact that our proposal is aimed at providing an infrastructure to data mediation where data resides at the original sources. However, for performance reasons, we store materialized views at some peers.

A peer to peer system called P-Grids [1] focuses on the construction and maintenance of the Grid or P2P system using randomized algorithm, as opposed to managing Information Systems which are connected using a P2P approach. At some starting point, the system assumes that no information regarding access paths between nodes is known. Thus, the entire search space is split into two sections where two peers, know the location of each other and then take responsibility for each half of the search space. Eventually, a Grid is formed as access paths between each set of pairs becomes known. This results in a graceful scaling in terms of both storage and communication costs and enable the access to both reliable and unreliable peers.

With respect to our research, the P-Grid approach concentrates on P2P issues while we are more concerned with data management issues such as querying and metadata. Furthermore, our approach does not take a binary approach to peer management as this causes an initial problem if the search space (or global information system) is very large. As It was shown in section 3, we divide the search space into a far greater number of sections, depending on the number of information system domains available.

6 Conclusions

In this paper we presented an architecture which is suited to large scale data integration. The architecture was designed using super-peer network features to cope with the issues caused by very large numbers of data sources and an environment in which nodes were either fixed or mobile and permanent or temporary. In our approach we view the network as a large searchable database, with special roles for super-peer elements. Specifically, a peer can be promoted to one of these three roles: (1) **cluster peer**: a mediator for its cluster; (2) **domain peer**: management of all cluster peers within a given domain; and (3) **global peer**: management of the domain set. By specifying client profiles (§4) and through the operation of a metadata service which models all system entities [3], it is possible to query all roles in an infinitely large system.

Our current research is focused on three primary areas. The first of these is the full deployment of our XML metamodel to represent all aspects of the system including mediated schema interfaces, metadata service repositories, domain management and unstructured data sources. The second task is to complete the current implementation of our system in order to test and optimize the performance of external queries. Finally, we are investigating the issue of selecting views for materialization and placement as part of the query optimization process.

Acknowledgments

The authors would like to acknowledge the contribution of Laurent Mignet in the section covering cluster management.

References

1. Aberer K. P-Grid: A Self-Organizing Access Structure for P2P Information Systems. *Proceedings of 9th International Conference on Cooperative Information Systems* (CoopIS), pp. 179-194, LNCS 2172, Springer, 2001.
2. Abiteboul S., Cluet S., Ferran G. and Rousset M. The Xyleme Project. *Computer Networks* Vol. 39, pp 225-238, 2002.
3. Bellahsène Z. and Roantree M. Large Scale Integration Using the XPeer Architecture. *Technical Report no. ISG-03-06*, Dublin City University, October 2003, http://www.computing.dcu.ie/~isg, October 2003.
4. Bernstein P.A., Giunchiglia F., Kementsietsidis A., Mylopoulos J., Serafini L., Zaihrayeu I.: Data Management for Peer-to-Peer Computing : A Vision. WebDB 2002: 89-94
5. Cali A., Calvanese D., DeGiacomo D., and Lenzerini M. Data Integration under Integrity Constraints. *Proceedings of 14th International Conference on Advanced Information Systems Engineering (CAiSE 02)*, LNCS 2348, pp. 262-279, Springer, 2002.

6. Conrad S., Hding M., Saake G., Schmitt I., and Trker C. Schema Integration with Integrity Constraints. *Proceedings of 15th BNCOD*, pp. 200-214, LNCS 1271, Springer, 1997.
7. Draper D., Halevy A., and Weld D. The Nimble XML Data Integration System. *Proceedings of the 17th International Conference on Data Engineering*, (ICDE 2001), IEEE Computer Society Press, 2001.
8. Delobel C., Reynaud C., Rousset M., Sirot J., and Vodislav D. Semantic Integration in Xyleme: a Uniform Tree-based Approach. To appear in *Journal on Data & Knowledge Engineering*, 2003.
9. Gribble S., Halevy A., Ives Z., Rodrig M., Suciu D. What Can Database Do for Peer-to-Peer? *Proceedings of the Fourth International Workshop on the Web and Databases*, WebDB 2001, in conjunction with ACM PODS/SIGMOD 2001.
10. Gnutella Website. http://www.gnutella.com, 2002.
11. Goasdoue F. and Rousset M. Querying Distributed Data through Distributed Ontologies: A Simple but Scalable Approach. In *Proceedings of IJCAI03 Workshop on Integration on the Web* (IIWeb 03), 2003.
12. Halevy A. Answering queries using views: a survey. *VLDB Journal* 10:4, pp 270-294, 2001.
13. Halevy A., Ives Z., Suciu D., and Tatarinov I. Schema Mediation in Peer Data Management Systems. To appear in 1*9th International Conference on Data Engineering* (ICDE), 2003.
14. Hull R. and Zhou G. A Framework for Supporting Data Integration Using the Materialized and Virtual Approaches. *Proceedings of ACM SIGMOD Conference*, pp. 481-492, ACM Press, 1996.
15. Kalnis P., Ng W., Ooi B., Papadias D., and Tan K. An Adaptive Peer-to-Peer Network for Distributed Caching of OLAP Results. *Proceedings of 2002 ACM Sigmod Conference*, 2002.
16. Lenzerini M. Data Integration: A Theoritical Perspective. PODS, *Proceedings of the 21st ACM Symposium on Principles of Database Systems* (PODS), pp. 233-246, 2002.
17. Morpheus Website. http://www.musiccity.com, 2002.
18. Manolescu I., Florescu D., and Kossmann D. Answering XML Queries on Heterogeneous Data Sources. *Proceedings of 27th International Conference on Very Large Data Bases*, Morgan Kaufmann 2001.
19. McBrien P. and Poulovassilis A. A Semantic Approach to Integrating XML and Structured Data Sources. *Proceedings of 13th International Conference on Advanced Information Systems Engineering (CAiSE 01)*, LNCS 2068, pp. 330-345, Springer, 2001.
20. Roantree M., Kennedy J., and Barclay P. Using a Metadata Software Layer in Information Systems Integration. *Proceedings of 13th International Conference on Advanced Information Systems Engineering (CAiSE 01)*, LNCS 2068, pp. 299-314, Springer, 2001.
21. Roantree M., Kennedy J., and Barclay P. Integrating View Schemata Using an Extended Object Definition Language. *Proceedings of 9th International Conference on Cooperative Information Systems* (CoopIS), pp. 150-162, LNCS 2172, Springer, 2001.
22. Saltor F. Castellanos M., and Garcia-Solaco M. Suitability of Data Models as Canonical Models for Federated Databases. *ACM SIGMOD Record* 20:4, 1991.
23. Tranier J., Baraer R., Bellahsène Z., and Teisseire M. Where's Charlie: Family based heuristics for Peer-to-Peer Schema Integration. To appear in *IDEAS 2004*.
24. Vermeer M. and Apers P. Behaviour Specification in Database Interoperation. *Proceedings of 9th International Conference on Advanced Information Systems Engineering* (CAiSE), pp. 61-74, LNCS 1250, Springer, 1997.
25. Wiederhold G. and Genesereth M. The Basis for Mediation. *Proceedings of the 3rd International Conference on Cooperative Information Systems* (CoopIS-95), pp. 140-157, 1995
26. Yang B., and Garcia-Molina H. Designing a Super-Peer Network. To appear in *19th International Conference on Data Engineering* (ICDE), 2003.

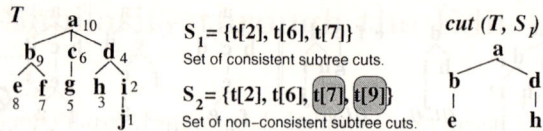

Fig. 2. An example of consistent subtree cuts on trees

3 The Forest Edit Distance

To allow the use of approximate pattern matching strategies, we have included the possibility of performing removal of irrelevant subtrees within the data tree. Following the Zhang *et al.* approach [10], we compute a modified edit distance, where the data tree can be simplified by cutting some of its subtrees with no associated cost. The idea is to make a more flexible matching mechanism possible, in which some structural details can be omitted and more general pattern trees can be managed.

We introduce $r\_keyroots(T)$ as the set of all nodes in a tree T which have a right sibling plus the root, $root(T)$, of T, indicated by arrows in the left-hand side of Fig. 1. The algorithm will proceed through the nodes, first determining mappings from all leaf r_keyroots, then all r_keyroots at the next higher level, and so on to the root.

We also define $r(i)$ as the rightmost leaf descendant of the subtree rooted at $t[i]$ in a tree T, and $T[i..j]$ as the ordered sub-forest of T induced by the nodes numbered i to j, inclusive, as is shown in the left-hand side of Fig. 1. In particular, we have $T[r(i)..i]$ as the tree rooted at $t[i]$, that we denote, in short, as $T[i]$.

The operation of cutting at node $t[i]$ means removing the subtree $T[i]$. A set S of nodes of $T[i]$ (resp. $T[i..j]$) is said to be a *set of consistent subtree cuts* in $T[i]$ (resp. $T[i..j]$) iff: (i) $t[k] \in S$ implies that $t[k]$ is a node in $T[i]$ (resp. $t[k]$ is a node in $T[i..j]$, that is $i \leq k \leq j$), and (ii) $t[k], t[l] \in S$ implies that neither is an ancestor of the other in $T[i]$ (resp. $T[i..j]$).

We denote by $cut(T, S)$ (resp. $cut(T[i..j], S)$) the tree T (resp. sub-forest $T[i..j]$) with subtree removals at all nodes in S, and we denote by $subtrees(T)$ (resp. $subtrees(T[i..j])$) the set of all possible sets of consistent subtree cuts in T (resp. $T[i..j]$). We illustrate these concepts in Fig. 2. Formally, given trees P and D, the *edit distance with cuts* is defined as

$$\delta_{cut}(P, D) = min_{S \in subtrees(D)} \delta(P, cut(D, S))$$

That is, δ_{cut} is the edit distance between the pattern and the data tree resulting from an optimal set of consistent cuts that yields a minimal distance. We now define the *forest edit distance with cuts* between a target P and a data tree D, generalizing δ_{cut} in the form

$$fd(P[s_1..s_2], D[t_1..t_2]) = \delta_{cut}(P[s_1..s_2], D[t_1..t_2])$$

that we denote $fd(s_1..s_2, t_1..t_2)$ when the context is clear. Intuitively, this concept computes the distance with cuts between two nodes, $p[s_2]$ and $d[t_2]$, in the context of their left siblings in the corresponding trees; while the tree distance, $\delta_{\text{cut}}(P[s_2], D[t_2])$, is computed only from their descendants. We compute the edit distance $td(P, D)$ applying the following three sets of formulae; the first one for initialization, numbered as (1), and the other two for distances between pairs of subtrees and for distances between pairs of actual sub-forests, identified as (2) and (3), respectively:

(1) $fd(\emptyset, \emptyset) = 0 \quad fd(\emptyset, r(j)..t) = 0 \quad fd(r(i)..s, \emptyset) = fd(r(i)..s - 1, \emptyset) + \gamma(p[s] \to \varepsilon)$

(2) $fd(r(i)..s, r(j)..t) = \min \begin{cases} fd(r(i)..s - 1, r(j)..t) + \gamma(p[s] \to \varepsilon) \\ fd(r(i)..s, r(j)..t - 1) + \gamma(\varepsilon \to d[t]) \\ fd(r(i)..s - 1, r(j)..t - 1) + \gamma(p[s]) \to d[t])) \\ fd(r(i)..s, \emptyset) \end{cases}$

iff $r(s) = r(i)$ **and** $r(t) = r(j)$

(3) $fd(r(i)..s, r(j)..t) = \min \begin{cases} fd(r(i)..s - 1, r(j)..t) + \gamma(p[s] \to \varepsilon) \\ fd(r(i)..s, r(j)..t - 1) + \gamma(\varepsilon \to d[t]) \\ fd(r(i)..r(s) - 1, r(j)..r(t) - 1) + td(s, t) \\ fd(r(i)..s, r(j)..r(t) - 1) \end{cases}$

otherwise

where nodes $p[s] \in P[i]$, $d[t] \in D[j]$, and $i \in r\_keyroots(P)$ and $j \in r\_keyroots(D)$. To compute $td(P, D)$ it is sufficient to take into account that

$$td(P, D) = fd(\text{root}(P)..r(\text{root}(P)), \text{root}(D)..r(\text{root}(D)))$$

Time bound is, in the worst case,

$$\mathcal{O}(|P| \times |D| \times \min(\text{depth}(P), \text{leaves}(P)) \times \min(\text{depth}(D), \text{leaves}(D)))$$

where $|T|$, $\text{depth}(T)$ and $\text{leaves}(T)$ are the number of nodes, the number of leaves and the depth in a tree T; respectively.

We extend the tree matching algorithm in a similarity parse measure taking into account the semantic proximity between words. In essence, we propagate a similarity measure at word level through the nodes in accordance with the syntactic distances computed by tree matching.

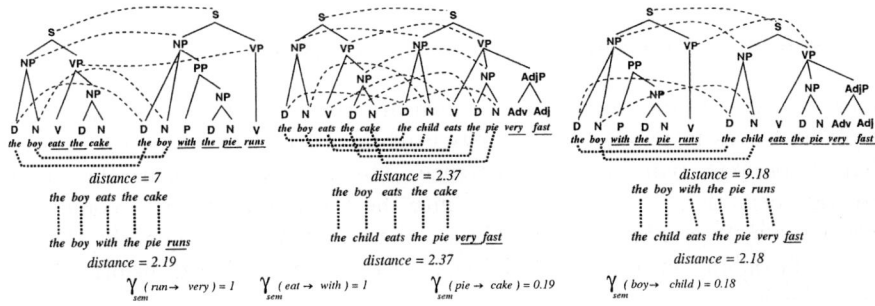

Fig. 3. String matching and tree matching mapping between words

3.1 Semantic Similarity at Word Level

Here, we have chosen to follow Lin's work [3], based on the use of the WORDNET [4] taxonomy, a computer dictionary that organizes its contents on a set of semantic relationships between structures called *synsets*. A *synset* is a set of words sharing the same, or, approximately the same, meaning. The semantic relationships are established between pairs of synsets, hyperonymy [1] being the most important one.

Lin assumes that the WORDNET taxonomy is a tree, and his approach is based on the information content of each synset. Given two words, w_1 and w_2, belonging to the synsets S_1 and S_2, respectively, let $P(S_i)$ be the probability that a randomly selected word from WORDNET belongs to synset S_i or one of its more specific synsets. So, if we assume that S_0 is the most specific synset that subsumes both S_1 and S_2, according to the hyperonymy relation, the similarity of w_1 and w_2 is computed as follows:

$$sim_{\text{Lin}}(w_1, w_2) = \frac{-2 \times logP(S_0)}{logP(S_1) \times logP(S_2)}$$

The resulting measure gives a value in $[0,1]$, where values closest to 1 mean a high semantical similarity, and values closest to 0 mean the greatest dissimilarity between words.

We use Lin's measure as a basis to compute the semantical cost, γ_{sem}, that we have to associate with the edit operations applied to the leaves of the parses we are comparing. Since we are dealing with a cost function, we must reverse the interpretation of the numerical values offered by this measure. Again, we denote the *insertion* of a word w_j as $\varepsilon \to w_j$, and the *deletion* of a word w_i as $w_i \to \varepsilon$. So, we compute $\gamma_{\text{sem}}(w_i \to w_j)$, as follows:

$$\gamma_{\text{sem}}(w_i \to w_j) = \begin{cases} 1 & \text{iff } w_i = \varepsilon \text{ or } w_j = \varepsilon \\ 1 - sim_{\text{Lin}}(w_i, w_j) & \text{iff } w_i \neq \varepsilon \text{ and } w_j \neq \varepsilon \end{cases}$$

When two words are close following Lin's measure, the cost will be near 0; and with non-similar words, the cost will be close to 1. This definition fulfills the properties of a metric.

3.2 Sentence Similarity Based on Edit Distance

Once we have established a way to measure the cost of the edit operations involving leaves in parses, we can extend it in order to compute a semantical distance between pairs of whole sentences. Our aim is to measure the cost of the transformation from one sentence into the other, taking into account both lexical and syntactic information. We use the function γ_{sem} to quantify the cost of the edit operations on the words needed to perform such a transformation.

---

[1] This is the classical *is-a* relationship, the semantic relation established between a general word and another more specific word.

As a first approach, we could use a variation of the classical string matching algorithm by Wagner and Fischer [9] to locate the operations to be applied over the words in the two sentences. The algorithm would identify the sequence of modifications needed to obtain one of them from the other with a minimum cost. We would simply treat each word in the sentences as if it were a character, measuring the cost of the edit operations with the γ_{sem} function.

However, as shown in Fig. 3, the correspondence between the words that the string matching approach yields can be rather odd. The approach simply tries to get an alignment between words with a minimum cost, without taking into account whether that correspondence makes sense or not at word level. So, in the first pair of sentences in Fig. 3, the algorithm aligns the verb "eat" with the preposition "with", adding a cost of 1 unit, which has no grammatical sense since the syntactic roles are different. The final measure results in a deviation masking the actual semantic distance between the sentences.

This justifies the consideration of tree matching to identify the transformations from which semantic proximity is computed. So, our approach integrates the algorithm to compute the minimum edit distance between trees by Zhang et al. [10], using the distances obtained to select which words have to be modified in order to transform the sentences.

In practice, the set of partial distances between parses are used to identify a minimal cost mapping, shown with dashed lines in Fig. 3. From this, we extract the edit operations applied over the leaves, and from them, we get the set of words whose semantical costs, computed by γ_{sem}, are accumulated. In the left-most pair of sentences in Fig. 3, we can see how using the tree matching approach the words "eats" and "with" are no longer related, due to their different structural context. So, both semantic costs and structural distances are computed in parallel, guided by the partial forest distances and following the same bottom-up strategy.

4 Semantic Similarity from Word to Sentence Level

Once we have sketched our proposal, we show now how the propagation of semantical measures is effectively performed, guided by the computation of partial structural distances.

4.1 The Semantic Distance

We first introduce a cost function, γ, to be used within the tree matching algorithm. This takes into account the semantic similarity between words implicated in tree edit operations. To do so, we extend a discrete function with the inclusion of the γ_{sem}. Formally, we define γ as

$$\gamma(a \to b) = \begin{cases} 1 & \text{iff } a = \varepsilon \text{ or } b = \varepsilon \text{ or } a \neq b \\ 0 & \text{iff } a = b \\ & \text{and } (a \notin \text{leaves}(P) \text{ or } b \notin \text{leaves}(D)) \\ \gamma_{sem}(word(a) \to word(b)) & \text{otherwise} \end{cases}$$

The two first cases define a discrete function. It assigns cost 1 to insert and delete operations. The cost of a relabeling is given by the γ_{sem} cost of the exchange between the corresponding words, which allows us to introduce a first notion of semantic similarity in tree matching.

We now introduce the *semantic forest distance*, fd_{sem}, as an extension of the concept at word level inspired by Zhang *et al.* [10]. Given two trees, P and D, $fd_{\text{sem}}(P[s_1..s_2], D[t_1..t_2])$ is the cost of the set of edit operations performed over the individual words belonging to the sub-forests $P[s_1..s_2]$ and $D[t_1..t_2]$. The selection of the operations to be applied on those words is made according to the current tree edit operation on the associated leaves, in order to obtain the optimal structural mapping that yields the $fd(P[s_1..s_2], D[t_1..t_2])$ value. In an analogous way, $td_{\text{sem}}(i,j)$ is equal to $fd_{\text{sem}}(r(i)..i, r[j]..j)$.

4.2 Computation of Semantic Distances

What our approach basically does is to make the computation of fd values and use them to decide which fd_{sem} values propagate in each case, according to the following set of formulae:

(1) $fd_{\text{sem}}(\emptyset, \emptyset) = 0$

$$fd_{\text{sem}}(\emptyset, r(j)..t) = \begin{cases} fd_{\text{sem}}(\emptyset, r(j)..t - 1) + \gamma_{\text{sem}}(\varepsilon \to word(d[t])) & \text{iff } r(t) = t \\ fd_{\text{sem}}(\emptyset, r(j)..t - 1) & \text{otherwise} \end{cases}$$

$$fd_{\text{sem}}(r(i)..s, \emptyset) = \begin{cases} fd_{\text{sem}}(r(i)..s - 1, \emptyset) + \gamma_{\text{sem}}(word(p[s]) \to \varepsilon) & \text{iff } r(s) = s \\ fd_{\text{sem}}(r(i)..s - 1, \emptyset) & \text{otherwise} \end{cases}$$

(2) $fd_{\text{sem}}(r(i)..s, r(j)..t) = \min \begin{cases} \begin{cases} fd_{\text{sem}}(r(i)..s - 1, r(j)..t) + \gamma_{\text{sem}}(word(p[s]) \to \varepsilon) & \text{iff } r(s) = s \\ fd_{\text{sem}}(r(i)..s - 1, r(j)..t) & \text{otherwise} \end{cases} \\ \text{iff } fd(r(i)..s, r(j)..t) = fd(r(i)..s - 1, r(j)..t) + \gamma(p[s]) \to \varepsilon) \\ \begin{cases} fd_{\text{sem}}(r(i)..s, r(j)..t - 1) + \gamma_{\text{sem}}(\varepsilon \to word(d[t])) & \text{iff } r(t) = t \\ fd_{\text{sem}}(r(i)..s, r(j)..t - 1) & \text{otherwise} \end{cases} \\ \text{iff } fd(r(i)..s, r(j)..t) = fd(r(i)..s, r(j)..t - 1) + \gamma(\varepsilon \to d[t]) \\ \begin{cases} fd_{\text{sem}}(r(i)..s - 1, r(j)..t - 1) + \\ \gamma_{\text{sem}}(word(p[s]) \to word(d[t])) & \text{iff } r(s) = s \text{ and } r(t) = t \\ fd_{\text{sem}}(r(i)..s - 1, r(j)..t - 1) & \text{otherwise} \end{cases} \\ \text{iff } fd(r(i)..s, r(j)..t) = fd(r(i)..s - 1, r(j)..t - 1) + \gamma(p[s]) \to d[t]) \\ fd_{\text{sem}}(r(i)..s, \emptyset) + \sum_k \gamma(\varepsilon \to d[k]), \ d[k] \in \text{leaves}(D[t]) \\ \text{iff } fd(r(i)..s, r(j)..t) = fd(r(i)..s - 1, \emptyset) \end{cases}$

iff $r(s) = r(i)$ **and** $r(t) = r(j)$

(3) $fd_{\text{sem}}(r(i)..s, r(j)..t) = \min \begin{cases} \begin{cases} fd_{\text{sem}}(r(i)..s - 1, r(j)..t) + \gamma_{\text{sem}}(word(p[s]) \to \varepsilon) & \text{iff } r(s) = s \\ fd_{\text{sem}}(r(i)..s - 1, r(j)..t) & \text{otherwise} \end{cases} \\ \text{iff } fd(r(i)..s, r(j)..t) = fd(r(i)..s - 1, r(j)..t) + \gamma(p[s] \to \varepsilon) \\ \begin{cases} fd_{\text{sem}}(r(i)..s, r(j)..t - 1) + \gamma_{\text{sem}}(\varepsilon \to word(d[t])) & \text{iff } r(t) = t \\ fd_{\text{sem}}(r(i)..s, r(j)..t - 1) & \text{otherwise} \end{cases} \\ \text{iff } fd(r(i)..s, r(j)..t) = fd(r(i)..s, r(j)..t - 1) + \gamma(\varepsilon \to d[t]) \\ fd_{\text{sem}}(r(i)..r(s) - 1, r(j)..r(t) - 1) + td_{\text{sem}}(s, t) \\ \text{iff } fd(r(i)..s, r(j)..t) = fd(r(i)..r(s) - 1, r(j)..r(t) - 1) + td(s, t) \\ fd_{\text{sem}}(r(i)..s, r(j)..r(t) - 1) + \sum_k \gamma(\varepsilon \to d[k]), \ d[k] \in \text{leaves}(D[t]) \\ \text{iff } fd(r(i)..s, r(j)..t) = fd(r(i)..s - 1, r(t) - 1) \end{cases}$

otherwise

where we use the notation $word(t[i])$, to reference the word associated with the $t[i]$ node in the tree T in the case of this node being a leaf. If $t[i]$ is not a leaf, we have that $word(t[i]) = \varepsilon$.

The computation of $fd_{\text{sem}}(r(i)..s, r(j)..t)$ is made in parallel with the computation of the $fd(r(i)..s, r(j)..t)$ values. As in the original tree matching case, we also have three sets of formulae: one for initialization, one for subtrees distances and one for sub-forests distance. These formulae reflect how the edit operation from which the current $fd(r(i)..s, r(j)..t)$ was obtained is identified,

$$"\text{the} \left\{ \begin{array}{c} \text{boy} \\ \text{child} \\ \text{girl} \end{array} \right\} \text{with the} \left\{ \begin{array}{c} \text{cake} \\ \text{pie} \end{array} \right\} \text{of} \left[\text{the} \left\{ \begin{array}{c} \text{friend} \\ \text{mate} \end{array} \right\} \text{of} \right]^i \text{Mary} \left\{ \begin{array}{c} \text{runs} \\ \text{walks} \end{array} \right\} \text{very fast"}$$

$$"\text{the} \left\{ \begin{array}{c} \text{boy} \\ \text{child} \\ \text{girl} \end{array} \right\} \left\{ \begin{array}{c} \text{eats} \\ \text{steals} \end{array} \right\} \text{the} \left\{ \begin{array}{c} \text{cake} \\ \text{pie} \end{array} \right\} \text{of} \left[\text{the} \left\{ \begin{array}{c} \text{friend} \\ \text{mate} \end{array} \right\} \text{of} \right]^i \text{Mary very fast"}$$

Fig. 4. Data sentences

and how the new fd_{sem} values are computed, propagating a previous semantic distance value or adding a semantic cost to such a previous value.

Zhang et al. [10] proceed through the trees in a bottom-up fashion, computing partial distances and increasing the sizes of the considered pairs of sub-forests. In each step, every possible way to obtain the current syntactic distance, one for each edit operation and one per subtree cut, is computed using the partial distances obtained in previous steps, and the one giving the minimum value is recorded. In our proposal, for each syntactic distance computed we identify which were the previous partial distances used to compute it. This allows us to determine whether the last nodes at the current sub-forests are involved in the optimal mapping or not, and which edit operations have been applied on them.

Once the best edit operation is identified, we compute $fd_{\text{sem}}(r(i)..s, r(j)..t)$ for the current pair of sub-forests. If no leaves are involved in this operation, we propagate the semantic distance associated with the syntactic distance fd from which the current $fd(r(i)..s, r(j)..t)$ was obtained. Otherwise, when $r(s) = s$ or $r(t) = t$, we add to the fd_{sem} value recovered from the previous step the semantic cost of the operation that has to be applied on the words present in the leaves. It must be noted that when case (3) is used, it only propagates previous fd_{sem} values. The reason is that if leaves were involved in that distance, the cost would have been taken into account in a previous step, when computing the corresponding $td_{\text{sem}}(s, t)$ value, through the tree-to-tree formulae, numbered as (2).

In the cases of subtree cuts, for both tree-to-tree and forest-to-forest distances, the previous values are incremented with the cost of deleting every leaf belonging to the cut subtrees, as shown in the last cases of the sets of formulae (2) and (3). In this way, we avoid deviations in the final semantic distance that subtree cuts could induce. So, although in the tree matching some parts of the data trees can be omitted and not taken into account in the final distance, our proposal does not miss out the deleted words at the cut leaves, which will be part of the semantic cost like any other delete operation.

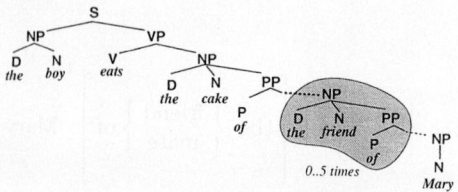

Fig. 5. Pattern trees

An additional refinement is required to deal with situations where a syntactic distance can be obtained using different edit operations. In the case of multiple ways to conform a minimal structural mapping we prefer the option with the least distance fd_{sem}. That is the reason why after having selected and computed all of the possible current $fd_{\text{sem}}(r(i)..s, r(j)..t)$ values, we select the minimum between all of them, as is shown in the formulae (2) and (3).

5 A Practical Example

Our aim now is to provide preliminary results illustrating how the tree matching based measure can give a more precise notion of semantic similarity than the classic string matching ones. To this end, we consider the pico-grammar of English as running example:

(1) S → NP VP   (4) PP → P NP   (7) NP → Det Name
(2) VP → Verb NP AdjP   (5) AdjP → Adv Adj   (8) NP → Det Name PP
(3) VP → Verb NP PP AdjP (6) NP → Name   (9) NP → Det Name PP PP

In accordance with this grammar, we have created a bank of data sentences generated as is shown in Fig. 4. All possible combinations of the words *"boy, child, girl"*, with *"eat, steal, run, walk"*, with *"cake, pie"* and with *"friend, mate"* have been considered to compose those sentences, where i represents the number of repetitions of the substrings enclosed in braces, with values ranging from 0 to 7. We have also created a set of pattern sentences in the following form, where i ranges from 0 to 5:

"the boy eats the cake of [the friend of]^i Mary"

The presence of a rule "NP → Det Name PP PP" implies that the number of possible parses grows exponentially with i, and it is given by:

$$C_0 = C_1 = 1 \quad \text{and} \quad C_i = \binom{2i}{i} \frac{1}{i+1}, \text{ if } i > 1$$

The described frame provides, in spite of its simplicity, a highly ambiguous environment to test our proposal. To deal with this, we have generated the parse trees using ICE [7], which represents them in a compact form as a shared forest. We have also incorporated the optimizations in the tree matching algorithm

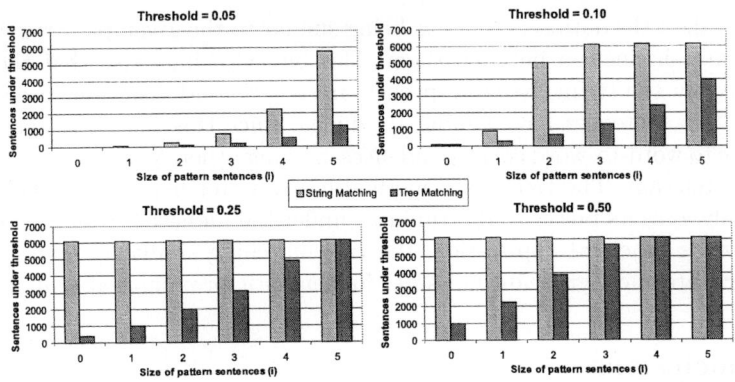

Fig. 6. Tree matching vs. string matching semantic measures

shown in [8], to take advantage of the structural sharing offered by ICE in order to avoid redundant computations.

In the case of tree matching, the pattern trees are deterministic sentences with the structure shown in Fig. 5. To test string matching, the pattern and data sentences were used directly, without parsing them, following the Lin's method [3]. To compare our proposal with Lin's one, we have normalized the resulting distances in [0, 1]. To normalize the similarity between sentences S_1 and S_2, we apply:

$$sim(S_1, S_2) = \frac{d(S_1, S_2)}{|S_1| + |S_2|}$$

where $d(S_1, S_2)$ is a semantic cost, and $|S_i|$ is the number of words in sentence S_i.

In this context, we calculate the number of sentences whose similarity values with respect to a pattern sentence fall under a given threshold, assuming that more precise approaches should provide reduced sets of sentences since they are based on stricter similarity criteria. We aim to determine whether the values obtained by both methods are able to make the semantic proximity between sentences evident, and to identify non-similar ones without deviations.

In Fig. 6 we compare the results obtained by both algorithms when considering thresholds 0.05, 0.10, 0.25 and 0.50; with values of i for the pattern sentences ranging from 0 to 5. As can be seen, under the four thresholds, the tree matching approach seems to be more precise, showing a higher power of discrimination, returning smaller numbers of sentences. Moreover, the string matching method tends to suffer from deviations when the sentences compared share the same words with different syntactic roles, as happens in our case. So, the number of sentences under every threshold is always greater when using the string based measure, showing that the tree based values provide a more accurate notion of semantic proximity.

We can also see in the four charts how the string based measure quickly degenerates when the thresholds become higher. In these cases this method identifies all of the data sentences as being similar to the given patterns, without making any distinction between them. This behavior indicates that the values computed by the string based approach are not a good criterion to determine whether two sentences have similar meanings, since this metric assigns a high relevance to word-to-word correspondences, making other syntactic and semantic aspects irrelevant. The tree based method has a better behavior in those cases, and it only loses its power to discriminate under the highest thresholds. So, with regard to its practical application, the tree matching similarity seems to offer more accurate and significant measures for semantic proximity at sentence level.

6 Conclusions

The increasing amount of information available in electronic format, placed on line, has created a growing need for effective similarity measures. Without this kind of tools, access to relevant documents becomes an inefficient task, with null practical interest. In this context, many strategies have been proposed and implemented, most of them based on single-term oriented approaches, which do not always convey local context information.

Our proposal exploits the meaning extracted from single-terms, integrating it into the edit distance construction. This allows us to deal with problems where we can take advantage of the use of semantic information in pattern-matching processes. In this sense, preliminary results seem to support the validity of the approach as opposed to solutions based exclusively on syntactic structures or single terms.

Acknowledgments

This research has been partially supported by the Spanish Government (projects TIC2000-0370-C02-01 and HF2002-0081, FPU grant AP2001-2545), the Autonomous Government of Galicia (projects PGIDIT-03SIN30501PR, PGIDIT-02SIN01E and PGIDIT-02PXIB3051PR) and the University of A Coruña.

References

1. K. Hammouda and M. Kamel. Phrase-based document similarity based on an index graph model. In *2002 IEEE Int. Conf. on Data Mining*, pages 203–210, Maebashi, Japan, 2002.
2. M. Montes-y-Gomez, A. Gelbukh, A. Lopez-Lopez and R. Baeza-Yates Flexible Comparison of Conceptual Graphs. In *2001 Database and Expert Systems Applications*, vol. 2113 of Lecture Notes in Computer Science, Springer-Verlag, 2001.
3. Dekang Lin. An information-theoretic definition of similarity. In *Proc. 15th International Conf. on Machine Learning*, pages 296–304, 1998.
4. G. Miller. WordNet: An online lexical database. *International Journal of Lexicography*, 3(4), 1990.

5. Mitchell. Machine learning and data mining. *CACM: Communications of the ACM*, 42, 1999.
6. Kuo-Chung Tai. The Tree-to-Tree Correction Problem. *Journal of the ACM*, 26(3):422–433, 1979.
7. M. Vilares and B.A. Dion. Efficient incremental parsing for context-free languages. In *Proc. of the 5th IEEE Int. Conf. on Computer Languages*, pages 241–252, Toulouse, France, 1994.
8. M. Vilares, F.J. Ribadas, and V.M. Darriba. Approximate pattern matching in shared-forest. *Lecture Notes in Computer Science*, 1873:322–333, 2000.
9. R.A. Wagner and M.J. Fischer. The string to string correction problem. *Journal of the ACM*, 21(1):168–173, 1974.
10. K. Zhang, D. Shasha, and J.T.L. Wang. Approximate tree matching in the presence of variable length don't cares. *Journal of Algorithms*, 16(1):33–66, January 1994.

A Document Model Based on Relevance Modeling Techniques for Semi-structured Information Warehouses

Juan Manuel Pérez, Rafael Berlanga, and María José Aramburu

Universitat Jaume I, Castellón, Spain
{martinej,berlanga,aramburu}@uji.es

Abstract. During the last decade, data warehouse and OLAP techniques have helped companies to gather, organize and analyze the *structured* data they produce. Simultaneously, digital libraries have applied Information Retrieval mechanisms to query their repositories of *unstructured* text-rich documents. In this paper we explain how XML allows for the convergence of these two approaches, making possible the development of warehouses for *semi-structured* information. So far, the proposals of extending data warehouse technology to manage semi-structured information have not been able to exploit the textual contents, mainly because they are not based on a proper document model. In our opinion, such a model must integrate IR and OLAP techniques. In this paper we present a set of requirements for semi-structured information warehouses, as well as a document model to support their construction. In this model, new Relevance Modeling mechanisms are used for ranking the facts described in the text of the documents according to their relevance to an IR-OLAP query. Preliminary evaluations show the usefulness of the document model.

1 Introduction

During the last decade, data warehouse [1] and OLAP [2] techniques have helped companies to gather, organize and analyze the *structured* data they produce (usually stored in their own databases) to support decisions at various levels. These organizations also produce huge amounts of *unstructured* documents such as e-mails, dossiers and reports. At the same time, the Web has become the largest source of companies external information. Unfortunately, although all these documents contain highly valuable information, current data warehouse technology cannot be applied to exploit their textual contents.

The ever increasing amount of information published on the Internet has provided us with new services like digital libraries. All these applications require of advanced techniques to store and manage huge amounts of *unstructured* information, in which large text sections predominate. Most solutions to query these repositories are based on Information Retrieval (IR) [3] techniques. More recently, the efforts in this field are focused on the definition of architectures for the integration of distributed and heterogeneous documents sources.

The acceptance of XML [4] as the standard for semi-structured data exchange over the Web, points out to a close future when information on the Internet will be published as XML documents, and exportation tools from most proprietary systems to XML-like formats will be available. This situation opens a novel and interesting range of possibilities where the efforts done in the warehouse and document retrieval areas can be joined to develop new systems able to integrate and analyze XML-like documents: *semi-structured information warehouses*.

In this paper we present a document model that supports the construction of text-rich XML document warehouses. In this document model the facts described at the text of documents are ranked by their relevance to an IR-OLAP query.

1.1 Related Work

In the recent literature, some works extend data warehouse technology towards XML. Some of these approaches [5] include techniques to gather and massively store XML documents, but they do not propose high level analysis mechanisms to exploit this information. The work presented in [6] introduces a new query language based on SQL and XPath [4] which allows for the execution of OLAP operations over the data contained in XML documents external to the warehouse. Although this language is valid to query highly structured XML data, we think it fails when considering other kinds of XML data, such as documents with large text sections describing the facts to analyze.

The documents storage community have proposed several models to store and retrieve text-rich XML documents (e.g. [7][8]). These approaches efficiently combine Information Retrieval (IR) [3] techniques with mechanisms for the evaluation of conditions over the structure of documents. It can be concluded that to properly exploit the textual contents of the documents, a warehouse for semi-structured information must be based on an underlying document model that integrates all these techniques.

A novel proposal in the field of IR is Language Modeling (LM) [9]. The works on LM consider each document D as a language model M_D, and each IR query Q as a string of text. Thus, documents are ranked according to the probability $P(Q \mid M_D)$ of obtaining a query Q when randomly sampling from the respective language model. An extension to the LM approach are the Relevance Models (RM) [10] which try to determine the probability $P(t \mid R_Q)$ of observing a term t in the set R_Q of the documents relevant to a query Q. In our document model, this last approach is adapted to estimate the relevance of a fact f to a given IR query Q, by its probability $P(f \mid R_Q)$.

The rest of the paper is organized as follows. In Section 2 we present an example scenario to explain a set of new requirements for semi-structured information warehouses. In Section 3 we propose the document model. Section 4 shows the results obtained in a preliminary evaluation of the document model. Finally, in Section 5 we discuss some conclusions and future research lines.

2 An Example Scenario

We consider a semi-structured information warehouse as a large collection of text-rich XML documents where information extraction techniques (see references in Section 4) have been applied to tag the facts described in the original documents contents. Figure 1 shows an example document in a warehouse of XML digital newspapers. Suppose we are interested in studying the weather conditions that caused the natural disasters described at the relevant documents. The tags **LOCATION**, **DATE** and **RAINFALL** contain values that can be considered as either measures of analysis, or dimension values. In addition, the **XW:FACT** tags of the document group measure and dimension values into facts.

```
<NEWSPAPER NAME="El País" PUBLICATION_DATE="Tuesday, 2nd July 2002"> ...
<LOCAL_SECTION>
<NEWS_ITEM>  <AUTHOR>Carlos García</AUTHOR>
<TITLE>
<XW:FACTS>
   <XW:FACT FREQUENCY="1">
      <XW:DIM NAME="LOCATION" VALUE="/Europe/Spain/Valencia"/>
   </XW:FACT>
</XW:FACTS>
<LOCATION XW:VALUE="/Europe/Spain/Valencia">Valencia</LOCATION> suffers the biggest storm
of July of the last 41 years
</TITLE>
<PARAGRAPH>
<XW:FACTS>
   <XW:FACT FREQUENCY="1">
      <XW:DIM NAME="DATE"  VALUE="/2002/07/01"/>
      <XW:DIM NAME="LOCATION" VALUE="/Europe/Spain/Valencia/Valencia"/>
      <XW:DIM NAME="RAINFALL" VALUE="128" UNIT="1/m2"/>
   </XW:FACT>
   <XW:FACT FREQUENCY="1">
      <XW:DIM NAME="DATE"  VALUE="/2002/07/01"/>
      <XW:DIM NAME="LOCATION" VALUE="/Europe/Spain/Valencia/Burjasot"/>
      <XW:DIM NAME="RAINFALL" VALUE="132" UNIT="1/m2"/>
   </XW:FACT>
   <XW:FACT FREQUENCY="1">
      <XW:DIM NAME="DATE"  VALUE="/2002/07/01"/>
      <XW:DIM NAME="LOCATION" VALUE="/Europe/Spain/Murcia"/>
   </XW:FACT>
   <XW:FACT FREQUENCY="1">
      <XW:DIM NAME="DATE"  VALUE="/2002/07/01"/>
      <XW:DIM NAME="LOCATION" VALUE="/Europe/Spain/Baleares"/>
   </XW:FACT>
</XW:FACTS>
The biggest storm of July of the last 41 years fell
<DATE XW:VALUE="/2002/07/01"> yesterday </DATE> over the city of
<LOCATION XW:VALUE="/Europe/Spain/Valencia/Valencia"> Valencia </LOCATION>, the
<RAINFALL XW:VALUE="128" XW:UNIT="1/m2">128 liters per square meter</RAINFALL> rained in
only 24 hours made firemen had to go on rescue more than 100 times. At
<LOCATION XW:VALUE="/Europe/Spain/Valencia/Burjassot">Burjassot</LOCATION> fell
<DATE XW:VALUE="/2002/07/01"> during the night </DATE>
<RAINFALL XW:VALUE="132" XW:UNIT="1/m2"> 132 liters per square meter</RAINFALL>, throwing
down a building. The strong rain on the East of Iberian Peninsula caused disasters in the
regions of <LOCATION XV:VALUE="/Europe/Spain/Murcia">Murcia</LOCATION> and
<LOCATION XW:VALUE="/Europe/Spain/Baleares">Baleares</LOCATION>.
</PARAGRAPH> ...
</NEWS_ITEM> ...
</LOCAL_SECTION> ...
</NEWSPAPER>
```

Fig. 1. A piece of a document of the warehouse

Next, we show an example query which could be used in the warehouse for building an OLAP cube to analyze the average of the amount of water collected per location when a storm occurred. Note that here, our purpose is not to propose a new query language, but to establish a set of key features that a warehouse must provide when managing semi-structured information.

```
SELECT Avg(Paragraph/Rainfall)
FROM //Local_Section//News_Item
WHERE Paragraph contains 'storm' > 0.5
GROUP BY CUBE (Paragraph/Location)
```

2.1 Documents Structure and Conceptual Analysis Schema

The example query uses path expressions to specify the document sections under study. In the FROM clause it is stated that we are studying the News_Item elements at the Local_Section parts of the documents. The SELECT clause provides the measure under analysis, that is, Rainfall values found at the Paragraph elements of these News_Item portions. Finally, in the GROUP BY clause the analysis dimension of the query is specified (Location values). In this way, the resulting OLAP cube will involve those facts described at the *news items* of the *local sections* of the documents which have values for the dimension *location* and the measure *rainfall*.

Note that since XML documents are self-describing, we consider that part of the conceptual analysis schema of the warehouse is implicitly represented in the own structure of documents. That is, measures and dimensions are tags in the documents. In this way, a semi-structured warehouse must be flexible enough to dynamically specify in the analysis queries the dimensions and measures included in the documents. The most natural way of specifying such measures and dimensions is by means of XPath [4]expressions.

2.2 IR Conditions and Facts Relevance

Following with the example query, an IR condition has been used in the WHERE clause to restrict the analysis to those news items whose paragraphs contain the term *"storm"* with a relevance index greater than 50%. In this way, only those facts described at the relevant paragraphs will be considered to build the OLAP cube. This kind of conditions are necessary when managing large repositories of documents which can include large texts about many different topics.

IR systems rank their answers according to their relevance to the retrieval condition. In the same way, a warehouse of XML documents should rank the facts in the OLAP cubes according to the relevance index of the textual document sections that include them.

A further feature to consider is that the same fact can be present at different parts of a document, which increases the importance of the fact at this document. For example, consider as facts the (DATE, LOCATION) pairs at the XW:FACT tags of the document shown in Figure 1. If we roll up to the second level of the hierarchy in the dimension LOCATION, the fact (2002/07/01, /Europe/Spain/Valencia) occurs twice whereas the facts (2002/07/01, /Europe/Spain/Murcia) and (2002/07/01, /Europe/Spain/Baleares) occur just once. This suggests that in this section of the document, the first fact is more relevant than the second and third one.

2.3 Summary of Requirements

In order to apply OLAP operations to exploit the textual contents of XML documents, the development of new semi-structured information warehouses must be based upon an underlying document model where:

- The structure of the documents is explicitly represented in the model, so that path expressions can be used to select the document parts under study, and to specify the dimensions/measures under analysis.
- IR queries are supported and the resulting facts are ranked by a relevance measure considering both the relevance of the textual document contents, and the number of times that the facts appear in these contents.

In the next section we propose a document model based on Relevance Modeling techniques that satisfies these requirements.

3 The Document Model

In our model a document is represented as a hierarchical tree built by nesting its elements. The leaves of the tree are either *textual contents, attribute values* or *facts collection* nodes. At the left-side of Figure 2 we show this representation for the example document of Figure 1. By choosing the usual tree representation of XML documents, all the previous works concerning the evaluation of path expressions over XML documents [4][8] can be directly applied to our document model.

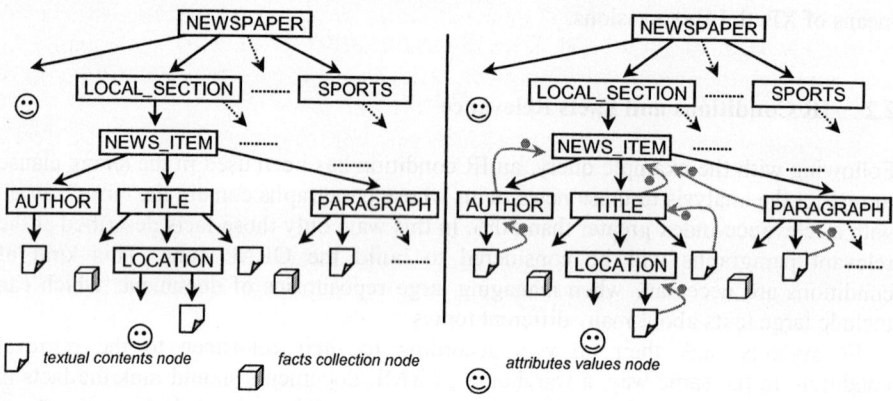

Fig. 2. Document example (left-side), and its aggregated term frequency calculus (right-side)

3.1 Textual Contents Nodes

A *textual contents node* represents the text contained into an element of the original document. For example, for each PARAGRAPH element in the document of Figure 1, we will have a corresponding PARAGRAPH node in the document tree with a child *textual contents node* representing the text contained in this paragraph (see Figure 2).

In the document model, we assign to each textual content node n a list of 2-tuples of the form $((t_1, tf_{1,n}), (t_2, tf_{2,n}), \ldots (t_k, tf_{k,n}))$, where t_i is a term appearing in the text represented by the node n and $tf_{i,n}$ is the frequency of the term t_i (i.e. the number of times the term occurs) in the node n.

We define the *aggregated term frequency* of a term t_i in any arbitrary node n as:

$$TF(t_i, n) = \begin{cases} tf_{i,n}, \text{ if } n \text{ is a textual contents node;} \\ \sum_{cn \in children(n)} TF(t_i, cn), \text{ otherwise} \end{cases}$$

Thus, in the document of Figure 2, the aggregated term frequency function can be used to represent the text contained by the NEWS_ITEM node or any of its descendants. That is, the text contained in the document subtree under the NEWS_ITEM node. At the right side of Figure 2 we show how this function is applied starting from the textual content nodes of the document subtree.

3.2 Facts Collection Nodes

Each *facts collection node* represents the facts described by an element of the document. Taking the previous example, for each PARAGRAPH element in the document of Figure 1, the corresponding PARAGRAPH node in the document tree will have associated a child *facts collection node* representing the facts described at this paragraph. Facts collection nodes can be considered as the formal representation of the **xw:FACTS** tags in the original documents.

In contrast to traditional warehouses, in our model measures are also considered dimensions. In this way, we add flexibility to the model by allowing, for example, to take **DATE** values as a measure in a OLAP query, and later to specify **DATE** as a dimension in a different query.

In the document model, a facts collection node n is represented as a list of 2-tuples of the form $((f_1, ff_{1,n}), (f_2, ff_{2,n}), \ldots (f_k, ff_{k,n}))$, where f_i is a fact and $ff_{i,n}$ its frequency in the node n (i.e. the number of times f_i is mentioned in n).

A fact f_i consists of a m-tuple, where m is the number of different dimension and measure types found in the documents of the warehouse. In the example of the Figure 1, there are three different types of measures/dimensions: **LOCATION**, **DATE** and **RAINFALL**. Other documents of the warehouse may add new dimensions/measures.

Thus, a m-tuple representing a fact f_i, will take values in $(D_1, D_2, \ldots D_m)$, where D_j is the domain of all the possible values in all the hierarchy levels of the dimension j. Given that the definition of dimension hierarchies is out of the scope of the document model, we simply consider the set of valid values that will be defined in the final warehouse model. It is important to point out that since incomplete facts may appear in the documents, all dimension domains D_j must include the *null* value. Next, we show the facts collection node that represents the facts described by the PARAGRAPH in the example of the Figure 1:

(((/2002/07/01, /Europe/Spain/Valencia/Valencia, 128), 1),
 ((/2002/07/01, /Europe/Spain/Valencia/Burjasot, 132), 1),
 ((/2002/07/01, /Europe/Spain/Murcia, *null*), 1),
 ((/2002/07/01, /Europe/Spain/Baleares, *null*), 1))

Finally, we define the *aggregated fact frequency* of a fact f_i in a node n as:

$$FF(f_i, n) = \begin{cases} ff_{i,n}, & \text{if } n \text{ is a facts collection node;} \\ \sum_{cn \in children(n)} FF(f_i, cn), & \text{otherwise} \end{cases}$$

As the aggregated term frequency function, the aggregated fact frequency function can be used to represent the facts described by any subtree of the document.

3.3 Fact Relevance Calculus

Given an IR query of the form $Q = q_1 q_2 \ldots q_n$, where q_i is a query term, we define the relevance of a fact f_i to the query Q as the probability of observing the fact f_i in the document nodes relevant to the query:

$$P(f_i | R_Q) = \sum_{n \in R_Q} P(f_i | n) P(n | Q) \quad (1)$$

The formula (1) is based on the RM formula presented in [10]. However, we have adapted it to estimate the relevance of facts instead of document terms. R_Q is the set of document nodes relevant to the query Q, as a consequence, R_Q will be a subset of all the nodes in all the documents of the warehouse.

$$P(n|Q) = \frac{P(Q|n)P(n)}{P(Q)} \quad (2) \qquad P(Q) = \sum_{n' \in R_Q} P(Q|n') P(n') \quad (3)$$

By applying the conditional probability formula (2), following the approach of [10] to estimate $P(Q)$ as (3), and considering that the probability of selecting a node $P(n)$ is constant, our fact relevance formula (1) can be rewritten as (4):

$$P(f_i | R_Q) = \frac{\sum_{n \in R_Q} P(f_i | n) P(Q | n)}{\sum_{n' \in R_Q} P(Q | n')} \quad (4)$$

Now, we take the LM approach [9] to calculate $P(Q | n)$ as (5), and propose (6) to estimate the probability of finding a term q_i in a document node n.

$$P(Q|n) = \prod_{q_i \in Q} P(q_i | n) \quad (5) \qquad P(q_i | n) = \lambda \frac{TF(q_i, n)}{|n|_t} + (1 - \lambda) \frac{ctf_{qi}}{coll\_size_t} \quad (6)$$

The formula (6) is also based on a LM proposal [9]. However, by including the aggregated term frequency in the formula, we adapt it to work with document nodes (document subtrees) instead of with entire documents. Here, $|n|_t$ is the total number of terms in the node n, ctf_{qi} is the total number of times that q_i occurs in all the documents of the warehouse, and $coll\_size_t$ is the total number of terms in all the documents of the warehouse. The value of λ is determined empirically.

In the same way, we propose (7) to estimate the probability of observing a fact f_i in a document node n. Here, $|n|_f$ is the total number of facts in the node n, cff_{fi} is the total number of times f_i occurs in all the documents of the warehouse, and $coll\_size_f$ the total number of facts in all the documents of the warehouse. The value of ω is determined empirically.

$$P(f_i | n) = \omega \frac{FF(f_i, n)}{|n|_f} + (1 - \omega) \frac{cff_{fi}}{coll\_size_f} \quad (7)$$

Summarizing, given an IR query Q, and a set of document nodes R_Q relevant to the query, our document model provides the formula (4) as a mechanism to estimate the relevance of the facts described at R_Q. Since the aggregated term and fact frequency functions have been used in the formulas (7) and (6), the nodes at R_Q can represent any document subtree in the warehouse. The latter means that the document model supports IR-OLAP queries, like the one presented in Section 2, where the user can arbitrary choose (for example, by using path expressions) which are the documents subtrees under analysis.

4 Experiments and Results

In order to validate the document model presented in Section 3, we designed some experiments. The objectives of these experiments were: first, to build an initial document corpus by following our document model; and second, given an IR query, to test if the proposed fact relevance ranking mechanism assigns the highest relevance index to the most relevant group of facts.

The initial corpus consists of a collection of 30 XML digital newspapers published during June 1999. By applying the shallow parsing and information extraction techniques presented in [11] and [12], we located and tagged the measure/dimension values described in the documents contents. As a result, we enriched the original documents with **LOCATION** and **DATE** tags, like those in Figure 1.

Finally, in order to group the measure/dimension values into facts (see the **XW:FACTS** tags in the document of Figure 1), we used a simple heuristics to know, the **LOCATION** and **DATE** values found in the same sentence will constitute a fact.

In our experiments we considered the news items contained in the International sections of the newspapers (a total number of 555 news items), and query them with a set of IR queries about different topics. In order to give more importance to the occurrence of the term and facts in the selected news items, rather than in the global collection, we set the parameters λ and ω of the formulas (6) and (7) to 0.9. However, for the future, we consider necessary a deeper study of their influence.

Then, for each IR query, we applied the formula (5) to estimate the relevance of the news items, and we chose the news items at the top of the relevance ranking to build R_Q.

Regarding the number of news items to include in R_Q, in our preliminary experiments we observed that a small size of R_Q led to imprecise results. In our opinion, this occurs because facts do not use to co-occur in different documents in a small set of samples. In addition, there are a set of important events which are transversally reported by many news items, independently of their main subject. If the size of R_Q is too big, these important events may become the main topic of the news items at R_Q. This last effect can be reduced by considering a larger document corpus. In our experiments, the best performance was obtained by keeping the size of R_Q between 20 and 60. Table 1 shows the top-ranked facts returned by our document model for different IR queries. As it can be noticed, all the returned facts are relevant to the stated queries, and they correspond to the dates and places where they actually occurred. However, in the results we also found a considerable number of incomplete facts (i.e. without the LOCATION or the DATE value). As a conclusion, a more elaborated technique to group measures/dimension values into facts must be studied.

Table 1. Example IR queries and facts at the top of the relevance ranking ($\lambda = \omega = 0.9$, size of R_Q between 20 and 60)

Facts	Q=civil, conflict	Relev.	Explanation
(10/06/1999, Kosovo)		0.0893	UNO finishes bombardments in Kosovo
(12/06/1999, Kosovo)		0.0882	Multinational NATO forces (KFOR) get into Kosovo
(15/06/1999, Kosovo)		0.0863	Serb radical party protests against KFOR
(31/03/1999, Macedonia)		0.0504	Three American soldiers were captured in Macedonia (*news items may describe facts from the past*)
(27/06/1999, Algeria)		0.0405	On 27th June, Government officials estimated that more than 100,000 Algerians died during the war against the Armed Islamic Group
(06/06/1999, Guatemala)		0.0381	Human Rights Organizations claim judgments for the crimes at the Guatemala's civil war
(16/06/1999, Kumanovo)		0.0263	The agreement on the retreat of the Serb forces from Kosovo is signed at Kumanovo
(09/06/1999, Serbia)		0.0185	Javier Solana's declarations about the Serbian situation
(07/06/1999, Brussels)		0.0143	NATO declarations at Brussels regarding the bombardments in Kosovo
Facts	**Q=election**	**Relev.**	**Explanation**
(1994, Holland)		0.0770	European Elections
(1994, Spain)		0.0753	
(1994, Ireland)		0.0709	
(2000, USA)		0.0599	Next USA Elections
(13/06/1999, Indonesia)		0.0411	Elections in Indonesia
(2/06/1999, South Africa)		0.0398	Elections in South Africa
Facts	**Q=summit**	**Relev.**	**Explanation**
(*/11/1999, La Habana)		0.0583	Summit of the Iberoamerican states in La Habana
(18/06/1999, Cologne)		0.0565	G-8 Summit in Cologne
(28/06/1999, Rio Janeiro)		0.0526	Meeting European Union and Latin American states in Rio Janeiro
(29/06/1999, Rio Janeiro)		0.0515	
(16/06/1999, Cologne)		0.0512	G-8 Summit in Cologne

5 Conclusions

In this paper we have described how a warehouse for semi-structured information can be used to analyze large collections of text-rich XML documents. Our main contributions are a set of new requirements for semi-structured warehouses, and a document model that supports their construction. The proposed document model adapts new Relevance Modeling techniques to rank the facts described in the documents according to their relevance to an IR-OLAP query.

In a preliminary evaluation of the model we have obtained satisfactory results. However a more rigorous study over a lager document corpus with more measure/dimension types needs to be done. Additionally, it would also be interesting to enrich the document model with some fact fusion operations able to derive initially incomplete facts. The model could also be extended to include the terms specified in the IR conditions as an additional analysis dimension. Thesaurus and ontologies could be used to define classification hierarchies over this dimension.

For the future, we plan to design a warehouse model over the proposed document model. In order to provide it with new OLAP operations, some concepts need to be meticulously revised as the facts relevance, incomplete facts, the semantics of the aggregation operations, etc. For this purpose the works [13] and [14] could be good reference points.

References

1. R. Kimball. *The Data Warehouse toolkit*. John Wiley & Sons, 2002.
2. E. F. Codd, S. B. Codd and C.T. Salley. *Providing OLAP to user-analysts: An IT mandate*. Technical Report, E.F. Codd & Associates, 1993.
3. R. Baeza-Yates and B.Ribeiro-Neto. *Modern Information Retrieval*. Addison-Wesley, 1999.
4. World Wide Web Consortium. http://www.w3.org
5. L. Xyleme. *A dynamic warehouse for XML data of the Web*. IEEE Data Engineering Bulletin 24(2), pp. 40-47, June 2001.
6. D. Pedersen, K. Riis, T.B. Pedersen. *XML-Extended OLAP Querying*. Proc of the 14th International Conference on Scientific and Statistical Database Management, pp 195-206, July 24-26, 2002
7. G. Navarro and R. Baeza-Yates. *Proximal Nodes: A Model to Query Document Databases by Contents and Structure*. ACM Trans. on Information Systems, 1997.
8. M.J. Aramburu and R. Berlanga. *A Temporal Object-Oriented Model for Digital Librares of Documents*. Concurrency: Practice and Experience 13 (11), John Wiley, 2001.
9. J.M. Ponte and W.B. Croft. *A Language Modeling Approach to Information Retrieval*. Proc. of ACM SIGIR' 98 conference, pp 275-281, 1998.
10. V. Lavrenko and W.B. Croft. *Relevance-based language models*. Proc. of ACM SIGIR' 98 conference, pp 267-275, 2001.
11. D.M. Llidó, R. Berlanga, M.J., Aramburu. *Extracting Temporal References to Assign Document Event-Time Periods*. Proc of. DEXA 2001, pp. 62-71, 2001.
12. A. Pons, R. Berlanga, J. Ruíz-Shulcloper. *Building a Hierarchy of Events and Topics for Newspaper Digital Libraries*. Proc of. ECIR 2003, pp. 588-596, 2003.
13. T.B. Pedersen, C.S. Jensen, and C.E. Dyreson. *Supporting Imprecision in Multidimensional Databases Using Granularities*. Proc. of the Eleventh International Conference on Scientific and Statistical Database Management, pp. 90–101, 1999.
14. E. Rundensteiner and L. Bic. *Evaluating Aggregates in Possibilistic Relational Databases*. DKE, 7(3):239–267, 1992.

Retrieving Relevant Portions from Structured Digital Documents

Sujeet Pradhan[1] and Katsumi Tanaka[2]

[1] Kurashiki University of Science and the Arts, Kurashiki, Japan
sujeet@soft.kusa.ac.jp
[2] Kyoto University, Kyoto, Japan
ktanaka@i.kyoto-u.ac.jp

Abstract. Retrieving relevant portions from structured documents consisting of logical components has been a challenging task in both the database and the information retrieval world, since an answer related to a query may be split across multiple components. In this paper, we propose a query mechanism that applies database style query evaluation in response to IR style keyword-based queries for retrieving relevant answers from a logically structured document. We first define an appropriate semantics of keywords-based queries and then propose an algebra that is capable of computing *every* relevant portion of a document, which can be considered answer to a set of arbitrary keywords. The ordering and structural relationship among the components are preserved in the answer. We also introduce several practically useful filters that saves users from having to deal with an overwhelming number of answers.

1 Introduction

Most digital documents consist of logical components of text namely title, sections, subsections, paragraphs, figures, tables and even multimedia objects such as images and video clips. There exists a natural hierarchical relationship among components within a document – the components at upper levels provide broader views on a topic compared to their lower level components. Generally, such a document is represented as a rooted ordered tree that suitably reflects both its natural hierarchical structure and the ordering of its contents.

Retrieving relevant portions from a structured document has been a challenging task in both the database and the information retrieval world since, an answer related to a query may be split across multiple components. Database style queries which heavily rely on schema conscious query languages such as SQL, OQL, or recently developed XQuery are capable of retrieving exactly matched components. However, these languages demand end users to be aware of the underlying structure of the document. On the other hand, the semantics of IR style keyword-based queries are generally ambiguous. This ambiguity becomes even more conspicuous when retrieving portions of structured documents, since not all the keywords specified in a query may be contained in a single component. In such a case, an answer needs to be composed from several logically related components. In this paper, we propose a query mechanism which integrates both IR and database approaches. While it allows users IR style query formulation, posing queries by simply specifying a set of keywords and thus relieving end users of having prior knowledge of schema or structure of the documents queried, it applies database-like query evaluation by transforming queries into algebraic expressions and then performing operations such as selection and join. Since the query semantics is imprecise, the operations need to produce *every* computable answer that can be considered relevant to a query.

In the rest of the paper, we next provide a motivating example that justifies our work. Section 3 explains the data model and some basic formal notations required for our query mechanism. In section 4, we formalize our query model and define algebraic operations required to compute all the answers relevant to a query. We also introduce some useful filters to select a certain subset of answers from a large set. Related work is provided in section 5, and finally we conclude by highlighting our contributions.

2 Motivating Example

One typical feature of digital document database is that the structures of documents are heterogeneous in nature. Moreover, there is also a heterogeneity in size and type even among the logical components within the same document. Some components such as a movie clip may be self contained while others such as a text paragraph may not be. As a result, a meaningful portion of a document not always necessarily means one physically indexed component. Furthermore, as stated before, there may not be a single component in which all the query keywords would appear, in which case the system should attempt to compose a meaningful portion from multiple components. Consider the following query informally stated in natural language.

Query 1. *Find meaningful portions related to 'Korakuen'[1] and 'Shibayaki'[2] in a collection of documents.*

In a typical IR system, when this query is posed to the document in Figure 1, its AND interpretation would return the fragment ⟨n8⟩ as the only answer, whereas its OR interpretation would return ⟨n4⟩,⟨n8⟩,⟨n9⟩ as three separate answers. However, the document fragment constituted by the logical components ⟨n4,n7,n8,n9⟩ (enclosed by dotted line in Figure 2; see also Figure 3 for a sample result) can also be considered a relevant answer to this query. Obviously such queries cannot be answered by simple boolean transformations due to the fact that an intuitive answer is split across multiple components of a document. One may consider using inverted indexing for preparing such intuitive answers beforehand for every possible query. However, as mentioned in [1], the index size would simply be too large to be practical. We need a mechanism that enables us to compose every intuitive answer from various logical components dynamically.

---
[1] Famous strolling garden in Japan.
[2] A Japanese festival involving the burning of grass.

An important issue here is that there may be many intuitive answers to a single query since the answer units are not decided beforehand. To our example query, 1. $\langle n4, n7, n8 \rangle$, 2. $\langle n4, n7, n8, n9 \rangle$, 3. $\langle n8 \rangle$ and 4. $\langle n8, n9 \rangle$ are four fragments that can be considered intuitive answers. However, there is no easy way to evaluate what is the most relevant among these answers since relevance largely depends on individual judgments. It is important to be able to enhance IR systems to return every intuitive answer. In the mean time, however, it is also important for one to be able to have some kind of control over the answer set so that one is not overwhelmed by an exploding number of answers. In a typical database system, such control is achieved with the help of a set of predicates. We believe a similar kind of mechanism must be provided to users who wish to select specific portions from a document. The formulation of selection predicates should, however, be as simple as possible and not be very schema conscious.

```
<document title="Around Okayama">#n1
  <chapter title="Historical Background">#n2
    <p>#n3
      Okayama, the mid-western prefecture of Japan
      ... main agricultural products ... grapes
      and peaches ... delicious seafood
      ... Seto Bridge ... access to Shikoku
    </p>
    <section title="Korakuen">#n4
      <p>#n5
        Also known as crow castle ... one of the
        three most famous national parks ...
        Greenery ... cherry blossom along the river
        <image title="Cherry Blossom"
               url="images/sakura.jpg" />#n6
      </p>
      <subsection title="Traditional Events">#n7
        <p>#n8
          Popular events in Korakuen are New Year
          koto music, shibayaki (burning of grass),
          komomaki (Manchurian rice) ...
          <movie title="korakuen spring festival"
                 url="movies/shibayaki.mpg" />#n9
          <movie title="komomaki"
                 url="movies/komomaki.mpg"
          />#n10
        </p>
      </subsection>
    </section>
  </chapter>
  <chapter title="Southern Okayama">#n11
    <p> ... </p>#n12
  </chapter>
</document>
```

Fig. 1. Sample document coded using XML-like tags. Tags, however, are unimportant in our model. Irrelevant text to the example query is shown as "...".

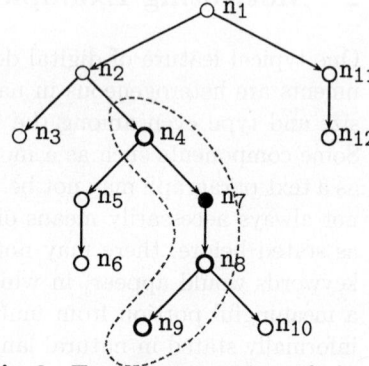

Fig. 2. Tree representation of the document in Figure 1. Each node is a logical component of the document. Nodes are numbered according to the depth-first-traversal of the tree preserving the topological order of the document.

```
<section title="Korakuen">#n4
  <subsection title="Traditional Events">#n7
    <p>#n8
      Popular events in Korakuen are New Year
      koto music, shibayaki (burning of grass),
      komomaki (Manchurian rice) ...
      <movie title="korakuen spring festival"
             url="movies/shibayaki.mpg" />#n9
    </p>
  </subsection>
</section>
```

Fig. 3. A possible answer to the query {korakuen, shibayaki}

3 Basic Definitions

Before we define and discuss our query mechanism, here we present some basic definitions and formally define our data model that we use as the basis for our query model. A digital document database is a collection of various documents. However, for simplicity, here we consider only one such document.

Definition 1 (Digital Document). *A digital document, or simply a document, is a rooted ordered tree* $\mathcal{D} = (\mathtt{N}, \mathtt{E})$ *with a set of nodes* $\mathtt{N}$ *and a set of edges* $\mathtt{E} \subseteq \mathtt{N} \times \mathtt{N}$. *There exists a distinguished root node from which the rest of the nodes can be reached by traversing the edges in* $\mathtt{E}$. *Each node except the root has a unique parent node.*

Each node $\mathtt{n}$ of the document tree is associated with a logical component of the document. There is a function $\mathtt{keywords(n)}$ that returns the representative keywords of the corresponding component in $\mathtt{n}$. The nodes are ordered in such a way that the topology of the document is preserved. We write $\mathtt{nodes}(\mathcal{D})$ for all the nodes $\mathtt{N}$ and $\mathtt{edges}(\mathcal{D})$ for all the edges $\mathtt{E}$. We write $\mathtt{n}_1 \downarrow \mathtt{n}_2$ to denote $\mathtt{n}_1$ is an ancestor of $\mathtt{n}_2$. The example document in Figure 1 can be represented by this data model as shown in Figure 2.

Definition 2 (Document Fragment). *Let $\mathcal{D}$ be a document. Then $\mathtt{f} \subseteq \mathcal{D}$ is a document fragment, or simply a fragment, iff $\mathtt{nodes}(\mathtt{f}) \subseteq \mathtt{nodes}(\mathcal{D})$ and the subgraph induced by $\mathtt{nodes}(\mathtt{f})$ in $\mathcal{D}$ is a tree. In other words, the induced subgraph is connected and has a distinguished root node.*

A fragment can thus be denoted by a subset of nodes in a document tree – the tree induced by which is also a rooted ordered tree. A fragment may consist of only a single node or all the nodes which constitute the whole document tree. In Figure 2, the set of nodes $\langle \mathtt{n4}, \mathtt{n7}, \mathtt{n8}, \mathtt{n9} \rangle$ is a fragment of the sample document tree. The subgraph enclosed by the dotted lines in Figure 2 is the tree induced by it, the root being the node $\mathtt{n4}$. Hereafter, unless stated otherwise, the first node of a fragment represents the root of the tree induced by it. For clarity, we refer to a single noded fragment simply as a node.

4 Query Mechanism

In this section, we formally present our query mechanism based on the data model described in the previous section. We assume that users are looking for meaningful fragments, which are logically inter-related components of a document.

4.1 Algebra

Users formulate queries simply by specifying a set of keywords. First, we informally define our interpretation of a query, which is different from the traditional boolean AND and OR. Intuitively, an answer to a query represented by a set of keywords (or terms) is a document portion that consists of at least one component associated with each query term. The ordering and the structural relationship among the components in the answer are preserved. Note that the answer may contain multiple components associated with any query term and no specific ordering is required for the terms to appear in the components. Next, we provide formal definition of a query and an answer to it.

Definition 3 (Query). *A query can be denoted by* $Q = \{k_1, k_2, ..., k_m\}$ *where for all* $j = 1, 2, ..., m$ k_j *is called a query term.*

We write $k \in \text{keywords}(n)$ to denote query term k appears in the textual contents associated with the node n.

Definition 4 (Query Answer). *Given a query* $Q = \{k_1, k_2, ..., k_n\}$, *answer* A *to this query is a set of document fragments defined to be* $\{f \mid (\forall k \in Q). \exists n \in f : k \in \text{keywords}(n)\}$.

To formally define the operational semantics of a query, we first need to define operations on fragments and sets of fragments. These operations will eventually be used to compute the intuitive answers that we discussed in our motivating example. The operations can be basically classified as (1) *selection* and (2) *join* operations.

Definition 5 (Selection). *Supposing* F *be a set of fragments of a given document, and* P *be a predicate which maps a document fragment into true or false, a selection from* F *by the predicate* P, *denoted by* σ_P, *is defined as a subset* F' *of* F *such that* F' *includes all and only fragments satisfying* P. *Formally,* $\sigma_P(F) = \{f \mid f \in F, P(f) = true\}$.

Hereafter, the predicate P is also called a filter of the selection σ_P.

The simplest filter is for the keyword selection of the type 'keyword = k' which selects only those document fragments having the word 'k'. Another selection predicate of the type 'size $< c$' is to have control over the size of the fragment. The size of a fragment is measured in terms of the number of nodes included in it. This means the predicate 'size < 5' would select only those fragments constituted by less than 5 nodes. Other complex but practically useful filters will be introduced in the following subsection. Next, we define various *join* operations on document fragments.

Definition 6 (Fragment Join). *Let* f_1, f_2, f *be fragments of the document tree* $\mathcal{D}$. *Then, fragment join between* f_1 *and* f_2 *denoted by* $f_1 \bowtie f_2$ *is* f *iff*

1. $f_1 \subseteq f$,
2. $f_2 \subseteq f$ *and*
3. $\nexists f'$ *such that* $f' \subseteq f \land f_1 \subseteq f' \land f_2 \subseteq f'$

Intuitively, the fragment join operation takes two fragments f_1 and f_2 of $\mathcal{D}$ as its input and finds the minimal fragment f in $\mathcal{D}$ such that the resulting fragment would contain both the input fragments f_1 and f_2, and there exists no other smaller fragment f' contained by f in $\mathcal{D}$, which would also contain the input fragments f_1 and f_2. Figure 4 (b) shows the operation between two fragments $\langle n5, n6 \rangle$ and $\langle n8, n10 \rangle$ (see Figure 4 (a)) which finds its minimal subgraph fragment $\langle n4, n5, n6, n7, n8, n10 \rangle$ (fragment inside dashed line in Figure 4 (b)). By its definition, the fragment join operation between arbitrary fragments f_1, f_2 and f_3 have the following algebraic properties.

Idempotency $f_1 \bowtie f_1 = f_1$
Commutativity $f_1 \bowtie f_2 = f_2 \bowtie f_1$
Associativity $(f_1 \bowtie f_2) \bowtie f_3 = f_1 \bowtie (f_2 \bowtie f_3)$
Absorption $f_1 \bowtie (f_2 \subseteq f_1) = f_1$

These properties not only enable an easy implementation of the operations but also reduce the cost of query evaluation, which will be explained below.

Next, we extend this operation to a set of fragments. called *pairwise fragment join*, which is the set-variant of fragment join.

Definition 7 (Pairwise Fragment Join). *Given two sets F_1 and F_2 of fragments of a document $\mathcal{D}$, pairwise fragment join of F_1 and F_2, denoted by $F_1 \bowtie F_2$, is defined as a set of fragments yielded by taking fragment join of every combination of an element in F_1 and an element in F_2 in a pairwise manner. Formally,*

$$F_1 \bowtie F_2 = \{f_1 \bowtie f_2 \mid f_1 \in F_1, f_2 \in F_2\}$$

Figure 4 (a),(c) illustrates an example of *pairwise fragment join* operation. For given $F_1 = \{f_{11}, f_{12}\}$ and $F_2 = \{f_{21}, f_{22}\}$, $F_1 \bowtie F_2$ produces a set of fragments $\{f_{11} \bowtie f_{21}, f_{11} \bowtie f_{22}, f_{12} \bowtie f_{21}, f_{12} \bowtie f_{22}\}$.

For arbitrary fragment sets F_1, F_2, and F_3, *pairwise fragment join* has the following algebraic properties.

Commutativity $F_1 \bowtie F_2 = F_2 \bowtie F_1$
Associativity $(F_1 \bowtie F_2) \bowtie F_3 = F_1 \bowtie (F_2 \bowtie F_3)$
Fixed Point $F_1 \bowtie F_1 = (F_1 \bowtie F_1) \bowtie F_1$

The *pairwise fragment join* operation does not satisfy the idempotency property as we can easily prove it by showing counter examples for it.

We now define *powerset fragment join* – another variant of *fragment join* operation.

Definition 8 (Powerset Fragment Join). *Given two sets F_1 and F_2 of fragments of a document $\mathcal{D}$, powerset fragment join of F_1 and F_2, denoted by $F_1 \bowtie^* F_2$, is defined as a set of fragments that are yielded by applying fragment join operation to an arbitrary number (but not 0) of elements in F_1 and F_2. Formally,*

$$F_1 \bowtie^* F_2 = \{\bowtie (F_1' \cup F_2') \mid F_1' \subseteq F_1, F_2' \subseteq F_2, F_1' \neq \phi, F_2' \neq \phi\}$$

$$\text{where} \bowtie \{f_1, f_2, \ldots, f_n\} = f_1 \bowtie \ldots \bowtie f_n$$

The above definition can be expanded as:

$$F_1 \bowtie^* F_2 = (F_1 \bowtie F_1) \cup (F_1 \bowtie F_1 \bowtie F_2) \cup (F_1 \bowtie F_2 \bowtie F_2) \cup (F_1 \bowtie F_1 \bowtie F_1 \bowtie F_2) \cup$$
$$(F_1 \bowtie F_1 \bowtie F_2 \bowtie F_2) \cup (F_1 \bowtie F_2 \bowtie F_2 \bowtie F_2) \cup \ldots$$

Figure 4 (a),(d) illustrates an example of *powerset fragment join* operation. It should be noted here that for the same two sets of fragments $F_1 = \{f_{11}, f_{12}\}$ and $F_2 = \{f_{21}, f_{22}\}$ in Figure 4 (a), *powerset fragment join* produces more fragments than *pairwise fragment join* (see Figure 4 (c)). It should also be noted that some of the fragments are produced more than once due to the algebraic properties of *fragment join* and *pairwise fragment join*.

Although the operation *powerset fragment join* looks complex, it can be transformed into the following equivalent expression:

$$F_1 \bowtie^* F_2 = (F_1 \bowtie F_1) \bowtie (F_2 \bowtie F_2)$$

The transformation of the *powerset fragment join* into three *pairwise fragment join* operations is possible due to certain algebraic properties that both *fragment join* and *pairwise fragment join* hold. For space constraints, we do not provide the formal proof.

One must note here that the transformed *powerset fragment join* is the operation that we actually use to compute all the document fragments relevant to a query. It is obvious that the transformation allows us to compute the answers in polynomial time.

4.2 Query Evaluation

Having defined all the necessary operations, we now return to the motivating example query and show how it is possible for us to evaluate the query that can return an appropriate set of intuitive answers. The Query 1 in section 2 can be represented as:

$$Q = \{\texttt{korakuen}, \texttt{shibayaki}\} = \sigma_{\text{keyword}=korakuen}(F) \bowtie^* \sigma_{\text{keyword}=shibayaki}(F)$$

Supposing this query is posed on the sample document data in Figure 1. We first find the set of nodes (or single node fragments) in the document tree (see Figure 1 and 2) for each query term in Q using the keyword selection operation.

- For the query term korakuen, let F_1 be the set of matching fragments. Then $F_1 = \sigma_{\text{keyword}=korakuen}(F) = \{\langle n4 \rangle, \langle n8 \rangle, \langle n9 \rangle\}$.
- Similarly, for the query term shibayaki, let F_2 be the set of matching fragments. Then, $F_2 = \sigma_{\text{keyword}=shibayaki}(F) = \{\langle n8 \rangle\}$.

Next, we compute the set of all possible answer fragments by applying the transformed *powerset fragment join* on set F_1 and F_2.

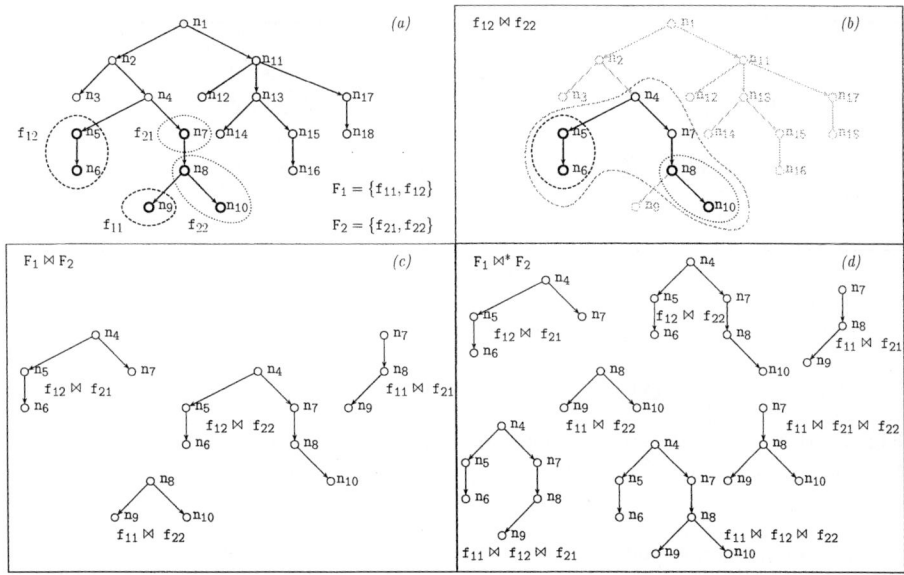

Fig. 4. (a) A Document Tree (b) Fragment Join (c) Pairwise Fragment Join and (d) Powerset Fragment Join Operations

$$F_1 \bowtie^* F_2 = (F_1 \bowtie F_1) \bowtie (F_2 \bowtie F_2)$$
$$= (\{\langle n4 \rangle, \langle n8 \rangle, \langle n9 \rangle\} \bowtie \{\langle n4 \rangle, \langle n8 \rangle, \langle n9 \rangle\}) \bowtie (\{\langle n8 \rangle\} \bowtie \{\langle n8 \rangle\})$$
$$= \{\langle n4 \rangle, \langle n8 \rangle, \langle n9 \rangle, \langle n4, n7, n8 \rangle, \langle n4, n7, n8, n9 \rangle, \langle n8, n9 \rangle\} \bowtie \{\langle n8 \rangle\}$$
$$= \{\langle n4, n7, n8 \rangle, \langle n8 \rangle, \langle n8, n9 \rangle, \langle n4, n7, n8, n9 \rangle\}$$

It is clear from the above example that we have successfully generated all four intuitive answers to our motivating example query in section 2.

4.3 Selection Predicates

One negative aspect of *powerset fragment join* operation is that it sometimes produces many large fragments that may be irrelevant to a user. However, with the combination of filters, users will be able to restrict the answer set effectively. We have already introduced one such useful filter, namely the filter to select fragments consisting of not more than a certain number of nodes. More powerful filters to select a subset of fragments, corresponding to the interests of a user, from a set of document fragments are introduced below.

Definition 9 (Equal Depth Filter). *For a set of fragments in which both a keyword* k_1 *and a keyword* k_2 *appear, an* equal depth filter *selects fragments in which every node having keyword* k_1 *is at the same distance as the node having*

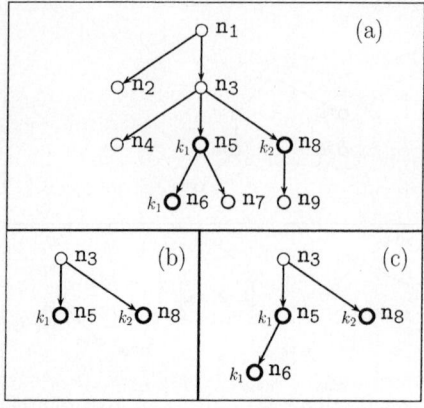
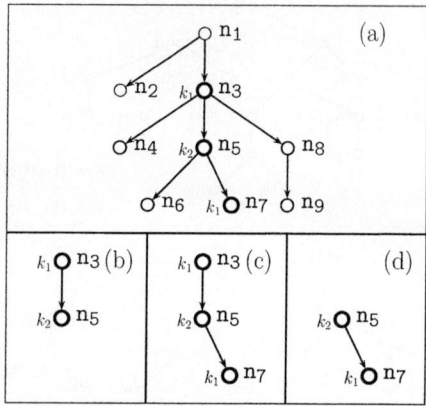

Fig. 5. (a) A Document Tree (b) Selected Fragment (c) Discarded Fragment

Fig. 6. (a) A Document Tree (b) Selected Fragment (c)(d) Discarded Fragments

keyword k_2 *from the root.*

$$\sigma_{\mathrm{depth}(n(k_1))=\mathrm{depth}(n(k_2))}(F)$$
$$= \{f \mid f \in F, (\forall n_1 \in N_{k1}, n_2 \in N_{k2}\ s.t.\ n_1, n_2 \in f)\ \mathrm{depth}(n_1) = \mathrm{depth}(n_2)\}$$

where N_k *denotes a set of all nodes containing the keyword* k *and the function* depth(n) *returns the depth of the node* n *in the tree.*

This filter is useful for selecting fragments that consist of components about two different topics under a common context. For example, one can assume that information regarding two different festivals celebrated at *'Korakuen'* might be available as two different subsections under a section titled *'traditional events'*. When applying this filter in the document in Figure 5 (a) for the keywords k_1 and k_2, the operation will select the fragment shown in Figure 5 (b) but not the fragment in Figure 5 (c).

Definition 10 (Ancestor Descendant Filter). *For a set of fragments in which both a keyword* k_1 *and a keyword* k_2 *appear, an* ancestor descendant filter *selects fragments in which every node having keyword* k_1 *is an ancestor of the node having keyword* k_2.

$$\sigma_{n(k_1)\downarrow n(k_2)}(F) = \{f \mid f \in F, (\forall n_1 \in N_{k1}, n_2 \in N_{k2}\ s.t.\ n_1, n_2 \in f)\ n_1 \downarrow n_2\}$$

where N_k *denotes a set of all nodes containing the keyword* k.

This filter is useful for selecting only those fragments that consist of a component with detail information on a certain subject under a certain contextual topic. For example, one can assume that information regarding *'Korakuen'* might be available as one subsection under a section titled *'Okayama's Gardens'*. When applying this filter in the document in Figure 6 (a) for the keywords k_1 and k_2, the operation will select the fragment shown in Figure 6 (b) but not the fragments in Figure 6 (c)(d).

5 Related Work

Most traditional IR assumes a whole document to be the basic unit of information to be queried and retrieved. However, extensive studies have been done on retrieval of logical units from structured documents[10][3][4][8][6]. Most of these studies are based on regional algebra, which first appeared in [10], and have been subsequently modified by [3][6] to allow overlapping and nested queries. Our work is different in the sense that their query formulations are mainly based on the specification of both structure and contents of a document. While their work provides more expressive power and more focussed retrieval, ours provides simplicity to end users. It is an extra burden for users to be aware of the underlying structure while posing queries.

Most of the above mentioned work uses position-based indexes[9], with queries being processed using word element and position. On the other hand, we deal with fragments in a document tree that is more complex than simple strings of text. Although path-based or even subtree-based indexing can be considered for each and every fragment in a document tree, the size of the index would be too large to be of any practical use[1]. That is the reason why answers need to be generated dynamically rather than decided statically beforehand.

The problem related to retrieval unit for keyword-based queries has been studied by many researchers in various contexts. [2] deals with this problem in the context of relational database management systems while [7] does that in the context of logical web documents consisting of multiple pages. In either of these papers, the underlying data is modelled as a graph and heuristic methods have been proposed to find out the most relevant answers from the graph. Both suffer from the problem of computational complexity. [5] proposes a method for integrating keyword queries in conventional XML queries, however, it is not solely based on keyword queries and therefore differs from our approach. We have stated the problem of computing retrieval unit in the context of structured documents and have provided an algebra that can compute all possible relevant answers in a reasonable computational time.

6 Conclusion

We discussed the issue of difficulty in structure-based query formulation and the ambiguity in generating answers from various indexed components in a document. A query mechanism with an integrated approach of IR and database for formulating and evaluating query has been proposed. The main contribution of this paper is the theoretical groundwork for a query mechanism for retrieving relevant portions of a document dynamically. We also provided several filters to enable users to select only specific portions of documents. Our ultimate goal, however, is to develop a theoretical framework for defining filters that would generalize various filters that we introduced, which would be capable of optimizing the overall query processing. Similar work was proposed in [11] for selection of video intervals. We are in pursuit of a similar kind of theoretical groundwork for our selection predicates.

Acknowledgments

This work was partially supported by the Ministry of Education, Culture, Sports, Science and Technology, Japan, under the grant 14780337.

References

1. Shurug Al-Khalifa, Cong Yu, and H. V. Jagadish. Querying structured text in an XML database. In *SIGMOD 2003*, pages 4–15, 2003.
2. G. Bhalotia, C. Nakhe, A. Hulgeri, S. Chakrabarti, and S. Sudarshan. Keyword searching and browsing in databases using BANKS. In *ICDE*, pages 431–440, 2002.
3. Forbes J. Burkowski. Retrieval activities in a database consisting of heterogeneous collections of structured text. In *Proc. of the 15th annual international ACM SIGIR conference on Research and development in information retrieval*, pages 112–125. ACM Press, 1992.
4. Charles L. A. Clarke, G. V. Cormack, and F. J. Burkowski. An algebra for structured text search and a framework for its implementation. *The Computer Journal*, 38(1):43–56, 1995.
5. D. Florescu, D. Kossman, and I. Manolescu. Integrating keyword search into XML query processing. In *International World Wide Web Conference*, pages 119–135, 2000.
6. Jani Jaakkola and Pekka Kilpelainen. Nested text-region algebra. Technical Report C-1999-2, Department of Computer Science, University of Helsinki, January 1999. Available at http://www.cs.helsinki.fi/TR/C-1999/2/.
7. Wen-Syan Li, K. Selcuk Candan, Quoc Vu, and Divyakant Agrawal. Retrieving and organizing web pages by 'Information Unit'. In *Tenth International WWW Conference, Hong Kong, China*, pages 230–244, 2001.
8. G. Navarro and R.A. Baeza-Yates. Proximal nodes: A model to query document databases by content and structure. *ACM Transactions on Information Systems*, 15(4):400–435, 1997.
9. R. Sacks-Davis, T. Arnold-Moore, and J. Zobel. Database systems for structured documents. In *International Symposium on Advanced Database Technologies and Their Integration*, pages 272–283, 1994.
10. A. Salminen and F. Tompa. Pat expressions: an algebra for text search. *Acta Linguistica Hungar*, 41(1-4):277–306, 1992.
11. Katsumi Tanaka, Keishi Tajima, Takashi Sogo, and Sujeet Pradhan. Algebraic retrieval of fragmentarily indexed video. *New Generation Computing*, 18(4):359–374, September 2000.

Parallel Hierarchical Data Cube for Range Sum Queries and Dynamic Updates

Jianzhong Li and Hong Gao

School of Computer Science and Technology
Harbin Institute of Technology, China
{lijz,gaohong}@mail.banner.com.cn

Abstract. While there are several studies on cube storage for range queries and dynamic updates, very few works have been done on addressing parallel cube storage structure in share nothing environments to improve the query performance. In this paper, we investigate the approach of how to answer range sum queries in a share nothing environment, and present an effective parallel hierarchical data cube storage structure (PHDC for short), which provides better load balancing for both range sum queries and updates. Analytical and experimental results show that PHDC have better load-balance and achieve optimum speedup for a very high percentage of range queries on multidimensional data cube.

1 Introduction

On-Line Analytical Processing[1] (OLAP) is a powerful tool in data warehouse to support decision making. An increasingly popular data model for OLAP applications is the data cube[2]. To build a data cube, certain attributes are chosen to be measure attributes, and other attributes, say d of them, are referred to as dimensions attributes. Thus, a data cube can be viewed as a d-dimensional array, indexed by the values of the d dimensional attributes, whose cells contain the values of the measure attributes for the corresponding combination of values of dimension attributes. Range queries are often used in analysis processing applications. A range query applies an aggregation operation (e.g., SUM) over all selected cells in a data cube. The cells are specified in the range query by providing ranges on several dimensions. Supposing $S=[l_1, h_1] \times [l_2, h_2] \times ... \times [l_d, h_d]$ being a sub-region in the d-dimensional Cube C, then the range query on S can be formulated as $f(S)=f(\{C(x_1, x_2, ..., x_d) \mid \forall (x_1, x_2, ..., x_d) \in S \})$, where f is an aggregate function.

Efficient methods of processing range query are becoming more important with the growing interest in database analysis, particularly in OLAP. The response time is crucial for OLAP applications that need user-interaction. Recently, various researches[3-8] have been made. However, those methods have some limitation in the context that they (1) still have the update propagation problem even though they have reduced it in some degree, such as the relative prefix sum cube (RPC), (2) sacrifice the search efficiency to reduce the update cost, or (3) bring high additional space overhead. With the explosion of massive data (which is larger than 10^{12} bytes) stored in data warehouses, it is becoming a pressing issue to develop innovative techniques to effectively deal with range queries and dynamic updates.

Key to the technique of cube storage structure is the ability to respond to both queries and updates on massive data in a timely fashion. I/O parallelism is considered to be a promising approach to achieving high performance in parallel database systems. This holds especially for data warehouses where huge amounts of data and complex analytical queries have to be dealt with. Several research works[9-15] have been done to improve the query performance by utilizing parallel technique. Most of the works are based on share-memory or share disk environments. To our best knowledge, there is no work on the range query and update processing in the share-nothing environment, such as PC-clusters. In addition, there is no parallel cube storage structure discussed special for range query processing in PC-clusters. In this paper, we investigate the approach of using PC clusters to process range queries and dynamic updates.

The main contribution of this paper is (1). It discusses the cube storage in a share nothing environment. (2). It proposes a data declustering method and the corresponding parallel data cube storage structure, which is proved to have better load-balance and achieve optimum speed-up for a very high percentage of range queries on data cubes. (3). It discusses the algorithms both for range sum queries and updates on parallel cubes. The technique proposed in this paper is also applicable to other aggregating functions, such as max.

The remainder of the paper is organized as follows. In section 2, we review the model for the range sum problems and the prefix sum technique proposed in [3]. In Section 3, we present a novel declustering method, called hierarchical partition declustering method(HPD), and corresponding storage structure for parallel data cube, which may achieve better load-balance and speed-up both for range sum queries and updates. The range sum query and update algorithms are discussed in Section 4 and Section 5. Section 6 gives the performance analysis of PHDC and the comprehensive experimental results. Finally, the summary of this paper is given in Section 7.

2 Reviews

In [3], a model was first proposed for range sum problems. In this paper, we also employ it. Assume that data cube C has one measure attribute and d-dimensional attributes. We can store C in a d-dimensional array A with size of $\prod_{i=1}^{d} n_i$, where $n_i=|Dom(D_i)|$. Without loss of generality and for simplicity, we assume that (1). A has a starting index 0 at each dimension, (2). Each dimension has the same size n, that is $n_1=n_2=\ldots=n_d=n$, and (3). For notational convenience, in the two-dimensional examples we will refer to cells in array A as $A(i,j)$. In this paper, our analysis of query and update costs are expressed in terms of the number of accessed cells in the data cube.

[3] presented an elegant algorithm, which is called the prefix sum method. In PS method, besides A, another d-dimensional array called Prefix Cube(PC for short) is introduced, which has the same size as A. PC is used to store various pre-computed prefix sums of A. Each cell indexed by $(x_1, x_2, \ldots, x_d)$ in PC contains the sum of all

cells up to and including itself in array A. Thus, the sum of the entire array A is found in the last cell of PC. In other words, we will precompute, for all $0 \leq x_i < n$ and $1 \leq i \leq d$, $PC(x_1, x_2, \ldots, x_d) = SUM(\{A(y_1, y_2, \ldots, y_d) \mid \forall 1 \leq i \leq d, 0 \leq y_i \leq x_i\})$.

Fig. 1 describes the essential idea about how PC can be used to answer a range query. The sum of all the data cells in the region selected by a range query can be computed by adding and subtracting the sums of various other regions until the interesting region is extracted. For example, sum(Area_E)=$PC(4,4)$-$PC(4,1)$-$PC(1,4)$+$PC(1,1)$. We note that all such regions begin at cell $A(0,0)$ and extend to some cell in A, thus, the prefix sum approach has reduced the range sum query problem to the problem of reading a single individual cell in PC that takes constant time.

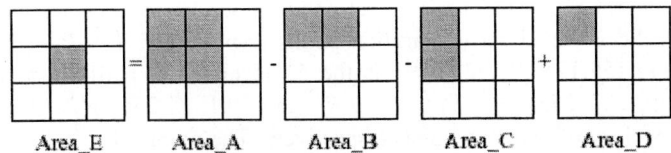

Fig. 1. A geometric illustration of the 2-dimensional case: Sum(Area_E)= Sum(Area_A)-Sum(Area_B)- Sum(Area_C)+Sum(Area_D)

3   Parallel Hierarchical Data Cube (PHDC)

3.1   Hierarchical Data Cube (HDC)

Definition 1 (Hierarchical Partition Point). Let $A = \bigtimes_{i=1}^{d} [0, n-1]$ be a d-dimensional array with size of n^d, P be the number of nodes in the PC cluster, $b_1, b_2, \ldots, b_d$ and $k_1, k_2, \ldots, k_d$ be two sets of non-negative integers. $m_i = n/(P \times b_i)$, $L_i = \log_{k_i}^{m_i}$ ($1 \leq i \leq d$). Then, we define the *hierarchical partition points* with different levels on each dimension of A as follows:

(1). $P_i^l = \{(j \times n/k_i^l) - 1 \mid 1 \leq j < k_i^l, j \bmod k_i \neq 0$ and $n/k_i^l \geq b_i \times P\}$ is defined to be the lth level set of *partition points* on the ith dimension of A.

(2). $P_i^{L+1} = \{ j \times n/(k_i^L \times P) - 1 \mid 1 \leq j < k_i^L \times P, j \bmod P \neq 0 \}$ is defined to be the $(L+1)^{th}$ level set of *partition points* on the ith dimension of A, and

(3.) $P_i^{L+2} = \{ j \times n/(k_i^L \times P \times b_i) - 1 \mid 1 \leq j < k_i^L \times P \times b_i, j \bmod b_i \neq 0\}$ is defined to be the $(L+2)^{th}$ level set of *partition points* on the ith dimension of A.

In the following discussion, we assume $b_1 = \ldots = b_d = b$, $m_1 = \ldots = m_d = m$ and $k_1 = k_2 = \ldots = k_d = 2$ for simplicity. By the definitions above, It is obvious that for $\forall i(1 \leq i \leq d)$, we get $L+3$ sets of *partition points* on the ith dimension of A: $P_i^0, P_i^1, \ldots$, and P_i^L, P_i^{L+1} and P_i^{L+2}. $P_i^0 \cup P_i^1 \cup \ldots, \cup P_i^L \cup P_i^{L+1} \cup P_i^{L+2}$ compose the domain of the ith dimension. That is $|P_i^0 \cup P_i^1 \cup \ldots, \cup P_i^L \cup P_i^{L+1} \cup P_i^{L+2}| = n$.

The points of $\sum_{i=1}^{d}(P_i^0 \cup P_i^1......\cup P_i^L)$ partition A into $(\lceil n/(b\times P)\rceil)^d$ non-overlapping regions. Each region has size of $(P\times b)^d$. We call each region a *hyper-rectangle block*. The points of $\sum_{i=1}^{d}(P_i^{L+1})$ further partition each hyper-rectangle block R into P^d disjoint boxes. Each dimension of the box has the same size b. We call each box a *hyper-rectangle box*. The box, which contains the highest index($P\times b-1$, $P\times b-1$,..., $P\times b-1$), is called the anchor of R.

For a 2-dimensional array $A=[0,255]\times[0,255]$, we can get $L=2$, assuming that $k=2$, $b=16$ and $P=4$. $P_1^0 = P_2^0 = \{255\}$ is the 0th level set of partition points on each dimension; $P_1^1 = P_2^1 = \{127\}$ is the 1th level set of partition points respectively; $P_1^2 = P_2^2 = \{63, 191\}$ is the 2th level set of partition points respectively; $P_1^3 = P_2^3 = \{15, 31, 47, 79, 95, 111, 143, 159, 175, 207, 223, 239\}$ is the 3th level set of partition points respectively and $\{0,1,..., 255\}-P_1^0 \cup P_1^1 \cup P_1^2 \cup P_1^3$ and $\{0,1,..., 255\}-P_2^0 \cup P_2^1 \cup P_2^2 \cup P_2^3$ are the 4th level set of partition points respectively. The points of $P_i^0 \cup P_i^1 \cup P_i^2$ on each dimension partition the array into 16 hyper-rectangle blocks, each of which is further partitioned into 16 hyper-rectangle boxes by the points of P_i^3 on each dimension. For example, $A[144:159;192:207]$ is a hyper-rectangle box. $R=A[128:191;64:127]$ is a hyper-rectangle block which has 16 hyper-rectangle boxes. Each hyper-rectangle block has an *anchor box* with it, i.e. $A[176:191; 112:127]$ is the anchor box of R.

Definition 2 (Hierarchical Data Cube). Let $A = \times_{i=1}^{d}[0, n-1]$ be a d-dimensional array with size of n^d, and $P_i^0, P_i^1,..., P_i^L, P_i^{L+1}, P_i^{L+2}$ be the sets of partition points on the ith dimension of $A(1\le i\le d)$. The HDC of A is an d-dimensional array which has the same size as A. Given a cell $c(x_1, x_2,..., x_d)$ in HDC, the value stored in c is determined as follows:

For each x_i, there must exist a k ($0\le k\le L+2$), satisfying $x_i \in P_i^k$. Then search p_i in $P_i^0 \cup P_i^1 \cup...\cup P_i^{k-1}$, such that: (1). $p_i < x_i$, and (2). $\forall p_i' \in P_i^0 \cup P_i^1 \cup...\cup P_i^{k-1}$, if $p_i' < x_i$, we have $p_i' \le p_i$.

Thus, c stores the sum of all cells in the region $[y_1,x_1]\times[y_2,x_2]\times...\times[y_d,x_d] \subseteq A$(if p_i not found, $y_i=0$, else $y_i = p_i+1$).

Details about the HDC, see[8].

3.2 Parallel Hierarchical Data Cube (PHDC)

Now we discuss how to decluster HDC to P nodes in the PC cluster to construct PHDC. According to the definition of HDC, it's clear that for $\forall i(1\le i\le d)$, $P_i^0, P_i^1,..., P_i^L, P_i^{L+1}, P_i^{L+2}$ are the sets of partition points on dimension i for both A and its HDC($1\le i\le d$). So all the points in $\bigcup_{i=1}^{d} P_i^0 \cup P_i^1 \cup...... \cup P_i^L$ partition HDC into several hyper-rectangle blocks, and further each hyper-rectangle block is partitioned into P^d

boxes by the points in $\bigcup_{i=1}^{d} P_i^{L+1}$. Each hyper-rectangle box can be considered as the allocation unit. That is the declustering of HDC is simply implemented by allocating each hyper-rectangle box to its corresponding node. For each hyper-rectangle block $R[l_1:h_1;l_2:h_2;...;l_d:h_d]$ in HDC, the hyper-rectangle boxes in R are distributed among P nodes uniformly according to the following rules:

For $\forall h_i$, $1 \leq i \leq d$, there must exist a k_i, satisfying $h_i \in P_i^{k_i}$, then

Rule (1):
If for each h_i, we have $(P_i^0 \cup P_i^1 \cup ... \cup P_i^{t_i-1}) \cap [0, h_i) = \Phi$,

Then search e_i in $P_i^{t_i} \cup ... \cup P_i^L$, such that : (i). $0 \leq e_i < h_i$, $\exists l_i$, $t_i \leq l_i \leq L$, $e_i \in P_i^{l_i}$ and (ii). $\forall e_i' \in (P_i^{t_i} \cup ... \cup P_i^L) \cap [0, h_i)$, if $e_i' \in P_i^{l_i'}$, then $l_i \leq l_i'$ must be satisfied.

If e_i is found

Then supposing that the anchor of hyper-rectangle block $R'[l_1:h_1;l_2:h_2;...l_{i-1}:h_{i-1}; e_i$-$P \times b +1:e_i; l_{i+1}:h_{i+1};...;l_d:h_d]$ is allocated to node p, then allocate the anchor of R to node $(p+1) \mod P$.

Else distribute the anchor box of R to node 0;

Else there must exist a j, $1 \leq j \leq d$, satisfying that $\exists y_j, k_j'$, $0 \leq y_j < h_j$, $y_j \in P_j^{k_j'}$, and $k_j' < k_j$ ($h_j \in P_j^{k_j}$). Search e_j in $P_j^0 \cup P_j^1 \cup ... \cup P_j^{k_j-1}$, such that :(i). $e_j < h_j$, and (ii). $\forall e_j' \in P_j^0 \cup P_j^1 \cup ... \cup P_j^{k_j-1}$, if $e_j' < h_j$, then we have $e_j' \leq e_j$.

Suppose the anchor of hyper-rectangle block $[l_1:h_1;l_2:h_2;...l_{j-1}:h_{j-1};e_j$-$P \times b+1:e_j;l_{j+1}:h_{j+1};...;l_d:h_d]$ is allocated to node p, then allocate the anchor of R to node $(p+1) \mod P$.

Rule (2): If the anchor of a hyper-rectangle block $R[l_1:h_1;l_2:h_2;...;l_d:h_d]$ is allocated to node v, then for each hyper-rectangle box $B[l_1':h_1';l_2':h_2';...;l_d':h_d'] \in R$, B will be allocated to node v', where

$v' = (\sum_{i=1}^{d}(h_i - h_i')/b + v) \mod P$.

Fig 2. distribution of hyper-rectangle boxes in $A[0,255]*[0,255](P=4)$

Fig. 2 shows the distribution of hyper- rectangle boxes of a 2-dimensional array $A=[0,255] \times [0,255]$, where $k=2$, $b=16$ and $P=4$. As an example, we will explain how hyper-rectangle boxes in $R[64: 127;64:127]$ are allocated. The anchor box of R is $B[112:127; 112:127]$. For the first dimension, $h_1=127 \in P_1^1$, For each $y_1 \in [0,127)$, $\exists k'$, $y_1 \in P_1^{k'}$, we have $k' \geq 1$. For the second dimension, $h_2=127 \in P_2^1$, For each $y_2 \in [0,127)$, $\exists k'$, $y_2 \in P_2^{k'}$, we have $k' \geq 1$. According to the allocation rule(1), the anchor box B is allocated to node 0. Then according to the allocation rule(2), the box $B[64:79;64:79]$

is allocated to node $((127-79)/16 + (127-79)/16+0)$ mod $4=2$; the box $B[64: 79;80:95]$ is allocated to node 1, and so on.

Lemma 1. Let $R[l_1:h_1;l_2:h_2;...;l_d:h_d]$ be a hyper-rectangle block, and be partitioned into P^d hyper-rectangle boxes, then these P^d boxes are uniformly distributed to P nodes. That is each node equally holds P^{d-1} hyper-rectangle boxes.

Proof: (omitted due to the limitation of space)

From lemma 1, we can easily get the following theorem:

Theorem 1. The distribution method of HDC is balanced.

4 Range Queries on PHDC

PHDC can be used to answer any prefix range sum query whose *target region* begins at $A(0,0)$ and ends at an arbitrary cell c in A. The range sum query algorithm consists of two phases: decomposing phase and computation phase. During the first phase, the algorithm decomposes the *target region* Q into a set of sub-regions $\{Q_1,Q_2,...,Q_t\}$ such that each sum(Q_j) can be obtained from a cell in PHDC. In the second phase, it accesses all these corresponding cells, which are distributed between P nodes, in parallel and calculates $\sum_{i=1}^{t} sum(Q_i)$.

Suppose that the target region is $Q[0,h_1]\times[0,h_2]\times...\times[0,h_d]$, the range sum query **PHDC_range_query(Q)** consists of two phases:

Decomposing phase: to decompose Q into a set of sub-regoins $Q_1, Q_2, ..., Q_t$, satisfying

(1). $Q= Q_1\cup Q_2\cup...\cup Q_t$, and $\forall i,j$, $1\leq i,j\leq t$, if $i\neq j$, then $Q_i\cap Q_j =\phi$;

(2). $\forall Q_i$, there must exist a cell PHDC($x_1, x_2,..., x_d$), such that sum(Q_i)=PHDC($x_1, x_2,..., x_d$).

Computation phase: for each Q_i, $1\leq i \leq t$, calculates Sum(Q_i) using PHDC in parallel.

In the PC cluster, one node is assigned to be the coordinate node, others to be the processing nodes. The coordinate node implements the first phase, and the processing nodes implement the second phase. During the decomposing phase: for each dimension i, beginning with the 0th level partition point set, try to search the maximal partition point $p\in P_i^0$, which falls in $[0,h_i]$, then continue to search the maximal partition point $p'\in P_i^1$, which falls in $[p+1, h_i]$. The processing stops when the maximal partition point found is h_i. At last, we get d ordering sets $T_1,T_2,...,T_d$, where $T_i =\{p_{i1}, p_{i2},..., p_{it_i}\}$. $\forall r,s$, if $r<s$, then $p_{ir}< p_{is}$. The points in $T_i(1\leq i\leq d)$ partition $[0:h_i]$ into t_i intervals $[0: p_{i1}],[p_{i1}+1: p_{i2}],......,[p_{it_i-1}: p_{it_i}]$. Thus, all intervals on the d dimensions compose $t_1\times t_2\times...\times t_d$ non-overlap sub-regions that enclose Q.

The correctness of **PHDC_range_query** is given in the long version[16].

5 Updates on PHDC

The value of a cell $c(x_1,x_2,...,x_d)$ in A can be easily updated by searching PHDC in bottom-up manner. The update algorithm first determines the difference Δ between the old and new values of c, and then updates all the cells in PHDC related to c. For any cell $c'(y_1,y_2,...,y_d)$ in PHDC, c' will be updated, if c' records the sum value of region $r \subseteq A$, and c is contained in r. Other cells that do not satisfy the condition are unaffected.

The update algorithm also consists of two phases: decomposing phase and updating phase. The coordinate node implements the first phase, and other processing nodes in parallel implement the second phase. The details of the update algorithm are omitted due to the limitation of space.

The correctness of **PHDC_update** is given in the long version[16].

6 Complexity and Experiments

6.1 Complexity

In this section, we analyze the complexities of PHDC_range_query and PHDC_update, including space complexity and I/O complexity. Given a d-dimensional cube C with size of n^d, it's obvious that the PHDC of C has the same size of n^d, according to the definition of PHDC. Thus, the space complexity of PHDC is n^d.

Now we analyze the I/O complexity of range query. PHDC_range_query_for_coordinate_node decomposes Q into a set of sub-regions. This phase doesn't need any I/O processing. In the worst case, on each dimension, the first phase may produce $\log n$ partition points, resulting $\log n$ intervals. So the $\log n$ intervals on each dimension may compose $\log^d n$ sub-regions. That means at most there will be $\log^d n$ cells in PHDC to be accessed by P nodes in parallel during the second phase. According to theorem 3 in section 4.1, we know each nodes will access $\log^d n /P$ cells approximately. Thus, in the worst case, the I/O complexity of PHDC_range_query is $O(\log^d n/P)$.

The analysis of PHDC_update is similar with PHDC_range_query. In the worst case, the I/O complexity of PHDC_update is also $O(\log^d n/P)$

6.2 Experimental Results

The range sum query algorithm is implemented and tested in this section. The standard measure of efficiency of a parallel processing is the speedup S, which is defined as follows:

Let $R(P)$ be the response time tested with P nodes, then $S=R(1)/R(P)$. The response time is defined as the number of the cells affected by range query and update operations on a processing node.

The test bed consists of 16 PCs. 100M-Ethernet connects all the PCs. The configuration of each PC is PIII 800, 120MBs main memory and 40GBs disk. The benchmark datasets were synthetic, being randomly generated. All the programs are written in C.

There are two factors that affect the performance of range queries and updates. The first one is the size of multi-dimensional cube; the second one is the dimensionality, the number of dimensions in a cube. In the following, we test the speedup of PHDC_Range_Query in terms of these two factors.

6.2.1 Speedup vs. Cube Size

First, we vary the size of the multidimensional cube while fixing the number of dimensions to verify the impact of the size of the multidimensional cube upon the speedup. We adjust the size of cube by varying the cardinality of each dimension. In this experiment, we generate three groups of datasets with $d=5$. Without loss of generality and for convenient, we assume that each dimension in each dataset has the same cardinality. We call the dataset large-scale dataset if it has over 10^{12} data cells. We call the dataset medial-scale dataset if it has over $10^{10} \sim 10^{11}$ data cells. We call the dataset small-scale dataset if it has less than 10^9 data cells. In this experiment, the size of the three kind of datasets are 2^{40}, 2^{36} and 2^{32} respectively.

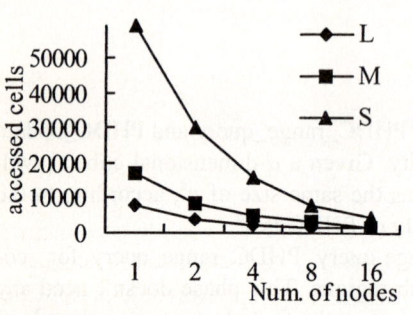

Fig. 3. Datasizes VS. number of nodes (d=5)

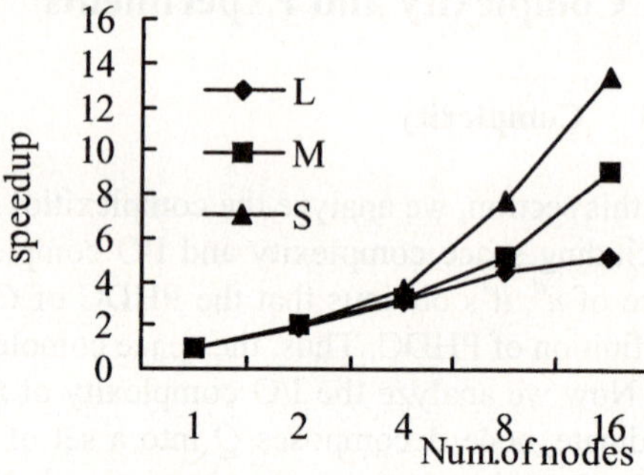

Fig.4. Speedup performance (d=5)

Fig. 3 and Fig 4 show the experimental results for different cube size, where the horizontal ordinate indicates the number of PCs in the cluster ranging from 1 to 16, the vertical ordinate indicates the speedup. The figures indicate that when the cube size is small the effect of number of nodes is not obvious, while for the datasets with larger amount of datas, the algorithm has better speeding up performance.

6.2.2 Speedup vs. Dimensionality

The second experiment exams how the dimensionality affects range query performance. We do the experiment on three kind of datasets with different dimensionality ranging from 3 to 5: 512×512×512, 512×512×512×512 and 512×512 ×512×512×512. The experimental results are depicted in Fig. 5 and Fig. 6. The figures show that varying the dimensionality can only incurs slow changes for speedup when d=3. But query performance will be improved faster as the increasing of dimensionality.

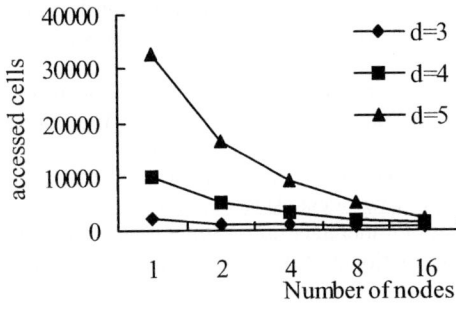

Fig. 5. Dimensionality VS. num. of nodes

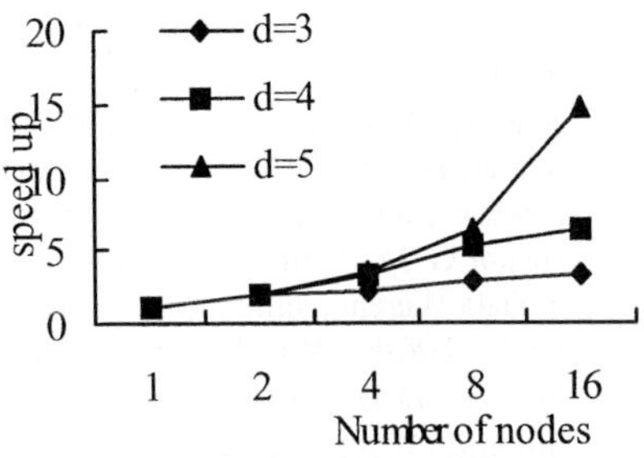

Fig. 6. Speedup performance

7 Conclusions

Due to an increasing demand for OLAP and data cube applications, efficient calculation of range queries has become more important in recent years. Several techniques have been developed to answer the range sum queries efficiently, however to our best knowledge, there is no literature to date how to deal with the range queries and update in a share-nothing environment. In this paper, we investigate the approach of using PC clusters to answer range sum queries, and present an effective parallel hierarchical data cube storage structure (PHDC for short), which provides better load balancing for both range sum queries and updates. The analytical and experimental results show that PHDC may have better load-balance and achieve optimum speed-up for a very high percentage of range queries on data cube.

Referencecs

1. Codd E.F.: Providing OLAP (on-line analytical processing) to user-analysts: An IT mandate, Technical report, E. F. Codd and Associates, 1993.
2. Gray J., Bosworth A., Layman A., Pirahesh H.: Data cube: A relational aggregation operator generating group-by, cross-tab and sub-total. In *Proc. Of the 12th ICDE Conf.* 1996. 152-159
3. Ho C.T., Agrawal R., Megiddo R., and Srikant R.: Range Queries in OLAP Data Cubes. In *Proceedings of the Intl. ACM SIGMOD Confference*, 1997, 73-88.
4. Geffner S., Agrawal D., Abbadi A., and Smith T.: Relative Prefix Sums: An Efficient Approach for Querying Dynamic OLAP Data Cubes. In *Proceedings of the 15th Intl. Conference on Data Engineering*, 1999, 328-335.
5. Chan C.Y. and Ioannidis Y.E.: Hierarchical Cubes for Range-Sum Queries. In *Proceedings of the 25th VLDB Conference*, 1999, 675-686.
6. Chun S.J., Chung C.W., Lee J.H., Lee S.L.: Dynamic update cube for range-sum queries In Proc. of 27th VLDB Conf. 2001,521-530.

7. Liang W., Wang H., Orlowska M.E. Range queries in dynamic OLAP data cubes. *Data and Knowledge Engineering 34*, 2000, 21-38.
8. Li J.Z., Gao H.: Hierarchical Data Cube for Range Queries and Dynamic Updates. In the East-European Conference on Advances in Databases and Information Systems(ADBIS), 2003.
9. Jens A., Wolfgang S.: Aggregate-based Query Processing in a Parallel Data Warehouse Server, In the 10th International Workshop on Database and Expert Systems Applications, Florence, Italy, September, 1999.
10. Hector G. M., Wilburt J.L., Janet L. W., et al..: Distributed and Parallel Computing Issues in Data Warehousing. http://www-db.stanford.edu/warehousing/ware-house.html.
11. Sun J., Grosky W.I.: Dynamic Maintenance of Multidimensional Range Data Partitioning for Parallel Data Processing, In ACM International Workshop on Data Warehousing and OLAP, 1998,.
12. Muto S., Kitsuregawa M.: A Dynamic Load Balancing Strategy for Parallel Datacube Computation. In ACM International Workshop on Data Warehousing and OLAP,1999.
13. Rohm U., Bohm K., et al.: OLAP query routing and physical design in a DB cluster. In International Conference on Extending Database Technology, 2000.
14. Dehne F., Eavis T., Rau-Chaplin A.: A Cluster Architecture for Parallel Data Warehousing. In IEEE International Conference on Cluster Computing and the Grid (CCGrid 2001), Brisbane, Australia, May 2001.
15. Goil S., Choudhary A.: An Infrastructure for Scalable Parallel Multidimensional Analysis, In the 11th International Conference on Scientific and Statistical Database Management, July, 1999.
16. J.Z. Li, H. Gao, Parallel Hierarchical Data Cube for Range Queries and Dynamic Updates, Technical report, ftp://211.93.34.108 ,2003.

A Bitmap Index for Multidimensional Data Cubes

Yoonsun Lim and Myung Kim

Dept. of Computer Science and Engineering, Ewha Womans University
11-1 Daehyun-Dong Seodaemun-Gu, Seoul 120-750 Korea
{lys96,mkim}@ewha.ac.kr

Abstract. Multidimensional arrays can be used to store multidimensional data cubes. One way of storing such array onto disk is to partition the array into a set of small chunks that can fit in a disk block. Chunks are usually of the same side length and are compressed before being stored, in order to achieve high query processing speed and space utilization. This scheme is called the chunk-based cube storage scheme. Although the scheme is considered to be a position based storage scheme, the chunks cannot be retrieved fast without using indexes since they are compressed. In this paper, we propose a bitmap index for such a storage scheme. The index can be constructed with the data cube in parallel. The relative positions of the chunks are retained in the index so that the chunk retrieval can be done in constant time. We placed in an index block as many chunks as possible so that the number of index searches is minimized for OLAP operations such as slice, dice, and range queries. We evaluated the proposed index by comparing it with existing multidimensional indexes such as UB-tree and grid file in terms of time and space.

1 Introduction

OLAP(On-line Analytical Processing) is a process and methodology that analyzes and queries multidimensional data stored in a data warehouse [6, 8]. With data mining and XML document processing technologies, OLAP is one of the fundamental technologies for today's business intelligence infrastructure. In order to provide timely responses, it is a common practice that OLAP systems summarize the given multidimensional data in advance. The performance of the system highly depends on how the summarized results are stored and accessed. In this paper, we consider an efficient index for the (summarized) multidimensional data.

Suppose that we are given a set of sales data for a national chain store. Our sales data represent how many items are sold in which store at what time. Common OLAP operations on this 3 dimensional data include how many items are sold during certain period of time, how good a store performs compared to other stores, and which time period certain items are sold better, etc. Note that the query results for such operations involve extensive searching and summarizing the entire multidimensional data. This is the main reason that OLAP systems summarize the multidimensional data by almost all combinations of the dimensions of the data. The resulting summary data are said to be stored in a 'multidimensional data cube'. The dimensionality of a cube is also a main factor that affects the performance of the OLAP system. In a situation where high query processing speed is required, no larger than 8~10 dimensions are recommended. In this paper, we focus on how to store such a multidimensional data cube onto disk, and how fast to retrieve data from disk.

Conceptually a multidimensional data cube can be stored in a multidimensional array. An efficient way of storing such array onto disk is to partition the array into small chunks that can fit in a disk block[10]. In order to give a fair chance to all the dimensions, the side lengths of a chunk are made equal. For space efficiency, sparse chunks are further compressed and stored. It is said that the resulting cube is stored by 'a chunk-based MOLAP (multidimensional OLAP) cube' storage scheme. Note that due to data compression, the position information on the chunks is destroyed, and efficient index schemes are required for fast access to the chunks.

In this paper, we propose an efficient index for chunk-based MOLAP cubes. The proposed index has the following advantages. Both the index and the cube are constructed in parallel. Only three bits are needed to index a chunk so that a large number of chunks can be indexed by one index block. Relative positions of the chunks are retained in the index so that index search for a specific chunk is done in constant time. Only a few index blocks are required to be read even for a range query that covers a wide region. Our index scheme is called 'the CBM index (index for a Chunk-Based MOLAP cubes)'.

We evaluated the CBM index in terms of query processing time and storage space efficiency by comparing it with the representative multidimensional indexes such as UB-tree[1] and Grid file[7]. The analysis result shows that the CBM index outperforms them even in cases that the cube is very sparse. The paper is organized as follows. In section 2, we describe the existing multidimensional indexes. In section 3, we propose the CBM indexing scheme. In section 4, we evaluated the CBM index. We conclude in section 5.

2 Multidimensional Indexes

Let us briefly explain some multidimensional indexes that can be used for chunk-based MOLAP cubes. We then describe the bitmap indexes. Here we use the terms, 'chunk', 'data', 'point', interchangeably.

Grid file[7], BANG file(balanced and nested grid)[3], and MLGF[9] belong to the category of hash-based multidimensional indexes. A Grid file consists of a set of linear scales, one per dimension, and a directory (or grid array) that partitions the multidimensional space according to the linear scales, as shown in Fig. 1(a). Each cell in the directory points to a bucket on disk that contains the addresses of the data belonging to the corresponding region. Data can be located in constant time, but incremental updates are not easily done. BANG file and MLGF are improved versions of the Grid file. The shape and size of the directory cells dynamically get adjusted according to the bucket density. Data updates can be easily processed. However, the hierarchical nature of the index slows down the index search.

R-Tree[4] and UB-Tree[1] are representative tree based indexes for multidimensional data. As with the B-tree, these are height balanced trees. A leaf node of an R-tree represents a rectangle in the multidimensional space. The regions represented by the leaf nodes can be overlapped one another. The internal nodes of the R-tree represent the smallest rectangle in the multidimensional space that covers all the rectangles represented by their children nodes. Multiple rectangles should be examined if the data items to be searched are not present. A UB-tree is a B-tree that is applied to a sequence of data items that are ordered by their Z indexes. It takes $O(\log n)$ index block searches to locate a data block, where n is the number of leaf nodes in the UB-Tree.

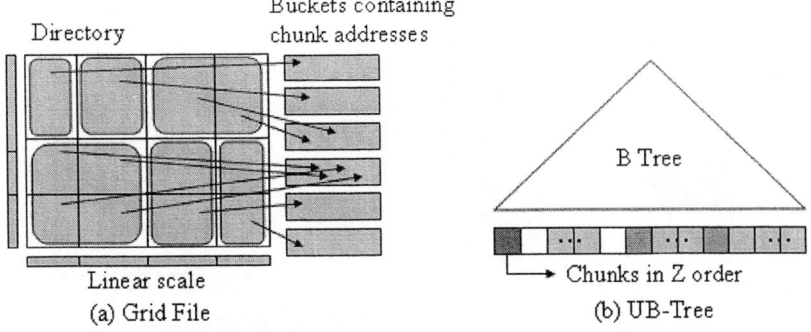

Fig. 1. Multidimensional indexes on a chunk based MOLAP Cube

A bitmap index [2] is a sequence of bits, where the i-th bit represents certain characteristics of the i-th data item. It is very useful for a dimension with small cardinality. For example, a bitmap index can be used to indicate a person's sexuality. They are especially useful to locate all the data items that satisfy certain conditions. Bitmap indexes are small, and they retain the position information on the data. These characteristics are what we used for our new index.

3 Chunk-Base MOLAP Cubes and the CBM Index

We first describe the chunk-based MOLAP cube storage scheme. We then propose our CBM index scheme, and explain how to use the index for data retrieval. Suppose that we are given a table of sales data set that consists of three dimensions, Product(P), Store(S), Time(T). Let us call the table *PST*. From this table, we can obtain 7 different summary tables such as *PS*, *PT*, *ST*, *P*, *S*, *T*, and *all*. Here we assume that each of them, including *PST* itself, is stored independently in a separate multidimensional array. In the chunk-based MOLAP cube storage scheme, these multidimensional arrays are partitioned into small chunks each of which can fit in a disk block whose typical size is 4K bytes. For example, Fig. 2 shows how to store *PST* onto disk. Dense chunks are stored as is. Sparse chunks are compressed as in the figure. That is, only the valid cells are stored with their offsets inside the chunk. Chunks with 40% or more valid cells are considered to be dense. Chunks can be ordered in various ways. Some possible orderings include row-major order, Hilbert order, and Z order. It is shown in [5] that the scheme that stores the dense chunks separately from the sparse chunks, and keeps each group in Z order performs very well. Our indexing scheme, the CBM index, stores the bits in the same order as the corresponding chunks are stored. Thus, it works for various chunk orders. However, for simplicity, we assume here that the chunks are stored in Z order and dense chunks are stored separately.

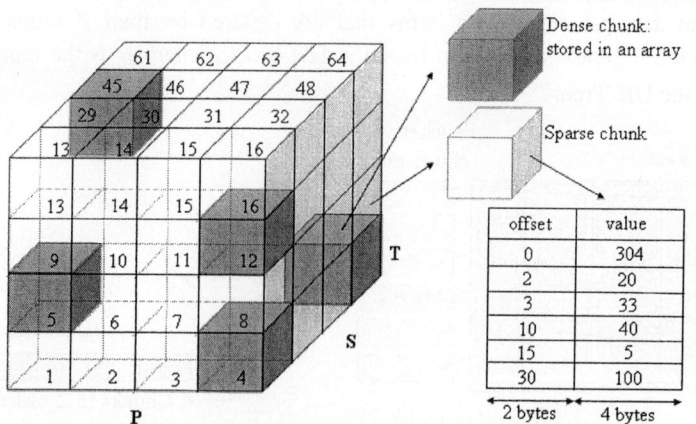

Fig. 2. An example of a 3-dim MOLAP cube

The CBM index is a bitmap index for a chunk-based MOLAP cube. Basically, it consists of three bit sequences such that the i-th bit of each sequence describes the i-th chunk of the cube. The CBM index allows us to locate the chunk of interest with at most one index block search. Range queries can also be processed very efficiently especially in case that the neighboring data chunks form a cluster on disk. Another advantage of the CBM index is that it can be constructed with the data cube construction, in parallel with a minimal cost.

Fig 3 shows an example of 2-dimensional data cube and its corresponding CBM index. Fig. 3(a) depicts a 2-dimensional cube that is partitioned into 64 chunks. For simplicity, here we use the Z order to number the data chunks. In the figure, dark colored chunks such as 0, 3, and 8 are dense chunks, and light colored chunks such as chunks 1, 4, and 6 are sparse chunks, and white chunks such as chunks 2, 5, and 7 are null (invalid) chunks. Fig. 3(b) shows the linearized version of the data cube. Fig. 3(c) shows the three bit sequences, B_0, B_1, and B_2, whose i-th bits are for chunk i of Fig. 3(b). The sequences in Fig. 3(c) are partitioned and stored onto disk in order as in Fig. 3(d), which is called the CBM index. We call each block in Fig. 3(d) an index block. Index block i contains two data items, AD_i and AS_i, where AD_i is the disk address of the first dense chunk that belongs to index block i, and AS_i is the address of the first sparse chunk that belongs to index block i. Note that we assume here that the dense chunks are stored separately from the sparse chunks in order to maximize the data clustering effect [5]. However, it is not a requirement to use the CBM index.

The contents of index block i is shown in Fig. 4. The j-th bit in each bit group, $B_0(i,j)$, $B_1(i,j)$, and $B_2(i,j)$, is for the j-th chunk indexed by index block i. $B_0(i,j)$ indicates whether the j-th chunk is null, and $B_1(i,j)$ indicates whether the j-th chunk is dense. In case the j-th chunk is sparse, $B_2(i,j)$ indicates whether it is the first chunk in a disk block. $B_2(i,1)$ is initially set to 1.

A Bitmap Index for Multidimensional Data Cubes

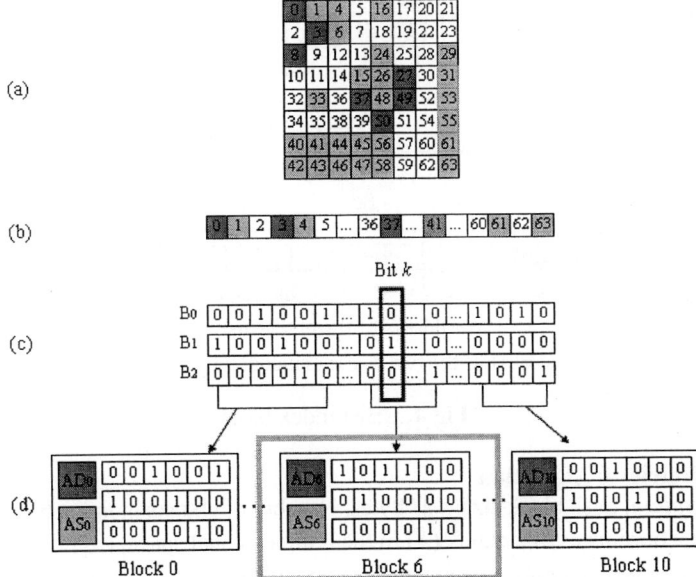

Fig. 3. The CBM Index: (a) data cube, (b) Z ordered chunks, (c) Bit sequences constituting the CBM index, (d) Index blocks of the CBM index

(1) Chunk Retrieval Algorithm

We explain here how to access a chunk, when given its ID (or the coordinates of the chunk in the data cube). For example, let us retrieve a chunk whose ID is x. First we compute the chunk's Z index, z, from x. Suppose that c is the number of chunks that are indexed by one index block. Chunk x is then indexed by $B_0(i,j)$, $B_1(i,j)$, and $B_2(i,j)$, if ($i = z$ div c) and ($j = z$ mod c). Thus, index block i is next read from disk, and the j-th bits ($B_0(i,j)$, $B_1(i,j)$, and $B_2(i,j)$) and AD_i and AS_i are examined to obtain the logical address of chunk x. For readability, we use the terms chunk (i, j) and chunk x, interchangeably.

The logical address of chunk x (or chunk (i, j)), X_{addr}, is computed as follows. First, $B_0(i,j)$ is examined to see if chunk (i, j) is null. If not null, $B_1(i,j)$ is next examined to see if it is dense. In case chunk (i, j) is dense, we count the number of 1's in between $B_1(i, 1) \sim B_1(i, j)$ that represents the number of dense blocks that precede chunk (i, j) and stored after AD_i. X_{addr} can be easily computed using the count, AD_i, and M, where M is the size of a dense block (or a disk block). In case chunk (i, j) is sparse, we also count the number of 1's in $B_2(i, 1) \sim B_2(i, j)$. The count gives us the information on how many disk blocks away chunk (i, j) is stored from AS_i, since $B_2(i,k)$ is set to 1 only if chunk (i, k) is the first chunk in a disk block. Thus, the count, AS_i, and M are used to compute X_{addr}. The algorithm is given below.

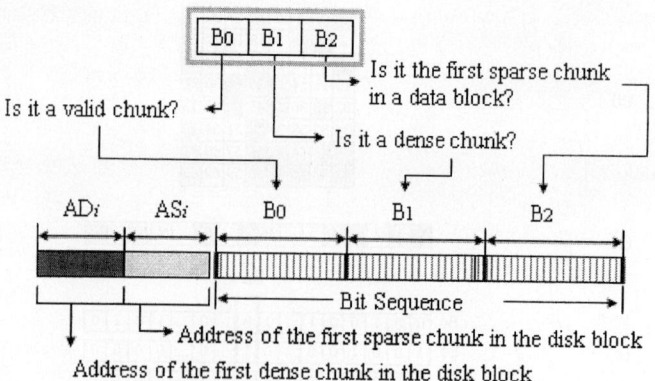

Fig 4. CBM index block i

Chunk Retrieval Algorithm
Assumption: Disk block size = M bytes, Number of chunks in index block = c.
Input: Coordinates of a chunk (X) in the n dimensional space, ($x_1, x_2, \ldots, x_n$).
Output: Address of the data block in which chunk X is stored, X_{addr}.
Step 1: compute the Z index of chunk X, z, from the given chunk coordinates.
Step 2: $i = z$ div c; $j = z$ mod c /* i:index block number, j:offset in the block*/
Step 3: read index block i.
Step 4: if $B_0(i,j) = 1$ then X_{addr} = NULL

$\quad$ else if $B_1(i,j) = 1$ then $X_{addr} = AD_i + M \times (\sum_{k=1}^{j} B_1(i,k) - 1)$

$\quad$ else $X_{addr} = AS_i + M \times \sum_{k=1}^{j} B_2(i,k)$

Step 5: Return (X_{addr})

(2) Range Query Processing Algorithm
Range query is a query that requests the data chunks whose dimension values belong to certain ranges. For example, a query that asks for the profit obtained from selling certain product that were sold during certain period in certain region of the country can be considered to be a range query. Assume that $c_{i_1}, c_{i_2}, \ldots, c_{i_k}$, $i_1 \leq i_2 \leq \ldots \leq i_k$, are the chunks requested by a range query. These chunks numbers can easily be obtained by parsing the query. The chunks can be retrieved as follows. First, the ID's of the chunks are transformed to their Z indexes, and sorted in their increasing order. Let us call the numbers $cz_{i_1}, cz_{i_2}, \ldots cz_{i_k}$, $cz_{i_1} < cz_{i_2} < \ldots < cz_{i_k}$. Second, the index block that contains the information on the first chunk, cz_{i_1}, is read into memory. All the requested chunks that belong to this index block are also retrieved. Let's assume that $cz_{i_1}, cz_{i_2}, \ldots cz_{i_j}$ are these chunks. Third, we use the chunk $cz_{i_{j+1}}$ to read the

corresponding index block, and retrieve the data chunks similarly. Remaining chunks are retrieved similarly until all the requested chunks are retrieved. A formal description of the range query processing algorithm is given below.

Range Query Processing Algorithm
  Assumption: Disk block size = M bytes, Number of chunks in index block = c.
    POP(*list*): returns the first number in the list, and removes it from the list.
  Input: Chunk numbers, $c_{i_1}, c_{i_2}, \ldots, c_{i_k}$, for range queries.
  Output : Array containing chunk addresses, Array(X_{addr})
  Step1: Transform $c_{i_1}, c_{i_2}, \ldots, c_{i_k}$ to the z indexes, $cz_{i_1}, cz_{i_2}, \ldots cz_{i_k}$.
  Step 2: *next_chunk* = POP($cz_{i_1}, cz_{i_2}, \ldots cz_{i_k}$); *index_block* = NULL
  Step 3: while (*next_chunk* != NULL) {
    if chunk *next_chunk* does not belong to index block *index_block*
      then *index_block* = *next_chunk* div c
        read index block *index_block* from disk
      else get the address of chunk *next_chunk* from the index block *index_block*
        and add it to Array(X_{addr});
    next_chunk = POP($cz_{i_1}, cz_{i_2}, \ldots cz_{i_k}$) }
  Step 4: Return Array(X_{addr})

4 Performance Analysis

In this section, we evaluate the CBM index by comparing it with the UB-tree and the Grid file in terms of space and time efficiencies. First, we assume that the chunk-based MOLAP cube does not allow incremental updates. Let us explain the other case later. Since no space is needed for incremental updates, and the indexes can be constructed with the cube generation in parallel, we do not have extra space for updates in the UB-tree and the Grid file, either. It means that we assume that the UB-tree and the Grid file have minimal space for indexing the cube. We further assume that the directory of the Grid file resides in memory.

(1) Space Efficiency
A CBM index needs only three bits for indexing a chunk. Thus we can index as many as 10K chunks using an index block of size 4K bytes. In a UB-tree and a Grid file, at least 9 bytes are needed to index a chunk to store the chunk number, the disk address of the chunk, and a flag representing the density of the chunk. It means that we can index at most 450 chunks using a leaf node of the UB-tree or a bucket of the Grid file. The number of internal nodes of a UB-tree depends on the number of leaf nodes. For the experiments, we used 3~6 dimensional cubes. The dimension cardinality of the 3, 4, 5, and 6 dimensional cube is assumed to be 1,280, 160, 128, and 48, respectively. The numbers of chunks in the cube are approximately 2M, 1M, 33M, and 17M,

respectively. The size of a chunk is assumed to be close to 4K bytes when they are 100% dense.

We first compared the sizes of the three indexes. The tests were performed on 3~6 dimensional cubes, by varying the ratio of valid chunks. As shown in Fig. 5, the size of the CBM index is fixed for all cases. On the other hand, the size of the UB-tree and the Grid file is linearly proportional to the valid chunk ratio. The space taken by the UB-tree and the Grid file are not distinguishable since the number of internal nodes of the UB-tree is negligible and the directory of the Grid file resides in memory. The CBM index takes less space for the cubes whose valid chunk ratio is 4% or above. This means that the CBM index may be smaller than the other two indexes for cubes with density lower than 4%, since in most cases the actual cube density can be a lot lower than the valid chunk ratio.

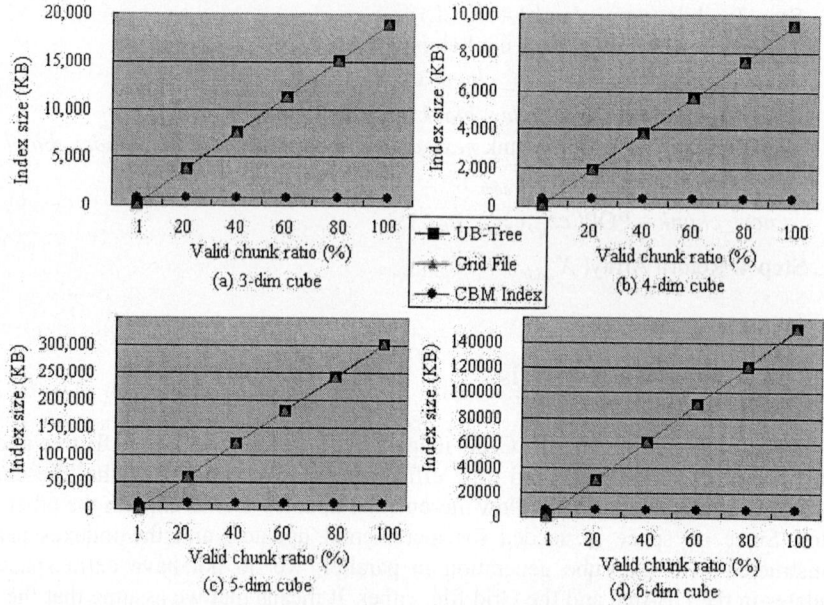

Fig. 5. Index sizes of the CBM, UB-Tree and Grid file

Let us now consider the case that incremental updates are allowed. For such case, some space in each chunk should be reserved, and it forces all the chunks to be valid, meaning that the valid chunk ratio becomes 100%. As shown in Fig. 5, the size of the CBM index does not change, but the other two indexes grow tremendously. We now compare the size of the CBM index with that of the data cube itself to see how small the index can be. The test results on our 3 dimensional data are shown in Fig. 6. We conducted the same test on our 4~6 dimensional data, and obtained similar results. For each value of data density, we obtained two values: Max and Min. Max is the ratio of data space to index space, when the data in the cube are uniformly distributed. Min is the ratio of the data space to the index space, when the data in the cube are all clustered so that all the valid chunks are of 100% dense. We can see that Min is 1,065 and Max is 1,613 when the data density is 10%. If the density of the data increases by

10%, the space for the relative space for the index becomes half. Note that Max and Min become the same, when the data density reaches 40% or above, since chunks of density 40% or above are not compressed.

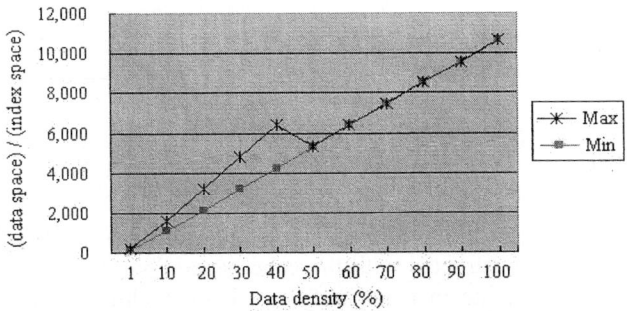

Fig. 6. Relative size of the CBM index

(2) Indexing Speed
The CBM index and the Grid file require only one index block search to locate a chunk. However, the UB-tree requires $O(\log_m n)$ disk block searches since all the nodes between the root and the leaf should be examined, where m is the number of fanouts of the UB tree and n is the total number of chunks. Also, note that the sizes of the CBM index for our 3-dim, 4-dim, and 5-dim data are only 788K bytes, 383K bytes, and 12M bytes respectively. Thus, the entire CBM index can reside in memory for such small or medium sized cubes.

Our CBM index performs very well for range queries. Suppose that Q is the total number of chunks that belong to the query range, and Q_1 is the number of valid chunks among them. The UB-tree requires $\lceil 2 \times Q_1 / M_1 \times O(\log_m n) \rceil$ index block searches, where M_1 is the number of chunks indexed by a leaf node, m is the total number of chunks indexed by the UB-tree, and n is the number of leaf nodes[1]. The number of leaf nodes to be searched is $\lceil 2 \times Q_1 / M_1 \rceil$[1]. The Grid-file requires $\lceil 2 \times Q_2 / M_2 \rceil$ index block searches, where Q_2 is the number of chunks that belong to the directory cell that overlaps with the query box and M_2 is the number of chunks in a bucket. However, the CBM index only requires $\lceil 2 \times Q / M_3 \rceil$ index block searches, where M_3 is the number of chunks indexed by an index block. For example, the index searches needed for our test data are shown in Table 2. Here we assumed that $Q = 3,000$, $M_1 = M_3 = 500$, $M_2 = 10,000$. In summary, the number of index blocks needed for range query is linearly proportional to the number of valid chunks. For the CBM index, there are 10,000 chunks inside an index block. For the UB tree and the Grid file, there are 500 chunks inside an index block. For the case that we allow data updates, the number of valid chunks becomes 100%. Thus, we can see that the CBM index outperforms the other two indexes.

Table 2. Number of index block accesses for a range query with $Q = 3,000$

Valid chunk ratio	CBM index	UB-tree	Grid file
100%	1	24	12
50%	1	12	6
10%	1	3	2

5 Conclusions

In this paper, we proposed an efficient index for chunk-based MOLAP cubes. The index can be easily constructed with the cube generation. The size of the index is small so that it can reside in memory for small or medium sized cubes. Relative positions of the chunks are retained in the index so that index search for a specific chunk is done by one index block search. Only a few index blocks are required to be searched even for a range query that covers a wide region. We evaluated the CBM index in terms of query processing time and storage space efficiency by comparing it with the representative multidimensional indexes such as UB-tree and Grid file. It is shown that the CBM index outperforms them even when the valid chunk ratio is as low as 4%. Note that the data cube density can be a lot lower than the valid chunk ratio.

References

[1] Rudolf Bayer, "The Universal B-Tree for Multidimensional Indexing", Technische Universitat München, TUM-I9637, November 1996.
[2] Chee-Yong Chan and Yannis E. Ioannidis, "Bitmap index design and evaluation," Proc. ACM SIGMOD, pp. 355-366, June 1998.
[3] Michael Freestone, "The bang file: A new kind of grid file," Proc. ACM SIGMOD, pp. 260-269, 1987.
[4] Antonin Guttman, "R-Trees: A Dynamic Index Structure for Spatial Searching," Proc. ACM SIGMOD, pp. 47-57, Boston, 1984.
[5] Myung Kim and Yoonsun Lim, "A Z index based MOLAP Storage Scheme", Journal of Korea Information Science Society, Vol. 29, No. 4, pp. 262-273, August 2002.
[6] Won Kim and Myung Kim, "Performance and Scalability in Knowledge Engineering: Issues and Solutions," *Journal of Object-Oriented Programming*, Vol. 12, No. 7, pp. 39-43, Nov/Dec. 1999.
[7] Jürg Neivergelt, Hans Hinterberger and Kenneth C. Sevcik, "The Grid File: An Adaptable, Symmetric Multikey File Structure," ACM Transactions on Database Systems, Vol. 9, No. 1, pp. 38-71, March 1984.
[8] Erick Thomsen, "OLAP Solutions: Building Multidimensional Information Systems," *John Wiley & Sons*, New York, 1997.
[9] Kyu-Young Whang and Ravi Krishnamurthy, "The Multilevel Grid File - A Dynamic Hierarchical Multidimensional File Structure", DSFAA, pp. 449-459, 1991.
[10] Yihong Zhao, Prasad Deshpande and Jeffrey Naughton, "An Array-Based Algorithm for Simultaneous Multidimensional Aggregates," Proc. ACM SIGMOD, pp. 159-170, 1997.

Analytical Synopses for Approximate Query Answering in OLAP Environments

Alfredo Cuzzocrea[1] and Ugo Matrangolo[2]

[1] DEIS Dept. - University of Calabria
87036 Rende, Cosenza, Italy
cuzzocrea@si.deis.unical.it
[2] ICAR Inst. - CNR
87036 Rende, Cosenza, Italy
matrangolo@icar.cnr.it

Abstract. In this paper we present a technique based on an *analytical interpretation* of multi-dimensional data and on the well-known *Least Squares Approximation* (LSA) method for supporting approximate aggregate query answering in OLAP environments, the most common application interfaces for a Data Warehouse Server (DWS). Our technique consists in building data synopses by interpreting the original data distribution as a set of discrete functions. These synopses, called Δ-Syn, are obtained by approximating data with a set of polynomial coefficients, and storing these coefficients instead of the original data. Queries are issued on the compressed representation, thus reducing the number of disk accesses needed to evaluate the answer. We also provide some experimental results on several kinds of synthetic OLAP data cubes.

1 Introduction

In modern advanced information systems, such as B2B and B2C *e*-commerce systems, transactional information systems and control systems the data layer is enormous. Data sources for these systems are often highly heterogeneous. Consequently, the use of a DWS for collecting, integrating, and making business-critical information available in a "transparent-for-user" way has become mandatory. Recently, DSS-based applications have become very popular (e.g. sales transaction databases, call detail repositories, customer service historical data etc), so that systems efficiently performing OLAP and Data Mining (DM) against a DWS have gained a leading role. In fact, on the basis of a multi-dimensional and multi-resolution interpretation of data stored in the DWS, managers and analysts can access and query the available information in order to make critical choices for their strategic business. The enormous size of the multi-dimensional data represents the main drawback of this analysis model: currently, tera-bytes and peta-bytes is the order of data magnitude, but astronomy, retail, economy, biology and health/medicine information systems are collecting with exponential increase massive and, above all, multi-dimensional data sets. Fortunately, the analysis required by decision support-oriented tasks is often qualitative, as in the querying and reporting phases decimal precision is not needed. In other words, managers and analysts are more interested in the "trend" analysis rather than in the "punctual" analysis.

Application fields in which multi-dimensional analysis has a leading role are manifold: transaction recording systems, data mining processors, intrusion detection systems, scientific databases, time-series databases, GIS systems, remote sensing systems, statistical databases etc. In some of them, dimensionality of data is very high. Dimension number, along with data size, is one of the most critical factors influencing the effectiveness of DSS-based applications, since it strongly affects the efficiency of the Query Engine.

From the above considerations, it follows that computing approximate answers is more convenient than providing exact answers, as it allows us to speed-up the throughput of DSSs without decreasing the quality and the effectiveness of querying and analyzing tasks.

In more detail, our attention is focused on *range-sum queries*, an important class of aggregate queries that are very often executed against OLAP data cubes[1]. They are defined as the application of the aggregation operator SUM over a set of selected contiguous ranges in the domains of the dimensional attributes (see Ho et al. in [5] for a more accurate definition).

In this paper we present a technique based on an analytical interpretation of multi-dimensional data and the well-known LSA method [14] for building analytical synopses, called Δ-Syn, in order to support approximate aggregate query answering in OLAP environments, the most common application interfaces for a DWS. Our technique consists in building data synopses by interpreting the original data distribution as a set of discrete impulsive functions[2]. The synopses are obtained by approximating the *Cumulative Distribution Functions* (CDF) of such functions with a set of polynomial coefficients by means of the LSA method, and storing these coefficients instead of the original data. This allows us to achieve a compact representation of the original data domain as the size of the polynomial coefficient set is bounded by the storage space B available for housing the synopses. We have developed an algorithm that takes the storage space B and builds Δ-Syn with low spatio-temporal complexity. Queries are issued on the compressed representation using an optimized procedure, thus reducing the number of disk accesses needed to evaluate the answer. We tested our proposed technique on several kinds of synthetic OLAP data cubes. Δ-Syn provide good performances, even in comparison with other well-known compression techniques presented in literature such as histograms, wavelet transforms, random sampling. Experimental results reported in Section 6 confirm this claim. So, the major contribution of this paper is outperforming previous important results in the context of approximate query answering, using a low spatio-temporal complexity technique.

The paper is organized as follows. In Section 2 we report related work on approximate query answering; in Section 3 we present the foundations of our work; in Section 4 we describe our technique for building Δ-Syn starting from a given data cube and present the related algorithm; in Section 5 we present the experimental results of the quality of our technique; finally, in Section 6 we draw conclusions and indicate future work.

---

[1] In the rest of the paper we use the term "data cube" instead of "OLAP data cube".
[2] In the rest of the paper we mutually use the terms "function" and "distribution".

2 Related Work

Recently research has devoted a great deal of attention on data reduction/compression and approximate query answering, by the Database and Data Warehousing research community. Many techniques for compressing data cubes and evaluating range queries over their compressed representation have been proposed. Several compression models, which had originally been defined in different contexts, have been used to this end. We provide a brief description of the most popular of these techniques: histograms, wavelets, and sampling.

Ioannidis and Poosala in [6] introduce the use of histograms for providing approximate answers to set-valued queries. Histograms are data structures obtained by partitioning a data distribution into a number of mutually disjoint blocks, called *buckets*, and then storing for each bucket some aggregate information, such as the sum of its items. Histograms were originally proposed for query size estimation inside Query Optimizers, and to summarize multi-dimensional data distributions [3,11,12]: in the latter case, the data distribution to be compressed consists in the frequencies of values of the attributes in a relation and queries are evaluated by performing linear interpolation on the stored aggregate values. Subsequently, histograms are also effectively used to estimate range queries in OLAP [13].

Vitter et al. in [16,17] introduce the idea of using a wavelet-based technique for approximating multi-dimensional data like data cubes. Previously, Matias et al. in [9] proposed using wavelets for improving *Selectivity Estimation*. Wavelets are a mathematical tool for the hierarchical decomposition of functions: they represent a function in terms of a coarse overall shape, plus details that range from coarse to fine. Wavelet-based techniques improve the histogram-based ones in to summarize multi-dimensional data.

Random sampling-based methods propose mapping the original multi-dimensional data domain in a smaller subset by sampling: this allows a more compact representation of the original data to be achieved. For instance, Gibbons and Matias in [2] present some experimental results that demonstrate how query performances can be significantly improved by applying sampling with very low computational overhead. Traditionally, random sampling-based techniques are not considered as performing as well as other more resource-intensive techniques such as multi-dimensional histograms and wavelet decomposition. However, they have recently been of renewed interest from the Database and Data Warehousing research community, due to their computational requirements, which are very low.

Hellerstein et al. in [4] propose a system for effectively supporting on-line aggregate query answering, also providing probabilistic guarantees about the accuracy of the answers in terms of confidence intervals. It allows a user to execute an aggregate query and to observe its execution in a graphical interface that shows both the partial answer and the correspondent (partial) confidence interval. The user can also stop the query execution when the answer has achieved the desired degree of approximation. Therefore, the whole process is interactive. No synopses are maintained since the system is based on a random sampling of the tuples involved in the query.

3 Foundations

Let $A = <D,M>$ be a data cube such that $D = \{d_0, d_1, \ldots, d_{N-1}\}$ is the set of dimensions, and $M = \{m_0\}$ the set of measures (for simplicity, in our analysis we assume we are dealing with only one measure, as in many real-life data cubes, but extending this analysis to more than one measure is straightforward). Without any loss of generality, we assume that A is stored according to a MOLAP data organization, and each data cell is represented by 32 bits. So, A is an N-dimensional array of size $S(A) = \prod_{i=0}^{N-1} |d_i|$ bits, where $|d_i|$ is the size of the dimension d_i and i belongs to the set $\{0,1,\ldots,N-1\}$.

A range-sum query Q over A can generally be formulated as follows:

$$Q(l_0 : u_0, \ldots, l_{N-1} : u_{N-1}) = \sum_{i_0=l_0}^{u_0} \cdots \sum_{i_{N-1}=l_{N-1}}^{u_{N-1}} A[i_0, i_1, \ldots, i_{N-1}] \quad (1)$$

where $<l_k:u_k>$ is the range defined on the dimension d_k and $A[i_0,i_1,\ldots,i_{N-1}]$ is the data cell located by the multi-dimensional entry $\{i_0,i_1,\ldots,i_{N-1}\}$.

The LSA method is a basic procedure of our technique. Given a discrete function f of n samples, it finds the "best" polynomial function $\tilde{f}$ approximating f by minimizing the sum of the squares of the distances between the points of f and $\tilde{f}$ [14]. $\tilde{f}$ is defined as the linear combination of T basis functions Φ_k belonging to Φ, such that Φ is the set of basis functions of the $\tilde{f}$ functional space [14], and T coefficients as follows:

$$\tilde{f} = \sum_{k=0}^{T-1} c_k \Phi_k \quad (2)$$

where each coefficient c_k is obtained as follows:

$$c_k = \frac{\Phi_k \times f}{\|\Phi_k\|^2} \quad (3)$$

In the LSA method, T is an input parameter and, intuitively, the greater T, the greater the degree of accuracy (i.e., the "quality") of $\tilde{f}$. In our algorithm, T depends on the storage space B available for representing Δ-Syn.

The key idea of the technique we propose is that given a data cube A, on the basis of an analytical interpretation of data, a set of polynomial functions $\mathcal{I}_A$ can be built applying the LSA method to the cumulative distribution of each row R of A. A compressed representation of $\mathcal{I}_A$, called $\langle \mathcal{I}_A \rangle$, is obtained by storing for each function belonging to $\mathcal{I}_A$ only its polynomial coefficients (the polynomial degree is directly derivable from the number of the coefficients) and, finally, $\langle \mathcal{I}_A \rangle$ is used at query time instead of the original domain A. Experimental results clearly show the efficiency of this approach.

In the following we provide some definitions for a better understanding of the proposed technique. According to the MOLAP data organization, the row number of an

N-dimensional data cube A is $RN(A) = \prod_{i=0}^{N-2} |d_i|$, and the discrete impulsive function representing the row selected by multi-dimensional entry $\{i_0=p_0, i_1=p_1, \ldots, i_{N-2}=p_{N-2}\}$ is defined as follows:

$$f_{\{p_0,\ldots,p_{N-2}\}}(x) = \sum_{k=0}^{|d_{N-1}|-1} A[p_0,\ldots,p_{N-2}][k]\delta(x-k) \quad (4)$$

where $\delta(x-k)$ is the Dirac impulsive function on k.

For instance, in the bi-dimensional case (i.e., $N=2$), the number of rows for a $|d_0| \times |d_1|$ bi-dimensional data cube A is $RN(A) = |d_1|$ and the discrete impulsive function representing the row R is:

$$f_R(x) = \sum_{k=0}^{|d_1|-1} A[R][k]\delta(x-k) \quad (5)$$

We highlight that the "definition" of a row in a MOLAP array (i.e., what a row is) depends on the particular storage strategy adopted by the OLAP server. Without any loss of generality, in the relation (4) we assume that rows are selected fixing the first $N-1$ i_k coordinates, but our technique is independent of the particular storage strategy. Usually, storage model (that can be ROLAP, that is based on a relational scheme, MOLAP, that is based on a multi-dimensional array, or HOLAP, that is based on an hybrid scheme derived from those relational and multi-dimensional) is maintained along with its particular storage strategy inside the Catalog of the OLAP server and can be easily accessed and queried.

In order to improve the quality of our approximate query answering technique, we build the cumulative distribution f_R^+ for each row R of A. f_R^+ is defined as follows:

$$f_R^+(x) = \begin{cases} f_R(x) & x = 0 \\ f_R^+(x-1) + f_R(x) & x \geq 1 \end{cases} \quad (6)$$

Introducing the function f_R^+ has two benefits. The first is reducing the computational overhead of the executions of the LSA method as f_R^+ is always an increasing function and consequently can be approximated with a polynomial function having a degree smaller than that obtained by approximating a skewed function. The second one is drastically reducing the time needed for computing the approximate answers in the compressed domain since the required disk I/Os are very few. Consider, for instance, a bi-dimensional data cube A and a range query $Q(l_0:u_0, l_1:u_1)$. Then, in the original domain the answer to Q is computed as follows:

$$A(Q) = \sum_{i_0=l_0}^{u_0} \sum_{i_1=l_1}^{u_1} A[i_0, i_1] \quad (7)$$

On the contrary, in the compressed domain the approximate answer is obtained as follows:

$$\tilde{A}(Q) = \sum_{i=l_0}^{u_0} \left[f_i^+(u_1) - f_i^+(l_1-1) \right] \quad f_i^+(-1) = 0 \forall i \in \{l_0,\ldots,u_0\} \quad (8)$$

that is, accessing only the boundary samples of the cumulative distributions.

4 Building Δ-Syn

A basic issue in our work is how to allocate the storage space B available for housing the compressed representation of the input data cube A (i.e., the Δ-Syn). This issue is common in techniques for compressing multi-dimensional data. Some approaches like that of Bruno et al. in [1], and Jagadish et al. in [7] propose allocating storage space according to the query workload against the OLAP server but this technique is affected by the so-called cold-start problem, that is the lack of information about queries during the boot-up phase of the server. Another class of techniques propose driving space allocation as a function of statistical properties of data. Our approach follows this guideline, and proposes a data-driven space allocation scheme.

Let R be a row of A and f_R be its representing function; in the remainder of this Section we denote by $\wp(R)$ a generic statistical property $\wp$ of f_R (i.e., $\wp(f_R)$). The skewness value $\gamma_1(R)$ is defined as follows [8]:

$$\gamma_1(R) = \frac{(\mu_3(R))^2}{(\mu_2(R))^3} \tag{9}$$

where $\mu_r(R)$ is the rth central moment of f_R, that is defined as follows [10]:

$$\mu_r(R) = \sum_{k=0}^{n-1} (k-\mu)^r f_R(k) \tag{10}$$

where n is the number of samples of f_R and μ is the mean value of f_R. An important result well-known in literature [15] claims that the skewness value of a data distribution is "significant" when it is greater than its standard deviation by a factor of 2.6. In this condition, it can be assumed that data are not distributed according to a normal distribution. The standard deviation of the skewness $\sigma_\gamma(R)$ can be computed as follows [15]:

$$\sigma_\gamma(R) = \sigma(\gamma_1(R)) = \sqrt{\frac{6}{n}} \tag{11}$$

where n is the number of samples of f_R.

In order to capture these statistical properties in a "global fashion", we have developed a space allocation scheme for efficiently storing Δ-Syn that is based on the optimal space allocation of each row of the input data cube A. This scheme aims to assign more storage space to those rows that are more difficult to approximate (thus, they require more polynomial coefficients, i.e. more storage space), and less storage space to those easy to approximate. The scheme is driven by the relation (9) and (11). We introduce the function $\Gamma(R)$ for detecting those rows for which the skewness value is significant:

$$\Gamma(R) = \begin{cases} 1 & \dfrac{\gamma_1(R)}{\sigma_\gamma(R)} > 2.6 \\ 0 & \text{otherwise} \end{cases} \tag{12}$$

We denote by $\lambda(R)$ the factor $\dfrac{\gamma_1(R)}{\sigma_\gamma(R)} - 2.6$. Then, we define the function $m(R)$ for providing the allocation for a given row R:

$$m(R) = \sigma^2(R) + \dfrac{abs[\gamma_1(R)]}{|R|} \qquad (13)$$

where $\sigma^2(R)$ is the variance of f_R, that is defined as follows:

$$\sigma^2(R) = \sum_{k=0}^{n-1}(k-\mu)^2 f_R(k) \qquad (14)$$

where n is the number of samples of f_R and μ is the mean value of f_R.

The first term (i.e., $\sigma^2(R)$) aims to capture the global behavior of f_R (i.e., how it oscillates around its average value) while the second term (i.e., $\dfrac{abs[\gamma_1(R)]}{|R|}$) captures the contribution of the asymmetric peaks of f_R, thus the local behavior of f_R, and mediates their effect among all the samples of f_R by dividing it by the sample number $|R|$. So, $m(R)$ assigns a smaller storage space when the variance of f_R is low, since f_R is "regular", and a larger one when the skewness value of f_R is high, since f_R is not "regular". Finally, it should be noted that the first term provides a "global metrics" for f_R whereas the second term a "local metrics" for f_R.

In conclusion, the storage space $B(R)$, as a portion of the whole available storage space B, to be allocated for the row R of a given data cube A, is provided by the following relation:

$$B(R) = \left\lfloor \dfrac{m(R) + \Gamma(R)\cdot\lambda(R)}{\sum_{k=0}^{RN(A)} m(k) + \sum_{k=0}^{RN(A)} \Gamma(k)\cdot\lambda(k)} \cdot B \right\rfloor \qquad (15)$$

and the data-driven allocation scheme of the storage space B for a given data cube A is obtained by computing the quantity (15) for all the rows of A.

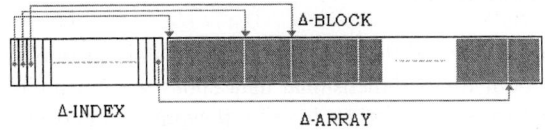

Fig. 1. Δ-Syn representation in secondary memory

Δ-Syn physical representation (see Fig. 1) consists of the set of the collections of coefficients representing all the approximating functions $\tilde{f}_R^+$, for each R belonging to the input data cube A. We denote each coefficient array for a given $\tilde{f}_R^+$ as Δ-BLOCK, and the collection of all the Δ-BLOCKs as Δ-ARRAY. In order to efficiently access Δ-Syn, we equip them with a simple indexing data structure, called Δ-INDEX allowing us, given a multi-dimensional entry $<i_0, i_1, \ldots, i_{N-1}>$, to retrieve the bounds of the correspondent Δ-BLOCK in secondary memory.

The following algorithm `buildΔSyn` codifies the technique we propose. Without any loss of generality, we assume that all the rows of the input data cube have the same size, but extending the algorithm for dealing with rows having different size is straightforward. For simplicity, in the code we assume that each T-degree polynomial function f is represented as an array of T elements such that each entry $F[k]$, being k belonging to the set $\{0,1,\ldots,T\text{-}1\}$, corresponds to the k-degree polynomial coefficient of f.

```
Algorithm buildΔSyn(A,B)
INPUT
A: The input data cube.
B: The storage space.
OUTPUT
D_Syn: The synopses.
int RN=OLAP_Util.getRowNum(A);
int RS=OLAP_Util.getRowSize(A);
int[] D_Index=new int[RN];
double[] D_Array;
double[][] R=new double[RN][RS];
double[][] C=new double[RN][RS];
double[][] Φ;
double[] Λ=new double[RN];
int[] Γ=new int[RN];
double[] M=new double[RN];
long[] S=new long[RN];
int[] T=new int[RN];
double[] coeffs;
double[] apxC;
int k,q,p,i;
for each k=0..RN do begin
  R[k]=OLAP_Util.getRow(A,k);
  C[k]=cumDist(R[k]);
end;
for each k=0..RN do begin
  Λ[k]=skw(R[k])/std_dev(R[k]);
  if (Λ[k]>2.6) then begin
    Γ[k]=1;
  else
    Γ[k]=0;
  end;
  M[k]=var(R[k])+(abs(swk(R[k]))/RS);
end;
for each k=0..RN do begin
  S[k]=(M[k]+Γ[k]*Λ[k])*B/
       (sum(M)+Γ[k]*sum(vetPro(Γ,Λ)));
  T[k]=S[k]/32;
end;
for each k=0..RN do begin
  coeffs=new double[T[k]];
  Φ=BasisFunctGen.get(RS,T[k]);
  for each q=0..T[k] do begin
    coeffs[q]=sclPro(Φ[k][q],C[k])/
              sqn(Φ[k][q]);
  end;
  apxC=linearComb(coeffs,Φ);
  D_Index[p]=i;
  p=p+1;
  i=i+T[k];
  D_Array.allocateCells(T[k]);
  D_Array.append(apxC);
end;
return
new D_Syn(D_Index,D_Array);
```

5 Experimental Results

In order to prove the effectiveness of the Δ-Syn, in this Section we present our experimental results both for bi-dimensional data cubes and for multi-dimensional data cubes. For the purpose of our tests, we have built synthetic multi-dimensional data sets taking two kinds of data cube into account: the data cube $A_{N,X}$ and the data cube $A_{N,Z}$, where N is the dimension number. The first one captures the situation in which the well-known *Continuous Values Assumption* (CVA) holds; CVA assumes that data are distributed according to a uniform distribution on the interval $[L_1,L_2]$, with $L_2 > L_1$. The second one describes a data cube for which data are distributed according to a Zipf distribution whose parameter is randomly chosen between z_{min} and z_{max}.

The data cube $A_{N,X}$ was built as follows. We iteratively used the procedure nextCVADataCell that takes the range $[L_1,L_2]$ and generates the value of the "current" data cell C_i such that C_i belongs to the range $[L_1,L_2]$. By varying the boundary values of the range $[L_1,L_2]$, different classes of CVA-aware data cubes can be obtained, that is data cubes more or less satisfying the CVA. The data cube $A_{N,Z}$ was built using a Zipf distribution with parameter z uniformly distributed on the range $[z_{min}, z_{max}]$. This realizes a totally random process for generating the data cells and, consequently, is more closer to real-life data cubes. A common feature for both the target synthetic data cubes is being sparse. Sparse data cubes are very popular in many real-life DSS-based applications and their sparsity coefficient s ranges between 0.0001% and 1%. Note that Δ-Syn are suitable with such situation, as data distributions with many zero values need few approximating coefficients and, thus, small storage space for housing their compact representation. This allows both the spatial complexity of Δ-Syn and the time complexity of the queries performed on them to be improved significantly.

For our experiments, we have engineered two kinds of range-sum query set: the query set $QS_{M,R}$ and the query set $QS_{M,S}$, where M is the number of ranges of the queries (i.e., the query dimensionality). The first one comprises queries having size $\Sigma_0 \times \Sigma_1 \times ... \times \Sigma_{M-1}$, such that each Σ_m is randomly generated, that is $\Sigma_m \neq \Sigma_q$ for each m, q belonging to the set $\{0,1,...,M-1\}$ with $m \neq q$ (in the bi-dimensional case, $QS_{M,R}$ contains rectangular queries). The second one is defined using the procedure buildEquiRangeQuerySet that takes a range size Σ^* and an integer W^* and builds a query set $Q_{M,S}^{\Sigma^*}$ having size W^* and containing queries with ranges of size Σ^*, that is $\Sigma_m = \Sigma^*$ for each m belonging to the set $\{0,1,...,M-1\}$. Queries belonging to $Q_{M,S}^{\Sigma^*}$ are isomorphic to the data cube and their central focus is the same as that of the data cube (in the bi-dimensional case, $Q_{M,S}^{\Sigma^*}$ contains square queries of side Σ^*). Then, the query set $QS_{M,S}$ is obtained by iteratively calling the procedure buildEquiRangeQuerySet on a defined set of couples $\left\{\left\langle \Sigma_0^*, W_0^* \right\rangle, \left\langle \Sigma_1^*, W_1^* \right\rangle, ..., \left\langle \Sigma_{P-1}^*, W_{P-1}^* \right\rangle\right\}$, such that $\Sigma_m^* \neq \Sigma_q^*$ for each m, q belonging to the set $\{0,1,...,P-1\}$, with $m \neq q$ and $\bigcup_{k=0}^{P-1} W_k^* = |QS_{M,S}|$. This allows to obtain queries with increasing ranges. The query set $QS_{M,R}$ tests the quality of our technique, that is its ability to answer randomly generated queries, and gives metrics about the accuracy of our technique. The query set $QS_{M,S}$ tests the scalability of our technique w.r.t. the input, as we submit it to queries with increasing ranges.

Finally, we have designed the generic test $T_{N,D,I}$, where N represents the dimension number of the data cube, D represents the kind of data cube (i.e., the CVA-aware kind, denoted by X, or the Zipf-based one, denoted by Z), and I represents the kind of query set (i.e., the "rectangular" kind, denoted by R, or the "square" one, denoted by S). $T_{N,D,I}$ defines an experiment in which a query set belonging to the class I is performed against a data cube of class D having N dimensions.

We have built four data cubes: $A_{2,X}$, $A_{2,Z}$, $A_{10,X}$, and $A_{10,Z}$. $A_{2,X}$ is a 2000 × 2000 CVA-aware bi-dimensional data cube, with $L_1 = 25$, $L_2 = 70$, containing about 35000 non zero data cells. $A_{2,Z}$ is a 2000 × 2000 Zipf-based bi-dimensional data cube, with $z_{min} = 0.5$, $z_{max} = 1.5$, containing about 42000 non zero data cells. $A_{10,X}$ is a CVA-aware 10-dimensional data cube, for which $|d_i|=10$ for each i belonging to the set $\{0,1,...,9\}$, with $L_1 = 15$, $L_2 = 80$, containing about 10^6 non zero data cells. $A_{10,Z}$ is a

Zipf-based 10-dimensional data cube, for which $|d_i|=10$ for each i belonging to the set $\{0,1,\ldots,9\}$, with $z_{min} = 0.5$, $z_{max} = 1.5$, containing about 5.3×10^6 non zero data cells. Then, we have built the query sets $QS_{2,R}$, $QS_{2,S}$, $QS_{10,R}$, and $QS_{10,S}$, according to the previous guidelines. Finally, we have defined the test set $TS = \{T_{2,X,R}, T_{2,X,S}, T_{2,Z,R}, T_{2,Z,S}, T_{10,X,R}, T_{10,X,S}, T_{10,Z,R}, T_{10,Z,S}\}$.

We have compared our technique with other well-known techniques in the context of data compression: *MaxDiff Histograms* [28], *Modified MaxDiff Histograms* [29], *Random Sampling* [14], and *Haar Wavelets* [33,34]. We considered the accuracy of the various techniques by looking at the size of the compact representation obtained for the input data cube, and the percentage average relative error of the approximate answers (i.e., the distance between exact answers and approximate answers). So, for each test belonging to the set *TS* we measured the average value of the *Relative Error* $\varepsilon_{rel} = |E(Q) - A(Q)| / \max\{1, E(Q)\}$, where $E(Q)$ is the exact answer to the query Q and $A(Q)$ is the approximate one, w.r.t. the *Space Gain G* (i.e., the memory amount gained thanks to the compression process). Note that G is indirectly proportional to the available storage space B, that is when G increases, B decreases and, consequently, the accuracy of the approximate answers decreases too.

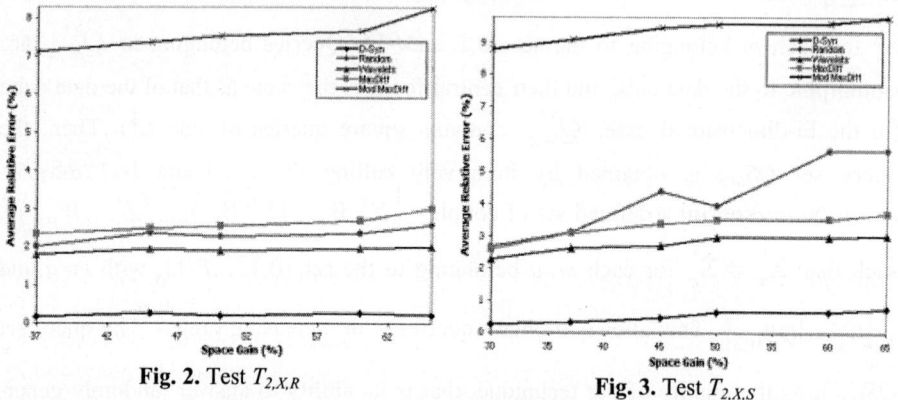

Fig. 2. Test $T_{2,X,R}$ **Fig. 3.** Test $T_{2,X,S}$

As shown in the figures from 2 to 9, Δ-Syn performs better than the other techniques, both for bi-dimensional data cubes and for multi-dimensional data cubes. This further confirms the effectiveness of our technique, as it is lowly dependent on the dimension number of the input data cube and it maintains good performances even when the dimension number is increased.

6 Conclusions and Future Work

In this paper we have presented Δ-Syn, analytical synopses for approximate aggregate query answering in OLAP environments. Δ-Syn are based on the well-known LSA method and provide an effective compression of data cubes for obtaining fast and approximate answers to range-sum queries. The main contributions of our proposal are: (*i*) low spatio-temporal complexity for building and querying Δ-Syn; (*ii*) good quality of the approximate answers; (*iii*) independence from any "a priori" assumption on the nature of the data distribution, which other similar techniques make (such as CVA).

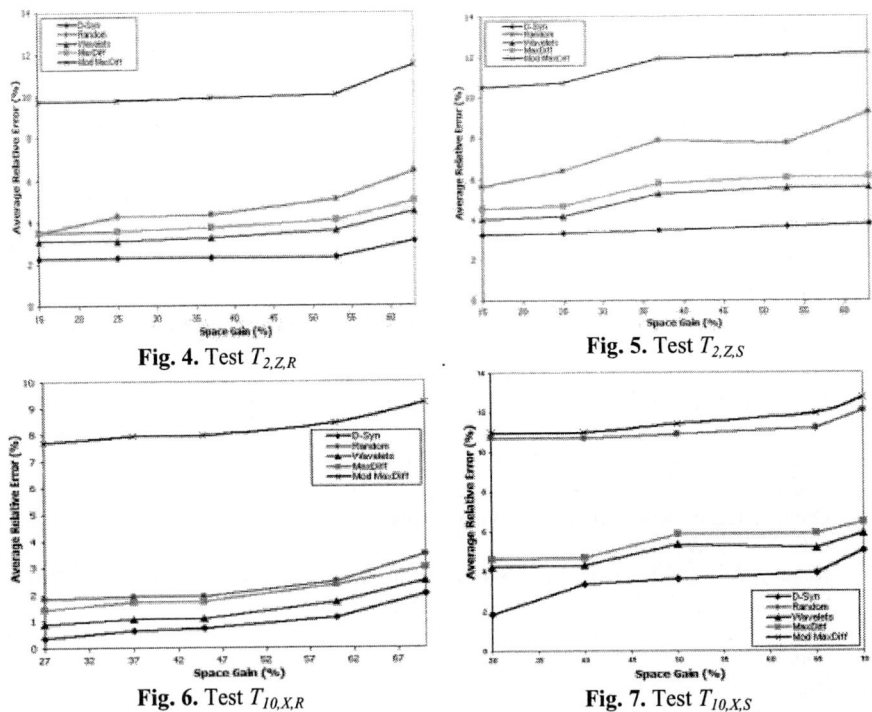

Fig. 4. Test $T_{2,Z,R}$

Fig. 5. Test $T_{2,Z,S}$

Fig. 6. Test $T_{10,X,R}$

Fig. 7. Test $T_{10,X,S}$

Experimental results clearly confirm the effectiveness of Δ-Syn on various classes of data cubes, outperforming other well-known similar techniques. Future work is focused on trying to will have two objectives. First, we want to make the Δ-Syn building task "adaptive", so that an intelligent agent near the client host would be able to interact with the remote approximate querying engine server in order to drive the Δ-Syn building task by taking into account only the portion of data which the user is interested in. On the other hand, we want to define and test several criteria for delineating strategies to select the optimal partition for a given data row in order to apply our technique to each bucket of the row partition instead of the entire row.

References

1. Bruno, N., Chaudhuri, S., and Gravano, L.: STHoles: A Multidimensional Workload-Aware Histogram. Microsoft Technical Report MSR-TR-2001-36 (2001)
2. Gibbons, P.B., and Matias, Y.: New Sampling-Based Summary Statistics for Improving Approximate Query Answers. In: Proc. of the 1998 ACM SIGMOD. Seattle, WA, USA (1998) 331-342
3. Gibbons, P.B., Matias, Y., and Poosala, V.: Fast Incremental Maintenance of Approximate Histograms. In: Proc. of the 23rd VLDB. Athens, Greece (1997) 466-475

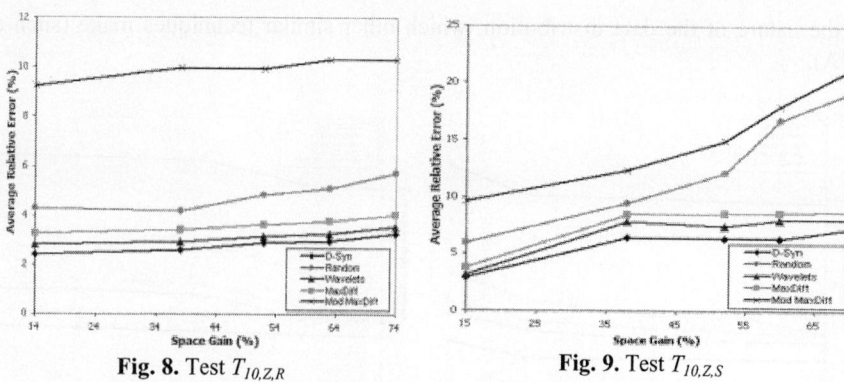

Fig. 8. Test $T_{10,Z,R}$ **Fig. 9.** Test $T_{10,Z,S}$

4. Hellerstein, J.M., Haas, P.J., and Wang, H.J.: Online Aggregation. In: Proc. of the 1997 ACM SIGMOD. Tucson, AZ, USA (1997) 171-182
5. Ho, C.-T., Agrawal, R., Megiddo, N., and Srikant, R.: Range Queries in OLAP Data Cubes. In: Proc. of the 1997 ACM SIGMOD. Tucson, AZ, USA (1997) 73-88
6. Ioannidis, Y.E., and Poosala, V.: Histogram-based Approximation of Set-Valued Query Answers. In: Proc. of the 25th VLDB. Edinburgh, Scotland (1999) 174-185
7. Jagadish, H.V., Koudas, N., Muthukrishnan, S., Poosala, V., Sevcik, K., and Suel, T.: Optimal Histograms with Quality Guarantees. In: Proc. of the 24th VLDB. New York City, NY, USA (1998) 275-286
8. Kenney, J.F., and Keeping, E.S.: Skewness. In: Mathematics of Statistics, Pt. 1, 3rd Edition, Van Nostrand. Princeton, NJ, USA (1962) 100-101
9. Matias, Y., Vitter, J.S., and Wang, M.: Wavelet-Based Histograms for Selectivity Estimation. In: Proc. of the 1998 ACM SIGMOD. Seattle, WA, USA (1998) 448-459
10. Papoulis, A.: Probability, Random Variables, and Stochastic Processes, 2nd Edition. McGraw-Hill, New York City, NY, USA (1984)
11. Poosala, V., Ioannidis, Y.E., Haas, P.J., and Shekita, E.: Improved Histograms for Selectivity Estimation of Range Predicates. In: Proc. of the 1996 ACM SIGMOD. Montreal, Canada (1996) 294-305
12. Poosala, V., and Ioannidis, Y.E.: Selectivity Estimation without the Attribute Value Independence Assumption. In: Proc. of the 23rd VLDB. Athens, Greece (1997) 486-495
13. Poosala, V., and Ganti, V.: Fast Approximate Answers to Aggregate Queries on a Data Cube. In: Proc. of the 11th SSDBM. Cleveland, OH, USA (1999) 24-33
14. Powell, M.J.D.: Approximation Theory and Methods. Cambridge University Press. Cambridge, England (1982)
15. Stuart, A., and Ord, J.K.: Kendall's Advanced Theory of Statistics, Vol. 1: Distribution Theory, 6th Edition. Oxford University Press. New York City, NY, USA (1998)
16. Vitter, J.S., Wang, M., and Iyer, B.: Data Cube Approximation and Histograms via Wavelets. In: Proc. of the 7th ACM CIKM. Bethesda, ML, USA (1998) 96-104
17. Vitter, J.S., and Wang, M.: Approximate Computation of Multidimensional Aggregates of Sparse Data Using Wavelets. In: Proc. of the 1999 ACM SIGMOD. Philadelphia, PA, USA (1999) 194-204

Morphological and Syntactic Processing for Text Retrieval[*]

Jesús Vilares[1], Miguel A. Alonso[1], and Manuel Vilares[2]

[1] Departamento de Computación, Universidade da Coruña
Campus de Elviña s/n, 15071 La Coruña, Spain
{jvilares,alonso}@udc.es

[2] Escuela Superior de Ingeniería Informática, Universidade de Vigo
Campus de As Lagoas, 32004 Orense, Spain
vilaress@uvigo.es

Abstract. This article describes the application of lemmatization and shallow parsing as a linguistically-based alternative to stemming in Text Retrieval, with the aim of managing linguistic variation at both word level and phrase level. Several alternatives for selecting the index terms among the syntactic dependencies detected by the parser are evaluated. Though this article focuses on Spanish, this approach is extensible to other languages by simply adapting the grammar used by the parser.

1 Introduction

Natural Language Processing (NLP) has frequently attracted the attention of the Information Retrieval (IR) community. This is because the task of deciding about the relevance of a given document with respect to a query basically consists of deciding whether the text of the document satisfies the information need expressed by the text of the query. To perform this task, IR systems have to deal with *linguistic variation*, that is, the different ways in which the same concept can be expressed. This way, textual information retrieval could be considered as a Natural Language Processing problem.

The research in this field has been mainly focused on English and its employment in other languages has not been studied enough, even when the possibilities of success in Spanish and other similar romance languages seem to be greater than those for English, since their syntax and morphology are more complex.

1.1 Dealing with Linguistic Variation

The lowest level of linguistic variation in natural language is *inflection*, those predictable changes a word undergoes as a result of gender, number, person,

---

[*] Supported in part by Ministerio de Ciencia y Tecnología (HF2002-81), FPU grants of Secretaría de Estado de Educación y Universidades (AP2001-2545), Xunta de Galicia (PGIDIT02PXIB30501PR, PGIDIT02SIN01E and PGIDIT03SIN30501PR) and Universidade da Coruña.

mood, time, tense, etc. This first level of variation is generally solved by means of *stemmers*, which reduce the word to its supposed grammatical root, or *stem*, through suffix stripping based on a list of frequent suffixes. In English, the results obtained are satisfactory enough since its inflectional morphology being very simple. Nevertheless, in the case of Spanish, its inflectional morphology is much more complex, with modifications at multiple levels and with many irregularities. The case of verbs also includes the possibility of having attached one, two or three clitic pronouns at the end, which confuses the stemmer. In this context, stemming does not seem to be an accurate solution due to many of these phenomena cannot be managed by such a simple tool. Instead, lemmatization seems to be a better solution.

For lemmatizing the documents, we employ MrTagoo [4], a high-performance part-of-speech tagger with lemmatization capability whose input is provided by a linguistically-motivated preprocessor module [2]. MrTagoo is based on a second order Hidden Markov Model whose core structure for storage and search has been implemented by means of finite-state automata [6]. Other advanced capabilities of our tagger are the management of unknown words, the possibility of integrating external dictionaries, and the possibility of managing ambiguous segmentations [5]. All these capabilities have been implemented using finite-state techniques in order to maintain linear complexity.

Once the viability of NLP techniques for managing morphological variation at word level has been established, the next step consists of applying phrase-level analysis techniques to reduce the *syntactic variation* present in both documents and queries. In order to do it, it is necessary to identify the syntactic structure of the text by means of parsing techniques. Nevertheless, full parsing of the text is non-viable because of its high computational cost, which makes non-practical its application on a large scale. Moreover, the lack of robustness of such approaches reduces their coverage to a grant extent, particularly in the case of Spanish, due to the lack of freely available resources such as grammars, treebanks, etc. In this context, the employment of *shallow parsing* techniques allows, on the one hand, to reduce the computational complexity and, on the other hand, to increase the robustness.

2 The Shallow Parser

We propose a shallow parser based on a cascade of finite-state transducers consisting of five layers, whose input is the output of the tagger-lemmatizer. Next, we will describe briefly the function of each of these layers.

Layer 0: Preprocessing. Its function is the management of certain linguistic constructions in order to minimize the noise generated during the subsequent parsing. Such constructions include *numerals in non-numerical format*, *quantity expressions (NumP)*, and *expressions with a verbal function*.

Layer 1: Adverbial phrases and first level verbal groups. This layer identifies, on the one hand, the *adverbial phrases (AdvP)* of the text, either those with an adverbial head —e.g., *rápidamente* (quickly)—, or those expressions which are not properly adverbial but having an equivalent function —e.g., *de forma rápida* (in a quick way). On the other hand, non-periphrastic verbal groups, which we call *first level verbal groups*, are processed, both their simple and compound forms, and both their active and passive forms.

Layer 2: Adjectival phrases and second level verbal groups. Adjectival phrases (*AdjP*) —e.g., *muy alto* (very high)— are managed here, together with periphrastic verbal groups —e.g., *tengo que ir* (I have to go)—, which we call *second level verbal groups*. Verbal periphrases are unions of two or more verbal forms working as a unit, giving attributing shades of meaning such as obligation, degree of development of the action, etc., to the semantics of the main verb.

Layer 3: Noun phrases. We have considered some complex phenomena in noun phrases (*NP*), such as the existence of *partitive complements* (*PC*) — e.g., *ninguno de* (none of)—, in order to cover complex nominal structures —e.g., *cualquiera de aquellos coches nuevos* (any of those new cars).

Layer 4: Prepositional phrases. Formed by a noun phrase (*NP*) preceded by a preposition (*P*), we have considered three different types according to this preposition: those preceded by the preposition *por* (by) or *PPby*, those preceded by *de* (of) or *PPof*, and the rest of prepositional phrases or *PP*.

These layers and the rules of the grammar employed by the parser are explained in detail in [17]. Each of the rules involved in the different stages of the parsing process has been implemented through a finite-state transducer. Unlike other tasks, such as Information Extraction or the extraction of lexical patterns [7], our goal is not to get as output a bracketed version of the input text, with the brackets delimiting its phrases, but to obtain, as pairs, a list of the syntactic dependencies of the text. The formation of such pairs only involves the heads of the phrases, so we only need to retain the lemma of the head, together with its corresponding morphosyntactic features. As a result, our parser behaves as a finite-state filter rather than as a finite-state marker.

2.1 Identification of Syntactic Roles and Syntactic Dependencies

Taking as our working hypothesis that for each verbal head there must exist an associated sentence, we will consider as an end of sentence the appearance of any of these elements: *punctuation marks, relatives, conjunctions*, and *verbal groups in personal form* when there is no other sentence boundary between such a verbal group and the previous one.

This limitation in the scope of the dependency extractor is not a severe problem in the context it has been designed for, index term extraction for IR, because we are not looking for exhaustivity but for reliability in the dependencies obtained, trying to minimize the noise introduced in the system. What we seek is to identify sentences with an underlying structure of the type:

- Active subject + active predicative verbal group + direct object.
- Active subject + copulative verbal group + attribute.
- Passive subject + passive predicative verbal group + agent.

According to the criteria established in Sect. 2.1, we show the syntactic roles of the phrases identified in our running example: an active subject (*SUBJact*), an active predicative verbal group (*Vact*), its prepositional verb complement (*PVC*), its direct object (*DO*), and the prepositional noun complement of the latter (*PNC*):

```
[ niño (child)        NCMP   NP ]   – 〈 SUBJact 〉
[ aprender (to learn) V3PRI  VG2 ]  – 〈  Vact   〉
[ hoy (today)         WI     AdvP ] – 〈         〉
[ colegio (school)    NCMS   PP ]   – 〈  PVC    〉
[ lección (lesson)    NCFS   NP ]   – 〈  DO     〉
[ historia (history)  NCFS   PPof ] – 〈  PNC    〉
```

Once the syntactic roles of each phrase have been identified, their associated dependencies are extracted according to Sect. 2.1:

```
ADJ      (niño      NCMP,  alegre   AQFP)
PNC      (lección   NCFS,  historia NCFS)
SUBJact  (aprender  V3PRI, niño     NCMP)
DO       (aprender  V3PRI, lección  NCFS)
PVC      (aprender  V3PRI, colegio  NCMS)
```

3 Evaluation

Our conflation approaches have been integrated in the well-known vector-based engine SMART [3], using an `atn-ntc` weighting scheme[2]. The corpus employed for their evaluation is the Spanish monolingual corpus corresponding to CLEF 2003 edition [15]. This corpus is formed by 454,045 news reports (1.06 GB) provided by EFE, a Spanish news agency, corresponding to the years 1994 and 1995. The set of topics consists of 60 queries, from 141 to 200, formed by three fields: a brief *title* statement, a one-sentence *description*, and a more complex *narrative* specifying the relevance assessment criteria. All these three fields have been employed to build the running queries, but giving double relevance to the *title* statement, because it summarizes the basic semantics of the query.

We have compared the behavior of four different conflation approaches:

Stemming (*stm*). This classical approach will be taken as baseline. The tool employed was Snowball Spanish stemmer [1], based on Porter's algorithm, and one of the most popular stemmers employed in research. The stopword list used was that one provided by SMART for Spanish.

Lemmatization (*lem*). The lemmas of the content words of the text —nouns, adjectives and verbs, the grammatical categories which concentrate the semantics of a text— are used as index terms. The corresponding stopword list was obtained by lemmatizing the content words of the SMART stopword list.

---

[2] Our aim is to investigate whether NLP techniques can be used to improve the performance of (non NLP-based) IR systems. Thus, we have chosen as working environment a classic configuration which can be considered, to a certain extent, standard.

Table 1. Experimental results on the CLEF 2003 collection

	Docs.	Rlv.	Precision N.I.	Precision Doc.	Precision R	5	10	15	20	30	100	200	500	1000
stm	57k	2216	.4577	.5145	.4372	.5754	.5070	.4585	.4175	.3567	.2247	.1422	.0702	.0389
lem	57k	2221	.4681	.5431	.4471	.5965	.5000	.4515	.4281	.3813	.2314	.1455	.0718	.0390
Δlem	57k	5	.0104	.0286	.0099	.0211	-.0070	-.0070	.0106	.0246	.0067	.0033	.0016	.0001
tsd1	57k	2218	.4014	.4647	.3961	.4842	.4333	.3860	.3632	.3205	.2053	.1368	.0692	.0389
tsd10	57k	2242	.4710	.5475	.4454	.6070	.5053	.4503	.4237	.3789	.2337	.1461	.0720	.0393
Δtsd10	57k	26	.0133	.0330	.0082	.0316	-.0017	-.0082	.0062	.0222	.0090	.0039	.0018	.0004
dsd1	57k	2256	.4741	.5538	.4425	.5825	.5070	.4561	.4211	.3731	.2328	.1486	.0733	.0396
dsd3	57k	2255	.4747	.5562	.4454	.5930	.5070	.4550	.4246	.3825	.2353	.1481	.0729	.0396
Δdsd3	57k	39	.0170	.0417	.0082	.0176	.0000	-.0035	.0071	.0258	.0106	.0059	.0027	.0007
					Experiments with pseudo-relevance feedback									
stm	57k	2253	.5048	.5908	.4749	.5754	.5281	.4772	.4456	.4000	.2426	.1519	.0733	.0395
lem	57k	2260	.5211	.6086	.4796	.6000	.5421	.4982	.4640	.4105	.2461	.1527	.0742	.0396
Δlem	57k	7	.0163	.0178	.0047	.0246	.0140	.0210	.0184	.0105	.0035	.0008	.0009	.0001
tsd10	57k	2266	.5125	.6011	.4681	.6070	.5439	.4901	.4500	.4012	.2437	.1542	.0742	.0398
Δtsd10	57k	13	.0077	.0103	-.0068	.0316	.0158	.0129	.0044	.0012	.0011	.0023	.0009	.0003
dsd3	57k	2258	.5151	.6047	.4752	.5965	.5421	.4901	.4535	.4058	.2418	.1530	.0741	.0396
Δdsd3	57k	5	.0103	.0139	.0003	.0211	.0140	.0129	.0079	.0058	.0008	.0011	.0008	.0001

Syntactic dependency pairs obtained from the topic (*tsd*). Based on the combined indexing of lemmatized simple terms —as in the case of *lem*— and complex terms derived from the syntactic dependencies existent in the documents. The dependencies containing stopwords are discarded. The final query submitted to the system is formed by the index terms obtained from the topic through the same process of lemmatization and shallow parsing.

Syntactic dependency pairs obtained from top documents (*dsd*). The indexing process is the same of *tsd*, but the querying process is performed in two stages:

1. The lemmatized query is submitted to the system.
2. The n top documents retrieved by this initial query are employed to select the most informative dependencies, which are used to expand the lemmatized query, but with no re-weighting. These dependencies are selected automatically using Rocchio's approach [16] to feedback. They are selected from the 10 best terms (both lemmas and dependencies) of the top 5 documents. In [9], relevance feedback is also used to select relevant noun phrases. However, our approach is more complete in the sense that we deal with all kind of syntactic dependencies and that our evaluation is performed on a large set of standard queries, which have not been specifically created for the experiments.

The expanded query is then submitted to the system in order to obtain the final set of documents retrieved.

3.1 Initial Experiments

Table 1 shows the results of the experiments performed. Each column contains one of the parameters employed to measure the performance: number of documents retrieved, number of relevant documents retrieved (2368 expected), average precision (non-interpolated) for all relevant documents (averaged over queries), average document precision for all relevant documents (averaged over relevant documents), R-precision, and precision at N documents retrieved.

The first row, *stm*, contains the results for the baseline, stemming. The second row, *lem*, shows the results of lemmatization, whereas the next row, *Δlem*, shows its improvement with respect to *stm*. As it can be seen, the improvement is clear. The next two rows, *tsd1* and *tsd10*, contain the results obtained using the syntactic dependency pairs obtained from the topic when the weight of simple terms is multiplied by 1 and 10 with respect to complex terms. As indicated in [13], when simple and complex terms are used together as index terms, the assumption of term independence is violated because words forming a dependency-pair also occur in the documents from which the dependency has been extracted. To address this problem, we must increase the weight of simple terms relative to the weight of complex terms. Training experiments were performed on the smaller CLEF 2001/2002 collection, consisting of 215,738 documents and 100 queries. We found that balance factors between *7 to 1* and *10 to 1* obtained the best results. Among them, the balance factor *10 to 1* obtained better precision at the top ranked documents. As we can observe, with the CLEF 2003 collection, *tsd10* obtains the best results for precision at N documents, and non-interpolated and document precision, being better than those obtained through stemming (*stm*) and lemmatization (*lem*). Its improvement with respect to *stm* is shown in *Δtsd10*.

The next two rows of table 1 correspond to syntactic dependency pairs obtained from top documents (*dsd*). As in the case of *tsd*, we have introduced a balance factor between the weight of simple and complex terms, The interferences introduced through this new approach due to the violation of term independence are much lesser than when using the dependencies from the topics, as we can immediately observe when we compare *tsd1* and *dsd1*. These new results are similar, and even better in some cases, to those reached with *tsd10*; the only exception is the precision at 5 top documents. The best behavior of *dsd* was obtained with a balance factor of *3 to 1*, whose corresponding results are shown in the row *dsd3*, together with its improvement with respect to *stm*, shown in *Δdsd3*.

From these experiments, we can conclude that the pairs chosen automatically by the system are much more accurate than those obtained directly from the topic, as it seems to be demonstrated when we compare *tsd1* and *dsd1*. Comparing the pairs obtained from topics and those obtained automatically from top documents, we have found that only a small set of pairs —28 to be precise, 5.92%— of the topic pairs were chosen by the system from top documents. This points at that the rest of them do not represent accurately the semantics of the topic. Nevertheless, these common terms represent more than a quarter —28.87%— of the terms selected automatically by the system, which indicates us that the contribution of the syntactic information of the topic continues to be important, but that it has to be adequately filtered and selected.

With respect to lemmatization, the approaches based on the employment of syntactic dependencies show a behavior not so good as expected, obtaining only slight improvements in recall, non-interpolated precision, and document precision.

3.2 Experiments Using Pseudo-relevance Feedback

A second group of experiments has been performed in order to compare the behavior of our NLP-based conflation approaches with respect to stemming during pseudo-relevance feedback (blind-query expansion). For these tests we have adopted Rocchio's approach [16], expanding the original topic with the best 10 terms of the 5 top ranked documents. As a result of a tuning process, the parameter α, which stands for the contribution of the original query vector, has been set at 1.40, whereas β, which stands for the contribution of the vectors of the relevant documents, has been set at 0.10. We have not considered any contribution from non-relevant documents, and so γ has been set to 0.

The results obtained for these new experiments are shown in the bottom part of Table 1. As we can see, NLP-based conflation techniques clearly outperform stemming (stm). The best behavior corresponds to lemmatization (lem) whereas the employment of syntactic dependencies in tsd and dsd, which outperform stemming, obtain quite similar results to those of lemmatization.

4 Conclusions

Throughout this article we have studied the employment of Natural Language Processing techniques in Text Retrieval as an alternative to stemming for managing linguistic variation. Their implementation by means of finite-state techniques result in a minimal overhead with respect to classical techniques, a key issue for their employment in practical environments.

Three different approaches have been tested. The first one employs lemmatization to solve linguistic variation derived from inflection. The other two approaches employ shallow parsing to manage syntactic variation by using syntactic dependencies as complex index terms.

The results obtained show that lemmatization seems to be, at this moment, the best option for Spanish conflation, since the improvement obtained using syntactic information is not so good as expected. Nevertheless, our experiments seem to indicate that the employment of syntactic information must not to be discarded, but the way it is employed should be reconsidered. Our experiences point at its employment for refining the results obtained through lemmatization, due to the noise introduced by syntactic dependencies when they are not accurately selected. As an alternative, syntactic dependencies could be used as a base to construct conceptual graphs representing the semantic of sentences [11, 12, 14, 10], paying the price of a higher computational cost.

References

1. http://snowball.tartarus.org (site visited October 2003).
2. F.M. Barcala, J. Vilares, M. A. Alonso, J. Graña, and M. Vilares. Tokenization and proper noun recognition for information retrieval. In *DEXA Workshop 2002*, pages 246–250. IEEE Computer Society Press, 2002.
3. C. Buckley. Implementation of the SMART information retrieval system. Technical report, Department of Computer Science, Cornell University, 1985.
4. J. Graña. *Técnicas de Análisis Sintáctico Robusto para la Etiquetación del Lenguaje Natural*. PhD thesis, University of La Coruña, La Coruña, Spain, 2000.
5. J. Graña, M.A. Alonso, and M. Vilares. A common solution for tokenization and part-of-speech tagging: One-pass Viterbi algorithm vs. iterative approaches. *Lecture Notes in Computer Science (LNCS)*, 2448:3–10, 2002.
6. J. Graña, F.M. Barcala, and M.A. Alonso. Compilation methods of minimal acyclic automata for large dictionaries. *LNCS*, 2494:135–148, 2002.
7. G. Grefenstette, A. Schiller, and S. Aït-Mokhtar. Recognizing lexical patterns in text. In F. Van Eynde and D. Gibbon, editors, *Lexicon Development for Speech and Language Processing*, pages 141–168. Kluwer Academic, Dordrecht, 2000.
8. C. Jacquemin and E. Tzoukermann. NLP for term variant extraction: synergy between morphology, lexicon and syntax. In T. Strzalkowski, editor, *Natural Language Information Retrieval*, pages 25–74. Kluwer Academic, Dordrecht, 1999.
9. M.S. Khan and S. Khor. Enhanced web document retrieval using automatic query expansion. *JASIST*, 55(1):29–40, 2004.
10. C.S.-G. Khoo. The use of relation matching in Information Retrieval. *LIBRES: Library and Information Science Research*, 7(2), 1997.
11. M. Montes-y-Gómez, A. Gelbukh, A. López-López and R. Baeza-Yates. Flexible Comparison of Conceptual Structures. *LNCS*, 2113:102–111, 2001.
12. M. Montes-y-Gómez, A. López-López and A. Gelbukh. Information Retrieval with conceptual graph matching. *LNCS*, 1873:312–321, 2000.
13. M. Narita and Y. Ogawa. The use of phrases from query texts in information retrieval. In *Proc. of ACM SIGIR 2000*, pages 318–320, Athens, Greece, 2000.
14. S. Nicolas, B. Moulin and G. W. Mineau. Sesei: A CG-based filter for Internet search engines. *Lecture Notes in Artificial Intelligence (LNAI)*, 2746:362–377, 2003.
15. C. Peters and F. Borri, editors. *Results of the CLEF 2003 Cross-Language System Evaluation Campaign, Working Notes for the CLEF 2003 Workshop*, Trondheim, Norway, August 2003.
16. J.J. Rocchio. Relevance Feedback in Information Retrieval. In G. Salton, editor, *The SMART Retrieval System–Experiments in Automatic Document Processing*. Prentice Hall, Englewood Cliffs, NJ, 1971.
17. J. Vilares, and M.A. Alonso. A Grammatical Approach to the Extraction of Index Terms. *Proceedings of International Conference on Recent Advances in Natural Language Processing (RANLP 2003)*, pages 500-504, Borovets, Bulgaria, 2003.
18. J. Vilares, F.M. Barcala, and M.A. Alonso. Using syntactic dependency-pairs conflation to improve retrieval performance in Spanish. *LNCS*, 2276:381–390, 2002.

Efficient Top-k Query Processing in P2P Network

Yingjie He[1], Yanfeng Shu[2], Shan Wang[1], and Xiaoyong Du[1]

[1] Information School, Renmin University of China, Beijing, 100872, China
{heyj,swang,duyong}@ruc.edu.cn
[2] Dept. of Computer Science, National University of Singapore, 117543, Singapore

Abstract. In this paper, we examine how to efficiently process top-k queries in pure P2P network. First, we propose a distributed algorithm to evaluate a top-k query in a hierarchical way. Each peer does its local top-k query, and top k results from different peers are merged hierarchically from bottom to the top (the root peer is the query initiator). Ranking and merging of results are distributed across the peers to exploit the computing resources in the network. Second, to improve performance, we maintain histograms at each peer according to the top k results returned by the peers. The histograms are used to estimate the possible upper bound scores of peers so that a query only needs to be forwarded to the most promising neighbouring peers. Our experimental study shows that the top-k query algorithm improves the query effectiveness, while the use of histograms enhances the query efficiency.

1 Introduction

In a Peer-to-Peer (P2P) system, a large number of nodes (e.g., PCs connected to the Internet) can potentially be pooled together to share their resources, information and services. However, existing P2P systems [5, 10, 7] only support simple title-based search, and users cannot search the data based on their content.

In this paper, we examine how top-k queries can be efficiently processed in pure P2P network. In a top-k query, the k results that best match the query, based on some ranking criterion, are returned. This class of queries is important as users are typically interested only in a small number of relevant results. Search engines like Google essentially operates with this concept - returning answers ordered based on some ranking criterion to users in batches/pages. Our domain is unstructured documents. Given a query which may be a phrase, a statement or even a paragraph, we look for the top k documents in the network that are semantically best match the query. Processing top-k query in P2P network is very challenging as there is no central controller and nodes can dynamically join and leave the network.

We first propose a basic distributed top-k query algorithm in a hierarchical way with the query initiator as the root of the hierarchy. Each peer evaluates the query locally and the top k results are transmitted to its parent node. The parent node merges these results using the CORI method [3] to get the top k results among its child nodes. As such, ranking and merging of results are distributed across the peers to exploit the computation power of the network. Moreover, top k results are merged from bottom to up, irrelevant results will be pruned in the early step, and bandwidth will be saved at the same time. Next, to avoid broadcasting the query to all neighbouring nodes, we use histogram to estimate the possible upper bound score of a peer, and selects the most possible peers to forward the query. Histogram is constructed for each peer according to its returned top k query results, so it doesn't need the peer to present its histogram in advance. Furthermore, The histogram is adaptive because it can be updated according to the query results. The maintaining cost of histogram is also very small. Our experiment results show that histogram greatly improves the query efficiency while keeping the query effectiveness.

Our work is related to distributed information retrieval systems like GLOSS [6] and CORI [3]. However, the context of these work is static. Moreover, they cannot guarantee the overall top k results. In [12], histogram-based distributed top-k query processing schemes are presented. However, the FQ histogram is only maintained by a centralized coordinator and is single level and stores the best match tuples for frequent queries only. In P2P context, PlanetP [4] and PeerSearch [11] have also addressed information retrieval. But these schemes are either not scalable or require global information to be maintained. Moreover, these systems do not consider the top-k queries.

The rest of paper is organized as follows. In section 2, we introduce hierarchical top-k query in P2P network. In section 3, we discuss the peer selection based on the histogram. In section 4, we conduct simulating experiments to evaluate the performance of the algorithm. At last, we give conclusion in section 5.

2 Hierarchical Top-k Query Processing

In this section, we first present our hierarchical top-k query processing algorithm, and then discuss how results are merged using the CORI method.

2.1 Top-k Query Processing in Pure P2P Network

In pure P2P networks, query is typically processed as follows. The query is flooded from the initiator to its neighbourhood until the TTL (Time-to-live) value of the query decreases to 0. The query processing flow can be represented as a tree. The initiator of the query is the root of the tree, and the nodes that receive the query with TTL value of 0 or have no neighbourhood are leaves of the tree. Figure 1 illustrates a query processing tree. Node a is the initiator of the query, acting as the root of the tree. The query is broadcast to child nodes b and c, which are the neighbour nodes of node a. Nodes j, k, l are the leaves of the tree. To eliminate the loop in the tree, every query message has a unique identification. When the node

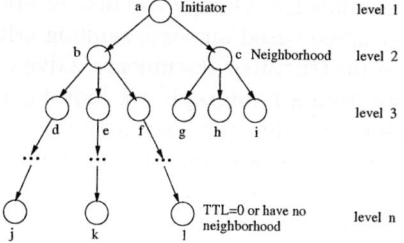

Fig. 1: Query processing tree

detects that the query id has already existed, it drops the query message and stops propagating it.

As noted, our context is to search for unstructured documents. As such, a top-k query essentially retrieves the k documents in the entire collection (among the nodes in the processing tree) that are most similar to the query.

In our work, we use the vector space model (VSM) [1]. In VSM, documents and queries are represented as vectors of term weights. The cosine of the angle between vectors is used to calculate the similarity between the document and the query. We use the similarity between the document and the query as the document score, and rank the documents according to their scores. The top k documents that have k highest scores are returned as results. The cosine similarity function is defined as:

$$Sim(d_j, q) = \frac{\vec{d_j} \cdot \vec{q}}{|\vec{d_j}| \times |\vec{q}|} = \sum_{i=1}^{n} w_{i,j} \times w_{i,q} \qquad (1)$$

Where $\vec{d_j}$ and $\vec{q}$ are vector representations of document d_j and query q, $\vec{d_j} = (w_{1,j}, w_{2,j}, \ldots, w_{n,j})$, $\vec{q} = (w_{1,q}, w_{2,q}, \ldots, w_{n,q})$. $w_{i,j}$ and $w_{i,q}$ are weights of term t_i in document d_j and query q. $|\vec{d_j}|$ and $|\vec{q}|$ are the norms of the document and query vectors. Assume $\vec{d_j}$ and $\vec{q}$ are all normalized, cosine of the angle between $\vec{d_j}$ and $\vec{q}$ is computed by the dot product of the two vectors.

Term weight in document is computed by TFxIDF rule, which is given by:

$$w_{i,j} = \frac{f_{i,j} \times \log N/n_i}{\sqrt{\sum_{t_i \in d_j} [f_{i,j} \times \log N/n_i]^2}} \qquad (2)$$

Where $w_{i,j}$ is the weight of term t_i in document d_j. $f_{i,j}$ is the term frequency (TF) of term t_i occurs in document d_j. N is the total number of documents in the collection, and n_i is the number of documents that contain term t_i. $logN/n_i$ represents the inverse document frequency (IDF) of term t_i. The term weight in document is normalized.

Term weight in query is either 1 if the term appears in the query or 0 if it doesn't. We also normalize the term weight in query.

In pure P2P network, there is no centralized controller, so we evaluate a top-k query in a decentralized way. Because query processing flow in pure P2P network can be represented as a tree, we can evaluate top-k query in hierarchical way based on the query processing tree. Essentially, a top-k query Q is broadcasted from node P to its neighbouring nodes $P_1, P_2, \ldots, P_n$ to do top-k query. Node P needs to merge the top k results from the child nodes $P_1, P_2, \ldots, P_n$ and its own local top k results to generate overall top k results. Leaf nodes ($TTL = 0$ or has no neighbourhood) only does local top-k query, and returns the top k results to its parent node. Top k results are merged from bottom to up, until it reaches the root (i.e., query initiator) to get the ultimate top k results. For example, in figure 1, leaf node j does local top-k query, and returns its top k results to its parent node. Node b merges its local results and the results from the nodes d, e, f to generate overall top k results, and then returns them to its parent node

a. Node a merges its local results and the results from the node b, c to generate the ultimate top k results.

In general cases, each node can use different local top-k function to do local top-k query. In our model, we assume that all nodes in the network use the cosine similarity function as defined in equation 1 as local top-k function.

We shall refer this hierarchical top-k query processing algorithm based on broadcast search as algorithm 1.

2.2 Merging Results

In our algorithm, we employ the CORI method to merge the results from child nodes. Because each peer does top-k query only according to its local collection information, the document scores returned by different peers often may not be comparable. For example, the word "computer" is frequent in technical collections, while it is infrequent in medical collections. If we can get the global information such as IDF for the whole collections in P2P network, the problem of incomparable scores can be solved. But it is very difficult to get this kind of global information in pure P2P network. Instead we use another simple strategy, weighted score, to solve to problem. Weighted score combines document score and collection score to get the comparable score. It favors documents from collections with high scores, but also enables a good document from a poor collection to be ranked highly.

CORI network is used in distributed information retrieval to do collection selection. It uses inference network to estimate the goodness of collections with respect to the query, and ranks the collections according to their goodness. We use CORI to compute the collection score of a peer. Suppose the user query contains k terms $t_1, t_2, \ldots, t_k$. Let N be the number of peers, each peer is considered as a collection. The belief that collection C_i contains useful documents due to the j-th query term is computed by:

$$p(t_j|C_i) = d_b + (1 - d_b) \cdot T \cdot I \tag{3}$$

$$T = d_t + (1 - d_t) \cdot \frac{\log(df + 0.5)}{\log(max\_df + 1.0)} \tag{4}$$

$$I = \frac{\log \frac{(N+0.5)}{cf}}{\log(N + 1.0)} \tag{5}$$

Where df is the number of documents in collection C_i contains term t_j. max_df is the number of the documents containing the most frequent term in C_i. cf is the number of collections containing term t_j. d_b and d_t are constants between 0 and 1, default value is 0.4. This is variation of TFxIDF rule to rank the collections.

We calculate the belief that collection C_i contains useful documents with respect to query by using one of INQUERY operators [2]:

$$p(q|C_i) = \frac{p_1 + p_2 + \ldots + p_k}{k} \tag{6}$$

Where p_j represents $p(t_j|C_i)$, assume that there are k terms in query q.

We use $p(q|C_i)$ as the score of collection C_i, and combine collection score and document score to get weighted score. The combining method we also adopt the method used by INQUERY system [2]. The weighted score is computed as follow:

$$D' = \frac{D + 0.4 \cdot D \cdot R_i'}{1.4}, \quad R_i' = \frac{(R_i - R_{min})}{(R_{max} - R_{min})} \tag{7}$$

Where D is the document score, and D' is the weighted score. R_i is the score of collection C_i, R_{max} and R_{min} are the maximum and minimum scores of the collections.

After getting the weighted scores, we can rank the documents based on their weighted scores, and output the top k documents as overall top k results. As equations 3, 4, 5 show, to compute the collection score, we need some collection information of the peer, such as document frequencies of the query terms. Because we do top-k query in hierarchical way, the results are merged from bottom to up. Each node not only returns its top k results to its parent node, but also returns its collection information. During merging the results, collection information also needs to be merged, i.e. the node needs to merge its local collection information and collection information from its child nodes to generate the overall collection information, which represents the overall collection information of subtree rooted at the node. For example, in figure 1, the document frequencies of term "computer" in node d, e, f are 3, 2 and 1, and the local document frequency of term "computer" in node b is 4, then the document frequency of term "computer" of subtree rooted at node b is $3+2+1+4 = 10$. Thus, the collection information returned by the node is in fact the overall collection information of the subtree rooted at the node.

3 Peer Selection Based on Histogram

Algorithm 1 broadcasts the query to all the neighbours, which is very inefficient. In this section, we introduce peer selection based on histogram. We construct histogram for the peer according to its returned top k results, and use the histogram to estimate the possible score upper bound of the peer, which represents the score upper bound of all documents in the subtree rooted at the peer. Then we rank the peers according to their score upper bounds, and select the most possible peers to send the query, which greatly prunes the search space and improves the search efficiency.

3.1 Histogram Construction

Before we discuss how to construct the histogram for the peer, we first introduce a property of cosine similarity function that is used to measure the similarity between documents and queries.

Property 1. Assume that the vectors of document d_j and query q are all normalized, then the cosine similarity function $Sim(d_j, q) = \sum_{i=1}^{n} w_{i,j} \times w_{i,q}$ is monotonic. i.e., given two documents d_1 and d_2, $\vec{d_1}$ and $\vec{d_2}$ are their vector representation, $\vec{d_1} = (w_{1,1}, w_{2,1}, \ldots, w_{n,1})$, $\vec{d_2} = (w_{1,2}, w_{2,2}, \ldots, w_{n,2})$. $\vec{q}$ is the vector representation of query q, $\vec{q} = (w_{1,q}, w_{2,q}, \ldots, w_{n,q})$. For each $w_{i,q} \neq 0$, if $w_{i,1} \geq w_{i,2}$, then $Sim(d_1, q) \geq Sim(d_2, q)$.

Assume the top k results returned by the peer contain not only document score but also vector representation of document. Base on *property 1*, we can construct histogram for the peer by its returned top k results. As the query is always associated with a TTL value in pure P2P network, we construct histograms with different TTL values for the peer. Assume TTL is the TTL value of query q in peer A. $\{d_1, d_2, \ldots, d_k\}$ are top k results of query q returned by peer A. $\vec{d_j} = (w_{1,j}, w_{2,j}, \ldots, w_{n,j})$ is the vector representation of document d_j, $\vec{q} = (w_{1,q}, w_{2,q}, \ldots, w_{n,q})$ is the vector representation of query q. Suppose that the document vectors and query vector are all normalized. We construct the peer A's histogram with TTL as follows. For each query term $t_i(w_{i,q} \neq 0)$, we compute t_i's term weight upper bound in the top k results and store it into the histogram. The peer A's histogram with TTL can be defined as:

$$Histogram_{A,TTL} = \{(t_i, w_{i,A,TTL} = \max_{1 \leq j \leq k} w_{i,j}) | w_{i,q} \neq 0\} \quad (8)$$

Peer A's score upper bound with respect to query q can be computed as $UpperScore_{q,A,TTL} = \sum_{w_{i,q} \neq 0} w_{i,A,TTL} \times w_{i,q}$. According to *property 1*, it is guaranteed that $UpperScore_{q,A,TTL} \geq Sim(d_j, q), 1 \leq j \leq k$. If $\{d_1, d_2, \ldots, d_k\}$ are the top k documents that have k highest scores in the subtree $QueryTree(A, q, TTL)$, $UpperScore_{q,A,TTL}$ must be no less than all document scores in the subtree $QueryTree(A, q, TTL)$.

After constructing histogram, we use the histogram to estimate the peer A's score upper bound for the following query q'. Let $\vec{q'} = (w_{1,q'}, w_{2,q'}, \ldots, w_{n,q'})$ to be the vector representation of q', TTL' is the TTL value of query q' in peer A. The score upper bound of peer A with respect to q' is computed as follow:

$$UpperScore_{q',A,TTL'} = \sum_{\substack{t_i \in Histogram_{A,TTL} \land \\ TTL = \min\{TTL | TTL \geq TTL'\}}} w_{i,A,TTL} \times w_{i,q'}$$

$$+ \sum_{\substack{\neg \exists Histogram_{A,TTL} \\ (t_i \in Histogram_{A,TTL} \land TTL \geq TTL')}} 1 \times w_{i,q'} \quad (9)$$

As discussed in section 2.2, the document scores from different peers are often not directly comparable. To get the comparable score upper bound of the peer, we also need to consider the collection score of the peer. Like merging results, we combine the collection score of the peer and the score upper bound estimated by the histogram to get the weighted score (as defined in equation 7), and rank the peers based on their weighted score.

Like top-k query, the histogram is also hierarchical. Parent node constructs histograms for each of its child nodes, and uses the histogram to estimate the possible score upper bound of the peer. The histogram is constructed by the top k results returned by the peer, so it doesn't need the child nodes to present their histograms in advance.

3.2 Hierarchical Top-k Query Processing Based on Histogram

Based on histogram, we can do peer selection to improve the search efficiency. First, we use the histogram to estimate the possible score upper bound of the peer. Then, we rank the peers in descending order according to their score upper bounds, and select the best peer one by one to send the query, until the minimum score of found top k results is larger than the score upper bounds of the left peers. We shall refer to this enhanced algorithm as algorithm 2.

Algorithm 2 avoids broadcasting the query to all the neighbours. If the peer's score upper bound is less than the minimal score of the found top k results, the subtree rooted at the peer may not contain any real top k results, and it will be pruned so as to improve the search efficiency. Experimental results show that the histogram is efficient. It can improve the query efficiency while keeping the query effectiveness.

3.3 Histogram Maintenance

As the histogram is constructed based on the top k results returned by the peer, it can be updated automatically during query processing. We compute the term weight upper bound for each query term t_i according to the top k results returned by peer A, denoted as $w'_{i,A,TTL}$. Assume $Histogam_{A,TTL}$ is already existed, If it still doesn't exist, we construct it as stated in section 3.1. If t_i is not contained in $Histogam_{A,TTL}$, we add the $(t_i, w'_{i,A,TTL})$ into $Histogam_{A,TTL}$, or else if $w'_{i,A,TTL}$ is larger than the term weight upper bound stored in $Histogram_{A,TTL}$ which is denoted as $w_{i,A,TTL}$, we replace $w_{i,A,TTL}$ with $w'_{i,A,TTL}$, otherwise keep $w_{i,A,TTL}$ not change. The maintenance of histogram is very small.

To reflect the dynamic change of the peer's content, each peer can refresh the histogram periodically to make sure that the histogram is up to date. The refreshing method is similar to query. For each term t_i in $Histogram_{A,TTL}$, we send query t_i with TTL to peer A, and update $Histogram_{A,TTL}$ according to the returned top k results. Histogram refreshing frequency is determined by the current load of the peer. It should be done when the load is not heavy.

3.4 Node Joining and Leaving

To do top-k query in P2P network, we should consider the dynamic of network. For a new joined node A, there is no histogram for the node, according to equation 9, the score upper bound of node A is $UpperScore_{q,A,TTL} = \sum_{i=1}^{n} 1 \times w_{i,q} \geq 1$. Because the document score is between 0 and 1, according to algorithm 2, node A is guaranteed to be visited. Node A's histogram will be established after the query is executed. If node A leaves from the network, according to algorithm 2, the query will be sent to other peers, until finding overall top k results.

4 Experiment

In this section, we report results of a simulation study to evaluate the effectiveness and efficiency of the top-k query algorithm.

All experiments were conducted on a WinXP with Pentium IV processor (1.6Ghz). Simulator is developed by java language. Table 1 shows some experiment parameters and their default settings. Study [9] shows that Gnutella follows power-law, so the simulated network topology in our experiments is also based on power-law, generated by the PLOD algorithm presented in [8] with average outdegree of 3.6.

Table 1. Parameter and settings

Parameter name	Default value	Description
NetworkTopology	Power-law	The topology of network, with outdegree of 3.6
NetworkSize	1000	The number of peers in the network
TTL	5	The time-to-live of a query message
K	10	The number of documents returned

In the following experiments, three collections, MED, CACM and CRAN, which are previously used by Buckley to evaluate SMART system, are used to measure performance of the algorithm. For the limited space, we only show the results for the MED collection, which represent the other two collections. Med collection consists of 1033 medical documents and 30 queries. We study performance of the algorithm under two different distributions of documents among the peers in the network: (a) even distribution which distributes documents uniformly across the peers, and (b) 80-20 distribution which distributes 80 percent of documents in 20 percents peers, and 20 percent of documents in 80 percents peers.

4.1 Effectiveness

We first examine the effectiveness of top-k query. We use two accepted metrics, precision and recall, to measure the effectiveness. We define the precision and recall in centralized index to be the optimal results, and compute the relative precision and recall to measure the effectiveness of top-k query, i.e.,

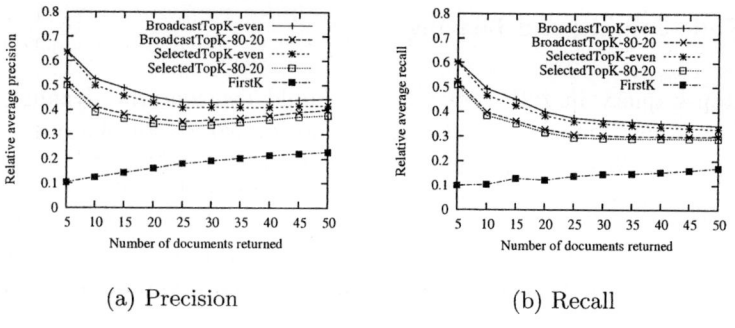

(a) Precision (b) Recall

Fig. 2. Effectiveness of top-k query against number of documents returned

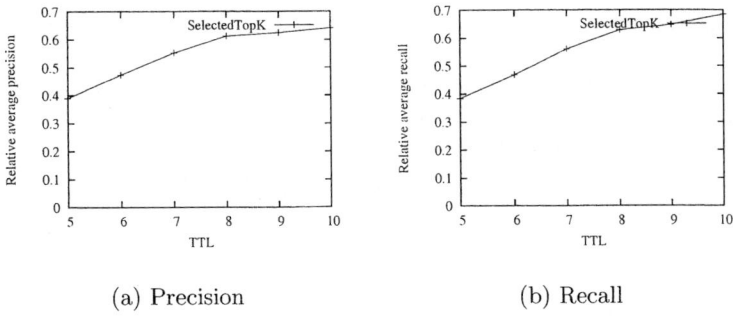

(a) Precision (b) Recall

Fig. 3. Effectiveness of top-k query against different TTL (K=10)

$$Relative\_Precision = Precision/Precision\_in\_centralized\_index \quad (10)$$
$$Relative\_Recall = Recall/Recall\_in\_centralized\_index \quad (11)$$

We execute all 30 queries of MED collection. Each query is executed 10 times at random peers in the network. At last, the relative average precision and recall are computed to measure the effectiveness of top-k query. Figure 2 shows the relative average precision and recall against number of returned results.

In figure 2, BroadcastTopK represents hierarchical top-k query processing algorithm based on broadcast search (algorithm 1), SelectedTopK represents the hierarchical top-k query processing algorithm based on histogram (algorithm 2), FirstK just finds the first k relevant results. First, we compare retrieval effectiveness between top-k query and FirstK. It shows that the top-k query is better than FirstK. Top-k query improves the query effectiveness. Second, we compare retrieval effectiveness of algorithm 1 and algorithm 2. The effectiveness of the two algorithms is very close. It shows that the histogram is efficient, which almost doesn't affect the effectiveness of the query. At last, we compare the effectiveness of top-k query under the even distribution and 80-20 distribution. It shows

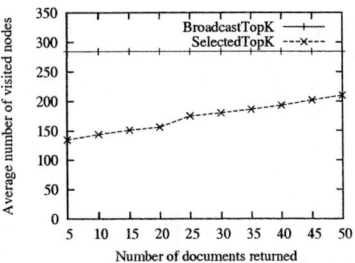

Fig. 4: Average number of visited nodes of top-k query

there is a little difference between them. Because top-k searches top k documents of all nodes within the TTL scope, different distribution will not influence the top-k query's effectiveness much. In the rest experiments, we will only consider the 80-20 distribution, as it is more conformable to the real data distribution in the P2P network.

Because the search scope of top-k query is limited by TTL, increasing TTL will improve the effectiveness of top-k query. Figure 3 illustrates the relative average precision and recall against different TTL.

4.2 Efficiency

We use the number of visited node to measure the efficiency of top-k query processing algorithm.

We also execute 30 queries of MED collection. Each query is executed 10 times at random peers in the network. At last we compute the average number of visited nodes. Figure 4 compare the average number of visited nodes for algorithm 1 which broadcast the query to all the neighbours and algorithm 2 which selects peers based on their histograms. Before executing the algorithm 2, we warm up the system to establish the histogram for each query. It shows that selecting peer based on the histogram is efficient, which greatly reduces the number of visited nodes and improves the search efficiency.

5 Conclusion

In this paper, we have addressed the issue of top-k query in pure P2P network. First, we propose evaluating a top-k query in a hierarchical way. Next, we use histogram to faciliate peer selection, which improves the search efficiency. Experimental results show that our method is efficient. Top-k query improves the query effectiveness, and histogram improves the query efficiency.

Acknowledgments

This research was partially supported by the grants from 863 High Technology Foundation of China (2002AA4Z3130), the Natural Science Foundation of China (60496325). We would like to thank professor Beng Chin Ooi and Kian-Lee Tan, for their support and guidance.

References

1. R. Baeza-Yates and B. Ribeiro-Neto. *Modern information retrieval.* Addison-Wesley, 1999.
2. J. Callan, W. Croft, and S. Harding. The inquery retrieval system. In *Proc. of DEXA*, 1992.
3. J. Callan, Z. Lu, and W. Croft. Searching distributed collections with inference networks. In *Proc. of ACM SIGIR*, 1995.
4. F. Cuenca-Acuna and T. Nguyen. Text-based content search and retrieval in ad hoc p2p communities. Technical report DCS-TR-483, Rutgers University, 2002.
5. Gnutella Development Home Page. http://gnutella.wego.com/.
6. L. Gravano, H. Garcia-Molina, and A. Tomasic. The effectiveness of gloss for the text database discovery problem. In *Proc. of ACM SIGMOD*, 1994.
7. Napster Home Page. http://www.napster.com/.
8. C. Palmer and J. Steffan. Generating network topologies that obey power law. In *Proc. of GLOBECOM*, 2000.
9. M. Ripeanu. Peer-to-peer architecture case study: Gnutella network. Technical report TR-2001-26, University of Chicago, July 2001.
10. I. Stoica, R. Morris, D. Karger, F. Kaashoek, and H. Balakrishnan. Chord: A scalable peer-to-peer lookup service for internet applications. In *Proc. of ACM SIGCOMM*, 2001.
11. C. Tang, Z. Xu, and M. Mahalingam. Peersearch: efficient information retrieval in peer-to-peer networks. Technical report HPL-2002-198, HP Labs, 2002.
12. C. Yu, G. Philip, and W. Meng. Distributed top-n query processing with possibly uncooperative local systems. In *Proc. of VLDB*, 2003.

Improved Data Retrieval Using Semantic Transformation

Barry G.T. Lowden and Jerome Robinson

Department of Computer Science, University of Essex
Colchester, Essex, CO4 3SQ, U.K.
robij@essex.ac.uk

Abstract. Semantic query optimisation uses knowledge about properties of the data, represented as a set of subset descriptor rules, to transform a query into another form that can be executed in a more efficient manner but still yields the same result as the original query. Commonly this 'semantic knowledge' in the form of rules is generated either during the query process itself or else is constructed in advance according to defined heuristics. Over a period of time the rule set may, therefore, become very large and the number of semantically equivalent queries that may be derived rises exponentially. Each rule use creates a new equivalent query. The problem is to identify one near optimal alternative query in a time that is minimal and also short relative to the overall query execution time. In this paper we propose a method for measuring the effectiveness of each rule and present a fast algorithm which selects the most cost effective transformations to directly yield the optimal alternative query. Experiments carried out on a large publicly available dataset show worthwhile savings using the approach.

1 Introduction

Semantic Query Optimisation (SQO) provides an intelligent interface between user and database. It uses association rules, derived from the data itself, to generate a set of alternative yet equivalent queries according to given transformation rules. A process of evaluation is then carried out to select, from this alternative query set, one which has a much lower execution cost than the original [5, 19]. SQO differs, therefore, from conventional optimisation in that it uses semantic information rather than the statistical data held within the DBM system catalogue [1, 2, 11].

Initially SQO rules were limited to knowledge provided by a person, e.g. integrity constraints and data dependencies [3] though later work focused on the automatic generation of database rules [20, 6] using techniques closely related to Data Mining [12, 21]. However, unlike data mining, the rules used in semantic optimisation are *exact*, rather than probability-based, in order to be used to create semantically equivalent queries producing exactly the same result as the original query.

As an example consider an **employee** relation whose attributes include *department, benefit, salary* and *status* to which the following rules apply:

      (i)   *department = 'computing'* → *benefit = 'car'*
      (ii)   *benefit = 'car'* ∧ *salary > 30K* → *status = 'executive'*

and the relation is *indexed* on *status*.

A query of the form *'retrieve all staff in computing who earn more than 35K'* may be transformed, using the above rules, into *'retrieve all executives who work in computing and earn more than 35K'*. If executives represent only 5% of the workforce then this semantically equivalent query should execute in around 5% of the time taken by the original since only 'executive' tuples need be checked for the two original conditions, instead of the whole table. The added condition shortlists relevant tuples. This means that the original conditions will be used to test only those tuples which satisfy the first condition.

In general, given a query Q with constraints (C_1, ...C_k), query transformation may be achieved by repeated use of the following reformulation operators:

(a) **Addition** – given a rule x → y, if a subset of constraints in Q implies x, then we can add constraint y to Q.
(b) **Deletion** – given a rule x → y, if a subset of constraints in Q implies x, and y implies C_i, then we can delete C_i from Q.
(c) **Refutation** – given a rule x → y, if a subset of constraints in Q implies x, and y implies ¬ C_i, then we can assert that Q will return NIL.

Based on these operators, the transformation process intercepts and rewrites the original query using a given rule set. It can also use other database information to estimate alternative query costs in order to select the optimum from the alternatives. Current query reformulation algorithms add new conditions to the user's query and then seek to remove all non-beneficial conditions [6]. (Only *one* extra condition is needed in the final version of the reformulated query, to provide rapid subset extraction).

However, generating and selecting the optimum reformulated query from the set of semantically equivalent queries, derived by alternative rewrite rules in various sequential orders, has traditionally been seen to be a very time-consuming task [17]. This led to research into improved techniques for rule generation [9, 7, 16, 19, 20], together with ways of limiting the size of rule sets and improving the quality of the rules [4, 13, 14, 10]. In this paper we show how semantic optimisation costs may be reduced to a linear function of the number of query conditions rather than the rule set cardinality.

The structure of the paper is as follows. In the next section we first review the standard reformulation approaches and then introduce our fast transformation and query selection technique in Section 3. This is further illustrated by an example and then in Section 4 we give the results of applying the method to 'real' data including part of a 'public domain' dataset. Section 5 outlines conclusions.

2 Query Reformulation

Given a user query Q, expressed in a language such as SQL, and a set of inference rules R, each of the form A → B, there is an exponential number of possible ways of applying **n** rules to the query yielding ($2^n - 1$) distinct alternative queries. To determine the optimum, each alternative would have to be evaluated using a standard cost estimation function [4] and the cheapest selected. Clearly this is impracticable in a realistic environment as even with the most efficient cost estimation procedures, it may be seen that the time taken to find the optimal alternative could easily exceed that of executing the original query.

A more practical approach is therefore needed and the one normally adopted is based on *best first* query generation. The essence of this strategy is to allocate a given amount of resource (time) in which to find a cheaper alternative to the original query. This allocation will usually be some function of the estimated time to execute the original query f(Q). The process is illustrated in Figure 1.

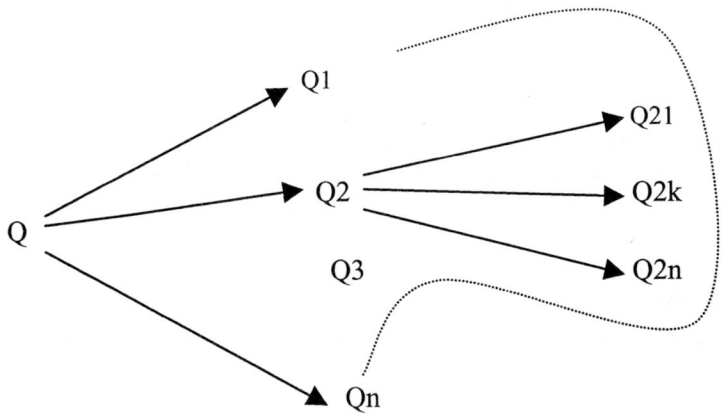

Fig. 1. Best First Query Generation

Q is reformulated with respect to each matching rule in the rule set yielding alternative queries $Q_1 \ldots Q_n$. The projected cost of each alternative is evaluated and the cheapest (Q_2 in the illustration) is further reformulated and then eliminated from the search. The process continues with repeated selection, reformulation and elimination until the resource allocation runs out. At this point the cheapest alternative is returned for execution.

The strategy may not necessarily identify the optimum alternative and is heavily dependent on the order in which the rules are applied since this will determine which subset of the full range of alternatives is generated.

Another area of difficulty is that estimating the full costs of constructing these alternatives must take into account both the cost of transformation and query selection. Although the method in [17] is of interest, it is not realistic for large numbers of matching rules.

3 A Direct Transformation Technique

In order to overcome the weaknesses prevalent in earlier approaches we have developed a transformation technique which runs in linear time by directly modifying the one original query. The method begins by identifying any rule whose antecedent or consequent matches a constraint in the original query.

The closure of these matching rules has been derived *in advance of query processing* using a graph-based model of the whole rule set [15, 16]. In this model, conditions are nodes, and edges correspond to attribute-pair rules [16]. The rule set therefore defines a graph (by listing its edges). An edge (or rule) A → B means A implies B, where A and B each represent single attribute conditions of the kind found in queries.

Query reformulation may be seen as path discovery in the rule graph. Query conditions map to condition nodes in the graph where paths can reveal redundant query conditions, lower cost equivalent conditions and conditions that can be added to the query.

For example, Figure 2 shows that it is possible to delete condition E from a query that contains conditions A and E and F. The path from A to E means that testing for condition A during query answering is sufficient for both conditions A and E. The pre-process of deriving transitive rules adds the direct rule A → E to the rule set, thereby eliminating the need for path traversal or search at query run-time. The old strategy of repeatedly adding conditions to the query (whose purpose is to build paths, such as that from A to E via 'added' conditions B, C, D) is now redundant. The process reduces, therefore, to a simple table lookup of query condition pairs.

Cycles in the rule graph identify equivalent conditions, which select the same set of tuples (because x ↔ y for any two nodes x, y in the cycle). So G, H or I could replace F in a query.

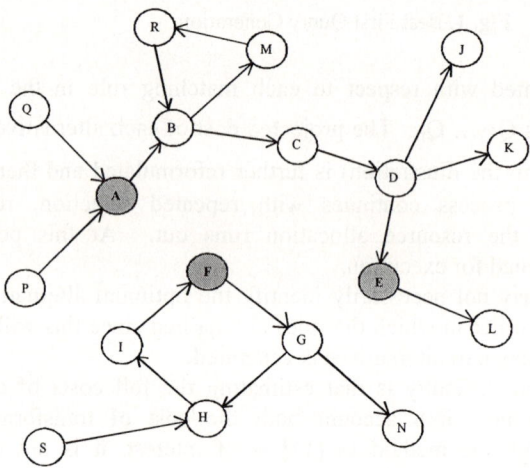

Fig. 2. Part of a Rule Graph

A check is first made to determine whether any matching condition is linked (by a forward or backward path) to a restriction condition that immediately refutes the query by contradicting another query condition, or else provides a single-value answer. If so the query process may be terminated without the need to access the database. This provides a very fast answer to the query.

If it is not possible to provide an immediate answer from the rules then the optimiser proceeds to identify redundant query conditions. Query condition y is redundant if a path x → y exists in the graph, where x is another condition in the query. All redundant conditions are immediately removed from the query.

If x forms part of a cycle in the rule graph with implied consequents y_i ($1 \le i \le n$) where n is the number of nodes apart from y in the cycle, then the cheapest $y_i = (y_i)_{min}$ is selected. If the evaluation cost of $(y_i)_{min}$ is less than that of x, then it is cost effective to replace x with $(y_i)_{min}$ since the cycle indicates that it is equivalent to x, i.e. $(y_i)_{min} \Leftrightarrow x$. Thus condition $(y_i)_{min}$ immediately replaces x in the query.

The final stage of query reformulation is to add zero or one implied condition. Any node reachable from a query node in the graph can be added to the query without affecting its meaning [15]. The choice is based on condition processing cost. It is only cost effective to add condition z from (non-cyclic) path w → z, where w is an existing query condition, if this reduces the combined cost of evaluating both w and z, since w must be retained in the query. In this case, therefore, the consequent cost is based on applying both conditions w and z to those tuples selected by z. A specific example would be where z was an indexed attribute condition with good selectivity and no indexed condition exists in the query.

The query optimisation process is now finished. The current version of the directly modified query is the optimised query, semantically equivalent to the original but perhaps *syntactically* unrelated to it.

It may be seen that the above process generates only one alternative query in linear time rather than all possible alternatives in exponential time. The method is not adversely affected by the size of the rule set, as in traditional approaches. The closure of the rule graph is held in an indexed lookup table, for fast query condition lookup. The method provides a fast and practical technique for semantic optimisation.

3.1 Estimating Condition Costs

The number of tuple instances identified by the antecedent and consequent conditions of a rule, together with the total number of the tuples in a table, are available because they were stored when the rule was initially derived [9]. We may use this information to determine whether a rule is cost effective for transforming a specific query. If the size of the result set is known in advance (as it is for each selection condition here) then it is not necessary to scan the whole table to retrieve all results. Search can terminate as soon as the correct number of items has been found.

Let the number of instances of a condition be R. This means R tuples are selected by the condition. Then the approximate number of disk blocks, A, retrieved for the R instances can be found using the following expression where B is the total number of disk blocks [8].

$$A = B*(1-(1-1/B)^R)$$

This assumes a random distribution of tuple instances across the relation space and 100% block packing density. If the condition is not indexed then it is necessary to calculate the number of disk blocks to be searched in order to retrieve those A blocks out of the total. Moreover, since there is no information about the location of the A blocks, we assume that C sequential blocks must be searched to retrieve the R instances where:

$$C = \frac{A*(B+1)}{A+1}$$ which for large A, B approximates to B.

Assuming N tuples per block, the number of tuples searched is therefore:

  N*A where the selection condition is indexed,
  N*C where the selection condition is not indexed.

The search cost will be the (number of tuples searched) * (the evaluation cost of the condition attribute). This latter is typically an implementation-defined function of the attribute length and type. In our examples evaluation costs are (for simplicity):

  strings = n bytes where n is the string length.
  integers = 1 byte.

Assume a rule:

$$Dcode= \text{`ACCT'} \ (30) \rightarrow Dname = \text{`Accounting'} \ (30)$$

where the number of condition instances is shown in brackets and the condition evaluation cost is defined as the number of bytes to be compared * number of condition instances. Assume further that the rule applies to a relation 'DEPARTMENT' consisting of 100 blocks, each consisting of 12 tuples.

Taking the antecedent as an example, we first compute approximately how many disk blocks need to be retrieved for the condition:

$$A = B*(1-(1-1/B)^R) = 100*(1-(1-1/100)^{30}) = 27 \text{ (rounded up to whole block)}$$

If the antecedent attribute is not indexed, we determine the expected number of disk blocks which need to be searched to retrieve the A blocks:

$$C = \frac{A*(B+1)}{A+1} = 27*(100+1)/28 \approx 98 \text{ (rounded up to whole block)}$$

giving:

  number of tuples to be tested $\cong$ C * N = 98 * 12 = 1176

where 'tested' means compared with the 4-byte string "ACCT", so total search cost of the antecedent condition $\cong$ 1176 * 4 = 4704.

In the same way we may compute the cost of the consequent condition since the number of instances is known.

3.2 A Transformation Example

Assume that we are looking for all information in the 'DEPARTMENT' relation where Dname = 'Marketing' and Manager = 'M3'. This query can be represented in SQL as query Q:

Q: select * from DEPARTMENT where Dname = 'Marketing' AND Manager = 'M3'

The following rules (edges) are found in the rule graph, for the two query conditions:

R1: Dname = 'Marketing' (40) → Project > 7 (60)   A → B
R2: Dname = 'Marketing' (40) → Project < 12 (90)   A → C
R3: Dname = 'Marketing' (40) → Dcode = 'MKTG' (40)   A → D
R4: Dname = 'Marketing' (40) → Manager = 'M3' (100)   A → E
R5: Manager = 'M3' (100)   → Salary > 30K (120)   E → F
R6: Dcode = 'MKTG' (40)   → Dname = 'Marketing' (40) D → A

where brackets indicate the number of tuples identified by each condition. The letters A to F can be used to represent the conditions. The two query conditions are A and E, for example. The column on the right represents each rule using the letters A to F in place of the corresponding conditions.

The part of the rule graph corresponding to these six rules, with query conditions A and E shaded, is as follows.

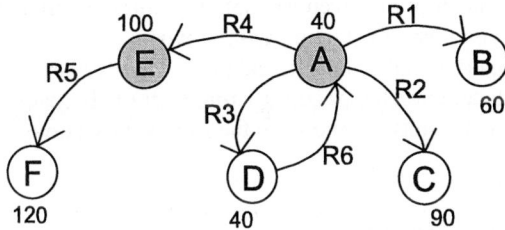

It may be seen that no rule causes a refutation of the given query or may be used to provide directly the answer to the query. Condition E can be removed immediately from the query, because it is implied by query condition A. D is equivalent to A, because of the cycle. It selects the same set of tuples. But the work to retrieve those tuples is greater for A than D, because the comparison of each examined tuple with the longer string 'Marketing' is slower than the 'MKTG' in condition D. Therefore D replaces A in the query. The query is now SELECT * FROM DEPARTMENT WHERE Dcode='MKTG' instead of WHERE Dname='Marketing' AND Manager='M3'. (No syntactic connection between WHERE clauses).

Any of the conditions B, C, D, E, F implied by A (or equivalently by D) could now be added to the query if it will act as a rapid retrieval mechanism for a super-set of the tuples selected by A (and also by D). The set of tuples selected by a rule's consequent condition always contains the set selected by the antecedent [16]. This is because if X implies Y (as asserted by rule X → Y) then 'all Xs are Ys'. Condition costs must be considered, to decide if one of the five conditions should be added to the query.

Condition costs, calculated from the formulae above, for all six conditions in the rule graph are shown in the table below. Only the Project attribute is indexed (affecting conditions B and C).

A	B	C	D	E	F
10692	552	720	4752	2400	1200

The rule graph shows that conditions A and D each imply all the other five conditions. In practice it is not necessary to calculate the cost of every condition. Often no calculation at all is required because the choice is obvious from condition properties. An indexed condition with good selectivity and fast tuple testing, for example, will speed up query processing. So the consequent of rule R1 is obviously the best choice for constraint addition, based on information visible in the rules themselves: relative selectivities, comparison costs and the existence of indices. The consequent of rule R1 is condition B. It is the most selective indexed condition, so cost calculation is not necessary to reformulate the query. The cost formulae explain why a heuristic decision provides the correct choice. Relative rather than absolute costs can be used to compare conditions.

The original query conditions: $A \wedge E$ have a combined cost of $2400 + 100*9 = 3300$, if condition E is used first and condition A applied to the 100 tuples which satisfy E. The cost would be $10692 + 40*2 = 10772$ if condition A was used first and the E tested the 40 tuples selected by A. In contrast, the new equivalent query: $D \wedge B$ will use the indexed condition B first, so cost is $552 + 60*4 = 792$.

It is possible to see from the given example that our method of query reformulation is simple, direct and fast. Cost comparison, when required, is usually based on comparison of properties rather than calculation. This further improves the speed of query processing, in addition to not constructing a set of alternative queries.

Some experimental results are shown in the following section.

4 Experimental Results

In order to measure the effectiveness of our approach, extensive experiments were undertaken on a publicly available dataset the 'General Household Survey Data, GN: 33124, Study number: 3170, Year: 1993-1994' provided by the UK ESRC Data Archive, held at the University of Essex. From this dataset was derived a 27266 instance relation 'HOUSEHOLD' encompassing 12 attributes, including three indexed, with a row length of 71 bytes. Total number of blocks was 6139, including pointer storage, in B-tree structure.

A typical experiment was as follows:

(1) A set of 500 sample queries was randomly generated, each query consisting of from 1 to 6 conjunctive terms with value domains drawn from the test relation.
(2) These queries were then run experimentally against the relation and execution times recorded. As a by-product of the execution process, a rule set consisting of 50 rules was constructed using the rule generation and selection techniques described in [9, 15].
(3) The same queries were then re-run using the semantic transformation approach introduced in section 3 of this paper.

Observations, as a result of semantic transformation, were as follows:

a) for all queries in the set, 6% were either refuted or the answer found by the matching rules alone. In the case of refutation the average saving was 99.15% and for direct query answering the saving on average was 99.53%.

b) in a further 8% of queries, semantic transformation introduced one or more indexed attributes leading to savings on average of 83.52% .

c) for the remaining 86% of queries the average saving was 2.13% due to reduced attribute matching time.

5 Conclusions

A method of semantic query optimisation by direct modification of the original query rather than choosing one of a set of alternative queries was presented.

The method is based on attribute-pair rules, which have a single antecedent and consequent condition, so that the rule set represents an inference graph whose closure can be computed before any queries are processed. Edges in the graph closure are stored in an indexed look-up table for fast access. Methods for 'matching' range conditions by sub-range containment have been discussed in a previous paper [15].

Rules are discovered or constructed from the data, rather than specified by people, so that rules with conditions relevant to queries are involved. The selectivity information stored with each antecedent and consequent condition was shown to allow cost estimation and early termination of query processing. It was indicated that computation of condition costs is rarely required because parameter-based comparison provides the same result.

Unlike more conventional approaches, our method combines the processes of query transformation and selection in such a way that the costs of optimisation are negligible, compared to query execution costs, even when the rule set is large.

References

[1] M.W. Blasgen and K.P. Eswaran. "Storage and access in relational data bases", IBM Systems Journal, 16 (4), 1977, pp. 363-377.

[2] A.F. Cardenas. *"Analysis and performance of inverted data base structures"*, Communications of the ACM, 18(5), May 1975, pp. 253-263.

[3] S. Chakravarthy, J. Grant and J. Minker, *"Logic-based approach to semantic query optimisation"*, ACM on Database Sys., 15(2), 1990, pp. 162-207.

[4] K.C. Chan and A.K.C. Wong, "*A statistical test for extracting classificatory knowledge from databases*", Knowledge Discovery in Databases, 1991, pp. 107-123.

[5] G. Graefe and D. Dewitt, *"The EXODUS optimiser generator"*, Proc. ACM SIGMOD Conference on Management of Data, 1987, pp. 160-171.

[6] J. Han, Y. Cai and N. Cercone, *"Data-driven discovery of quantitative rules in relational databases"*, IEEE Trans. Knowledge and Data Eng., 5 (1), 1993, pp. 29-40.

[7] C. Hsu and C.A. Knoblock, *"Rule induction for semantic query optimization"*, Proceedings of the 11th International Conference on Machine Learning, 1994, pp. 112-120.

[8] B.G.T. Lowden, *An Approach to Multikey Sequencing in an equiprobable keyterm retrieval situation*, Proceedings of the 8th ACM SIGIR International Conference on Research and Development in Information Retrieval, 1985, pp 92-96.

[9] B.G.T. Lowden, J. Robinson and K.Y. Lim, *"A semantic query optimiser using automatic rule derivation"*, Proc. WITS'95, 5th Annual Workshop on Information Technologies and Systems, 1995, pp. 68-76.

[10] B.G.T. Lowden and J. Robinson, *"A statistical approach to rule selection in semantic query optimisation"*, Proc. ISMIS'99, 11th Intl Symposium on Methodologies for Intelligent Systems, 1999, pp 330-339. LNCS 1609.

[11] L. F. Mackert and G. M. Lohman, *"R* optimizer validation and performance evaluation for local queries"*, Proc. ACM SIGMOD Conference, 1986, pp. 84-95.

[12] H. Mannila, *"Methods and problems in data mining"*, Proc. 6th Intl Conference on Database Theory, 1997, pp. 41-55.

[13] G.Piatetsky-Shapiro and C. Matheus, *"Measuring data dependencies in large databases"*, Proc. AAAI Workshop on Knowledge Discovery in Databases, 1993, pp. 162-173.

[14] J. Robinson and B.G.T. Lowden, *"Data analysis for query processing"*, Proc. 2nd International Symposium on Intelligent Data Analysis, London, 1997, pp 447-458.

[15] J. Robinson and B.G.T. Lowden, *"Semantic optimisation and rule graphs"*, Proc. 5th KRDB Workshop, 1998.
http://sunsite.informatik.rwth-aachen.de/Publications/CEUR-WS/Vol-10/

[16] J. Robinson and B.G.T. Lowden, *"Attribute-pair range rules"*, Proc. DEXA'98, 1998, pp 680-691,

[17] S. Shekhar, J. Srivastava and S. Dutta, *"A formal model of trade-off between optimisation and execution costs in semantic query optimization"*, Proc. 14th VLDB Conference, 1988, pp. 457-467.

[18] S. Shekhar, B. Hamidzadeh and A. Kohli. "Learning transformation rules for semantic query optimisation: A data-driven approach", IEEE Trans. Data & Knowledge Engineering, 5 (6), December 1993, pp. 950-964.

[19] S.T. Shenoy and Z.M. Ozsoyoglu, *"Design and implementation of semantic query optimiser"*, IEEE Transactions on Knowledge and Data Eng., 1(3), 1989, pp. 344-361.

[20] M. Siegel, E. Sciore and S. Salveter, *"A method for automatic rule derivation to support semantic query optimisation"*, ACM Trans. Database Systems, 17(4), 1992, pp. 563-600.

[21] Yu C. and Sun W., *Automatic knowledge acquisition and maintenance for semantic query optimisation*, IEEE Trans. Knowledge and Data Engineering, 1 (3), pp. 362-375, 1989.

A Structure-Based Filtering Method for XML Management Systems

Olli Luoma

Department of Information Technology, University of Turku, Finland
olli.luoma@it.utu.fi

Abstract. To answer queries, many XML management systems perform structural joins, i.e., they determine all occurences of parent/child or ancestor/descendant relationships between node sets. These joins are often one of the most time-consuming phases in query evaluation, so it is desirable to reduce the size of the node sets before performing the joins. This problem has earlier been approached by using signatures built on the content of the nodes, but in this paper, we propose a novel method in which the nodes are filtered based on the structural properties of their subtrees. To achieve this, we use a schema graph which summarizes the structures of XML documents more accurately than conventional summarization methods.

1 Introduction

Because of its simplicity and flexibility, Extensible Markup Language (XML) [1] has proved very useful in many application areas. Today, XML is used not only as a standard for data exchange, but also as a core for development and deployment platforms, such as Microsoft .NET. Furthermore, there are many application areas, such as bioinformatics, where XML serves as a format to store heterogeneous information [2]. Storing, querying, and updating XML documents presents an interesting research area and there has indeed been a significant amount of research on XML data management.

Every well-formed XML document can be represented as an XML tree, a partially ordered labeled tree in which each element, attribute, and text node[1] corresponds to an element, attribute, or piece of text in the document, and the ancestor/descendant relationships between the nodes correspond to the nesting relationships between elements, attributes, and pieces of text [3]. XML trees can be modeled using several different methods, such as parent/child indexes, ancestor/descendant indexes, pre-/postorder encoding [4], absolute or relative region coordinates [5], and virtual nodes [6]. All of these methods encode the information of parent/child or ancestor/descendant relationships which is needed to perform structural joins.

---

[1] According to the original XPath recommendation there are seven different node types, four of which have been omitted here to simplify the discussion.

In many systems, query processing is speeded up by using a *schema tree*, a structural summary which partitions the nodes of an XML tree into equivalence classes according to their label paths. In [7], however, we proposed a schema graph as an alternative way to summarize the structures of XML documents. Since a schema graph creates a more precise, structure-based partitioning of the nodes, it can be used for two purposes. Firstly, queries that select nodes based only on their structural properties, such as "find all employees who have children", can be evaluated very quickly [7]. Secondly, queries that select nodes based on both structure and content, can be speeded up by using the schema graph as a filtering structure. For example, when evaluating query "find all employees who have a child named Alina", we can filter out those employees who do not have any children in the first place.

The remainder of this paper is organized as follows. Section 3 explores the possibilities of a schema graph as a filtering structure. Section 4 describes Xeek, our prototype system, and in Section 5, the results of experimental evaluation are presented. Section 6 concludes this article and discusses our future work.

2 Related Work

A lot of work has been carried out to develop methods to manage XML documents. The proposed methods can be divided into three categories. In the *flat streams approach*, the documents are considered as byte streams. Large streams are distributed on disk pages using the file system or a BLOB manager in a database management system. Since accessing the structures of the documents requires parsing, this method is hardly suitable for XML management systems. In the *metamodeling approach*, the documents are first represented as trees which are then stored into a database. This provides fast access to the XML trees and, consequently, this method has been used in many XML management systems [8] [9]. The *mixed approach* aims to combine the previous two approaches. Some systems store the data in two redundant repositories, one flat and one metamodeled, which allows fast retrieval but creates significant storage overhead [10]. The other option is the hybrid approach in which the coarser structures of the documents are modeled as trees and finer structures as flat streams [11].

Many content-based filtering methods derived from information retrieval have been applied to structured documents [6] [12]. However, a structure-based filtering method for XML management systems has previously been proposed only by Park and Kim [13]. Their idea is to attach a signature built over the labels of the descendants to each node of the XML tree. This signature can then be used to filter out the nodes which cannot satisfy the conditions set by a query. However, since their method requires accessing the XML tree before filtering, it is fundamentally different from the method proposed in this paper. Furthermore, our schema graph partitions the nodes of an XML tree very accurately, so nodes can be filtered based on complex structural conditions. This can often reduce the size of joined node sets more than a filtering method that relies on simple label signatures.

3 Using a Schema Graph as a Filtering Structure

As mentioned above, a *schema graph* creates an accurate, structure-based partitioning of the nodes of an XML tree, which makes it possible to filter the nodes based on their structural position. To define a schema graph formally we first need to define two concepts for the nodes of an XML tree, namely a *label* (Definition 1), and a *label path* (Definition 2).

Definition 1. *A label $l(n)$ for node n is the name of the corresponding element if n is an element node and the name of the corresponding attribute preceded by an @-sign if n is an attribute node.*

Notice that Definition 1 does not define any label for text nodes. However, text nodes, as well as element and attribute nodes, do have a label path which is defined in Definition 2.

Definition 2. *Let $s(n)$ denote the parent of node n. The label path $p(n)$ of an element or attribute node n is $/l(n)$ if n is a root node, and $p(s(n))/l(n)$ otherwise. The label path of a text node n is $p(s(n))$.*

Many XML management systems, such as Lore [8], BUS [9], and XRel [14], summarize the documents using a *schema tree*, an index structure which partitions the nodes according to their label paths[2]. A schema tree allows fast retrieval of the nodes based on their label paths, but to achieve structure-based filtering on the summary level we need a summarization method which creates more accurate partitioning. Thus, our filtering method takes advantage of a schema graph, an acyclic, directed graph, which allows fast retrieval of the nodes based not only on their label paths, but also on the structures of their subtrees. The partitioning created by a schema graph is described formally in Definition 3; the difference between schema tree and schema graph is illustrated in Fig. 1.

Definition 3. *Let N denote the set of nodes in an XML tree and let $C(n)$ denote the set of attribute and element nodes that are children of node n. A vertex in a schema graph corresponds to an equivalence class $[n]_g$ induced by an equivalence relation $\equiv_g$ on N such that for any $n_1, n_2 \in N$, $n_1 \equiv_g n_2$, iff*

$$C(n_1) = \emptyset \wedge C(n_2) = \emptyset \wedge p(n_1) = p(n_2), \text{ or}$$

$$C(n_1) \neq \emptyset \wedge C(n_2) \neq \emptyset \wedge (\forall c_1 \in C(n_1) : \exists c_2 \in C(n_2) : c_1 \equiv_g c_2) \wedge (\forall c_2 \in C(n_2) : \exists c_1 \in C(n_1) : c_2 \equiv_g c_1).$$

In simple terms, two nodes in an XML tree are equivalent if their label paths are identical and their subtrees are structurally similar. Notice that according to Definition 3 there cannot exist two nodes $n_1, n_2 \in N$ such that $p(n_1) \neq p(n_2)$ and $n_1 \equiv_g n_2$, so we can define a label path also for a vertex in a schema graph in Definition 4.

---

[2] In Lore, for example, this index is called a *DataGuide*, but in the current paper, any structure that partitions the nodes according to their label paths is called a schema tree.

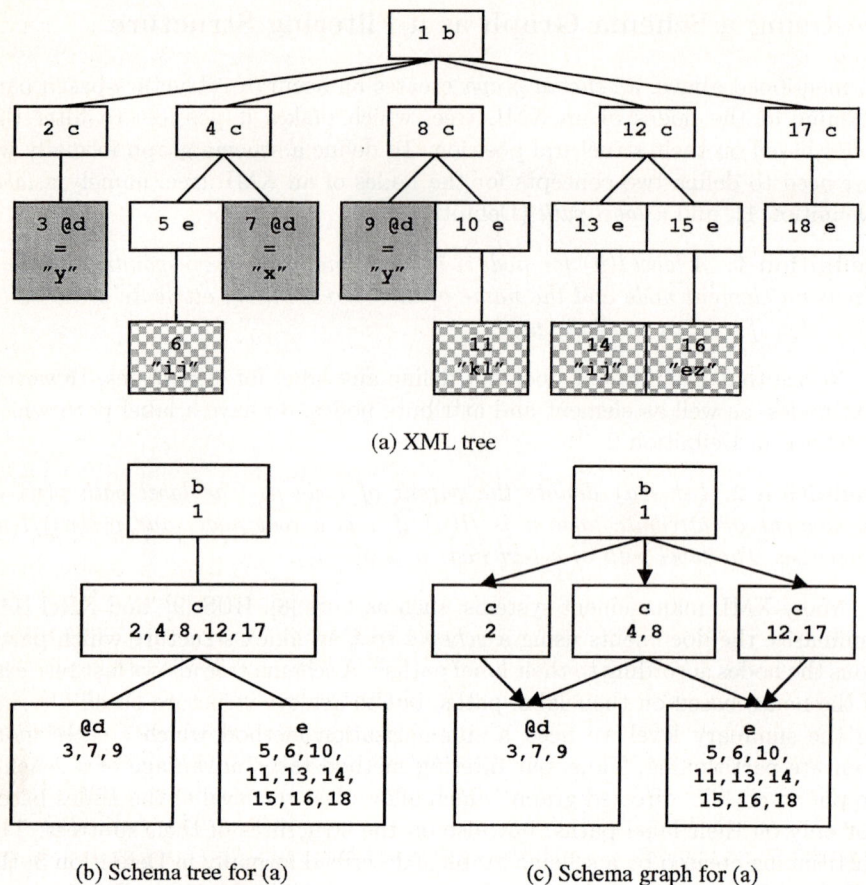

Fig. 1. An XML tree, a schema tree, and a schema graph

Definition 4. *A label path $p(v)$ for a vertex v in a schema graph is the label path of any node belonging to the equivalence class corresponding to v.*

Consider, for example, evaluating XPath query /b/c[//@d="y"] using the XML tree and the schema tree presented in Fig. 1. We first use the schema tree to find the set $N_1 = \{2, 4, 8, 12, 17\}$ of element nodes with the label path /b/c and then the set $N_2 = \{3, 7, 9\}$ of attribute nodes with label path matching /b/c//@d. Both of these operations can be performed very quickly. After this, we scan N_2 to find the set $N_3 = \{3, 9\}$ of attribute nodes with label path matching /b/c//@d and value "y". Sets N_1 and N_3 are then structurally joined to find all nodes in N_1 that have a descendant in N_3, so the result of this query is $\{2, 8\}$.

Let us now consider evaluating the same query using the schema graph presented in Fig. 1 to filter the nodes. First, we use the schema graph to find the set $N_1 = \{2, 4, 8\}$ of element nodes that satisfy the condition /b/c[//@d], i.e., the set of nodes that belong to the equivalence class corresponding to a vertex v in the schema graph such that $p(v)$ = /b/c, and from which a vertex with label path matching /b/c//@d can be reached. Notice that this set is now smaller than the set N_1 obtained using the schema tree. We then proceed similarly as in our first example to find the set $N_3 = \{3, 9\}$ of attribute nodes with label path matching /b/c//@d and value "y". After this, we structurally join sets N_1 and N_3 to get the final result $\{2, 8\}$.

The algorithms needed for evaluating queries using a schema graph as a filtering structure are presented in Fig. 2. As in XRel [14], for example, queries have to be first represented as query trees in which exactly one node is active and each node has two features, a label path and a value; for element nodes, the value is defined as an empty string. Notice that algorithm nodeVertexMatch is intrinsically complex as such[3], but this problem can be avoided rather easily. In our prototype system Xeek, for example, we achieved good results by using a relational database system to implement the schema graph redundantly as a set of pairs (v_1, v_2), where vertex v_2 is reachable from vertex v_1.

Notice also that our filtering method can take full advantage of the structural conditions involved in complex queries, which sets it apart from the method proposed by Park and Kim [13]. For example, to answer XPath query //s[s[d/n= "Aino"][s/n="Aapo"]], we join four node sets, set N_1 of nodes that satisfy the condition //s[s[d/n][s/n]], set N_2 of nodes that satisfy the condition //s/s[d/n][s/n], set N_3 of nodes with label path //s/s/d/n and value "Aino", and set N_4 of nodes with label path //s/s/s/n and value "Aapo". Assuming that every label present in our query is part of the signature, the filtering method proposed by Park and Kim would have resulted in N_1 satisfying a much looser condition //s[//s][//d][//n] and N_2 satisfying //s/s[//d][//n][//s]. Furthermore, in our method, the filtering actually takes place on the summary level, i.e., before accessing the XML tree.

4 Xeek - A Prototype System

To test our idea of structure-based filtering, we implemented Xeek, a prototype system based on a relational database. The basic Xeek schema consists of five relations:

```
Element(DocId, Start, End, VertexId)
Attribute(DocId, Start, End, VertexId, Value)
Text(DocId, Start, End, VertexId, Value)
Vertex(VertexId, PathExp)
ReachVertex(VertexId, ReachVertexId)
NodeSet(NodeSetId, DocId, Start, End)
```

---

[3] Since implementing the schema graph as a graph is hardly practical, we actually did define the schema graph as a partitioning criterion, not as a graph structure, in Definition 3.

5   Experimental Results

We evaluated the effectiveness of our method using three different sets of XML documents: the 7.65 MB collection of Shakespeare's plays marked up in XML [15], a synthetic 111 MB XMark document generated using XMLgen [16], and a 127 MB XML document generated from the DBLP database [17]. We stored these documents into a MySQL database using Xeek; the sizes of the relations in each case are presented in Table 1.

Notice that, although Xeek models the schema graph redundantly, the sizes of relations Vertex and ReachVertex are rather modest for the Shakespeare collection and the DBLP document. The structure of the deeply nested XMark document, in contrast, is much more irregular, so the combined size of the relations Vertex and ReachVertex is rather large, about 10 % of the database. It is worth noticing, however, that the best-case and worst-case sizes of both schema tree and schema graph are identical [7]. The best-case behaviour of both structures is yielded by an XML tree where all element nodes that share the same label path also share the same subtree structures. The worst-case behaviour is yielded by an XML tree where every node has a different label.

Table 2 shows our small but versatile query set for the different collections and Table 3 the materialization and the join times for each query, both with filtering and without filtering. Notice that the materialization times with filtering are seldom much longer than without filtering, although the filtering requires more accesses to the schema graph in the materialization phase. In many cases, the materialization times with filtering are even shorter, because filtering reduces the amount of tuples that have to be written in the NodeSet table.

As our results demonstrate, the small penalty paid in the materialization phase usually pays off in the join phase. In the best case, structural filtering can improve the query evaluation time by an order of magnitude. When evaluating query Q6, for example, filtering reduces the sizes of node sets to be structurally joined to 713, 2210, and 14314 from 21750, 2210, and 14314, respectively, which reduces the time needed for structural joins considerably.

One interesting detail in the results is the relatively good join performance while evaluating queries using the Shakespeare collection. Since the Shakespeare collection consists of many XML documents, the structural joins can partially be performed using equijoins on document identifiers. In contrast, the joins on the XMark and DBLP documents have to be completely performed using much slower nonequijoins on the region coordinates.

6   Conclusion and Future Work

In this paper, we proposed a new structure-based filtering method for XML management systems which is utilizes an accurate, structure-based partitioning created by a schema graph. Our filtering method can take advantage of even the most complex structural conditions set by queries, which sets it apart from previous proposals. We implemented our method using a relational database and presented the positive results of our performance studies.

Table 1. Database sizes

	Shakespeare		XMark		DBLP	
Relation	Tuples	Size(MB)	Tuples	Size(MB)	Tuples	Size(MB)
Element	179618	11.0	1666315	112	3332130	164
Attribute	0	0	381878	30.9	404276	32.9
Text	147383	16.4	988027	145	3003323	234
Vertex	232	0.02	52747	3.75	552	0.04
ReachVertex	3231	0.08	1041318	29.3	3779	0.13
Total	330464	27.5	4130285	321	6744060	431

Table 2. Query set

#	Data	Query
Q1	Shak.	/PLAY/ACT[//SPEAKER='EDMUND']
Q2	Shak.	//SPEECH[SPEAKER='HAMLET']/STAGEDIR
Q3	Shak.	//SPEECH[SPEAKER='KING LEAR'][STAGEDIR='Aside']
Q4	XMark	//person[//interest/@category='category620']
Q5	XMark	//item[@featured='yes']
Q6	XMark	//item[@featured='yes']//mail//keyword
Q7	DBLP	//article[author='Jukka Teuhola']
Q8	DBLP	//inproceedings[crossref='conf/safecomp/1998']
Q9	DBLP	//article[@rating='SUPERB']/author

Table 3. Query performance

	With filtering		Without filtering	
#	Mat.(sec)	Join(sec)	Mat.(sec)	Join(sec)
Q1	0.60	0.00	0.77	0.00
Q2	1.36	0.03	0.57	0.52
Q3	1.33	0.02	0.57	0.35
Q4	0.49	0.45	0.64	1.09
Q5	1.53	6.13	0.98	61.02
Q6	1.64	14.36	1.10	>600
Q7	2.19	1.48	2.18	1.48
Q8	2.09	4.05	4.28	7.83
Q9	3.67	7.06	9.88	11.27

We plan to extend Xeek to a full-fledged XML storage system. To achieve this, we need to develop ways to efficiently construct the result documents from the result sets. During the performance studies we encountered some cases where the join order of the tables determined by the MySQL query optimizer was far from optimal. Thus, we will seek ways to avoid the pitfalls of bad query optimization by studying how different optimization and join methods used in RDBMSs affect the performance when the database is used to manage XML trees.

References

1. World Wide Web Consortium. Extensible Markup Language (XML) 1.0. http://www.w3c.org/TR/REC-xml, 2000.
2. A.B. Chaudri, A. Rashid, and R. Zicari. *XML Data Management: Native XML and XML-Enabled Database Systems*. Addison-Wesley, 2003.
3. World Wide Web Consortium. XML Path Language (XPath) Version 1.0. http://www.w3c.org/TR/xpath, 2000.
4. P.F. Dietz. Maintaining order in a linked list. In *Proc. of the 14th ACM Symposium on Theory of Computing*, pages 122-127, 1982.
5. D.D. Kha, M. Yoshikawa, and S. Uemura. An XML indexing structure with relative region coordinate. In *Proc. of the 17th IEEE Intl Conf. on Data Engineering*, pages 212-220, 2001.
6. Y.K. Lee, S. Yoo, K. Yoon, and B. Berra. Index structures for structured documents. In *Proc. of the 1st Intl Conf. on Digital Libraries*, pages 91-99, 1996.
7. O. Luoma. Indexing XML data with a schema graph. In *Proc. of the IASTED Intl Conf. on Databases and Applications*, pages 274-279, 2004.
8. J. McHugh, S. Abiteboul, R. Goldman, R. Quass, and J. Widom. Lore: A database management system for semistructured data. *SIGMOD Record*, 26(3): 54-66, 1997.
9. D. Shin, H. Jang, and H. Jin. BUS: An effective indexing and retrieval scheme in structured documents. In *Proc. of the 3rd ACM Intl Conf. on Digital Libraries*, pages 235-243, 1998.
10. T.W. Tak and J. Annevelink. Integrating a structured-text retrieval system with an object-oriented database system. In *Proc. of the 20th Intl Conf. on Very Large Databases*, pages 740-749, 1994.
11. C.C. Kanne and G. Moerkotte. Efficient storage of XML data. Poster abstract in *Proc. of the 16th Intl Conf. on Data Engineering*, page 198, 2000.
12. Y. Chen and K. Aberer. Combining pat-trees and signature files for query evaluation in document databases. In *Proc. of the 10th Intl Conf. on Database and Expert Systems Applications*, pages 473-484, 1999.
13. S. Park and H.J. Kim. A new query processing techique for XML based on signature. In *Proc. of the 7th Intl Conf. on Database Systems for Advanced Applications*, pages 22-31, 2001.
14. M. Yoshikawa, T. Amagasa, T. Shimura, and S. Uemura. XRel: A path-based approach to storage and retrieval of XML documents using relational databases. *ACM Transactions on Internet Technologies*, 1(1): 110-141, 2001.
15. J. Bosak. The complete plays of Shakespeare marked up in XML. http://www.ibiblio.org/xml/examples/shakespeare
16. R. Busse, M. Carey, D. Florescu, M. Kersten, I. Manolescu, A. Schmidt, and F. Waas. XMark - an XML benchmark project. http://monetdb.cwi.nl/xml/index.html
17. M. Ley. Digital bibliography library project. http://dblp.uni-trier.de/

Uncertainty Management for Network Constrained Moving Objects*

Zhiming Ding and Ralf Hartmut Güting

Praktische Informatik IV
Fernuniversität Hagen, D-58084 Hagen, Germany
{zhiming.ding,rhg}@fernuni-hagen.de

Abstract. One of the key research issues with moving objects databases (MOD) is the uncertainty management problem. In this paper, we discuss how the uncertainty of network constrained moving objects can be reduced by using reasonable modeling methods and location update policies. Besides, we present a framework to support variable accuracies in presenting the locations of moving objects. The operation design issues with uncertainty involved are also discussed.

1 Introduction

Uncertainty management is an important research issue in the moving objects database (MOD) technology. As stated in [8, 13], due to network delays, measuring errors, and the limitations of sampling methods, uncertainty is an inherent aspect of MOD.

The uncertainty management problem in MOD is actually two-fold – first, how to reduce uncertainty through reasonable modeling methods and location update policies; and second, how to express uncertainty and deal with uncertain data in databases by introducing suitable data types, operations, and index structures.

In recent years, a lot of research has been focused on the uncertainty management problem for moving objects, especially on the second aspect of the problem. In [8], Pfoser and Jensen et al. have analyzed the sources of uncertainty in presenting the locations of moving objects, and a representation framework has been proposed to deal with uncertain data. The work in [9] has explored the uncertainty and fuzziness in managing moving objects, and a mechanism is provided to deal with temporal, spatial, and spatio-temporal indeterminacies. In [12, 13], Trajcevski and Wolfson et al. have discussed the uncertainty management strategies in the DOMINO system. By applying an uncertainty threshold, the trajectory of a moving object is extended from a curve to a tube in the X×Y×T space and the operations, such as **inside**, are extended by introducing the uncertainty semantics such as "sometimes", "always", "possibly", and "definitely". In [11], a set of data types and operations have been proposed for the uncertainty management of moving objects. However, nearly none of these works have treated the interactions between moving objects and the underlying transportation networks in anyway. The works in [4, 7, 10] have discussed the uncertainty man-

---

* This research was supported by the Deutsche Forschungsgemeinschaft (DFG) research project "Databases for Moving Objects" under grant number Gu293/8-1.

agement problems with transportation networks involved. However, transportation networks are only used to reduce sampling noises from GPS or to predict future positions of moving objects.

In this paper, we discuss how the uncertainty of network constrained moving objects can be reduced through reasonable modeling methods and location update policies. We will mainly focus on the uncertainty caused by sampling methods so that we assume the uncertainty caused by other factors to be negligible.

The remaining part of this paper is organized as follows. Section 2 describes the basic methodologies in managing the uncertainty of network constrained moving objects; Section 3 deals with variable granularities in uncertainty management; Section 4 analyzes operation design issues with uncertainty involved; and Section 5 finally concludes the paper.

2 Basic Uncertainty Management Strategies for Network Constrained Moving Objects

In this section, we first present the basic data model for network constrained moving objects and the corresponding location update policies, and then we analyze the uncertainty problem under this framework.

2.1 The Basic Data Model to Present Network Constrained Moving Objects

Let's first deal with the underlying transportation networks. For simplicity, we model the whole transportation network as one single graph (for a more complete model, see [3]), and we will use "transportation network" and "transportation graph" interchangeably throughout this paper.

Definition 1 (Transportation Graph). A transportation graph G is defined as a pair:

$$G = (R, J)$$

where R is a set of routes and J is a set of junctions.

Definition 2 (Route). A route of graph G, denote by r, is defined as follows:

$$r = (rid, route, len, fdr)$$

where rid is the identifier of r, $route$ is a polyline which describes the geometry of r, len is the length of r, and $fdr \in \{0, 1, 2\}$ is the direction of the traffic flow allowed in r.

The polyline $route$ in the above definition can be defined as a series of points in the Euclidean space. For simplicity, we suppose that the graph is spatially embedded in the $X \times Y$ plane so that the polyline can be presented as a series of points of the (x, y) form. The polyline is considered directed, which enables us to speak of the beginning point (or 0-end) and the end point (or 1-end) of the route.

The direction of traffic flow allowed in a route can have three possibilities, which are specified by fdr, whose value can assume 0, 1, 2, which corresponds to "from 0-end to 1-end", "from 1-end to 0-end", and "both directions allowed" respectively.

Definition 3 (Junction). A junction of graph G, denoted by j, is defined as follows:

$$j = (jid, loc, ((rid_i, pos_i))_{i=1}^{n}, m)$$

where jid is the identifier of j, loc is the location of j which can be represented by a point value in the X×Y plane, m is the connectivity matrix [3] of j and $((rid_i, pos_i))_{i=1}^{n}$ describes the routes connected by j, where rid_i is the identifier of the ith route and $pos_i \in [0, 1]$ describes the position of the junction in the ith route. We suppose that the total length of any route is 1, and then every location in the route can be presented by a real number $p \in [0, 1]$.

Based on the above definitions for transportation networks, we can then define some useful data types – graph point, graph route section, and graph region, which form the basis for the modeling and querying of moving objects.

Let $junct(jid)$, $route(rid)$ be functions which return the junction and the route corresponding to the specified identifiers respectively. Let $juncts(G)$ and $routes(G)$ be the set of junctions and the set of routes of G respectively.

Definition 4 (Graph Point). A graph point is a point residing in the graph. The set of graph points of graph G, denoted by GP, is defined as follows:

$GP = \{(rid, pos) \mid route(rid) \in routes(G), \text{ and } pos \in [0, 1]\}$

In this definition, we only cite the route information since the locations of junctions can be represented by the locations in routes.

Definition 5 (Graph Route Section). A graph route section is a part of a route. The set of graph route sections of graph G, denoted by GRS, can be defined as follows:

$GRS = \{(rid, S) \mid route(rid) \in routes(G), \text{ and } S \subseteq [0, 1]\}$.

Definition 6 (Graph Region). A graph region is defined as a set of junctions and a set of route sections. The set of graph regions of graph G, denoted by GR, is defined as follows:

$GR = \{(V, W) \mid V \subseteq GJ, W \subseteq GRS\}$

where $GJ = \{jid \mid junct(jid) \in juncts(G)\}$.

Based on the above definitions of network constrained data types, we can then model network constrained moving objects. Since in most cases a moving object can be viewed as a point, moving objects are modeled as moving graph points. A moving graph point, mgp, is a function from time to graph point, that is:

$mgp = f: T \to GP$

where T is the domain of time, and GP is the domain of graph point of the graph.

In implementation, this function should be translated into a discrete representation. That is, a moving graph point is expressed as a set of moving units, and each moving unit describes one single moving pattern of the moving object for a certain period of time.

Definition 7 (Moving Graph Point). A moving graph point, *mgp*, is defined as a sequence:

$$mgp = (t_i, (rid_i, pos_i), vm_i)_{i=1}^{n}$$

where t_i is a time instant, $(rid_i, pos_i) = gp_i$ is a graph point describing the location of the moving object at time t_i, and vm_i is the speed measure of the moving object at time t_i. We call $(t_i, (rid_i, pos_i), vm_i) = \mu_i$ the *i*th "moving unit" of *mgp*. For a running moving object, its last moving unit, μ_n, contains predicted information so that it is called "active moving unit", which contains key information for location update algorithms (see Subsection 2.2).

The speed measure *vm* is a real number value. Its abstract value is equal to the speed of the moving object, while its sign (either positive or negative) depends on the direction of the moving object. If the moving object is moving from 0-end towards 1-end, then the sign is positive. Otherwise, if it is moving from 1-end to 0-end, the sign is negative.

For a valid moving graph point value, the following conditions should be met:
(1) $\forall i \in \{1, \ldots n\text{-}1\}$ $(rid_i = rid_{i+1}) - (gp_{i+1}$ geographically coincides with a junction which connects gp_i and gp_{i+1});
(2) $\forall i \in \{1, \ldots n\text{-}1\}$ viable(gp_i, gp_{i+1});
(3) $\forall i \in \{1, \ldots n\text{-}1\}$ $t_i < t_{i+1}$, and the moving object is assumed to move at even speed between t_i and t_{i+1}.

In the above definition, viable(gp_i, gp_{i+1}) means that through route(rid_i) or the junction which connects gp_i and gp_{i+1}, moving objects can transfer from gp_i to gp_{i+1}.

The main benefit of modeling moving objects on networks is that inside a certain route, the movement of the moving object is reduced to 1-demensional so that the index structures, the location update policies, and the related uncertainty management issues can be simplified.

2.2 The Location Update Policy for Network Constrained Moving Objects

In Definition 7, we assume that between two consecutive moving units, the moving object moves at even speed so that the position of the moving object at any time instant is a precise graph point. However, this is only an ideal situation. In real-world MOD applications, moving units are generated by location updates. If every speed change corresponds to a location update, the communication and computation cost can be too much expensive. To balance precision and communication costs, the system typically uses some predefined threshold to trigger location updates [14] so that the moving object between two consecutive location updates only moves at roughly even speed, which yields uncertainty (see Subsection 2.3).

In the network constrained MOD system, we suppose that every moving object is equipped with a portable computing platform and a GPS. The GPS enables the moving object to measure its current position in the (x, y) form (suppose that the MOD application is based on X×Y plane). With the support of some algorithms, the computing platform of the moving object can transform this location information to the (*rid*, *pos*) form, where *rid* is the identifier of the route where the moving object is located, and pos ∈ [0, 1] is the location of the moving object inside the route.

When a moving object *mo* initiates its journey in the MOD system, it needs to send to the server a location update message of the following form:

$msgu = (mid, t_u, (rid_u, pos_u), vm_u)$

where *mid* is the identifier of *mo*, t_u is the time when the location update is triggered, $(rid_u, pos_u) = gp_u$ is the location (expressed as a graph point) of *mo* at time t_u, and vm_u is the speed measure of *mo* at time t_u.

Whenever receiving a location update message, the server will simply extract the information contained in it and generate a corresponding moving unit. This moving unit is then appended to the moving graph point value of the moving object as the active moving unit. The moving object will also keep the active moving unit for location update purposes.

During its move, the moving object will compare its actual location with the computed location derived from the active moving unit. Whenever certain conditions are met, a location update will be triggered. In the network constrained MOD system, there are three kinds of location updates – the ID-Triggered Locations Update (ITLU), the Distance-Threshold-Triggered Location Update (DTTLU), and the Speed-Threshold-Triggered Location Update (STTLU), as shown in Figure 1.

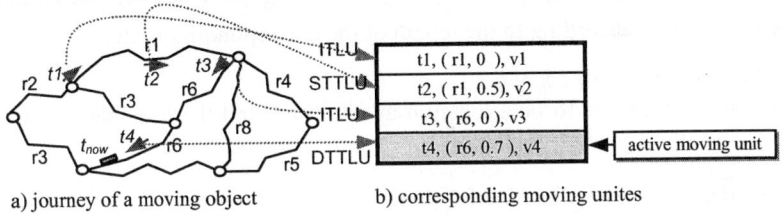

a) journey of a moving object   b) corresponding moving unites

Fig. 1. An example moving graph point value

(1) ITLU. Whenever the moving object changes from one route to another via a junction, a location update will be triggered, and a new moving unit corresponding to the entering point to the new route will be appended to the corresponding moving graph point value of the moving object.

(2) DTTLU. A location update will be triggered whenever the difference between the computed position derived from the active moving unit and the actual position measured by the milemeter exceed a certain predefined distance threshold ⑤. The computed location of the moving object is as follows (suppose the active moving unit is $(t_n, (rid_n, pos_n), vm_n)$):

$pos_{now} = pos_n + vm_n \times (t_{now} - t_n)$

(3) STTLU. Whenever the difference between the current speed of the moving object and the speed recorded in the active moving unit exceeds a certain predefined speed threshold ψ, a location update will be triggered.

2.3 Computing the Locations of Moving Objects with Uncertainty Considered

As stated in Subsection 2.2, since inside a moving unit, a moving object moves only roughly at even speed, its location is no longer a precise graph point at any time instant. Actually, its position other than the location update times becomes uncertain, and we can only describe its position by the concept of "possible location". In this subsection, we discuss how the possible location of the moving object at any given time instant can be computed through its moving unit and the thresholds predefined in the system.

We suppose that the corresponding moving units of an active moving object, mo, is as follows:

$$mgp = ((t_i, (rid_i, pos_i), vm_i))_{i=1}^{n}$$

Let $\mu_i = (t_i, (rid_i, pos_i), vm_i)$ ($1 \leq i \leq n$) be the ith moving unit of the moving object, and $gp_i = (rid_i, pos_i)$ be the location of the moving object at time t_i. For the sake of simplicity, we assume that the speed measure vm_i is positive, which means that the moving object is moving from 0-end towards 1-end along route(rid_i). The methodology can be easily adapted to the situation when the speed measure is negative.

Let $v_{max}^i = vm_i + \psi$ and $v_{min}^i = vm_i - \psi$, where ψ is the speed threshold. In the following discussion, we suppose that ξ, v_{min}^i, and v_{max}^i have already been transformed to the [0, 1] scope according to the length of the corresponding route.

Case 1. $\exists i \in \{1, ..., n\} : t_q = t_i$

In this case, t_q happens to be a location update time, and the possible location of the moving object is a precise graph point $gp_q = (gid_i, rid_i, pos_i)$.

Case 2. $\exists i \in \{1, ..., n-1\} : t_i < t_q < t_{i+1}$

If $rid_i = rid_{i+1}$, we can be assured that the moving object is on route(rid_i) at time t_q. Suppose its position in route(rid_i) is $p_q \in [0, 1]$. p_q satisfies the following conditions:

1) $pos_q^* - \xi \leq p_q \leq pos_q^* + \xi$, where $pos_q^* = pos_i + vm_i \times (t_q - t_i)$. Otherwise there would be a DTTLU between t_i and t_{i+1};

2) $pos_i + v_{min}^i \times (t_q - t_i) \leq p_q \leq pos_i + v_{max}^i \times (t_q - t_i)$. Otherwise there would be an STTLU between t_i and t_{i+1};

3) $pos_{i+1} - v_{max}^i \times (t_{i+1} - t_q) \leq p_q \leq pos_{i+1} - v_{min}^i \times (t_{i+1} - t_q)$. Otherwise, the moving object would not be able to arrive at gp_{i+1} in time without triggering an STTLU.

Therefore, the possible location of the moving object at time t_q is a graph route section $grs_q = (gid_n, rid_n, [p_{qmin}, p_{qmax}])$, where p_{qmin}, p_{qmax} can be computed in the following way:

$$p_{qmin} = \max(0, pos_q^* - \xi, pos_i + v_{min}^i \times (t_q - t_i), pos_{i+1} - v_{max}^i \times (t_{i+1} - t_q))$$

$$p_{qmax} = \min(1, pos_q^* + \xi, pos_i + v_{max}^i \times (t_q - t_i), pos_{i+1} - v_{min}^i \times (t_{i+1} - t_q))$$

where $pos_q^* = pos_i + vm_i \times (t_q - t_i)$.

If $rid_i \neq rid_{i+1}$, then we know that μ_{i+1} is generated by an ITLU, and gp_{i+1} geographically coincides with a junction. In this case, before proceeding with the above procedure, we need first to transform gp_{i+1} to the corresponding graph point in route(rid_i).

Case 3. $t_n < t_q \leq t_{now}$
In this case, we know that the moving object is still on route(rid_n), and its location in route(rid_n) at time t_q, denoted by p_q ($p_q \in [0,1]$), satisfies the following conditions:

1) $pos_q^{\diamond} - \xi \leq p_q \leq pos_q^{\diamond} + \xi$, where $pos_q^{\diamond} = pos_n + vm_n \times (t_q - t_n)$. Otherwise there would be a DTTLU triggered after t_n;

2) $pos_n + v_{min}^n \times (t_q - t_n) \leq p_q \leq pos_n + v_{max}^n \times (t_q - t_n)$. Otherwise there would be a STTLU triggered after t_n;

Therefore, the possible location of the moving object at time t_q is a graph route section $grs_q = (gid_n, rid_n, [p_{qmin}, p_{qmax}])$, where p_{qmin}, p_{qmax} can be computed as follows:

$$p_{qmin} = \max(0, pos_q^{\diamond} - \xi, pos_n + v_{min}^n \times (t_q - t_n))$$

$$p_{qmax} = \min(1, pos_q^{\diamond} + \xi, pos_n + v_{max}^n \times (t_q - t_n)),$$

where $pos_q^{\diamond} = pos_n + vm_n \times (t_q - t_n)$.

As described above, the possible location of the moving object is a moving graph route section, as shown in Figure 2 (for simplicity, we only depict the situation when the moving objects is moving inside one route. For the whole trajectory covering multiple routes, see Figure 4).

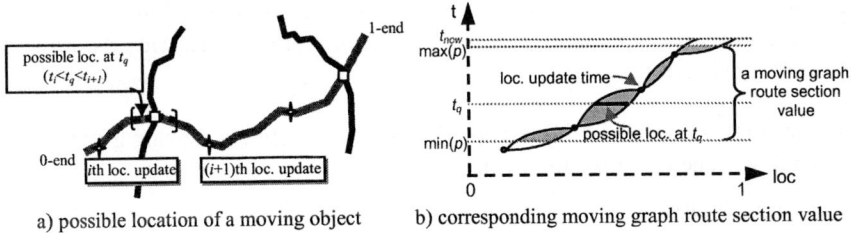

a) possible location of a moving object

b) corresponding moving graph route section value

Fig. 2. Possible location of a moving object

As illustrated in Figure 2, when uncertainty is considered, the possible location of the moving object at any time instant can be computed, which is a graph route section. This is a main advantage compared with the model of moving objects on free X%Y plane, where the possible location of a moving object is a region. To generalize the concept of moving graph route section for the design of operators, we define it as follows.

Definition 8 (Moving Graph Route Section). A moving graph route section, $mgrs$, is defined as the following form:

$$mgrs = ((t_i, (rid_i, pos_i), vm_i)_{i=1}^n, p)$$

where $(t_i, (rid_i, pos_i), vm_i)_{i=1}^{n}$ includes all the moving units of the moving object generated by location updates, and p is a period value which is composed of a set of disjoint time intervals. Figure 2(b) illustrates an example moving graph route section value (the shaded part).

For a valid moving graph route section value, the following conditions should be met (suppose $gp_i = (rid_i, pos_i)$):

(1) $\forall i \in \{1, \ldots n-1\}$ $(rid_i = rid_{i+1}) - (gp_{i+1}$ geographically coincides with a junction which connects gp_i and gp_{i+1});
(2) $\forall i \in \{1, \ldots n-1\}$ viable(gp_i, gp_{i+1});
(3) $t_1 \le \min(p) < \max(p) \le t_{now}$ (if the moving object is still active in the system)
  $t_1 \le \min(p) < \max(p) \le t_n$ (if the moving object has finished its trip)

3 Multiple Granularities in Uncertainty Management

By adjusting the distance threshold ξ and the speed threshold ψ, the framework presented in Section 2 can support variable precisions in presenting the locations of moving objects. However, sometimes this is still "too precise". In a lot of cases, much lower precisions in presenting the locations of moving objects, for instance, "from 8:00 to 10:00, I was traveling in the city center; after that until 13:00 I was visiting the museum area; and from 13:00 to 15:00 I was in the university area" is quite acceptable.

To better support variable precisions in presenting the locations of moving objects, we define a new data type, discretely moving graph region, to describe the possible locations of moving objects.

Definition 9 (Discretely Moving Graph Region). A discretely moving graph region is defined as a sequence of the following form:

$$dmgr = ((t_i, gregion_i))_{i=1}^{n}$$

where t_i is a time instant, $gregion_i$ is a graph region value. For $\forall i \in \{1, \ldots n-1\}$, $t_i < t_{i+1}$, and the moving object is assumed to move inside $gregion_i$ between t_i and t_{i+1}. For simplicity, we also call $((t_i, gregion_i))$ $(1 \le i \le n)$ a "moving unit" of the moving object.

The locations of moving objects can be tracked in the following way. First, the whole transportation network is partitioned into a group of areas with each area to be a graph region. To support multiple granularities in uncertainty management, the system can have multiple partitions on the same traffic network, which form a hierarchical structure (as shown in Figure 3(a)). The graph regions are uniquely numbered, and both the server and the moving object need to keep the partition information. To avoid frequent location updates when moving objects are moving near the border between two partitions, these partition areas should overlap each other to some extent, as shown in Figure 3(b).

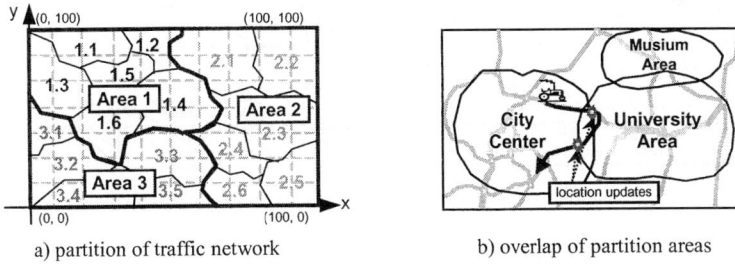

a) partition of traffic network b) overlap of partition areas

Fig. 3. Partition of the underlying traffic network

When a moving object starts its trip, it needs to send to the server its current region number. During its life time, whenever it crosses the border of the current region, a location update will be triggered. The location update message includes the time and the number of the new graph region where the moving object is located. When the server receives a location update message, it will simply generate a moving unit and append it to the discretely moving graph region value of the moving object. Under this framework, the possible location of a moving object at any given time instant t_q is a graph region. If $t_i \leq t_q < t_{i+1}$, then the possible location of the moving object is $gregion_i$. If $t_n \leq t_q < t_{now}$, then the possible location is $gregion_n$.

By selecting a suitable granularity, the moving object can control the communication and computation costs caused by location updates.

4 Taking Uncertainty into the Design of Operations

In [5], Güting *et al.* have defined a rich set of operations for network constrained moving objects and the related data types. Through some extension, these operations can be upgraded to support uncertainty. In this section, we do not aim to present a full design of operations with uncertainty involved. Instead, we only outline some general ideas behind the design.

First let's see the "trajectories" of moving objects. If a moving object is modeled directly in the Euclidean space, its trajectory is a curve (or a tube when uncertainty is considered) in the X×Y×T space [8, 13]. However, in network constrained moving objects databases, the trajectory of a moving object can have totally different forms, as shown in Figure 4.

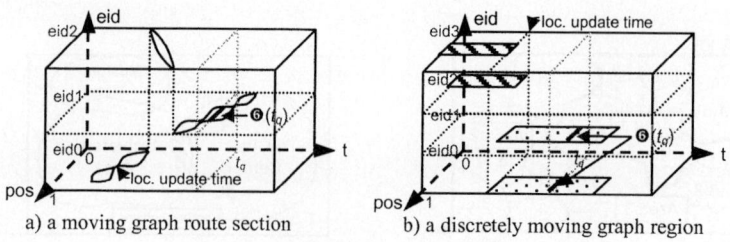

a) a moving graph route section

b) a discretely moving graph region

Fig. 4. "Trajectories" of moving objects

As illustrated in Figure 4, the possible location of a moving object at any given time instant t_q, denoted by $\omega(t_q)$, is the intersection of its trajectory and the plane corresponding to t_q (which is vertical to the t–axis). $\omega(t_q)$ can be either a graph route section (see Figure 4(a)), or a graph region (see Figure 4(b)).

Let $\partial\omega(t_q)$ be the set of points contained in $\omega(t_q)$. In designing an operation which involves the whole trajectory or part of the trajectory, say **inside**, we need to extend it to **inside_possibly** and **inside_definitely** with the following semantics:

inside_possibly$(\omega(t_q), A)$ $\Leftrightarrow$ $\exists p \in \partial\omega(t_q) :$ **inside**$(p, A) \Leftrightarrow$ **intersects**$(\omega(t_q), A)$
inside_definately$(\omega(t_q), B)$ $\Leftrightarrow$ $\forall p \in \partial\omega(t_q) :$ **inside**$(p, B) \Leftrightarrow$ **inside**$(\omega(t_q), B)$

Figure 5 illustrates the semantics of the extended **inside** operation.

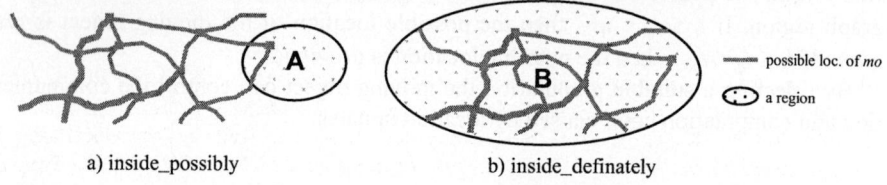

a) inside_possibly

b) inside_definately

Fig. 5. Semantics of **inside_possibly** and **inside_definately**

Following the strategy described above, we can extend other operations, such as **at**, **intersect**, **atperiod**, and **atinstant**, with uncertainty involved. For instance, the signature of the **atperiod** and **atinstant** operations can be extended as follows (_mgrs_, _dmgr_, _grs_, _gr_ are the data types corresponding to moving graph route section, discretely moving graph region, graph route section, and graph region respectively):

atperiod: _mgrs_ × _period_ → _mgrs_   **atinstant:** _mgrs_ × _instant_ → _grs_
           dmgr × _period_ → _dmgr_   _dmgr_ × _instant_ → _gregion_

5 Conclusion

One of the key research issues with moving objects databases (MOD) is the uncertainty management problem. In this paper, we have discussed how the uncertainty of network constrained moving objects can be reduced by using reasonable modeling methods and location update policies. Besides, we have presented a framework to support variable accuracies in presenting the locations of moving objects. The operation design issues with uncertainty involved have also been discussed.

The above mechanism is designed for implementation in the Secondo system [1]. We have designed a rich set of data types and operations for moving objects and the underlying transportation graphs [5, 2], which are under development as three algebra modules, spatial algebra, transportation graph algebra, and moving object algebra, in the Secondo system.

The future research includes the full design of the operations with uncertainty considered, the index structures for the uncertain trajectories of the network constrained moving objects, and the corresponding query processing techniques.

References

[1] Dieker S., Güting R.H. Plug and Play with Query Algebras: SECONDO. A Generic DBMS Development Environment. *Proc. of IDEAS 2000*, Yokohoma, Japan, 2000.
[2] Ding Z., Güting R.H. Modeling Temporally Variable Transportation Networks. *Proc. of DASFAA 2004*, Jeju Island, Korea, March 2004.
[3] Ding Z., Güting R.H. Managing Moving Objects on Dynamic Transportation Networks. *Proc. of SSDBM 2004*, Santorini, Greece, June 2004.
[4] Gowrisankar H., Nitte S. Reducing Uncertainty in Location Prediction of Moving Objects in Road Networks. *Proc. of GIScience 2002*, Colorado, 2002.
[5] Güting R.H., Almeida V.T., Ding Z. Modeling and Querying Moving Objects in Networks, Technical Report 308, Fernuniversität Hagen, 2004.
[6] Güting R.H., Böhlen M.H., Erwig M., Jensen C.S. et al. A Foundation for Representing and Querying Moving Objects. *ACM Transactions on Database Systems*, 25(1), 2000.
[7] Meratnia N., Kainz W. et al. Spatio-temporal Methods to Reduce Data Uncertainty in Restricted Movement on a Road Network, *Proc. of joint ISPRS, IGU and CIG Symp.on Geospatial theory, Processing and Applications*, Canada, 2002.
[8] Pfoser D., Jensen C.S. Capturing the Uncertainty of Moving Object Representations. *Proc. of SSD'99*, Hong Kong, China, July, 1999.
[9] Pfoser D., Tryfona N. Capturing Fuzziness and Uncertainty of Spatiotemporal Objects. *ADBIS 2001*, Vilnius, Lithuania, Sept. 2001
[10] Schlenoff C., Madhavan R., Balakirsky S. An Approach to Predicting the Location of Moving Objects during On-Road Navigation. *IJCAI 2003*, Mexico, August, 2003.
[11] Tøssebro E., Nygård M. Uncertainty in Spatiotemporal Databases, *Proc. 2nd Biennial Int. Conf. on Advances in Information Systems (ADVIS)*, Turkey, Oct., 2002.
[12] Trajcevski G., Wolfson O., Cao H., Lin H., Zhang F., Rishe N. Managing Uncertain Trajectories of Moving Objects with Domino. *ICEIS'02*, Spain, April, 2002
[13] Trajcevski G, Wolfson O, Chamberlain S, Zhang F. The Geometry of Uncertainty in Moving Objects Databases, *Proc. of EDBT'02*, Prague, Czech Republic, 2002.
[14] Wolfson O, Xu B, Chamberlain S, Jiang L. Moving Object Databases: Issues and Solutions. *Proc. of SSDBM'98*, Capri, Italy, July 1998.

Towards Context-Aware Data Management for Ambient Intelligence

Ling Feng, Peter M.G. Apers, and Willem Jonker

Dept. of Computer Science, University of Twente
PO Box 217, 7500 AE Enschede, The Netherlands
{ling,apers,jonker}@cs.utwente.nl

Abstract. *Ambient Intelligence* (AmI) is a vision of future Information Society, where people are surrounded by an electronic environment which is sensitive to their needs, personalized to their requirements, anticipatory of their behavior, and responsive to their presence. It emphasizes on greater user-friendliness, user-empowerment, and more effective service support, with an aim to make people's daily activities more convenient, thus improving the quality of human life. To make AmI real, effective data management support is indispensable. High-quality information must be available to any user, anytime, anywhere, and on any lightweight device. Beyond that, AmI also raises many new challenges related to context-awareness and natural user interaction, entailing us to re-think current database techniques.

The aim of this paper is to address the impact of AmI, particularly its *user-centric context-awareness* requirement on data management strategies and solutions. We first provide a multidimensional view of database access context. Taking diverse contextual information into account, we then present five context-aware data management strategies, using the most fundamental database operation - context-aware query request as a case in point. We execute the proposed strategies via a two-layered infrastructure, consisting of *public data manager*(s) and a *private data manager*. Detailed steps of processing a context-aware query are also described in the paper.

1 Introduction

Developments in *ubiquitous computing* and *ubiquitous communication*, together with *intelligent user friendly interfaces*, will eventually lead to a world in which computing functionality will be embedded in all kinds of objects, which are capable of recognizing and responding to individual human needs in a seamless, unobtrusive and often invisible way. An example is a hotel room that can adapt automatically to its customer's favorite room temperature and music choice. Such a vision of the future was coined **Ambient Intelligence** (AmI) by the European Community's Information Society Technology (IST) Program, whose aim is to sustain and extend the objectives of the eEurope 2002 Action Plan of bringing IST applications and services to everyone, every home, every school, and every business [4].

The aim of this paper is to address the impact of AmI, particularly its *user-centric context-awareness* requirement on data management strategies and solutions. Unlike conventional data management paradigms, ambient data management frees users from the constraint of stationary desktops, enabling data sharing and dissemination throughout the ambience of users. The database access in an AmI environment will not occur at a single location in a single context, as in desktop computing, but rather span a multitude of contexts covering the office, plane, meeting room, home, hotel, and so on.

Till now, decades of efforts have been made in improving *content*-based database access, due to the long-historical stationary database constraint. Nevertheless, AmI promotes us to go further for *context*-based data access. *"Get the report which I prepared last night before dinner in the hotel for this afternoon's meeting"* and *"Find restaurants nearby which I have not visited for half a year"* are two examples of such queries. Identifying data items by context has great potential, especially for the coming AmI era. On the one hand, it facilitates users to make the best of data through a flexible query-answering mechanism. On the other hand, it provides hints on how to process data requests in the most optimal way, as it carries a kind of semantics related to what, why, when, where, and how to use data sources. We believe that by context awareness, the interaction between data managers and users can be enriched than ever.

To deliver context-aware data management solutions raises a number of interesting and challenging questions as follows.
a) By context-awareness, can we make data managers more adaptable, responsive, personalized, dynamic, and anticipatory, as charted by AmI, than before?
b) Compared with traditional data management, what are the fundamental issues underlying context-aware data management?
c) To bring context-awareness feature into data management, how to acquire, categorize, and model contextual information?
d) How to exploit contexts to answer a user's data request?
e) What are context-aware data management strategies? How to support, manage, and execute these strategies?
f) How to provide context-aware data management supports to users? How to design a friendly and easy-to-use context-aware query language for users? How to effectively and efficiently communicate with users, given a handheld device which is much smaller than conventional desktop devices?

The purpose of this study is to propose potential ways to tackle the above problems. In Section 2, we review some closely related work. A multidimensional view of context is described in Section 3. Taking the diverse contexts into account, five context-aware data management strategies are proposed in Section 4. To execute these strategies, a two-layered infrastructure is given in Section 5. We overview different steps of processing a context-aware query in Section 6. We conclude the paper in Section 7.

2 Related Work

Context awareness is being actively studied in different fields. In this section, we review related work from a data management perspective. More comprehensive good survey on context-aware computing can be found in [3, 20].

Location-Dependent Query Processing. Location is an important kind of context. The concept of location constrained queries, i.e., queries whose answers depend on the locations of mobile users, was first introduced in [16]. [7, 26] presented a location-dependent query processing architecture. An approach of querying the nearest services in a multi-cell mobile environment was given in [32]. [27] designed a Moving Objects Spatial-Temporal data model for querying moving objects. [28, 17] investigated dynamic queries over mobile objects, where the locations of query issuers themselves are changing with the time.

Conceptual Modeling of Context Information. [23] proposed to model contextual information using *key-value* pairs. [13] structured contextual information based on entity-relationship paradigm. An object-oriented modeling technique was explored to model networked environments [12]. [11] represented sensed context using first-order predicate logic, composed into more complex sensed context expressions and associated with meta-propositional properties.

Context-Aware Computing Frameworks. Early attempts included Active Badge Infrastructure [24] and Stick-e Notes framework [2]. The *widget, server,* and *interpreter* components in the Context Toolkit separated context acquisition from the delivery and use of context [6]. A four-layered model, consisting of *sensors, cues, context profiles,* and *an application layer*, was further proposed [25]. [15] developed a Situated Computing Service to encapsulate context acquisition from applications. A middleware approach [14], as well as an agent-based architecture [21], was also presented for context-aware computing.

Context-Aware Applications. Most currently existing applications use identity, location, and time. The sensors used are mainly short range IR and RF signals, and GPS. These applications include Active Badge [30], office assistant ParcTab [31], shopping guide [1], In/Out registration board [22], Conference Assistant [6], tour-guide [6, 5], the reminder and memory aid system [10, 19].

3 Context Categorization, Acquisition, and Modeling

In this study, we are aiming at context-aware database support for AmI. The term *context* here refers to the situation under which user's database access happens. We categorize context into two kinds, namely, *user-centric context* and *environmental context*, as depicted in Figure 1. We view context as an n-dimensional space, constructed by n contextual attributes. Each dimension of the context is represented by one contextual attribute, describing one perspective of context. The domain of a contextual attribute can be either a scalar value, a string value, a set of scalar/string values, or an empty or a NULL value, depending on the application semantics. For example, the domain of the contextual attribute *trafficJam* can be a set of strings, specifying the names of sites where a traffic jam happens. When there is no traffic jam, *trafficJam*=∅.

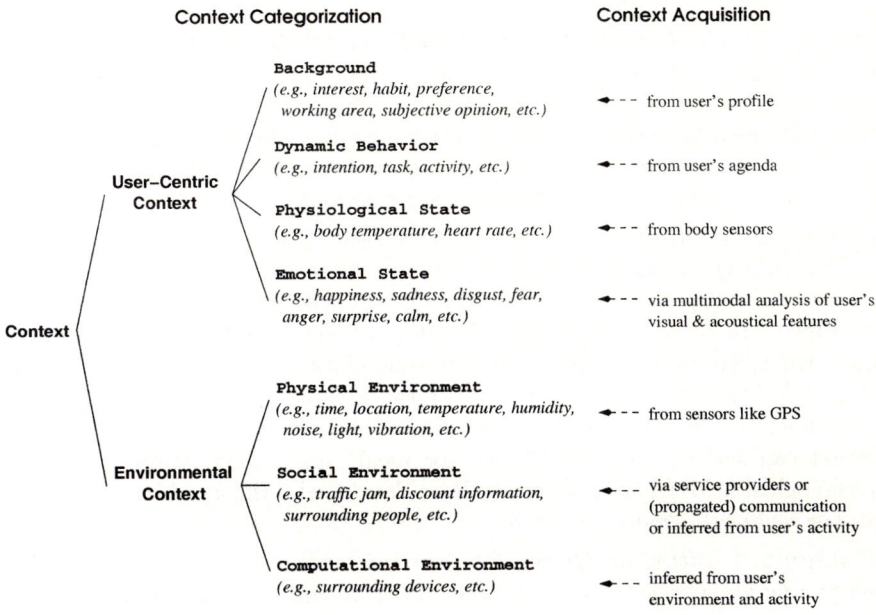

Fig. 1. Context categorization and acquisition

Formally, let $\{a_1, a_2, \ldots, a_n\}$ be a set of contextual attributes, whose domains are represented as $Dom(a_1)$, $Dom(a_2)$, ..., $Dom(a_n)$. An *n-dimensional context*, denoted as $[\![Context]\!]$, is the cartesian product $[\![Context]\!] : a_1 \times a_2 \times \ldots \times a_n$ of these contextual attributes. According to application requirements, abstract operators can be defined on compatible contextual attributes. To support operations conducted on different types of operands, we can define functions, whose parameters may involve contextual attributes as well. For instance, given the address (like the street, area code, etc.) of a restaurant, its distance from a current location, measured in a geographic pair of latitude and longitude, can be implemented via function of the form *float Distance(address: string, location: (float, float))* (Thanks to GIS systems, which enable the translation from an implicit reference (such as address) to explicit geographic reference (such as latitude and longitude) [9].) Throughout the paper, we call these privately-defined abstract operators/functions uniformly **contextual operators/functions**.

4 Context-Aware Data Management Strategies

Taking diverse contexts into account, we present the following five context-aware data management strategies.

Strategy 1: *Context as Present On-the-Spot Query Condition.* The highly dynamic, intelligent, and responsive ambient environments prompt users to ask ad hoc queries anytime and anywhere. Such on-the-spot queries usually involve the current context like time, location, traffic, etc. as the query referential points, like *"look for the earliest flight that I can catch"* and *"look for the fastest route to the airport, given the current traffic status."*.

Strategy 2: *Context as Past Recall-Based Query Condition/Target.* For human users, context under which data was accessed in the past is always easier to remember than detailed data content itself. For example, a user might feel difficult to recall the headline of a piece of news. By contrast, the context under which to read the news, such as the place where the news was read, the people present when it was read, or the activity being carried out at the same time, etc., can be easier to remember. In fact, such an observation that context can serve as a powerful cue for recall has a solid foundation in the psychological field, where researchers have developed a theory about *episodic* or *autobiographical memory* [29, 18, 8].

Strategy 3: *Context as Query Constraint.* From context, we can also infer background knowledge, which can be explored to constrain data requests.

I) <u>Understanding user's real query intention</u>. When a user issues a query, s/he usually has some purpose in mind. Database access should be directed by user's specific task. For example, s/he retrieves restaurant information in the city because s/he wants to invite the clients to lunch in a few minutes according to his/her agenda. In this case, only *open* restaurants are meaningful to the user.

II) <u>Personalizing user's data request</u>. The usefulness of data is often subjective to the context. For example, for safety reason, a user driving at *mid-night* does not like the database showing him/her the routes, which need to pass through a dark wood. Also, during the daytime *rush hours*, the database system should be considerate enough not to return the routes going through the city center, or the sites that have traffic jams at that moment.

III) <u>Tuning the level of query content</u>. The desired abstract level of data to be queried relies on the context as well. For example, a user with a big screen nearby would prefer to display a picture at high-resolution, while with only a tiny handheld PDA, a low-resolution requirement is enough. Also, aggregate/summarized data would be more appropriate than detailed one for small-sized displays.

Apart from assisting query formulation, another important use of context is to determine the manner regarding what, when, where, and how to pass the query output to the user.

Strategy 4: *Context as Criteria for Query Result Measurement.* Given the limitation of small devices, it would be convenient for users if the query answer could be sorted in such a way that the most potentially useful items shown in front. Such a sorting can be performed based on user's interests, obtained from the profile. For example, if the user likes oriental food, the restaurants serving asian meals can be displayed ahead of others.

Strategy 5: *Context as Guide to Query Result Delivery.* The output modality should also be adapted to user's current context. For instance, if the user is driving, it would be convenient to have a speech query output. However, if the user is talking with someone, postponing the delivery of query results by giving a vibration alert, or screen-displaying the query results will be more appropriate. The presentation of query results on a big screen would be welcomed for a group of people who are interested in the query answer.

5 Context-Aware Data Management Infrastructure

We execute the presented context-aware data management strategies via a two-layered architecture, consisting of *public data manager*(s) and a *private data manager*.

5.1 Public Data Manager vs. Private Data Manager

Public data managers can be of any kind of conventional database managers, which support users to access *public databases*, as long as these users have the appropriate rights. In contrast, a *private data manager* behaves like a personal assistant in satisfying user's information needs. It runs on user's private side, say PDA, knows, stores, and manages user's personal information like working area, agenda, profile, data access history, etc. within a *personal/private database*. While conventional public data managers aim essentially at *efficiency* of data management support; the private data manager targets at *usability* aspect by providing the most desirable information to its user in carrying out his/her daily activities. To deliver to the user the right information at the right time in the right way, the private data manager, however, must collaborate with one or more public data managers. As conventional public data managers have been extensively studied in the literature, here, we concentrate on the private data manager, and examine its roles in context-aware data management, particularly context-aware query processing throughout the rest of discussions.

5.2 Major Components of the Private Data Manager

Figure 2 shows the major components of the private data manager. They cooperate as follows.
1) The ***context manager*** defines and maintains the contextual space. It facilitates the use of context by real-time acquiring and instantiating contextual attributes from various external sources.
2) The ***profile manager*** is responsible for managing and supplying user's profile information, including user's interest, working area, habit, preference, etc.

3) The *agenda manager* manages user's daily agenda. Given a user's historical database access record, it evokes from the agenda the past associated activities and context for the data access. User's intention in accessing the database can also be predicted based on his/her near-future activities on the agenda.

4) User's database access histories are uniformly stored and managed by the *log manager*, which collaborates with the agenda manager for recalling the past context and providing support to the context-ware query coordinator.

5) The *database service communicator* serves as a bridge between the private data manager and external public data managers. Public data managers must register to it as database service providers in order to be used by the private user. The database service communicator deals with the heterogeneity of different public data managers, while providing to the private user an intermediate uniform view of data model and database schemas in use [1].

6) The *multi-modal interface* to external functions/services offers input and output modalities that adaptable to contexts. One such kind of functions is to transform textual output into an audio speech output, when a user is driving.

7) The *context-aware query coordinator* enforces and monitors the execution of five context-aware query strategies, presented in Section 4.

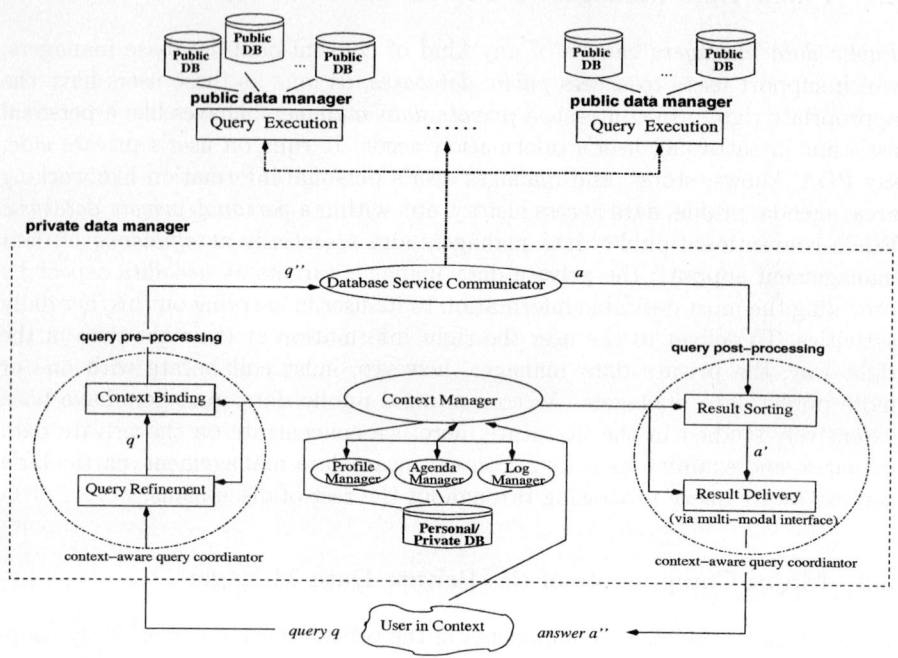

Fig. 2. Steps and components involved in context-aware query processing

---

[1] In this study, we assume a relational data model is used.

6 Context-Aware Query Processing Framework

A context-aware query is a query whose query answering depends not only on the database, but also on the context under which the query is issued. We can thus view a context-aware query as a parameterized query with two parameters - *database* and *context*, denoted as $CQ(db, \llbracket Context \rrbracket) \Longrightarrow A$. The same query, raised by different users, or by the same user under different contexts, may result in different answers. For example, a query on the database relation **Route** from city "A" to city "B" will return different answers, depending on different contexts. If the query is issued at *mid-night*, the query answer will preclude the route that bypasses an wood for safety reason; however, if the query is issued at *day-time* during the rush hours, the routes that avoid sites having traffic jams *at the moment* will be considered to be useful and thus returned. In this study, we explicate such users' assumptions implicitly behind queries through a set of privately-defined rules, associated with the relations like **Route**. We call these relations **context-sensitive database relations**. Note that, the rules defined here are highly personal, varying from user to user. They are managed and enforced at query time by the context manager at the private data manager's side.

In comparison, a traditional non-context-aware query answering depends only on the database, i.e., $NCQ(db) \Longrightarrow A$.

Given a context-aware query, we divide context-aware query processing into three phases, i.e., *query pre-processing, query execution,* and *query post-processing,* as shown in Figure 2. Except for the *query execution* by the public data manager(s), the rest is performed at the private data manager's side by the *context-aware query coordinator*. The query pre-processing phase proceeds in two steps, i.e., *query refinement* and *context binding*. Before *query execution* can begin, a user's query, which may incorporate context as query condition/target (Strategy 1 & 2), must go through a *query refinement* step whose task is to further constrain the query condition by means of different contextual information (Strategy 3). The *context binding* contacts the context manager to instantiate with exact values all the contextual attributes involved in the refined query, like the current traffic jam, the current time, etc. In this way, the request sent to the public data manager(s) via the database service communicator to execute contains no contextual attributes, and looks like any conventional database query acceptable by the public data manager(s). After the *query execution*, the query post-processing phase will sort the query answer based on user's context via the *result sorting* step (Strategy 4). The *multi-modal interface* component will then invoke external functions/services for the *result delivery* to the user (Strategy 5).

7 Conclusion

In response to *adaptability, dynamicity, personalization,* and *anticipation* demands from AmI, we present five *context-aware* data management strategies. A two-layered infrastructure is outlined to execute the proposed strategies. Different steps and components involved in processing a context-aware query, as well as the query language, are also addressed in the paper. In collaboration with other services like context acquisition component, we are currently building a prototype system which will serve as a user-friendly database frontend.

References

1. A. Asthana, M. Cravatts, and P. Krzyzanowski. An indoor wireless system for personalized shopping assistance. In *Proc. of the IEEE Workshop on Mobile Computing Systems and Applications*, pages 69–74, CA, USA, December 1994.
2. P. Brown, J. Bovey, and X. Chen. Context-aware applications: From the laboratory to the marketplace. *IEEE Personal Communications*, 4(5):58–64, 1997.
3. G. Chen and D. Kotz. A survey of context-aware mobile computing research. Technical Report TR2000-381, Dartmouth College, November 2000. http://www.cs.dartmouth.edu/~dfk/papers/chen:survey-tr.pdf.
4. European Commission. Scenarios for ambient intelligence in 2010. http://www.cordis.lu/ist/istag.htm, 2001.
5. N. Davies, K. Mitchell, K. Cheverst, and G. Blair. Developing a context sensitive tourist guide. Technical Report Technical Report, Computing Department, Lancaster University, 1998.
6. A. Dey, D. Salber, and G. Abowd. A conceptual framework and a toolkit for supporting the rapid prototyping of context-aware applications. *Human Computer Interaction*, 16(2-4):97–166, 2001.
7. M. Dunham and V. Kumar. Location dependent data and its management in mobile databases. In *Proc. of the 9th Intl. Conf. on Database and Expert Systems Applications*, pages 414–419, Vienna, Austria, August 1998.
8. M. Eldridge, P. Barnard, and D. Bekerian. Autobiographical memory and daily schemas at work. *Memory*, 2(1):51–74, March 1994.
9. ESRI. ESRI: GIS and mapping software, 2003. http://www.esri.com/library/gis/abtgis/giswrk.html.
10. F. Flynn, D. Pendlebury, C. Jones, M. Eldridge, and M. Lamming. The Satchel system architecture: Mobile access to documents and services. *Mobile Networks and Applications*, 5(4):243–258, 2000.
11. P. Gray and D. Salber. Modeling and using sensed context in the design of interactive applications. In *Proc. of the 8th IFIP Conf. on Engineering for Human-Computer Interaction*, pages 317–336, Toronto, Canada, May 2001.
12. A. Harter, A. Hopper, P. Steggles, A. Ward, and P. Webster. The anatomy of a context-aware application. In *Proc. of the 5th ACM/IEEE Intl. Conf. on Mobile Computing and Networking*, pages 59–68, Washington, USA, August 1999.
13. K. Henricksen, J. Indulska, and A. Rakotonirainy. Modeling context information in pervasive computing systems. In *Proc. of the 1st Intl. Conference on Pervasive*, pages 167–180, Zurich, Switzerland, August 2002.
14. J. Hong and J. Landay. An infrastructure approach to context-aware computing. *Human Computer Interaction*, 16(2-4):287–303, 2001.
15. R. Hull, P. Neaves, and J. Bedford-Roberts. Towards situated computing. In *Proc. of the 1st Intl. Symposium on Wearable Computers*, pages 146–153, Boston, USA, October 1997.

16. T. Imielinski and B. Badrinath. Querying in highly mobile distributed environments. In *Proc. of the 18th Intl. Conf. on Very Large Data Bases*, pages 41–52, Vancouver, Canada, 1992.
17. I. Lazaridis, K. Porkaew, and S. Mehrotra. Dynamic queries over mobile objects. In *Proc. of the 8th Intl. Conf. on Extending Database Technology*, pages 269–286, Prague, Czech Republic, March 2002.
18. Barsalou L.W. The content and organization of autobiographical memories. In Remembering reconsidered: Ecological and Traditional Approaches to the Study of Memory (U. Neisser and E. Winograd eds.), Cambridge University Press, 1988.
19. N. Marmasse and C. Schmandt. Location-aware information delivery with ComMotion. In *Proc. of the 2nd Intl. Symposium on Handheld and Ubiquitous Computing*, pages 157–171, UK, September 2000.
20. K. Mitchell. A survey of context-awareness. Technical Report, Lancaster University, UK, March 2002, http://www.comp.lancs.ac.uk/~km/papers/ContextAwarenessSurvey.pdf.
21. J. Riekki, J. Huhtinen, P. Ala-Siuru, P. Alahuhta, J. Kaartinen, and J. Röning. Genie of the net: Context-aware information management, 2000. http://www.pbol.org/projects/genie/~publications/infomanageme.pdf.
22. D. Salber, A. Dey, and G. Abowd. The context toolkit: Aiding the development of context-enabled applications. Technical Report Technical Report GIT-GVU-98-33, USA, 1998.
23. B. Schilit, M. Theimer, and B. Welch. Customizing mobile applications. In *Proc. of USENIX Mobile & location-Indepedent Computing Symposium*, pages 129–138, Cambridge, Massachusetts, August 1993.
24. W.N. Schilit. System architecture for context-aware mobile computing. PhD thesis, Columbia University, USA, MAY 1995.
25. A. Schmidt, K. Aidoo, A. Takaluoma, U. Tuomela, K. Laerhoven, and W. Van de Velde. Advanced interaction in context. In *Proc. of the 1st Intl. Symposium on Handheld and Ubiquitous Computing*, pages 89–101, Karlsruhe, Germany, September 1998.
26. A. Seydim, M. Dunham, and V. Kumar. An architecture for location dependent query processing. In *Proc. of the 12th Intl. Conf. on Database and Expert Systems Applications*, pages 549–555, Muich, Germany, September 2001.
27. A. Sistla, O. Wolfson, S. Chamberlain, and S. Dao. Modeling and querying moving objects. In *Proc. of the 12th IEEE Intl. Conf. on Data Engineering*, pages 422–432, Birmingham, UK, April 1997.
28. Z. Song and N. Roussopoulos. K-nearest neighbor search for moving query point. In *Proc. of the 7th Intl. Symposium on Advances in Spatial and Temporal Databases*, pages 79–96, USA, July 2001.
29. E. Tulving. *Elements of Episodic Memory*. Oxford University Press, 1983.
30. R. Want, A. Hopper, V. Falcao, and J. Gibbons. The active badge location system. *ACM Transactions on Information Systems*, 10(1):91–102, 1992.
31. R. Want, B. Schilit, N. Adams, R. Gold, K. Petersen, D. Goldberg, J. Ellis, and M. Weiser. An overview of the PARCTAB ubiquitous computing experiment. *IEEE Personal Communications*, 2(6):28–43, December 1995.
32. B. Zheng and D. Lee. Processing location-dependent queries in a multi-cell wireless environments. In *Proc. of the 2nd ACM Intl. Workshop on Data Engineering for Wireless and Mobile Access (MobiDE01)*, pages 54–65, CA, USA, May 2001.

TriM: Tri-Modal Data Communication in Mobile Ad-Hoc Networks*

Leslie D. Fife[1] and Le Gruenwald[2]

[1] Computer Science Department, Brigham Young University – Hawaii, Laie, HI 96762
ldfife@cs.byuh.edu
[2] School of Computer Science, University of Oklahoma, Norman, OK 73019
ggruenwald@ou.edu

Abstract. A Mobile Ad-Hoc Network (MANET) is a group of wireless, mobile, battery-powered clients and servers that autonomously form temporary networks. Three data communication modes can be provided in a MANET, data broadcast, data query, and peer-to-peer messaging. Currently, no MANET data communication protocol provides the ability to use all MANET data communication modes. The objective of this research is to develop a MANET data communication protocol, TriM (for Tri-Modal communication), capable of providing all three data communication methods. TriM was designed to accommodate node disconnection and reconnection through periodic synchronization. Each part of the protocol has minimum power consumption as a goal. Simulation showed TriM minimizes the average power consumption of servers and clients while accommodating node disconnection.

1 Introduction

A MANET is a collection of mobile, wireless and battery powered servers and clients [5]. The topology of a MANET changes frequently as nodes move. A MANET is a potential solution whenever a temporary network is needed and no fixed infrastructure exists. MANETs differ from traditional mobile networks. In traditional mobile networks the servers, and potentially some clients, are stationary and powered by a fixed power grid. The servers communicate with the mobile clients over a wireless link. A MANET provides the traditional wireless network capabilities of data push and data pull as well as allowing clients to communicate directly in peer-to-peer communication without the use of a server, unless necessary for routing [1]. Due to servers having a larger capacity than clients [5], we assume that servers contain the complete database management system (DBMS) and bear the responsibility for data broadcast and satisfying client queries.

Nodes (clients and servers) may not remain connected to the MANET throughout their life. To be connected to the network, a node must be able to hear the transmission of at least one other node on the network and have sufficient power to function.

---

* This material is based in part upon work supported by the National Science Foundation under grant No. IIS-0312746.

We assume a fixed transmission power level. Network nodes (clients and servers) may operate in any of the three modes that are designed to facilitate the reduction in power used [8]. These are: **transmit** – this mode uses the most power, allowing transmission and reception of messages, **receive** – this mode allows the processing of data and reception of transmissions, and **standby** – in this mode, the CPU does no processing, transmitting or receiving.

Traditional mobile network research must address the limitations of the wireless bandwidth as well as the mobility and battery power of clients. MANET must consider these issues for both clients and servers. This prevents the use of current traditional mobile network data communication protocols, which assume stationary servers with unlimited power.

The majority of research in MANET has centered on routing issues [1][7]. Over the past few years, interest in data communication has been increasing [5][16][17]. However, current MANET data communications protocols have provided only one or two modes of data communication. Unlike TriM, no current protocol provides the ability for a MANET to use all three modes of data communication.

The rest of this paper is organized as follows. Section 2 will present the current research in MANET data communication. In Section 3 TriM, a MANET data communication protocol allowing all three modes of data communication is proposed. Section 4 describes the scenarios simulated and the results of the simulations for the TriM protocol. Section 5 provides conclusions and outlines future work.

2   Current MANET Data Communication Research

The data communication research issues in MANET center around two areas. These issues are covered in detail in [3][4]. The first area concerns the limitations of the environment (wireless, limited bandwidth, battery powered, mobile) for both clients and servers. The second area concerns the three ways in which MANET data communication may take place. Within this area, concerns due to data push, data pull and peer-to-peer communications exist.

Some work in MANET data communication has been scenario specific. In the work of Jung [9], location dependent queries in urban areas are addressed. Tang [13] adapts MANET data broadcasting to power controlled wireless ad-hoc networks. In these networks, servers have the ability to broadcast at one of several discrete power levels. The work of Tseng [14] deals with the broadcast storm.

Wieselthier, et al, have been working on MANET data broadcast. Their approach is the construction of a minimum-energy tree rooted at the broadcast source [15][16]. Two algorithms, one for broadcast and one for multicast were described [15]. The algorithms were tested and showed that by utilizing broadcast in a mobile environment, energy savings can be achieved. However, the networks tested were small and node mobility was not addressed. The cost of building the tree is considered negligible by the authors [15]. However, it has been shown that tree-based protocols do poorly when there is node mobility [6] The problems of limited bandwidth, the need for tree maintenance, and node mobility also remain.

Two protocols to handle data push and data pull within the MANET were proposed by Gruenwald, et al. [5]. They use a global network where all servers in a region know the location and power of all other servers in the region and full replication of the database is assumed. Periodically, each server broadcasts its location and power level. This begins the broadcast cycle [5]. Data deadlines are used to determine which data requests to service. The protocols include a leader selection protocol. The leader coordinates the broadcast responsibilities of other servers in its region by determining which portion of the broadcast each server transmits. No server transmits the entire broadcast unless it is the only server in a region. Between broadcast transmissions, clients are permitted to query the servers [5]. These algorithms have a potentially large overhead as mobility may cause the leader selection protocol to run frequently. While selecting a leader, less popular items may starve or be broadcast too late [5]. In addition, servers with no clients still broadcast, wasting power.

The second protocol includes the use of a popularity factor (PF), as suggested by Datta [2]. The PF is a measure of the importance of a data item. The PF increases each time a request is made for a data item [5]. An additional factor, Resident Latency (RL) also affects the PF. If it has been too long, the need to broadcast the item may be gone. RL is system and scenario specific [5]. The PF decreases whenever request age exceeds the RL [5]. If a server has not received any requests for a certain number of broadcasts, it will sleep rather than broadcast to an empty audience [5]. Finally, to localize data delivery, the lead server assigns each server the amount of data to broadcast but not which items [5]. In addition to leader selection costs, calculation of the PF and comparison to the RL add to the overhead, further delaying data delivery.

3 TriM Data Communication Protocol

In the following subsections, the TriM data communication protocol is presented. The specific parameters used to control the protocol are not listed but are available in [4]. This paper describes the overall design of TriM. In Figure 1 we see an overview of TriM. This figure shows a single iteration. The protocol will cycle through these stages repeatedly. A single time through these stages is referred to as a service cycle (SC). Here we see the relationship of each data communication mode within the protocol. Prior to the first iteration of the SC, the network is initialized. At this time, all protocol parameters are set. Currently, these parameters are static.

Synchronization Stage	Data Push Stage	Data Pull Stage	Idle Stage
	Data Broadcast	Data Request Peer-to-Peer	

Fig. 1. TriM Data Communication Protocol

In two of the four stages, data communication can take place. These are the data push stage and the data pull stage. The synchronization stage allows servers/clients to synchronize and detect the other nodes in their immediate vicinity. The idle stage allows the setting of a period of time during which all nodes are inactive. This gives the network designer the ability to set the frequency of data communication within the network. By setting this parameter carefully, we can avoid too frequent repetition of broadcasts or the other energy expensive portions of data communication. The service cycle repeats until the network is taken out of service or all nodes fail.

3.1 Network Initialization and Control

There are four stages, synchronization, data push, data pull and idle, in TriM. The first three are active while the last one is inactive. Within each active stage there are tasks associated with the servers and tasks associated with the clients.

Network initialization is accomplished when deploying a MANET. The network designer determines the length of each of the network stages according to the needs of the network and the characteristics of that particular deployment. Network initialization involves a variety of parameters. Each node in the network (server and client) is initialized using the same parameter values. These values are static throughout the MANET deployment. The database maintained by the servers is assumed to be fully replicated. Each server and client independently monitors its location in the SC based on these common parameters and uses them for synchronization with other nodes.

3.2 TriM Synchronization Stage

The synchronization stage has two parts. The first part is restricted to the transmission of information by servers (LMHs). Servers transmit their unique ID and location. This information is necessary to perform peer-to-peer message routing and is used by clients (SMHs) during data query to select the nearest LMH to query. There are generally fewer LMHs and their individual presence is critical to the protocol. Sufficient time is allocated during LMH synchronization to allow all LMHs to transmit their information independently. Each LMH knows the number of LMHs that were deployed during network initialization. The unique IDs are numbered from 1 to n. Each LMH transmits its information in turn, waiting the appropriate period of time before transmitting its information. The importance of the LMH information to the protocol prohibits transmission in parallel. Collisions in the limited bandwidth of wireless networks could cause the loss of critical information from neighboring LMHs. The amount of time a LMH must wait is determined by the number of LMHs having smaller IDs and the time needed for it to transmit its ID and location.

The second stage is for transmission of information by clients (SMHs). Each SMH transmits their unique ID and location. To perform routing of peer-to-peer messages during the data pull stage, the location of each SMH is needed. However, the number of SMHs is potentially large and it may not be possible to reserve sufficient time for each SMH to transmit independently. SMHs transmit their information when the transmission channel is clear. SMH location information is updated when synchronization provides new information; otherwise the most recent data available is used.

The synchronization stage is important as it synchronizes all nodes in the MANET. By regularly synchronizing all nodes, each node will be in the same protocol stage at the same time. This prevents contention over the limited network bandwidth. This is especially important during data broadcast, which immediately follows synchronization. The results of synchronization also play a role in data query and peer-to-peer communication. The synchronization stage occurs once per SC. During synchronization, nodes can determine if they are currently disconnected from the network. If a node detects no other nodes during synchronization, it will sleep until the next service cycle.

3.3 TriM Data Push Stage

The second stage of the service cycle is the data push or broadcast stage. The data push stage occurs before data pull so that the maximum number of potential data needs can be served before a server becomes too weak to transmit data. Separating data push and data pull reduces the contention for the limited bandwidth. When the data needs of a client are satisfied by the broadcast, the need for data query is eliminated. This results in a power savings.

Servers – Data Push Stage. The autonomous and mobile nature of this self-organizing network suggests independent LMHs. This eliminates the need for and energy consumption of a leader selection protocol. The decision of whether to transmit a data broadcast is a local one, made by each server. The contents of the broadcast are also partially determined by each server. The data broadcast will be composed of both a pre-selected set of data items and a set of dynamically selected items. The pre-selected items are determined at MANET deployment by the network designer. These are data items that each client needs frequently. The fixed portion of the broadcast is the same for each LMH. The dynamic portion of the data broadcast will vary, depending on the unserved data queries of the SMHs within transmission range of each LMH during the previous service cycle.

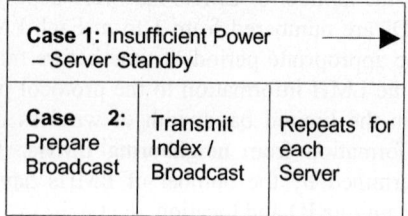
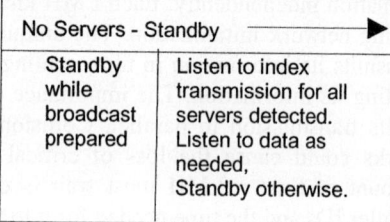

Fig. 2. TriM Data Push Stage – Server   **Fig. 3.** TriM Data Push Stage - Client

Figure 2 shows the broadcast portion of the service cycle for servers. Two possible situations are shown. In the first situation, the server has insufficient power to transmit an index and data broadcast. The LMH will go into standby mode. In the other case, the index and broadcast are transmitted in server ID order with each server being allocated a broadcast slot to prevent collision. As the size of the MANET broadcast is meant to be of minimal size, a single transmission of the index is preferred as transmission of the index takes time and consumes power. Servers do not listen to the broadcast transmissions of other servers. As several servers may broadcast in the same region, duplication of the broadcast static portion is a waste of power. To some extent, this cannot be prevented. A client may be in the transmission range of several or only one of the servers, depending on its geographic location.

Clients – Data Push Stage. Clients, like servers, have two potential situations during data push. If a client detects no servers during synchronization, it will be in standby. The client behavior is shown in Figure 3. Each SMH knows from the synchronization stage which LMHs will transmit in their region. The SMHs can then tune into receivable transmissions. The SMH will receive the static portion from any of the LMH transmissions it receives, but need only listen to the static portion once. A SMH will also check the index for any needed dynamic data items. It will use the index to determine when the data item will be transmitted. The index contains a list of all data items that will be transmitted as a part of the broadcast, and the order in which they will be transmitted. A SMH needs only listen to transmitted indices, the static data portion once and dynamic data items of interest. To listen to these items, the SMH must be in receive mode. The remainder of the time, the SMH may be in sleep mode.

3.4 TriM Data Pull Stage

During the data pull stage, both data query and peer-to-peer communication occur. During data query, servers respond to data requests from clients. A server may also be asked to do routing of peer-to-peer communications. In data query, clients request data from servers when the data they need was not in the recent broadcast. In peer-to-peer communication, clients communicate directly with other clients. Selection of peer-to-peer communication partners is determined by the application rather than TriM. If the client contacted is disconnected from the network, the message is dropped. During data pull, all nodes are aware that their transmission may not be heard as nodes detected during synchronization may now be out of transmission range. For this reason, clients will not retransmit the same query or peer message twice during the data pull stage in a single service cycle.

Servers – Data Pull Stage. The actions of servers during the data pull stage of the service cycle are shown in Figure 4. The servers have two primary tasks during the data pull stage. First they must respond to data queries. Any data query that is not serviced during this data pull stage is added to the dynamic data portion of the broadcast in the next service cycle. Second, servers must route client peer communications when requested.

Clients – Data Pull Stage. A SMH has only a few potential tasks during data pull as shown in Figure 5. The first situation is when a client needs to make a data request. The client will be in transmit mode while transmitting the data query and will be in receive mode as it awaits a response. Second, a client may need to communicate directly with another client. If the target client is detected during the most recent synchronization stage, it will transmit to the target directly. Otherwise, a routing request will be sent to a server. Finally, a client may receive a peer message. If this

4.1 Evaluation Criteria

- **Average Power Consumption.** The average power consumed by clients and the average power consumed by servers are calculated. For each client and server the power consumed per time unit is calculated by multiplying the percentage of time a node spends in each mode by the cost in power dissipation of each power mode.
- **Percentage of Coverage.** The effect of mobility that we measure is the percentage of SMHs out of range of all data broadcast transmissions. This demonstrates the effect of network mobility and implies the level of node disconnection in the network.
- **Broadcast Effectiveness.** The broadcast portion of the MANET is important, as data push is energy efficient. The measure for this portion of data communication will be broadcast effectiveness, which is the ratio of items of interest in a broadcast to the total number of items transmitted.
- **Query Efficiency.** The data pull section will rely on the measurement of query efficiency. This is a measure of the percentage of data queries that get served during an entire simulation.
- **Peer Efficiency.** Peer-to-peer communication is a time when clients can communicate directly with clients. Peer efficiency is measured as a percentage of the messages sent to peers by the number of messages received by peers.

4.2 Simulation Results

The initial scenario simulated was a comparison between the Leader Selection protocol [5] and TriM. The Leader Selection protocol is a soft real-time MANET data broadcast protocol. Data query, as described in this paper does not exist. Rather, data requests help inform the building of subsequent data broadcasts. Individual data items are not served interactively and no peer-to-peer communication occurs. This protocol is selected for comparison to TriM as it is one of the few MANET data communication algorithms that allow multiple data communication methods while providing sufficient data for comparison. This protocol provides 4 measures for evaluation, which are energy consumed by LMHs, energy consumed by SMHs, access time and broadcast hit ratio. A complete comparison cannot be made due to protocol differences. However a partial comparison is possible.

Energy consumption is measured for both LMHs and SMHs in both protocols. In Leader Selection, 6 variations of the protocol were tested, providing the range of values shown in Table 2. In addition, our Broadcast Effectiveness (BE) is similar to the Broadcast Hit Ratio (BHR) of [5] when the probability that dynamic items in the broadcast are of interest is 1. To make the comparison as accurate as possible, the simulation used as many of the parameters of [5] as possible, including number of SMHs and LMHs, CPU power, bandwidth, and transmission radius, size of simulation region and database size. Each LMH transmitted 20% of the database in each data broadcast. Table 2 shows the comparison between Leader Selection and TriM. Peer Efficiency and Query Efficiency were not calculated, as they have no corresponding value in [5].

Table 2. TriM Comparison to Leader Selection Protocol

	TriM	Leader Selection
SMH Avg Power Consumption (watts)	0.19	20-60
LMH Avg Power Consumption (watts)	18.99	15-24
Percent SMH Hearing Broadcast	95.9	Not applicable
Broadcast Effectiveness/Broadcast Hit Ratio	70.36 BE	60-100 BHR

The behavior of TriM was similar to the Leader Selection protocol. The major departure is in the SMH power consumption. This is due to a difference in how SMHs are used in the two protocols. In Leader Selection, SMHs drive the contents of the data broadcast. In TriM, the SMHs only request what was not received in a recent data broadcast. The primary advantage of TriM over Leader Selection is the addition of peer messaging and interactive data query, which are not available in Leader Selection. TriM compares favorably with Leader Selection.

The remainder of the data presented is for the 9 workloads described above. It should be noted that when a LMH must choose between routing peer messages and serving data queries, routing takes precedence. The rationale is that data queries can be added to the next data broadcast while peer messages are dropped at the end of data pull. Figure 6 shows the average client power consumption simulation results for all 9 variations of broadcast size and pull frequency. Figures 7, 8, 9, 10, and 11 show the average LMH power consumption and the percentage of SMHs hearing a broadcast, Broadcast Effectiveness, Query Effectiveness and Peer Effectiveness, respectively.

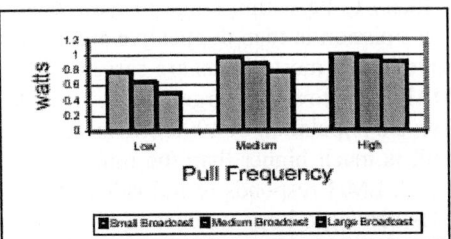

Fig. 6. Avg. Client Power Consumption

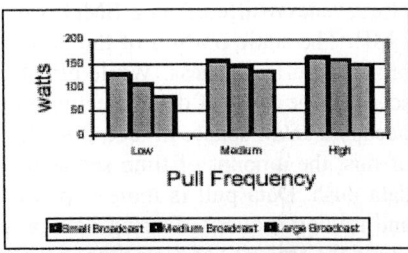

Fig. 7. Avg. Server Power Consumption

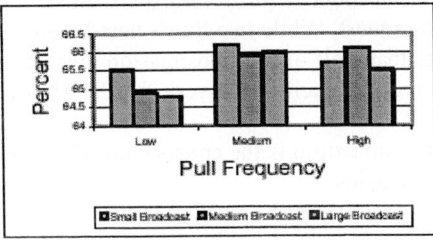

Fig. 8. % of SMHs hearing Data Broadcast

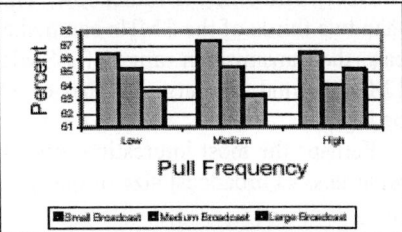

Fig. 9. Broadcast Effectiveness

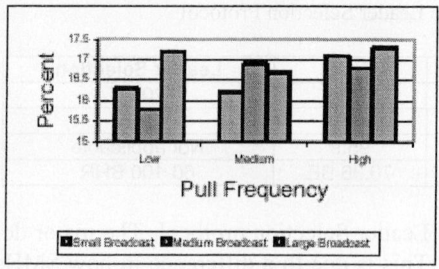
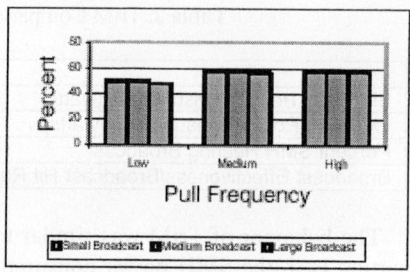

Fig. 10. Query Efficiency   **Fig. 11.** Peer Efficiency

To understand the results, it is important to know that the length of each stage of the service cycle changes from one workload to the next. For instance, as the maximum size of the data broadcast increases, so does the length of the data push stage. When the pull frequency increases, the data push stage is also increased in length. As the length of the service cycle increases because of a larger data broadcast, the average power consumption for LMH decreases as less time is spent transmitting. While each broadcast transmission is longer, the amount of time waiting for the other LMHs to transmit also increases. As the length of a service cycle increases due to a larger pull frequency, the average power consumption increases due to the increase of transmission by each LMH. A larger pull frequency requires a greater number of data queries to be processed per second.

The average power consumption for SMHs is nearly at the receive level. Nearly two thirds of the SMHs were within the reach of a LMH transmission. The broadcast effectiveness suffered as a SMH was more likely to be within range of more than 1 LMH. The static portion of the broadcast transmission is then duplicative and lowers broadcast effectiveness. While effectiveness is lower, most clients are served. In this scenario the level of disconnection in the MANET is low as a large number of nodes occupy a small space. In fact, the 6 LMHs serve a population of 1000 SMHs. Because of this, the amount of time spent in data pull is much higher than the time spent in data push. Data pull is more expensive as each LMH responds to individual queries and routing requests. During data pull, LMHs serving a large number of SMHs may spend the majority of their time in transmit mode.

Query efficiency is rather low. This can be accounted for in two ways. First, less than two thirds of the SMHs can make a data request. While two thirds heard a broadcast, the transmission range of a SMH is less than half of the transmission range of a LMH. Second, the large number of SMH served by each of the very few LMHs will be high.

Perhaps the most interesting result from the simulation is the consistency of results, regardless of broadcast size or query/peer frequencies.

5 Conclusions and Future Work

This paper presented a protocol that allows all three forms of MANET data communication, preserving power and accommodating limited bandwidth and mobility. The proposed protocol, TriM, compared favorably to the Leader Selection MANET data communication protocol while providing the additional capability of peer-to-peer messaging. In the scenarios simulated, data query and peer messaging were reasonably successful and TriM performed well in simulation.

The development of additional MANET scenarios is needed. Some MANET applications suggested in the literature have parameters different from those used. Included in future work is the development of appropriate mobility models. When the movement characteristics of nodes within the scenario are better parameterized, it may be found that current protocols need additional modification. In addition to mobility models, the effect of increased transmission ranges should be investigated. The ability to increase coverage through data relay and greater node cooperation should be studied. Currently, no standard method exists for the study and evaluation of MANET data communication protocols. The development and acceptance of a standard benchmark is recommended. Further work on the protocol itself is in order. Adding real-time capabilities, directional antennas, variable power transmissions, etc. provide a list of items that can be added to a new or modified protocol.

References

1. Das, S., Castañeda, R., and Yan, J., "Simulation-Based Performance Evaluation of Routing Protocols for Mobile Ad Hoc Networks," *Mobile Networks and Applications*, 5(3): pp. 179-189, 2000.
2. Datta, A., VanderMeer, D., Kim, J., Celik, A., and Kumar, V., "Adaptive Broadcast Protocols to Support Efficient and Energy Conserving Retrieval from Databases in Mobile Computing Environments." A TimeCenter Technical Report (University of Arizona), 1997.
3. Fife, L. and Gruenwald, L., "Research Issues for Data Communication in Mobile Ad-Hoc Network Database Systems," *ACM SIGMOD Record*, 32(2): June 2003.
4. Fife, L., "TriM: Tri-Modal Data Communication in Mobile Ad-Hoc Network Database Systems," Dissertation, University of Oklahoma, 2003.
5. Gruenwald, L., Javed, M., and Gu, M., "Energy-Efficient Data Broadcasting in Mobile Ad-Hoc Networks," In *Proc. International Database Engineering and Applications Symposium (IDEAS 2002)*, Edmonton, Canada, July 2002.
6. Guo, Y., Pinotti, M., and Das, S., "A New Hybrid Broadcast Scheduling Algorithm for Asymmetric Communication Systems," *ACM Mobile Computing and Communications Review*, 5(4): pp. 39-54, 2001.
7. Johansson, P., Larsson, L., Hedman, N., Mielczarek, B., and Degermark, M., "Scenario-based Performance Analysis of Routing Protocols for Mobile Ad-hoc Networks," In *Proc. 5th International Conference on Mobile Computing and Networking (MOBICOM'99)*, Seattle, Washington, USA, August 1999.
8. Jones, C., Sivalingam, K., Agrawal, P., and Chen, J., "A Survey of Energy Efficient Protocols for Wireless Networks," *Wireless Networks*, 7 pp. 343-358, 2001.
9. Jung, I., You, Y., Lee, J., and Kim, K. Broadcasting and Caching Policies for Location-Dependent Queries in Urban Environments. In *Proc. Second International Symposium on Mobile Commerce (WMC 2002)*, pp. 54-60, Atlanta, Georgia, USA, September, 2002.
10. Kunz, T. and Cheng, E. On-Demand Multicasting in Ad-Hoc Networks: Comparing AODV and ODMRP. In *Proc. 22nd International Conference on Distributed Computing Systems (ICDCS 2002)*, Vienna, Austria, July, 2002.

11. O'Reilly, J. and Lilegdon, W. Introduction to AweSim. In *Proc. 1999 Winter Simulation Conference*, pp. 196-200, 1999.
12. Pritsker, A. and O'Reilly, J. *Simulation with Visual SLAM and AweSim,* 2nd ed. New York: John Wiley & Sons, 1999.
13. Tang, C., Raghavendra, A., and Prasanna, V. Energy Efficient Adaptation of Multicast Protocols in Power Controlled Wireless Ad Hoc Networks. In *Proc. International Symposium on Parallel Architectures, Algorithms and Networks (ISPAN 2002)*, Manila, Phillipines, May, 2002.
14. Tseng, Y., Ni, S., Chen, Y., and Shue, J., "The Broadcast Storm Problem in a Mobile Ad Hoc Network," *Wireless Networks*, 8 pp. 153-167, 2002.
15. Wieselthier, J., Nguyen, G., and Ephremides, A., "Algorithms for Energy-Efficient Multicasting in Static Ad Hoc Wireless Networks," *Mobile Networks and Applications*, 6(4): pp. 251-263, 2001.
16. Wieselthier, J., Nguyen, G., and Ephremides, A. Resource-Limited Energy-Efficient Wireless Multicast of Session Traffic. In *Proc. 34th Hawaii International Conference on System Sciences (HICSS-34)*, Wailea, Maui, Hawaii, USA, January 2001.
17. Williams, B. and Camp, T., "Comparison of Broadcasting Techniques for Mobile Ad Hoc Networks," In *Proc. International Symposium on Mobile Ad Hoc Networking and Computing (MOBIHOC 2002)*, Lausanne, Switzerland, June 2002.

Efficient Rule Base Verification Using Binary Decision Diagrams

Christophe Mues[1,2] and Jan Vanthienen[1]

[1] K.U.Leuven, Naamsestraat 69, B-3000 Leuven, Belgium
{Christophe.Mues,Jan.Vanthienen}@econ.kuleuven.ac.be
[2] University of Southampton, School of Management
Southampton, SO17 1BJ, United Kingdom

Abstract. As their field of application has evolved and matured, the importance of verifying knowledge-based systems is now widely recognized. Nevertheless, some problems have remained. In this paper, we address the poor scalability to larger systems of the computation methods commonly applied to rule-chain anomaly checking. To tackle this problem, we introduce a novel anomaly checking method based on binary decision diagrams (BDDs), a technique emanating mainly from the hardware design community. In addition, we present empirical evidence of its computational efficiency, especially on rule bases with a deeper inference space.

1 Introduction

As knowledge-based systems (KBS) technology is being deployed in business settings where errors may have serious financial consequences or cause considerable damage, the importance of ensuring the quality and reliability of those systems is now widely recognized. As a result, verification and validation (V&V) have become key activities in the KBS development cycle. What's more, with the growing attention that the business rules paradigm is currently receiving from information systems practitioners, the potential scope of application for V&V techniques and tools developed in the KBS realm has broadened even more in recent years.

Especially during the late eighties and early nineties, the traditional view on the V&V of KBS was established. In fact, many of the techniques and tools commonly accepted today can be traced back to that period. Nevertheless, some problems have remained. In this paper, we will address one such outstanding issue: the scalability of the computation methods applied to rule-chain anomaly checking towards larger-scale systems.

Checking for logical anomalies in a given knowledge description (most often a rule base) is a widely applicable KBS verification method. In general, an *anomaly* involves a particular use or rather abuse of the applied formalism that may indicate a mistake on the part of the human expert or knowledge engineer – in other words, anomalies should be interpreted not as errors, but as symptoms of possible errors. According to a popular classification by Preece and Shinghal [6], four main classes of rule base anomalies can be distinguished:

- *redundancy*: a rule can be omitted without affecting the system's inferences;
- *conflict*: incompatible inferences can be made from valid initial data;
- *circularity*: an inference depends on itself;
- *deficiency*: no useful conclusions are produced for some valid input set.

To detect the most complex class of anomalies, i.e., those occurring over inference chains, arguably the predominant computation technique at present is rooted in de Kleer's assumption-based truth maintenance system (ATMS). Its core idea is to represent the input conditions under which an output is true as a set (*label*) of valid input sets (*environments*) [2, 7, 8]. In order to detect anomalies, the computed labels (which are essentially disjunctive normal form expressions) are to be checked against each other. In theory however, the required unfolding process can easily result in an exponential number of environments, with the exponent being in the depth of the reasoning induced by the rule base. In practice, the – albeit rather scarce – reports of case studies on real-world rule bases indeed tend to reveal a rapid increase in the number of generated environments for inference spaces of a larger scale. For example, in [2], the unfolding of knowledge bases of approximately 50, 150 and 370 rules in size took about 700, 4000 and 35000 environments, respectively. Hence, the actual deployment of many of the proposed verification techniques and tools has so far suffered from their limited scalability from toy example to practice [9].

In order to deal with this scalability issue, we will introduce a novel KBS anomaly detection technique, which uses *Binary Decision Diagrams* (BDDs) to encode and analyze KBS behavior. BDDs provide a canonical class of rooted, acyclic digraph representations of Boolean functions, accompanied by a set of graph algorithms implementing operations on these functions [1]. Until now, they have been studied and applied mainly by the hardware design community, where they contributed to a breakthrough in the scale of digital systems eligible for automatic optimization and verification. There are, on the other hand, few reported applications so far in the domain of artificial intelligence [3], while their use for rule anomaly checking has, to our knowledge, not been proposed before.

The organization of this paper is as follows. Firstly, ATMS-derived checks will be discussed in section 2. In section 3, the BDD representation will be explained. Subsequently, section 4 will show how the latter can be used to check a rule-based system for anomalies. Next, in section 5, the efficiency of this approach will be validated on a set of real-world test cases. Section 6 concludes the paper.

2 Rule Base Verification: ATMS-Based Methods and Tools

To detect the most general types of rule base anomalies, one must account for anomalies occurring over rule chains. Ginsberg [2] and Rousset [8] originally proposed a technique rooted in ATMS label calculus to do so. Their systems were named KB-Reducer and COVADIS, respectively. Further developments were implemented in Preece's COVER tool (e.g. [7]). The core idea of the approach is to unfold the rule base into a series of so-called *labels*, which explicitly state the dependencies between the inputs and outputs of the reasoning. The label of an output is basically a set of *environments* (the latter being defined as valid sets of input facts that may be supplied to the system), from (a superset of) each of which the output can be inferred. Each label is computed by forward or backward chaining through the rule base, substituting intermediate hypotheses in partial labels until only inputs remain. During this process, these labels are checked against each other for anomalies. A path of rules is associated with each environment for reporting purposes.

Let us illustrate this using the following example rule base for determining a person's academic status (for a more detailed explanation, we refer to [7]):

$$univMember(X) \land enrolled(X) \rightarrow student(X) \qquad (r1)$$
$$student(X) \land \neg hasDegree(X, bSc) \rightarrow undergraduate(X) \qquad (r2)$$
$$student(X) \land hasDegree(X, bSc) \rightarrow graduate(X) \qquad (r3)$$
$$enrolled(X) \land \neg hasDegree(X, bSc) \rightarrow undergraduate(X) \qquad (r4)$$
$$\neg student(X) \rightarrow staff(X) \qquad (r5)$$

Let $univMember(a)$, $enrolled(a)$, $hasDegree(a, bSc)$ be the possible inputs to the system. Accordingly, let $undergraduate(a)$, $graduate(a)$ and $staff(a)$ be (mutually incompatible) goal outputs.

In order to check this rule base, we build labels for its respective outputs. For example, $undergraduate(a)$ can be inferred via two different inference paths: either directly from rule r_4, resulting in a first environment, viz. $\{enrolled(a), \neg hasDegree(a, bSc)\}$, or using r_1 and r_2, that is, through the intermediate hypothesis $student(a)$. By substituting the literal $student(a)$ in the antecedent of r_2 by the antecedent of r_1, we are able to trace back the firing of the latter path to a certain combination of inputs, viz. $\{univMember(a), enrolled(a), \neg hasDegree(a, bSc)\}$. Both sets can then be joined as members of a tentative label for $undergraduate(a)$. At that point however, we observe that the second set is a superset of the first one, so it can as well be eliminated in the final label (cf. Table 1). Accordingly, the rule path (r_1, r_2) does not contribute to the reasoning of (r_4), and is thus found redundant.

Table 1. ATMS labels for the academic rule base

goal	label	rule paths
$undergraduate(a)$	$\{\{enrolled(a), \neg hasDegree(a, bSc)\}\} \lor \{\{univMember(a), enrolled(a), \neg hasDegree(a, bSc)\}\}$ $= \{\{enrolled(a), \neg hasDegree(a, bSc)\}\}$	(r_4), (r_1, r_2)
$graduate(a)$	$\{\{univMember(a), enrolled(a), hasDegree(a, bSc)\}\}$	(r_1, r_3)
$staff(a)$	$\{\{\neg univMember(a)\}, \{\neg enrolled(a)\}\}$	(r_1, r_5)

Apart from this redundancy, the rule base also contains a case of conflict, as the conjunction of the labels for $staff(a)$ and $undergraduate(a)$ includes the valid combination $\{enrolled(a), \neg hasDegree(a, bSc), \neg univMember(a)\}$.

The efficiency of such an approach clearly depends on the compactness of these generated label expressions. It is however well known that these may require exponential size, with the exponent being in the depth of the rule set (see, e.g., [4] for a detailed treatment on the issues of decidability and complexity). Therefore, we have investigated a potentially more time- and space-efficient representation for the functional behavior of a KBS, viz. binary decision diagrams.

3 Binary Decision Diagrams

A *binary decision diagram* (BDD) is a rooted, directed acyclic graph, with two sink nodes labelled by the constants 0 and 1, and whose internal nodes are of out-degree two. Each internal node v is labelled by a binary variable $var(v) = x_i$ ($i = 1, ..., n$). Its two outgoing edges are labelled by 0 and 1, and are usually depicted as dotted and solid lines, respectively. Let the two corresponding successor nodes of v be denoted by $low(v)$ and $high(v)$, respectively.

A BDD is *ordered* (OBDD), iff, on all paths through the graph, the variables respect a given linear order $x_1 \prec x_2 \prec ... \prec x_n$; i.e., for each edge leading from a node labelled by x_i to a node labelled by x_j, it holds that $x_i \prec x_j$.

An OBDD is meant to represent an n-variable Boolean function, $\{0,1\}^n \to \{0,1\}$. For a given assignment to the variables, the function value is determined by tracing a path from the root to a sink, thereby following the edges indicated by the values assigned to the variables. The label of the sink node specifies the function value assigned for that input case. Fig. 1(a) displays an example of an OBDD for a three-variable function given by the Boolean formula $(x_1 + x_2) \cdot x_3$, with respect to the variable order $x_1 \prec x_2 \prec x_3$.

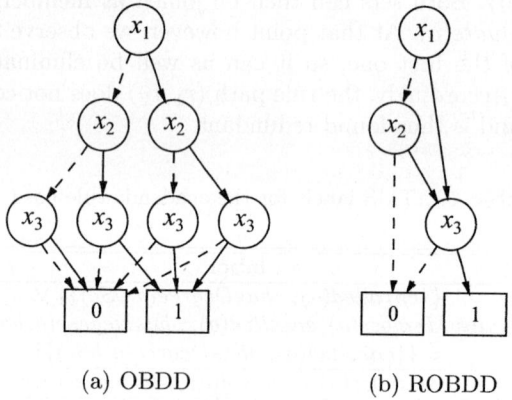

(a) OBDD (b) ROBDD

Fig. 1. BDD examples

Up to here, OBDDs are not yet uniquely determined for each function. However, by further restricting the representation, a canonical form of BDDs is obtained, namely *reduced* OBDDs (ROBDD). An OBDD is said to be reduced, iff it does not contain a node v whose successor nodes are identical (i.e., $low(v) = high(v)$), and no two distinct nodes u, v exist such that the subgraphs rooted in u and v are isomorphic, i.e., for which: $var(u) = var(v)$, $low(u) = low(v)$, and $high(u) = high(v)$. In Fig. 1(b), the ROBDD representation is depicted that can be obtained from Fig. 1(a). For a given variable ordering, the ROBDD representation of any function is uniquely determined (up to isomorphism), so that several properties (e.g., functional equivalence, constant functions, etc.) become easily testable. Conceptually, a reduced diagram can be interpreted as the result of the repeated application of two types of transformations: one reduction rule is to bypass and delete redundant nodes (*elimination rule*), the other is to share isomorphic subgraphs (*merging rule*). Note that, from here on, we will use the term 'BDD' to denote ROBDDs in particular.

When using BDDs to represent a (set of) function(s), some total ordering of the input variables must be selected. Since the size of a BDD is very sensitive to this choice, finding a suitable ordering is critical: inability to do so will in general lead to unacceptable running times or even memory overflow. Several exact minimization algorithms have been proposed, but, considering that finding an optimal order is an NP-hard problem, they are often too costly for larger problem instances. Hence, heuristic approaches (selecting some ordering based on available problem data) or local search techniques (which aim at improving a given variable order, e.g., by moving variables up or down the graph) have been widely investigated as well.

A number of operations on Boolean functions can be implemented as graph algorithms applied to their corresponding BDDs. For example, binary operations such as the Boolean sum and product can be implemented by the same general procedure, APPLY, which takes as arguments two BDDs representing functions f and g, and a binary operator op, and which produces the BDD representing the function f op g. It operates by traversing the argument graphs in a depth-first manner, returning a node of the result graph at every recursive call. Apart from APPLY, other typical operations include: taking the complement of a function (COMPLEMENT); the restriction of a certain variable to 0 or 1 (RESTRICT); the composition operation, where a function is substituted for a variable of another function (COMPOSE); finding a satisfying input assignment for the represented function (SATISFY_ONE). Importantly, the devised algorithms are such that, during the computations, the size of the BDD under construction remains bounded, as a reduced form is produced directly, not in a separate step. In fact, all operations listed above have time and space complexities that are at most polynomial in the sizes of their operand graphs.

Over the years, several highly efficient BDD packages have been implemented, which provide interfaces for the manipulation of BDDs. In our experiments (cf. infra, section 5), we have applied David Long's package, developed at Carnegie Mellon University (http://www-2.cs.cmu.edu/~modelcheck/bdd.html).

4 Rule Base Verification Using Binary Decision Diagrams

In order to apply BDDs to the problem of checking a rule-based system for anomalies, what we need to do, is:

- encode its input space into binary form;
- traverse the rule base, thereby constructing BDDs (instead of ATMS labels) that describe the input/output dependencies of the system;
- check the resulting BDD labels against each other, and report anomalies.

Revisiting the academic rule base, we can, e.g., represent its input space by a three-bit encoding, letting x_1, x_2, x_3 denote the presence (value 1) or absence (value 0) of the inputs $univMember(a)$, $enrolled(a)$ and $hasDegree(a, bSc)$, respectively. We can then traverse the inference space, either by forward or backward chaining through the rule base, and, using the selected encoding scheme, compute BDD labels for every hypothesis. For any rule instance in the inference space, a BDD, referred to as the rule label, is constructed using the BDD labels of the literals in its antecedent, and the APPLY or COMPOSE operation (cf. section 3). The label of the corresponding hypothesis is obtained by computing the logical sum (again by means of the APPLY operation) of the rule labels of all rule instances having that hypothesis as a consequent. If a backward strategy is applied, the required subgoal labels of the rule's antecedent literals are recursively constructed using the same method; this process stops at any input literal, whose (trivial) label derives its BDD from the agreed input encoding. In contrast, a forward strategy starts at the other end of the inference space, computing rule labels that can be readily built from inputs solely. Then, it typically advances through the rule base on a level-by-level basis, making sure that the labels of all subgoals whereupon the computation of a new rule label depends, are completed beforehand. For the example rule base, this process results in the BDD labels depicted in Fig. 2.

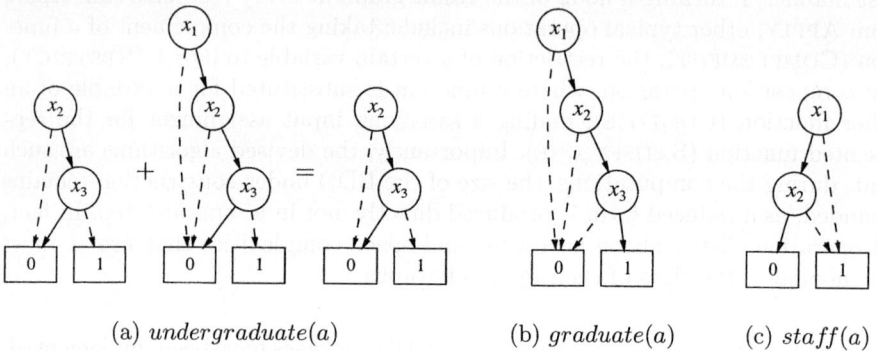

(a) $undergraduate(a)$ (b) $graduate(a)$ (c) $staff(a)$

Fig. 2. BDD labels for the academic rule base

During and after the BDD label computations, various checks can be applied to detect anomalies; only now, we are using BDDs, not ATMS labels, to perform these analyses. For example, checking for the general case of redundant rules again involves a test for label containment, which can be implemented by applying the logical implication operation to two argument BDDs (e.g., the labels for rules r_2 and r_4) and verifying whether the result reduces to the single-node BDD $\boxed{1}$ (representing the tautology function). Similarly, we can establish that the incompatible outputs $undergraduate(a)$ and $staff(a)$ can be simultaneously inferred, by computing the Boolean product of their corresponding BDD labels, again using the APPLY-procedure. Since the outcome is different from the single-node BDD $\boxed{0}$, a conflict is indicated for the input combinations encoded by the satisfying input assignments of the result BDD (cf. Fig. 3). Note that a more detailed explanation of the suggested approach is provided in [5].

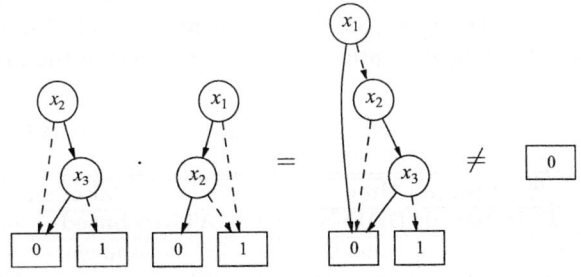

Fig. 3. Checking for conflict; $undergraduate(a)$ vs. $staff(a)$

5 Empirical Evaluation

In this section, we will empirically assess the computational efficiency and scalability advantages of the proposed BDD-based approach over a representative ATMS-inspired procedure, viz. COVER's rule chain check. To conduct our experiments, we selected three real-life rule bases, largely on account of availability:

- Tapes (3M Corp, help-desk; 101 rules; depth (min.–avg.–max.): 0–2–6);
- DMS1 (Bell Canada, fault diagnosis/repair; 405 (used) rules; depth: 0–1–2);
- Handirules (K.U.Leuven, legal advice system; 264 rules; depth: 1–8.5–11).

The former two are public-domain knowledge bases that have served as test cases before in the V&V literature – they were verified using the COVER-tool. The third rule base originates from a development effort that involved our own modelling and verification tool environment, PROLOGA [10].

5.1 Experiment 1: Comparing Time and Space Requirements

The first experiment that we conducted was to run the ATMS-inspired rule chain check for redundancy and conflict implemented in COVER, as well as a

BDD-based check, on the three aforementioned rule bases, and to compare their performance on them in terms of running times and memory consumption.

Firstly, where the input encoding method for the BDD-based procedure is concerned, we have, in all three cases, applied a compact encoding where yes/no-attributes were encoded by a single variable (1 for yes, 0 for no). To other single-valued attributes with any number of categories, a logarithmic encoding variant was applied where spare code points were dissolved by taking together some of the adjacent higher-end combinations. Set-valued attributes, finally, were encoded by standard positional notation (i.e., allocating one variable per value).

Secondly, a relatively simple static variable ordering scheme is adopted, based on goal-oriented, depth-first rule dependency graph traversal, whereby the encoding variables for a certain input attribute are added to the order as soon as it is encountered for the first time in some visited rule's antecedent. No additional heuristic for sorting alternatives was implemented: intermediate hypotheses are pursued in the (textual) order by which they appear in rule antecedents. The experiment was executed on an IBM SP2 workstation. Table 2 shows the running times, together with the aggregate label size at the end of the process.

Table 2. Time and space requirements for ATMS- vs. BDD-based checks

rule base	running time		label size	
	ATMS-based	BDD-based	ATMS-based	BDD-based
Tapes	0 min. 26.9 sec.	0 min. 0.3 sec.	167 environments	996 nodes
DMS1	3 min. 10.9 sec.	0 min. 3.6 sec.	1626 environments	2492 nodes
Handirules	> 24 hrs.	0 min. 1.1 sec.	> 28532 environments	8863 nodes

First of all, one must be cautious in interpreting the presented running times, since they are produced by very different implementations. Specifically, COVER is for the most part written in Prolog, whereas the BDD package is composed of highly efficient C-code. Furthermore, there is no common measurement unit available with regard to label size (number of environments versus number of nodes). Therefore, rather than at the absolute figures, one should mainly look at the relative differences in requirements over the three sample rule bases.

In so doing, probably the most striking result is COVER's breakdown on the Handirules-case, set against the relative performance of the BDD-based procedure on the same case. More in particular, when compared to the DMS1-case, COVER's performance drastically deteriorates to the point of failure to complete within 24 hours, whereas the BDD-based computations are in fact roughly three times faster on Handirules than they are on DMS1. This result shows that the scalability concerns expressed earlier were warranted. The ATMS-procedure indeed turns out to be infeasible on the deepest of the three rule bases, whereas there is considerably less performance variability, both in terms of running time and label size, on the part of the BDD-based procedure. For example, while the BDD node count scales up rather nicely from 996 nodes for Tapes, over 2492 for DMS1, to 8863 for Handirules, the corresponding increase in the number of

ATMS label environments is much more prominent (note that, although it could not be obtained, the ultimate environment count for Handirules will most likely lie well above 28532, which is the last reported figure).

5.2 Experiment 2: Growth Analysis of Computed Labels

In the second experiment, we were interested in the evolution of ATMS- vs. BDD-label size in the course of computations. More specifically, we considered the number of environments and BDD nodes, respectively, after processing each rule. In theory, we may apply any rule processing order, but in order to make a fair comparison, we should at least apply the same rule order in both instances. In addition, to provide an insightful picture of how label growth relates to reasoning depth in specific, we have chosen to partition the rules into levels according to the inference dependencies among them, and then use a forward strategy that processes the rules level by level. This has been done for both the ATMS- and BDD-computations. As could be expected, for Tapes and DMS1, being rather 'flat' rule bases, the perceived trends for both methods were not too disparate. The results for the more involved Handirules-case are plotted in Fig. 4.

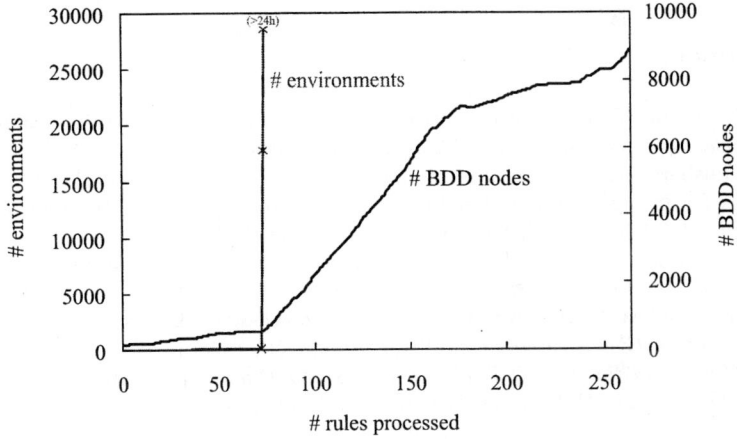

Fig. 4. Handirules; ATMS- vs. BDD-label growth plot

Upon closer inspection of the latter, COVER runs over a CPU time limit set at 24 hours after having processed 74 out of a total of 264 rules. After a slow initial build-up, an abrupt increase in the growth rate (indicated by a sharp knee in the plot) is observed when the ATMS label computations enter inference level 3. The BDD node count, on the other hand, appears less affected. Roughly around the same point, the BDD size curve becomes steeper as well, but this change in the slope is far less dramatic than that of the ATMS curve. Moreover, after this bend, the graph reassumes a more or less linear trajectory.

6 Conclusions

In this paper, drawing from a technique studied extensively by the hardware design community, we have put forward a novel rule-chain anomaly checking method for KBS verification, based on binary decision diagrams (BDDs). To that end, it was explained how to: (1) encode the input space of a KBS into binary form; (2) compute BDD labels (as opposed to classic ATMS-labels) for its outputs; (3) apply the resulting BDDs to the detection of rule anomalies. Subsequently, we investigated the computational efficiency of our approach on a test set of real-life rule bases. Firstly, we compared the time and space consumption of an ATMS- and a BDD-based procedure for detecting general redundant or conflicting rule anomalies. Here, we found that the ATMS-derived tool failed to terminate on the 'deepest' of the three rule bases, whereas the BDD-based procedure showed relatively little performance variability over the three test cases. In the second experiment, the respective growth of the ATMS- and BDD-labels during these computations was examined. This analysis showed that the generated ATMS-labels, unlike their BDD-counterparts, rapidly blow up beyond a certain level in the inference structure. Hence, the presented empirical evidence suggests that BDDs provide an efficient technique for anomaly checking, which scales up well to knowledge bases with a deeper inference structure.

References

1. R.E. Bryant. Graph-based algorithms for Boolean function manipulation. *IEEE Transactions on Computers*, C-35(8):677–691, 1986.
2. A. Ginsberg. Knowledge-base reduction: a new approach to checking knowledge bases for inconsistency and redundancy. In *Proc. of the 7th National Conf. on Artificial Intelligence (AAAI-88)*, pages 585–589, 1988.
3. T. Horiyama and T. Ibaraki. Ordered binary decision diagrams as knowledge-bases. *Artificial Intelligence*, 136(2):189–213, 2002.
4. A. Levy and M.-C. Rousset. Verification of knowledge bases based on containment checking. *Artificial Intelligence*, 101(1-2):227–250, 1998.
5. C. Mues. *On the Use of Decision Tables and Diagrams in Knowledge Modeling and Verification*. PhD thesis, K.U.Leuven, Dept. of Applied Econ. Sciences, 2002.
6. A. Preece and R. Shinghal. Foundation and application of knowledge base verification. *Intl. Journal of Intelligent Systems*, 9(8):683–701, 1994.
7. A. Preece, R. Shinghal, and A. Batarekh. Principles and practice in verifying rule-based systems. *The Knowledge Engineering Review*, 7(2):115–141, 1992.
8. M.-C. Rousset. On the consistency of knowledge bases: the COVADIS system. *Computational Intelligence*, 4:166–170, 1988.
9. W.-T. Tsai, R. Vishnuvajjala, and D. Zhang. Verification and validation of knowledge-based systems. *IEEE Transactions on Knowledge and Data Engineering*, 11(1):202–211, 1999.
10. J. Vanthienen, C. Mues, and A. Aerts. An illustration of verification and validation in the modelling phase of KBS development. *Data and Knowledge Engineering*, 27(3):337–352, 1998.

How to Model Visual Knowledge: A Study of Expertise in Oil-Reservoir Evaluation

Mara Abel [1], Laura S. Mastella[1], Luís A. Lima Silva [1],
John A. Campbell [2], and Luis Fernando De Ros [3]

[1] Federal University of Rio Grande do Sul - UFRGS
Instituto de Informática - Porto Alegre, Brazil
{marabel,mastella,llima}@inf.ufrgs.br

[2] University College London
Dept. of Computer Science - London, UK
j.campbell@cs.ucl.ac.uk

[3] Federal University of Rio Grande do Sul - UFRGS
Instituto de Geociências - Porto Alegre, Brazil
lfderos@inf.ufrgs.br

Abstract. This work presents a study of the nature of expertise in geology, which demands visual recognition methods to describe and interpret petroleum reservoir rocks. In an experiment using rock images we noted and analyzed how geologists with distinct levels of expertise described them. The study demonstrated that experts develop a wide variety of representations and hierarchies, which differ from those found in the domain literature. They also retain a large number of symbolic abstractions for images. These abstractions (which we call visual chunks) play an important role in guiding the inference process and integrating collections of tacit knowledge of the geological experts. We infer from our experience that the knowledge acquisition process in this domain should consider that inference and domain objects are parts of distinct ontologies. A special representation formalism, kgraphs+, is proposed as a tool to model the objects that support the inference and how they are related to the domain ontology.

Keywords: Knowledge acquisition, knowledge representation, expertise, visual knowledge, petroleum exploration.

1 Introduction

Knowledge about the evaluation of oil-reservoir rocks is crucial in petroleum exploration, since it can substantially decrease the risks of exploration and increase the efficiency of hydrocarbon production. Most of the data relevant for geological interpretation of oil reservoirs consist of visual information that cannot be described only through geometric components, such as size and format. Many of the aspects recognized by a geologist during the interpretation task have no formal denomination and are learnt through an implicit process during training and field experience.

The use of features without names in supporting problem-solving is a current practice in many natural domains. These objects constitute the implicit body of knowledge, also called *tacit knowledge* by Nonaka and Takeuchi [1] when referring to the unarticulated knowledge that someone applies in daily tasks but is not able to describe in words. The articulated or *explicit knowledge* refers to the consciously recognized objects and how these objects are organized. This portion of knowledge in the context of artificial intelligence is called *ontology*. Tacit and explicit knowledge should be seen as two separate aspects of knowledge and not different sorts of it. Extracting the ontology of a domain is one important objective of knowledge acquisition techniques; sometimes, it is misunderstood to be the only one. Along with the ontology, which represents the explicit part of knowledge, it is necessary to identify the tacit knowledge applied by experts and propose knowledge representations for it.

In geology, as in many other natural domains, the role of tacit knowledge in the expert problem-solving process has a dominating influence on the results achieved. Therefore, it deserves special attention in knowledge engineering. This paper describes a study in the petroleum domain that identifies what kind of tacit knowledge is applied by geologists in the evaluation of oil reservoirs, as part of the *PetroGrapher* project for the development of an expert system to support reservoir-rock interpretation. The study acknowledges and identifies differences between the cognitive mechanisms of novice and expert geologists during the rock interpretation process. Further, we discuss how these differences can influence the choice and application of knowledge-acquisition techniques.

2 Knowledge Acquisition and Knowledge Elicitation Techniques

Knowledge acquisition refers to the process of collection, elicitation, interpretation and formalization of the data regarding the functioning of expertise in a particular domain. Its objective is to reduce the communication gap between the expert or knowledge worker and the knowledge engineer, allowing the knowledge to become independent of its sources.

The main classes of knowledge acquisition techniques are described briefly below.
- Interviews, observation and protocol analysis: A grouping of many different techniques that demand direct interaction with experts. In retrospective interviews, the expert narrates a memory of how a problem was solved. This description commonly omits many crucial details. In concurrent interviewing, e.g. via observation and protocol analysis, the expert verbalises his/her reasoning *during* the problem-solving process while it is being recorded and observed. The result is more trustworthy, but the expert is usually unable to verbalize what he/she is doing when the inference requires both a high level of abstract reasoning and a low (i.e. concrete) level of sensorial activity. The collected information is commonly imperfect and needs to be complemented through further techniques.
- Classification techniques aim to identify the terms and concepts of the domain and how these concepts are organized in classes, groups or components, according to the expert. These include card-sorting and multidimensional scaling techniques [2].
- Collecting cases: A general label for all techniques that exploit recorded cases in knowledge acquisition, such as scenario analysis, event recovering, and the analysis of legacy cases for use in case-based reasoning systems.

- Extracting cause-effect relations. This includes techniques used to extract causal relations among concepts of the domain (such as evidence for conclusions, or problems and their applicable solutions). Variations on repertory grids [3], rule-extraction, knowledge graphs [4, 5] and conceptual graphs [6] belong in this class.
- Identifying the reasoning path. Problem-solving methods (PSM) [7] and inference structures [8] are graphical representations of the inference process involved in problem solving, described at an abstract (though not generic) level.

The accepted knowledge acquisition techniques are effective in revealing the ontology (explicit knowledge) underlined in expert reasoning. However, little progress on elucidating the unarticulated parts of expert knowledge has occurred, e.g. visual recognition or the integration of sensorial objects in the domain ontology. These issues are the main focus of the present work.

3 Investigation of the Cognitive Abilities of Experts in Petrography

Geological interpretation is strongly based on visual interpretation of features imprinted in rocks or landscape by physical phenomena. Since this process is improved mainly by practical experience, and not by supervised learning, geology is one of the areas in which experts develop themselves as strategic sources of knowledge.

The most familiar achievements in knowledge acquisition for geological domains are the development of the PROSPECTOR system [9]; the XEOD expert system to identify detrital depositional environments [10]; and the knowledge acquisition project SISYPHUS III, concerning igneous petrography [11]. The influence of the domain on the efficacy of the knowledge acquisition technique is significant, as was discussed by [12]. The common aspect of all these projects is that they have drawn attention to the development of dealing with visual diagnostic features and also have shown the necessity of representing the objects that support inference within a separate ontology.

In the present study, our intention has been to elucidate the cognitive process and objects that support the expertise in sedimentary petrography, by using tests similar to those found occasionally in cognitive psychology, e.g. in [13].

The investigation was conducted over a group of 19 geologists with distinct levels of expertise in sedimentary petrography. The group was selected among lecturers, undergraduate and graduate students of the Geosciences Institute of UFRGS and geologists from a petroleum company. Practical experience, instead of only theoretical knowledge, was a fundamental prerequisite for the selected group. The members of this group were first classified as novices, intermediates or experts. Novices were students or geologists who had received at least 100 hours of training in sedimentary petrography. Intermediates were geologists who used petrography as a daily tool in their work. Experts possessed at least 10 years of experience in the subject and directly utilized sedimentary petrography for more than 10 hours per week.

The group was requested to carry out 5 different tests, based on the presentation of images from rocks, using a high-definition video system attached to an optical microscope. The first experiment was designed to evaluate long-term memory. They were requested to describe fully a thin section that had been examined one hour before. The second test requested a full description of a thin section without time restriction, in order to evaluate the richness of technical vocabulary. The third test investigated short-term memory, by requiring description of a rock image shown just previously for a very short time. In the fourth experiment, recall of a first set of pictures of common objects (animals, landscapes and people) and a second set of sedimentary rocks was requested just after these had been shown for a short time. In the fifth experiment, the geologists were asked to divide another set of pictures into subsets (i.e., classify them) and explain their criteria for this subdivision. The pictures were basically reservoir images under microscope and, in a second experiment, common scenes, such as people, landscapes, etc.

The set of experiments was conceived in order to measure the association of 3 indicators with the predefined class of expertise. The indicators were:
1. amount of significant information in the description obtained after or during image exposition: it was expected that experts knew more about the domain and that their knowledge would be expressed through the use of technical and precise vocabulary;
2. intensity of use of interpreted features, instead of features having objective geometrical properties: it was expected that experts would develop image recognition at a more abstract level than novices and would be able to demonstrate this in recognizing features that needed only a short process of inference for their identification;
3. efficiency of organization and indexing of the domain: it was expected that experts would be more effective in grouping and classifying new information related to the domain and could demonstrate this ability in experiments involving their memory.

In the results of the experiment, we found no relation between the quantities of words or even of significant words (which are the words really related to the domain) in descriptions produced by experts and by novices. On the average, experts record more efficiently the details of the rock inspected, but the overall relation is not so simple: some novices exhibit an expert level of performance and some experts perform like novices.

When considering the use of interpreted features in the description, experts clearly demonstrate a higher average, as shown in Fig 1. The vertical axis in this figure indicates how many clearly interpreted features were used in describing the rock. The general pattern was the same in the short-term memory experiments involving sedimentary rock samples: the faster the expert is requested to classify or interpret rocks, the more he/she will try to recognize diagnostic features.

Our experimental picture changes completely when another kind of rock is used, such as a metamorphic rock sample. The result can be seen in Fig 2, where no relation between level of expertise and interpreted features can be identified. The sample here includes a professor of metamorphic petrology, classified as a novice in the context of sedimentary petrography. As expected, the geologist exhibited an expert pattern of behaviour in his own domain of knowledge.

Another significant result was obtained from the experiments with the set of images. Experts show a worse memory for common photographs than the novices, but obtain excellent results when the pictures concern their domain of expertise.

Evidence for the ontological support for memorisation was demonstrated when experts were requested to organise pictures of common objects and rocks. In the classification of rock pictures, the experts utilised evidently interpreted aspects of the rock, such as the quality of porosity or the kind of cementation. The novices organised the pictures mainly in terms of colour, texture or abundance of minerals. The organisation of the domain in the expert's mind relies on aspects that make the *problem-solving process* easier or more effective, rather than the taxonomy commonly used for teaching of students.

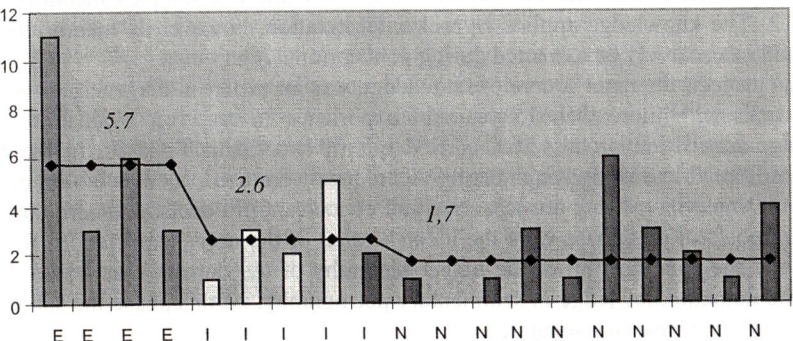

Fig 1. Relation between the level of expertise and the usage of interpreted features in information extracted from thin-section rock images by geologists in their descriptions of rock samples. The bars indicate the number of interpreted features and the line represents the median for each class (experts (E), intermediate (I) and novices (N))

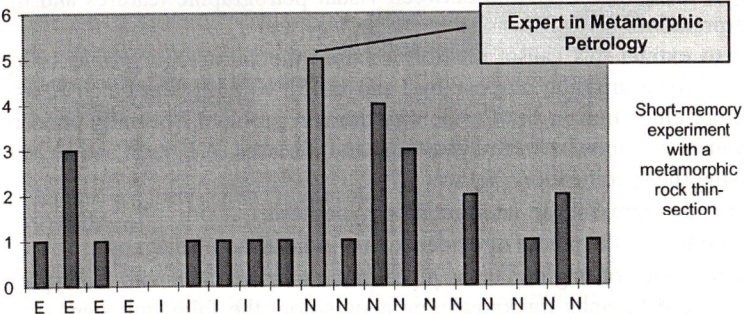

Fig 2. The same experiment as covered in Fig 1, but using a metamorphic rock sample. The relation between expertise and amount of features is not longer perceived. The highest bar refers to a professor of metamorphic petrology, who exhibits an expert behaviour in this experiment.

The experiments were able to identify that experts apply interpreted features more often than novices do in the problem-solving process. These features not only provide ontological support which improves memorisation of pictures concerning the domain of expertise, but also make the expert's problem-solving process more effective, even though in most instances the geologist can not give them a proper name. Given the observed importance of these cognitive objects for the process of interpretation, further cognitive research to establish methods tuned specifically for acquisition and representation of such knowledge is desirable.

3. Gaines, B.R. and M.L.G. Shaw, *Personal Construct Psychology and the Cognitive Revolution.* 2003, University of Calgary - Knowledge Science Institute: Cobble Hill. p. 30.
4. Abel, M., J.M.V. Castilho, and J. Campbell. *Analysis of expertise for implementing geological expert systems.* in *World Conference on Expert Systems.* 1998. Mexico City: Cognizant Communication Offices.
5. Leão, B.F. and A.F. Rocha, *Proposed methodology for knowledge acquisition: a study on congenital heart disease diagnosis.* Methods of Information in Medicine, 1990(29): p. 30-40.
6. Sowa, J.F., *Conceptual structures: information processing in mind and machine.* 1984, Reading: Addison Wesley.
7. Benjamins, V.R. and D. Fensel, *Editorial: problem-solving methods.* International Journal of Human-Computer Studies, 1998. **49**(4): p. 305-313.
8. Schreiber, G., H. Akkermans, A. Anjewierden, R.d. Hoog, N. Shadbolt, W.v.d. Velde, and B. Wielinga, *Knowledge engineering and management - The CommonKADS methodology.* 2000, Cambridge: The MIT Press: p. 104.
9. Duda, R.O., P.E. Hart, P. Barret, J. Gaschnig, K. Konolige, R. Reboh, and J. Slocum, *Development of the PROSPECTOR consultation system for mineral exploration.* 1978, Stanford Research Institute International: Menlo Park.
10. Schultz, A.W., J.H. Fang, M.R. Burston, H.C. Chen, and S. Reynolds, *XEOD: an expert system for determining clastic depositional environments,* in *Geobyte.* 1988: [S.l]. p. 22-32.
11. Gappa, U. and F. Puppe. *A study of knowledge acquisition - experiences from the SISYPHUS III experiment for rock classification.* in *Workshop on Knowledge Acquisition, Modeling and Management.* 1998. Alberta, Canada: Voyager Inn.
12. Wagner, W.P., Q.B. Chung, and M.K. Najdawi, *The impact of problem domains and knowledge acquisition techniques: A content analysis of P/OM expert system case studies.* Expert Systems with Applications, 2003. **24**(1 January 2003): p. 79-86.
13. Ericsson, K.A. and J. Smith, *Toward a general theory of expertise: prospects and limits.* 1991, New York: Cambridge University Press.
14. VanLehn, K., *Problem-solving and cognitive skill acquisition,* in *Foundations of Cognitive Science,* M.I. Posner, Editor. 1989, The MIT Press: Cambridge. p. 526-579.
15. Abel, M., L.A.L. Silva, L.S. Mastella, J.A. Campbell, and L.F.D. Ros, *Visual knowledge modelling and related interpretation problem-solving method.* Conferencia Latinoamericana de Informática - CLEI2002, 2002.
16. Silva, L.A.L., M. Abel, L.F.D. Ros, J.A. Campbell, and C.S.d. Santos. *An Image-Based Reasoning Model for Rock Interpretation.* in *Workshop on Intelligent Computing in the Petroleum Industry - 18th International Joint Conference in Artificial Intelligence, 2003.* 2003. Acapulco - Mexico: Proceedings of the Second Workshop Intelligence Computing in the Petroleum Industry: p. 27-32.
17. Abel, M., L.A.L. Silva, L.F.d. Ros, L.S. Mastella, J.A. Campbell, and T. Novello, *PetroGrapher: managing petrographic data and Knowledge using an intelligent database application.* Expert Systems with Applications, 2004.
18. Mastella, L.S., *Análise de Formas de Representação para Modelar Conhecimento Inferencial - Research Report (000405143).* 2002, Universidade Federal do Rio Grande do Sul: Porto Alegre. 72 p.

A New Approach of Eliminating Redundant Association Rules

Mafruz Zaman Ashrafi, David Taniar, and Kate Smith

School of Business Systems, Monash University, Clayton, Vic 3800, Australia
{Mafruz.Ashrafi,David.Taniar,Kate.Smith}@infotech.monash.edu.au

Abstract. Two important constraints of association rule mining algorithm are support and confidence. However, such constraints-based algorithms generally produce a large number of redundant rules. In many cases, if not all, number of redundant rules is larger than number of essential rules, consequently the novel intention behind association rule mining becomes vague. To retain the goal of association rule mining, we present several methods to eliminate redundant rules and to produce small number of rules from any given frequent or frequent closed itemsets generated. The experimental evaluation shows that the proposed methods eliminate significant number of redundant rules.

1 Introduction

Association rule mining is an iterative and interactive process that explores and analyzes voluminous digital data to discover valid, novel and meaningful rules, using computationally efficient techniques. It searches for interesting relationships among items in a given dataset. The main advantage of association rule mining is that it has ability to discover hidden associations with in the digital data.

Two important constraints of association rule mining are *support* and *confidence* [1]. Those constraints are used to measure the interestingness of a rule. Therefore, most of the current association rule mining algorithms use these constraints in generating rules. However, choosing support and confidence threshold values is a real dilemma for association rule mining algorithms. For example, discovering association rules with high support threshold removes rare item rules without considering the confidence value of these rules. On the other hand, when support threshold is low, it generates large number of rules, and consequently it becomes very difficult, if not impossible, for end user to utilize these rules.

It is widely recognized that number of association rules grows as number of frequent itemsets increases. In addition, most of the traditional association rules mining algorithms consider all subsets of frequent itemsets as antecedent of a rule [7]. Therefore, when resultant frequent itemsets is large, these algorithms produce large number of rules. However, many of these rules have identical meaning or are redundant. In fact, the number of redundant rules is much larger than the previously expected. In most of the cases, number of redundant rules is significantly larger than that of essential rules [4]. In many cases such enormous redundant rules often fades away the intention of association rule mining in the first place.

To reduce redundant rules, there are number of frameworks that have been proposed [4-8]. Most of the proposed frameworks have several prior assumptions. Based on these assumptions, the frameworks identify redundant rules and prune them subsequently. However, these prior assumptions are not suitable in many situations, and subsequently redundant rules may still exist in the resultant rule set. Furthermore, some of the proposed frameworks [4, 8] mark rule r as redundant and eliminate it, in the presence of another rule R (consider r, $R \in R'$, where R' is resultant ruleset) without considering whether rule R characterizes the knowledge of rule r. For example, an algorithm will mark rule $AB \Rightarrow C$ as redundant in the presence of rule $A \Rightarrow C$. However, it is apparent from this example that rule $A \Rightarrow C$ is not fully characterized the knowledge of rule $AB \Rightarrow C$.

In order to eliminate redundant rules, in this paper, we propose several methods that remove redundant rules from the resultant ruleset without losing any important knowledge. We are motivated by the fact that one can only utilize association rules efficiently when resultant rule set is small in size. However, without an efficient redundant rule reduction technique, one cannot achieve this goal. The proposed methods mark a rule as redundant when it finds a set of rules that also convey the same knowledge. For example, the proposed method will mark rule $A \Rightarrow BC$ as redundant, if and only if the rule such as $A \Rightarrow B$ and $A \Rightarrow C$ are present in that set. Our experimental evaluation shows that the proposed method generates only small number of rules. Therefore it becomes very convenient for end users to make use of this knowledge.

The rest of paper is organized as follows: In Section 2 we describe the background of association mining and summarize the reasons of rule redundancy. We describe related work in section 3. In Section 4 we present our proposed algorithms. The performance evaluation and comparison are described in section 5 and we conclude at Section 6.

2 Redundant Rules: A Background

One of the key issues of association rule mining is redundant rule [4-8]. Before further discussion on redundant rules is carried out, let us briefly discuss some of the key tasks of association rule mining algorithms.

2.1 Association Rule Mining: A Brief Overview

Algorithms for association rule mining usually have two distinct phases *(i) frequent itemset* and *(ii) rule generation* [2]. In order to find all *frequent itemsets*, we need to enumerate the support of all itemsets of the database. The support of an itemset can be defines as follows:

Definition: Let D be a transaction database has n number of items and I is a set of items such that $I = \{a_1, a_2, a_3, \ldots\ldots\ldots a_n\}$, where $a_i \subset n$. Consider N be the total number of transactions and $T = \{t_1, t_2, t_3, \ldots\ldots\ldots t_N\}$ be the sequence of transaction, such that $t_i \subset D$. The support of each element of I is the number of transactions in D containing I and for a given itemset $A \subset I$.

Itemset A is *frequent* if and only if *support*$(A) \geq$ *minsup* where *minsup* is a user-defined support threshold value. However, the enumeration of itemsets is computationally and I/O intensive [1]. For example, if the database has m number of distinct items, the search space for enumerating all frequent itemsets is 2^m. If m is large, then generating support for all itemsets requires long period of time and may exhaust the main memory limit.

Since frequent itemset generation is considered as an expensive operation, an approach known as Frequent Close Itemset (*FCI*) [7] was introduced. Itemset A is *closed* if there exists no itemset A' such that A' is a proper superset of A and all transactions containing A also contain A'. The total number of frequent *closed* itemsets generated from a given dataset is smaller than the total number of frequent itemsets, especially when the dataset is dense and have enough information so one can generate association rules from it [7]. For example, if "*B*" and "*B C*" are two frequent itemsets that have occurred in the same number of times in a given dataset, then only the itemset "*B C*" will be considered as FCI.

In the frequent itemset approach, *rule generation* task is relatively straightforward. Association rule mining algorithms use *frequent* itemsets in order to generate rules. An association rule R is an implication of two frequent itemsets $F_1, F_2 \in I$; such that $F_1 \cap F_2 = \{\}$ and can be expressed as $F_1 \Rightarrow F_2$.

Using the FCI approach, association rules are generated in the same manner as it does for the frequent itemsets. However, when the rules are generated from FCI, there is a chance that it will not consider some of the important rules. For example, in a given dataset if itemsets such as "*A*", "*A B*", "*A C*" and "*A B C*" have the same support, then the *closed* itemset will only consider itemset "*A B C*" as *frequent*. Therefore one cannot generate $A \Rightarrow B$, $A \Rightarrow C$ or $A B \Rightarrow C$, even though these rules have very high confidence value.

2.2 Overview of Rule Redundancy

The frequent itemsets based association rule mining framework produces large a number of rules, because it considers all subsets of frequent itemsets as antecedent of a rule. Therefore, the total number of rules grows as the number of frequent itemsets increases. Number of redundant rules is larger than the previously suspected and often reaches in such extend that sometimes it is significantly larger than number of essential rules.

Rule	Support	Confidence
$X \to YZ$	$S(X \cup Y \cup Z)$	$S(X \cup Y \cup Z)/S(X)$
$XY \to Z$	$S(X \cup Y \cup Z)$	$S(X \cup Y \cup Z)/S(X \cup Y)$
$XZ \to Y$	$S(X \cup Y \cup Z)$	$S(X \cup Y \cup Z)/S(X \cup Z)$
$X \to Y$	$S(X \cup Y)$	$S(X \cup Y)/S(X)$
$X \to Z$	$S(X \cup Z)$	$S(X \cup Z)/S(X)$

Fig. 1. Redundant Rules

Consider five different rules generated from a frequent itemset '*XYZ*' at a given support and confidence threshold s and c as shown in the figure 1. However, Aggarwal et al. [4] argue that if rule $X \Rightarrow YZ$ meet s and c, then rules such as $XY \Rightarrow Z$,

$XZ{\Rightarrow}Y$, $X{\Rightarrow}Y$, and $X{\Rightarrow}Z$ are redundant. This is because the support and confidence values $X{\Rightarrow}YZ$ are less than the support and confidence values for the rules $XY{\Rightarrow}Z$, $XZ{\Rightarrow}Y$, $X{\Rightarrow}Y$, and $X{\Rightarrow}Z$.

Furthermore, by observing at abovementioned scenario one may think that if the FCI method is used instead of frequent itemset, then one can avoid those redundant rules. However, the FCI will also consider those itemset as frequent if itemsets "X" "XY" "XZ" and "XYZ" do not occur the same number of times in the dataset. Therefore we cannot avoid these kinds of redundant rules, should we generate rules by using FCI. Based on this rationale, we can define redundancy rules as follows:

Definition: In the context of association rule mining, a set of rules R which is generated from a set of frequent itemsets F, such that each element $r \in R$ satisfy both *support* and *confidence* thresholds. A rule r in R is said to be **redundant** if and only if a rule or a set of rules S where $S \in R$ possess same intrinsic meaning of r.

For example, consider a rule set R has three rules such as $milk{\Rightarrow}tea$, $sugar{\Rightarrow}tea$, and $milk, sugar{\Rightarrow}tea$. If we know the first two rules i.e. $milk{\Rightarrow}tea$ and $sugar{\Rightarrow}tea$, then the third rule $milk, sugar{\Rightarrow}tea$ becomes redundant, because it is a simple combination of the first two rules and as a result it does not covey any extra information especially when the first two rules are present.

2.3 Why Does Redundancy Occur?

It is very important to have a clear idea how current support and confidence based association mining algorithms work in order to identify the reasons that cause redundancy. In the current approach, first we enumerates all frequent itemsets, and then we find all candidate rules (i.e. rules those confidence value are not verified) by combining subsets of every frequent itemset in all possible way.

The validity of association rules (i.e. rules that meet a given *confidence* value) is verified simultaneously during the time of candidate rules generation. All traditional association rule mining algorithms subsequently prune away candidate rules that do not meet the *confidence* threshold. Due to the fact that the traditional algorithms generate association rules in two phases based on *support* and *confidence* values, they generate a large number of rules especially when the user-specified threshold values of support and confidence are low. It is worth to mention that the total number of subset elements grows proportionally as the length of frequent itemset increases. Consequently the number of rules may increase unwieldy when the average length of frequent itemset is long.

From the above discussions one may think that if user-specific *support* and *confidence* threshold values are high, the rule redundancy problem should be solved. Indeed such assumption reduces the ratio of redundant rules but is not able to eliminate redundant rules completely. Because traditional algorithms find association rules based on confidence value, they consider all candidate rules as valid rules when these rules have confidence above the threshold value. Nevertheless from a frequent itemset we can construct different rules. And many of these rules may meet the high support and confidence values. However, when a frequent itemset generates many valid rules then without a doubt we can say that many of those rules will fall under redundant rules category. For example a simple rule $(A{\Rightarrow}B)$ can be represent in two different ways ($A \Rightarrow B$, $B \Rightarrow A$), if we interchange the antecedent and confidence itemset. Furthermore the confidence value is changed as we interchange the *antecedent* and *consequence* itemset of a rule. The traditional approach only checks whether the confidence is above the user-specified threshold or not. Swapping the *antecedent* itemset with *consequence* itemset of a rule will not give us any extra information or knowledge.

However, choosing the support and confidence threshold values is a real dilemma for all association rules mining algorithms. If the *support* value is set too high, we will not find rules from rare itemsets although there might be some rules with very high confidence. On the other hand when the support and confidence threshold value is low then one can find many rules that do not make any sense.

3 Related Work

One of the main drawbacks of association rule mining is redundant rule. To overcome redundant rules a number of research works [4-7] had been found in the data mining literature. In this section, we discuss some of the previously proposed redundant rule reduction techniques.

Aggarwal et al. [4] classify the redundant rule in two groups, such as: *simple redundant* and *strict redundant*. The authors proposed different methods to remove redundant rules. They proposed that a rule bears *simple redundancy* in the presence of other rules if and only if those rules are generated from same frequent itemset and the support values for the those rules are the same but the confidence value for one of them is higher than the others. For example, the rule $AB \Rightarrow C$ bears simple redundancy with respect to rule $A \Rightarrow BC$. But this approach recognizes rule $BC \Rightarrow A$ as non-redundant with respect to $AB \Rightarrow C$ because item $BC \not\subset AB$. Notice that both rules are generated from same itemset ABC. Furthermore, rule $BC \Rightarrow A$ does not convey any extra information, if rule $A \Rightarrow BC$ is present, because it only swaps the antecedent and consequent itemset.

The authors considered rules as *strict redundancies* that are generated from two different frequent itemsets but one is the subset of another. For example, this approach consider rule $C \Rightarrow D$ as redundant with respect to $A \Rightarrow B$ if $A \cup B = X_i$ and $C \cup D = X_j$ and $C \supseteq A$, where $X_i \supset X_j$. But we argue that this property is not true in all situations. Consider two rules such as $R1: AC \Rightarrow BDE$; $R2: ACD \Rightarrow B$ (where $X_i = ABCDE$; $X_j = ABCD$ so $X_j \supset X_i$ and $ACD \supseteq AC$), and if we say rule $R2$ is redundant with respect to $R1$ and remove it, we then might lose a important rule because rule $R2$ does not fully characterize the knowledge of rule $R1$.

Jaki et al. [7] present a framework based on FCI (Frequent Close Itemset) that reduces number of redundant rules. The authors used FCI to form a set of rules and inferred all other association rules from that. Since FCI is used for choosing a set of rules based on the confidence value, the number of rules grows as the number of FCI increases. Therefore, it becomes difficult for end-users to infer other rules when there is a large number of FCI. Additionally, since this approach uses FCI, it may prune some important rules without considering the confidence and support value of those rules.

Liu et al. [5] present a technique to summarize the discovered association rules. It selects a subset of rules called direction-setting rules, in order to summarize the discovered rules. For example, we have rules such as $R1: A \Rightarrow C$, $R2: B \Rightarrow C$ and $R3: A, B \Rightarrow C$. Rule $R3$ intuitively follows $R1$ and $R2$ and for this reason rule $R3$ is nonessential. The main drawback of this algorithm is that it focuses only on those association rules that have a single item in the consequence. Therefore, it is not able to remove redundant rules that have multiple items in the consequence. This algorithm also selects the target attributes (i.e. consequence) before the algorithm starts the rule mining task. Consequently it fails to find rules that have different consequence itemset. Since association rule mining is an unsupervised learning approach, if we choose the target attributes earlier, we may unable to generate some useful rules that do not belong to the target groups. Liu et al [6] also propose another algorithm known as multilevel organization and summarization of discovered rules. In this algorithm, rules are summarized in a hierarchical order, so that end users can browse all rules at different levels of details. However, this algorithm only summarizes the rules and redundant rules may still exist in the final model.

Similar to all of the abovementioned redundant rule reduction algorithms, our main objective of this paper is to eliminate redundant rules. However, our proposed methods have *two distinct features* that distinguish it from all other existing algorithms.

- The proposed methods are not based on any bias assumptions. In addition it verify each rule with set of rules in order to find redundant rule. Hence it eliminates redundant rules without losing any important knowledge from the resultant rule set.
- The proposed methods are case independent. It verifies all rules that have one or more items in the consequence. Therefore, it has the ability to eliminate redundant rules that contain single or multiple items in the consequence.

4 Proposed Methods

One can classify association rules in two different types based on the number of items in the consequence: rules having single items in the consequence and rules having multiple items in the consequence. Depending on the application requirements, association rule mining algorithms produce ruleset, which may contains rules of both types. However, it is worth to mention that redundant rules exist in both types. To eliminate redundant rules of these two types, we propose two methods: removing redundant rules with fixed *antecedent* rules, and with fixed *consequent* rules. The proposed methods not only remove redundant rules that are generated from frequent itemset but also have the ability to remove redundant rules when rules are being generated from the frequent closed itemset.

4.1 Finding Redundant Rules with Fixed Antecedent Rules

To remove redundant rules with fixed antecedent, we propose following theorem:
Theorem 1: Consider rule $A \Rightarrow B$ satisfying the minimum confidence threshold such that antecedent A has i items and consequent B has j items where $i \geq 1$ and $j > 1$. The

rule $A \Rightarrow B$ is said to be redundant if and only if n number of rules such as $A \Rightarrow e_1$, $A \Rightarrow e_2, \ldots A \Rightarrow e_n$ satisfy minimum confidence threshold where $\forall e \subset B$ and $n=j$.

Proof: Since $\forall e \subset B$
Then, $Support(A \cup e) \geq Support(A \cup B)$
$$\therefore \frac{Suppport(A \cup e)}{Suppport(A)} \geq \frac{Suppport(A \cup B)}{Suppport(A)}$$
$\therefore Confidence(A \Rightarrow e) \geq Confidence(A \Rightarrow B)$

Hence, if the rule $A \Rightarrow B$ is true in a certain level of support and confidence, then same must be true for all rules $A \Rightarrow e$ where $\forall e \subset B$.

Example: Let us apply this theorem to a ruleset R that has three rules such as $\{AB \Rightarrow X, AB \Rightarrow Y$ and $AB \Rightarrow XY\}$. Consider the rule $AB \Rightarrow XY$ has $s\%$ support and $c\%$ confidence. Then, the rules such as $AB \Rightarrow X$ and $AB \Rightarrow Y$ will also have at least $s\%$ support and $c\%$ confidence because $X \subset XY$ and $Y \subset XY$. Since $AB \Rightarrow X$ and $AB \Rightarrow Y$ dominate $AB \Rightarrow XY$ both in support and confidence, for this reason $AB \Rightarrow XY$ is redundant.

4.2 Finding Redundant Rules with Fixed Consequence Rules

The traditional association rule mining algorithms produce many rules that have the same consequence but have different antecedents. To remove this kind of redundant rules, we propose following theorem:

Theorem 2: Consider rule $A \Rightarrow B$ that satisfies minimum confidence threshold such that antecedent A has i items and consequent B has j items where $i > 1$ and $j \geq 1$. The rule $A \Rightarrow B$ is said to be redundant if and only if n number of rules such as $e_1 \Rightarrow B$, $e_2 \Rightarrow B, \ldots e_n \Rightarrow B$ satisfy minimum confidence threshold where $\forall e \subset A$, $n=i$ and each e has $(i-1)$ items.

Proof: Since, $\forall e \subset A$ and $e_1 \cup e_2 \cup \ldots \cup e_n = A$
So, $support(e) \geq support(A)$
$\therefore Support(e \cup B) \geq Support(A \cup B)$

Thus if rules such as $e_1 \Rightarrow B$, $e_2 \Rightarrow B, \ldots e_n \Rightarrow B$ have a certain confidence threshold, then rule $A \Rightarrow B$ is redundant because $A = e_1 \cup e_2 \cup \ldots \cup e_n$.

Example: Let us apply this theorem to a rule set R that has three rules such as $\{XY \Rightarrow Z, X \Rightarrow Z$ and $Y \Rightarrow Z\}$. Suppose rule $XY \Rightarrow Z$ has $s\%$ support and $c\%$ confidence. If n (i.e. number of items in the antecedent) number of rules such as $X \Rightarrow Z$ and $Y \Rightarrow Z$ also satisfy s and c then, the rule $XY \Rightarrow Z$ is redundant because it does not convey any extra information if rule $X \Rightarrow Z$ and $Y \Rightarrow Z$ are present.

4.3 Proposed Algorithms

Based on the abovementioned theorems, we propose two algorithms to discover redundant rules. The pseudocode of these algorithms is shown in figures 2 (a) and (b). The first algorithm finds those redundant rules that have multiple items in the consequence but have the same antecedent itemset in the antecedent. It first iterates through the whole rule set and finds those rule that have multiple itemsets in the consequence. Once it comes across such a rule, checking is carried out to see whether n number of $(n-1)$-*itemset* of the consequence are in the rule set with the same antecedent. If it finds n number of rules in the rule set then we delete that rule from the rule set otherwise that rule remains in the rule set.

The second algorithm finds those redundant rules that have multiple items in the antecedent but have the same antecedent itemset in the consequence. It is similar to first algorithm except that it finds antecedent that have multiple itemset. Once it comes across such rule a check is made to see whether n number of $(n-1)$-*itemset* of the antecedent are in the rule set with the same consequence. If it finds n number of rules in the rule set then we delete that rule from the rule set otherwise that rule remains in the rule set.

```
for all rules r ∈ R
  r = ∪{A, C}
  n = length(A)
  if (n ≻ 1)
    for all (n−1)−subsets e ∈ A
      if (r_i = ∪{e, C})
        e.i++;
    end for
    if (i == n)
      R = R − r
  end if
end for
```
(a)

```
for all rules r ∈ R
  r = ∪{A, C}
  n = length(C)
  if (n ≻ 1)
    for all (n−1)−subsets e ∈ C
      if (r_i = ∪{A, e})
        e.i++;
    end for
    if (i == n)
      R = R − r
  end if
end for
```
(b)

Fig. 2. Pseudo Code for finding redundant rules that have (a) same antecedent but different consequence (b) same consequence but different antecedent

5 Performance Study

We have done performance study on our proposed methods to conform our analysis of its effectiveness in eliminating redundant rules. We have chosen four datasets for this performance study. Table 1 shows the characteristics of those datasets. It shows the total number of items, average size of transaction and the total number of transactions of each dataset. It is worth to mention that many association rule mining algorithms had used all of these datasets as a benchmark.

Table 1. Dataset Characteristics

Name	Avg. Transaction Length	No. of Items	No. of Transactions
pumsb*	74	7117	49046
Connect-4	43	130	67557
T40I10D100K	20	1000	100000
BMS-WEB-View-1	2	497	59602

The pumsb* and Connect-4 [9] datasets are very dense (there are large number of items very frequently occurred in the transaction) and are able to produce very large itemsets when the support threshold is high. Therefore, we use very high support threshold for generating rules from those datasets. The T40I10D100K and BMS-Web-

View-1 [10] datasets are relatively sparse (total number of items are large but only few of them are occurred frequently in the transaction) and due to this we generate rules from those datasets using low support threshold value.

In following experiments we examine the level of redundancy (i.e. redundant rules) present in the resultant rule set. The benchmark for measuring the level of redundancy is referred to the redundancy ratio [4] and is defined as follows:

$$\text{Redundancy Ratio } (\partial) = \frac{\text{Total Rules Generated (T)}}{\text{Essential Rules (E)}} \ldots \ldots \ldots (1)$$

$$\text{Essential Rules (E)} = T - R \ldots \ldots \ldots (2)$$

where R is the total number of redundant rules present in the resultant rule set.

To find redundancy ratio in the traditional approach, at first we used those datasets to generate frequent itemsets using the Apriori [11] association rule-mining algorithm. Since we use different support threshold values, the total number of frequent itemsets varies for different support values. After generating frequent itemsets we use those itemsets for the rule generation purpose. To generate association rules in traditional approaches, we choose a publicly available a third party rule generation program developed by Bart Goethals [11]. We have implemented our proposed methods and compare them with the traditional approaches as shown in the Figure 3.

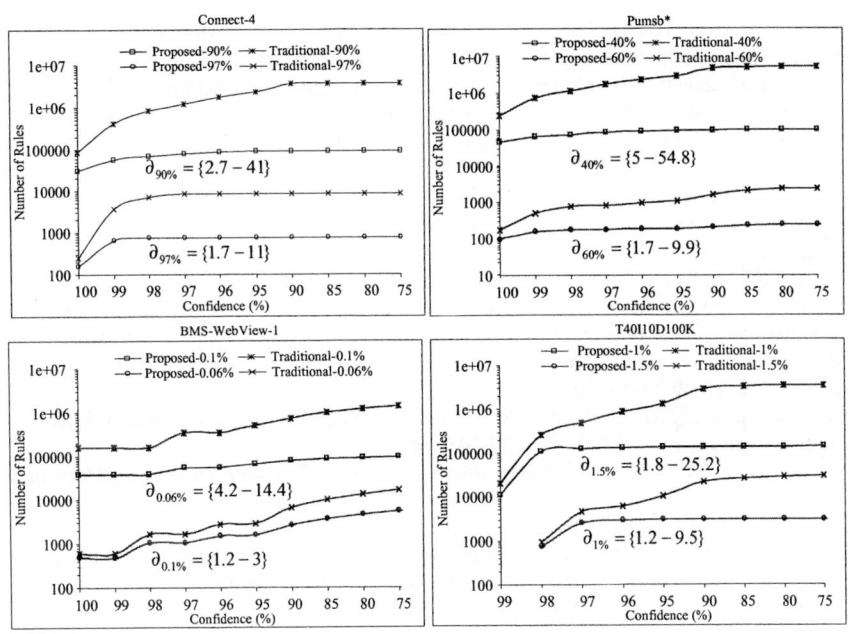

Fig. 3. Number of rule Proposed vs. Traditional

Figure 3 compares the total number of rules generated by the traditional methods with our proposed methods. It also depicts the redundancy ratio. From the above graph it is clear that the proposed methods reduce the total number of rules drastically. It generates 1.2 to 55 times less number of rules in compare with traditional approach. Since the traditional approach considers all possible subsets of a frequent itemsets as antecedent of a rule, it produces a large number of rules in all datasets regardless of the support threshold. However, our proposed methods check every rule with a set of rules in order to find redundant rule. Therefore it only generates only few rules from each frequent itemset. In addition, the total number of rules grows as the support threshold decreases therefore the proposed methods reduce more number of redundant rules when support thresholds are low.

6 Conclusion

In this paper we examine various reasons that cause the redundancy problem in association rule mining. We also proposed several methods to eliminate redundant rules. The proposed methods rigorously verify every single rule and eliminate redundant rules. Consequently it generates a small number of rules from any given frequent itemsets in compare to all traditional approaches. The experimental evaluation also suggests that the proposed methods not only theoretically eliminate redundant rules but also reduce redundant rules from real datasets.

References

1. Rakesh Agrawal, Tomasz Imielinski and Ramakrishnan Srikant "Mining Association Rules between Sets of Items in Large Databases", *ACM SIGMOD*, pp 207-216, May 1993.
2. Mohammed Javeed Zaki, "Parallel and Distributed Association Mining: A Survey", *IEEE Concurrency*, pp. 14-25, October-December 1999.
3. Mohammed Javeed Zaki, "Scalable Algorithms for Association Mining" *IEEE Transactions on Knowledge and Data Engineering*, Vol. 12 No.2 pp. 372-390 (2000).
4. Charu C. Aggarwal and Philip S. Yu, "A new Approach to Online Generation of Association Rules". *IEEE TKDE*, Vol. 13, No. 4 pages 527- 540.
5. Bing Liu, Minqing Hu and Wynne Hsu "Multi-Level Organization and Summarization of the Discovered Rules". *In the proc. KDD*, pp. 208-217, 2000.
6. Bing Liu, Wynne Hsu and Yiming Ma, "Pruning and Summarize the Discovered Associations". *In the proc. of ACM SIGMOD* pp.125 134, San Diego, CA, August 1999.
7. Mohammed Javed Zaki, "Generating non-redundant association rules" *In Proceeding of the ACM SIGKDD*, pp.34-43, 2000.
8. Bing Liu, Wynne Hsu and Yiming Ma, "Mining Association Rules with Multiple Minimum Supports". *In the proc. KDD*, pp. 337-341, 1999.
9. C.L. Blake and C.J. Merz. *UCI Repository of Machine Learning Databases*, University of California, Irvine, Dept. of Information and Computer Science, 1998, http://www.ics.uci.edu/~mlearn/MLRepository.html.
10. Ron Kohavi and Carla Brodley and Brian Frasca and Llew Mason and Zijian Zheng "KDD-Cup 2000 organizers report: Peeling the onion" , *SIGKDD Explorations*, Vol. 2 No.2 pp.86-98, 2000, http://www.ecn.purdue.edu/KDDCUP/ .
11. Bart Goethals, *Frequent Pattern Mining Implementations*, University of Helsinki-Department of Computer Science, http://www.cs.helsinki.fi/u/goethals/software/.

An a Priori Approach for Automatic Integration of Heterogeneous and Autonomous Databases

Ladjel Bellatreche, Guy Pierra, Dung Nguyen Xuan,
Dehainsala Hondjack, and Yamine Ait Ameur

LISI/ENSMA - Futuroscope - FRANCE
{bellatreche,pierra,nguyenx,hondjack,yamine}@ensma.fr

Abstract. Data integration is the process that gives users access to multiple data sources through queries against a global schema. The semantic heterogeneity has been identified as the most important and toughest problem when integrating various sources. The mapping between the global schema and local schemas was done manually in the first generation of integrated systems, when ontologies are not used to make explicit data meaning. It is semi automatic when ontologies and ontology mappings are defined at integration level. In this paper, we propose a fully automatic integration approach based on ontologies. It supposes that each data source contains a formal ontology that references a shared ontology. The relationships between each local ontology and the shared ontology are defined at the *database design time* and also *embedded in each source*. We assume that a domain ontology exists, but each source may extend it by adding new concepts and properties. Our approach is currently prototyped in various environments: OODB, ORDB, and RDB.

1 Introduction

The overwhelming amount of heterogeneous data stored in various data repositories emphasizes the relevance of data integration methodologies and techniques to facilitate data sharing. Data integration is the process by which several autonomous, distributed and heterogeneous information sources (where each source is associated with a local schema) are integrated into a single data source associated with a global schema. It recently received a great attention due to many data management applications : examples are data warehouse [1], and e-commerce [10] and represents a significant challenge to the database community.

Any integration system should consider both integration at schema level (schema integration consists in consolidating all source schemas into a global or mediated schema that will be used as a support of user queries) and at data level (global population). Constructing a global schema from local sources is difficult because sources store different types of data, in varying formats, with different meanings, and reference them using different names. Consequently, the construction of the global schema must handle different mechanisms for reconciling both data structure (for example, a data source may represent male and female in the same entity type, when another splits them into two different entities), and data meaning (for example synonymous). The main task of integrating data sources is identifying the equivalent concepts (and properties). To do so, different categories of conflicts should be solved. Goh et al. [5] suggest the following taxonomy: *naming conflicts, scaling conflicts, confounding conflicts* and *representation conflicts*. These conflicts may be encountered at *schema level* and at *data level*.

Various integration systems have been proposed in the literature [2, 8, 4, 13, 9]. Their fundamental drawbacks is their inability to integrate automatically at the meaning level several *heterogeneous* and *autonomous* data sources. In the first generation of integration systems (e.g., TSIMMIS [4]), data meaning was not explicitly represented. Thus, concept meaning and meaning mapping were manually encoded in a view definitions (e.g., SQL views). The major progress toward automatic integration resulted from the explicit representation of data meaning through ontologies. Various kinds of ontologies were used, either linguistic [3] or more formal [7]. All allowed some kind of partially automatic integration under an expert control. In a number of domains, including Web service, e-procurement, synchronization of distributed databases, the new *challenge* is to perform a fully automatic integration of autonomous databases. We claim that: *if we do not want to perform human-controlled mapping at integration time, this mapping shall be done a priori at the database design time*. This means that some formal shared ontologies must exist, and each local source shall embedded some ontological data that references explicitly this shared ontology. Some systems are already developed based on this hypothesis: Picsel2 project for integrating Web services [13], and the COIN project for exchanging for instance financial data [5]. Their weakness is that once the shared ontology is defined, each source shall used the common vocabulary. The shared ontology is in fact a global schema and each source is not autonomous. Our approach gives more autonomy to various data sources by assuming that: (1) each data source participating in the integration process *shall* contain its own ontology, we call that source an ontology-based database (OBDB); (2) each local source references a shared ontology, and (3) a local ontology may extend the shared ontology as much as needed. Consequently, the automatic integration process involves two steps: automatic integration of ontologies and then an automatic integration of data (contents of sources).

One of the target domains of our work is automatic integration of industrial component databases [12]. Our approach requires target domains to be already modeled by ontologies (as in e-commerce applications). We have already contributed to the development of such ontologies at the international standardization level (e.g., IEC61630-4:1998). A number of other initiatives are based on the same assumptions [13].

In this paper, we present a novel ontology-based data integration approach. Contrary to linguistic ontologies, ontologies used in our integration process are conceptual (no linguistic), consensual, embedded with each data source (consequently it can be exchangeable), extensible using the subsumption relationship (each source may add whatever property or class). Like COIN [5] (where the ontology represents a contextual information of values), our ontology *also* represents the context of the ontology definition. To the best of our knowledge, the proposed work is the first article that addresses the integration problem supposing that a conceptual ontology is embedded in each data source.

The rest of this paper is organized as follows: in section 2, we present an overview of the ontology model that will be used as a basic support for our integration algorithms, in section 3, we present the concept of ontology-based database and its structure, in section 4; integration algorithms for two real scenarios are presented, and section 5 concludes the paper.

2 The PLIB Ontology Model

To describe the meaning and the context of each data source, any ontology language like OWL, PSL, DAML+OIL, Ontolingua, etc can be used. In this paper we use the PLIB ontology model because of number of domain ontologies based on this model already exist or are emerging (e.g., IEC, JEMIMA, CNIS, etc. see http://www.plib.ensma.fr) and also because it was precisely designed to promote data integration [11]. A PLIB ontology model has the following characteristics:

- *Conceptual*: each entity and each property are unique concepts completely defined. The terms (or words) used for describing them are only a part of their formal definitions.
- *Multilingual*: a globally unique identifier (GUI) is assigned to each entity and property of the ontology. Textual aspects of their descriptions can be written in several languages (French, English, Japanese, etc.). The GUI is used to identify *exactly* one concept (property or entity).
- *Modular*: an ontology can reference another one for importing entities and properties without duplicating them. Thus providing for autonomy of various sources that do reference a shared ontology.
- *Consensual* : The conceptual model of PLIB ontology is based on an international consensus and published as international standards (IEC61630-4:1998, ISO13584-42:1998) (for more details see [11]).
- *Unambiguous* : Contrary to linguistic ontology models [11], where partially identical concepts are gathered in the same ontology-thesaurus with a similarity ratio (affinity) [3, 14], each concept in PLIB has with any other concepts of the ontology well identified and explicit differences. Some of these differences are computer-interpretable and may be used for processing queries, e.g., difference of measure units, difference of evaluation context of a value.

2.1 An Automatic Resolution of Naming Conflicts in PLIB

One of the utilization of the GUI is solving naming conflicts as shown in the following example. Let S_1 be a source referencing the PLIB ontology model describing a Person (Figure 1). This source has the autonomy to use different names for its attributes (it may use nom instead of name). For the integrated system these two attributes are similar because they have the same GUI. More generally, if several sources use different names; we can identify easily whether they are different or identical using the following procedure: (1) these two properties have the same GUI, for the integration system, these properties are identical (they represent the same thing, i.e., the family name of a person) even if they have different names. (2) They have different GUIs, for the integration system, they are different, even if they have the same name.

Note that unlike other integration systems based on linguistic ontologies, where affinity measurements and thresholds are used to compute the similarity between concepts [3, 14], the orthogonality of PLIB ontologies and the use of GUI make the resolution of naming conflicts *deterministic* and *fully automated*.

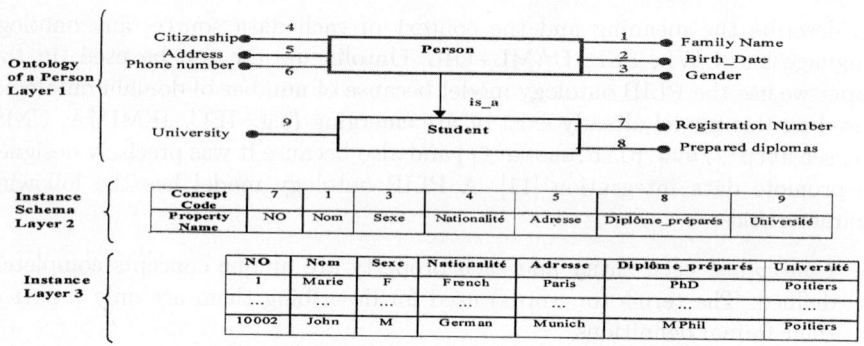

Fig. 1. An example of specializing a global ontology

2.2 PLIB Class Properties

The PLIB ontology model is represented by a tree of classes, where each class has its own properties. Three types of properties are distinguished: (1) *characteristics* are rigid properties (a rigid property is a property that is essential to all instances of a class [6]) (e.g., the Birth-date of a person), (2) a *context dependent property* is an instance property whose value is a function of its evaluation context (e.g., the *balance* of a bank account depends on the *date* where it is computed), and (3) a *context parameter* is a property that defines the evaluation context of a context dependent property (e.g., the *date* where an *account* balance is computed). Such a context explication gives more autonomy to databases that reference a common shared ontology [11].

2.3 Extension Possibilities Offered by PLIB

When a PLIB ontology model is shared between various sources (because these sources commit to ontological definitions that were agreed and possibly standardized (e.g.,JEMIMA)), each source remains autonomous and may extend the shared ontology using subsumption relationship. To ensure modularity, the subsumption may be implemented by two mechanisms called is-a and case-of.

In the *Is-A Relationship*, a local source can extend the shared ontology by specializing class(es) of the shared ontology. Through this relationship, properties are inherited. Figure 1 considers a shared ontology describing a Person with six properties Family name, Birth date, Gender, Citizenship, Address and Phone number. A local source may specialize this shared ontology in order to define its own ontology describing Student with three more properties.

In the *Case-Of Relationship*, properties are not inherited but may be explicitly (and partially) imported. Figure 3 shows an extension of the shared ontology Person using the case-of relationship. The local ontology PhD Student imports some properties of the shared one (Family name, Religion, Citizenship, Address). Note that this local ontology does not import some properties of the shared ontology like Birth date, and Birth Citizenship. To respond to its need, it adds other properties describing a PhD student, like registration number, advisor and thesis subject.

3 Ontology-Based Databases

Contrary the existing database structures (that contain two parts: data according to a logical schema and a meta-base describing tables, attributes, Foreign keys, etc), an ontology-based database contains four parts : two parts as in the conventional databases, plus the ontology definition and meta-model of that ontology. The relationship between the left and the right parts of this architecture associates to each instance in the right part its corresponding meaning defined in the left part. This architecture is validated by a prototype developed on Postgres.

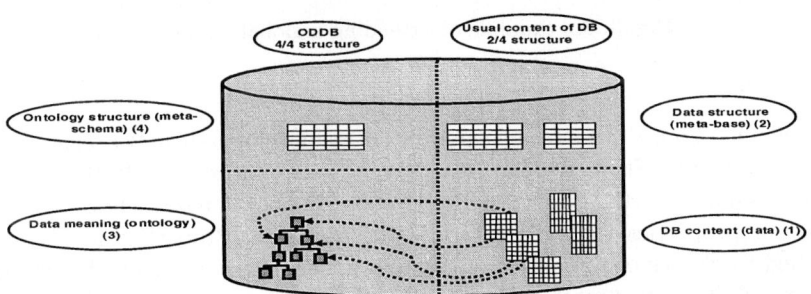

Fig. 2. The ontology-based database architecture

3.1 A Formal Definition of an Ontology-Based Database

Formally, a PLIB ontology is defined as the quadruplet $O < C, P, Sub, Applic >$. C is the set of the classes used to describe the concepts of a given domain (like travel service [13], equipment failures, etc). P is the set of properties used to describe the instances of the C classes. Note that it is assumed that P defines a much greater number of properties that are usually represented in a database. Only a subset of them might be selected by any particular database [1]. Sub is the subsumption function (Figure 1, 3) defined as $Sub : C \to 2^C$ [2], where for a class c_i of the ontology it associates its direct subsumed classes [3]. Sub defines a partial order over C. Finally, $Applic$ is a function defined as $Applic : C \to 2^P$. It associates to each ontology class those properties that are applicable (i.e., rigid) for each instance of this class. Applicable properties are inherited through the is-a relationship and partially imported through the case-of relationship.

Note that, as usual, ontological definitions are intentional: the fact that a property is rigid for a class does not mean that value will be explicitly represented for each instance of the case. In our approach, this choice is made among applicable properties at the schema level.

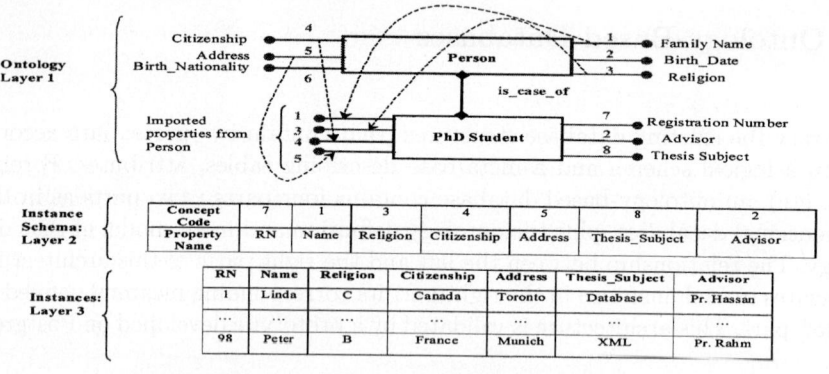

Fig. 3. An example of extending a global ontology

Example 1. Figure 3 gives an example of an ontology with two classes $C = $ {Person and PhD Student}. Let P = {Family_Name, Citizenship, Birth_Date, Religion, Address, Birth_Citizenship, Registration_Number, Advisor, Thesis_Subject}}. be set of properties that characterizes these classes. Properties in P will be assigned to classes of the ontology (therefore, each class will have its own rigid properties). The subsumption function Sub defines a case-of relationship between classes (for example, the class *Person* subsumes the class *Phd Student*).

---

[1] Through the case-of relationship, a particular database may also extend the P set.
[2] We use the symbol 2^C to denote the power set of C.
[3] C_1 subsumes C_2 iff $\forall x \in C_2, x \in C_1$.

An ontology-based database $OBDB$ allows to record together with an ontology a set of instances of ontology classes. Thanks to the subsumption relationship, an instance belongs to several classes. We assume that the set of classes to which an instance belongs ordered by the subsumption relationship has a unique minimal class (called instance *basis class*). Moreover, for the purpose of simplicity, we assume in this paper that instances are defined only at the level of some leaf classes (non-leaf classes are "abstract" and thus only leaf classes are basis classes). Formally, an $OBDB$ is a quadruplet $< O, I, Sch, Pop >$, where: O is an ontology ($O :< C, P, Sub, Applic >$); I is the set of instances of the database; each one represented as an instance of its basis class; $Sch : C \rightarrow 2^P$ associates to each ontology class c_i of C the properties which are effectively used to describe the instances of the class c_i; Sch has two definitions based on the nature of each class (a leaf or a no-leaf class).

Schema of each leaf class c_i is explicitly chosen. It shall only ensure the following: $\forall c_i \in C, Sch(c_i) \subset Applic(c_i)$ (1). (Only applicable properties of c_i may be used for describing instances of c_i).

Schema of a no-leaf class c_j is computed as the intersection between the applicable properties of c_j and the intersection of properties associated with values in all subclasses $c_{i,j}$ of c_j. $Sch(c_j) = Applic(c_j) \bigcap (\bigcap_i Sch(c_{i,j}))$ (2)

An alternative definition may also be used to create the schema of a no leaf class where instances are completed with null values:
$Sch'(c_j) = Applic(c_j) \bigcap (\bigcup_i Sch(c_{i,j}))$ (3).

$Pop : C \rightarrow 2^I$ associates to each class (leaf class or not) its own instances.

Example 2. Let's consider the class tree in Figure 4 where A is a no-leaf class and B, C and D leaf-classes. We assume that each class has it own applicable properties, and the DBA (database administrator) has chosen its schema for B, C and D and a formula (2) or (3) for all non-leaf classes. To find the schema of the class A using equation 2, we first perform the intersection operation among all properties of the schema of the leaf-classes. We obtain a set $U = \{b, c\}$, then we perform the intersection operation between U and the applicable properties of A ($\{a, b, c, g\}$). As result the schema of A contains two properties b and c (see figure 4). By using Sch' definition (equation 3), $Sch'(A)$ would be (a, b, c). The instances from C and D will be associated with NULL value for property a.

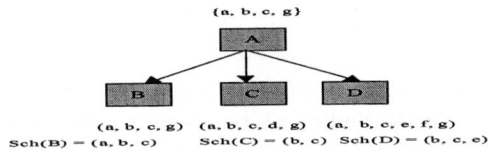

Fig. 4. An example of a no-leaf class schema

4 Algorithms for Integrating OBDB Sources

In this section, we present algorithms to integrate various ontology-based database sources that correspond to the same domain. A typical scenario is the one of Web-services of a particular domain like traveling [13]. Each supplier references the same domain ontology and adds its own extensions. Let $S = \{SB_1, SB_2, ..., SB_n\}$ be the set of data sources participating in the data integration process. Each data source SB_i ($1 \leq i \leq n$) is defined as follows: $SB_i =< O_i, I_i, Sch_i, Pop_i >$. We assume that all sources have been designed referencing as much possible a common shared ontology O. *As much possible* means that (1) each class of a local ontology references explicitly (or implicitly through its parent class) its lowest subsuming class in the shared ontology and (2) only properties that do not exist in the shared ontology may be defined in a local ontology, otherwise it should be imported through the case-of relationship. This requirement is called smallest subsuming class reference requirement (S2CR2). Each source is designed following three steps: (i) the DBA of each source defines its own ontology $O_i :< C_i, P_i, Sub_i, Applic_i >$, (ii) the DBA of each source chooses for each leaf class properties that are associated with values by defining $Sch_i : C_i \rightarrow 2^{P_i}$; (iii) she chooses an implementation of each leaf c_i class (e.g., to ensure the third normal form), and then she defines $Sch(c_i)$ as a view over c_i implementation.

We may distinguish two different integration scenarios associated with automatic integration algorithms: **FragmentOnto**, where each local ontology of each source is a fragment of the shared ontology, and **ExtendOnto**, where each local ontology may be an extension of the shared ontology O (to ensure the autonomy of a local source). This extension is done through explicit subsumption using case-of relationship (Figure 3) and should respect the S2CR2.

4.1 An Integration Algorithm for FragmentOnto

[4] This integration approach assumes that the shared ontology is complete enough to cover the needs of all local sources. Such an assumption is done for instance in the Picsel2 project [13] for integrating web service (travel agency) or in COIN [5]. Source autonomy consists (1) in selecting the pertinent subset of the shared ontology (classes and properties), and (2) designing the local database schema. The ontology O_i ($1 \leq i \leq n$) of each source SB_i is defined as a fragment of the common ontology O. It is defined as quadruplet $O_i :< C_i, P_i, Sub_i, Applic_i >$, where : $C_i \subseteq C$; $P_i \subseteq P$; $\forall c \in C_i, Sub_i(c) \subseteq Sub(c)$; $\forall c \in C_i, Applic_i(c) \subseteq Applic(c)$. Integrating these n sources ($SB_i :< O_i, I_i, Sch_i, Pop_i >$), means finding an ontology, a schema and a population of the integrated system. Therefore, the integrated system $OInt$ is defined as a 4-tuple $OInt :< O_{OInt}, I_{OInt}, Sch_{OInt}, Pop_{OInt} >$. Now the question that we should answer is how to find the structure of each element of $OInt$?

---

[4] This approach corresponds to formula (2). An approach based on formula (3) is also possible.

- The ontology of the integrated system is O ($O_{OInt} = O$).
- The schema of the integrated system Sch_{OInt} is defined for each class c as follows: $Sch_{OInt}(c) = (\cap_{i \in \{1..n \mid Sch_i(c) \neq \phi\}} Sch_i(c))$ (4). This definition ensures that instances of the integrated system are not expanded with null values to fit with the more precisely defined instances. In place, only properties which are provided in all data sources are preserved. In some data sources may incur empty classes. These classes are removed from the set of classes used to compute the common provided properties.
- The population of each class of the integrated system Pop_{OInt} is defined as follows: $Pop_{OInt}(c) = \bigcup_i proj_{Sch_{OInt}(c)} Pop_i(c)$ (5), where $proj$ is the projection operation as defined in classical databases, and $I_{OInt} = \bigcup_{(1 \leq i \leq n)} I_i$.

4.2 An Integration Algorithm for ExtendOnto

In a number of cases, including the target application domains of the PLIB approach namely an automatic integration of electronic catalogues/databases of industrial components, more autonomy is requested by various sources:
- classification of each source needs to be completely different from the shared ontology (or ontologies);
- some classes and properties do not exist at all in the shared ontology and need to be added in the local ontologies.

This case differs from the previous one by the fact that each data source has its own ontology and the classes of each ontology are specific (no class of the shared ontology are directly used in local ontology's). But all the ontologies reference "as much possible" (i.e., S2CR2) a shared ontology $O :< C, P, Sub, Applic >$. Therefore, each source SB_i maps the referenced ontology O to its ontology O_i. This mapping can be defined as follows: $M_i : C \rightarrow 2^{C_i}$, where $M_i(c) = \{$greatest classes of C_i subsumed by c$\}$. Contrary to the previous case, each data source SB_i is defined as quintuple: $SB_i = < O_i, I_i, Sch_i, Pop_i, M_i >$. In such as case also an automatic integration is possible. To do so, we should find the structure of the final integrated system $F :< O^F, I^F, Sch^F, Pop^F >$. Note that the structure of O^F is $< C^F, P^F, Sub^F, Applic^F >$, where elements of these structures are defined as follows: Integrated classes $C^F = C \bigcup_{(i \mid 1 \leq i \leq n)} C_i$; $P^F = P \bigcup_{(i \mid 1 \leq i \leq n)} P_i$; $\forall c \in C$, $Sub^F(c) = Sub(c) \bigcup_{(i \mid 1 \leq i \leq n)} M_i(c)$;

$$Applic^F(c) = \begin{cases} Applic(c), \text{ if } c \in C \\ Applic(c_i), \text{ if } c \in C_i \wedge c \notin C \end{cases}$$

Then, $I^F = \bigcup_{(i \mid 1 \leq i \leq n)} I_i$, and the population Pop^F of each class (c) is computed recursively using a post-order tree search. If c belongs to one C_i and does not belong to C, its population is given by: $Pop^F(c) = Pop_i(c)$.
Otherwise (i.e., c belongs to the shared ontology tree), $Pop^F(c)$ is defined as follows: $Pop^F(c) = \bigcup_{(c_j \in Sub^F(c))} Pop^F(c_j)$ (6)

Finally, the schema of each class c of the integrated system is computed following the same principle as the population of c by considering leaf nodes and non-leaf nodes. If c does not belong to C but to one C_i, $sch(c)$ is computed

using the formula (2) (resp. 3). Otherwise (if c belongs to the shared ontology), its schema is computed recursively using a poster-order tree search by :
$$Sch^F(c) = Applic(c) \bigcap (\bigcap_{(c_j | c_j \ \in \ Sub^F(c) \wedge Pop^F \neq \phi)} Sch^F(c_j)) \quad (7)$$
This shows that it is possible to leave a large autonomy to each local source and compute in a fully automatic, deterministic and exact way the corresponding integrated system. To the best of our knowledge our ontology based database approach is the first approach that reconciles these two requirements.

It is important to note that when all data sources use independent ontologies without referencing a shared ontology the task of mapping these ontologies onto a receiver ontology may be done manually, by the DBA of the receiving system. But then integration process will be performed automatically as in ExtendOnto.

5 Conclusion

In this paper, we present a fully automated technique for integrating heterogeneous sources. This approach assumes the existence of a shared ontology and guarantees the autonomy of each source that may extend the shared ontology to define its local ontology. This extension is done by adding new concepts and properties. The ontologies used by our approach are modeled according to a formal, multilingual, extensible, and standardized (ISO 13584) ontology model known as PLIB. The fact that an ontology is embedded with each data source helps in capturing both the domain knowledge and the knowledge about data, schema, and properties. Therefore it allows a complete automation of the integration process contrary to the existing systems. Finally, two integration algorithms are presented: (1) when all sources only use a fragment of a shared ontology, and (2) when sources extend the shared ontology by specific classes and properties.

In addition to its capability for automating the integration process of heterogeneous databases (note that several prototypes of ontology-based databases are currently in progress in our laboratory), there are many other future directions that need to be explored. Some of the more pressing ones are: (1) extending our ontology model to capture functional dependencies between properties, (2) *schema evolution*, and (3) considering the query optimization aspect to see how an ontology can be used for indexing query (semantic indexing).

References

1. L. Bellatreche, K. Karlapalem, and M. Mohania. Some issues in design of data warehousing systems. In *Developing Quality Complex Data Bases Systems: Practices, Techniques, and Technologies*, pages 125–172. Idea Group Publishing, 2001.
2. S. Castano and V. Antonellis. Semantic dictionary design for database interoperability. *Proceedings of the International Conference on Data Engineering (ICDE)*, pages 43–54, April 1997.
3. S. Castano, V. Antonellis, and S.D.C. Vimercati. Global viewing of heterogeneous data sources. *IEEE Transactions on Knowledge and Data Engineering*, 13(2):277–297, 2001.

4. S.S. Chawathe, H. Garcia-Molina, J. Hammer, K. Ireland, Y. Papakonstantinou, J.D. Ullman, and J. Widom. The tsimmis project: Integration of heterogeneous information sources. *Proceedings of the 10th Meeting of the Information Processing Society of Japan*, pages 7–18, Marsh 1994.
5. C.H. Goh, S. Bressan, E. Madnick, and M.D. Siegel. Context interchange: New features and formalisms for the intelligent integration of information. *ACM Transactions on Information Systems*, 17(3):270–293, 1999.
6. N. Guarino and C.A. Welty. Ontological analysis of taxonomic relationships. *in Proceedings of 19th International Conference on Conceptual Modeling (ER 2000)*, pages 210–224, October 2000.
7. F. Hakimpour and A. Geppert. Global schema generation using formal ontologies. *in Proceedings of 21th International Conference on Conceptual Modeling (ER 2002)*, pages 307–321, October 2002.
8. R. Lawrence and K. Barker. Integrating relational database schemas using a standardized dictionary. *in Proceedings of the ACM Symposium on Applied Computing (SAC)*, pages 225–230, Marsh 2001.
9. A.Y. Levy, A. Rajaraman, and J.J. Ordille. The world wide web as a collection of views: Query processing in the information manifold. *Proceedings of the International Workshop on Materialized Views: Techniques and Applications (VIEW 1996)*, pages 43–55, June 1996.
10. B. Omelayenko and D. Fensel. A two-layered integration approach for product information in b2b e-commerce. *Proceedings of the Second International Conference on Electronic Commerce and Web Technologies*, pages 226–239, September 2001.
11. G. Pierra. Context-explication in conceptual ontologies: The plib approach. *in Proceedings of 10th ISPE International Conference on Concurrent Engineering: Research and Applications (ce 2003) : Special Track on Data Integration in Engineering*, pages 243–254, July 2003.
12. G. Pierra, J.C. Potier, and E. Sardet. From digital libraries to electronic catalogues for engineering and manufacturing. *International Journal of Computer Applications in Technology (IJCAT)*, 18:27–42, 2003.
13. C. Reynaud and G. Giraldo. An application of the mediator approach to services over the web. *Special track "Data Integration in Engineering, Concurrent Engineering (CE 2003) - the vision for the Future Generation in Research and Applications*, pages 209–216, July 2003.
14. G. Terracina and D. Ursino. A uniform methodology for extracting type conflicts and & subscheme similarities from heterogeneous databases. *Information Systems*, 25(8):527–552, December 2000.

PC-Filter: A Robust Filtering Technique for Duplicate Record Detection in Large Databases

Ji Zhang[1], Tok Wang Ling[2], Robert M. Bruckner[3], Han Liu[1]

[1]Department of Computer Science, University of Toronto,
Toronto, Ontario, M5S 3G4, Canada
{jzhang,hanliu}@cs.toronto.edu
[2]School of Computing, National University of Singapore, Singapore 117543
lingtw@comp.nus.edu.sg
[3]Microsoft Research, Redmond, WA, USA
robruc@microsoft.com

Abstract: In this paper, we will propose PC-Filter (PC stands for Partition Comparison), a robust data filter for approximately duplicate record detection in large databases. PC-Filter distinguishes itself from all of existing methods by using the notion of partition in duplicate detection. It first sorts the whole database and splits the sorted database into a number of record partitions. The Partition Comparison Graph (PCG) is then constructed by performing fast partition pruning. Finally, duplicate records are effectively detected by using internal and external partition comparison based on PCG. Four properties, used as heuristics, have been devised to achieve a remarkable efficiency of the filter based on triangle inequity of record similarity. PC-Filter is insensitive to the key used to sort the database, and can achieve a very good recall level that is comparable to that of the pair-wise record comparison method but only with a complexity of $O(N^{4/3})$. Equipping existing detection methods with PC-Filter, we are able to well solve the "Key Selection" problem, the "Scope Specification" problem and the "Low Recall" problem that the existing methods suffer from.

1 Introduction

Data cleaning is of crucial importance for many industries over a wide variety of applications. Aiming to detect the duplicate or approximately duplicate records that refer to the same real-life entity, duplicate record elimination is a very important data cleaning task. The naïve method is to pair-wisely compare all record pairs in the database in order to detect the duplicate records. Obviously, this method is practically infeasible due to its intolerable complexity of $O(N^2)$, where N is the number of records in the database. To lower the complexity, various techniques have been proposed. We can broadly classify the state-of-the-art methods into two major categories: *window-based methods* [4, 5, 9, 10] and *clustering-based methods*[7]. The window-based methods typically sorts the whole database based on a key and use the notion of *sliding window* to delimit the scope of record comparison: record comparison is only carried out within the scope of sliding window. The clustering-based methods group the records into clusters with unfixed sizes, and record comparison is performed within each of the clusters independently.

Though they can, to some different degree, improve the efficiency of detecting duplicate records, the existing methods suffer from three major problems: the *"Key*

Selection" problem, the *"Scope Specification"* problem and the *"Low Recall"* problem. Firstly, methods involving database sorting are very sensitive to the key chosen to sort the database. In addition, the optimal size of the window (for window-based methods) or the clusters (for clustering-based methods) is hard to determine, making it difficult to specify the optimal scope for record comparison for the given database. Given the typically small size of the window or clusters, the existing methods cannot produce results with very satisfactory recall level.

In order to solve the abovementioned problems, we will propose PC-Filter, a novel filtering technique for effective and efficient duplicate record detection. The major contribution of our proposed PC-Filter is that it is able to solve the three major that the existing methods suffer from. Specifically:

(1) PC-Filter uses the notion of partition instead of a window or cluster to detect duplicate records in a database. PC-Filter will not only compare records within each partition, but also compare records across different partitions. This strategy makes it possible for PC-Filter to detect duplicate records even when they are located far apart from each other under a sorting based on an improperly chosen key. Therefore, the result of PC-Filter is insensitive to the sorting order of the database under different keys and a single sorting of the whole database will suffice in our work.

(2) By using a process called Inter-Partition Comparison, PC-Filter is able to globalize the scope of record comparison in the whole database. Therefore, even the duplicate record pair that is far apart from each other in the database can be detected. PC-Filter is able to achieve a very good recall that is even comparable to the pair-wise comparison method.

(3) The size of the partition has been optimized in our work to give the best possible speed performance.

2   Related Work

[5] has proposed the *Sorted Neighborhood Method (SNM)*, serving as the basis of many existing duplicate detection methods. SNM is able to speed up the data cleaning process by only examining neighboring records that is in the sliding window for a relevant record. Among the variants of SNM are *Duplicate Elimination SNM (DE-SNM)* [4], *Multi-pass-SNM* [4], *Clustering-SNM* [5] and *SNM-IN/OUT* [9]. In *DE-SNM*, the records are first divided into a duplicate list and non-duplicate list. The SNM algorithm is then performed on the duplicated list to produce the lists of matched and unmatched records. The list of unmatched records is merged with the original non-duplicate list using SNM again. *Multi-pass-SNM* uses several different keys to sort the records and perform the SNM algorithm several times, rather than only one pass of SNM based on a single key. Generally, combination of the results of several passes over the database with small window sizes will be better than the result of the single pass over the database. *Clustering-based SNM* clusters records into a few clusters and the record merging process is performed independently for every cluster using SNM. *SNM-IN/OUT*, which is probably the most related method

to our PC-Filter, uses several properties, namely the lower and upper bounds of the Longest Common Subsequence (LCS) and Anchor Record (AR), to save record comparisons in SNM without impairing accuracy. The *priority Queue method* [7] clusters the records and uses a priority of set of records belonging to the last few clusters already detected. The database is sequentially scanned and each record is tested as whether it belongs to one of the clusters residing in the priority queue.

In addition to the above window-based and clustering-based methods, [3] presents an on-the-fly detection scheme for detecting duplicates when joining multiple tables. This method, however, is not directly applicable for detecting duplicates in a single table where no join operation will be involved. A fuzzy duplicate match method is also proposed to detect duplicate for online data in [1] and [2]. A knowledge-based method is proposed in [6] based on a number of rules. However, using rules to detect duplicates in large database is rather expensive.

3 Measurements of Record Similarity

The fields of records are treated as strings and we utilize the similarity measure used in [10] in our work.

Field Similarity: Suppose a field F in record A has the character set $A_F=\{x_1, x_2, ..., x_m\}$ and the corresponding field in record B has the character set $B_F=\{y_1, y_2, ..., y_n\}$, where x_i, $1 \leq i \leq m$, and y_j, $1 \leq j \leq n$, are characters with association numbers. For example, for a string "abcabd", it is transferred to the character set {a1, b1, c1, a2, b2, d1}. The field similarity of the field F for A and B is computed as:

$$Sim_F(A,B) = \min(\frac{|A_F \cap B_F|}{|A_F|}, \frac{|A_F \cap B_F|}{|B_F|})$$

Suppose a table consists of fields $F_1, F_2,..., F_n$, and the field weightings are $W_1, W_2,..., W_n$, respectively, $\bullet W_i=1$. The TI-similarity of two records, A and B, is computed as:

$$Sim(A,B) = \sum_{i=1}^{n}(W_i * Sim_{F_i}(A,B))$$

Two records are treated as duplicate pair if their similarity value exceeds a user-defined threshold, denoted as σ.

Next, we will discuss the transitive closure properties of TI-Similarity, which will be intensively used in generation of Partition Comparison Graph and partition comparison in PC-Filter to achieve a remarkable efficiency improvement. The *Upper Bound (UB)* and *Lower Bound (LB)* of the similarity between two records using TI-Similarity is unveiled in Lemma 1 by [10].

Lemma 1: When the distance measure satisfies the triangle inequity, the *LB* and *UB* of the similarity between two records A and C, denoted as $LB_B(A,C)$ and $UB_B(A,C)$, can be computed as follows using record B as an Anchor Record:

$$LB_B(A,C) = sim(A,B) + sim(B,C) - 1$$
$$UB_B(A,C) = 1 - |sim(A,B) - sim(B,C)|$$

The properties utilized by PC-Filter, based on *LB* and *UB* of the similarity between two records using TI-Similarity are called Record-Record (R-R) Properties and Record-Partition (R-P) Properties. These properties provide heuristics for deciding the duplication or non-duplication between two records and between a record and a record partition, respectively.

(1) Record-Record Properties (R-R Properties)
Record-Record Properties (R-R Properties) are the properties used for deciding duplication/non-duplication between two records using AR. Suppose we have three records, *A, B* and *C. B* is chosen as the Anchor Record. We have two R-R Properties regarding duplication/non-duplication between records *A* and *C*.
Property 1: *If $sim(A,B)+sim(B, C)-1 \geq \sigma$, then A and C are duplicate records.*
Property 2: *If $1-|sim(A, B)-sim(B, C)| < \sigma$, then A and C are non-duplicate records.*

Using record *B* as the AR, the duplication/non-duplication between records *A* and *C* can be decided immediately if they satisfy either Rule 1 or 2, and the expensive record comparison between *A* and *C* can thus be avoided.

(2) Record-Partition Properties (R-P Properties)
Based on the two R-R Properties presented above, we devise the following R-P Properties (Properties 3-4) regarding the duplication/non-duplication decision for a single record and a partition of records.

Property 3: *If $sim(R, AR)+MinSim-1 \geq \sigma$, then R is definitely duplicate with all the records residing in the partition, where MinSim is the minimum similarity value between AR and records in the partition.*
Proof: Since for any record in the partition R_i, we have $sim(R, AR)+ sim(R_i, AR)-1 \geq sim(R, AR)+MinSim-1$. Then if $sim(R, AR)+MinSim-1 \geq \sigma$, then we have $sim(R, AR)+ sim(R_i, AR)-1 \geq \sigma$. From Property 1, we can conclude that record *R* is duplicate with all the record residing in the partition. Thus Property 3 is proved. ∎

Property 4: *For every record R_i in the partition, if $(1-min\{| sim(R, AR)- sim(R_i, AR)|\}) < \sigma$), then R is definitely not duplicate with any records residing in the partition.*
Proof: For each record R_i in the partition, we have $min\{|sim(R, AR)-sim(R_i, AR)|\} \leq |sim(R, AR)-sim(R_i, AR)|$. So $1-Min\{|sim(R, AR)-sim(R_i, AR)|\} \geq 1-|sim(R, AR)-sim(R_i, AR)|$. If $1-Min\{|sim(R, AR)-sim(R_i, AR)|\} < \sigma$, then $1-|sim(R, AR)-sim(R_i, AR)| < \sigma$, which means that every record in the partition satisfies Property 2. Thus we conclude *R* is definitely not duplicate with any records residing in the partition. Property 4 is proved. ∎

The advantage of R-P Properties (Properties 3-4) is that they provide heuristics greatly facilitating the decision of duplication/non-duplication between a single record and a whole partition of records, without comparing this particular record with each record in the partition using TI-Similarity.

4   PC-Filter

PC-Filter performs duplicate record detection in 3 steps described below: database sorting and partitioning, construction of Partition Comparison Graph (PCG) and partition comparison. The overview of PC-Filter is given in Figure 1.

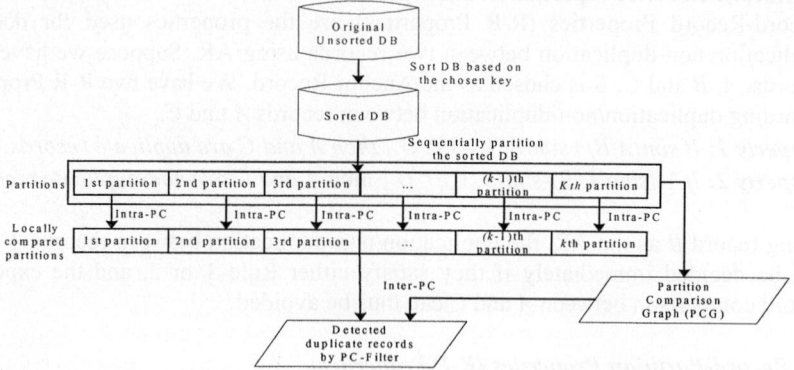

Fig. 1. Overview of PC-Filter

(1) Database Sorting and Partitioning

A key is computed for each record in the database by extracting relevant fields or portions of fields for discriminating records. The whole database is sorted based on the chosen key. We then divide the sorted database into k sequential partitions. To perform fast database partition and balance the computation load of record comparison in each of the partitions, all partitions are set to have the same size in our work. The partitions to which a record R does not belong are called the *outer partitions* of R.

Other pre-processing work involves choosing the median record in each partition as the Anchor Record of the partition and computing the similarity between each record in the partition and the AR that will be maintained in a similarity list. The similarity list is sorted to provide efficient support to the evaluation of Property 3 and 4 in PC-Filter.

(2) Construction of Partition Comparison Graph (PCG)

It is observed that, in most cases, the outer partitions that needed to compare for records within the same partition actually falls into a relatively small range. Based on this observation, we will construct the Partition Comparison Graph (PCG) for the whole database such that the records in a particular partition will only be compared with the records of its immediate neighboring outer partitions in this graph rather than with all the partitions in the database.

Partition Comparison Range (PCR) for each partition is first constructed and then converted to Partition Comparison Graph (PCG). To construct PCR, the first and last $N_{dr}/2$ records in a partition will be selected as the *Delimiting Records (DRs)*, the records used to delimit the PCR of this partition. N_{dr} is the number of DRs specified by users and should be an even number. To construct the PCR of a partition, pruning of outer partitions using Property 4 is performed based on each of the DRs, whereby the lower and upper bounds of the range can be specified. More precisely, let $F_1, F_2, ..., F_{Ndr/2}$ be the first $N_{dr}/2$ records in a partition P and $L_1, L_2, ..., L_{Ndr/2}$ be the last $N_{dr}/2$ records in this partition. These N_{dr} records constitute the *DRs* of this partition. Each *DR* is associated with a set of outer partitions that are left after pruning using Property 3, denoted as $PartList(F_1)$, ..., $PartList(F_{Ndr/2})$, and $PartList(L_1)$, ..., $PartList(L_{Ndr/2})$. For a Delimiting Record *dr*, we have

$PartList(dr)$=I- $\{P_{dr}\}$ - $\{P \mid P$ is an outer partition of *dr*, and *P* and *dr* satisfy Property 3$\}$

where *I* denotes the complete set of partitions in the database and P_{dr} denotes the partition to which *dr* belongs. The lower and upper bounds of the PCR of a partition are determined by the non-empty post-pruning partition sets of the first and last $N_{dr}/2$ DRs in the partition, respectively. Specifically, let *k* be the number of DRs that have non-empty post-pruning partition sets, where $0 \leq k \leq N_{dr}$. There are 3 cases in constructing the PCR of a partition:

(1) If $k=N_{dr}$, then the lower and upper bounds of the PCR of the partition *P*, denoted as $Range_{LB}(P)$ and $Range_{UB}(P)$, are defined as

$PCR_{LB}(P)=min\{min\{PartList(F_1)\}, ..., min\{PartList(F_{Ndr/2})\}\}$
$PCR_{UB}(P) = max\{max\{PartList(L_1)\}, ..., max\{PartList(L_{Ndr/2})\}\}$

The *max()* and the *min()* functions return the maximum and minimum *sequence number* of partitions in the sorted order;

(2) If $0<k<N_{dr}$, the lower and upper bounds of the PCR of the partition *P* are specified in a similar way to (1), but they will only use the non-empty partition sets of the DRs;

(3) If $k=0$, then all the partition sets of all DRs are empty, thus we write the PCR of this partition as [$, $], where "$" is a special symbol.

Definition 1: *Partition Comparison Graph (PCG)* is an undirected graph $G=<V, E>$, where *V* denotes the node set, representing all the partitions in the database, and *E* denotes the edge set. Two nodes (partitions) are directly connected if the sequence number of at least one partition is in the PCR of the other partition. More precisely, for two nodes p_1 and p_2, connect (p_1, p_2)=true if $SequNo(p_1) \in PCR(p_2)$ or $SequNo(p_2) \in PCR(p_1)$ or both.

Sequence No. of partitions	PCR
1	[2, 4]
2	[1, 3]
3	[1, 4]
4	[3, 3]
5	[3, 4]
6	[$, $]

Table 1. The Partition Comparison Ranges (PCR) of the partitions

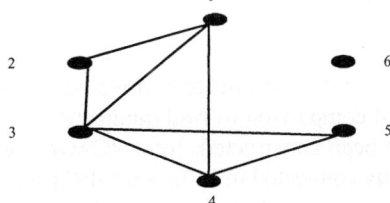

Fig.2. The corresponding Partition Comparison Graph (PCG)

Note that it is possible that there exits one or more singleton nodes in the PCG, the nodes that are not connected with any other nodes in the graph. These singletons are those partition whose PCR is [$, $].

E.g. Let's suppose that there are 6 partitions in a database and their PCRs are given in Table 1. Their corresponding PCG is presented in Figure 2. The 6th partition is an example of singleton node that is not directly connected with any other nodes in the PCG.

The general steps of constructing PCG are as follows:
  (1) The set of outer partitions that are left after pruning using Property 4 for each Delimiting Record of a partition is computed;
  (2) The PCR of the partition is obtained by using all the post-pruning list of Delimiting Records in the partition in Step (1);
  (3) Step (2) and (3) are repeated until the PCRs of all partitions in the database have been found.
  (4) PCRs of all partitions are converted to PCG.

(3) Partition Comparison
After we obtain the PCG of each partition in the database, partition comparison will be performed. The record comparison in PC-Filter involves an Intra-Partition Comparison process (Intra-PC) and an Inter-Partition Comparison process (Inter-PC).

Intra-PC
Intra-PC involves the record comparison in each of the partitions. R-R Properties (Property 1 and 2) are used in Intra-PC to avoid the record comparison of two records if they can satisfy either Property 1 or Property 2. Intra-PC is performed in 3 steps as follows:
(1) Using Property 1 and 2, pair-wise similarity evaluations are performed among all the records within each partition. A record pair is detected duplicate (or not duplicate) if Property 1(or Property 2) is satisfied.
(2) All the records of a partition, whose duplication or non-duplication decision cannot be made using Property 1 and 2, are compared using TI-Similarity. Also, duplicate pairs of records are detected if their similarities exceed the similarity threshold.
(3) Repeat Step (1) and (2) until all partitions of the database have been compared internally.

Inter-PC
Instead of finding duplicate records only within each partition, Inter-PC globalizes the record comparison to find duplicate records across different partitions. After the PCG has been constructed, Inter-PC will compare the records of the partitions that are directly connected in PCG. Inter-PC performs 4 steps for the whole database:
(1) For each record R, the similarities are computed between R and ARs of R's immediate neighboring outer partitions in the PCG. R is detected duplicate with all the records in an outer partition if Property 3 is satisfied for R and the outer

partition. If Property 4 is satisfied for R and an outer partition, the outer partition, which impossibly contains any duplicate records with R, can be safely pruned.
(2) For those neighboring partitions that do not satisfy either Property 3 or 4, we will evaluate R with each record in these partitions. R is detected duplicate (or not duplicate) with a record in an outer partition if Property 1 (or Property 2) is satisfied for this pair of records. For those records that cannot be evaluated using Property 1 or 2, Inter-PC will perform detailed comparisons between R and these using TI-Similarity.
(3) Repeat Step (1) and (2) until all the record in a partition have been evaluated. When a whole record partition has been evaluated, this partition will be deleted from the PCG, together with all the edges associated with this partition in the PCG.
(4) Repeat Step (1)-(3) until there are not any nodes left in the PCG.

5   Complexity Analysis

Let N be the number of records in the database, s be size of each partition, k be the number of partitions, p be the average number of neighboring outer partitions in PCG of each partition, a be the percentage of total record pairs that have to be compared using TI-Similarity in Intra-PC, b be the percentage of records in neighboring outer partitions that each examined record has to compare with using TI-Similarity in Inter-PC, C_{sim} be the average cost of comparison of a pair of records using TI-Similarity and C_{flop} be the cost other than C_{sim} for float point operations such as additions, deletions, multiplications and judgments.

In database sorting, the cost will be $N*logN*C_{flop}$ for a database of N records.

In the pre-processing step, similarities between AR and other records within each partition will be computed, so the cost will be $N*C_{sim}$. These similarity values will be sorted within each of the partitions with a cost of $k*s*logs* C_{flop} = N*logs *C_{flop}$. The total cost for this step is thus approximately $N*C_{sim}$ given $s<<N$ and $C_{flop}<< C_{sim}$.

To construct PCR of each partition, similarities between each DR of the partition and ARs of its outer partitions will be computed, with a cost of $N_{dr}*k^2*C_{sim}$. Then, one scan of the PCRs of all partitions is required in the conversion from PCR to PCG, which requires a cost of $k* C_{flop}$. In sum, the cost of constructing PCG is $N_{dr}*k^2*C_{sim}+ k* C_{flop}$. Given $C_{flop}<< C_{sim}$, the cost of constructing PCG can be simplified as $N_{dr}*k^2*C_{sim}$.

In Intra-PC, the similarities of all record pairs will be examined in terms of Property 1 and 2, which requires a cost of $s^2* C_{flop}$. The cost of comparing record pairs using TI-Similarity will be $a*s^2*C_{sim}$. In summary, the total cost to perform k such processes will be $k*(s^2* C_{flop}+ a*s^2*C_{sim})$. Given $C_{flop}<< C_{sim}$ and $N=k*s$, the cost of Intra-PC can be simplified as $k*a*s^2*C_{sim}= a*(k* s^2)* C_{sim}= a*s*N* C_{sim}$.

In Inter-PC, each record R will compare with all the ARs in its neighboring outer partitions in PCG, requiring a cost of $p* C_{sim}$. Inter-PC will then draw on R-P and R-R Properties to evaluate pairs of records, with a cost of $p* C_{flop}$ and $p*s*C_{flop}$, respectively. Finally, R will compare with the records in the partitions that have not been pruned using TI-Similarity, with a cost of $b*p*s*C_{sim}$. In sum, the total cost for examining N records in inter-PC will be $N*(p* C_{sim}+ p* C_{flop} +p*s*C_{flop}+b*p*s*C_{sim})$. Given $C_{flop} \ll C_{sim}$, the cost of Inter-PC can be simplified to $b*p*s *N*C_{sim}$.

Combining the cost of all the above steps, the total cost of PC-Filter will approximately be $N*\log N*C_{flop}+(N+ N_{dr}*k^2)*C_{sim}+ a*s*N* C_{sim} +b*p*s* *N*C_{sim}$. Given $k=N/s$, the cost will be $N*\log N*C_{flop}+(1+(a+b*p)*s+ N_{dr}*N/s^2)*N*C_{sim}$. This cost can be minimized to $N*\log N*C_{flop}+(1+1.89\ (a+b*p)^{2/3}N^{1/3}+N_{dr}^{1/3}N^{1/3})*N*C_{sim} \sim O(N^{4/3})$ when $s=2^{1/3}*N_{dr}^{1/3}*N^{1/3}*(a+b*p)^{-1/3}$. This analysis shows that the complexity of PC-Filter can be ideally reduced to the order of $O(N^{4/3})$ by picking an optimized value of s.

6 Experimental Results

In our experiments, the pair-wise comparison method, Multi-pass SNM, Priority Queue method [7] and RAR [10] are used for comparative study on the performance in duplicate record detection.

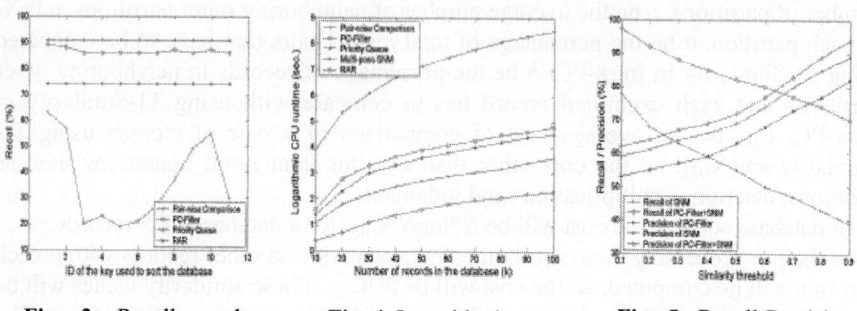

Fig. 3. Recall results when varying the keys

Fig. 4. Logarithmic CPU runtime

Fig. 5. Recall-Precision graph of SNM and PC-Filter+SNM

At first, we will vary the key to sort the database in order to evaluate its effect on the recall level of PC-Filter. Specifically, we sort the database based on each of the 11 fields of the records in the synthetic dataset and compute the recall of duplicate record detection using each of these 11 sorted databases. The keys are 1. Social Security No. 2. Name 3. Gender 4. Martial status 5. Race 6. Nationality 7. Education 8. Office phone number 9 Home phone No. 10. Mailing address 11. Position. The result is shown in Figure 3. We can see that the recalls of PC-Filter, pair-wise comparison method and Priority Queue method have very stable recalls while RAR is very sensitive to the key selected to sort the database. Pair-wise comparison method and Priority Queue method do not require database sorting, thus their recalls are not affected by the key chosen to sort the database. Using a fix-sized window in RAR, the recall will be relatively higher when using more discriminating keys to let the truly duplicate records locate close to each other, but will be lower when using less discriminating ones in which the truly duplicate records will probably stay far apart from each other. Without using a window of fixed size, PC-Filter is able to compare two records even when they are far apart from each other in the sorting list. This experiment justifies that PC-Filter is able to solve the "Key Selection" problem the existing methods suffer from.

We are also interested in exploring the efficiency of PC-Filter against other four methods. Figure 4 shows the logarithmic CPU runtime of different methods. The CPU time of PC-Filter is higher than the time of Multi-pass SNM ($O(k*w*N)$) and RAR ($O(w*N)$), but comparable to the time of Priority Queue method ($O(NlogN)$) and significantly less than the time of the pair-wise comparison method ($O(N^2)$), where w is the window size and N is the number of records in the database. By taking advantage of the transitive closure properties of record similarity, PC-Filter saves a noticeable amount of expensive record comparisons and therefore is able to well scale to large databases due to its computational complexity of $O(N^{4/3})$.

Finally, we will experimentally show that the framework of PC-Filter+X (incorporating PC-Filter into a compare method X with a different similarity measure, such as edit distance), will enable us to achieve better recall and precision than only using X. Recall that the major role of PC-Filter is to return a relatively small set of duplicate records efficiently with a high recall level. However, there may be many false-positives in this result, thus the method X is used to refine the result by pruning away these false-positives from the result. In our experiment, we choose X as SNM using edit distance and compare the effectiveness of PC-Filter+SNM and SNM. The recall-precision graph is presented in Figure 5. We can see, from the figure, that (i) The recall of PC-Filter+SNM is much higher than SNM, this is because PC-Filter outperforms SNM in terms of recall; (ii) The precision of the result of PC-Filter is slightly lower than that of SNM. This is understandable since when more record are needed to compare, there will be a higher chance for some false-positives to be included in the result. (iii) The precision of the result of PC-Filter+SNM is, however, higher than that of SNM. This is because using two similarity measures, TI-Similarity in PC-Filter and edit distance in SNM, PC-Filter+SNM can be more effective in detecting duplicate records than only using one kind of similarity measure. Put simply, by incorporating PC-Filter to SNM, we can achieve better recall and precision performance than performing SNM alone.

7   Conclusions

A robust filtering technique, called PC-Filter, is proposed in this paper for duplicate record detection in large database. In PC-Filter, the database is first sorted and sequentially split into a number of partitions. These partitions will be internally and externally compared in order to detect duplicate records. We utilize the transitive closure of record similarity and devise four properties, used as heuristics, based on such transitive closure to achieve a remarked efficiency of the filter. Experimental results verify PC-Filter is able to well solve a number of critical problems the existing methods suffer from.

References

[1] R. Ananthakrishna, S. Chaudhuri and V. Ganti. Eliminating Fuzzy Duplicates in Data Warehouses. In *Proceedings of VLDB' 2002*, pages 586-597, Hong Kong, China, 2002.

[2] S. Chaudhuri, K. Ganjam, V. Ganti and R. Motwani. Robust and Efficient Fuzzy Match for Online Data Cleaning. In *Proceedings of ACM SIGMOD 2003*, pages 313-324, San Diego, USA, 2003.

[3] L. Gravano, P. G. Ipeirotis, N. Koudas, D. Srivastava: Text Joins for Data Cleansing and Integration in an RDBMS. In *Proceedings ICDE'03*, pages 729-731, 2003.

[4] M. Hernandez. A Generation of Band Joins and the Merge/Purge Problem. *Technical Report CUCS-005-1995, Columbia University*, Feb 1996.

[5] M. A. Hernandez and S. J. Stolfo. The Merge/Purge Problem for Large Documents. In *Proceedings of the 1995 ACM-SIGMOD*, pages 127-138, 1995.

[6] W.L. Low, M.L. Lee and T.W. Ling. A Knowledge-Based Framework for Duplicates Elimination. In *Information Systems: Special Issue on Data Extraction, Cleaning and Reconciliation*, Volume 26, Issue 8, Elsevier Science, 2001.

[7] A.E. Monge and C.P. Elkan. An Efficient Domain-independent Algorithm for detecting Approximately Duplicate Document Records. In *Proceedings of SIGMOD Workshop on Research issues and Data Mining and Knowledge Discovery*, 1997.

[8] A.E. Monge and C.P. Elkan. The Field Matching Problem: Algorithms and Application. In *Proceedings of SIGKDD'96*, pages 267-270, 1996.

[9] Z. Li, S.Y. Sung, P. Sun and T. W. Ling, A New Efficient Data Cleansing Method. In *Proceedings DEXA'02*, Aix-en-Provence, France, 2002.

[10] S.Y. Sung, Z. Li and S. Peng. A Fast Filtering Scheme for Large Document Cleansing. In *Proceedings of CIKM'02*, pages 76-83, 2002.

On Efficient and Effective Association Rule Mining from XML Data

Ji Zhang[1], Tok Wang Ling[2], Robert M. Bruckner[3], A Min Tjoa[4], and Han Liu[1]

[1]Department of Computer Science, University of Toronto,
Toronto, Ontario, M5S 3G4, Canada
{jzhang,hanliu}@cs.toronto.edu
[2]Department of Computer Science, National University of Singapore, Singapore 117543
lingtw@comp.nus.edu.sg
[3]Microsoft Research, Redmond, WA, USA
robruc@microsoft.com
[4]Institute of Software Technology, Vienna University of Technology, Vienna, Austria
tjoa@ifs.tuwien.ac

Abstract: In this paper, we propose a framework, called XAR-Miner, for mining ARs from XML documents efficiently and effectively. In XAR-Miner, raw XML data are first transformed to either an Indexed Content Tree (IX-tree) or Multi-relational databases (Multi-DB), depending on the size of XML document and memory constraint of the system, for efficient data selection in the AR mining. Concepts that are relevant to the AR mining task are generalized to produce generalized meta-patterns. A suitable metric is devised for measuring the degree of concept generalization in order to prevent under-generalization or over-generalization. Resultant generalized meta-patterns are used to generate large ARs that meet the support and confidence levels. An efficient AR mining algorithm is also presented based on candidate AR generation in the hierarchy of generalized meta-patterns. The experiments show that XAR-Miner is more efficient in performing a large number of AR mining tasks from XML documents than the state-of-the-art method of repetitively scanning through XML documents in order to perform each of the mining tasks.

1 Introduction

The fast-growing amount of XML-based information on the web has made it desirable to develop new techniques to discover patterns and knowledge from the XML data. Association Rule (AR) mining is frequently used in data mining to reveal interesting trends, patterns, and rules in large datasets. Mining ARs from XML documents thus has become a new and interesting research topic. Association rules have been first introduced in the context of retail transaction databases [1]. Formally, an AR is an implication in the form of $X \rightarrow Y$, where X and Y are sets of items in database D that satisfy $X \cap Y = \Phi$, where D is a set of data cases. X and Y are called the antecedent and subsequent of the rule, respectively. The rule $X \rightarrow Y$ has support of s in D if $s\%$ of the data cases in D contain both X and Y, and the rule has a confidence of c in D if $c\%$ of the data cases contain Y if they also contain X. Association rule mining aims to discover all large rules whose support and confidence exceed user-specified minimum support and confidence thresholds: *minsup* and *minconf*.

A recent trend of mining ARs is the development of query language to facilitate association rule mining. The MINE RULE operator is introduced in [8] and extended in [9]. In addition, [7] introduced a SQL extension, called MSQL, which is equipped with various operators over association rules such as generation, selection, and pruning. DMSQL [5] is another query language used for association rule specification. There has already been research in mining ARs from semi-structured documents [2, 4, 12, 13], among which the works in [2, 4] use unsupervised procedures and [12, 13] use single and multi-constraints in mining ARs. The constraint-based methods, compared to the non-constraint ones, are able to achieve better efficiency in the mining process and generate a manageable number of rules. In the domain of XML data, the work in [3] uses the MINE RULE operator introduced in [8] for AR mining purposes in native XML documents. The Predicative Model Markup Language (PMML) is proposed to present various patterns such as association rules and decision trees extracted from XML documents [10]. [15] presents a XML-enable AR mining framework, but does not give any details on how to implement this framework efficiently. [16] claims that XML AR can be simply accomplished using XQuery language.

However, the major problems with the state-of-the-art methods, i.e. [3], [10] and [16], are two-fold: (i) they select data from native XML data, thus the efficiency of these approaches is low because of the normally huge volume of XML data need to scanned in the process of AR mining. This becomes even worse when performing a large number of AR mining tasks. Data organization in XML format inherently renders the data selection inefficient. (ii) They do utilize generalization (e.g. group or cluster operations) of data. However, they lack the mechanism to control the degree to which generalization is performed. Under-generalization or over-generalization will seriously affect the effectiveness of the AR mining.

To address the above problems, we will propose a framework, called XAR-Miner, to efficiently and effectively mine ARs from XML documents in this paper. In this framework, XML data are extracted and organized in a way that is suitable for efficient data selection in the AR mining. Concepts relevant to the AR mining task are generalized, if necessary, to a proper degree in order to generate meaningful yet nontrivial ARs.

2 Overview of the Framework

The framework of AR mining of XML data consists of three major parts: (1) Pre-processing (i.e., construction of the Indexed XML Tree (IX-tree) or Multiple Relational Databases (Multi-DB)); (2) Generation of generalized meta-patterns; and (3) Generation of large ARs of generalized meta-patterns.

In the pre-processing module, data in the XML document are extracted and the IX-tree or Multi-DB will be built. Choice of IX-tree or Multi-DB is made based on the size of XML data and the main memory constraint of the system. IX-tree will be used when the XML data can be fully loaded into the main memory of the system while Multi-DB will be used otherwise. The transformed XML data will be indexed using sorting method to facilitate efficient data selections during the mining process.

Secondly, the AR mining task issued by user is analyzed and properly formulated by the system. Because of the sparsity of the XML data, especially in the AR mining tasks that involve multiple concepts, concept generalization will usually be performed to generate generalized meta-patterns. Two constraints, called Min_gen and Max_gen, are used to specify the allowed degree of generalization, which help avoid under-generalization or over-generalization of the meta-patterns.

Large ARs of the generalized meta-patterns that meet the support and confidence requirements are then mined using Apriori algorithm, a typical AR mining algorithm, in the AR Mining Module.

In this paper, a sample XML document of employee information, *EmployeeInfo.xml* (shown in Figure 1), is used to illustrate the ideas, definitions and algorithms of XAR-Miner, as appropriate.

```
<EmployeeInfo>
    <Employee>
        <Name> James Wang </Name>
        <Education>
            <Major> Computer Science </major>    <Degree> B.S </Degree>
            <Major> Computer Science </major>    <Degree> M.Sc </Degree>
        </Education>
        <TypeOfJob> System Analyst </TypeOfJob>
    </Employee>
    <Employee>
        <Name> Ghai Vandana </Name>
        <Education>
            <Major> Accounting </major>    <Degree> B.A </Degree>
        </Education>
        <TypeOfJob> Accountant </TypeOfJob>
    </Employee>
    <Employee>
        <Name> Linda Lee </Name>
        <Education>
            <Major> Mathematics </major>    <Degree> B.S </Degree>
            <Major> Management </major>    <Degree> M.B.A </Degree>
            <Major> Economics </major>    <Degree> Ph.D </Degree>
        </Education>
        <TypeOfJob> Project Manager </TypeOfJob>
    </Employee>
</EmployeeInfo>
```

Fig. 1. Sample XML document (EmployeeInfo.xml)

3 XML Data Extraction and Transformation

The preprocessing work of XAR-Miner is to extract information from the original XML document and transform them into a way that is suitable for efficient AR mining. Specifically, we build *Indexed XML Tree* (IX-tree) when all the XML data can be loaded into main memory, and build *Multi-relational Databases* (Multi-DB) otherwise. We will evaluate the size of the XML data involved and the main memory available to select the proper strategy for XML data transformation and storage before AR mining tasks are preformed.

3.1 Construction of Indexed XML Tree (IX-Tree)

Definition 1. *Indexed XML Tree (IX-tree)*: An Indexed XML Tree (IX-tree in short) is a rooted tree IX-tree=<V, E, A>, where V is the vertex set, E is the edge set and A is the indexed array set. V is set of nodes appearing in the XML document. The intermediate nodes in the IX-tree store the addresses of its immediate parent and children. An edge $e(v_1, v_2)$ in the IX-tree connects the two vertices v_1 and v_2 using a bi-directional link. The set of indexed arrays A positioned at the bottom level in the IX-tree stores the data in the leaf element or attribute nodes in the original XML document.

The IX-tree of EmployeeInfo.xml is shown in Figure 2. The IX-tree can be seen as a sort of hybrid of hierarchical and array-like structure. The hierarchical structure maintains the inherent parent-child and sibling relationships of the extracted XML data while the arrays store their indexed structural values. The construction of the IX-tree consists of the following two steps:

(1) Hierarchical structure building of IX-tree

The XML document will be scanned to get hierarchical information and structural values in the leaf nodes of the document. The moment an element or attribute is scanned in the XML document, a new node will be created in the corresponding IX-tree. Two pointers, *ParentNode* and *ChildNode* are used in this scanning process. If *ParentNode* is currently not a leaf node, the next node (its child node) will be read and these two nodes will be connected using a bi-directional link in the IX-tree. When the leaf node has been reached, the data in this leaf node will be retrieved and stored in an array. This process will be terminated when the end of the XML document is reached.

(2) Indexing of data in the arrays

The arrays storing the extracted data from the XML document are indexed by sorting the data to facilitate fast selection of relevant data for the AR mining task.

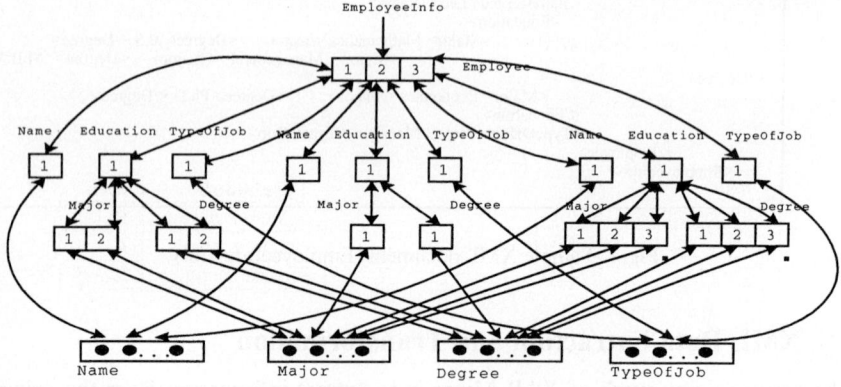

Fig. 2. IX-tree of EmployeeInfo.xml

3.2 Construction of Multi-relational Databases of XML Data

Under the circumstance that the size of XML data exceeds the main memory available, it is impossible to build an in-memory IX-tree. Therefore, we alternatively choose to construct Multi-relational Databases to accommodate the extracted XML data. In this architecture, an XML document will be transformed to a few relational databases, each of which will store the indexed structural values of a concept in the XML document. Unlike using hierarchical structure to maintain the inherent parent-child and sibling relationships of XML data, we use the notion of Serial Xpath String (SXS) to identify each XML data in relational databases.

Definition 2. *Serial Xpath String (SXS) of XML data*: The Serial Xpath String of an XML data x, denoted as SXS(x), is a string that gives the ordinal numbers of concepts of different levels along the path from the root to the leaf node of x. Any

SXS will start with the root node and the ordinal number of concepts along the path will be delimited by dashed lines.

For example, the SXS of the data "Economics" in Figure 1 is "R-3-1-3". R in the SXS denotes the root node of the hierarchy. 3, 1 and 3 are the ordinal number of the concepts along the path, i.e. Employee, Education and Major. Please note an SXS with in a relational database is unique but not so across different databases since an SXS itself does not hold any information regarding the concepts along the path. To uniquely identify XML data stored in the multi-relational databases, we use the complete path in the XML tree starting from the root to the leaf node of the XML data, called *Xpath*, and associate it with each of the relational databases. In this particular example, the complete path of "Economics' which is associated with Major.db is Employeeinfo/Employee/Education/Major, thus the SXS of "R-3-1-3" is equivalent to Employinfo-Employee(3)-Education(1)-Major(3), meaning that Economics is the third major (i.e. PhD) in the education information of the third employee in the XML document. The salient feature of SXS is that it is compact and, together with the Xpath associated with each relational database, it is able to uniquely identify an XML data in the whole XML document using the ordinal occurrence number of concepts in SXS. In addition, by using a string format, it is able to well maintain the hierarchical relationships of XML data. The Multi-relational databases transformation of the Employeeinfo.xml is given in Figure 3.

Name.db (XPath: Employeeinfo/Employee/Name)

Name	SXS
James Wang	R-1-1
Ghai Vandana	R-2-1
Linda Lee	R-3-1

TypeOfJob.db
(XPath: Employeeinfo/Employee/TypeOfJob)

TypeOfJob	SXS
System Analyst	R-1-1
Accountant	R-2-1
Project Manager	R-3-1

Major.db(XPath: Employeeinfo/Employee/Education/Major)

Major	SXS
Computer Science	R-1-1-1
Computer Science	R-1-1-2
Accounting	R-2-1-1
Mathematics	R-3-1-1
Management	R-3-1-2
Economics	R-3-1-3

Degree.db
(XPath: Employeeinfo/Employee/Education/Degree)

Degree	SXS
B.S	R-1-1-1
M.Sc	R-1-1-2
B.A	R-2-1-1
B.S	R-3-1-1
M.B.A	R-3-1-2
Ph.D	R-3-1-3

Fig. 3. Multi-relational database transformation of Employeeinfo.xml

3.3 Advantages of XML Data Transformation

The major advantage of performing XML Transformation into either IX-tree or Multi-DB architecture is that this transformation can ideally satisfy the requirements of AR mining as follows: firstly, AR mining often involves selecting data that are only relevant to the AR mining task. These data are usually only a fragment of the whole XML document. Information indexing in each of the arrays or relational databases helps to greatly facilitate the retrieval of relevant data from the relational databases for AR mining. The selection of data from these indexed structures is much more efficient than selecting data from the original XML document that usually requires a scan through the whole XML document. Secondly, the relationships among data in the XML document, such as a parent-child relationship or a sibling relationship, are perfectly maintained in the transformation by using either hierarchical structure in IX-tree or SXSs in each of the relational databases, enabling us to meet any AR mining requirement on the inherent hierarchical structure of the XML document.

4   Generate Large AR Rules

4.1   Data Selection from IX-Tree and Multi-DB

One of key problems we have to deal with in the AR mining from XML document is the selection of data that are relevant to the AR mining task. In this step, we will select all the instances of involved concepts that meet the WHERE specification. This step resembles the answering of queries. Since all the data in IX-tree and the Multi-relational databases have been indexed, the retrieval of qualified data from them can be very efficient. This efficiency is very significant when the number of AR mining tasks to be performed is large. If the WHERE statement involve multiple concepts, then the query results of multiple database will be joined to generate the final result of this step.

(a) Data Selection in IX-Tree

Recall that in IX-tree, we take advantage of the bi-directional linking between parent and child nodes in the tree hierarchy to realize fast top-down and bottom-up traversal. This fast traversal can facilitate the retrieval of the value of the concepts involved in AR mining. We classify the concepts in the AR mining as *queried concepts* if they are used to specify the scope of data in the WHERE clause and *non-queried concepts* otherwise. We will use the path connecting the queried concepts used in the WHERE clause for data retrieval of non-queried concepts. To create such a path, the Nearest Common Ancestor Node (NCAN) of these concepts must first be found.

Definition 3. *Nearest Common Ancestor Node (NCAN)*: The NCAN of elements $e_1, e_2, ..., e_n$ in the hierarchy of an XML document H, denoted as $NCAN_H(e_1, e_2, ..., e_n)$, is defined as the common ancestor element node in H that is the closest to e_i ($1 \leq i \leq n$).

The NCAN in the hierarchy serves as the common information bridge semantically linking together data of the elements involved in an AR mining task. It is also called the *most informative subsumer* [11] of nodes in the tree structure. For example, the NCANs of the various nodes in the hierarchy in Figure 2 are as follows: $NCAN_H$(Education, TypeOfJob)=Employee and $NCAN_H$(Major, Degree)=Education.

Searching a NCAN of concepts in a XML hierarchy involves path comparison for these concepts. The searching of NCAN can be divided into two sub-steps. The first step is to find the common nodes of all the paths and the second step is to find the node from these common nodes that is closet to the leaf nodes of all these paths.

After the NCAN has been determined, instances of non-queried concepts will be retrieved by first performing a bottom-up traversing from the queried concepts to their NCAN and then a top-down traversing from their NCAN to the non-queried concepts.

(b) Data Selection in Multi-DB

Unlike IX-tree, Multi-DB architecture does not have the bi-directional link among nodes for traversal. However, we have created SXS for each XML data and Xpath for each relational database that perfectly maintains the hierarchical information of concepts in the original XML document. It is noticed that the related XML data have the identical substring of varied lengths in their SXSs. This identical substring is the Xpath from the root to the NCAN of these related concepts. The ordinal number of the NCAN of the concepts can be used to identify data uniquely. This observation can help retrieve the value of related concepts easily. The system finds data value of related concepts in two substeps: (1) The format of SXS of the non-queried concepts will be decided by using the Xpath associated with the databases of the concepts; (2) Search in the relevant databases for the data whose SXS meets the format specified in the first step.

Consider, for example, if we want to find the name of employees whose has B.S degree. The SXSs of the data valued "B.S" are "R-1-1-1" and "R-3-1-1" in Major.db. The NCAN of Name and Degree are Employee, so the SXS of name value of the employee who has B.S degree should be in the format of "R-1-*" and "R-3-*" in the Name.db, where * denotes the substring after the employee node in the complete SXS. We then search in the Name.db for the name value whose SXS matches the above two formats, which are "James Wang" and "Linda Lee".

4.2 Generate Generalized Meta-patterns

After the raw XML data that are relevant to the AR mining task have been retrieved, they will be usually generalized in order to generate ARs that are significant enough. The generalization of XML data is necessitated by the sparsity of the XML data involved in the AR mining task

It is worthwhile mentioning that the data should be generalized properly in order to find significant yet nontrivial ARs. On one hand, under-generalization may not render the data dense enough for finding patterns which extract significant ARs that can meet support or confidence level. On the other hand, over-generalization may lead to patterns which extract trivial ARs that are not depended on the minimum support and confidence.

Definition 4. *Primitive Meta-patterns*: A *primitive meta-pattern* for single-concept AR mining is a tuple $p: \{X, a\}$, where X is the XML data source (IX-tree or Multi-DB) and a is the concept involved in the AR mining. A *primitive meta-pattern* for multi-concept AR mining is a tuple $p: \{X, a_1,...,a_i, s_1,...,s_j\}$, where X is the XML data source (IX-tree or Multi-DB), $a_1,..., a_i$ are the concepts for the antecedent of the AR, and $s_1,...,s_j$ are the concepts for the subsequent of the AR.

Definition 5. *Generalized Primitive Meta-patterns*: Single-concept generalization involves the generalization of only a concept while in multi-concept generalization more than one concept will be generalized. A *generalized primitive meta-pattern* for single-concept generalization is a tuple p': $\{X, a \rightarrow a'\}$, meaning that concept a is generalized to concept a'. A *k-generalized primitive meta-pattern* for multi-concept generalization ($1 \leq k \leq n$), denoted as p_k', is a pattern in which k concepts are generalized. n is the number of concepts in this meta-pattern.

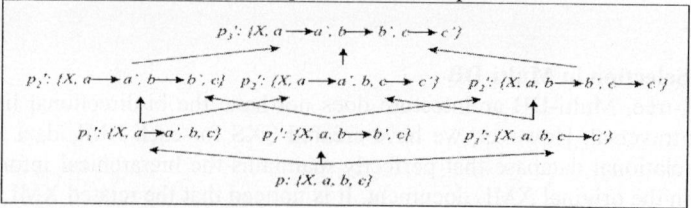

Fig. 4. Generalization lattice of a primitive meta-pattern

Note that there are a combinatorial number of k-generalized primitive meta-patterns for a primitive meta-pattern. To depict all the generalized primitive meta-patterns, we use a structure of generalization lattice. Consider, for example, a primitive meta-pattern in the form of p: $\{X, a, b, c\}$. The corresponding generalization lattice of p is shown in Figure 4.

Now, we will present the quantitative generalization metric for measuring the degree of concept generalization. We denote the generalization degree of a generalized meta-patterns p' as $Gen(p')$ and is defined as follows:

$$Gen(p') = \frac{1}{k} \prod_{i=1}^{k} \overline{D}_i / D_i$$

where $\overline{D}_i$ denotes the average number of distinct values in each record of the ith concept, D_i denotes the total number of distinct values of the ith concept, and k denote the number of concepts that have been generalized. When $k=1$, we will obtain the *Gen* value of single-concept generalization.

Now, we will propose the algorithm of finding all the generalized meta-patterns whose generalization degrees fall into the range of [*Min_gen*, *Max_gen*] in multi-concept generalization (the AR mining of single-concept generalization is relatively quite simple since there will be only one generalized meta-pattern). It is known that if p_2 is a derived generalized meta-pattern of p_1, then $Gen(p_1) \cdot Gen(p_2)$. This theorem can be applied to facilitate the pruning of the excessively generalized meta-patterns: if the generalization degree of a meta-pattern exceeds *Max_gen*, then all its derived generalized meta-patterns are definitely excessively generalized and are therefore pruned away.

Algorithm Find_Generalized_Meta_Patterns (p, k)
p—a primitive meta-pattern, k—the number of concepts in p.
Step 1: Initialize a full lattice of p. Compute the generalization degree *Gen* of the primitive meta-pattern p.
  IF $Gen(p) \leq Min\_gen$, THEN p is pruned from the lattice;
  ELSE IF $Gen(p) \geq Max\_gen$, THEN return an empty set of generalized meta-patterns and whole algorithm is terminated.
Step 2: FOR $i= 1$ to k DO

Compute generalization degree *Gen* of *i*-generalized meta-patterns p_i' of p that has not been pruned from the lattice.
IF $Gen(p_i') \geq Min\_gen$, THEN p_i' is pruned from the lattice;
ELSE IF $Gen(p_i') \geq Max\_gen$, THEN p_i' and all its derived generalized meta-patterns in the lattice are pruned;
Step 3: Output all the meta-patterns that are not pruned in the lattice.

4.3 Generate Large AR Rules

After the generalized meta-patterns have been obtained, XAR-Miner will generalize the raw XML data based on the meta-patterns and generate large ARs w.r.t. the user-specified minimum support (*minsup*) and confidence (*minconf*) requirements using Apriori algorithm.

Theorem 1: Consider two ARs R_1 and R_2. If R_2 is the generalized AR of R_1, then $Support(R_1) \leq Support(R_2)$. ∎

Based on the above theorem, we can infer that if R_2 is not a large AR, then it is definite that R_1 is not a large AR either. This observation helps us devise an efficient algorithm to perform AR generation of generalized meta-patterns, which adopts a top-down strategy to traverse the generalization meta-patterns. The basic idea is that, instead of directly working on the raw generalized data to generate large ARs for a certain meta-pattern, we can first draw on the large ARs of its higher generalized meta-pattern in order to obtain the candidate ARs and then verify the largeness of these candidate ARs. Obviously, verifying the largeness of ARs is much cheaper than mining all the large AR directly from the data.

Algorithm Find_Large_ARs (*M, n*)

M—the set of generalized meta-patterns obtained, *n*—the number of meta-patterns in *M*.
Step1: Sort *M* in descending order based on the number of generalized concepts of the meta-patterns;
Step 2: FOR *i* =1 to *n* do
IF there exists the derived meta-pattern of the ith meta-pattern in the sorted *M*, THEN candidate ARs of this i^{th} meta-pattern are generated based on the large ARs of its derived meta-pattern and the largeness of candidate ARs is verified;
ELSE mine large ARs of this i^{th} meta-pattern using Apriori algorithm;
Step 3: Output the large ARs of all meta-patterns.

5 Experimental Results

In order to evaluate the performance of XAR-Miner, a comparative study is conducted between XAR-Miner and the method using the MINE RULE operator for AR mining purposes in native XML documents [3] (called MineRule Operator Method), which has to scan the whole XML document in order to select the qualified data for AR and incremental AR mining. The IBM XML Generator [6] is used to generate synthetic XML documents with varying sizes specified by user in our experiments.

To study the efficiency of XAR-Miner in AR mining, we first investigate the execution time of performing an AR mining task from XML documents with varied sizes. From the observation of the experimental results as shown in Figure 5, we can see that the execution time of XAR-Miner using IX-tree and Multi-DB is much smaller than that of the MineRule Operator method. The main reason for this is that each AR mining task in the MineRule Operator method entails a full scan of the XML document while the AR mining in XAR-Miner only requires retrieval of relevant data directly from the IX-tree or Multi-DB, which is obviously more efficient.

Because efficient AR mining in XAR-Miner benefits from the construction of the IX-tree or Multi-DB, the comparison will be more fair if we take into account the cost in this pre-processing step and investigate the total execution time of performing 1-10 and 10-100 AR mining tasks. The total time for performing n AR mining is $T_{average}*n + T_{pre-processing}$, where $T_{average}$ denotes the average time spent in each of the AR mining and $T_{pre-processing}$ denotes the time spent in the pre-processing step, i.e. construction of IX-tree or Multi-DB.

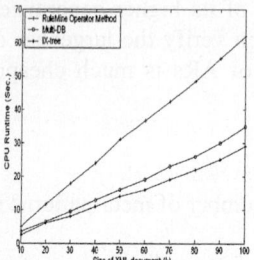
Fig. 5. Mining large ARs from XML document with varied sizes

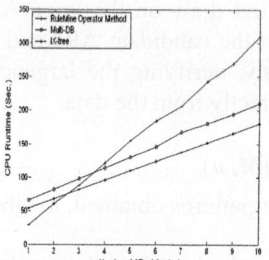
Fig. 6. Performing small number of AR mining tasks (1-10)

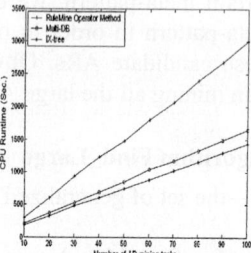
Fig. 7. Performing large number of AR mining tasks (10-100)

The results are presented in Figures 6 and 7. We can see that the execution time of XAR-Miner using IX-tree or Multi-DB is larger than that of MineRule Operator method when the number of AR mining tasks to be performed is small (1-3). But as the number of AR mining tasks continues to increase, MineRule Operator begins to require more time than XAR-Miner. This is because that the speedup of XAR-Miner by using IX-tree and Multi-DB overwhelms the cost of constructing IX-tree and Multi-DB when the number of AR mining tasks becomes large. Figure 7 shows that result comparison when performing larger number of AR mining tasks (10-100), in which the efficiency of XAR-Miner is much better than MineRule Operator method.

6 Conclusions

In this paper, we propose a framework, called XAR-Miner, to mine ARs from XML documents efficiently and effectively. XAR-Miner transform data in the XML document and constructs an Indexed XML Tree (IX-tree) if the XML data can be fully loaded into main memory or Multi-relational databases (Multi-DB) otherwise. The IX-tree and Multi-DB perfectly maintain the hierarchical information of XML data and perform indexing of the data to realize efficient retrieval of data in AR mining. Concepts that are relevant to the AR mining task are generalized to produce generalized meta-patterns. A suitable quantitative metric is devised for measuring the degree of concept generalization in order to prevent under-generalization or over-generalization. An efficient AR mining algorithm is also presented based on candidate AR generation.

References

[1] R. Agrawal and R. Srikant. Fast Algorithms for Mining Association Rules in Large Databases, in Proceedings of *VLDB '94*, pp. 487-499, Santiago de Chile, Chile, Sept. 1994.
[2] A. Amir, R. Feldman and R. Kashi. A New and Versatile Method for Association Generation, in *Information Systems*, Vol. 22(6/7), pp. 333-347, 1997.
[3] D. Braga, A. Campi, M. Klemettinen and P. Lanzi. Mining Association Rules from XML Data, in Proceedings of *DaWaK 2002*, Springer LNCS 2454, pp. 21-30, Aix-en-Provence, France, Sept. 2002.
[4] R. Feldman and H. Hirsh. Mining Associations in the Presence of Background Knowledge, in Proceedings of *the 2nd International Conference on Knowledge Discovery in Databases*, pp. 343-346, Portland, Oregon, USA, 1996.
[5] J. Han and M. Kamber. *Data Mining Concepts and Techniques*, Morgan Kaufmann, 2000.
[6] IBM XML Generator. http://www.alphaworks.ibm.com/tech/xmlgenerator .
[7] T. Imielinski and A. Virmani. MSQL: A Query Language for Database Mining, *Data Mining and Knowledge Discovery*, Vol. 3(4), pp. 373-408, Dec. 1999.
[8] R. Meo, G. Psaila and S. Ceri. A New Operator for Mining Association Rules, in Proceeding of *VLDB '96*, pp. 122-133, Bombay, India, Sept. 1996.
[9] R. Meo, G. Psaila and S. Ceri. A Tightly-coupled Architecture for Data Mining, in Proceedings of *ICDE '98*, pp. 316-323, Orlando, FL, USA, Feb. 1998.
[10] PMML 2.0: Predicative Model Makeup Language. Available at http://www.dmg.org , 2000.
[11] P. Resnik. Semantic Similarity in a Taxonomy: An Information-based Measure as its Application to Problems of Ambiguity in Natural Language, in *Journal of Artificial Intelligence Research*, Vol. 11, pp. 95-130, 1999.
[12] L. Singh, B. Chen, R. Haight, and P. Scheuermann. An Algorithm for Constrained Association Rule Mining in Semi-structured Data, in Proceedings of *PAKDD '99*, Springer LNCS 1574, pp. 148-158, Beijing, China, April 1999.
[13] L. Singh, P. Scheuermann and B. Chen. Generating Association Rules from Semi-structured Documents Using an Extended Concept Hierarchy, in Proceedings of *CIKM '97*, pp. 193-200, Las Vegas, Nevada, Nov. 1997.
[14] G. Psaila, and P.L. Lanzi. Hierarchy-based Mining of Association Rules in Data Warehouses, in Proceedings of *ACM SAC 2000*, Como, Italy, 2000.
[15] L. Feng, T. S. Dillon, H. Weigand, E. Chang. An XML-Enabled Association Rule Framework. In Proceedings of *DEXA 2003*, pp 88-97, Prague, Czech Republic, 2003.
[16] W.W. Wan, G. Dobbie. Extracting association rules from XML documents using XQuery. In Proceedings of *WIDM 2003*, pp.94-97, New Orleans, Louisiana, USA, 2003.

Support for Constructing Theories in Case Law Domains

Alison Chorley and Trevor Bench-Capon

Department of Computer Science, The University of Liverpool, UK
{alison,tbc}@csc.liv.ac.uk

Abstract. Reasoning with cases has been a central focus of work in Artificial Intelligence and Law since the field began in the late eighties. Reasoning with cases is a distinctive feature of legal reasoning and is of interest because such reasoning is both inherently defeasible, and because it is an example of practical reasoning in that it aims to provide a rational basis for a *choice* rather than to deduce some conclusion from premises. As reasoning with cases has developed, it has moved beyond techniques for matching past cases to the current situation to consider how arguments for a position are constructed on the basis of past cases. Recently it has been argued that this should be seen as a process involving the construction, evaluation and application of theories grounded in the phenomena presented by the past cases. Our aim is to develop and refine this idea, with the ultimate goal of building a system which is able to reason with cases in this manner. This paper describes the implementation of a theory construction tool (CATE) to aid in the construction and evaluation of theories to explain the decisions obtained in legal cases, so as to give an understanding of a body of case law. CATE gives a rapid way of creating and testing different theories. Use of CATE is illustrated by showing the construction of alternative theories in a small case study. CATE is useful in itself for anyone wishing to explore their understanding of a set of cases, such as lawyers practising in the domain and knowledge engineers tasked with constructing a rule based system in the domain. We also believe that it offers good prospects for automating the process of theory construction.

1 Introduction

Although there has been some limited success with legal expert systems developed solely on the basis of rules derived from legislation, it is now generally accepted that such systems require knowledge derived from case law if they are to make any real contribution to legal problem solving. Even where there are clear rules, problems of interpretation, under specification and conflict remain. Although cases are used differently in civil and common law jurisdictions this point applies to both styles of legal system. This can be illustrated by [7]: although in their system the Restatement of Torts appear to offer some clear rules, in order to apply these rules to specific cases, the experience of past cases must be drawn upon.

The implication of this is that if one is to understand a piece of law, whether with a view to applying it unaided, or to building a decision support system, it is first necessary to come to an understanding of the relevant case law. Recent work, most fully described in [5], has revived an idea originally proposed by McCarty (eg. [11]) and suggests that coming to this understanding is best seen as represented as the construction of a theory of the domain, developed from, and intended to explain, the phenomena presented by decisions in precedent cases. Once constructed, the theory can be evaluated according to both internal considerations of coherence and by its effectiveness in accounting for the decisions in the precedent cases.

In this paper we describe CATE (CAse Theory Editor), a tool developed to provide support to this process of understanding a legal domain through theory construction. CATE is intended to be useful both to lawyers exploring their understanding of a set of cases, and to knowledge engineers desirous of building an automated system. By providing a means rapidly to develop and execute theories, the task of exploring alternatives and refining initial intuitions is greatly eased.

Section 2 of this paper gives an overview of what we see as a theory of a body of case law, and section 3 describes CATE, which effectively realises the theoretical specification of [5]. Section 4 illustrates the use of CATE through stepping through a well known case study, which although small is sufficiently rich to show many of the important features. Section 5 discusses an extension to CATE which supports a further stage of domain analysis. Section 6 offers some discussion, and considers the prospects for automating the process of constructing legal decision support systems from case data.

2 A Theory of Case Law Domain

Our notion of a theory is taken from [5], which in turn derives from the style of legal case base reasoning developed in the HYPO system and its descendants, e.g. [2], [1] and [7]. The starting point for theory construction is the background of *cases* and the *factors* with which to describe them, which we represent as two files: the *factor background* and the *case background*. Factors are particular patterns of facts which may be present in a case and which if present, will provide a prima facie reason for deciding for one or other of the parties to a case. For example in US Trade Secrets Law, the domain of HYPO, if the plaintiff took security measures his case is strengthened. Thus taking security measures is a factor favouring the plaintiff. Factors are additionally linked to *values*: our account takes a consequentialist view of legal theory, so that we view decisions as justified by the purposes they effect. Here a *value* associated with a factor is some desired purpose, which will be promoted by deciding for the party favoured by the factor when the factor is present. The factor background thus consists of a set of 3-tuples of the form <*factor-name, outcome-favoured, value-promoted*>.

These factors are used to describe the cases which form the case background. Each case will contain a set of factors in the factor background, and as a past case will have an outcome. The case background thus comprises a set of 3-tuples of the form <*case-name, factors-present, outcome*>.

From this background theories are constructed. A theory is a 5-tuple comprising: a selection of cases from the case background; a selection of factors from the factor background; a set of rules linking the factors to outcomes; a set of preferences amongst those rules; and a set of preferences over values promoted by the factors within the rules.

[5] construes the construction of a theory from the background as the application of a number of constructors which enable the inclusion of elements from the background, the formation of rules from included factors and the expression of preferences between rules and between values. It is this process of applying constructors that CATE supports.

3 Description of CATE

Figure 1 gives a screen shot of CATE. It is designed to embody the set of theory constructors as described in [5] and has been implemented in Java. There are panels to show case and factor backgrounds, and the theory under construction. The various theory constructors can be used by clicking on the appropriate button on the screen. For example, to include a case into the theory, the *Include Case* button is selected and the user is prompted to choose which case they want. CATE also provides some checking on the legality of use of the constructors: when a user specifies preferences over rules or values, CATE checks that the resulting theory is consistent and if adding the preference would make the theory inconsistent then a warning is issued and the preference is not added. If the user of CATE still wishes to include the preference then the existing preference causing the conflict must first be removed. CATE also tracks where the rule preferences came from, so that we can distinguish those derived from cases from those derived from a value preference, by labelling each rule preference depending on which theory constructor was used.

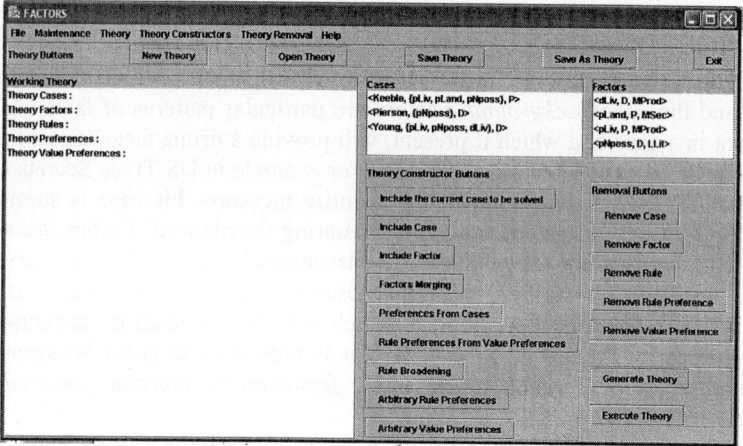

Fig. 1. This figure shows CATE before the Theory is constructed

The *Execute Theory* button can be used to generate Prolog code representing the theory which can be executed to give the outcome which results from applying the theory to each case included in the theory. These case outcomes can then be used to evaluate how the theory performs with respect to the actual decisions for the cases, so as to verify that the theory does indeed explain the selected cases.

CATE requires that a domain analysis has already been completed, so as to supply the case and factor backgrounds. CATE is not restricted to any particular domain and so can be used with any domain once the analysis to supply the requisite background has been completed.

4 Wild Animal Case Study

In much of our work we have used as a test domain US Trade Secret law, drawing on the analysis of [2], [1] and [7]. This domain is substantial containing twenty six factors and five values, and up to one hundred and eighty six cases. For the purposes of illustration, however, we will discuss here a small case study. This case study has been discussed in a number of papers in the AI and Law domain, such as [6], [12], [4], and [3], and is widely used as an example for teaching Law students.

The example consists of three cases involving the pursuit of wild animals. In all of those cases, the plaintiff was chasing wild animals, and the defendant interrupted the chase, preventing the plaintiff from capturing those animals. The issue to be decided is whether the plaintiff has a legal remedy (a right to be compensated for the loss of the game) against the defendant or not. In the first case, *Pierson v Post*, the plaintiff was hunting a fox on open land in the traditional manner using horse and hound when the defendant killed and carried off the fox. In this case the plaintiff was held to have no right to the fox because he had gained no possession of it. In the second case, *Keeble v Hickeringill*, the plaintiff owned a pond and made his living by luring wild ducks there with decoys, shooting them, and selling them for food. Out of malice the defendant used guns to scare the ducks away from the pond. Here the plaintiff won. In the third case, *Young v Hitchens*, both parties were commercial fisherman. While the plaintiff was closing his nets, the defendant sped into the gap, spread his own net and caught the fish. In this case the defendant won. The cases are interesting because many people intuitively feel that the final case should have been decided for the plaintiff rather than the defendant, and the challenge is to come up with a convincing rationale of the actual decision.

We must first give a domain analysis. There are several variants in the literature. Here we follow that given in [5]. First we identify four factors:
1. whether the plaintiff had possession of the animal,
2. whether the plaintiff owned the land on which the chase was taking place,
3. whether the plaintiff was engaged in earning his living and
4. whether the defendant was engaged in earning his living.

We abbreviate these factors to *pNposs* (plaintiff had no possession), *pLand* (it was the plaintiff's land), *pLiv* (plaintiff earning his living) and *dLiv* (defendant earning his living.

We can now identify the values associated with these factors. By requiring the plaintiff to be actually in possession of the animal we give a clear line following which will tend to reduce litigation in this area. The first factor thus promotes this value, which we abbreviate as *LLit* (less litigation). The second factor promotes respect for property rights, offering more security (*MSec*). The final two factors will protect economic activity, which should enable more production (*MProd*).

Our initial starting point thus comprises a case background consisting of:

```
<Keeble, {pLiv, pLand, pNposs}, P>
<Pierson, {pNposs}, D>
<Young, {pLiv, pNposs, dLiv}, D>
<Young, {pLiv, pNposs, dLiv}, P>
```

and a factor background consisting of:

```
<dLiv, D, MProd>
<pNposs, D, LLit>
<pLand, P, MSec>
<pLiv, P, MProd>
```

Two versions of the as yet undecided Young case are included in the background, as suggested in [5], so that the outcome being argued for is available for use in the theory.

We now use CATE to construct the theories. Figure 1 shows the initial state. *Theory 1* is constructed for the defendant. First the *Include Case* Constructor is used to include the *Pierson* case and the defendant based *Young* case. Then the *Include Factor* Constructor is used to include the *pNposs* factor in the theory.

The theory produced by CATE is this:

```
Theory Cases :
   <Pierson, {pNposs}, D>
   <Young, {pLiv, pNposs, dLiv}, D>
Theory Factors :
   pNposs
Theory Rules :
   <{pNposs}, D>
Theory Preferences :
Theory Value Preferences :
```

This theory can be used to generate Prolog code which is executed to produce the outcome for the cases according to the theory. We show the case, the outcome and the decisive rule.

```
pierson | d | outcome(X, d) :- factor(X, pnposs).
young   | d | outcome(X, d) :- factor(X, pnposs).
```

Both cases have been decided for the defendant as there was only a defendant factor present in the theory. This theory adopts a very straightforward approach: considering only a single factor, possession being seen as the whole of the law. *Theory 2* is next constructed for the plaintiff. It extends *Theory 1* by including the *Keeble* case using the *Include Case* Constructor and then the *Include Factor* Constructor is used to include the *pLiv* factor. This gives us two conflicting rules applying to *Keeble*. We know, however, how this conflict was resolved: *Keeble* was found for the plaintiff. We can therefore use this case to give a rule preference which prefers *pLiv* factor over the *pNposs* factor. This rule preference also generates a value preference which is also included in the theory.

```
Theory Cases :
  <Young, {pLiv, pNposs, dLiv}, P>
  <Pierson, {pNposs}, D>
  <Keeble, {pLiv, pLand, pNposs}, P>
Theory Factors :
  pLiv
  pNposs
Theory Rules :
  <{pLiv}, P>
  <{pNposs}, D>
Theory Preferences :
  pref(<{pLiv}, P>, <{pNposs}, D>)        <|<Keeble, {pLiv,
pLand, pNposs}, P>|>
Theory Value Preferences :
  valpref({MProd}, {LLit})
```

The theory can be executed to produce the following outcomes for the cases. *Young* and *Keeble* have been decided for the plaintiff because the plaintiff factor is preferred over the defendant factor.

```
pierson  |  d  |  outcome(X, d) :- factor(X, pnposs).
keeble   |  p  |  outcome(X, p) :- factor(X, pliv).
young    |  p  |  outcome(X, p) :- factor(X, pliv).
```

Theory 3 is constructed for the defendant and adds *pLand* to *Theory 2*. This factor is merged with *pLiv* to produce a rule with *(pLand, pLiv)* as antecedent. The preference in *Keeble* can now be explained in terms of this rule, giving the rule preference of *(pLand, pLiv)* over *pNposs* instead of *pLiv* over *pNposs* as in *Theory 2*. However, this will not explain how *Young* should be decided. To do this we need to include an arbitrary rule preference of *pNposs* preferred over *pLiv*.

```
Theory Cases :
  <Pierson, {pNposs}, D>
  <Keeble, {pLiv, pLand, pNposs}, P>
  <Young, {pLiv, pNposs, dLiv}, D>
Theory Factors :
  pLand
  pLiv
  pNposs
Theory Rules :
  <{pLand, pLiv}, P>
  <{pLand}, P>
  <{pLiv}, P>
  <{pNposs}, D>
Theory Preferences :
  pref(<{pLand, pLiv}, P>, <{pNposs}, D>)
<|<Keeble, {pLiv, pLand, pNposs}, P>|>
  pref(<{pNposs}, D>, <{pLiv}, P>)        <|Arbitrary Rule
Preference|>
Theory Value Preferences :
```

```
valpref({LLit}, {MProd})
valpref({MProd, MSec}, {LLit})
```

This theory decides *Young* in the way we wanted but has resorted to an arbitrary rule preference, which is not desirable.

```
pierson  | d | outcome(X, d) :- factor(X, pnposs).
keeble   | p | outcome(X, p) :- factor(X, pland), factor(X,
pliv).
young    | d | outcome(X, d) :- factor(X, pnposs).
```

An alternative to *Theory 3* is *Theory 4* which is constructed by including *dLiv* instead of *pLand* and merging it with the *pNposs* factor to give a rule with antecedent *(dLiv, pNposs)*. We now add the value preference of *(LLit, MProd)* over *MProd* (which seems justifiable as the preferred value is a superset of the less preferred value) and from this we derive the rule preference of *(dLiv, pNposs)* over *pLiv*.

```
Theory Cases :
  <Pierson, {pNposs}, D>
  <Keeble, {pLiv, pLand, pNposs}, P>
  <Young, {pLiv, pNposs, dLiv}, D>
Theory Factors :
  dLiv
  pLiv
  pNposs
Theory Rules :
  <{dLiv, pNposs}, D>
  <{dLiv}, D>
  <{pLiv}, P>
  <{pNposs}, D>
Theory Preferences :
  pref(<{dLiv, pNposs}, D>, <{pLiv}, P>)        <|From Value
Preference|>
  pref(<{pLiv}, P>, <{pNposs}, D>)        <|<Keeble, {pLiv,
pLand, pNposs}, P>|>
Theory Value Preferences :
  valpref({LLit, MProd}, {MProd})
  valpref({MProd}, {LLit})
```

When executed, this theory gives the required decision for *Young*.

```
pierson  | d | outcome(X, d) :- factor(X, pnposs).
keeble   | p | outcome(X, p) :- factor(X, pliv).
young    | d | outcome(X, d) :- factor(X, dliv),
factor(X, pnposs).
```

A screen shot of CATE in this final state is shown in Figure 2. This example illustrates the benefits of using CATE to assist in coming to an understanding of the domain. By incrementally constructing the theory we can develop a broad understanding and then refine it to accommodate cases not yet explained. At any point we have a clear statement of the theory and can check its implications by executing it. This ensures that we can recognise when additional preferences are required to complete the theory; and that the theory has the desired effects, and if it does not, the reasons for the undesired effects are identified. Adding preferences is constrained by the need to keep the theory consistent. The ability to experiment with different theories also helps to identify false moves: in [6] it is said that students are often misled into incorporating the fact about the ownership of land in *Keeble,* which leaves them unable to explain *Young.* This move corresponds to *Theory 3* above, in which the need for an arbitrary preference shows the deficiencies of the theory, allowing us to explore the more acceptable alternative of *Theory 4.*

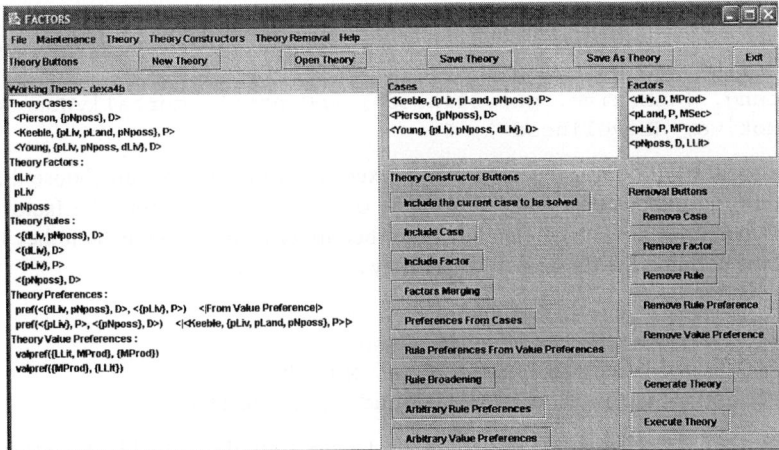

Fig. 2. CATE displaying the complete Theory 4

5   Dimensions

As described above, CATE supports case based reasoning in the style of CATO [1] and IBP [7]. The original conception, however, as described in HYPO [2] used dimensions instead of factors. A factor is either present in the case or not, and if present, favours either the plaintiff or the defendant, However, the features of a case can be thought of more as a particular point on a range or dimension. For example, above the factor *pNposs* represents the fact that the plaintiff was not in possession of the animal and favours the defendant. Possession can, however, be seen as a point on a range of positions starting from just seeing the animal, through chasing it, all the way to having caught and killed it. One end of the dimension favours the defendant strongly and as one moves along the dimension the defendant is less strongly supported and the plaintiff is more strongly supported

CATE has been extended to deal with dimensions and works in much the same way as the factor based version. The starting point is now a dimension background, giving a range of possibilities for each of the four factors.

```
<pControl, <noContact, seen, started, wounded, mortally-
Wounded, captured>, <D, P>, <LLit, Prop>>
```

```
<pOwn, <dProperty, dLease, otherPeopleProperty, communalProp-
erty, pLease, pProperty>, <D, P>, <MFreedom, Prop>>
<pMotive, <pMalice, pSport, pLivelihood>, <0, P>, <0, MProd>>
<dMotive, <dMalice, dSport, dLivelihood>, <0, D>, <0, MProd>>
```

The case background is now expressed in terms of <dimension, point> pairs instead of factors.

```
<Keeble, {<pMotive, pLivelihood>, <pOwn, pProperty>, <pCon-
trol, mortallyWounded>}, P>
<Pierson, {<pControl, mortallyWounded>}, D>
<Young, {<pMotive, pLivelihood>, <pControl, mortallyWounded>,
<dMotive, dLivelihood>}, D>
<Young, {<pMotive, pLivelihood>, <pControl, mortallyWounded>,
<dMotive, dLivelihood>}, P>
```

Now instead of being presented with a fixed set of factors, we can choose different points on the dimensions so as to produce our own set of factors. The factor background therefore now has the factors described in terms of the dimension they belong to and the point on the dimension where they are.

```
<dLiv, dMotive, dLivelihood, D, MProd>
<pLand, pOwn, pProperty, P, MSec>
<pLiv, pMotive, pLivelihood, P, MProd>
<pNposs, pControl, mortallyWounded, D, LLit>
```

Once we have selected the desired set of factors from the available dimensions, we can proceed as above. The importance of this extension is that it allows for disagreement as to where the crucial points on dimensions should be fixed. The need to be able to represent arguments of this sort is argued in [3]. This extension thus allows a further level of theory construction to be supported.

6 Prospects for Automation

We believe that it should be possible to automate the process of constructing and evaluating theories. The theory constructors of CATE are available for an automated program to use, although it will need guidance on how to construct the theory, so that the theory constructors and the cases, factors and preferences to use can be selected according to some fixed strategy. In previous work [8], [9] and [10] we have explored and evaluated different principles for theory construction. Current work involves determining suitable heuristics for case and factor selection. These methods will be used to construct a program which will drive the CATE so as to create its own theories. These theories will then be evaluated to see how well they explain the outcomes for the cases in both the training set and a set reserved to test how well the theory generalises to new cases.

7 Conclusion

In this paper we have described CATE, a tool which supports the construction of theories to explain a set of legal cases. We see this process as a central part of the work both of a lawyer who wishes to apply the cases, and of a knowledge engineer constructing a system to represent and apply knowledge of cases. The process of theory construction is not simple, and we believe there is a real need for support tools. CATE embodies a particular theory of case based reasoning using factors (or dimensions) and of theory construction (as described in [5]). It enables the rapid development of theories, and enhances the process through checks for consistency and by providing a means to execute the theory so as to explore its implications. Although CATE is designed for human use, we hope in future to add functions to automate the process, by providing strategies for theory construction and heuristics for case selection. This could be deployed either as a stand alone program capable of reasoning with legal cases, or as part of a semi-automated knowledge engineering methodology.

References

[1] Aleven, V. (1997). *Teaching Case Based Argumentation Through an Example and Models.* PhD Thesis. The University of Pittsburgh.
[2] Ashley. K.D., (1990). Modelling Legal Argument. Bradford Books, MIT Press, Cambridge, Mass.
[3] Bench-Capon, T.J.M., and E.L., Rissland, 2001. Back to the Future: Dimensions Revisited. In B. Verheij, A.R. Lodder, R.P. Loui, and A. J. Muntjewerff (eds.) *Legal Knowledge and Information Systems*, IOS Press, Amsterdam, pp41-52.
[4] Bench-Capon, T.J.M., 2002. The Missing Link Revisited: The Role of Teleology in Representing Legal Argument, *Artificial Intelligence and Law*, volume 10, 1-3, pp 79-94.
[5] Bench-Capon, T., and Sartor, G. 2003. A model of legal reasoning with cases incorporating theories and values. *Artificial Intelligence*. Vol 150 1-2 pp97-143.
[6] Berman, D.H., and C.L. Hafner. 1993. Representing Teleological Structure in Case Based Reasoning: The Missing Link. In *Proceedings of the Fourth International Conference on AI and Law,* 50-59. ACM Press, New York.
[7] Brüninghaus, S and Ashley, K.D. 2003. Predicting Outcomes of Case-based Legal Arguments. *Proceedings of the Ninth International Conference on AI and Law*: ACM Press, New York, 2003, pp233-42.
[8] Chorley, A and Bench-Capon, T. 2003. *Developing Legal Knowledge Based Systems Through Theory Construction.* Technical Report ULCS-03-013, Department of Computer Science, The University of Liverpool, 2003.
[9] Chorley, A., and Bench-Capon, T. 2002. Developing Legal Knowledge Based Systems Through Theory Construction. *Proceedings of the Ninth International Conference on AI and Law*: ACM Press, New York, 2002, pp85-6.
[10] Chorley, A., and Bench-Capon, T. 20023. Reasoning With Legal Cases as Theory Construction: Some Experimental Results. In D. Bourcier (ed.) *Legal Knowledge and Information Systems: Jurix 2003.* IOS Press: Amsterdam.
[11] McCarty, L.T. 1995. *An Implementation of Eisner v Macomber.* In Proceedings of the Fifth International Conference on AI and Law, 276-286. ACM Press: New York.
[12] Prakken, H. 2000. An exercise in formalising teleological case based reasoning. In J. Breuker, R. Leenes and R. Winkels (eds*.), Legal Knowledge and Information Systems: Jurix 2000,* 49-57. IOS Press, Amsterdam.

Identifying Audience Preferences in Legal and Social Domains

Paul E. Dunne and Trevor Bench-Capon

Dept. of Computer Science, University of Liverpool
Liverpool L69 7ZF, United Kingdom
{ped,tbc}@csc.liv.ac.uk

Abstract. Reasoning in legal and social domains appears not to be well dealt with by deductive approaches. This is because such reasoning is open-endedly defeasible, and because the various argument schemes used in these domains are often hard to construe as deductive arguments. In consequence, argumentation frameworks have proved increasingly popular for modelling disputes in such domains. In order to capture a third phenomenon of these domains, however, namely that rational disagreement is possible due to a difference in the social values of the disputants, these frameworks have been extended to relate the strengths of arguments in the dispute to the social values promoted by their acceptance.
If we are to use such frameworks in computer systems we must be aware of their computational properties. While we can establish efficiently the status of an argument for a particular audience, deciding the status of an argument with respect to all potential audiences is known to be intractable. The main result of this paper is an algorithm which identifies the audiences for which some set of arguments is coherently cotenable. The usefulness of this algorithm is particularly evident in the dialectical settings in which these value based frameworks are most naturally deployed.

1 Introduction

Although deductive techniques have proved successful in many areas, legal and social applications seem less amenable to this style of approach. In domains relating to practical reasoning, such as law, politics and ethics, it is not possible to demonstrate the acceptability of a position absolutely. Rationality in such fields depends on having an argument (not necessarily a proof) which provides a *prima facie* justification of the position, and then defending this argument against any counter arguments that may be offered. The process is thus open ended, and dependent on the context, which is supplied by arguments advanced against the position on the particular occasion.

While a variety of non-monotonic logics have been proposed which address problems arising from uncertain and incomplete information, these are not ideal for legal and social domains. There are two reasons for this. First, in legal and social domains counter arguments arise not only from additional and clarified information, but also from the perspective taken on existing information, the interpretation to be given to the available data. Second, arguments in legal and social domains typically exhibit a variety of argument schemas (for example, [15] identifies sixteen such schemes) and so are not always easily cajoled into some standard form.

For these reasons those modelling rationality in legal and social domains have increasingly been attracted to argumentation frameworks, as originally proposed in [6]. For example, in the legal domain [1], [12], and [10] all use these frameworks in particular ways. The usefulness of argumentation frameworks is that they have a very abstract notion of argument which allows them to accommodate the plurality of possible argumentation schemes, and that they consider conflict between a body of arguments, so as to identify arguments that are plausibly co-tenable, accounting for the notions of defeat and reinstatement that are typical of these areas of reasoning.

However, argumentation frameworks do not in general give a definitive answer as to which arguments should be accepted. This is as should be expected. As Searle remarks in [13, p. xv]

> Assume universally valid and accepted standards of rationality. Assume perfectly rational agents operating with perfect information, and you will find that rational disagreement will still occur; because, for example, the rational agents are likely to have different and inconsistent values and interests, each of which may be rationally acceptable.

The point is also made by Perelman [11]:

> If men oppose each other concerning a decision to be taken, it is not because they commit some error of logic or calculation. They discuss *apropos* the applicable rule, the ends to be considered, the meaning to be given to values, the interpretation and characterisation of facts.

Since typically there are several sets of arguments which could be accepted, we need to try to motivate the choice between these positions in some principled way. We do this by recognising that legal and social arguments depend for their persuasiveness not only on their intrinsic merits, but also on the audience to which they are addressed. Which arguments are found persuasive depends, as Searle and Perelman suggest, on the opinions, values and, perhaps, even the prejudices of the audience to which they are addressed. Consider an example: it is an argument in favour of raising income tax that it promotes equality, and for decreasing income tax that it promotes enterprise. Most people would acknowledge that both arguments are valid, but which they will choose to follow depends on the importance they ascribe to equality as against enterprise in the given situation. Thus which of the arguments is found persuasive by a given audience will depend on the ordering of these two values by that audience. So if I claim that income tax should be raised to promote equality, I can defend my claim against the attack that so doing would discourage enterprise not only by attacking this counter argument but instead by declaring my preference for equality over enterprise. Whether this defence will be persuasive will depend on whether the audience shares my preference as to the values promoted by acceptance of the argument.

Having recognised that the acceptability of arguments in these domains is dependent on values and needs to accommodate the notion of audiences with different values, Dung's original framework was extended in [2] and [3] to give what are termed there Value Based Argumentation Frameworks (VAFs). In those papers a number of properties of VAFs are demonstrated. For example, given an argument system, H, within which each distinct argument promotes one of a finite number of "values" and an ordering, α, of these values representing an individual's preferences, there is a unique maximal subset, $P(\alpha)$, of the arguments in H that is internally consistent and can defend itself against attacks from arguments of H that are not in $P(\alpha)$: in [2] an efficient algorithm for identifying the set $P(\alpha)$ given an value-based argument system H and value ordering α is also described.

Within VAFs arguments can be classified according as to whether they are accepted by at least one audience (so-called *subjective acceptance*); accepted by any audience, that is acceptable whatever the ordering of values, (so-called *objective acceptance*); or indefensible, that is unacceptable whatever the ordering on values. Ideally we would wish to have an efficient way of determining the status of a particular argument within a VAF: Unfortunately it is shown in [8] that this is unlikely to admit an efficient algorithmic solution: subjective acceptance being shown NP–complete, and objective acceptance CO-NP–complete.

These results raise the concern that the approach of using argumentation frameworks with values may, despite their attractions for modelling rationality in legal and social domains, present computational problems if applied to realistically large scale problems. Our aim in this paper is to present further indications that, notwithstanding the negative consequences of [8], the VAF formalism provides a practical model for the study and analysis of persuasive argument. This case is promoted by describing efficient algorithms that could be exploited in arenas such as dialogue processes on VAFs, in particular in uncovering points of disagreement regarding value precedence between the different audiences participating in the dialogue.

The remainder of this paper is structured as follows: section 2 reviews the definition of Argumentation Systems from [6] and their development into the Value Based Argumentation Frameworks of [2, 3], noting the computational properties established. In section 3 we discuss and motivate a number of algorithmic problems for VAFs and describe efficient solution methods for these: these problems relate to determining those values whose ranking is disputed. Finally, section 4 will offer some discussion and concluding remarks.

2 Basic Definitions: Argument Systems and VAFs

The basic definition below of an Argument System is derived from that given in [6].

Definition 1. *An* argument system *is a pair* $\mathcal{H} = \langle \mathcal{X}, \mathcal{A} \rangle$, *in which* $\mathcal{X}$ *is a finite set of arguments and* $\mathcal{A} \subset \mathcal{X} \times \mathcal{X}$ *is the* attack relationship *for* $\mathcal{H}$. *A pair* $\langle x, y \rangle \in \mathcal{A}$ *is referred to as 'y is attacked by x' or 'x attacks y'. For R, S subsets of arguments in the system* $\mathcal{H}(\langle \mathcal{X}, \mathcal{A} \rangle)$, *we say that*

a. $s \in S$ *is* attacked *by R if there is some* $r \in R$ *such that* $\langle r, s \rangle \in \mathcal{A}$.
b. $x \in \mathcal{X}$ *is* acceptable with respect to S *if for every* $y \in \mathcal{X}$ *that attacks x there is some* $z \in S$ *that attacks y.*
c. S *is* conflict-free *if no argument in S is attacked by any other argument in S.*
d. *A conflict-free set S is* admissible *if every argument in S is acceptable with respect to S.*

e. *S is a* preferred extension *if it is a maximal (with respect to $\subseteq$) admissible set.*
f. *S is a* stable extension *if S is conflict free and every argument $y \notin S$ is attacked by S.*
g. *$\mathcal{H}$ is* coherent *if every preferred extension in $\mathcal{H}$ is also a stable extension.*

An argument x is credulously accepted *if there is some preferred extension containing it; x is* sceptically accepted *if it is a member of every preferred extension.*

Abstracting away concerns regarding the internal structure and representation of arguments affords a formalism which focuses on the relationship between individual arguments as a means of defining divers ideas of acceptance. In particular preferred extensions are of interest as these represents maximal coherent positions that can be defended against all attackers.

While this approach offers a powerful tool for the abstract analysis of defeasible reasoning, there are, however, several potential problems. While every argument system has *some* preferred extension, this may simply be the empty set of arguments and although the use of *stable* extensions avoids such problems these in turn have the problem that there are systems which contain no stable extension. An additional problem is the computational complexity of a number of the associated decision problems that has been shown to range from NP–complete to Π_2^p–complete. A summary of these is given in Table 1 below. The classification of problems (3–5) follows from [5]; that of (6) and

Table 1. Decision Problems in Argument Systems

	Problem	Decision Question	Complexity
1	ADM($\mathcal{H}, S$)	Is S admissible?	P
2	STAB($\mathcal{H}, S$)	Is S stable?	P
3	PREF-EXT($\mathcal{H}, S$)	Is S *preferred*?	CO-NP-complete.
4	CA($\mathcal{H}, x$)	Is x in a *preferred S*?	NP-complete
5	STAB-EXIST($\mathcal{H}$)	Has $\mathcal{H}$ a stable extension?	NP-complete
6	SA($\mathcal{H}, x$)	Is x in *every* preferred S?	$\Pi_2^{(p)}$-complete
7	COHERENT($\mathcal{H}$)	Preferred$\equiv$stable?	$\Pi_2^{(p)}$-complete

(7) has recently been demonstrated in [7]. Related problems arise with proof-theoretic mechanisms for establishing credulous acceptance, e.g. for the TPI-dispute mechanism proposed in [14], Dunne and Bench-Capon [9] show that this defines a weak propositional proof system under which proofs that arguments are not credulously accepted require exponentially many steps.

While the issues discussed above concern algorithmic and combinatorial properties of the standard argument system framework, there is also one interpretative issue of some importance. A typical argument system may contain many distinct preferred extensions and, in some cases, two different preferred extensions may define a partition of the argument set. Thus a single argument system can give rise to a number of disjoint internally consistent admissible argument sets. The abstract level at which Dung's formalism operates avoids any mechanism for distinguishing notions of the relative merit of such mutually incompatible outcomes. Thus the situation arises in which we appear to have several coherent positions that could be adopted, and no well motivated way of choosing between them.

As mentioned above, [2] and [3] extend Dung's framework to provide a semantics for distinguishing and choosing between consistent but incompatible belief sets through the use of *argument values*. Thus arguments are seen as grounded on one of a finite number of abstract values and the interpretation of which of a set of arguments to "accept" is treated in terms of preference orderings of the underlying value set according to the views held by a particular *audience*. Thus while in the standard Argumentation system the choice between preferred extensions is arbitrary, in a VAF we are able to motivate such choices by reference to the values of the audience. The formal definition of such *value-based argumentation frameworks* is given below.

Definition 2. *A* value-based argumentation framework *(VAF), is defined by a triple* $\langle \mathcal{H}(\mathcal{X}, \mathcal{A}), \mathcal{V}, \eta \rangle$, *where* $\mathcal{H}(\mathcal{X}, \mathcal{A})$ *is an argument system,* $\mathcal{V} = \{v_1, v_2, \ldots, v_k\}$ *a set of k values, and* $\eta : \mathcal{X} \to \mathcal{V}$ *a mapping that associates a value* $\eta(x) \in \mathcal{V}$ *with each argument* $x \in \mathcal{X}$. *An* audience, α, *for a VAF* $\langle \mathcal{H}, \mathcal{V}, \eta \rangle$, *is a total ordering of the values* $\mathcal{V}$. *We say that* v_i *is preferred to* v_j *in the audience* α, *denoted* $v_i \succ_\alpha v_j$, *if* v_i *is ranked higher than* v_j *in the total ordering defined by* α.

Using VAFs, ideas analogous to those of admissible argument in standard argument systems are defined in the following way. Note that all these notions are now relative to some audience.

Definition 3. *Let* $\langle \mathcal{H}(\mathcal{X}, \mathcal{A}), \mathcal{V}, \eta \rangle$ *be a VAF and* α *an audience.*

a. *For arguments x, y in* $\mathcal{X}$, *x is a* successful attack *on y (or x defeats y) with respect to the audience* α *if:* $\langle x, y \rangle \in \mathcal{A}$ *and it is* not *the case that* $\eta(y) \succ_\alpha \eta(x)$.
b. *An argument x is* acceptable to the subset S with respect to an audience α *if: for every* $y \in \mathcal{X}$ *that successfully attacks x with respect to* α, *there is some* $z \in S$ *that successfully atttacks y with respect to* α.
c. *A subset R of* $\mathcal{X}$ *is* conflict-free with respect to the audience α *if: for each* $\langle x, y \rangle \in R \times R$, *either* $\langle x, y \rangle \notin \mathcal{A}$ *or* $\eta(y) \succ_\alpha \eta(x)$.
d. *A subset R of* $\mathcal{X}$ *is* admissible with respect to the audience α *if: R is conflict free with respect to* α *and every* $x \in R$ *is acceptable to R with respect to* α.
e. *A subset R is a* preferred extension for the audience α *if it is a maximal admissible set with respect to* α.
f. *A subset R is a* stable extension for the audience α *if R is admissible with respect to* α *and for all* $y \notin R$ *there is some* $x \in R$ *which successfully attacks y.*

A standard consistency requirement which we assume of the VAFs considered is that every directed cycle of arguments in these contains *at least two* differently valued arguments. We do not believe that this condition is overly restricting, since the existence of such cycles in VAFs can be seen as indicating a flaw in the formulation of the framework. While in standard argumentation frameworks cycles arise naturally, especially if we are dealing with uncertain or incomplete information, in VAFs odd length cycles in a single value represent paradoxes and even length cycles in a single value can be reduced to a self-defeating argument. Given the absence of cycles in a single value the following important property of VAFs and audiences was demonstrated in [2].

Fact 1. *For every audience, α, $\langle \mathcal{H}(\langle \mathcal{X}, \mathcal{A} \rangle), \mathcal{V}, \eta \rangle$ has a unique non-empty preferred extension, $P(\mathcal{H}, \eta, \alpha)$ which can be constructed by an algorithm that takes $O(|\mathcal{X}|+|\mathcal{A}|)$ steps. Furthermore $P(\mathcal{H}, \eta, \alpha)$ is a stable extension with respect to α.*

From Fact 1 it follows that, when attention is focused on one specific audience, the decision questions analogous to those described in Table 1 become much easier. There are, however, a number of new issues that arise in the value-based framework from the fact that that the relative ordering of different values promoted by distinct audiences results in arguments falling into one of three categories.

C1. Arguments, x, that are in the preferred extension $P(\mathcal{H}, \eta, \alpha)$ for some audiences but not all. Such arguments being called *subjectively acceptable*.
C2. Arguments, x, that are in the preferred extension $P(\mathcal{H}, \eta, \alpha)$ for *every* audience. Such arguments being called *objectively acceptable*.
C3. Arguments, x, that do not belong to the preferred extension $P(\mathcal{H}, \eta, \alpha)$ for *any* choice of audience. Such arguments being called *indefensible*.

To show the advantages of taking values into account, consider the following ethical debate, discussed in, e.g. [4]. Hal, a diabetic, loses his insulin and can save his life only by breaking into the house of another diabetic, Carla, and using her insulin. We may consider the following arguments:

A. Hal should not take Carla's insulin as he may be endangering her life.
B. Hal can take the insulin as otherwise he will die, whereas there is only a potential threat to Carla.
C. Hal must not take Carla's insulin because it is Carla's property.
D. Hal must replace Carla's insulin once the emergency is over.

Now B attacks A, since the permission licensed by the actual threat overrides the obligation arising from the potential threat. A does not attack B, since the immediate threat represents an exception to the general rule which A instantiates. C attacks B, construing property rights as strict obligations whereas possible endangerment is a defeasible obligation. D attacks C. since it provides a way for the insulin to be taken whilst property rights are respected. Further, Christie argues in [4] that B attacks D, since even if Hal were unable to replace the insulin he would still be correct to act so as to save his life, and therefore he can be under no strict obligation to replace the insulin. The argumentation system can be depicted as a directed graph as shown in Figure 1.

Considered as a standard Argumentation System there is no non-empty preferred extension, and it seems we have no coherent position, which is why it is seen and discussed as an ethical dilemma. If, however, we consider it as a VAF, we can see that arguments A and B rely on the importance of preserving life, whereas C and D depend on respect for property. We will now have two preferred extensions, depending on whether life or property is preferred. If we prefer life, we will accept $\{B,C\}$: whilst we respect Carla's property rights, we regard Hal's need as paramount. In contrast if we prefer property to life, the preferred extension is $\{B,D\}$: the property claim can be discharged if restitution is made. Thus B is objectively acceptable, C and D are subjectively acceptable and A is indefensible. This small example shows how we can

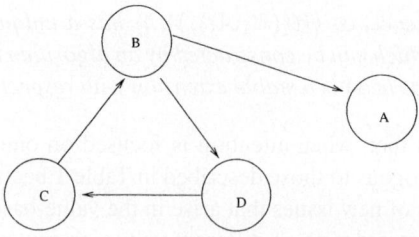

Fig. 1. VAF Example Argument System

use explicit value preferences to cut through what would otherwise be an irresolvable dilemma.

In [8] the following questions specific to the value-based setting are considered.

Definition 4. *The decision problem* Subjective Acceptance *(SBA) takes as an instance a VAF* $\langle \mathcal{H}, \mathcal{V}, \eta \rangle$ *and an argument x in this. The instance is accepted if there is at least one audience, α, for which $x \in P(\mathcal{H}, \eta, \alpha)$. The decision problem* Objective Acceptance *(OBA) takes as an instance a VAF* $\langle \mathcal{H}, \mathcal{V}, \eta \rangle$ *and an argument x in this. The instance is accepted if $x \in P(\mathcal{H}, \eta, \alpha)$ for every audience α.*

Let $\langle \mathcal{H}(\mathcal{X}, \mathcal{A}), \mathcal{V}, \eta \rangle$ *be a VAF, and* $\langle v, v' \rangle$ *be an ordered pair of distinct values from* $\mathcal{V}$*. The pair* $\langle v, v' \rangle$ *is* critical *with respect to an argument* $x \in \mathcal{X}$ *if there is an audience α for which $v \succ_\alpha v'$ and $x \in P(\mathcal{H}, \eta, \alpha)$, but for every audience β for which $v' \succ_\beta v$ it holds that $x \notin P(\mathcal{H}, \eta, \beta)$. The decision problem* Critical Pair *(CP) takes as an instance a triple $\langle \langle \mathcal{H}, \mathcal{V}, \eta \rangle, \langle v, v' \rangle, x \rangle$ comprising a VAF, ordered pair of values $\langle v, v' \rangle$ within this, and argument x. An instance is accepted if $\langle v, v' \rangle$ is critical with respect to x.*

In [8] evidence is presented that these are intractable: SBA is NP–complete, OBA is CO-NP–complete; and, CP is D^p–complete.

We have now arrived at the position where we can detect efficiently the arguments acceptable to any particular given audience, but cannot guarantee that we will be able to determine the status of an argument with respect to the totality of audiences. In the next section we consider another problem relating to VAFs which admits of an efficient solution, namely finding an audience for whom a subset of arguments represents a preferred extension, if one exists.

3 Efficient Algorithms for VAFs

We begin by giving a formal statement of our problem:

a. Given a VAF $\langle \mathcal{H}(\mathcal{X}, \mathcal{A}), \mathcal{V}, \eta \rangle$ and a *subset S* of $\mathcal{X}$ find an *audience* α for which $S = P(\mathcal{H}, \eta, \alpha)$ or report that no such audience exists.

In this section we address this problem raised and some related applications. On first inspection, it might appear that, given the status of SBA, this too would be an intractable problem. We will show, however, that this pessimistic view is ill-founded: the critical difference between the two problems is that subjective acceptance concerns the existence of an audience with respect to which a *single* given argument is accepted; whereas the current problem asks for an audience with respect to which a given *set* of arguments defines the totality of what that audience accepts. In the context of standard argument systems, subjective acceptance is analogous to deciding *credulous acceptance* whereas (a) to deciding if a given set defines a *preferred extension*. While there is no reduction in difficulty in moving from the standard to value-based frameworks, it turns out that the nature of acceptance following the introduction of value associations allows (a) to be solved by an efficient method. To see this we consider the following algorithm:

FIND AUDIENCE
Instance: VAF $\langle \mathcal{H}(\mathcal{X}, \mathcal{A}), \mathcal{V}, \eta \rangle$; $S \subseteq \mathcal{X}$.
Returns: Audience α for which $S = P(\mathcal{H}, \eta, \alpha)$ or FAIL if no such audience exists. The audience is returned as a set of pairs of $\langle v_i, v_j \rangle$ for which $v_i \succ_\alpha v_j$ must hold.

1. PARTIAL-$\alpha := \emptyset$;
2. **for each** $\langle x, y \rangle \in S \times S$:
   2.1. **if** $\langle x, y \rangle \in \mathcal{A}$ **then**
      a. **if** $\eta(x) = \eta(y)$ **then** report FAIL **else**

      PARTIAL-$\alpha :=$ PARTIAL-$\alpha \cup \{\langle \eta(y), \eta(x) \rangle\}$
3. Replace PARTIAL-α with the transitive closure of PARTIAL-α.
4. **if** PARTIAL-α is "inconsistent" **then** report FAIL **else**
   5. **for each** $z \notin S$
      a. **if** $\eta(z) = \eta(x)$ for some $x \in S$ **then**
         Find some $y \in S$ for which $\langle y, z \rangle \in \mathcal{A}$ *and* for which $\langle \eta(z), \eta(y) \rangle \notin$ PARTIAL-α.
         report FAIL if no suitable $y \in S$ is found.
      b. **else** – $\eta(z)$ does not occur as the value of any $x \in S$
         Choose any $y \in S$ for which $\langle y, z \rangle \in \mathcal{A}$ and add $\langle \eta(y), \eta(z) \rangle$ to PARTIAL-α.
         report FAIL if no $y \in S$ attacks z.
6. **return** any audience that is consistent with the (partial) ordering given by PARTIAL-α.

Theorem 1. *Given an instance $\langle \mathcal{H}(\mathcal{X}, \mathcal{A}), \mathcal{V}, \eta \rangle$ and $S \subseteq \mathcal{X}$ the algorithm* FIND AUDIENCE *returns an audience α for which $S = P(\mathcal{H}, \eta, \alpha)$ or reports* FAIL *if no such audience exists. Furthermore the time taken is $O(|\mathcal{X}|^2)$.*

Proof. Steps (2) and (3) of FIND AUDIENCE construct a partial ordering of the values in S that satisfies the requirement that S must be conflict-free with respect to the audience: thus each $\langle x, y \rangle \in \mathcal{A}$ for which both x and y are in S forces an ordering of the values $\{\eta(x), \eta(y)\}$ according to the constraints specified in Definition 3(c). All constraints arising thus are added by the loop comprising (2), resulting in the set of constraints PARTIAL-α upon completion. At step (3), this set is extended to include all of the additional pair-wise orderings arising through the property that if $\langle \eta(x), \eta(y) \rangle \in$ PARTIAL-α and $\langle \eta(y), \eta(z) \rangle \in$ PARTIAL-α then any audience α consistent with PARTIAL-α must have $\eta(x) \succ_\alpha \eta(z)$: constructing all of the pair-wise ordering that should be included simply involves computing the transitive closure of the relations identified after (2) has completed. Step (4) deals with the requirement that any audience α for which $S = P(\mathcal{H}, \eta, \alpha)$ defines a *total* ordering of the value set $\mathcal{V}$ and thus the set of pairs PARTIAL-α cannot contain both $\langle v_i, v_j \rangle$ and $\langle v_j, v_i \rangle$: this would happen if, for example, there where $\{x, y, z\} \in S$ with $\langle x, y \rangle \in \mathcal{A}$, $\langle y, z \rangle \in \mathcal{A}$ and $\eta(x) = \eta(z)$. Since (3) has formed the transitive closure of the constraint relationship identified in (2), the "consistency" test in (4) involves checking that for each $x \in S$ the pair $\langle \eta(x), \eta(x) \rangle$ has not been added to PARTIAL-α. Step (5) is concerned with checking that S is *maximal* with respect to the partial audience that has been constructed in the earlier stages. Again, from Definition 3, this simply involves testing for each argument $z \notin S$, that z cannot be added to S without creating a conflict. There are two possibilities. The value $\eta(z)$ is among those considered in S: in which case it suffices to ensure that z is successfully attacked by some $y \in S$. The value $\eta(z)$ is distinct from any value used in S: in which case it suffices to find any $y \in S$ that attacks z.

4 Discussion

Considered abstractly it is tempting to see the problem of resolving a dispute as a matter of computing a "grand" VAF - the union of the VAFs recognised by every participant to the dispute - with a fixed ordering of values for each of the audiences. This picture is, however, inappropriate for many practical settings in two ways. First, as Searle [13] says, participants do not always come to a dispute with a fixed value order; rather they work out what values they prize the most as the dispute progresses. Second the argumentation framework relevant to the dispute is typically constructed during the dispute as the participants introduce arguments.

In this setting we can see the importance of the algorithm established in section 3. When contributing an argument to the growing framework representing the dispute, the contributor knows which of the arguments already put forward he wishes to accept, but is perhaps unsure as to his exact values preferences. Given a state of the dispute, before contributing an additional argument, a participant should first consider if he is content with the current state. If the arguments he favours form a preferred extension for some audiences, and he is willing to accept a value ordering that this requires, he should contribute no further. Should a contribution be necessary, he must be sure that the argument added to the dispute will produce a preferred extension containing the arguments he desires: otherwise the opponents could choose to terminate the dispute by remaining silent leaving him with a less that optimal preferred extension.

Given the ability efficiently to compute the audience for which a given subset of the current arguments is a preferred extension, we can suggest the following strategy.

Suppose H to be the current argumentation framework. Let S be the set of arguments desired to be the preferred extension Is S a preferred extension of H? If yes, remain silent. If no, consider arguments, p, which extend the current framework If $S \cup \{p\}$ yields a preferred extension of $H \cup \{p\}$, advance p. Otherwise consider arguments, q, such that S is a preferred extension in $H \cup \{q\}$. Advance any such q.

Now the participant can be sure that he is only contributing when it is necessary to so, and that any contributions he makes will successfully defend his preferred set of arguments. The algorithm in section 3 ensures that the required information can be calculated efficiently.

5 Conclusion

In this paper we have argued that VAFs are suitable to capture the features characteristic of argumentation in legal and social domains. Additionally, we have shown that there is an efficient algorithm to supply the information required to drive an heuristic for deciding whether to continue to contribute to a dispute, and if so what would make a sensible continuation.

References

1. T.J.M. Bench-Capon 'Representation of Case Law as an Argumentation Framework' in *Legal Knowledge and Information Systems*, eds., T. Bench-Capon, A. Daskalopoulu and R. Winkels, IOS Press: Amsterdam. 103-112 (2002)
2. T.J.M. Bench-Capon, 'Agreeing to differ: modelling persuasive dialogue between parties with different values', *Informal Logic*, **22** 3 (2003).
3. T.J.M. Bench-Capon, 'Persuasion in Practical Argument Using Value Based Argumentation Frameworks', *Journal of Logic and Computation*, **13** 3 429-48 (2003).
4. G. Christie, *The Notion of an Ideal Audience in Legal Argument*, Kluwer Academic, Dordrecht, (2000).
5. Y. Dimopoulos and A. Torres, 'Graph theoretical structures in logic programs and default theories', *Theoretical Computer Science*, **170**, 209–244, (1996).
6. P.M. Dung, 'On the acceptability of arguments and its fundamental role in nonmonotonic reasoning, logic programming, and N-person games', *Artificial Intelligence*, **77**, 321–357, (1995).
7. P.E. Dunne and T.J.M. Bench-Capon, 'Coherence in finite argument systems', *Artificial Intelligence*, **141**, 187–203, (2002).
8. P.E. Dunne and T.J.M. Bench-Capon, 'Complexity in value-based argument systems'. Technical Report, Dept. of Comp. Sci., Univ. of Liverpool, February 2004.
9. P.E. Dunne and T.J.M. Bench-Capon, 'Two party immediate response disputes: properties and efficiency', *Artificial Intelligence*, **149**, 221–250, (2003).
10. H. Jakobovits and D. Vermeir, 'Dialectic semantics for argumentation frameworks', in *Proceedings of the Seventh International Conference on Artificial Intelligence and Law (ICAIL-99)*, ACM SIGART, pp. 53–62, N.Y., (June 1999). ACM Press.
11. C. Perelman, *Justice, Law and Argument*, Reidel: Dordrecht, 1980.
12. H. Prakken, *Logical Tools for Modelling Legal Argument*, Kluwer Academic Publishers, 1997.
13. J.R. Searle, *Rationality in Action*. MIT Press, Cambridge Mass., 2001
14. G. Vreeswijk and H. Prakken, 'Credulous and sceptical argument games for preferred semantics.', in *Proceedings of JELIA 2000, The 7th European Workshop on Logic for Artificial Intelligence.*, pp. 224–238, Berlin, (2000). Springer LNAI 1919, Springer Verlag.
15. D.N. Walton, *Argumentation Schemes for Presumptive Reasoning*, Erbaum: Mahwah, NJ.

Characterizing Database User's Access Patterns

Qingsong Yao and Aijun An[*]

Department of Computer Science, York University, Toronto M3J 1P3 Canada
{qingsong,aan}@cs.yorku.ca

Abstract. Much work has been done on characterizing the workload of a database system. Previous studies focused on providing different types of statistical summaries, and modeling the run-time behavior on the physical resource level. In this paper, we focus on characterizing the database system's workload from the view of database users. We use *user access patterns* to describe how a client application or a group of users accesses the data of a database system. The user access patterns include a set of *user access events* that represent the format of the queries and a set of *user access graphs* that represent the query execution orders. User access patterns can help database administrators tune the system, help database users optimize queries, and help to predict and cache future queries. In this paper, we present several approaches to using user access patterns to improve system performance, and report some experimental results.

1 Introduction

Database workload characterization is usually based on the database traces. The traces are a collection of measures, such as pages read/written, the number of locks and the number of SQL statements, produced by all transactions being processed by the DBMS within a time interval. Database workload characterization can be based on the three abstract levels: application level, transaction or session level, and physical resource level [7]. Previous studies focus on providing different kinds of statistical summaries and run-time behavior on the physical resource level. Most of the work is from the view of database servers. We are interested in database user behaviors in the session level, i.e., the queries submitted by a user within a user session. In this paper, we propose the idea of *user access patterns* to characterize the database's workload from the view of database users. The main components of the user access patterns are a collection of user access events which represent the format of the queries, and a collection of user access graphs which represent the query execution orders. We suggest several ways to improve system performance by applying user access patterns.

The rest of the paper is organized as follows. We discuss the concepts of user access events and user access graphs in Section 2. In Section 3 , we propose several

---

[*] This work is supported by research grants from Communications and Information Technology Ontario (CITO) and the Natural Sciences and Engineering Research Council of Canada (NSERC).

approaches to improving system performance by using user access patterns. We give experimental results in Section 4. Related work is discussed in Section 5. We conclude the paper 6.

2 User Access Event and User Access Graph

Given an SQL query, we can transform it into two parts: an **SQL template** and a set of **parameters**. We treat each data value embedded in the query as a parameter, and the SQL template is obtained by replacing each data value with a wildcard character (%). In many situations, the SQL queries submitted by a user have the same SQL template and are only different in the data value part. In this paper, we use a **user access event** to represent the queries with a similar format. A user access event contains an SQL template and a set of parameters. The value of a parameter is either a constant or a variable. For example, event *"select name from customer where id =% "*, *'c101'* represents a single query which retrieves the name of a customer *'c101'*, while event *"select name from customer where id ='%' "*, g_cid represents a set of similar queries.

From the view of database users, in order to execute a certain task, a sequence of queries is submitted to the server. A **database user session** consists of a sequence of queries that performs a certain function or task. Given a collection of user sessions of the same type, we use a *user access graph* to represent the corresponding query execution order. A **user access graph** is a directed graph $G_p(V_p, E_p, F_p)$. $F_p = (f_1, ..., f_n)$ is a set of variables/constants. $V_p = (v_1, ..., v_m)$ is a set of nodes, and each node has a support value ρ_{v_i}, which is the occurrence frequency within the set of user sessions. A directed edge $e_k = (v_i, v_j, \sigma_{v_i \to v_j})$ means that v_j follows v_i with a probability of $\sigma_{v_i \to v_j}$, and it is called the confidence of the edge. There are two types of user access graphs depending on the granularity of the nodes. The first type is called the basic user access graph, whose nodes represent only events. The second type is a high level user access graph, in which each node is represented by a basic user access graph. A high level user access graph is used to describe the execution orders among sessions that are performed by the same user. For example, in a client application, there is a patient-information model that helps an employee to retrieve a patient's treatment history and treatment schedules. When a user logs in, the corresponding profile is retrieved. Then he/she can either retrieve the treatment history information or treatment schedules. Figure 1 shows two user access graphs for the patient-information model. Graph *P*, illustrated on the left side, is a high-level user access graph that describes the execution orders of five sub-models. Table 1 is an instance of the treatment-history sub-model containing five consecutive SQL queries. The corresponding user access graph *P3* is shown on the right side in Figure 1.

A parameter in an event can be a constant, a dependent variable or an independent variable. The value of a constant parameter cannot be changed by any of the events in the user access graph. An independent variable can take different values and its value does not depend on any other variable in the

The performance of these rewriting solutions depends on the internal query process mechanism of DBMS. We create necessary indices according to the definition of *TPC-W* benchmark, and test the system performance under two different database servers: *Microsoft SQL Server 2000*[2] and *MySQL 4.0*. The benchmark does not specify the frequency of the valid users and the frequency of the users who have at least one order, we set them as *0.95* and *0.80* respectively. The client application is implemented in *Java*, which has a connection speed of *56K bps* with the server. Table 4 illustrates the experimental results, and case *0* corresponds to the original queries. The two servers have different results since they have different query processing mechanisms. For *SQL Server 2000*, cases *4* and *5* generate fewer requests to the server and have faster response time than the other cases. However, they have more server *I/Os*. Meanwhile, cases *2* and *3* have a shorter response time than case *0*, and they have the same amount of server *I/Os* as case *0*. Case *1* has no significant improvement over case *0*. *MySQL* server does not support sub-queries, thus cases *4* and *5* are not applicable. Cases *2* and *3* have shorter response time than cases *0* and *1*. And cases *1* and *3* have less server *I/O* than cases *0* and *2*, while case *1* has the lowest network traffic[3].

Table 4. Performance for Order Display Interaction (per 100 instances)

	queries per instance	SQL Server 2000			MySQL 4.0		
		response time (s)	server I/O (pages)	sent/received (packets)	response time (s)	server I/O (pages)	sent/received (Kbytes)
case0	5	518	3557	1810/1810	259	2259	611/ 53
case1	5	501	3576	1810/1810	206	1965	596/ 49
case2	4	464	3557	1510/1510	190	2259	567/ 90
case3	4	470	3556	1510/1510	189	1965	571/ 86
case4	3	401	3648	1210/1210	N/A	N/A	N/A
case5	3	407	3721	1210/1210	N/A	N/A	N/A

5 Related Work

A survey of the techniques and methodologies for the construction of workload models in different application domains is presented in [2]. Some previous workload studies focused on describing the statistical summaries and run-time behavior [3,15,6], clustering database transactions[16,9], predicting the buffer hit ratio [4,5], and improving caching performance [10,14]. Chaudhuri *et al* [3] suggest to use SQL-like primitives for workload summarization, a few examples of workload summarization and the possible extensions to SQL and the query engine to support these primitives are also discussed in the paper. In [15], a

---

[2] SQL Server 2000 is registered trademark of the Microsoft Corporation.
[3] The experimental results presented in the paper should not be used for the benchmark performance comparison between the two database servers

relational database workload analyzer (REDWAR) is developed to characterize the workload in a DB2 environment. In [6], Hsu et al analyze the characteristics of the standard workloads TPC-C and TPC-D, and examine the characteristics of the production database workloads of ten of the world's largest corporations. Yu et al [16] propose an affinity clustering algorithm that partitions the transactions into clusters according to their database reference patterns. Nikolaou et al [9] introduce several clustering approaches by which the workload can be partitioned into classes consisting of units of work exhibiting similar characteristics. Dan et. al. [4, 5] analyze the buffer hit probability based on the characterization of low-level database access (physical pages). They make distinctions among three types of access patterns: locality within a transaction, random access by transactions, and sequential accesses by long queries. Sapia [10] discusses the PROMISE (Predicting User Behavior in Multidimensional Information System Environment) approach that provides the cache manager with transaction level access patterns to make prediction for OLAP systems. In [14], we propose algorithms to analyze the semantic relationship between the queries, and rewrite and cache queries based on the semantic relationship.

6 Conclusion

In this paper, we use user access events to represent the static features of a database workload, and use user access graphs to represent the dynamic features. To our knowledge, this is the first attempt to analyze and make use of database users' dynamic access patterns systemically. The experimental results presented in this paper show that the application of user access patterns can improve system performance greatly. Database vendors can also use the idea of *SQL-Relay* proposed in the paper to develop intelligent database gateways.

References

1. Todd Bezenek, Harold Cain, Ross Dickson, Timothy Heil, Milo Martin, Collin McCurdy, Ravi Rajwar, Eric Weglarz, Craig Zilles, and Mikko Lipasti. Characterizing a Java implementation of TPC-W. In *Third CAECW Workshop*, 2000.
2. Maria Calzarossa and Giuseppe Serazzi. Workload characterization: A survey. *Proc. IEEE*, 81(8):1136–1150, 1993.
3. Surajit Chaudhuri, Prasanna Ganesan, and Vivek Narasayya. Primitives for workload summarization and implications for SQL. In *VLDB 2003*, pages 730–741. Morgan Kaufmann, 2003.
4. Asit Dan, Philip S. Yu, and Jen-Yao Chung. Database access characterization for buffer hit prediction. In *Proc. of the Ninth ICDE, 1993*, pages 134–143. IEEE Computer Society, 1993.
5. Asit Dan, Philip S. Yu, and Jen-Yao Chung. Characterization of database access pattern for analytic prediction of buffer hit probability. *VLDB Journal*, 4(1):127–154, 1995.
6. W.W. Hsu, A. J. Smith, and H. C. Young. Characteristics of production database workloads and the TPC benchmarks. *IBM Systems Journal*, 40(3), 2001.

7. O. Klaassen. Modeling data base reference behavior. In *Computer Performance Evaluation: Modelling Techniques and Tools*, page 47. NorthHolland, 1992.
8. Qiong Luo and Jeffrey F. Naughton. Form-based proxy caching for database-backed web sites. In *Proceedings of VLDB 2001*, pages 191–200, 2001.
9. Christos Nikolaou, Alexandros Labrinidis, Volker Bohn, Donald Ferguson, Michalis Artavanis, Christos Kloukinas, and Manolis Marazakis. The impact of workload clustering on transaction routing. Technical Report TR98-0238, 1998.
10. Carsten Sapia. PROMISE: predicting query behavior to enable predictive caching strategies for OLAP systems. In *DAWAK*, pages 224–233, 2000.
11. Transaction Processing Performance Council (TPC). TPC Benchmark-W (Web Commerce) - standard specification revision 1.6, Feb 2002.
12. Wayne D. Smith, Intel Corporation. TPC-W: Benchmarking an ecommerce solution, Feb 2000.
13. Qingsong Yao and Aijun An. SQL-Relay: An event-driven rule-based database (demonstration). In *International Conference on Web-Age Information Management*, 2003.
14. Qingsong Yao and Aijun An. Using user access patterns for semantic query caching. In *Database and Expert Systems Applications*, 2003.
15. Philip S. Yu, Ming-Syan Chen, Hans-Ulrich Heiss, and Sukho Lee. On workload characterization of relational database environments. *Software Engineering*, 18(4):347–355, 1992.
16. Philip S. Yu and Asit Dan. Performance analysis of affinity clustering on transaction processing coupling architecture. *IEEE TKDE*, 6(5):764–786, 1994.

Using Case Based Retrieval Techniques for Handling Anomalous Situations in Advisory Dialogues

Marcello L'Abbate, Ingo Frommholz, Ulrich Thiel, and Erich Neuhold

Fraunhofer-IPSI, Dolivostr. 15, 64293 Darmstadt, Germany
{labbate,frommhol,thiel,neuhold}@ipsi.fraunhofer.de

Abstract. The efficacy of expert systems often depends on the accuracy and completeness of the problem specification negotiated with the user. Therefore, efficient user interfaces are needed, in order to assist the user in identifying and supplying the required data. Our approach presented in this paper is based on the utilisation of conversational interfaces, giving users the possibility of interacting with the system by means of natural language. Through the use of flexible dialogue management plans and an advanced problem solving strategy based on case based reasoning and information retrieval, efficient user guidance during the interaction with an expert system can be achieved. Thus, the user can interactively develop a comprehensive and coherent specification of his problem, based on clarifications, explanations, and context-based factual information provided by the system. As an application framework we introduce the EU-funded Project VIP-Advisor whose objective is the development of a virtual insurance and finance assistant capable of natural language interaction.

1 Introduction

Expert Systems aim at simulating human expertise in well defined problem domains [6]. Usually, they consist of programs closely resembling human logic in which abstract information is used for the computation of a result. Therefore, the correctness and precision of the achieved results mainly depend on the quality and soundness of the submitted information. This is acceptable as long as domain experts use the system, but casual or naïve users frequently fail to be complete and concise during the input phase. They either get overwhelmed by the complexity of the required data or have problems in fulfilling unclearly specified requests for input. Therefore, efficient user interfaces are needed, supporting the user during the problem specification phase. By means of a natural language based interaction, a twofold effect can be achieved: the user can benefit from a certain degree of freedom while choosing a formulation of the data to supply, and the conversational nature of a dialogue can be used for improving the user guidance and minimizing the risk of loosing the orientation. Moreover, whenever a wish for clarification or a need for assistance arises, the user can submit her request in an intuitive way, without having to use or even learn unfamiliar formalisms. Indeed, the grammar of a natural language provides enough expressive power for formulating interaction steps in many different alternatives.

Common conversational systems such as chatterbots or other more sophisticated conversational agents frequently rely on the same underlying technology [5]: user utterances are interpreted and, by means of a pattern matching approach, an applicable rule is selected out of a predefined rule base. The chosen rule also defines the system response to be delivered back to the user. If no relevant rule can be found, a standard answer like "Please reformulate your input" is given. In order to cope with the sequential nature of the data collection phase of expert systems, in our approach we extend the basic technology of conversational systems with flexible dialogue management plans: rules are hierarchically organized into structured sequences in order to adapt the dialogue flow to the application's interaction scheme. User utterances causing a deviation to the currently applied plan are treated as dialogue "problems": instead of returning the standard request for reformulation, the problematic sentence is used as input to a case-based reasoning based problem solver. This approach consists of solving the new problem by adapting solutions that were used to solve old and similar problems [2]. For this aim, a memory of specific prior episodes, called case base, is built. It contains structured recordings of previous successful dialogues (i.e. the cases) including the used dialogue rules. They describe prototypical sequences of dialogue steps which serve to fulfill a task. If an applicable case is found, it is temporarily substituted to the currently used dialogue plan. Once fulfilled, the original state is restored, i.e. the previous plan in which the problem occurred is processed again. In this way, not only a clarification of concepts can be given, but also a user's request for advice can be handled. The gathered information will be considered during the generation of the final problem solution, to be presented to the user. The approach outlined above has been used in the EU-funded Project VIP-Advisor, described in the following section.

2 VIP-Advisor

The key objective of the EU-funded Project VIP-ADVISOR (IST-2001-32440) was the development of a virtual personal insurance and finance assistant specialized in risk management counseling for Small and Medium Enterprises (SMEs). The interface supports speech recognition and synthesis in order to make the advisor easier and more convenient to use. Through online translation mechanisms it is possible to use the advisor in different languages. The project builds upon an existing static expert system (the Risk Manager Online) provided by the user organisation (Winterthur insurances). The existing tool takes the user through a Q&A session with predefined questions before producing a risk analysis matrix. The first steps of the Risk Manager Online (RMO) target the generation of an enterprise profile. For this aim, the pertaining business sector is identified out of a list of 15 entries. Afterwards, the main business activities have to be selected. For every business sector a different set of activities is generated. On the base of the produced profile, the system generates a list of generic assertions, which are evaluated by the user according to different levels of appropriateness (Fig. 1a).

For instance, the user may have to provide the level of dependency on its suppliers (in the case of a business pertaining to the sector "retail trade" and exercising the activity "purchasing"). Finally, the evaluated sentences are used for the generation and visualization of a risk portfolio. The identified risks are grouped to five categories and their weighting is shown by means of a diagram (Fig. 1b).

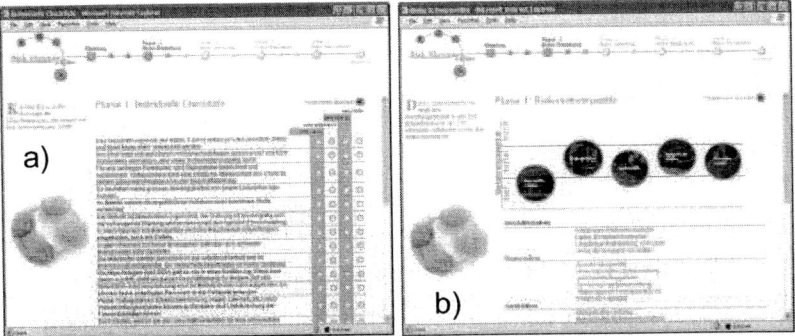

Fig. 1. Screenshots of the Risk Manager Online

In the successive steps of the RMO the user can view and select appropriate measures to counter the presented risks and, finally, build a personalized risk plan. Within the VIP-Advisor project, only the steps up to the presentation of the risk analysis are considered. The standard interaction means of the RMO are augmented by the usage of natural language for both input and output. The virtual assistant guides the user during the elicitation of the needed data and provides help in unclear or problematic situations (Figure 2).

Fig. 2. A screenshot of the VIP-Advisor system prototype

Therefore, the user can always take over the initiative, by asking questions or expressing his uncertainty during the fulfillment of a specific task. An Interaction Manager component is responsible for coordinating and synchronizing the multi-modal interaction with the system, as the user can simultaneously talk via a microphone and make selections directly on the Risk Manager Forms via the pointing device and keyboard. Whenever a user's intervention causes a deviation from the current plan, a new one has to be selected and substitutes the no longer valid plan. This process is deeper described in the following Section.

3 Dialogue Management

The main aim of the dialogue management components of VIP-Advisor is to control the evolution of the conversation. This is achieved by following the active dialogue strategy, defined within the currently adopted dialogue management plan. A plan can be represented in terms of a decision tree whose nodes stand for the system's output states and the edges represent user inputs (usually annotated by patterns). Therefore, if at a specific state one edge can be applied (i.e. the pattern annotating it matches the user input) the destination node is set as the new current state, and the related system utterance is outputted. If, instead, no matching edge can be identified, the user utterance is analyzed by a Problem Identifier component. Its aim is to check whether the user input can be interpreted as a dialogue problem. Four problem classes in which the system recognizes the need to apply a new dialogue plan are identified: concept definitions, process descriptions, concept clarifications and arbitrary knowledge requests. A *concept definition* may consist of a straightforward question from the user seeking a definition e.g., "What is a fire risk?". *Process descriptions* entail the user asking for explanation of a process, e.g., "How can I prevent a fire risk?". In both of these cases a direct answer to the question usually suffices so that FAQ-like dialogue plans (consisting of one question and a related answer) are used for solving the problem. *Concept clarification* is more complex than the first two problem classes since the solution consists of more than a straightforward sequence of questions and answers. A user may, for instance, ask "Why should I prevent a fire risk?". More information needs to be elicited from the user so that the system can present the user with a process as its answer. The dialogue cases here are manual-like (troubleshooting) rather than FAQ-like. Finally, an arbitrary knowledge request is not part of the dialogue, for example, a user may enquire as to possible payment modes or ask for the location of an office. The solution is provided by general information retrieval, information sources being either the enterprise portal or the Web, whereas problems of the first three classes are handled by the Case Based Reasoner Module.

Internally, system and user actions are described by a semantic language based on communicative acts for representing both the meaning and the intention of an interaction step. The used communicative acts are derived from Searle's theory of speech acts [4] and adapted to the system's needs. Actions performed by means of the pointing device or English sentences exchanged between user and system are all represented by a communicative act, such as "request", "inform", "confirm", "authorize" and so on. All acts are extended by a set of parameters which specify the meaning and contents of the performed interaction step. For instance, the signature for "request" is:

```
request (type, matter, subject, content)
```

This communicative act is used to represent a situation in which one of the speakers requires the other speaker to provide some information. The parameter "type" is used for determining the kind of information requested. Usual values are "data", "explanation" or "comparison". The parameter "matter" specifies what exactly is being requested. For instance, common values are "definition", "process", "feature" or "lastAction". The last two parameters provide a deeper characterization of the communicative act: "subject" is used for specifying the topic of conversation and "content" refers to the object of the request. Analogously, the communicative act "inform" provides the same signature as "request". It is used when information (not necessarily new in the dialogue) is provided in a sentence. In the case of a user utterance, the choice of a communicative act, as well as the assignment of values to its pertaining parameters is carried out by both analyzing the grammatical structure of the sentence and by considering contextual information. For instance, during the business sector selection phase, the user may post the question "What is meant by manufacturing?". The standard dialogue management plan only expects the selection of a business sector at this stage (it includes patterns such as "please select *" or "I choose *"), therefore no valid matching can be found, and the Problem Identifier has to be invoked. This module ascertains that the sentence is indeed a "request" for an "explanation" (typically expressed by the formulation "What is meant by"). Particularly, a "definition" is sought, referring to a "business sector" (as defined by the context, i.e. the currently processed interaction step), namely "manufacturing". As a result, the communicative act "request (explanation, definition, business sector, manufacturing)" is generated. As we will see in the following section, this communicative act will be used as a "problem definition", entailing the Case Base Reasoner Module to search for a new strategy, which aims at a solution of the problem. In Table 1 you can see a summary of the criteria used by the Problem Identifier for the assignment of a recognized problem to a specific problem class (in case of a request communicative act).

Table 1. Values for „type" and „matter" attributes of the „request" communicative act and their relation to problem classes. For the last column refer to section 4.

Problem Class	Type	Matter	Case Type	Relevant Case Categories
Concept Definition	Explanation, Comparison, ...	Definition, Feature, ...	FAQ-like	All
Process Description	Explanation, Description, ...	Process, Operation, Procedure, ...	FAQ-like	Interviews, RMO usage, System Usage
Concept Clarification	Instruction, Clarification, ...	Process, Feature, Operation, Procedure, ...	Manual-like	Interviews, Business Sectors and Activities

4 Case-Based Retrieval

Case-based reasoning techniques are applied in VIP-Advisor whenever an unexpected dialogue situation occurs, causing a deviation from the original dialogue plan. The estimation of the suitability of a new plan is based on *pragmatic relevance*: a dialogue plan is relevant to a certain problem if its application helped solving the problem in similar situations happened before. Cases establish a repository of problems which occurred previously, together with the solutions which were applied to solve the according problem. A problem solution contained in a case was useful (and used) in the past; hence, the more the current problem is similar to the old one, the more likely the old solution applies. The initial case base utilized for VIP Advisor contained about 500 different problem definitions and related solutions. For the collection of the cases, several knowledge sources have been used, including the FAQs and glossaries of various insurance and financial web portals as well as interviews carried out with professional advisors. The interviews had the aim of recognizing problems and questions that users normally have during a risk management advisory session. The cases are divided into different categories, according to the topic they refer to.

```
<problemDefinition>
    <ComActList>
        <request>    <type>explanation</type>
            <matter>definition</matter>
            <subject>business sector</subject>
            <content>Manufacturing</content>
        </request>
        <text>Can you explain to me what the business
            sector Manufacturing is?</text>
    </ComActList>
</problemDefinition>
<problemSolution>
    <ComActList>
        <inform>    <type>explanation</type>
            <matter>definition</matter>
            <subject>business sector</subject>
            <content>Manufacturing</content>
        </inform>
     <text>By the business sector manufacturing we mean
            the trade which produces goods and machines
            of every kind.</text>
    </ComActList>
</problemSolution>
```

Fig. 3. An example Case

For instance, cases about pertinent laws, risk factors, and insurance types are included, but also FAQs about business sectors and activities, general financial and insurance concepts and explanations to specific processes and functions of the Risk Manager Online tool can be found. The case base will be regularly updated by examining the system log files: problems which could not be solved will be considered as a new case after the identification of an appropriate solution. In VIP Advisor, the cases are coded using XML. An example case is shown in Figure 3.

The *problem definition* part consists of a communicative act and a representative user utterance causing the problem. The *problem solution* part contains the dialogue plan to apply in order to solve the problem. The figure shows a simple problem solution, consisting of only a single answer. This case would be relevant for the user mentioned in the previous section, asking for the meaning of "manufacturing".

Analogously to the problem definitions contained in cases, a problem representation p resulting from the user input which caused the deviation to a current plan consists of attribute-value-pairs and text. The retrieval of a suitable case is carried out by finding cases whose problem definition is topically similar to the representation of problem p. So we map our dialogue problem dealing with pragmatic relevance onto a retrieval problem dealing with *topical relevance*. Our assumption is that the more (topical) relevant a problem definition is w.r.t. a problem representation, the more (pragmatic) relevant is the according dialogue plan for the given problem. We apply uncertain inference to retrieve topical relevant cases. For this, we adapt the framework proposed by van Rijsbergen for information retrieval [1]. In our case, we seek $P(pd \rightarrow p)$, the probability that a problem definition pd implies a problem representation p. Uncertain inference like described above can be implemented using the probabilistic inference engine HySpirit [3]. HySpirit is an implementation of probabilistic datalog based on Horn clauses, used for modelling uncertain facts and rules (similar to Prolog).

In order to perform retrieval of cases, we have to index the problem definitions in the case base. As we have shown, problem definitions consist of certain attributes and text. Both are indexed and represented as probabilistic facts within HySpirit. In our example above, we have the attributes type, matter, subject and content. These are indexed using a special predicate `attribute`. The attributes of the example case in Figure 3 (having the ID c1) would be indexed as

```
attribute(type, c1, explanation).
attribute(matter, c1, definition).
etc.
```

Besides attributes, we also find text in a problem definition. We create a full-text index in HySpirit using the two predicates `term` and `termspace`. The first one draws the connection between cases and terms, whereas the latter one contains information about all terms in the index. Each `term` or `termspace` fact is given a certain probability, determined by two well-known measures from information retrieval, the normalised term frequency (tf) and the inverse document frequency (idf). The term frequency of a term t in a case c is higher the more frequent it appears in the text of the problem definition of c; on the other hand, the inverse document frequency of t is higher the lesser it appears in other cases. As an example,

```
0.3 term(water, c1).
```

states that the term "water" appearing within the text tag of the problem definitions, has a term frequency of 0.3 in c1, while

```
0.2 termspace(water).
```

indicates the inverse document frequencies of "water", 0.2.

As mentioned before, each case is represented by a problem definition pd and we estimate $P(pd \rightarrow p)$ for each problem representation p and each problem definition. The resulting probability is used as the retrieval weight to rank the cases in the case base and deliver the according dialogue plan. Problem definitions are described as probabilistic facts like above. Case-based retrieval is performed in two steps: first, we match the attribute values of the problem definitions in the case base against the attribute values of the problem representation. If we can uniquely identify a case with the best relevance weight (i.e. there are no other cases also having the best weight), we present this case as the one containing the solution for the problem. If there are more top-ranked cases having the same retrieval weight, we use the full text of both problem definition and problem representation to determine the best-matching case. This way we lay the focus on matching the attributes, but consider the free text when attribute matching does not yield a unique result. The underlying assumption for this retrieval strategy is that problem definitions and problem representations can correctly be classified into the attributes and that the matching of attributes has the higher priority than the matching of text. In the ideal case the result will be unique and we can stop. If not, we have to choose a case out of the top ranked cases, i.e. the cases with the highest retrieval weight. In our framework this means we neglect all cases not having the highest retrieval weight and recalculate the weight for all remaining cases. For these, the new inference process is based on rules reflecting the terms which can be extracted from the text of the problem definition. Out of the user's utterance we extract the terms "meant" and "manufacturing" (stop words are eliminated). We now calculate a probability for the predicate *ptext*:

```
ptext(C) :- term(meant, C) & termspace(meant).
ptext(C) :- term(manufacturing, C) &
            termspace(manufacturing).
? - ptext(C).
```

The probability for the predicate `ptext` is calculated by applying the Sieve formula (see [3] for details on the calculation of probabilities in HySpirit). If we still do not have a unique top-ranked case after the 2nd step, we randomly chose a case among those with the highest weight based on `ptext`.

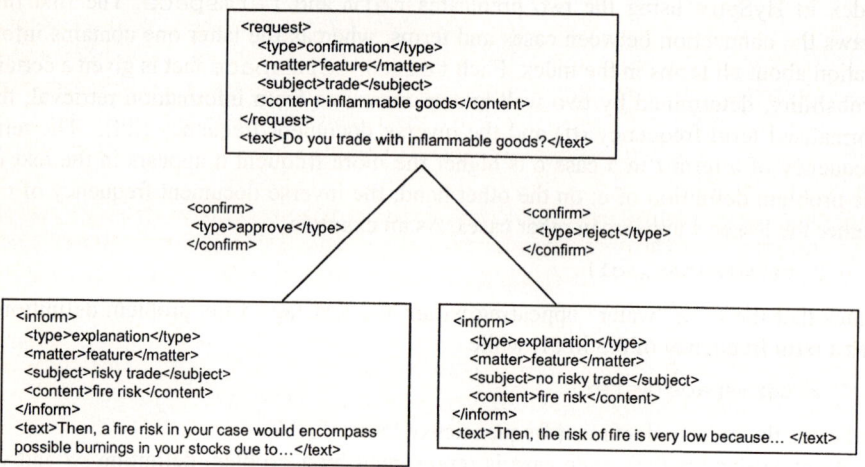

Fig. 4. The problem solution part of a concept clarification case

The problem solutions of cases solving problems pertaining to the concept clarification class have a more complex structure than simple FAQ-based cases. Instead of a single answer, they require the processing of an entire dialogue plan before producing a final answer. Within the plan, the system may ask counter questions, evaluate the user's answer and finally generate a dynamic output, based on the data collected during the processing of the plan. For instance, consider the following user question: "Should I care about a fire risk in my stock?" (coded by the communicative act "request(clarification, feature, risk, fire in stock)"). A direct answer to this question would be inappropriate, as it depends on whether the user's business is trading with flammable goods or not. Therefore, before delivering a final statement, the system should investigate about the inflammability of the goods. This is achieved by processing the plan contained in Figure 4. The actual branch of this plan is processed according to the user's response to the counter question. The communicative acts annotating the edges stand for patterns of user input. For the sake of simplicity in this example we considered a counter question allowing only for a simple answering scheme (e.g. a confirmation or a rejection). This approach can also be applied (thus raising in interest) in the case of counter questions enabling for multiple responses.

5 Context-Based Retrieval

So far we based the calculation of $P(pd \rightarrow p)$ on topical relevance and assumed that its degree is proportional to the degree of pragmatic relevance. Within our retrieval framework we have the chance to go a step further towards pragmatic relevance by incorporating non-topical context information into the retrieval process. We consider two different sources for contextual information, namely the user profile and the utterances exchanged so far between user and system, called dialogue history. The former is generated at runtime by analyzing the contents of the user input (both performed actions with the pointing device and spoken text). The latter is extracted out of the interaction log files. For the generation of context-aware system responses, cases contain a section called "contextual Data". It consists of a sequence of attribute-value pairs, expressing the suitability of a case to a certain contextual state. This approach allows for a flexible extension of the cases with context-relevant data. For instance, to avoid repeated trials to execute the same plan, the already used cases are available as part of the context.

During the interaction with the system, the user input can be analyzed for inferring user characteristics, thus building a profile. Once a problem solution is found, it can be checked if the retrieved case matches the current profile. Otherwise, a new case has to be identified. For instance, the country of origin can be used for providing a more adapted problem solution. This is especially appropriate for problems whose solution depends on local information, such as legal rule or used terminology. Furthermore, by analyzing the user behaviour, her level of expertise can be determined. Cases more suitable to experts can be avoided as a response to less skilled users, and vice versa.

While building the Case Base of VIP-Advisor, experts of various domains obviously needed to be involved. A thorough research was carried out and the results carefully evaluated. Comparisons about legal systems of different countries, as well as deep reviews of definitions and explanations were performed. The aim was to achieve an efficient diversification and personalization of the cases, according to different user properties. The interviews with risk management advisors resulted in both the identification of an evaluation scheme for identifying the level of expertise of users and the specification of appropriate problem solutions.

6 Summary and Outlook

In this paper we presented an extension to the dialogue management capabilities of conversational interfaces to expert systems. By the use of a goal-oriented dialogue strategy defined within flexible management plans, we minimized the risk of orientation loss and improved user guidance by offering support and advice in both problematic and unclear situations. In order to cope with dialogue plan deviations caused by user interventions we devised a case-based retrieval approach accessing a repository of prototypical problem occurrences and their related solutions. Within the project activities, several functionality and usability tests have been performed. Real users with different levels of expertise were involved in the evaluation, carrying out risk management sessions on the basis of predefined scenarios. While slight improvements to the interface components such as the voice recognition and the translation engine are still needed, the outcome of the tests showed a positive impact of the system's problem solving capabilities.

Future work will also consider the implementation of a more proactive dialogue behavior. It will be analyzed if problems occurring stereotypically for a given context and for users having similar profiles can be anticipated. In this case, the system might take over the initiative suggesting a solution to a problem most likely to appear in the next interaction steps. The aim is to provide a more efficient support to users not able to generate a focused problem description or even not capable of recognizing on their own the existence of an advisory need.

References

1. C.J. van Rijsbergen, A non-classical logic for Information Retrieval. The Computer Journal, 29(6):481-485, 1986.
2. D. Leake, CBR in context: The present and future. In: Leake, D. (ed), 1996, Case-based Reasoning: Experiences, Lessons, and Future Directions. AAAI Press/MIT Press, 1996.
3. N. Fuhr and T. Roelleke, HySpirit - A probabilistic inference engine for hypermedia retrieval in large databases. Extending Database Technology (EDBT), Valencia, Spain, 1998.
4. J.R. Searle, Speech Acts: An Essay in the Philosophy of Language. Cambridge Press, 1969.
5. Wilks, Y. (editor): Machine Conversations. Kluwer Academic Publishers, Dordrecht, 1999.
6. E.A.Feigenbaum. A personal view of expert systems: Looking back and looking ahead. Expert Systems with Applications, 5, 193-201, 1992

A Probabilistic Approach to Classify Incomplete Objects Using Decision Trees

Lamis Hawarah, Ana Simonet, and Michel Simonet

TIMC-IMAG
Institut d'Ingénierie et de l'Information de Santé
Faculté de Médecine , 38700 La Tronchet
http://www-timc.imag.fr
{Lamis.Hawarah,Ana.Simonet,Michel.Simonet}@imag.fr

Abstract. We describe an approach to fill missing values in decision trees during classification. This approach is derived from the *ordered attribute trees* method, proposed by Lobo and Numao in 2000, which builds a decision tree for each attribute and uses these trees to fill the missing attribute values. It is based on the Mutual Information between the attributes and the class. Our approach primarily extends this method on three points: 1) it does not impose an order of construction; 2) a probability distribution is used for each missing attribute instead of the most probable value; 3) the result of the classification process is a probability distribution instead of a single class. Moreover, our method takes the dependence between attributes into account. We present Lobo's approach and our extensions, we compare them, and we discuss some perspectives.

1 Introduction

Decision Trees are one of the most popular classification algorithms currently in use in Data Mining and Machine Learning. Decision Trees belong to supervised classification methods and are built from a training data set, according to the divide-and-conquer approach [13]. Once built, decision trees are used to classify new cases. A case is classified by starting at the root node of the tree, testing the attribute specified by this node, then moving through the tree until a leaf is encountered; the case is classified by the class associated with the leaf. It may happen that some objects do not have any value for some attributes. This problem, known as the problem of missing values, may occur during the building phase of the decision tree, when calculating the information gain between an attribute and the class to decide which attribute to select to branch on, and also when partitioning the training set according to the selected attribute. This problem may also occur during the classification phase: when classifying an object, if the value of a particular attribute which was branched on in the tree is missing, it is not possible to decide which branch to take in order to classify this object, and the classification process cannot be completed.

Our objective is to classify an object with missing values. We aim at using the dependencies between attributes to predict missing attribute values; when we estimate the values of an unknown attribute from its dependent attributes, we use the maximum amount of information contained in the object in order to fill the missing values of this attribute. Replacing an unknown attribute by only one value eliminates some other possible values; therefore, we will give a probability distribution for each unknown attribute instead of a single value, because that seems to us closer to reality, like Quinlan's method [13] which gives a probability result. In our work, we are interested in the type of approaches which use decision trees to fill in missing values [7,11], because if a decision tree is able to determine the class of an instance thanks to the values of its attributes, then it can be used to determine the value of an unknown attribute from its dependent attributes. Decision trees are suitable for representing relations among the most important attributes when determining the value of a target attribute [7]. The idea to start by dealing with the attribute which is the less dependent on the class [7,8,9] is interesting, because it is the attribute which has least influence on the class. Our work extends the *Ordered Attribute Trees* method (*OAT*), proposed by Lobo and Numao [7], on three points: 1) it does not impose an order of construction of attribute trees; 2) it uses for each missing attribute a probability distribution instead of the most probable value calculated from its attribute tree; 3) the result of classification is a probability distribution instead of a single class. We make the assumption that the limits of *Lobo's approach* are mainly due to two factors: 1) it does not take into account the dependence between attributes when constructing the attribute trees and 2) an object with missing values is associated with a single leaf in the tree.

In this paper, we first present the work in the domain, and particularly Lobo's approach. We then describe our approach to estimate missing values, that uses the dependencies between attributes and gives a probabilistic result, and finally, we present some perspectives.

2 Related Work

We present in this section the methods to deal with missing values using decision trees. The general idea in filling missing values is to infer them from other known data. We can distinguish several approaches to deal with missing values. The simplest one is to ignore instances containing missing values [6]. The second type of technique consists in replacing a missing value with a value considered as adequate in the situation. For example, [4] proposes a method that uses class information to estimate missing attribute values during the training phase; the idea is to assign the attribute's most probable value to the missing value, given the class membership of the case concerned. [10] fills in an attribute's missing values with its most common known value in the training set during the classification phase.

The third type of technique replaces missing values with a distribution of probability. For example, Quinlan's method [13] assigns *probability distributions* to each node of the decision tree when learning from training instances. The probability distribution, for the values of the attribute involved in the test in a node, is estimated from the relative frequencies of the attribute values among the training instances collected at that node. The result of the classification is a class distribution instead of a single class. This approach works well when most of the attributes are independent, because it depends only on the prior distribution of the attribute values for each attribute being tested in a node of the tree [12,13].

The fourth type of technique focuses on the classification phase and uses another attribute instead of the one that is unknown in order to keep on classifying the current case, and the selected attribute is correlated with the unknown attribute. For example, the CART method [2], which constructs binary decision trees, consists in using a *surrogate split* when an unknown value is found in the attribute originally selected. A surrogate split is a split that is similar to the best split in the sense that it makes a similar partition of the cases in the current node. Algorithms for constructing decision trees, such as [2,13], create a single best decision tree during the training phase, and this tree is then used to classify new instances.

The fifth type of technique constructs the best classification rule instead of constructing the whole decision tree. For example, the *dynamic path generation* method [6] produces only the path (i.e., the rule) needed to classify the case currently under consideration, instead of generating the whole decision tree beforehand. This method can deal with missing values in a very flexible way. Once a missing value is found to be present in an attribute of a new instance, such an attribute is never branched on when classifying the instance. Similarly, the *lazy decision tree* method [5] conceptually constructs the best decision tree for each test instance. In practice, only a classification path needs to be constructed. Missing attribute values are naturally handled by considering only splits on attribute values that are known in the test instance. Training instances with unknowns filter down and are excluded only when their value is unknown for a given test in a path.

The last type of approach uses decision trees to fill in missing values. For example, Shapiro's method [11] constructs a decision tree for an unknown attribute by using the subset of the original training set consisting of those instances whose value of the unknown attribute is defined. The class is regarded as another attribute and it participates in the construction of the decision tree for this attribute. This method is used only in the building phase.

We now present the Ordered Attribute Trees (OAT) method [8], which also deals with missing values and which we have studied in more detail.

Lobo's Approach: It is a supervised learning method for filling missing values in categorical data. It uses decision trees as models for estimating unknown values. This method constructs a decision tree for each attribute, using a training subset that contains instances with known values for the attribute. These cases in the training subset, for a target attribute, are described only by the attributes whose relation with the class has lower strength than the strength of the relation between the target attribute and the class. The resulting decision tree is called an *attribute tree*. This method uses *mutual information* [15] as a measure of the strength of relations between the attributes and the class. Mutual information between two categorical random variables X and Y is the average reduction in uncertainty about X that results from learning the value of Y; it is defined by:

$$IM(X,Y) = - \sum_{x \in Dx} P(x) \log_2 P(x) + \sum_{y \in Dy} P(y) [\sum_{x \in Dx} P(x|y) \log_2 P(x|y)] \quad (1)$$

D_x and D_y are the domains of the categorical random variables X and Y. $P(x)$ and $P(y)$ are the probability of occurrence of $x \in Dx$ and $y \in Dy$, respectively. $P(x|y)$ is the conditional probability of X having the value x once Y is known to have the value y. There is an order for the construction of the attribute trees. This order is guided by the mutual information between the attributes and the class. The method orders the attributes from low mutual information ones to high mutual information ones. The method constructs attribute trees according to this order and determines unknown values for each attribute. The first attribute tree constructed is a one-node tree with the most frequent value among the values of the attribute. An attribute tree is constructed for an attribute A_i using a training subset, which contains instances with known values for the attribute A_i and the attributes whose missing values have already been filled before. Then, the attributes A_k for which $IM(A_i, C) < IM(A_k, C)$ are excluded [7]. During the calculation of $IM(A_i, C)$, the instances that have missing values for the attribute A_i are ignored [9]. The *OAT* method uses a standard decision tree learning algorithm to construct its attribute trees. This method is not general enough to be applicable to every domain [9]. The domains in which there are strong relations between the attributes appear to be the most suitable to apply the *OAT* method.

We illustrate the *OAT* method using an example taken from [13] with four attributes and the class. The attributes are ordered incrementally according to mutual information between the class and the attributes as follows: *Temperature, Windy, Humidity, and Outlook*. Their trees, presented in fig.1 and fig.2, are constructed using two standard decision tree algorithms: ID3 [11] and C4.5[1] [13]. The number of training cases at each node is shown in brackets, e.g., sunny (2) and rain (3), and at each leaf, this number indicates the number of objects belonging to the class nominated by this leaf. The first tree built according to the *OAT* method is the *Temperature* tree; it has only one node, with its most probable value. The *Windy* tree in fig.1 is built using *Temperature* according to the mutual information order.

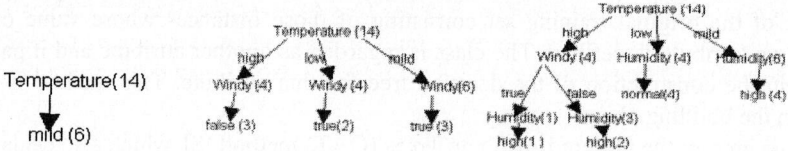

Fig. 1. Ordered attribute trees for *Temperature, Windy* and *Humidity* using ID3[2]

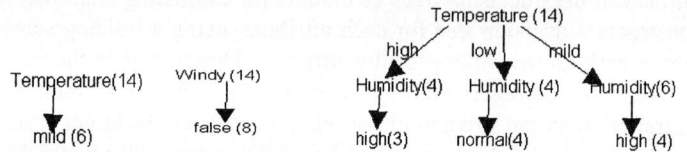

Fig. 2. Ordered attribute trees for *Temperature, Windy* and *Humidity* using C4.5[3]

But when *Temperature* is low, we have 2 objects where *Windy* is false and two objects where *Windy* is true, the ID3 algorithm [11] chooses randomly the value *true*. In fig.2,

---

[1] Java Implementations of ID3 and C4.5: www.cs.waikato.ac.nz/ml/weka/index.html .
[2] ID3 here builds the full tree (stops when all the training cases have been classified or all the attributes have been used).
[3] C4.5 constructs a pruned decision tree.

C4.5 [13] constructs the *Windy* Tree without using *Temperature*, so the *Windy* tree has only one node, with its most probable value; therefore the value of *Windy* is always false.

Humidity and *Windy* are independent because mutual information between them is null. Using ID3, the *Humidity* tree is built using *Temperature* and *Windy* (fig.1), but according to C4.5, which constructs a pruned decision tree, it is built using only *Temperature* (fig.2). In both cases, we notice that associating the most probable value with a leaf eliminates some other possible values. For example, this method replaces the missing values for the attribute *Temperature* with the value *mild* in any object which has an unknown *Temperature*. We also observe that the order imposed by this method discards the possibility of constructing an attribute tree using its dependent attributes.

2.1 Conclusion

We observe that the methods above have some drawbacks. For example, [4,10,13] determine the missing attribute values only once for each object with this unknown attribute. The *Dynamic path generation* method and the *lazy decision tree* method [5,6] do not resolve the missing values problem during the construction of the tree, but they classify the object using only its known attribute. Shapiro's method [11] makes good use of all the information available from the class and all the other attributes, but there is a difficulty that arises if the same case has missing values on more than one attribute [6,14]: during the construction of a tree to predict an unknown attribute, if a missing value is tested for another attribute, another tree must be constructed to predict this attribute, and so on. This method cannot be used practically, because this recursion process of constructing a decision tree once we find missing values for an attribute, leads to eliminating too many training cases when there are many unknown attributes. [9] By constructing the attribute trees according to an order relying only on mutual information between the attributes and the class, Lobo and Numao provide a solution which can work in every situation. However, it may happen that an attribute tree is built using attributes which are not dependent on it, which is somewhat paradoxical. It seems to make sense to build an attribute tree from the attributes which are dependent on it, which we have proposed in [EGC'04][3]. However, this is not possible when there is a cycle, i.e., mutually dependent missing attributes. Therefore, in the next section, we start by presenting a proposal which extends the *OAT* method given a probabilistic result; it is *OAT* method enriched with probabilistic information. Then we present the *probabilistic attribute trees* approach, which takes into account the dependencies between attributes and gives a probabilistic result, it also contains a solution to deal with the cycle problem.

3 Probabilistic Approach

To estimate missing values during classification we use a decision tree to predict the value of an unknown attribute from its dependent attributes. This value is represented by a probability distribution. We have two proposals. The first one simply extends

Lobo's *OATs* with probabilistic data; the second uses the dependence between attributes and also gives a probabilistic result.

3.1 First Proposal: Probabilistic OATs

For each attribute we propose to construct an attribute tree using Lobo's *OAT* approach, enriched with probabilistic information. We call these trees *Probabilistic Ordered Attribute Trees (POAT)*. The *POAT* method extends *OATs* in that each leaf in such an attribute tree is associated with a probability distribution for the possible attribute values. The result of classifying an object with missing values using *POAT* is a class distribution instead of a single class. The *POATs* for the attributes *Temperature*, *Windy* and *Humidity* are shown in fig.3:

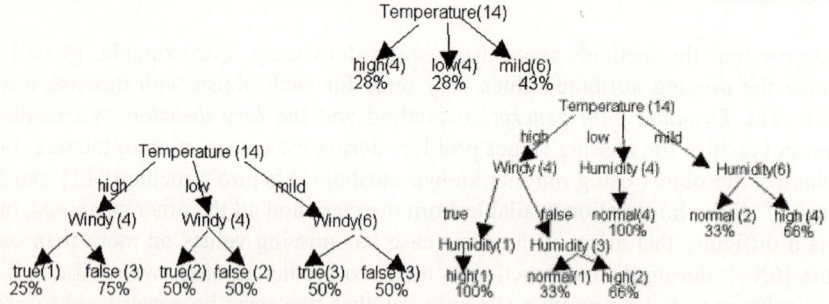

Fig. 3. Probabilistic Ordered Attribute Trees for *Temperature*, *Windy*, and *Humidity*

We use these trees when an unknown attribute is encountered during the classification of an object with missing values; each missing value is replaced by a distribution of probability. For example, assuming that *Humidity* is unknown, if *Temperature* is high and *Windy* is false, then *Humidity* is normal with the probability 0.33 and high with the probability 0.66. These trees give a probabilistic result which is more refined than Lobo's initial *OATs*. However, they do not take into account the dependencies between attributes, because they are built in an ordered manner. Therefore, we suggest another approach (*Probabilistic Attribute Trees*) which is based on the dependencies between attributes.

3.2 Second Proposal: Probabilistic Attribute Trees (PAT)

To take into account the dependencies, we calculate the mutual information between each pair of attributes in order to determine for each attribute its dependent attributes. Then, a *Probabilistic Attribute Tree (PAT)* is constructed for each attribute, using all the attributes depending on it. A *PAT* is a decision tree whose leaves are associated with distributions of probability for the attribute values.

For an attribute A_i we first determine its set of dependent attributes $Dep(A_i) = \{A_j \mid IM(A_i, A_j) > 0.01^4\}$. Then we construct for A_i a Probabilistic Attribute Tree (*PAT*) according to its A_j. We use a standard algorithm to construct a decision tree[5] with a small extension: we associate with each leaf a probability distribution for the values of A_i, instead of a single value.

According to the example taken from [13],
  Dep(*Humidity*) = {*Temperature, Outlook*}
  Dep(*Outlook*) = {*Temperature, Humidity*}
  Dep(*Temperature*) = {*Humidity, Outlook, Windy*}
The *PAT* for *Humidity* is shown in fig. 4 and the *PAT* for *Outlook* in fig. 5.

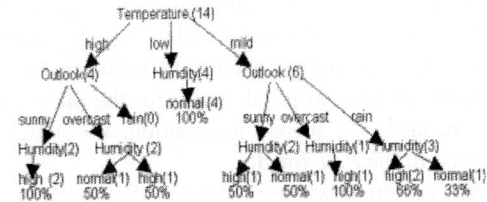

Fig. 4. Probabilistic Attribute Tree for *Humidity*

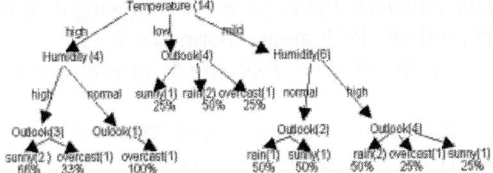

Fig. 5. Probabilistic Attribute Tree for *Outlook*

When *Temperature* is mild and *Outlook* is rain (fig. 4): instead of associating its most probable value (high) with the *Humidity* leaf, we keep the two possible values with their probability distribution, i.e., high with 66% and normal with 33%. To classify an object where *Humidity* is unknown, we can use its *PAT* provided that *Temperature* and *Outlook* are known (fig.4). Depending on the current values of *Temperature* and *Outlook*, *Humidity* is assigned a probability distribution. For example, from the fig.4: if *Temperature* is low, then *Humidity* is normal with probability 1 and high with probability 0. If *Temperature* is mild and *Outlook* is rain, *Humidity* is normal with probability 1/3 and high with probability 2/3.

The *PAT* and *POAT* approaches both give a probabilistic result. The *PAT* approach is more satisfactory because it takes into account the dependence between attributes. We

---

[4] 0.01 is an arbitrary value we have chosen to test the system. However, the choice of a threshold has important consequences on cycles.

[5] The standard approaches to construct a decision tree from a training set of cases, like ID3, C4.5, CART, associate with each leaf a single class (the most probable class among the subset).

have tested the *PAT* approach on the data sets[6] [1]. The trees built according to the *PAT* approach give a better result than the *POAT* trees. The results of the comparison of our approach with other methods are not presented in this paper.

We now examine some problems which may occur during the classification of an object with missing values or during the construction of a *PAT*.

4 Problems with PAT

1) The Cycle Problem: This problem occurs when two attributes *A* and *B*, which are dependent, are missing at the same time. To resolve the cycle problem between *A* and *B*, the idea is to deal first with the attribute which is less dependent on the class; let it be the attribute *B*. To calculate the probability distribution for *B*, we use its *POAT* constructed according to the first proposal. Then, for the other attribute *A*, we use its *PAT* constructed according to the second proposition. We notice that the probability distribution for *B* is used in the *PAT* for *A*.

For example, to classify an object where the values of *Humidity* and *Outlook* are missing, according to our first solution (Lobo's *OAT* enriched with probability information), we choose the attribute less dependent on the class, which is *Humidity*, and we use its *POAT* (fig. 3 on the right) to determine its value. Assuming that *Windy* is false and *Temperature* is high, the *Humidity POAT* gives the following distribution:

P(Humidity= high) = 0.66, P(Humidity=normal) = 0.33

These values are then used in the *Outlook PAT* (fig.5) to estimate the probabilistic distribution of *Outlook*:

P(Outlook=rain) = 0, P(Outlook=sunny) = 0.66*0.66 = 0.435
P(Outlook=overcast) = 0.33*0.66+0.33*1 = 0.547

2) Indeterminate Leaves Problem: This problem occurs when a leaf contains no case when constructing a *PAT*; in this situation, we do not know which class will be associated with this leaf. In standard decision trees construction algorithms, this leaf is associated with the most probable class at its parent node. In our approach, when classifying an object with missing values, if we reach such a leaf in a *PAT* for an unknown attribute, we use the *POAT* for this attribute instead of its *PAT*. For example, assume that we classify an object where *Windy* is false, *Temperature* is high and *Outlook* is rain, but *Humidity* is missing. If we use the *Humidity PAT* (fig.4), we find no leaf corresponding to this case. Therefore, we use the *Humidity POAT* (fig.3 on the right), which gives the following distribution:

P (Humidity= high) = 0.66, P (Humidity=normal) = 0.33

3) If an attribute is independent of all the other attributes, its *PAT* consists of only one root node whose leaves are the values of the attribute with their probabilities in the whole training set.

---

[6] The data sets were obtained from UCI Machine Learning Repository [1].

5 Discussion and Perspectives

Using a *POAT* to resolve the cycle problem is not entirely satisfying because a *POAT* is constructed without taking into account the dependence between attributes.

We have considered constructing all the probabilistic attribute trees for each attribute according to its dependent attributes and use these trees instead of *POATs* when a cycle problem is encountered during classification. This would solve the cycle problem because when two missing attributes *A* and *B* are mutually dependent, we use for *B* (the less dependent on the class) its tree constructed using all dependent attributes expecting *A*; this tree is better than the *POAT* for *B* because we make sure that it is built using the attributes which depend on *B*. As this solution is combinatorially explosive we have tried to construct only useful probabilistic attribute trees. For example, we construct only one *PAT* for the attribute which is the most dependent on the class. On the other hand, assuming there are, among the attributes which depend on an attribute *B*, two attributes *A* and *C* which are more dependent on the class than *B*, we build successively two probabilistic attribute trees for *B* without *A* and *C*; and we also build another tree for *B* without *A* and *C* together. These trees can be used instead of *POAT* to resolve the above problems because we always start by treating the attributes which are the least dependent on the class. Of course, a *PAT* is constructed for *B* using all its dependent attributes. Theoretically, this algorithm gives a better result than the results given by the first and second proposals because all the trees are built by taking into account the dependence between attributes, but if there are a lot of attributes which depend on *B* and which are more dependent on the class than *B*, then the number of constructed trees become greater.

6 Conclusion

In the real world, an incomplete object can potentially belong to several classes and therefore should be associated with several leaves in the decision tree. Moreover, in a critical domain like medicine, making a single decision when some of the information needed is not available or is missing could be dangerous. In this paper, we have introduced a probabilistic approach to fill missing values in decision trees during classification. We have proposed two solutions. The first one consists in using the trees constructed according to Lobo's *Ordered Attribute Trees* method, enriched with probabilistic information. The result of classification is a probability distribution. This solution is not satisfactory because the trees are built in an ordered manner, without using the dependence between the attributes. The second solution consists in constructing for each attribute a *probabilistic decision tree* that takes into account the dependence between attributes; each probabilistic attribute tree is constructed using only its dependent attributes and each leaf is associated with a probability distribution. To resolve the cycle and indeterminate leaves problems, we use the *POAT* approach.

We are currently trying out our approach to choose the best solution. We are comparing our approach to other methods like *OAT*'s method [7] and Quinlan's method [13], by using the data sets [1] used by Lobo and Numao in their study of *OATs* [9]. The scenario, it is important to consider also for semistructured temporal data models the formalization of the set of constraints needed to manage in the correct way the semantics of the represented time dimension(s), as it was deeply studied in the past years in the literature for the classical temporal database field [11]. Such an issue has not yet been completely considered in the literature related to semistructured data.

We propose an original graphical temporal data model general enough to include the main features of semistructured data representation, by considering also the issues of modeling the semantics of a given time dimension. In particular, in this work we consider *transaction time* (TT), which is system-generated and represents the time when a fact is current in the database and may be retrieved [10, 11]: we focus on the specification of the main constraints and operations needed for a correct handling of this temporal aspect.

The structure of the paper is as follows: in the next Section we describe the main proposals dealing with time for semistructured data. Section 3 introduces the Graphical sEmistructured teMporal (GEM) data model, and Section 4 describes and discusses constraints and operations when dealing with transaction time. In Section 5 we sketch some conclusions and possible lines for future work.

2 Related Work

Recently, some research contributions have been concerned with temporal aspects in semistructured databases. While they share the common goal of representing time-varying information, they consider different temporal dimensions and adopt different data models and strategies to capture the main features of the considered notion of time.

The Delta Object Exchange Model (DOEM) proposed in [5] is a temporal extension of the Object Exchange Model (OEM) [14], a simple graph-based data model, with objects as nodes and object-subobject relationships represented as labeled arcs. Change operations (i.e. node insertion, update of node values, addition and removal of labeled arcs) are represented in DOEM by using *annotations* on nodes and arcs of an OEM graph for representing the history. Intuitively, annotations are the representation of the history of nodes and edges as it is recorded in the database. This proposal takes into account the *transaction time* dimension of a graph-based representation of semistructured data. DOEM graphs (and OEM graphs as well) do not consider labeled relationships between two objects (actually, each edge is labeled with the name of the unique pointed node).

Another graph-based model proposed in the literature is described in [8]. This model uses labeled graphs to represent semistructured databases and the peculiarity of these graphs is that each edge label is composed by a set of descriptive properties (e.g. name, transaction time, valid time, security properties of relationships). This proposal is very general and extensible: any property may be used and added to adapt the model to a specific context. In particular, the model allows one to represent also temporal aspects: to this regard, some examples of constraints which need to be suitably managed to correctly support semantics of the time-related properties are provided, both for querying and for manipulating graphs.

The Temporal Graphical Model (TGM) [13] is a graphical model for representing semistructured data dynamics. This model uses *temporal elements*, instead of simple intervals, to keep trace of different time intervals when an object exists in the reality. In [13] the authors consider only issues (e.g. admitted operations and constraints) related to *valid time* representation.

The Temporal XPath Data Model [2] is an extension of the XPath Data Model capable of representing history changes of XML documents. In particular, this approach introduces the *valid time* label only for edges in the XPath model.

3 The Graphical sEmistructured teMporal Data Model

In this Section we propose the Graphical sEmistructured teMporal (GEM) data model, which is able to represent in a uniform way semistructured information by considering also their time dimension. We focus on the classical notion of transaction time studied in the past years in the context of temporal databases [10, 11] and formalize the set of constraints that the considered time dimension imposes.

Our proposal is based on rooted, connected, directed, labeled graphs. The transaction time is represented by means of an interval belonging to both node and edge labels. A GEM graph is composed by two kinds of nodes, *complex* and *simple* nodes, which are graphically represented in different ways. Complex nodes are depicted as rectangles and represent abstract entities, while simple nodes are depicted as ovals and represent primitive values.

Formally, a *GEM graph* is a rooted labeled graph $\langle N, E, r, \ell \rangle$, where:

1. N is a (finite) set of nodes (actually, it is the set of object identifiers).
2. E is a set of labeled edges.
3. $r \in N$ is the unique root of the graph and it is introduced in order to guarantee the reachability of all the other nodes.
4. Each node label is composed by the node name, the node type (complex or simple), the content and the time interval[1]. The *label* function ℓ is such that for each node $n_i \in N$, $\ell(n_i) = \langle Nname_i, Ntype_i, Ncontent_i, Ntime_i \rangle$ where $Nname_i$ is a string, $Ntype_i \in \{complex, simple\}$, $Ncontent_i$ is a value for simple nodes and the null value $\bot$ for complex nodes (see constraints in Figures 1(a) and 1(b)), and $Ntime_i$ is a half-open interval.
5. Each edge label is composed by the relationship name and the time interval. Each edge $e_j = \langle (n_h, n_k), label_j \rangle$, with n_h and n_k in N, has a label $label_j = \langle Ename_j, Etime_j \rangle$. We do not suppose to have an identifier for edges: an edge can be identified by its label and the two connected nodes, because between two nodes we suppose to have only one edge with a particular name and a particular time interval.

---

[1] In the figures related to GEM graphs, we report only the name label of nodes and edges and the related time intervals, because we graphically represent the different types of nodes by means of their shape (rectangle or oval). Moreover, we specify the content label only for simple nodes.

It is worth noting that, differently from other proposals [5, 8], we choose to associate labels both to edges and to nodes: this way, we can have a more compact, graph-based representation of semistructured databases.

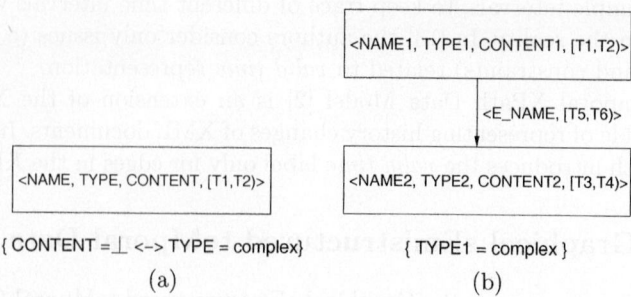

Fig. 1. (a) Complex nodes do not have a specified content label (b) Each simple node is a leaf

There are some constraints for a GEM graph: indeed, we do not allow a complex node to have a primitive value as a content (it could be equivalent to not allowing mixed elements in XML [15], the widely known language for semistructured data); on the other hand, a simple node must be a leaf of the graph and must have a (primitive) content. Thus, a GEM graph must satisfy the following two basic constraints, not related to temporal aspects.

1. The content label of a node is ⊥ if and only if the node is complex (this is due to the fact that complex nodes represent abstract entities without a primitive value). We show this property in Figure 1(a).
2. If a node is simple, then it is a leaf. Figure 1(b) depicts this property by specifying that each node with outgoing edges must be a complex node.

The graphical formalism we use in these two figures has been defined in [7, 12]. In this graphical formalism a constraint is composed by a *graph*, which is used to identify the subgraphs (i.e. the portions of a semistructured database) where the constraint is to be applied, and a set of *formulae*, which represent restrictions imposed on those subgraphs.

In the following Section we will focus on the constraints we have to introduce on GEM graphs, to suitably represent transaction time. In [6] the complete formalization of constraints for both valid time and transaction time is described. We preferred to adopt a semistructured data model, instead of dealing directly with XML: this way, as mentioned in the introduction and according to other proposals [5, 8, 13], the proposed solution can be considered as a logical model for temporal semistructured data, which can be translated into different XML-based languages/technologies.

To the best of our knowledge, the only other work which explicitly addresses the issue of time-related semantics for semistructured data is [8]. In [8], the authors propose a framework for semistructured data, where graphs are composed by nodes and labeled edges: edge labels contain properties (i.e., meta-data), as valid and transaction times, the name of the edge, quality, security, and so on. Edges can have different properties: a property can be present in an edge and missing in another one. Nodes have no labels and are identified by paths leading to them. The focus of that work is on the definition of suitable operators (i.e., collapse, match, coalesce, and slice), which allow one to determine the (different) semantics of properties for managing queries on such graphs. As for the temporal aspects, even though in [8] some examples are provided about special semantics for update to accommodate transaction time, a detailed and complete examination of all the constraints for modeling either transaction or valid times is missing and is outside the main goal of that work. Moreover, the authors claim that they "leave open the issue of how these constraints are enforced on update" [8]. With respect to the proposal described in [8], we thus explicitly focus on the semantics of temporal aspects and do not consider the semantics of other properties; this way, even though we are less general than the authors in [8], we are able to provide a complete treatment of the constraints when representing either transaction or valid times [6], facing some important aspects which have not been completely considered in [8], such as, for example, the problem of the presence of nodes/subgraphs which could become unreachable from the root of the graph after some updates. Moreover, another novel feature of our work is that we explicitly address the issue of providing users with powerful operators for building GEM graphs consistent with the given temporal semantics.

4 Managing Transaction Time with the GEM Data Model

Transaction time allows us to maintain the graph evolutions due to operations, such as insertion, deletion, and update, on nodes and edges. From this point of view, a GEM graph represents the changes of a (atemporal) graph, i.e. it represents a sequence of several *atemporal graphs*, each of them obtained as result of some operations on the previous one. In this context, the *current* graph represents the current facts in the semistructured database, and is composed by nodes and edges which have the transaction time interval ending with the special value *now*.

Our idea is that operations on nodes and edges of a GEM graph must have as result a rooted, connected graph. Thus, the *current* graph, composed by current nodes and edges must be a rooted connected graph, i.e. a GEM graph. Changes in a GEM graph are timestamped by transaction time in order to represent the graph history which is composed by the sequence of intermediate graphs resulting from the operations. In the next Section we define the set of constraints temporal labels must satisfy in order to guarantee that the current (atemporal) graph, resulting after each operation, is still a GEM graph.

From the other point of view, each operation on the graph corresponds to the suitable management of temporal labels of (possibly) several nodes and edges on the GEM graph.

4.1 Constraints for Transaction Time

The following constraints on a GEM graph allow us to explicitly consider the append-only feature of semistructured data timestamped by the transaction time.

1. The time interval of a generic edge connecting two nodes must be related to the their time intervals. Intuitively, a relation between two nodes can be established and maintained only in the time interval in which both nodes are present in the graph. For each edge $e_j = \langle (n_h, n_k), \langle Ename_j, [t_{js}, t_{je}] \rangle \rangle$ where $\ell(n_h) = \langle Nname_h, Ntype_h, Ncontent_h, [t_{hs}, t_{he}] \rangle$ and $\ell(n_k) = \langle Nname_k, Ntype_k, Ncontent_k, [t_{ks}, t_{ke}] \rangle$, then it must hold $t_{js} \geq max(t_{hs}, t_{ks})$ and $t_{je} \leq min(t_{he}, t_{ke})$. In Figure 2 we report an example of this constraint: in part a) we show two nodes and the generic edge connecting them, while in part b) we show a possible set of nodes and edge time intervals that satisfy the constraint. The time interval $[t_{js}, t_{je}]$ of the edge does not start before that both the node-related time intervals started and does not end after that one of the node-related time intervals ended.

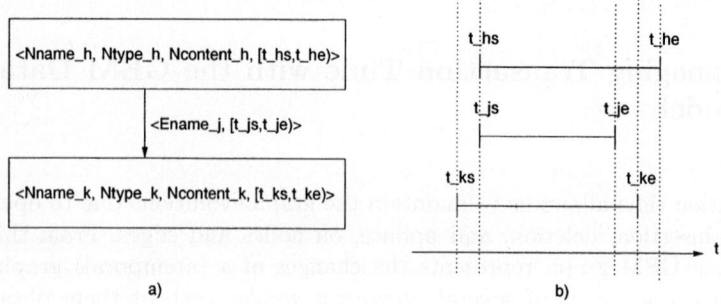

Fig. 2. The TT constraint on the time interval of a generic edge

2. The time interval of each node is related to the time interval of all its ingoing edges. Intuitively, a node (different from the root) can survive only if it is connected at least to one current complex node by means of an edge. For each node n_k with $\ell(n_k) = \langle Nname_k, Ntype_k, Ncontent_k, [t_{ks}, t_{ke}] \rangle$ and for the set of its ingoing edges $e_{j_i} = \langle (n_{h_i}, n_k), \langle Ename_{j_i}, [t_{j_is}, t_{j_ie}] \rangle \rangle$ (with $i = 1, \ldots, n$) it must hold $t_{ks} = min(t_{j_is})$ and $t_{ke} = max(t_{j_ie})$. Part a) of Figure 3 shows three complex nodes and a node (simple or complex) connected by means of three edges; part b) depicts an example of time intervals

satisfying this constraint, by showing three possible edge-related time intervals $[t_{j_i s}, t_{j_i e}]$ (with $i = 1, 2, 3$). The pointed node-related time interval cannot start before that the first edge-related time interval starts (according to the insertion order) and cannot end after that the last one ends (according to the deletion order).

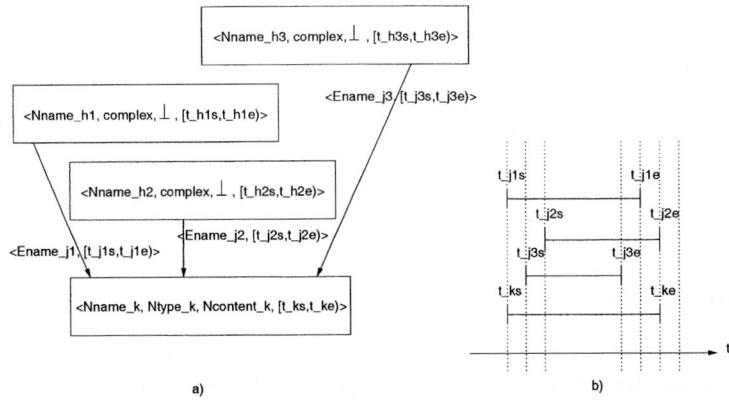

Fig. 3. The TT constraint on the time interval of a node

3. For each complex node n_h with label $\langle Nname_h, complex, \perp, [t_{hs}, t_{he}] \rangle$ and for all the simple nodes n_{k_i}, with $i = 1, \ldots, n$ and $\ell(n_{k_i}) = \langle Nname, simple, Ncontent_{k_i}, [t_{k_i s}, t_{k_i e}] \rangle$, related to n_h by means of the edges $e_{j_i} = \langle (n_h, n_{k_i}), \langle Ename, [t_{j_i s}, t_{j_i e}] \rangle \rangle$, it must hold $\bigcap_{i=0}^{n} [t_{j_i s}, t_{j_i e}] = \emptyset$. Note that all the edges e_{j_i} have the same name $Ename$, and all the simple nodes n_{k_i} have the same name $Nname$. Intuitively, at a specific time instant, a complex node can be related to at most one simple node named $Nname$ by means of a relation named $Ename$. This is due to the fact that a simple node represents a property and a complex node cannot have, at a given time, different values for the same property. For example, at a given time instant, the complex node $Person$ can be connected at most to one simple node $City$ by means of the edge $Lives\_in$. Part a) of Figure 4 shows a complex node and three simple nodes connected by means of edges with the same label; part b) shows the edge-related time intervals $[t_{j_i s}, t_{j_i e}]$ (with $i = 1, 2, 3$), which satisfy this constraint, being without intersection.

With these restrictions we do not allow one to represent multi-valued attributes of a complex node. In order to overcome this limitation, multi-valued properties could be represented, for example, by a set of complex nodes with the same name connected to the referring complex node by edges (possibly having the same name). Each complex node representing a value of the considered property has a single simple node storing the value of the property.

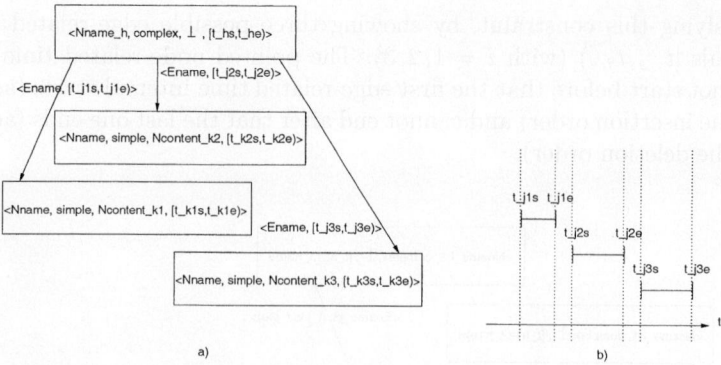

Fig. 4. The TT constraint on time interval of edges pointing to simple nodes

4.2 Operations

Let us now consider how node and edge insertions, deletions, and updates modify a GEM graph: the result of each operation is a GEM graph which satisfies the previous constraints. By considering single operations, each of them producing a GEM graph, we obtain that any sequence of the defined operations is correct, thus we avoid the problem of having incorrect sequences of operations [5].

1. **Insert the root node**
   $obj_r = insert\text{-}root\text{-}node(Nname)$ inserts at time t_s the root node with label $\langle Nname, complex, \perp, [t_s, now] \rangle$ and gives as result the object identifier obj_r of the node itself. The time interval $[t_s, now]$ is system-generated.

2. **Insert a complex node**
   $obj_c = insert\text{-}complex\text{-}node(Nname, obj_k, Ename)$ inserts at time t_s the complex node with label $\langle Nname, complex, \perp, [t_s, now] \rangle$ connected to the node with object identifier obj_k by means of an edge starting from obj_k. The operation gives as result the object identifier obj_c of the inserted node. The inserted edge is $\langle (obj_k, obj_c), \langle Ename, [t_s, now] \rangle \rangle$ and is added in order to avoid the possibility that the node obj_c cannot be reached from the root. If the node obj_k is not current (i.e., its time interval does not end with the special value now), then the operation fails (for example, it returns NULL) and the GEM graph is not modified.

3. **Insert a simple node**
   $obj_s = insert\text{-}simple\text{-}node(Nname, Ncontent, obj_k, Ename)$ inserts at time t_s the simple node with label $\langle Nname, simple, Ncontent, [t_s, now] \rangle$ connected to the node obj_k by means of an edge starting from obj_k. This operation checks whether there is another current simple node obj_h, with label $\langle Nname, simple, Ncontent_h, [t_{hs}, now] \rangle$, connected to the same node obj_k by means of an edge with the same name $Ename$. If this is the case it calls the operation $remove\text{-}edge(obj_k, obj_h, Ename)$, which (logically) deletes the old value of the considered property, which is updated by the new insertion.

This restriction is added in order to avoid the possibility to store for a given node two properties with the same label at the same time. The operation gives as result the object identifier obj_s of the inserted node. The inserted edge is $\langle(obj_k, obj_s), \langle Ename, [t_s, now)\rangle\rangle$. If the node obj_k is not current, then the operation fails.

4. **Insert an edge**
   $insert\text{-}edge(obj_h, obj_k, EName)$ inserts at time t_s the edge $\langle(obj_h, obj_k), \langle EName, [t_s, now)\rangle\rangle$. This operation fails when at least one of the two nodes is not current or there is already a current edge $Ename$ between the two considered nodes.

5. **Remove a node**
   $remove\text{-}node(obj_k)$ removes at time t_e the node obj_k, if it is current, otherwise the operation fails. Suppose that the node obj_k has as label $\langle Nname, Ntype, Ncontent, [t_s, now)\rangle$: the operation changes the label into $\langle Nname, Ntype, Ncontent, [t_s, t_e)\rangle$. Moreover, it removes also all its ingoing edges, i.e., for each edge $\langle(obj_h, obj_k), \langle Ename, [t_s, now)\rangle\rangle$ it calls $remove\text{-}edge(obj_h, obj_k, Ename)$. It removes also all outgoing edges, i.e., for each edge $\langle(obj_k, obj_x), \langle Ename, [t_s, now)\rangle\rangle$ it calls $remove\text{-}edge(obj_k, obj_x, Ename)$.

6. **Remove an edge**
   $remove\text{-}edge(obj_h, obj_k, Ename)$ removes at time t_e the edge $\langle(obj_h, obj_k), \langle Ename, [t_s, now)\rangle\rangle$, which becomes $\langle(obj_h, obj_k), \langle Ename, [t_s, t_e)\rangle\rangle$. Note that this operation fails when there is not a current edge labeled $Ename$ between the nodes obj_h and obj_k. Moreover, in order to avoid the possibility to have nodes that cannot be reached from the root, this operation implies another check on the node obj_k by calling the operation $garbage - collection(obj_k)$.

7. **Garbage collection**
   $garbage\text{-}collection(obj_k)$ checks whether obj_k is current and there is at least one edge $\langle(obj_h, obj_k), \langle Ename, [t_s, now)\rangle\rangle$. If such edge exists, then the operation terminates, otherwise it removes the node with object identifier obj_k by calling the operation $remove\text{-}node(obj_k)$.

5 Conclusions

In this paper we presented the new graph-based GEM model for semistructured temporal data. It allows us to model in a homogeneous way temporal dimensions of data. More particularly we discussed in some detail constraints and operations on GEM graphs dealing with transaction time, the well-known time dimension of data [10]. We showed how a GEM graph can represent a sequence of timestamped atemporal graphs. GEM can also be used to represent the valid time; in this case, the time dimension is given by the user, being the valid time related to the description of the considered real world. Thus, constraints and operations must be able to guarantee that the history of the given application domain is consistent.

As for future work, the GEM data model will be extended to deal with both valid and transaction times together: further issues should be considered when both the temporal dimensions are represented on the same graph. Moreover, different approaches, such as the logic-based or the algebraic ones, will be considered and studied in order to provide the GEM data model with a language for querying, viewing, and "transforming" GEM graphs.

References

1. S. Abiteboul. Querying Semi-Structured Data. In *Proceedings of the International Conference on Database Theory*, volume 1186 of *Lecture Notes in Computer Science*, pages 262–275, 1997.
2. T. Amagasa, M. Yoshikawa, and S. Uemura. Realizing Temporal XML Repositories using Temporal Relational Databases. In *Proceedings of the Third International Symposium on Cooperative Database Systems and Applications*, pages 63–68. IEEE Computer Society, 2001.
3. P. Atzeni. Time: A coordinate for web site modelling. In *Advances in Databases and Information Systems, 6th East European Conference*, volume 2435 of *Lecture Notes in Computer Science*, pages 1–7. Springer-Verlag, Berlin, 2002.
4. S. Ceri, S. Comai, E. Damiani, P. Fraternali, S. Paraboschi, and L. Tanca. XML-GL: a Graphical Language for Querying and Restructuring XML Documents. *Computer Network*, 31(11–16):1171–1187, 1999.
5. S.S. Chawathe, S. Abiteboul, and J. Widom. Managing historical semistructured data. *Theory and Practice of Object Systems*, 5(3):143–162, 1999.
6. C. Combi, B. Oliboni, and E. Quintarelli. A Unified Model for Semistructured Temporal Data. Technical Report 2003.11, Politecnico di Milano, February 2003.
7. E. Damiani, B. Oliboni, E. Quintarelli, and L. Tanca. Modeling semistructured data by using graph-based constraints. In *OTM Workshops Proceedings*, Lecture Notes in Computer Science, pages 20–21. Springer-Verlag, Berlin, 2003.
8. C.E. Dyreson, M.H. Böhlen, and C.S. Jensen. Capturing and Querying Multiple Aspects of Semistructured Data. In *VLDB'99, Proceedings of 25th International Conference on Very Large Data Bases*, pages 290–301. Morgan Kaufmann, 1999.
9. M. Fernandez, D. Florescu, J. Kang, A. Levy, and D. Suciu. STRUDEL: A web site management system. In *Proceedings of the ACM SIGMOD International Conference on Management of Data*, volume 26,2 of *SIGMOD Record*, pages 549–552. ACM Press, 1997.
10. C.S. Jensen, C.E. Dyreson, and M.H. Bohlen et al. The consensus glossary of temporal database concepts - february 1998 version. In *Temporal Databases: Research and Practice*, volume 1399 of *Lecture Notes in Computer Science*, pages 367–405. Springer, 1998.
11. C.S. Jensen and R. Snodgrass. Temporal data management. *IEEE Transactions on Knowledge and Data Engineering*, 11(1):36–44, 1999.
12. B. Oliboni. *Blind queries and constraints: representing flexibility and time in semistructured data*. PhD thesis, Politecnico di Milano, 2003.
13. B. Oliboni, E. Quintarelli, and L. Tanca. Temporal aspects of semistructured data. In *Proceedings of The Eighth International Symposium on Temporal Representation and Reasoning (TIME-01)*, pages 119–127. IEEE Computer Society, 2001.
14. Y. Papakonstantinou, H. Garcia-Molina, and J. Widom. Object Exchange Across Heterogeneous Information Sources. In *Proceedings of the Eleventh International Conference on Data Engineering*, pages 251–260. IEEE Computer Society, 1995.
15. World Wide Web Consortium. Extensible Markup Language (XML) 1.0, 1998. http://www.w3C.org/TR/REC-xml/.

Effective Clustering Schemes for XML Databases

William M. Shui, Damien K. Fisher, Franky Lam, and Raymond K. Wong

School of Computer Science & Engineering
University of New South Wales
Sydney, NSW 2052, Australia

Abstract. Although clustering problems are in general NP-hard, much research effort on this problem has been invested in the areas of object-oriented databases (OODB) and relational databases systems (RDBMS). With the increasing popularity of XML, researchers have been focusing on various XML data management including query processing and optimization. However, the clustering issues for XML data storage have been disregarded in their work. This paper provides a preliminary study on data clustering for optimizing XML databases. Different clustering schemes are compared through a set of extensive experiments.

1 Introduction

A number of native XML and semi-structured databases have been developed over the past decade. These databases share many similarities with the object oriented databases popular in the early 1990s, although their simpler data model should make their task considerably easier. Research into OODB clustering techniques has shown that effective clustering can improve the performance of some OODBs by up to several hundred percent [2]. Apart from the obvious effect of reducing number of disk accesses per query execution, clustering related objects together yields other performance improvements. For instance, better locality of reference can reduce locking contention in highly concurrent systems. It could be expected that clustering would have a similar effect on XML databases.

As an example of the potential effect of clustering, consider the database shown in Figure 1. A typical XML database may load the data in using a SAX parser, and hence the nodes would be clustered in the order indicated in Figure

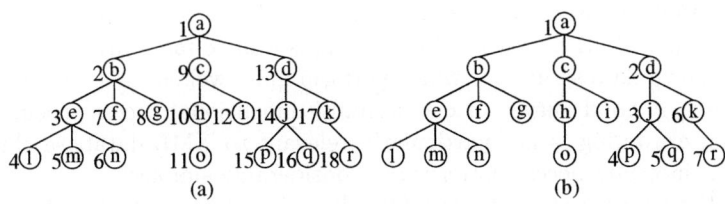

Fig. 1. A sample XML database

1(a). However, suppose we run the XPath query /a/d//* over this database. If the nodes were clustered in the order indicated by Figure 1(b), it is clear that the average distance between consecutive nodes is smaller, because nodes which are not accessed by the query are stored in another part of the database. More dramatic improvements could be anticipated for real world database systems, which very often have large portions that are rarely queried.

While XML databases have many similarities to traditional the OODBs, there are some differences which mean that existing OODB clustering strategies may not be utilized directly. The most important difference is that XML is ordered, whereas in object databases unordered sets of objects are common. This difference is particularly crucial as the most popular query languages for XML, such as XPath and XML Query, both deal with ordered queries explicitly.

A second significant difference is that XML databases store trees of objects, whereas object databases store general graphs[1]. Thus, we expect that many of the algorithms designed for object oriented databases could possibly be made considerably simpler, by restricting them to the case where the data is a tree. For the rest of this paper, we will treat XML databases as trees.

The rest of this paper is organized as follows: Section 2 covers the plethora of related work from OODB research. Section 3 lists five different clustering strategies of varying degrees of complexity and characteristics, some of which are adapted from object oriented clustering strategies. Section 4 presents our experimental results. It shows that clustering strategies do indeed have a positive effect on overall query time. Finally Section 5 concludes the paper.

2 Related Work

The Natix native XML database system [6] is, to the best of the authors' knowledge, the only system to have considered the problem of clustering in XML bases. The basic Natix strategy is to store sub-trees of a certain size together as tuples at the physical level. Our methods work at a finer granularity — instead of grouping nodes together into a single tuple, we continue to treat nodes individually. This simplifies the system, and as we show in our experimental results still yields a performance improvement.

Database clustering has been thoroughly investigated in both relational and object oriented databases. Relational clustering is relatively simple; generally, the clustering is performed along one or more attributes of the relation. If a single attribute is used, then the standard structure is a B-tree or one of its many variants. Multi-dimensional clustering is a little more involved, but there are well known data structures which perform quite well, such as the R-tree and its variants. A good survey of classic multi-dimensional access schemes is [4]. Relational clustering is not particularly relevant to XML database clustering, due to the fact that access patterns are considerably simpler.

OODB clustering is a far more difficult and well-researched problem. Given that XML databases can be thought of as fairly simple object oriented databases,

---

[1] We ignore here the use of ID and IDREF, which is not common in practice.

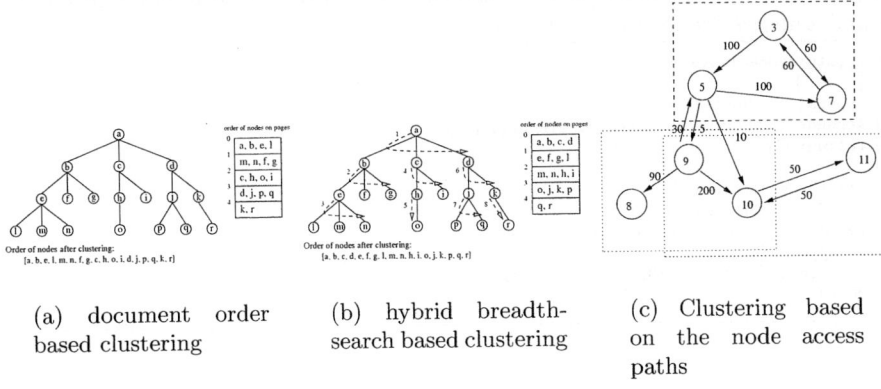

(a) document order based clustering

(b) hybrid breadth-search based clustering

(c) Clustering based on the node access paths

Fig. 2. Static clustering of XML database

it is clear that OODB clustering should be applicable to XML databases. Generally speaking, the research into OODB clustering can be classified into *static* and *dynamic* strategies. While all static strategies are *offline* [7–9], dynamic strategies can be further partitioned into *offline* [1,3,10] and *online* strategies [11,12].

3 Clustering Strategies

This section proposes several clustering strategies that are based on the availability of different database information such as query statistics and schema information (here we assume a DataGuide [5] is available). These clustering strategies range from static offline clustering algorithms to dynamic offline clustering algorithms.

3.1 Scheme A: Document Order Clustering

In general, we can categorize XML databases into *document*-centric and *data*-centric databases. While in the latter case many queries will have access patterns not corresponding to document order, we expect that in the former case document order will be heavily relied upon. As it was mentioned earlier, XML query languages such as XPath 2.0 and XQuery require all query result nodes to be sorted in document order. Therefore, we might expect that a sensible approach for the query processor to return node sets in document order is to actually search through the document in document order. This clustering strategy is designed based on this assumption.

Of course, if there were indexing support for document order built in to the database system or if the queries executed rely on other properties of the data, for example, searching for records with an element whose numerical value lies within some range, then clustering in document order may not be the most efficient way of ordering. However, even in the event that queries are executed

Algorithm 1 Document Order Clustering: *Re-clustering of a database $\mathcal{D}_1$ into a new ordered set $\mathcal{D}_2$ based on document*

```
DocumentOrderRecluster(D₁)
1  D₂ ← ∅
2  Append(D₂, Root(D₁))
3  Append(D₂, DocumentOrderRecurse(Root(D₁)))
4  return D₂

DocumentOrderRecurse(n)
1  {C, D} ← {Children(n), C}
2  for each  c  in  C  in document order do
3      Append(D, c)
4      Append(D, DocumentOrderRecurse(c))
5  return D
```

on document-centric databases which do not follow document order, it is still likely that the results of these queries will have to be materialized in document order.

Figure 2(a) shows how a small database is arranged in document order, and how the nodes are stored in the pages, assuming each page stores four objects. We believe this clustering scheme is particularly effective at speeding up queries which contain the descendant operator (//). The pseudo code for clustering the database into document order is given by Algorithm 1.

3.2 Scheme B: Hybrid Breadth-Search Clustering

Our second static clustering scheme is based upon observations of real world XML documents such as MEDLINE[2] and DBLP[3]. The majority of large XML documents tend to have a similar structure, with very broad breadth and shallow depth. In fact, many XML documents can easily be visualized as a large relational database; the key advantage to using XML in these cases is that each record has a high degree of irregularity. For example, DBLP is only five levels deep, but it contains more than 300000 records (in fact, the vast majority of these records are only two levels deep). Therefore, we can reasonably assume that the number of children of each node is generally quite high.

To cater for the pseudo-relational nature of many XML documents, a possibly effective clustering scheme is to cluster in breadth-first order. The effectiveness of this strategy is predicated upon the assumption that the data is accessed like a relational database, with many horizontal scans of the records. However, we expect breadth-first clustering will tend to slow down materialization queries, such as //*, which will typically be executed when returning portions of the database.

Figure 2(b) shows the order of traversal used by our clustering scheme. The arrows indicate the order in which the nodes are rearranged. Note that we do not use an actual breadth-first based ordering of nodes, but instead a hybrid

---

[2] See http://www.nlm.nih.gov/bsd/licensee/data_elements_doc.html.
[3] See http://dblp.uni-trier.de/xml/.

Algorithm 2 Hybrid Clustering: *Re-clustering of a database $\mathcal{D}_1$ into a new ordered set $\mathcal{D}_2$ based on hybrid breadth-depth ordering*

```
HybridOrderRecluster(D₁)
1  D₂ ← ∅
2  Append(D₂, Root(D₁))
3  Append(D₂, HybridOrderRecurse(Root(D₁)))
4  return D₂

HybridOrderRecurse(n)
1  {C, D} ← {Children(n), C in document order}
2  for each  c  in  C  do
3     Append(D, HybridOrderRecurse(c))
4  return D
```

between pre-order (document order) and breadth-first based ordering of nodes. We expect that in general, when horizontal scans are performed, they will only be performed on the set of all children of a node, instead of the set of all nodes at a particular level. Hence, by grouping children together instead of entire levels, we strike a balance between navigational and materializational accesses. The pseudo code for re-clustering the database using this strategy is described in Algorithm 2.

3.3 Scheme C: Schema-Based Static Clustering

In this scheme, we consider a static clustering strategy which takes advantage of schema information. While we cannot expect it to be as accurate as the previous scheme, we can expect the scheme to be considerably easier to implement, and faster to run. The scheme clusters the database by clustering by DataGuide type.

We assume each DataGuide node keeps a count of the number of nodes in its target set (this information is trivial to maintain). The algorithm proceeds by picking the DataGuide node that has the highest count of corresponding document nodes. For each DataGuide node, we cluster its target set by document order. Hence, the nodes are clustered in a hierarchy of clusters: at the top level, they are clustered by type, and then clustered by document order. Thus, this algorithm is an adaptation of the ORION database's clustering strategy [7] to ordered XML. This approach differs from the previous two static clustering strategies in that it assumes, like the dynamic schema algorithm discussed next, that access patterns for XML nodes remain approximately the same for all nodes of the same type. The algorithm is described by Algorithm 3.

3.4 Scheme D: Schema-Based Dynamic Clustering

The last three clustering schemes were all static, in the sense that they did not adapt to the query workload of the database. Our next algorithm is inspired by McIver and King's dynamic use of breadth-first and depth-first traversals [12]. Their algorithm keeps track of two quantities, *heat* and *tension*. The heat of an object is the number of references made to it, and hence is a measure of that

Algorithm 3 Static Schema-based Clustering: *Re-clustering of a database $\mathcal{D}_1$ into a new ordered set $\mathcal{D}_2$ based on static schema-based clustering*

```
DataguideNodesRecluster(𝒟₁)
1  𝒟₂ ← ∅
2  for each  n in DataGuideNodes(𝒟₁) in decreasing order of access frequency do
3      S ← TargetSet(n)
4      Append(𝒟₂, DocumentOrderRecluster(S))
5  Append(𝒟₂, 𝒟₁-𝒟₂)
6  return 𝒟₂
```

object's popularity. The tension is the number of co-references made navigating from one object to another, and measures the correlation between accesses to different objects.

The novel insight of McIver and King was to split the heat metric into two values, the *navigational* heat and the *materialization* heat. Navigational heat measured the references that were made to an object during a navigation-like query, such as a scan over a set of objects. Materialization heat measured the references that were made to an object during a query which accessed an object and all of its sub-objects (for instance, to print the object on screen). Using these two different quantities, their algorithm then clustered the children of each object as follows: if the navigational heat was greater than the materialization heat, a breadth-first traversal of the children was used, otherwise, a depth-first traversal was used.

McIver's algorithm has one particularly significant disadvantage: we must store a reference count for each node and edge. This overhead is typical of virtually all OODB dynamic clustering algorithms. We can alleviate this to a significant degree in an XML database due to the properties of real world XML data. We make the assumption that elements of an XML document which share the same "type" will most likely be accessed in similar ways. Hence, if we only store the relevant information per type, instead of per node, then we should be able to render the storage overhead of the clustering algorithm insignificant, whilst maintaining a reasonable degree of optimality. We make use of DataGuides, which provide a structural summary that can be efficiently computed and stored. A particularly appealing property of a DataGuide is that they mesh well with simple regular path expressions, whose navigation axes correspond to traversal of the DataGuide. Thus, we expect that if the statistical information is stored per DataGuide node instead of per database node, the loss in accuracy should be minimal, due to the fact that access patterns should remain relatively constant across the target set of a DataGuide node.

For each node of the DataGuide, our algorithm maintains a reference count, which is incremented every time an object in the target set of that node is accessed. We do *not* store co-reference information, for several reasons. Firstly, in an XML database there are typically only a few access paths that can be taken from a node; this contrasts with OODBs where access paths can be far richer. As we are restricting our statistics to DataGuide nodes only, this is made even worse by the fact that sibling information is essentially lost. Hence, we do

Algorithm 4 Dynamic Schema Based Clusteirng: *Re-clustering a database $\mathcal{D}_1$ into an ordered set $\mathcal{D}_2$ using the schema based dynamic clustering algorithm*

```
DynamicSchemaRecluster(D₁)
1  {D₂, Q} ← {∅, ∅}
2  Append(Q, Root(D₁))
3  while Q ≠ ∅ do
4      n ← RemoveFirst(Q)
5      C ← Children(n)
6      Sort C by decreasing DataGuide node reference count
7      c₁ ← RemoveFirst(C)
8      Append(D₂, {n, c₁})
9      Append(Q, C)
10 return D₂
```

not expect that maintaining co-reference information would add much accuracy to the algorithm. Our approach is thus much simpler than that of McIver, and has considerably less overhead.

To perform our re-clustering pass, we traverse the database in a single pass, beginning with the root node. We maintain a queue of nodes to visit; for each node, we examine its direct children, through whichever access paths the database implementation supports. We sort these nodes by the reference count of their DataGuide node, with ties broken by favoring depth-first traversals (such as accessing child nodes) over breadth-first traversals (such as accessing sibling nodes). We favor depth-first traversals because we expect these to occur more frequently in practice, however, we also do not believe that this choice substantially affects the performance of the algorithm.

Our algorithm is given in pseudo-code in Algorithm 4. At each step of the algorithm, the most expensive step is the sort. However, as we expect the number of nodes to be sorted to be very small, this step can be regarded as constant time. Hence, the entire algorithm runs in approximately one linear pass over the database, which is the best that can be hoped for.

3.5 Scheme E: Clustering Based on Access Patterns

The previous dynamic clustering scheme in section 3.4 made approximations based on assumptions about standard XML query access patterns. In this approach, we remove these assumptions, and instead process data about access patterns directly. We store information from the most popular database queries and re-cluster the database system periodically, in order to optimize it for these popular queries. In between re-clustering runs, we store the access paths of all queries. An example of such an access path is `firstchild 2 -> 3`, denoting that we accessed node 3 from node 2 through the `firstchild` operator.

Clustering is then performed based on the frequencies of the access paths appearing in the *access log* (above), which can be visualized as a graph as shown in Figure 2(c), with the nodes of the graph being the nodes in the database, and the edges of the graph annotated with their access frequencies. In the figure, we assume each page can hold at most three nodes; if this is the case, then for the access patterns given, the following clustering is optimal according to most OODB clustering schemes [1]: {{3, 5, 7}, {8}, {9, 10, 11}}. Although this has proved to be effective on object databases, this clustering scheme is extremely expensive unless heuristics are employed. For instance, using a greedy algorithm one might instead cluster the graph into: {{3, 5, 7}, {8, 9, 10}, {11}}.

In order to cluster vast amounts of XML data in a very short time, we partition the nodes by their access frequencies. Note that this has been proved to be optimal for database with independent and identically distributed accesses [13]. To compute the frequencies from the access log file efficiently, we combine the following steps and perform them at the same. First, let us assume the links in the access log are written as $(x, y)_i$ (i.e., the i-th entry is operation $x \to y$) and that each page can hold P nodes.

1. Swap x and y if necessary so that $x \leq y$.
2. Sort the access log by (x, y), so that $(x_i, y_i) < (x_j, y_j)$ if and only if either $x_i < x_j$ or $x_i = x_j$ and $y_i < y_j$.
3. Scan the access log, merging duplicates by computing the frequencies of their occurrences (note that this can be performed at the same time with step 1 and 2 above).
4. Partition the nodes into pages of P nodes each based on their frequencies, using a simple greedy algorithm.

One aspect of this method is that the first two steps above treat the graph as an undirected graph, even though the access paths are directed. Our reason for doing so is that, in terms of clustering, it makes little difference whether node A accesses node B or vice-versa; we are instead interested in the total number of co-references between A and B.

We demonstrate our technique on the example of Figure 2(c), with the results appearing in Figure 3. As described above, once we have obtained the final result we use a simple greedy algorithm to partition the nodes into pages. We note that, as proved in [13] under the assumption of i.i.d. accesses, this scheme is optimal under an LRU buffer management scheme. Since most operating systems and database systems use algorithms very similar to LRU for their buffer management, grouping nodes with high access frequencies together is likely to increase the effectiveness of LRU.

4 Experimental Results

We performed our experiments on a dual Pentium III 750MHz box running Linux with 50 GB 7200 rpm SCSI hard-drive and 1000 * 8KB cache pages. The experiment used the native XML database SODA4 from Soda Technologies[4] on a cut-down version of the DBLP database, which had 50000 bibliographic records.

The data was first loaded into an empty database with a SAX-based XML parser, such that the XML data was stored according to the order of how the

---

[4] http://www.sodatech.com.

(a) Raw Data

x	y	Freq
3	7	60
7	3	60
3	5	100
5	7	100
9	5	30
5	9	5
5	10	10
9	10	200
...	...	...

(b) After Step 2

x	y	Freq
3	7	60
3	7	60
3	5	100
5	7	100
5	9	30
5	9	5
5	10	10
9	10	200
...	...	...

(c) After Step 3

x	y	Freq
9	10	200
3	7	120
3	5	100
5	7	100
5	9	35
5	10	10
...	...	...

```
9
10
3
7
5
...
```

(d) Final Result

Fig. 3. Scheme E applied to Figure 2(c)

Table 1. Queries used in experiments

Query	Result Size	Path Expression
Q1	50,000	dblp/*
Q2	533	/dblp/article
Q3	100	/dblp/*[position() >= 1 and position() <= 100]
Q4	250	/dblp/*[publisher='Springer'] [year >= 1998 and year <= 2002]
Q5	14	/dblp/*[author='Hector Garcia-Molina']
Q6	27	/dblp/*[author='Hector Garcia-Molina'] /author[.!='Hector Garcia-Molina']
Q7	77	//school

SAX-based parser performed the parsing. Different queries, as described in Table 1, were then sent to and processed by the database system.

Figure 4 shows the performance of different clustering schemes. As shown in the figure, most of our clustering algorithms improved the overall performance of each query over the default scheme A. In particular, Scheme E performed significantly better than the other clustering schemes on some queries. This is due to the fact that it uses substantially more data than the other schemes to perform its clustering, and hence can produce considerably more accurate results. However, on simple queries, it is interesting to note that the relative difference between the clustering schemes is much less, which indicates that the assumptions made by the simpler static clustering schemes are appropriate for primitive XML queries.

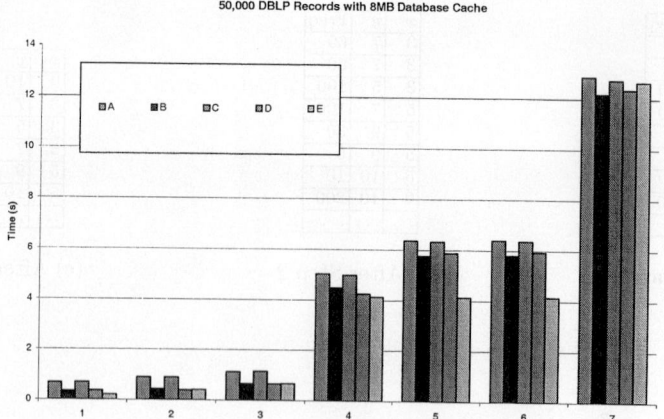

Fig. 4. Results (in seconds)

Apart from Scheme E, the most consistent performer was Scheme D. Recall that the main assumption that this clustering scheme made was that access patterns remained the same for nodes which had the same DataGuide node. It is clear from our experimental results that this assumption seems to hold fairly well in practical queries. It is particularly interesting to note that Queries 4 and 5, where Scheme E comfortably beat Scheme D, are queries which do not just access structural information, but also data values (the author's name). This is exactly the kind of access path which Scheme D's assumption implicitly ignores.

For static schemes, it is interesting to see that scheme B's performance is close to scheme D and it out-performs other two static schemes. This can possibly be explained by the way each data nodes are visited (a mix of pre-order and breadth-first order), which allows maximal usage per page without run-time optimization.

5 Conclusion

In this paper, we have adapted some of the standard OODB clustering techniques to XML databases. We have investigated the applicability of various assumptions about standard access paths in XML. We have shown that clustering has a dramatic effect on essentially all queries. Just as with OODB clustering, partitioning-based clustering schemes (e.g., Scheme E) can perform dramatically better than other, simpler schemes, particularly as query complexity increases, but require substantially more data to achieve accurate results.

We have shown that by making some simple assumptions about XML access methods we can adapt these schemes to achieve respectable performance (e.g., Scheme C). We suspect that in practice it will be these schemes that are used, as the amount of data required for the re-clustering pass is an order of magnitude less than for the full partitioning-based strategies.

References

1. Christoph Kilger Carsten A. Gerlhof, Alfons Kemper and Guido Moerkotte. Clustering in object bases. Technical Report 6, Universitität Karlsruhe, 1992.
2. E. E. Chang and R. H. Katz. Exploiting inheritance and structure semantics for effective clustering and buffering in an object-oriented dbms. In *Proceedings of SIGMOD 1989*, pages 348–357. ACM Press, 1989.
3. Jia-Bing R. Cheng and A.R. Hurson. Effective clustering of complex objects in object-oriented databases. In *Proceedings of SIGMOD 1991*, pages 22–31. ACM Press, 1991.
4. Volker Gaede and Oliver Gnther. Multidimensional access methods. *ACM Computing Surveys (CSUR)*, 30(2):170–231, 1998.
5. Roy Goldman and Jennifer Widom. DataGuides: Enabling Query Formulation and Optimization in Semistructured Databases. In *Proceedings of VLDB*, pages 436–445, East Sussex - San Francisco, August 1997. Morgan Kaufmann.
6. Carl-Christian Kanne and Guido Moerkotte. Efficient storage of XML data. In *ICDE*, 2000.
7. W. Kim, J.F. Garza, N. Ballou, and D. Woelk. Architecture of the ORION next-generation database system. *tkde*, 2(1):109–124, March 1990.
8. Charles Lamb, Gordon Landis, Jack Orenstein, and Dan Weinreb. The objectstore database system. *Communications of the ACM*, 34(10):50–63, 1991.
9. David Maier, Jacob Stein, Allen Otis, and Alan Purdy. Development of an object-oriented dbms. In *Conference proceedings on Object-oriented programming systems, languages and applications*, pages 472–482. ACM Press, 1986.
10. Manolis M. Tsangaris and Jeffrey F. Naughton. On the performance of object clustering techniques. In *Proceedings of SIGMOD 1992*, pages 144–153. ACM Press, 1992.
11. Chao-Ming Wang. *Dynamic Online Data Clustering for Object-Oriented Databases*. PhD thesis, University of Illinois at Urbana-Champaign, 2000.
12. Jr. William J. McIver and Roger King. Self-adaptive, on-line reclustering of complex object data. In *Proceedings of SIGMOD 1994*, pages 407–418. ACM Press, 1994.
13. P.C. Yue and C.K. Wong. On the optimality of the probability ranking scheme in storage applications. *Journal of the ACM (JACM)*, 20(4):624–633, 1973.

Detecting Content Changes on Ordered XML Documents Using Relational Databases

Erwin Leonardi[1], Sourav S. Bhowmick[1], T.S. Dharma[1], and Sanjay Madria[2]

[1] School of Computer Engineering, Nanyang Technological University, Singapore
{pk909134,assourav}@ntu.edu.sg
[2] Department of Computer Science, University of Missouri-Rolla, Rolla, MO 65409
madrias@umr.edu

Abstract. Previous works in change detection on XML focused on detecting changes to text file using ordered and unordered tree model. These approaches are not suitable for detecting changes to large XML document as it requires a lot of memory to keep the two versions of XML documents in the memory. In this paper, we take a more conservative yet novel approach of using traditional relational database engines for detecting *content* changes of *ordered* large XML data. First, we store XML documents in RDBMS. Then, we detect the changes by using a set of SQL queries. Experimental results show that our approach has better scalability, better performance, and comparable result quality compared to the state-of-the-art approaches.

1 Introduction

Over the next few years XML is likely to replace HTML as the standard format for publishing and transporting documents over the Web. Since online information changes frequently, being able to quickly detect the changes in XML documents (hereafter called *XML deltas* or *XDeltas*) is an important problem. Such change detection tool is important to incremental query evaluation, trigger condition evaluation, search engine, data mining applications, and mobile applications [1]. In this paper, we focus on detecting *content* changes on the *ordered* XML documents.

Let us illustrate changes to ordered XML with an example. Suppose we have two versions of an XML document that is used for storing the contents of a book. These XML documents are represented as trees as depicted in Figure 1. These XML documents are classified into ordered XML since the content of a book must be ordered. The highlighted ellipses in Figure 1 indicate the different types of changes. The "XML Syntax" chapter is moved to be the second chapter of the book because of insertion of "XML Introduction" chapter.

The changes on ordered XML documents can be classified into two types: *changes occur in the internal element* and *changes occur in the leaf element*. An *internal element* is the element which does not contain textual data and is not a leaf element. For example, nodes 5 and 6 in Figure 1(a) are the internal elements. The changes occur in the internal elements (which are called as *structural*

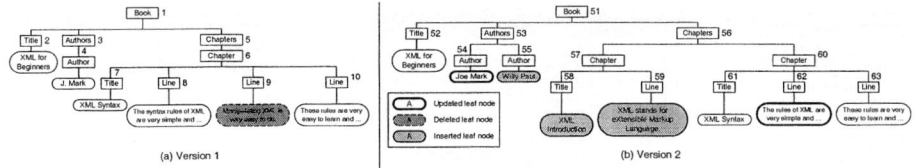

Fig. 1. Tree representation of Ordered XML Documents

changes) modify the structure and do not change textual data content. The types of changes which are classified as *structural changes* are as following: *insertion of internal element, deletion of internal element,* and *internal element movement*. For instance, node 57 in Figure 1(b) is the new inserted element. Node 60 is moved from being the first child of node 56 to be the second child of node 56. A *leaf element* is the element/attribute which contains textual data. For example, node 52 is a leaf element which has name "Title" and textual content "XML for Beginners". The changes in the leaf elements (which are called as *content changes*) modify textual data content. There are four types of *content changes* as following: *leaf element insertion, leaf element deletion, content update of leaf element,* and *leaf element movement*. A leaf element "Line" which has value "Manipulating XML is very easy to do." is a new inserted leaf element. In this paper, we present a technique for detecting *content* changes (changes to the leaf element) on the *ordered* XML documents using relational database.

Some previous works [1–3] have been proposed to solve the problem of detecting changes on XML documents. Cobena et al. [2] proposed an algorithm, called XyDiff, for detecting changes on ordered XML documents. The changes are detected by using the signature and weight of nodes. XMLTreeDiff [3] is also proposed for solving the problem of detecting changes for ordered XML documents by using DOMHash. In [1], the authors presented X-Diff, an algorithm for detecting the changes on unordered XML documents. The algorithm assigns XHash value for each node in the trees. The XHash value of a node is calculated from the XHash values of its descendants. The algorithm tries to find a minimum-cost matching between two documents before generating the edit script in order to find the minimum edit script.

Our approach is different from the previous approaches in the following ways. First, our approach focuses on the *content change*, while the state-of-art approaches detect both *structural changes* and *content changes*. Second, we detect the changes on XML documents by using relational database. The state-of-art approaches detect the changes on XML documents stored in main memory after they are parsed. Our approaches give the opportunities to have more scalable change detection system since we depend on the secondary storage rather than the main memory. We store the XML documents in a relational database. Then, we detect the changes by using a set of SQL queries.

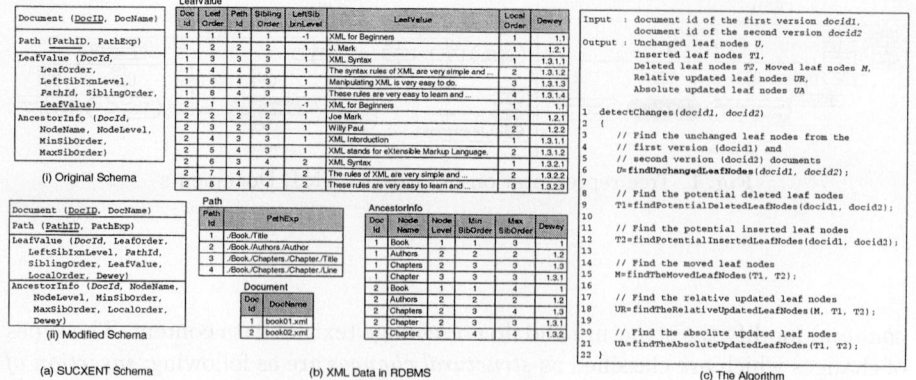

Fig. 2. SUCXENT

2 Storing XML Data

There are two approaches for storing XML documents in relational database: the *structure-mapping* and the *model-mapping* approaches [5, 7]. In this paper, we have decided to adopt the model mapping approach.

We now discuss how XML documents are stored in relational database by using SUCXENT (Schema UnConcious XML ENabled sysTem) schema [7]. SUCXENT is a model-mapping, path-oriented approach. We choose SUCXENT because it outperforms significantly current state-of-the-art model mapping approaches like XParent [5] as far as storage size, insertion time, extraction time, and path expression queries are concerned [7]. SUCXENT schema is shown in Figure 2(a)(i). The details of the schema can be found in [7].

We modify the SUCXENT schema by adding the attribute *LocalOrder* in the LeafValue table to store the position of a leaf element among its siblings. We also need to know the ancestors' local orders of each leaf and internal elements. We adopt the Dewey Order Encoding [6]. Let us name this attribute *Dewey*. We add attribute *Dewey* in the LeafValue and AncestorInfo tables. The modified SUCXENT schema is depicted in Figure 2(a)(ii). Suppose we have two versions of an XML document that are represented as trees depicted in Figure 1. The XML documents stored in RDBMS by using SUCXENT schema are depicted in Figure 2(b).

3 Content Changes Detection

In this section, we discuss how to detect the content changes by using our approach. The algorithm of our approach is shown in Figure 2(c).

3.1 Unchanged Leaf Elements Detection Phase

In the first phase, we find the leaf elements that are not changed during the transition. The unchanged leaf elements must have the same paths (*PathID*),

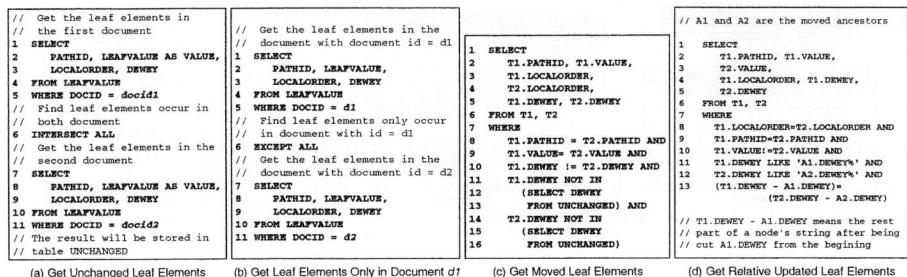

Fig. 3. SQL Queries

values (*LeafValue*), local orders (*LocalOrder*), and the ancestors' local orders (*Dewey*).

Given a set of tuples in the `LeafValue` table which correspond to leaf elements of two versions of an XML document, we are able to detect the unchanged leaf elements by using the SQL query shown in Figure 3(a). The SQL query is encapsulated in function `findUnchangedLeafNodes` (line 6) in Figure 2(c). Note that *docid1* and *docid2* are the document ids of the first and second versions respectively. Basically, the query tries to find the common leaf elements of the first and the second versions. We use "INTERSECT ALL" SQL operator because we want to preserve the duplicate tuples of two tables. The results of the queries are stores in the table, namely `UNCHANGED` table as depicted in Figures 4(a)(i).

3.2 Potential Inserted and Deleted Leaf Elements Detection Phase

The objective of the second phase is to find the *potential* inserted and *potential* deleted leaf elements. This phase is useful to filter out data which are not used for detecting changes in the subsequent phases. We call them *potential* inserted and *potential* deleted leaf elements because they are not only the deleted and inserted leaf elements respectively, but also the updated leaf elements which are detected as pairs of deleted and inserted leaf elements respectively. For example, the corresponding tuples in the T1 and T2 tables of *potential* deleted and *potential* inserted leaf elements as depicted in Figures 4(a)(ii) and (iii) respectively. The first tuples in the T1 and T2 tables are the corresponding tuples of an updated leaf element which is detected as a pair of *potential* deleted and *potential* inserted leaf elements respectively.

Given a set of tuples in the `LeafValue` table which correspond to leaf elements of two versions of an XML document, we can detect the *potential* deleted and *potential* inserted leaf elements by using the SQL query as depicted in Figures 3(b). The SQL query is encapsulated in functions `findPossibleDeletedLeafNodes` (line 9) and `findPossibleInsertedLeafNodes` (line 12) in Figure 2(c). We use "EXCEPT ALL" SQL operator in order to preserve the duplicate tuples of two tables. If we want to find the *potential* deleted nodes, we set the value of *d1* and *d2* to the document ids of the first and second versions respectively. The

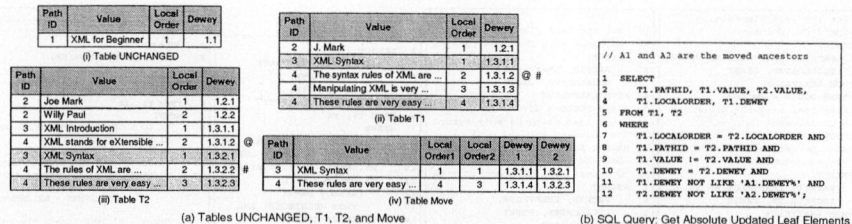

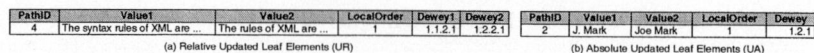

Fig. 4. Tables and SQL Query

PathID	Value1	Value2	LocalOrder	Dewey1	Dewey2	PathID	Value1	Value2	LocalOrder	Dewey
4	The syntax rules of XML are ...	The rules of XML are ...	1	1.1.2.1	1.2.2.1	2	J. Mark	Joe Mark	1	1.2.1

(a) Relative Updated Leaf Elements (UR)   (b) Absolute Updated Leaf Elements (UA)

Fig. 5. Updated Leaf Elements Detection

value of *d1* and *d2* are set to the document ids of the second and first versions respectively if we want to get the *potential* inserted nodes. In the subsequent phases, we are going to detect the content changes of these XML documents by using the UNCHANGED, T1 and T2 tables.

3.3 Moved Leaf Elements Detection Phase

Next, we search for the moved leaf elements (if any) by using the results of the first and second phases. There are three types of moved leaf elements as follows. First, the leaf elements are moved because of the movement of their ancestors. Second, they are moved because of the insertions or deletions of their siblings. Third, the leaf elements are moved among their siblings.

Give two sets of tuples in the T1 and T2 tables, we execute a SQL query as depicted in Figure 3(c) in order to detect these moved leaf elements. The SQL query is encapsulated in function findTheMovedLeafNodes (line 15) in Figure 2(c). Basically, the query tries to find tuples in the T1 and T2 tables which have the same paths (*PathID*), and values (*Value*), but have different *Dewey* value. If the local order of a leaf element is changed, the *Dewey* value of this node will also be changed. Similarly, the *Dewey* value of this node will be changed if the ancestors' local orders of a leaf element are changed. The results of this query are stored in the Move table which is depicted in Figure 4(a)(iv). Since these leaf elements have been detected as moved leaf elements, we have to delete the corresponding tuples of these leaf elements in the T1 and T2 tables. The highlighted rows in the T1 and T2 tables in Figures 4(a)(ii) and (iii) respectively are the deleted rows.

3.4 Relative Updated Leaf Elements Detection Phase

There are two types of updated leaf elements, namely, *absolute updated leaf elements* and *relative updated leaf elements*. If a leaf element which has the *same* absolute position in the first and second versions is updated, then we classify it as an *absolute updated leaf element*. We classify a leaf element as a *relative updated leaf element* if it is updated and has *different* absolute positions in the first and second versions. For example, the leaf element "Line" which has value "The syntax rules of XML are ..." is updated to "The rules of XML are ...". This leaf element has different absolute positions in the first and second versions. Detecting *absolute updated leaf elements* will be after detecting *relative updated leaf elements* in our approach in order to avoid misdetection.

We illustrate misdetection with an example. Suppose we have two sets of leaf elements which are stored as tuples in the T1 and T2 tables as depicted in Figure 4(a)(ii) and (iii) respectively after the highlighted rows are deleted. If we detect the absolute updated leaf elements first, the leaf element which is stored as tuple in the T1 table with "1.3.1.2" as the value of its *Dewey* attribute (denoted by "@" at the right of the rows) will be detected as an updated leaf element from "The syntax rules of XML are ..." to "XML stands for eXtensible ..." since they have the same absolute position in both XML documents. The leaf element which has value "The syntax rules of XML are ..." should be updated to "The rules of XML are ..." (denoted by "♯" at the right of the rows). The leaf element which has value "XML stands for eXtensible ..." should be detected as an inserted leaf element.

We now discuss how we detect the relative updated leaf elements. The discussion on how we detect the absolute updated leaf elements will be presented in the later section. Before finding the relative updated leaf elements, we have to do some preprocessing on the *Dewey* values. The aim of this preprocessing is to find the ancestor nodes of the moved leaf elements which are moved. We need to find these moved ancestor nodes in order to know which subtrees in XML trees are moved. To find these moved ancestor nodes, we use the values of attributes *Dewey1* and *Dewey2* in the Move table. For example, the first tuple in the Move table has "1.3.**1**.1" and "1.3.**2**.1" in attributes *Dewey1* and *Dewey2* respectively. We notice that the parent of the corresponding leaf elements is moved to be the second child. The *Dewey* values of these moved ancestors are "1.3.**1**" and "1.3.**2**". The algorithm for finding the moved ancestors is depicted in Figure 6(a).

After finding the moved ancestors, we are able to find the relative updated leaf elements. The SQL query shown in Figures 3(d) is used to detect the relative updated leaf elements. The SQL query is encapsulated in function findTheRelative UpdatedLeafNodes (line 18) in Figure 2(c). The query tries to find the tuples belong to first and second versions of an XML document which have the same local orders (*LocalOrder*), path (*PathID*), but have different value (*Value*) (Figures 3(d), lines 8-10). The prefix of *Dewey* attributes of the tuples corresponding to first and second versions of the XML document are equal to the moved ancestors' *Dewey* in the first and second versions respectively (Figures 3(d), line 11-12). We also have to make sure that the position of the corresponding leaf elements of these tuples are not changed (Figures 3(d), line 13).

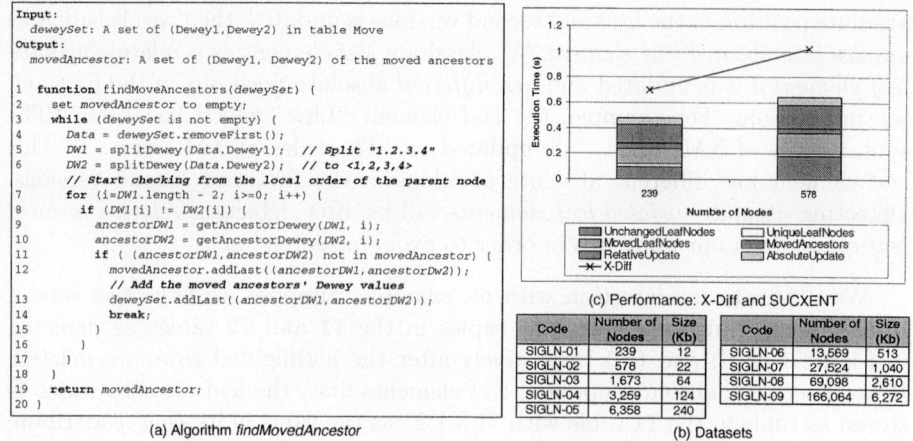

Fig. 6. Algorithm, Datasets, and Experimental Results

After we detect the relative updated leaf elements, we need to delete the corresponding tuples of the updated leaf elements which are in the T1 and T2 tables. The deleted rows in the T1 and T2 tables in Figure 4(a) are indicated with "⌗" at the right of the rows. The results of this query are stored in the UR table as shown in Figure 5(a).

3.5 Absolute Updated Leaf Elements Detection Phase

Now, the T1 and T2 tables may only consist of the deleted and inserted leaf elements respectively, and the *absolute updated leaf elements* which are detected as a pair of deleted and inserted leaf elements respectively. The objective of this phase is to find the *absolute updated leaf elements*. Intuitively, the *absolute updated leaf elements* are the updated leaf elements which are not the descendants of the moved ancestors. If the prefix of *Dewey* value of a leaf element is equal to the *Dewey* value of a moved ancestor, it must be under that moved ancestor. The *absolute updated leaf elements* are the leaf elements whose corresponding tuples have the same *LocalOrder* values, *PathID* values, *Dewey* values, but have different *Value* values.

Based on the above requirements, we are able to find the *absolute updated leaf elements* by using the SQL query as depicted in Figure 4(b). The SQL query is encapsulated in function findTheAbsoluteUpdatedLeafNodes (line 21) in Figure 2(c). After we detect the absolute updated leaf elements, we need to delete the corresponding tuples of these leaf elements in the T1 and T2 tables which are already detected as absolute updated leaf elements. The results will be stored in the the UA table as depicted in Figure 5(b).

3.6 Inserted and Deleted Leaf Elements Detection Phase

After detecting the absolute updated leaf elements, the T1 and T2 tables will only consist of the corresponding tuples of deleted and inserted leaf elements

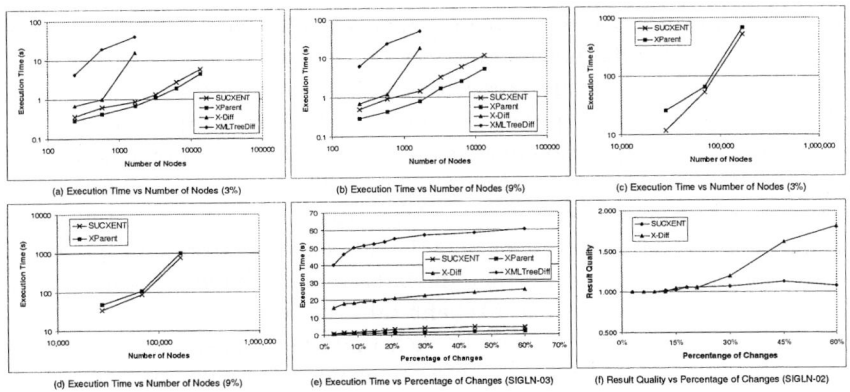

Fig. 7. Datasets and Experimental Results

respectively. Hence, we do not need an SQL query to detect the inserted and deleted leaf elements.

4 Experimental Results

We now present the results of our experiments to study the performance of our database approaches for detecting changes on ordered XML documents.

4.1 Experimental Setup and Data Set

We have implemented our approach entirely in Java. The Java implementation and the database engine were run on a Microsoft Windows 2000 Professional machine with a Pentium 4 1.7 GHz with 512 MB of memory. The database system we used was IBM DB2 UDB 8.1. We also created appropriate indexes on the relations to expedite query processing. We used a set of synthetic SIGMOD Record XML documents. Figure 6(b) shows the characteristics of our data sets. Note that we focus on numbers of nodes in our data sets. The higher number of nodes in a tree will increase the query cost since the database engine will join more tuples. We generated the second version of each XML document by using our own change generator.

We also studied the performance of the state-of-the-art approaches. We could not find the Java version of XyDiff [2][1] which was proposed to solve the problem of detecting changes on ordered XML documents. Hence, we compared our approach to X-Diff [1][2] and XMLTreeDiff [3][3] which are implemented in Java.

---

[1] Unfortunately, despite our best efforts (including contacting authors), we could not get the Java version.
[2] Downloaded from http://www.cs.wisc.edu/~yuanwang/xdiff.html.
[3] Available at http://www.alphaworks.ibm.com.

Since X-Diff was proposed for detecting changes in unordered XML documents, our change generator did not permute the order of any nodes.

We also implemented our approach using XParent schema [5] by doing some modifications. XParent outperforms some model-mapping approaches in some cases as far as path expression queries are concerned. We add one more relation for storing the information on the documents. The Document table consists of two tuples: *DocID* and *DocuName* which records the unique id and filename of XML documents respectively. Hence, XParent is able to store multiple versions of XML documents. We notice that the Data table in XParent stores information on leaf elements, while the Element table stores information on all nodes (including leaf elements). We modify such that the Element table only stores information on internal elements in order to avoid data redundancy. We use preorder traversal rather than level-order traversal for node id in XParent because we use SAX Parser that works in depth-first search fashion. We also added attribute *Dewey*, that has the same function as that in modified SUCXENT schema, in the Element and Data tables. Due to space constraints, we do not show the SQL queries for detecting changes using XParent.

4.2 Execution Time vs Number of Nodes

In this experiment, we analyze the execution time of our approach implemented in SUCXENT and XParent on different numbers of nodes.

Figures 7(a) and (b) depict the execution times of SUCXENT, XParent, X-Diff, and XMLTreeDiff on small datasets (the number of nodes is less than 20,000 nodes) when the percentages of changes are set to 3% and 9% respectively. We notice that XParent has better performance compared to other approaches. XParent is about 2 to 25 times faster than X-Diff, and is about 15 to 70 times faster than XMLTreeDiff. Compared to SUCXENT, XParent performs better in terms of execution time. XParent is about 1.2 to 2 times faster than SUCXENT for small datasets. Figures 7(c) and (d) depict the execution times of SUCXENT, and XParent on large datasets (the number of nodes is more than 20,000 nodes) when the percentages of changes are set to 3% and 9% respectively. We notice that SUCXENT is about faster 1.3 to 2 times faster than XParent for large datasets. We also notice that SUCXENT and XParent have better scalability and performance compared to X-Diff and XMLTreeDiff. X-Diff and XMLTreeDiff fail to detect large XML documents due to lack of main-memory. In this experiment, X-Diff and XMLTreeDiff are only able to detect the changes on XML documents which have around 2000 nodes.

The difference of execution time between SUCXENT and X-Diff increases as number of nodes increased. Recall the complexity of X-Diff as discussed in [1]. The performance of X-Diff is significantly influenced by the number of nodes and the out-degrees of nodes. X-Diff performs more numbers of node comparisons when the number of nodes and out-degree of nodes are increased. That is, the increment of the numbers of nodes from 400 to 2000 significantly influences the performance of X-Diff. In the first two phases of our approach, we query from the LeafValue table. The query plans of these queries show that RDBMS uses the indexed access method. In other phases, we only query from the T1, T2, UNCHANGED, MOVE, UR, and UA tables that are relatively much smaller than the LeafValue table. We also create appropriate indexes on these tables to expedite query processing. Figure 6(c) depicts the comparison between X-Diff and each phase in our approach using the first two datasets. We observe that most of the execution time of our approach is taken by finding the unchanged leaf nodes, detecting moved leaf nodes, and detecting the relative updated leaf nodes. Even then, it is faster than X-Diff.

The execution times of first and second steps (*unchanged leaf elements detection* phase and *potential deleted and inserted leaf elements detection* phase respectively) of SUCXENT and XParent are significantly different. The execution times of other steps are same because we use the same tables and the same SQL queries. XParent is faster than SUCXENT for small XML documents because XParent does not perform θ-joins while SUCXENT does. When the number of nodes is increased, the performance of XParent becomes slower than SUCXENT because the size of the Ancestor table in XParent becomes very large. Consequently, the cost of θ-joins performed by SUCXENT is cheaper that one of joining the Ancestor table in XParent.

4.3 Execution Time vs Percentage of Changes

In this experiment, we analyze the execution time of our approach implemented in SUCXENT and XParent on different percentages of changes.

Figure 7(e) depicts the execution times of SUCXENT, XParent, X-Diff, and XMLTreeDiff on different percentages of changes. We use dataset "SIGLN-03" in this set of experiments. We observed that the execution times of SUCXENT, XParent, and X-Diff are affected insignificantly to the changes of percentages of changes. When we vary the percentages of changes from "3%" to "60%", the execution times of SUCXENT and XParent are less than 5 seconds. If the percentages of changes are increased from "3%" to "60%", the execution times of X-Diff are between 15 and 25 seconds. We also notice that the execution times of XMLTreeDiff are affected to the changes of percentages of changes. The execution times of XMLTreeDiff are between 40 and 60 seconds if the percentages of changes are increased from "3%" to "60%".

4.4 Result Quality vs Percentage of Changes

In this set of experiments, we study the result quality [1] of our approach compared to the X-Diff. The results of SUCXENT and XParent are same because we use the same queries against the same tables. In X-Diff, we may have insertions and deletions of subtrees. In this case, we only count numbers of leaf elements which are in the inserted and deleted subtrees. We use dataset "SIGLN-02" in this set of experiments.

Figure 7(f) depicts the result quality of our approach compared to X-Diff of different percentages of changes. We notice that if the percentage of changes is less than 10%, both approaches results the optimal deltas. When the percentage of changes becomes larger, our approach has better quality results compared to the X-Diff. This happens because when the XML documents are changed significantly, some subtrees in the XML trees are also changed significantly. Hence, X-Diff may detect these subtrees as inserted and deleted subtrees. Note that X-Diff does not focus only on the leaf elements changes.

5 Conclusions

In this paper, we present an approach to detect the content changes on ordered XML documents stored in relational databases. This approach focuses on the changes to the leaf elements. This approach is motivated by the scalability problem on the native approaches and the necessity of detecting the changes on the leaf elements for several applications. In our approach, first, it tries to find the *unchanged*, *potential* inserted, and *potential* deleted leaf elements from the XML documents. These leaf elements are kept in tables. From these tables, the SQL queries are issued in order to find the *moved*, the *relative updated*, and *absolute updated* leaf elements. The experimental results indicate that our approach has better performance and scalability compared to the native approaches. We also show that our approach has better result quality for the XML documents which are changed significantly. We also notice that the performance of our approach is schema dependent, while the result quality of our approach is schema independent.

References

1. Y. Wang, D. J. DeWitt, J. Cai. X-Diff: An Effective Change Detection Algorithm for XML Documents. *Proceedings of 19th ICDE, India*, 2003.
2. G. Cobena, S. Abiteboul, A. Marian. Detecting Changes in XML Documents. *Proceedings of 18th ICDE, San Jose, California, USA*, 2002.
3. Curbera, D. A. Epstein. Fast Difference and Update of XML Documents. *XTech'99, San Jose*, 1999.
4. D. Florescu, D. Kossmann. Storing and Querying XML Data using an RDMBS. *IEEE Data Engineering Bulletin, Volume 22, Number 3*, 1999.
5. H. Jiang, H. Lu, W. Wang, J. Xu Yu. XParent: An Efficient RDBMS-Based XML Database System. *Proceedings of the 18th ICDE 2002 (Poster Paper), San Jose, California, USA*, 2002.
6. Online Computer Library Center. Introduction to the Dewey Decimal Classification. http://www.oclc.org/oclc/fp/about/about_the_ddc.htm.
7. S. Prakash, S. S. Bhowmick, S. Mardia. SUCXENT: An Efficient Path-based Approach to Store and Query XML Documents. *Proceedings of the 15th DEXA, Zaragoza, Spain*, 2004.

Timestamp-Based Protocols for Synchronizing Access on XML Documents

Sven Helmer, Carl-Christian Kanne, and Guido Moerkotte

Fakultät für Mathematik und Informatik, D7, 27
Universität Mannheim, 68131 Mannheim, Germany
phone: +49 621 181 2585, fax: +49 621 181 2588
{helmer,cc,moerkotte}@informatik.uni-mannheim.de

Abstract. The eXtensible Markup Language (XML) is well accepted in many different application areas. As a consequence, there is an increasing need for storing XML documents persistently. As soon as many users and applications work concurrently on the same collection of XML documents — i.e. an XML base — isolating accesses and modifications of different transactions becomes an important issue.
We discuss two different timestamp-based protocols for synchronizing access on XML document collections. These core protocols synchronize structure traversals and modifications. Further, we extend the protocols to handle node contents and IDREF jumps, so that they can be integrated into a native XML base management System (XBMS).

1 Introduction

The popularity of the eXtensible Markup Language (XML [10]) results in a rapidly growing number of XML documents. This is especially true in web-based applications where semi-structured data makes markup languages ideal. We believe that users will soon work concurrently on XML documents employing general purpose applications like XML editors and stylesheet processors as well as specialized tools. Consequently, isolating different concurrent applications (i.e. preventing them from having unwanted effects on each other) becomes important.

The database community has developed successful protocols for isolating different applications. One of the key concepts is the notion of serializability, i.e. that the outcome of concurrently executed transactions is equivalent to a strictly serial execution of the transactions. Most of the protocols that guarantee serializability already found their way into textbooks more than a decade ago [1, 4, 7]. During the last decade, some researchers have concentrated on defining weaker notions than serializability and developed protocols that allow a less restrictive cooperation between users. For a survey on cooperating transactions and synchronization in general see [8].

We believe that serializability is an essential requirement for any database management system (DBMS), including an XBMS. This motivated us to start with the development of protocols that guarantee serializability. After we introduced lock-based protocols in [5], we now turn to timestamp-based protocols. Timestamps have the advantage that for low-conflict environments they avoid the overhead for locking. Also, timestamp-based schedulers are easier to distribute, since each scheduler can act independently of the others. Thus, no communication for coordination between the distributed schedulers is necessary.

The paper is organized as follows. In Section 2 we give some basic definitions on XML documents needed for the remainder of the paper. We present the core protocols in Section 3 and show results of an evaluation in Section 4. Section 5 covers extensions to our protocols and Section 6 wraps up the paper with a conclusion and an outlook.

2 Traversing and Modifying XML Documents

Semi-structured data, such as XML documents, is often represented as ordered, labeled trees. The nodes of the tree store the tag names or textual data. For an example of a tree representation of an XML document see Figure 1.

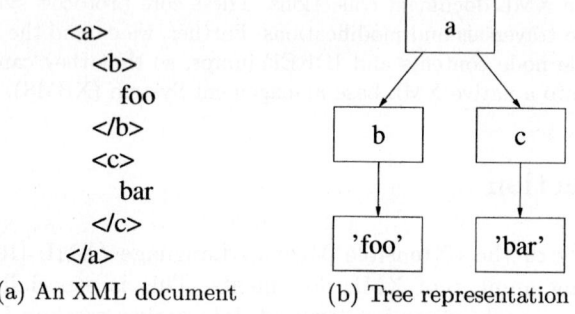

(a) An XML document (b) Tree representation

Fig. 1. An XML document and its tree representation

The operations of a typical API for XML documents (e.g. DOM [2]) fall into four categories: mutators and observers of the contents of a node and mutators and observers of the structure of a document (for a list of some operations provided by DOM see Figure 2).

In order not to overburden the discussion, we work with a small representative set of general operations that are sufficient to implement the navigational part of a DOM API. Missing parts are addressed in Section 5.

We assume that a transaction first selects a document to work on. This is done via a *select document* (**sd**) operation. The result is a reference to the selected document's root node. From there on, the transaction traverses and modifies the document structure using a sequence of the following operations:

mutator	structure	insertBefore	observer	structure	firstChild
		replaceChild			lastChild
		removeChild			previousSibling
		appendChild			nextSibling
	contents	appendData			getNodeById
		deleteData			getElementByTagName
		insertData		contents	getTextContents
		replaceData			nodeName
		setAttribute			getAttribute

Fig. 2. Some DOM Operations

nthP retrieves the n-th child in the child list
nthM retrieves the n-th child counting from the end of the child list backwards
insA inserts a new node after a given node
insB inserts a new node before a given node
del deletes a given node (and the associated subtree)

The operations nthP and nthM are conceptually on the same level, as both allow navigation to child nodes. Practically they allow more concurrency by allowing different transactions to take different non-conflicting paths to child nodes. The distinction between attribute, element, and other node types is not important for synchronization purposes. Therefore, we talk about nodes in general.

3 Protocols

In this section we give a brief review of basic timestamp ordering (TO) as described in textbooks before presenting our two core protocols, XML timestamp ordering (XTO) and XML Dynamic Commit Ordering (XCO). It is important to note that all core protocols require that document access start at the root node and traverse documents top down. This requirement is relaxed in Section 5.

3.1 Basic Timestamp Ordering (TO)

In the basic timestamp ordering (TO) protocol, the transaction manager assigns a unique timestamp to each transaction at the start of the transaction. A timestamp can be generated by a clock or some other kind of running counter. (For further details on TO, see e.g. [1].) Each operation associated with a transaction is also attributed with the transaction's timestamp. Schedulers that respect TO use the timestamps to order conflicting operations. Thus, if $p_i[x]$ and $q_j[x]$ are conflicting operations (issued by the transactions T_i and T_j, respectively) on data element x, then $p_i[x]$ is processed before $q_j[x]$, iff the timestamp of T_i is lower than the timestamp of T_j (that is $ts(T_i) < ts(T_j)$).

The basic version of a TO scheduler processes incoming operations immediately in a first-come-first-served manner. It guarantees the processing in timestamp order by rejecting operations that arrive too late. An operation $p_i[x]$ is too late if a conflicting operation $q_j[x]$ with a larger timestamp has already been processed. In that case, the transaction T_i has to be aborted and restarted with a new, higher timestamp.

In order to recognize tardy operations, a TO scheduler stores the timestamp of the most recent operation on data element x for each operation type q in max-q-scheduled(x), which is an attribute of x. When the scheduler receives an operation $p_i[x]$, it compares $ts(T_i)$ to max-q-scheduled(x) for all operation types q that conflict with p. If $ts(T_i) <$ max-q-scheduled(x), then $p_i[x]$ is rejected, otherwise $p_i[x]$ is processed and max-p-scheduled(x) is updated.

It is also possible to create recoverable schedules by delaying the commit operations of a transaction T_i until all transactions from which T_i has read data items have committed. Checking this read/write relationship between transactions is usually done with a dependency graph that stores all read/write dependencies between transactions. With this graph we can determine whether a transaction may commit or, in the case of an aborting transaction, find all transactions that also have to abort. Thus, the timestamp order also defines the commit order.

3.2 XML Timestamp Ordering (XTO)

While (basic) TO is not difficult, there are some pitfalls in extending it to navigational queries and structural changes. Before delving into details, let us briefly describe the main idea of our approach. We achieve serializability by altering the visibility of nodes to different transactions. Deleted nodes are not immediately removed from the document, but marked as deleted. Older transactions may still traverse these nodes, while younger ones just skip them. Newly inserted nodes are handled similarly: older transactions just skip them, while younger ones traverse them. This bears some similarity to multiversion timestamp ordering as introduced by [9].

Let us start by defining the structural operations possible on an XML node. A transaction can traverse (via nthP or nthM), insert (via insA or insB), or delete a node (via del). We use the abbreviations T, I, and D, respectively. When deleting a node, we mark it as deleted. The actual deletion is deferred until all transactions with an older timestamp than the deleting transaction have committed.

For each node, we have values for max-T-scheduled, max-I-scheduled, and max-D-scheduled. T-operations are compatible with other T-operations, while I- and D-operations are in conflict with all other operations. Furthermore, consider two operations $op_1 \in \{T, I, D\}$ of transaction T_1 and $op_2 \in \{T, I, D\}$ of transaction T_2 applied to node n. We assume that op_1 has already been executed and op_2 is about to be scheduled. We have to distinguish two different cases: $ts(T_1) < ts(T_2)$ and $ts(T_1) > ts(T_2)$. Considering all possible combinations op_1 and op_2 gives us eighteen different cases (see Table 1(a) for an overview).

We will now take a closer look at the eighteen cases presented in Table 1(a):

Table 1. Overview of XTO/XCO protocol (The superscript numbers refer to the case numbers below)

op_1	op_2	$ts(T_1) < ts(T_2)$	$ts(T_1) > ts(T_2)$
T	T	no conflict[1]	no conflict[2]
D	T	ignore[3]	traverse[4]
I	T	traverse[5]	ignore[6]
T	D	mark as deleted[7]	abort T_2[8]
D	D	not possible[9]	abort T_2[10]
I	D	window[11]	not possible[12]
T	I	not possible[13]	ignore/abort T_2[14]
D	I	not possible[15]	ignore/abort T_2[16]
I	I	not possible[17]	ignore/abort T_2[18]

(a) XTO protocol

$ts(T_1) <>_{DCO} ts(T_2)$
no conflict[19]
choice[20]
choice[21]
$ts(T_1) <_{DCO} ts(T_2)$[22]
not possible[23]
not possible[24]
choice[25]
choice[26]
choice[27]

(b) XCO protocol

Cases 1 and 2: Two traversal operations are never in conflict with each other.

Case 3: T_2 can ignore the node marked as deleted by T_1, i.e., T_2 just traverses to the next sibling not counting node n. However, if T_1 aborts, T_2 also has to abort, as the node n was not deleted after all and T_2 should not have ignored it.

Case 4: As the deletion takes place after the traversal, T_2 just traverses the node (marked as deleted by T_1). This is the reason why we have to keep the deleted node as long as transactions with an older timestamp than the deleting transaction are still active. Otherwise, a transaction may miss a node that should have been traversed.

Case 5: T_2 traverses the node inserted by T_1. However, if T_1 aborts, T_2 also has to abort.

Case 6: T_2 just ignores the node, as the insertion takes place after the traversal.

Case 7: T_2 marks the node as deleted.

Case 8: T_2 has to abort because the node was already traversed by a transaction with a newer timestamp.

Case 9: Not possible: before deleting the node, T_2 has to navigate to it via a T-operation. However, this T-operation will ignore the node (see Case 3).

Case 10: T_2 has to abort because the node was already deleted by a transaction with a newer timestamp (similar to Case 8).

Case 11: The newly inserted node is marked with the two timestamps $ts(T_1)$ and $ts(T_2)$. A third transaction T_3 traversing the node will see it if $ts(T_1) < ts(T_3) < ts(T_2)$, otherwise it will ignore it. (Note that this may also lead to cascading aborts.)

Case 12: Not possible: (see Case 9).

Case 13: Not possible: T_1 cannot traverse a node that is not there yet.

Case 14: This is a very problematic case. There may have been a traversal in the immediate vicinity of the newly inserted node that should have been able to see the node. So when inserting a node, we have to look at max-T-scheduled and max-I-scheduled of the two neighboring nodes. If both of them are younger than $ts(T_2)$, we have to abort T_2, as it is possible that a traversal (e.g. by T_1) going from one to the other should have seen the inserted node.

If at least one of them is older, no transaction with a timestamp newer than $ts(T_2)$ (including T_1) has passed the place of the newly inserted node.

Case 15: Not possible: we cannot delete a node before inserting it.

Case 16: In that case, T_1 should have deleted the node inserted by T_2. As there are no delete operations without prior traversals, this is covered by the subcases of Case 14. That means, if the timestamps of the neighboring nodes are both younger than $ts(T_2)$, we have to abort T_2. Otherwise, T_1 has deleted the correct node (which is different from the one inserted by T_2).

Case 17: Not possible: the same node cannot be inserted twice.

Case 18: This is analogous to the cases 14 and 16. Again we need to find out if the insertion of T_1 should have considered the node inserted by T_2. If yes, T_2 has to be aborted.

3.3 XML Dynamic Commit Ordering (XCO)

The main disadvantage of XTO is that (as in basic TO) the dependency graph forces the commit order of transactions. As shown in Table 1, we have several cases where conflicting operations with incompatible timestamps lead to the abortion of a transaction. Determining the commit order of transactions dynamically is the basic idea of the *dynamic commit ordering protocol* XCO. As we will see, this reduces the abortion rate considerably. A similar approach has been successfully applied to optimistic concurrency control in real-time databases [6].

We do not assign a fixed timestamp to a transaction when it starts. Instead, we wait until we detect conflicting operations between two transactions for the first time, and only then we order them. XCO maintains a dependency graph representing the dynamic commit order $<_{DCO}$. How the order is assigned to two transactions not ordered yet (represented by $<>_{DCO}$) is shown in Table 1(b) for each operation pair op_1/op_2. Once we have fixed an order between two transactions, XCO behaves in essentially the same way as XTO. Let us look at the cases 19 to 27 in more detail:

Case 19: Two traversal operations are never in conflict with each other. In this case, we do not even have to decide on the DCO-order of the transactions T_1 and T_2 yet.

Case 20: We can order $ts(T_1)$ and $ts(T_2)$ in both ways here. That means we fall back on Case 3 or Case 4 with all the consequences (possible cascading aborts) mentioned there.

Case 21: Similar to Case 20, we also have two options here. Depending on our choice, it will all boil down to Case 5 or Case 6.

Case 22: This is the only order that does not force T_2 to abort.

Case 23: Not possible: as a delete operation is always preceded by a corresponding traversal operation, the transactions T_1 and T_2 were already ordered by Case 20.

Case 24: Not possible: similar reasons as in Case 23, T_1 and T_2 were already ordered by Case 21.

Cases 25, 26 and 27: While $ts(T_1) <_{DCO} ts(T_2)$ is not possible, since we cannot work with a node before inserting it or insert the same node twice, we should take a look at the timestamps of the nodes neighboring the newly inserted node. As long as we can guarantee that $ts(T_2)$ is newer than the timestamp of at least one neighboring node, we avoid all conflicts. Thus, whether we choose $ts(T_1) <_{DCO} ts(T_2)$, $ts(T_1) >_{DCO} ts(T_2)$, or delay the choice further, depends on the timestamps that T_1 has left at the neighboring nodes.

4 Evaluation

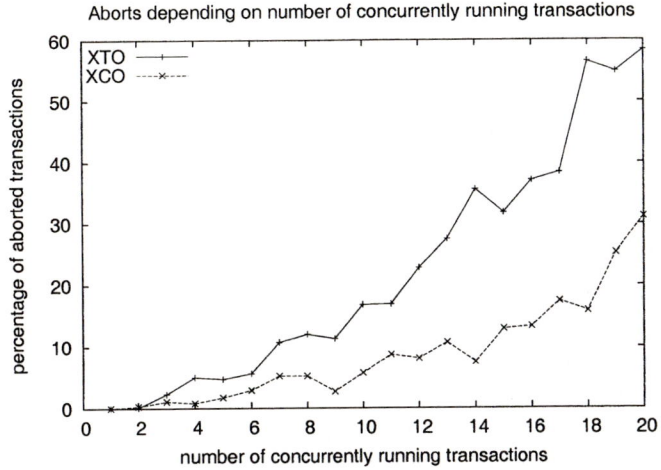

Fig. 3. Abortion rate of XTO vs. XCO

We have implemented a simulation environment in which we tested the performance of the XTO and XCO protocols. In this environment we generated 50 XML documents with a depth of four and a fan-out of each node that is between three and five. As its first operation, a transaction selects a document randomly. It then continues by choosing randomly any of the following operations (the number after each operation indicates the probability with which this operations is chosen): nthP (40%), nthM (40%), insA (5%), insB (5%), and del (10%). Each transaction consists of 50 operations. The probabilities do not apply to root nodes, as we neither allow the deletion of roots nor the insertion of siblings of roots. When a transaction tries to access a child of a leaf node, it randomly selects a new document instead.

The excerpt in Figure 3 taken from our evaluation summarizes our results. First, the higher the number of concurrently running transactions, the higher the percentage of aborted transactions. This comes as no surprise, as a higher number of transactions leads to a higher probability of interference between the transactions. Second, the XCO protocol aborts fewer transactions than the XTO provide real-time response to user requests. Incidentally, it is now well-known that most peers in a P2P system do *not* offer any data i.e., a majority of the peers typically download data from a small percentage of peers that offer data[1]. As a result of such skews in the initial data distribution among the peers, a disproportionately high number of queries need to be answered by a few 'hot' peers, thereby leading to severe load imbalance throughout the system. The job queues of the 'hot' peers keep increasing, thereby resulting in significantly increased waiting times and consequently high response times for queries directed to them. This decreases the *dependability* of the system. The sheer size of P2P networks and the inherent heterogeneity and dynamism of the environment pose significant challenges to the improvement of dependability in P2P systems. This paper focuses on improving the dependability of unstructured P2P systems via dynamic data replication. The main contributions of our proposal are two-fold.

1. We propose a dynamic data placement strategy involving data replication, the objective being to reduce the loads of the overloaded peers.
2. We present a dynamic query redirection technique which aims at reducing response times.

Our performance evaluation demonstrates that our proposed technique is indeed effective in reducing user response times significantly, thereby increasing the dependability of P2P systems. The remainder of this paper is organized as follows. Section 2 discusses related work, while Section 3 presents an overview of our proposed system. Section 4 presents the proposed replication and query redirection strategy, while Section 5 reports our performance evaluation. Finally, we conclude in Section 6 with directions for future work.

2 Related Work

Existing P2P systems such as Pastry [11] and Chord [12] emphasize specifically on query routing, while the work in [3] proposes routing indices, the primary objective being to forward a query *only* to those peers which are likely to contain the answers to the query. Unlike broadcast approaches, routing indices attempt to avoid flooding the network with queries. Replication has also been studied in P2P systems primarily for improving search operations. The proposal in [6] investigates optimal replication of content in P2P systems and develops an adaptive, fully distributed algorithm which dynamically replicates content in a near-optimal manner. Notably, replication strategies for P2P systems have also been presented in [2,8], but since the objective of replication in these works is to facilitate search, these works do *not* specifically address issues concerning dependability.

Dependability via load-balancing in structured P2P systems (using distributed hash tables or 'DHTs') has been addressed in [4,10]. Moreover, the work in [13] discusses dependability via inter-cluster and intra-cluster load-balancing in a P2P system which is divided into clusters based on semantic categories. Note that our work differs from these works in that we address dependability issues in unstructured P2P systems which neither impose a logical structure on the P2P system (as in [13]) nor assume DHT abstraction (as in [4, 10]).

Incidentally, our previous work [9] concerning load-balancing in spatial GRIDs has some similarity with this work in that they both aim at reduction of response times in wide-area environments. However, there are several major differences. First, in contrast to this work, the proposal in [9] imposes a structure on the system by dividing the entire system into sets of clusters. Second, replicating one tuple of a spatial database in a spatial GRID entails data movement at most in the Kilobyte range, while P2P data movements are usually in the Megabyte range (e.g., for music files) or even in the Gigabyte range (e.g., for video files), the implication being that the communication cost of data movement can be expected to be significantly higher in case of P2P systems. Third, for spatial GRIDs, prevention of data scattering is a major concern, which is *not* really a concern in case of P2P systems. Fourth, in case of spatial GRIDs, individual nodes are usually dedicated and they may be expected to be available most of the time, while for P2P systems, nodes may join or leave arbitrarily at any point of time. Fifth, the work in [9] aims at load-balancing, while this work investigates dynamic replication issues in detail without any explicit load-balancing aims.

3 System Overview

In our proposed system, each peer is assigned a globally unique identifier *PID* and for search, we adopt a broadcast-based approach[5]. For detecting hotspots, every peer maintains its own access statistics i.e., the number of accesses made to each of its data files. Moreover, for each data file D_i, each peer keeps track of all the peers which have downloaded D_i from itself. Additionally, every peer provides a certain amount $Space_i$ of its disk space to the P2P system for storing the replicas of other peers' 'hot' data files. In other words, $Space_i$ is the available disk space at each peer that can be used for replication purposes, whenever the need arises. To optimize the usage of $Space_i$ at each peer, we adopt the commonly used LRU (Least Recently Used) scheme. To address dynamically changing popularities of files in P2P systems, each peer checks the number of accesses N_k (for recent time intervals) for each data file replicated at itself and deletes files, for which N_k falls below a pre-specified threshold. Additionally, in consonance with most existing works concerning replication in P2P systems, we sacrifice replica consistency for improving response times.

We define *distance* between two peers as the communication time τ between them and two peers are regarded as neighbors if they are directly connected to each other. Messages concerning load status and available disk space are periodically exchanged between neighboring peers. Additionally, we define the load L_{P_i} of a peer P_i as the number of queries waiting in P_i's job queue. Given that the loads of two peers P_i and P_j are L_{P_i} and L_{P_j} respectively and assuming without loss of generality that $L_{P_i} > L_{P_j}$, the normalized load difference Δ between P_i and P_j is computed as follows:

$$\Delta = ((L_{P_i} \times CPU_{P_i}) - (L_{P_j} \times CPU_{P_j}))/(CPU_{P_i} + CPU_{P_j}) \qquad (1)$$

where CPU_{P_i} and CPU_{P_j} are the processing capacities of P_i and P_j respectively. Moreover, we assume that peers know transfer rates between themselves and other peers and every peer has knowledge concerning the availability information of its neighboring peers. In practice, after the system has been in operation for a significant period of time, the peers will have exchanged several messages between themselves and over a period of time, such information can be obtained by the peers. Given that very 'hot' files may be aggressively replicated across hundreds of peers in a very transitive manner and some peers may quickly become out of reach of the primary copy owner, each peer keeps track *only* of the replications that it has performed i.e., whenever a peer replicates any of its data files at other peers, it notes the PIDs of those peers. For example, when a 'hot' data file D_i is replicated by peer P_i to another peer P_j, P_i will note that D_i has been replicated at P_j. However, if subsequently P_j replicates D_i at another peer P_k, P_j (and *not* P_i) would note this replication information.

4 Proposed Replication and Query Redirection Strategy for P2P Systems

This section presents our proposed strategy for replication and query redirection in P2P systems.

Initiation of Replication

Each peer P_i periodically checks the loads of its neighboring peers and if it finds that its load exceeds the average loads of its neighboring peers by 10%, it decides that it is overloaded and initiates replication by selecting the 'hot' data files. For hotspot detection purposes, P_i maintains its own access statistics comprising a list, each entry of which is of the form ($dataID, f$), where $dataID$ represents the identifier of a specific data file and f indicates the number of times the data file had been queried. Notably, in order to deal with the inherent dynamism of P2P environments where the popularity of data files typically change from time to time, we take *only* recent access statistics information into consideration for detecting hotspots. P_i sorts all its data files in descending order of the access frequencies of the files. For identifying hotspots, P_i traverses this sorted list of data files and selects as 'hot' files the top N files whose access frequency exceeds a pre-defined threshold T_{freq}. The number of replicas to be created for each 'hot' data file D_i is decided by the number of accesses to D_i. In particular, for every N_d accesses to D_i, a new replica is created for D_i. Notably, the values of T_{freq} and N_d are pre-specified by the system at design time. Now the destination peer(s) where D_i should be replicated must be determined efficiently. Hence, we shall now discuss how the destination peer(s) for D_i are selected.

Proposed Replication Strategy

The 'hot' peer P_{Hot} considers the following selection criteria for selecting a destination peer P_{Dest} for replication of D_i.

- P_{Dest} should have a high probability of being online (available).
- P_{Dest} should have adequate available disk space for replication. If P_{Dest} does not have sufficient disk space, D_i's replica at P_{Dest} may be subsequently deleted by the LRU scheme used at P_{Dest} in favor of hotter data items.
- Load difference between P_{Hot} and P_{Dest} should be significant enough to call for replication at P_{Dest}.
- Transfer time T_{Rep} between P_{Hot} and P_{Dest} should be minimized. T_{Rep} can be computed as $F_i \div T_i$, where F_i is the size of the file to be replicated and T_i is the transfer rate of the network connection between P_{Hot} and P_{Dest}. Since files in P2P systems are typically in the range of Megabytes (for music files) and Gigabytes (for video files), T_{Rep} can be expected to be a significant cost. Interestingly, D_i is a 'hot' data file, the implication being that D_i is likely to exist in the disk of at least some of the peers which had earlier queried for D_i and downloaded D_i from P_{Hot}. Hence, we propose that P_{Dest} should be chosen from the peers which have already downloaded D_i. This has the advantage of making T_{Rep} effectively equal to 0.

Based on the above criteria for selecting P_{Dest}, we shall now present our replication strategy. For each 'hot' data file D_i, the 'hot' peer P_{Hot} sends a message to each peer which has downloaded D_i during recent time intervals, enquiring whether a copy of D_i is *still* stored in them. (Some of the peers which have downloaded D_i may have subsequently deleted D_i.) The peers in which a copy of D_i exists reply to P_{Hot} with their respective load status information as well as the amount of available disk space that they have for replication purposes. Among these peers, only those with high availability and sufficient available disk space for replication of D_i are candidates for being the destination peer. Now, among these candidate peers, P_{Hot} first puts the peer with the lowest load into a set which we designate as *Candidate*. Additionally, peers whose normalized load difference with the least loaded peer is less than δ are also put into *Candidate*. Note that δ is a small integer, the significance of δ being that two peers are considered to be having approximately the same load if the load difference between them is less than δ. Then the peer in *Candidate* whose available disk space for replication is maximum is selected as the destination peer. Figure 1 depicts the algorithm for selecting the destination peer.

Proposed Technique for Query Redirection

When a peer P_{Issue} issues a query Q for data item D_i to a 'hot' peer P_{Hot}, P_{Hot} needs to make a decision concerning the redirection of Q to a peer containing D_i's replica, if any such replica exists. The peer $P_{Redirect}$ to which Q should be redirected must be selected such that Q's response time is minimized. In our proposed strategy, P_{Hot} checks the list L_{Rep} comprising the PIDs of the peers where it had replicated D_i and selects $P_{Redirect}$ based on the following criteria:

- $P_{Redirect}$ should have a high probability of being online (available).
- Load difference between P_{Hot} and $P_{Redirect}$ should be significant.
- Transfer time between $P_{Redirect}$ and P_{Issue} should be low.

Algorithm *Select_DestPeer*

P_{Hot}: The 'hot' peer which needs to select a destination peer for its 'hot' data file D_i
$SetP_{Download}$: Set of peers which have downloaded D_i from P_{Hot}

P_{Hot} sends a message to each peer in set $SetP_{Download}$ enquiring whether they still have a copy of D_i and if so, their load and available disk space information.

Upon receiving the replies, P_{Hot} deletes those peers from $SetP_{Download}$ that do *not* have a copy of D_i.
P_{Hot} deletes the peers with low availability from $SetP_{Download}$.
P_{Hot} deletes the peers, whose available disk space is not adequate for D_i, from $SetP_{Download}$.
if ($P_{Download}$ is an empty set) {
  end
} else {
  P_{Hot} selects the peer P_{min} with the least load from $SetP_{Download}$ and puts it into a set *Candidate*.

  Peers of $SetP_{Download}$ whose normalized load difference with P_{min} falls below δ are put into *Candidate*.
  Among the members of *Candidate*, the peer with maximum available disk space for replication is selected as the destination peer.
}
end

Fig. 1. Algorithm for selecting the destination peer

In consonance with the above criteria, our query redirection technique works as follows. The 'hot' peer P_{Hot} first selects a set of peers which contain a replica of the data file D_i associated with the query Q and whose load difference with itself exceeds T_{Diff}. T_{Diff} is a parameter which is application-dependent and also depends on how one considers the system to be imbalanced. A small value of T_{Diff} would encourage replications (albeit at the cost of disk space), while a large value of T_{Diff} would possibly result in lesser number of replications. Note that the normalized load difference is compared with T_{Diff} to take the heterogeneity in processing capabilities of different peers into consideration. Among these selected peers, the peer with the *maximum* transfer rate with the query issuing peer P_{Issue} is selected for query redirection. Notably, this is in consonance with our objective of reducing response times. Figure 2 depicts the query redirection algorithm.

5 Performance Study

We conducted extensive simulation experiments to evaluate the performance of our proposed replication strategy. Our simulation environment comprised a machine running the Solaris 8 operating system. The machine has 4 CPUs, each of which has a processing power of 900 MHz. Main memory size of the machine

Algorithm Query_Redirect

L_{Rep}: List comprising the PIDs of peers which contain a replica of the 'hot' data file D_i associated with the query Q.
P_{Issue}: The peer which originally issued the query.
P_{Hot}: The 'hot' peer which needs to redirect Q.

for each peer P_j in L_{Rep} {
    P_{Hot} checks the normalized load difference L_D between itself and P_j.
    if ($L_D \geq T_{Diff}$) {
        P_{Hot} puts P_j into a set $Set_{Redirect}$.
    }
}

P_{Hot} selects the peer, whose transfer rate with P_{Issue} is maximum from $Set_{Redirect}$.
end

Fig. 2. Query redirection algorithm

is 16 Gigabytes, while the total disk space is 2 Terabytes. We used a maximum of 4 neighboring peers corresponding to each peer. The interarrival time for queries arriving at each peer was fixed at 1 millisecond. Table 1 summarizes the parameters used for our performance study. In Table 1, z is a parameter whose value equals **(1 - zipf factor)**. This implies that when $z=0.1$, the skew is high and when $z=0.9$, the skew is low. Note that in all our experiments, in order to model free-riders, we directed queries *only* to 1% of the total number of peers in the system and these peers become the 'hot' peers (data providers), the rest of the peers being free-riders. For all our experiments, the system was allowed to run for sometime for collection of access statistics information and we started recording the results only after the system had reached a stable state. Hence, all our experimental results indicate the performance of our proposed strategy during the stable state. Additionally, in all our experiments, the 'hot' peers always remained available (*online*), while the availability of other (non-hot) peers was randomly selected in the range of 10% to 90%. Our main performance metric is query response time. For the sake of convenience, we shall henceforth refer to our proposed dynamic replication scheme as **DRep** (Dependability via Replication) and the policy of *not* performing replications as **NoRep** (no replication).

Performance of DRep

Figure 3 indicates the results for the default values of the parameters i.e., the case in which the total number of peers was 1000, queries were directed to only 10 of these peers, the number of replicas initially being 4 and $z=0.1$. Figure 3a depicts the *average response times* at each of the 10 'hot' peers. Observe that there is significant reduction of average response times at each of the 'hot' peers, the reduction in average response time being maximum for the hottest peer. Further investigation of the experimental log files revealed that DRep was able to reduce the average response time of the hottest peer by upto 50%. Such reduction in

Table 1. Parameters used in Performance Study

Parameter	Default value	Variations
No. of peers	1000	5000, 10000
No. of peers to which queries are directed	10	50, 100
No. of queries	20000	100000, 200000
z	0.1	0.5, 0.9
Number of replicas	4	
Interarrival time between queries	1ms	
Transfer rate between peers	0.5 Mb/s to 1 Mb/s	
Latency	10 ms to 20 ms	
Size of a file	1 MB to 10 MB	

average response time is possible owing to load reduction at the 'hot' peers as shown in Figures 3b and 3c, which present two snapshots (taken at different points in time) of the load distribution at the 'hot' peers.

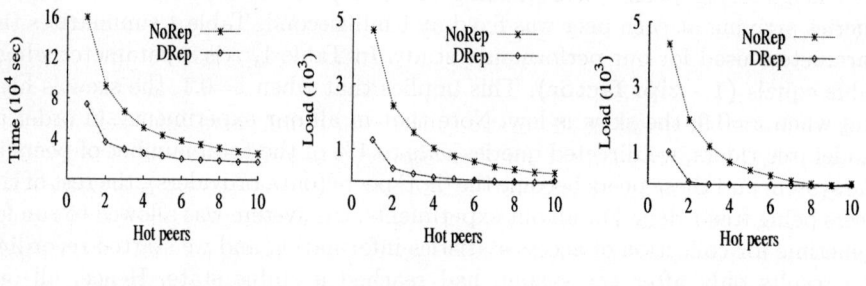

(a) Average Response times at the hot nodes

(b) Snapshot of Load distribution

(c) Snapshot of Load distribution

Fig. 3. Performance of DRep

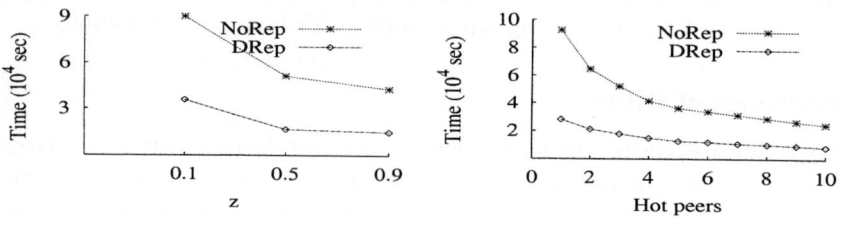

(a) Average Response times at the hot nodes

(b) Average Response times at the hot nodes for z=0.5

Fig. 4. Effect of varying the Workload Skew

Variations in Workload Skew

Now let us examine the effect of variations in workload skews among the 10 'hot' peers on the average query response times. For this purpose, we varied z to 0.5 and 0.9. Figure 4a displays the average response time of all the queries in the system for different values of z. The results show that DRep significantly outperforms NoRep for variations in workload skews. However, the gain in terms of average response time is higher in case of highly skewed workload (i.e., $z=0.1$) and the gain in average response time keeps decreasing as the workload skew decreases. This occurs because as the workload skew decreases, the load becomes more evenly distributed among the 'hot' nodes, the implication being that the load at the hottest peer also decreases, thereby reducing the waiting times of queries at the hottest peer. Figure 4b depicts the average response times at the hot peers when z was fixed at 0.5, the explanations for these results being essentially the same as the explanations for Figure 3.

Variation in the Number of Peers

Now we shall investigate the scalability of DRep with respect to the total number of peers in the system. For this experiment, as the total number of peers in the system is increased, the number of queries in the system is increased in a proportional manner. This is in consonance with real-life situations because as the number of peers in the system increases, more peers are likely to issue queries, thereby increasing the number of queries circulating in the system. The number of queries for systems comprising 1000, 5000 and 10000 peers was 20000, 100000 and 200000 respectively. Moreover, the number of 'hot' peers for systems consisting of 1000, 5000 and 10000 peers was fixed at 10, 50 and 100 respectively i.e., in each case, the number of 'hot' peers was 1% of the total number of peers in the system. The number of replicas was initially 4. Figure 5 shows the average response time of *all* the queries when the total number of peers was varied. The results in Figure 5 demonstrate the scalability of DRep and indicate that DRep provides more performance gain over NoRep as the number of peers increases primarily because increased number of peers implies more options for performing replication and more possibilities for query redirection. The implication is that the load imposed on the 'hot' peers by queries on the 'hot' data files can be distributed among a larger number of peers by replicating the 'hot' data files at those peers.

6 Conclusion

The sheer scale, dynamism and heterogeneity of P2P environments coupled with the presence of disproportionately large number of 'free-riders' pose significant challenges to dependability (in terms of data availability) of P2P systems. In this regard, we have proposed a novel strategy for enhancing the dependability of P2P systems via dynamic replication. Our performance evaluation demonstrate

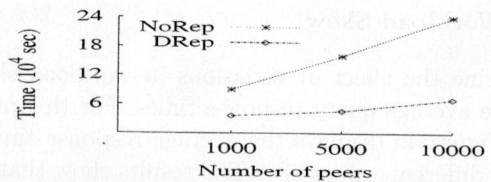

Fig. 5. Effect of varying the number of peers

that our proposed technique is indeed able to enhance the dependability of P2P systems by reducing response times significantly. In the near future, we plan to extend this work by considering issues concerning replication of very large data items such as video files.

References

1. Adar and Huberman. http://news.bbc.co.uk/1/hi/sci/tech/948448.stm.
2. E. Cohen and S. Shenker. Replication strategies in unstructured peer-to-peer networks. *Proc. ACM SIGCOMM*, 2002.
3. A. Crespo and H. G. Molina. Routing indices for Peer-to-Peer systems. *Proc. ICDCS*, 2002.
4. F. Dabek, M.F. Kaashoek, D. Karger, R. Morris, and I. Stoica. Wide-area cooperative storage with CFS. *Proc. SOSP*, 2001.
5. Gnutella. http://www.gnutella.com/.
6. J. Kangasharju, K. W. Ross, and D. A. Turner. Optimal content replication in P2P communities. *Manuscript*, 2002.
7. Kazaa. http://www.kazaa.com/.
8. Q. Lv, P. Cao, E. Cohen, K. Li, and S. Shenker. Search and replication in unstructured peer-to-peer networks. *Proc. ACM ICS*, 2002.
9. A. Mondal, K. Goda, and M. Kitsuregawa. Effective load-balancing via migration and replication in spatial GRIDs. *Proc. DEXA*, 2003.
10. A. Rao, K. Lakshminarayanan, S. Surana, R. Karp, and I. Stoica. Load balancing in structured P2P systems. *In Proc.IPTPS*, 2003.
11. A. Rowstron and P. Druschel. Pastry: Scalable, decentralized object location and routing for large-scale peer-to-peer systems. *Proc. IFIP/ACM*, 2001.
12. I. Stoica, R. Morris, D. Karger, M. F. Kaashoek, and H. Balakrishnan. Chord: A scalable peer-to-peer lookup service for internet applications. *Proc. ACM SIGCOMM*, 2001.
13. P. Triantafillou, C. Xiruhaki, M. Koubarakis, and N. Ntarmo. Towards high performance peer-to-peer content and resource sharing systems. *Proc. CIDR*, 2003.

Processing Ad-Hoc Joins on Mobile Devices

Eric Lo[1], Nikos Mamoulis[1], David W. Cheung[1],
Wai Shing Ho[1], and Panos Kalnis[2]

[1] The University of Hong Kong
{ecllo,nikos,dcheung,wsho}@cs.hku.hk
[2] National University of Singapore
kalnis@nus.edu.sg

Abstract. Mobile devices are capable of retrieving and processing data from remote databases. In a wireless data transmission environment, users are typically charged by the size of transferred data, rather than the amount of time they stay connected. We propose algorithms that join information from non-collaborative remote databases on mobile devices. Our methods minimize the data transferred during the join process, by also considering the limitations of mobile devices. Experimental results show that our approach can perform join processing on mobile devices effectively.

1 Introduction

Recently, mobile devices such as Personal Digital Assistants (PDAs) and mobile phones are fast emerging as components of our daily life. Many applications of mobile devices access data on remote servers through a wireless network. For example, some people may ask for stock ticks through their PDAs wirelessly. In addition to querying a single remote information source, some mobile users may wish to combine information from different remote databases. Consider for example a vegetarian, who visits Hong Kong and looks for some restaurants recommended by both the HK tourist office and the HK vegetarian community. He may issue a query that joins the contents of two relations in Figure 1(a) hosted by the two different services:

SELECT R1.Name, R1.Address, R2.Cost FROM R1, R2 WHERE R1.Name = R2.Name

This query is an example of an *ad-hoc* join (where the join key is "Name"), with few results compared to the large volume of input data, and the joined relations are located at different non-collaborative servers. Since the target relations are non-collaborative and users may pose queries on arbitrary sets of data sources, distributed mediator systems like HERMES [1] may not be applicable. Also, remote servers would only accept simple input like selection queries, expressed in SQL through public interfaces, like Web services, etc. Thus traditional distributed query processing techniques that involve shipments of data structures like semijoin [2] and bloomjoin [3] are not applicable.

Downloading both relations entirely to perform a join operation on the mobile device may not be the best solution. First, some devices (e.g., mobile phones) do not have enough memory to hold the large volume of data locally. Second, the network traffic or QoS of various wireless data networking technologies such as CDMA [4], IEEE 802.11 [5], WAP (www.wapforum.org) and 3G (www.nokia.com/3g/index.html) are all strongly dependent on many factors such as the network workloads and the availability of various network stations. As a result, mobile service providers often charge their customers in terms of the amount of data transferred, rather than the amount of time they stay connected to the service or the query processing cost on the data host. Therefore, the cost of joining relations from different remote databases does not involve the traditional I/O and CPU costs, but the *transfer cost*.

Name	Address	Cuisine	Quality
Alpha Food	Address 1	ThaiFood	3
Beta Food	Address 2	Chinese	4
...	...	...	2

HK Tourist Office (R1)

Name	Address	Cost
Beta Food	Address A	100
Bay SeaFood	Address B	200
Delta	Address C	150
...	...	...

HK vegetarian community (R2)

(a) Relations hosted by different services

Bucket	Count
A	5001
B	2350
...	...
Y	231
Z	125

Histogram on R1.Name

Bucket	Count
A	3121
B	2
...	...
Y	160

Histogram on R2.Name

(b) Histograms of R1 and R2

Fig. 1. Examples relations and histograms

In this paper, we study the evaluation of joins on mobile devices, taking those issues (independent data sources, limited memory size and transfer-cost based optimization) under consideration. We propose *RAMJ* (*R*ecursive and *A*daptive *M*obile *J*oin) algorithm that runs on a mobile device and joins two relations located on non-collaborative remote servers. RAMJ partitions the data space and downloads *statistical* information from the servers for each partition, before downloading the data to be joined. Based on the statistics of a partition, RAMJ may *adaptively* choose to download data that fall into that partition and join them using a join technique, or to apply RAMJ *recursively* for retrieving more refined statistics there.

The rest of the paper is organized as follows. Section 2 describes various basic approaches and RAMJ for evaluating equi-join queries on mobile devices. Section 3 describes how RAMJ can be applied on other query types. Section 4 reports the experiment result. Section 5 describes the related work and we conclude in Section 6 with some directions for future research.

2 Processing of Ad-Hoc Equi-Joins

2.1 Basic Approaches

A Late-Projection Strategy. In highly selective joins, most tuples fail to contribute to the result. One naive way to reduce the transfer cost and memory requirements of the join is to download and join the *distinct values of join keys* only. Subsequently, only tuples belonging to the join result entails downloading the rest of non-key attributes from both sites. The late projection strategy avoids downloading the non-key attributes which do not contribute to the result, and can be applied to all types of join queries. Therefore we adopt this strategy in the rest of the paper.

Block-Merge Join (BMJ). The late-projection technique is better than downloading all relations and joining them locally, but it is still insufficient when the results of the projections of join keys do not fit into the memory. A straightforward method to evaluate the equi-join with limited memory is sort-merge join, by assigning the sorting part to the servers. Then, only one block from each server is required to be in memory and computational cost on the client is saved by forcing the servers to sort the data. The idea is to download one block of *ordered* join keys from each relation (using the ORDER BY SQL statement) and merge them, until one block is exhausted. Then a new block is retrieved from the corresponding server and the process continues until one relation is scanned.

Ship-Data-as-Queries Join (SDAQ). If two target relations R1 and R2 have large size difference (e.g., $R1 \ll R2$), the join can be evaluated by downloading *all* join keys of R1 to the device and sending each of them as a selection query to R2. Before that, two SQL queries are sent to count the number of tuples on the join attributes in each server, in order to identify the relation with smaller cardinality. This method resembles the semijoin [2] approach in System R* [6], with the only difference that the join keys are expressed as queries and shipped through the mobile devices indirectly. If the set of join keys of the smaller relation does not fit into the device, SDAQ can be implemented by downloading the join keys from R1 and sending them to R2, in a block-wise fashion, like the block-merge join.

2.2 RAMJ: A Recursive and Adaptive Approach

BMJ requires that all data from both relations are downloaded. SDAQ, on the other hand, can only do better if the sizes of the relations differ much. In fact, when the data distributions of the join keys are different, there may be empty key value ranges in one relation that are densely populated in the other. Such knowledge may help avoid downloading data in these ranges, as we know that they do not participate in the join result. Figure 1(b) shows two histograms summarizing the "Name" attribute of our example relations. If the value ranges which are empty in one relation (e.g., bucket "Z" of R2), they are pruned and their contents are not downloaded from the other relation (e.g., R1).

In general, remote services accept *selection* queries only, i.e., we cannot create any temporary relation on remote servers to facilitate the collection of statistics. In view of this, the intuition behind our method is to apply some cheap queries first, in order to obtain some information about the distribution of the data values of join attributes in both datasets. A simple way to construct a histogram on an attribute is to pose an aggregate query. For this, we can use the SUBSTRING function and `ROUND` function. An example SQL statement that returns the left histogram of Figure 1(a) (grouped by first character) is given below. Notice that the `HAVING` clause avoids fetching value ranges with no data to reduce data transferred.

```
SELECT SUBSTRING(Name,1,1) AS Bucket, COUNT(Name) AS Count FROM R1
GROUP BY SUBSTRING(Name,1,1) HAVING COUNT(Name) > 0
```

Retrieving and comparing histograms prior to actual data contents not only reduces the join space; in fact, histogram buckets are also employed as the basic unit of our recursive solution. Essentially, we divide the problem into G smaller ones. Subsequently, each smaller join can be processed by a different method. Thus, for each pair $\langle \alpha_i, \beta_i \rangle$ of buckets (where α_i comes from R1 and β_i comes from R2), we consider *one* of the following actions according to the bucket size:

Direct Join. This method applies the merge-join algorithm for the current partition. Essentially, the data in the partition are downloaded from R1 and R2 and then joined on the mobile device, using BMJ.

Ship-Join-Keys Join. This method shares the same idea of ship-data-as-queries join that downloads the join keys of the *smallest* partition and sends them as selection queries to the other service. It can be cheaper than direct join, if the data distributions in the two buckets are very different.

Recursive Partitioning. This method breaks a partition into more refined ones and requests histograms for them. Essentially, it further breaks a bucket into smaller ones, hoping that some smaller buckets will be eliminated or cheap ship-join-keys joins will be applied on them. However, if partitions' data are uniform, it could be more expensive than direct join, given the overhead for retrieving the histograms.

To illustrate, consider the level-1 histograms of Figure 1(b) again. After obtaining the histograms, bucket Z of R1 can be pruned immediately, since the corresponding one of R2 is empty. For bucket Y, as the number of join keys that fall into this bucket for both relations is quite small and balanced, downloading them and applying direct join may be the best choice because (i) the ship-join-keys join will have a larger overhead (for downloading the data from R2, sending them to R1 as queries and then retrieving the results) and (ii) the overhead of repartitioning and retrieving further statistics may not pay-off for this bucket size. For bucket A, we may want to apply recursive partitioning, hoping that data distribution in the refined buckets will be more skewed, helping to prune the join space. The finer histogram of bucket A may consist of 26 sub-buckets ("AA","AB",...,"AZ") by issuing a SQL statement that group by the first two characters. Finally, for bucket B, ship-join-keys is arguably the best method since only two join keys from R2 will be downloaded and shipped to R1.

2.3 The Cost Model

We provide formulae which estimate the cost of each of the three potential actions that RAMJ may choose. Our formulae are parametric to the communication cost of the wireless network services. In general, $T(B)$ bytes are transmitted through a network for B bytes of data because some overhead are spent in each transfer unit (e.g., MTU in TCP/IP). Let λ_1 and λ_2 be the per-byte transfer cost (e.g., in dollars) for accessing R1 and R2 respectively. Sending a selection query Q to a server needs $T(B_{SQL} + B_{key})$ bytes, where B_{SQL} denotes the size of a SQL statement (different query types have different B_{SQL} values) and B_{key} reflects the cost of sending the key value that defines the selection. Due to space constraints, details of derivation of the following cost equations are omitted and interested readers are referred to [7].

Direct Join. Let α_i and β_i be the i-th histogram bucket summarizing the same data region of R1 and R2 respectively. Further, let $|\alpha_i|$ and $|\beta_i|$ be the number of tuples represented by α_i and β_i. The total transfer cost of downloading all key values represented by α_i and β_i and joining them on the mobile device is:

$$C_1(\alpha_i, \beta_i) = (\lambda_1 + \lambda_2)T(B_{SQL} + B_{key}) + \lambda_1 T(|\alpha_i|B_{key}) + \lambda_2 T(|\beta_i|B_{key}) \quad (1)$$

The first term is the transfer cost of two outgoing queries and the last two terms are the transfer cost of downloading the data contents represented by α_i and β_i.

Ship-Join-Keys Join. Assuming $|\alpha_i| \leq |\beta_i|$, the total transfer cost C_2 of joining α_i and β_i using ship-join-keys join is:

$$C_2(\alpha_i, \beta_i) = \lambda_1(T(B_{SQL} + B_{key}) + T(|\alpha_i|B_{key})) + \lambda_2(T(B_{SQL} + 2|\alpha_i|B_{key})) \quad (2)$$

The first term is the transfer cost of the selection query sent to R1 and its query result. The second term is the transfer cost of the selection query sent to R2 for checking existence of R1 keys and its query result.

Recursive Partitioning. The cost C_3 of applying recursive partitioning on α_i and β_i composes of three sub-costs:

1. $C_h(G, R1)$: The cost of retrieving G bucket-count pairs $\lambda_1(T(G(B_{key} + B_{int})))$ that refine bucket α_i by submitting an aggregate COUNT query $\lambda_1(T(B_{SQL} + B_{key}))$ to R1.

2. $C_h(G, R2)$: The cost of retrieving G-bucket-count pairs from R2: $\lambda_2(T(G(B_{key} + B_{int}))) + \lambda_2(T(B_{SQL} + B_{key}))$

3. Let $\alpha_{i,j}$ and $\beta_{i,j}$ ($j = 1 \cdots G$) be the set of sub-buckets of α_i and β_i respectively. After downloading the refined histograms, each pair of sub-buckets are examined recursively to determine the next optimal transfer cost action. Therefore, the last sub-cost of C_3 is: $C_{RP}(\alpha_i, \beta_i) = \sum_{j=1}^{G} \min_{l \in \{1,2,3\}} C_l(\alpha_{i,j}, \beta_{i,j})$

Since we have no knowledge on how the data are distributed in the sub-buckets, we cannot directly determine the last sub-cost $C_{RP}(\alpha_i, \beta_i)$ (observe that it contains a C_3 component), we introduce two different models to estimate this last sub-cost.

Optimistic Estimation. When the join is highly-selective, the data distribution of the two datasets is quite different; thus, one way to deal with the unknown component is to optimistically assume all buckets are pruned in next level:

$$C_3(\alpha_i, \beta_i) = C_h(G, R1) + C_h(G, R2) \quad (3)$$

This model tends to obtain finer statistics in each level. It is a simple approach with small computation demand and shown to be quite effective in the experiment section.

Estimation by Linear Interpolation. This model estimates the last sub-cost $C_{RP}(\alpha_i, \beta_i)$ more accurately, but with higher computation cost on the client device. The idea is to exploit the histograms in the coarser level to speculate the local data distribution in the next level. To estimate the last sub-cost $C_{RP}(\alpha_i, \beta_i)$, the counts of sub-buckets $\alpha_{i,j}$ and $\beta_{i,j}$ have to be determined. Take α_i as an example. We propose to distribute the count of α_i to its sub-buckets $\alpha_{i,j}$ by linear interpolation. Adjacent buckets are selected to be the interpolation points because they are more related to local skew. Thus, to estimate the data distribution in the buckets of the finer level, only two adjacent buckets (α_{i-1} and α_{i+1}) of the current bucket (α_i) at the current level are selected. The sub-buckets are then weighted by the following formulae:

When G is even $\begin{cases} W_{\alpha_{i,j}} = |\alpha_i| + (|\alpha_{i+1}| - |\alpha_i|)(2(j - G/2) - 1)/2G \text{ if } j > G/2 \\ W_{\alpha_{i,j}} = |\alpha_i| + (|\alpha_{i-1}| - |\alpha_i|)(2(G/2 - j) + 1)/2G \text{ if } j \leq G/2 \end{cases}$

When G is odd $\begin{cases} W_{\alpha_{i,j}} = |\alpha_i| + (|\alpha_{i+1}| - |\alpha_i|)(j - \lceil G/2 \rceil)/G \text{ if } j > G/2 \\ W_{\alpha_{i,j}} = |\alpha_i| + (|\alpha_{i-1}| - |\alpha_i|)(\lceil G/2 \rceil - j)/G \text{ if } j \leq G/2 \end{cases}$

After weighting, the count of bucket α_i is distributed to the sub-buckets according to the weights, i.e. $|\alpha_{i,j}| = |\alpha_i| W_{\alpha_{i,j}} / \sum_{j=1}^{G} W_{\alpha_{i,j}}$. Now, for each bucket pair of the next level, the cost of direct join ($C_1(\alpha_{i,j}, \beta_{i,j})$) and ship-join-keys join ($C_2(\alpha_{i,j}, \beta_{i,j})$) can be determined using the estimates, according to equations 1 and 2. However, the sub-cost $C_{RP}(\alpha_{i,j}, \beta_{i,j})$ cannot be estimated, as those sub-buckets may recursively be partitioned and there is no more information to further estimate their recursive actions. Fortunately, the lemma below provides an appropriate upper-bound for our estimation.

Lemma 1. *Let α_i and β_i be the i-th bucket of the G-bucket equi-width histograms downloaded from R1 and R2 respectively. The cost $C_{RP}(\alpha_i, \beta_i)$ is bounded by the inequality: $C_{RP}(\alpha_i, \beta_i) \leq \sum_{j=1}^{G} min(C_1(\alpha_{i,j}, \beta_{i,j}), C_2(\alpha_{i,j}, \beta_{i,j}))$* □

A proof of the lemma can be found in [7]. Using Lemma 1, we can estimate an upper bound for $C_{RP}(\alpha_i, \beta_i)$. Hence, C_3 becomes:

$$C_3(\alpha_i, \beta_i) = C_h(G, R1) + C_h(G, R2) + \sum_{j=1}^{G} min(C_1(\alpha_{i,j}, \beta_{i,j}), C_2(\alpha_{i,j}, \beta_{i,j})) \quad (4)$$

2.4 The RAMJ Algorithm

Although the action and the cost estimation of every bucket are determined in runtime, RAMJ defers all bucket actions and execute them in batches according to their action types. Thus a constant number of queries is sent out in each level and reduces the packet headers overhead, since multiple requests are "compressed" in a single statement.

Algorithm RAMJ($R1, R2, G, L$)
/* G is the partition granuality; L is the list of buckets currently served*/
1. $H_{R1} := \text{BuildHist}(R1, G, L)$;
2. $H_{R2} := \text{BuildHist}(R2, G, L)$;
3.   For each bucket pair $\langle \alpha_i, \beta_i \rangle, \alpha_i \in H_{R1}, \beta_i \in H_{R2}, \alpha_i = \beta_i$
4. $C_{min} := \min(C_1(\alpha_i, \beta_i), C_2(\alpha_i, \beta_i), C_3(\alpha_i, \beta_i))$;
5.   If $C_{min} = C_1(\alpha_i, \beta_i)$, add current bucket to L_{C1};
6.   If $C_{min} = C_2(\alpha_i, \beta_i)$, add current bucket to L_{C2};
7.   If $C_{min} = C_3(\alpha_i, \beta_i)$, add current bucket to L_{C3};
8.   If $L_{C1} \neq \emptyset$, execute direct join $\forall$ buckets $\in L_{C1}$;
9.   If $L_{C2} \neq \emptyset$, execute ship-join-keys join $\forall$ buckets $\in L_{C2}$;
10. If $L_{C3} \neq \emptyset$, RAMJ($R1, R2, G, L_{C3}$);

The above shows the RAMJ algorithm. RAMJ follows the bucket-wise approach and it is recursive; given two remote relations R1 and R2, the algorithm first draws two G-bucket equi-width histograms H_{R1} and H_{R2} that summarize the distribution of join key in R1 and R2 (Lines 1–2). In BuildHist, L is the set of buckets from the previous level that are currently refined as a batch. When RAMJ is called for the first time, L corresponds to a single bucket that covers the whole domain of the join attribute. For each refined bucket range that exists in both relations, RAMJ employs the cost model to estimate the cost of each of the three potential actions for the current bucket. The action of each bucket is deferred until the costs of all buckets have been estimated. Finally, Lines 8–10 execute each of the three actions (if applicable) for the corresponding set of bucket ranges, as a batch. We note here, that if the memory of the device is limited, the device may not be able to support action deferring or even direct join or ship-join-keys join for a specific bucket (or set of buckets). In this case, recursive partitioning is directly used without applying the cost model to choose action.

3 Processing of Other Join Queries

We have discussed RAMJ for the case where there is a single join attribute. In case of multiple attributes, RAMJ can be simply adapted by retrieving multidimensional histograms and adjusting the cost formulae accordingly.

Sometimes, users may apply some selection constraints on the joined relations. Constraints are usually expressed by (allowed) value ranges on the attribute domain. Consider the example query in the introduction, assume that the user is now only interested in restaurants with cost lower than $20 recommended by both HK tourist office and vegetarian community:

SELECT R1.Name, R1.Address, R2.Cost FROM R1,R2 WHERE R1.Name=R2.Name and $R2.Cost< 20$

RAMJ can efficiently process such queries by "pushing" the selections as early as possible, following the common optimization policy of database systems. The selections are sent together with the histogram requests to avoid including disqualified tuples in the bucket counts. Therefore, only tuples that satisfy all conditions are summarized and the adaptivity of our algorithm is not affected.

RAMJ is also useful for iceberg semijoin queries. As an example, consider the query "find all restaurants in R1 which are recommended by at least 10 users in a discussion group R2". Such queries require joining two remote relations and retrieving only the tuples in one (e.g., R1) that join with at least t tuples in the other (e.g., R2). The result is usually small, making it useful to the mobile user. RAMJ can easily handle such queries by modifying the aggregate COUNT query in BuildHist procedure; buckets with count less than the threshold t are not included in the histogram. This can be achieved by modified the HAVING predicate from "HAVING COUNT (Attribute) > 0" to "HAVING COUNT (Attribute) > t". As a result, large parts of the data space can be pruned by the cardinality constraint early.

4 Performance Experiments and Results

To evaluate the effectiveness of the proposed RAMJ algorithm, we have conducted experiments on both real and synthetic datasets. The remote datasets resided on two Oracle 8i servers. We have implemented RAMJ on mentioned cost models, i.e., optimistic (RAMJ-OPT) and linear interpolation (RAMJ-LI). In addition, we also report results for an optimal version of RAMJ (OPTIMAL) that pre-fetches the next-level histograms to determine the "optimal" action for each bucket. This version is only of theoretical interest, and serves as a lower bound for our cost model. The mobile device is simulated by a Pentium PC with 8MB memory available to RAMJ. We compare all versions of RAMJ with the basic approaches, i.e., block-merge join (BMJ) and ship-data-as-query join (SDAQ). For fairness, all implemented algorithms employ the late-projection strategy (i.e., joining the set of join attributes only).

Table 1. Experimental results

Algorithm	Real Data		NegExp-Gaussian		Zipf-Gaussian		Zipf-NegExp	
	Transferred (Bytes)	No. of joined keys	Transferred (Bytes)	No. of joined keys	Transferred (Bytes)	No. of joined keys	Transferred (Bytes)	No. of joined keys
BMJ	266.22K		80116		80124		80120	
SDAQ	180.15K		181944		139728		143580	
RAMJ-OPT	116.67K	163	48654	420	35056	184	77114	1148
RAMJ-LI	n/a		40956		25680		67092	
OPTIMAL	66.2K		35100		21436		34848	

The real data set contains information of 152K restaurants crawled from restaurantrow.com. We split the restaurant data into different (overlapping) sets according to the cuisine they offered. We then joined these sets to retrieve restaurants offering more than one type of cuisine. We present an illustrative experiment that joins relation *steaks* (4573 tuples) with *vegetarian* (2098 tuples) to identify the restaurants that offer both steak and vegetarian dishes. Experiments joining different cuisine combinations have similar results. Table 1 shows that the data transferred by RAMJ-OPT are only 44% and 65% compared to BMJ and SDAQ respectively. SDAQ transferred less bytes than BMJ because the size differences between the two input relations of the restaurant datasets are significant. RAMJ-OPT is more close to OPTIMAL than both BMJ and SDAQ because of its adaptivity. RAMJ-LI was not tested on string data joins since the distribution of characters is independent at different levels.

Next, we study the performance of our algorithms on synthetic data, under different settings. In particular, we studied the amount of data transferred on joining relations in different data distribution by RAMJ. Each input relation consists of 10,000 tuples of integers with domain size 100,000, and G is set to 20.

Overall Performance. To model the real scenario of ad-hoc joining, we generated data with 3 different distributions: Gaussian, Negative Exponential (Neg-Exp) and Zipf (with skew parameter $\theta = 1$). Table 1 shows that RAMJ outperforms BMJ and SDAQ even when the data have similar distribution (e.g., when joining Negative Exponential data with Zipf data). RAMJ-LI is better than RAMJ-OPT, and closer to OPTIMAL, because RAMJ-LI employs a more accurate cost model.

The Impact of Data Skew. Since RAMJ is designed for highly selective join, we study how data skew affects the performance of RAMJ. We generated 6 relations with different Zipf distribution by varying the skewness (θ) from 0 (uniform distribution) to 1. Each of them was joined with the Gaussian data relation. Figure 2(a) shows that the total number of bytes transferred by RAMJ decreases when the join selectivity (θ) increases. It is because when the data distribution is skewed, parts of the search space are pruned and for some buckets cheap ship-join-keys joins are performed, hence, the histograms retrieved by RAMJ pay-off. BMJ transfers a constant amount of bytes because it downloads all tuples, independent of the data skew. If the data are near-uniform, BMJ outperforms RAMJ-OPT because RAMJ-OPT optimistically retrieves more statistics unsuccessfully hoping to prune the search space. On the other hand, RAMJ-LI outperforms BMJ and SDAQ in all cases because it is less sensitive to data skew.

The Impact of Memory Size. We evaluate how memory of mobile devices affects the transfer cost. Figure 2(b) shows the performance of joining the Gaussian and Zipf ($\theta=1$) distributions by RAMJ again, under different memory settings. As expected, the transfer cost increases when the memory is very limited (less than 20K). It is because many buckets cannot execute their optimal actions, but need to apply recursive partitioning if those actions cannot be performed with the available memory. Note that the transfer cost stabilizes to a constant when the memory is larger than 20K memory. This figure shows that only a small memory on the mobile device suffices for RAMJ to perform the speculated optimal actions.

Summary of Other Experiments. We also ran RAMJ:
i) in different granularities, results show that the performances of RAMJ is unaffected by G, if G is not very small ($G < 5$).
ii) in different input relation sizes, which draw similar conclusions as the experiments we presented.
iii) on another real dataset, the DBLP bibliography, results show that RAMJ-OPT transferred 66% of BMJ and 69% of SDAQ respectively.

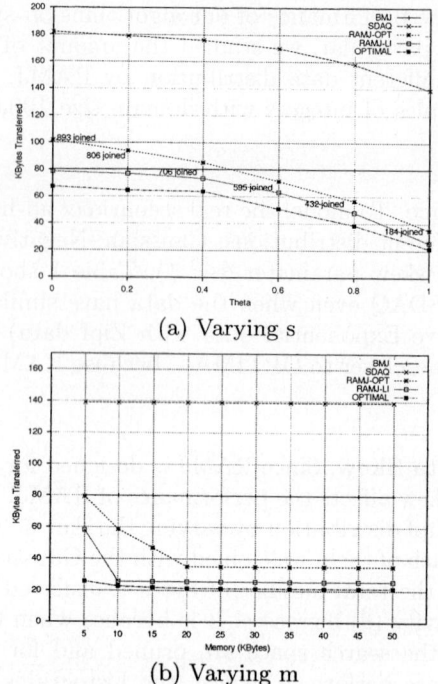

Fig. 2. Synthetic data experiments

Readers that interest on the detail of these experiment results and the query processing time of RAMJ (all finished with seconds) are referred to [7].

5 Related Work

We are aware of no work in the area of transfer-cost based query optimization (measured in dollars/byte) in the context of join queries on mobile devices. Nonetheless, query processing in a decentralized and distributed environment has been studied extensively in the past two decades [8, 2, 6]. Transfer cost optimization is discussed in some of these works. However, the traditional distributed database model assumes cooperative servers (in a trusted environment), which is not the case in our problem. Notice that, although we have adapted the semi-join [8] approach for this problem, its cost is higher than the other methods in practice.

Our work is also related to distributed query processing using mediators (e.g., [1]). Nevertheless we study queries that combine information from ad-hoc services, which are not supported by mediators. Join processing on mobile devices considering transfer-cost minimization has been studied in [9, 10]. In [9] the mobile clients are distributed database nodes (pairs of nodes are collaborative in nature). On the other hand, [10] applies similar techniques with this paper, but considers spatial joins only.

6 Conclusions and Future Work

Emerging mobile devices such as PDAs and mobile phones are creating opportunities for users to access information from anywhere and at any time. However, mobile devices have some limitations that make traditional query processing technology inappropriate. In this paper, we studied join queries on remote sources which are non-collaborative and are not logically connected via mediators. We addressed two issues: (i) the limited resources of the device and (ii) the fact that users are charged by the amount of transferred information, rather than the processing cost on the servers. Indeed, users are typically willing to sacrifice a few seconds in order to minimize the query cost in dollars. Furthermore, we proposed RAMJ, an adaptive algorithm that recursively partitions the data space and retrieves statistics that dynamically optimize equi-join queries. We also discussed how RAMJ can be extended to answer other types of joins including iceberg semijoins and constrained equi-joins. Finally, we evaluated RAMJ on several synthetic and real datasets. Our experiments reveal that RAMJ can outperform the basic approaches for a wide range of highly-selective joins.

RAMJ evaluates the basic equi-join efficiently. Indeed, RAMJ provides a basic framework to evaluate many highly-selective query types that may also involve joining (e.g., evaluating skyline and top-k query over a set of attributes that resided in different non-collaborative servers). In future, we will extend our approach for multi-way join queries, by utilizing the histograms to estimate the size of intermediate join results.

References

1. Adali, S., Candan, K.S., Papakonstantinou, Y., Subrahmanian, V.S.: Query caching and optimization in distributed mediator systems. In: Proc. of ACM SIGMOD. (1996) 137–148
2. Bernstein, P.A., Goodman, N.: Power of natural semijoin. SIAM Journal of Computing **10** (1981) 751–771
3. Mullin, J.K.: Optimal semijoins for distributed database systems. IEEE Tran. on Software Engineering **16** (1990) 558–560
4. Knisely, D.N., Kumar, S., Laha, S., Nanda, S.: Evolution of wireless data services: IS-95 to CDMA2000. IEEE Comm. Magazine (1998) 140–149
5. Kapp, S.: 802.11: Leaving the wire behind. IEEE Internet Computing **6** (2002)
6. Mackert, L.F., Lohman, G.M.: R* optimizer validation and performance evaluation for distributed queries. In: Proc. of VLDB. (1986) 149–159
7. Lo, E., Mamoulis, N., Cheung, D.W., Ho, W.S., Kalnis, P.: Processing ad-hoc joins on mobile devices. Technical report, The University of Hong Kong (2003) Available at http://www.csis.hku.hk/~dbgroup/techreport.
8. Bernstein, P.A., Chiu, D.M.W.: Using semi-joins to solve relational queries. Journal of the ACM (JACM) **28** (1981) 25–40
9. Lee, C.H., Chen, M.S.: Processing distributed mobile queries with interleaved remote mobile joins. IEEE Tran. on Computers **51** (2002) 1182–1195
10. Mamoulis, N., Kalnis, P., Bakiras, S., Li, X.: Optimization of spatial joins on mobile devices. In: Proc. of SSTD. (2003)

Preserving Consistency of Dynamic Data in Peer-Based Caching Systems

Song Gao[1], Wee Siong Ng[2], and Weining Qian[3]

[1] Department of Computer Science
National University of Singapore, Singapore
gaosong@comp.nus.edu.sg
[2] Singapore-MIT Alliance, 4 Engineering Drive 3
National University of Singapore, Singapore
smangws@nus.edu.sg
[3] Department of Computer Science Engineering
Fudan University, China
wnqian@fudan.edu.cn

Abstract. On-line decision making often involves significant amount of time-varying data, which can be regarded as dynamic data. Maintaining dynamic data consistency in existing P2P systems is often inefficient. Most of the previous P2P research works are predominantly remaining at the static files management. In this paper, we focus on the problem of maintaining consistency of dynamic data items in an overlay network of cooperating peers. We present CC-Buddy, an adaptive framework for efficiently disseminating dynamic data in P2P environments. Our approach combines application-level multicasting and demand-driven dissemination filtering techniques. We evaluate CC-Buddy with a prototype system built on top of BestPeer infrastructure. We examine our approach using real-world traces of dynamically changing data items. The results show our techniques can efficiently satisfy the consistency requirements by different users.

1 Introduction

Data caching is a well-understood technology deploying in distributed systems to achieve easy data access, minimize query response time and raise system performances. However, all the benefits that caches and replications can bring are due to the assumption that the cached objects are static without being modified rapidly. In contrast to static data, on-line decision-making often involves significant amount of dynamic data. Dynamic data is data which varies rapidly and unpredictably. Examples of such data include financial information such as stock prices and current exchange rates, real-time traffic, weather information, and sensors data. Most of these data are acquired and stored in a centralized server. Clearly, maintaining dynamic data in a centralized system would suffer from heavy workload and scale problems. A viable option is to deploy a peer-to-peer architecture that takes advantages of content distribution and utilizes idle bandwidth in order to serve content scaling with demand.

Many data replications and caching systems have been deployed or proposed for P2P data sharing environments [4, 13, 1]. Replicating and caching create numerous copies of data objects scattered throughout the P2P networks. They promise high data availability in P2P systems, minimize response latency to query and reduce the network traffic. Unfortunately, most of the proposals suffer from dynamic data inconsistency. Peers happen to join the network and might leave gracefully or ungracefully[1]. Moreover, messages disseminating scope is limited by TTL (e.g., Gnutella-like systems) coverage, which leads to a large number of peers may not be reachable by messages and therefore cause data inconsistency among peers. In this paper, we present the design of CC-Buddy, an adaptive framework for maintaining dynamic data consistency in P2P systems.

We have implemented an adaptive data consistency framework CC-Buddy layered on the BestPeer [9] infrastructure. We provide user-interactive mechanism for them to specify their consistency preferences. Furthermore, peers are cooperating with each other in order to maintain the consistency of cached data. CC-Buddy deploys filtering and application-level multicasting delivery techniques to reduce the source peer workload and achieve the scalability. CC-Buddy is formed as a graph overlay with numerous trees, each particular dynamic data item has a corresponding logically connected data dissemination tree. The source peer of the data item forms the root of the tree. To build the trees efficiently, we present two different policies, randomized policy and locality-based policy. Since considering the peer capacity and network locality factors and introducing redundant peer nodes as backups, CC-Buddy can guarantee high fidelity in peer local cached data, high scalability and minimize network resources usage in P2P environment.

2 Cooperative Consistency Model

The challenge of our work is to provide content distribution to clients with a good *Quality of Service (QoS)* while retaining efficient and balanced resource consumption of the underlying infrastructure based on peers cooperation.

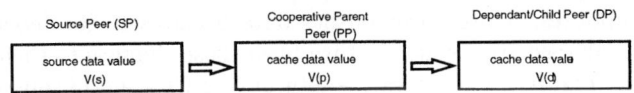

Fig. 1. Distributed cooperative consistency maintenance

As shown in Figure 1, in a distributed cooperative approach, dependant peer (DP) may not be informed about the item updates from the source peer (SP). The set of updates received by dependant peer is a subset of that received at its parent peer (PP), which in turn is a subset of unique data values at the source peer. Let v_i^s, v_{i+1}^s, v_{i+2}^s ... denote a sequence of updates (i.e., in an unit of time) to v at the SP. Let v_j^p, v_{j+1}^p, v_{j+2}^p ... denote the updates received by

---
[1] Measured activity in Gnutella and Napster indicates that the median up-time for a node is 60 minutes [2].

PP and v_k^d, v_{k+1}^d, v_{k+2}^d ... denote the updates received by the child peer DP. In order to guarantee the consistency requirement, each PP should forward the update to its children or dependent peer, if $|v_j^p - v_k^d| > c^d$, where c^d denotes the consistency requirement specified by dependent peer DP. Meanwhile, each peer (PP or DP) should ensure the conditions of $|v_i^s - v_j^p| < c^p$ and $|v_i^s - v_j^d| < c^d$ are hold. By combining the above conditions, the updates pushing mechanism must be initiated if the inequation $|v_j^p - v_k^d| \leqslant c^d - c^p$ is violated. The conditions must be checked by any parent peer to see if an update should be disseminated to its child peers. The detailed proof can be referred to [12].

2.1 CC-Buddy Architecture

We assume *source peers* have the authority for updating data items and disseminating dynamic data. Besides that, all *source peers* are considered as long-running nodes. The peers who cache the dynamic data items for querying, are called *client peers*. A peer in CC-Buddy network can play as a source peer or a client peer simultaneously.

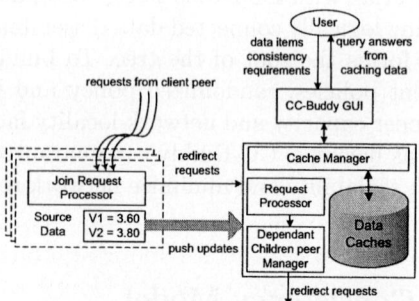

Fig. 2. CC-Buddy system architecture

CC-Buddy provides filtering and pushing services by organizing the peer members into a self-organized, source-specific, logical spanning tree that is maintained as nodes join and leave. CC-Buddy framework uses a push approach to disseminate updates. Source peer pushes data updates to its dependent peers via a logical multicast tree, which in turn push these changes to their dependent children peers. Figure 2 illustrates the internals of CC-Buddy source peer node and client peer node. There are essentially four components that are loosely integrated. The first component is a dependant children peer management system that facilitates immediate dependant peers management, maintains the data values pushed to the client peers last time and checks the push condition satisfaction upon receiving data updates from upper level peers. The second component is a redirection process manager. The policy adopted by the redirection mechanism decides the topology of dissemination tree. The third component is a cache manager. Cache manager takes charge of all the cached data. The last component is the graphic user interface. This provides a user-friendly environment for users to specify their data items of interest, and set the associated consistency requirements.

3 System Design

In this section, we discuss CC-Buddy framework design issues, and present alternative data dissemination tree construction policies, self-adaptive procedure, and the strategies to address peer leave and recovery problems.

Dissemination Tree Construction Policies. Any peer who is interested in maintaining the consistency of dynamic data item e_i has to submit a join request to the source peer of e_i, and receives the data updates via the dissemination tree after participating the network. The source peer serves an incoming peer by registering its entry, and establishing a logical connection if and only if there is enough connection slots to handle the request. Otherwise, it redirects the request by choosing one or more candidates from its immediate peers. The redirection procedure recurs until a qualified peer is discovered. In order to become the parent peer of the incoming peer, the qualified peer must fulfill the consistency needs of the new incoming peer. If the incoming peer's requirement is more stringent than all of the existing peers, it will swap with one of the existing peer and lets that peer becomes its dependant child. In this way, the incoming peer with stringent consistency requirement to certain data item is guaranteed to be placed much closer to the source peer of that data item than other peers who have lower requirements. There are two dissemination tree construction policies:
1. *Randomized Policy* - When there is no available capacity to serve a new incoming peer, peer n chooses one (or several) of its immediate child peers by using a randomized approach. The request is then being redirected to the selected peer. Such a policy requires minimal state and computation cost. The submission entry of the new incoming peer includes dynamic a data item identity e_i and associated its consistency requirement cr_i. Since the computation cost is minimized, the first response delay to new coming client peer is also expected to be small.
2. *Locality-Biased Policy* - This policy helps to construct the data dissemination tree by considering the network proximity (i.e., network locality property). In order to reduce the number of ping messages and round-trip latency, CC-Buddy uses the Group-based Distance Measurement Service (*GDMS*) [8] to improve the performance. The inter-group and intra-group estimation can be figured out by the *GDMS* service, in this way, peer n chooses the redirect target based on the knowledge of distance estimation offered by *GDMS* service. The locality property of tree construction naturally leads to the locality of CC-Buddy, i.e., parent peer and its immediate children tend to be close to each other. This provides CC-Buddy near-optimal data updates delivery delay and leads to high data fidelity.

The new client peer sets the metric *max_waiting_time* after receiving the first answer. Client peer computes an optimal parent peer from the collected answers using the metric preference factor (which is decided by workload, data availability, etc.), and takes the rest of peer nodes which satisfy the consistency requirement as backups.

We collected 10 traces, which were the most active stocks in Nasdaq. The details of the traces are listed in Table 2 to suggest the characteristics of the traces used. We simulated the typical peer-to-peer network topology. The nodes were connected either through a slow WAN or a fast LAN line to the network. We employed the power-law topology, and the model for the physical network was randomly generated. It consisted of 10 corresponding source peers, each took responsibility for a specific stock data update disseminating to numerous client peers. For our experiments, we varied the size of the network N from 100 nodes to 1000 nodes. Meanwhile, we setup $\lfloor \sqrt{N} \rfloor$ peer groups in the locality-biased tree construction policy. Each group has inter-group and intra-group distance estimations, which would affect the average transfer rate between remote peers or local peers. We used the proportional rates to simulate the inter-group and intra-group network locality factors. The computational delay incurred at the peer to disseminate an update to a dependant child peer is totally taken to be 12.5 ms, which is derived from the [12]. It includes the time to perform any checks to examine whether an update needs to be propagated to a dependent and the time to prepare an update for transmission to a dependent.

Table 2. Characteristics of all the traces used for the experiments

Symbol	Interval	Min	Max	Symbol	Interval	Min	Max
Microsoft	2-Jan-03:31-Dec-03	22.81	57.0	SINA	2-Jan-03:31-Dec-03	5.6	45.6
INTEL	2-Jan-03:31-Dec-03	13.0	29.01	SUN	2-Jan-03:31-Dec-03	30.0	52.5
ORACLE	2-Jan-03:31-Dec-03	10.65	13.92	YAHOO	2-Jan-03:31-Dec-03	17.5	46.44
IBM	2-Jan-03:31-Dec-03	75.25	93.9	SAP	2-Jan-03:31-Dec-03	18.85	44.75
CISCO	2-Jan-03:31-Dec-03	12.87	24.83	AMD	2-Jan-03:31-Dec-03	4.95	18.23

We have simulated static network and dynamic network. Static network simulation was used to examine the scalability. Dynamic network simulation was used to evaluate the peer autonomy effect. We modelled node failure by assigning each node an up-time picked uniformly at random from [0, *maxlifetime*], *maxlifetime* was set the same with the simulation time. Nodes disconnect from their neighbors, shutdown, and immediately rejoin the system by connecting initially to a random number of neighbors. Then, we setup the environment of [6] in order to compare between our method and theirs to show the efficiency of CC-Buddy.

The key metrics for our experiments were the fidelity of the cached data and query false ratio. Fidelity of cached data is a degree to which a peer user's consistency requirements are met and is measured as the total length of time for which the difference between local cached data value and source peer data value kept within user's consistency requirements. Our results were plotted using loss fidelity of cached data. Query false ratio is referred to the ratio of querying the stale cached data.

4.2 Experimental Results and Analysis

Each client peer was interested in all the 10 stocks. However, the consistency requirements for each specific stock were different. We set the T% of the cached data in client peers with high stringent consistency requirements. The consistency requirement was uniform randomly picked from [0.01, 0.099], and the other 100 - T% data are less stringent requirement, picked randomly from [0.1, 0.99]. We set the T% value equals 50% initially, which means each peer user was interested in half of all the provided stock with high attention.

Our first experiment examined the cost comparison of two alternative CC-Buddy dissemination tree construction policies. The topology of the dissemination tree has a significant impact on fidelity, the larger the end-to-end delay, the greater the loss in fidelity. As illustrated in Figure 4, the locality-biased construction takes more message consumption and bandwidth cost than the randomized construction. It is because randomized construction policy can generate balanced tree. In contrast, locality-biased construction policy should use numerous multicast ping messages to generate peer groups to estimate the distance between nodes. Totally, locality-biased tree construction policy consumes far more network resources, however, we can see from the later experiments, it brings more benefits than randomized constructed tree.

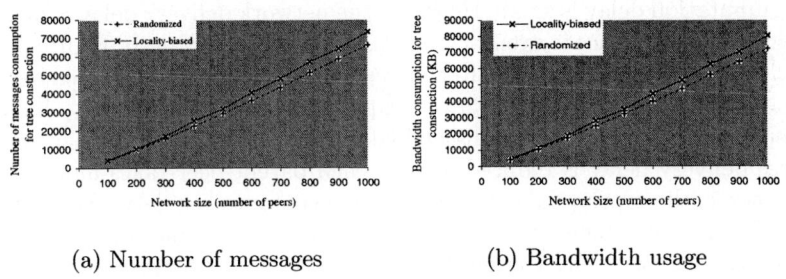

(a) Number of messages   (b) Bandwidth usage

Fig. 4. Tree construction cost

Second experiment was to compare the performance of overlay constructed by randomized approach and overlay constructed by locality-biased approach, taken the centralized approach as the baseline. In Figure 5, locality-biased construction performs better as we had expected. Due to taking network proximity into account, it takes less delay to disseminate the data updates. Although centralized approach could take minimum communication latency, it suffers from large computational delay.

Third experiment shows the impact of bandwidth of client peer capacity. Since each peer filters and forwards the data updates to its children peers, the performance of the CC-Buddy framework is sensitive to the available bandwidth at the nodes participating in the system. We characterize the bandwidth

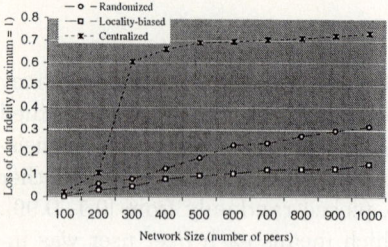
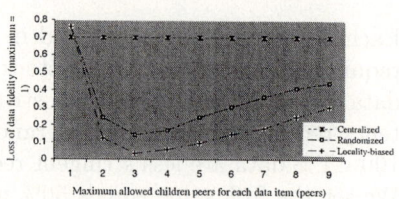

Fig. 5. Performance comparison **Fig. 6.** Peer bandwidth capacity

which nodes can contribute to CC-Buddy by the number of maximum children, $number_{max}$. We can see from Figure 6 that centralized approach presents as a horizontal line. Because it does not take the advantage of client peer cooperation. CC-Buddy has great performance fluctuation with the variety of client peer capacity. We can see that the performance fluctuation of them is both like a V-curve with the increment of the max-allowed children.

Due to the computation delay and network dissemination delay, when the dependent children number to a specific data item increases, the computation delay will enlarge. It will take more time to finish assembling the updates to deliver in the waiting queue. When $number_{max}$ equals 1, tree is formed as a chain. The computation delay is small. However, the network delivery delay is increased so that the performance is even worse than centralized approach. Figure 6 shows that it brings no more benefits after increasing the cooperative degree beyond a threshold. The threshold was 3 in our experiment. When $number_{max}$ increases, the depth of the corresponding dissemination tree decreases. Although the data updates delivery delay is reduced, due to each parent peer takes more children peer to serve, the overlay suffers from the large computation delay. Since updates from different data items arrive asynchronously, peers should adopt an optimal cooperative degree to any specific item to achieve better performance.

Peer frequent departure does negative effect to the performance of CC-Buddy because of the disconnection of the dissemination tree. Upon parent peer ungracefully leaves, it can only be detected via periodical submitting "heartbeat" message by children peer. If the children peer can not get the response in a systematic time threshold. It is regarded that parent peer fails or ungracefully leaves, meanwhile, recovery policies are adopted. The ratio of ungraceful leave and repair interval can have a significant impact on the CC-Buddy performance. As illustrated in Figure 7, we present the effect of repair interval and ratio of ungraceful departure. If 10% departure are ungraceful leave, the performance is still acceptable from the results. Initially, we set all the client peers take 50% dynamic data items with stringent consistency requirements. In this experiment, we increased the proportion of high consistency requirements, as illustrated in Figure 8, we can find that with more stringent consistency requirements, the loss of fidelity is increased. However, increment the number of stringent consistency items also reduce the benefit of data cache.

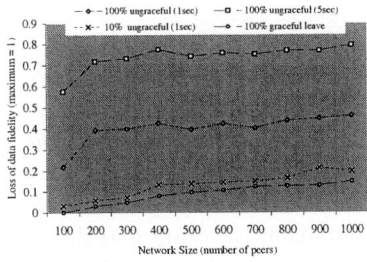 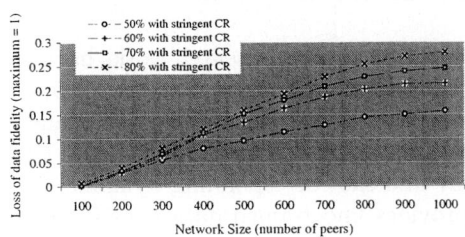

Fig. 7. Peer departure **Fig. 8.** Different consistency requirements

Gtk-Gnutella protocol is designed for cache consistency maintenance in P2P environment [6]. It presents three methods: push, adaptive pull and push with adaptive pull. Lastly, we evaluated the performance of CC-Buddy with comparison to Gtk-Gnutella protocol. We ran three strategies of Gtk-Gnutella and CC-Buddy to collect the results. We fixed the update interval to 1 second, and average query interval to 1 second. Message TTL value was set to 10. Network size was varied from 100 to 2500 nodes. Figure 9 plotted the performance comparison between CC-Buddy and Gtk-Gnutella. The performance of push invalidation approach is poor when the network size is over 700. It is because the scope of invalidation message is limited by the TTL value. Likewise, adaptive pull policy is suffered by the scalability. Since data updates happen unpredictably, it is hard to when and how frequently to poll the source peer for checking. Push with adaptive pull and CC-Buddy can achieve satisfactory query fidelity. As shown in Figure 10, push with adaptive pull method imposes two orders of magnitude larger overhead than CC-Buddy, since it combines the advantages of the pull and push methods, which results in huge network traffic consumption. From the results analysis, CC-Buddy outperforms the previous work.

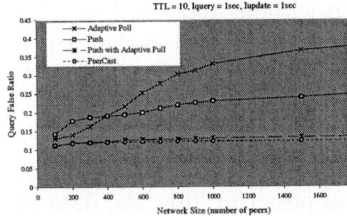 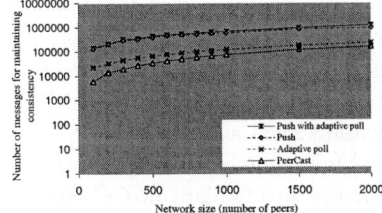

Fig. 9. CC-Buddy vs. Gtk-Gnutella

Fig. 10. Bandwidth consumption

5 Related Works

Most consistency research works have been done on web proxy caching and content distribution network scenarios [5, 7, 11]. Jiang Lan et al.'s work [6] focuses on the problem of consistency maintenance among multiple replicas in the presence of updates. Shetal Shal et al.'s work [12] proposes cooperative repositories overlay and the corresponding dynamic data dissemination techniques. The system provides fine-grained data consistency and an intelligent filtering and dissemination techniques based on each repositories coherency requirement. Yan Chen et al.'s work [3] proposes a dynamic replica placement for scalable content delivery, which is proposed to address the problem how to achieve maximum benefits by placing minimum replicas in Tapstry, meanwhile satisfy all the client peer's query latency.

Our work differs from previous research works in three aspects. First, each peer manages its local cache data, which is used to raise query performance. The data consistency is on the peer node granularity. Peers maintain the cached data consistency with cooperation with each other. Peer possessing data item with high stringent consistency can push the updates to the peers with lower requirements based on their demands. Second, we provide an adaptive dissemination overlay with numerous trees inside. Source data peers and client peers cooperate to choose the optimal parent peer for new coming client peer, taking peer workload and network locality into account. What's more, the overlay can adjust itself according to consistency requirement changing of peer users, the initially-setup dissemination tree can adapt to demands without administration. Third, we introduce redundancy techniques to backup potential parent peers for each client peer when it joins the consistency overlay without any manual administration.

6 Conclusion

We present our framework CC-Buddy to address the major problems in maintaining dynamic data consistency in P2P caching systems. We have proposed dissemination overlay with two alternative tree construction policies: randomized construction and locality-biased construction without replying low infrastructure knowledge. Our approach has been experimentally proved that it is far more efficient than the conventional centralized approaches. We have extended the bounded cache techniques which have been proposed in previous centralized systems such as TRAPP [10] into peer-to-peer environment, without decentralized management or any centralized computing [12]. Due to the demand driven delivery mechanism in CC-Buddy, the upper level peer can filter the data updates so as to disseminate them to dependant peers selectively. In this way, our approach can also outperform the recent approaches proposed to multicast media streams on P2P systems in aspects of scalability and relative delay penalty.

References

1. S. Bakiras, P. Kalnis, T. Loukopoulos, and W.S. Ng. A general framework for searching in distributed data repositories. In *Proceedings of IPDPS*, 2003.
2. Y. Chawathe, S. Ratnasamy, L. BresLau, N. Lanham, and S. Shenker. Making Gnutella-like P2P System Scalable. In *Proceedings of ACM SIGCOMM*, 2003.
3. Y. Chen, R. Katz, and J. Kubiatowicz. Dynamic Replica Placement for Scalable Content Delivery. In *1st International Workshop on P2P Systems*, May 2002.
4. E. Cohen and S. Shenker. Replication Strategies in Unstructured Peer-to-Peer Networks. In *Proceedings of ACM SIGCOMM*, August 2002.
5. V. Duvvuri, P. Shenoy, and R. Tewari. Adaptive Leases: A Strong Consistency Mechanism for the World Wide Web. *IEEE TRANSACTION ON KNOWLEDGE AND DATA ENGINEERING*, 15, August 2003.
6. Jiang Lan, Xiaotao Liu, Prashant Shenoy, and Krithi Ramamritham. Consistency maintenance in peer-to-peer file sharing networks. In *Proceedings of the 10th International Conference on Database and Expert Systems Applications*, August 2003.
7. C. Liu and P. Cao. Maintaining Strong Cache Consistency in the World-Wide Web. In *Proceedings of ICDCS*, May 1997.
8. J. Liu, X. Zhang, B. Li, Q. Zhang, and W. Zhu. Distributed Distance Measurement for Large-scale Networks. *The International Journal of Computer and Telecommunications Networking*, 41:177 – 192, 2003.
9. W.S. Ng, B.C. Ooi, and K L. Tan. BestPeer: A Self-Configurable Peer-to-Peer System. In *ICDE*, page 272, 2002.
10. C. Olston and J. Widom. Offering a Precision-Performance Tradeoff for Aggregation Queries over Replicated Data. In *Proceedings of VLDB*, pages 144–155, 2000.
11. P. Rodriguez and S. Sibal. SPREAD: Scalable Platform for Reliable and Efficient Automated Distribution. In *Proceedings of WWW*, pages 223–227, 2000.
12. S. Shah, K. Ramamritham, and P. Shenoy. Maintaining Consistency of Dynamic Data in Cooperating Repositories. In *VLDB*, 2002.
13. B. Yang and H. Molina. Improving Search in Peer-to-Peer Systems. In *Proceedings of ICDCS*, 2002.

Efficient Processing of Distributed Iceberg Semi-joins

Mohammed Kasim Imthiyaz, Dong Xiaoan, and Panos Kalnis

Department of Computer Science
National University of Singapore
3 Science Drive 2, Singapore 117543
{iscp1134,dongxiao,dcskp}@nus.edu.sg

Abstract. The Iceberg SemiJoin (ISJ) of two datasets $\mathcal{R}$ and $\mathcal{S}$ returns the tuples in $\mathcal{R}$ which join with at least k tuples of $\mathcal{S}$. The ISJ operator is essential in many practical applications including OLAP, Data Mining and Information Retrieval. In this paper we consider the distributed evaluation of Iceberg SemiJoins, where $\mathcal{R}$ and $\mathcal{S}$ reside on remote servers. We developed an efficient algorithm which employs Bloom filters. The novelty of our approach is that we interleave the evaluation of the Iceberg set in server $\mathcal{S}$ with the pruning of unmatched tuples in server $\mathcal{R}$. Therefore, we are able to (i) eliminate unnecessary tuples early, and (ii) extract accurate Bloom filters from the intermediate hash tables which are constructed during the generation of the Iceberg set. Compared to conventional two-phase approaches, our experiments demonstrate that our method transmits up to 80% less data through the network, while reducing the disk I/O cost.

1 Introduction

Many practical applications, including Data Warehousing [2], Market-basket Analysis [5] and Information Retrieval [6], rely on Iceberg queries. Such queries compute aggregate functions over a set of attributes and return the aggregate values which are above some threshold. They are called *Iceberg* queries because the result is usually very small (i.e., the tip of an Iceberg) compared to the input set.

Here, we deal with the evaluation of Distributed *Iceberg SemiJoins* (ISJ). Consider the following scenario: Server S stores the transactions of a supermarket's cashiers in a table $\mathcal{S}(pID, rest)$, where pID identifies the product and $rest$ is a set of attributes containing the details of the transaction (e.g., cashier ID, timestamp, etc). A remote server R contains a set $\mathcal{R}(pID)$ of "interesting" products. The user at site R wants to find which of the products in $\mathcal{R}$ sold at least T items in supermarket S. For the dataset of Figure 1 and assuming that $T = 2$, the only qualifying product is coffee (notice that some of the products in $\mathcal{R}$ may not appear in $\mathcal{S}$ and visa versa). Formally, the ISJ query corresponds to the following SQL statement (Query 1):

Query 1:   SELECT S.pID, COUNT(S.rest)
            FROM R, S

pID
coffee
toothpaste
cola

pID	rest
coffee	Cashier 2, 10:01
fruit	Cashier 1, 10:02
fruit	Cashier 1, 10:02
cola	Cashier 3, 10:03
coffee	Cashier 1, 10:30

(a) Dataset $\mathcal{R}$ (b) Dataset $\mathcal{S}$

Fig. 1. Two datasets to be joined

```
WHERE R.pID = S.pID
GROUP BY S.pID
HAVING COUNT(S.rest) >= T
```

Since the datasets reside in remote servers, a straight-forward way to evaluate the ISJ is to employ a two-steps algorithm: (i) Execute Query 2 in server S to find the set of tuples $\mathcal{S}_{ICE}$ which appear at least T times[1] in $\mathcal{S}$.

Query 2:
```
SELECT S.pID, COUNT(S.rest)
FROM S
GROUP BY S.pID
HAVING COUNT(S.rest) >= T
```

(ii) Transfer $\mathcal{S}_{ICE}$ to server R and evaluate the join $\mathcal{R} \bowtie \mathcal{S}_{ICE}$. We call this method *Naïve Iceberg SemiJoin* (nIS).

The simplest way to evaluate Query 2 is to maintain one counter per group in the main memory (i.e., 3 counters in our example). Using this method, we can compute the answer by reading $\mathcal{S}$ only once. However, this is inapplicable in practice, since the number of groups is usually larger than the available memory. Another approach is to sort $\mathcal{S}$ on the *pID* attribute by employing external sorting; subsequently, Query 2 can be answered by reading the sorted data from the disk. External sorting, however, may require several passes over the data if the available memory is limited. Moreover, in some applications (e.g., Information Retrieval [6]) $\mathcal{S}$ is computed on-the-fly from other relations and is impractical to be materialized. The implicit drawback of both methods is that they generate all possible groups, although (by the definition of Iceberg queries) only few of them are expected to satisfy the threshold. Fang et.al [8] solved this problem by designing a family of algorithms based on sampling and multiple hashing. We call their method *Efficient Iceberg Computation* (EIC).

In this paper we present the *Multiple Filter Iceberg SemiJoin* (MulFIS) algorithm. MulFIS exploits the intermediate steps of EIC in order to minimize the cost of Distributed ISJ. Specifically, instead of computing $\mathcal{S}_{ICE}$ and $\mathcal{R} \bowtie \mathcal{S}_{ICE}$ in two independent steps, MulFIS interleaves the execution in the remote servers. Therefore it can access the internal hash tables which are generated by EIC; these

---

[1] In our examples we use COUNT for simplicity. However, our methods are also applicable to more complex criteria (e.g., HAVING SUM(S.price * S.itemsSold)>=T).

are used to construct accurate Bloom filters [3] (i.e., compact representations of the tables' contents) with minimal extra cost. The resulting Bloom filters are exchanged between the processing sites enabling the elimination of unnecessary tuples at the early stages. We developed a prototype and performed extensive experimentation with standard industry benchmarks. Our results revealed that MulFIS can reduce the network cost of the Distributed ISJ by 80% compared to nIS, while the Disk I/O cost also decreases. We also show that MulFIS is better than alternative implementations which employ Bloom filters at various stages of the query execution.

The rest of this paper is organized as follows: In Section 2 we present the related work together with some essential background; the EIC method is described in more details in Section 3. Next, in Section 4 we discuss several variations of our approach and explain the MulFIS algorithm. Our experimental results are presented in Section 5, while Section 6 concludes the paper.

2 Related Work

A common technique to reduce the network cost of joins in distributed databases is the *SemiJoin* [1]. Assume that relation $\mathcal{R}$ at site R is joined with relation $\mathcal{S}$ at site S on attribute a (i.e., $\mathcal{R} \bowtie_a \mathcal{S}$). SemiJoin reduces the amount of data transferred between the two sites as follows: (i) At site R, it computes $\mathcal{R}' = \pi_a(\mathcal{R})$ and sorts the result. (ii) $\mathcal{R}'$ is sent to site S, where it is used to compute $\mathcal{S}' = \pi_{\mathcal{S}.*}(\mathcal{R}' \bowtie_a \mathcal{S})$. (iii) $\mathcal{S}'$ is transferred back to site R. There, the final join $\mathcal{R} \bowtie_a \mathcal{S}'$ is executed and the results are presented to the user.

BloomJoin [4] is another approach which uses Bloom filters [3] to eliminate non-matching tuples. Bloom filters are bitmap vectors representing the contents of a relation in a compact way. BloomJoin works as follows: (i) A k-bit-vector (i.e., Bloom filter) is initialized to 0 at site R. Then, each tuple of $\pi_a(\mathcal{R})$ is hashed in the vector, setting the corresponding bit to 1. (ii) The vector is sent to site S. By using the same hash function, the values of $\pi_a(\mathcal{S})$ that correspond to 0-bits in the vector, are eliminated. Let $\mathcal{S}'$ be the subset of $\mathcal{S}$ which was not eliminated (i.e., the candidate tuples). (iii) $\mathcal{S}'$ is sent to site R. Finally the join $\mathcal{R} \bowtie_a \mathcal{S}'$ is evaluated at R. BloomJoin typically outperforms SemiJoin in terms of network cost since the filter is generally smaller than the projection on the join attribute. Observe that due to hash collisions in the filter, BloomJoin performs lossy compression. Therefore, the candidate set $\mathcal{S}'$ may contain non-matching tuples which would have otherwise been eliminated by SemiJoin.

Iceberg queries were introduced by Fang et.al. [8] who proposed a family of evaluation techniques based on sampling and multiple hashing. The advantage of these algorithms is that they are output sensitive; therefore, they avoid generating all possible groups of tuples. We will discuss the method further in the next section. Iceberg queries have also been studied in the context of Data Warehousing. The problem in this case is the efficient evaluation of an entire *Iceberg Cube* (i.e., multiple Group-Bys). Beyer and Ramakrishnan [2] proposed a bottom-up computation strategy (BUC). BUC is based on the anti-monotonic property which assures that if a cell of a group-by does not satisfy the threshold T, then none of the descendent cells can satisfy T. This idea was extended by

Han et.al. [9] for iceberg cubes with complex measures which do not satisfy the anti-monotonic property (e.g., AVERAGE).

Ng et.al [11] focus on the parallel computation of iceberg cubes. They assume a cluster of interconnected workstations and design parallel variations of BUC which aim at reducing the I/O cost and achieve good load balancing. This is different from our work, since they do not consider joins. Several papers also discuss the evaluation of *Top-K* queries in distributed environments. In the work of Fagin et.al [7] for instance, the measure function is evaluated by a distributed join involving several sites. Yu et.al. [12], on the other hand, focus on selecting the appropriate sites which contribute to the answer from a large set of remote sources. Notice, however, that the requirements of distributed Top-K queries are very different from the Distributed ISJ. To the best of our knowledge, Distributed ISJ is discussed only by Mamoulis et.al. [10]; the authors consider spatial datasets and propose a recursive partitioning algorithm to prune the 2-D space. Nevertheless, this paper focuses on spatial joins and requires a middleware evaluation site.

3 Efficient Iceberg Computation (EIC)

In this section we present in details the EIC method [8] since it is the basis of our algorithms. Recall from Section 1 that S_{ICE} is the answer set for the Iceberg query (i.e., Query 2). We call the tuples in S_{ICE} *heavy targets*, since they satisfy the threshold T. The aim of EIC is to select a set $\mathcal{F}$ of *potentially* heavy targets by eliminating fast many groups which cannot satisfy the threshold T. Observe that $\mathcal{F}$ does not necessarily contain the correct answer. There are two types of errors: (i) If $\mathcal{F} - S_{ICE} \neq \emptyset$ then the algorithm generates *false positives*, meaning that $\mathcal{F}$ contains tuples which do not satisfy T. (ii) If $S_{ICE} - \mathcal{F} \neq \emptyset$, there are *false negatives* meaning that some heavy targets are missed. EIC uses two techniques to compute $\mathcal{F}$:

- *Sampling*: A set S_{rnd} of random samples is selected from S. Then we calculate the count of each target in the sample, scaled by $\frac{|S|}{|S_{rnd}|}$. If it satisfies the threshold, the target is added into $\mathcal{F}$. Obviously the result may contain both false positives and false negatives.
- *Course Count*: This technique uses an array $A[1..m]$ of m counters initialized to zero and a hash function h which maps the grouping attributes v of a tuple to a cell of A. The algorithm works as follows: (i) For each tuple in S with grouping attributes v, the counter $A[h(v)]$ is incremented by one. After scanning the entire S the algorithm generates a bitmap vector $BMAP[1..m]$. A bit $BMAP[i], 1 \leq i \leq m$ is set if $A[i] \geq T$. Intuitively, $BMAP$ indicates which hash values correspond to *potential* heavy targets. Notice that $BMAP$ is much smaller than A. (ii) *Candidate Selection*: S is scanned, and a target with grouping attributes v is added to $\mathcal{F}$ if $BMAP[h(v)] = 1$. Observe that $\mathcal{F}$ may contain false positives but no false negatives. (iii) $Count(\mathcal{F})$: S is scanned again to explicitly count the frequency of targets in $\mathcal{F}$. The targets that occur less than T times (i.e., false positives) are eliminated, while the remaining targets are the final answer S_{ICE}.

Algorithm 1 Multiple Filter Iceberg SemiJoin (MulFIS)
_____
1. Generate a Bloom filter BF_1 for $\mathcal{R}$
2. Send the query and BF_1 to site S
3a. Perform sampling in $\mathcal{S}$. Use BF_1 to prune tuples during sampling
3b. Perform hash scanning h_1 in $\mathcal{S}$. Use BF_1 to prune tuples during scanning
4. Use the hash table from 3b to generate a Bloom filter BF_2
5. Send BF_2 to site R
6a. Scan $\mathcal{R}$ and use BF_2 to eliminate unmatching tuples
6b. Generate a Bloom filter BF_3 from the qualifying tuples of $\mathcal{R}$
7. Send BF_3 to site S
8a. Perform hash scanning h_2 in $\mathcal{S}$. Use BF_3 to prune tuples during scanning
8b. Perform Candidate Selection. Use BF_3 to prune tuples while generating $\mathcal{F}$
8c. Generate S_{ICE} by executing Count($\mathcal{F}$). Use BF_3 to prune tuples
9. Send S_{ICE} to site R
10. Evaluate the join $\mathcal{R} \bowtie S_{ICE}$ in site R
_____

5 Experimental Evaluation

In order to evaluate the effectiveness of the proposed algorithms, we developed a prototype in C++ running on Sun UltraSparc III machines. The servers were physically connected to a 100Mbps LAN and the communication between them was achieved through Unix sockets. We extracted our datasets from the industry standard TPC-H benchmark. The $\mathcal{S}$ relation consists of around 1.3M tuples from the LineItem table. We generated three instances of $\mathcal{R}$ denoted as $\mathcal{R}_{10}, \mathcal{R}_{30}, \mathcal{R}_{60}$. All instances contain 10K tuples, but only a subset of them (i.e., 10%, 30% and 60%, respectively) joins with at least one tuple of $\mathcal{S}$. We executed Query 1 for several threshold values T. We selected T such that the cardinality of the iceberg result S_{ICE} varied from around 130 to 35,000.

We measured the network cost of each algorithm by counting the number of bytes transmitted through the network. The largest amount of data that can be transferred in one physical frame is referred to as MTU (Maximum Transmission Unit); for Ethernet, $MTU = 1500$ bytes. Each packet consists of a header and the actual data. The largest segment of TCP data that can be transmitted is called MSS (Maximum Segment Size). Essentially, $MTU = MSS + B_H$, where B_H is the size of the TCP/IP headers (typically, $B_H = 40$ bytes). Let D be a set of data. The size of D in bytes is $B_D = |D| \cdot B_{obj}$, where B_{obj} is the size of each object in bytes (e.g., 4 bytes for an integer attribute). Thus, when the whole D is transmitted through the network, the number of transferred bytes is: $T_B(B_D) = B_D + B_H \cdot \lceil \frac{B_D}{MSS} \rceil$, where the second component of the equation is the overhead of the TCP/IP headers.

In the first set of experiments (Figure 3), we measured the performance of the algorithm for varying threshold T. For fairness, we used the $\mathcal{R}_{60}$ dataset, which represents the worst case for MulFIS, while we set the size of the Bloom filters to 60KB. MulFIS clearly outperforms the other algorithms in terms of transfer cost for most values of T. This is due to the multiple filters which manage to eliminate early most unnecessary tuples. Notice that while ISIF achieves some improvement over nIS, it is still much worse than MulFIS due to the lack of feedback from the intermediate hash tables in server S. Observe, however, that

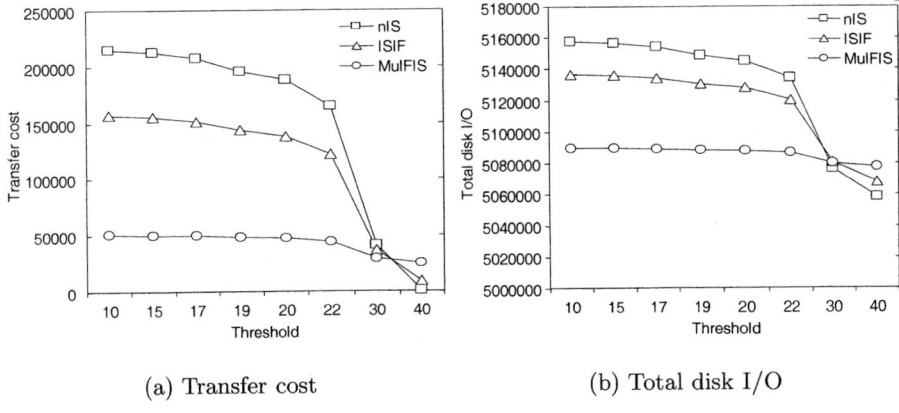

Fig. 3. Performance vs. the threshold T for the $\mathcal{R}_{60}$ dataset

for large values of T, nIS performs slightly better. In this case, the cardinality of $\mathcal{S}_{ICE}$ is so small that does not justify the overhead of the Bloom filters. In practice, we can minimize the performance loss of MulFIS by using smaller filters, as we discuss below. In terms of disk I/O the trend is similar, although the relative difference is considerably smaller. This is due to the fact that the I/O cost is dominated by the scanning of $\mathcal{S}$. Improving this aspect of MulFIS is part of our on-going work. Notice, finally, that we do not present the results of nFIS because the transfer and I/O cost are the same as these of ISIF.

In the next experiment we set $T = 20$ and vary the size of the Bloom filter. In Figure 4.a we present the transfer cost. If the Bloom filter is very small (i.e., 10KB), there are many hash collisions; therefore MulFIS cannot prune enough tuples. For larger values, the collisions decrease fast; thus MulFIS performs similarly for 40-60KB large filters. Obviously, nIS is constant since it does not employ any filter. Notice that the performance of ISIF also does not vary significantly. This indicates that the most important factor for the performance gain of MulFIS is the feedback mechanism from the internal hash tables of S. To investigate this further, we show in Figure 4.b the size of the iceberg result $\mathcal{S}_{ICE}$ (bars) and the number of false positives (lines). As expected, both metrics decrease in MulFIS when we use more accurate (i.e., larger) filters due to the feedback, while ISIF is almost unaffected.

Next (Figure 5.a) we draw the transfer cost for each of the three datasets $\mathcal{R}_{10}, \mathcal{R}_{30}, \mathcal{R}_{60}$; we used 60KB Bloom filters and T was set to 20. nIS is constant since it always transmits the same $\mathcal{S}_{ICE}$ result (i.e., no pruning). As expected, ISIF performs better when more tuples of $\mathcal{R}$ join with $\mathcal{S}$, since a larger percentage of the Bloom filter contains accurate information. Observe, however, that the trend for MulFIS is different. This happens because there is an overhead of the additional Bloom filters, while the feedback step of MulFIS does not depend on the number of matching tuples. Nevertheless, the overhead is very small and MulFIS still outperforms significantly the other algorithms.

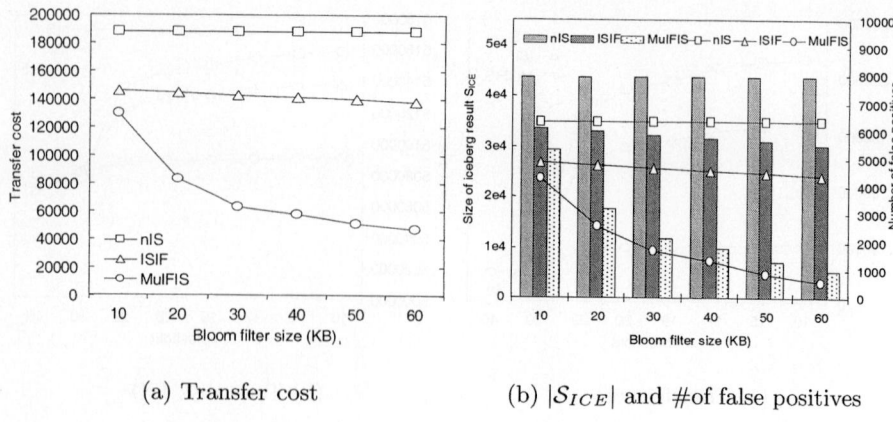

(a) Transfer cost

(b) $|S_{ICE}|$ and #of false positives

Fig. 4. Performance vs. the Bloom filter size ($T = 20$, $\mathcal{R}_{60}$ dataset)

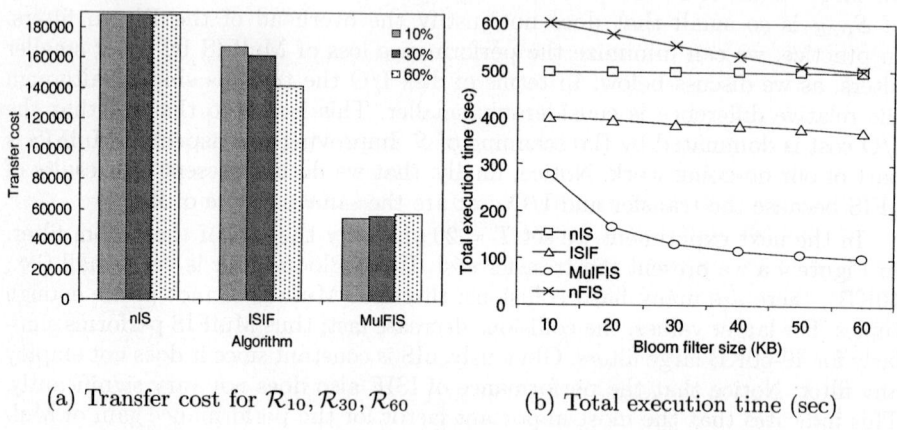

(a) Transfer cost for $\mathcal{R}_{10}, \mathcal{R}_{30}, \mathcal{R}_{60}$

(b) Total execution time (sec)

Fig. 5. Performance vs. $\mathcal{R}$ and total execution time ($T = 20$)

In the final experiment (Figure 5.b) we show the actual running time of the algorithms. The trend is similar to this of the transfer cost (compare with Figure 4.a). Here we also present the nFIS algorithm. Recall that the transfer cost of nFIS is the same as ISIF, since both algorithms employ only one Bloom filter. The difference is that the filter is used at the intermediate steps of ISIF but only at the last step of nFIS. Observe that the actual running time is affected considerably, due to the larger set of intermediate results in nFIS. The performance is even worse than nIS, due to the additional overhead of the filter.

6 Conclusion

In this paper we dealt with the evaluation of the Distributed Iceberg Semi-Join operator. This operator is essential in numerous real-life applications. It is used, for instance, to analyze information from two independent datamarts, or to extract correlated documents from a remote digital library. We developed MulFIS, an efficient algorithm which interleaves the execution of the iceberg query and the join in the two servers and uses the internal hash tables to prune the non-qualifying groups. We developed a prototype and used an industry standard benchmark to validate that MulFIS provides significant advantages over its competitors. Currently, we are working towards two directions: (i) to improve further the disk I/O cost and (ii) to describe formally the behavior of our algorithm by developing an accurate cost model.

References

1. P. Bernstein and D. Chiu. Using semijoins to solve relational queries. *Journal of the ACM*, 28(1):25–40, 1981.
2. K.S. Beyer and R. Ramakrishnan. Bottom-up computation of sparse and iceberg cubes. In *Proc. of the Int. Conf. on Management of Data (ACM SIGMOD)*, pages 359–370, 1999.
3. B.H. Bloom. Space/time trade-offs in hash coding with allowable errors. *Communications of the ACM*, 13(7):422–426, 1970.
4. K. Bratbergsengen. Hashing methods and relational algebra operations. In *Proc. of the 10th Int. Conf. on Very Large Data Bases (VLDB)*, pages 323–333, 1984.
5. S. Brin, R. Motwani, J. Ullman, and S. Tsur. Dynamic itemset counting and implication rules for market basket data. In *Proc. of the Int. Conf. on Management of Data (ACM SIGMOD)*, pages 255–264, 1997.
6. A. Broder, S. Glassman, and M. Manasse. Syntactic clustering of the web. In *Proc. of the 6th Int. World Wide Web Conference*, 1997.
7. R. Fagin, A. Lotem, and M. Naor. Optimal aggregation algorithms for middleware. In *Proc. of the 20th ACM SIGMOD-SIGACT-SIGART Symposium on Principles of Database Systems (PODS)*, pages 102–113, 2001.
8. M. Fang, N. Shivakumar, H. Garcia-Molina, R. Motwani, and J. D. Ullman. Computing iceberg queries efficiently. In *Proc. of the 24th Int. Conf. on Very Large Data Bases (VLDB)*, pages 299–310, 1998.
9. J. Han, J. Pei, G. Dong, and K. Wang. Efficient computation of iceberg cubes with complex measures. In *Proc. of the Int. Conf. on Management of Data (ACM SIGMOD)*, 2001.
10. N. Mamoulis, P. Kalnis, S. Bakiras, and X. Li. Optimization of spatial joins on mobile devices. In *Proc. of the 8th Int. Symposium on the Advances in Spatial and Temporal Databases (SSTD)*, pages 233–251, 2003.
11. R.T. Ng, A. Wagner, and Y. Yin. Iceberg-cube computation with pc clusters. In *Proc. of the Int. Conf. on Management of Data (ACM SIGMOD)*, pages 25–36, 2001.
12. C.T. Yu, G. Philip, and W. Meng. Distributed top-n query processing with possibly uncooperative local systems. In *Proc. of the 29th Int. Conf. on Very Large Data Bases (VLDB)*, pages 117–128, 2003.

Definition of Derived Classes in ODMG Databases

Eladio Garví[1], José Samos[1], and Manuel Torres[2]

[1] Dept. de Lenguajes y Sistemas Informáticos, Universidad de Granada, España
{egarvi,jsamos}@ugr.es
[2] Dept. de Lenguajes y Computación, Universidad de Almería, España
mtorres@ual.es

Abstract. The ODMG standard does not include the 'definition of derived classes', characteristic that has been recognized as a fundamental aspect for the development of object-oriented applications in order to customize existent classes. For the purpose of not subtracting functionality to object-oriented databases (OODB) with respect to relational databases, a mechanism to define derived classes must be offered. Such a mechanism, which allows the dynamic selection of objects, can be used as a shorthand in queries, and makes easier the integration of heterogeneous databases. Besides, to define derived classes, the problem of obtaining the identifiers of their objects must be solved. In this paper, we propose a mechanism to define derived classes in ODMG. In our mechanism, the identifiers of the new objects are defined according to their *core attributes* only.

1 Introduction

The conceptual schema of an OODB consists of a set of classes. These classes, called *non-derived classes*, describe the initial requirements of information of users. In OODB, *derived classes* are similar to *relational views*, and they are defined from other existent classes to customize them in some way (e.g., hiding information). However, the current specifications of the ODMG (*Object Data Management Group*) standard [5] does not include the possibility of defining derived classes.

The ODMG standard basically consists of an object model, an Object Definition Language (ODL), an Object Query Language (OQL), and several bindings to object-oriented programming languages.

The ODMG object model allows the definition of *interfaces*, *classes* and *literals*: an *interface* specifies the abstract behaviour of an object type; a *class* specifies the abstract behaviour and state of an object type; finally, a *literal* only specifies the abstract state of a literal type. In this object model, the definition of *named queries* was proposed as a basis to define views. However, a *named query* cannot be used to define others *named queries*. Therefore, *named queries* are not enough as a mechanism to define views (i.e., derived classes).

In this work, we present a proposal for the definition of derived classes in ODMG databases, and our main contributions are:
 1. A solution for obtaining identifiers of objects in derived classes.

2. A syntax, based on OQL, for the definition of derived classes that allows both object preserving and generating semantics.
3. An extension of ODMG metadata that allows to include in the ODMG schema repository information about derived classes.

The paper is organized as follows. In Section 2, related work is revised. In Section 3, the object identifiers and its impact in the definition of derived classes is introduced. In Section 4, our proposal to define derived classes to ODMG is described, and an example is shown. In Section 5, the ODMG metadata and ODL extensions required by our proposal are put forward. Finally, Section 6 conclusions and future work are presented.

2 Related Work

A derived class is defined from one or several *base classes*, which may be derived or non-derived; the set of attributes that are used in its definition are called *base attributes*. The objects in a derived class are called *derived objects*, while the objects in base classes, which participate in the definition of a derived object, are called *base objects*. Like in relational views, a query language can be used to define derived classes in OODB.

The definition of a derived class can be carried out using two kinds of semantics: (1) *Object preserving semantics* [14, 18, 23] if it only contains objects of their base classes; and (2) *Object generating semantics* [1, 2, 4, 13] if it contains new objects generated from objects of their base classes. The object preserving semantics allows that derived classes provide a new view of existing classes. The object generating semantics allows reorganizations of the information stored in the database that would be impossible otherwise (e.g., transforming values into objects, or making an aggregation of objects in order to obtain a new one).

When derived classes are created, the schema where they will be integrated, and the position in such a schema must be determined. *The positioning problem* deals with finding the most appropriate place in the class hierarchy to locate them [2, 11]. Several approaches have been proposed to solve this problem: generating intermediate classes to integrate the derived class [18, 23]; defining new relationships between derived classes and their base classes in user schemas with the purpose of making easier the integration [11, 14, 22], extending so the object-oriented paradigm. These solutions serve as reference for our work, which is based on the use of the *derivation relationship* proposed in [20].

With respect to the schema where derived classes are integrated, in [2, 6, 15, 21], derived classes are directly integrated in external schemas; in [9] they are integrated in the conceptual schema, while in [18, 23] they are integrated in the *global schema*, which includes all classes of the conceptual schema, all classes in external schemas, and intermediate classes generated to integrate derived classes. Our work is based on [19], where the integration in the repository is proposed, allowing the reutilization of existing definitions, and keeping intact the conceptual schema.

The above mentioned proposals define their mechanisms on particular models instead of defining them on a standard. The development of the ODMG standard has lead to some researchers to define their proposals according to this standard [7, 8, 17]. However, they allow only the definition of derived classes with object preserving semantics. Recently, an ODMG extension to define external schemas [25] has been presented; this extension includes the basic support to define derived classes and interfaces in ODMG databases. Our proposal is based on this extension.

3 Object Identification in OODB and Derived Classes

The *umbral model* [16] establishes that an essential property for an OODB system is the *object identity*. This property is based on the fact that the existence of an object is independent of its content. Furthermore the *identity* [10] allows us to distinguish between an object and another one.

The unique identification is included in the logical level by an *object identifier* (OID); this OID is usually transformed in the physical level by another one generated by the system, which has the responsibility about its uniqueness and its use (e.g., for relating some objects with others). Currently, most of the OODB management systems allow us to distinguish between *objects* and *literals* [6]; each object has an immutable OID, while a literal does not have OID, and it is represented by itself. Other systems also allow us to create complex structured values without necessity of an identifier.

The most important characteristic of an OID is the *immutability*, i.e., the value of an identifier for a particular object cannot change. In consequence, the concept of object identifier is different from the notion of key in the relational model, because an OID is independent of the value of a state of the object, and a key is defined by the value of one or more attributes. Furthermore, two different objects can have different identifiers although their states are identical. The ODMG object model supports the concept of key as a restriction of semantic integrity, but it is not used for object identification.

The support to *object identity* allows us to share objects among classes. In previous systems, the most used forms for sharing objects among derived classes were the same that were used among non-derived classes (by inheritance) or between non-derived and derived classes (by derivation with object preserving semantics).

To give support to *object identity* derived classes must be defined with object generating semantics, where each new object must have its own OID. Some authors [3, 12, 13] use Skolem functions for generating new identifiers. In these proposals a different Skolem function is used for each new derived class; so that, derived classes defined with object generating semantics cannot share objects with previous existent classes, since these functions generate values which depend on the derived class.

In our case, we follow the proposal given in [20], so that each derived or non-derived object is represented by an identifier. With respect to a derived object with object preserving semantics, the identifier is the same as its base objects, but if the derived object is obtained with object generating semantics, its identifier will be obtained from their *core attributes* [2, 24, 26]. The set of *core attributes* will be a subset of the set of base attributes; however, it is not necessary that all attributes of *core attributes* are included in the derived class; furthermore, a subset of object identifiers of the different base classes can also be included among them.

Thus, two derived classes defined with object generating semantics can share objects without being related by inheritance or derivation. For such a purpose, it will be enough that they have the same set of *core attributes*.

4 A Proposal to Define Derived Classes in ODMG

When a derived class is defined, a name must be provided to identify it in order to define its attributes and operations. Also, as it has been mentioned in the previous section, it is essential to have a mechanism for assigning identifiers to their objects.

In this section, we propose a mechanism to define derived classes in ODMG databases with object preserving and generating semantics. For the latter, we use an object identifier generation method, which does not depend on the base classes, and it allows to share easily objects between derived classes defined with object generating semantics. Our proposal is illustrated with an example.

4.1 Syntax for the Definition of Derived Classes in ODMG

To generate a new derived object and its corresponding identifier, one needs to specify the name of the derived class and its attributes, the names of base classes and the attributes that define the identity of the derived class, as well as values of considered base attributes and the set of base objects that take part in the definition of the derived object.

Taking into account this situation, we propose a syntax (see Figure 1) that allows us to define a derived class in ODMG. This syntax is based on OQL, and on the works of Kifer *et al.* [13] and Bertino [11]. Boldface words correspond to reserved words, and words in italics represent information that must be provided by the definer of the derived class.

```
define derivedClass derivedClassName [([parameterList])]
  as query
  [identityFrom baseClass |
   identityFunctionOf coreAttributes];
  [derivedClassOperations opSpecifications]
```

Fig. 1. Syntax for the definition of a derived class in ODMG

With this syntax, the creation of a derived class, called `derivedClassName`, is specified. The option `parameterList` represents a list of couples (data type, attribute name) separated by commas; if this option is not used, then attribute names of the derived class are the same as the attribute names of their base classes; the use of parenthesis is also optional. The `query` syntax is the same of OQL; in this clause a query can be specified, and the attributes of the new derived class will be selected from the attributes of derived or non-derived classes previously defined; these classes will be the *base classes* of the derived class.

The semantics of the new derived class can be specified by some of the options in brackets at the end of the Figure 1. If no option is given, the semantics of the new derived class will be object preserving semantics obtained from a single base class. We suppose that a derived class with object preserving semantics may also be defined from several base classes by selecting objects of them, but taking its identity from only one of them; in such a case, we can use the option **identityFrom** baseClass, where it is specified that object identifiers of the derived class objects are obtained from the class specified in baseClass. If the option **identityFunctionOf** coreAttributes is used, a derived class will be defined with object generating semantics, using for the identification of the new objects the attributes of base classes specified in coreAttributes. Like in [13], it will be addressed as a Skolem function, which will generate the new identifiers from the values of the attributes expressed in coreAttributes; these attributes can also be identifiers. So, derived classes can share derived objects if those have the same coreAttributes, although common attributes have not been chosen in the definition of these classes.

Operations may also be included using **derivedClassOperations**. In this case, opSpecifications indicates the list of operations of the derived class separated by commas. Like in [11], each operation will match with one of the following ways:

a) operationName. It specifies the name of an existing operation in a base class.

b) opName1 **renameOperation** opName2. In this case, the operation opName1 renames to the operation opName2 of a base class; the operation opName1 will have the same parameters and the same definition as the operation opName2 in the base class.

c) opName (...). It indicates that opName is a new operation of a derived class. Its definition is carried out in ODL, like operations defined on non-derived classes. So, new operations can be defined in derived classes, and a new definition for an operation existing in a base class can be provided in the derived class too.

d) allOperations [of baseClassesList]. It indicates that all operations in all base classes or only operations of base classes specified in baseClassesList will be included in the derived class.

If **derivedClassOperations** is not specified, a derived class does not include the operations of their base classes, because, in general, these operations will not be valid in the derived class. In consequence, the user will specify what operations are allowed in the derived class.

In the definition of a derived class, name conflicts with attributes and operations can be found. In order to solve these conflicts and to avoid the ambiguity, we can apply the form given in OQL for the qualifiedName element.

4.2 Example of Derived Classes Definition in ODMG

Let us suppose a conceptual schema that includes the class Person and, for each object of this class, we know her name, her year of birth, and her credit card type, the credit card number and the expiration date. We will use this class for illustrating the derived classes definition method proposed in this work, obtaining, from it, two derived classes, Person' and CreditCard, as illustrates Figure 2.

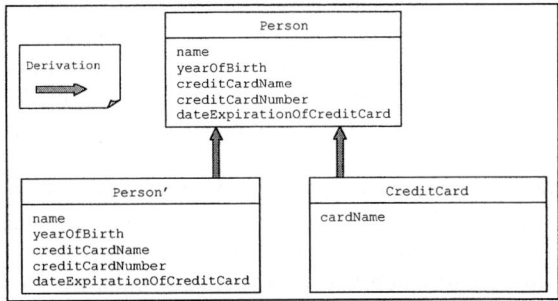

Fig. 2. Example of derived classes

Using the syntax proposed in Figure 1, we will obtain the derived class Person' with object preserving semantics (see Figure 3). This new class will have Person as base class; its attributes and its operations will be the same as the ones of base class and their objects will be all the persons born before 1970; moreover, the identifiers of their objects will be the same as those in its base class, because the identity is taken from Person as states **identityFrom**.

```
define derivedClass Person' as
    select *
    from Person
    where yearOfBirth < 1970
    identityFrom Person
    derivedClassOperations allOperations;
```

Fig. 3. Example of derived class with object preserving semantics

Next, we define the other derived class, CreditCard, using object generating semantics (see Figure 4).

```
ne derivedClass CreditCard(string cardName) as
select distinct creditCardName
from Person
identityFunctionOf Person.creditCardName
derivedClassOperations findCardName implementationOfFindCardName;
```

Fig. 4. Example of derived class with object generating semantics

This new derived class also has the class Person as base class, and the only existing attribute in it will allow us to know the various types of credit cards that people use. In this class, a new operation, findCardName, is defined and the objects will have a new identifier, which will be based on the value of the attribute creditCardName in the base class.

5 Extension of the ODMG Metamodel

To define derived classes with object preserving and generating semantics in ODMG databases, it is necessary to include new metadata in the ODMG repository. The extension that we propose is based on [25], which provides the basic support to define derived classes and interfaces, and it uses the *derivation relationship* to integrate derived classes in the repository. This relationship is modeled as an ODMG relationship, and it describes the relationship between a derived classes and its base classes.

Figure 5a shows the extension of the ODMG repository related with derived classes, proposed in [25]. In this extension, besides new metaclasses for *derived classes* and *interfaces*, abstractions *generic classes* and *generic interfaces* have been included. These abstractions describe characteristics common to non-derived and derived classes and interfaces, respectively. As can be observe, a derived class (or derived interface) can be defined from several existing generic classes (i.e., derived or non-derived), and from an existing class (or interface), several derived classes (or interfaces) can be defined too.

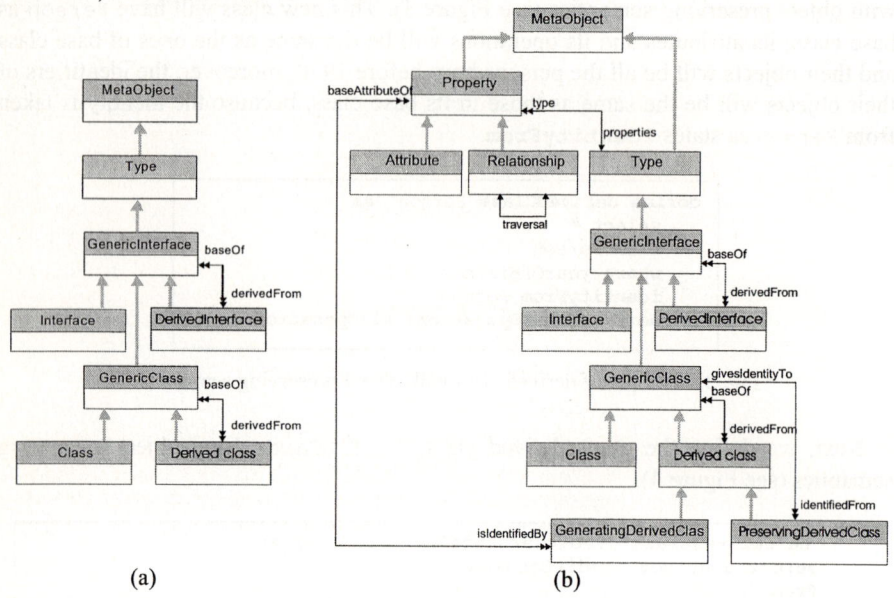

Fig. 5. ODMG metadata extensions

The extension shown in Figure 5a allows us to generate external schemas in a semiautomatic way, and to place derived classes in an automatic way into the repository. However, it only allows us to define derived classes with object preserving semantics. Our proposal uses this extension as a framework and incorporates new elements to complete the information stored in the repository. These new elements describe the following aspects: the semantics used to define the derived class, its base classes and the attributes that are used to identify derived objects. This new extension is shown in Figure 5b.

Before, we have to indicate how the information described in Figure 1 is stored in the repository: the name and parameters of the derived class and its operations are stored in it; `identityFrom` and `identityFunctionOf` are obtained from the new relationships between metaclasses.

In the new extension (Fig. 5b) two new specialized metaclasses of `DerivedClass`, called `PreservingDerivedClass` and `GeneratingDerivedClass`, have been included. These metaclasses allow us to distinguish, whether derived classes are defined with object preserving or generating semantics respectively.

To obtain OIDs for derived objects, two new relationships are added. One of them, between `GenericClass` and `PreservingDerivedClass` with cardinality 1:N. In this relationship, the role `givesIdentityTo` allows us to know which derived classes with object preserving semantics have used it in the identification of their objects for a concrete base class; the role `identifiedFrom` makes easier knowing, for a derived class, which base class the identifiers will be taken from. Other relationship with cardinality M:N is added between `Property` and `GeneratingDerivedClass`. Here, the role `baseAttributeOf` allows us to know, for a concrete attribute, which derived classes with object generating semantics have used it as one of their *core attributes* in the identification of their derived objects; the role `isIdentifiedBy` specifies, for a derived class defined with this semantics, which are its *core attributes*.

Changes introduced in the metamodel involve the introduction of some modifications that affect to definitions given in ODL for the metadata `GenericClass` and `Property` (see Figure 6). These modifications appear in italics.

```
interface GenericClass: GenericInterface {
  attribute list<string> extents;
  attribute list<string> keys;
  relationship set<ModuleClasses> extender
    inverse ModuleClasses::correspondsToSubclasses;
  relationship set<ModuleClasses> extensions
    inverse ModuleClasses::correspondsToSuperclasses;
  relationship set<DerivedClass> baseOf
    inverse DerivedClass::derivedFrom;
  relationship set<PreservingDerivedClass> givesIdentityTo
    inverse PreservingDerivedClass::identifiedFrom;
  ... ...
};

interface Property: MetaObject {
  ... ...
  relationship set<GeneratingDerivedClass> baseAttributeOf
    inverse GeneratingDerivedClass::isIdentifiedBy;
  ... ...
};
```

Fig. 6. Definitions modified in ODL

Also, it is essential to add the definition in ODL of `PreservingDerivedClass` and `Generating-DerivedClass` (see Figure 7).

```
interface PreservingDerivedClass: DerivedClass {
  relationship set<GenericClass> identifiedFrom
    inverse GenericClass::givesIdentityTo;
  ... ...
};

interface GeneratingDerivedClass: DerivedClass {
  relationship set<Property> isIdentifiedBy
    inverse Property::baseAttributeOf;
  ... ...
};
```

Fig. 7. New definitions in ODL

Therefore, with this proposal we have the required framework that enables the definition of derived classes in ODMG with object preserving and generating semantics.

6 Conclusions and Future Work

The ODMG object model does not include support to define derived classes. Some proposals have been defined in order to incorporate such functionality into the standard. However, these proposals only allow the definition derived classes with object preserving semantics.

In this paper we have put forward an approach to define derived classes in ODMG databases with object preserving and generating semantics, which includes: A syntax to define derived classes based on OQL, and an extension of the ODMG schema repository that implies the modification of related metadata. Another distinctive characteristic of our proposal with respect to others is that identifiers of derived objects are obtained from their *core attributes* only, without specifying a function name. This idea makes easier that two derived classes can share objects without being related by inheritance or derivation; other systems do not allow this.

Currently, we are working on the transmission of modifications at instance level between derived classes defined with object preserving and generating semantics and their corresponding base classes.

Acknowledgements

This work has been supported by the Spanish CICYT under project TIC2000-1723-C02-02. We would like to thank the anonymous reviewers for their helpful comments on earlier versions of this paper.

References

1. Abiteboul, S., Kanellakis, P.C.: Object Identity as A Query Language Primitive. In: Bancilhon, F. et al. (eds.): Building an Object-Oriented Databases Systems. The Story of O_2. Morgan Kaufmann Publishers (1992) 98-127
2. Abiteboul, S., Bonner, A.: Object and Views. ACM SIGMOD Int. Conf. on Management of Data (1991) 238-247
3. Abiteboul, S. et al.: Data on the Web: From Relations to Semistructured Data and XML. Morgan Kaufmann (2000)
4. Bellahsene, Z.:Updates and object-generating views in ODBS. Data & Knowledge Engineering, Vol. 34. Elsevier (2000) 125-163
5. Cattell, R.G.G.: The Object Database Standard: ODMG 3.0. Morgan Kaufmann (2000)
6. Diskin, Z., Kadish, B.: Variable set semantics for keyed generalized sketches: formal semantics for object identity and abstract syntax for conceptual modeling. Data & Knowledge Engineering, Vol. 47, **1**. Elsevier (2003) 1-59
7. Dobrovnik, M., Eder, J.: Adding View Support to ODMG-93. ADBIS (1994) 62-73
8. García-Molina, J. et al.: Extending the ODMG Standard with views. Information and Software Technology, Vol. 44. Elsevier (2002) 161-173
9. Geppert, A. et al.: Derived Types and Subschemas: Towards Better Support for Logical Data Independence in Object-Oriented Data Models. TR 93-27. Univ. Zürich (1993)
10. Guarino, N., Welty, C.: Identity, Unity, and Individuality: Towards a Formal Toolkit for Ontological Analysis. ECAI. IOS Press (2000) 219-223
11. Guerrini, G. et al.: A formal Model of Views for Object-Oriented Database Systems. TAPOS, Vol. 3, **3** (1997) 157-183
12. Hull, R. et al.: On Data Restructuring and Merging with Object Identity. IEEE Data Engineering, Vol. 14, **2** (1991) 18-22
13. Kifer, M. et al.: Querying Object-Oriented Databases. ACM SIGMOD Int. Conf. on Management of Data (1992) 393-402
14. Kim, W., Kelley, W.: On View Support in Object Oriented Database Systems. In: Modern Database Systems (1995) 108-129
15. Lacroix, Z. et al.: Object Views. Networking and Information Systems, Vol. 1, **2-3** (1998) 231-250
16. Meyer, B.: Construcción de software orientado a objetos. Prentice Hall (1999)
17. Roantree, M. et al.: Providing Views and Closure for the Object Data Management Group Object Model. Information and Software Technology, Vol. 41 (1999) 1037-1044
18. Rundensteiner, E. A.: Multiview: A Methodology for Supporting Multiple Views in Object-Oriented Databases. VLDB (1992) 187-198
19. Samos, J.: Definition of External Schemas in Object Oriented Databases. OOIS (1995) 154-166
20. Samos, J.: Definition of External Schemas and Derived Classes in Object-Oriented Databases. PhD. Thesis. Univ. Politècnica de Catalunya, Barcelona (1997)
21. Santos, C.S. et al.: Virtual schemas and bases. EDBT (1994) 81-94
22. Santos, C.S.: Design and Implementation of Object-Oriented Views. DEXA (1995) 91-102
23. Scholl, M.H. et al.: Updatable Views in Object-Oriented Databases. DOOD (1991) 189-207
24. Tejada, S. et al.: Learning object identification rules for information integration. Information Systems, Vol. 26, **8** (2001) 607-633
25. Torres, M., Samos, J.: Extending ODMG Metadata to Define External Schemas. Journal of Object Technology, Vol. 2, **2** (2003) 183-202
26. Welty, C., Guarino, N.: Supporting ontological analysis of taxonomic relationships. Data & Knowledge Engineering, Vol. 39. Elsevier (2001) 51-74

methods are to prove cardinality faithful and terminating. For example, when an entity is inserted, all associated binary relationships are studied to see whether their cardinality constraints are not violated. So, asking the user for all relationships related to the inserted entity is required and this process is repeated until constraints are satisfied. In order to terminate propagation a null entity could be inserted.

Our work addresses the issue of insert operations because an inserted instance in the database needs to satisfy the cardinality constraints with all associated elements, and to insert more than one instance at a time could be required. Therefore, in this paper a method to divide the relational schema of a database into several subschemata is proposed. This solution will reduce the number of objects in each subschema and consequently to reduce the number of objects that must be verified when an insert operation is performed. The final objective is to simplify the complex implementation of verifying cardinality constraints. We believe that an insertion operation could be easier controlled if few associated elements are verified whatever approach is used. We will do this by taking advantage of the definition of the optional and fuzzy participations [12]. So, we consider that the optional and the fuzzy participation roles are end points of verifying the cardinality constraints in a relational schema. The fuzzy participation roles are used in many works such as [13] where several fuzzy conditions on each instance have been defined and a trigger that checks the value of a quantifier is used to verify these conditions. If this value is less than the minimum percentage that constraints must satisfy in a database, then the DBMS must produce an error message informing about the non-fulfilment of this constraint.

3 Total/Partial and Fuzzy Participations

Let $R = (r_1E_1, \ldots, r_nE_n, A_1, \ldots, A_s)$ be a n-ary relationship with s attributes, where each r_i is the role that plays an entity E_k in the relationship R (Figure 2).

We define R^t as a set of instances in R. An element r^t in R^t is a vector of n components, where each r_i position in the n-vector represents a participation role, and it contains an instance of the entity identifier which participates with that role. Thus, a set of the instances R^t of R is a subset of the Cartesian product of the identifier instances of the entities that participate in R and the attribute domains that belong to it.

$$R^t \subseteq r_1E_1 \times \ldots \times r_n E_j \times dom(A_1) \times \ldots \times dom(A_s) \qquad (1)$$

Therefore:
$|R^t|$ = Number of instances that belong to R.
$|E_1|$ = Number of instances that belong to E_1.

According to the definition of cardinalities in [3], we define the cardinality constraints of an entity E_i as;

$$Card(E_i, R^t) = (n,m), \text{ IFF } n \le |\{a_1,\ldots, a_{i-1}, a_{i+1},\ldots,a_n \in E_1,\ldots,E_{i-1}, E_{i+1}, \ldots E_n \:/\: (a_1,\ldots, a_{i-1}, a_i, a_{i+1},\ldots,a_n) \in R^t\}| \le m \quad (2)$$

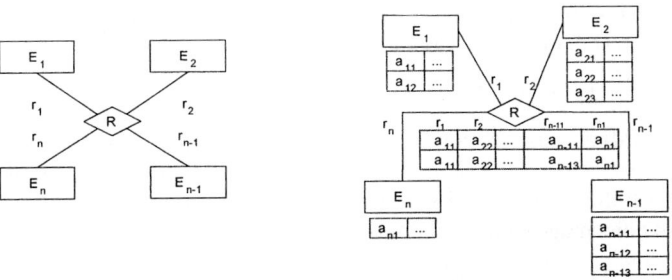

Fig. 2. Representation of a n-ary relationship R and the set of instances associated to it

A set of instances that fulfils the minimum and maximum cardinality constraints (n, m), is defined as;

$$C_i = \{a_1,\ldots, a_{i-1}, a_{i+1},\ldots,a_n \in E_1,\ldots,E_{i-1}\ldots, E_{i+1}, \ldots E_n \:/\: n \le |\{(a_1,\ldots, a_{i-1}, a_i, a_{i+1},\ldots,a_n) \in R^t\}| \le m\} \quad (3)$$

Therefore:
$|C_i|$ = Number of instances that fulfil the cardinality constraints of E_i.

$|C'_i|$ = Number of instances that not fulfil the cardinality constraints of E_i.

We propose to use a relative quantifier Q_{ri} that shows the percentage of instances that not fulfil the cardinality constraint in the role r_i of the entity E_k in a relationship R, as shown:

$$Q_{ri} = |C'_i| * |R^t|^{-1} \quad (4)$$

The quantifier Q_R shows the percentage of semantic loss in a n-ary relationship R and be calculated as shown:

$$Q_R = \sum_{i=1}^{n} (|C'_i| * |R^t|^{-1}) \quad (5)$$

We can easily calculate this quantifier in a real database applying directly the previous equation (4) on each element associated with a relationship. This will give us an idea about the percentage of the instances that do not fulfil the cardinality constraints in this role, and help us to decide improving the verification of the cardinality constraints. It is possible to predefine a maximum limit to semantic loss, but when this value increases significantly, the improvement mechanisms could be enabled to recover the semantics. These mechanisms could be enabled or disabled depending on the actual cardinality semantics. For example, in certain relationships if the predefined limit is ($Q_R <= 0.002$) then the improvement mechanisms should be activated when ($Q_R > 0.002$).

In the total participation it is necessary to ensure that all instances must fulfill the cardinality constraints of the role r_i, that is, ($|C'_i|=0$), whenever an insertion operation is performed, the semantic loss percentage in this role must be $Q_{ri}=0$.

$$Q_{ri} = |C'_i| * |R^t|^{-1} = 0 * |R^t|^{-1} = 0$$

With the partial participation we could have instances that do not fulfil the cardinality constraints of the role r_i. Therefore, the cardinality constraint of r_i could be consistent when the value ($|C'_i|>0$), whenever an insertion operation is performed, the semantic loss percentage of this relationship could be $Q_{ri}>0$.

$$Q_{ri} = |C'_i| * |R^t|^{-1} > 0$$

We define the fuzzy participation similarly to the partial participation i.e., let R be a relationship and E_i, E_j are the entities involved in this relationship. If the role r_i corresponds to total participation in R and there is an instance in E_i which does not satisfy the constraints then we define this case as fuzzy participation role. Therefore, the cardinality constraint of r_i could be consistent when the value ($|C'_i|>0$), whenever an insertion operation is performed, the semantic loss percentage of this relationship could be $Q_{ri}=[0,1]$.

$$Q_{ri} = |C'_i| * |R^t|^{-1} \in [0, 1]$$

4 Relaxing Cardinality Constraints

Taking into account the designer's point of view, there are two types of elements that can be distinguished in a EER schema; first order elements are the most important in the model and they always need mechanisms to verify its constraints, especially for these objects, it would be very useful applying the fuzzy participation; and second order elements, less important in the schema and which do not requiere to verify its constraints at the same time when a modification is done, so it would be useful applying a polling system and periodically verification.

Our method could be used on an actual database, where the developer or the administrator of a database can periodically gathers statistics about each element in it, these statistics are used to know exactly where the semantic losses are produced. A quantifier Q_{ri} is calculated for each role in the schema, if the value of any quantifier is greater than the predefined limit, a verification tool such as triggers system or others could be activated. It is not a good way to increases the number of ends points because this produces a high loss of cardinality semantics.

A partial view of a schema for a university is used to illustrate the approach of verifying cardinality constraints, figure (3). The two relationships in the ER schema are translated into relations containing as foreign keys the primary keys of the associated entities. The foreign key options (***On Delete Cascade*** and ***On Update Cascade***) are available to both relations.

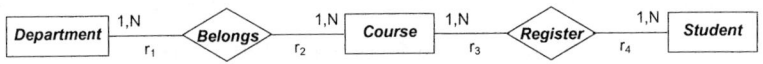

Fig. 3. ER schema for the case study

The cardinality constraints are verified by using a trigger-based approach [5] when deleting or updating the PKs, FKs are produced. But, the insertion operations need more effort to verification. For example, when inserting a tuple into ***Course***, it is very necessary to satisfy the roles r_2, r_3 because each course belongs to at least one department and one or several students have to be registered in each course. But, what happen if we need to relate the inserted course to a new student or a new department?. So, we must satisfy also the roles r_1, r_4. In such model, controlling the cardinality constraints needs complex predefined systems, and this may be produce other problems in the execution model of these systems or an impact on the database performance.

So, we suggest here that achieving more precise verification is very important whenever a high percentage of semantic loss is produced. In a real database, we can calculate this percentage in each element. These percentages give us an image of the semantic loss in the schema, as well as the elements that need to be verified. So, we need to gather statistics at time *t* about the instances participating in each entity and each role. In our example, at *t* there are 28 departments, 1244 courses, 16538 students, 3318 tuples in ***Belongs***, and 114564 tuples in ***Register***. From these, 4 courses in r_2, 6 courses in r_3, and 13 students in r_4 are not participating in any relationships. The semantic loss percentage in each relationship objects $Q_{Belongs}$ and $Q_{Register}$ are calculated from equation 5, as shown:

$$Q_{Belongs} = (|C'_{r1}| + |C'_{r2}|) * |R^t._{Belongs}|^{-1}$$
$$= (0*3318^{-1} + 4*3318^{-1})*100 \cong 0.12\%$$

$$Q_{Register} = (|C'_{r3}| + |C'_{r4}|) * |R^t._{Register}|^{-1}$$
$$= (6*114564^{-1} + 13*114564^{-1})*100 \cong 0.017\%$$

The quantifier $Q_{Belongs}$ shows the percentage of the instances that do not satisfy the cardinality constraints in ***Belongs***. While $Q_{Belongs}$ shows the percentage of the instances that do not satisfy the cardinality constraints in ***Register***. Here, the database designer would decide if the semantic loss percentages are high or not. According to his decision, the cardinality constraints could be verified. Nevertheless, we think that as priority, we must do the best in those elements which have high semantic loss such as ***Belongs***.

But yet, in large database schemata the verification needs to be more simply. Moreover, we can consider only those roles that have high quantifier. The semantic loss percentage in each participations roles r_1, r_2, r_3 and r_4 are calculated from equation 4, as is shown below:

$$Q_{r1} = |C'_{r1}| * |R^t._{Belongs}|^{-1} = 0 * 3318^{-1} *100 = 0$$

$$Q_{r2} = |C'_{r2}| * |R^t._{Belongs}|^{-1} = 4 * 3318^{-1} *100 = 0,12\%$$

$$Q_{r3} = |C'_{r3}| * |R^t._{Register}|^{-1} = 6 * 114564^{-1} *100 = 0,005\%$$

$$Q_{r4} = |C'_{r4}| * |R^t._{Register}|^{-1} = 13 * 114564^{-1} *100 = 0,011\%$$

When the previous results are compared, we find that r_2 has the highest percentage of semantic loss. Although the participation type in all roles is total, the developer should give the priority to r_2 when he wants to verify the constraints. In such a way, we propose a method to select only those roles that need to be verified, saving much effort and time, reducing the errors, and getting better results when we evaluate the database performance.

Let the relation **Department** with 28 tuples and let each department associated to the same number of **Course**, then this number ($n_{i.r1}$) is calculated by dividing the total number of the tuples in **Belongs** by the total number of departments in **Department**, and let us do the same to find ($n_{i.r2}$, $n_{i.r3}$, $n_{i.r4}$) as is shown below:

$$n_{i.r1} = |R^t._{Belongs}| * |E_{DEPRTS}|^{-1} = 3318 * 28^{-1}$$
$$\cong 118$$
(each department is related to 118 Courses).

$$n_{i.r2} = |R^t._{Belongs}| * |E_{COURSES}|^{-1} = 3318 * 1244^{-1}$$
$$\cong 3$$
(each course is related to 3 departments).

$$n_{i.r3} = |R^t._{Register}| * |E_{COURSES}|^{-1} = 114564 * 1244^{-1}$$
$$\cong 92$$
(each course is related to 92 students).

$$n_{i.r4} = |R^t._{Register}| * |E_{STUDENTS}|^{-1} = 114564 * 16538^{-1}$$
$$\cong 7$$
(each student is related to 7 Courses).

This example shows clearly that the major semantic losses are produced in r_2, r_4, therefore, more efforts are required to verify it than to verify r_1, r_3. But, in the case of deletions or updates the verification of r_1, r_3 should be more important than r_2, r_4, because if an old department is deleted without semantic verification many relationships ($\cong 118$) may be deleted from **Belongs** because of the referential integrity actions. This deletion may be lead to damage in cardinalities semantics more than if an old student and his relationships ($\cong 7$) are deleted.

These results can be extended to database design phase, i.e., the designer of the database who has the better knowledge about the Universe of Discourse, could consider the following aspects during the database design:

- It is possible to leave without verification the roles that have total participation if the associated elements to these roles have a fixed number of instances or the insertion operations that are produced in these objects are very limited. But, in this case we must carefully verify the remaining operations such as deleting and updating. For example, **Department** has a fixed number of departments and consequently the insertion operations on it are very limited.

- In a binary relationship if the entities have approximately the same number of instances, then we can verify the entity, which gets more modifications (insert, delete, and update) at t. For example, if the numbers of instances in E_1, E_2, R^t are $|E_1|$, $|E_2|$, $|R^t|$ respectively, and ($|E_1| \cong |E_2|$). Let we suppose that 30% and 5% of the instances are modified in E_1, E_2 respectively. The total instances in R^t that are modified by the referential integrity rules are ($e_{i.r1} = 0.3 * (|R^t| * |E_1|^{-1})$) and ($e_{i.r2} = 0.05 * (|R^t| * |E_2|^{-1})$). Because of ($|E_1| \cong |E_2|$), we find that ($e_{i.r1} > e_{i.r2}$). So we can say that E_1 has more modifications at t and consequently its cardinality constraints need more verification.

5 Conclusions

The cardinality constraint is one of the most important constraints that can be established in a conceptual schema but the verification of these constraint is very difficult, especially in the case of insertions due to logical model constructs are not coincident with the conceptual model ones. Therefore, our work is addressed to the issue of the insertion operations. Some research prototypes have performed different and complex methods to solve this problem. Some solutions would lead to other problems such as the complex execution model or the impact on the database performance.

We propose a method to simplify the verification of cardinality constraints although three aspects have to be considered; (1) a minimum threshold of temporarily semantic loss in cardinality constraints could be allowed, it is measured periodically as a relative quantifier, and calculated by dividing the total number of the instances which do not fulfil the constraints by the total number of the instances in the associated relationship; (2) the designer should trust in his own design, because he must decide this threshold depending on the importance of each element; (3) the database must be periodically submitted to a polling system to recover the losses of cardinality constraints.

References

1. Elmasri, R. Navathe, S.: Fundamentals of Database Systems, Third Edition, Addison-Wesley, 2000.
2. Toby J. Teorey: Database Modeling & Design, third edition, Morgan Kaufmann Series in data management systems, 1999.
3. Teorey, T., Yang, D., Fry, J. A Logical Design Methodology for Relation Databases Using the Extended Entity-Relationship Model. Computer Surveys, Vol. 18. No. 2. 1986.
4. Il-Yeol Song, Mary Evans, E.K. Park, A Comparative Analysis of Entity-Relationship Diagrams, Journal of Computer and Software Engineering, 3(4), 427-459, 1995.
5. Chen, P.: The Entity-Relationship Model – Toward a Unified View of Data, ACM Transactions on Database Systems, Vol. 1, N. 1. 1976.

6. D. Cuadra, C. Nieto, E. Castro, P. Martínez M. Velasco: Preserving relationship cardinality constraints in relational schemata, Database Integrity: Challenges and Solutions, Ed: Idea Group Publishing, 2002.
7. H. Al-Jumaily, D. Cuadra, P. Martínez. PANDORA CASE TOOL: Generating triggers for cardinality constraints verification in RDBMS. IADIS International Conference, Portugal, 2003.
8. H Al-Jumaily, D. Cuadra, P. Martínez. Incorporando Técnicas Activas para la Conservación de Semántica en la Transformación de Esquemas. VIII Jornadas de Ingeniería del Software y Bases de Datos 12-14 Noviembre 2003, Alicante.
9. Norman W. Paton, Active Rules in Database Systems, Springer-Verlag, New York, 1998.
10. Lazarevic, B., and Misic. Extending the entity-relationship model to capture dynamic behaviour. European Journal Information Systems 1 (2) pp. 95-106. 1991.
11. Balaban, M., and Shoval, P. MEER - An EER model enhanced with structure methods. Information Systems 27, pp 245-275, 2002.
12. Guoqing Chen, Fuzzy Logic in Data Modeling; Semantic, Constraints, and Database Design. Kluwer Academic Publishers, London 1998.
13. Galindo J., Urrutia A., Carrasco R., Piattini M.: Fuzzy Constraints using the Enhanced Entity-Relationship Model. XXI International Conference of the Chilean Computer Science Society, (Chile). 2001.

In Support of Mesodata in Database Management Systems

Denise de Vries[1], Sally Rice[1,2], and John F. Roddick[1]

[1] School of Informatics and Engineering
Flinders University of South Australia
PO Box 2100, Adelaide, South Australia 5001
{Denise.deVries,Sally.Rice,roddick}@infoeng.flinders.edu.au
[2] School of Computer and Information Science
University of South Australia,
Mawson Lakes, South Australia 5095,
sally.rice@cis.unisa.edu.au

Abstract. In traditional relational database modelling there is a strict separation between the definition of the relational schema and the data itself. This simple two level architecture works well when the domains over which attributes are required to be defined are relatively simple. However, in cases where attributes need to be defined over more complex domain structures, such as graphs, hierarchies, circular lists and so on, the aggregation of domain and relational definition becomes confused and a separation of the specification of domain definition from relational structure is appropriate. This aggregation of domain definition with relational structure also occurs in XMLS and ontology definitions. In this paper we argue for a three level architecture when considering the design and development of domains for relational and semi-structured data models. The additional level facilitating more complete domain definition - mesodata - allows domains to be engineered so that attributes can be defined to possess additional intelligence and structure and thus reflect more accurately ontological considerations. We argue that the embedding of this capability within the modelling process augments, but lies outside of, current schema definition methods and thus is most appropriately considered separately.

1 Introduction

The common view of relational data modelling and relational database structures (and as a result database languages) is to consider the specification of attributes, normally defined over a restricted set of domains, as part of table definition. When the user's requirements indicate that attributes need only be defined over relatively simple (normally DBMS-supplied) domains this is generally adequate. However, in more complex applications, domain structure becomes an important issue and even for some simpler applications, there is often advantage to be gained from utilising more sophisticated domains, such as concept graphs [1], hierarchies [2], intervals [3], and so on. In practice, this rarely occurs and where it

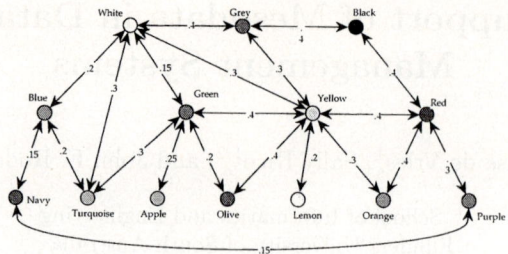

Fig. 1. Example Colour Chart as Weighted Graph

```
RelA                                RelB
   PartId            CHAR(5)           PartId           CHAR(5)
   Description       CHAR(20)          ItemDesc         CHAR(20)
   Colour            CHAR(8)           ItemCol          CHAR(6)
   Category          CHAR(10)          ItemType         CHAR(12)
   SupplierCategory  NUM(5)
```

does, design decisions often mean that implementations are inconsistent and not transferable. This research focuses on the utility of augmenting the information capacity of the attribute domain in a reusable and systematic manner. This also has the advantage of reducing the size of ontology definitions and allowing them to focus on the specific characteristics of the concept.

Our approach is thus to retain the overall structure and operations of the relational model and to enhance the capability of the attribute domain to handle more advanced semantics. We do this by more clearly delineating between domain definition - mesodata - and schema definition - metadata. This approach can be considered as falling between the basic relational (minimalist) approach in which there are only a very limited number of common domains, and the object-relational model in which commonality is facilitated through reuse. This pragmatic, middle-ground approach reflects the approach taken in research areas such as temporal, spatial and multi-dimensional modelling which argue for a flexible but unified way of handling common modelling problems. Indeed, using mesodata may facilitate better accommodation of such extensions.

As an example, consider the problems resulting from the logical integration of data from two databases defined over different schemata for the purposes of executing database queries, as shown in Figure 1. While Description and ItemDesc may be semantically equivalent (and thus simply merged), Category may exist within a product hierarchy in which ItemType is a non-leaf node, Colour and ItemCol may take their values from nodes of a graph of colours (such as that in Figure 1) and SupplierCategory may have no equivalent attribute. Consider now the following query executed over the combined data and using a hybrid schema RelAB:

```
SELECT    PartId, Colour
FROM      RelAB
WHERE     Category = 'Electrical'
AND       Colour = 'Green'
```

One response could be to utilize the colour graph to *translate* ItemCol to the closest defined Colour and to use the product hierarchy to convert instances of ItemType to Category. Moreover, this could be achieved automatically if the DBMS had access to appropriate domain definitions. Unfortunately, in many cases the overhead of creating these definitions is large and other options, such as coercing data to a common format, is adopted. Indeed in practice, the constraints imposed by DBMS often have a large impact on design decisions.

In addition to the simplifications inherent for design and implementation issues, if we adopt the accommodation of 'intelligent' domains we can also utilise them to provide richer querying capability. For example, if an attribute is defined over a hierarchy or a graph, we can entertain advanced semantic concepts such as *descendant, closeness* and so on [1, 4]. In the example below, the operators INTREE and CLOSETO are defined to operate over specific mesodata types[1].

```
SELECT    PartId, Colour
FROM      RelAB
WHERE     Category INTREE 'Electrical'
AND       Colour CLOSETO 'Green'
```

To extend our example further, if we consider the different aspects of colour that interest us – the shade, the intensity and so on – then the context will determine the interpretation of which colours are considered close but the overall structure of the domain as a graph is context-independent, eg.

```
SELECT    PartId, Colour
FROM      RelAB
WHERE     Category INTREE 'Electrical'
AND       Colour CLOSETO(Intensity) 'Green'
```

In short, what is important is that any ontology/data model for an attribute should permit the user to determine the interpretation in isolation from the representation used, and to do this an ontology might need to adopt a more complex underlying data structure such as (in the case of colour) a typed graph.

In this work we suggest that common domain structures, such as graphs, queues, circular lists, and so on, if available as mesodata *complete with appropriate operations and associated DBMS support*, would both simplify and enhance data modelling. We argue that the inclusion of a mesodata layer in the definition of attribute domains introduces more flexibility into the modelling process, promotes re-use, increases the level of abstraction, and simplifies the implementation of schema change. A further aspect discussed in this paper (but not covered in depth) is that of multiply-typed attributes. Such a concept would allow attributes to be *physically* represented in two or more different formats, which would more seamlessly facilitate heterogeneous data management and schema integration. Space precludes a full discussion of this aspect of the work with the paper focussing on the definition and use of mesodatatypes.

The paper is structured as follows. In Section 2 we argue that this approach is not dissimilar to other extensions to the relational model. It also discusses ontologies and conceptual graphs while Section 3 outlines in detail our proposals. Section 4 outlines some modifications to SQL and our implementation. A conclusion is given in Section 5.

---

[1] We have adopted the convention of using alphabetic operators for our extensions for clarity.

2 Related Work

Much research has concentrated on dealing with important domains in special-purpose data models which incorporate common operations for their domains and their effects on the relational operations. Ontologies and concept graphs are other techniques for including more semantic information in domains. The development of these techniques has highlighted the need for common languages to allow the exchange of knowledge between similar representations and underly much of the research into the *semantic web*. This section presents a brief overview of some of this work.

2.1 Intelligent Domains

The success of the relational model has led to many attempts to extend it to accommodate additional semantics. Some of these extensions, such as semi-structured data models, do not entail specific changes to domain definition and will not be further considered here. Of those entailing changes to domains, some have been successfully developed into well-accepted data models that have progressed from research-only to varying levels of deployment, such as temporal and, to a lesser extent, spatial, while others are still largely experimental. In this research we adopt the term *intelligent domains* for our enhanced mesodata generated domains because of the increased semantic content that they provide. This mirrors work in a number of areas which attempt to extend the relational model to capture the semantics of a particular aspect of reality. Some of these domains are described below.

Temporal. The development of temporal databases to support various aspects of time has led to a general consensus on the requirements for any temporal data model. This includes the definition of a standard temporal query language TSQL2 with a data model which supports both point (*instant timestamp*) and interval (*period timestamp*) time values [5]. Within this model the underlying time domain can be viewed as either continuous, dense or discrete (i.e. isomorphic to real, rational or integer numbers respectively) [6]. Algebras describing the possible binary relationships between time points and intervals have also been formally defined [3, 7].

Spatial. Spatial data modelling is becoming an increasingly important for GIS, environmental modelling and image processing. Spatial data, usually existing in 2- or 3-dimensional space, is inherently more complex than 1- or 2-dimensional temporal data, and this complexity has given rise to formal definition methods based on *point set theory, point set topology, algebraic topology* and *order theory* [8]. It is conceptually more difficult to formally describe relationships between two spaces than between two times. Egenhofer and Franzosa [9] introduce a set of binary spatial relations for formally describing relationships between spatial regions using point-sets and the topological concepts of *boundary* and *interior*.

Probabilistic. The probabilistic relational model proposed by Dey and Sarkar [10] introduces a probability stamp pS for tuples where $0 < pS \leq 1$. This probability represents the likelihood of the tuple to be true. The basic algebra operations are redefined for this model, and the concept of the primary key is altered to cope with the fact that unique real world objects may have more than one set of values in a probabilistic relation.

Each of these domains entails change to the underlying domain of attributes as well as a set of operators over them. We can generalise these and other applications by defining underlying domain structures such as graphs, circular lists, interval and so on. Moreover, it is also important to consider these domains in combination with each other. For example, the interaction of time and space has lead to research into spatio-temporal databases [11], and the need to accommodate imperfect information exists with all the basic data types. For example, for temporal intervals Freksa [12] introduces the concept of a temporal *semi-interval*, where only the start or the end of the interval is known. We believe that the inclusion of a mesodata layer within which these domain structures and their operations can be defined will facilitate their use, thus encouraging more semantic information to be included in databases.

2.2 Ontologies

An ontology is a formal, explicit description of concepts in an area of interest (domain of discourse). It is *a vocabulary of such terms (names of relations, functions, individuals), defined in a form that is both human and machine readable.* [13]. The three areas that benefit from using ontologies, as identified by Jasper and Uschold [14], are *Communication* - by providing consistency, lack of ambiguity, and integration of different perspectives, *Inter-operability* - by providing computer systems with an interchange format for translation between languages, representations and paradigms, and *Software Engineering* - by providing a shared understanding for specification, resulting in re-use and improved reliability. The main components of an ontology are *concepts* or *classes* of the domain which are often organised in taxonomies, *relations* describing the types of interaction between concepts, *functions* such as definitions of calculated attributes, *axioms* specifying rules and/or constraints, and *instances* to represent specific elements.These components are then defined in an ontology in terms of *Concepts*, (a.k.a. classes, categories, types, terms, entities, sets and things),*Slots*, (a.k.a. roles, properties, relations, relationships, associations, functions and attributes), and*Facets*, (a.k.a. role restrictions, criteria, constraints, features and predicates). As can be inferred from the alternative labels and terms for the constituent parts of an ontology, there is no single standard for the structure and design of an ontology. Ontology representations are broadly categorised by Wache *et al.* [15] as one of frame-based systems, description logics, formal concept analysis, object languages or annotated logics.

The strength of ontologies lies in their being a shared computer-based resource. As Meersman and Jarrar point out [16] *an ontology needs to be even more generic, across tasks and even task types, than a data model is for a number of given applications. Justadding a mere is_a-taxonomy of terms is not sufficient, as the literature sometimesseems to suggest. An ontology needs to include (the meaning of) a much richer set of relationships, such as* instance_of, part_of, ..., *which depending on the domain allmight deserve a 'generic semantics'.* Thus,

$$Vocabulary + Structure \Rightarrow Taxonomy \qquad (1)$$

and

$$Taxonomy + Relationships + Rules + Constraints \Rightarrow Ontology. \qquad (2)$$

Although it may seem desirable to have a single ontology to simplify sharing and integration of concepts, this is not always possible. An ontology may serve multiple users' perspectives and their applications, and striving to be all things to all users can produce an ontology that is difficult to build, maintain and use. Many, for example, run to many hundreds of lines of definition.

We propose a model where multiple ontologies may be utilised to represent the mesodata layer. An ontology created for an attribute domain, in whichever representation is preferred, will hold the structure as well as the processing logic for mesodatatype's deployment. For example, an ontology for a weighted graph with the CLOSETO operator as described in Section 1.

2.3 Concept Graphs

Concept Graphs are another medium by which concepts can be represented in a human and computer readable way. The Conceptual Graph Standard [17] provides a guide for the implementation of conceptual graphs in systems. The conceptual graph is *an abstract representation for logic with nodes called concepts and conceptual relations linked together by arcs*. These provide an abstract model which can be used at different levels; conceptual and implementation. Conceptual graphs (CG) were developed for the representation of natural language semantics and are designed for communication with humans or between humans and machines. Sowa [18] contends that CGs *...can help form a bridge between computer languages and the natural languages that everyone reads, writes, and speaks*. The conceptual graph is generally in a visual format and is represented in machine-readable text format using CGIF (Conceptual Graph Interchange Format) syntax. The CGIF syntax is specified in terms of the Extended BNF (EBNF) rules and metalevel conventions. This syntax and structure also provides the basis for the construction of a mesodatatype.

2.4 Knowledge Interchange

Common Logic (CL) is currently being proposed as a new language standard for knowledge interchange. It aims in providing a superset for other interchange formats, such as KIF, CGIF, CLML (Common Logic Markup Language), and DL (Description Logics) so that content exchanged between Common Logic conformant languages has the same semantics in each language. The World Wide Web Consortium (W3C) is developing standards for two logic-based content languages for the semantic web: RDF (Resource Definition Facility), a language for expressing relationships and OWL (Web Ontology Language), a language for expressing constraints. People involved in the W3C project are also involved in CL development ensuring that the Common Logic semantics are inherited by RDF and OWL. An RDF graph, for example, is represented in an N-triple format which translated readily to a relation in a relational database.

There has been a significant amount of work done in recent years in the research and development of techniques for utilising ontologies and conceptual graphs for the semantic web. The aim being for highly distributed systems to share, relate and combine information over the web. We envisage that these techniques are also applicable to relational database development. Currently ontologies and interchange formats are viewed as resources that are positioned *outside* a user's information system and are used as an aid for the design of metadata, for the translation of concepts or for transformation of related concepts. However, they could be an integral part of an RDMS with an interface positioned between data and metadata, ergo *mesodata*. The slots (attributes) already defined in an ontology can be a valuable resource for databases if they are accessed through *mesodata*, with ramifications for attribute domain evolution, data integration and querying.

Schema evolution and ontology evolution share many of the same problems and solutions which are discussed by Roddick [19] and Klein [20] respectively. Extending the relational model to utilise these methods adds a powerful new dimension to database information systems.

3 Mesodata and Multiply-Typed Attributes

Currently, when defining an attribute within a schema, elementary types, such as integer, string and so on, are available together with operators for comparison and manipulation. Such types are supplied as they are both common and useful. However, there are many other instances of domain structures for which standardised and supplied definitions would be a practical enhancement, particularly to facilitate data integration, schema and domain evolution processes.

3.1 Multiply-Typed Attributes

It is often the case that the data stored exists in a variety of types, one of which is chosen to be the storage representation. We argue that this can result in information loss and thus our overall model aims to accommodate multiply-typed attributes (MTAs). For example, colours could be stored as a three-byte hexadecimal value or a 10 character standard description with a mesodatatype *translating* between the two. This would mean that the original semantics of the value are maintained. It would also facilitate domain evolution (such as in the lazy conversion method of Tan and Katayama [21]).

Note that the concepts of complex mesodata domains and that of multiply-typed attributes are somewhat independent — it can be conceived of an attribute being defined over a single mesodata domain and an attribute over multiple base domains. We discuss them together in this paper as they mutually support each

Domain Structure	Operations (Extended SQL Op.)	Source Relation(s)
Unweighted Graph (GRAPH)	Adjacency (NEXTTO)	Binary relation (FROM, TO)
Weighted Graph (WGRAPH)	Adjacency, Proximity (CLOSETO)	Ternary relation (FROM, TO, WEIGHT)
Directed Graph (DGRAPH)	Adjacency	Binary relation (FROM, TO)
Directed Weighted Graph (DWGRAPH)	Adjacency, Proximity	Ternary relation (FROM, TO, WEIGHT)
Tree (TREE)	In subtree (DESCENDENT), Parent(PARENT), Ancestor(ANCESTOR), Child(CHILD), Sibling(SIBLING)	Binary Relation(PARENT, CHILD)
Weighted Tree (WTREE)	In subtree, Parent, Ancestor, Sibling, Proximity	Ternary Relation(PARENT, CHILD, WEIGHT)
List (LIST)	Next (NEXT), Previous (PREV), First(FIRST), Last(LAST), Between(BETWEEN)	Binary Relation(SEQUENCE, ITEM)
Circular List (CLIST)	Next, Previous, Between	Binary Relation(SEQUENCE, ITEM)
Synonyms (SYNONYM)	Primary Term (PRIMARY)	n-ary Relation(PRIMARYTERM, SECONDARYTERMS)
Set (SET)	In Set(INSET)	Unary Relation(ITEM)
Tri-State Logical	Maybe Equal (MAYBE)	None

Table 1. Partial List of domain structures suitable for adoption as mesodata types. This list is deliberately abbreviated as it is beyond the aim of this paper to discuss which domains would be appropriate for inclusion. Note that the SYNONYM mesodatatype is the only one that handles multiple basetypes

other in terms of the semantics and functions they provide. However, we do not discuss MTA's in this paper in depth.

3.2 Mesodata Definition

The usual practice when using, for instance, graphs is to include code in the application for depth-first or breadth-first traversal, topological ordering, finding the shortest path between selected nodes, calculating nearest and furthest nodes, and so on. We maintain that those operations that relate to the domain rather than the data value or the application should reside closer to the structure of the database than to the populated values of the database. However, it is difficult to position them in the metadata. We therefore argue that there should be *mesodata* layer between the metadata and the data. The metadata holds the 'intelligence' for the data type and provides the link between the base data type, an optional ontology and the database application. Note that it is not the goal of this paper to exhaustively list the types of mesodata that might be made available, although a partial list is given in Table 1. However, any candidate mesodata type would be commonly used and have a generally agreed and stable semantics.

An important distinction must be made between the provision of, say, a graph as a mesodata type and the provision of a graph as a data type. In the former, the attribute would take as its value an instance of an elementary type that exists *within a graph* while in the latter the type is a graph. Unlike the provision of libraries of ADTs, the graph itself is not directly accessible or manipulable through the attribute.

3.3 Formal Specification

The semantics of information held in a database can be considered as a function of the data value. That is,

$$S = F(v) \tag{3}$$

where F is a function external to the database that maps the (strongly typed) data value v to its meaning S. An example would be mapping the day number 1 to the understood concept of the first day of the working week. The introduction of a mesodata layer allows regularly used mappings to be accommodated in the database. Conceptually, you can have mappings of mappings, ie.

$$S = F(M_1^i(M_2^i(\ldots M_k^i(v^i)\ldots))) \qquad (4)$$

where the M^i are mesodata layer mappings for the value when in base type i. For our example we could have $S = F(M_1^i(M_2^i(1))$ where $M_2^i(1) = \text{'Monday'}$ and $M_1^i(\text{'Monday'}) = \text{'Lundi'}$. Formally, a mesodata domain D_k^i is a set of identically typed values $\{v_1^i, \ldots, v_n^i\}$ taken from either a simple domain or another mesodata domain D_j^i such that $M : D_j^i \rightarrow D_k^i$ is a mapping that provides a relationship based on the semantics of the structure between the instances. An instance d^i of D_k^i is either one of the enumerated values $\{v_1^i, \ldots, v_j^i\}$ or, if permitted, another value of the same base type. Implicit in this is that a domain defined over a mesodata type, as for base domains such as CHAR, INT etc., is:

- a DBMS-supplied structure consisting of a uniformly agreed data structure consisting of either other mesodata types or elementary data types;
- a set of common and uniformly agreed operators over the structure.

An attribute defined over such a domain would take an *instance* of an elementary value which would exist within the mesodata structure. Thus, in our previous example for the attribute 'colour', the base type would remain unchanged (eg. CHAR(8)). However, the value might exist within a graph of colours and operations such as *Find all parts with a colour close to red* would not then require specific code within the application but would be handled by the DBMS through reference to the mesodata type.

Note that in many implementations, for a multiply-typed attribute, the base type used in a mesodata domain M^i might be the same as one of the base representations and a synonym of another thus allowing some resilience to existing applications when the base representation changes. Thus to extend the example above, the storage of new "colours" as a three-byte RGB value could have a mesodata domain of SYNONYM which translated new values to the older CHAR(8) format.

Mesodata can be represented in an ontology, using one of the aforementioned forms, which describes the concept, its operations, rules and constraints. As with all ontologies this can be re-used, shared, linked with other ontologies and can evolve.

4 Proof-of-Concept Implementation

In this section we illustrate our ideas by showing the relatively simple extensions that can be accommodated into a database language such as SQL and discuss our implementation.

A major argument of this work is the separation of domain and schema definition. This is reflected in the use of the (extended[2]) CREATE DOMAIN statement which allows for the creation of domains which can then be referenced in CREATE TABLE statements. The basic format is as follows:

```
CREATE DOMAIN    dom
                 AS          mesodatatype
                 OF          basedom
                 (RETURNS    returndom)
                 OVER        sourcerel {(attributes)}
                 EXCLUSIVE | NONEXCLUSIVE
```

where `mesodatatype` is one of the supplied mesodata domains, as suggested in Table 1, `basedom` is either a simple domain, such as INT, CHAR, etc. or a previously definition mesodata domain and `relname` is the relation, defined as required by `mesodatatype`. The EXCLUSIVE | NONEXCLUSIVE option indicates whether values not present in `sourcerel`, but still consistent with `basedom` are to be rejected or allowed. We take the view that maintaining the source as user tables facilitates both reuse and amendment. The term `attributes` allows flexibility in what columns are chosen from existing `sourcerel`s. The RETURNS clause is used only by the SYNONYM type which returns values of type `returndom` but uses `basedom` as a storage representation. A similar DROP DOMAIN statement can be defined as follows:

```
DROP DOMAIN      dom
                 CASCADE | RESTRICT
```

The CASCADE | RESTRICT option indicates whether the `sourcerel` is to be deleted or retained. Using the example in Section 1, we could define the Category attribute as:

```
CREATE DOMAIN    categories
                 AS          tree
                 OF          CHAR(12)
                 OVER        categoryrel
CREATE DOMAIN    colours
                 AS          weightedgraph
                 OF          CHAR(8)
                 OVER        colourgraph
CREATE DOMAIN    hexcolours
                 AS          synonym
                 OF          CHAR(3)
                 RETURNS     COLOURS
                 OVER        hextotext
CREATE TABLE     RelAB
                 PartId              CHAR(5) NOT NULL
                 Description         CHAR(20)
                 Colour              COLOURS, HEXCOLOURS
                 Category            CATEGORIES
                 SupplierCategory    NUM(5)
                 PRIMARY KEY ...
```

Regarding the definition of the domains, if they did not already exist, the tables `categoryrel` and `colourgraph` would be defined (but not populated)

---

[2] The CREATE DOMAIN statement is an existing, but largely ignored extension present in SQL2 and SQL99.

according to the requirements of the mesodata types. If the tables already existed they would be checked for conformity with the mesodata requirements. Moreover, we envisage that these tables could be augmented as long as the minimum requirements for the operation of the types were maintained. Note also the multiple domains defined for Colour. Having defined an attribute over a mesodata type, additional operations would become available according to the mesodatatype selected. It is beyond this paper to enunciate an exhaustive list but some are provided in Table 1. These would be used in the same way as current operations are provided as illustrated in Section 1.Note that more complex domain structures could be built. For example:

```
CREATE DOMAIN   coloursets
                AS              list
                OF              colours
                OVER            listrel
```

would create a list of graphs. In this case listrel would contain the names of relations holding the colourgraphs.

We have implemented these changes using wrappers over the MySQL software [22]. Two additional metarelations were required – an ATTDOM relation to correlate attributes to their mesodata domains (this would not be required in an embedded implementation) and a DOMREL relation to hold the domain definitions.

5 Conclusion and Future Directions

The principle idea argued in this paper is the logical and pragmatic separation of schema definition from domain definition. While the idea has been used implicitly in a number of previous research efforts, the contribution of this paper is the formalisation of an explicit split between metadata and mesodata. We believe that this approach has many benefits, not the least of which is the simplification of complex database design. The enunciated changes to SQL are examples only, but they do serve to show that such an enhancement is backwards compatible with current methods of definition and also serve to illustrate the simplicity of what is a relatively major change in database design.

Further work in this area is progressing, particular in using mesodata to alleviate some of the problems encountered in schema evolution and integration and in the accommodation of imperfect data. Other work, not currently being tackled by our group, includes extending the mesodata concept to other aspects of conceptual modelling such as, for example, UML, XMLS and the semantic web.

References

1. Roddick, J.F., Hornsby, K., deVries, D.: A unifying semantic distance model for determining the similarity of attribute values. In Oudshoorn, M., ed.: 26th Australasian Computer Science Conf. (ACSC2003). Volume 16 of CRPIT., Adelaide, Australia, ACS (2003) 111–118

2. Rice, S., Roddick, J.F.: Lattice-structured domains, imperfect data and inductive queries. In Ibrahim, M.T., Küng, J., Revell, N., eds.: 11th Int. Conf. on Database and Expert Systems Applications (DEXA2000). Volume 1873 of LNCS., Greenwich, London, UK, Springer (2000) 664–674
3. Allen, J.: Maintaining knowledge about temporal intervals. CACM **26** (1983) 832–843
4. Kedad, Z., Metais, E.: Dealing with semantic heterogeneity during data integration. In Akoka, J., Mokrane, B., Comyn-Wattiau, I., Metais, E., eds.: Eighteenth Int. Conf. on Conceptual Modelling. Volume 1728 of LNCS., Paris, France, Springer (1999) 325–339
5. Snodgrass, R., ed.: The TSQL2 Temporal Query Language. Kluwer Academic Publishing, New York (1995)
6. Dyreson, C.E., Soo, M.D., Snodgrass, R.T.: The data model for time. In Snodgrass, R.T., ed.: The TSQL2 Temporal Query Language. Kluwer Academic Publishers (1995) 97–101
7. Vilain, M.: A system for reasoning about time. In: National Conf. on Artificial Intelligence, Pittsburg (1982) 197–201
8. Schneider, M.: Spatial Data Types for Database Systems. Volume 1288 of LNCS. Springer (1997)
9. Egenhofer, M., Franzosa, R.: Point-set topological spatial relations. Int. Journal of Geographical Information Systems **5** (1991) 161–174
10. Dey, D., Sarkar, S.: A probabilistic relational model and algebra. ACM Transactions on Database Systems **21** (1996) 339369
11. Abraham, T., Roddick, J.F.: Survey of spatio-temporal databases. Geoinformatica **3** (1999) 61–99
12. Freksa, C.: Temporal reasoning based on semi-intervals. Artificial Intelligence **54** (1992) 199–227
13. Gruber, T.R.: A translation approach to portable ontology specifications. Knowledge Acquisition **5** (1993) 199–220
14. Jasper, R., Uschold, M.: A framework for understanding and classifying ontology applications. In: IJCAI99 Workshop on Ontologies and Problem-Solving Methods(KRR5), Stockholm, Sweden (1999)
15. Wache, H., Vogele, T., Stuckenschmidt, H., Schuster, G., Neumann, H., Hubner, S.: Ontology-based integration of information a survey of existing approaches (2002)
16. Meersman, R., Jarrar, M.: Formal ontology engineering in the dogma approach. In Meersman, R., Tari, Z., eds.: CoopIS/DOA/ODBASE 2002. Volume 2519., Springer-Verlag (2002) 1238–1254
17. Sowa, J.F.: Conceptual graph standard (2001)
18. Sowa, J.F.: Knowledge Representation: Logical, Philosophical, and Computational Foundations. Brooks Cole Publishing Co., Pacific Grove, CA, USA (2000)
19. Roddick, J.F.: A survey of schema versioning issues for database systems. Information and Software Technology **37** (1995) 383–393
20. Klein, M., Fensel, D., Kiryakov, A., Ognyanov, D.: Ontology versioning and change detection on the web. In Gmez-Prez, A., Benjamins, V.R., eds.: Knowledge Engineering and Knowledge Management. Ontologies and the Semantic Web, 13th Int. Conf. LNCS, Siguenza, Spain, Springer (2002) 197–212
21. Tan, L., Katayama, T.: Meta operations for type management in object-oriented databases - a lazy mechanism for schema evolution. In Kim, W., Nicolas, J.M., Nishio, S., eds.: First Int. Conf. on Deductive and Object-Oriented Databases, DOOD'89, Kyoto, Japan, North-Holland (1989) 241–258
22. MySQL: SQL shareware software, MySQL AB Co. (2003)

Moderate Concurrency Control in Distributed Object Systems

Yohsuke Sugiyama, Tomoya Enokido, and Makoto Takizawa

Dept. of Computers and Systems Engineering
Tokyo Denki University
{sugi,eno,taki}@takilab.k.dendai.ac.jp

Abstract. Objects are concurrently manipulated by multiple transactions in object-based systems. We newly introduce availability and exclusion types of conflicting relations among methods. Then, we define a partially ordered relation on lock modes showing which modes are stronger than others. We newly propose a moderate locking (ML) protocol. Here, an object is initially locked in a weaker mode than an intrinsic mode of the method. Then, the lock mode is escalated to the method mode. The weaker the initial mode is, the higher concurrency is obtained but the more frequently deadlock occurs. The ML protocol is evaluated in terms of throughput and deadlock compared with the pessimistic and optimistic locking protocol.

1 Introduction

In object-based systems [6], each object is an encapsulation of data and methods for manipulating the data. A method is a procedure which is more complex than *read* and *write*. An object is allowed to be manipulated only through methods. Multiple transactions issue methods to an object. There are two issues on conflicting relation, "a method conflicts with another method on an object *o*." One means that the result obtained by performing a pair of methods depends on the computation order from the serializability point of view [7]. Another type of conflicting relation means that multiple methods cannot be concurrently performed. Locking protocols are a synchronization means to realize the mutual exclusion of methods. An asymmetric lock mode *update* is introduced in addition to *read* and *write* modes [8] to increase the concurrency and reduce deadlocks. We introduce *exclusion* and *availability* relations among methods. The exclusion relation shows how exclusively each method can be performed. The availability relation indicates how frequently an object can be locked to perform each method. Based on the conflicting relations, we discuss what a *stronger* lock mode means.

In *pessimistic* approaches [2,4], an object is locked before manipulated by a transaction. An object is locked in *write* and *read* modes before the object is written and read, respectively. In *optimistic* approaches [5], a transaction manipulates an object without locking the object. It is validated that every object manipulated by a transaction has not been manipulated in a conflicting way by other transactions when the transaction commits. The transaction aborts unless validated.

An object is first read and then written by a transaction in order to update the object in typical transactions. In order to increase the throughput, every object is first locked in a *read* (r) mode in stead of *write* (w) mode. Then, a transaction reads the object. On writing the object, the lock mode of the object is changed up to w mode. If successfully changed, the transaction writes the object. Otherwise, the transaction waits. This way is *moderate* in between the pessimistic and optimistic ways. In this paper, we extend the way to methods on objects. An object is first locked in a *weaker* mode before manipulated in a method. Then, the object is locked in an intrinsic mode of the method on commitment of the transaction.

In section 2, we present a system model. In section 3, we discuss lock modes. In section 4, we discuss a moderate locking protocol. In section 5. we evaluate the protocol.

2 System Model

A system is composed of clients and servers $D_1, \cdots, D_n$ ($n \geq 1$) which are interconnected in reliable communication networks. Each server D_i supports applications with a collection of objects [6]. An object is an encapsulation of data and methods. An object is allowed to be manipulated only through its own methods. A method *conflicts* with another method on an object o iff the result obtained by performing the methods depends on the computation order. If some pair of methods are concurrently performed on an object, output or object state obtained by performing the methods is inconsistent. Here, each of the methods should be exclusively performed on the object. Thus, there are two aspects on conflicting relations; the serializability [2] of transactions and mutual exclusion of multiple methods on an object.

Transactions are performed on clients and application servers in 2-tier and 3-tier client server models, respectively. An transaction issues a method to manipulate an object in a server. The method is performed on the object. Then, the response with the result obtained by performing the method is sent back to the transactions. A *transaction* shows execution state of an application program which manipulates objects in servers. A transaction is modeled to be an atomic sequence of methods issued to objects, which satisfies ACID (atomicity, consistency, isolation, durability) properties [1]. A transaction T_1 *precedes* another transaction T_2 ($T_1 \rightarrow T_2$) iff T_1 and T_2 issue conflicting methods op_1 and op_2 to an object o, respectively, and op_1 is performed before op_2. A collection **T** of transactions $T_1, \cdots, T_n$ are *serializable* iff both $T_i \rightarrow T_j$ and $T_j \rightarrow T_i$ do not hold for every pair of transactions T_i and T_j in the transaction set **T** [1,2]. That is, the precedent relation is asymmetric. Objects are consistent if a set of transactions are serializable.

3 Lock Modes

3.1 Availability and Exclusion Sets

In traditional theories [2], a conflicting relation among *read* and *write* lock modes on a simple object like *table* is symmetric. For example, *read* conflicts with *write* while *write* conflicts with *read*. Korth [4] discusses an asymmetric conflicting relation with a new *update* (u) mode in addition to *read* (r) and *write* (w) modes. Here, w and u modes conflict with one another. However, the mode u is compatible with r but r conflicts with u so that r mode can be escalated to w mode without deadlock in a transaction. A transaction first locks an object in u mode and reads the object. Then, the transaction escalates the lock mode u to w mode to write the object. Even if other transactions lock the object in r mode, the transaction can lock the object in u mode. However, any transaction can neither lock the object in r mode nor w mode after the transaction holds the u lock. Transactions can update objects without deadlock.

Let $\mathbf{P}_o$ be a set of methods supported by an object o. Let $\mu(op)$ denote a lock mode of a method op on an object o. Let $\mathbf{M}_o$ be a set of modes on an object o, $\{\ \mu(op)\ |\ op \in \mathbf{P}_o\ \}$.

[Definition] A mode $\mu(op_1)$ *conflicts* with a mode $\mu(op_2)$ on an object o ($\mu(op_1) \triangleright \mu(op_2)$) iff op_1 cannot be performed while op_2 is being performed.

The conflicting relation $\triangleright$ on the mode set $\mathbf{M}_o$ may be neither symmetric nor transitive. A mode μ_1 is *compatible* with a mode μ_2 ($\mu_1 \not\triangleright \mu_2$) if μ_1 does not conflict with μ_2, i.e. $\mu_1 \not\triangleright \mu_2$. The compatibility relation $\not\triangleright$ is not symmetric either. Relations $\Diamond$ and $\Box$ show symmetric conflicting and compatibility relation on $\mathbf{M}_o$, respectively, i.e. $op_1 \Diamond op_2$ iff $op_1 \triangleright$ and $op_2 \triangleright op_1$, and $op_1 \Box op_2$ iff $op_1 \Diamond op_2$ does not hold.

We define an *availability* set $A(op)$ ($\subseteq \mathbf{P}_o$) and *exclusion* set $E(op)$ ($\subseteq \mathbf{P}_o$) of methods for every method op on an object o as $A(op) = \{op_1\ |\ \mu(op)$ conflicts with $\mu(op_1)$ ($\mu(op) \triangleright \mu(op_1)$)$\}$ and $E(op) \equiv \mu(op_1) \triangleright \mu(op)$. If the *conflicting* relation $\triangleright$ is symmetric, a *conflicting* set $C(op)$ is $\{op_1\ |\ \mu(op_1) \Diamond \mu(op)\}$ ($= A(op) = E(op)$).

First, a method op is issued to an object o. If any method in the availability set $A(op)$ is being performed on the object o, the method op cannot be performed, i.e. blocks. The larger the availability set $A(op)$ is, the less frequently a method op can be performed. Suppose $A(op_1) \subseteq A(op_2)$ for a pair of methods op_1 and op_2 on an object o. Here, op_2 cannot be performed on the object o if op_1 cannot be performed, i.e. some method conflicting with op_1 is being performed on an object o. However, even if op_2 cannot be performed, op_1 may be performed. Here, op_1 is *more available* than op_2 ($op_1 \succ_A op_2$). op_1 is *equivalent* (*A-equivalent*) with op_2 with respect to the available set A ($op_1 \equiv_A op_2$) iff $A(op_1) = A(op_2)$. $op_1 \succeq_A op_2$ iff $op_1 \succ_A op_2$ or $op_1 \equiv_A op_2$.

Next, suppose a method op is now being performed on an object. Even if a method op_1 in the exclusion set $E(op)$ is issued to the object o, op_1 cannot be performed. The larger $E(op)$ is, the more exclusively a method op is performed, i.e. the fewer number of methods can be concurrently performed with the method op. Suppose $E(op_1) \subseteq E(op_2)$ for a pair of methods op_1 and op_2 on an object and $\top$ be *bottom* and *top* modes, i.e. $\bot = \cap \{ \mu \mid \mu \in \mathbf{M}_o \}$ and $\top = \cup \{\mu \mid \mu \in \mathbf{M}_o \}$. The top mode $\top$ shows the most exclusive lock mode such that no other method can be performed on an object o with the mode $\top$ if the object o is locked in the mode $\top$. On the other hand, the bottom mode $\bot$ indicates the least exclusive mode such that every method can be performed on an object o even if the object o is locked in $\bot$. Here, $CM(\bot) = \phi$ and $CM(\top) = \mathbf{M}_o$. If an object supports only *read* and *write*, $\top = w$ and $\bot = r$.

Suppose a transaction T issues a method op_i to the object o. The object o is locked and then manipulated in the method op by the transaction T as follows:

[Locking Protocol]

1. The object o is locked in an initial mode β where $\bot \preceq \beta \preceq \mu(op)$
2. If locked, the method op is performed on the object o. Otherwise, the transaction T waits.
3. When the transaction T terminates, the initial lock mode β is escalated to the mode $\mu(op)$. If succeeded, T commits. Otherwise, T aborts. □

If $\beta = \bot$, the protocol is the most optimistic. If $\beta = \mu(op)$, the protocol is the most pessimistic. $\bot \prec \beta \prec \mu(op)$ in the moderate approach. The stronger the initial mode β is, the more pessimistic the protocol is. Let $NM(\mu)$ be a set of lock modes compatible with a lock mode μ. Here, $CM(\mu) \cap NM(\mu) = \phi$ and $CM(\mu) \cup NM(\mu) = \mathbf{M}_o$. In the protocol, $CM(\beta)$ should be a subset of $CM(\mu(op))$, i.e. $CM(\beta) \subseteq CM(\mu(op))$. We have to discuss which subset of $CM(\mu(op))$ to be selected as an initial lock mode β.

The weight $|\mu|$ shows the usage ratio, i.e. probability that a method of a mode μ is issued. The more frequently methods of the mode μ are issued, the larger $|\mu|$ is. $|\mathbf{M}_o| = |\mu_1| + \cdots + |\mu_h| = 1$ for $\mathbf{M}_o = \{\mu_1, \cdots, \mu_h\}$. Now, suppose that an object o is locked in a mode $\mu_1 \in \mathbf{M}_o$ and then the lock mode will be escalated to another mode $\mu_2 \in \mathbf{M}_o$ where $\mu_2 \succeq \mu_1$ by a transaction. The more number of lock modes are compatible with the mode μ_1, the more number of transactions can manipulate the object o. However, if transactions lock the object o in lock modes which are compatible with the mode μ_1 but conflict with μ_2, the lock mode μ_1 cannot be escalated to μ_2. Here, deadlocks may occur. $|NM(\mu_1)|$ shows probability that an object o can be locked by a method issued by another transaction after an object o is locked in a mode μ_1. $|NM(\mu_1) \cap CM(\mu_2)|$ indicates probability that a lock mode held after an object o is locked in a mode μ_1 conflicts with μ_2, i.e. the lock mode μ_1 on the object o cannot be escalated to μ_2. For example, suppose $|ini| = 0.01$, $|chk| = 0.59$, $|inc| = 0.2$, and $|dec| = 0.2$. $|CM(dec)| = |\{ini, chk\}| = |ini| + |chk| = 0.6$ and $|NM(dec)| = |\{dec, inc\}| = 0.4$. After the transaction T locks a *counter* object c in a *dec* mode, 40% of all transactions can lock the object c. $NM(ini) = \{\phi\}$ and $CM(ini) = \{ini, chk, inc, dec\}$. $|NM(dec) \cap CM(inc)| = |\{ini, chk\}| = 0.6$. A transaction T can escalate *dec* into *ini* with probability 0.6.

An initial lock mode $\beta \subseteq CM(\mu(op))$ is taken as follows:

- $|NM(\beta)|$ is the maximum, i.e. $|NM(\beta)| \geq |NM(\alpha)|$ for every mode $\alpha \in CM(\mu(op))$ and $|NM(\beta) \cap CM(\mu(op))| \leq \tau$ for the maximum allowable conflicting ratio τ (≤ 1).

The larger τ is, the fewer number of transactions are concurrently performed but the less frequently deadlocks occur. τ is given by the designer.

A transaction may manipulate an object o through multiple methods. For example, a transaction *increments* a *counter* object after *checking*. Suppose that a transaction T issues a lock of mode μ_2 to an object o after a mode μ_1. The lock mode of the object o is changed as follows:

1. If $\mu_1 \succeq \mu_2$, the lock mode μ_1 on the object o is not changed.
2. If $\mu_1 \preceq \mu_2$, the lock mode is escalated to μ_2.
3. Otherwise, the lock mode μ_1 is escalated to the least upper bound $\mu_1 \cup \mu_2$.

The lock mode on an object is monotonically escalated but never descended in a transaction [4].

5 Evaluation

We evaluate the moderate concurrency control protocol in terms of throughput and number of transactions aborted due to deadlocks. A system includes m objects $o_1, \cdots, o_m$ ($m \geq 1$) and each object o_i supports k_i ($k_i \geq 1$) types $op_{i1}, \cdots, op_{ik_i}$ of methods. Here, let $\mathbf{P}$ be a set of all methods $\mathbf{P}_{o_1} \cup \cdots \cup \mathbf{P}_{o_m}$. A conflicting relation $\Diamond_i$ among methods is assumed to be symmetric on every object o_i ($i = 1, \cdots, m$). The conflicting relation $\Diamond_i$ is randomly created. Here, the conflicting ratio σ_i is $|\Diamond_i| / k_i^2$. It is randomly decided whether or not every pair of methods op_s and op_t conflict with one another on the object o_i given the conflicting ratio σ_i. We assume $k_1 = \cdots = k_m = k$ and $\sigma_1 = \cdots = \sigma_m = \sigma$.

Each transaction T_s serially invokes l_s methods on the objects ($s = 1, \cdots, h$). A transaction T_s randomly selects a method op^{sj} in the mode set $\mathbf{P}$ and issues the method op^{sj} to the server ($j = 1, \cdots, l_s, l_s \geq 1$). The transaction T_s waits for the response. Here, we assume $l_1 = \cdots = l_h = l$. Suppose a transaction T_s issues a method op^{sj} to an object o_i. Here, the object o_i is first locked in an initial mode β_{sj} ($\preceq \mu(op^{sj})$). If succeeded, the object o_i is manipulated by the method op^{sj} and then T_s issues a succeeding method $op^{s,j+1}$. Otherwise, T_s waits. Finally, T_s terminates. Here, a lock mode on the object o_i for each method op^{sj} issued by T_s is changed to the mode $\mu(op^{sj})$. If succeeded, all the locks held by T_s are released. Otherwise, T_s waits. If transactions are deadlocked, one of the deadlocked transactions is randomly selected and aborted.

In this simulation, ten objects are assumed to be stored in one server ($m = 10$). Each object supports ten types of methods ($k = 10$). There are ten types of transactions ($h = 10$) and each transaction issues totally ten access requests ($l = 10$). ML stands for the moderate protocol. 2PL and OL indicate the pessimistic and optimistic protocols, respectively. The 2PL protocol is an ML protocol with $\beta = \mu(op)$ for each method op. OL is an ML protocol with $\beta = \bot$.

We measure the throughput [methods/time unit] and the number of transactions aborted due to deadlock for ML and 2PL protocols. We assume it takes one time unit to perform one method in presence of no other transaction. The maximum throughput is 1[methods/time unit]. One transaction is randomly selected at each time unit. One method of the transaction is performed. If an object is locked, the transaction waits. If some transactions are deadlocked, one of the deadlocked transaction is aborted. The transaction aborted is restarted. If all transactions commit, the simulation terminates. Figures 1 and 2 show the throughput and deadlocked transactions of ML, 2PL, OL for the conflicting ration σ [%]. In the simulation, the maximum allowable conflicting ration τ is 1.0. The larger σ is, the more number of conflicting methods. Following the figures, the moderate protocol ML implies larger throughput OL implies the fewer number of transaction aborted than ML and 2PL for $\sigma < 80$[%]than 2PL. In ML, fewer number of transactions are aborted for $\sigma < 30$[%] than 2PL. ML supports large throughput than OL for $\sigma > 20$ [%].

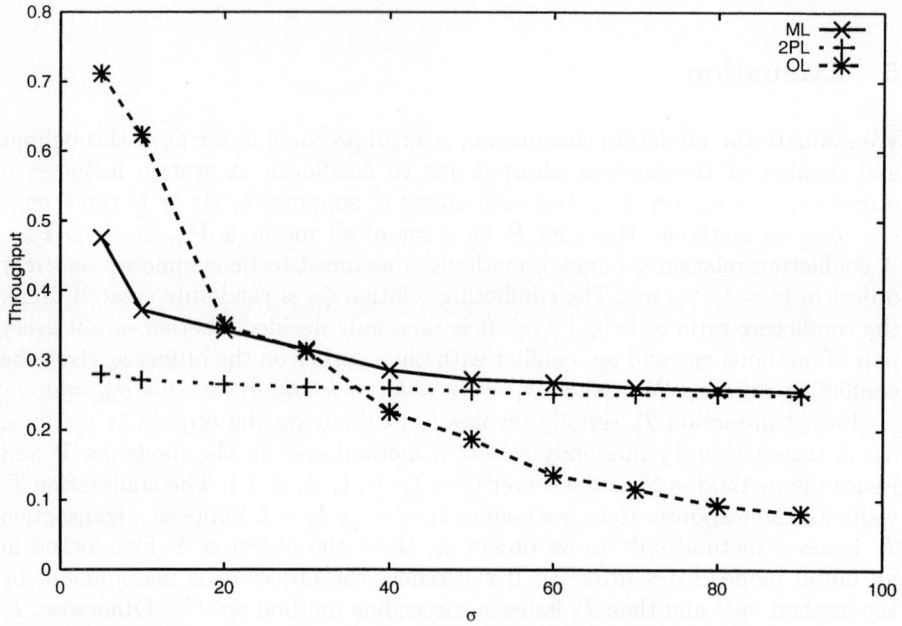

Fig. 1. Throughput [methods/time unit]

6 Concluding Remarks

We discussed the moderate type of locking protocol for objects. The moderate approach takes a position in between the pessimistic like two-phase locking protocol one and the optimistic one. A transaction initially locks an object in a weaker mode before manipulating the object by a method and escalates the initial mode to a mode of the method on commitment of the transaction. We discussed the moderate concurrency control protocol by extending the traditional pessimistic and optimistic protocols for read and write to objects with meth-

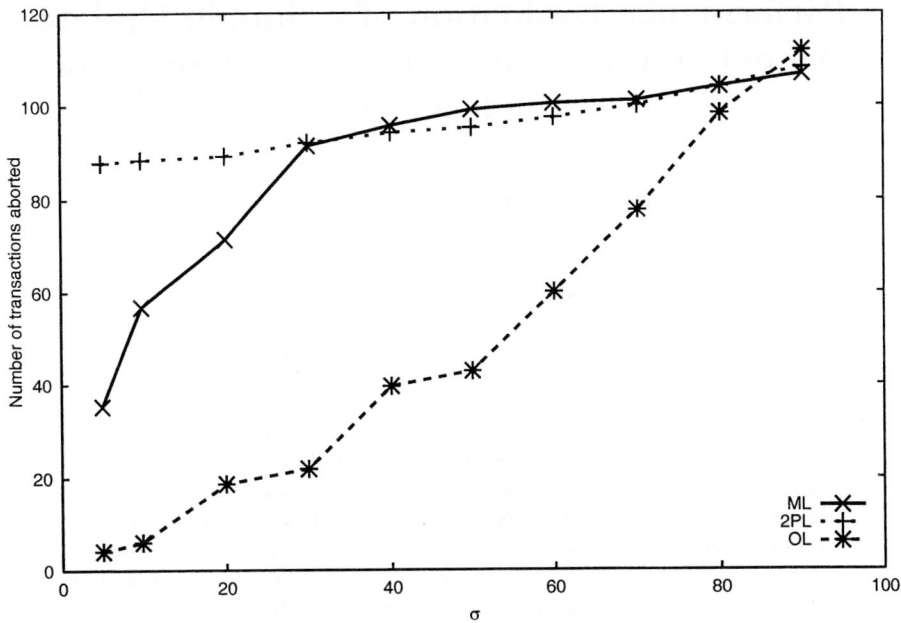

Fig. 2. Number of transactions aborted due to deadlock

ods. We showed the throughput can be increased and deadlocks can be reduced compared with traditional two-phase locking and optimistic protocols.

References

1. P. A. Bernstain, V. Hadzilaces, and N. Goodman. *Concurrency Control and Recovery in Database Systems.* Addison-Wesley, 1987.
2. J. Gray. Notes on Database Operating Systems. *Lecture Notes in Computer Science,* (60):393–481, 1979.
3. J. Jing, O. Bukhres, and A. Elmagarmid. Distributed Lock Management for Mobile Transacitons. *Proc. of the 15th IEEE International Conf. on Distributed Computing Systems (ICDCS-15),* pages 118–125, 1995.
4. H. F. Korth. Locking Primitives in a Database System. *Journal of the Association for Computing Machinery,* 30(1):55–79, 1983.
5. H. T. Kung and J. T. Robinson. On Optimistic Methods for Concurrency Control. *ACM Transactions on Database Systems,* 6(2):213–226, 1981.
6. J. Niwbray and R. Zahari. *The Essential CORBA.* Wiley, 1995.
7. K. Tanaka and M. Takizawa. Quorum-based Locking Protocol for Replicas in Object-based Systems. *Proc. of the 5th IEEE International Symp. on Autonomous Decentralized Systems (ISPADS 2001),* pages 196–203, 2001.
8. S. Yasuzawa and M. Takizawa. Uncompensatable Deadlock in Distributed Object-Oriented System. *Proc. of IEEE International Conf. on Parallel and Distributed Systems (ICPADS'92),* pages 150–157, 1992.

Performance Evaluation of a Simple Update Model and a Basic Locking Mechanism for Broadcast Disks

Stephane Bressan and Guo Yuzhi

School of Computing
Department of Computer Science
National University of Singapore
{steph,g0201747}@nus.edu.sg

Abstract. Broadcasting architectures in general and broadcast disks in particular outperform traditional client/server architectures when many clients read data from few servers. Yet several issues arise when the broadcasting model allows updates by the clients. These issues, most of which are related to the control of the concurrent access (isolation and consistency), are rooted in the asynchronous nature of the broadcast model and in the replication of data on the broadcast channel and in the caches of the clients.
In this paper we study the design and evaluate the performance of a simple update model controlled by a basic locking mechanism for broadcast disks architecture that involves replication on the broadcast channel and client caches.

1 Introduction

Broadcasting fits the requirement of more and more modern applications for the distribution of data. This is due to the nature of data (multimedia data or more generally streamed data, e.g. movies and radio programs [1]), to the ubiquity and multiplicity of devises consuming and producing data (personal computers in peer-to-peer environment, mobile phones and portable devices, and sensors, e.g. [2]) converging with the development of a global network infrastructure.

Broadcasting architectures in general and broadcast disks in particular outperform traditional client/server architectures when many clients read data from few servers (see e.g. [3]). Yet several issues arise when the broadcasting model allows updates by the clients. These issues, most of which are related to the control of the concurrent access (isolation and consistency), are rooted in the asynchronous nature of the broadcast model and in the replication of data on the broadcast channel and in the caches of the clients.

We study in this paper the design and evaluate the performance of a simple update model controlled by a basic locking mechanism for a broadcast disks architecture that involves replication on the broadcast channel and client caches

In the next section we review the related work. In section 3 we present the model we propose. After recalling the architecture of the reference client-server model, we incrementally introduce a model using a broadcast channel for updates and lock table at the server, a model using a multi-level broadcast disk, i.e. replication on the broadcast channel, and finally the complete multi-disk broadcast disks model with client cache. In section 4 we analyze the performance of the model and its variants. Finally we conclude.

2 Related Work

In the late nineteen eighties, a group of researchers proposed a radically new architecture for database management systems intended to maximize throughput. In this architecture, called the Datacycle [4, 5], the server cyclically broadcasts database objects on a broadcast channel. The clients monitor the broadcast channel for the objects they want to manipulate. Other communications with the server such as the management of update and concurrency control utilize an upstream channel from the clients to the server.

More recently in [3], the authors proposed in a read-only environment a cyclic broadcast mechanism using replication called the multi-level broadcast disks. Objects identified as being more frequently accessed have more replicas. From the clients' viewpoint - clients see the broadcast channel as a disk - the broadcast channel simulates a disk whose speed is commensurate to the frequency of access of each object. The authors showed that the multi-level broadcast disks can outperform a flat broadcast. In [6] the authors studied prefetching and caching at the clients' side and compared different replacement policies such as *LRU* and *LIX*. In [7], the same group incorporated an upstream channel in the broadcast disks architecture and studied the performance improvement yield by the balancing of the pushing of objects on the broadcast channel by the server and the pulling of objects by the clients. [7] also studied the tradeoffs between allowing updates on the server side and maintaining consistency in a broadcast disks model.

[8] proposed a complete concurrency control model for cyclic broadcast environment. The strategy is based on the broadcasting of a control matrix whose size is quadratic in the number of objects whose access is to be controlled (possibly the size of the database). Before a client reads an object from the broadcast channel, it must check the control matrix. The transactions are first executed locally on the client. They are then committed on the server. This method assumes a notion of broadcast cycle, i.e. some kind of guarantee about the order of messages.

In other architectures the control of concurrency in the presence of update and replication in clients caches has been studied. For instance, [9] proposed to maintain the consistency while allowing the replication and multiple versions. A client accesses objects whose latest access is within an interval that guarantees cache consistency. [10], in a mobile computing environment, proposed a solution to the problem of inconsistency in the client cache based on invalidation reports.

Since, in the mobile case, cache invalidation strategies are affected by the disconnection of the mobile clients, a taxonomy of cache invalidation strategies is also proposed and the performance of techniques in this classification studied.

3 Broadcasting Models with Updates at Client

Without loss of generality we consider in the discussions below a single server and several clients. Ultimately every computer in the network can play both roles simultaneously thus yielding a peer-to-peer architecture.

3.1 Client-Server Model

In the traditional client/server model the server manages objects. Such objects are often pages containing data elements. If a client needs to read or update a data element, it reads or updates the object or page that contains it. Clients must request to the server the objects for a read or a write operation. Read- and write-requests are sent by clients to the server by an upstream channel. The server controls the concurrent accesses by maintaining a lock table. Each entry in the lock table indicates, for any given currently accessed page, the type (read or write) and number of locks on the object as well as a queue of requests waiting on this object. If no potential conflict is detected in the lock table, the server delivers the requested object to the client on a downstream channel, otherwise the request is queued. Locks are set when requests are granted and released when responses are completed.

Such a standard mechanism is the basis for the implementation of concurrency control strategies for the interleaved execution of transactions. For instance it is the basis of the implementation of the classic two phase locking strategies guarantying serializability and recoverability properties for transactions.

3.2 Broadcast Channel with Updates and Locking

We now replace the upstream channel used by the clients to send their read- and write-requests and the updated objects by a single cyclic channel, which we call the broadcast channel.

Client. A client needing to read an object sends a read-request to the server on the broadcast channel. It then monitors the broadcast channel until the object to be read is at hand. The client removes the object from the channel, reads it, and places it back on the channel.

A client needing to update an object sends a write-request to the server on the broadcast channel. The client monitors the broadcast channel until the object to be updated is at hand. The client removes the object from the channel, updates it, and places it back on the channel. A client is allowed to read or update an object if it is tagged with a note identifying the client as the recipient. A client is not allowed to read or update an object tagged with a note identifying a different client as the recipient. A client is allowed to read any untagged object.

Server. The server maintains a lock table identical to the one used in the client-server model. When the server receives a read- or write-request it grants the request according to the lock table, i.e. updates the lock table and sends the object on the broadcast channel, else it queues the request. In the case of a write request the object sent is tagged with the identifier of the recipient (i.e. the client requesting the page for update). Read- and write-locks are released as untagged and tagged pages, respectively, come back to the server. The pages themselves serve as lock-release notices.

Discussion. There can be several copies of an untagged object, i.e. an object requested for read, on the broadcast channel. It is not necessary to indicate the recipient of the copy of an object requested for read and any client having requested an object for read can read any copy of the object. This is a potential source of higher throughput. There can however only be one copy of a tagged object, i.e. an object requested for update, exclusively of untagged objects on the broadcast channel. This is a potential bottleneck that we try to avoid with the extension presented in the next subsection.

3.3 Broadcast Disks with Updates and Locking

Except for a possible simultaneous copy of untagged objects, our model so far does not allow the replication of objects on the broadcast channel. In particular we it does not a controlled a priori replication of objects. In other words, our previous broadcast disk model had a single disk spinning at the lowest possible speed and we now present a model extending a multi-disk and multi-speed broadcast disks model following [3] to update and locking. We later refer to this model as the *broadcast disks* model.

Client. A client needing to read an object need not send a read-request to the server on the broadcast channel. It just monitors the broadcast channel until the object to be read is at hand. The client removes the object from the channel, reads it, and places it back on the channel.

As previously, a client needing to update an object sends a write-request to the server on the broadcast channel. The client monitors the broadcast channel until the object to be updated is at hand. The client removes the object from the channel, updates it, and places it back on the channel. The client must wait for an acknowledgment before it can read the same object again. This prevents it from reading an older version still on the broadcast channel. Otherwise, a client is allowed to read or update an object if it is tagged with a note identifying the client as the recipient. A client is not allowed to read or update an object tagged with a note identifying a different client as the recipient. A client is allowed to read any untagged object.

Server. The server sends one or more untagged copies of each object on the broadcast according to a predetermined policy (see [3] for details) thus simulating several disks spinning a different speed (the more copies the higher the speed).

The server maintains a lock table in which it records, for each object being used, the write-locks and the number of untagged copies currently on the broadcast channel. Write-locks are set as write-requests arrive. The copy counter is incremented as an untagged copy is sent on the channel and decremented as an untagged copy comes back to the server. When the server receives a write-request it grants it if there is no write lock for the requested object and sends the object on the broadcast channel, else it queues the request. The object sent is tagged with the identifier of the recipient (i.e. the client requesting the page for update). Write-locks are released as tagged pages come back to the server. The server resends every untagged object on the broadcast channel unless there is a write lock for the object. If there is a write lock untagged copies cannot be resent. An untagged copy can only be sent after the counter for the object has reached zero, i.e. all untagged copies have come back to the server, the updated page has come back to the server, and an acknowledgment of update has been sent to the client performing the update and has returned. When the condition is met the server can start resending the untagged copies of the new version of the object.

Discussion. In the case of an update, the client sends on the broadcast channel a write-request for an object. The server, after receiving the request, locks the object and sends a tagged copy (the tag indicating the recipient client) on the broadcast channel. The copy reaches its recipient which performs the update and places the (tagged) updated object on the channel. The server waits for the updated objects and all the untagged copies to return. It then sends an acknowledgment to the client. When the acknowledgment comes back the server can resume the broadcasting of the object, now in its updated version.

This policy guaranties that there is on the broadcast channel only one version of an object that can be read. As before the pages themselves serve as lock-release notices.

The model has no read-lock. Although the untagged copy counter plays a similar role to the one of the read-locks, the model does not seem to be able to cater for read-write conflicts. Indeed the counter is not involved in the granting of write-request. We remember that no synchronization among the clients is assumed. In particular there is no global clock and time. Furthermore the clients do not send read-requests. We can therefore freely consider that every read-request corresponding to a read made between the granting of a write request and the moment at which the updated page has arrived at the server and all the untagged pages have come back has virtually been sent before the write-request. We can also consider that the actual read occurs before the write. Since there are no read-locks, we can consider that prior to resuming the sending of the updated objects, the server releases all the read-locks before it releases the write-lock. Therefore the system is free of read-write conflicts.

There can now be, on the broadcast channel, several copies of the same object available for read as well as one copy available for update by one identified client or and exclusively one already updated copy not available for read or write.

Clients can read the previous version of an object while the current version is being updated.

3.4 Broadcast Disks with Client Cache, Updates, and Locking

To complete the model we now consider the clients' caches. We now assume that clients may perform read and write operations directly on the data in their cache. We later refer to this model as the *broadcast disks with cache* model.

Client. A client needing to read an object need not send a read-request to the server on the broadcast channel. If the object is in the cache it is used. Otherwise the client monitors the broadcast channel until the object to be read is at hand. The client removes the object from the channel, reads it, and places it back on the channel. When an object is read from the channel it is also loaded in the cache. An object currently in the cache may be sacrificed according to the replacement policy. We use both *LRU* (Least Recently Used) as in [3], and *LIX* as in [6].

As previously, a client needing to update an object sends a write-request to the server on the broadcast channel. The client monitors the broadcast channel until the object to be updated is at hand. The client removes the object from the channel, updates it, and places it back on the channel. The updated object is also loaded in the cache. An object currently in the cache may be sacrificed according to the replacement policy. The updated object is temporarily pinned in the cache. It is unpinned when the client receive acknowledgment of the update on the server and of the guarantee that no older copies of the object can be read. This acknowledgment comes in the form of an invalidation message for this object sent by the server.

A client is allowed to read or update an object if it is tagged with a note identifying the client as the recipient. A client is not allowed to read or update an object tagged with a note identifying a different client as the recipient. A client is allowed to read any object in the cache and any untagged object on the broadcast channel.

Server. The server functions as in the previous subsection: upon receiving the updated object, it waits for the invalidation message and all copies of the object to come back. It then sends an invalidation message to all clients and waits for the message to come back before it releases the write-lock and resumes the broadcasting of the tagged copies of the new version of the object.

Discussion. Similarly to the model in the previous subsection this policy guaranties that there is on the broadcast channel and in the caches - except in the cache of the client having performed an update - only one version of an object that can be read. The client performing the update must however wait until it receives the invalidation report before it unpins the updated object and before it can let the replacement policy sacrifice the updated object from the cache. This prevents a subsequent read of an older version of the updated object.

4 Comparative Performance Analysis

4.1 Experimental Set-Up

For the purpose of the performance evaluation, we simulate the models using the CSIM [11] discrete event simulator. A unit of time is the time the server takes to process one incoming message on the up- or downstream channel and to reply by sending one object, request, or notice on the downstream channel (or the broadcast channel). The performance metrics we use is the throughput, i.e. the number of (read and write) operations executed per unit of time. The higher the throughput, the better the performance. We subsequently plot the throughput in number of operations per 5000 units of time.

To measure the relative performance of the reference model and the models we proposed under different conditions, we use several parameters. The parameter ρ indicates the ratio of read- overwrite-requests for any object. In our experiments it varies from one (there are as many read-requests as there are write-requests in average for any given object) to sixteen (there is sixteen times more read- than there are write-requests for any object). The parameter θ controls the popularity of objects or the distribution of the probability for objects to be requested (i.e. for a read- or write-operation following the previous parameter ρ). In some experiment we use two independent distributions for read- and write-requests parameterized by θ_r and θ_w, respectively. θ is the parameter of a Zipfian distribution of the form: $p_i = (1/i)^\theta$. A value of zero for θ indicates a uniform distribution, i.e. every object is equally popular. A value of one indicates a skewed distribution (a small group of objects is highly popular). The server serves 30 distinct objects. We vary the number of clients from 8 to 64.

4.2 Results

Broadcasting versus Client-Server. To confirm our approach and validate our simulation with respect to the previous work on broadcast channels we first verify that the comparative performance of the broadcast channel model versus the client-server model is maintained in the presence of update with locking. It is the case provided there are sufficiently enough opportunities for sharing objects on the broadcast channel for reading among the clients and few chances of operations being queued and delayed because of locks.

As the ratio of read to write operations increases, the opportunity for sharing objects for read-operation increases for the broadcast channel model. For a mildly skewed popularity distribution Figure 1 shows that, as the number of reads over the number of writes varies from 1 to 16 the performance of the broadcast channel model increases significantly while the one of the client-server model remains practically unchanged.

Similarly, as the number of clients increases, the opportunity for sharing objects for read-operation increases for the broadcast channel model. In conditions mildly favorable to the broadcast channel, Figure 2 shows that, as the number of

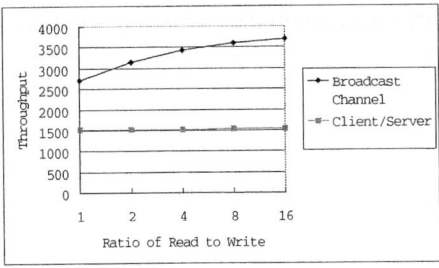
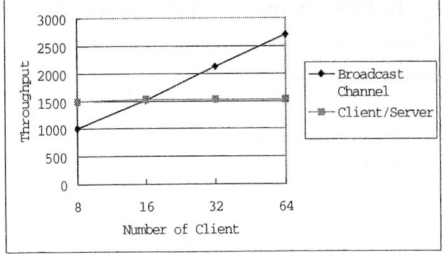

Fig. 1. $\theta = 0.5$, 64 clients

Fig. 2. $\theta = 0.5$ and $\rho=1$

clients increases, the performance of the broadcast channel model increases significantly while the one of the client-server model remains practically unchanged. The broadcast channel model outperforms the client-server model for 16 clients and more.

As the distribution of popularity of objects becomes skewed, the opportunity for sharing objects for read-operation increases for the broadcast channel model. However, there is potentially a higher risk of requests being queued and delayed because of locks for both models. Figure 3 shows that, as the distribution of the popularity of objects becomes skewer, the performance of the broadcast channel model increases significantly while the one of the client-server model remains practically unchanged.

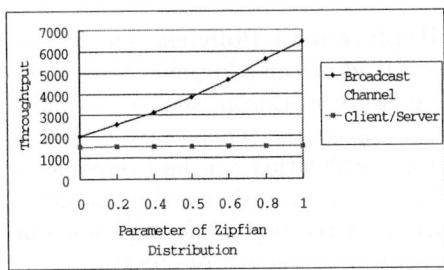

Fig. 3. $\rho=4$, 64 clients

Broadcast Disks versus Broadcast Channel. Broadcast disks improve on a read-only broadcast channel by simulating several disks spinning at different speeds. We compare in this subsubsection the broadcast channel model with several versions of the broadcast disks model with different combinations of speeds. We use three different sets of broadcasts, two of which simulate three disks spinning at 5/3/1 and 7/4/1, respectively, and the third one a single disk.

In this group of experiments we use different distributions for the popularity of objects for read and write. This separation is important since, as the experiments demonstrate, the best performing model depends on these distributions.

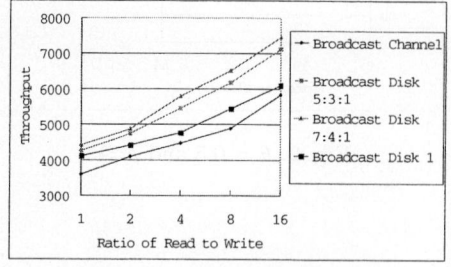
Fig. 4. $\theta_r=1$, $\theta_w=0.5$, 64 clients

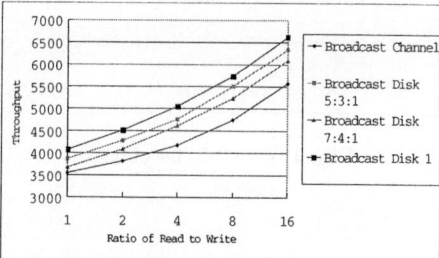
Fig. 5. $\theta_r=0.5$, $\theta_w=1$, 64 clients

A series of experiments, some of which are reported on Figures 4 and 5 confirm that broadcast disks require a good (a priori) knowledge of the distribution of the popularity of objects (we remark that it would be interesting to devise an adaptive strategy for the replication of objects). Our contribution, however, is a model for client update and server locking in the broadcast disks model in spite of the replication inherent to the concept of multi-speed broadcast disks. Under the above model, our experiments show that both popularity distributions for read and for write separately but not independently influence the performance.

Client Cache and Replacement Policies. The broadcast disks model with cache at the client side introduces an additional need for synchronization among the clients and the server: the cache inconsistencies invalidation. Our experiments confirm the results of [3] about the replacement policy. We therefore use LIX to show that the cost of invalidation can be overcome by the gain of caching when there are sufficiently more read than write operations. Figure 6 shows, for varying read-write ratio that the best performance is obtained for the biggest client cache. The size is given in number of objects.

5 Conclusions

We have presented an update and locking mechanism for a broadcast disks model with client's cache. In order to introduce and study the features of our model we presented three different incremental versions: a model using a broadcast channel, a model using a broadcast disk, and a model using a broadcast disk and allowing caches at the clients side. We have demonstrated that broadcasting remains a viable alternative even in the presence of updates at the client. The models we devised and studied can support the implementation of schedulers or lock-based concurrency control strategies.

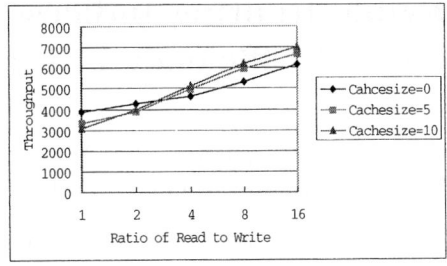

Fig. 6. 64 clients, $\theta_r = \theta_w = 0.5$

Further details can be found in [12]. The thesis includes the algorithms in pseudo code as well as further experiments and discussions.

References

1. S. Viswanathan and T. Imielinski. Pyramid broadcasting for video-on-demand service. In *SPIE Multimedia Computing and Networking Conference*, 1995.
2. Y. Zhao, R. Govindan, and D. Estrin. Residual energy scans for monitoring wireless sensor networks. In *Technical Report 01-745, May*, 2001.
3. S. Acharya, R. Alonso, Franklin M., and S. Zdonik. Broadcast disks: Data management for asymmetric communication environments. In *SIGMOD*, pages 199–210, 1995.
4. T.F. Bowen, G. Gopal, G. Herman, T. Hickey, K.C. Lee, W.H. Mansfield, J. Raitz, and A. Weinrib. The datacycle architecture. *Communications of the ACM*, 35(12), 1992.
5. G. Herman, K.C. Lee, and A. Weinrib. The datacycle architecture for very high throughput database systems. In *SIGMOD*, 1987.
6. S. Acharya, M. Franklin, and S. Zdonik. Prefetching from broadcast disks. In *ICDE*, pages 276–285, 1996.
7. S. Acharya, M. Franklin, and S. Zdonik. Balancing push and pull for data broadcast. In *SIGMOD*, pages 183–194, 1997.
8. J. Shanmugasundaram, A. Nithrakashyap, R. Sivasankaran, and K. Ramamritham. Efficient concurrency control for broadcast environments. In *SIGMOD*, pages 85–96, 1999.
9. R. Alonso, D. Barbara, and H. Garcia-Molina. Data caching issues in an information retrieval system. *TODS*, 15(3), 1990.
10. D. Barbara and T. Imielinski. Sleepers and workaholics: Caching strategies in mobile environments. In *SIGMOD*, 1994.
11. J. Hlavicka, S. Racek, and P. Herout. C-sim v.4.1. In *Research Report DC-99-09, Sep*, 1999.
12. G. Yuzhi. The network is the database. Master's thesis, National University of Singapore, 2004.

Adaptive Double Routing Indices: Combining Effectiveness and Efficiency in P2P Systems

Stephane Bressan[1], Achmad Nizar Hidayanto[2],
Chu Yee Liau[1], and Zainal A. Hasibuan[2]

[1] School of Computing, Department of Computer Science
National University of Singapore
{steph,liaucy}@comp.nus.edu.sg
[2] Faculty of Computer Science, University of Indonesia
{nizar,zhasibua}@cs.ui.ac.id

Abstract. Unstructured peer-to-peer systems rely on strategies and data structures (Routing Indices) for the routing of requests in the network. For those requests corresponding to information retrieval queries, the emphasis can be either put on the effectiveness of the routing by privileging the relevance of the documents retrieved, or on the efficiency of the routing by privileging the response time. We propose in this paper a novel routing strategy based on adaptive Routing Indices. The Routing Indices are adaptive to the environment, i.e. network traffic, location, as well as relevance of the documents indexed, thanks to a reinforcement learning approach to their maintenance. The strategy can be used to tune the compromise between efficient and effective routing. It combines the estimation of the response time of routes with the estimation of the relevance of routes to keywords. We study performance and the tuning of the compromise offered by this novel strategy under various characteristics of the network and traffic.

1 Introduction

In unstructured peer-to-peer architectures such as those of [1, 2] peers are connected to each other as they join the network and objects are generally not moved. Searching for an object requires the broadcasting of the request to all or some of the neighboring peers. The order in which the peers are contacted depends on the search strategy. The selection of the peers to which the request is forwarded can leverage routing information maintained, for instance, in local Routing Indices. Because of the autonomy of the peers, of the users, and of the underlying network, a routing strategy for a peer-to-peer system in general and for an unstructured peer-to-peer system in particular needs to deal with a continuously changing environment. It must be able to adapt simultaneously to several phenomena: changes in the amount of traffic of requests, responses, system messages and possibly other packets on the network, availability of objects such as documents being stored at users discretion, peers freely joining and leaving the system, etc.

In this paper, we are interested in studying the routing of keyword-based requests for documents in an unstructured peer-to-peer system. We propose to extend the adaptive Routing Indices that we introduced in [3]. While in [3] we focused on routing of definite requests, i.e. request to retrieve documents by their identifier or name, we are now interested in search by keyword. Therefore while, as we have shown, the former strategy yielded efficient routing, the new strategy must combine efficiency and effectiveness. It must minimize the response time and maximize the relevance to keywords of the documents retrieved, or at least allow the control of the compromise between the two conflicting factors.

We present Routing Indices that are adaptive to the environment, i.e. network traffic, location, and relevance of the documents indexed, thanks to a reinforcement learning approach to their maintenance. The corresponding routing strategy combines the optimization of both relevance and response time routing thanks to a double dual-reinforcement learning. We study the tuning of the compromise offered by this strategy under various characteristics of the network and traffic.

In the next section we present a brief overview of the main related work on searching and routing strategies in unstructured peer-to-peer systems. We briefly recall the principles underlying reinforcement learning in section 3. We present the new Routing Indices and the proposed routing strategy with its algorithms and variants in section 4. In section 5 we evaluate and analyze the performance of the approach we propose under various parameters of the system and environment. In the last section we present our conclusions.

2 Related Work

Different routing strategies for unstructured peer-to-peer networks have been proposed. Gnutella is one of the most popular peer-to-peer systems. Gnutella belongs to the category of unstructured peer-to-peer systems. Its search algorithm simply requires every node to broadcast the search request to its neighbors. Matei presents a performance evaluation of Gnutella in [4].

Yang and Garcia-Molina [5] have studied various strategies to improve the performance of search in unstructured peer-to-peer systems and distributed information retrieval systems. They studied three techniques: Iterative Deepening, Directed BFS and Local Indices. Iterative deepening uses BFS at depths specified in the policy. The next iteration is applied when the request is not answered. Directed BFS selects a subset of the neighbors to broadcast the request using heuristics techniques. The authors also consider maintaining some routing information in Local Indices. The selection of the neighbors to which a request is forwarded is based on the Local Index. Local Indices maintain a table of pairs (object, neighbor) such that the object is reachable via the peer in the minimum number of hops. The table contains entries for objects reachable within a maximum number of hops. This threshold limits the size of the index.

The Routing Indices by Arturo and Garcia-Molina [6] extend the idea of Local Indices to keyword or topic search. The authors propose several variants in which such information as the estimate of the number of documents per topic when routing to a given neighbor and the distance in hops to documents of a given topic is maintained. The authors demonstrate that Routing Indices yield significantly better performance than flooding or random forwarding strategies. The Routing Indices are created and maintained using (this is not acknowledged by the authors of [6]) the propagation principle of the Bellman-Ford algorithm.

Bellman-ford propagation limits the evaluation of the response time to the evaluation of number of hops ignoring the traffic and network load. Similarly to all algorithms estimating or computing the number of hops (shortest path), it is not capable of identifying and adapting to such phenomenon as traffic jams. In practice, it and all algorithms estimating or computing the number of hops even create traffic jams at bottlenecks by sending similar requests through the same routes. This has been studied in the context of packet routing in communication networks. In this context adaptive routing algorithms such as Q-routing [7] and its variants have been developed.

We have shown in [3] that such adaptive algorithms can be used in the context of peer-to-peer systems to maintain Local Indices, i.e. indices suitable for searching objects by reference. They yield a better performance than existing routing algorithms and adapt to various traffic conditions. We have also shown that Local Indices can be pruned more effectively, i.e. for a better routing performance, based on the popularity of the objects rather than on topological information such as furthest or nearest (as in [6]) located objects.

3 Reinforcement Learning

A reinforcement learning agent [8] learns from its interactions with its environment. In a given state, the reinforcement learning agent selects the next action according to a model it constantly constructs and updates based on the reward that it receives when trying the different actions. A routing agent could, for instance, favor an action that yields the minimum estimated time to destination. Notice that, in order to continuously learn about its environment, the agent must occasionally depart from its base strategy and try random actions.

Reinforcement learning has been successfully applied to many domains, among which network routing. There are numerous forms and variants of reinforcement learning that have been proposed for various network routing problems: Q-Routing [7], Dual Q-Routing [9], Confidence-based Q-Routing and Dual Confidence-based Q-Routing [10], etc. Dual Q-Routing extends the idea of Q-Routing by incorporating backward propagation that yields better performance. Confidence-based Q-Routing in other hand extends the idea of Q-Routing by adding a table that stores the confidence level of Q-value. Experiment in [10] showed that confidence-based yields the best performance among all of them but requires large storage. For the sake of simplicity and scalability we chose Dual Reinforcement Q-Routing. Further refinement of the reinforcement learning strategy can only improve the results presented in this paper.

In Q-Routing, a node that receives a request for a resource and hosts the resource then provides the resource to the original requester otherwise forwards the request according to the reinforcement learning strategy. It adopts forward propagation strategy to estimate the status of the network by maintaining a table called Q-table that contains Q-value $Q(n,r)$ which quantifies the expected reinforcement when a request for a resource r is sent to n. Dual Q-routing incorporates the idea of propagation of Bellman-Ford algorithm into Q-routing. A node n not only forwards a request to resource r to its neighbor but also transmits the value of $Q(n,r)$ which is used by the neighbor to update its Q-table. The Q-table is updated by forward and backward propagation hence the name of *Dual Q-learning*.

Such algorithms can outperform shortest-paths algorithms such as Bellman-Ford for they are able to estimate routing time taking into account the traffic.

4 Design

The peer-to-peer model we study is following the architecture proposed by [6]: we consider an unstructured system in which peers store documents and hold Routing Indices used for by routing strategy. As in [6], we consider requests to documents by topics or keywords. We aim at a design that combines the optimization of the response time to a request with the optimization of the relevance of the retrieved documents to the topics in the request. For the relevance we assume that each peer embeds a local mechanism capable of evaluating the relevance of a document to a topic. We assume the availability of a function rf maps pairs of documents and list of topics to a number that we call the relevance. This function can, for instance, be the cosine similarity in a vector space model.

4.1 Routing Indices

We implement the Routing Index as a Q-table of a dual Q-routing algorithm. The Routing Index maintained by a peer o contains, for each neighbor n of the peer and for each topic t values denoted $T_o(n,t)$ (we call them T-values) which represent the estimated minimum time to retrieve a document relevant to t by forwarding a query to n. The Routing Index therefore estimates the response time instead of just the number of hops as in other systems. The Routing Index of each peer o also maintains for each neighbor n of the peer and for each topic t values denoted $R_o(n,t)$ (we call them R-values) which represents the estimated maximum relevance to t of a document obtained by forwarding a query to n.

Peers can seamlessly join and leave the network without necessity to tell to the whole network. The peers joining the network can initialize the content of the Routing Index to the default and initial values, which is 0. Peers leaving the network inform their direct neighbors to delete the corresponding entries in the Routing Index. If a peer leaves the network on a failure, i.e. without informing its neighbors, its absence will be eventually discovered from its estimated performance in the Routing Index.

For a peer o each entry in the Routing Index is of the form:

$$(n, (T_o(n, t_1), R_o(n, t_1)), \ldots, (T_o(n, t_m), R_o(n, t_m)))$$

for each direct neighbor peer n, where m is the number of topics.

Values in the Routing Index, i.e. T- and R-values, are updated from both forward and backward propagation of the neighbors T- and R-values respectively upon sending or forwarding or receiving a query.

T-values for a peer o and a topic t are updated according to the following Q-routing formula:

$$T_o(n,t)^{new} = T_o(n,t)^{old} + l(T_n(t) + q_{o,n} - T_o(n,t)^{old})$$

where n is the neighbor of o transmitting its best T-value for t, namely $T_n(t) = \min_{p \in neighbor(n) \wedge p \neq o} (T_n(p,t))$, $q_{o,n}$ is the overhead communication cost from o to n, l is a number between zero and one which determines the learning rate. The bigger l, the more sensitive to changes the system. When l is set to 1, the equation becomes:

$$T_o(n,t)^{new} = T_n(t) + q_{o,n}$$

which updates the T-value without considering the old value.

R-values for a peer o and a topic t are updated according to the following formula:

$$R_o(n,t)^{new} = R_n(t)$$

where n is the neighbor of o transmitting its best R-value for t, namely

$$R_n(t) = max(\max_{p \in neighbor(n) \wedge p \neq o} (R_n(p,t)), \max_{d \in doc(n)} (rf(d,t)))$$

It is a learning process with a rate of 1 and an overhead cost of zero. The relevance function rf is used to compute the actual relevance (retrieval status value) of stored documents.

Clearly the estimated R-values are expected to be less subject to fluctuation than the T-values. Indeed, although both values depend on the network structure (peers leaving and joining) the T-value depends on the traffic (requests and responses) while the R-value depends on the documents content and location. We expect the traffic to be most dynamic element of the system.

As we have shown in [3] for Local Indices, we expect to be able to most effectively prune Routing Indices without damaging their routing performance using the popularity of information, i.e. in this case, the frequency of topics. We will not study this pruning in this paper to concentrate on the adaptive combination of response time and relevance indices.

4.2 Routing Strategy

The general routing strategy generally routes a request to the neighbor[1] with the smallest T-value for that request for a strategy seeking to optimize the response time and to the neighbor with the highest R-value (while the local R-value is smaller than the neighbors R-value) for that request for a strategy seeking to optimize the relevance. Occasionally, requests are randomly routed to allow the correction of the estimated values. Also, in practice requests are deleted from the system after they have traveled a predetermined number of hops known as the Time-to-Live or TTL.

A strategy seeking the combined optimization of the response with the relevance of the retrieved documents clearly calls for a trade-off. The more exhaustive, therefore the longer the search and the higher the chances to locate and retrieve more relevant documents. Such a strategy combines the T-values and the R-values into a single value obtained as follow.

First the T-and R-values are normalized as follow:

$$norm\_R_o(n,t) = \frac{R_o(n,t)}{\max\limits_{y \in neighbor(o)} (R_o(y,t))}$$

and

$$norm\_T_o(n,t) = 1 - \frac{T_o(n,t)}{\max\limits_{y \in neighbor(o)} (T_o(y,t))}$$

For every pair of T- and R-values in the Routing Index a weighted sum, $V(o,t)$, of their normalized values called the V-value or routing value is computed as follow:

$$V(o,t) = w \times norm\_T_o(n,t) + (1-w) \times norm\_R_o(n,t)$$

Queries are forwarded to the neighbor with the highest routing value. A value close to 0 for w emphasizes higher relevance, while a value close to 1 emphasizes better response time.

The reader notices that the weight w needs not be a parameter fixed globally to the system nor locally to the machines but can be associated to each individual request thus allowing users to indicate their preference for the combination of efficiency or response time and effectiveness or relevance.

In the general case, unless the TTL limit is reached, a document d at a peer n is returned as the answer to a query on a topic t and the search is stopped when its relevance is equal or greater than

$$(1-w) \times \max\limits_{p \in neighbor(n)} (R_n(p,t))$$

---

[1] Without loss of generality we will evaluate the strategy in the simpler case in which queries are forwarded to a single neighbor. The scheme naturally extends to forwarding queries to several neighbors.

The reader has noticed that we implicitly defined as relevant a document with non-zero relevance. This hypothesis can easily be changed to a minimum acceptable relevance. The model can also be generalized to allow a set of result to be returned and sorted.

4.3 Dynamically Controlling Effectiveness and Efficiency

Numerous and various functions can be used to combine the T- and the R-values into a single value used for the routing strategy. A simple weighted function can achieve some level of direct control but leave some risks of divergence of the response time (i.e. the response time increases as the elapsed time increases), as experiments presented in the next section show. To demonstrate the opportunity to define functions adaptive to various parameters of the environment lets us try and design a function which is adaptive to the network load.

Obtaining information about the network level of activity requires information from other peers participating in the system. However, the local activity may be a good estimate of the network activity as far as the routing of queries is concerned. We locally measure the load of each machine o as:

$$l_o = \frac{N_m}{C_p}$$

where N_m represents the number of messages (requests and system messages) in the queue of the peer o and C_p represents the number of messages that peer o can process in a unit of time (which for instance can be assumed to be commensurate to its processor speed and other hardware and system features).

We now define a function of l_o, returning the weight w. We want to design a function that takes the network load into account when choosing a compromise between efficiency and effectiveness or response time. When the network in low load the function should favor effectiveness or relevance with a small value of w: the function is decreasing. When the network in high load the function should favor efficiency with a large value of w: the function is increasing. In summary, we wish to design a function such that:

- The value of the function is between 0 and 1 (since the w expected is within this range)
- The function is continuous (to be able to display a gradual effect)
- The function follows l_o monotonically.

There are many such functions. As an example, we propose the following function:

$$w = \begin{cases} 1, & if\ \frac{N_m}{C_p} > \theta + \varphi \\ 0, & if\ \frac{N_m}{C_p} < \theta - \varphi \\ \frac{\left(\frac{N_m}{C_p} - (\theta - \varphi)\right)}{2\varphi} & otherwise \end{cases}$$

As shown in figure 1, θ is used to control the inflection point of the function. θ takes its values between zero and infinity. θ reflects the normal value of l_o.

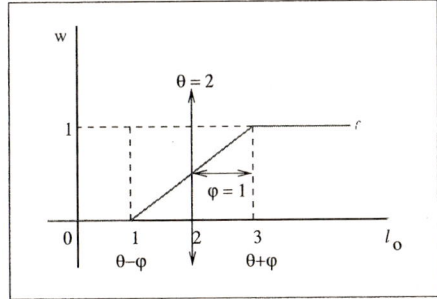

Fig. 1. A Function Adaptive to the Network and Machine Load

If the value of l_o is equal to θ then w is equal to 0.5 therefore giving equal weight to efficiency and effectiveness. Setting θ to a large value relatively to l_o is expected to increase relevance because the w becomes small. φ is used to control the gradient of the function. The value of φ ranges between zero and infinity. When setting φ tends towards zero, the slope of the function near its inflection tends towards vertical. When the value of φ is large the slope of the function tends toward the horizontal making the function less sensitive to variation of l_o and thus striking a balance between effectiveness and efficiency.

Although the proposed function has now two parameters θ and φ instead of one w, our experiments (some of which are discussed in the next section) have shown that the proposed function is capable of adapting to the network and machine load. In that sense the two parameters are secondary fine tuning parameters. As with w the two parameters θ and φ can be set for individual queries and need not be global to the system or to a peer.

5 Performance Analysis

[2]We implemented a discrete event simulation of our proposed strategies to evaluate their performance. In our experiments, we use a re-wired ring lattice network topology as suggested by I. Clark et. al. in [2] for the simulation of a peer-to-peer network. A ring lattice is a graph with n vertices (peers), each of which is connected to its nearest k neighbors. In our experiments we use a k value of 4. The rewiring is done by randomly choosing m vertices to connect with each other. We use an m value of 10% of n. The network we use for these experiments contains 36 peers without loss of generality since we have shown in [3] it can be scaled to larger number of nodes.

We consider 500 documents and 1000 topics. For each document, we chose 10% of the topics. For each document and for each of these chosen topics, we randomly chose a relevance value. For each document d, we randomly choose 10% of the peers to store it. The number of queries on a given topic is determined by a

---

[2] The figures in this section can be viewed better with colors.

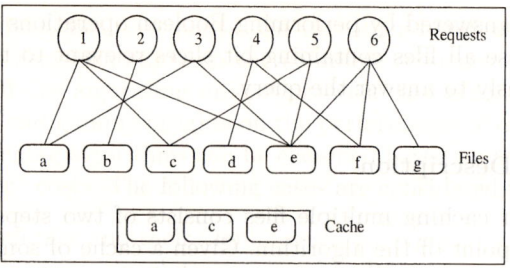

Fig. 1. A bipartite graph depiction of a set of jobs and their file requests

3. Analysis of the heuristics and derivation of tight bounds from the optimal solution
4. Extensive simulation results comparing the new algorithm with the traditional first come first serve.

The rest of the paper is organized as follows. In Section 2 we formally describe the MFC problem and discuss its complexity. In Section 3 a heuristic greedy algorithm, called *Greedy Request Value (GRV)* is proposed and its bounds from the optimal solution are shown using Linear Programming (or LP) relaxation. In Section 4, we present a simulation framework for evaluating the performance of the proposed *GRV* algorithm. Results of the simulation studies, i.e., workload characterization and measurements of performance metrics are presented in Section 5. Conclusions and future work are presented in Section 6.

2 Related Problems and Approximation Complexity

The Multi-File Caching (MFC) problem is defined as follows: Given a collection of requests $R = \{r_1, r_2, \ldots, r_n\}$, each with associated value $v(r_i)$, defined over a set of files $F = \{F_1, F_2, \ldots, F_m\}$, each with size $s(F_i)$ and a constant M, find a subset R' of the requests, $R' \subseteq R$, of maximum total value such that the total size of the files needed by R' is at most M. It is easy to show that in the special case that each file is needed by exactly one request the MFC problem is equivalent to the knapsack problem. The MFC problem is NP-hard even if each request has exactly 2 files. This is done by reduction from the Dense k-subgraph (DKS) problem [9]. An instance of the DKS problem is defined as follows: Given a graph $G = (V, E)$ and a positive integer k, find a subset $V' \subseteq V$ with $|V'| = k$ that maximizes the total number of edges in the subgraph induced by V'. Given an instance of a DKS problem, the reduction to an instance of MFC is done by making each vertex $v \in V$ correspond to a file $f(v)$ of size 1. Each edge (x, y) in E corresponds to a request for two files $f(x)$ and $f(y)$. A solution to the MFC instance with a cache of size k corresponds to a solution to the instance of the DKS where the k files loaded into the cache correspond to vertices of the subgraph V' in the solution of the DKS instance. We also note that any approximation algorithm for the MFC problem can be used to approximate a DKS problem with the same bound from optimality. Currently the best-known approximation for the DKS problem [9] is within a factor of $O(|V|^{1/3-\epsilon})$ from optimum for some $\epsilon > 0$. It is also conjectured in [9] that an approximation to DKS with a factor of $(1+\epsilon)$ is NP-hard. It is also interesting to note that in case each request can start its service when at least one of its files is in the cache (but not necessarily all), the problem becomes equivalent to the Budgeted Maximum Coverage Problem (BMC) [10, 11]. Using the above terminology, in the BMC problem we are given a budget L (cache size) and the goal is to select a subset of the files $F' \subseteq F$ whose total size is at most L such that the total value of the requests using files from F' is maximized. It turns out that BMC is easier to approximate. In [10], an approximation algorithm is given for the BMC with a factor of $(1 - 1/e)$ from optimal.

3   A Greedy Algorithm and Bounds from Optimality

Next, we will describe a simple greedy algorithm called Algorithm GRV (Greedy Request Value) and later prove the relationship between the request value produced by this algorithm and the optimal one. First we need some definitions. For a file f_i, let $s(f_i)$ denote its size and let $d(f_i)$ represent the number of requests served by it. The adjusted size of a file f_i, denoted by $s'(f_i)$, is defined as its size divided by the number of requests it serves, i.e., $s'(f_i) = s(f_i)/d(f_i)$. For a request r_i, let $v(r_i)$ denote its value and $F(r_i)$ represent the set of files requested by it. The adjusted relative value of a request, or simply its relative value, $v'(r_j)$, is its value divided by the sum of adjusted sizes of the files it requests, i.e.

$$v'(r_j) = \frac{v(r_j)}{\sum_{f_i \in F(r_j)} s'(f_i)}$$

Algorithm GRV below attempts to service requests in decreasing order of their adjusted relative values. It skips requests that cannot be serviced due to insufficient space in the cache for their associated files. The final solution is the maximum between the value of requests loaded and the maximum value of any single request.

3.1   Linear Programming Relaxation

We now proceed to analyze the quality of the solution produced by this algorithm. The MFC problem can be modeled as a mixed-integer program as follows. Let

$$z_i = \begin{cases} 1 & \text{if the file} f_i \text{ is in cache} \\ 0 & \text{otherwise} \end{cases}$$

and let

$$y_j = \begin{cases} 1 & \text{if all files used by } r_j \text{ are in cache} \\ 0 & \text{otherwise} \end{cases}$$

Then the mixed integer formulation, $\mathcal{P}$, of MFC can be stated as:

$$\mathcal{P}: \quad \max \sum_{j=1}^{n} v(r_j) y_j$$

> **input** : A set of n requests $R = \{r_1, \ldots r_n\}$, their values $v(r_j)$, a set of n files F, the sets $F(r_i)$, a cache C of size $s(C)$ and the sizes $s(f_i)$ of all files in F.
> **output**: The *solution* - a subset of the requests in R whose files must be loaded into the cache.
> **Step 0:** /* Initialize */
> *Solution* $\leftarrow \phi$; //set of requests selected
> $s(C') \leftarrow \phi$; // $s(C')$ keeps track of unused cache size
> **Step 1:** Sort the requests in R in decreasing order of their relative values and renumber from $r_1, \ldots, r_n$ based on the this order
> **Step 2:**
> for $i \leftarrow 1$ *to* n do
>   if $s(C') \geq s(F(r_i))$ then
>   Load the files in $F(r_i)$ to the cache
> $s(C') \leftarrow s(C') - s(F(r_i))$; // update unused cache size
>   *Solution* $\leftarrow$ *Solution* $\cup r_i$; // add request r_i to the solution
>   end
> end
> **Step 2:** Compare the total value of requests in *Solution* and the highest value of any single request and choose the maximum

Algorithm 1: GRV

subject to

$$y_j - z_i \leq 0, \forall i \in F(r_j), \text{ and } \forall j$$

$$\sum_{i=1}^{m} s(f_i) z_i \leq s(C), \quad z_i \in \{0,1\}$$

The linear relaxation of this problem, $\mathcal{P}_\infty$, and its associated dual problem, $\mathcal{D}$, are not only easier to analyze but also provide a useful bound for a heuristic solution procedure.

$$\mathcal{P}_\infty : \quad \max \sum_{j=1}^{n} v(r_j) y_j$$

subject to

$$y_j - z_i \leq 0, \forall i \in F(r_j), \text{ and } \forall j$$

$$\sum_{i=1}^{m} s(f_i) z_i \leq s(C), \quad 0 \leq z_i \leq 1.$$

$$\mathcal{D} : \quad \min s(C)\lambda + \sum_{i=1}^{m} \lambda_i$$

subject to

$$\sum_{i \in F(r_j)} \lambda_{ji} = v(r_j) \text{ for } j = 1, 2, \ldots, n \tag{1}$$

$$\lambda s(f_i) + \lambda_i - \sum_{j: f_i \in F(r_j)} \lambda_{ji} \geq 0, \text{ for } i = 1, 2, \ldots, m, \quad \lambda, \lambda_i, \lambda_{ji} \geq 0, \quad (2)$$

where λ_{ji} are the dual variables corresponding to the first set of primal constraints, λ is the dual variable corresponding to the cache size constraint, and the λ_i's correspond to the last set of constraints bounding the z's to be less than one.

To avoid trivialities, we assume that for each request j, $\sum_{i \in F(r_j)} s(f_i) \leq s(C)$. That is, each request can be addressed from the cache, otherwise we can eliminate such requests in the problem formulation.

Theorem 1. *Let V_{GRV} represent the value produced by Algorithm GRV and let V_{OPT} be the optimal value. Let d^* denote the maximum degree of a file, i.e., $d^* = \max_i d(f_i)$ then*

$$\frac{V_{OPT}}{V_{GRV}} \leq 2d^*$$

Proof Outline: For lack of space, we provide only an outline of the proof. The full version is in [12]. Consider the algorithm $GRV(LP)$ such that it stops with the last request that can only be accommodated partially (or not at all). It then compares the solution produced to the value of the last request that could not be accommodated and outputs the larger of the two solutions. We can also show, from a detailed analysis, that the integral solution produced by the modified $GRV(LP)$ is at least $1/2d^*$ times the optimal solution. Algorithm GRV can be adapted to produce equivalent or a better solution then $GRV(LP)$ □

4 The Simulation Framework for Multi-file Caching

To evaluate various alternative algorithms for scheduling jobs in a Multi-File caching environment, we developed an appropriate machinery for file caching and cache replacement policies that compares GRV and FCFS job admissions each in combination with the least recently used (LRU) replacement policy. Although cache replacement policies have been studied extensively in the literature, these only address transfers between computing system's memory hierarchy, database buffer management and in web-caching with no delays. The model for cache replacement assumes instantaneous replacements. That is that the request to cache an object is always serviced immediately and once the object is cached, the service on the object is carried out instantaneous. As a result the literature gives us very simplistic simulation models for the comparative studies of cache replacement policies. Such models are inappropriate in the practical scenarios for MFC. For instance, once a job is selected for service, all its files must be read into the cache and this involves very long delays.

We present an appropriate simulation model that takes into account the inherent delays in locating a file, transferring the file into the cache and holding the file in the cache while it is processed. The sizes of the files we deal with impose these long delays. We capture these in the general setup of our simulation machinery. The machinery considers the files to exist in various states and undergo state transitions conditionally from state to state, when they are subjected to certain events.

4.1 The States of a File in a Disk Cache

Each file object associated with the cache is assumed to be in some state. If the file has not been referenced at all it is assumed to be in state S_0. When a reference is made to the file (an event which we characterize subsequently), the file makes a transition to state S_1. A file in state S_1 implies that it has been referenced with at least one pending task waiting to use it but has neither been cached nor in the process of being cached. A file is in state S_2 if it has been previously referenced but not cached and there are no pending tasks for the file. A file is in state S_3 if it has been cached but not pinned and it is in state S_4 if space reservation has been made for the file, but it is still in the process of being cached. A file is in state S_5 if it is cached and pinned. Each of these states is characterized by a set of conditions given by the file status, number of waiting tasks, the last time the file was cached, the job identifier that initiated the caching of the file, and the setting of a cache index.

At some intermittent stages, all files in state S_2 that have not be used for a specified time period are flushed from memory. At this stage all accumulated information, such as the number of reference counts accumulated since its first reference, is lost. The file is said to be set back into state S_0. For our simulation runs all files in state S_2 that have not been referenced in the last five days are cleared. Any subsequent reference to the file would initiate a new accumulation of historical information on the references made to the file. The various states of a file is summarized as follows:

S_0: Not in memory and not-referenced.
S_1: Referenced, not cached but has pending tasks.
S_2: Referenced, not cached and has no pending tasks.
S_3: Cached but not pinned.
S_4: Space reserved but not Cached. Caching in progress.
S_5: Cached and pinned.

4.2 The Event Activities of the Disk Cache

A file that is referenced, cached, processed and eventually evicted from the cache is considered to undergo some state changes. The events affecting the state changes of the files are caused by the actions of the tasks that are invoked by the jobs and other related system actions. Jobs that arrive at a host are maintained in either a simple queue or a balanced search tree depending on the algorithm for processing the jobs.

A job scheduling policy is used to select the job whose files are to be cached next. For FCFS, the job in front of the queue is selected next. In the GRV algorithm, we evaluate the selection criterion for all waiting jobs and select the recommended one based on the potential available cache space. When a job is selected, all its files are then scheduled to be brought into the disk cache. For each such file of a job a task event is initiated by creating a task token that is inserted into an event queue. Each task token is uniquely identified by the pair of values of the job and file identifiers. A task token is subjected to five distinct events at different times. These events are: *Admit-File* (E_0) *Start-Caching* (E_1), *End-Caching* (E_2), *Start-Processing* (E_3) and *End-Processing* (E_4). Two other events are the *Cache-Eviction* (E_5) and the *Clear-Aged-file* (E_6). The special event, *Clear-Aged-file* (E_5), when it occurs, causes the all the information (e.g., history of references to a file) for files that have been dormant for a stipulated period to be deleted. The entire activities within this framework are executed as a discrete event simulation. The activities of the simulation may be summarized by the finite state machine, with conditional transitions. This is depicted as a state transition diagram of Figure 2. The simulation is event driven and the

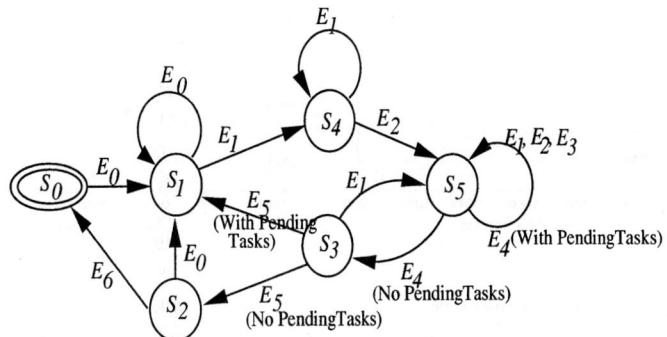

Fig. 2. A Finite State Machine Diagram with Conditional Transitions

three different file processing orders are modeled accordingly with the order of insertions and deletions of files in the data structure T_4.

4.3 File Processing in MFC with Delays

The event selected next is an admission if the arrival time of the next job is earlier than the time of the earliest event. If a job arrival is earliest, it is inserted into the admission structure. On the other hand if the top event of the event queue is earlier, it is removed and processed accordingly. The processing of the event may reinsert an event token into the event queue unless the event is the completion of a task. Each time a job completes, we determine the potential available free cache space and schedule the next job to be processed. In GRV, the potential available cache space is used in the algorithm and not the actual free space. The *potential available free cache space* is the sum of unoccupied space and total size of all unpinned files.

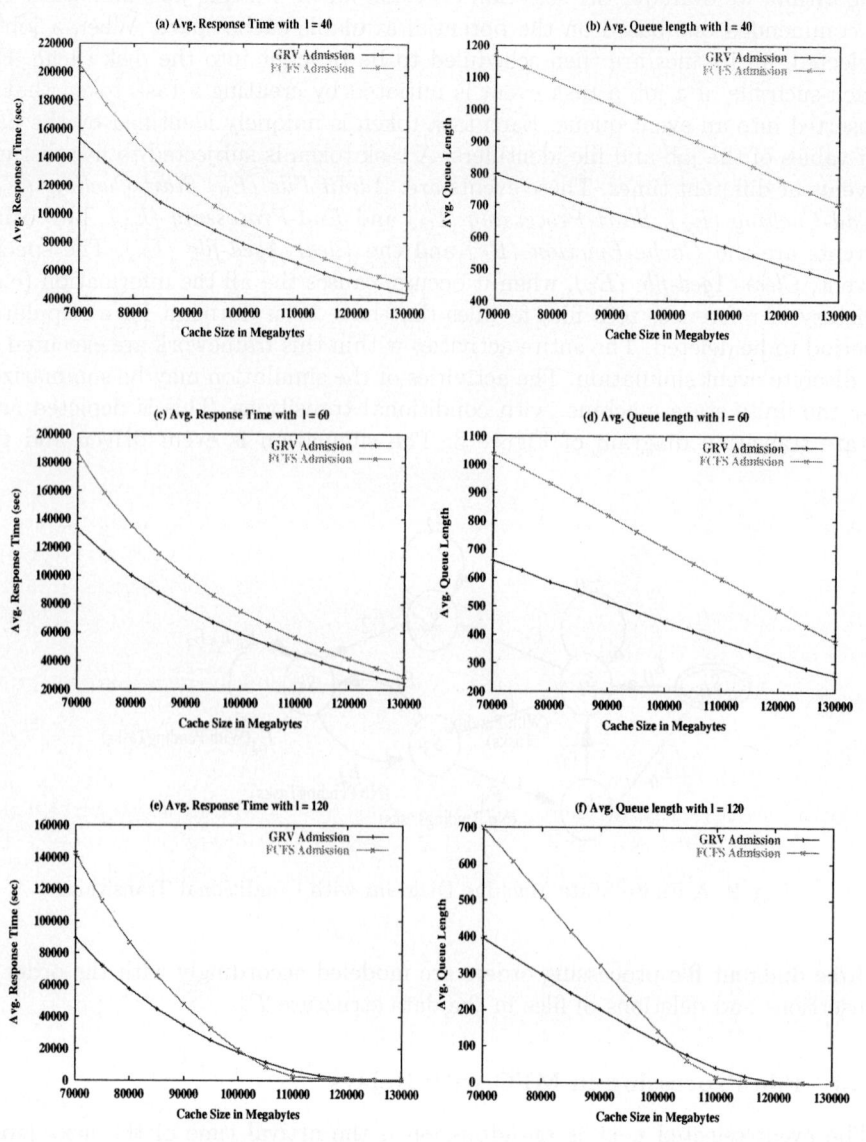

Fig. 3. Graphs of GRV vs FCFS in Multi-file Caching for Average Response Times and Average Queue Lengths

We evaluate the jobs admission policy and the cache replacement policy separately but not independently. In evaluating GRV, a file in the cache is assigned a zero file size and in evaluating a replacement policy, all files that appear in the batch of files to be cached are first pinned by restricting them from being candidates for eviction.

5 Experimental Setup

We conducted experiments using the simulation framework described above to compare the GRV algorithm with a naive FCFS job scheduling of the Multi-file Caching problem when the cache replacement algorithm is LRU. Two performance metrics were used: the average response time of a job and the average queue length jobs with workloads of varying jobs arrival rates. Our implementation is a straight forward translation of the *Finite State Machine (FSM)*, with conditional transitions, to a C++ code. When all the files of a job are cached the tasks associated with the jobs, process the files at a steady rate of 10 MBytes per second. This implies that the processing time of a job is the time to process the file with the largest size.

5.1 Workload Characteristics and Simulation Runs

We subjected the simulation model to workloads in our experiments where the job inter-arrival times are exponentially distributed with mean inter-arrival times of 40, 60 and 120 seconds. Each job makes a request for n files where n is a uniform number between 1 and 25. The file sizes are also uniformly distributed between 500KB and 4GB.

The simulation runs were carried out on a Redhat Linux machine with 512 MBytes of memory. We evaluated the performance metrics of the average response time per job and the average queue length when the cache replacement policy is LRU. For each configuration and for each workload, a number of runs were done with cache sizes varying from 70 to 130 Gigabytes. For each run and for each cache size, we applied a variance reduction method by averaging the statistics that we compute independently for 5 segments of the workload.

5.2 Discussion of Results

Figures 3a, 3c and 3e show the graphs of the response times of synthetic workloads with respective mean inter-arrival times of 40, 60 and 120 seconds. These graphs indicate that the GRV clearly gives a better response time than a simply FCFS job scheduling. GRV performs even better for higher arrival rates. However, as the disk cache sizes increase the graphs of the two algorithms converge.

The graphs of the average queue length shown in Figures 3b, 3d and 3f show similar trends as the graphs of the average response times. This was expected since the average queue length is strongly correlated with the response time for a fixed arrival rate. FCFS admission policy cannot be discarded entirely. As Figures 3e and 3f illustrate, for sufficiently low rate of arrivals and significantly large disk cache size, FCFS job scheduling can perform competitively with GRV. Using different cache replacement policies, e.g., greedy dual size, the same relative results are likely to be achieved. This is left for future work.

6 Conclusions and Future Work

We have identified a new type of caching problem that appears whenever dependencies exist among files that must be cached. This problem arises in various scientific and commercial applications that use vertically partitioned attributes in different files. Traditional caching techniques that make caching decisions one file at a time do not apply here since a request can only be processed if all files requested are cached. Since the problem of optimally loading the cache to maximize the value of satisfied requests is NP hard, we settled on approximation algorithms that were shown analytically to produce solutions bounded from the optimal one. The MFC problem is also of theoretical interest in its own right because of its connection to the well known dense k-subgraph and the fact that any approximation to MFC can be used to approximate the latter problem with the same bounds from optimality.

The simulation studies show that the new algorithms outperform ($FCFS$) scheduling of requests with multiple file caching. The system throughput using schedules based on Algorithm GRV is consistently higher than the FCFS schedules and the queue length is correspondingly shorter. Future work to be conducted involves detailed simulations using real workloads derived from file caching activities of data intensive applications. We also intend to pursue these studies for both synthetic and real workloads for multiple file replacements at a time rather than one file at a time.

Acknowledgment

This work is supported by the Director, Office of Laboratory Policy and Infrastructure Management of the U. S. Department of Energy under Contract No. DE-AC03-76SF00098. This research used resources of the National Energy Research Scientific Computing (NERSC), which is supported by the Office of Science of the U.S. Department of Energy.

References

1. Cao, P., Irani, S.: Cost-aware WWW proxy caching algorithms. In: USENIX Symposium on Internet Technologies and Systems. (1997)
2. Hahn, U., Dilling, W., Kaletta, D.: Adaptive replacement algorithm for disk caches in hsm systems. In: 16 Int'l. Symp on Mass Storage Syst., San Diego, California (1999) 128 – 140
3. Otoo, E.J., Rotem, D., Shoshani, A.: Impact of admission and cache replacement policies on response times of jobs on data grids. In: Int'l. Workshop on Challenges of Large Applications in Distrib. Environments, Seatle, Washington, IEEE Computer Society, Los Alamitos, California (2003)
4. Tan, M., Theys, M., Siegel, H., Beck, N., Jurczyk, M.: A mathematical model, heuristic, and simulation study for a basic data staging problem in a heterogeneous networking environment. In: Proc. of the 7th Hetero. Comput. Workshop, Orlando, Florida (1998) 115–129

5. Wang, J.: A survey of web caching schemes for the Internet. In: ACM SIG-COMM'99, Cambridge, Massachusetts (1999)
6. Young, N.: On-line file caching. In: SODA: ACM-SIAM Symposium on Discrete Algorithms (A Conference on Theoretical and Experimental Analysis of Discrete Algorithms). (1998)
7. Shoshani, A.L.B., Nordberg, H., Rotem, D., Sim, A.: Multidimensional indexing and query coordination for tertiary storage management. In: Proc. of SSDBM'99. (1999) 214 – 225
8. Wu, K., Koegler, W.S., Chen, J., Shoshani, A.: Using bitmap index for interactive exploration of large datasets. In: SSDBM'2003, Cambridge, Mass. (2003) 65–74
9. Feige, U., Peleg, D., Kortsarz, G.: The dense k-subgraph problem. Algorithmica **29** (2001) 410–421
10. Khuller, S., Moss, A., Naor, J.S.: The budgeted maximum coverage problem. Information Processing Letters **70** (1999) 39–45
11. Krumke, S.O., Marathe, M.V., Poensgen, D., Ravi, S.S., Wirth, H.C.: Budgeted maximum graph coverage. In: int'l. Workshop on Graph Theoretical Concepts in Comp. Sc., WG 2002, Cesky Krumlov, Czech Republic (2002) 321 – 332
12. Rotem, D., Seshadri, S., Otoo, E.J.: Analysis of multi-file caching problem. Technical report, Lawrence Berkeley National Laboratory (2003)

A System for Processing Continuous Queries over Infinite Data Streams

Ehsan Vossough

Department of Computing and InformationTechnology
University of Western Sydney, Campbelltown
NSW 2560, Australia
e.vossough@uws.edu.au

Abstract. This paper investigates the use of an off the shelf database management system for the processing of continuous queries. It describes the utilization of existing features in a DBMS and their adoption to synchronize processing of unlimited data streams and discusses the performance of the proposed solution. It provides a solution for the inherent limitations in the architecture of a DBMS to be able to react to continual inputs from several sources. The outcome of this paper shows that it is possible to process continuous data streams from several sources and in some ways a better performance is also achievable.

1 Introduction

Traditional database management systems (DBMS) process data physically stored on disk drives and at a logical level visible as a collection of persistent datasets. The datasets are accessed by DBMS only if a database application running on behalf of an end user submits an explicit request to do so. A class of new database applications that violate this principle has recently emerged. These applications require the continuous access to a new kind of data objects referred to as data streams. A data stream is a continuously expanding and theoretically unlimited sequence of data items. Data streams are typical for medical monitoring systems, sensor networks, satellite monitoring systems, financial stock markets, weather monitoring systems, network tracking systems and many other real-time sensing systems. A common belief is that traditional DBMSs are not geared toward processing of data streams. They are generally geared toward the processing of individual transactions generated by humans. A data stream needs to be processed by a modified form of a query that is called a continuous query and requires a special approach to both the management and processing of data. We believe that the current DBMSs have many useful features that can be adapted to perform the tasks needed to process data streams. These features include transaction management, concurrency control, query optimization and indexing.

Data stream processing techniques has its roots in the earlier developed methods for adaptive, incremental, and continuous query processing. A comprehensive review of the works and the results achieved can be found in [2], [4], [5], [6], [8], [16], [18], [21], [23].

The recent work [4] reviews the research issues and unsolved problems in this area. The computational models suitable for data stream processing fit either into the categories of incremental or dataflow processing models. Continuous data processing model originates from the techniques developed for incremental [11], [24], adaptive [12], [13], [22] and continuous query processing [7], [21].

The remaining sections of the paper are organized as follows. Section 2 provides the motivation for the development of a data stream management system. Section 3 presents a brief description of our data stream management system using a stream processing system called a *tandem*. Section 4 describes the synchronization of streams for several tandems. Section 5 provides synchronization issues relating to tandem propagation delays. Section 6 provides some experimental results. The paper concludes with a general vision and plans for future developments.

2 Motivation

In the scientific world, electronic sensors are connected to a computer to collect data, to automate record keepings, to ensure that some critical limits in the data are not exceeded and to minimize human errors. Such data must be analyzed immediately as they are collected. A typical example is a weather monitoring system that checks temperature, atmospheric pressure, rainfall, humidity, wind speed, wind direction and solar energy. A data logger collects the information to be processed, displays them on the monitor and archives them on a hard disk. Collected data could be logged either to a local or to a remote machine using a data acquisition system, e.g. YSI 6600 Data Acquisition System [25], [26].

We believe that it is possible to adapt a conventional DBMS for stream processing through appropriate selection of transaction processing techniques, query optimizations, physical database design and fine tuning of the system parameters. DBMSs operate on a passive repository that stores large amounts of data. The human operators perform manual data processing tasks on such a repository. This is normally referred to as Human Active DBMS Passive (HADP) approach [17]. In the latter case, repository data is processed when all the information has been collected from various sources. Data stream applications, however, are systems that monitor and process continuous streams of data. They must be able to continuously process large amounts of data as they arrive from many sources.

Our system is implemented with a standard SQL language and is generally designed to process many types of data streams. Synchronization is handled with the existing transaction processing management and concurrency control in a DBMS. Existing memory management for operations on tables is utilized. Existing rules in the relational algebra is also adapted to process a single data element in the same way as single row of data from a table. Existing relational integrity rules, indexing techniques and Query optimization techniques in DBMS also play an important role. Existing SQL99 is adopted.

3 A Stream Processing System

A model for processing of infinite data streams presented in [23] is for three basic binary operations; join α_{join}, union α_{union} and difference α_{diff}. This model considers a building block called a tandem that processes two data streams over a number of sequential windows. A cascading system containing several tandems is used to process several streams concurrently. Each tandem is represented as a block α_{AB}, α_{ABC}, ... and a number of sequential windows as W_{SA} ... W_{SM}.

Extension of a single operator to more than one stream using several tandems can also be viewed as follows.

Stream A: $(((\delta A <\alpha_{AB}> W_{SB}) <\alpha_{ABC}> W_{SC}) .. <\alpha_{A..N}> W_{SN}) \rightarrow JIT_{A..M}$
Stream B: $(((W_{SA} <\alpha_{AB}> \delta B) <\alpha_{ABC}> W_{SC}) .. <\alpha_{A..N}> W_{SN}) \rightarrow JIT_{A..M}$ ... and so on.

4 Synchronization of Tandems

If we allow data elements arrive from different streams in any order then there are instances when the delays in the arrival of data elements on the input of a tandem produce erroneous results. The following scenario sheds some light on this problem.

Consider the first tandem with inputs A and B in a cascading system of tandems. At any instance in time two data elements δ_a and δ_b arrive from streams A and B and are recorded in windows W_{SA} and W_{SB} at the same instance of time, respectively. α_a and α_b begin operating on δ_a and δ_b, concurrently. At this moment, W_{SA} contains data elements ($W_{SA}+\delta_a$) and W_{SB} contains data elements ($W_{SB}+\delta_b$). Since operators α_a and α_b operate independently, the immediate tendency is for α_a to operate data element δ_a with ($W_{SB}+\delta_b$) and for α_b to operate data element δ_b with ($W_{SA}+\delta_a$). Consequently, result S_{outAB} would contain two duplicated instances of data elements $\alpha_a(\delta_a\delta_b)$ and $\alpha_b(\delta_b\delta_a)$ with the same identifier and attribute values. Ordinarily, we should have α_a operating on W_{SB} that excludes δ_b, followed by α_b operating on ($W_{SA}+\delta_a$).

This scenario can be viewed in a different context by treating all the execution steps in the consummation of a tuple in a stream as a transaction and by applying the traditional correctness criteria to the execution of several transactions. A transactional view of data stream processing is as follows. The transaction starts immediately after a data element is collected from a stream and ends when the results of processing of the data element are recorded in a temporary container, JIT_{AB}. Figure 1 demonstrates the operations in the execution of a transaction in a chronological order of execution for elementary operators α_A and α_B in a tandem α_{AB}.

The columns in schedule show transactions T_A and T_B performed by the elementary operators α_A and α_B, respectively. Rows in each schedule show the instructions that are executed in the transaction. Latter schedule is not serial because transactions do not interleave their operations. Moreover latter schedule is not serializable because of a possible conflict in the executions of instructions Write (W_{SA}, δ_a) and Write (W_{SB}, δ_b) followed by Read (W_{SB}) and Read (W_{SA}). A second conflict can also arise from the operation in the execution of Write(S_{outAB}, Y) and Write(S_{outAB}, X) instructions, shaded in gray. If schedule is to be conflict equivalent to a serial schedule then the order of any two conflicting operations must be the same in both schedules. To prove that schedules are conflict serializable we must prove that they are also conflict equivalent.

α_{AB}	
Transaction T_A, α_A	Transaction T_B, α_B
Write (W_{SA}, δ_a)	
	Write (W_{SB}, δ_b)
Read (W_{SB})	
X ← α_A (δ_a, WS_B)	
	Read (W_{SA})
	Y ← α_B (δ_b, W_{SA})
	Write (S_{outAB}, Y)
Write (S_{outAB}, X)	

Fig. 1. A non-serial schedule for transactions T_A and T_B

To ensure that tandem schedule is conflict serializable we use timestamps in the form of sequence numbers on all data elements from a stream. Each new data element is given a unique sequence number before it is recorded. A solution in the executions of Write(W_{SB}, δ_b) followed by Read(W_{SB}) or Write(W_{SA}, δ_a) followed by Read(W_{SA}) is reached by imposing the rule that a new data element is only operated with the data elements in a window that have arrived *earlier* and have a *smaller* sequence number.

We also prove that the order of the execution of instructions Write(S_{outAB}, X) and Write(S_{outAB}, Y) can be swapped without any conflict. To do this we apply the set interpretation of a temporary container that stores the results of Write(S_{outAB}, X) and Write(S_{outAB}, Y) instructions and consider how the results from a data element are stored in a temporary container.

Suppose that a result from a data element δ_a produces a set result Res(δ_a) and the result from a data element δ_b produces a set result Res(δ_b). The final result will be the union of the set results as Res(δ_a) + Res(δ_b) which can also be interpreted as Res(δ_b) + Res(δ_a); this is true since the order in which set results are written to a temporary container can be changed without affecting the final answer. Consequently, the set interpretation of a temporary container can be used to show that the order of Write(S_{outAB}, X) and Write(S_{outAB}, Y) can be changed and the execution would be conflict serializable. Ability to swap the instructions Write(S_{outAB}, X) and Write(S_{outAB}, Y) eliminates the conflicts arising from the Write(S_{outAB}, X) and Write(S_{outAB}, Y).

5 Synchronizations Issues Relating to Tandem Propagation Delay

Several cascading tandems with different propagation delays may process a data element. There are occasions when a result from an earlier data element arrives on the first input of a succeeding tandem when a later data element on the second input of latter tandem has already been processed. Consequently, results from the earlier data element will not be operated with the latter data element. This would lead to missing data elements in the final results. The following scenario illustrates this problem.

Consider the data elements δ_a and δ_b arriving on the input of a tandem α_{AB} and produce a composite result δ_{ab}. This result is consumed on the first input of a following tandem, α_{ABC}. It may happen that a data element δ_c with a higher sequence number than δ_a and δ_b arrives earlier on the second input of α_{ABC}. At this point in time, a delayed result δ_{ab} has not yet been stored in JIT_{AB}. Consequently, operations on δ_c and JIT_{AB} will not *see* δ_{ab} having a smaller time stamp than δ_c and the output of α_{ABC} will not include a result $(\delta_{ab})\alpha_{ABC}(\delta_c)$.

A general solution to this problem is performed by α_{ABC} as follows. After δ_{ab} is recorded, α_{ABC} obtains an exclusive lock on JIT_{AB}, immediately, so that δ_{ab} cannot be operated with any new data elements arriving from stream C. At this point in time α_{ABC} looks in the temporary container JIT_{AB}, on the first input of the next tandem, for a data element with a higher sequence number δ_{ab}. This means that a data element with a higher sequence number than δ_{ab} may have already been processed and recorded in JIT_{ABC}. Since processing of δ_c by α_{ABC} consumes a small amount of time, α_{ABC} must wait for this time interval to elapse until all results $\alpha_{ABC}(\delta_c)$ are recorded in JIT_{ABC}. At this moment in time if α_{ABC} finds a result $\alpha_{ABC}(\delta_c)$ in JIT_{ABC} with a higher sequence number than δ_{ab}, it would release the lock on JIT_{AB} and include δ_c in its next operation; it would operate δ_{ab} with all elements in W_{SC} that have a time stamp less than *or equal* to the highest sequence number in W_{SC}. This operation would include δ_c with δ_{ab}. This solution is attractive, since stream operations are bound to the same tandem.

A second solution to this problem is by allocating *new* sequence numbers to each data element, including δ_{ab}, before it is recorded. This means that a delayed data element on the first input of a succeeding tandem would obtain a higher sequence number relative to an earlier data element on the second input of the latter tandem. Consequently, the delayed data element *will* include the earlier data element in tandem operations and will eliminate any missing results.

This solution relies on the condition that the order of processing streams does not influence the final result. From our previous discussions, using the set interpretation of a temporary container data, elements from a tandem may be stored in any order as they arrival regardless of their sequence numbers and the final result would be correct i.e. $\{\alpha_{ABC}(\delta_{ab}), \alpha_{ABC}(\delta_c)\}$ would be the same as $\{\alpha_{ABC}(\delta_c), \alpha_{ABC}(\delta_{ab})\}$.

6 Experiments

Experimental platform uses windows XP professional on a Pentium 4, 1.7GHz machine with 256 megabytes of memory. Simulations were performed using a standard off the shelf DBMS and a standard Structured Query Language. Two groups of random orders were created each with 100,000 orders. Group A contains order values of between $40 and $50 rounded to the nearest dollar value and group B contains order values of between $1 and $100 rounded to the nearest dollar value. Group A provides denser clusters of order values than group B and provides a more processor intensive environment where indexing and search criteria are critical to the performance of the system. Group B has a more widespread range of order values providing less intensive stream operations and smaller results.

Metadata for a typical purchase order is as follows; order_value INTEGER, ordID INTEGER, ordName CHAR(20), ordDetails CHAR(30), ordAddress CHAR(50), ordPhNo CHAR(20), SeqNo INTEGER, flag INTEGER. Another attribute for a *balance* of an order was later added to a data element for operations that involved a mix of relational and equality operators. For example, to test if a purchase order from one stream has a higher order balance than a purchase order from another stream. This attribute was designated BAL as a FLOAT.

		1	2	3	4	5
Stream A	Order Number (ordID)	1	2	3	4	5
	Order_Value $	25	34	49	25	55
Stream B	Order Number (ordID)	1	2	3	4	5
	Order_Value $	12	43	43	25	54

Fig. 2. Transaction orders in two streams

In Figure 2, each stream contains orders with unique order IDs. However, order ID 4 from stream A has the same order value $25 as an order from stream B with an order ID of 4. A sequential window on a stream has a sequence of data elements with incrementally ascending order numbers. Sequence number of each data element is assumed the same as the order number, which is unique for all data elements in a stream. We used the "normal" method of operations on relational tables to provide some feel for the performance of stream operations, i.e. how long would it take if blocks of data from several data sources were to be stored in relational tables and then the tables were processed in the traditional way. A block of data is the same size as a sequential window over a stream from the same data source. Relational tables were then processed and results compared with stream operations that operate on the streams of data obtained from the same data sources.

6.1 Union Tandem

Experiments with group A database used different sequential window sizes and "read uncommitted" transaction isolation level.

Results of normal union operation on group A and group B tend to overlap with minor differences, as shown in Figure 3.

In stream operations, differences for group A and group B are more significant. Processing time for a sequential window increases with increasing JIT size. This is also reflected in the increasing processing time for each data element. This is related to the random differences in the order values in each group.

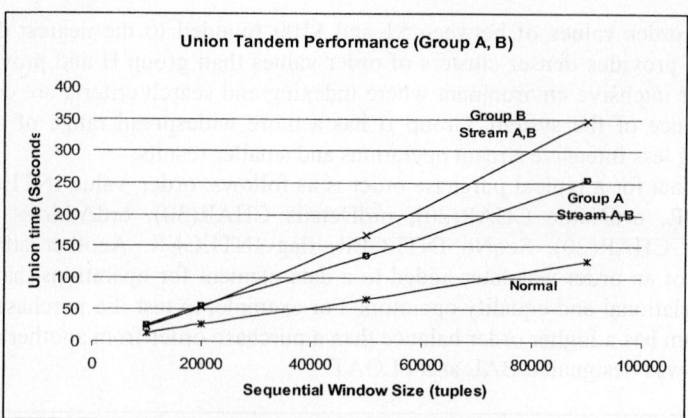

Fig. 3. Performance of a union tandem

6.2 Join Tandem

Results in Figure 4 show that consummation time for tuples increases in a non-linear manner with the increase in the window size. This relates to several tuples produced as the result of the consummation of an atomic tuple and consequent exponential rise in the size of JIT_{AB}. An interesting point to note is the time measured for a normal join operation with a window of 5,000 tuples. The performance becomes more inferior to a stream operation from this point onward. Reason for this difference can be pinpointed in the logging behavior of the DBMS. As the size of log file increases it becomes more costly to maintain. Unlike a normal join, at any moment in time, a join tandem consumes only one single tuple within a transaction. Once it is consumed the log for this transaction is truncated. Consequently, the size of the log file remains virtually unchanged during the whole operation. Results in Figure 5 show that normal performance outruns the stream operation performance. This is result of overhead associated with transferring of processed data from one JIT to the next, until the last JIT is populated.

7 Conclusions

General limitations of the system describes in this work relate to performance of DBMS to cope with data elements that arrive quickly and in large numbers and application to aggregate functions. Current DBMSs are optimized internally to perform basic relational type operations, such as join, very quickly, whereas, a system described here is not. However, if the latter system were to be optimized for stream operations then it may outperform similar hardware designed for the same purpose.

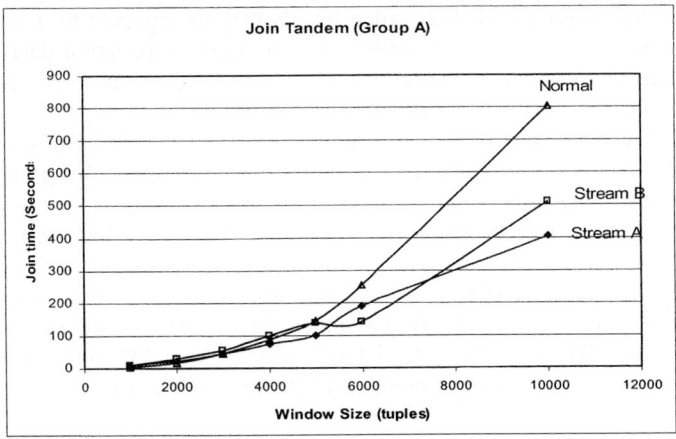

Fig. 4. Join Tandem performance for group A, category A

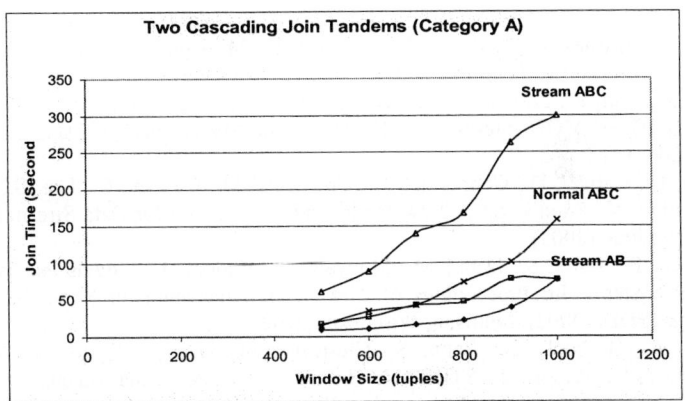

Fig. 5. Performances of two cascading join tandems for category A join operation

Future work will look into the extension of a cascading system of tandems to a model with several tandems connected as a web of tandems. This means that inputs to a tandem could receive streams from any two tandems or a combination of a single stream and another tandem or from any two streams. Development of such a system would necessitate improved synchronization methods and a reevaluation of the system performance. Another main objective is to eliminate as many JITs as possible and perform direct and transparent piping of data between any two tandems. An example is a selection followed with a join operation, which could be performed as a single operation.

A future research looks into a distributed network of tandems focusing on what method can best be used for synchronization of stream operations other than applying time stamps in the form of sequence numbers from a global table. Several issues may need to be closely investigated, as follows. What would be effects of network propagation delays on tandem operations? This question relates to a case when a result from a tandem arrives at the next JIT with some delay. How to process a tuple with an earlier sequence number when results that are injected to a remote JIT are delayed over the network? One would expect a larger propagation delay than having two tandems in the close proximity of each other, and the correctness of the final result would be delayed in proportion to the network delays.

Would there be a need for a central scheduler to perform different scheduling tasks for different tandems? Since tandems perform their *own* synchronization and operate *independently*, there is no need for such a scheduler and this system does not use an adaptive approach. This is what clearly distinguishes our system from other similar systems such as [2], [4], [7] and [13]. However, a scheduler may be useful for optimization processes and memory management issues relating to queuing of large sequences of data (not sets) from one tandem to another. It may also be possible to share the same JIT between several tandems to reduce I/O cost, in which case a scheduler's task would be to monitor and synchronize the process of populating the shared JITs.

References

1. Abadi, D., Carney, D., Cetintemel, U., Cherniack, M., Convey, C., Erwin, C., Galvez, E., Hatoun, M., Hwang, J., Maskey, A., Rasin, A., Singer, A., Stonebraker, M., Tatbul, N., Xing, Y., Yan, R., Zdonik, S.: A data stream management system. In: Proceedings of the 2003 ACM SIGMOD International Conference on Management of Data, San Deigo, CA, June (2003) 663–663
2. Abadi, D., Carney, D., Cetintemel, U., Cherniack, M., Convey, C., Lee, S., Stonebraker, M., Tatbul, N., Zdonik, S.: A New Model and Architecture for Data Stream Management. VLDB Journal (2003)
3. Babcock, B., Babu, S., Datar, M., Motwani, R., Widom, J.: Models and Issues in Data Stream Systems. In: Proceedings of 21st ACM Symposium on Principles of Database Systems (PODS 2002), Madison, Wisconsin (2002) 1-16
4. Arasu, A., Babcock, B., Babu, S., Cieslewicz, J., Datar, M., Ito, K., Motwani, R., Srivastava, U., Widom, J.: STREAM: The Stanford Stream Data Manager, In: Bulletin of technical committee on Data Engineering, IEEE Computer Society (2003) 19-26
5. Babcock, B., Babu, S., Datar, M., Motvani, R.: Chain: Operator scheduling for memory minimization in data stream systems. In: Proceedings of the 2003 ACM SIGMOD International Conference on Management of Data (2003) 253–264
6. Carney, D., Cetintemel, U., Rasin, A., Zdonik, S., Cherniack, M., Stonebraker, M.: Operator Scheduling in a Data Stream Manager. In: proceedings of the 29th International Conference on Very Large Data Bases (VLDB'03) (2003)
7. Chen, J.: NiagraCQ: A scalable continuous query system for Internet databases. In: Proc. of the 2000 ACM SIGMOD Intl. Conf. on Management of Data (2000) 379–390
8. Cranor, C., Johnson, T., Spatscheck, O., Shkapenyuk, V.: The Gigascope Stream Database. In: Bulletin of technical committee on Data Engineering, IEEE Computer Society, (2003) 27-32
9. Cola, J.L., Pouzet, M.: Type-based Initialization Analysis of a Synchronous Data-flow Language. Electronic Notes in Theoretical Computer Science 65 No. 5 (2002)
10. Hellerstein, J.M., Hass, P. J., Wang, H.: Online Aggregation. In: Proceedings of the 1997 ACM SIGMOD International Conference on Management of Data, (1997) 171-182
11. Lars, B., Mark, L.: Incremental Computation of Time-Varying Query Expressions. IEEE Transactions on Knowledge and Data Engineering, vol. 7, No. 4, (1995) 583-590

12. Madden, S., Shah, M., Hellerstein, J.M., Raman, V.: Continuously adaptive continuous queries over streams. In: Proceedings of the 2002 ACM SIGMOD International Conference on Management of Data, Madison, Wisconsin, June 4-6, (2002) 49–60
13. Krishnamurthy, S., Chandrasekaran, S., Cooper, O., Deshpande, A., Franklin, M. J., Hellerstein, J., Hong, W., Madden, S. R., Reiss, F., Shah, M. A.: TelegraphCQ: An architectural status report. Bulletin of the Technical Committee on Data Engineering, (2003) 11–18
14. Shanmugasundaram, J., Tufte, K., DeWitt, D. J., Naughton, J. F., Maier, D.: Architecting a network query engine for producing partial results. In: Proc. of the 2000 Intl. Workshop on the Web and Databases, (2000) 17–22
15. Srinivasan, V., Carey, M.J.: Compensation-Based On-Line Query Processing. In: Proceedings of the 1992 ACM SIGMOD International Conference on Management of Data, (1991) 331-340
16. Zdonik, S., Stonebraker, M., Cherniack, M., Cetintemel, U., Balazinska, M., Balakrishnan, H.: The Aurora and Medusa Projects. In: Bulletin of technical committee on Data Engineering, IEEE Computer Society, (2003) 3-10
17. Abadi, D., Carney, D., Cetintemel, U., Cherniack, M., Convey, C., Lee, S., Stonebraker, M., Tatbul, N., Zdonik S.: Aurora: A New Model and Architecture for Data Stream Management. VLDB Journal, Vol. 12, No. 2, (2003)
18. Motwani, R., Widom, J., Arasu, A., Babcock, B., Babu, S., Datar, M., Manku, G., Olston, C., Rosenstein, J., Varma, R.: Query Processing, Resource Management, and Approximation in a Data Stream Management System. CIDR (2003)
19. Sumii, E., Kobayashi, N.: Online-and-Offline Partial Evaluation: A Mixed Approach. PEMP00, ACM 2000, (2000) 12-21
20. Vossough E., Getta, J.: Block Level Query Scrambling Algorithm within Distributed Multi-Database Environment, In: Proceedings of the DEXA 2001 12th International Workshop on Database and Expert Systems Applications, (2001) 123-127
21. Vossough, E., Getta, J.: Processing of Continuous Queries over Unlimited Data Streams. In: Proceedings of the DEXA 2002 14th International Workshop on Database and Expert Systems Applications (2002) 123-127
22. Vossough, E.: Adaptable Processing of Large Data Sets in Distributed Environments. In: Proceedings of the EDBT 8th International Conference on Extending Databases Technology, (2002) 101-110
23. Vossough, E., Getta, J.: Processing of Data Streams in Relational Database Systems. The 7th IASTED International Conference on Software Engineering and Applications, Marina del Rey, LA, USA, (2003) 341-346
24. Yellin, D. M.: INC: A Language for Incremental Computations, IBM T. J. Watson Research Center. ACM Transactions on Programming Languages and Systems, No. 2, (1991) 211-236
25. http://www.sontek.com/ysi.htm , http://www.ysi.com/index.html
26. http://www.srl.caltech.edu/compastro/comp_disp.html
27. http://www.traderbot.com.
28. http://www.unitracking.com
29. http://www.yahoo.com
30. http://www-3.ibm.com/software/data/informix/pubs/whitepapers.html

Outer Join Elimination in the Teradata RDBMS

Ahmad Ghazal, Alain Crolotte, and Ramesh Bhashyam

NCR Corporation, Teradata Division
100 N. Sepulveda Blvd., El Segundo, CA, 90245

{ahmad.ghazal,alain.crolotte,ramesh.bhashyam}@ncr.com

Abstract. Queries in relational DBMS are getting more and more complex especially in the decision support environment. Also, tools generate most SQL queries received by commercial DBMS engines with not much user control. Query rewrite plays an important role in optimizing these complex and tool-generated queries. One important such technique is eliminating redundant joins whenever possible. In this paper, we present a new solution for outer join elimination. This solution was implemented in the Teradata DBMS part of V2R5.1. As an example, we show how applications based on vertical partitioning and universal views can greatly benefit from our outer join elimination technique. Finally, we describe performance improvement results of applying these techniques to the TPC-H benchmark.

1 Introduction

Complex analytics and data mining applications on large data warehouses with large volumes of data are becoming common. Query optimization is critical in complex analytic systems. The difference between a decent plan and bad one is the difference between a query that executes in meaningful time and one that fails to complete.

[1, 10 - 13] discuss query optimization in relational and deductive databases, while [23] provides a good overview of query optimization in relational databases. Query optimization can be split into plan optimization and rewrite optimization. Plan optimization is about determining the optimal plan for a query such as the optimal join algorithms to use, the appropriate join order to pursue, and the efficient way to access a table. Rewrite optimization transforms the original query into a semantically equivalent query that can be processed more efficiently [13, 22]. There are two techniques for query transformation − algebraic transformation and semantic transformation. Algebraic transformations include techniques such as predicate push down, various forms of transitive closure, predicate derivation and some forms of magic sets. Semantic query transformations use structural constraints to rewrite the query [1, 13, 15, 16, 20]. [13] describes five different transformations. [2, 6] mention techniques implemented in commercial databases. [13, 22] discuss other forms of query transformations.

Our paper is about a form of semantic transformation called join elimination [1, 2, 6, 4, 7]. Joins can be eliminated when the result of a join can be determined without having to perform the join. For example, Primary Key – Foreign Key joins can be eliminated if there is a referential integrity (RI) constraint among the two relations and no attributes are projected from the primary key relation. Performing the join would only revalidate the RI and that is unnecessary.

There is not much by way of literature on join elimination. In [2], inner join elimination is discussed. The authors eliminate joins across explicit RI relations. The idea here is to not perform the join when columns from the primary key table are not required. They also discuss techniques to infer redundant joins when multiple tables are joined. The idea is to combine query conditions with RI conditions in order to determine unnecessary intermediate joins. Finally they present a real world example of a view that projects columns from all the tables but the query itself does not require all the view columns. Such views are common in large warehouses where users are allowed access to generic views and the user has no way of tuning the view since access to base tables is often disallowed. Optimizer driven join elimination is important in such cases. The elimination techniques discussed in [2] all relate to inner joins. The algorithm presented in [2] infers redundant joins from analyzing the query and from constraints on table definitions. The idea is to replace the primary key table and the join to it by the foreign key table. Note that eliminating an inner join may not always be beneficial. Therefore join elimination decisions based on cost are preferable to decisions based on heuristics

There is not much discussion in the literature about techniques to determine outer joins as being redundant and mechanisms to eliminate them. This paper hopes to fill this gap. We discuss join elimination techniques that remove unnecessary left outer joins and equivalent right outer joins. For the rest of the paper we refer to both left/right outer joins simply as outer joins.

The paper is organized as follows. Section 2 provides a detailed description of the outer join elimination problem. Section 3 discusses two practical applications of Join Elimination – Vertical Partitioning and Universal Views. Section 4 describes the algorithm for outer join elimination. Finally, section 5 provides experimental results quantifying the benefits of outer join elimination.

2 Problem Description

The main question is: "When can an outer join be eliminated?" We discuss below four cases where outer join elimination can occur (for a formal description of the join elimination algorithm see section 4). In all these cases it should be understood that the inner table attributes (columns) couldn't occur anywhere other than in the ON clause of the join. In each of these cases the outer table can replace the outer join and the inner table can be removed from the query.

1) The set of equi-join columns from the inner table are declared to be unique. This means that a join will not add more rows than there are in the outer table. Note that uniqueness automatically implies that the inner table column value

cannot be a NULL. As an example consider the following query to determine the suppliers and parts for items greater than a certain quantity.

```
SELECT  l_orderkey, l_suppkey, l_partkey
FROM    LINEITEM LEFT JOIN ORDERTBL ON l_orderkey = o_orderkey
WHERE   l_quantity > 20;
```

O_orderkey is unique. Therefore all the rows of the outer table will be selected once either as matching rows or as non-matching rows. This query can be therefore rewritten as:

```
SELECT  l_orderkey, l_suppkey, l_partkey
FROM    LINEITEM WHERE  l_quantity > 20;
```

2) Same as #1 where the inner table is a view with 3 sub cases.
   a. The view is an aggregate and the inner join columns contain the entire group by columns. It is obvious that the group by columns is implicitly unique in this case.
   b. The view is an aggregate with no group by clause in which case the view reduces to a single row thus insuring uniqueness trivially.
   c. The view is defined with select distinct and the inner join columns contain the entire select distinct columns. In this case the uniqueness is insured by the distinct clause. Note that there are cases where uniqueness can be exploited to eliminate distinct clauses but this is another subject (see [14] for example).

3) The query makes the join cardinality to be no more than the number of rows in the outer table by an explicit DISTINCT clause on the select list. Consider the following query:

```
SELECT DISTINCT l_orderkey, l_suppkey
FROM LINEITEM LEFT OUTER JOIN PARTSUPP
ON l_partkey = ps_partkey;
```

There is a many to one relationship between the partsupp and lineitem tables such that the same lineitem row will be selected multiple times. However the DISTINCT clause limits the selection to just one instance of the outer row. Therefore this query will also be rewritten as:

```
SELECT DISTINCT l_orderkey, l_suppkey
FROM    LINEITEM;
```

4) The outer join conditions are such that there are no matching rows from the inner table. Such conditions can occur in the real world when the query conditions are inferred to be contradictory. It is important to note that such contradictions may not be immediately apparent to the user and often, applications

of techniques such as transitive closure to derive new conditions are necessary to reveal underlying contradictions in complex queries.

The following query illustrates the above case where the ON clause conditions are contradictory. The contradiction is a result of empty range on l_shipdate.

```
SELECT   l_orderkey, l_suppkey, l_partkey
FROM     LINEITEM LEFT JOIN ORDERTBL
ON       l_orderkey = o_orderkey
AND      l_shipdate >= '2003-03-28' and l_shipdate <= '2003-03-25';
```

In contrast with inner join elimination, outer join elimination decisions, whenever possible, are always cost effective. Indeed, performing an outer join will require, at a minimum, scanning the qualifying rows of the outer table either as matching or non matching rows. Removing the join will therefore be beneficial unlike in the case of inner joins which require a cost-based algorithm since, depending on where clause restrictions, joining may actually be more efficient.

There are other issues to consider when comparing inner joins and outer joins: Inner join elimination requires explicit RI constraints. The maintenance of these constraints could be expensive (see section 5) especially if the update volumes are high. Outer join elimination has no cost and is always beneficial. On one hand we have outer joins which are by nature more expensive than inner join but could be eliminated in some cases and one the other hand inner joins which can possibly be removed at a cost and not always with benefit. These issues are particularly important to consider in cases where outer joins could be replaced by inner joins.

There are cases in which RI maintenance is not necessarily expensive. Vertical partitioning provides such an example (see section 3.1). In vertical partitioning the system is aware of the partitioning and therefore RI maintenance could be optimized, resulting in a trivial cost. In such cases an inner join between the partitions of the table would be better.

3 Applications of Join Elimination

As the main focus of the study we used the TPC-H benchmark [16] because its data model and its associated 22 queries and 2 refresh functions are well-understood and the TPC-H data easy to materialize in a reliable fashion. Whether such techniques would be useful or even allowed under TPC-H rules is a question not addressed in this paper. The motivations behind the use of vertical partitioning and universal views are quite different yet they both benefit greatly from outer join elimination.

3.1 Vertical Partitioning

The problem addressed by vertical partitioning is performance. The potential advantages of vertical partitioning for performance are fairly obvious. Since any given query accesses only a few fields, if these fields were isolated in a separate table, the access cost would be lower because the rows would be smaller. The problem is that all fields are usually accessed so there are tradeoffs for splitting the fields into groups but the general basis for choice is frequency of access and size. In the TPC-H case for instance, an obvious choice is to split the lineitem fields into 2 sets, one not containing l_comment and one containing l_comment only since no TPC-H query uses this particular field. Similarly, we could split the ordertbl fields before o_comment since only one query (Q13) uses it and it is the largest field. Another alternative would be to include the fields most used and smallest in both derived tables or even use three tables. These are just examples of the many possible choices. In order to make the experiment interesting and yet not too complicated, we isolated l_comment into a separate table but split ordertbl differently. Then we defined views based on outer joins. This resulted in the following table definitions (notice the need to include the set l_orderkey, l_linenumber as a unique identifier for lineitem1 and lineitem2 and o_orderkey for ordertbl1 and ordertbl2):

Lineitem1:l_orderkey,l_linenumber,l_comment

Lineitem2:l_orderkey,l_linenumber,l_suppkey,l_quantity,l_extendedprice,l_discount, l_tax,l_returnflag,l_linestatus,l_shipdate,l_commitdate,l_receiptdate,l_shipinstruct, l_shipmode

Ordertbl1:o_orderkey,o_custkey,o_orderdate

Ordertbl2:o_orderkey,o_orderstatus,o_totalprice,o_orderpriority,o_clerk, o_shippriority ,o_comment

Views are defined as follows in Teradata SQL:

CREATE VIEW LINEITEMVIEW AS SELECT
L2.*, L1.L_COMMENT
FROM LINEITEM1 L1 LEFT JOIN LINEITEM2 L2 ON
L1.L_ORDERKEY=L2.L_ORDERKEY AND
L1.LINENUMBER=L2.LINENUMBER;

CREATE VIEW ORDERTBLVIEW AS SELECT
O2.*,O1.O_CUSTKEY,O1._ORDERDATE
FROM ORDERTBL1 O1 LEFT JOIN ORDERTBL2 O2 ON
O1.O_ORDERKEY=O2.O_ORDERKEY;

Queries are then rewritten using lineitemview instead of lineitem and ordertblview instead of ordertbl leaving to the optimizer the task of deciding whether the outer table or both tables should be used. Most importantly we want the optimizer to perform the actual join only if both tables ordertbl1 and ordertbl2 are involved in the join.

Another possibility for vertical partitioning would consist of using an inner join technique. Unfortunately, although very feasible, this technique requires the use of referential integrity (RI) and hence poses related performance problems. RI constraints need to be maintained and the cost of maintenance could be prohibitive if database updates involve a large amount of data. In the case above, for instance, table lineitem2 would be augmented with an RI constraint to lineitem1. Ordertbl1 and ordertbl2 would be modified in a similar fashion to include RI and the views would be based on inner joins instead of outer joins. The enforcement of RI would have a negative impact on both the load time and the refresh functions in addition to the obvious impact of having two tables instead of one. Notice that the refresh functions in TPC-H consist of one set of inserts and one set of deletes of orders and their associated lineitem and each function involves 0.1% of the total amount of data. One fact worth mentioning is that inner joins are usually preferable to outer joins as they are simpler. In the particular case chosen however, all the outer joins can be converted into inner joins by the optimizer. Performance tradeoffs are outlined in section 5 along with the outer join results.

3.2 Universal Views

The main use of universal views is security. Users are assigned views that contain all the fields they need and are allowed to access and only those. For example, a user may be allowed to see individual lineitem prices but not the total price of the order. In the case of the TPC-H schema this could possibly translated into access to all lineitem fields, all the ordertbl fields except o_totalprice. Another user could have access to all the lineitem fields but only to a few of the ordertbl fields such as for example, o_orderstatus, o_orderpriority and o_clerk depending on the job description. Users will then be given access to views covering these fields. The SQL will be rewritten to use the view instead of the individual tables. The main performance issue is to make sure that the join is performed only when necessary to satisfy a query.

From an experimental standpoint we chose to look at a situation where a view is defined with all fields of both lineitem and ordertbl tables as follows:

CREATE VIEW LINEITEM_VIEW AS SELECT L.*, O.* FROM LINEITEM LEFT JOIN ORDERTBL ON L_ORDERKEY=O_ORDERKEY;

In the case of universal views, operational restrictions impose looking at the data through the view. The drawback is that every query which accesses both underlying tables lineitem and ordertbl will join the tables through the view but all queries which access fields from the outer table only will also perform the join which presents a serious drawback. This explains the need for outer join elimination. Performance data for this case is presented in section 4.

4 Outer Join Elimination Algorithm

The Teradata optimizer performs two phases of query optimization, namely query re-write and join planning[1]. This is similar to DB2 UDB optimizer [4] and the Startbust optimizer [5]. The queries re-write phase involves a rule-based semantic transformation of the query into a simpler or more efficient form. Prior to Teradata V2R5.1, the query re-write phase included: predicate push-down, de-correlating subqueries, transitive closure, satisfiability test, view flattening, outer join to inner join transformation, inner join elimination and many more. In Teradata V2R5.1, outer join elimination was added as part of the query re-write phase.

The previous section described in a high level the types of outer joins that the Teradata optimizer considers redundant. In this section, we formally present the algorithm. Program OuterJoinElimination below receives a SQL query 'Q' and applies outer join elimination to it when applicable. The main idea behind the procedure is to look for outer joins that satisfy one of the four possibilities mentioned before and replaces the join with the outer table.

```
program OuterJoinElimination (Q)
   begin
      Construct a binary tree 'T' that represents the
      outer joins of Q. An outer join is represented by
      a node where the left child is the outer part and
      the right child is the inner part.

      Traverse all parts of the query and identify all
      tables in T that are not referenced in other parts
      of Q. Other parts include SELECT, ORDER BY,
      GROUP BY, HAVING, … etc. Denote this set of tables
      as S.

      Traverse T bottom up. For an outer join, if the
      inner table InnerTab belongs to S and InnerTab is
      not referenced in other outer joins, remove the
      outer join by replacing it with the outer table if
      following conditions is true:
      1. Q has the distinct option in the SELECT
      2. The outer join condition is not satisfiable[2].
      3. The outer join condition contains equality
      join conditions based on a unique column(s) of the
      InnerTab. A special case is when InnerTab is an
      aggregate view and its join columns contain the
      group by column.

   end.
```

---

[1] The join planning phase also has some query re-write processing that are cost based.
[2] Note that Teradata performs a check for satisfiability of conditions prior to outer join elimination.

Here are some notes about the above program:
- The processing is done to the innermost outer joins up-ward. This provides efficiency to the process since eliminating some outer joins may trigger eliminating others.
- The group by columns of a view is implicitly unique and hence the special case of the third case above.
- The join conditions in 3 relevant to the InnerTab should be conjuncts of the ON clause condition. A conjunct in this context is a condition connected by AND with other conditions. The whole ON clause conditions still may not be conjunctive.

A final note about OuterJoinElimination is that no costing is required to eliminate the redundant outer joins. This is true since outer joins always require accessing the whole outer table to get un-matching rows. This may not be the case for inner join elimination based on referential integrity constraints. It is possible that it is more costly to access the foreign key table (child table) than performing the join between it and the primary key table (parent table). This could happen if the query has a good access path on the primary key that helps avoiding scanning the foreign key table.

5 Experimental Results

This section presents two sets of experimental results: one for vertical partitioning and one for universal views as described in section 2. We used the 100GB scale factor for experiments on a 4-node system with 4 disk array modules under MP-RAS, the NCR version of UNIX. This machine is 3 generations old so comparisons with actual TPC-H benchmarks published by Teradata would be meaningless. In addition, the techniques presented here would not necessarily apply. In fact, explicit vertical partitioning is strictly prohibited by TPC-H benchmark rules.

Table 1 shows which of two tables ordertbl1 and ordertbl2 is accessed by a given query and the performance difference between base and vertical partitioning (- means an improvement in performance). Notice that queries 2, 11 and 16 are not included in this study since they do not involve lineitem or order. All queries in the table except 13 and 20 (which do not use lineitem) will benefit from using lineitem1, which is significantly smaller than lineitem. All queries benefit from vertical partitioning with the exception of 12, 13, 18 and 21. For these queries the slip in performance is due to the extra join between ordertbl1 and ordertbl2. While the join is unavoidable for 13 and 18, it could be avoided for 12 and 21. In the case of queries 3 and 4, although there is also an unavoidable extra join, its negative effect is somewhat mitigated by the positive effect of using lineitem1 (smaller than lineitem) while query 13 does not use the lineitem table and therefore receives full negative impact. In the same vein, queries 18 and 21 (21 very heavily) use lineitem so the negative impact of the extra join is also mitigated, resulting in a performance drop lower than that of query 13. These results were obtained using the new V2R5.1 software with outer join elimination and the SQL for the queries was rewritten using the views instead of the tables and collecting statistics on primary indexes, foreign keys and dates.

Table 1. Experimental Results for Vertical Partitioning

	ordertbl1	ordertbl2	100g
Q1			-2%
Q3	x	x	-8%
Q4	x	x	-15%
Q5	x		-20%
Q6			-22%
Q7	x		-12%
Q8	x		-17%
Q9	x		-2%
Q10	x		-21%
Q12		x	20%
Q13	x	x	32%
Q14			-20%
Q15			-18%
Q17			-1%
Q18	x	x	19%
Q19			-19%
Q20			-12%
Q21	x	x	2%
Q22	x		-6%

The RF1 and RF2 functions hardly suffer any drop in performance due to the fact that 4 tables are updated instead of 2 resulting in an overall performance improvement of 7% in the TPC-H power metric. With the RI-based inner join approach the RF1/RF2 functions suffer a significant degradation bringing down the overall benefit to a wash.

Table 2. Experimental Results for Universal Views

	100g
Q1	-71%
Q6	-28%
Q14	-25%
Q15	-33%
Q17	-53%
Q19	-21%
Q20	-32%

The load time saw a minor increase due to the fact that 4 extra tables needed to be loaded with an insert/select, an operation quite fast on Teradata. Overall, the increase in load time was about 30% including the load and extra statistics collection operations that need to be included in the load time. With RI, the increase in load time is more significant since the materialization of the RI constraints comes on top of the 30% increase.

The result of join elimination on universal views is even more compelling. With the framework described in section 2.2, table 2 shows the performance improvements provided by join elimination on all queries that use only the lineitem table.

With an average 48% performance improvement for these queries and considering that the effect on RF1/RF2 is non-existent, the overall TPC-H power metric improves by 16%.

6 Conclusion

We have presented the problem of outer join elimination and a solution based on semantic query optimization implemented in the Teradata RDBMS. This solution is applicable to real-life situations such as vertical partitioning and universal views. A set of controlled experiments on TPC-H data has shown significant performance enhancements.

References

1. U. Chakravarty, J.J.Grant and J Minker. Logic Based approach to semantic query optimization. ACM TODS, 15(2):162-207, June 1990.
2. Qi Cheng, Jack Gryz, Fred Koo, et al. Implementation of two semantic query optimization techniques in DB2 Universal Database. Proc. 25th VLDB, pages , September 1999.
3. César A. Galindo-Legaria, Arnon Rosenthal: How to Extend a Conventional Optimizer to Handle One- and Two-Sided Outer join. ICDE 1992: 402-409
4. César A. Galindo-Legaria: Outerjoins as Disjunctions. SIGMOD Conference 1994: 348-358.
5. César A. Galindo-Legaria, Arnon Rosenthal: Outerjoin Simplification and Reordering for Query Optimization. TODS 22(1): 43-73 (1997).
6. A. Ghazal and R, Bhashyam. Dynamic constraints derivation and maintenance in the Teradata RDBMS, DEXA 2001.
7. A. Ghazal, R. Bhashyam and A. Crolotte: Block Optimization in the Teradata RDBMS, DEXA 2003.
8. J. Gryz, L. Liu, and X. Qian. Semantic query optimization in DB2: Initial results. Technical Report CS-1999-01, Department of Computer Science, York University, Toronto, Canada, 1999.
9. L. M. Haas et al. Starbust Mid-Flight: As the dust clears. IEEE TKDE, pages 143-160, March 1990.
10. M. T. Hammer and S. B. Zdonik. Knowledge based query processing. Proc. 6th VLDB, pages 137-147, October 1980.
11. M. Jarke, J. Clifford, and Y. Vassiliou. An optimizing PROLOG front end to a relational query system. SIGMOD, pages 296-306, 1984

12. M. Jarke, J. Koch, Query Optimization in Database Systems. ACM Computing Surveys 16 (1984), 111-152
13. J.J. King. Quist: A system for semantic query optimization in relational databases. Proc. 7th VLDB, pages 510-517, September 1981.
14. G. Paulley and P. Larson. Exploiting uniqueness in query optimization. In *Proceeding of ICDE*, pages 68-79, 1994.
15. H. Pirahesh, J.M. Hellerstein, and W. Hasan. Extensible/rule based query rewrite optimization in Starbust. In Proc. Sigmod, pages 39-48, 1992.
16. H. Pirahesh, T Y. Leung, and W Hassan. A rule engine for query transformation in Starburst and IBM DB2 C/S DBMS. ICDE, pages: 391-400, 1997.
17.] Jun Rao, Bruce G. Lindsay, Guy M. Lohman, Hamid Pirahesh, David E. Simmen: Using EELs, a Practical Approach to Outerjoin and Antijoin Reordering. ICDE 2001: 585-594.
18. Arnon Rosenthal, César A. Galindo-Legaria: Query Graphs, Implementing Trees, and Freely-Reorderable Outerjoins. SIGMOD Conference 1990: 291-299.
19. Arnon Rosenthal, David S. Reiner: Extending the Algebraic Framework of Query Processing to Handle Outerjoins. VLDB 1984: 334-343.
20. S.T. Shenoy and Z.M. Ozsoyoglu. Design and implementation of a semantic query optimizer. IEEE transactions on Knowledge and data Engineering, Sep 1989 1(3) 344-361
21. S.T. Shenoy and Z Meral Ozsolyoglu. A System for Semantic Query Optimization. Proceedings of the ACM SIGMOD Annual Conference on Management of data 1987, 181-195.
22. M. Siegel, E. Scorie and S. Salveter. A method for automatic rule derivation to support semantic query optimization. ACM TODS, 17(4):563-600, December 1992.
23. Surajit Chaudhuri, An overview of query optimization in relational systems. Proceedings of the 17th ACM SIGACT-SIGMOD-SIGART symposium on Principles of database systems, 1998, 34-43
24. TPC-H specification – Transaction Performance Council www.tpc.org

Formalising Software Quality Using a Hierarchy of Quality Models

Xavier Burgués Illa and Xavier Franch

Universitat Politècnica de Catalunya (UPC)
Jordi Girona 1 - 3 (Campus Nord, C6). 08034 Barcelona (Spain)
Phone +34 93401{7006, 6965} FAX +34 4017014
{diafebus,franch}@lsi.upc.es
http://www.lsi.upc.es/~gessi/

Abstract. The success of any activity relies on its quality. There are many approaches to quality assessment and management related to software activities like specification, modelling and design of all kind of artifacts (from large systems to small Java applets, from custom-made applications to commercial software). Unfortunately, these approaches are difficult to compare, combine or select because of the lack of a widespread quality reference framework. In this paper we propose three kinds of hierarchically structured quality models in order to formalise software quality issues and deal with quality information modelling. A *generic model* that represents the fundamental concepts related to software quality is the root of this hierarchy. Starting from this generic model, many *reference models* that specialise it may be derived. Finally, reference models are refined into *domain models* that adapt them to a particular domain of software. In the paper, we define as example a reference model that adopts the ISO/IEC 9126-1 quality standard, classical proposals about metrics and the quality-related QML language. We then refine this model into three different domain models, for a kind of component libraries, databases and web services.

1 Introduction

Quality assessment and management (QA&M) plays currently a crucial role in all the facets of software development. This means that not only the software process and the system-to-be are targets of QA&M, but also subprocesses such as specification, design and testing, and software-related artifacts such as system requirements, specifications and software architectures. As a result, we may find a great deal of proposals aiming at the study of QA&M issues in those contexts, so diverse in nature such as software process assessment and improvement [22, 15], analysis of data models like UML class diagrams [17] or ER models [19], measurement of OO designs [4], quality of services (QoS) [6, 25], and so on. Furthermore, the tendency seems not to converge into more compact, general-purpose frameworks but on the contrary, to provide new, specialized proposals.

All of these proposals share a core of common concepts, e.g. metrics, quality factor, etc., but it is not obvious to identify similarities and differences between them. This difficulty hampers the understanding of the quality frameworks, their further extension or evolution, and their comparison when it becomes necessary to choose one in a given context. As a result, it becomes necessary to work on the foundations, to obtain a set of widely accepted general concepts with a clear structure to be used as the basis of particular methods and tools.

The goal of this paper is to define a framework to contribute to this process by means of the definition of a hierarchy of three kinds of quality (meta)models to be applicable to different kind of artifacts:

- Generic model. The root of the hierarchy. It introduces the fundamental concepts that are present in every single approach to QA&M. It is abstract enough to be used in several software engineering activities: specification, modelling, development, certification, selection, etc.
- Reference models. They provide particular interpretations of the generic model fundamental concepts in a particular setting for a particular type of artifact, such as system requirements, software architectures or software products. Reference models are more concrete than the generic model but still abstract enough to be used in a variety of domains.
- Domain models. They refine the concepts that exist in a reference model to tailor them to a particular domain. Examples of domains could be real-time systems, web services, component libraries, databases, particular types of office information systems (word processors, workflow tools, etc.) and so on.

Although diverse, all these models are structured into four different parts:

- Context. It has to do with the software domains which the quality models will be attached to; the structure of artifacts to be measured; and the environment in which they operate (a type of organisation, a particular one, a department, a project, etc.). Domains may be structured as a taxonomy as it is proposed in [12, 5]. The artifacts may be aggregations or compositions of others.
- Conceptual framework. It embraces the concepts and relationships that form the quality models and system requirements about quality. The concepts therein stem from general quality standards [13, 14, 16] and widespread catalogues of quality factors [23] and requirements.
- Metrics. Here we define the types of metrics to be used to measure the items defined by the model and to state the satisfaction of requirements. Classic proposals [10, 27] and quality standards again [16] are the foundations of this part.
- Language. This part is related to the notation used to formally express the elements of the three preceding ones. The language may be used as the basis for a (semi)automation of certain tasks as the evaluation of quality requirements. We consider adaptable general-purpose languages as XML [26] or DAML [7] as well as software quality-specific languages as QML [9], NoFun [11] or QRL [21].

Figure 1 illustrates the evolution from the generic model to the domain models passing through the reference ones. In each step some or all of the four parts of the source model are refined. A single source model may be refined into several new models that may share the same refinement of some part. In the figure, two reference models sharing the metrics (MET) and context (CON) parts are defined. Starting from the second one two domain models arise: the first one could correspond to a very specific domain and, thus, it defines its own context, metrics and language (LAN). On the other hand, the second one only refines the context part of the reference model. In both cases, the conceptual framework (C.FR) is the same.

In this paper, we present a reference model that we have used in the selection of both office information systems such as ERP systems, workflow tools and document management tools, and development support tools such as requirements management tools. This reference model combines a context allowing the composition of artifacts and a hierarchical arrangement of environments; the ISO/IEC 9126 standard [16] as conceptual framework; classical notions of metrics coming from [10, 18]; the quality-related language QML [9]. We also roughly explain the refinement of this model into 3 domains: a kind of component libraries, database systems and web services.

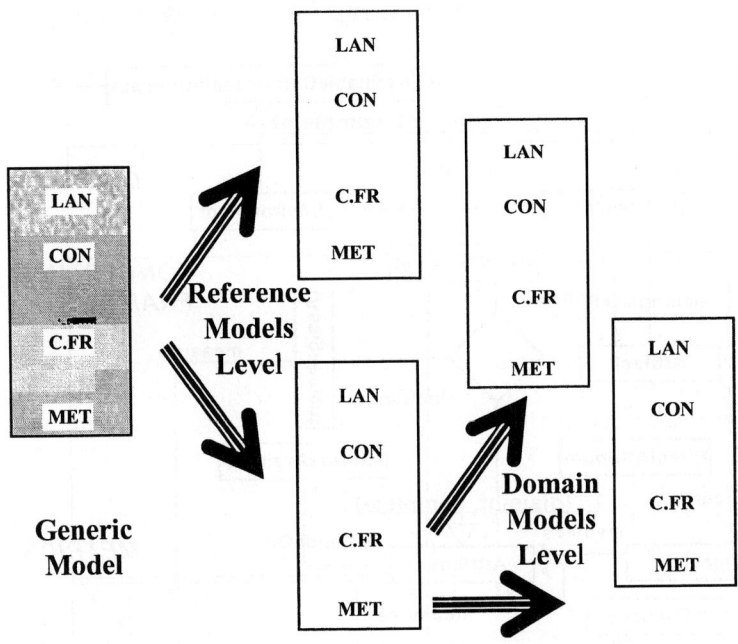

Fig. 1. Three levels to deal with software quality

2 The Generic Model

Figure 2 describes the generic model as a UML class diagram. Most of the concepts that we use in this model are refinable and composable as it is represented by the *RefinableComposableConcept* class.

2.1 Context

The class *Domain* captures the knowledge about any kind of software artifacts.

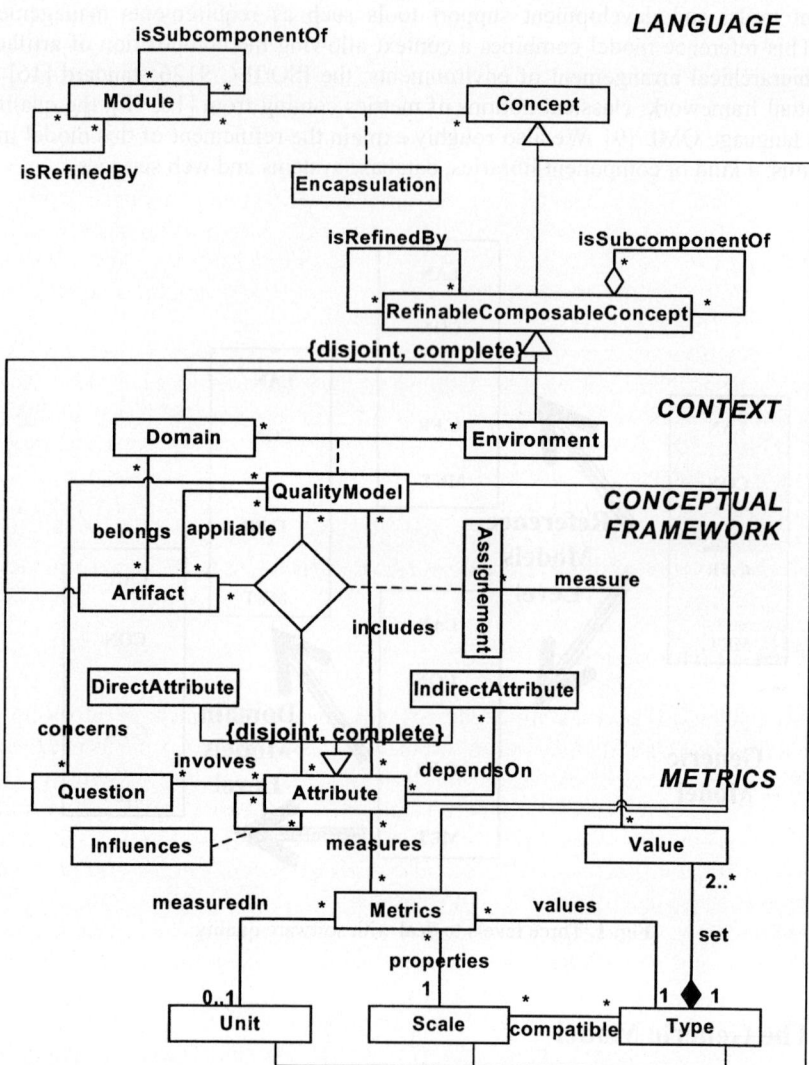

Fig. 2. UML class diagram representation of the generic model; for the sake of clarity, integrity constraints (UML notes) and dependency relations between model elements do not appear

The concept of "artifact" is utterly comprehensive, embracing different things that can be as general as the notion of "office tool", as specific as a "sorting algorithm", or related not to the software itself but to software descriptions and documentations as models or specifications. The refinement association between two elements of this class (note that is a subclass of *RefinableComposableConcept*) allows to construct a taxonomy of artifacts. As an example, if we derive a domain model for Office Information Systems, the domain of text processing tools may be a refinement of the domain of office tools, allowing some degree of reusability of quality models [5]. The component-subcomponent association allows the definition of hierarchical metrics, which relate measures of the component with measures of its subcomponents. It will be possible, for instance, to define the reliability of the component as a combination of the reliability of the subcomponents in a reference or domain model. Each *Artifact* belongs to one or more domains: on the one hand, if a domain (text editors, for instance) is a specialisation of another one (text-processing tools, for instance), all artifacts belonging to the first one belong also to the second one. That is, all text editors are also text-processing tools. On the other hand, an artifact may be classified in several domains. For instance, the quality of a geographical information system may be viewed from the point of view of information systems and from the point of view of geographical software. In fact, software domains may be arranged not in a perfect hierarchy but in a directed acyclic graph structure.

The class *Environment* represents the circumstances in which the artifacts are used, taking into account the existence of external attributes (whose measure depends not only in the artifact itself but also in other factors). The environment may define the kind of organisation (for instance: a huge supermarket, the main secretariat of a non-governmental organization, ...), a kind of project (like a CMM level 3 one), etc. *Environment* is also refinable (we may have a quality model tailored for a given organisation and derive models for its departments) and composable (we may relate quality from the point of view of the organisation with the points of view of its departments).

2.2 Conceptual Framework

A quality model will be used for a domain in a given environment. That's why we represent the class *QualityModel* as an association class. Thus, refinements of *Domain* and *Environment* cause a refinement of *QualityModel*. For instance, there will be a quality model for groupware systems in medium-size companies and a quality model for mail servers in ISPs. This means that more than a single quality model will be applicable to a given artifact depending not only on the environment but also on the domain (an artifact may belong to many of them) that we choose as a reference.

As stated in [14], a quality model is a hierarchy of quality attributes. The class *Attribute* is the core of this part of the generic model. The reflexive association class *Influences* allows the representation of relationships between attributes (synergies, conflicts, dependencies, ...). The hierarchical structure of attributes is reflected by the existence of two subclasses of *Attribute* (*DirectAttribute* and *IndirectAttribute*) and the *dependsOn* association. Direct attributes are those that are introduced in the model whose semantics does not depend on others while indirect ones are defined in terms of other attributes. Note that for an attribute being direct or indirect is sometimes subjective as in the following example: the attribute "number of errors" has a clear meaning by itself but may also be defined as the sum of "severe errors" and "light errors".

Measurement appears as the assignment of values to the attributes of the artifacts under consideration. Note that several quality models may be applicable to an artifact and note also that the same attribute may appear in different models (maybe with different metrics). That's why the class *Assignment* is defined as a ternary association class between *Attribute, Artifact* and *QualityModel*. Finally, the class *Question* represents quality requirements, constraints, criteria and other elements needed to use the model in an evaluation process. We have chosen this name because we expect the process to be an implicit or explicit application of some inquiry-based methods such as the Goal-Question-Metric paradigm [3].

2.3 Metrics

The class *Metrics* introduces how an attribute will be measured. An important restriction that should be included in figure 2 as a UML note is the following: given a quality model, an attribute is associated to (at most) one metrics. Metrics are mainly characterised by the scale type, the unit of measure and the type of values. The types of scales are taken from the theory of measurement [24]. Declaring the type of scale may be useful to avoid erroneous conclusions about the attributes. For instance, thinking in the quality of programs, we may introduce an attribute *TestLevel* with possible values 0 (not tested), 1 (tested only by author) and 2 (tested also by other programmers). In this case, it has no sense to state that a program with value 2 has a double degree of testing than another one with value 1. If we select the proper type of scale (ordinal in this case) this kind of reasoning is not admissible because it does not fit the scale. We prefer not to fix the set of types in the generic model although the set of five types from [24] (also adopted in [10]) is the most frequently used. The type of values states the domain of values and the set of operations over it. The classes *Scale, Type, Unit* and *Value* and the related associations (for instance, one between scales and types denoting compatible pairs) introduce these concepts in the UML class diagram. This part is connected with the evaluation one by an association between *Value* and *Assignment*. Metrics, depending on their direct or indirect nature, state how to find the value to assign: directly measuring (this will be the general case for direct attributes) or performing some calculation involving other attributes (the general case for indirect attributes).

2.4 Language

Our generic model states that the above quality concepts may be encapsulated in modules. This is done introducing the superclass *Concept* that generalises the previously presented classes and the association with the class *Module*. The reflexive associations between concepts induce analogous associations between modules. For instance, as an attribute may be decomposed in several attributes, an association between modules must exist to reflect this decomposition. Modules and concepts may be related in several ways: the concept generates a module or is included in a module generated by another concept, a module contains a single instance of a concept or several ones, etc. This is represented by the association class *Encapsulation*.

3 Reference Models

We have conceived the generic model presented in the previous section in order to allow the refinement of its four parts depending on the methodology that is going to be used. Each refinement results in a reference model. As an example, we present below the refinement corresponding to the methodology of software package selection defined in [8] that we have used in several experiences.
The reference model to attain must be useful to, given a set of candidates, evaluate them with respect to the stated quality requirements to select the best one. We could think on general questions embracing quality widely enough to discover general attributes relevant to the task of selection. Instead, we take advantage of the existence of the ISO/IEC 9126-1 standard [16] in order to define the hierarchy of attributes. For each domain, this reference model will be refined to obtain a domain model introducing the questions over attributes that are relevant to the selection goal in that domain.
In the ISO/IEC 9126-1 standard, a model is defined by software *characteristics* refined in terms of *subcharacteristics* which, in turn, are decomposed in *attributes*. This leads to a multilevel hierarchical structure. At the bottom of the structure we find direct attributes. Quality requirements are defined as restrictions on the model.
The questions are classified in this reference model in two categories: quality requirements on which the selection process relies and universal properties related to some attributes. This second kind refers to constraints related to attributes coming from the reality captured by the model. For instance, the attribute "number of errors" must have a value not less than the attribute "number of severe errors".
The context part of the generic model is refined to allow the decomposition of domains specified by regular expressions (for instance, one may define an office package to be composed by exactly one text processing tool and one or more calculators).
In the area of metrics, we use Steven's five types of scale [24] and usual types of values: numeric, sets, and enumeration-defined types. The last one gives an example of the convenience of choosing a compatible pair of scale and type: sometimes, we want enumeration types to be ordered (as in the case of qualitative scales) but sometimes we simply consider the values of the enumeration as labels. In the first case we will use the *ordinal* scale type but in the second one we will use the *nominal* one.
We use QML [9] as the supporting language for the quality model. It is based on the existence of contract types, contracts and profiles. Contract types introduce several dimensions, which may represent the ISO/IEC 9126-1 quality factors (attributes, subcharacteristics and characteristics). Contracts define requirements constraining the valid values of the dimensions. Profiles connect contracts with artifacts and are twofold: on the one hand, they specify the quality required by a client; on the other hand, they specify the quality offered by a server. Contracts, contract types and profiles may be structured, refined, inherited and may fit in UML specifications.
One key observation for defining reference models is that the selection of an existing language does not simply serve as a vehicle to express the concepts of the other three parts of the reference model but it also influences them. For instance, the types of values discussed in the metrics section come from the types in QML. We have observed this also using NoFun [11].

4 Domain Models

In this section we study the specialisation of a reference model depending on the software domain of interest. Not all the domains require such a specialisation, but in the general case it is necessary to adapt the reference model to the software components and systems of the domain. The result of this specialisation is a domain model.

4.1 A Domain Model for Component Libraries

Component libraries are widely used in the developing of software applications. They prevent programmers to implement basic algorithms and data structures again and again. There are a lot of them and, thus, it is useful to define a quality model related to them. As a first example, we outline some of the adaptations to apply to the reference model presented in the previous section in order to specialise it to the domain of data type libraries as JCF [1] and STL [20]:

- Conceptual framework: the standard ISO/IEC 9126 defines the subcharacteristic *Attractiveness* as "the capability of the software product to be attractive to the user - this refers to attributes of the software intended to make the software more attractive to the user, such as the use of colour and the nature of the graphical design". This subcharacteristic has nothing to do with data type libraries and must be removed from the model.
- Metrics: the reference model includes integer, real, boolean and enumeration-defined types of values. Real values may be used for the subcharacteristic *Time Behaviour* defined by the standard ISO/IEC 9126-1 if we measure it by means of some benchmarks. But considering data types, this subcharacteristic may be measured examining the implementation using asymptotic notations [2]. If we prefer this approximation, none of the value types of the reference model may be used and we need to introduce a new one with the operations and properties of asymptotic notations (for instance, $n + n$ and n are equivalent as asymptotic expressions).
- Context: we should define the structure of the artifacts (libraries); a library is decomposed in types and algorithms, a type is decomposed in data structures and operations, and so on. We should also define the relations between attributes of a part and attributes of its subparts.
- Language: the new type of values for efficiency should be introduced in the language QML.

4.2 Other Domain Models

We finish this section outlining two additional examples of adaptation of the reference model. We address the domains of database servers and web services.

In the domain of databases, focusing on the server side, the following refinements should be performed:

- Conceptual framework: as in the domain of component libraries, the subcharacteristic *Attractiveness* must be removed from the model.

- Metrics: general-purpose metrics to deal with efficiency are not well-suited to databases servers; specific ones based on number of disk accesses should be defined.
- Context: it would be useful to define the structure of database servers, which may be decomposed into storage and algorithms, storage is decomposed in tables which are in turn composed by intensional and extensional data, etc.

Concerning web services, there are, among others, two issues to deal with:

- Temporal conscience. This refers to changes on the quality of a service and on the requirements over the service.
- Automated negotiation. Many times a web service is found that does not match completely the requirements. In this case, the existence of a negotiation framework to check if it is possible to make some requirements weaker making some others stronger is crucial.

QRL [21], a language specifically designed for the web services domain, includes solutions to these problems. In the domain model, the language of the reference model should be enriched with them.

5 Conclusions

The variety of approaches to software quality that can be found in the literature may cause some confusion. We have tried to contribute to solve this problem by defining a hierarchical structure of quality models that structure the quality concepts at three different levels of abstraction. The contributions of our proposal may be summarised as follows:

- We integrate several issues that are often addressed separately: definition of quality factors, quality requirements, software product and other artifacts structure, environment, metrics and formal notation.
- We state three levels to work with software quality: the generic model furnishes a universal and unified framework. Reference models allow the definition of operational frameworks that may be directly applied because all the concepts coming from the generic model are refined. Domain models adapt reference models to the specificities of software domains. These three levels conveniently combine the properties of abstraction, reusability and concretion that are needed at different moments to address software quality in an efficient manner.

Our proposal expands the approach of Kitchenham *et al* [18]. In this work, the necessity of metadata (information about collected data during software evaluation) is claimed and a generic model for measurement issues is proposed in order to capture this information and obtain other benefits. We go beyond this idea with a model that covers not only measurement but the rest of quality-related concepts. Moreover, while [18] defines a generic level from which the metadata for each project is derived, we think in a multilevel development. In fact, it is possible to capture [18] in a reference model as a refinement of our generic model. As future work, we aim at linking our generic model with the UML metamodel in a way similar to the work in [25].

References

1. K. Arnold, J. Gosling, D. Holmes. *The Java Programming Language*. Addison-Wesley, 2000.
2. Brassard, G. Bratley, P. *Fundamentals of Algorithmics*. Prentice Hall, 1996.
3. V. Basili, C. Caldiera, H. Rombach. "Goal Question Metric Paradigm". In *Encyclopedia of Software Engineering*, volume 1, John Wiley & Sons, 1994.
4. A. Burton-Jones, P. Meso. "How good are these UML diagrams? An empirical test of the Wand and Weber good decomposition model". In *Procs. 23rd International Conference on Information Systems* (ICIS'02), 2002.
5. J.P. Carvallo, X. Franch, C. Quer, M. Torchiano. "Characterization of a Taxonomy for Business Applications and the Relationships among them". Int. Conf. COTS Based Software Systems, 2004.
6. J. Aagedal. *Quality of Service Support in Development of Distributed Systems*. PhD thesis, University of Oslo, 2001.
7. Defense Advanced Research Projects Agency. *The DARPA Agent Markup Language Homepage*. Available at http://www.daml.org/. Last accessed on March 2004
8. X. Franch, J.P. Carvallo. "Using Quality Models in Software Package Selection". IEEE Software, 20(1), January/February 2003, pp. 34-41.
9. S. Frølund, J. Koistinen. "Quality-of-service specification in distributed object systems". *Distributed Systems Engineering Journal*, 5(4), 1998.
10. N.E. Fenton, S.L. Pfleeger. *Software Metrics: A Rigorous and Practical Approach*. PWS, 1998.
11. X. Franch. "Systematic Formulation of Non-Functional Characteristics of Software". *Procs of the 3rd IEEE International Conference on Requirements Engineering* (ICRE), 1998.
12. R. Glass, I. Vessey. "Contemporary Application Domain Taxonomies". *IEEE Software*, 12(4), 1995.
13. IEEE Standard 1061-1992. *Standard for a software quality metrics methodology*, 1992.
14. ISO Standard 8402: *Quality management and quality assurance-Vocabulary*, 1986.
15. ISO/IEC 15504: *Information Technology - Software Process Assessment*, 1998.
16. ISO/IEC Standard 9126-1 *Software Engineering - Product Quality - Part 1*, 2001.
17. H. Kim, C. Boldyreff. "Developing Software Metrics Applicable to UML Models". 6th Workshop on Quantitative Approaches in O.O. Software Engineering, (QAOOSE), 2002.
18. B. Kitchenham, R. Hugues, S.G. Linkman. "Modeling Software Measurement Data". *IEEE Transactions on Software Engineering*, 27(9), 2001.
19. D.L. Moody. "Metrics for Evaluating the Quality of Entity Relationship Models". In *Procs. 17th International Conference on Conceptual Modeling* (ER), LNCS 1507, 1998.
20. D.R. Musser, A. Saini. *STL Tutorial and Reference Guide*. Addison-Wesley, 1996.
21. A. Ruíz, R. Corchuelo, A. Durán, M. Toro. "Automated negotiation of quality requirements". *Procs. VII Jornadas de Ingeniería Software y Bases de Datos* (JISBD), 2002.
22. Software Engineering Institute (CMU). *The Capability Maturity Model: Guidelines for Improving the Software Process*. Addison-Wesley, 1995.
23. S.E. Keller, L.G. Kahn, R.B. Panara. "Specifying Software Quality Requirements with Metrics". IEEE Computer, 1990.
24. S.S. Stevens. "On the theory of scale types and measurement". Science 103, 1946.
25. J.I. Asensio, V.A. Villagrá. A UML Profile for QoS Management Information Specification in Distributed Object-based Applications. HP-OVUA Workshop,, 2000.
26. World Wide Web Consortium (W3C). *Extensible Markup Language (XML)*. Available at http://www.w3.org/XML/. Last accessed on March 2004.
27. H. Zuse. Framework of Software Measurement. De Gruyter, 1998.

RgS-Miner: A Biological Data Warehousing, Analyzing and Mining System for Identifying Transcriptional Regulatory Sites in Human Genome

Yi-Ming Sun[1], Hsien-Da Huang[2], Jorng-Tzong Horng[1,3],
Ann-Ping Tsou[4], and Shir-Ly Huang[3]

[1] Department of Computer Science and Information Engineering
National Central University, Chung-Li 320, Taiwan
{horng,felix}@db.csie.ncu.edu.tw
[2] Department of Biological Science and Technology, Institute of Bioinformatics
National Chiao Tung University, Hsin-Chu 300, Taiwan
bryan@mail.NCTU.edu.tw
[3] Department of Life Science, National Central University, Chung-Li 320, Taiwan
[4] Insititute of Biotechnology in Medicine, National Yang-Ming University
Taipei 112, Taiwan

Abstract. Recently, biological databases and analytical methods have become available for analyzing gene expression and transcriptional regulatory sequences. However, users must make the complicated analyses to query the data in various databases, and then they must analyze the gene upstreams using various predictive tools, before finally converting date among formats. Beyond methods for predicting transcriptional regulatory sites, new automated and integrated methods for analyzing gene upstream sequences on a higher level are urgently required. Efficient and integrated data management methods are essential, too. We present an integrated system, namely RgS-Miner, to predict transcriptional regulatory sites and detect co-occurrence of these regulatory sites. RgS-Miner comprises a biological data warehousing system, pattern discovery programs, pattern occurrence association detectors and user interfaces. The system is available at http://rgsminer.csie.ncu.edu.tw/.

1 Introduction

Genome-wide gene expression data provides a unique set of genes and are used to decipher the mechanisms that underlie the common regulations of transcriptional response. Gene regulation is one of the most challenging and exciting areas in molecular genetics. The large amount of information gained from the projects for sequencing and elucidating gene expression of the human genome enables researchers to use a computational approach to investigating the mechanism by which genes are regulated. Not only do the identification of transcription factor (TF) binding sites yield valuable information on gene expression and regulation, but also detection of the co-occurrence of regulatory sites facilitates the determination of regulation mechanisms. Recently, biological information and analytical methods have become available for analyzing gene expression and transcriptional regulatory sequences. However, users must make the complicated analyses to query the data in various databases, and then they must analyze the gene upstreams using various predictive tools, before finally converting date among formats. Beyond methods for predicting transcriptional regulatory sites, new automated and integrated methods for analyzing gene upstream sequences on a higher level are urgently required. Identifying regulatory sites requires many biological databases, so efficient and integrated data management methods are essential.

Generally speaking, the analyzing processes for the investigation of the gene transcriptional regulations are mainly described as shown in Fig. 1, the analysis for gene expression profiles are considered to be potentially co-regulated. Intuitively, the analysis of regulatory sequences searches in the upstreams of co-regulated genes for highly conserved patterns which are possible to be regulatory sites. The co-occurrences of putative regulatory sites are detected to decipher the cooperation or synergisms between transcription factors.

An integrated system for analyzing transcriptional regulatory sites in the human genome was designed and implemented. Users can input a gene group or a set of upstream sequences, and then work on the analysis of the transcriptional regulatory sequences stepwise. The system returns putative regulatory sites, as well as co-occurrences of sites. The specific aim is to develop a predictive system that automatically performs the gene upstream analysis to predict transcriptional regulatory sites. The predictive system facilitates the detection of regulatory sites in upstream regions of the genes and help to discover co-occurrence of the regulatory sites.

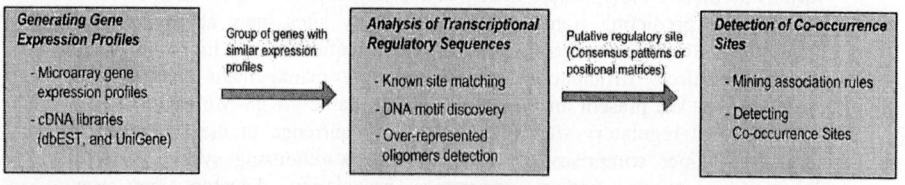

Fig. 1. The analyzing process in gene transcriptional regulation

2 Designs Goals

The research goal in this work is mainly to establish a predictive system, namely RgS-Miner, for the analyses of transcriptional regulatory sequences in the gene upstream sequences. The system facilitates the comprehensive *in silico* gene regulation analyzing processes of correlating co-regulated gene groups from gene expression profiles, predicting regulatory sites in co-regulated gene upstreams, and detecting the co-occurrence of putative sites.

Since the analyses in the system require multiple biological databases in various types of data sources, a biological data warehouse based on a Relational Database Management System (RDBMS) is designed and constructed to integrate and maintain a variety of heterogeneous biological databases.

The system enables the functions as follows. (1) Extraction of gene information and tailoring the upstream regions. (2) Predicting regulatory sites. (3) Detecting site co-occurrences. (4) The visualization tools showing the synergy between transcription factors. (5) User profiles and historical pages. Additionally, RgS-Miner integrates multiple regulatory site prediction methodologies and proposes an approach to combine the result regulatory site into non-redundant ones.

Another design goal in this work is to design and implement the interface of the RgS-Miner system. Users can input a set of gene groups in the data input page to access the biological data warehouse to obtain the biological information. All the analyzing steps are processed on the web interface step by step and the results of each step are stored in the data warehouse. The system provides both text formats and visualizing formats to show the analyzed results.

3 Architectural Overview of RgS-Miner

The system is designed to record information about human genomic sequences, gene information, the transcription factors (TF) and TF binding sites, gene transcriptional start sites (TSS), repetitive elements, and CpG islands in the database. The system facilitates the detection of regulatory sites in human genome by inputting a gene group, which can be constructed based on the cluster analysis of gene expression data or the genes considered potentially co-regulated under particular transcriptional regulation mechanisms. Additionally, graphical web interfaces are designed to show the upstream regions where regulatory sites or site combinations occurs. User profiles and analyzing histories are also maintained in the database.

3.1 Biological Data Management

A lot of biological databases in different formats provide valuable information in each molecular biology research field. In order to efficiently manage the information from multiple biological databases to facilitate the implementation of the proposed system, we incorporate the concept of data warehousing system to construct a biological data warehouse, which maintains, updates and integrates all the required biological databases in the proposed system. Especially, this study incorporates the repetitive sequences in eukaryotic genomes to detect over-represented repeats during the analysis of transcriptional regulation of gene expression.

As shown in Fig. 2, we design and implement a data warehouse to integrate the RgS-Miner databases and multiple heterogeneous biological data sources such as GenBank at NCBI [1], Ensembl [2], TRANSFAC [3], Eponine [4], and Tandem-Repeat-Finder [5]. The relational database model is incorporated in the internal database model of the biological data warehouse. Wrappers and monitors are designed for each type of biological database, which the wrappers are capable of converting the external data into the internal data model and the monitors monitor and update the states of the external data sources. The proposed data warehousing system also provides a uniform query interface for easily retrieving the biological information required in the analysis of transcriptional regulatory sites in RgS-Miner system.

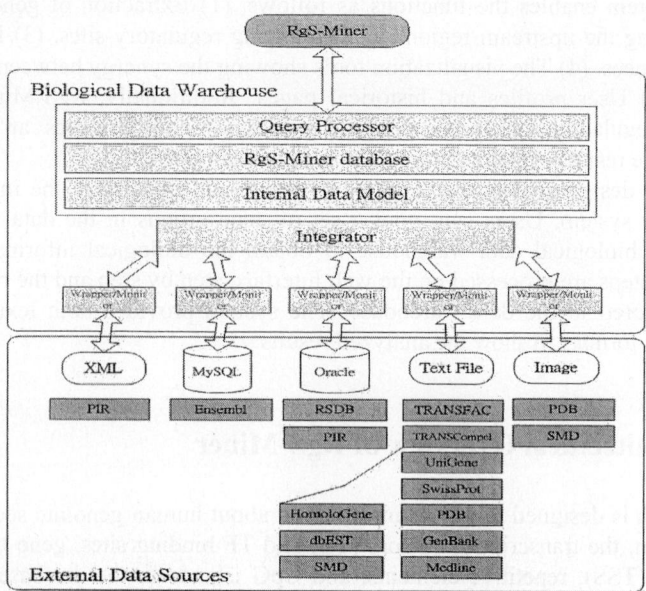

Fig. 2. The biological data warehouse overview

Each external data sources are categorized into different types in biological meaning, as well as the different storing data types. The data types of the external data sources are text-file, XML, image, MySQL database model, and Oracle database model. Especially, some external data sources contain more than one data types, e.g., the protein structures in the protein data bank (PDB) is in text-file as well as structural images. Generally, most of the external data sources provide the data files which can be downloaded freely and directly.

The data warehouse can convert various data formats into the relational database model and store the data into the warehouse. The internal database schema based on relational database model is designed to maintain the required biological information from different databases. To maintain the user profiles and analyzing histories, the RgS-Miner system stores the user input cases and the analyzing results of each steps in the database in the biological data warehouse. For each analyzing case, users can submit a gene group for the analysis of regulatory sequences. The case descriptions, putative regulatory sites, and site co-occurrences are stored in the relations of "Site", "Cases", "Patterns", and "Rules", respectively.

In order to integrate the external data sources into the internal database in the warehouse system, the integrator is responsible for bringing source data into the data warehouse, propagating changes in the source relations to the data warehouse, and maintaining the data extracted in the data warehouse, which may include merging, filtering and summarizing information from different information sources. When storing integrated data, it may need to obtain further information from the same or different information sources. Then it would send requests to the appropriate wrapper modules below it.

The wrapper/monitor for each biological database are designed and implemented. The major tasks of the wrapper/monitor are the translation and change detection. The wrapper is responsible for translating the schema of the information source it concerns to the schema which is used by the data warehouse system. The monitor module is in charge of detecting any change from the information source it connects to, and reporting those changes to the component above, the integrator. Any change from information sources will be propagated to the integrator.

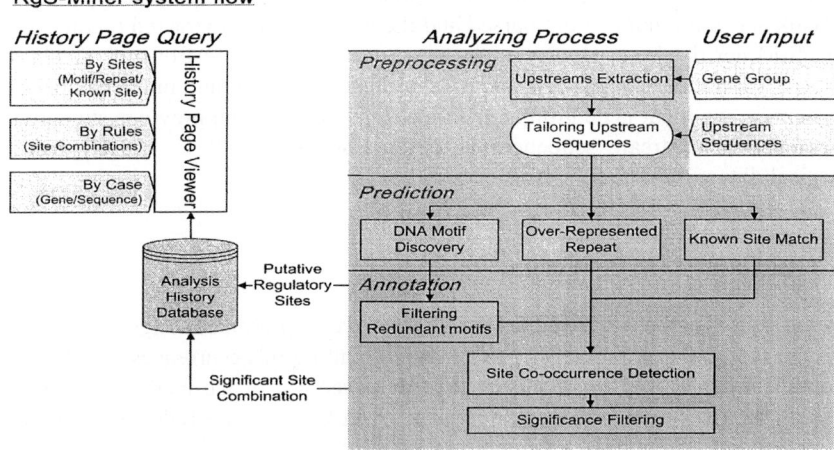

Fig. 3. The system flow

3.2 System Flow

Fig. 3 shows the system flow for analyzing transcriptional regulatory sequences. Users first input a set of genes or a set of upstream sequences. The preprocessing phase returns a set of upstream regions. In the subsequent prediction phase, statistical and computational methods, known site matching, detection of over-represented (OR) oligonucleotides and DNA motif discovery, are provided to predict regulatory sites. Users separately run each predictive method to detect the regulatory sites in the upstream regions. Many highly similar regulatory motifs are thus detected. The system has the function to group the redundant motifs; a representative motif is selected in each such group.

The annotation phase for identifying the co-occurrence of regulatory sites follows the detection of the putative regulatory sites and motif groups in the prediction phase. For each site found in a particular group of gene upstreams, a statistical measurement, the cumulative hyper-geometric distribution, is determined to filter out insignificant sites. The putative regulatory sites and site co-occurrences are presented in both textual and graphical formats. The results of each step of the analysis are automatically stored in the database. User can login the system to query user profiles and history pages, which are then displayed on the web pages.

3.3 Preprocessing

The gene upstreams can be from our database through a query or from user submitted sequences if the gene instances are not found in the database. Since some of the genes without the annotation of the predicted TSS, the users can tailor the upstream regions by referring the gene coding region start positions. To prepare the user specified region of gene upstreams, formats described genes including gene symbol, and GenBank accession number are parsed and the upstreams are extracted by querying in the RgS-Miner database. However, the gene upstreams can be from the database or from user submitted sequences if the gene instances are not found in the database. For each gene in the input gene groups, the identifiers passed from previous step are used to retrieve the upstream sequences in DNA alphabet set {A, T, C, G} from the biological data warehousing system.

3.4 Regulatory Site Prediction

Olio-analysis has been developed to detect over-represented oligonucleotides in upstream regions. It is based on a systematic counting of occurrences of all possible oligonucleotides in a given sequence [6]. An advantage of the method is that it can detect all the over-represented patterns of a given length in a single run. The system applies a statistical method to discover statistically significant oligonucleotides, which are DNA sequences of small length within the upstream regions of genes by comparing their frequencies of occurrence to their background frequencies of occurrence throughout human genome: the frequencies of occurrence of oligonucleotides yield a pre-constructed index.

The experimentally identified transcription factor binding sites were obtained from TRANSFAC (professional 5.4), which contains 11,537 sites and 4,774 factors [3]. In the system, 3,294 vertebral TF binding sites are matched to upstreams of human genes. A program is implemented to match the consensus patterns of the TRANSFAC known sites to the upstream sequences. The program allows mismatching by considering a mismatch penalty. The known TF binding sites are matched to the prepared upstreams both in double strands; the positions of each known site homologues are stored in the database for further analysis in the annotation phase.

Three popular regulatory sites prediction program - Gibbs sampler [7], MEME [8] and AlignACE [9] – were integrated to discover DNA motifs and thus identify the binding sites in a group of upstream regions. The motifs obtained by the DNA motif discovery methods are stored in the format of consensus pattern, which includes the site sequences that occur in each upstream region.

3.5 Filtering out Redundant Regulatory Motifs

Some of the DNA motifs detected by various approaches are highly similar to each other and so are redundant for further analysis for detecting site co-occurrence. The CompareACE score [9], based on the Pearson correlation coefficient between the nucleotide base frequencies of two motif alignments, is used to measure the similarity between pairs of motifs. The occurrence sequences of a motif are used to compute the

CompareACE scores. The similarities between each pair of motifs are then used to perform clustering. The K-means clustering method is used to combine similar motifs into groups. The motif groups are used to detect the co-occurrences of sites. The motif group nearest to the centroid of the motif cluster is selected as the representative motif of the motif group.

3.6 Mining Co-occurrences of Sites

A previous study of regulatory site prediction by Horng et al. presented a data mining method to mine the associations between site occurrences with combinations of known TF binding site homologues and over-represented oligonucleotides [10, 11]. That method is herein extended to three categories of potentially regulatory sequences. Accordingly, the implemented algorithm detects sites that occur concurrently in the upstream regions of a considered gene group, and the found site co-occurrences is also called site combinations, which are with both a support value and a confidence value. In the system, a user can specify the minimum support value, the minimum confidence value and the maximum number of sites in a site combination.

In the step, the RgS-Miner detect the site occurrence associations from the combinations of the TF binding site homologues, over-represented repetitive sequences, and DNA motifs by implemented algorithm Apriori and AprioriTid algorithm [12]. The site co-occurrence detection detects co-occurring site combinations in the upstream regions. The cumulative hyper-geometric probability has been used to assess the functional significance of computationally derived motifs [13, 9, 14]. A motif pair is considered to co-occur significantly if the hyper-geometric P-value is less than the reciprocal of the total number of motif pairs tested; that is, if $P(C>c') < 1/MP$, where MP is the total number of site pairs considered in the analysis.

3.7 Interfaces

The system requires users to input the case name and description to enable the result of the analysis of each user's input case to be stored. The result in text format contains the consensus pattern of TF binding sites, the number of the upstream sequences in which the TF binding sites occur, and the description of the TF binding sites. RgS-Miner also provides the detailed information about site occurrences in the upstream regions, obtained by clicking on links on the web pages. The interface shows the over-represented (OR) oligonucleotides (also called repeats) and their corresponding p-values, which measure the over-representation of the oligonucleotides.

The system has two output pages to present site combinations - a tree-like view and a circular synergy map - to elucidate the relationship among site combinations. The tree-like view presents the site combinations that contain the pattern either on the right or left. The circular synergy map shows the synergism between putative regulatory sites.

4 Implementation

The biological data warehouse is implemented by using the MySQL relational database management system version 3.23, which is running on a PC server under the Linux Red Hat 8.0 operating system. The wrapper and monitors are written by C/C++ programming language. Typically, the lengths of the query oligonucleotides in the application of regulatory site prediction do not exceed 25 bps. We construct the suffix-array and support the querying of occurrences of oligonucleotides whose length from 4 to 25 bps. For the sake of efficiently providing the analysis requirements in RgS-Miner system, the index of whole genome sequences are implemented. The query forms and output pages on the web are created dynamically by CGI scripts written in PHP programming language, which accesses the database via the PHP-MySQL module.

5 Related Works

Many experimentally identified TF binding sites have been collected in TRANSFAC [3], which is the most complete and well maintained database of transcription factors, their genomic binding sites and DNA-binding profiles. van Helden et al. systematically searched promoter regions of potentially co-regulated genes for over-represented repetitive oligonucleotides, which could perhaps be transcription factor binding sites, involved in regulating genes [15]. Numerous methods including Consensus [16], MEME [8], Gibbs Sampler [7] and ANN-Spec [17], for multiple local alignment have been employed to tackle the problem for identifying individual TF binding site patterns. In many cases in which binding sites for transcription factors are experimentally determined. Brāzma et al. [18] developed a general software tool to find and analyze combinations of transcription factor binding sites that occur in upstream regions of the genes in the yeast genome. Their tool can identify all the combinations of sites that satisfy the given parameters with respect to a given set of gene in promoter regions, their counter sets and the chosen set of sites.

RSA tools [6] is a web site for performing computational analysis of regulatory sequences, focusing on yeast. A series of computer programs have been developed and integrated for the analyzing transcriptional regulatory sequences. The TOUCAN system is a Java application for predicting cis-regulatory elements from a set of co-expressed or co-regulated genes [19]. Putative sites of known transcription factors are detected using a database of known site and a probability background model.

6 Discussions

The system facilitates the analysis of gene transcription regulatory sequences in a set of potentially co-regulated genes. Many computational and statistical methods have been previously developed to compare the gene expression profiles obtained from microarray experiments or cDNA libraries, and thus elucidate the gene co-expression.

DNA motif discovery methods represent the occurrence sequences of a pattern as a consensus pattern and a position weight matrix (PWM). The system currently supports only consensus patterns in the analyses, but the PWM will be supported in the future. Limited by computational power, the system is currently restricted in its application to up to 25 genes in a submitted group, and each the length of the sequences may not exceed 3000 bps.

Comparing the predictions that pertain to multiple gene groups in various biological considerations is interesting and important work. Statistical and computational methods are designed to examine the group-specificity of the putative regulatory sites as well as the co-occurrence of regulatory sites. The authors plan to support the development of functionality to asses the group-specificity of the putative regulatory sites and co-occurrence sites in the future.

We present a novel system to integrate different approaches for detecting putative transcriptional regulatory sites in the upstream regions of genes. The system as several characteristics addressed as follows: (i) The required gene annotation information, human genome sequences, and upstream features are *prior* storing in the RgS-Miner database which is comprised in the proposed biological data warehouse. (ii) The sequences of the gene upstream regions can be tailored easily by just specifying the start and end positions. (ii) Cross-species comparison of known TF binding sites between human and other vertebrates is also provided. (iii) To efficiently obtain the background frequency of an oligonucleotide, we establish a special data structure to index whole genomic sequences. (iv) to merge the redundant motifs predicted by different methods, we propose a motif grouping methodology to result non-redundant motif groups. (v) Investigating the synergism of putative regulatory sites, the system implements a data mining algorithm to detect the site co-occurrences, and adapt statistical methods to filter insignificant site combinations. In addition to the tree-like view and the circular synergy map facilitates the representation of the regulatory site synergisms.

Acknowledgements

The authors would like to thank the National Science Council of the Republic of China for financially supporting this research under Contract No. NSC93-3112-B-008-002. Prof. Ueng-Cheng Yang and Prof. Yu-Chung Chang are appreciated for their valuable discussions regarding molecular biology. We also thank Prof. Cheng-Yan Kao for his valuable suggestions and comments.

References

1. Pruitt, K.D. and Maglott, D.R.: RefSeq and LocusLink: NCBI gene-centered resources. Nucleic Acids Res, Vol. 29. 1 (2001) 137-140
2. Hubbard, T., et al.: The Ensembl genome database project. Nucleic Acids Res, Vol. 30. 1 (2002) 38-41
3. Wingender, E., et al.: The TRANSFAC system on gene expression regulation. Nucleic Acids Res, Vol. 29. 1 (2001) 281-283
4. Ohler, U. and Niemann, H.: Identification and analysis of eukaryotic promoters: recent computational approaches. Trends Genet, Vol. 17. 2 (2001) 56-60

5. Benson, G.: Tandem repeats finder: a program to analyze DNA sequences. Nucleic Acids Res, Vol. 27. 2 (1999) 573-580
6. Van Helden, J., et al.: A web site for the computational analysis of yeast regulatory sequences. Yeast, Vol. 16. 2 (2000) 177-187
7. Lawrence, C.E., et al.: Detecting subtle sequence signals: a Gibbs sampling strategy for multiple alignment. Science, Vol. 262. 5131 (1993) 208-214
8. Bailey, T.L. and Elkan, C.: Fitting a mixture model by expectation maximization to discover motifs in biopolymers. Proc Int Conf Intell Syst Mol Biol, Vol. 2. (1994) 28-36
9. Hughes, J.D., et al.: Computational identification of cis-regulatory elements associated with groups of functionally related genes in Saccharomyces cerevisiae. J Mol Biol, Vol. 296. 5 (2000) 1205-1214
10. Horng, J.T., et al.: Mining putative regulatory elements in promoter regions of Saccharomyces cerevisiae. In Silico Biol, Vol. 2. 3 (2002) 263-273
11. Horng, J.T., et al.: The repetitive sequence database and mining putative regulatory elements in gene promoter regions. J Comput Biol, Vol. 9. 4 (2002) 621-640
12. Srikant, R., et al.: Mining Generalized Association Rules., Vol. (1995) 407-419
13. Jensen, L.J. and Knudsen, S.: Automatic discovery of regulatory patterns in promoter regions based on whole cell expression data and functional annotation. Bioinformatics, Vol. 16. 4 (2000) 326-333
14. Sudarsanam, P., et al.: Genome-wide co-occurrence of promoter elements reveals a cis-regulatory cassette of rRNA transcription motifs in Saccharomyces cerevisiae. Genome Res, Vol. 12. 11 (2002) 1723-1731
15. Van Helden, J., et al.: Extracting regulatory sites from the upstream region of yeast genes by computational analysis of oligonucleotide frequencies. J Mol Biol, Vol. 281. 5 (1998) 827-842
16. Hertz, G.Z. and Stormo, G.D.: Identifying DNA and protein patterns with statistically significant alignments of multiple sequences. Bioinformatics, Vol. 15. 7-8 (1999) 563-577
17. Workman, C.T. and Stormo, G.D.: ANN-Spec: a method for discovering transcription factor binding sites with improved specificity. Pac Symp Biocomput, Vol. (2000) 467-478
18. Brazma, A., et al.: Data mining for regulatory elements in yeast genome. Proc Int Conf Intell Syst Mol Biol, Vol. 5. (1997) 65-74
19. Aerts, S., et al.: Toucan: deciphering the cis-regulatory logic of coregulated genes. Nucleic Acids Res, Vol. 31. 6 (2003) 1753-1764

Effective Filtering for Structural Similarity Search in Protein 3D Structure Databases*

Sung-Hee Park and Keun Ho Ryu

Database Laboratory, Chungbuk National University
Cheongju, 361-763, Korea
{shpark,khryu}@dblab.chungbuk.ac.kr

Abstract. Similarity search for protein 3D structure databases is much more complex and computationally expensive than sequence comparison. In most cases, existing comparison systems such as DALI and VAST do not provide search results on time. Therefore, we propose a fast filtering method for structural similarity search considering spatial features and chemical properties of protein. In our approach, the structural similarity search composes of a filter step to generate small candidate set and a refinement step to compute structural alignment. This paper describes discovery of spatial topological patterns of SSEs in 3D space and the construction of histograms for chemical properties. To improve the accuracy of the filter step, we combine similarity of histograms on chemical properties using Euclidean form distance function together with the similarity of topological patterns. Our system is fully implemented using Oracle 8i spatial. Experimental results show that our method is approximately three times faster than DALI.

1 Introduction

The prediction of protein function has become the hot topic and major concern in bioinformatics. Protein 3D structures present a strong determination of their functionality. Thus, the analysis of protein structures is important in several activities like understanding evolutionary processes, rational drug design, and etc.

One of approaches for predicting protein structures is to compare a new protein with those proteins whose functions are already known. To compare protein structures, structural similarity search is more useful technique in case of attempting to identify structurally similar protein even though their sequences are not similar at the level of amino acids.

The diversity of the techniques which involve molecular atomic distance [1, 2, 3], clustering [4, 5] and topology [6] demonstrate that the comparison problem is much more complex and computationally expensive. Some methods are quite efficient for the

---

*This work was supported by KISTEP, University IT Research Center for Project, and the RRC of MOST and KOSEF in Korea.

pairwise comparison of structures. However, when performing similarity search on a database, all these methods practice exhaustive searches.

The major crucial issues of the existing methods are as follows: 1) many methods mentioned above perform a single step of similarity search at the atomic coordinate level by running a whole scan of entire structure databases. They are simply too slow for automatic similarity searching and all-against-all neighboring of known structures. In most cases, existing comparison systems such as DALI [1] and VAST [7] do not provide search result on time. 2). Most methods lack of simultaneously considering a series of defined molecular properties (geometry, topology, and chemical properties) and do not consider multiple levels of structural features in comparison. Associated properties of the conventional comparison methods are mainly geometry features such as intra-molecular distance.

The objective of our work is to develop a fast filtering method for similarity search in a 3D protein structure database. We adopt two-phase query processing, composed of a filter step and refinement step. Our approach focuses on reducing candidate set and improving the accuracy of filtering for more delicate structural alignment. In the computational geometry, it is the fact that the topological properties are invariant even if geometric features such as length and angle are easily changed. We induce that computation cost for topology relations is less expensive than that for evaluation of geometry matching. Therefore, topological properties of proteins are suitable for the filtering.

In this paper, we describe discovery of topological patterns based on spatial relations and the construction of histograms for chemical properties. Multi-levels of the geometry of proteins are represented by spatial data types such as points and lines. Geometry features are indexed using Rtrees in a spatial database for fast retrieval. In order to find similar topological patterns of proteins, spatial topological operators discover the topological patterns of SSEs in 3D space based on Rtree index join in a spatial database. An algorithm of the fast similarity search compares patterns of a query protein with those of proteins in the structure database. The search results can be aligned by publicly available alignment tools such as DALI, SSAP and LOCK. We consider using alternative filters to reduce the number of candidates rather than applying them sequentially. Therefore, it enhances the overall performance of similarity search.

2 Preprocessing and Representation

Proteins have the multi-levels of geometry representations, which directly affect the algorithmic complexity of comparing these the geometry. This section introduces shape representation of structures by spatial objects and how to store them into a structure database indexed by Rtree.

2.1 Representation of Geometry of Proteins

The geometry of proteins means the shape of 3D structures in proteins. Each amino acid can be approximated to a central $C\alpha$ atom and a protein can be viewed as a folded

3D-curve of amino acids. The protein functions exposed via surface residues, while the internal residues supply the structural scaffold. Thus, our aim of similarity search is to detect similar spatial pattern in the protein folds, and we represent the geometry of different levels in protein structures with spatial types.

We represent a Cα atom of each amino acid by a spatial 3D point and handle a protein sequence as an ordered set of 3D points. Each secondary structure element consists of a sequence of consecutive amino acids. SSEs (Secondary Structure Elements) have two ending Cα atoms and the list of Cα atoms between them, and each of them is approximated to a vector of a starting point, length and direction. Therefore, SSEs are modeled as line strings that have the 10–20 connected points connected by straight line segments from start and end points. A 3D structure of a protein could be considered as mixed set of points and segments.

The SSE representation of proteins reduces the size of the input data and can facilitate fast retrieval of folds from the 3D protein structure database at the filtering step. The atomic description of proteins can be used in the refinement step.

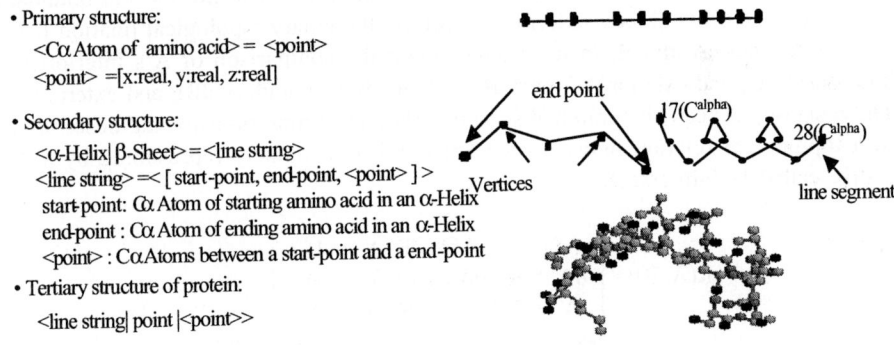

- Primary structure:
  <Cα Atom of amino acid> = <point>
  <point> =[x:real, y:real, z:real]

- Secondary structure:
  <α-Helix| β-Sheet> = <line string>
  <line string> =< [start-point, end-point, <point>] >
  start-point: Cα Atom of starting amino acid in an α-Helix
  end-point : Cα Atom of ending amino acid in an α-Helix
  <point> : CαAtoms between a start-point and a end-point

- Tertiary structure of protein:
  <line string| point |<point>>

Fig.1. The spatial representation of protein structures

R-tree indexes [8] allows fast access to spatial data of coordinates that are defined relative to a particular representation of shape of roads and lands. An R-tree index is constructed for SSE vectors represented by line string. An R-tree index approximates each geometry with the minimum bounding rectangle that encloses the geometry of line string. An R-tree index consists of a hierarchical index on MBR(Minimum Bounding Rectangle). In Fig.2, green rectangles are nodes of each R-trees.

2.2 Topological Relations of Proteins

A biological meaning of topology refers to the spatial relations of 3D folds. More specifically, for given spatial arrangement of secondary structure elements (SSEs), the topology describes how these elements are connected.

We consider SSEs' order along the backbone, SSE direction that are up and down representation in topology diagram. In terms of spatial patterns, we emphasize SSE proximity and spatial relations in 3D space between binary SSEs. Topological relations are only a subset of the large variety of spatial relationships and are preserved under topological transformation such as translation, rotation, and scaling. Therefore, spatial relation is represented by eight topological relations, which are defined as 9IM (Intersection Matrix)[9]. As described in the previous section, ending points of a line will be referred to as the boundary of the line. Points that are an endpoint of more than one point are interior points. The exterior is the difference between the embedding space and the closure of the lines.

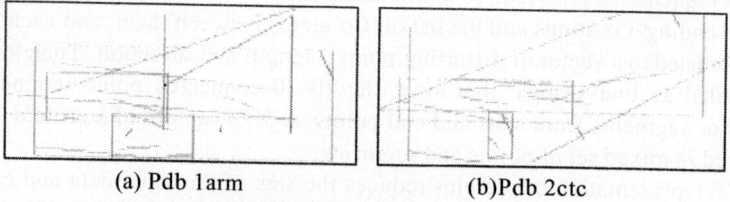

(a) Pdb 1arm   (b) Pdb 2ctc

Fig. 2. Rtree Index of SSEs

The 9-Intersection Matrix is defined as the location of each interior and boundary with respect to other objects exterior. Therefore, the binary topological relation R between two lines, A and B, in R^2 is based upon the comparison of A's interior($A°$), boundary(∂A), and exterior(A^-) with B's interior($B°$), boundary(∂B), and exterior(B^-). These six objects can be combined such that they form nine fundamental descriptions of a topological relation between two lines and be concisely represented by a 3×3 matrix, called the 9-intersection.

$$R(A, B) = \begin{bmatrix} A° \cap B° & A° \cap \partial B & A° \cap B^- \\ \partial A \cap B° & \partial A \cap \partial B & \partial A \cap B^- \\ A^- \cap B° & A^- \cap \partial B & A^- \cap B^- \end{bmatrix}$$

Each intersection is characterized by two values; value empty($\emptyset$) or non-empty($\neg\emptyset$), which allows one to distinguish $2^9 = 512$ different configurations. Eight different types of topological relations can be induced two lines in R^2 as shown in Fig.3. The relations are 2D topological operators computed by the join operation of two Rtree indexes.

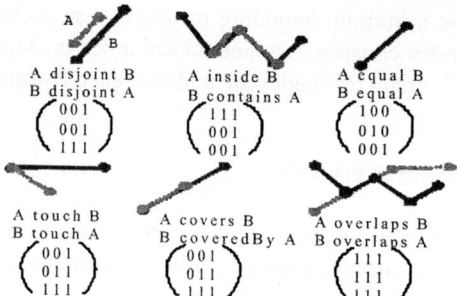

Fig. 3. Spatial topological relations

2.3 Histograms of Chemical Properties

One of the important principles in the studies of protein structures is that the amino acids in the interior of the protein form almost exclusively hydrophobic side chain. The main driving force for folding protein molecule is to pack hydrophobic side chains into interior of the molecule, thus creating a hydrophobic core and a hydrophilic surface. Therefore, it is important to identify position of hydrophobic core in protein structure and their shape.

Frequently on top of the geometric information, a lot of thematic information is used to describe spatial objects. Thematic information along with spatial properties is provided by histograms. Therefore, we map chemical properties of protein structures to thematic information of spatial objects and represent chemical properties by histograms.

A histogram on an attribute column in Table 1 is constructed by partitioning data distribution of chemical properties into partition classes. The proportion of residues that is the specific chemical characteristics is represented by frequency. A chemical property is represented by sum of histograms of SSEs. Therefore, the matter of similarity for chemical property of SSEs is inferred from similarity of histograms.

Table 1. Chemical properties

Attribute	Class	Description
1. SSE type	SSE Type	Helix, Sheet, Turn and Loop
2. charged residue	Negatively charged residues	Proportion of negatively charged residues in a SSE
	Positively charged residues	Proportion of positively charged residues in a SSE
	Polar residues	Proportion of polar residues in a SSE
3. hydrophoicity	Hydrophobic residues	Proportion of hydrophobic residues in a SSE
	Neutral residues	Proportion of neutral residues in a SSE
	Hydrophilic residues	Proportion of hydrophilic residues in a SSE

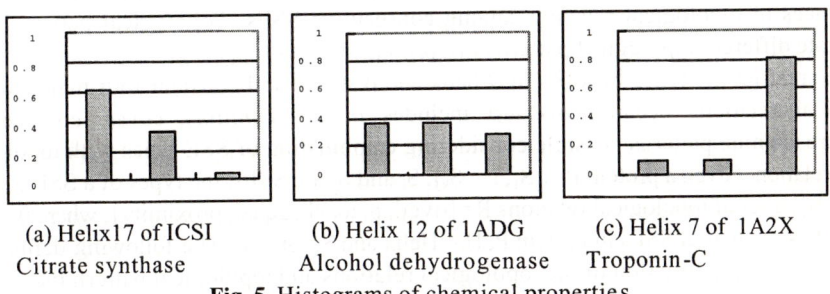

(a) Helix17 of ICSI Citrate synthase   (b) Helix 12 of 1ADG Alcohol dehydrogenase   (c) Helix 7 of 1A2X Troponin-C

Fig. 5. Histograms of chemical properties

The proportion of hydrophobic residues is marked by left bin, neutral residues by middle bin and hydrophilic residues by right bin in each histogram.

Compared with the existing methods, this method uses spatial characteristics of protein structures, which are purely represented by using the existing spatial databases. This approach also has an advantage of speed in performance. In addition, the representation of protein structures with spatial objects can provide a framework for management of chemical properties and spatial features together using index structures and spatial operations. Thus, we recognize that advanced conventional data management systems such as spatial databases can be applied to search for newly emerging protein structure data. Future work includes investigating comparison of more complex structures as well as biological meaningfulness of our result sets.

References

1. L. Holm, C. Sander: Proein structure comparison by alignment of distance matrices, J. of Mol. Biol.,Vol. 233. (1993) 123-138
2. C.A. Orengo, W.R. Taylor: SSAP: Sequential structure alignment program for protein structure comparison. J. of *Methods in Enzym.*, Vol.266. (1996) 617.635
3. I. N. Shindyalov, P.E. Bourne: Protein structure alignment by incremental combinatorial extension of the optimal path, *Protein Eng.,Vol.*11. (1998) 739-747
4. N. Alexandrov, D. Fisher: Analysis of topological and nontopological structural similarities in the PDB: New examples with old structures, Protein,Vol.25.(1996) 354-365
5. I. Koch, T. Lengauer, E. Wanke: An algorithm for finding maximal common subtopologies in asset of protein structures,. J. comput. Biol., Vol.3.(1996) 289-306
6. D. Gilbert, D.R. Westhead, N. Nagano, J.M. Thornton: Motif-based searching in TOPS protein topology databases.,J. of Bioinformatics, Vol. 15. Oxford University Press New York (1999) 317-326
7. J.-F. Gibrat, T. Madej, H. Bryant: Surprising similarities in structure comparison, *Current Opinion in Structural Biology*,Vol. 6 (1996) 377-385
8. Guttman: A. R-Trees: A Dynamic Index Structure for Spatial Searching, In Proc. ACM SIGMOD Intl. Symp. on the Management of Data(1984) 45-47
9. E. Clementini, P. Felice, P. van Oostrom: A small set of formal topological relationships suitable for end-user interaction. In: Proc. of Spatial Databases Symp., Singapore (1993) 277-295
10. Amit P. Singh, Douglas L. Brutlag: Protein Structure Alignment: A Comparison of Methods, Dept. of Biochemistry, Stanford Univ (2000)
11. L. Holm, J. Park: DaliLite workbench for protein structure comparison, *Bioinformatics, Vol. 16.* Oxford University Press New York (2000) 566-567
12. S.H. Park, K.H. Ryu, H.S. Son: Modeling Protein Structures with Spatial Model for Structure Comparison, LNCS, Vol. 2690. Springer-Verlag Berlin Heidelberg .(2003) 490-497

Fast Similarity Search for Protein 3D Structure Databases Using Spatial Topological Patterns

Sung-Hee Park and Keun Ho Ryu

Database Laboratory, Chungbuk National University
Cheongju, 360-763, Korea
{shpark,khryu}@dblab.chugnbuk.ac.kr

Abstract. It becomes too expensive computationally to compare a query protein with protein structures in a 3D structure databases for determining their similarity. Therefore, we emphasize that solving structural similarity search is to develop fast structure comparison algorithms. We propose a new method for comparing the structural similarity in protein structure databases with a given query protein by using topological pattern of proteins. In our approach, the geometry of SSEs(Secondary Structure Elements) is represented by spatial data types and indexed using an Rtree. We discover topological patterns of SSEs in 3D space using 9IM topological relations accelerated by Rtree index join to all the structures in 3D structure databases. A similarity search algorithm compares topological patterns of a query protein with those of proteins in the structure database. Experimental results show that execution time of our method is 3 times faster than DALITE while keeping the accuracy similar. This study identifies that similarity search based on spatial databases can find the similar structures rapidly and generate small candidate sets for the generalized alignment tools such as DALI and SSAP.

1 Introduction

The number of known structures has increased rapidly either by crystallography or by NMR experiment. However, the biology techniques to decide their functions are still limited and time consuming. Therefore, it is desirable to describe the relationships between known structures and new structures, and to classify them in a systematic and automatic way. The first step to solve this problem is to develop fast structure comparison algorithms. The problem of protein structure comparison is grouped into some categories. One is pairwise comparison of protein structures. It is to figure out how similar two protein structures are.. The other is similarity search in 3D protein structure databases that finds the most similar structures in a database. Then we predict the function based on these similar structures.

The major crucial issue of the existing methods[4, 5, 6, 13] is that algorithms to find superposed substructures would stop if the alignment does not change much or

---

This work was supported by KISTEP, University IT Research Center for Project, and the RRC of MOST and KOSEF in Korea.

iteration count exceeds some maximal values. To reach the convergence of the structural alignment should search a configuration space. They cause exhaustive search and heuristic algorithms used in calculation. In most cases, existing comparison systems such as DALI[6] and VAST[9] do not provide search result on time.

The goal of this work is to develop a method for rapid similarity search in 3D protein structure databases. Our approach toward this goal is to adopt two-phase query processing, a well-known technique from spatial database systems such as a filter and a refinement step. This work is based on a filter step of similarity search in order to reduce size of input for existing structural alignments.

This paper describes a new method for comparing topological patterns of 3D structures in a database with a given query structure using spatial topological operators based on the Rtree index. We approximate SSEs to vectors and represent them with spatial types. Spatial representation of SSE vectors is indexed by the Rtree.

Topological relations of SSEs in proteins are discovered by topological operators defined as 9IM(Intersection Matrix)[7]. Similarity search compares the topological patterns of 3D structures in a database with those of a given query structure.

This work contributes to provide a fast filter for similarity search using a method for discovery of topological patterns of SSEs in 3D space based on spatial database systems. Computation cost to discover the topology relations is less costly than calculation cost for searching completely superposed the geometry.

2 Representation of Protein Structure

Structural features of proteins consist of geometry, topology and physico-chemical properties. The representations of the geometry at the different levels of protein directly affect both the size of the input and the algorithmic complexity of handling the geometry. This section describes the approximation and the shape representation of structures with spatial types.

2.1 Spatial Representation of 3D Structures

Primary structure of a protein is the ordered list of amino acids. We represent a $C\alpha$ atom of each amino acid in a sequence by a spatial 3D point and handle a sequence as an ordered set of points.

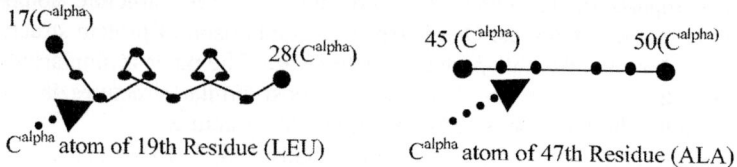

Fig.1. Approximation of SSEs and representation with spatial types

The most common secondary structures are the helices and sheets, consisting of strands. A SSE includes two ending Cα atoms and a list of Cαa atoms between them. A SSE is approximated to a vector between two ending position of the SSE. Therefore, SSEs are modeled as line segments of 10- 20 points. Proteins could be considered as mixed sets of points and segments. Fig. 1 shows examples for approximation of an Helix and a sheet and representation of them with spatial type line segment.

The approximation of protein structures to SSEs reduces the size of the input data for fast similarity search and can facilitate fast retrieval of folds or motifs from the 3D protein structure database. The atomic description of proteins can be used in the refinement step. Representation of multi levels of the geometry can improve efficiency of comparison algorithms. Detailed information for the representation of protein structures with spatial types is referred to [1]. To store the shape representation of SSEs into databases, preprocessing step extracts coordinates of a Cαa atom in SSEs from PDB flat files, and represents them with spatial type of line segment based on oracle 8i spatial. Then, the Rtree index is built on line segments and stored them into oracle 8i database.

2.2 Topology of Protein Structures and Representation

Biologically topology refers to the three-dimensional fold. More specifically, for the given spatial arrangement of secondary structure elements(SSEs), the topology describes how these elements are connected. For examples, Fig.2 shows a 3D structure of a protein while its topology diagram is shown in Fig.3.

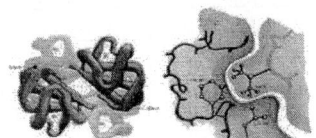

Fig. 2. 3D structure of a protein human growth hormone

Fig. 3. Topological Diagram

The topology of protein structures is diverse from that of structure levels. We group the topology of proteins into three categories; primary, secondary and tertiary topology. Primary topology includes SSE's type and length. In Fig.3, secondary topology includes SSEs' order along the backbone, SSE direction and SSE proximity. Tertiary topology includes the spatial arrangement of SSEs in 3D space.

In terms of spatial topology, we emphasize SSE proximity and the spatial arrangement of SSEs. The spatial topology is represented by eight topological relations, which are defined as 9IM (Intersection Matrix)[7]. Spatial arrangement between SSEs is represented by topological relations shown in Fig. 4 and inferred by topological operators from coordinates of two ending Cα atom in SSE vectors. Here, we use four major relations such as crossover, equal, touch and overlap among eight relations and these relations are accelerated by join operation of two Rtree index.

The SSE proximity[10] describes the nearest neighbor SSEs which satisfy the minimum distance from a given line segment encoding the SSE vector to end points of SSEs vectors under threshold distance. Proximity of an SSE to the preceding element denotes packing information of SSEs. As each minimum point-to-line distance is calculated, the position on the nearest line segment to point is calculated. Given an element with endpoints c, d and a preceding elements with end points a, b, the minimum distances between points a and b and the line described by cd are calculated.

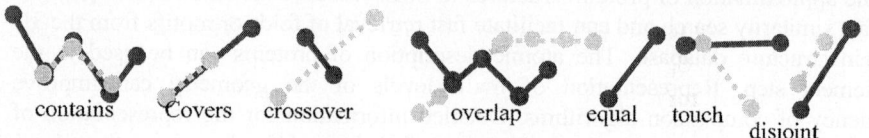

contains Covers crossover overlap equal touch disjoint

Fig .4. Topological relations

In Fig. 5, (X) is considered proximal if dc, db are < 12.0 Å. (Y) is not proximal because the nearest points to a, b, c and d are not between the secondary structure end points.

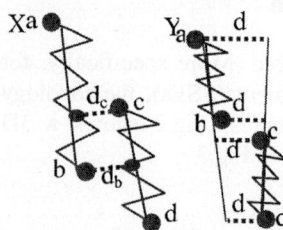

Fig.5. Proximity of a SSE

Table 1. Topology string

Topological Relation(⊙)	SSE types of Secondary Structure		
	Helix⊙Helix	Helix⊙Strand	Strand⊙Strand
Overlap	A	E	J
Cross over	B	F	K
Equal	C	G	L
Touch	D	H	M
Proximity	E	I	N

3 Discovery of Topological Patterns

To facilitate similarity search for databases, we discover topological pattern from all the structures in a database and store the discovered patterns into a database. With the representation scheme described in the previous section, a discovery algorithm constructs topological pattern lists by investigating topological relations that have occurred in protein structures.

A topological pattern list composes a combination of binary and n-ary topological relations sorted by SSE's order along the backbone. Each type of the binary topological relations in the topological pattern list is mapped to each character as shown in Table 1. Thus, the topological pattern lists are those of topology strings. To find similar structures, a similarity search algorithm ultimately compares the lists of topology strings for a given query with those of structures in a database.

There are fifteen possible topological relations considering SSE types to join a binary topological relation. Given a protein P ={ S_1, ... S_k}, S_i and S_j are SSEs, a type of a SSE belongs to the set $S^T =$ {H, S}, and a set of topological relations R={overlap, touch, crossover, equal, proximity}, where 0 < i, j ≤ k, k is number of SSEs in Protein P, H = Helix and S= Strand. The binary and n-ary topological relations and topological pattern list are defined as follows:

Definition 1 (binary topological relation) Let R^2 = {$S_i \odot S_j$} be a binary topological relation, where $S_i \neq S_j$, |R|=2 (number of SSE), $\odot \in R$ and $S_i^T, S_j^T \in$ {H, S}.
Definition 2 (n-ary topological relation) Let R^n = {($S_1 \odot S_2$), ($S_2 \odot S_3$), ...,($S_i \odot S_q$), ($S_q \odot S_j$),... ($S_{n-1} \odot S_n$)} be n-ary topological relation, where 0 < i < q < j ≤ n, the order of all SSEs is sequence in n-ary topological relation, binary topological relations R^2 must be sequence, |R| = n, $\odot \in R$ and $S_i^T, S_j^T \in$ {H, S}.
Definition 3 (topological pattern list) Let T = <($S_1 \odot S_2$), (($S_i \odot S_q$), ($S_q \odot S_j$)), ($S_{n-1} \odot S_n$)> be topological pattern list, where T= {$R^2, R^3, ..., R^n$}, 1 < i < q and q < n ≤ k and |T| is number of all the topological relations in a protein P

The n-ary topological relation indicates consecutive contact patterns of SSEs. Topological pattern lists present data structure to express combination patterns of the binary and n-ary topological relations for the purpose of comparison of similar proteins. In fact, topological pattern lists reflect spatial arrangement of SSEs in 3D space and their proximity.

To make the comparison algorithm efficient, all the binary topological relations are mapped to the characters as shown in Table 1. and the n-ary topological relations are converted into a string, so it is called a topology string. The topological pattern list is a set of topology string.

4 Similarity Search

When a query structure is submitted, geometric features are extracted and represented in the same manner as described in section 2. All the topological relations in the query structure are explored and the list of topology strings is built in the same way. Then we compare the list of topology strings.

The matter of similarity search is inferred from the comparison of lists of topology strings between a query protein and proteins in the 3D structure database. Proteins are ranked by frequencies of matched topology strings among database objects against the query protein.

Searching Database: Similar structure matching problems can be generally defined as follows: Given two sets of geometric features like line segments, determine the largest common subsets that are geometrically similar. In our approach, similarity between two proteins is determined by frequencies of matched pairs of topology strings between two topological pattern lists. To consider geometry similarity as well as topological relations, we prune proteins with constraint of difference of length of SSE together with topological relations in comparison.

Our similarity score is based on calculation of intersection frequency. Intersection frequency is calculated as follows: Given topology string sets for query protein $Q=\{a_1, \{a_2, a_3\}, \ldots, \{\ldots a_{n-1}, a_n\}\}$ and a protein in the database $D=\{b_1, b_2, \ldots, b_m\}$, compute the number of the matched pairs of topology strings between two topological pattern lists, such that the difference rate of the length between a pair of the matched SSEs included in a common strings is at most δ $(0.5<\delta<2)$. The two topology strings a_1 and b_1 are regarded as matched if and only if:

$(P \cap Q \neq \Phi) \wedge (0.5 < (SSELen(a_1)/SSELen(b_1)) < 2)$, where $a_1 = b_1$, $a_1 \equiv (Sq_1 \odot Sq_2)$, $b_1 \equiv (Sd_1 \odot Sd_2)$, $Sq_1^T = Sd_1^T$, $Sq_2^T = Sd_2^T$.

the similarity score S between query protein Q and a protein D in a 3D structure database is calculated as follows;

$$S(Q,D) = \frac{1}{W_d} \cdot \sum_{s \in q \wedge d} (W_{q,s} \cdot W_{d,s}),$$

$$W_{q,s} = \log(f_{q,s}+1) \cdot \log(\frac{N}{f_s}+1),$$

$$W_{d,s} = \log(f_{d,s}+1) \cdot \log(\frac{N}{f_s}+1),$$

$$W_d = \log(1 + \sum_{s \in d} f_{d,s})$$

where $f_{d,s}$ is intersection frequencies of a topology string s in a topological pattern list d of a protein D in the 3D structure database, N is the number of proteins in the 3D structure database, f_s is the number of proteins in the 3D structure database, which includes a topology string s, $W_{d,s}$ and $W_{q,s}$ denote weight of topology string s in the query protein Q and a protein D in the database. W_d is length of topology pattern list for the target protein D in the database.

Similarity function mentioned above comes from similarity-based information retrieval. We use similarity measure in a vector space model[14], which supposes that information retrieval systems find similar documents based on a set of common keywords. Similar documents are expected to have similar relative term frequencies and similarity among a set of documents and a query (as a set of keywords) is based on similar relative term occurrences in the frequency table.

Scoring and Ranking: The results are ranked according to similarity score S and then reported. We calculate the scores of all the proteins in the database simultaneously and report the top 10 scores and top 1,000 scores rather than set the cutoff scores for S.

5 Experiments and Evaluation

To evaluate the efficiency and effectiveness of our method, We used the PDB Release #101. The database we used in our experiments is a subset of PDB and contains 586 proteins which are representative proteins from difference SCOP(Structural Classification of Proteins) Classes. We used the same query proteins that Singh and Brutlag[8] used for assessing the existing structure comparison programs as shown in Table 2.

Table 2. Query Proteins

PDB id	Name	# Residue	SCOP Class	SCOP fold
1mbd	Sperm whale myglobin	153	All-α	Globin-like
1tph-2	Triose phosphate isomerase, chain 2	245	α and $\beta(\alpha/\beta)$	β/α (TIM) barrel
8fab-A	Immunoglobulin, chain A	106-208	All-β	Immunoglobulin-like β sandwich

Our similarity search algorithms were run on a Compaq ProliantML330e server with an 800 MHz CPUs and 512bytes memory. We used the spatial types and topological operators in ORACLE 8i DBMS.

5.1 Experiment 1: Performance

Execution time for similarity search for three query proteins is shown in Fig 6. The results show that our method can be approximately up to 3 times faster than DaliLite[7].

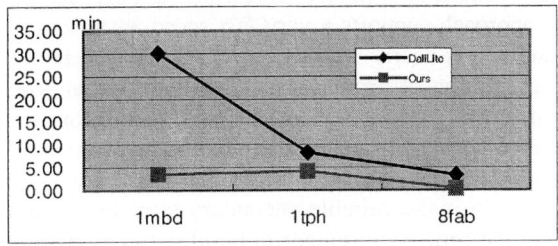

Fig. 6. Comparison of execution time

5.2 Experiment 2: Accuracy

We compared our results of similarity search with those of the SCOP classification hierarchy. If a protein belongs to the same family of the SCOP database, it is counted as a true positive. We calculated the positive predictive value(PPV) for evaluating the accuracy of the comparison as follows.

PPV=(number of True Positives/ True Positive(TP) +False Positive(FP))* 100

Table 2. Accuracy evaluation

query protein	num. of TP	num. of FP	PPV
1mbd	10	1	90.9%
1tph	45	6	88.2.%
8fab	20	18	52.6 %

It is observed that the matched proteins are almost the same as those of the SCOP family as shown in Table2. However, the cases where PDB flat files lack SSEs or have missing values for SSEs even though proteins in PDB flat files actually have enough SSEs , do not denote exact results. The reason is that we implemented a parsing algorithm to extract SSEs from PDB flat files. For examples, the number of true positive for protein 8fab is worse than that of the other two proteins. The overall results of our method are similar to those of the SCOP classification hierarchy. The accuracy of comparison of structures is reasonable to be accepted as a filtering step for structure similarity search.

5.3 Advantages and Disadvantages

Previous studies show that approximation of protein structure performs rapid comparison. The main difference between ours and other methods is that spatial characteristic of protein structures is purely represented through use of the existing spatial database. This approach supports a very fast speed advantage while keeping accuracy of search results. It is nearly 3 times faster than the current implementation of DaliLite. The representation of protein structures with spatial types and index also provides the framework for management and analysis of proteins structures.

On the contrary, our method has several disadvantages compared with other methods. The first disadvantage is that it is most likely to fail when the parser of PDB flat files is unable to make reliable secondary structure assignments. The second disadvantage is the time requirement to build topology pattern list. In our experiment, representing protein structure with spatial types and building the topology pattern list on around 586 proteins took 1 hour and 23 minutes. Most of time consumption is in the parsing step for extracting SSEs. However, the construction of topology pattern lists dose not require online processing. It does not affect execution time of similarity search.

6 Conclusions

To improve performance of existing structural similarity search for protein 3D structure databases, we described a new approach for structural similarity search based on topological pattern discovery. We approximated protein structures to SSEs and represent geometry of SSEs with spatial data types. We discovered topological patterns of SSEs in 3D space using 9IM topological relations accelerated by Rtree index join. A similarity searching algorithm compared topological patterns of a query protein with those of proteins in the structure database. The experimental results show that our method was faster than DaliLite. Search results also can be used in input of algorithms of more accurate structural alignment.

This paper indicates that topological properties of protein structures are proper to be used as a filter step in a fast structural similarity search because the topology of protein structures is invariant even though the geometry of protein is sensitive to its changes. We also recognize that spatial database theory can be applied to manage the newly emerging protein structure data. In future work, we will evaluate comparison of more complex structures and biological meaningfulness of their result sets.

References

1. S. H. Park, K. H. Ryu, H. S. Son: Modeling Protein Structures with Spatial Model for Structure Comparison, LNCS, Vol. 2690. Springer-Verlag Berlin Heidelberg .(2003) 490-497
2. O.Camoglu, T. Kahveci, A. K. Singh: PSI: indexing protein structures for fast similarity search, Bioinformatics, Vol. 19. Oxford University Press New York (2003) 81i-83i
3. Oracle Spatial User's Guide and Reference: Loading and Indexing Spatial Object Types. Release8.1.5, Oracle (2001)
4. L. Holm, J. Park : DaliLite workbench for protein structure comparison, *Bioinformatics, Vol. 16.* Oxford University Press New York (2000) 566-567
5. L. Holm , C. Sander: Proein structure comparison by alignment of distance matrices, J. of Molecular Biology,Vol. 233 (1993) 123-138
6. L. Holm , C. Sander: Proein structure comparison by alignment of distance matrices, J. of Molecular Biology,Vol. 233 (1993) 123-138
7. E. Clementini, P. Felice, P. van Oostrom: A small set of formal topological relationships suitable for end-user interaction. In: Proc. of Spatial Databases Symp., Singapore (1993) 277-295
8. Amit P. Singh, Douglas L. Brutlag: Protein Structure Alignment: A Comparison of Methods, Dept. of Biochemistry, Stanford Univ (2000)
9. J-F. Gibrat, T. Madej, H. Bryant: Surprising similarities in structure comparison, *Current Opinion in Structural Biology*,Vol. 6 (1996) 377-385
10. A. Martin: The ups and downs of protein topology: rapid comparison of protein structure, *Protein Engineering*, Vol. 13 (, 2000) 829-837
11. H. M. Berman, J. Westbrook, Z. Feng, G. Gilliland, T. N. Bhat, H. Weissig, I. N. Shindyalov, P. E. Bourne: The Protein Data bank. J. Nucleic Acids Research., Vol. 28. Oxford University Press, New York (2000) 235-242

12. P. Rigaus, M. School, A. Voisard: Spatial Databases with application to GIS. Academic Press, San Diego (2002) 29-61
13. D. Higgins, W. Tailor: Bioinfomatics: Sequence, Structure, and databanks, 1st edn. Oxford University Press, New York (2000)
14. I.H. Witten, A. Moffat, T.C. Bell: Managing Gigabytes: Compressing and Indexing Documents and Images, The Second Edition, Morgan Kaufmann Publishing, San Francisco (1999)

Ontology-Driven Workflow Management for Biosequence Processing Systems

Melissa Lemos[1], Marco Antonio Casanova[1], Luiz Fernando Bessa Seibel[1], José Antonio Fernandes de Macedo[1], and Antonio Basílio de Miranda[2]

[1] Department of Informatics, Pontifical Catholic University of Rio de Janeiro, Brazil
Rua Marquês de S. Vicente, 225 - Rio de Janeiro, RJ - Brazil - CEP 22453-900
{melissa,casanova,seibel,jmacedo}@inf.puc-rio.br
[2] Oswaldo Cruz Institute, Brazil
antonio@fiocruz.br

Abstract. Researchers typically need to combine Bioinformatics processes to perform larger, more complex tasks, expressed as workflows. However, there is a strong indication from users that running complex workflows is an addition burden that must be alleviated. Motivated by this observation, this paper first introduces an ontology that defines classes and instances of Bioinformatics projects, processes, resources and data. Then, it argues that it is fruitful to design the workflow tool around the ontology, thereby creating an ontology-driven Bioinformatics workflow management system.

1 Introduction

The ultimate goal of the Human Genome Project is to generate a high-quality reference DNA sequence for the human genome – some 3 billion base pairs – and to identify all human genes. Other important goals include sequencing the genomes of model organisms to interpret human DNA, enhancing computational resources to support future research and commercial applications, exploring gene function, studying human variation, and training future scientists in Genomics [1].

Experimental data in what follows means raw molecular data - DNA or protein sequences - and will be referred as *biosequences*. Because experimental data carry no meaning, genome projects usually include an *annotation* phase whose goal is to convert biosequences into biologically relevant information [2]. An annotation is a meta-information or a description of high level features of the biosequence. Useful information includes characteristics of a known gene, such as its name and function[2].

After researchers isolate new biosequences in the laboratory, usually they proceed to analyze and annotate the biosequence with the help of a variety of computer tools or processes. However, given the rate at which researchers now generate biosequences, on one hand, careful human analysis is becoming increasingly difficult and, on the other hand, automatic annotation presents a computational challenge.

One of the main analysis processes used in the annotation phase is to check whether other researchers have already studied biosequences similar to the new biosequence obtained in laboratory. The FASTA [21] and BLAST [3] (Basic Local Alignment

Tool) program families are examples of sequence comparison tools. Probably the most widely used computational tool in Biology, BLAST searches databases for all biosequences similar to a target biosequence.

Indeed, Molecular Biology databases have been proliferating rapidly. Some databases concentrate on specific molecules or specific functions and provide highly detailed information, while others try to cover broader areas with less detailed information. Researchers therefore need effective tools to mine large sets of biosequences.

In addition to biosequence comparison, there are tools for gene prediction, gene classification, comparative genomics, structure prediction, phylogenetic analysis, pattern discovery, pattern recognition, sequence assembly and others.

In summary, researchers now have access to a rich set of databases, as well as a variety of data analysis processes. They also need to combine processes to perform larger, more complex tasks. That is, a collection produced by one process can, given the appropriate semantics, act as an input collection to another process. In the context of this paper, process compositions will be expressed as workflows [4].

The public databases are heterogeneous, store large data volumes, are in constant growth, but do not usually have a detailed documentation of the database schema. Also, the analysis programs do not always have good documentation that describes the execution parameters and the input and output data formats, which makes it difficult to integrate them into more complex workflow processes. Therefore, there is a strong indication from users that defining complex workflows is an addition burden that must be alleviated. This context reveals the importance of creating a tool to help users define and execute Bioinformatics workflows.

In addition, since the set of Bioinformatics processes and databases is continuously growing, it becomes interesting to design an ontology that captures the major data and process characteristics, including quality properties, and design the tool around the ontology. We call such a tool an *ontology-driven* [5] *Bioinformatics workflow management system*.

This paper describes the design of the ontology-driven Bioinformatics workflow component of Bionotes [6], a biosequence annotation system under development at the Catholic University of Rio de Janeiro and in use at Oswaldo Cruz Institute [7] and at RioGene [8].

The paper is organized as follows. Section 2 provides a summary of the major requirements for a Bioinformatics workflow management. Section 3 presents the ontology used. Section 4 outlines the ontology-driven Bioinformatics workflow management system. Finally, Section 5 contains the conclusions.

2 Requirements for Workflow Management Systems

Briefly, a workflow defines a composition of tasks. We assume that workflows are written in a suitable workflow language, which we leave unspecified for the sake of brevity.

Briefly, a workflow management system should:
R1. Include commonly used tasks or processes and offer extensibility mechanisms to accommodate new processes.

R2. Guide users throughout the process of workflow definition or re-definition (when intermediate or final results are judged not be useful or interesting)
R3. Support workflow validation and optimization.
R4. Support workflow execution scheduling.
R5. Support unsupervised workflow execution, as well as supervised workflow execution that allows user intervention.
R6. Store the provenance of workflow definitions and executions, and of the data generated by workflow executions, and help users access such metadata.
R7. Help users analyze workflow results.

These requirements are fairly general and apply to most application domains. We comment only on the last two requirements.

Briefly, by *workflow provenance* we mean metadata capturing aspects of workflow definition, such the user who created the workflow, or aspects of workflow execution, such total execution time, the start time, end time, status (finished successfully, finished with errors, in execution, not started). Likewise, by *workflow data provenance*, we mean metadata indicating what workflow executions generated which data.

As for the last requirement, in the context of Bioinformatics, an example would be as follows. In the annotation phase of the genome project of a bacterium, researchers need to identify genes. This may be accomplished using Glimmer, a process designed to identify ORFs – Open Read Frames. Based on the punctuation Glimmer generates for each ORF it detects, researchers may indicate if they believe the ORF is indeed a gene or not. Researchers also typically compare each ORF with the data stored in several databases, with the help of BLAST, to confirm the results from Glimmer.

In this case, the system should organize the results produced by Glimmer and by the several runs of BLAST in a way that facilitates comparing ORFs and identifying which of them are most likely genes, as well comparing the results of the several runs of BLAST for the same ORF. A table with a line for each ORF and a column for Glimmer and a column for each BLAST run would be a good candidate for the combined presentation of the results.

3 An Ontology of Bioinformatics Workflow

In this section, we outline our proposal for an ontology that drives the Bioinformatics workflow management system. We first describe the overall structure of the ontology and then informally introduce the major classes and their properties. Although we adopt the concepts in [9], a formal definition of the ontology in OWL is beyond the scope of this paper.

Our ontology defines classes and instances of Bioinformatics processes, resources, data and projects. It also defines object properties that relate processes to projects, resources and data, and datatype properties that map processes to quality properties.

We classify processes as constructive, filter, format transformation and workflow control. *Constructive* processes build new collections of objects, and include the Bioinformatics processes. A constructive process is just a process that is actually implemented by the system. A constructive process class is a generic name for a set of process instances or, recursively, a set of process classes, so that process classes and process instances form a hierarchy. For example, the Process View panel in Figure 1 (at the end of the paper) displays the roots of the process class hierarchy and the process class hierarchy rooted at Sequence Alignment process class. BLASTP and BLASTN are examples of process instances.

A *filter* process extracts parts of an existing collection for further processing.

A *format transformation* process applies format transformations to a collection. A format transformation can be *simple*, such as a mere syntactical transformation, or *complex*, such as a transformation of a nucleotide sequence into an amino acid sequence.

A *control* process governs workflow execution. Control processes include sequential and parallel composition, stop points and tests to inspect the result of process execution (failure or success).

The behavior of a process can be modified by the setting of *parameters*. In addition, a process may have a *description* and *quality properties*. Parameters, descriptions and quality properties are part of the process definition and are included in the ontology with default values, which can be updated.

Our ontology includes the following quality properties: *performance,* which measures the amount of computational resources consumed by the process; *popularity*, which measures the percentage of the user community that knows and uses the process; *cost*, which measures the (financial) cost of running the process; *default*, which indicates if the process is the default option for the process hierarchy it belongs to; *fidelity*, which is the percentage of "false positives" and "false negatives" (applicable only to certain classes of processes); and *availability*, which is the percentage of time a service is available (in the context of a process implemented as a Web service).

The system can help the user decide what is the best process instance to use, based on quality properties he specifies. For example, suppose the user wants to compute the local alignment of a sequence against a given database. This process may be implemented by variants of BLAST or FAST, depending on the quality properties the user determines. If the user privileges efficiency, the system should use BLAST. If he emphasizes fidelity, the system should choose FAST.

The ontology also contains class hierarchies for the genome projects, input and output data and for the resources accepted by the Bioinformatics processes.

Genome projects can be classified as EST and Complete. ESTs are typically unedited, automatically processed, single-read sequences produced from cDNAs (small DNA molecules reverse-transcribed from the cellular mRNA population). Libraries of cDNAs are routinely prepared that contain tens of thousands of clones, represent a variety of specific tissues types and represent a snapshot of gene expression during defined developmental stages and following specific biotic and abiotic challenges.

The relative cheapness of EST sequencing and its associated automation often makes EST sequencing the most attractive route for eukaryotic genomes, whereas complete projects for prokaryotic genomes [20]. Indeed, EST projects are more appropriated if one desires to focus on the coding sequences, thereby reducing cost and time, which is the case of eukaryotic genomes, composed mostly of non-coding sequences.

Determining the class of the genome project is important because it influences the choice of the processes. For example, Phrap [10] and CAP3 [11] are both fragment assembly processes, but Phrap is the best choice for complete genome projects, whereas CAP3 is the best choice for EST genome projects.

By specifying a project, a resource, an input or an output data class, the system can guide users to decide what is the best process instance to use.

Data and resource quality properties are somewhat more difficult to define and are typically related to the hierarchy of abstract processes. For example, curatedness and redundancy are resource quality properties. SWISSPROT [12] is a curated database, meaning that it contains data that was manually checked, whereas TrEmbl[19] is not curated.

4 Using the Ontology-Driven Workflow Management System

4.1 How the System Works

The system is organized as follows. The *ontology management module* is responsible for storing the ontology and for performing inferences. The module also facilitates updating the ontology to accommodate new classes, properties and rules pertaining to Bioinformatics processes, resources, data and projects.

The *workflow assistant* helps researchers construct workflows by selecting constructive, filter and control process one at a time. The necessary inspection control and format transformation processes are automatically inserted by the system.

The *optimizer* first verifies the coherence of the workflow the user defined. That is, it checks, with the help of the ontology, if the output data class of one process instance is an expected object property of the next process instance. If this checking fails, the optimizer includes a format transformation process to make process instance composition viable. Then, the optimizer applies the optimization rules, discussed in more detail in Section 4.2, to transform the workflow into its final form.

The optimizer outputs an XML file which defines the workflow to the last module, the *workflow interpreter*.

The system's interface, shown in Figure 1, is organized as follows. The rightmost panel, called the workflow view, displays a tree view of the current workflow; the symbols ";" and "//" indicate sequential and parallel composition, respectively. The center panel, called the process view, exhibits the hierarchy of process classes and instances, perhaps pruned as explained below. The leftmost panel is divided into four sub-panels. The topmost sub-panel, called the project view, displays the project classes and instances hierarchy, and the second panel from the top, called the resource view, the hierarchy of resource classes and instances. The last two sub-panels display the input and output data class hierarchies. These are called the input and output views, respectively.

The researcher directly access the process view, select a process instance and move it to the current workflow. If he is unsure about which process instance to select, he may use the views on the leftmost panel to prune the process view as follows. If he selects a specific project class on the project view, the assistant will remove from the process view the process classes and instances that do not apply to the project class selected. Likewise, if the researcher selects a class or instance from the resource view, the assistant will remove from the process view the process classes and instances that cannot use the resource class or instance selected. The assistant will behave similarly when the researcher selects a data class from the input or output views.

The researcher may also access the quality properties. He can click on the process class name and the assistant will show, in a window, quality process properties that will help him choose between the process instances. He can also look at a process description clicking on the process name in the Process View.

In general, the researcher may modify the default configuration parameters of the process instance to adjust the quality of the results. The system displays all configuration parameters of a process if the user clicks on its name in the Workflow View. The researcher may change the default value of a parameter by clicking on its name. Besides parameter configuration, user can also bind the input, resource and output data instances of the processes to external files or to other process outputs.

The system also displays filter parameters as children of their process instances in the Process View. We note that some process instance already have an input parameter that restricts the output and, therefore, do not require an explicit definition of an output filter.

Moreover, the researcher can ask the system to verify the coherence of the process instance composition and, if it is necessary, include a format transformation process to make the composition viable. Furthermore, the user can ask the system to insert inspection control processes and optimize the workflow. The final result is an XML file which defines the workflow and will be processed by the workflow interpreter.

4.2 Workflow Optimization

Experience has shown that, in the context of biosequence processing systems, workflows are not too complex and, therefore, they are not amenable to complex optimization procedures, such as those found in current object-relational database systems. Yet, several simple optimization procedures can be profitable employed, as discussed in what follows. Again, the optimization rules are part of the ontology and stored in the ontology management module.

Process Pipelining. Suppose that the workflow contains a sequential composition of two programs, denoted S1;S2, and that the output of S1 is a set of biosequences (that must then be passed to S2). Then, depending on the semantics of S1 and S2, the system pass to S2 the sequences output by S1, as S1 produces them, without having to wait for S1 to produce the full set of output sequences. For example, consider the composition of Glimmer and BLAST, shown in Figure 1. The ORFs resulting from Glimmer may be immediately passed to BLAST. By contrast, the composition of Phred [13] and Phrap cannot be pipelined because Phrap can assemble the fragments only when Phred generates all reads.

Process Parallelization. Suppose now that the workflow contains a sequential composition of two programs, S1;S2, such that S2 does not use any data output by S1. Then, obviously, their execution may be fully parallelized, that is, S1;S2 may be replaced by S1//S2. Note that process pipelining can also be used in combination with process parallelization, for example, in a workflow fragment of the form S1;(S2//S3), if S1 satisfies the conditions for pipelining with respect to S2 and S3.

Data Parallelization. Consider the following simple data parallelization strategy:
- Distribute an input sequence set S among different processors, or assume that the input sequence set is already stored in different processors.
- Apply the same program P, in parallel, to the sequence sets stored in the different processors, obtaining local results.
- Move the local results to a central processor.
- Combine the local results, in the central processor, using some combination procedure C, to obtain the final result.

The strategy would be correct if the final result is the same as applying P to S.

As an example, consider again the scenario of Figure 1. It is viable to distribute a set of contigs among several processors and then run Glimmer in each of them to parallelize ORF discovery. The final result is simply the union of the local results. This is, therefore, an example of a very simple combination procedure.

Global Optimization. By global optimization, we mean optimizing together several workflows that work on approximately the same data, at approximately the same time, to reduce the volume of data accesses or data moves across different processors. This might involve simultaneous access to cached data, or even caching data across different transactions, as implemented in object oriented databases.

4.3 An Example of a Workflow

Figure 1 depicts the system interface corresponding to the example discussed in this section. As a first step, suppose that a researcher starts with a set of chromatograms and that he wants to identify the bases of the sequences. If the user does not know which process to select, he may select Chromatogram Set (the input data class) in the Input View and then click on the ">" button. The system will show all processes which accept chromatograms as input class in the Process View. In this case, the tree will have the Bases Identification as process class with Phred and Abiview as process instances. The researcher may select one of them or, if he is unsure, he may click on the Bases Identification class process. The assistant will show, in a window, quality process properties that will help him choose between the Phred and Abiview process instances. For example, cost differentiates these process instances since Phred is a free software and Abiview is licensed. If the user indicates that cost is relevant, the assistant will suggest Phred as the best option. In this example, suppose that Phred is selected, as shown in the Workflow View.

Next, the researcher has to select a process to obtain contigs by assembling the reads. CAP3 and Phrap are process instances designed to perform this task. The user may select one of these process instances directly from the Processes View or he may indicate the input data class, the output data class and the project class he is working on. If he indicates Read Set as the input data class, the system will list a large number of process classes and process instances which accept this input data class as an object property, direct or indirectly. For example, the system will include Sequence Assembly in the list, since it accepts Read Set as an object property, as well as Sequence Alignment, which accepts any sequence as an object property, including Read Sets. If the user indicates Contig Set as output data class, the assistant will restrict the possibilities and will only display a tree with Sequence Assembly as process class and Phrap and CAP3 as process instances. If the user is still in doubt, he may indicate the project class he is working on. In our example, the project type is Complete, which implies that Phrap is the best process.

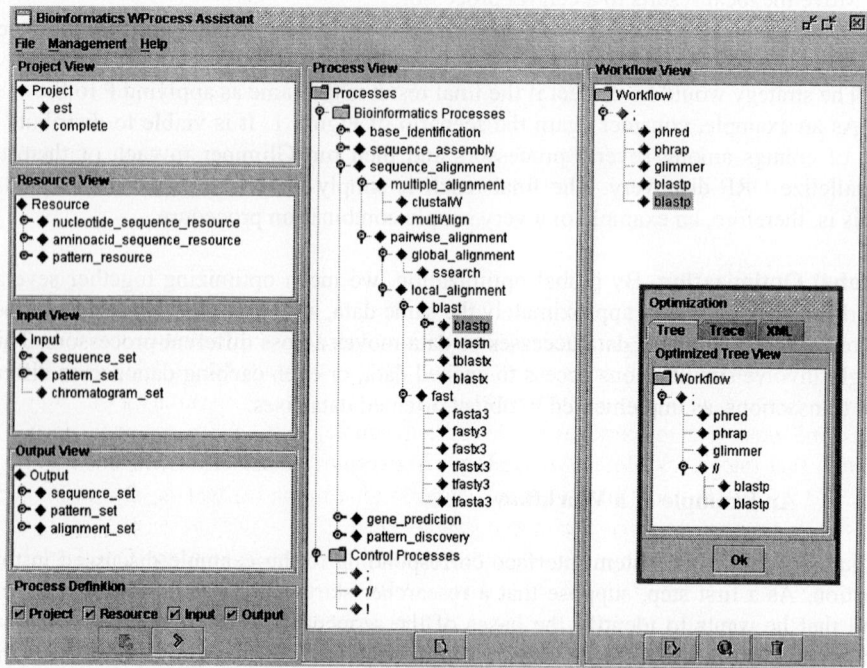

Fig. 1. The workflow management system interface

The goal of the next step is gene prediction, which may be carried out using different process instances, such as Glimmer and ORF Finder. The user may indicate Contig Set as input data class, ORF Nucleotide Sequence Set as output data class and Complete as project type. The assistant will suggest Glimmer as the best option.

The next task is to compare the ORFs, generated by the previous step, with NR [14], an amino acid sequence public database. The user has to choose ORF Amino acid Sequence Set as input data class, NR as resource instance (using the Resource View) and Alignment Set as output data class. The assistant will display Sequence Alignment / Global Alignment / ssearch and Sequence Alignment / Local Alignment / BLAST and FAST as possible processes. The researcher will have to choose between global and local alignment. This choice is left entirely to the researcher, i.e., it does not depend on the input/output data class and quality properties. Suppose that the researcher chooses local alignment. Then, he has to decide between BLAST and FAST. The system may help him by displaying the performance and fidelity quality properties, which indeed indicates that BLAST is faster, but it is less precise than

FAST. The researcher may indicate weights for each quality property that differentiates BLAST and FAST. The assistant computes the punctuation of each process and indicates the best process class. Suppose that the researcher chooses high for performance and low for fidelity. In this case, the assistant will indicate BLAST, which has five process instances. As the input data class and the resource class are amino acid sequence sets, the assistant will indicate BLASTP as the best possibility.

The researcher may also want to compare the ORFs with the SWISSPROT resource. This comparison may use BLASTP since the input and output data classes are both amino acid sequence sets.

To conclude, we observe that the last two comparisons may be executed in parallel, since they use different databases. The workflow optimizer will automatically detect this alternative and modify the workflow appropriately. Additionally, the optimizer may decide to pipeline the composition of Glimmer and BLAST. That is, the ORFs resulting from Glimmer are immediately passed to BLASTP, without having to wait for Glimmer to produce the full set of output sequences.

5 Conclusions

We first argued that it becomes interesting to define a Bioinformatics ontology that captures the major Bioinformatics data and process characteristics. This ontology is used to create a workflow management system that will help researchers define, optimize and execute their workflows. This system can be positioned as a new layer over a system that integrates Molecular Biology data resources and processes, such as BioAXS [15], that already contain the necessary infrastructure, that is, Bioinformatics process instances and input and output data instances.

Large molecular biological ontologies already exist, such as Gene Ontology [16] and EcoCyc [17], which provide consistent definitions and interpretations of biological concepts. In addition, there are Bioinformatics ontologies, such as that discussed in Section 3 or used in the myGrid Project [18], that define knowledge of Bioinformatics processes and their input and output data type. myGrid is a project targeted at developing open source high-level middleware to support personalized in silico experiments in Biology on a (computational) Grid. Our assistant uses an ontology to guide the researcher during the process of workflow definition, whereas the myGrid components use an ontology to classify and retrieve services and workflows registered in the myGrid catalog.

Acknowledgments

We would like to thank Paulo Ferreira, Orlando Martins, Marcelo Bertalan, Marcelo Alves and Wim Degrave, for the many discussions. This work was partially supported by CNPq under grant no. 141938/2000-5 for Melissa Lemos.

References

1. D.K.Casey, Human Genome Program, U.S. Department of Energy, Genomics and its Impact on Science and Society: A 2003 Primer, (2003), http://www.ornl.gov/sci/techresources/Human_Genome/publicat/primer/index.shtml .
2. J.Kim, Computers are from Mars, Organisms are from Venus, Computer, 35(7) (2002), 25-32.
3. S.F.Altschul, W.Gish, W.Miller, E.W.Myers, and D. J. Lipman, A basic local alignment search tool, Journal of Molecular Biology, 215 (1990), 403-410.
4. Workflow Management Coalition (WfMC), Workflow Management Coalition Terminology and Glossar, Technical Report WFMC-TC-1011 3.0. Brussels, (1999).
5. N. Guarino, Formal Ontology and Information Systems, Formal Ontology in Information Systems, Ed. Amsterdam, Netherlands: IOS Press, (1998).
6. M.Lemos, L.F.B.Seibel, M.A.Casanova, BioNotes: A System for Biosequence Annotation, DEXA Workshops, (2003), 16-20.
7. Department of Biochemistry and Molecular Biology, Oswaldo Cruz Institute, (2004), http://www.dbbm.fiocruz.br .
8. Department of Medical Biochemistry, Federal University of Rio de Janeiro, (2004), http://www.bioqmed.ufrj.br/ .
9. OWL Web Ontology Language Overview. W3C Proposed Recommendation 15 Dec 2003. D. L. McGuinness and F. v. Harmelen eds. http://www.w3.org/TR/owl-features/ .
10. P. Green, Documentation for Phrap, March 2003, http://bozeman.mbt.washington.edu/phraps.docs/phrap.html .
11. X.Huang and A.Madan, CAP3: A DNA sequence assembly program, Genome Research, 9 (1999), 868-877.
12. B.Boeckmann, et al., The SWISS-PROT protein knowledgebase and its supplement TrEMBL in 2003, Nucleic Acids Research, 31 (2003), 365-370.
13. B.Ewing, et al., Base-Calling of Automated Sequencer Traces using Phred. I. Accuracy Assessment, Genome Research, 8 (1998),175-185.
14. National Center of Biotechnology Information, The BLAST Databases, (2004), ftp://ftp.ncbi.nih.gov/blast/db/ .
15. L.F.B. Seibel, S.Lifschitz, A Genome Database Framework, DEXA (2001), 319-329.
16. Gene Ontology, (2004), http://www.geneontology.org/ .
17. Encyclopedia of Escherichia coli K12 Genes and Metabolism, (2004), http://ecocyc.org/.
18. R.D. Stevens, A.J.Robinson and C.A.Goble, myGrid: personalised bioinformatics on the information grid, Bioinformatics, 19 Suppl. 1, (2003), (Eleventh International Conference on Intelligent Systems for Molecular Biology).
19. T. Kulikova, et al, The EMBL Nucleotide Sequence Database, Nucl. Acids. Res., (2004) 32, D27-D30.
20. S. Rudd, Expressed sequence tags: Alternative or complement to whole genome sequences?, Trends in Plant Science (2003), 8 (7), 321-329.
21. W. R. Pearson and D. J. Lipman, Improved Tools for Biological Sequence Comparison, (1988), PNAS 85, 2444-2448.

Towards Integration of
XML Document Access and Version Control

Somchai Chatvichienchai[1], Chutiporn Anutariya[2],
Mizuho Iwaihara[3], Vilas Wuwongse[4], and Yahiko Kambayashi*

[1] Department of Info-Media, Faculty of Global Communication
Siebold University of Nagasaki, Nagasaki, Japan
somchaic@sun.ac.jp
[2] Computer Science Program, Shinawatra University, Pathumthani, Thailand
chutiporn@shinawatra.ac.th
[3] Department of Social Informatics, Graduate School of Informatics
Kyoto University, Kyoto, Japan
iwaihara@i.kyoto-u.ac.jp
[4] Computer Science and Information Management Program
Asian Institute of Technology, Pathumthani, Thailand
vw@cs.ait.ac.th

Abstract. Due to an increasing popularity of employing XML documents in various application domains, there arises a demand for an efficient XML document database management. Thus, development of effective mechanisms for manipulating access and version control has become a major research area. However, well-developed access and version control mechanisms alone do not suffice because they are closely interrelated. An update to a document (resulting in a new version of that document) may have a side effect to its associated access control policy, and vice versa. Thus, different document versions can be assigned different access authorizations. This paper gives an insight into the problems of access and version control of XML documents and proposes an approach to overcoming them by integrating these two essential mechanisms into a single framework. It employs RDF as a unified representation of access control policies and version information, and formalizes their interrelationships by means of *RDF Declarative Description Theory*.

1 Introduction

With an increasing popularity of employing XML documents in a variety of applications, a demand for efficient XML document database management has hence arisen. Since a single document may be edited and accessed concurrently by many different users, development of effective mechanisms for manipulating versions and access control has become a major research area. Version control keeps track of changes of evolving XML documents and maintains appropriate version information, including the identities of users who modify the documents, date/time and modification details; hence enabling the documents to be reverted back to their previous versions. Access

---

* Prof. Kambayashi passed away on February 6th, 2004.

control, on the other hand, deals with granting or denying particular accesses to the specified documents, mostly to their latest versions. The development of suitable authorization for XML documents poses new protection requirements with respect to conventional object-oriented databases [11]. These new requirements arise because of the richer structure of XML documents with respect to HTML documents and the possibility of attaching a DTD to XML documents, which has similarity with the notion of type in the object-oriented context.

However, well-developed access and version control mechanisms alone do not suffice because they are closely interrelated. An update to a document (resulting in a new version of that document) may lead to a change of the document's access policy. Thus, different document versions can be assigned different access authorizations. For instance, insertion of certain confidential data may require addition of new access policies for the inserted data. To accommodate such requirements, a management framework with fine-grained access control mechanisms on multi-version XML documents is demanded. This framework will be useful to various applications. However, to the best of our knowledge, there does not exist such a framework

This paper not only analyzes essential features and requirements of both access and version control mechanisms but also explores in depth their interrelationships. Based on the analysis, an approach to integrating them into a single framework is developed.

Section 2 gives insight into access and version control problems, Section 3 discusses their interrelationships and points out the benefits gained from their integration, Section 4 proposes an integrated framework by employment of *RDF* [12] and *RDF Declarative Description (RDD)* theory [1], and Section 5 concludes with a summary and a list of future work.

2 Access and Version Control Problems

2.1 Access Control Problems

Various XML access control models [2,4,15] have been proposed. These models enforce access restrictions directly on the structure and content of XML documents. In this way, information in XML format can be protected at a finer level of granularity (e.g., the element level) rather than the whole document. Each document is associated with a set of authorizations specifying access rights of users on information within the document. By employment of an RDF rule-based declarative language, the approach proposed in [2] has incorporated facilities which allow derivation of implicit, complex authorizations on the basis of other authorizations.

The structure of XML documents changes by various reasons (such as information exchange between organizations that use different document formats). When a document is transformed to a new format (schema), the associated authorizations must also be translated for the transformed document. Algorithms for translating authorizations of source documents into those of transformed documents by using document-node and schema-node mapping have been proposed in [5,6].

2.2 Version Control Problems

Version management of XML documents has recently been discussed in [13,7]. A change-centric method proposed in [13] stores the latest version of a document and the sequence of forward completed deltas. The *Reference-Based Version Model* (*RBVM*) [7] focuses on the storage performance of multi-version documents.

Let d_i and d_j be documents of versions i and j, respectively. Assume that d_j is established by applying a number of changes (insertions, deletions or updates) to d_i. In a typical *RCS (Revision Control System)* scheme [16], these changes are stored in a script denoted by *Delta* $\Delta d_{i,j}$. Such a script could be generated directly from the edit commands of a structured editor or obtained by applying the pair (d_i, d_j) to a structured diff package, such as XyDiff [9] and Microsoft XML Diff [14].

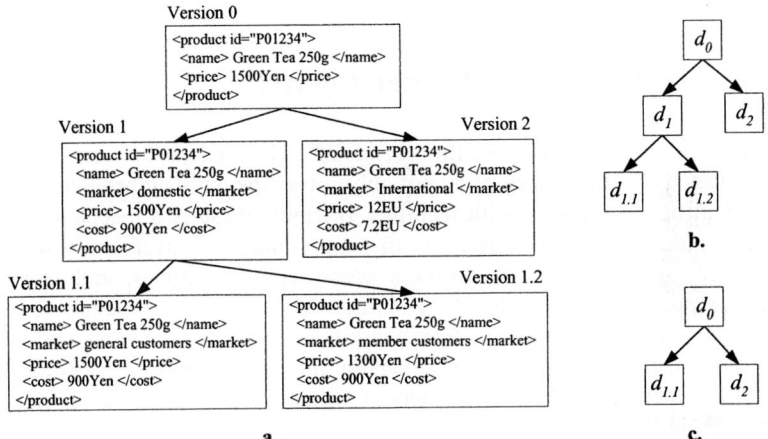

Fig. 1. Version evolution of a product catalog "catalog.xml" and its corresponding version trees

2.3 Integrating Access and Version Control Requirements

The problems that arise when both access and version controls are not integrated into XML document database management will be now discussed. As a document changes, some information of the changed document should not be disclosed to some users.

As an example, consider Fig. 1-a which illustrates version evolution of a product catalog, and Fig. 1-b which depicts its corresponding *version tree*[1], where $d_0, d_1, d_{1.1}, d_{1.2}$, and d_2 denote product catalogs of versions 0, 1, 1.1, 1.2 and 2, respectively. Firstly, d_0 is evolved into d_1 and d_2 for domestic market and international market, respectively, and d_1 is next evolved into $d_{1.1}$ and $d_{1.2}$ for general customers and member customers, respectively. After d_1 is evolved into $d_{1.1}$ and $d_{1.2}$, general customers who are allowed to access d_1 and $d_{1.1}$ should not be allowed to access $d_{1.2}$ which is only accessible by member customers. A lack of proper access control over documents of new versions results in confidential information disclosure problem. Fur-

---

[1] For simplicity, version trees are employed but they can be readily generalized to *version graphs*.

thermore, a user may have different access authorizations on different document versions. For instance, a general customer is allowed to read the entire d_0 but not allowed to read some part (e.g., *cost*) of $d_{1.1}$ and the whole part of $d_{1.2}$. Thus, fine-grained access control is essential for defining access rights of users to information inside each version of a document. Assuming that a member customer is not allowed to access d_1, $d_{1.2}$, a version tree of this customer is depicted in Fig.1-c.

On the other hand, a lack of multi-version concept makes schema design and access authorization policy of a document become very complex and error-prone. For instance, integration of $d_{1.1}$, $d_{1.2}$ and d_2 into a single document requires redefining price elements for all types of markets. In addition, since the schema of a combined single-version document tends to be more complicated, authorization control policy of each user on a database of such documents will be more complex. Integration of access and version control can simplify schema and access control policy definitions.

3 Integrating Access and Version Control

The previous section has analyzed the strong interrelationships between access and version control. Thus, their integration not only solves the outlined problems, but also results in a unified framework with facilities to handle these two mechanisms effectively and simultaneously. It allows one to simply and straightforwardly model the side effect of document versions towards access control policies, and vice versa. Moreover, because version information and access control policies themselves can be represented as XML documents, the framework then provides a complete and uniform solution to the manipulation of schemas, version information and access control policies of XML documents. Issues of concern, when developing such an integrated framework are as follows:

- *Inference Problems*: As a rule, unauthorized users should not be aware of the existence of confidential information contained in a document. Hence, proper mechanisms that prevent users from inferring contents and/or structures of protected data should be implemented.
- *Version History*: Public view of version history and version tree could let users yield some conclusions about protected data. Thus, it is preferable to represent version information as an XML document so that fine-grained access control over such version information can be simply defined. Moreover, the use of a number sequence as a version ID may let users deduce the existence of some versions that they are not allowed to access, hence one could simply use a document's timestamp as its version ID.
- *Version Control over Schemas*: Version control mechanisms could be used to manage not only versions of XML documents but also their schemas. To avoid consistency and integrity problems, all versions of a document in a version tree should conform to the same version of schema. That is, when a schema of a document is modified, a new version tree should be created.
- *Temporal Features*: The association of *timestamps* (or *temporal data*) with various attributes of version information, e.g., editing and valid time, is fundamental to version management. They play an important role in sophisticated access control models by allowing definition of policies with certain condi-

tions on timestamp attributes, e.g., a policy which states that all documents will be disclosed to public after ten years from the date of document creation. Broad sets of queries related to temporal information are also enabled.
- *Improper Disclosure of Confidential Data*: When a modification of a document results in a change of access policies, the framework should have a warning mechanism to ensure that it does not lead to improper disclosure of confidential data, which usually happens when an update by a particular user inadvertently gives that user an authorization to access protected data.

4 Proposed Framework

The developed framework employs *RDF* [12] as a unified representation of access control policies and version information, and formalizes their interrelationships by means of *RDF Declarative Description (RDD) Theory* [1].

4.1 Authorization Model

Managing access to a protected document is expressed in terms of *access control policies* [2]. A policy is simply described by a set of authorization rules, a conflict resolution and a default policy. An authorization specifies for each user (or group of users) the types of accesses that the user can/cannot exercise on each object. An authorization either positive (granting access) or negative (denying access) on an element can be propagated to all of its sub-elements (by *cascade* option), or to only its attributes (by *no_propagation* option). The *read* privilege allows a subject to view an element and its attributes. The *write* privilege allows a subject to update and delete information in an element. A *priority* is an integer value which specifies the priority level of an authorization. An authorization with a higher priority can prevail over lower ones. The default value of a priority is zero.

The possibility of specifying both positive and negative authorizations introduces potential conflicts among authorizations with the same priority levels. Hence, a conflict resolution policy must be specified. Examples of conflict resolution policies include *instance-*, *descendant-*, *denial-* and *grant-take-precedence*. In addition, there might exist an element without an associated authorization, either defined explicitly or propagated along the document structure by means of the cascade option. In such a case, a default authorization could be applied. Two main types of default policies are *open* and *close*. Formal definitions of policies and authorizations follow.

Definition 1 (Access Control Policy). An access control policy is simply described by a set of *authorizations*, a *conflict resolution* and *default policy*. An authorization consists of the following properties:
- *subject*: a user, a user group, a role or credentials describing properties (e.g., age, gender, domain) of the user to whom the authorization is specified;
- *target*: specifying the baseline version of a document;
- *path*: an *XPath* [8] expression identifying an element or attribute within the target document;

rates facilities to model interrelationships between authorization and version management and to automate such a complex process.

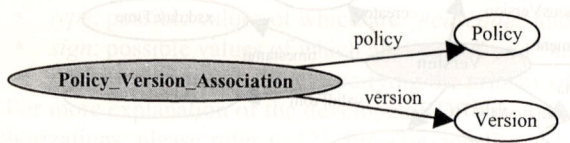

a. RDF schema for policy and version association.

```
<Policy_Version_Association>
   <policy rdf:resource="#p1"/>
   <version rdf:resource="#d1.1"/>
</Policy_Version_Association>
```

b. Example: associating policy p_1 to the document version $d_{1.1}$.

Fig. 4. Policy-version-association schema and example.

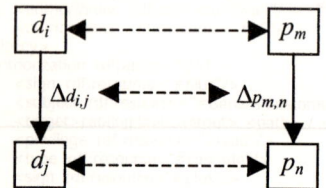

d_i: document version i
d_j: document version j, a successive version of d_i
p_m: policy document version m
p_n: policy document version n
$\Delta d_{i,j}$: modification applied to d_i to obtain d_j
$\Delta p_{m,n}$: modification applied to p_m to obtain p_n

Fig. 5. Access and version control interrelationships

First, consider the modeled interrelationships of Fig. 5. Assume that authorization of a document version d_i is regulated by a policy p_m. An update $\Delta d_{i,j}$ made to d_i resulting in a newer version d_j may lead to a change of its associated policy, i.e., accesses to d_j will then be regulated by another policy p_n. In particular, there are three possible alternatives to select an appropriate policy for d_j, depending on the type of changes occurred in $\Delta d_{i,j}$:

- A user manually defines an appropriate policy p_n for d_j;
- The system automatically assigns an existing policy p_n, or instantly generates a new policy p_n based on some predefined relationships between $\Delta d_{i,j}$ and $\Delta p_{m,n}$;
- If the above two cases are not applied, by default d_j will be assigned with the same policy as its previous version d_i.

These three methods can be formulated as *RDF clauses* [1], hence allowing the framework to determine the appropriate policy for each version based on some predefined application-specific rules.

Definition 3 (Policy-Version-Association Clause). A policy-version-association clause is represented as an *RDF clause* of the form $H \leftarrow B_1, \ldots, B_n$, where

- H is an RDF expression describing a derived policy-version-association and conforming to the schema of Fig. 4-a,
- B_i is an RDF expression or an RDF constraint restricting a certain condition on the derived association. ❑

As an example of a policy-version-association clause, consider again the running example of product catalog document. Suppose that in this scenario, the catalog version d_1 is the latest version and is manually associated with the policy p_1 of Fig. 2-a by a security officer. After that d_1 is evolved into $d_{1.1}$ and $d_{1.2}$ with Deltas $\Delta d_{1,1.1}$ and $\Delta d_{1,1.2}$, respectively. The description of version $d_{1.2}$ together with $\Delta d_{1,1.2}$ are given by Fig. 3-b. Since d_1 is evolved into $d_{1.2}$ by updating the value of market-element to "member customers", based on the definition of the policy-version-association clause of Fig. 6-a, the framework can automatically yield an element of Fig. 6-b. That is, the access control of document version $d_{1.2}$ is regulated by the policy p_2.

```
<Policy_Version_Association>                            // This RDF clause formalizes that
    <policy rdf:resource="#p2"/>                        // if a document catalog.xml of
    <version rdf:resource=$S:Y/>                        // version Y is evolved from ver-
</Policy_Version_Association>                           // sion X by changing the value of
    ← <Version rdf:about=$S:Y>                          // market-element to "member
        <document rdf:resource="catalog.xml"/>          // customers" and that document
        <previousVersion rdf:resource=$S:X/>            // version X is associated with
        <delta>                                         // policy p₁, then policy p₂ will be
            <xd:xmldiff rdf:parseType="Literal">        // assigned to the new version Y.
                <xd:change match=$S:anynode>
                    member customers </xd:change>
                $E:otherchanges
            </xd:xmldiff>
        </delta>
        $E:versionProperties
    </Version>,
    <Policy_Version_Association>
        <policy rdf:resource="#p1"/>
        <version rdf:resource=$S:X/>
    </Policy_Version_Association>
```
a. Policy-version-association clause example.

```
<Policy_Version_Association>
    <policy rdf:resource="#p2"/>
    <version rdf:resource="#d1.2"/>
</Policy_Version_Association>
```
b. Derived Policy_Version_Association element.

Fig. 6. Policy-version-association clause

5   Conclusions

This paper has addressed the problems that arise when access and version control of XML documents are handled separately, such as the complexity of designing a single policy for enforcement of authorization over all versions of a document. To deal with these problems, a framework which integrates both access and version control mechanisms has been developed. This unified framework has facilities to handle these two essential mechanisms effectively and simultaneously. Moreover, because access control policies and version information themselves can be represented as XML documents, the framework then provides a complete and uniform solution to easily manipulating schemas, version information and access control policies of XML document databases. Further work includes the following issues:
- incorporation of a mechanism to handle version control over document schemas;
- development of an appropriate technique to solve inference problems (i.e., a situation that allows users to infer certain information about protected data);
- in-depth analysis and refinement of the representation of temporal features to deal with temporal XML document databases and temporal query processing;

- application of the framework to XML data warehouses-repositories of data coming from several sources (e.g., web sites) in which many important issues such as security, consistency and maintenance/querying of history of or changes in document versions are interwoven; and
- implementation of the framework by *RDD's inference engine* [3].

References

1. Anutariya, C., Wuwongse, V., Akama, K., and Nantajeewarawat, E.: RDF Declarative Description: A Language for Metadata. *J. Digital Information*, Vol. 2, Issue 2 (2001).
2. Anutariya, C., Chatvichienchai, S., Iwiahara, M., Wuwongse, V., and Kambayashi, Y.: A Rule-Based XML Access Control Model. *Proc. Rules and Rule Markup Languages for the Semantic Web Workshop*, LNCS #2762, Springer Verlag, pp. 92-103 (October 2003).
3. Anutariya, C., Wuwongse, V., and Wattanapailin, V.: An Equivalent-Transformation-Based XML Rule Language. *Proc. Int'l Workshop Rule Markup Languages for Business Rules in the Semantic Web*, Sardinia, Italy (2002)
4. Bertino, E., Castano, S., Ferrari, S., and Mesiti, M.: Specifying and Enforcing Access Control Policies for XML Document Sources. *World Wide Web*, Vol. 3, No. 3, Baltzer Science Publishers, Netherlands (2000).
5. Chatvichienchai, S., Iwaihara, M., and Kambayashi. Y.: Translating Content-Based Authorizations for XML Documents. *Proc. 4th Int. Conference on Web Information Systems Engineering*, IEEE CS, pp.103–112, Roma, Italy (Dec. 2003).
6. Chatvichienchai, S., Iwaihara, M., and Kambayashi. Y.: Authorization Translation for XML Document Transformation. *J. World Wide Web*, Vol. 7, No. 1, pp. 111-138 (2004).
7. Chien, S.Y., Tsotras, V.J., and Zaniolo. C.: Efficient Management of Multiversion Documents by Object Referencing. *Proc. VLDB 2001* (Sep. 2001).
8. Clark, J., and DeRose, S.: XML Path Language (XPath) Version 1.0 (November 1999). http://www.w3c.org/TR/xpath
9. Cobena, G., Abiteboul, S., and Marian, A.: XyDiff Tools Detecting changes in XML Documents. http://wwwrocq.inria.fr/cobena
10. Cuppens, F., and Gabillon, A.: Cover story management. *Data Knowledge Engineering*, Vol. 37, No. 2, pp. 177-201 (2001).
11. E. Fernandez, E. Gudes, and H. Song.: A Model for Evaluation and Administration of Security in Object-Oriented Databases. *IEEE Transactions on Knowledge and Data Engineering*, Vol. 6, pp. 275-292 (April 1994).
12. Lassila, O., and Swick, R.R.: Resource Description Framework (RDF) Model and Syntax Specification. *W3C Recommendation* (Feb. 1999) http://www.w3.org/TR/REC-rdf-syntax/
13. Marian, A., Abiteboul, S., Cobna, G., and L. Mignet. Change-centric management of versions in an XML warehouse. *Proc. VLDB 2001* (Sep. 2001).
14. Microsoft XML Diff and Patch 1.0, Microsoft Corporation (2002). http://apps.gotdotnet.com/xmltools/xmldiff/overview.html
15. OASIS XACML Technical Committee: XACML 1.0 Specification Set. *OASIS Standard* (Nov. 2002). http://www.oasis-open.org/committees/xacml
16. Tichy, W.F.: RCS A System for Version Control. *Software Practice and Experience*, Vol. 15, No. 7, pp. 637-654 (July 1985).

Prefix Path Streaming: A New Clustering Method for Optimal Holistic XML Twig Pattern Matching

Ting Chen, Tok Wang Ling, and Chee-Yong Chan

School of Computing, National University of Singapore
Lower Kent Ridge Road, Singapore 119260
{chent,lingtw,chancy}@comp.nus.edu.sg

Abstract. Searching for all occurrences of a twig pattern in a XML document is an important operation in XML query processing. Recently a class of holistic twig pattern matching algorithms has been proposed. Compared with the prior approaches, the holistic method avoids generating large intermediate results which do not contribute to the final answer. The method is CPU and I/O optimal when twig patterns only have ancestor-descendant relationships.The holistic twig-pattern matching method proposed earlier [1] operates on element streams which cluster all XML elements with the same tag name together. In this paper we introduce a clustering method called *Prefix Path Streaming* (PPS) and new holistic twig pattern matching algorithms based on *PPS*. *PPS* clusters elements of XML documents according to the paths from root to the elements. This clustering approach avoids unnecessary scanning of irrelevant portion of XML documents.More importantly, we develop optimal algorithms based on *PPS* streaming which can process a large class of twig patterns consisting of both ancestor-descendant and parent-child relationships.

1 Introduction

XML data is often modelled as labelled and ordered tree or graph. Naturally twig (a small tree) pattern becomes an essential part of XML queries. A twig pattern can be represented as a node-labelled tree whose edges are either *Parent-Child* (P-C) or *Ancestor-Descendant* (A-D) relationship. For example, the following twig pattern written in XPath[7] format:

section[title]/paragraph//figure   ...(Q1)

selects *figure* elements which are descendants of some *paragraph* elements which in turn are children of *section* elements having at least one child element *title*.

Prior work on XML twig pattern processing usually decomposes a twig pattern into a set of binary parent-child or ancestor-descendant relationships. After that, each binary relationship is processed using *structural join* techniques[8][5] and the final match results are obtained by "stitching" individual binary join results together. This approach may generate large and possibly unnecessary intermediate results. Bruno et al.[1] propose a novel *holistic* method of XML path and twig pattern matches which avoids storing intermediate results unless they contribute to the final results. The method is CPU and I/O optimal for all path(with no branching) patterns and twig patterns whose edges are entirely ancestor-descendant edges. However the approach is found to be suboptimal if there are parent-child relationships in twig patterns.

The original holistic method groups all elements in XML document with the same tag name together. We call this clustering method *Tag Streaming*. Choi et al.[3] show that it is not possible to develop an optimal holistic twig join algorithm for twig patterns having both ancestor-descendant and parent-child relationships using Tag Streaming. In this paper, we propose a new XML document clustering scheme: *Prefix-Path Streaming* (PPS), which groups XML document elements with the same root-to-element tag sequence into the same stream (we call such a stream *Prefix-Path Stream*). Prefix-Path Streaming is simple and it can avoid unnecessary scanning of portions of XML documents which do not contribute to final matching results. More importantly,we demonstrate that for twig patterns with only P-C edges or only A-D edges and twig patterns with only one node having fan-out factor larger than 1(or *1-branch* twig pattern), PPS streaming can provide I/O and CPU optimal solution. To the best of our knowledge, this is the first method which can process all the above classes of twig pattern optimally.

The rest of this paper is organized as follows: Section 2 is the preliminary who introduces XML data model, twig pattern query and notations used in this paper. In section 3, we review the current holistic methods for twig pattern matching and discuss its problems. In section 4 we introduce our new clustering method: Prefix-Path Streaming (PPS). Section 5 explains how to prune unnecessary streams given a twig pattern. Section 6 shows our holistic pattern matching algorithms based on PPS: *PPS-TwigStack*. Section 7 shows the performance of our new methods. Section 8 concludes the paper.All the proofs of results are omitted in this paper and can be found in a full version on line[2].

2 Preliminary

A XML document is commonly modelled as a rooted, ordered and labelled tree. In this paper wherever the word "element" appears, it refers to either element or attribute in a XML document. Many XML query processing algorithms rely on certain numbering schemes. [4] uses *(startPos: endPos, LevelNum)* to label elements in a XML file.*startPos* and *endPos* are calculated by performing a preorder(document order) traversal of the document tree; *startPos* is the number in sequence assigned to an element when it is first encountered and *endPos* is equal to one plus the *endPos* of the last element visited. Leaf elements have *startPos* equal to *endPos*. *LevelNum* is the level of a certain element in its data tree. Element A is a descendant of Element B if and only if $startPos(A) > startPos(B)$ and $endPos(A) < endPos(B)$. A sample XML document tree labeled with the above scheme is shown in Fig.1.

A *twig pattern match* in a XML database can be represented as an n-ary tuple $< d_1, d_2, \ldots, d_n >$ consisting of the database nodes that identify a distinct match of Q with n nodes in D. The problem of twig pattern matching is defined as:

Given a twig pattern query Q, and an XML database D that has index structures to identify database nodes that satisfy each of Q's node predicates, compute ALL the matches to Q in D.

As an example, the matches to twig pattern $Q1$ of Section 1 in Fig.1 are tuples $< s_1, t_1, p_4, f_3 >$ and $< s_2, t_2, p_2, f_1 >$.

In the remaining sections of this paper, we use Q to denote a twig pattern and Q_A denote the subtree of Q rooted at node A. We use *node* to refer to a query node in twig pattern and *element* to refer to a data node in XML data tree. We use M or $M :< e_1, e_2, \ldots, e_n >$ to denote a match to a twig pattern or sub-twig pattern where e_i is an element in the match tuple.

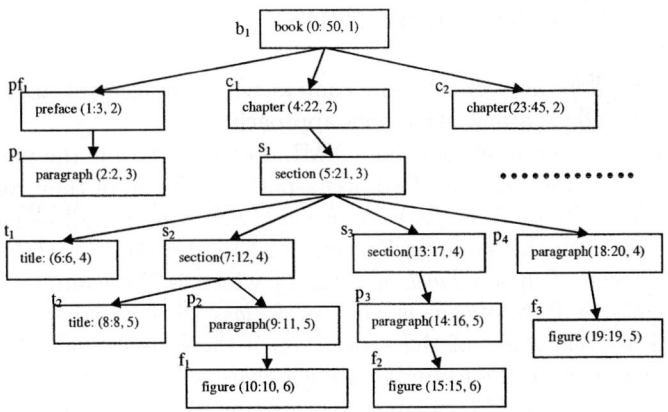

Fig. 1. A sample XML document with node labels in parentheses. Each element is also given an identifier (e.g. s_1) for easy reference

3 Related Work

The holistic method *TwigStack*, proposed by Bruno et al[1], is CPU and I/O optimal for all path patterns and A-D only twig patterns. It associates each node q in the twig pattern with a stack S_q and an element stream T_q containing all elements of tag q. Elements in each stream are sorted by their *startPos*. Each stream has a cursor which can either move to the next element or read the element under it. The algorithm operates in two phases:

1. *TwigJoin*. In this phase a list of element paths are output as intermediate results. Each path matches one path of the twig pattern.
2. *Merge*. In this phase, the list of paths are merged to produce the final output.

When all the edges in the twig are A-D edges, *TwigStack* ensures that each path output in phase 1 not only matches one path of the twig pattern but is also part of a match to the entire twig. Thus the algorithm ensures that *its time and I/O complexity is independent of the size of partial matches to any root-to-leaf path of the descendant-only twig pattern*. However, with the presence of P-C edges in twig patterns, the TwigStack method is no longer optimal.

Example 1. Let us evaluate the twig pattern $section[title]/paragraph//figure$ on the XML document in Fig.1. In order to know that element s_1 is in a match, we have to advance $T_{paragraph}$ to p_4 and T_{figure} to f_3. By doing so, we skip nodes p_2, p_3, f_1 and f_2 and miss the matches involving p_2 and f_1. However, since s_2 and s_3 have not been seen, we have no way to tell if any of the above four elements might appear in the final match results. The only choice left is to store all the four elements in which only two are useful (unnecessary storage).

4 Prefix-Path Streaming (PPS)

Tag Streaming does not consider the context where an element appears. In this section, we introduce a new streaming approach.

The *prefix-path* of an element in a XML document tree is the path from the document root to the element. Two prefix-paths are equal iff they consist of the same sequence of tags. A *prefix-path stream(PPS)* contains all elements in the document tree with the same prefix-path, ordered by their *startPos* numbers. Each PPS stream T has a *label* or *label(T)* which is the common prefix-path of its elements. A PPS stream is said to of *class N* if its label ends with tag N. Two PPS streams are of the same class if their labels end with the same tag. Referring again to the example in Fig.1 there will be 11 streams using PPS streaming compared with 7 streams generated by Tag Streaming. For example, instead of a single stream $T_{section}$ in Tag Streaming, now we have two PPS streams: $T_{book-chapter-section}$ and $T_{book-chapter-section-section}$.

4.1 Differences between Tag and Prefix-Path Streaming

We first discuss why CPU and I/O optimal solutions can be devised over descendant-only twig queries and Tag Streaming.

Definition 1 (Match Order). *Given a twig pattern Q, a match M_A to Q_A is said to be ahead of a match M_B to Q_B or $M_A \leq M_B$ if for each node $q \in (Q_A \cap Q_B)$, $e_q^A.startPos \leq e_q^B.startPos$ or e_q^A and e_q^B are placed on different streams, where e_q^A and e_q^B are of tag q and belong to match M_A and M_B respectively.*

PPS streaming allows comparison of many more match pairs under the definition of *Match Order* because it divides elements with the same tag into different streams according to their prefix paths. As an example,for twig pattern $Q1 : section[title]/paragraph//figure$, the two matches $M_1 :< s_1, t_1, p_4, f_3 >$

and $M_2 :< s_2, t_2, p_2, f_1 >$ in Fig.1 are incomparable under Tag Streaming because $t_1.startPos < t2.startPos$ but $p_4.startPos > p_2.startPos$. However under PPS streaming, we have both $M_1 \leq M_2$ and $M_2 \leq M_1$ simply because the eight elements in M_1 and M_2 are placed on eight different streams.

Definition 2. *Given a twig pattern Q and two elements a with tag A and b with tag B, $a \leq_Q b$ if a is in a match M_A to Q_A such that $M_A \leq M_B$ for any match M_B to Q_B containing element b.*

Intuitively, $a \leq_Q b$ implies that we can determine if a is in a match to Q_A without skipping any matches of b to Q_B. For example, given the twig pattern $Q : section[//title]//paragraph//figure$, $s_1 \leq_Q s_2$ in Fig.1 under Tag Streaming because s_1 has a match (s_1, t_1, p_2, f_1) which is ahead of any match s_2 for Q.

Lemma 1. *For two elements a of tag A and b of tag B in a A-D only twig pattern Q, suppose a has matches to Q_A and b has matches to Q_B, either $a \leq_Q b$ or $b \leq_Q a$ under Tag Streaming.*

However, for $Q1 : section[title]/paragraph//figure$, the only match of s_1 is $< s_1, t_1, p_4, f_3 >$ and the only match of s_2 is $< s_2, t_2, p_2, f_1 >$. Since the two matches are not "comparable", Lemma 1 does not hold anymore for the query and in general twig patterns having both A-D and P-C edges. On the other hand, we have $s_1 \leq_Q s_2$ as well as $s_2 \leq_Q s_1$ under PPS streaming.

Analogous to Lemma 1, PPS-streaming has similar properties for a larger classes of twig patterns.

Lemma 2. *For two elements a of tag A and b of tag B in a A-D only or a P-C only or a 1-branch twig pattern Q, if a has matches to Q_A and b has matches to Q_B, either $a \leq_Q b$ or $b \leq_Q a$ under PPS streaming.*

Lemma 1 is the crucial reason why a forward scan algorithm like $TwigStack$ can find all matches to an A-D only twig pattern without using excessive storage. Lemma 2 shows that it is possible to design efficient twig pattern matching algorithms for a larger class of twig patterns using PPS streaming.

5 Pruning PPS Streams

Using labels of PPS streams, we can statically prune away PPS streams which contain no match to a twig pattern. For example, the stream $T_{book-preface-para}$ of the XML document in Fig.1 is certainly not useful for the twig pattern $section[title]/paragraph//figure$. Although all the elements in the PPS stream have element name $paragraph$, they do not have $section$ parents!

A PPS stream T_1 is an *ancestor PPS stream* of PPS stream T_2 if label(T_1) is a prefix of label(T_2). T_1 is the *parent PPS stream* of T_2 if label(T_1) is a prefix of label(T_2) and label(T_1).length = label(T_2).length -1. The following recursive formula helps us determine the useful streams for evaluating a twig pattern Q.

For a PPS stream of class N with label l, we define S_l to be the set of all descendant PPS streams of l (including l) which are useful for the sub-twig of Q_N except that we only use stream T_l (not its descendant streams) to match node N.

$$S_l = \begin{cases} \{l\} & \text{if N is a leaf node;} \\ \{l\} \cup \{\bigcup_{N_i \in child(N)} C_i\} & \text{if none of } C_i \text{ is null;} \\ null & \text{if one of } C_i \text{ is null.} \end{cases}$$

where $C_i = \bigcup S_{l_i}$ for each child stream label l_i of l if the edge $< N, N_i >$ is a P-C edge ;or $C_i = \bigcup S_{l_i}$ for each descendant stream label l_i of l if the edge $< N, N_i >$ is a A-D edge. Function $child(N)$ returns the children nodes of N in the twig.

The base case is simple because if N is a leaf node, any PPS stream of class N must contain matches to the trivial single-node pattern. As for the recursive relationship, note that for a PPS stream with label l of class N to be useful to the sub-twig pattern rooted at N, for each and every child node N_i of N, there should exist some non-empty set S_{l_i} which are useful to the sub-twig rooted at N_i AND the structural relationship of l and l_i satisfies the edge between N and N_i. In the end the set $\bigcup S_{l_r}$ contains all the useful PPS streams to a query pattern Q, where l_r is the PPS streams of class $root(Q)$.

6 Holistic Twig Join Based on PPS

Similar to the idea of simulation of a single sorted array by multiple sorted arrays, any operation on a stream T_q in Tag Streaming can be translated to operations on the set of PPS streams of class q. This allows $TwigStack$ to run on PPS streams for all twig patterns correctly. However the method again is optimal only for A-D only twig patterns.

With Lemma 2, we can devise the following more efficient searching strategy to process twig patterns which are A-D only, P-C only or 1-branch on PPS streams:

In each step, we repeatedly find element a of tag A with the following properties in the remaining portions of streams:

1. a is in a match to Q_A and $a \leq_Q e$ for each e in the remaining portions of streams.
2. $a.startPos < d.startPos$ for each d of tag D which is in a match to $Q_D (D \in Q_A)$.
3. For each sibling node S_i of A, there is an element s_i of tag S_i which satisfies property (1) and (2) w.r.t. S_i.
4. $a.startPos < s_i.startPos$ for each sibling node S_i.
5. There is no element a' in streams of class $parent(A)$ such that $a' \leq_Q a$ and a' is parent(ancestor) of a if the edge $< A, parent(A) >$ is a P-C(A-D) edge.

After such element a is found, it will be pushed into its stack S_A and the stream T_A is advanced. The way to maintain elements in stacks is identical to that of $TwigStack$.

Notice that in searching such an element a we do not skip any potential matching elements because of property (1). Properties (2)-(4) ensure that whenever an element is popped out of its stacks, all matches involving it have been found. Property (5) guarantees that ancestor element of a match to Q or sub-twig of Q is always found before any descendant element in the same match. The existence and searching of element a satisfying the above five properties is explained together with the algorithm *PPS-TwigStack*.

The algorithm *PPS-TwigStack* reports all the matches in a XML document to a twig pattern. *PPS-TwigStack* is also a stack-based algorithm. It associates a *stack* for each query node in the twig pattern. A stack S_{q_1} is the parent stack of S_{q_2} if q_1 is the parent node q_2 in Q. Each item in the stack S is a 2-tuple consisting of an element e and a pointer to the *nearest* ancestor of e in the parent stack of S. The parent pointer is used to reconstruct result paths. This idea is first used in [1]. A query node N is also associated to *all* the useful PPS streams of class N. A PPS stream has the same set of operations as a stream in Tag Streaming. Fig.2(a) shows the main data structures used.

Algorithm 1 *PPS-TwigStack*

1: **while** ¬end(q) **do**
2:    $<q_{min}, \{T_{q_{min}}\}> =$ getNext(q);
3:    T_{min} = the PPS-stream in set $\{T_{q_{min}}\}$ whose head element has the smallest startPos;
4:    **if** ¬isRoot(q_{min}) **then**
5:      cleanStack(parent(q_{min}),nextL(q_{min}))
6:    **if** isRoot(q_{min}) ∨ ¬empty($S_{parent(q_{min})}$) **then**
7:      cleanStack(q_{min},next(q_{min}))
8:      moveStreamToStack(T_{min},$S_{q_{min}}$,pointer to top of $S_{parent(q_{min})}$)
9:      **if** isLeaf(q_{min}) **then**
10:        showSolutionWithBlocking($S_{q_{min}}$,l)
11:        pop($S_{q_{min}}$)
12:    advance(T_{min})
13: mergeAllPathSolutions()

At the heart of our algorithm, the method **getNext** implements the basic searching strategy. Lines 2-3 in the *main* routine find the element satisfying the two conditions. Lines 4-12 maintain the states of matching in stacks(which are identical to those of *TwigStack*). The **getNext()** method returns two things:

1. a node q_x in the sub-twig Q_q;and
2. a set of PPS streams $\{T_{q_x}^i\}$ of class q_x whose head elements are in matches to Q_{q_x}. Moreover, among head elements of streams in $\{T_{q_x}^i\}$, the one with the smallest *startPos* satisfies all the five properties w.r.t. sub-twig Q_q.

getNext() works recursively. For a node q, it makes recursive calls for all child nodes of q(lines 3-4 of textsf(getNext()).

- If getNext(q_i) = q_i for all child nodes q_i, we are able to find an element e which satisfies the first four properties. Then in lines 7-16 we try to find if there is an element of tag q which is in match of Q_q and parent(ancestor) of e. If such an element exists,e does not satisfy property (5) and we return $< q, T_q >$ in lines 18-19 and keeps on searching. Otherwise, e is the element satisfying all five properties and can be returned(line 20).
- Otherwise getNext(q_i) $\neq q_i$ for some child nodes q_i, which suggests the element satisfying the five properties have been found. Therefore we just return what getNext(q_i) returns.

Example 2. Consider the twig pattern query *section[title]/paragraph//figure* on the XML document in Fig.1. The call stack of the first getNext(section) is shown in Fig.2(b). We find s_1 in a match because we recursively find the first two *paragraph* elements and the first two *title* elements from their respective PPS-streams which are in matches to *paragraph//figure* and */title*. After considering the four combinations of the *title* and *paragraph* elements (2x2), we find two match elements s_1 and s_2 push s_1 into its stack $S_{section}$. The subsequent calls find $t_1,s_2,t_2,p_2,f_1,p_3,f_2,p_4$ and f_3 in order.

Algorithm 2 *getNext(q)*

1: **if** isLeaf(q) **then**
2:    return $< q, \{T_q\} >$ /* T_q contains PPS streams of class q not yet end*/
3: **for** q_i in children(q) **do**
4:    $< n_i, \{T_{c_i}\} > \;=\;$ getNext(q_i)
5:    **if** $n_i \neq q_i$ **then**
6:      return $< n_i, \{T_{c_i}\} >$
7: **for** $< T_{c_1}^{\alpha_1}, T_{c_2}^{\alpha_2}, \ldots, T_{c_n}^{\alpha_n} >\in \{T_{c_1}\} \times \{T_{c_2}\} \times \ldots \times \{T_{c_n}\}$ **do**
8:    **for each** T_q^j of class q satisfying the P-C or A-D relationship with each $T_{c_i}^{\alpha_i}$ **do**
9:      T_{min} = the stream in $< T_{c_1}^{\alpha_1}, T_{c_2}^{\alpha_2}, \ldots, T_{c_n}^{\alpha_n} >$ whose head has the smallest startPos
10:     T_{max} = the stream in $< T_{c_1}^{\alpha_1}, T_{c_2}^{\alpha_2}, \ldots, T_{c_n}^{\alpha_n} >$ whose head has the largest startPos
11:     **if** $\neg$mark[T_q^j] **then**
12:       **while** head(T_q^j).endPos $<$ head(T_{max}).startPos **do**
13:         advance(T_q^j);
14:       **if** head(T_q^j).startPos $<$ head(T_{min}).startPos **then**
15:         mark[T_q^j] = true;
16:         add T_q^j to set $\{T_q\}$
17: $T_1 = \min(T_q); T_2 = \min(\cup\{T_{c_i}\})$; /* min is a function which returns the PPS-stream in the input set whose head has the smallest startPos */
18: **if** head(T_1).startPos $<$ head(T_2).startPos **then**
19:    return $< q, \{T_q\} >$
20: return $< c_i, \{T_{c_i}\} >$ /*T_2 is of class c_i */

PPS-TwigStack performs a single forward scan of all useful PPS streams. It never stores any paths which are only partial matches to one branch of the twig pattern but do not appear in the final match results. Therefore, the worst case I/O complexity is linear in the sum of sizes of the useful PPS streams and the output list. The worst case CPU complexity is $O((|max\_PPSStreams\_per\_tag|)^{|Q|} \times (|Input\_list| + |Output\_list|))$ where $|Q|$ is the twig pattern size, which is also independent of the size of partial matches to any root-to-leaf path of the twig. The factor of $|max\_PPSStream\_per\_tag|^{|Q|}$ is because getNext() needs to enumerate PPS stream combinations. The space complexity is the maximum length of a root-to-leaf path.

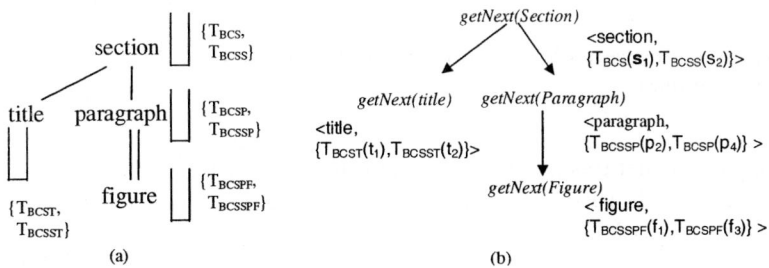

Fig. 2. Illustration of Algorithm $PPS - TwigStack$ (a) Main data structures used. We use a shorter form to denote PPS streams. E.g. $T_{book-chapter-section}$ is represented as T_{bcs} (b) The call stack of the first getNext() call with return values

7 Experiments

All our experiments were run on a 2.4GHz Pentium 4 processor with 512MB memory. We first measure the effect of PPS pruning on the following five twig queries in XMark[6] benchmark. For each twig pattern, Fig.3 shows the execution time and the total number of pages read using $TwigStack$ and $PPS-TwigStack$ with pruning on a XMark document of size 130MB.

1. /site/people/person/name
2. /site/open_auctions/open_auction/bidder/increase/
3. /site/closed_auctions/closed_auction/price
4. /site/regions//item
5. /site/people/person[//ageand//income]/name

PPS-TwigStack is optimal for A-D or P-C only twig patterns and 1-branch twig patterns. Even without pruning, PPS-TwigStack still outperforms TwigStack in these classes of queries. We build XML documents of 1 million nodes with tags A, B, C, D, E such that no PPS stream will be pruned away. The XML data generated has two sub-trees: the first contains only partial matches while the second contains full matches. We vary the size of the second sub-tree from 5% to 30% of the total document size and run the twig query $A/B[C//D]//E$.

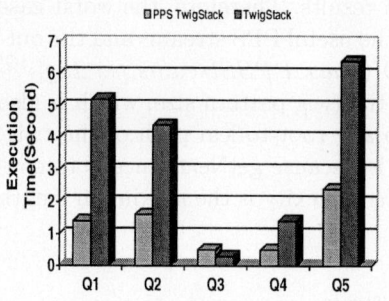 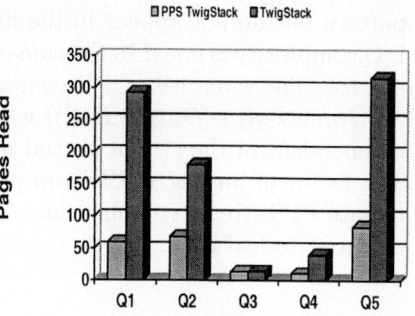

Fig. 3. Comparison of execution time and I/O cost of TwigStack and PPS-TwigStack on a 130MB XMark data

$PPS - TwigStack$ generates much smaller intermediate result sizes. As an example, when the ratio is 10%, $PPS - TwigStack$ produces 9,674 paths whereas $TwigStack$ produce 121,532.

8 Conclusion

In this paper, we address the problem of holistic twig join on XML documents. We propose a novel clustering method Prefix-Path Streaming (PPS) to group XML elements. The benefits of PPS streaming include reduced I/O cost and optimal processing of a large class of twig patterns with both A-D and P-C edges. In particular we show that A-D and P-C only twig and 1-branch twig patterns can be evaluated optimally using PPS.

References

1. N. Bruno, D. Srivastava, and N. Koudas. Holistic twig joins: Optimal xml pattern matching. In *ICDE Conference*, 2002.
2. T. Chen, T.W. Ling, and C.Y. Chan. Prefix path streaming: A new clustering method for optimal holistic xml twig pattern matching. Technical report, National University of Singapore, http://www.comp.nus.edu.sg/~chent/dexapps.pdf.
3. B. Choi, M. Mahoui, and D. Wood. On the optimality of the holistic twig join algorithms. In *In Proceeding of DEXA*, 2003.
4. M.P. Consens and T.Milo. Optimizing queries on files. In *In Proceedings of ACM SIGMOD*, 1994.
5. S. Al-Khalifa, H.V. Jagadish, Nick Koudas, J.M. Patel, Y. Wu, N. Koudas, and D. Srivastava. Structural joins: A primitive for efficient xml query pattern matching. In *In Proceedings of ICDE*, pages 141–152, 2002.
6. XMARK. Xml-benchmark. http://monetdb.cwi.nl/xml.
7. XPath. http://www.w3.org/TR/xpath.
8. C. Zhang, J.F. Naughton, D.J. DeWitt, Q. Luo, and G.M. Lohman. On supporting containment queries in relational database management systems. In *SIGMOD Conference*, 2001.

A Self-adaptive Scope Allocation Scheme for Labeling Dynamic XML Documents

Yun Shen[1], Ling Feng[2], Tao Shen[3], and Bing Wang[1]

[1] Department of Computer Science, University of Hull
Hull, HU6 7RX, United Kingdom
{Y.Shen, B.Wang}@dcs.hull.ac.uk
[2] Department of Computer Science, University of Twente
PO Box 217, 7500 Enschede, The Netherlands
{ling}@cs.utwente.nl
[3] School of Management, UESTC, 610054,P.R.China

Abstract. This paper proposes a self-adaptive scope allocation scheme for labeling dynamic XML documents. It is general, light-weight and can be built upon existing data retrieval mechanisms. Bayesian inference is used to compute the actual scope allocated for labeling a certain node based on both the prior information and the actual document. Through extensive experiments, we show that the proposed Bayesian allocation model can practically and significantly improve the performance of the conventional fixed scope allocation models.

1 Introduction

It is increasingly expected that XML [1] will become the de facto standard of the Web, ultimately replacing HTML. An XML document consists of data enclosed by user defined tags, and its nested tree structure is described by DTD. Figure. 1 shows an example of an XML document and figure. 2 illustrates the corresponding DTD.

To allow efficient querying of XML data, each node in the XML data trees is typically given a unique label, such that given the labels of two nodes, we can determine whether one node is an ancestor of the other. Till now, many indexing structures have been proposed to process structural queries efficiently based on certain coding schemes [9,13,4]. [9] "stitches" the binary twigs to obtain final results based on range labeling scheme. [4] improves [9] by using a stack-based algorithm to efficiently join root-to-leaf paths. [13] treats both document and query as sequences, and matches the query as a whole unit when querying.

However, to fully evolve XML into a universal data representation and exchange format, the capability of modifying XML document is indispensable. It thus arises an important aspect to XML indexing: how to support dynamic data insertion, deletion, and update with corresponding index structure.

Cohen et al. [6] firstly proposed a dynamic labeling scheme for XML documents to support updating operations. The children of a node v have the label concatenated with the string s attached to their incoming edge. Given s(1)=0, to obtain s(i+1), the binary number represented by s(i) is increased 1 and if the

```
<prices>
  <book>
    <title>Algorithms</title>
    <information>
      <source>bstore2.example.com</source>
      <price>31.99</price>
    </information>
  </book>
  <book>
    <title>Data on the Web</title>
    <information>
      <source>bstore2.example.com</source>
      <price>34.95</price>
    </information>
    <author>Serge Abiteboul</author>
    <author>Peter Buneman</author>
    <author>Dan Suciu</author>
  </book>
  <book>
    <title>TCP/IP Illustrated</title>
    <information>
      <source>bstore2.example.com</source>
      <price>65.95</price>
    </information>
    <author>W. Richard Stevens</author>
  </book>
</prices>
```

Fig. 1. Example of an XML Document

```
<!ELEMENT prices (book*)>
<!ELEMENT book (title?, information+, author*)>
<!ELEMENT information (source, price)>
<!ELEMENT author (#PCDATA)>
<!ELEMENT price (#PCDATA)>
<!ELEMENT source (#PCDATA)>
<!ELEMENT title (#PCDATA)>
```

Fig. 2. Example of DTD

representation of s(i)+1 consists of all ones, its length is double. The problem with this approach is that the size of labeling will grow fast with the increase of degree of the nodes for its the dependency on the fan-out of a node.

State-of-the-art research efforts [13, 14, 9] have been proposed to cope with the problem of allocating scope for dynamic XML documents. [9, 14] considered to give some extra scope while allocating the labels. But as for how much to allocate, they did not address it. [13] considered to allocate scope for each node on the basis of the probability of its occurrences from statistical information. The deficiency is that the probability of allocating space for a certain node is fixed and is considered as a constant. To summarize, these methods are not self-adaptive to real document environment where the probability of a node's occurrence varies in difference XML documents.

In this paper, we improve the conventional scope allocation scheme using Bayesian inference technique. Combining the prior information (i.e DTD and statistical information) and the actual documents, better performance in scope allocation for dynamic XML documents is achieved. we propose Bayesian Allocation Model (BAM), a general, self-adaptive scope allocation model that addresses the above important challenges for dynamic XML data. It is general, light-weight and can be adapted to existing data retrieval mechanisms [5, 4, 8, 16, 7, 13, 9]. The scope allocated for each node depends on the probability it will be updated. Thus we can guarantee a better performance than the traditional allocation methods when updating.

Outline of the Paper. The rest of the paper is organized as follows. Our proposed method, Bayesian allocation model, is introduced and theoretically proved in section 2. The corresponding algorithms are shown in section 3. The performance is demonstrated in section 4 through a set of experiments. Finally, our work is concluded in Section 5.

2 Bayesian Allocation Model

Notations: Let u be a node in a DTD, which has t child nodes. Let $nodetype_i$ denote the type of the ith child node ($1 \leq i \leq t$), which occurs x_i times under the node u in corresponding XML document. $\sum_{i=1}^{t} x_i = z$, where z equals to the total number of children under node u. Assume all sibling nodes of different $nodetype_i$ occur independently with probability θ_i. Let $\bar{\theta}_i$ denote estimators of θ_i, which can be obtained from semantic of our XML document or the statistics of a sample dataset. Let n denote the *range* scope allocated for the z nodes under node u. In the paper, n = c × z, where c denotes the *range enlarging factor*.

2.1 Scope Allocation Overview

The scope allocation scheme works as follows; 1) parse DTD to obtain prior information for each name type; then during the breadth first traversal of an XML document, embed the tree into a complete K-ary tree, 2) root node of an XML document is put in level 0 and labeled 1 in the complete K-ary tree; 3) for each non-leaf node, calculate the number of children, denoted as z, and the types of its children, denoted as t; 4) allocate scope for each child node using Bayesian allocation model in lth level below its parent, satisfying $l \geq \lceil \log_k(c \times z) \rceil$, c denotes a range enlarging factor; 5) repeat 3) and 4) till breadth-first traversal finishes.

2.2 Bayesian Allocation Model

Self-adaptive Bayesian allocation model is proposed to allocate scope for dynamic XML documents on the basis of K-ary tree and Breadth-First Traversal. Pre-allocating scope for dynamic XML data is a natural solution. The core of Bayesian allocation model is on efficiently allocating scope for each node in actual dynamic XML documents in a self-adaptive manner.

Bayesian Allocation Model. The core of our work is on estimating probability θ_i. In ViST [13], Haixun Wang et al. calculate θ_i only from available DTD or statistics from sample set of XML documents, and consider θ_i as a constant, which is fixed without considering the actual documents. Our objective is self-adaptively allocating dynamic scope for each node according to its actual probability in each document, not just using a fixed constant probability, which is simply calculated from DTD or sample set of datasets.

Our proposed Bayesian allocation model considers θ_i as a random variable not a constant, and chooses a proper prior distribution for θ_i, which reflects the observer's beliefs about the proper value θ_i may take, and then updates these beliefs on the basis of the actual data observed. Thus estimators of θ_i can accord with the real world data in a self-adaptive manner. To summarize, the heuristics guiding the allocation model is that the more child nodes of $nodetype_i$ a node u has, the more likely for these child nodes being updated.

Given a node u with t children in a DTD. Each of them occurs x_i times, i = (1, ..., t), in the corresponding XML document. x_i may be zero in an actual XML document if a certain node is optional in DTD. Assume 1) all sibling nodes of different $nodetype_i$ occur independently with probability θ_i (i=1, ..., t) and 2) the probability of data insertion/deletion on these nodes occurs according to the same probability. Thus, given scope range n for the z nodes in an XML document, if we know θ_i (i = 1, ..., t) for the z nodes, a natural idea is that we allocate scope for each node type according to probability θ_i. For instance, if all the sibling nodes with $nodetype_i$ occur x_i times under a node u, and update probability is θ_i, then we allocate $\frac{n\theta_i}{x_i}$ for each node with $nodetype_i$.

In general our Bayesian allocation model is based on the following hypothesis below:

- Sibling nodes of different $nodetype_i$ occur independently with probability θ_i (i=1, 2, ..., t), where t denotes the node name types in the correspond DTD. And all data insertion/deletion/update on the nodes of different $nodetype_i$ occurs independently with the same probability θ_i.
- θ_i is a random variable ,we use $\pi(\theta_i)$ to denotes prior distribution of θ_i , which reflects our beliefs about what values parameters θ_i may take. We assume that θ_i is a $beta(\alpha_i, \beta_i)$ distribution

Whether or not using prior distribution in statistical inference is not only a problem of mathematical technic but a problem of philosophy [3] as well. Thus we do not discuss necessity of using prior distribution here, and use it by the way of Bayesian inference theory. However, how to choose prior distribution is another problem. We choose beta distribution as prior distribution because: 1) density curve of beta distribution is plane curve when $\alpha \gg 1, \beta > 1$, and $0 \leq$ value of beta distribution ≤ 1, matching the definition of probability. Thus we consider $\bar{\theta}_i$, prior information of θ_i, as mean value of beta distribution, which means that the probability of $node_i$ occurs around $\bar{\theta}_i$ is greater than in other zone, matching our hypothesis; 2) from lemma 1 we know posterior distribution $\theta_i|x_i$ is also a beta distribution which is convenient to compute the posterior estimators of θ_i. Using other prior like norm distribution will result in complicated monte carlo simulations and the computational complexity. In fact, using beta distribution as prior distribution of parameter θ_i in binomial distribution is very common in practice [3].

Theoretical Proof. In our model we consider sample information of θ_i as occurrence times x_i under a certain node u since we assume a node with $nodetype_i$ occurs with same probability θ_i in our hypotheses. From the Hypotheses x_i observes binomial distribution, denoted as $b(z, \theta_i)$. The updating procedure is performed using Bayesian theorem, which states that the posterior distribution $\theta_i|x_i$, representing our beliefs on the observed data, is proportional to the product of the prior distribution and the likelihood function.

The following two lemmas are proved for the correctness of our Bayesian allocation model:

Lemma 1 *Assume $\pi(\theta_i)$ is $beta(\alpha_i, \beta_i)$ ($\alpha_i \gg 1, \beta_i > 1$), and sample information variable $x_i \sim b(z, \theta_i)$ (binomial distribution) with parameter θ_i. Thus, the posterior distribution function $p(\theta_i|x_i)$ is also a $beta(\alpha_i^*, \beta_i^*)$ distribution, and $beta(\alpha_i, \beta_i)$ is called conjugate prior distribution. We have the following result:*

$$E(\theta_i|x_i) = \lambda_i E(x_i|\theta_i) + (1-\lambda_i)\frac{x_i}{z}$$

where

$$E(x_i|\theta_i) = \frac{\alpha_i}{\alpha_i + \beta_i}$$

Proof: Given

$$\pi(\theta_i) \sim beta(\alpha_i, \beta_i)$$

and it's density function

$$\pi(\theta_i) = \frac{\Gamma(\alpha_i + \beta_i)}{\Gamma(\alpha_i)\Gamma(\beta_i)} \theta_i^{\alpha_i - 1}(1-\theta_i)^{\beta_i - 1}$$

because x_i is binomial distribution, density function of x_i given parameter θ_i is:

$$f(x_i|\theta_i) = C_z^{x_i} \theta_i^{x_i}(1-\theta_i)^{z-x_i}, where 0 \leq \theta_i \leq 1$$

Thus, according to Bayesian theorem posterior distribution of θ_i is:

$$p(\theta_i|x_i) = \frac{f(x_i|\theta_i)\pi(\theta_i)}{\int_0^1 f(x_i|\theta_i)\pi(\theta_i)d\theta_i}$$

$$= \frac{\theta_i^{\alpha_i+x_i-1}(1-\theta_i)^{z+\beta_i-x_i-1}}{\int_0^1 \theta_i^{\alpha_i+x_i-1}(1-\theta_i)^{z+\beta_i-x_i-1}d\theta_i}$$

$$= k_i \theta_i^{x_i+\alpha_i-1}(1-\theta_i)^{z+\beta_i-x_i-1})$$

where

$$k_i = \frac{\Gamma(\alpha_i+x_i)\Gamma(\beta_i+z-x_i)}{\Gamma(\alpha_i+\beta_i+z)}$$

hence:

$$p(\theta_i|x_i) \sim beta(\alpha_i+x_i, \beta_i+z-x_i)$$

and:

$$E(\theta_i|x_i) = \frac{\alpha_i+x_i}{\alpha_i+\beta_i+z} = \frac{\alpha_i}{\alpha_i+\beta_i}\lambda_i + (1-\lambda_i)\frac{x_i}{z}$$

$$= E(\theta_i)\lambda_i + (1-\lambda_i)\frac{x_i}{z}$$

where

$$\lambda_i = \frac{\alpha_i+\beta_i}{\alpha_i+\beta_i+z}$$

λ_i reflects on the importance balance between prior information and sample information.

Lemma 2 *Assume prior distribution $\pi(\theta_i)$, sample information x_i and square loss function $L(\delta_i, \theta_i)$ is given. The Bayesian estimators of θ_i, $\delta^\pi(x_i)$, is the expectation (or mean value) of posterior distribution $\pi(\theta_i|x_i)$ which is written as:*

$$\delta^\pi(x_i) = E(\theta_i|x_i)$$

Proof: The posterior risk of any decision function $\delta_i = \delta(x_i)$ given square loss function is :

$$E((\delta_i - \theta_i)^2|x_i) = \delta_i^2 - 2\delta_i E(\theta_i|x_i) + E(\theta_i^2|x_i)$$

obviously the function value is minimized *iff*:

$$\delta_i = E(\theta_i|x_i)$$

From Lemma 1 we know that

$$\delta_i = \frac{\alpha_i+x_i}{\alpha_i+\beta_i+z} = E(\theta_i)\lambda_i + (1-\lambda_i)\frac{x_i}{z}$$

In our model we assume that $E(\theta_i) = \bar{\theta}_i$ which means that the prior probability of node i occurs around $\bar{\theta}_i$ is greater than in other zone. And from lemma 1 we get posterior expectation of θ_i. So we use $E(\theta_i|x_i)$ as estimators of θ_i according to Lemma 2.

Let $\lambda_i = 0.5$, which implies that importance of prior information is the same as that of sample information. Let θ'_i denote estimators of θ_i given prior information $\bar{\theta}_i$. From Lemma 1 and Lemma 2, we have:

$$\theta'_i = \frac{1}{2}\bar{\theta}_i + \frac{1}{2} * \frac{x_i}{z} \qquad (1)$$

Eq(1) proves that the prior information and posterior information both contribute to the final probability a node will be updated, which is better than ViST allocation method which only utilizes prior information only.

3 Algorithms

We call the above process of allocating scope in a complete K-ary tree with Bayesian allocation model *Bayesianization*. After a brief description of how to compute the prior information from DTD, we present Algorithm. BAYESIANIZATION and Algorithm. BAYESINFERENCE which describe the labeling process that combines with the Bayesian theorem in detail. Figure. 3 gives an example of our proposed Bayesian allocation model. We show how to compute these p_i (i=1, 2, 3, ...) in the following section.

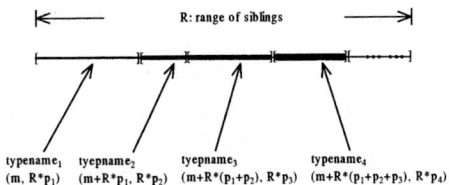

Fig. 3. Example of Bayesian Allocation Model

3.1 Prior Information

Prior information about the occurrence probability of all the children below a node u in DTD, denoted by $\bar{p}_{DTD_u}$, is defined as follows:

$$\bar{p}_{DTD_u} = (\bar{p}_{c_1}, \bar{p}_{c_2}, ..., \bar{p}_{c_t})$$

where t is the number of different child nodes u has. Each $\bar{p}_{c_i}$, i = 1, 2, ...,t, can be computed based DTD Table.1, which defines the proportion of the scope among the different cardinality.

For example, the value 0.08 at (?, +) in Table 1 specifies the proportion relationship 0.08:1 between child node type with "?" and child node type with "+". Also the proportion 1.25:1 between child node type with "+" and the one with "*". Thus we have 0.08:1:0.8 having three child nodes with type "?", "+" and "*". Notice that the data in Table. 1 can be calculated from the statistic information of the sample XML documents.

Actually, table.1 reflects our belief on prior information. (a|b) is transformed into (a,b) to minimize the computational complexity. Consider, for example, given <!ELEMENT book (title?, information+, author*)>, the proportion among these three nodetypes is 0.08:1:0.8, to normalize, $\bar{p}_{title?} = \frac{0.08}{0.08+1+0.8} = 0.043$, $\bar{p}_{information+} = \frac{1}{0.08+1+0.8} = 0.532$ and $\bar{p}_{author*} = \frac{0.8}{0.08+1+0.8} = 0.425$. Therefore, $\bar{p}_{DTD_{book}} = (0.043, 0.532, 0.425)$.

Table 1. Prior information on the cardinality proportion

	*	+	?
*	1	0.8	10
+	1.25	1	12.5
?	0.1	0.08	1

3.2 Algorithms

As we can see in Algorithm. BAYESIANIZATION and Algorithm. BAYESINFERENCE, our specific Bayesian allocation model is light-weight and self-adaptive for each node in the XML document tree (Line 1 - 11 in Algo.BAYESINFERENCE). The time complexity of the algorithms is O(n), depending on the number of the nodes in a tree, and the space complexity is linear as well. It implies that our algorithm guarantees both time and space complexity efficiency while allocating self-adaptive scope for each node, which is not provided by the previous methods. The performance results are shown in section 4.

Algorithm BAYESIANIZATION
Input: T: Data tree of XML document; Queue: queue of nodes; p_{DTD}: the DTD prior distribution generated
1.
Output: BAM Allocated Document
2. Queue.insert(T.root)
3. **while** (!Queue.empty())
4.   **do** u ← Queue.fetch()
5.   list ← listofchildren(u)
6.   z ← numofchildren(list)
7.   t ← typeofchildren(list)
8.   BAYESINFERENCE($\bar{p}_{DTD_u}$, z, t, list)
9.   Queue.insert(list)

Algorithm BAYESINFERENCE
Input: $\bar{p}_{DTD_u}$: prior information of node u; z: number of child nodes; t: number of child node types, list: list of nodes

Output: BAM allocated scope of u
1. level = $\lceil \log_k(c \times z) \rceil$
2. n = k^{level}
3. **for** i ← 1 to t
4.   **do** $p_i \leftarrow \frac{\bar{p}_{DTD_{u_i}} + x_i/z}{2}$
5. $subrange_i \leftarrow$ n × p_i
6.   **for** j ← 1 to z in list
7.   **do** $subrange_{node_j} \leftarrow subrange_i / t_i$
8. $seqnum_{node_j} \leftarrow (\sum_1^{i-1} subrange_i + \sum_1^{j-1} subrange_{node_j})$

Consider, for example, given <!ELEMENT book (title?, information+, author *)>, we get $p_{DTD_{book}} = (0.043, 0.532, 0.425)$. If in an actual XML document, a node named "book" has 1 "title" child node, 2 "information" child nodes, however, 10 "author" child nodes. Suppose the range enlarging factor is 100, thus we allocate scope 13*100 = 1300 (n = c × z, section 2) for these 13 child nodes. Thus their actual probability should be <0.0599 = $((0.043 + \frac{1}{13})/2)$, 0.4198 = $((0.532 + \frac{2}{13})/2)$, 0.5971 = $((0.425 + \frac{10}{13})/2)$ >, and the scope allocated for each node are 0.0599*1300 = 77 for "title" node, 0.4198 * 1300 = 545 for "information" nodes, and 0.5971 * 1300 = 776 for "author" nodes. We notice that the allocation scopes of these three nodes accord to their actual occurrence probability.

4 Performance Experiments

4.1 Experiments

The experiments were conducted on a PC with Pentium III CPU 1.2GHZ and 512 MB main memory. We implemented the proposed method Bayesian allocation model and the conventional fixed allocation scheme for comparison purpose. Our synthetic XML documents are generated using Sun XML instance generator [12] utilizing various DTDs, i.e. ACM Sigmod Record DTD [2], and public XML benchmark database XMARK [15].

Update Performance. We focus on studying the update performance in dynamic XML documents. We generate 200 XML documents with maximum depth 8 for experiments. Five different experiments are performed with different range enlarging factors. In the experiments, we respectively set the range enlarging factor $c = 50, 75, 100, 125$ and 150 for these documents in the set of experiments. We then implement an allocation scheme similar to ViST and our allocation scheme tailored to ViST. In ViST, it allocates scope for each type of child nodes directly from DTD without constructing trie-like tree. However, for comparison purpose, we first construct the trie-like tree physically, and then apply BAM to allocate scope for each node in the trie-like tree.

In the experiments, we randomly choose m nodes the datasets we generated. Suppose each $node_i$ (i = 1, ..., m) has t different node name types. Firstly we compute the prior information for each $node_i$ from the corresponding DTD, denoted as $\bar{p}_{DTD_{node_i}} = (\bar{p}_1, \bar{p}_2, ..., \bar{p}_t)$. Then we use t independent beta distribution to generate t random numbers, denoted as $(r_1, r_2, ..., r_t)$. We can

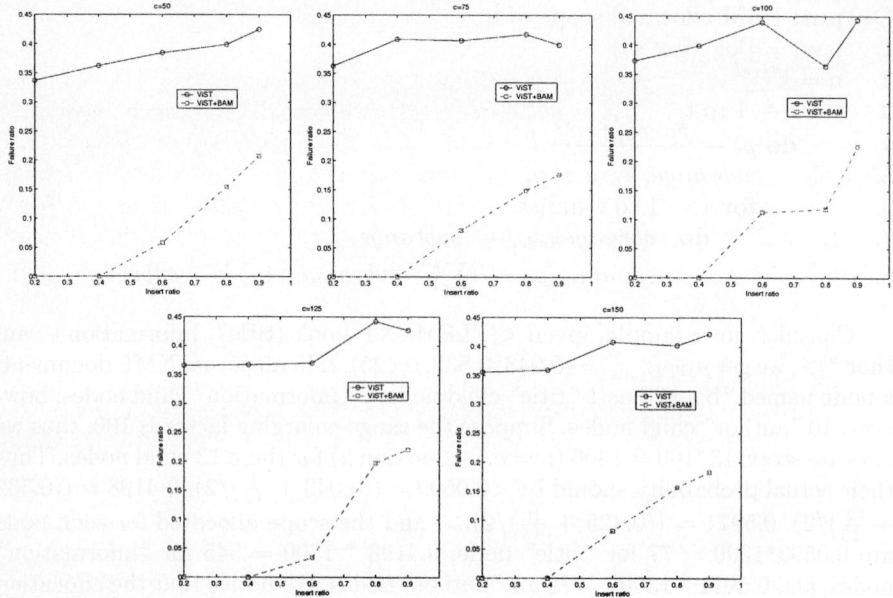

Fig. 4. Insert ratio vs. failure ratio

prove that $0 \leq r_1, r_2, ..., r_t < 1$. Thirdly we generate the insertion/deletion probability for each node type: $p_i = \frac{r_i}{s}$, where $s = \sum_{i=1}^{t} r_i$, which obeys our hypotheses and is fair to both ViST and ViST with BAM when the probability of insertion/deletion is concerned. Finally we random generate the position a node should be inserted/deleted.

We define that a "failure" occurs when a position has been allocated during inserting, and an "overflow" when pre-allocated space for a certain node is used up. During the experiments, we record the "failure"times. eq(2) and eq(3) are presented to clarify the experimental results shown in figure 4.

$$failure_{ratio} = \begin{cases} 1, & \text{when "overflow" occurs,} \\ \frac{times_{failure}}{times_{insert}}, & \text{otherwise.} \end{cases} \quad (2)$$

$$insert_{ratio} = \frac{times_{insert}}{Space_{free}} \quad (3)$$

We can see that BAM improves at least 49.34% comparing to the conventional ViST method, for the scope allocated for each node accords to the probability it would be updated, which further depends not only on the prior information, i.e. statistical information from sample datasets, but combining the actual probability of its occurrence as well. Especially, when the probability of inserting/deleting a node in an XML document is much greater than the average prior information, BAM performs much more better than ViST method.

```
<!ELEMENT Info (Course+, Student+)>
<!ELEMENT Course (CName, Description?)>
   <!ATTLIST Course Number ID #REQUIRED>
<!ELEMENT CName (#PCDATA)>
<!ELEMENT Description (#PCDATA)>
<!ELEMENT Student (SName, Major)>
   <!ATTLIST Student StudentID ID #REQUIRED
                     Courses IDREFS #IMPLIED>
<!ELEMENT SName (#PCDATA)>
<!ELEMENT Major (#PCDATA)>
```

```
<Info>
   <Course Number="CMPS200">
      <CName>Intro. Programming</CName>
   </Course>
   <Course Number="CMPS212">
      <CName>Data Structures</CName>
   </Course>
   <Student StudentID="s20021234"
            Courses="CMPS200 CMPS212">
      <SName>Fatmé</SName>
      <Major>Computer Science</Major>
   </Student>
   <Student StudentID="s20021235"
            Courses="CMPS200">
      <SName>Khaled</SName>
      <Major>Mathematics</Major>
   </Student>
</Info>
```

Fig. 2. Document info.xml with its DTD

In the F2/XML method, we store intra-document references in the database as follows. XMLID is a predefined class which has three attributes: value of domain String, inDoc of domain Document, and IDatt of domain ATTRIBUTE (metaclass). It contains objects which represent ID values and which are described by a value (e.g. "CMPS200"), a document in which they appear (e.g. info.xml document), and an ID attribute on which they are taken (e.g. Number attribute). The key of class XMLID is the set of attributes {value, inDoc} since ID values are unique within a document. As we said before, an XML element A is mapped into a database class named A. An XML attribute of type ID or IDREF(S) in element A is mapped into a database attribute from the class named A to the class XMLID. The database storing the document info.xml is given in Figure3. As we can see, XMLID is an intermediate class which contains objects that are referenced through ID and IDREF(S) attributes. For an object x in XMLID, att:=IDatt(x) gives the ID attribute through which x is referenced, and ref:=att^{-1}(x) gives the object that references x through the ID attribute. Computing the inverse of an attribute is an easy operation in the F2 DBMS, since F2 supports transposed storage of objects [1].

Navigating in a document corresponds to navigating in the database where the document is stored. If an object o has an IDREF attribute att1, and x:=att1(o) (x is an object in class XMLID), then we get the ID attribute att2:=IDatt(x), and the object ref:=att2^{-1}(x). In other words, we traverse the reference from the element represented by object o to the element represented by object ref. In our example, if we take s in Student (Khaled student), Courses(s) gives the object x in XMLID (of value "CMPS200"), IDatt(x) gives the Number attribute, and Number^{-1}(x) gives the object c in Course (Intro. Programming course).

4 Inter-document Links

XLink allows to create links between documents. These links are expressed in XML. There are two kinds of links: simple links and extended links. A simple link deals with

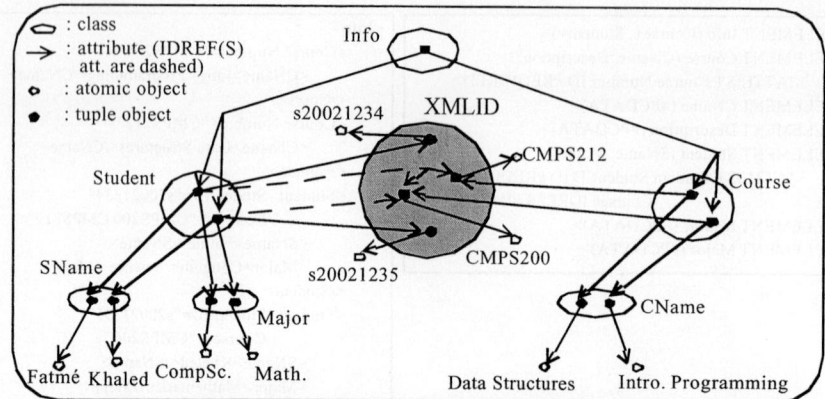

Fig. 3. Database storing the info.xml document (the attributes XMLID.inDoc and XMLID.IDatt, and the class Description are omitted)

only two resources, and is unidirectional (like HTML hyperlinks). An extended link can involve more than two resources, and allows to specify traversal rules between the various resources.

4.1 Simple Links

An existing XML element is made into a simple link by adding to it the XLink attributes `xlink:type` (whose value is "simple") and `xlink:href`.[1] The value on the `xlink:href` attribute specifies the target element (which is in another document or in the same document). It is expressed in the XPointer language which identifies an element: (i) by its value on an ID attribute (e.g. courses.xml#CMPS200), or (ii) with an XPath expression (e.g. courses.xml#xpointer(Course[position()=1])) returns the first element named "Course", or (iii) with a child sequence that defines its position in the document hierarchy (e.g. courses.xml#/1). Our current XPointer implementation allows to identify elements only by their ID value.

For example, we have now two documents courses.xml and students.xml. The document courses.xml (see Figure4) stores the courses offered by the computer science department. The document students.xml (see Figure5) stores the students with the courses they are enrolled in. In the DTD, the Student element does not have any more the IDREFS attribute. Instead, it has a child Courses (with cardinality '*' since the IDREFS attribute was #IMPLIED), which is defined as an empty element. The Courses element is a simple link, it has the two XLink attributes `xlink:type` (set to "simple") and `xlink:href`. The namespace xlink is first defined with the attribute `xmlns:xlink`. In the document, the Courses child of the second Student element takes the value "courses.xml#CMPS200" on the `xlink:href` attribute, which means that it references the element in the document courses.xml which takes "CMPS200" on an ID attribute.

---

[1] Simple links can have other optional XLink attributes (xlink:role, xlink:arcrole, xlink:title, xlink:show, xlink:actuate).

```
<!ELEMENT CourseList (Course+)>
<!ELEMENT Course (CName, Description?)>
    <!ATTLIST Course Number ID #REQUIRED>
<!ELEMENT CName (#PCDATA)>
<!ELEMENT Description (#PCDATA)>
```

```xml
<CourseList>
    <Course Number="CMPS200">
        <CName>Intro. Programming</CName>
    </Course>
    <Course Number="CMPS212">
        <CName>Data Structures</CName>
    </Course>
</CourseList>
```

Fig. 4. Document courses.xml with its DTD

```
<!ELEMENT StudentList (Student+)>
<!ELEMENT Student (SName, Major, Courses*)>
    <!ATTLIST Student StudentID ID #REQUIRED>
<!ELEMENT SName (#PCDATA)>
<!ELEMENT Major (#PCDATA)>
<!ELEMENT Courses EMPTY>
    <!ATTLIST Courses  xmlns:xlink   CDATA #FIXED "http://www.w3.org/1999/xlink"
                       xlink:type    (simple | extended | locator | arc) #FIXED "simple"
                       xlink:href    CDATA #REQUIRED>
```

```xml
<StudentList>
    <Student StudentID="s20021234">
        <SName>Fatmé</SName>
        <Major>Computer Science</Major>
        <Courses xlink:href="courses.xml#CMPS200"/>
        <Courses xlink:href="courses.xml#CMPS212"/>
    </Student>
    <Student StudentID="s20021235">
        <SName>Khaled</SName>
        <Major>Mathematics</Major>
        <Courses xlink:href="courses.xml#CMPS200"/>
    </Student>
</StudentList>
```

Fig. 5. Document students.xml with its DTD

In the F2/XML method, the way we store a simple link is similar to the way we store an intra-document reference. The $\texttt{xlink:href}$ attribute in the link element A is mapped into a database attribute $\texttt{xlink\_href}$ from the class named A to the class $\texttt{XMLID}$. Both documents courses.xml and students.xml are stored in the same database shown in Figure6. Navigating through the two documents corresponds to navigating in the database. If an object o has an $\texttt{xlink\_href}$ attribute, and $x:=\texttt{xlink\_href}(o)$ (x is an object in class $\texttt{XMLID}$), then we get the ID attribute $att2:=\texttt{IDatt}(x)$, and the object $ref:=att2^{-1}(x)$. In other words, we traverse the link from the source element represented by object o to the target element represented by object ref.

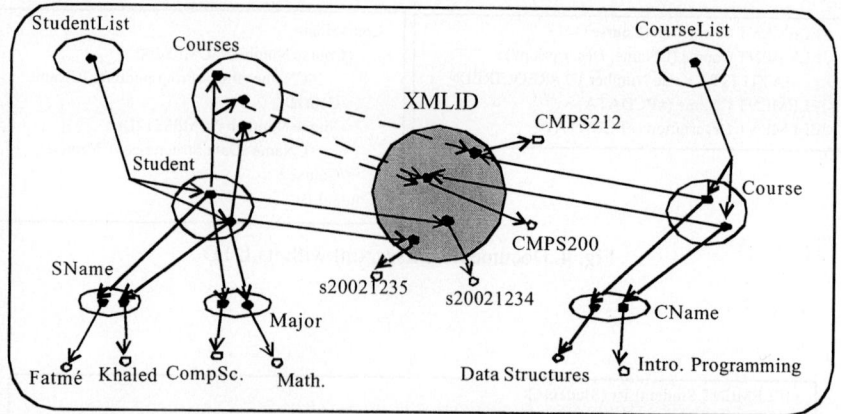

Fig. 6. Database storing the documents courses.xml and students.xml, and the simple links between them (href attributes are dashed)

4.2 Extended Links

An extended link can link any number of source elements to any number of target elements. It can be viewed as a set of links. An extended link is defined as a new auxiliary element with the XLink attribute xlink:type set to "extended". This element has children, called locators, which specify the elements (source and target elements) that participate in the extended link.[2] A locator is an element with the following XLink attributes: xlink:type which is set to "locator", xlink:href whose value specifies an element in an XML document, and xlink:label. The auxiliary element has other children, called arcs or traversals, which specify which elements are linked to which elements. An arc is an element with the XLink attributes xlink:type, set to "arc", and xlink:from and xlink:to whose value must be a value taken by a locator element on the xlink:label attribute.[3]

For example, we take our previous document courses.xml as it is, and take another document students2.xml (see Figure 7). In the latter, the Student elements do not have any more Courses children. Instead, there is a new element Registrations which is an extended link. It has five locators which specify two Student elements (in the document itself) and three Course elements (in the document courses.xml). It has two arcs, the first links the student Fatmé to both courses CMPS200 and CMPS212, while the second links the student Khaled to the course CMPS200.

In the F2/XML method, we store extended links as follows. We introduce two predefined classes: XMLLocator and XMLArc. The class XMLLocator has three attributes: xlink__type, xlink__href (of domain XMLID), and xlink__label (of domain String). The class XMLArc has the attribute xlink__type, and two multi-valued attributes xlink__from and xlink__to (of domain XMLLocator). A locator

---

[2] The auxiliary element can also have another kind of children called resources.
[3] Extended links and locators can have other optional XLink attributes (xlink:role, xlink:title), and arcs can have other optional XLink attributes (xlink:arcrole, xlink:title, xlink:show, xlink:actuate).

```
<!ELEMENT StudentsInfo (Registrations?, StudentList)>
<!ELEMENT Registrations (Loc+, Go+)>
    <!ATTLIST Registrations    xmlns:xlink CDATA #FIXED "http://www.w3.org/1999/xlink"
                               xlink:type (simple | extended | locator | arc) #FIXED "extended">
<!ELEMENT Loc EMPTY>
    <!ATTLIST Loc      xlink:type    (simple | extended | locator | arc) #FIXED   "locator"
                       xlink:href    CDATA         #REQUIRED
                       xlink:label   NMTOKEN       #REQUIRED>
<!ELEMENT Go EMPTY>
    <!ATTLIST Go       xlink:type    (simple | extended | locator | arc) #FIXED   "arc"
                       xlink:from    NMTOKEN       #REQUIRED
                       xlink:to      NMTOKEN       #REQUIRED>
<!ELEMENT StudentList (Student+)>
<!ELEMENT Student (SName, Major)>
    <!ATTLIST Student StudentID ID #REQUIRED>
<!ELEMENT SName (#PCDATA)>
<!ELEMENT Major (#PCDATA)>
```

```
<StudentsInfo>
    <Registrations>
        <Loc xlink:href="#s20021234" xlink:label="A"/>
        <Loc xlink:href="#s20021235" xlink:label="B"/>
        <Loc xlink:href="courses.xml#CMPS200" xlink:label="C"/>
        <Loc xlink:href="courses.xml#CMPS212" xlink:label="C"/>
        <Loc xlink:href="courses.xml#CMPS200" xlink:label="D"/>
        <Go xlink:from="A" xlink:to="C"/>
        <Go xlink:from="B" xlink:to="D"/>
    </Registrations>
    <StudentList>
        <Student StudentID="s20021234">
            <SName>Fatmé</SName>
            <Major>Computer Science</Major>
        </Student>
        <Student StudentID="s20021235">
            <SName>Khaled</SName>
            <Major>Mathematics</Major>
        </Student>
    </StudentList>
</StudentsInfo>
```

Fig. 7. Document students2.xml with its DTD

element in the DTD is mapped into a subclass of XMLLocator which consequently inherits the attributes of the latter. An arc element in the DTD is mapped into a subclass of XMLArc which consequently inherits the attributes of the latter. Figure 8 shows the database storing both documents courses.xml and students2.xml. Note that objects in class Go are associated directly to locator objects (and not to labels).

Navigating through the two documents corresponds to navigating in the database. For an object o, the first step is to find the arcs in which it participates as source. Let o belong to a class which has the ID attribute att, so x:=att(o) gives the corresponding object in class XMLID. The locators referencing x are obtained by L:=xlink__href^{-1}(x) (L is a set of objects). For each l in L, the arcs taking l as source are obtained by A:=xlink__from^{-1}(l) (A is a set of objects). The second step is to find the target elements of the found arcs. For each a in A, L2:=xlink__to(a) gives the target locators of the arc (L2 is a set of objects). For each l2 in L2, x2:=xlink__href(l2). The ID attribute is obtained as before by

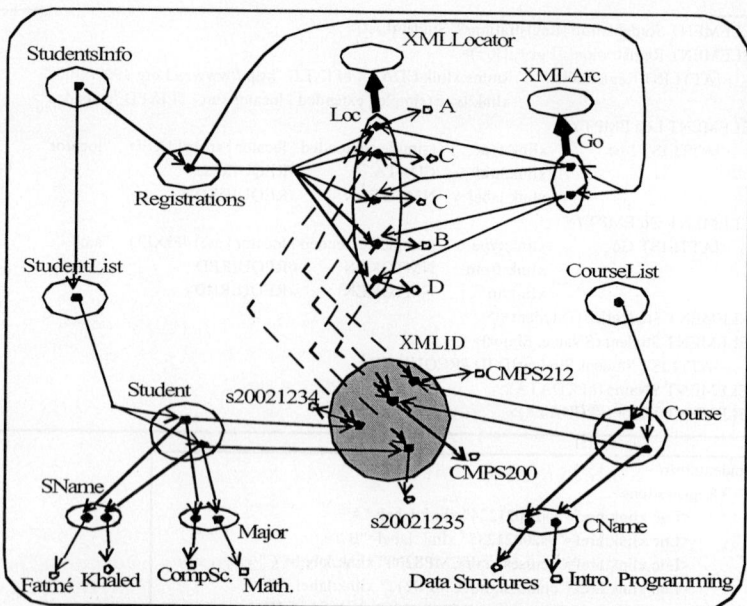

Fig. 8. Database storing the documents courses.xml and students2.xml, and the extended link between them (href attributes are dashed)

att2:=IDatt(x2). Finally ref:=att2^{-1}(x2) gives the target objects. In other words, we traverse a set of links from the source element represented by object o to the target elements represented by the objects ref. In our example, if we take s in Student (Khaled student), StudentID(s) gives the object x in XMLID (of value "s20021235"), xlink__href^{-1}(x) gives the object 1 in Loc (of label "B") and xlink__from^{-1}(1) gives the object a in Go. Then xlink__to(a) gives the object 12 in Loc (of label "D"), xlink__href(12) gives the object x2 in XMLID (of value "CMPS200"), IDatt(x2) gives the Number attribute, and Number^{-1}(x2) gives the c object in Course (Intro. Programming course).

5 F2Web Browser

The additional XLink attributes xlink:show and xlink:actuate are used in simple and extended links for browsing purposes. They specify the behavior of a link when browsing. xlink:show determines the triggered action, i.e. where the target element should appear. The "replace" value replaces the current document with the target element, the "embed" value includes the target element in the current page, and the "new" value displays the target element in a new window. xlink:actuate determines the activating event, i.e. when the link will call the target element. The value "onRequest" requires a user action, like a mouse click, to activate the link, and the value "onLoad" activates the link when the document loads into the browser.

For example, in the DTD of document students.xml (fig. Figure5), we replace the attribute list declaration of the Courses element (the link) by the following:

```
<!ATTLIST Courses       xmlns:xlink    CDATA                                   #FIXED   "http://www.w3.org/1999/xlink"
                        xlink:type     (simple | extended | locator | arc)     #FIXED   "simple"
                        xlink:href     CDATA                                   #REQUIRED
                        xlink:show     (replace | embed | new)                 #FIXED   "embed"
                        xlink:actuate  (onLoad | onRequest)                    #FIXED   "onRequest">
```

Similarly, in the DTD of document students2.xml (fig. Figure7), we replace the attribute list declaration of the Go element (the arc) by the following:

```
<!ATTLIST Go            xlink:type     (simple | extended | locator | arc)     #FIXED   "arc"
                        xlink:from     NMTOKEN                                 #REQUIRED
                        xlink:to       NMTOKEN                                 #REQUIRED
                        xlink:title    CDATA                                   #IMPLIED
                        xlink:show     (replace | embed | new)                 #FIXED   "new"
                        xlink:actuate  (onLoad | onRequest)                    #FIXED   "onRequest">
```

The xlink:title attribute indicates a human-readable description of the link.

We implemented the enhanced F2/XML method and integrated it with the F2Web interface. F2Web is a Java applet which has an XML menu with five items. It allows the user to map a DTD/document to an F2 database schema/instance, retrieve a DTD/document from the database, and browse an XML document stored in the database by giving its tree representation. Linked XML documents can be browsed as illustrated in Figure9 and Figure10. Figure9 shows that both documents courses.xml and students.xml are stored in the database. Clicking on students.xml displays its tree representation. Clicking on the first Courses element (simple link, icon in red) shows the referenced Course element as its child (embed and onRequest mode). Figure10 shows the document students2.xml in the F2Web browser. Clicking on the first Student element (icon in red) displays a pop-up window with all the arcs from this element (in our case, only one). Clicking on the arc entitled "enrolled in" shows the two referenced Course elements in a new window (new and onRequest mode).

6 Conclusion

In this paper, we proposed the F2/XML method to store/retrieve linked XML documents in/from an object database and navigate through them. We implemented our method in the F2 DBMS. We integrated it with the F2Web interface to browse the linked documents. F2/XML can also be used to change the schema of XML documents [3]. Future work includes enhancing our XPointer implementation, addressing performance issues, and querying linked documents. Currently, neither XPath nor XQuery support navigation along XLink references.

References

1. Al-Jadir L., Léonard M., "Transposed Storage of an Object Database to Reduce the Cost of Schema Changes", Proc. Int. ER Workshop on Evolution and Change in Data Management, ECDM'99, Paris, 1999.
2. Al-Jadir L., El-Moukaddem F., "F2/XML: Storing XML Documents in Object Databases", Proc. Int. Conf. on Object-Oriented Information Systems, OOIS'02, Montpellier, 2002.

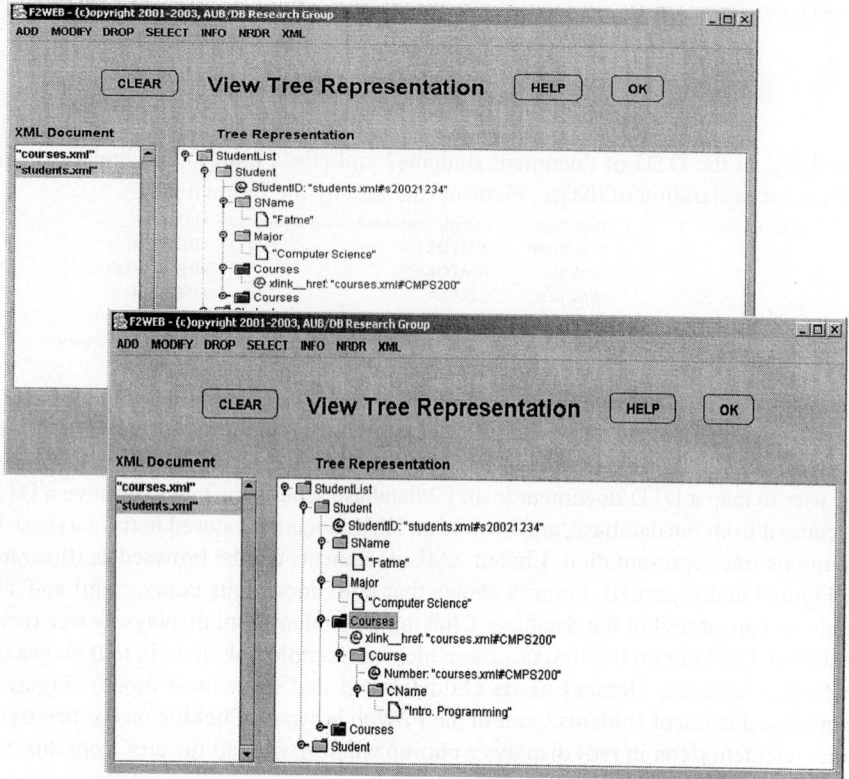

Fig. 9. Traversing a simple link (embed and onRequest mode). The top and bottom show before and after clicking on the first Courses element

3. Al-Jadir L., El-Moukaddem F., "F2/XML: Managing XML Document Schema Evolution", Proc. Int. Conf. on Enterprise Information Systems, ICEIS'04, Porto, 2004.
4. Chung T-S., Park S., Han S-Y., Kim H-J., "Extracting Object-Oriented Database Schemas from XML DTDs Using Inheritance", Proc. Int. Conf. on Electronic Commerce and Web Technologies, EC-Web'01, Munich, 2001.
5. Florescu D., Kossmann D., "Storing and Querying XML Data Using an RDBMS", IEEE Data Eng. Bulletin, vol. 22, no 3, pp. 27-34, sept. 1999.
6. Hunter D., Cagle K., Dix C. et al., "Beginning XML", 2nd edition, Wrox Press, 2003.
7. Kappel G., Kapsammer E., Rausch-Schott S., Retachitzegger W., "X-Ray - Towards Integrating XML and Relational Database Systems", Proc. Int. Conf. on Conceptual Modeling, ER'00, Salt Lake City, 2000.
8. Klettke M., Meyer H., "XML and Object-Relational Databases - Enhancing Structural Mappings Based on Statistics", Proc. Int. Workshop on the Web and Databases, WebDB'00, Dallas, 2000.
9. May W., Malheiro D., "A Logical, Transparent Model for Querying Linked XML Documents", Proc. Datenbanksysteme für Business, Technologie und Web, BTW'03, Leipzig, 2003.
10. Schmidt A., Kersten M., Windhouwer M., Waas F., "Efficient Relational Storage and Retrieval of XML Documents", Proc. Int. Workshop on the Web and Databases, WebDB'00, Dallas, 2000.

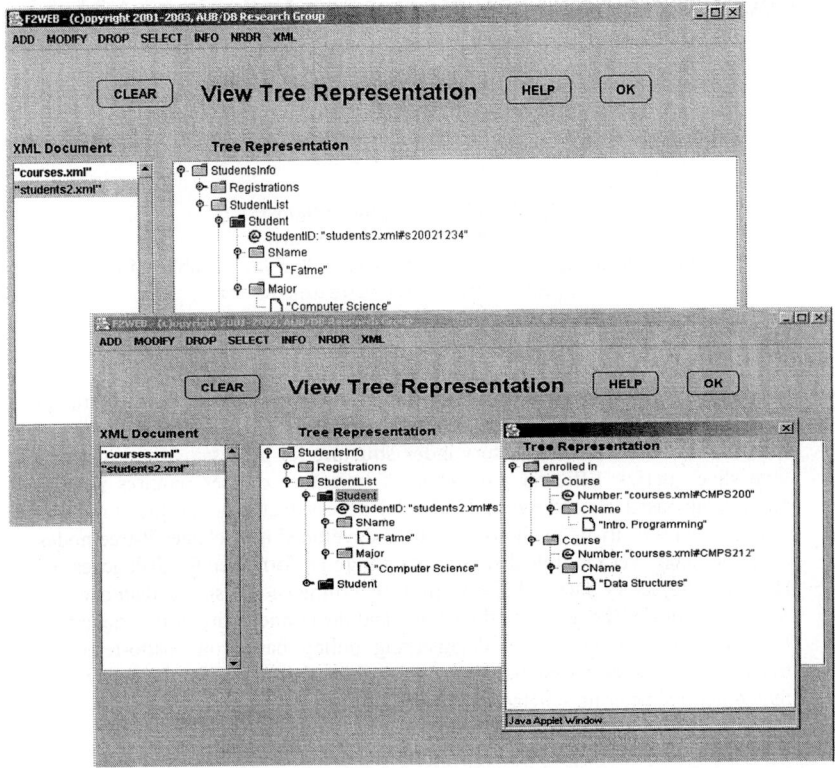

Fig. 10. Traversing an extended link (new and onRequest mode). The top and bottom show before and after clicking on the first Student element

11. Shanmugasundaram J., Tufte K., He G., Zhang C., DeWitt D., Naughton J., "Relational Databases for querying XML Documents: Limitations and Opportunities", Proc. Int. Conf. on Very Large DataBases, VLDB'99, Edinburgh, 1999.
12. Shimura T., Yoshikawa M., Uemura S., "Storage and Retrieval of XML Documents using Object-Relational Databases", Proc. Int. Conf. on Database and Expert Systems Applications, DEXA'99, Florence, 1999.
13. Tian F., DeWitt D.J., Chen J., Zhang C., "The Design and Performance Evaluation of Alternative XML Storage Strategies", SIGMOD Record, vol. 31 (1), 2002.
14. W3C, Bray T., Paoli J., Sperberg-McQueen C.M., Maler E. (eds), "Extensible Markup Language (XML) 1.0 (2nd Edition)", W3C Recommendation, http://www.w3.org/TR/2000/REC-xml-20001006, Oct. 2000.
15. W3C, DeRose S., Maler E., Orchard D. (eds), "XML Linking Language (XLink) Version 1.0", W3C Recommendation, http://www.w3.org/TR/2001/REC-xlink-20010627, Jun. 2001.
16. W3C, Grosso P., Maler E., Marsh J., Walsh N. (eds), "XPointer Framework", W3C Recommendation, http://www.w3.org/TR/2003/REC-xptr-framework-20030325, Mar. 2003.
17. XLip (Fujitsu XLink Processor), http://www.labs.fujitsu.com/free/xlip/en/download.html, Nov. 2002.

Declustering of Trajectories for Indexing of Moving Objects Databases*

Youngduk Seo and Bonghee Hong

Department of Computer Engineering
Busan National University
30 Jangjeon-dong, Geumjeong-gu, Busan 609-735, Republic of Korea
{ydseo,bhhong}@pusan.ac.kr

Abstract. Efficient storage and retrieval of trajectory indexes has become an essential requirement for moving objects databases. The existing 3DR-tree is known to be an effective trajectory index structure for processing trajectory and time slice queries. Efficient processing of trajectory queries requires parallel processing based on indexes and parallel access methods for the trajectory index. Several heuristic methods have been developed to decluster R-tree nodes of spatial data over multiple disks to obtain high performance for disk accesses. However, trajectory data is different from two-dimensional spatial data because of peculiarities of the temporal dimension and the connectivity of the trajectory. In this paper, we propose a declustering policy based on spatio-temporal trajectory proximity. Extensive experiments show that our STP scheme is better than other declustering schemes by about 20%.

1 Introduction

One of the most challenging and encouraging applications of state-of-the-art technology is the field of traffic control systems. It combines techniques from the areas of telecommunications and computer science to establish traffic information and various assistance services. The support of the system requires a moving objects database system (MODB) that stores moving objects efficiently and performs spatial or temporal queries with time conditions. The management of spatio-temporal data is one of the most exciting current research areas. [1, 9] are examples of this trend.

The data obtained from moving objects is trajectory data. It is different from spatial data in the following ways. First, in a MODB, all past trajectories are stored, and objects are generally never deleted. The result is large amount of data, which we also want to be able to query. Very large numbers of moving objects make performance issues important. The second property is the connectivity of multiple trajectories for a given object. This disturbs the randomness of the MODB dataset, making it highly skewed. The last property is the unbalanced distribution of trajectories because most moving objects (cars, trains...) travel along a street or other fixed path. Thus, they

---

* This work was supported by grant No. (R05-2003-000-10360-0) from the Basic Research Program of the Korea Science & Engineering Foundation.

have a high probability of having the same spatial distributions and tend to be crowded on roads or tracks.

In previous literature, several approaches for processing spatial data using indexes have been proposed. [8] suggests a method based on R-trees. The methods, the STR-tree and the TB-tree, are based on R-trees, supporting efficient query processing of three-dimensional trajectories of spatial data. [11] proposed a method based on R-trees to store trajectories. This literature adapts R-trees to index either spatial, temporal or spatio-temporal occurrences of actors and the relationships between them.

Even with an efficient index structure, the I/O bandwidth of the storage system can be a bottleneck. To provide the necessary computing power and data bandwidth, a parallel architecture is necessary. Single-disk architectures are not truly scalable, so our primary interest is in multiple-disk systems. With the advent of high-performance computers, we expect high performance on query processing of trajectory indexes.

Declustering is the distribution of data over multiple disks. The primary goal of declustering is to maximize throughput and minimize workload on any given disk. To achieve the goals, there are two requirements: minLoad and uniSpread [5]. MinLoad implies that queries should touch as few nodes as possible, and uniSpread implies that the nodes qualifying for a query should be distributed over the disks as uniformly as possible. However, these schemes offer only limited performance improvement on the declustering of trajectory indexes.

There have been many studies on how to organize traditional index structures (especially B-trees) on multi-disk or multi-processor machines. For the B-tree, [7] proposed a PNB-tree, which uses a 'super-node' ('super-page') scheme on synchronized disks. [3] proposed an algorithm to distribute the nodes of the B-tree on different disks and offered the idea that when a new page is created, it should be assigned to a disk that does not contain nearby pages.

To distribute the index nodes of a temporal or spatial database, several approaches have been proposed [2, 5, 10]. The work by [10], which is concerned with declustering of temporal data, is based on a hierarchy of one-dimensional index structures. They addressed the issues of declustering a temporal index and access structures for a single-processor multiple independent disk architecture. In [5], the authors studied multi-disk architectures, and proposed the so-called 'proximity index' (PI) to measure the dissimilarity of two rectangles, to decide the unit to which each rectangle should be assigned. A comparison with other intuitive schemes (Round robin (RR), Minimum area (MA) and Minimum Intersection (MI)) was also presented.

The definition of the proximity index is based on the following assumptions:
- the address space is normalized to the unit hypercube;
- the queries are posed uniformly on the address space.

However, the issues related to declustering a trajectory index have not been addressed. Here, we focus on the parallelization of R-trees storing trajectories (e.g., 3DR-trees, STR-trees, TB-trees). Because trajectory data have different characteristics from spatial data, such as the connectivity of trajectories and unbalanced distributions mentioned above, previous studies on the declustering of spatial data offer only limited performance improvement. There have been no studies on spatio-temporal proximity of trajectories. Moreover, there has been no work on the parallelization of trajectory indexes.

In this paper, we propose a new declustering scheme (based on trajectory proximity) to distribute trajectory index nodes to multiple disks. The key idea of this paper is to assign a new node to a disk based on the trajectory proximity, taking the properties of trajectories into account. The scheme measures a trajectory's proximity dynamically, and utilizes the connectivity of trajectories based on spatio-temporal proximity to decluster nodes of a trajectory index. Experimental results show that the scheme outperforms previous schemes and reflects the properties of trajectories well.

The remainder of this paper is organized as follows. Section 2 presents the problems of declustering trajectory indexes and range querying. The trajectory proximity mechanism is presented in Section 3. Section 4 presents the experimental results of our declustering scheme based on trajectory proximity. Finally, Section 5 contains our conclusions and contributions.

2 Problem Definition

To distribute trajectory index nodes to multiple disks properly, we require a spatio-temporal proximity model of a trajectory index. The model should have different characteristics from existing spatial indexes. These properties can be categorized in two parts. The first category concerns the temporal axis of a trajectory. The other category concerns the distribution and shapes of trajectories.

The first problem in making a proximity model of trajectory indexes using declustering is the different characteristics of the time and spatial axes. The temporal axis of a trajectory grows by the process of insertion. Thus, the temporal axis cannot be normalized into a unit space before the insertions. From this property, we will define two types of domain in Definition 1.

Definition 1.
Static domain: A domain that can be defined as a limited boundary when a database is created.
Dynamic domain: A domain that grows as time increases, and cannot be defined as a limited boundary when a database is created.

The two domains have different characteristics. A static domain has a unique domain space. Its datasets can be normalized to a unit space, and measurements of proximity can be produced while inserting data. However, dynamic domains cannot have static boundaries. Thus, the proximity of a dataset with the dynamic domain property cannot be measured while inserting data.

The declustering schemes based on known declustering functions are appropriate only for datasets based on static domains and having normal distributions, i.e., the datasets can be normalized to a unit space before insertion. When the data cannot be normalized to a unit hypercube space, these schemes are unusable. Spatial databases have static domains, so a distance metric can easily be determined. However, trajectories dynamic domains, because the time space is continuously extended. Thus, a time distance metric should be determined dynamically.

The other property of the categories is the connectivity of trajectories. Trajectories are connected to each other for a given object. This disturbs the randomness of the MODB dataset, and makes the dataset highly skewed. Previous studies concentrated on the proximity of spatial localities of static datasets, and did not consider the locality of connected line segments. However, range and trajectory queries require parallel loading of connected pages or nodes because of locality in those queries. Thus, we should distribute connected nodes to different disks using a specific scheme.

According to the existing spatial proximity index method[5], the spatial proximity of A_1 and B_1, in Fig.1., is greater than that of A_1 and A_2. Thus, when we try to store the two, A and B, trajectories over two disks(A_1,D_2), we should distribute the trajectories of the object $A(A_1,A_2,A_3)$ to D_1 and those of $B(B_1, B_2)$ to D_2. Thus, if we distribute the trajectories using spatial proximity, all connected trajectories will be distributed to the same disk.

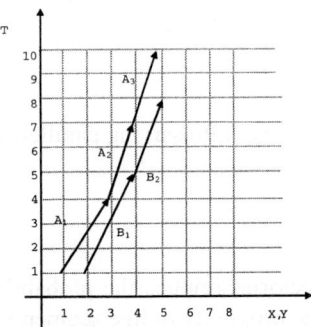

Fig. 1. Trajectory of moving objects

3 Declustering of Trajectory Indexes

In this section, we describe a method to distribute trajectory nodes to disks. The scheme overcomes the limitations of static declustering schemes and is suited to the properties of trajectories.

3.1 Dynamic Domain

To define spatio-temporal proximity, we require a normalized unit space for the time domain. However, the time dynamic domain cannot be normalized while inserting. In spite of good heuristics for declustering schemes for static databases, we cannot determine the proximity of a trajectory statically in the time domain. Thus, we will make a static normalization from the dynamic domain of the temporal dimension of trajectories.

The trajectory O_{t2} of the moving object O can be represented as $(x_1, y_1, t_1) - (x_2, y_2, t_2)$. The spatial coordinates (x, y) can be normalized easily and the time axis (t_1, t_2) can be converted into (t_1, T_N) where T_N is the current time. Thus, using T_N, t_1 can be normalized dynamically. To make a semi-static normalization from the dynamic time domain, we propose Lemma 1.

Lemma 1: *The nth normalization of the extended time axis preserves the parallelism of (n-1)th normalization.*

For example, preservation of parallelism can be demonstrated using Fig. 2. Angles X and Y are transformed to X', Y', respectively. The line ab is relocated to a' b', and lines ac and bd are resized. Thus, the ratio of X' to Y' is preserved.

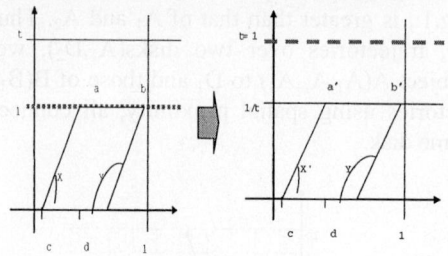

Fig. 2. Preserving parallelism

3.2 Proximity of Trajectories

The proximity of two trajectories implies the probability of concurrent access for a given query. To measure the proximity of line segments, we assume that the leaf node of index contains trajectories. That is, we will measure the proximity of two trajectories by the proximity of two leaf nodes in the dynamic domain space. To measure the proximity in the dynamic domain, we must modify the proximity model from [6]. They proposed a method to calculate the probability of selecting a node using the inflated area of the node for any given query Q. For example, in Fig. 3, from the two-dimensional normalized spatial domain, the probability of selection of node N_0 for query $Q(q_x, q_y)$ is the area of N_0 inflated with Q. i.e., (q_x, q_y).

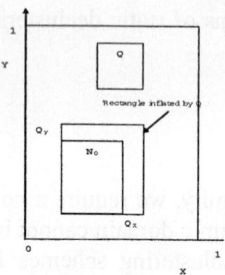

Fig. 3. Probability of selecting a node

From the study, we will define the probability of concurrent access of two different nodes in spatio-temporal space. For any two given rectangles, the probability of parallel loading can be measured by the overlapped area of the inflated rectangle when the space of the domain is normalized to the unit space. For example, in Fig. 4, the spatial proximity P_A of the two nodes N_0 and N_1 is the overlap of their inflated areas. Because the spatial domain is normalized to the unit space, the probability of concurrent loading of two different nodes can be measured by (1) from Fig. 4.

$$P_A = A(O(I(N_0), I(N_1))). \tag{1}$$

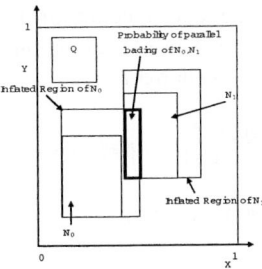

Fig. 4. Probability of accessing two nodes simultaneously

Table 1. Summary of symbols and definitions

Name	Description
N	Node, consisting of $(x_0, t_0) - (x_1, t_1)$, $t_1 > t_0$
C	Capacity of index node
N_C	Number of connected trajectories from N
A(N)	Area of N
I(N, Q)	Object N inflated by Q
O_X	Overlap ratio on dimension x
O(I, J)	Overlap area of rectangles I, J

The proximity of trajectories (STP:P_T) should account for the properties of trajectories described previously. In this paper, we will account for both the connectivity and temporal effects of trajectories with the spatial proximity. The variable NC determines the ratio of the connected trajectory to the total trajectory in two nodes, and the temporal effect EC is a ratio of temporal duration to spatial distance. It converts a relatively long rectangle to a square rectangle. Because the STP can be measured by the product of the variables, the proximity of connected trajectories of nodes (P_T) can be measured by their product. Thus, we can depict the STP in (2) by P_A, which is the spatial proximity of the spatial domain measured by (1), NC, and EC.

$$P_T = P_A * \text{ratio of trajectory connection (NC)} * \text{Temporal Effect (EC)} \tag{2}$$

$$= P_A * (\text{Connected nodes} + 1)/\text{Nodes capacity} * EC.$$

From (2) and Lemma 1, we can dynamically measure proximity. At any increasing time t_N, a newly created node N_0 has a spatio-temporal proximity P_T with the previously created node N_1 for query Q given by (3).

$$P_T = PA * (NC + 1)/C * EC \tag{3}$$

$$= \{A(I(N_0, Q) \bullet I(N_1, Q))/T_N\} * (1 + NC)/(C + 1) * EC.$$

However, we cannot determine static values from P_T, because query Q cannot be determined when a node splits. If we consider all possible random queries, we can integrate queries of all sizes, as shown in (4). Thus, we extend (3) to general queries, i.e., for any sized query Q, we have a trajectory proximity (STP) for two-dimensional movement of trajectories as shown in (4). Equation (4) shows the proximity of the trajectory node in the dynamic time domain.

$$P_T = \int_0^1\int_0^1\int_0^{T_N} \left\{ \frac{A(I(N_0,Q) \cap I(N_1,Q))}{T_N} * \frac{1+N_C}{C+1} * E_C \right\} d_{qt} d_{qx} d_{qy} \qquad (4)$$

$$= \frac{1+N_C}{C+1} E_C (\frac{1}{2}+O(x))(\frac{1}{2}+O(y))(\frac{1}{2}T_N+O(t))$$

For example, a node N_0 is created from the node N_1 in Fig. 5. In [5], the authors state that the proximity of N_0 with N_1 and N_2 has the same value, 0.14, because the overlap areas are the same. However, the connectivity-based proximity of N_0 and N_1, $STP(N_0, N_1)$, is 0.87, whereas $STP(N_0, N_2)$ is 0.29, because node N_0 has more connected trajectories with N_1 than N_2. Thus, node N_0 has a higher probability of concurrent access with N_1 than with N_2.

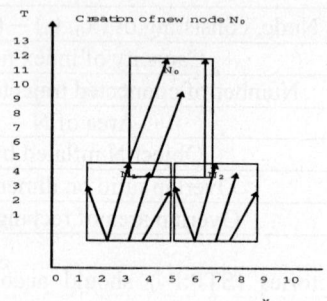

Fig. 5. Creation of new node

The determination of the disk on which to store a new node occurs when the node is created. At that time, we determine the STP value from P_T with its sibling nodes using (5) The node is stored on the disk that has a node with minimum STP value. Ideally, we should consider all the nodes that are on the same level with N_0, before we decide where to store it. However, this would require too many disk accesses. Thus, we consider only the sibling nodes $N_1, ..., N_k$, that is, the nodes that have the same parent. Accessing the parent node comes at no extra cost, because we must bring it into main memory anyway.

4 Experimental Results

We now evaluate the performance of our new multidimensional STP scheme and compare it with previously proposed schemes. The comparisons are made with the proximity index (PI) and round-robin (RR) schemes described in [5]. The PI scheme has been shown to give the best performance among existing schemes.

To assess the merit of STP over the other heuristics, we ran experiments on two-dimensional trajectories. All tests were run using synthetically generated trajectories based on the network of Oldenburg using a traffic data generator [4]. We created 119,044 trajectories. We augmented the 3DR-tree code with some routines to handle multiple disks. The code was written in C++ under Microsoft Windows® and the experiment ran on an Intel Pentium IV System. For all experiments, we considered various disk configurations (1, 2,..., 12).

There are many factors that affect the performance of a declustered index. Among them, we chose the following representative factors as experimental variables: NB, the number of buffers; SB, the buffer size and page size; D, the number of disks; SQ, the size of a query; and DD, the distribution of data.

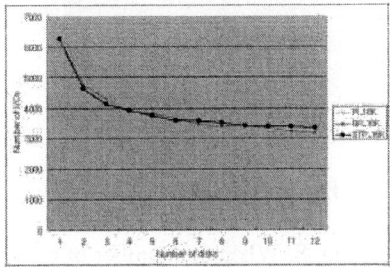

Fig. 6. The number of I/O of RR, SP, STP

In our first experiment, we assessed the speedup of STP over the PI and RR schemes using the following parameters: NB = 0, SB = 8k, D = 1, ..., 12, SQ = 1% and DD = random. As shown in Fig. 6, we found that declustering based on the STP scheme gives about 18% performance increment over the RR or PI schemes for the trajectory index of a randomly distributed moving object. However, when the number of disks is larger than 10, the performance of these schemes is about the same. This is because of the selectivity of child nodes: for any given query, each node has a limited number of child nodes that satisfy the query.

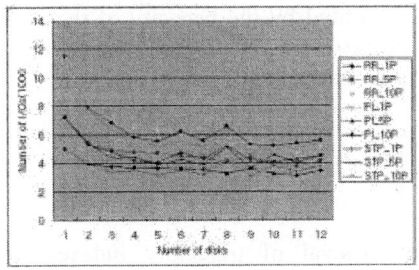

Fig. 7. The number of I/Os by query size

Figure 7 shows the number of I/Os for query sizes 1%, 5% and 10% of total data. With a single disk, the number of I/Os varies greatly with query size. However, the difference and speedup become smaller with increasing numbers of disks. This indicates that the candidate nodes are evenly distributed over all disks. Thus, the performance increment reduces as the number of disk increases.

In our second experiment, we assessed the effect of the number of buffers and the size of index nodes (pages). To do this, we varied the page size and the number of buffers. This experiment has the following parameters: NB = 100, 200, 400, 800; SB = 8 K, 16 K; D = 12; SQ = 1%, 5%, 10%; and DD = random.

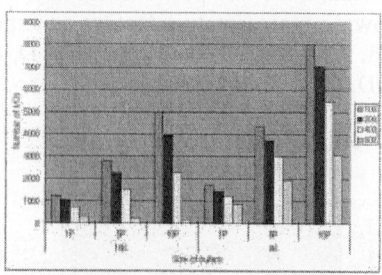

Fig. 8. The effect of buffers

The results are shown in Fig. 8. When the number of buffers is doubled but the size kept the same, the number of I/Os is reduced by about 30% for all sizes of query. However, there is a noteworthy result when the size of the buffers is doubled but the number is kept the same. For the query size of 1%, there is a small performance increment, but for the query size of 10%, we can achieve a performance increment of about 50%. This means that the critical factor for performance is the size of the buffers (node capacity) for large queries, whereas for small queries the number of buffers is more critical. We know that large nodes have a higher parallelism than small nodes.

From these comparisons, we conclude that the proposed method gives better response time than the proximity index method, at least for large queries. Both results agree with our intuition, and indicate that the proposed method will offer a higher throughput for a spatial object server. The experiments also show that the parallelism of index declustering is limited by the capacity of the nodes and the selectivity of queries. The number of disks limits the distribution of nodes, but the ability to load in parallel is limited by the number of child nodes selected.

5   Conclusions

Efficient storage and retrieval of trajectory indexes has become an essential requirement for many moving object databases. However, spatio-temporal data, in the context of trajectories of n-dimensional moving objects, is somewhat different from $(n + 1)$-dimensional spatial data because of the dynamic property of the time domain and connectivity.

Efficient processing of such queries requires parallel processing based on indexes and access methods for spatio-temporal data. In this paper, we have proposed a spatio-temporal proximity model to distribute trajectory index nodes to multiple disks. A modification of declustering based on spatial proximity, namely STP, is proposed for declustering the indexes of trajectories of moving point objects. The performance study presents results from experiments involving declustering schemes based on round robin and spatial proximity. The experiments show that the STP scheme is better than other declustering schemes by about 20%. STP proves to be a declustering scheme well suited for a range of queries on trajectory indexes, especially large queries. Moreover, we drew the following conclusions.

- The parallelism of index declustering is limited by the capacity of nodes and the selectivity of queries.
- Large nodes have higher parallelism than small nodes for the same number of parallel loading nodes.
- The critical factor for performance is the buffer size for large queries, whereas the number of buffers is more critical for small queries.

Although recent literature includes related work on declustering spatial indexes and relational databases, the work presented in this paper is the first to propose a declustering method (STP) that clearly addresses the requirements and peculiarities of this context by considering temporal domain proximity. However, the proposed scheme has limitations with large numbers of disks. Our future research will therefore focus on extending the proximity concept to aid parallelization for large numbers of disks and to reduce the cost of the STP proximity model.

References

[1] Andrew U. Frank and Stephan Winter. "CHOROCHRONOS Consortium", First CHOROCHRONOS Intensive Workshop CIW'97, TECHNICAL REPORT CH-97-02.
[2] Bernd Schnitzer and Scott T. Leutenegger. Master-Client R-Trees: A New Parallel R-Tree Architecture. SSDBM 1999: pp. 68–77.
[3] Bernhard Seeger and Per-Ake Larson. Multi-disk btrees. Proc. ACM SIGMOD, pp. 138–147, May 1991.
[4] T. Brinkhoff. "Generating Traffic Data", Bulletin of the Technical Committee on Data Engineering, IEEE Computer Society, vol. 26, no. 2, 2003, pp. 19–25.
[5] Ibrahim Kamel and Christos Faloutsos, "Parallel R-trees", ACM SIGMOD 1992 pp. 195-204.
[6] Ibrahim Kamel and Christos Faloutsos, "On Packing R-trees", CIKM, pp. 490–499, 1993.
[7] S. Pramanik and M.H. Kim. "Parallel processing of large node b-trees". IEEE Transactions on Computers, vol. 39, no. 9, pp. 1208–1212, 1990.
[8] Dieter Pfsor, Yannis Theodoridis, and Christian S. Jensen. "Indexing Trajectories of Moving Point Objects", Chorochoronos TR CH-99-03.
[9] T. Sellis. "Research Issues in Spatio-temporal Database Systems," Advances in Spatial Databases, 6th International Symposium, SSD'99, pp.5-11, 1999.
[10] Vram Kouramajian, Ramez Elmasri, and Anurag Chaudhry. "Declustering Techniques for Parallelizing Temporal Access Structures," IEEE ICDE 1994, pp. 232-242.
[11] Yannis Theodoridis, Michael Vazirgiannis, and Timos Sellis. "Spatio-Temporal Indexing for Large Multimedia Applications," 'Proceedings, IEEE ICMCS 1996, pp. 441-448.

Computing the Topological Relationship of Complex Regions

Markus Schneider[*]

University of Florida
Department of Computer & Information Science & Engineering
Gainesville, FL 32611, USA
mschneid@cise.ufl.edu

Abstract. *Topological predicates* between spatial objects have always been a main area of research on spatial data handling, reasoning, and query languages. The focus of research has definitely been on the design of and reasoning with these predicates, whereas implementation issues have been largely neglected. Besides, design efforts have been restricted to simplified abstractions of spatial objects like single points, continuous lines, and simple regions. In this paper, we present a general algorithm which is based on the well known plane-sweep paradigm and determines the topological relationship between two given *complex* regions.

1 Introduction

For a long time, *topological predicates* on spatial objects like *overlap*, *disjoint*, or *inside* have been a focus of research on spatial data handling and reasoning in a number of disciplines like artificial intelligence, linguistics, robotics, and cognitive science. They characterize the relative position between two (or more) objects in space. In particular, they support the design of suitable query languages for spatial data retrieval and analysis in geographical information systems (GIS) and spatial databases. Two important approaches are the *9-intersection model* [4] based on point set topology as well as the *RCC model* [3] based on spatial logic. Whereas the predicates in these two models operate on simplified abstractions of spatial objects like simple regions, we are interested in the design and implementation of topological predicates for *complex* regions, which may consist of several components (faces) and which may have holes. Implementation issues for these predicates, regardless of whether they operate on simple or complex geometries, have so far been rather neglected. Hence, the goal of this paper is to show how topological predicates for complex regions can be efficiently implemented on the basis of the well-known plane-sweep paradigm. This algorithm copes with region objects whose segments are non-interesting or allowed to intersect.

Section 2 discusses related work. Section 3 describes a database-compatible data structure for complex regions. In Section 4 we present the algorithm *TopRel* which determines the topological relationship for a given pair of complex regions. Finally, Section 5 draws some conclusions.

---
[*] This work was partially supported by the National Science Foundation under grant number NSF-CAREER-IIS-0347574.

2 Related Work

Spatial data types (see [7] for a survey) like *point, line,* or *region* have turned out to provide fundamental abstractions for modeling the structure of geometric entities, their relationships, properties, and operations. Whereas in older models the geometric structure of spatial data has been restricted (only simple regions, continuous lines, single points), in the meantime a few models also allow complex spatial objects which may consist of several disjoint components. Additionally, a region object may have holes. The reasons for defining complex geometric structures are the maintenance of closure properties for geometric operations (simple spatial data types are not closed under these operations) and application-specific requirements (e.g., to be able to model Italy with its offshore islands and the Vatican as a hole).

A well known, mathematical model for characterizing topological relationships between simple regions is the *9-intersection model* [4]. Eight well known topological predicates have been identified for two simple regions. They are named *disjoint, meet, overlap, equal, inside, contains, covers, coveredBy*. All predicates are mutually exclusive and cover all topological situations. This paper is based on a generalization of these eight predicates to *complex* regions [8]. The generalized predicates inherit the properties of the simple predicates but take into account multi-component regions possibly containing holes. Informally, two complex regions A and B are *disjoint* if they do not share any points. They *meet* if their boundaries share points and their interiors are disjoint. They are *equal* if both their boundaries and their interiors coincide. A is *inside* B (B *contains* A) if A is a proper subset of B and if their boundaries do not touch. A *is covered by* B (B *covers* A) if A is a proper subset of B and if their boundaries touch. Otherwise, A and B *overlap*.

The algorithm *TopRel* is based on the plane-sweep paradigm and on the ROSE algebra [6] which has the requirement of non-intersecting spatial objects. This is ensured by the so-called *realm* concept [5] providing a discrete, numerically robust, and consistent geometric basis upon which all spatial objects are constructed. Hence, different spatial objects are only allowed to have line segments meeting in end points or being disjoint. This makes an understanding and implementation much easier if we compare it, e.g., to the classical Bentley-Ottmann algorithm [2]. But our algorithm also covers the general case of intersecting segments by reducing it to the ROSE case.

3 Data Structures

For reasons of efficiency and performance, our region data structure does not use main memory pointer structures but a small number of memory blocks that can be transferred efficiently between secondary and main memory. It is represented by a *root record* which contains some fixed size components and one or more components which are references to arrays. Arrays are used to represent the varying size components of the data structure and are allocated to the required size. All internal pointers are expressed as array indices. Of course, the data structure supports plane-sweep algorithms very well.

In the following, we represent an array as a sequence $\langle \cdot \rangle$ with additional, direct access to its elements. A *subarray* shall denote a specific subrange (subsequence) within an array. Coordinates are given as rational numbers of a certain precision[1]. A value of type *point* is represented by a record $p = (x, y)$ where x and y are coordinates. We assume the usual lexicographical order on points.

Conceptually, complex regions can be considered from a "structured" and a "flat" view. The structured view defines an object of type *region* as a set of edge-disjoint faces. A face is a simple polygon possibly containing a set of edge-disjoint holes. A hole is a simple polygon. Two spatial entities are edge-disjoint if they share perhaps single boundary points but not boundary segments. The flat view defines an object of type *region* as a collection of line segments which altogether preserve the constraints and properties of the structured view. For a formal definition see [6].

The implementation of a *region* object is given as an *ordered* sequence (array) of *halfsegments*. The idea of halfsegments is to store each segment twice. Let $S = point \times point$ be the set of segments. We normalize S by the requirement that $\forall s \in S : s = (p, q) \Rightarrow p < q$. This enables us to speak of a *left* and a *right end point* of a segment. We define $H = \{(s, d) \mid s \in S, d \in \{left, right\}\}$ as the set of *halfsegments* where flag d emphasizes one of the segments' end points, which is called the *dominating point* of h. If $d = left$, the left (smaller) end point of s is the dominating point of h, and h is called *left halfsegment*. Otherwise, the right end point of s is the dominating point of h, and h is called *right halfsegment*. Hence, each segment s is mapped to two halfsegments $(s, left)$ and $(s, right)$. Let dp be the function which yields the dominating point of a halfsegment. For two distinct halfsegments h_1 and h_2 with a common end point p, let α be the enclosed angle such that $0° < \alpha \leq 180°$ (an overlapping of h_1 and h_2 is excluded by the prohibition of self-intersections of *region* objects). Let a predicate rot be defined as follows: $rot(h_1, h_2)$ is *true* if and only if h_1 can be rotated around p through α to overlap h_2 in counterclockwise direction. We can now define a complete order on halfsegments which is basically the (x, y)-lexicographical order on dominating points. For two halfsegments $h_1 = (s_1, d_1)$ and $h_2 = (s_2, d_2)$ we obtain:

$$h_1 < h_2 \Leftrightarrow dp(h_1) < dp(h_2) \vee$$
$$(dp(h_1) = dp(h_2) \wedge$$
$$((d_1 = right \wedge d_2 = left) \vee (d_1 = d_2 \wedge rot(h_1, h_2))))$$

An example of the order on halfsegments is given in Figure 1. An ordered sequence of halfsegments is given as an array $\langle (h_1, a_1, nsic_1), \ldots, (h_m, a_m, nsic_m) \rangle$ of m halfsegments $h_i \in H$ with $h_i < h_j$ for all $1 \leq i < j \leq m$. Each *left* halfsegment $h_i = (s_i, left)$ has an attached set a_i of *attributes*. Attributes contain auxiliary information that is needed by geometric algorithms. Each left halfsegment h_i also has an additional pointer $nsic_i$ (next segment in cycle) indicating

---

[1] To ensure consistency among operations, we currently plan to replace the fixed size rationals by varying length rationals and explore the costs that this could have regarding the performance.

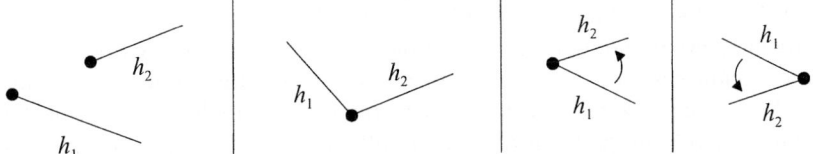

Fig. 1. Examples of the order on halfsegments: $h_1 < h_2$

the array index of the next segment in the cycle it belongs to[2]. We assume clockwise order for the traversal of the segments of outer and hole cycles. An example is given in Figure 2. Those *left* halfsegments of a region object r carry an associated attribute *InsideAbove* where the interior of r lies above or left of their respective (normalized) segments.

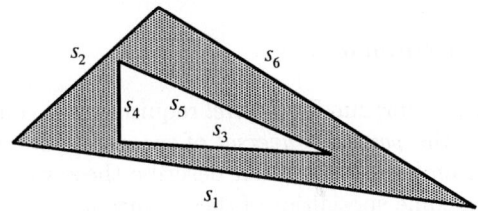

Fig. 2. Example of the halfsegment sequence of a region. If $h_i^l = (s_i, \textit{left})$ and $h_i^r = (s_i, \textit{right})$ denote the left and right halfsegments belonging to the segments s_i for $1 \leq i \leq 6$, then $\textit{halfsegments} = \langle (h_1^l, \{I\}, 2), (h_2^l, \varnothing, 8), (h_3^l, \varnothing, 4), (h_4^l, \{I\}, 6), (h_4^r, \varnothing, 0),$ $(h_5^l, \{I\}, 0), (h_2^r, \varnothing, 0), (h_6^l, \varnothing, 0), (h_5^r, \varnothing, 0), (h_3^r, \varnothing, 0), (h_6^r, \varnothing, 0), (h_1^r, \varnothing, 0) \rangle$. For right halfsegments, the second and third component of a triple are always the empty set and zero, so that they are omitted in our implementation. For left halfsegments, I stands for the attribute *InsideAbove* and a zero in the third component indicates the end of a segment list of a cycle. Index counting in an array is assumed to start at 1

Since inserting a halfsegment at an arbitrary position needs $O(m)$ time, in our implementation we use an AVL-tree embedded into an array whose elements are linked in sequence order. An insertion then requires $O(\log m)$ time.

4 The Algorithm *TopRel*

The description of implementation strategies for topological predicates both on simple and complex spatial data types has been rather neglected in the literature. This fact is surprising since such an implementation is required especially in GIS and spatial databases for the realization of spatial joins and spatial selections.

---

[2] It is unnecessary to attach attributes and pointer information to *right* half segments since their existence in an ordered halfsegment sequence only indicates to plane sweep algorithms that the respective segment has to be removed from the *sweep line status*.

Let T be the set of eight generalized topological predicates between two complex regions. We do not consider the implementation of a specific predicate $p \in T$ with $p : region \times region \to bool$ (leading to eight algorithms) but a single function $TopRel : region \times region \to T$ which determines the topological relationship for a given spatial configuration of two complex regions. An adaptation to an individual implementation of topological predicates can be easily performed since $p(r_1, r_2) \Leftrightarrow (TopRel(r_1, r_2) = p)$.

A specialty of our implementation is that it is able to process two regions with either possibly *intersecting* line segments (the general case) or with *exclusively non-intersecting* line segments (the ROSE case). The reason for our interest in the second case is that we integrate the algorithm *TopRel* into our ROSE algebra implementation [6], which so far only offers a rudimentary treatment of topological predicates. We will indicate the necessary modifications.

4.1 Geometric Preliminaries

The description of the algorithm for *TopRel* requires three concepts: (i) the *plane sweep* paradigm, (ii) the *parallel traversal* of two complex regions, and (iii) the concept of *overlap numbers*. We will not describe these well-known concepts in general but focus on some specialties of these concepts in our setting.

Plane Sweep. The well-known plane-sweep works as follows: A vertical *sweep line* sweeping the plane from left to right stops at special points called *event points* which are generally stored in a queue called *event point schedule*. The event point schedule must allow one to insert new event points discovered during processing; these are normally the initially unknown intersections of line segments. The state of the intersection of the sweep line with the geometric structure being swept at the current sweep line position is recorded in vertical order in a data structure called *sweep line status*. Whenever the sweep line reaches an event point, the sweep line status is updated. Event points which are passed by the sweep line are removed from the event point schedule.

Whereas a general plane sweep requires an efficient, fully dynamic data structure to represent the event point schedule and often an initial sorting step to produce the sequence of event points in (x, y)-lexicographical order, in the ROSE case an explicit event point schedule is implicitly given by the two ordered halfsegment sequences of the operand objects. The event point schedule is even static since no two segments intersect within their interiors. There is even no initial sorting necessary, because the plane sweep order of segments is the base representation of *region* objects anyway.

For the general case, to preserve these benefits, it is our strategy to reduce it to the ROSE case. In case that two segments from different *region* objects intersect, partially coincide, or touch each other within the interior of a segment, we pursue a splitting strategy which we call *realmification*. If the segments intersect, they are split at their common intersection point so that each of them is replaced by two segments (i.e., four halfsegments) (Figure 3a). If two segments

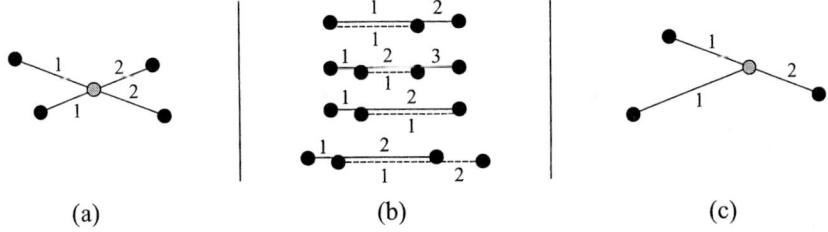

Fig. 3. Splitting of two intersecting segments (a), two partially coinciding segments (without symmetric counterparts) (b), and a segment whose interior is touched by another segment (c). Digits indicate part numbers of segments after splitting

partially coincide, they are split each time the endpoint of one segment lies inside the other segment. Depending on the topological situations, which can be described by Allen's thirteen basic relations on intervals [1], each of the two segments either remains unchanged or is replaced by up to three segments (i.e., six halfsegments). From the thirteen possible relations, eight relations (four pairs of symmetric relations) are of interest here (Figure 3b). If an endpoint of one segment touches the interior of the other segment, the latter segment is split and replaced by two segments (i.e., four halfsegments) (Figure 3c).

For each *region* object, besides a static part, the halfsegments obtained by the realmification are stored in an additional dynamic part of the halfsegment sequence. This part is also organized as an AVL tree which is embedded in an array and whose elements are linked in sequence order. Assuming that k splitting points are detected during the plane sweep, we need additional $O(k)$ space, and to insert them requires $O(k \log k)$ time.

Parallel Object Traversal. During the planesweep we traverse the halfsegment sequences of both region operands. We know that each sequence is already in halfsegment sequence order. Hence, it is sufficient to check the current halfsegments of both sequences and to take the lower one with respect to halfsegment sequence order for further computation.

The order definition on halfsegments given in Section 3 is referring to the halfsegment sequence of *individual* regions. In the ROSE case, this order definition is also sufficient for the parallel object traversal of two regions since any two halfsegments stemming from different regions may not intersect each other or partially coincide. For the general case, however, Figure 4 shows additional situations. The first three constellations are covered by the existing order definition on halfsegments. The fourth constellation requires an extension of the definition. For two halfsegments $h_1 = (s_1, d_1)$ and $h_2 = (s_2, d_2)$ we define:

$$h_1 < h_2 \Leftrightarrow dp(h_1) < dp(h_2) \lor (dp(h_1) = dp(h_2) \land \\ ((d_1 = right \land d_2 = left) \lor (d_1 = d_2 \land rot(h_1, h_2)) \lor \\ (d_1 = d_2 \land collinear(h_1, h_2) \land len(h_1) < len(h_2))))$$

The function *collinear* checks whether h_1 and h_2 are located on the same infinite line, and the function *len* computes the length of a halfsegment.

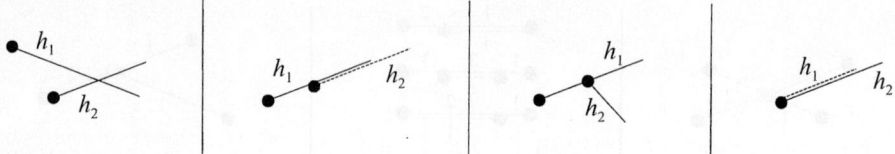

Fig. 4. Some examples of additional constellations of two halfsegments from different regions in the general case for $h_1 < h_2$

Overlap Numbers. Overlapping of region parts is important for determining the topological relationship between two complex regions. For this purpose we introduce the concept of *overlap numbers*. A point obtains the overlap number 2 if it is covered by (or part of) two *region* objects. This means that for two intersecting simple polygons the area outside of both polygons gets overlap number 0, the intersecting area gets overlap number 2, and the other areas get overlap number 1. Since a segment of a region separates space into two parts, an inner and an exterior one, each (half)segment is associated with a pair (m/n) of overlap numbers, a lower (or right) one m and an upper (or left) one n. The lower (upper) overlap number indicates the number of overlapping *region* objects below (above) the segment. In this way, we obtain a *segment classification* of two *region* objects and speak of (m/n)-segments. Obviously, $m, n \leq 2$ holds. Of the nine possible combinations only seven describe valid segment classes. This is because a $(0/0)$-segment contradicts the definition of a *region* object, since then at least one of both regions would have two holes or an outer cycle and a hole with a common border. Similarly, $(2/2)$-segments cannot exist, since then at least one of the two regions would have a segment which is common to two outer cycles of the object. Hence, possible (m/n)-segments are $(0/1)$-, $(0/2)$-, $(1/0)$-, $(1/1)$-, $(1/2)$-, $(2/0)$-, and $(2/1)$-segments. An example is given in Figure 5.

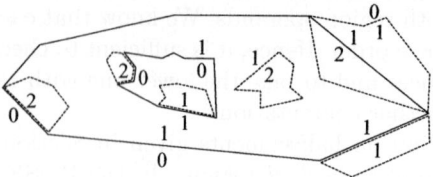

Fig. 5. Example of the segment classification of two *region* objects

4.2 The Algorithm *TopRel*

Using the three aforementioned concepts, we perform a characterization of the eight topological predicates that is based on the segment classification of both argument objects and is a unique translation of the respective predicate specifications shown in [8]. The characterizations of all predicates together are also complete since their specifications in [8] are complete. The question is here: To which segment class(es) must the segments of both objects belong so that a given topological predicate is fulfilled? The computation of the segment classes itself is performed "on the fly" during the plane sweep. Let F and G be two *region* objects, and let $H(F)$ and $H(G)$ be functions which yield the elements of the halfsegment sequences of F and G, respectively, as sets. For a halfsegment h let (m_h, n_h) be its associated pair of overlap numbers. A function *point_in_common* checks whether two halfsegments stemming from two different *region* objects share at least a common point. In the ROSE case, this can only be a common end point. In the general case, this can in addition also indicate a touching point (i.e., an end point of one halfsegment touches the interior of another halfsegment), an intersection point, or a partial overlapping of two halfsegments. We obtain the following characterization for the predicates:

$$disjoint(F,G) \Leftrightarrow \forall h \in H(F) \cup H(G) : (m_h, n_h) \in \{(0/1), (1/0)\} \land$$
$$\forall h \in H(F) \; \forall g \in H(G) : \neg point\_in\_common(h, g)$$
$$meet(F,G) \Leftrightarrow \forall h \in H(F) \cup H(G) : (m_h, n_h) \in \{(0/1), (1/0), (1/1)\} \land$$
$$(\exists h \in H(F) \cup H(G) : (m_h, n_h) \in \{(1/1)\} \lor$$
$$\exists h \in H(F) \; \exists g \in H(G) : point\_in\_common(h, g))$$
$$inside(F,G) \Leftrightarrow \forall h \in H(F) : (m_h, n_h) \in \{(1/2), (2/1)\} \land$$
$$\forall g \in H(G) : (m_g, n_g) \in \{(1/0), (0/1)\} \land$$
$$\forall h \in H(F) \; \forall g \in H(G) : \neg point\_in\_common(h, g)$$
$$contains(F,G) \Leftrightarrow inside(G, F)$$
$$equal(F,G) \Leftrightarrow \forall h \in H(F) \cup H(G) : (m_h, n_h) \in \{(0/2), (2/0)\}$$
$$coveredBy(F,G) \Leftrightarrow \forall h \in H(F) : (m_h, n_h) \in \{(1/2), (2/1), (0/2), (2/0)\} \land$$
$$\forall g \in H(G) : (m_g, n_g) \in \{(1/0), (0/1), (0/2), (2/0)\} \land$$
$$\exists h \in H(F) : (m_h, n_h) \in \{(1/2), (2/1)\} \land$$
$$\exists g \in H(G) : (m_g, n_g) \in \{(1/0), (0/1)\} \land$$
$$((\exists h \in H(F) : (m_h, n_h) \in \{(0/2), (2/0)\} \land$$
$$\exists g \in H(G) : (m_g, n_g) \in \{(0/2), (2/0)\}) \lor$$
$$\exists h \in H(F) \; \exists g \in H(G) : point\_in\_common(h, g))$$
$$covers(F,G) \Leftrightarrow coveredBy(G, F)$$
$$overlap(F,G) \Leftrightarrow \exists h \in H(F) : (m_h, n_h) \in \{(2/1), (1/2)\} \land$$
$$\exists g \in H(G) : (m_g, n_g) \in \{(2/1), (1/2)\}$$

The predicate *disjoint* yields *true* if both objects do not share common areas, common segments, and common points. The *meet* predicate is similar to *disjoint* but, in addition, it requires the existence of at least one (1/1)-segment or a common point. Note that each object cannot exclusively consist of (1/1)-segments so that each object must automatically have (0/1)- or (1/0)-segments. For the *inside* predicate we must especially ensure that no segment of F shares a common point with any segment of G. The evaluation of the *equal* predicate amounts to a comparison of the two halfsegment sequences which have to be identical and hence all to be (0/2)- or (2/0)-segments. The specification of the *coveredBy* predicate is a little more complicated. The reason is that we must exclude the case that all segments from both objects are (0/2)- or (2/0)-segments, which would correspond to equality. The *overlap* predicate requires a test for the existence of a (2/1)- or (1/2)-segment in each object.

The characterizations can be read in both directions. If we are interested in a specific topological predicate, we have to look from left to right and check the

Table 1. Possible segment class constellations between two consecutive segments in the sweep line status

n_s	1	2	1	2	1	2	0	1	2	0	1	2	0	1	2	0	1	0	1
m_s	0	0	0	0	0	0	1	1	1	1	1	1	1	1	1	2	2	2	2
n_p	–	–	0	0	0	0	1	1	1	1	1	1	1	1	1	2	2	2	2
m_p	–	–	1	1	2	2	0	0	0	1	1	1	2	2	2	0	0	1	1

respective right side of the predicate's characterization. This corresponds to an explicit implementation of each individual predicate. In our case, where we aim at deriving the topological relationship from a given spatial configuration of two regions, we have to look from right to left. That is, we traverse the two regions in parallel by a plane sweep, simultaneously register the arising segment classes of halfsegments as well as possibly common points, and match the result against the right sides of all predicate characterizations. For the characterization that matches we look on its left side to obtain the name of the predicate.

The algorithm for determining the topological relationship between two complex regions runs in three phases. In the first phase, in $O(1)$ time, we apply a bounding box test as a filter condition to the two *region* argument objects. If the bounding boxes do not intersect, the two regions must be disjoint.

Otherwise, in the second phase, we have to perform a more detailed analysis. For each region operand, we define a vector $v(i, j, k)$ which stores a boolean value for each triple (i, j, k). If region k contains an (i/j)-segment, $v(i, j, k)$ is set to *true* and otherwise to *false*. In this way, v records the segment classes found during the parallel traversal. The parallel object traversal visits the halfsegments of both *region* argument objects according to their halfsegment order and computes for each left halfsegment its segment class. In order to be able to determine the correct segment class, each (half)segment is inserted into the sweep line status according to the y-order of its dominating point and the y-coordinates of the intersection points of the current sweep line with the segments momentarily in the sweep line status. The possible 19 segment class constellations between two consecutive segments in the sweep line status are shown in Table 1. The table shows which segment classes (m_s/n_s) a new segment s to be inserted into the sweep line status can get, given a certain segment class (m_p/n_p) of a predecessor segment p. The first two columns show the special case that at the beginning the sweep line status is empty and the first segment is inserted. This segment can either be shared by both region objects ($(0/2)$-segment) or stems from one of them ($(0/1)$-segment). In all these cases $n_p = m_s$ must hold.

If F has l and G m halfsegments, at most $n = l + m$ halfsegments are visited in the ROSE case and $n = l + m + k$ times in the general case (where k is the number of splitting points detected during the plane sweep). Each of these (half)segments are inserted into and removed from the sweep line status. Since at most n elements can be contained in the sweep line status, the worst time complexity of the parallel object traversal and the plane-sweep is $O(n \log n)$.

The third and last phase is the evaluation phase. The vector v contains the found segment classes. By checking its different boolean values, the matching topological relationship can be identified in $O(1)$ time. This is done by comparing with the aforementioned characterizations of the predicates and excluding all other cases, i.e., v must yield false for all kinds of halfsegments not belonging to a predicate's characterization. In total, the time complexity of the algorithm *TopRel* is $O(n \log n)$.

5 Conclusions

In this paper, we have presented an efficient algorithm, called *TopRel*, which computes the topological relationship between two regions. It is general in the sense that (i) it operates on complex regions, (ii) it is applicable both to intersecting as well as exclusively non-intersecting regions, and (iii) it can be easily leveraged to explicitly compute a single topological relationship. This implementation is part of SPAL2D which is a *spatial algebra* under development for two-dimensional applications.

References

1. J.F. Allen. Maintaining Knowledge about Temporal Intervals. *Communications of the ACM*, 26:832–843, 1983.
2. J.L. Bentley and T. Ottmann. Algorithms for Reporting and Counting Geometric Intersections. *IEEE Trans. on Computers*, C-28:643–647, 1979.
3. Z. Cui, A.G. Cohn, and D.A. Randell. Qualitative and Topological Relationships. *3rd Int. Symp. on Advances in Spatial Databases*, LNCS 692, pp. 296–315, 1993.
4. M.J. Egenhofer, A. Frank, and J. P. Jackson. A Topological Data Model for Spatial Databases. *1st Int. Symp. on the Design and Implementation of Large Spatial Databases*, LNCS 409, pp. 271–286. Springer-Verlag, 1989.
5. R.H. Güting and M. Schneider. Realms: A Foundation for Spatial Data Types in Database Systems. *3rd Int. Symp. on Advances in Spatial Databases*, LNCS 692, pp. 14–35. Springer-Verlag, 1993.
6. R. H. Güting and M. Schneider. Realm-Based Spatial Data Types: The ROSE Algebra. *VLDB Journal*, 4:100–143, 1995.
7. M. Schneider. *Spatial Data Types for Database Systems - Finite Resolution Geometry for Geographic Information Systems*, volume LNCS 1288. Springer-Verlag, Berlin Heidelberg, 1997.
8. M. Schneider. A Design of Topological Predicates for Complex Crisp and Fuzzy Regions. *Int. Conf. on Conceptual Modeling*, pp. 103–116, 2001.

A Framework for Representing Moving Objects

Ludger Becker, Henrik Blunck, Klaus Hinrichs, and Jan Vahrenhold

Westfälische Wilhelms-Universität Münster
Institut für Informatik, 48149 Münster, Germany
{beckelu,blunck,khh,jan}@math.uni-muenster.de

Abstract. We present a framework for representing the trajectories of moving objects and the time-varying results of operations on moving objects. This framework supports the realization of discrete data models of moving objects databases, which incorporate representations of moving objects based on non-linear approximation functions.

1 Introduction

The need for storing and processing continuously moving objects arises in a wide range of applications, including traffic control, physical simulation, or mobile communication systems. Most of the existing database systems, which assume that the data is constant unless it is explicitly modified, are not suitable for representing, storing, and querying continuously moving objects because either the database has to be continuously updated or a query output will be obsolete. A better approach would be to represent the position of a moving object as a function $f(t)$ of time, so that the position changes without any explicit change in the database system, and the database needs to be updated only when the function $f(t)$ changes. Recently, there has been a collection of results on extending existing database systems to handle moving-object databases (e.g., [5,6,8]).

In their approach to modeling moving objects, Erwig et al. [5] distinguish the abstract and the discrete data model. The abstract model defines the data model a user of the system sees. A crucial point in modeling moving objects is the kind of motion, e.g., linear or non-linear motion. While the abstract model allows for general "smooth curves" [8], their discrete model [5,6] only considers piecewise linear motion. They approximate continuous motion of objects by assuming piecewise linear motion, interpolating an object's position or shape between static snapshots [14]. Furthermore, most indexing methods for handling moving objects assume that objects have piecewise linear trajectories (e.g., [1, 7, 10, 13]). The discrepancy between smooth curves and their approximation by polygonal lines has been recognized, and several authors indicate that a discrete model ultimately should allow for representing non-linear motion [4, 12, 15].

In this paper, we develop a framework for representing moving objects that simultaneously addresses three important issues. First, the representation of moving objects' trajectories should be as natural as possible. In moving object databases, not only the trajectory itself but also higher-order derivatives can be of interest, e.g., to obtain information about change of direction or about acceleration. Hence, we require that these quantities should be continuous and non-trivial. The second issue is to be able to derive a discrete model closed under (concatenation of) all operators. For example, in a model based on linear motion, the distance between two moving objects is a quadratic function. Applying the distance operator to moving objects whose construction is based on the result of previous applications of the distance operator (we call this the concatenated distance operator) can result in functions of arbitrarily high complexity, which obviously are not captured by a model using linear motion. Because the second issue cannot be resolved using both constant-size information and exact representation, the final issue addressed is to develop a compact representation with bounded space requirements and best possible approximation of the trajectory in question. Objects modeled in specific applications will impose quite different requirements for how these issues may be addressed. Consequently, being "best" is not a global property of any fixed representation but heavily depends on the application at hand, and we present our approach in an extensible manner.

2 Representing Trajectories for Moving Objects

We will use the notation of the abstract model by Forlizzi et al. and Güting et al. [6,8]. The abstract model provides basic constant types like int, real, string, and bool, spatial data types point$\langle d \rangle$, line$\langle d \rangle$, and region$\langle d \rangle$, where d is the number of dimensions of the underlying space, and timevariant types. In principle, each of the constant and spatial data types can be lifted to a timevariant type [8]. In most applications objects of type line$\langle d \rangle$ are polylines and extended geometric objects of type region$\langle d \rangle$ are polygonal regions which both can be described by a set of timevariant vertices. Therefore we concentrate on the representation of d-dimensional timevariant points denoted as mpoint$\langle d \rangle$ and on onedimensional timevariant datatypes, especially mreal. For all data types there are constructors, which can be used to initialize corresponding objects, e.g., there is a constructor which initializes an object of type mpoint$\langle d \rangle$ based upon d objects of type mreal. All operators defined on constant types can be lifted to timevariant types and thus be applied to timevariant objects. In addition, other operators for moving objects of type mpoint$\langle d \rangle$ can be defined, e.g., trajectory, derivative, speed, velocity, and acceleration [8].

2.1 Requirements for Moving Object Trajectories

The motion of real-world objects is usually recorded in discrete steps, e.g. by radar-, radio-, or GPS-based tracking devices. Hence any attempt to model the motion has to respect this discrete set of spatial information. A central concept will be what we call a *constraining fact*, a pair (t_i, f_i), which indicates information (e.g., a spatial position) f_i valid for an object at a specific point in time t_i. The motion of an object can then be modeled by a discrete collection of constraining facts and an appropriate interpolation function which gives the trajectory of the object as the graph of the interpolation function in the $(d+1)$-dimensional space (d spatial dimensions, one temporal dimension). The information f_i can consist of, e.g., the spatial position, speed, direction, acceleration, or higher-order derivatives at time t_i. Current models usually use the spatial position. A *concept of representation* is given by one or more kinds of trajectories (e.g., piecewise linear curves or splines), a construction algorithm for deriving an appropriate interpolation function, and an algorithm for evaluating this function.

There is an obvious trade-off between the size of the representation and its precision. A representation of arbitrary precision would not only incur increased overhead for evaluating interpolating functions but, more important, due to unpredictable differences in the objects' sizes, organizing data layout and data accesses becomes more expensive. Therefore Cao et al. [3] consider algorithms for compressing trajectories which select from the facts known about a moving point the most relevant ones which are then used for interpolation by a (compressed) trajectory. We abstract from this by using as defining facts those which have to be interpolated, but we require, however, that the amount of storage needed for the result of an operation on timevariant data is bounded as follows:
Bounded Size Requirement: The size $|I(mp)|$ of the interpolating function's representation $I(mp)$ linearly depends on the number $F(mp)$ of constraining facts, that is $|I(mp)| \leq c \cdot F(mp)$, where the constant c is global for the concept of representation. When applying an operator, the maximum allowed size for the representation of the result is bounded by the maximum size for the representation of any of the operands, that is, if an operator op is applied to operands $mp_1, \ldots, mp_n$, we have $|I(\text{op}(mp_1, \ldots, mp_n))| \leq \max\{|I(mp_1)|, \ldots, |I(mp_n)|\}$.

2.2 Trajectory Types for Specific Requirements

Different applications impose different requirements on the kind of interpolation function, and there are several classes of interpolation functions available.

If only discrete positions of a moving object are known, but not speed, moving direction, and acceleration, the trajectory can be represented by piecewise linear interpolation, i.e., by a polyline in $(d+1)$-dimensional space, which is given as a sequence of points, e.g., for 2-dimensional (x, y)-space by a sequence $(x_1, y_1, t_1), (x_2, y_2, t_2), \ldots, (x_n, y_n, t_n)$. This representation has the disadvantage that the first-order derivative of the trajectory is a non-continuous function, i.e., speed and direction may change only in discrete steps. Furthermore, acceleration which is represented by the second-order derivative is always zero, i.e., piecewise linear interpolation cannot capture non-zero acceleration.

If continuous first- and second-order derivatives are needed to enforce smooth changes of speed and direction, (higher-degree) splines can be used. For representing smooth curves, B-splines [11] form a well-investigated concept with numerous applications in numerical analysis, geometric modeling, computer graphics and other areas. Besides continuous first- and second-order derivatives cubic splines have a nice balancing property: they have a nearly optimal, minimal average quadratic curvature and therefore are inherently smoother and oscillate less than other interpolation functions like higher-order polynomials. In our context this means that changes of direction and speed are minimized and uniformly distributed between constraining facts. The interpolating spline function of a trajectory does not deviate too much from the polygonal chain connecting the sample points, and its local behavior can be predicted [11].

Besides location information, speed and direction of movement may also be available, e.g., by GPS-based tracking devices. In the context of Hermite-interpolation [11] not only given time/space positions can be prescribed, but also the first-order derivatives of the resulting trajectory in these points, i.e., speed and direction. In certain applications, it may be useful to adapt the representation of moving objects to reflect additional properties of an object's motion. For example, an airplane performs turns only very close to sample points and otherwise moves almost linearly. This can be modeled by ν-splines [9] for which the amount of change in the second continuous derivative can be (even locally) prescribed. This amount is determined by the turning radius of the airplane. This exact prescription can be necessary, e.g., in modeling airport approach procedures where airplanes approach two parallel runways in a butterfly-shaped flight pattern.[1] Other applications may require mixed representations, i.e., the representation of a trajectory uses different types of interpolation functions for different time intervals, e.g., circular arcs and piecewise linear curves.

3 Representing Results of Operations on Moving Data

Our goal is to represent the timevariant results of operations on moving data, i.e., to represent results of operations on trajectories, such that the requirements for a representation are not violated. In terms of the abstract model described in Section 2, this demands the closure of the types $\mathtt{mpoint}\langle d\rangle$ and $\mathtt{mreal}$ under operations, in particular under the concatenation of lifted operations. The following examples illustrate the major problems that can arise with respect to the closure under operations (mp_i denoting an instance of class $\mathtt{mpoint}\langle d\rangle$):

Example 1: Compute the distance $\mathtt{mdistance}(mp_1, mp_2)$.

If mp_1 and mp_2 are represented by piecewise linear trajectories, the exact result is given piecewise by the root of a polynomial of degree two. Erwig et al. [5] observed this problem in the linear model, and Forlizzi et al. [6] proposed an extended model using piecewise linear interpolation. They propose to extend the datatype $\mathtt{mreal}$ for moving reals to also represent timevariant roots of polynomials of degree 2. However, this is not sufficient if the results obtained by applying the $\mathtt{mdistance}$ function are used in further calculations. The result in the next example cannot be represented in the extended model by an $\mathtt{mreal}$ since it cannot be described piecewise by the root of a polynomial of degree 2.

Example 2: Compute the concatenated distance $\mathtt{mdistance}(\mathtt{mdistance}(mp_1, mp_2), \mathtt{mdistance}(mp_3, mp_4))$, the timevariant absolute value of a difference.

---

[1] The European Organization for Safety of Air Navigation maintains a database http://www.eurocontrol.fr/projects/bada of the inflight behavior, e.g., velocity or descent speed, of over 250 aircraft types to support exact modeling.

This computation is useful when analyzing the timevariant distances of pairs of planes flying in formation or the timevariant distances of particles to a nucleus. Other applications may use the results of the mdistance function to construct new instances of class mpoint⟨d⟩. In Forlizzi et al.'s extended model these instances cannot be represented because they cannot be described piecewise by a line or a root of a polynomial. To make things worse, the mdistance function as well as other functions may even be applied to such constructed instances. This shows that the representation model should be closed under unlimited number of lifted operations. Applications using the results of the mdistance function to construct new instances of class mpoint⟨d⟩ can be found, e.g., in object tracking. Distance-based tracking systems (e.g., GPS or sonar tracking) use distance measurements with respect to a fixed number of sites to reconstruct the movements of objects. If these timevariant distances are of interest in their own right, they should be appropriately interpolated over time (and thus be stored as mreals). If it cannot be guaranteed that the distances are measured synchronously at the same points-in-time it becomes necessary to interpolate the timevariant distances in order to reconstruct and store the recorded motion.

Example 3: Compute the timevariant center of gravity of a set $\{mp_1, \ldots, mp_n\}$.

This operation requires the closure of the model under addition and scalar multiplication of the data type mpoint⟨d⟩. This requirement is already fulfilled for a model based upon piecewise linear trajectories, but, in general, the bounded size requirement will be violated: To exactly represent the result, each constraining fact of the operands has to contribute to the representation of the result. More precisely, if for each mp_i the number of constraining facts $F(mp_i)$ is at most s, then the following holds for the result m_r: $s \leq F(m_r) \leq n \cdot s$.

The discussion shows that no concept of representation is known to exactly represent the results of relevant lifted geometric operations since the representation size for the exact results obtained by iterated applications of the mdistance operator cannot be bounded. Additionally, it is impossible to maintain the bounded size requirement for the application of non-unary operators while at the same time respecting all constraining facts of all operands. To resolve this conflict while maintaining the closure of the model, we propose that the construction algorithm included in the concept of representation must support a size reduction of the representation of the interpolation function, which preserves the main characteristics of the trajectory. We propose to classify and to process the constraining facts of the operands according to their relevance.

Application of Operators and Recruitment Strategies. In the following, we describe how a construction algorithm can proceed to select constraining facts from the set of constraining facts given by all operands. Such a recruitment strategy first has to determine a bounded number of points in time for which either reliable spatial information is known, or which are necessary for preserving the main characteristics of the trajectory. If these points result in more spatial information than can be accommodated in the maximum allowed space (given by the bounded size requirement), the strategy has to select the most relevant points, if there are less such points, the strategy may choose to include additional points of less reliability. This process is guided by assigning to each point-in-time t_i given by a constraining fact (t_i, f_i) a relevance score $v(t_i)$, and then selecting a bounded number of points-in-time according to these scores. The result of an operator is then computed using the following two steps: (i) For each chosen point-in-time, retrieve the spatial information of all operands valid at that point-in-time and apply the operator to this spatial information. (ii) Interpolate the results of Step (i) using the given interpolation method.

A *first-class point-in-time* has an associated spatial information that has to be accounted for in the representation of the trajectory, whereas a *second-class point-in-time* has an associated spatial information considered less relevant. We can restate the bounded size requirement in the context of an operator's result:

Definition 1. *Let* op *be an n-ary operator and let* $\{mp_1, \ldots, mp_n\}$ *be the set of its operands. The bounded size requirement for* op *is fulfilled if and only if the size of the representation for* $op(mp_1, \ldots, mp_n)$ *is bounded by a (global) constant times the maximum number of first-class points-in-time for any of the operands.*

As long as we can bound the size of the representation by a (global) constant times the number of first-class points-in-time, this definition exactly matches our earlier requirement that the maximum allowed size for the representation of the result is bounded by the maximum allowed size for the representation of any of the operands, and we will demonstrate below how to obtain these bounds. This definition also subsumes the construction of an instance of class mpoint$\langle d \rangle$ from a set of m constraining facts if we consider the constructor as an operator that takes an argument of size m and if we consider each timestamp of a constraining fact as a first-class point-in-time. Second-class points-in-time will not occur in trajectories initially constructed from a set of constraining facts as all facts are exactly known and thus reliable. They may occur, however, in the representation of an operator's result, e.g., if, at a given point-in-time t, reliable information is known for only one of the operands. Consequently, the spatial information of the operator's result at point-in-time t may be less relevant for the (overall) representation than the spatial information at any point-in-time t' where reliable information is known for all operands. In the following description, we assume that all operands are defined on a (time) interval $[a, b]$.

We propose to implement a skeleton for a recruitment strategy as follows:

Step 1: Select $t = a$ and $t = b$ as first-class points-in-time. Assign these points-in-time a score of $v(t) = 5 \cdot n$ (always select interval end points).

Step 2: Collect all first- and second-class points-in-time given by the operands and label them as follows: Each point-in-time t is assigned a score of $v(t) = 3 \cdot fc(t) + sc(t)$ where $fc(t)$ denotes the number of operands considering t as a first-class point-in-time and where $sc(t)$ denotes the number of operands considering t as a second-class point-in-time. Consequently $v(t) \leq 3 \cdot n$.

Step 3: [Optional] Select points-in-time according to a strategy-specific heuristic and assign each such point-in-time t a score of $v(t) = 4 \cdot n$ (a recruiting heuristic, e.g., uniform sampling, is allowed to override the operand-given classification), a score of $v(t) = 2 \cdot n$ (respect points that coincide with many first-class points), or a score of $v(t) = 0$ (supply additional points as needed).

Step 4: Let m be the maximum number of points-in-time that can be accounted for according to the bounded size requirement. Of the m recruited points-in-time with the highest assigned scores, the m' points-in-time with the highest assigned scores are labeled first-class points-in-time, where m' is the maximum number of first-class points-in-time of any single operand. The remaining $m - m'$ points-in-time are labeled second-class points-in-time.

It is easy to realize that this strategy does not violate the bounded size requirement. Note, that the global constant c allows for an application-specific trade-off between exactness and storage costs. The third step (selection according to a heuristic) can prove useful, e.g., when computing the distance. In this situation, the points-in-time corresponding to local extremal points of the distance function may be chosen to ensure that all such extremal points are accounted for in the representation of the operator's result. In addition to the flexibility in handling operator-specific requirements, the third step of the recruitment strategy facilitates extending the framework: If a specific interpolation function is known to work best for, say, equidistant interpolation points, it can use this step to enforce a corresponding (over-)sampling of all operands. Neglecting a possible overriding due to the recruiting heuristics in Step 3, our concept creates a representation of an operator's result that is derived from "relevant" (e.g. exactly known) information, i.e. the (important) constraining facts of the argument trajectories. The categorization of the result's constraining facts according to their relevance guarantees this property also for results of operations applied to operation results—a main advantage over standard curve simplification algorithms.

4 Implementing the Framework

We are currently implementing a framework with the following properties:

- Encapsulation of various interpolation methods.
- Incorporation of construction/evaluation algorithms for each trajectory type.
- Closure with respect to an arbitrary concatenation of operators.
- Incorporation of different kinds of recruitment strategies.
- Capability of handling different kinds of constraining facts.

Our approach (Fig. 1) associates a moving object of class mpoint$\langle d \rangle$ with a representation of its interpolation function, which consists of d objects of class Function, each representing the motion in one spatial dimension. There are subclasses of class Function for each kind of trajectory. An mpoint$\langle d \rangle$ object also references the constraining facts interpolated by its trajectory. Each constraining fact is represented by an object of class InTimeData. This object at least has attributes for a timestamp and a classification, which in turn may be used to guide recruitment strategies. We may derive subclasses from InTimeData to represent different kinds of constraining facts, e.g., the class InTimePositionData represents the spatial position corresponding to a point-in-time. Other subclasses may be derived to represent other kinds of information, e.g., speed, direction, or acceleration. Depending on the concrete subclass of Function, the information part f of a constraining fact (t, f) can be provided efficiently by the Function object. Then, constraining facts are represented by instances of subclasses of class InTimeData, and getInTimeData() uses the method Function::evaluate() to determine f.

The construction algorithm and the evaluation algorithm corresponding to a concept of representation are realized by a factory method createTrajectory() and by a method evaluate(), both operations of a subclass of FunctionRules to which construction and evaluation is delegated. Each Function object, which is responsible for the representation of the interpolation function associated with a moving object, has an associated FunctionRules-object. This design allows interpolation functions to be combined with different construction and evaluation algorithms in the form of subclasses of FunctionRules.

To construct moving objects resulting from the application of an operator, an object of class Heuristics and an object of class Bindings are required. The

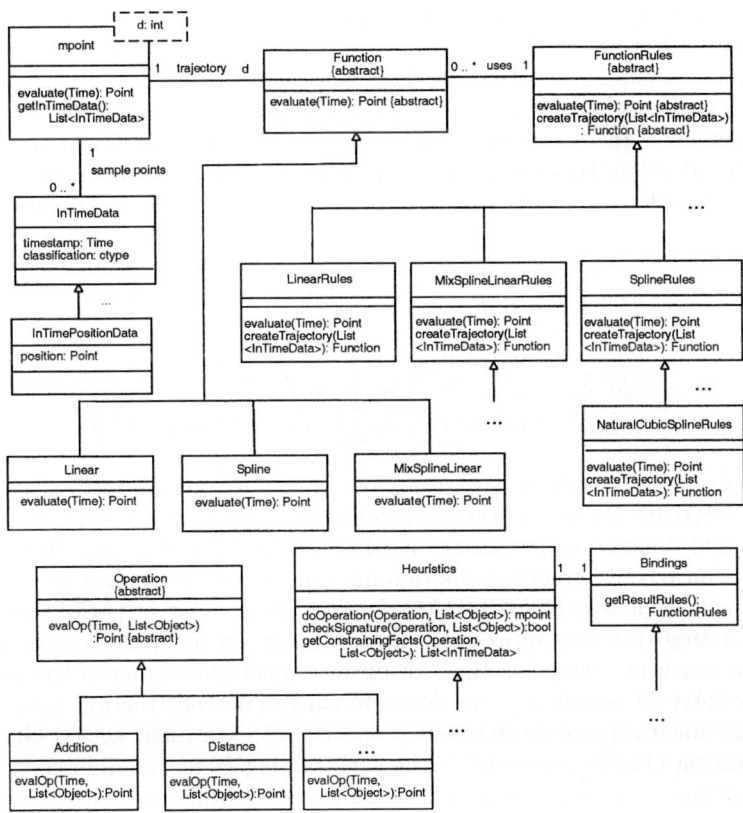

Fig. 1. Class diagram for representing and handling objects of class mpoint$\langle d \rangle$

Heuristics-object provides the recruitment algorithm (see Section 3) and the Bindings-object selects the concept of representation (i.e., the subclass of class FunctionRules), which is used to represent the resulting object.

Operations are implemented as subclasses of class Operation. Each Operation-object has a signature, which is used to check the type of each operand. If an object of class mpoint$\langle d \rangle$ is constructed as the result of an operation, the method doOperation() of the responsible object of class Heuristics is activated by a message containing the responsible object of class Operation and the corresponding operands. The referenced Bindings-object determines for each dimension the kind of the resulting trajectory, i.e., a subclass of class FunctionRules is selected depending on the operation and the trajectory types of the arguments. The construction algorithm realized by that class finally constructs an object of the corresponding subclass of class Function.

5 Experimental Evaluation

We have implemented the class structure described above as an extension of the GIS-database-kernel GOODAC, developed at the University of Münster [2] on top of the object-oriented database system OBJECTSTORE. We have conducted a small set of experiments to examine the practical relevance of the proposed model. The focus of our interest was on the extra cost for using trajectories that allow for higher-order derivatives. We created piecewise linear trajectories and cubic B-spline trajectories for randomly generated constraining facts and compared construction and evaluation time for randomly selected points in time.

No. of Facts	Construction			Evaluation		
	Linear	Spline	Ratio	Linear	Spline	Ratio
40	0.314s	0.510s	1.61	0.793ms	0.933ms	1.33
160	0.693s	1.219s	1.76	0.892ms	1.174ms	1.32
320	1.461s	2.722s	1.86	0.964ms	1.307ms	1.36
640	5.783s	8.814s	1.52	1.014ms	1.518ms	1.50

The results given above have been obtained on a Sun Enterprise 250 (2 ∗ 400 MHz, 1.5 GB RAM) and reflect the timings averaged over five runs. Evaluation timings additionally have been averaged over sequences of 10 and 1000 evaluations. A non-trivial amount of the running time, however, is spent on allocating or accessing (persistent) GOODAC-objects. Thus, relative performance may change if only transient objects are involved, e.g., in main-memory databases. The non-constant evaluation time for linear trajectories is due to having to locate the interval containing the elevation time. The construction time for the piecewise linear representation mainly consists of time spent within GOODAC for allocating objects representing the constraining facts: the difference in construction time is the time actually needed for computing the spline coefficients.

The important conclusion that can be drawn from this small set of experiments is that there is only a moderate loss in construction and evaluation performance when going from piecewise linear to spline interpolation. In our setting, evaluating the (more powerful) spline representation takes no more than 150% of the evaluation time for piecewise linear trajectories.

6 Conclusions

We have presented a framework that supports the realization of discrete data models of moving objects databases, which allow for representations of moving objects based on non-linear approximation functions and of results of time-variant operators. We also have stated general and strategy-dependent requirements for non-linear approximations. The framework is closed with respect to arbitrary concatenation of operators and can be extended easily. Preliminary experiments show that evaluation performance diminishes only moderately when switching from linear to a (more powerful and complex) spline representation.

References

1. P.K. Agarwal, L.A. Arge, J. Erickson. Indexing moving points. *Symp. Principles of Database Systems*, 175–186, 2000.
2. L. Becker, A. Voigtmann, K.H. Hinrichs. Developing applications with the object-oriented GIS-kernel GOODAC. *Symp. Spatial Data Handling*, 5A1–5A18, 1996.
3. H. Cao, O. Wolfson, G. Trajcevski. Spatio-temporal data reduction with deterministic error bounds. *Symp. Mobile Ad Hoc Networking and Comp.*, 33–42, 2003.
4. J. Chomicki, P.Z. Revesz. A general framework for specifying spatiotemporal objects. *Workshop Temporal Representation and Reasoning*, 41–46, 1999.
5. M. Erwig, R.H. Güting, M. Schneider, M. Vazirgiannis. Spatio-temporal data types: An approach to modeling and querying moving objects in databases. *GeoInformatica*, 3(3):269–296, 1999.
6. L. Forlizzi, R.H. Güting, E. Nardelli, M. Schneider. A data model and data structures for moving objects databases. *SIGMOD Int. Conf. Management of Data*, 319–330, 2000.
7. L.J. Guibas, J.S.B. Mitchell, T. Roos. Voronoi diagrams of moving points in the plane. *Workshop Graph-Theoretic Concepts in Computer Science, LNCS* 570, 113–125, 1992.
8. R.H. Güting, M.H. Böhlen, M. Erwig, C.S. Jensen, N.A. Lorentzos, M. Schneider, M. Vazirgiannis. A foundation for representing and quering moving objects. *ACM Trans. Database Systems*, 25(1):1–42, 2000.
9. G.D. Knott. *Interpolating Cubic Splines*. Birkhäuser, Boston, MA, 1999.
10. G. Kollios, D. Gunopulos, V.J. Tsotras. On indexing mobile objects. *Symp. Principles of Database Systems*, 261–272, 1999.
11. G. Nürnberger. *Approximation by Spline Functions*. Springer, New York, 1978.
12. D. Pfoser, C.S. Jensen. Querying the trajectories of on-line mobile objects. *Workshop Data Engineering for Wireless and Mobile Access*, 66–73, 2001.
13. S. Saltenis, C.S. Jensen, S.T. Leutenegger, M.A. López. Indexing the positions of continously moving objects. *SIGMOD Conf. Management of Data*, 331–342, 2000.
14. E. Tøssebro, R.H. Güting. Creating representations for continuously moving regions from observations. *Symp. Spatial and Spatio-Temporal Databases, LNCS* 2121, 321–344, 2001.
15. T.-S. Yeh, B. De Cambray. Modeling highly variable spatio-temporal data. *Australiasian Database Conference*, 221–230, 1995.

Temporal Functional Dependencies with Multiple Granularities: A Logic Based Approach*

Carlo Combi and Rosalba Rossato

Dipartimento di Informatica
Università degli Studi di Verona
Ca' Vignal 2 - Strada Le Grazie 15 - 37134 Verona (Italy)
{combi,rossato}@sci.univr.it

Abstract. Functional dependencies allow one to define semantic constraints on relational databases without focusing on data dynamics. Some efforts have been devoted in these last twenty years to extend functional dependencies to support temporal aspects of data; the existing proposals capture temporal features which are slightly different one from each other. In this paper we propose a logic based approach for the problem of modeling and managing temporal data dependencies, and we show how our proposal allows one to express in a homogeneous way the temporal functional dependencies previously proposed in the literature.

1 Introduction

Central to the design of database schemata is the idea of *data dependency*, which is a constraint on the allowable relations that can be instantiated for a relational schema. Functional dependencies (FD) are widely used dependencies in the framework of logical design of relational databases [5]. These dependencies are static, in the sense that they are intended for snapshot databases which do not manage any temporal dimension of data. Temporal databases allow us to store and access temporal-related information [3]: in a temporal database, integrity constraints can place restrictions on the evolution of data in time. To this regard, the need of extending functional dependencies to support temporal aspects of data, has received increasing attention [1, 3, 7, 8, 9]. Different temporal functional dependencies have been proposed [3, 6, 8], which capture temporal features slightly different one from each other. All the considered temporal features must be taken into account: indeed, it is important, as we will discuss in this paper, both to constraint a database to verify at each time point a specific functional dependency (for example, each employee can belong to a single department) and to define constraints on updates (for example, if an employee gets a promotion, then his salary must increase).

---

* This work has been partially supported by contributions from the Italian Ministry of University and Research (MIUR) under program COFIN-PRIN 2003 "Representing and managing spatial and geographical data on the Web".

In the real world, when we describe a fact we use specific temporal units: for example, in the context of business applications the activities are organized in business weeks or business months while university courses are scheduled on semesters. In order to describe this information with the suitable abstraction level, the concept of *temporal granularity* [2, 7, 9] has been introduced. A time granularity can be viewed as a partitioning of a temporal domain in groups of indivisible units (granule). The possibility of representing different temporal units is a first step towards the capability of defining integrity constraints which can include different user-defined calendars (i.e. finite sets of temporal granularities). Few proposals deal with the problem of describing temporal functional dependencies with multiple granularities [7, 9].

This paper proposes a new approach for the problem of modeling and managing temporal dependencies which can involve multiple granularities; we show how our proposal allows one to express in a homogeneous way the other proposals for the same topic. We will introduce the concept of *labeled linear time structure* for representing temporal relations and will explain how *temporal linear logic* can be used in order to describe temporal functional dependencies (TFDs) with multiple granularities.

2 Background and Related Work

Relations and Functional Dependencies. Let be $\mathcal{A}$ a set of the attributes and $\mathcal{D}$ a set of domains each of them containing atomic values for the attributes. The map $dom : \mathcal{A} \to \mathcal{D}$ associates a domain in $\mathcal{D}$ to each attribute in $\mathcal{A}$. A *relation schema* is defined by a relation name and a set of attributes; in the follow we describe dependencies over a temporal relation with schema $R(Z)$. A *tuple over* Z is a total function from Z ($Z \subseteq \mathcal{A}$) into Z. In general, if t is a tuple of a relation r, and A is an attribute of the same relation, then $t[A]$ represents the value of the attribute A in the tuple t.

Definition 1. *A functional dependency (FD) is a statement $X \to Y$, where X and Y are sets of attributes. The functional dependency $X \to Y$ is satisfied by a relation r over Z, with $X, Y \subseteq Z$, if and only if for every $s, t \in r$, if $s[X] = t[X]$ then $s[Y] = t[Y]$.*

Temporal Functional Dependencies without Granularities. In the work of Vianu [6], a temporal relation is viewed as a sequence of snapshot relations in time. Each new snapshot is obtained from the previous one by global updates, which affect several or all tuples simultaneously. A tuple is perceived as an object representation and preserves its identity through updates. *Static* and *dynamic* constraints are used in order to describe FDs and constraints that the database has to respect during its evolution (i.e. a sequence of updates), respectively. In their work [3], Jensen et al. propose a bitemporal conceptual data model, which associates, by means of *bitemporal elements* (t, v), the *transaction time* t and the *valid time* v to each tuple. The construct of FDs for temporal relations is extended in this way: if X and Y are sets of traditional attributes of a temporal relation schema $R(Z)$, a *temporal functional dependency*, $X \to^T Y$ exists on R if, for all instances r of R, all snapshots of r satisfy the functional dependency $X \to Y$. In the work of Wijsen [8], the time (discrete and bounded) is incorporated in snapshot relations by associating each tuple with a set of time points which represent its *valid time*. The timeslice T_i at time i of a valid-time relation T over a set of attributes Z, is the smallest snapshot relation over Z containing t[Z] whenever $t \in T$ and i is contained in the valid time of the tuple t ($i \in t(VT)$). In this context, a FD $X \to Y$ is said to be satisfied by a valid-time relation T at time i, if and only if it is satisfied by T_i. The author defines two kinds of functional dependencies which involve temporal aspects. A *temporal functional dependency* (TFD) is a statement of the form $X\,G\,Y$ and it is satisfied by a valid-time relation T at time i, if and only if $X \to Y$ is satisfied by $T_i \cup T_{i+1}, \ldots \cup T_{maxTime}$. A *dynamic functional dependency* (DFD), is a statement of the form $X\,N\,Y$ and it is satisfied by a valid-time relation T at time i, if $X \to Y$ is satisfied by $T_i \cup T_{i+1}$, and by $T_{maxTime}$ if $i = maxTime$.

Temporal Functional Dependencies with Multiple Granularities. In the work of Wang et al. [7], the notion of temporal functional dependency with multiple granularities (TFD) is formalized. The concept of temporal granularity is obtained with a mapping μ from the set of time points $\mathbb{N}$ (*index set*) to $\mathcal{P}(\mathbb{R})$. A TDF is a proper extension of the traditional functional dependency and takes the form $X \to_\mu Y$, meaning that there is a unique value for Y during one granule of the temporal granularity μ for one particular X value. In [9] Wijsen defines temporal functional dependencies (TFD) for temporal databases that include the object-identity; the concept of temporal granularity is similar to that in the proposal of Wang et al. [7].

3 Representing Temporal FDs

3.1 Representing Time Granularities

We model time granularities according to the following standard definition [2].

Definition 2. *A granularity is a mapping $G : I \to 2^T$ such that:*

1. *for all $i < j$, for any $n \in G(i)$ and $m \in G(j)$, $n < m$;*
2. *for all $i < j$, if $G(j) \neq \emptyset$, then $G(i) \neq \emptyset$.*

T is the *time domain* and I is the domain of a granularity G, called *index set*. The elements of the codomain of G are called *granules*. The first condition of the previous definition states that granules in a granularity do not overlap and that their order is the same as their time domain order. The second condition states that the subset of the index set that maps to nonempty granules forms an initial segment. In the following, we assume that both the index set I and the time domain T are in the linear discrete domain $(\mathbb{N}, <)$. Let $\mathcal{G} = \{G_1, G_2, \ldots, G_n\}$

be a finite set of granularities (*calendar*) and let $\mathcal{P}_\mathcal{G} = \{P_{G_i}, Q_{G_i} | 1 \leq i \leq n\}$ be a set of propositional symbols associated with the calendar $\mathcal{G}$. Given an alphabet of propositional symbols $\mathcal{P} \supseteq \mathcal{P}_\mathcal{G}$ (which contains at least the symbols describing the calendar $\mathcal{G}$) the $\mathcal{P}$-labeled (discrete) linear time structure has the form $(\mathbb{N}, <, V)$, where $(\mathbb{N}, <)$ is the set of natural numbers with the usual ordering modeling the time domain, and $V : \mathbb{N} \to 2^\mathcal{P}$ is a labeling function mapping the natural number set to sets of propositional symbols. The idea is to identify the starting point of an arbitrary granule of G in the structure with the propositional symbol P_G and the ending point of an arbitrary granule of G in the structure with the symbol Q_G. The formal notion of *consistency* of a labeled linear structure with respect to a granularity G can be expressed by means of a suitable logical formula [2] which describes that every point labeled with P_G has to match with a unique point labeled with Q_G and viceversa.

3.2 Representing Temporal Relations and Functional Dependencies

In order to represent a temporal relation over the labeled structure, the idea is to use a set of symbols which describe, at each time point, the set of valid tuples. As previously mentioned, the propositional symbols P_G and Q_G are used to identify the granules of the granularity G, which is expressed in the labeled linear structure as a PPLTL (Past Propositional Temporal Linear Logic) logical formula. In addition, we use symbols $r(a_1 : v_1, \ldots, a_n : v_n)$ in order to represent the valid tuple over a relation r (a_i is an attribute and v_i the associated value).

Example 1. Let us to consider the temporal relation *Patient*, which represents the name and the assumed drugs of a set of patients. The attribute *VT* is associated to each tuple in order to describe the corresponding valid-time, i.e. the time during which the patient assumes the prescribed drug. The (atemporal) schema of this temporal relation is *Patient(Name, Drug)*.

Let us assume that the temporal domain associated to the labeled linear structure is the time domain $\mathbb{N}$ of days. We can associate to each point (each day) in the structure, the set of symbols which describe the valid tuples at the given time (day). Let us suppose to have a PPLTL formula ϕ_{month}, which defines the month granularity on the labeled structure (P_{month} and Q_{month} identify the granules). The tuple (*Ed, Nimesulide*) is valid during October, 2000; for this reason, we will associate the symbol *Patient(Name:Ed, Drug:Nimesulide)* to each time point which describes a day of October, 2000. In a similar way we can describe the other tuples with respect to their temporal validity. The linear labeled structure for the considered example is shown in Figure 1.

Let us now consider the problem of expressing temporal functional dependencies in the proposed labeled structure. For example, with respect to the *Example 1*, we would be able to describe the following constraint: "*a patient cannot assume different drugs during the same month*". The instance of the relation *Patient* shown in Figure 1 satisfies this temporal dependency. In order to describe the required temporal dependency, we need to check the absence of tuples, related to the same patient, which store the assumption of different drugs during the same month. As we will describe in the following, the meaning of functional dependencies and temporal functional dependencies can be easily expressed by a formula in the temporal linear logic, suitably extended to deal with tuple values with a notation analogous to that of the tuple-oriented relational calculus [5].

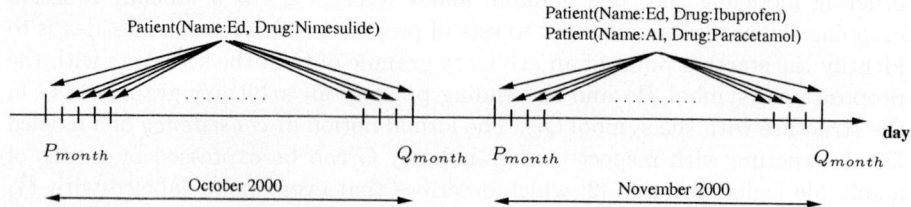

Fig. 1. The linear labeled structure which describes the valid tuples

3.3 The Proposed Logic

The proposed logic is a *temporal logic* where expressions are built up from *variables*, used to denote tuples of a relation, *constants* used to denote values of attributes, and *functions* that, given a tuple and the name of one of its attributes, return the corresponding value. Starting from the fact that FDs describe properties which have to be satisfied by all the tuples, in the following we assume that there is an implicit *universal quantification* over the variables (i.e. over the tuples of a temporal relation).

Let $\mathcal{A}, \mathcal{D}$ be a set of attributes and their associated set of domains respectively, $\Theta = \{<, =, >, \leq, \geq, \neq\}$ a set of comparing operators for the tuple values and $\mathcal{V}$ a set of variables which refer to tuples of the temporal relation. A tuple of r, having schema $R(X)$, is described by a sequence $(a_1 : v_1, \ldots, a_n : v_n)$, which associates to each attribute $a_i \in X$ the corresponding value v_i. $\mathcal{L}$ is the extended alphabet which contains the propositional symbols to denote granules and symbols which describe the valid tuples of temporal relations. If $i \in \mathbb{N}$, then the set of objects which can be associated to the time point i is:

$$L(i) = \begin{cases} P_G, Q_G & \text{where G is a defined granularity;} \\ r(a_1 : v_1, a_2 : v_2, \ldots, a_n : v_n) & \text{where } r \text{ is the name of a relation,} \\ & a_i \in X \text{ and } v_i \text{ is its associated value.} \end{cases}$$

The $\mathcal{L}$-labeled (discrete) linear time structure $\mathcal{M}$ has the form $(\mathbb{N}, <, L)$, where $L : \mathbb{N} \to 2^{\mathcal{L}}$ is a labeling function mapping natural numbers to sets of symbols to denote granules and valid tuples.

The set of logical formulae is defined according to the following definition:

Definition 3. *The set of formulae is inductively defined as follows:*

1. *any symbol $p \in \mathcal{P}_G$ is a formula;*
2. *if r is the name of a relation and $t \in \mathcal{V}$, then $r(t)$ is a formula;*

3. *if* $t_i, t_j \in \mathcal{V}$, $c_k \in \mathcal{D}$, *and* $a_h, a_k \in \mathcal{A}$ *then* $t_i[a_h]\theta t_j[a_k]$, $t_i[a_h]\theta c_k$ *are formulae;*
4. *if* ϕ *and* ψ *are formulae, then* $\phi \wedge \psi$, $\neg \psi$, $\mathbf{X}\phi$, $\phi \, \mathbf{U} \, \psi$, $\mathbf{X}^{-1}\phi$ *and* $\phi \, \mathbf{S} \, \psi$ *are formulae.*

As mentioned at point 2, if r is the name of a relation and t is variable, then $r(t)$ is an atomic formula stating that the variable t represents a tuple of a relation r. The point 3 states that $t_i[a_h]\theta t_j[a_k]$ and $t_i[a_h]\theta c_k$ are formulae describing that the attribute a_h of the tuple represented by the variable t_i (denoted with $t_i.a_h$) is in θ-relation with the attribute a_k of the tuple t_j ($t_j.a_k$) and with the value c_k, respectively. At point 4 are described the formulae which can be obtained by the usage of logical and temporal logical operators.

Let t a variable which is associated to a tuple of a relation r (defined on the set Z of attributes) by means of the atomic formula $r(t)$. The function $t[a]$ is *legal* for each attribute $a \in Z$. In order to describe the semantic of the proposed formulae, we need to a *valuation function* φ assigning to each variable $t \in \mathcal{V}$ a tuple. Thus, if t is a variable associated to the relation r, the function $\varphi(t)$ returns a tuple in r which is described by the variable t.

The semantics of the formulae is as follows.

Definition 4. *Let* $\mathcal{M} = (\mathbb{N}, <, L)$ *be a $\mathcal{L}$-labeled linear time structure and* $i \in \mathbb{N}$. *The truth of a formula* ψ *in* $\mathcal{M}$ *with respect to the point* i, *denoted* $\mathcal{M}, i \models \psi$, *is defined as follows:*

$\mathcal{M}, i \models p$	iff	$p \in L(i)$ for $p \in \mathcal{P_G}$;
$\mathcal{M}, i \models r(t)$	iff	$t \in \mathcal{V}$ and $\varphi(t) \in L(i)$;
$\mathcal{M}, i \models t_i[a_h] \, \theta \, t_j[a_k]$	iff	$t_i[a_h], t_j[a_k]$ are legal and $\varphi(t_i).a_h \theta \varphi(t_j).a_h$
$\mathcal{M}, i \models t[A] \, \theta \, c_k$	iff	$t_i[a_h]$ is legal and $\varphi(t_i).a_h \theta c_k$
$\mathcal{M}, i \models \phi \wedge \psi$	iff	$\mathcal{M}, i \models \phi$ and $\mathcal{M}, i \models \psi$;
$\mathcal{M}, i \models \neg \phi$	iff	it is not the case that $\mathcal{M}, i \models \phi$;
$\mathcal{M}, i \models \phi \mathbf{U} \psi$	iff	$\mathcal{M}, j \models \psi$ for some $j \geq i$ and $\mathcal{M}, k \models \phi$ for each $i \leq k < j$;
$\mathcal{M}, i \models \mathbf{X}\psi$	iff	$\mathcal{M}, i+1 \models \psi$;
$\mathcal{M}, i \models \phi \mathbf{S} \psi$	iff	$\mathcal{M}, j \models \psi$ for some $j \leq i$ and $\mathcal{M}, k \models \phi$ for each $j < k \leq i$;
$\mathcal{M}, i \models \mathbf{X}^{-1}\psi$	iff	$i > 0$ and $\mathcal{M}, i-1 \models \psi$.

Remark: The semantics of the formula $t_i[a_h] \, \theta \, t_j[a_k]$ requires that the functions $t_i[a_h]$ and $t_j[a_k]$ are legal, i.e. in the past or in the future they have to be associated to the relation r.

Notation: In the following, if $X = \{X_1, X_2, \ldots, X_n\}$ is a set of atomic attributes $X_1, X_2, \ldots, X_n$, then the notation $t_1[X]\theta t_2[X]$, stands for $t_1[X_1]\theta t_2[X_1] \wedge t_1[X_2]\theta t_2[X_2] \wedge \ldots \wedge t_1[X_n]\theta t_2[X_n]$.

4 Expressing TFDs

4.1 Motivating Example

We consider here chemotherapies for oncological patients who undergo several chemotherapy cycles. Each cycle can include the administration of several drugs: the temporal administration of each drug is usually predefined and a cycle can be repeated several times. As an example, consider the following chemotherapy recommendation [4]: *"the recommended CEF regimen consists of 14 days of oral cycloshosphamide and intravenous injection of epirubicin and 5-fluorouracil on days 1 and 8. This is repeated every 28 days for 6 cycles"*. According to this scenario, it is possible to identify some definitions of granularities. Let us assume that OC (cyclophosphamide), IE (intravenous epirubicin) and FI (5-fluorouracil) are the granularities corresponding to drugs of the CEF regimen. Figure 2 shows the granularities involved in a chemotherapy treatment.

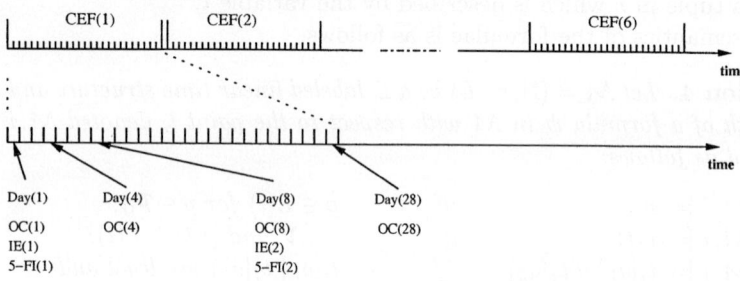

Fig. 2. Granularities involved in a chemotherapy treatment

The formula ϕ_{CEF} defines, on the time domain $\mathbb{N}$ of days, the granularities CEF, OC, IE and FI.

FinerThan$(IE, CEF) \wedge$ **FinerThan**$(OC, CEF) \wedge$ **FinerThan**$(FI, CEF) \wedge$
$Count(P_{CEF}, 6) \wedge$ **Uniform**$_{28}(CEF) \wedge \mathbf{G}((Q_{CEF} \wedge \mathbf{F}P_{CEF}) \rightarrow \mathbf{X}P_{CEF}) \wedge$
$\mathbf{G}(P_{CEF} \rightarrow (\forall[0,13](P_{OC} \wedge P_{IE} \wedge Q_{OC} \wedge Q_{IE}) \wedge P_{FI} \wedge Q_{FI} \wedge$
$\mathbf{X}^7(P_{FI} \wedge Q_{FI}) \wedge \forall[1,6](\neg P_{FI} \wedge \neg Q_{FI}) \wedge \forall[8,13](\neg P_{FI} \wedge \neg Q_{FI}) \wedge$
$\forall[14,27](\neg P_{OC} \wedge \neg P_{IE} \wedge \neg P_{FI} \wedge Q_{OC} \wedge \neg Q_{IE} \wedge \neg Q_{FI})))$.

The first three conjuncts say that the three granularities related to the assumption of the prescribed drugs are finer than the CEF granularities and that all the four granularities are internally continuous. These relationships between granularities are expressed by means of the formula **FinerThan**(G, CEF) described in detail in [2] (G stands for IE, OC, or FI). The next three conjuncts, in the second line, say that the granularity CEF consists of 6 granules (cycles) ($Count(P_{CEF}, 6)$), each of 28 elements (day) (**Uniform**$_{28}(CEF)$), and each cycle starts one time unit after the end of the previous one (in [2] all the previous notations are detailed and discussed). The other conjunctions associate the drugs with each day in the cycle, according to the recommendations.

In the following, we consider the temporal relation *Patient* which stores some information about patients who underwent chemotherapies. The atemporal schema of the relation is $Patient(\lambda, Chemo, P\text{-}Id, BG, Drug, Qty)$. In particular, the attributes *Chemo, P-Id, BG, Drug* describe the type of therapy, the patient's identifier, the blood group, and the assumed drugs, respectively. The attribute *VT* describes the specific assumption time and is expressed in term of therapy-day while the attribute λ is used in order to refer to the same object (i.e. tuple) before and after the updates. In the next Section we consider some kinds of temporal functional dependencies over the relation *Patient*.

4.2 Temporal Functional Dependencies without Granularities

With respect to the considered clinical example, we can express the following dependencies:

A1. each new drug is determined uniquely on the basis of the current type of chemotherapy and the assumed drug;

A2. at one time, a patient can undergo only one chemotherapy;

A3. every patient has a unique value of blood group which remains unchanged over all time;

A4. if the value of the attributes P-Id and Drug are preserved between times i and i+1, then the associated type of chemotherapy (Chemo attribute) must be preserved as well.

Dynamic Functional Dependencies of Vianu. The constraint **A1** is an example of Vianu's *dynamic constraint* because it requires the satisfaction of the dependency after global updates. Using the notation of Vianu, this dependency can be described as $\overset{\vee}{Chemo}, \overset{\vee}{Drug} \longrightarrow \overset{\wedge}{Drug}$, and it can be expressed with the following logical formula:

$$\mathbf{G} \, (\, (Patient(t_1) \wedge Patient(t_2) \wedge (t_1[Chemo] = t_2[Chemo]) \wedge$$
$$(t_1[Drug] = t_2[Drug]) \wedge \mathbf{X}(Patient(t'_1)) \wedge$$
$$\mathbf{X}(Patient(t'_2)) \wedge (t_1[\lambda] = t'_1[\lambda]) \wedge (t_2[\lambda] = t'_2[\lambda]))$$
$$\longrightarrow (t'_1[Drug] = t'_2[Drug]) \,).$$

The formula states that if we have two tuples t_1 and t_2 with the same values for the attributes *Chemo* and *Drug*, then they must have the same value for the attribute *Drug* after the updates (represented by t'_1 and t'_2 respectively).

Remark: In this case the dependency involves only two consecutive instances of the database, before and after an update respectively. In order to compare the objects according to the required dynamic functional dependency, we suppose that all the cycles related to the same kind of chemotherapy start together.

Temporal Dependencies of Jensen et al. The constraint **A2** is an example of Jensen et al.'s *temporal dependency* because it describes a dependency which has to be satisfied in each time slice of the considered temporal relation. This property, described by using the notation of Jensen et al. as $P\text{-}Id \to^T Chemo$, can be easily expressed in our logic with the following formula:

$$\mathbf{G}\ (\ (Patient(t_1)\ \wedge\ Patient(t_2)\ \wedge\ (t_1[P\text{-}Id] = t_2[P\text{-}Id]))$$
$$\to (t_1[Chemo] = t_2[Chemo])\ ).$$

Remark: In this case we check the required condition between all the tuples which are valid at the same time; unlike the previous case, synchronization assumptions are not necessary.

Dynamic Temporal Dependencies of Wijsen. The dependency **A3** describes a *temporal dependency* of Wijsen because it involves all the timeslices and it can be identified with the notation: $\{P\text{-}Id\}G\{BG\}$. This temporal functional dependency can be expressed in our logic with the following formula:

$$\mathbf{G}\ (\ (Patient(t_1)\ \wedge\ \mathbf{F}(Patient(t_2)))\ \wedge\ (t_1[P\text{-}Id] = t_2[P\text{-}Id])$$
$$\longrightarrow (t_1[BG] = t_2[BG])\ ).$$

The dependency **A4** describes a *dynamic functional dependency* of Wijsen because it involves only two consecutive timeslices and will be expressed assuming that all the cycles related to the same kind of chemotherapy start together. With the notation of Wijsen, the dependency **A4** can be described as $\{P\text{-}Id, Drug\}N\{Chemo\}$ and can be expressed, in our logic, with the formula:

$$\mathbf{G}\ (\ ((Patient(t_1) \wedge \mathbf{X}(Patient(t_2)))\ \wedge\ (t_1[P\text{-}Id] = t_2[P\text{-}Id])\ \wedge$$
$$(t_1[Drug] = t_2[Drug]))\ \longrightarrow (t_1[Chemo] = t_2[Chemo])\ ).$$

Remark: Also in this case we assume that all the cycles related to the same kind of chemotherapy start together. The temporal and dynamic dependencies are not related to a particular granularity.

4.3 Temporal Functional Dependencies with Granularities

A temporal functional dependency which refers to specific temporal granularities, related to the considered clinical example is:

B1. *A patient can not assume different quantities of the same drug within a therapy cycle.*

The proposed temporal dependency can be represented by means of a suitable logical formula in the linear structure, where the CEF granularity is described as mentioned in Section 4.1. The dependency **B1** can be identified by using the notation of Wang et al. as $P\text{-}Id, Drug \longrightarrow_{CEF} Qty$. The logical formula which translates it is the following:

$$\phi_{CEF} \wedge \mathbf{G} \ (\ ((\neg(P_{CEF} \vee Q_{CEF})\mathbf{S}(P_{CEF} \wedge \neg Q_{CEF})) \wedge \ Patient(t_1) \ \wedge$$
$$\mathbf{G}(\neg(P_{CEF} \vee Q_{CEF})\mathbf{U}(Patient(t2) \ \wedge \ (t_1[P\text{-}Id] = t_2[P\text{-}Id]) \ \wedge$$
$$(t_1[Drug] = t_2[Drug]))) \ \longrightarrow (t_1[Qty] = t_2[Qty]) \ ).$$

The first and second conjuncts state that the tuples t_1 and t_2 are valid in the same cycle and that they have the same value for the attribute $P\text{-}Id$ and $Drug$. If these conditions are satisfied, then these tuples must have the same value for the attribute Qty, as required in the third conjunct of the previous formula.

5 Conclusions and Future Work

In this paper, we propose a new approach to represent and manage temporal relations and associated temporal functional dependencies. Valid tuples of a temporal relation are represented by means of atomic formulae in the context of a temporal linear logic. Our proposal allows one to model and describe sets of time granularities and temporal functional dependencies which involve multiple granularities. As for future work, we aim to analyze the complexity of the satisfiability problem for our logic: given a structure $\mathcal{M}$ and a temporal functional dependencies σ, does $\mathcal{M}$ define a model of σ? A further research direction is towards the description of a new kind of temporal constraints, called *trend dependencies*, which involve multiple granularities and which require the satisfaction of complex temporal patterns.

References

[1] T. Calders, R.T. Ng, and J.Wijsen. Searching for dependencies at multiple abstraction levels. *ACM TODS*, 27(3):229–260, 2002.
[2] C. Combi, M. Franceschet, and A. Peron. Representing and reasoning about temporal granularities. *JLC*, 14(1):51–77, 2004.
[3] C.S. Jensen, R.T. Snodgrass, and M.D. Soo. Extending existing dependency theory to temporal databases. *IEEE TKDE*, 8(4):563–581, 1996.
[4] M. Levine, C. Sawka, and D. Bowman. Clinical practice guidelines for the care and treatment of breast cancer: 8. adjuvant systemic therapy for women with node-positive breast cancer (2001 update). *Canadian Medical Association journal*, page 164, 2001.
[5] J.D. Ullman. *Principles of Database and Knowledge-Base Systems*. Computer Science Press, 1988.
[6] V. Vianu. Dynamic functional dependency and database aging. *Journal ACM*, 34(1):28–59, 1987.
[7] X. Sean Wang, C. Bettini, A. Brodsky, and S. Jajodia. Logical design for temporal databases with multiple granularities. *IEEE TKDE*, 22(2):115–170, 1997.
[8] J. Wijsen. Design of temporal relational databases based on dynamic and temporal functional dependencies. In J. Clifford and A. Tuzhilin, editors, *Workshop on Temporal Databases*, pages 61–76. Springer, 1995.
[9] J. Wijsen. Temporal FDs on complex objects. *ACM TODS*, 24(1):127–176, 1999.

Device Cooperative Web Browsing and Retrieving Mechanism on Ubiquitous Networks

Yutaka Kidawara[1], Koji Zettsu[1,2],
Tomoyuki Uchiyama[2], and Katsumi Tanaka[1,2]

[1] Interactive Communication Media and Contents Group
National Institute of Information and Communications Technology
3-5 Hikaridai, Seika-cho, Soraku-gun,Kyoto, 619-0289, Japan
TEL: +81-774-98-6886, FAX: +81-774-98-6959
{kidawara,zettsu}@nict.go.jp

[2] Department of Social Informatics, Graduate School of Informatics
Kyoto University
Yoshida-Honmachi, Sakyo-ku, Kyoto, 606-8501 Japan
TEL: +81-75-753-5385, FAX: +81-75-753-4957
{tomoyuki,tanaka}@dl.kuis.kyoto-u.ac.jp

Abstract. We propose a new concept for displaying, browsing, and retrieving web content in public spaces via a ubiquitous network. The new type of content operation, described in this paper, is semantically synchronized and based on *Device Cooperative Browsing* and *Device Cooperative Retrieval*. These are interactive methods of browsing and retrieving content related to that currently being viewed by the user. The operating mechanism is based on multiple devices connected via a peer-to-peer network. The mechanism operates cooperatively to find each user's individual interests and it maintains information about them. Multiple devices sharing common information might thus have common topics of interest listed on various user devices. When new devices are connected in this environment, they detect the required information through filtering, and obtain it from other devices in the local ubiquitous network. In addition to describing this concept, we also discuss the *WebBoard*, which is a successful implementation of our novel approach.

1 Introduction

Various network-accessible devices are expected to be installed ubiquitously, indoors and out, in the not too distant future. The evolution of communication and device technologies will enable us to progress onto the next-generation communications tool, called the "ubiquitous Internet". Many researchers have already studied technologies for ubiquitous and pervasive computing. They have focused on the development of an infrastructure and framework for dealing with several types of devices. Far less attention has been paid to what content should be browsed and how information from physical material in the real world should be obtained. Ubiquitous and pervasive computing technology enables physical materials to be distributed via information directories on a network. Various physical materials have RFID tags and small microprocessors attached, which can be annotated and browsed for their characteristic descriptions. Moreover, we can use various suitable cooperative devices for browsing and manipulating the characteristics of content to do more effective research. In this paper, we describe the concept behind Device Cooperative Content and its operating mechanism, which enable us to extract personalized information from common public content and monitor that which has captured our interest. We propose the *WebBoard*, which is a browsing system used cooperatively in some devices, outdoors or indoors. Section 2 explains the operating concept behind ubiquitous content. We also describe Device Cooperative Browsing and Device Cooperative Retrieval. Section 3 describes their implementation and experiments we did with the WebBoard. Section 4 discusses related work and Section 5 is the conclusion.

2 Operating Concept behind Digital Content on Ubiquitous Network Environment

A ubiquitous network requires a more complex network configuration. The network is not only a global network connected with the Internet, but also a local network that is not connected to it. Various devices have network connection capabilities and distribute various kinds of content on it. The information in devices is transmitted to other locations, connects with other local P2P networks, and is distributed to other devices.

For instance, a user can connect to the Internet in his/her home. However, when they get on a bus or train, they may not be connected and can only connect their devices to a local network and access local information from this.

When this happens, the user's devices and those connected locally make up a local P2P network. Information should be shared by users with common profiles. Some of the devices distribute their own information to other devices and share common interests. Information delivery is like the evaporation and solidification of materials. Information evaporates, or is disseminated, from stored devices into the network and is solidified, or incorporated, in appropriate devices.

In public areas, we find various kinds of information emanating from real objects (e.g. flowers, animals, and signboards). Each object has characteristic information and various related information, which depend on the location and the objects's properties. We often understand what the real object means and discuss this referring to related content, which is based on the context. In such cases, people retrieve related content and demonstrate their understanding within the context. A ubiquitous network enables such procedures to work on various digital devices cooperatively. The necessary devices are connected and information is shared by peer-to-peer networks. We have to develop not only ubiquitous computing technology, but also content distribution and operation management on ubiquitous devices to be able to use them practically in the ubiquitous Internet age. We will describe our concept for manipulating content with cooperative devices in what follows.

2.1 Device Cooperative Browsing

We often search for surrounding or related content, which is not only web content but also various multimedia content, when we browse for material we are interested in. In such situations, we open many windows so that we can see them all on the display. We expect that such a browsing style will change on the ubiquitous Internet. Users can browse for surrounding or related content on different devices connected to a network when the main web content is being displayed on the main devices.

In particular, web content displayed on public display monitors like sign boards and bulletin boards in public areas cannot be changed based on the requests of a few people. These monitors are only for public and not for private use. Current mobile network technology enables us to obtain more information from the Internet on handy phones when we are interested in content on public monitors. However, content synchronization is based on users' activities. We have to read, search for, and understand the content topic when we are interested in information. We also have to try to connect to the Internet, search for related content, and browse for this when we want to obtain more information quickly. If we do not have time to browse in the field, we might want to record observations and browse these later at home. In such situations, however, we can only take pictures with digital cameras and send them as e-mail attachments at present.

If our personal devices provided a directory for content on monitors, we could browse not only the displayed content but also a variety of related content. The peer-to-peer (P2P) network technology, which has been proposed by many researchers, enables us to use such communications. The web content on network-accessible monitors should have functionality in providing not only displayed but also additional information. The content can be influenced by the location the monitor is mounted in. Reliability is important and essential information behind web content that is dependent on the location is necessary. This content and related material should be able to be passed to users' personal devices when they request more information. *Cooperative Device Browsing* is where a device displays some content, manages each related content item by itself, distributes these when other devices are browsing, and requests one item from the content shown. The concept also applies to real physical objects that have RFID tags or small microprocessors attached. Users can browse related information while looking at real objects instead of digital representations on the monitor.

2.2 Device Cooperative Retrieval

Device Cooperative Retrieval is the opposite of *Device Cooperative Browsing*. The *Device Cooperative Browsing* mechanism provides not only the original, but also surrounding and related information based on context, which the information owners intended to provide.

The mechanism works effectively when an information provider has the capability of arranging information clearly in cases like advertisements. His/her own context is often displayed so that the specified information can be explained.

However, we try to understand the meaning using our own knowledge and context when we find unknown information. If we cannot understand it, we discuss it with other people within our own context, which consists of the keywords and content that is retrieved. We compare the unknown information and well known information involved within our context. We try to understand it searching for similar content from the content set within our context.

Device Cooperative Retrieval depends on the user knowing his/her context in order to retrieve information. He/she stores@the context on his/her personal device, which distributes this to public display monitors that reveal the retrieved content set located by his/her context keywords. He/She compares the retrieved information and searches similar content. Each personal device distributes various contexts to other devices. All the devices on the P2P network share and operate content based on the context cooperatively.

3 Implementation and Experiment with WebBoard

We have already developed the middleware for extended SMIL content, which we proposed as *Device Cooperative Content* [1]. We extended it to the *WebBoard* so that the *WebBoard Controller* could communicate with the *Owner's PC*. The extended middleware supports the new SOAP protocol. Furthermore, the related-content-retrieval function is also supported by the latest version of the middleware.

The *WebBoard* supplies related content to that pasted to the browsing device to which the user is connected through P2P networks. The function to retrieve related web content searches it automatically through the following steps.

It obtains the URL of the pasted Web content in the region, and calls Google-API to retrieve related content with its search engine (Step 1). All the retrieved web content is temporarily placed in the storage area (Step 2). The retrieval result does not consider profiles. The function then calculates their relevance according to the profiles. The document feature vector over all profile keywords is calculated for every item of stored content with a tf-idf ranking (Step 3). Cosine similarity is calculated between the query feature vector and every stored content feature vector (Step 4). The function ranks content according to similarities (Step 5). These functions are provided by the middleware.

We developed a prototype system to confirm the usefulness of Device Cooperative Content on a ubiquitous network. The *WebBoard* displays web content from the semantic region on the screen for the public area, which is based on the *Device Cooperative Browsing* concept. The basic concept is the application of data distribution in the real world to the digital world. The system consists of the following equipment (See Fig.1).

- **Device to Provide Content:** The device requests that it wants to paste specific web content on the *WebBoard controller*. The application, which

works on a PC or PDA, manages user profiles and semantical group information. Every piece of information and request is communicated to the the WebBoard Controller by SOAP.
- **WebBoard Monitor and Controller:** The *WebBoard Monitor* consists of a large-screen display, a touch panel, and a PC that manages the arranged content on the screen. The *WebBoard Controller* is a PC that regulates the pasted content and annotation management applications. The controller also manages related content, the owner's profile information, regional information on the board, and pasted web content. The software communicates with the owner's *WebBoard Controller*, which controls the display items and distributes information. User profile information, pasted web page information, and regional information are shared between the controller and personal devices. Several groups, which the board owner creates semantically on his/her PC, can appear as planes on the board. For instance, if the owner creates a *"hobby"* group to classify his interests on the WebBoard Controller, an *"hobby"* plane appears on the screen of the *WebBoard Monitor*. Also, a web page, which is annotated by the owner, appears on the *"hobby"* plane of the screen when he/she places it into the group window on the *WebBoard Controller*. Furthermore the *WebBoard Controller* retrieves related content from the Internet automatically. The retrieval function is not as complicated in the current version. The controller just retrieves the related pages through Google API and prepares a content list with profile keywords. In addition, the controller creates a tf-idf weighting feature vector for every content item. The controller calculates and compares each feature vector for pasted content and other content retrieved by Google. Similarity is calculated by the *Cosine Correlation*. The retrieved content information, user profile, and regional profile are managed by an XML database, Xindice.
- **Personal Browsing Device:** Users looking at the *WebBoard* may be interested in some of its content. The *Personal Browsing Device* works when he/she is not satisfied with the information because it is too limited. His/Her *Personal Browsing Device* has functions that communicate with the *WebBoard Controller* and exchange user requests and selected content information with it on the local P2P network. Furthermore, the device stores query keywords as context, which is shared between devices and the *WebBoard*.

3.1 Device Cooperative Browsing

We conducted experiments browsing *WebBoard* content based on *Device Cooperative Browsing* (see Fig.2). We found that all functions worked effectively on our prototype system. A board owner could select and place content of interest (computer) into the "hobby" and "work" groups. No sooner was the selected page placed into the group windows, than it was shown as content on the WebBoard screen. The *WebBoard Controller* found that the content took on two meanings as hobby and work. The controller resized both regions and laid them out on the overlapping area. The user could therefore establish that the item

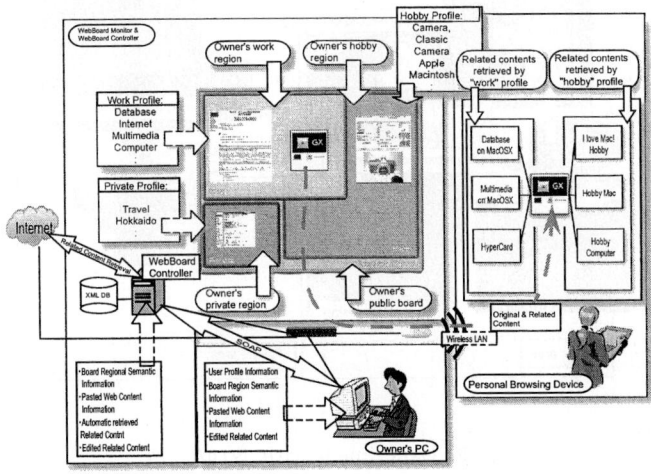

Fig. 1. System Configuration for *WebBoard*

had a couple of meanings and this enabled him/her to browse related content from two different perspectives on his/her browser.

The user then looked at the pasted web content and pointed to it on the board. The *WebBoard Controller* selected this and distributed content information, which involved the related content list and original content, to the *Personal Browsing Device*. If the user understood the importance of the information after browsing related content, he/she could store and bring it back to his/her office. Here, they could find the most important content because various related content had been browsed and differences found. Users returning to their offices could also paste this on their *WebBoards*. They could edit related content or retrieve more automatically based on their individual profile information. Selection depended on their decisions.

We confirmed useful and intuitive content distribution in the real world. The distribution method was based on the fact that we bring our interests with us everywhere at all times.

3.2 Device Cooperative Retrieval

We conducted experiments retrieving similar content based on *Device Cooperative Retrieval* (See Fig.3). We used some of our own contexts in searching for similar content from specified content. The Personal Browsing Device (PBD) stores its owner's context, which means the user's property information to retrieve content. We defined that context is a keyword set, which can be explained by the user's interest. If a person is interested in "Formula-one Car Racing", his/her context for the interest may be explained by keywords, e.g. "F1","Ferrari","

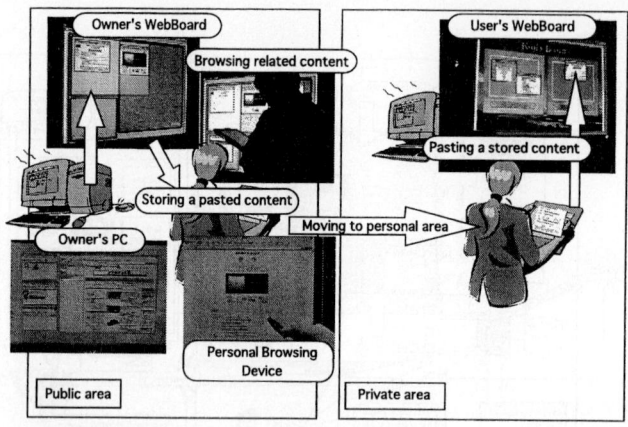

Fig. 2. Experiment with *WebBoard*

Schumacher", and "F2004". We expect that he/she will try to find information related to the "Ferrari Formula-one Team" when he/she retrieves content on his/her interest. His/her friend may be interested in travel and the context may also be explained by keywords, e.g. "Europe", "France", and "Paris". He/She may retrieve European travel information as a result. When people try to go on trips together, they may search common information of interest using their contexts. The contexts are provided by his/her keywords to the *WebBoard* system, which are explained by his/her interests. When the context is provided to the *WebBoard controller*, the display shows it as a context plane. The controller prepares a content set based on the context so that it can send query keywords to Google API. The Google search engine provides the retrieved content lists to the controller, which creates a tf-idf weighting feature vector for every item of content. Pasted content that the *Content Providing Device* provides to the *WebBoard* can be moved onto the context plane. The controller recalculates the feature vector and searches similar content using the *Cosine Correlation* between the feature vector for pasted content and other content when they overlap the plane. In addition, the controller provides a content list to each PBD that distributes the context. A user can browse similar content on his/her PBD and on the *WebBoard*, cooperatively. If users select content on their PBD, it is highlighted on the *WebBoard*. The context plane can be operated intuitively in order to change the retrieved results. Two types of intuitive operations have been done, which are "stretching plane" and "overlapping plane". Stretching changes the similarity ranking level of content to be displayed. As a result, this changes the amount of content displayed. Overlapping means the intersection between content sets. If one overlaps some context planes, the *WebBoard* creates a content set based on the common properties of the selected contexts. The controller, in fact, selects common content included in each context. The user can search similar content using his/her context and other people's when the selected content is moved onto the overlapping context plane.

The operations, in practice, are worked on the *WebBoard* intuitively. (See Fig.3). First, the user selects his/her context information (1) and distributes his/her context for the interest (motor sport) in the PBD to the *WebBoard Controller*. The *WebBoard* displays the hobby context plane (2) including the keywords ,"F1", "Ferrari", "Schumacher", and "F2004". He/She also distributes his/her content of interest on his/her *Content Providing Device* to the *WebBoard*, which appears on the screen. After the user has dragged it onto the context plane, the *WebBoard Controller* calculates the feature vector and shows similar content (3). Six types of content can be shown by default plane size. Users can browse more content when they stretch the plane size (4). Next, another user can distribute another context plane with the context of "travel". The context is included the keywords, "Europe", "France", "Paris", and "Spain". His/Her context can be shown as another context plane (5). Users can drag the content onto the plane because they are browsing similar content using other contexts. The *WebBoard* shows similar content on another plane (6). After browsing this, the user can overlap both planes. If they move a plane onto another, the planes overlap and the *WebBoard Controller* selects common content. This means the intersection of both contexts. The controller recalculates every feature vector and searches similar content. As a result, the *WebBoard* displays a similar content set from the intersection of both context content sets (7). They can find travel information to watch the "F1 Grand Prix in Spain". The *WebBoard* and all PBDs that are provided with a context plane work cooperatively. Selected content is displayed on each plane and the content is shown on the PBD storing the context (8).

4 Related Work

Our proposed mechanism works on a peer-to-peer network. A variety of approaches have already been proposed. In the ubiquitous computing area, the main issue is the synthesis of network services. Wapplet[4] and STONE[5] have also focused on synthesizing network services. These proposed technologies aim at functional integration on a ubiquitous network. Our main objective is creating useful content on a ubiquitous network, which is quite different from their objective. Development of devices on a ubiquitous network is also the main concern in this area. Our proposed application," *WebBoard* ", uses a device that browses and stores content on a board. The device has to have functions that enable communications, storage of content, and browsing capabilities. MediaBox [6, 7] and Personal Server [8] also have communications and content-storage functions. However, these are portable communications attachments mounted on ubiquitous devices. They only provide content to other devices through networks or wireless communications methods and do not allow the capability of browsing related content. *WebBoard* has the potential of organizing material from mixed digital and physical environments. This organization has recently focused on the

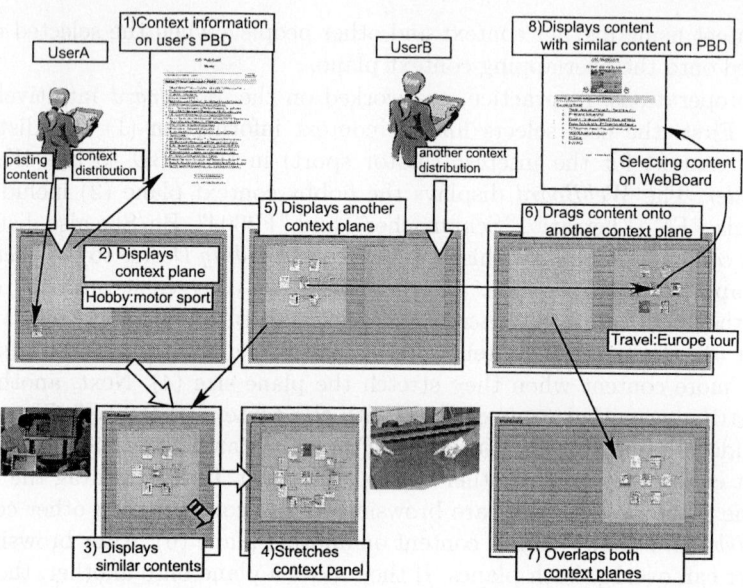

Fig. 3. Experiment on Device Cooperative Retrieval with *WebBoard*

Hypermedia research area. Physical Hypermedia [9] uses three kinds of tags that combine physical material with digital objects. Simple object tags and collectional tags are linked to the digital object. Tool tags are linked to operations in the digital world. HyperReal [10] provides a hypermedia framework to construct context aware and mixed realities. The proposed model specifies the relation between real and virtual space. The Ambient Wood Journal [11] aims to facilitate learning experiments in outdoor environments. It can record children's activities on detailed logs in portable devices. The recorded logs are displayed as journals on the web. This research is extremely interesting. *WebBoard* should be of tremendous help in assisting us to organize physical material in the real world.

5 Conclusion

Device cooperative operation is the most@useful function in ubiquitous computing. However, as content has not been stressed, we proposed *Device Cooperative Content* as being the most useful, ubiquitously. Furthermore, we also proposed an operating mechanism for this. We believe content is very important with the new computing technology. The World Wide Web (WWW) is a killer content and is an application of the Internet. However, if the WWW had not developed about ten years ago, the Internet could not have become as popular as it is today. The *WebBoard* is a new type of content browser, distribution, and retrieval application. The data distribution and retrieval procedures are intuitive. There are people walking currently about with handyphones, PDAs, and digital music players. Storing a variety of information within the city in personal devices is a very intuitive and natural activity. Furthermore, intuitive retrieval and seeing related content makes us understand what the content means. This application is obviously suitable for educational areas. No sooner do students raise questions, than they can browse a variety of content and search for answers. If they cannot find this, they have reached a rich communications environment and can search for additional information later. We confirmed the usefulness of the prototype. The content service, which the prototype provided, had never been experienced. We found the possibility of new content operation on the ubiquitous Internet. However, we discovered new concerns affecting our proposed content and operating mechanism. The *WebBoard* can browse for content related to that on the board. Although the current automatic retrieval function is very simple, we developed complicated context-based retrieval to browse for more useful content. The development of additional functions remains as future work.

References

1. Y. Kidawara, K. Zettsu, and M. Katsumoto: A Distribution Mechanism for an Active User Profile in a Ubiquitous Network Environment Laboratory, PACRIM, 2003.
2. S. Shinomiya, Y. Kidawara, T. Sakurada, S. Tsuchiike, and S. Nakagawa: "NADIA: Network Accessible Device on the Internet Architecture", IEEE ICOIN-16, Vol. III, pp. 8D-4.1-4.11, Jan. 2002
3. Y. Kidawara, S. Shinomiya, T. Sakurada, H. Nagata, and S. Nakagawa: "Device Cooperation and Content Management for Remote-control Microscope for Medical Use", IEEE AINA, Mar. 2003.
4. M. Murase, T. Iwamoto, T. Nagata, N. Nishio, and H. Tokuda: "Implementation and Evaluation of Wapplet Framework" IEEE International Workshop on Networked Appliances (IWNA), pp. 275-284, Jan. 2002.
5. M. Minami, H. Morikawa, and T. Aoyama: Ad-hoc Service Composition Framework for Networked Functions - STONE: Service synThesizer On the NEt , JPSJ DICOMO, pp. 13-18, Jun. 2000.
6. B. Ullmer, H. Ishii, and D. Glas: MediaBlocks: Physical Containers, Transports, and Controls for Online Media, In Computer Graphics Proceedings of SIGGRAPH'98, pp. 379-386, Jul. 1998.
7. B. Ullmer and H. Ishii: MediaBlocks: Tangible Interfaces for Online Media. In Extended Abstracts of CHI'99, pp. 31-32, May 1999.
8. R. Want,T. Pering, G. Danneels, M. Kumar, and M. Sundar, J. Light: The Personal Server: Changing the Way We Think about Ubiquitous Computing, In Proceedings of UBICOMP2002, pp. 194-209, Sep.-Oct. 2002.
9. K. Gronbak, J. F. Kristensen, P. Orbak, and M. A. Eriksen: Physical Hypermedia: Organizing Collections of Mixed Physical and Digital Material, In Proceedings of ACM HyperText '03, pp. 10-19, Aug. 2003.
10. L. Romero and N. Correia: HyperReal: A Hypermedia Model for Mixed Reality, In Proceedings of ACM HyperText '03, pp. 2-9, Aug. 2003.
11. M. J. Weal, D. T. Michaelides, M. K. Thompshon, and D. C. DeRoure: The Ambient Wood Journals - Replaying the Experience, In Proceedings of ACM HyperText '03,pp. 20-27, Aug. 2003.

A Flexible Security System for Enterprise and e-Government Portals

Torsten Priebe, Björn Muschall, Wolfgang Dobmeier, and Günther Pernul

Department of Information Systems
University of Regensburg, D-93040 Regensburg, Germany
{torsten.priebe,bjoern.muschall,guenther.pernul}@wiwi.uni-regensburg.de
wolfgang.dobmeier@gmx.de

Abstract. Web-based systems like enterprise and e-government portals pose special requirements to information security. Today's portal platforms provide some security functionality, mainly targeting at supporting a single-sign-on for the underlying applications. We argue that single-sign-on is not sufficient, but rather a mature security service is needed as a central authorization instance. As access control is needed on different levels of a portal architecture, only this allows an integrated approach to security management. We present CSAP (Communication Security, Authentication, and Privacy), a flexible security system for enterprise and e-government portals. CSAP was originally developed within the EU-funded research project "Webocracy". Meanwhile, various enhancements to CSAP have been made, which are being discussed in this paper. The major enhancement is a Metadata-based Access Control facility (MBAC) which allows more flexibility in highly open and heterogeneous systems. We use CSAP within two portal prototypes, one in an enterprise one in an e-government context, which are being presented as case studies.

1 Introduction

The use of Web-based portals has become a popular approach for providing an integrated user interface for different information sources and application systems in an intranet as well as Internet context. This is particularly true for an enterprise environment where employees, customers or suppliers are accessing such portals. However, also the public sector is employing similar technologies as part of its e-government initiatives. While portals integrate the applications by combining several user interface components (so called portlets) on a single portal webpage the backend integration has to be performed by other means. Technologies like Enterprise Application Integration (EAI) are evolving here. At the same time it is being recognized that in such global and integrated environments also (and in particular) security aspects cannot be properly addressed in an isolated fashion, either. Portals are required to provide a single-sign-on facility to avoid the necessity for users to authenticate themselves multiple times. However, single-sign-on is not enough. The administration of users, roles, etc. and their permissions on security objects also needs to be supported in an integrated way.

As an answer to these issues, we present CSAP, a flexible security system for enterprise and e-government portals. The CSAP security module was originally developed within the EU-funded research project "Webocracy" (IST-1999-20364). Meanwile, the Metadata-based Access Control (MBAC) model presented in section 3.2, as well as its implementation and further enhancements to the CSAP security module have been developed within the project "SEWISS", funded by the Bavarian Research Cooperation for Information Systems (FORWIN)[1].

The remainder of this paper is organized as follows: Section 2 introduces portal systems and gives an overview on security aspects, identifying authorization and access control as major issues. Section 3 discusses two access control models, the well established Role-based Access Control model (RBAC) as well as the novel Metadata-based Access Control model (MBAC). Both have been implemented within our CSAP security module which is being used in two portal prototypes. These are covered by section 4. Finally, section 5 concludes the paper by discussing possible future work.

2 Security in Portal Systems

Enterprise portals focus on corporate information and services being provided to employees (B2E, business-to-employee portals) or customers and suppliers (B2C/B2B portals). The goal is to provide the user with a consolidated, personalized user interface to all information he needs. Recently the term enterprise knowledge portal is more and more used instead of enterprise information portal. Advanced techniques try to help the user with accessing the right information at the right time. This implies the support of organizational learning and corporate knowledge processes.

In an e-government context similar techniques are being utilized to provide citizens with administrative information and to allow them to participate in democratic processes (G2C, government-to-citizen portals). In addition, G2B (government-to-business) portals support processes like public tendering.

One important property of such portals (in both, an enterprise and public context) is their openness. The number of users accessing the portal – consuming or publishing content – is usually very high. The same is true for the number of information objects (e.g. documents), possibly containing sensitive information. Obviously, these conditions lead to special security requirements. Like for most information systems the major security services needed are user identification and authentication and authorization and access control. When a user has been identified (e.g. by a username) and authenticated (e.g. by a password) authorization deals with managing the permissions which define which users can access certain information or system functions. Access control checks these permissions at run time avoiding unauthorized access.

Access control in portals has to be applied on different levels. Firstly, portal platforms provide access control on a structural level, defining which users can

---

[1] http://www.forwin.de.

access which parts of the portal (i.e. which portlets can be viewed, configured, etc.). On the other hand, access control for the actual content, e.g. individual documents, is performed within the portlets. Often this access control is even enforced by the underlying applications rather than the portlets themselves which represent only user interface components. The portlets usually use only the authentication (login) feature of the portal to provide a single-sign-on capability. However, a truly integrated approach to authorization and access control is highly desirable in order to be able to provide centralized and integrated security management.

3 Access Control Models

A security system that can be used portal-wide (and possibly even by the underlying applications) needs to be flexible enough to support different environments. For many applications with structured security requirements (especially in an organizational context) the well-established Role-based Access Control model (RBAC) is very suitable and can be seen as a de-facto standard. Section 3.1 gives a short overview of this model.

However, in rather open and heterogeneous applications the security requirements are hard to model in form of structured role hierarchies. To address such environments we have developed a more flexible Metadata-based Access Control model (MBAC) which will be described in section 3.2. We argue that a flexible security system for enterprise and e-government portals should support both role- and metadata-based access control.

3.1 Role-Based Access Control

The concept of Role-based Access Control (RBAC) [7] has evolved to the de-facto standard in enterprise multi-user systems, involving a large (but structured) number of users with different rights and obligations as well as a large amount of sensitive data. In contrast to simpler earlier access control approaches RBAC simplifies the administration of access permissions by means of roles which can be derived from the organizational structure.

Experiences in organizational practice show that the definition of roles as part of the organizational structure can be seen as relatively stable while the assignment of users to roles in comparison changes more frequently. This assignment can be abolished without affecting the definition of a role itself while on the other hand the role's definition can be modified without interfering with the assignment. Furthermore, by assigning different users to the same role and different roles to the same user, redundancy can be avoided.

In [7] a standard for Role-based Access Control has been proposed. The RBAC reference model is divided into submodels which embody different subsets of the functionality.

Core RBAC covers the essential aspects such that permissions are assigned to roles and roles are assigned to users. It comprises five basic element sets. Users are active elements that can be human beings as well as software artefacts. Roles correspond to fields of activities of users. These activities are bound to permissions needed to carry them out. Only such permissions should be assigned to a role that are absolutely necessary to fulfill the corresponding activities. A permission is a certain operation (e.g. read) that can be executed on a certain object. Objects and operations reflect arbitrary system objects and methods at different levels of granularity. A session represents the context in which a sequence of activities is executed.

In addition to Core RBAC, Hierarchical RBAC introduces a partial order between the roles, an inheritance relation where senior roles acquire the permissions of their juniors and junior roles acquire the user membership of their seniors. There may be general permissions that are needed by a large number of users and consequently may be assigned to a more general role. Finally, Constraint RBAC assumes that there are relations or exclusions between some fields of activity and allows to define separation of duty constraints to enforce conflict of interest policies.

3.2 Metadata-Based Access Control

The Role-based Access Control model presented in the previous subsection simplifies the administration of authorizations. However, for very large open systems such as digital libraries, enterprise or e-government portals, or hospital systems, the role hierarchies can become very complex. When the number of protected objects also increases, a manual assignment of authorizations becomes very expensive and error-prone. Furthermore, in many situations access depends on contents of an object and the environment the subject is acting in. In these applications we need to deal with users not previously registered. The Metadata-based Access Control model provides a more convenient and efficient way to manage access rights for these situations.

The basic idea is to utilize (possibly dynamic) properties of subjects and objects as the basis for authorization, rather than directly (and statically) defining access rights between users, roles, and objects. On the user side, an attribute could be his position within an organization, quite similar to a role. Especially for external users however, acquired credentials (e.g. subscriptions, customer status) or attributes such as age or shipping address may need to be used instead. For the security objects, the content, e.g. of documents, can be described by means of metadata. Such metadata elements should be used for authorization purposes.

Two primary directions of research have evolved. The first derives from research on security for digital libraries. [1] propose a Digital Library Access Control Model (DLAM), which defines access rights according to properties associated with subjects and objects. The second important direction of research has its origin in the area of public key infrastructures (PKI) and is based on the use of certificates for authentication. A widespread standard for certificates is X.509 [8], which enables the user to employ his private key for authentication, while the respective addressee is using the certified corresponding public key for checking the claimed identity. In addition to the public key, also other attributes can be assigned to the owner of a certificate. [2] proposes to use these attributes for authorization and access control purposes.

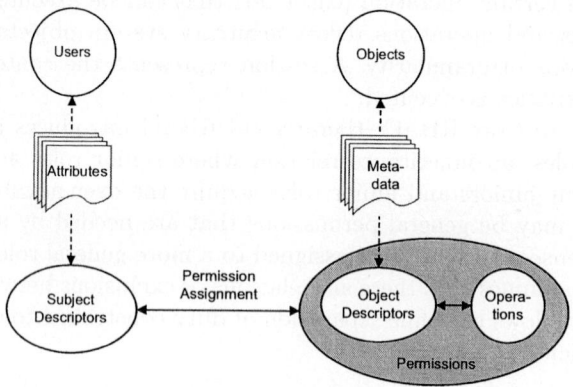

Fig. 1. MBAC model

Figure 1 shows the elements of the Metadata-based Access Control model. A subject is represented by a number of attributes (also called credentials). Similarily, an object (i.e. a resource to be protected) is described by a number of properties. The permissions are no longer assigned between subjects and objects but between subject and object descriptors. A subject descriptor consists of a number of attribute qualifiers (e.g. age > 18, ZIP code begins with "93") and can be seen as a "virtual subject" that can possibly relate to multiple real subjects. The same is true for the object descriptors. Here qualifiers are defined on the basis of object properties, e.g. concerns a certain project, published by a certain publisher.

The MBAC model has been described in detail as a security pattern in [9]. In order to reach more flexibility, enhanced (more complex) versions of the MBAC model have been developed. These enhancements have also been described as security patterns reusing the basic MBAC pattern.

The first enhancement concerns the principle of "least privileges" and introduces a session concept as known from RBAC. The user has the option to activate only a subset of the attributes assigned to him within a session. This might also help to enhance user privacy. A user will potentially only want to disclose personal data (e.g. age or sex) if it is indispensable for the task he intends to perform[2]. For example, an e-commerce system selling adult entertainment needs to know the age of a customer before granting him access to its products. If attributes are assumed to be centrally stored and managed, users have only

---

[2] See also the controlled disclosure of personal properties on the Internet in P3P (Platform for Privacy Preferences) [12].

limited control over the use of their personal data. The idea of storing user attributes in attribute certificates rather than in a central database may help to overcome this issue.

A second enhancement to the MBAC model introduces predicates. While the basic MBAC model only allows the use of constant values to define subject and object descriptors, predicates allow comparisons between attribute and property values. For example an object within a digital library might have the property "publisher". A user might pay a subscription fee for accessing content by a certain publisher, represented by an attribute "subscribed for". A predicate could define that a certain permission can only be utilized if the user's "subscribed for" attribute matches the "publisher" property of the object to be accessed.

4 Implementation and Prototypes

4.1 Enhanced CSAP Security Module

As mentioned before the authors have been involved in the EU-funded project "Webocracy" in which the "Webocrat" e-government portal has been developed (presented in section 4.2). Within this project our primary task was to implement a security management module called CSAP (Communication Security, Authentication and Privacy) whose purpose is to form the basis of trust for the whole system by offering "practical and consistent" security. This has been achieved by providing services for user identification and authentication, access control and authorization, auditing, and session management.

CSAP was designed to satisfy differing requirements by providing alternative implementations of security services via a plug-in concept. The original version of CSAP developed within "Webocracy" [4] implements a password-based authentication scheme and an RBAC access control capability. In order to be more flexible and applicable for a wider range of applications, we have enhanced CSAP to provide also an MBAC access control service. An authentication mechanism based on X.509 certificates [8] is subject to current work (see section 5). The goal is to provide a security system that is suitable as a central security component for enterprise and e-government portals addressing the demands stated in section 2.

The overall architecture of CSAP is shown in figure 2. It consists of two layers: the service layer where the actual security services are implemented, and a data layer that defines a generic interface in order to access the security metadata independently of the storage technology of choice. Note that the dashed lines in the figure symbolize components that have not yet been fully implemented.

CSAP is implemented as a Java class library but has also been designed for being used in a distributed environment. That is, it offers RMI access to its services via the API. All data objects like a user or a session object can be serialized and sent over a network as parameters to the remote services. This allows the distribution of services to different machines, e.g. for balancing system load. Moreover, it allows CSAP to be accessed remotely by different applications at the same time as a single central security instance.

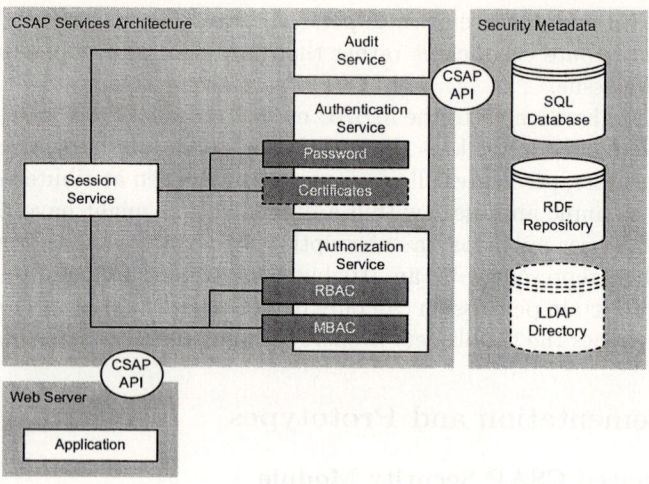

Fig. 2. CSAP architecture

Another aspect in this context is the multiple use of sessions. After a user has been authenticated, a session object is created. This session can be used by different applications independently of each other. This way, a session that is globally established by the authentication dialog of a portal can be reused on various levels by other components, i.e. portlets or underlying application systems, providing a single-sign-on facility.

As mentioned earlier, we extended CSAP by an MBAC access control service. In the current version the implementation covers the MBAC model in its basic form, i.e. it does not support predicates and sessions. The implementation is done as an additional authorization service which can be accessed via corresponding API methods. It can be used together with the RBAC service, thus multiple access control models are available in a single instance of CSAP. This facilitates a deployment in environments with the need for different access control methods.

The implementation is based on the MBAC pattern presented in [9]. Its structure was converted into an ER model and integrated into the CSAP database design for the security metadata. To improve the performance when a large number of access control requests needs to be executed in a short time (e.g. by a search engine, where the search results are to be checked before being presented to the user), we implemented the option to precalculate and store all subject descriptors that match a certain subject. We plan to expand this caching approach to the object descriptors and objects, respectively.

4.2 e-Government Portal "Webocrat"

As mentioned before the authors have been involved in the research project "Webocracy". The "Webocrat" portal developed within the project is an example of innovative use of state-of-the-art technologies to provide citizens, businesses, and government agencies with more convenient access to governmental information and services. The project's main goal is to develop and investigate Internet and Web technologies which increase the quality of the offered services, improve efficient and transparent access and consequently provide greater opportunities to participate directly in democratic processes.

The "Webocrat" e-government portal provides a central user interface, which integrates several application systems like discussion and opinion polling rooms, components for knowledge management, tools for content management and publishing, and finally systems for intelligent retrieval of information and explorative analysis of data. All modules share common access to the central CSAP security module. For details see [6].

Within "Webocrat" we are now evaluating the enhancements (e.g. the MBAC access control service) that have been made to the original CSAP module.

4.3 Enterprise Knowledge Portal "INWISS"

A prototype of an integrative enterprise knowledge portal called "INWISS" [10] is in development within another project of the authors' group. In this project we integrate various knowledge management components through a portal in such a way that user actions within one portlet can be propagated to others. For example, if a user navigates in an OLAP report through slicing/dicing or drilling, a search engine can evaluate the user's current query context to offer relevant documents from the Internet or a document management system. We use context-related metadata based on RDF [11] for that purpose. An overview of the architecture is provided in figure 3.

The Apache Jetspeed framework[3] provides the basis for the portal user interface for which we developed an OLAP portlet to display OLAP reports accessing a data warehouse, a search portlet to perform semantic (metadata-based) searches, and a news portlet as an example for native portal content.

The CSAP Security Module is the central instance where users are authenticated and access control is performed, triggered from various layers of the architecture. We modified the login service in Jetspeed to use CSAP to perform the desired authentication and create a user session. The session data is put into the Jetspeed environment, ready to be used by other components of the portal. We also connected the user administration of Jetspeed to CSAP in a way that the management of a user's properties (e.g. password) or adding new users can be done via the Jetspeed security administration portlet. This way, one security module can be used for almost all components of the portal, avoiding heterogeneous and decentralized security administration.

The semantic search engine provides a possibility to (explicitly and implicitly) search for documents on the basis of metadata and an enterprise ontology. For access control, we use our metadata-based approach as described in section 3.2. While the metadata for the subjects (i.e. the user attributes) is kept in the CSAP

---

[3] http://jakarta.apache.org/jetspeed/.

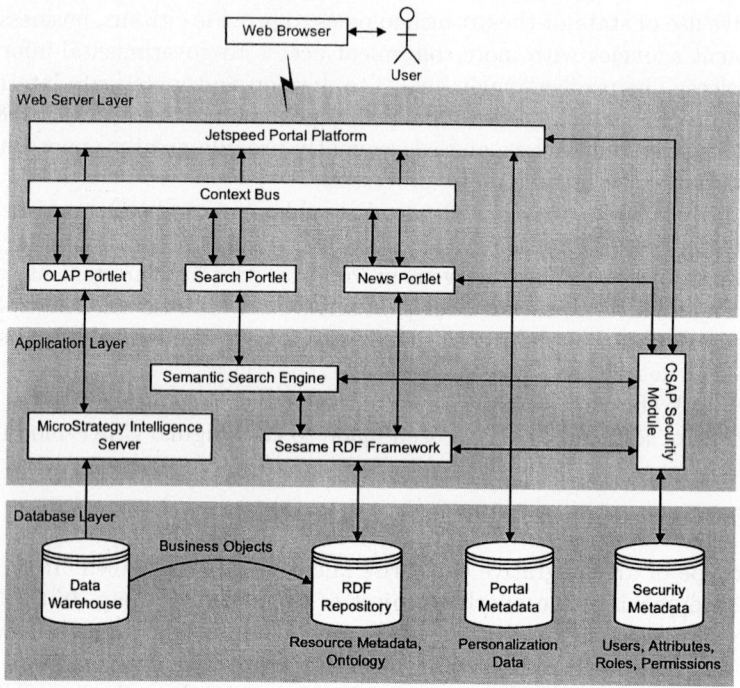

Fig. 3. "INWISS" enterprise knowledge portal prototype architecture

database, the object metadata is stored in a repository that is maintained by the Sesame RDF framework[4] [3].

5 Conclusions and Future Work

We have presented CSAP, a flexible security system for enterprise and e-government portals. We discussed two sample prototype portals that utilize the system as well as several enhancements to the system that have been made since the original version that has been implemented within the "Webocracy" project. The main enhancement was the Metadata-based Access Control (MBAC) facility. Some further technical improvements we are currently working on are an XML-based import/export facility for the security metadata and advanced analysis mechnisms for the audit trail.

As mentioned before an important motivation for an integrated security system like CSAP is to have a central point for security management. Users and security objects, as well as authorization entities like roles and subject or object descriptors, should be managed centrally. A first approach for such a security

---

[4] http://www.openrdf.org.

administration console has been presented in [5]. We are currently porting this console to a portlet implementation which allows integrating it into the portal user interface. The support for RDF-based object metadata has been another step towards application interoperability. On the user side we are working on supporting an LDAP directory for storing the users and user attributes respectively.

A further enhancement concerns the support for X.509 certificates for authentication as well as for attribute storage. PKI support, standardized interfaces (like LDAP) and additional security services (like timestamping) might turn CSAP into a service component suitable also for distributed authentication and authorization infrastructures (AAI).

References

1. Adam, N.R., Atluri, V., Bertino, E., Ferrari, E.: A Content-based Authorization Model for Digital Libraries. IEEE Transactions on Knowledge and Data Engineering, Volume 14, Number 2, March/April 2002.
2. Biskup, J.: Credential-basierte Zugriffskontrolle: Wurzeln und ein Ausblick. 32. Jahrestagung der Gesellschaft für Informatik e.v. (GI), Dortmund, Germany, September/October 2002, pp. 423-428.
3. Broekstra, J., Kampman, A., van Harmelen, F.: Sesame: A Generic Architecture for Storing and Querying RDF and RDF Schema. Proc. of the First International Semantic Web Conference (ISWC 2002), Sardinia, Italy, June 2002.
4. Dridi, F., Fischer, M., Pernul, G.: CSAP an adaptable security module for the e-government system Webocrat. Proc. of the 18th IFIP International Information Security Conference (SEC 2003), Athens, Greece, May 2003.
5. Dridi, F., Muschall, B., Pernul, G.: Administration of an RBAC System. Proc. of the 37th Annual Hawaii International Conference on System Sciences (HICSS'04), Big Island, Hawaii, USA, January 2004.
6. Dridi, F., Pernul, G., Sabol, T.: The Webocracy Project: Overview and Security Aspects. In: Schnurr, H.-P. et al. (Eds.): Professionelles Wissensmanagement: Erfahrungen und Visionen. Aachen, Germany, 2001.
7. Ferraiolo, D.F., Sandhu, R., Gavrila, S., Kuhn, D., and Chandramouli, R.: Proposed NIST Standard for Role-based Access Control. ACM Transactions on Information and Systems Security, Volume 4, Number 3, August 2001.
8. ITU-T Recommendation X.509: The Directory – Public Key and Attribute Certificate Frameworks. 2000.
9. Priebe, T., Fernandez, E.B., Mehlau, J.I., Pernul, G.: A Pattern System for Access Control. To appear in: Proc. of the Proc. 18th Annual IFIP WG 11.3 Working Conference on Data and Application Security, Sitges, Spain, July 2004.
10. Priebe, T., Pernul, G.: Towards Integrative Enterprise Knowledge Portals. Proc. of the Twelfth International Conference on Information and Knowledge Management (CIKM 2003), New Orleans, LA, USA, November 2003.
11. Resource Description Framework (RDF) Model and Syntax Specification. W3C Recommendation, 1999.
    http://www.w3.org/TR/1999/REC-rdf-syntax-19990222/
12. The Platform for Privacy Preferences 1.0 (P3P1.0) Specification. W3C Recommendation, 2002. http://www.w3.org/TR/2002/REC-P3P-20020416/

Guiding Web Search by Third-Party Viewpoints: Browsing Retrieval Results by Referential Contexts in Web

Koji Zettsu[1,2], Yutaka Kidawara[1], and Katsumi Tanaka[1,2]

[1] National Institute of Information and Communications Technology
3-5 Hikaridai, Seika-cho, Soraku-gun, Kyoto, 619-0289 Japan
TEL: +81-774-98-6887, FAX: +81-774-98-6959
{zettsu, kidawara}@nict.go.jp
[2] Department of Social Informatics, Graduate School of Informatics,
Kyoto University
Yoshida-Honmachi, Sakyo-ku, Kyoto, 606-8501 Japan
TEL: +81-75-753-5385, FAX: +81-75-753-4957
tanaka@dl.kuis.kyoto-u.ac.jp

Abstract. In a typical web search session, a user starts with partially defined queries which are refined as the user finds out more about the search domain. Conventional approaches emphasize narrowing the search, but pay little attention to outlining the scope of search, in which the user aggregates the retrieval results in a bottom-up approach. Although the standard technique is to cluster the page contents, this becomes difficult as the results contain a wide spectrum of page contents due to the fragmentary queries. In this paper, we propose an approach for outlining the scope of search based on "third-party viewpoints" on retrieval results. A web page is referred to by other web pages in various contexts through hyperlinks. The proposed method extracts an appropriate range of web contents surrounding the page as the referential context. By clustering similar contexts, web page "aspects" are discovered as generalized descriptions of the page references. Visualizing correlations between the page contents and the aspects helps a user find coherent semantic units of the retrieval results, which are classified into acknowledged pages, versatile pages, and alternative pages. We explain the details of the proposed method and a prototype implementation.

1 Introduction

As the web becomes widely used in our daily lives, people search the web for a wide spectrum of information related to, for example, business, travel, shopping, and education. Today, a web search engine, such as Google or Altavista, is the most popular tool for retrieving web information. However, it is often hard or impossible for a user to formulate a query precisely, because the user may not be familiar with the vocabulary appropriate for describing a topic of interest, or may wish to discover the general information. In such a situation, a user starts with partially defined queries which are refined as the user finds out more about the search domain. However, the user often fails to obtain the web page satisfying all of the queries. Even worse, the user should formulate another query by trial-and-error in order to find the alternative pages. Conventional approaches put the emphasis on narrowing the search, but pay little attention to figuring out the scope of search. It is important to discover the *context* in which the partially defined queries can be aggregated.

Our basic idea is to make use of *surrounding contents* of web pages for aggregation of retrieval results. A web page is linked to other web pages through various contexts, and the web contents surrounding a link anchor indicate a particular context. For example, a company's page might be referred to by a message on a discussion board about "secure jobs with good pay" or by a collection of links entitled "innovative research activity", while the company's page itself might contain only product and service information. We call context-based semantics, such as "secure jobs with good pay" and "innovative research activity", the *aspects* of the page to distinguish them from the page contents. Aggregating retrieval results according to their aspects facilitates positioning a search with respect to "third-party viewpoints", such as the reputations, roles, or subjects associated with the current scope of a search.

In this paper, we propose an approach for browsing through retrieval results based on their aspects. The rest of this paper is organized as follows. Section 2 explains the basic concept of our approach. Section 3 explains the mechanism for discovering the aspects of a web page. Section 4 explains the method for browsing through retrieval results by visualizing correlations between their page contents and aspects. Section 5 describes related work. Section 6 provides our conclusions and plans for future work.

2 Basic Concepts

2.1 Aspect of Web Page

A referential context of a web page is defined as a particular range of web contents "surrounding" the link anchor. Since the web consists of structured documents and hyperlinks, the referential context is represented not only by texts close to a link anchor, but also by the upper paragraphs of the link anchor and, possibly, the secondary link source pages. For example, if a web page is cataloged in a web directory, such as the Open Directory Project, the referential context is represented by the link anchor text and the category labels appear in the upper paragraphs and/or the index pages.

By clustering similar contexts, we can obtain more abstracted viewpoints regarding the references to web pages than we would from the individual contexts. An *aspect* of a web page means a generalized description of the referential contexts. Figure 1 shows an aspect discovery result. In Fig. 1, each set of keywords shows an aspect of a web page, and each edge indicates the association between the web page and the aspect. The edge label shows the strength of the association (see Section 3 for details).

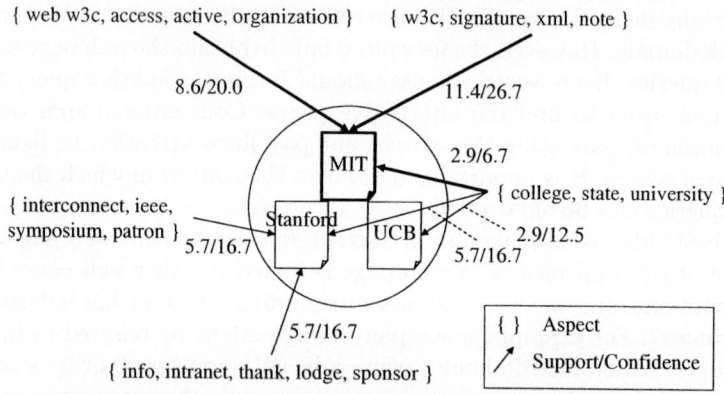

Fig. 1. Aspects of web pages. All pages, from three universities notable in computer science, are associated with the aspect {college, state, university}, which generally characterizes the universities' web pages. On the other hand, two aspects {web, w3, access, active, organization} and {w3c, signature, xml, note} are only associated with MIT's page. This means MIT's page is distinguished from the other two pages by these aspects. Considering that MIT is a core member of the W3C organization, which specializes in Web technology, and that the W3C office is located at MIT, this is a reasonable result

2.2 Characterization of Retrieval Results by Aspect

For each iteration of a query, the proposed approach discovers the aspects of the retrieval results accumulated throughout the search session. A user browses the association between the result page contents and the aspects in order to outline current scope of search. It facilitates local and relative positioning of the search in regard to the surrounding contents.

According to the aspects, the retrieval results are characterized as follows (as illustrated in Fig. 2).

(1) **Acknowledged pages:** Retrieval results that are similar with respect to both page contents and aspects indicate a strong correlation between the page contents and the aspects. For example, our preliminary experimental result says that "nature sounds" pages are typically associated with the aspect "CD, video sales". According to the aspect, a user can evaluate appropriateness of current scope of search. Moreover, the query can be localized with regard to the aspect.

(2) **Versatile pages:** Retrieval results similar with respect to page contents but dissimilar with respect to aspects indicate that the results are referred to differently by other users. Each aspect provides a hint for navigating the search to a particular domain. For example, when a user searches company pages for a new job, the user typically starts with the type of business. Although the retrieval results will be for the same type of business, some results might be referred to by the aspect "secure jobs with good pay" and other

results might be referred to by the aspect "innovative research activity". If the aspect "secure jobs with good pay" provokes the user's interest, the user will examine the pages with that aspect and refine the query to focus on such pages.

(3) **Alternative pages:** Retrieval results that are dissimilar regarding page contents, but similar regarding aspects indicate that various kinds of page are referred to in similar contexts. This means that the pages can be regarded as alternatives or competitive with each other. For example, when a user searches product pages while shopping, the user will often retrieve various product pages in parallel. Although each page contains individual product information, some product pages are referred to by similar aspects, such as "enterprise customers" or "business use". The user focuses on the product pages with a particular aspect and compares them with each other.

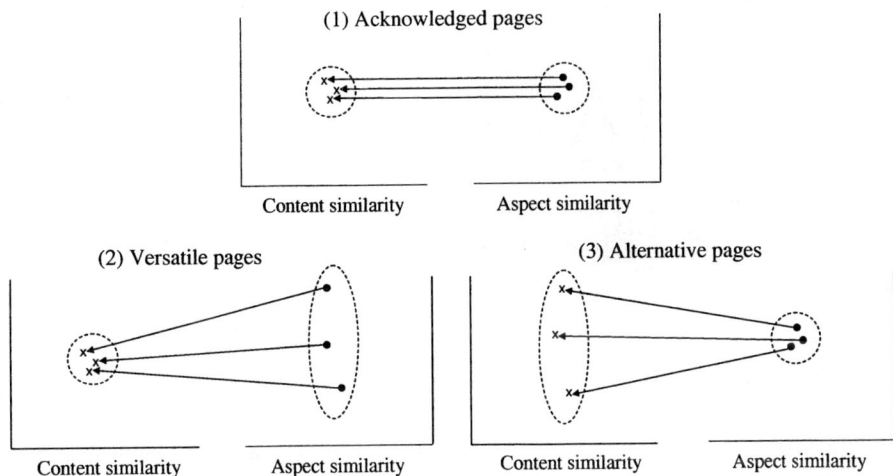

Fig. 2. Characterizing retrieval results by aspects

3 Aspect Discovery

The web is modeled as a directed graph $G = (V, E)$, in which each node $v \in V$ represents a document element defined by HTML/XML tags, and each edge $e \in E$ represents either a parent-child relation or a link between document elements (Fig. 3). The logical structure of the web can be viewed as recursive aggregations of document elements. This means a parent element aggregates its child elements and a link anchor element aggregates the target element. According to graph G, each document element on the path to the target page is treated as a potential aggregation element for the target page (the shaded node in Fig. 3). Once a document element on the aggregation path is set to be an aggregation element, the context of the target page is represented by the sub-tree rooted by the aggregation element (the shaded region in Fig. 3), and the reference to the page is represented by the aggregation path from the aggregation element to the page (the bold path in Fig. 3). Let $c(p)$ denote the context of web page p, where $c(p) = (V_c, E_c)$ $(V_c \subset V, E_c \subset E)$.

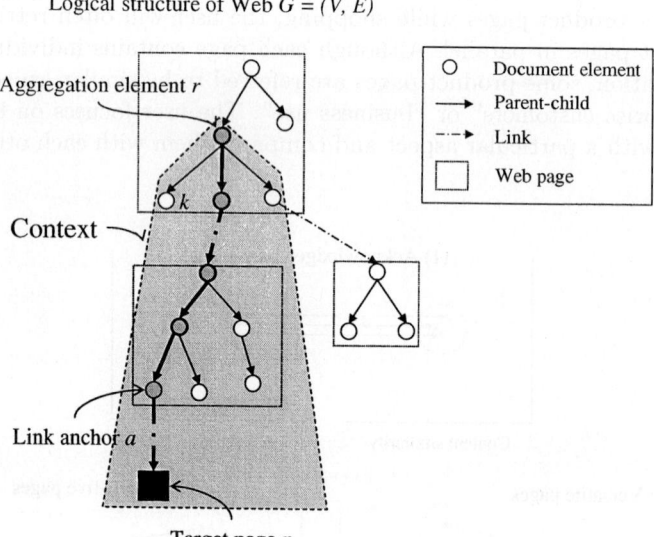

Fig. 3. Context of a media object in the web

The semantic content of a context $c(p)$ is characterized by the keywords that (1) appear close to the page p and (2) appear frequently in the context $c(p)$ but less frequently in other contexts. The first criterion is evaluated using the distance between the page and each keyword in the context. In Fig. 3, the distance between the target page p and the keyword k, denoted by $d(k,p)$, is indicated by the length of the path connecting p and the document element containing k. The second criterion is evaluated by the *tficf* degree, which is analogous to the tfidf degree [1]. The tficf degree of keyword k, denoted by $tficf(k)$, is calculated as the product of the tem frequency of keyword k (tf) in the context and the inverted context frequency of keyword k (icf). According to the above two criteria, the *context-contribution degree* of a keyword is defined to evaluate the significance of the keyword characterizing the context. It is calculated as follows:

$$ccd(k) = \frac{1}{d(k,p)} \cdot tficf(k). \qquad (1)$$

From each context, a set of keywords with the most significant context contribution degrees are extracted as the *context keywords*.

The range of context is determined by detecting significant changes in context keywords while extending the range from the target page. The resulting context represents a coherent semantic unit of the web contents aggregating the page. The process is conducted as follows:

1. Set the link anchor element of page p to the initial aggregation element r_0.
2. Set either the parent element or the link anchor element of the current aggregation element r_{i-1} to the new aggregation element r_i .
3. Extract the context $c_i(p)$ rooted by the aggregation element r_i.
4. Evaluate the change in context keywords between the previous context $c_{i-1}(p)$ and the current context $c_i(p)$ as follows:

$$shift(c_i(p)) = 1 - similar(\mathbf{K}(c_{i-1}(p)), \mathbf{K}(c_i(p))) \qquad (2)$$

Here, $\mathbf{K}(c_i(p))$ represents the keyword vector of the context keywords in the context $c_i(p)$, in which each element indicates the context contribution degree of the corresponding keyword. The function $similar(\mathbf{K}(c_{i-1}(p)), \mathbf{K}(c_i(p)))$ calculates the cosine similarity measure [2] between the context keyword vectors: $\mathbf{K}(c_{i-1}(p))$ and $\mathbf{K}(c_i(p))$.

5. Evaluate the magnitude of change from the previous context $c_{i-1}(p)$ to the current context $c_i(p)$ as follows:

$$\delta_{shift}(c_i(p)) = max(\ (shift(c_{i-1}(p)) - shift(c_i(p))),\ 0) \qquad (3)$$

6. If the magnitude of the change $\delta_{shift}(c_i(p))$ exceeds a given threshold θ, return the current context $c_i(p)$ as the result. Otherwise, repeat from 2.

Each context is characterized by the set of context keywords extracted from the document elements on the aggregation path.

Finally, the aspect discovery method clusters similar contexts. Figure 4 illustrates the basic idea. Each cluster (Z_i) corresponds to an aspect (A_i). The aspect is characterized by the set of context keywords which appear at the cluster centroid $(\mathbf{z}_i)$. These keywords, called aspect keywords, intuitively represent a coherent description of the contexts in the cluster. The strength of association between a page and an aspect is evaluated with respect to two measures:

Aspect support: The web page p_i is associated with the aspect A_j with *support* of $supp(p_i \Rightarrow A_j)$, if $supp(p_i \Rightarrow A_j)$ % of all contexts is contained both in the p_i's contexts and the cluster Z_j corresponding to A_j. For example, in Fig. 4, $supp(p_1 \Rightarrow A_2) = |\{c_2, c_3\}|/|\{c_1, \ldots, c_8\}| = 25\%$

Aspect confidence: The web page p_i is associated with A_j with *confidence* of $conf(p_i \Rightarrow A_j)$, if $conf(p_i \Rightarrow A_j)$ % of the p_i's contexts is contained in the Z_j corresponding to A_j. For example, in Fig. 4, $conf(p_1 \Rightarrow A_2) = |\{c_2, c_3\}|/|\{c_1, c_2, c_3\}| = 67\%$

The basic idea is inspired by the use of support and confidence for making association rules in conventional data mining [3].

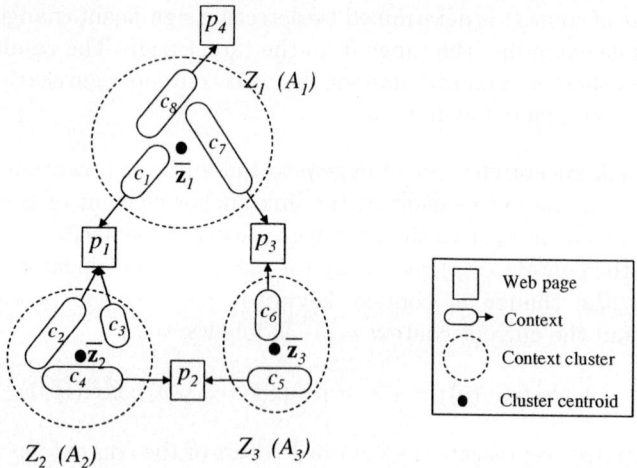

Fig. 4. Discovering aspects by clustering contexts

4 Browsing Retrieval Results with Aspects

4.1 Visualizing Correlation between Contents and Aspects

In order to discover the types of retrieval results shown in Fig. 2, the proposed approach simultaneously visualizes (1) similarity between pages, (2) similarity between aspects, and (3) the strength of associations between the pages and the aspects. An example based on a survey plot technique [4] is shown in Fig. 5. There are four plot areas, each of which plots the associations between the pages and the aspects on a different discrimination scale. Each point in the plot area represents an association between the page and the aspect. The horizontal axis indicates the pages, while the vertical axis indicates the aspects. Each page is represented by a content keyword vector, whose dimensions are reduced to the two most significant principal components (content PCA #1 and #2) through principal component analysis. In a similar way, each aspect is represented by an aspect keyword vector (aspect PCA #1 and #2). The brightness of each point indicates the strength of association, which is gray-scaled in proportion to the product of the aspect support and the aspect confidence.

According to the visualization result, the types of pages shown in Fig. 2 are found as follows:

(1) **Acknowledged pages:** Pages similar in both page contents and aspects are shown as a point group in the shape of a square.
(2) **Versatile pages:** Pages similar in page contents but dissimilar in aspects are typically shown as a point group in the shape of a vertically long rectangle.
(3) **Alternative pages:** Pages dissimilar in page contents but similar in aspects are typically shown as a point group in the shape of a horizontally long rectangle.

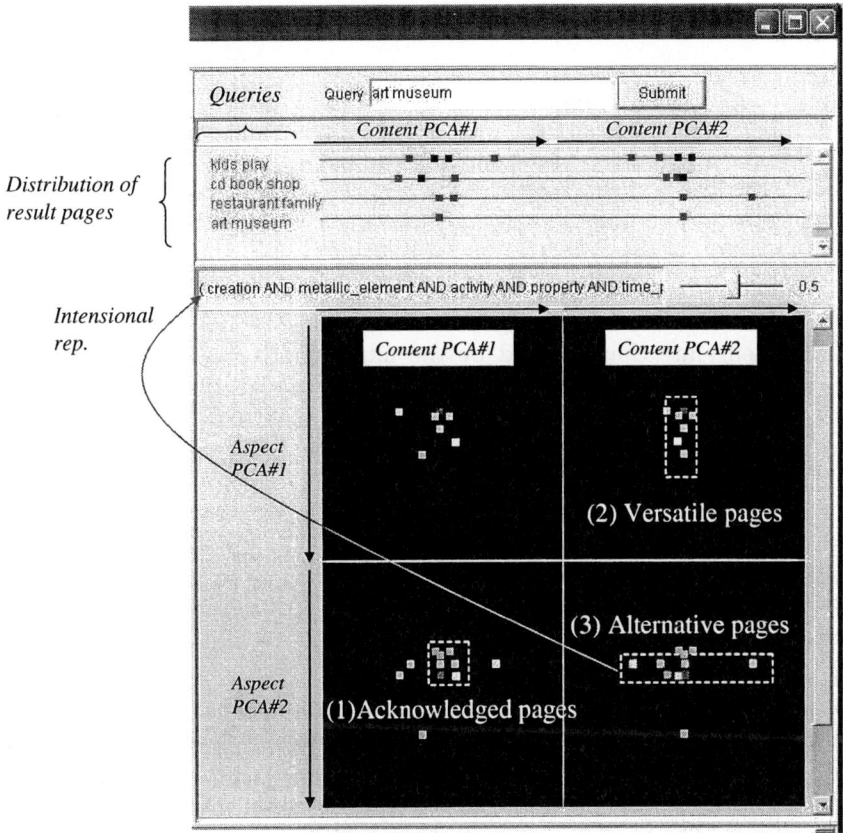

Fig. 5. Visualizing association between page contents and aspects

To provide an overview of the web pages corresponding to a point group, the visualization method also generates an intensional representation of the page contents. The intensional representation consists of a Boolean expression (AND/OR) of content keywords, like a query for most conventional web search engines. It is not only a concise description of the pages, but also provides a direct hint regarding succedent queries. The generation method is based on word-intersection clustering[5]. It is an unsupervised hierarchical clustering algorithm that clusters web pages which share the same content keywords. The web pages in each cluster can be represented by the conjunction of (i.e., AND-ing) the keywords of the cluster centroid. The entire set of the selected web pages can be represented by the disjunction of (i.e., OR-ing) the conjunctive expressions of the clusters (i.e., the disjunctive normal form). The more strictly the clustering algorithm evaluates keyword intersection (i.e., evaluates the intersections of more keywords), the more precise the expression becomes. Alternatively, the expression becomes more complicated and longer.

4.2 A Sample Scenario

Let us consider that a user is organizing a weekend with his family. Since each family member has different wishes, the user starts with the individual queries: "kids, play", "cd, book, shop", "restaurant, family", and "art, museum". In Fig. 5, the upper part of the prototype window plots the retrieval results for each query with respect to the page content (corresponding to the horizontal axis of the association plot area). Although there is no retrieval result satisfying all of the queries, the cluster of *alternative pages* can be found in the association plot area, which aggregates the result pages for all of the queries under the aspects {activity, leaf, time} and {design, creating by mental acts, typography}. The page contents are characterized by the intensional representation: "creation" AND "metallic element" AND "activity" AND "property" AND "time period". In order to find web contents satisfying the wishes as many as possible, the user may refine the query so as to reflect the intensional representation.

The preliminary experiment was conducted against relatively small collection of web pages (about 20,000 pages randomly gathered by our prototype). Although the aspect description and the intensional representation were still less meaningful due to the poor test collection, the sample scenario was validated.

5 Related Work

Browsing web search results by clustering page contents has been extensively researched and exploited in several commercial services, such as Teoma[1], Vivisimo[2], and Grokker[3]. However, most approaches focus on narrowing down the retrieval results, while few address the aggregation of retrieval results for partially defined queries. The Scatter/Gather technique [6, 7] helps a user interactively aggregate (gather) and cluster (scatter) documents for the purpose of gaining an overview of a document collection. Our approach extends the concept of the Scatter/Gather technique to exploit the "surrounding contents" of web pages in order to aggregate fragmented retrieval results based on third-party viewpoints.

The contents surrounding web pages have been used to improve the performance of traditional web information retrieval[8–11]. Conventional approaches aim to complement the page contents with the surrounding contents. In contrast, we focus on analyzing the associations between web pages and their usage as represented by the surrounding contents. Therefore, our approach extracts surrounding contents as the referential contexts of web pages, and then summarizes them to discover generalized descriptions of the contexts (i.e., aspects).

6 Conclusion and Future Work

In this paper, we propose an approach for browsing through web search results based on referential contexts of web pages. Our main purpose has been

---
[1] Teoma, http://www.teoma.com/.
[2] Vivisimo, http://vivisimo.com/.
[3] Grokker2, http://www.groxis.com/service/grok.

to discover coherent semantic units consisting of retrieval results with respect to page contents and references. The context extraction mechanism determines the appropriate range of web contents to aggregate the web page by examining the web document structure and link structure. By clustering similar contexts, generalized descriptions of the contexts, called web page aspects, are discovered. The browsing mechanism visualizes correlations between the page contents and aspects so that a user can easily find following types of retrieval results: acknowledged pages, versatile pages, and alternative pages.

The goals of our future work include (1) a more abstract description of aspects, (2) automatic detection of the three types of retrieval results, and (3) automatic query refinement using the generated intensional representation.

References

1. Salton, G., Buckley, C.: Term weighting approaches in automatic retrieval. In: Information Processing and Management. Volume 24. (1988) 513–523
2. Salton, G., McGill, M.: Introduction to modern information retrieval. In: McGraw Hill. (1983)
3. Han, J., Kamber, M.: Data Mining: Concepts and Techniques. Morgan Kaufmann (2000)
4. Lohninger, H.: Inspect, a program system to visualize and interpret chemical data. In: Chemometrics and Intelligent Laboratory Systems. Volume 22. (1994) 147–153
5. Zamir, O., Etzioni, O., Madani, O., Karp, R.M.: Fast and intuitive clustering of web documents. In: Proceedings of the 3rd International Conference on Knowledge Discovery and Data Mining (KDD-97), Newport Beach, California, USA (1997) 287–290
6. Cutting, D.R., Karger, D.R., Pedersen, J.O., Tukey, J.W.: Scatter/gather: a cluster-based approach to browsing large document collections. In: Proceedings of the 15th annual international ACM SIGIR conference on Research and development in information retrieval, ACM Press (1992) 318–329
7. Hearst, M.A., Pedersen, J.O.: Reexamining the cluster hypothesis: scatter/gather on retrieval results. In: Proceedings of the 19th annual international ACM SIGIR conference on Research and development in information retrieval, ACM Press (1996) 76–84
8. Glover, E.J., Tsioutsiouliklis, K., Lawrence, S., Pennock, D.M., Flake, G.W.: Using web structure for classifying and describing web pages. In: Proceedings of the WWW2002 International World Wide Web Conference. (2002) 562–569
9. Chakrabarti, S., Dom, B., Raghavan, P., Gibson, S.R.D., Kleinberg, J.: Automatic resource list compilation by analyzing hyperlink structure and associated text. In: Proceedings of the 7th International World Wide Web Conference. (1998)
10. Attardi, G., Gullí, A., Sebastiani, F.: Automatic Web page categorization by link and context analysis. In Hutchison, C., Lanzarone, G., eds.: Proceedings of THAI-99, European Symposium on Telematics, Hypermedia and Artificial Intelligence, Varese, IT (1999) 105–119
11. Pant, G.: Deriving link-context from html tag tree. In: Proceedings of the 8th ACM SIGMOD workshop on Research issues in data mining and knowledge discovery, ACM Press (2003) 49–55

Algebra-to-SQL Query Translation for Spatio-temporal Databases

Mohammed Minout and Esteban Zimányi

Department of Informatics & Networks, Faculty of Engineering CP 165/15,
Université Libre de Bruxelles
50 av. F.D. Roosevelt, 1050 Brussels, Belgium
{mminout,ezimanyi}@ulb.ac.be

Abstract. Although many spatio-temporal conceptual models has been proposed in the last years, users must express their queries on the underlying physical data structures. In the context of the European project MurMur we developed a Query Editor tool that allows the creation of queries visually from the conceptual schema as well as the visualization of the query result. In this paper we describe the Query Translator module that is in charge of transforming the queries expressed for the conceptual schema into an operational query for a target DBMS or GIS (e.g., an SQL query or a PL/SQL program). It is composed of a Transformation module that translates a conceptual query into an equivalent logical query using only the concepts provided by the target software, and a Wrapper module that expresses the query in the Data Manipulation Language of the target platform.

1 Introduction

Spatio-temporal databases have been the focus of considerable research activity over a significant period. Many spatio-temporal models have been proposed in the literature, stemming from either the entity-relationship (e.g., [3,12]) or the object-oriented approach (e.g., [9,1]). Spatial and temporal data types provide the building blocks for developing such models. While the definition of standard spatial data types [10] has reached a good level of consensus, there is no such agreement for temporal data types. As for spatio-temporal data types, the work in [2] is foundational.

However, there exists very few prototypes or products providing effective support for applications tracking changes of spatial and non-spatial data over time. Therefore, while users may use a conceptual spatio-temporal model for developing their applications, such specifications must be translated into the operational model of current DBMS or GIS, and this usually induces a reduction of expression power. Further, when the resulting model needs to be queried users must delve into the physical model of their application and use the Data Manipulation Language of the target platform (e.g., SQL) for expressing the queries. This places a burden on users, especially those who have little technical knowledge of the underlying DBMS or GIS software.

The MurMur project aimed at provide a complete conceptual approach for spatio-temporal data management. We developed a spatio-temporal conceptual model called MADS that includes in addition multi-representation features. This data model is complemented with an associated Data Manipulation Language (DML) based on the same modeling paradigm. Thus, users can reason about their world of interest using a single set of concepts all over the lifespan of their applications, from designing, loading, to querying and updating the database.

While the MADS DML is based on an algebraic approach, a visual query editor allows users formulating a query by direct manipulation on the screen mainly through point and click interactions. This hides the algebraic specifications to users and frees them from the burden of learning the complex rules that usually govern textual languages. All available usability studies show the superiority of visual query languages over textual (usually SQL-like) languages. The visual query editor also ensures the automatic translation of the visual queries into equivalent MADS algebra expressions.

In this paper we describe the Query Translator module that is in charge of transforming queries expressed as algebraic expressions on the conceptual schema into operational queries that can be executed on a target DBMS or GIS (e.g., an SQL query or a PL/SQL program). It is composed of a Transformation module that translates a conceptual query into an equivalent logical query using only the concepts provided by the target software, and a Wrapper module that expresses the query in the Data Manipulation Language of the target platform.

The remainder of the paper is organized as follows. Section 2 presents the MADS conceptual model while Section 3 briefly describes the associated MADS algebra. Section 4 shows the query editor architecture and Section 5 presents the Query Translator. Finally, Section 6 concludes and points to directions for future research.

2 The MADS Data Model

MADS [7] is a conceptual spatio-temporal model based on an extended ER model. MADS includes several modeling dimensions: structural, spatial, temporal and multi-representation. These modeling dimensions are *orthogonal*, meaning that spatial, temporal, and multi-representation features can be freely added to any construct of the schema: object and relationship types, aggregation types, attributes, methods, etc.

Spatial and Temporal Dimensions. To describe the spatiality of real-world phenomena, MADS provides several spatial Abstract Data Types organized in a generalization hierarchy [8]: generic (Geo), simple (Point, Line, Simple Area, Oriented Line), and complex types (Point Set, Line Set, Complex Area, Oriented Line Set). Each spatial type has an associated set of methods to define and handle the instances of the type.

MADS also enables to describe continuous fields with the concept of *space-varying attribute*, i.e., attributes whose values are defined by a function having as domain any non-punctual spatial extent, i.e., any spatial ADT but Point. Phenomena described by space-varying attributes can be *continuous* (like elevation), *stepwise* (like the type of crop in a cultivated area), or *discrete* (like mines in a minefield). Each type of function defines the kind of interpolation, if any, used to compute the value(s) of the attribute.

Temporality associated to object or relationship types concerns their lifecycle, i.e., the existence of instances in their type: objects or relationships are created, can be temporarily suspended, then reactivated, and finally removed. The lifecycle is described by a particular time-varying attribute that can take one of four values: not-yet-existing, active, suspended, or disabled. An attribute is said to be *time-varying* if it keeps track of the value changes over time. Like space-varying attributes, time-varying attributes are defined as a function of time to the value domain. Each value of the attribute is associated with a temporal element that describes its validity as seen by the application (valid time) or known to the database (transaction time). This temporal element is described with one of the temporal Abstract Data Types in MADS, which are also organized in a hierarchy: generic (Temporal), simple (Instant, Interval), and complex types (Point Set, Interval Set). MADS also allows attributes varying simultaneously in both space and time. An example arises when keeping track of rainfall values in a given area over time.

In MADS *constrained relationship types* are relationship types conveying spatial and temporal constraints on the objects they link. MADS includes three types of *constrained spatial relationships*: topological, orientation, and metric. They define a spatial constraint between the geometry of the objects linked. For example, a topological relationship type Inside may link object types Station and River, expressing that the geometry of a Station is within the geometry of the related River. MADS proposes a range of predefined topological relationships, such as disjoint, adjacent, intersects, cross, inside, and equal.

Similarly, *synchronization relationships* allow specifying constraints on the lifecycle of the participating objects. They convey useful information even if the related objects are not timestamped. They allow in particular to express constraints on schedules of processes. The semantics of the synchronization relationships is based on Allen's operators, namely before, equals, meets, overlaps, during, starts, and finishes, extended to complex temporal types.

Multiple Representations. There is no natural unique way to look at some phenomenon and there is no natural unique way to represent it. Usually, the same database must serve many different purposes, each of them requiring different data or the same data but with different representations. The multiple representation facilities supported by MADS rely on a simple idea [13]: the possibility to stamp any element of a schema with a *representation stamp* (or *r-stamp*) that identifies for which scale, time frame, viewpoint, etc. the element is valid. Object types, relationship types, attributes (including geometry and lifecycle), methods, etc., can be r-stamped and therefore have different representations.

Representations may vary according to different criteria. In the MurMur project, we focused on two criteria. The first, *viewpoint*, is the materialization of user's needs. For example different user profiles see different information in the database. The second criteria, *resolution* specifies the level of detail for representing spatial information. However, any other criteria can be used for defining the representations. Stamping may apply on *data*, whether it is object and relationship instances, or attribute values, and on *metadata*, whether object and

relationship type definitions or attribute definitions. Stamping allows users to personalize object and relationship types by changing their attribute composition according to their stamps, and to keep several values for the same attribute.
Example. We illustrate the concepts explained in the previous paragraphs with an example. Figure 1 shows the MADS schema for a river monitoring applica-

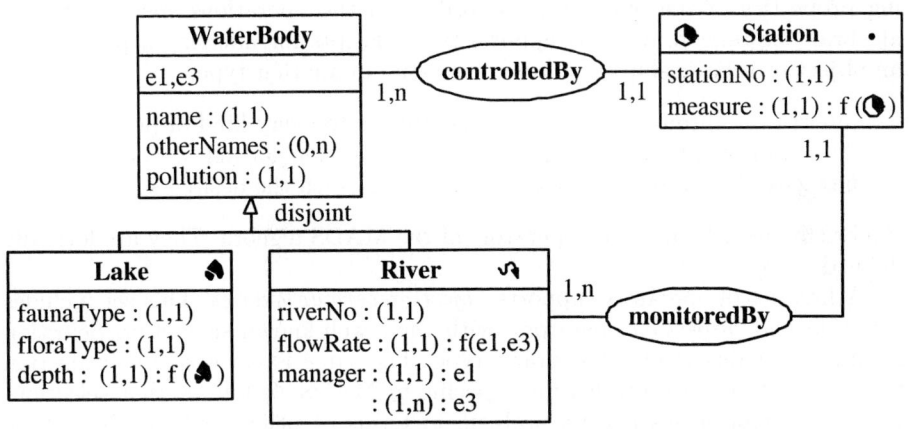

Fig. 1. An example of a MADS schema

tion. The spatial, temporal, and multi-representation characteristics are visually represented by icons. We refer to [13] for the complete list of spatial and temporal types available in MADS.

Temporal and spatial icons are embedded into object or relationship types. The temporal icon (symbolizing a clock) on the left-hand side of the object/relationship type expresses that the lifecycle information is to be kept. Spatial icons are shown on the right-hand side. In the example the object types River and Lake are subtypes of WaterBody. The Station type keeps water quality information about the rivers. The stations may not operate continuously: their lifecycle information allows to records periods of operation. Each station provides several values for the attribute measure, each one associated with its validity period. Each lake records its depth which is a space-varying attribute. The WaterBody object type has two representations e1 and e3. The manager attribute has two definitions, one for e1 and another for e3. Both definitions of manager have the same domain but have different cardinalities: one value is kept for the stamp e1 while several values for stamp e3.

3 The MADS Algebra

The MADS algebra is a two-sorted algebra defined on object and relationship types: The operands and the results of the operators are object types, relationship types, or both. To be able to write expressions involving any sequence of operators, the result of any operator must be a full object or relationship type, with the only exception that they are virtual types, i.e., they need not to be materialized by creating the associated population in the database. Resulting object or relationship types behave like regular types of the database. In particular, they have properties, i.e., attributes (including geometry and lifecycle), methods, roles, and links. All their properties are inferred from the corresponding properties of the operand(s) according to the operations specified in the algebraic expression. MADS supports two concepts for inferring a property of an object or relationship type from properties of another type:

- inheritance through is-a links, which applies to every kind of property;
- derivation of attribute values through derivation formulas. Formulas may navigate the database structure in order to reach the desired source values.

We briefly describe next the operators of the MADS algebra. They are formally defined in [6].

A first set of operators supports *object-preserving queries*. This set includes *selection* and *projection* operators, with their well-known semantics. Selection results in a subtype of the operand type. The same is achieved for projection thanks to the inheritance features specific to MADS. It follows that selection-projection expressions rise no problem in terms of placing the resulting type in the schema, solving one of the issues that object-oriented systems cannot face. Another object-preserving operator is the *extend* operator, which allows dynamically adding to a type derived features. Extend is a traditional alternative to providing join operations, and is likely to be easier to manipulate and leading to simpler algebraic expressions: extend directly picks up what is needed, while joins need further pruning to discard all unwanted items that were generated by the join operation. Other object-preserving operators as those of set theory: *union, difference, intersection*, as long as these are defined to result in instances of a single result type (which does not need to be identical to operand types).

MADS also includes *object-generating operators*. One of them is the *Cartesian product* of two or more object types, whose result is a new relationship type linking the operands. As in the relational algebra, the Cartesian product is likely to be combined with a subsequent selection operation, this combination allowing to enrich the schema with dynamically-defined relationships. Experience proves indeed that schema evolution is unavoidable, and dynamic enrichment copes with simple situations where some requirements had not been taken into account but the data in the database is sufficient to infer the missing constructs. *Objectify* is another object-generating operator that uses an algebraic expression to form values that are subsequently turned into instances of a new object type. Properties of the resulting type, should be defined within the specification of the objectify operation.

4 Query Editor Architecture

One goal of the MurMur project was to provide a set of tools allowing users to visually define queries at the conceptual level, automatically translate such visual queries into algebraic expressions, execute them on a database, and finally display their result both in graphical (spatial) and in textual (thematic) form.

Figure 2 shows the general architecture of the Query Editor. It is composed of the following modules:

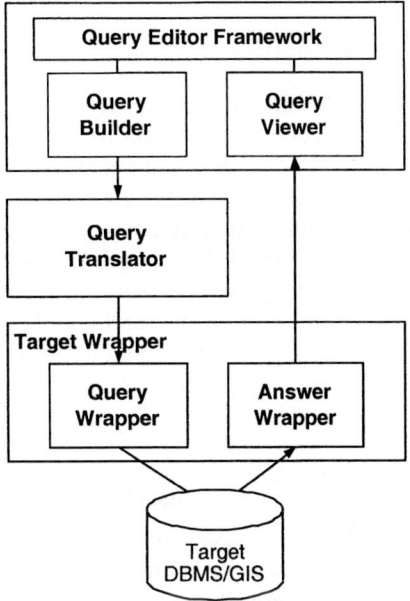

Fig. 2. Query Editor Architecture

1. The Query Builder in which, based on the conceptual database schema expressed in MADS, the visual query is built interactively. The Query Builder also translates the visual query into an algebraic expression.
2. The Query Viewer used to display the query result, both its spatial and its thematic parts. It provides capabilities to manipulate time-varying and representation-varying data. In particular, it implements intelligent zoom capabilities for multi-resolution spatial databases.
3. The Query Translator in charge of transforming the query expressed on a conceptual schema into a preformatted query for a target DBMS or GIS.
4. The Query Wrapper for a particular target DBMS or GIS (e.g., Oracle) that rewrites the output of the Query Translator into an executable query expressed in the DML provided by the target platform (e.g., SQLPlus and/or PL-SQL). There are as many wrappers as they are target platforms.
5. The Answer Wrapper that translates the result set of the target DBMS or GIS into GML 3.0, the exchange format recommended by the Open GIS Consortium [5]. This result set is supplied as input to the Query Viewer.

Among these five modules, only the Query Builder and the Query Viewer are directly manipulated by the user. The three other modules are in charge of all the intermediate steps and thus, their actions are transparent to the user. Within the scope of the project, only the Oracle DBMS has been implemented as target but the current modular structure makes it easy to add other targets.

5 Query Translation Tool

Since many concepts of the MADS model are not provided by the target platform, we have developed a schema translator tool [4] that transforms a conceptual MADS schema into an equivalent logical schema that only employs the subset of MADS concepts provided by the target system.

We show an example of schema transformation using an excerpt of the schema in Figure 1. The transformation of the object type Station into a logical schema for an object-relational model is given in Figure 3. The logical schema defines the Station object type with attributes statusNo, and geometry, as well as the DMeasure domain, representing the time-varying attribute measure.

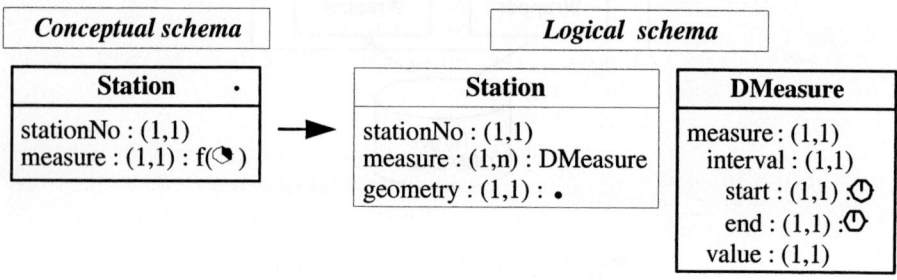

Fig. 3. Conceptual and logical schemas

As a consequence of the schema translation, it is necessary to transform user queries on the conceptual schema (expressed as algebra expressions) into equivalent algebra expressions on the logical schema. Then, the transformed algebra expressions must be rewritten into the Data Manipulation Language (DML) provided by the target implementation platform. Based on the example in Figure 3, we will present the translation the following query: find all stations having a measure greater than 1000 m^3 at date 01/05/2000.

5.1 Transformation Mechanism

The MADS algebra allows to use all methods and operators provided by the spatial and temporal ADTs when formulating queries. For example, the above query is expressed in the MADS algebra as follows:

```
select [measure.atTime(01/05/2000) > 1000] Station
```

The atTime method allows to extract the value of a time-varying attribute at a particular point in time. However, many spatial and temporal operators provided by MADS have no equivalence in the DML of current implementation platforms. Therefore, the query translation process must take into account not only the transformation of the conceptual schema into the logical schema, but also the transformation of the spatial and temporal methods and operators.

As already shown in Figure 3, since traditional DBMSs do not provide support for time-varying attributes, measure is translated into a multivalued attribute defined on the complex domain DMeasure. Therefore, when translating our example query an existential quantifier must be added to take into account the multivalued attribute. Further, the atTime method is translated by testing that the required date is included in the interval defined by start and end. The result of the translation will be as follows:

select [$\exists$d $\in$ measure | d.measure.start $\leq$ 01/05/2000 $\wedge$ d.measure.end $\geq$ 01/05/2000 $\wedge$ d.measure.value $\geq$ 1000] Station

The core of the translation module is composed of transformation rules. Each rule seeks in the query tree the nodes concerned by the rule and applies various transformations to these nodes. Since each rule is applied only once to the query tree, a strict scheduling of the rules is needed. Further, as the expression power of the different target platforms varies, a driver allows to select the set of transformation rules to be activated.

Our implementation of the schema translator [4] is also based on transformation rules. However, the rules of the schema translator are simpler since they just modify the schema tree. The rules of the query translator are more complex because they must seek how the different elements of the conceptual schema were translated by the schema translator when obtaining the logical schema.

5.2 Query Wrapper

The Query Wrapper module transforms a MADS algebra expression on the logical schema into an equivalent DML expression (or a program containing DML expressions) for the target DBMS or GIS. For instance, the translation of a MADS algebra expression for Oracle will generate either an SQL query or a PL/SQL program. Thus, our example query will be written as follows:

```
SELECT * FROM Station s, TABLE(s.measure) m
WHERE m.measure.interval.start <= '01-05-2000'
  AND m.measure.interval.end >= '01-05-2000'
  AND m.measure.value > 1000
```

The result obtained from the execution of the query (or program) on the target system must be expressed as defined by the original user query on the original conceptual schema. This implies that the query (or program) may have to construct this result by iterations and aggregations of several partial results.

5.3 Query Translator Implementation

We use XML as an exchange format for expressing queries and GML 3.0 for expressing query results. Each MADS query produced by the Query Builder is exported to the Translator in XML format respecting a Data Type Description (DTD). In the Translator the different drivers selecting the transformation rules to be activated are also expressed in XML. The result of the translation expressed also in XML is sent to the Wrapper.

The Translator has been implemented using the Java platform. We used the JAXP (Java API for XML Parsing) package to implement the transformation rules. This package enables applications to parse and transform XML documents using an API that is independent of a particular XML processor implementation.

The Query Translator tool is divided in three fundamental packages:

1. `QueryTranslator` is the main translator class whose task consists in the management of the translation process by reading input files (tree and schema info), executing the translation by applying the rules, and writing the result.
2. `TranslationRule` is an abstract class, parent of all other `translationRule` classes. It defines common translation functions, and a specific abstract function `translateNode` whose role is to transform a given node. This is the method whose behavior changes for different translation rules and different query contexts.
3. `VisualTranslation` is a visual tool that enable users to select some translation properties, like the target database, as well as to select the location to find database schema.

6 Conclusions and Future Work

Many spatio-temporal models have been proposed in the literature. They allow users to design their applications at a conceptual level. However, since operational DBMS or GIS provide little support for spatio-temporal data management, such conceptual specifications must be translated into the operational model provided by such implementation platforms. In addition, users must express their queries using the physical schema of the application. This situation is far from ideal since users must understand the intricacies and particularities of the different platforms.

This paper presents a tool for translating conceptual queries expressed in MADS algebra into operational queries that can be executed on a DBMS or GIS. The translation is made in two steps. First, the conceptual query is translated into a logical query, involving only the concepts available in the target data model. Second, the logical query is rewritten into a query expressed with the Data Manipulation Language provided by the target system. This two-step strategy allows to reuse most of the code when adding a new target data model.

We continue to study the problem of query translation, in particular the translation of spatial and temporal operators. Although we have validated our strategy using Oracle 9i, we plan to support other platforms such as ArcInfo and MapInfo. We are also continuing the development of the other modules of the Query Editor, and we plan to include support for integrity constraints.

Acknowledgments

The authors would like to thanks Christine Parent and Stefano Spaccapietra, our colleagues of the MurMur project, for our fruitful collaboration. In particular, Christine Parent is the initiator of the MADS model and provided the original definition of the MADS algebra.

References

1. E. Camossi, M. Bertolotto, E. Bertino, and G. Guerrini. A multigranular spatiotemporal data model. In *Proc. of the 11th ACM International Symposium on Advances in Geographic Information Systems, ACM GIS 2003*, pages 94–101, 2003.
2. R.H. Güting, M.H. Böhlen, M. Erwig, C.S. Jensen, M. Schneider, N.A. Lorentzos, and M. Vazirgiannis. A foundation for representing and querying moving objects. *ACM Trans. on Database Systems*, 25(1):1–42, 2000.
3. V. Khatri, S. Ram, and R.T. Snodgrass. ST USM: Bridging the semantic gap with a spatio-temporal conceptual model. Technical report, TimeCenter Research Report TR-64, 2001.
4. M. Minout and E. Zimányi. A tool for transforming conceptual schemas of spatiotemporal databases with multiple representations. In *Proc. of the IASTED Int. Conf. on Database Applications, DBA '2004*, 2004.
5. Open GIS Consortium, Inc. OpenGIS Geography Markup Language (GML) Implementation Specification. Version 3.0, January 2003.
6. C. Parent. Query language specification for the MADS model. Technical Report MM-WP3-DLA-008, INFORGE, Université de Lausanne, Switzerland, January 2001. Deliverable 8, MurMur Project.
7. C. Parent, S. Spaccapietra, and E. Zimányi. Spatio-temporal conceptual models: Data structures + space + time. In *Proc. of the 7th ACM Symposium on Advances in Geographic Information Systems, GIS'99*, pages 26–33, 1999.
8. C. Parent, E. Zimányi, M. Minout, and A. Aissaoui. Implantation d'un modèle conceptuel avec multi-représentation. In Ruas [11], chapter 7, pages 131–147.
9. R. Price, N. Tryfona, and C.S. Jensen. Extended spatiotemporal UML: Motivations, requirements, and constructs. *Journal of Database Management*, 11(4):14–27, 2000.
10. P. Rigaux, M. Scholl, and A. Voisard. *Introduction to Spatial Databases: Applications to GIS*. Morgan Kaufmann, 2000.
11. A. Ruas, editor. *Traité IGAT sur la représentation multiple et la généralisation*. Hermès, 2002.
12. N. Tryfona and C.S. Jensen. Conceptual data modeling for spatiotemporal applications. *GeoInformatica*, 3(3):245–268, 1999.
13. C. Vangenot, C. Parent, and S. Spaccapietra. Modélisation et manipulation de données spatiales avec multi-représentation dans le modèle MADS. In Ruas [11], chapter 5, pages 93–112.

Visualization Process of Temporal Data

Chaouki Daassi[1], Laurence Nigay[2], and Marie-Christine Fauvet[2]

[1]Laboratoire SysCom, Université de Savoie, Chambéry, France
Chaouki.Daassi@univ-savoie.fr
[2]Laboratoire CLIPS-IMAG BP 53-38041, Grenoble cedex 9, Grenoble, France
{Laurence.Nigay,Marie-Christine.Fauvet}@imag.fr

Abstract. Temporal data are abundantly present in many application domains such as banking, financial, clinical, geographical applications and so on. Temporal data have been extensively studied from data mining and database perspectives. Complementary to these studies, our work focuses on the visualization techniques of temporal data: a wide range of visualization techniques have been designed to assist the users to visually analyze and manipulate temporal data. All the techniques have been designed independently. In such a context it is therefore difficult to systematically explore the set of possibilities as well as to thoroughly envision visualization techniques of temporal data. Addressing this problem, we present a visualization process of temporal data. We adapt the Ed Chi's visualization process to the case of temporal data. We illustrate the steps of our visualization process by considering the design of the Star Representation Technique that we have developed. By identifying and organizing the various aspects of design, our process serves as a basis for classifying existing visualization techniques and should also help the designer to address the right design questions and to envision future systems.
Keywords: Visualization Technique, Visualization Process, Temporal Data.

1 Introduction

A temporal data denotes the evolution of an object characteristic over a period of time. The value of a temporal data is called a history. For the sake of simplicity, we define a history as a collection of instant time-stamped or interval time-stamped data items, although there are many other ways of representing a history [10]. Fig. 1, shows a history of numeric values (a monthly production of a firm), where each time-stamp denotes a month. The set of timestamps is the temporal domain of the observed data.

Several visualization techniques of temporal data such as the ThemeRiver technique [13] have been proposed in the literature. In this paper, we present a visualization process for temporal data to structure the design space of these visualization techniques. We aim at defining the steps and their parameters that the designer should consider during the design. We adapt the Ed Chi's visualization process to the case of a temporal data.

[<400, 01/1985>, <500, 02/1985>, <450, 03/1985>, <460, 04/1985>, <480, 05/1985>, <510, 06/1985>, <600, 07/1985>, <700, 08/1985>, <720, 09/1985>, <610, 10/1985>, ...<3240, 01/2001>, <3250, 02/2001>]

Fig. 1. A collection of timestamped items

This paper is organized as follows: First (in Section 2), we briefly describe the Ed Chi's visualization process. In section 3, we show how Ed Chi's visualization process can be applied to temporal data. Finally, in section 4, we illustrate our visualization process by considering the design of the Star Representation Technique that we have developed.

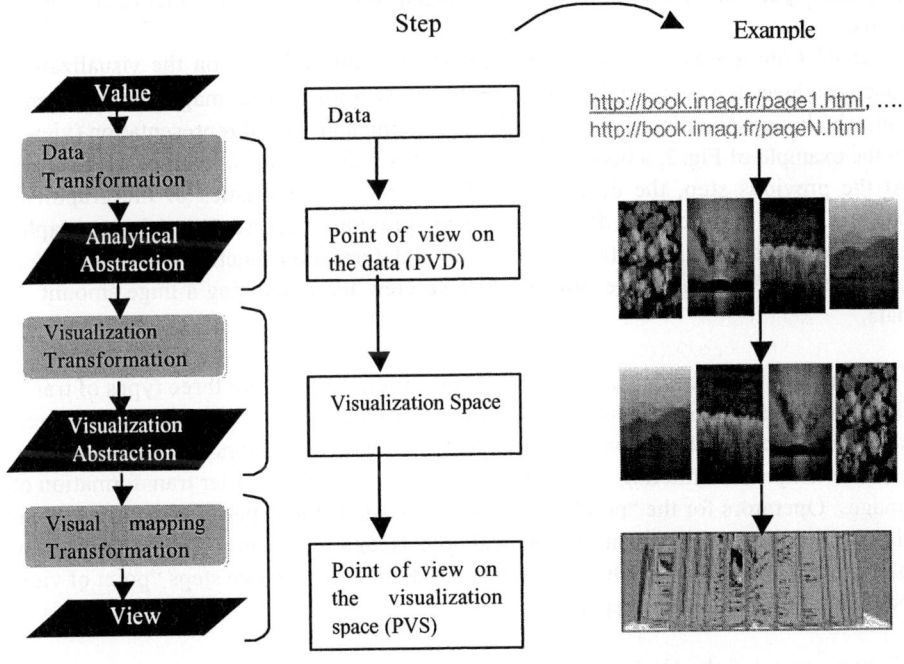

a. Ed Chi's decomposition   b. Four steps of a visualization process

Fig. 2. Ed Chi visualization process

2   Ed Chi's Visualization Process

As shown in Fig. 2, Ed Chi [8] decomposes the visualization process into three types of transformations manipulating four types of data.

In this paper, we adopt the point of view of Vernier [16] that structures the visualization process of Ed Chi into four steps namely: (1) data, (2) point of view on the data, (3) visualization space and (4) point of view on the visualization space. *Data.* This step is related to the data to be visualized. For example, as illustrated in Fig. 2, the data could be a set of URLs.

Point of View on the Data. At this stage of the process, the data are transformed onto an analytical representation. The point of view on the data is obtained by defining an analytical abstraction, in other words by obtaining meta-information, information related to the data such as their organization (hierarchical, sequential, etc.) or by filtering the initial space. For example, in Fig. 2, the web pages are retrieved from the list of URLs (initial data space), then an image is generated for each web page.

Visualization Space. The visualization space is defined by a transformation of visualization which maps an analytical representation onto values ready to be displayed. In the visualization process shown in Fig. 2, the images (the point of view on the data) are ordered (ordered list of images). This transformation fixes the characteristics of the graphical space in which the data are visualized in terms of the number of its dimensions.

Point of View on the Visualization Space. The point of view on the visualization space produces the perceptible rendering. It results from a visual mapping transformation which maps the directly displayable values onto a graphical representation (view). In the example of Fig. 2, a book is defined for presenting the list of web pages as in [7]. At the previous step, the designer decides on the characteristics of the graphical space. During this step, the data values of the previous step are mapped onto graphical representations. In addition, at this step, a deformation function of the graphical space could be applied, for example a fisheye view for visualizing a huge amount of data.

In addition to the decomposition of the visualization process into three types of transformations manipulating four types of data, Ed Chi defines operators. We present some of these operators along the four steps of Fig. 2. Operators for the "data" step are for example data filtering, adding new sets of data and the Fourier transformation of images. Operators for the "point of view on the visualization space" step include rotation, translation, enlargement of graphical objects, and the positioning and orientation of a camera in a 3D scene. Other operators are defined for the two steps "point of view on data" and "visualization space".

Having presented the Chi's visualization process, we now apply this process to visualize temporal data.

3 Visualization Process of Temporal Data

Fig. 3 distinguishes the two dimensions of a temporal data: structural dimension and temporal dimension. The structural dimension is characterized by a given data type. For example, we can distinguish one dimensional, two-dimensional and three-dimensional data. One dimensional data could be either quantitative, nominal or ordered as defined by Card and Mackinlay [6]. Two dimensional data are for example images or geographical maps. Three-dimensional data are for example real world objects.

Based on these two dimensions of a temporal data (i.e., structural and temporal dimensions), we define the visualization process as an association between two visualization processes dedicated to the two dimensions of the temporal data. The visualization process of the structural dimension is dependent on the type of data. Studying this process consists of studying the visualization process of data in general, which is out of the scope of this paper. We therefore only focus on the visualization process of the temporal dimension.

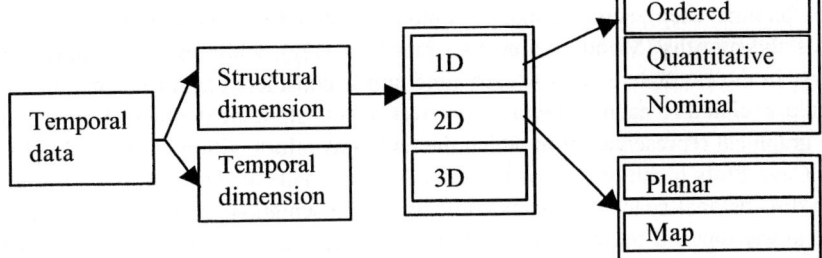

Fig. 3. Two dimensions of a temporal data

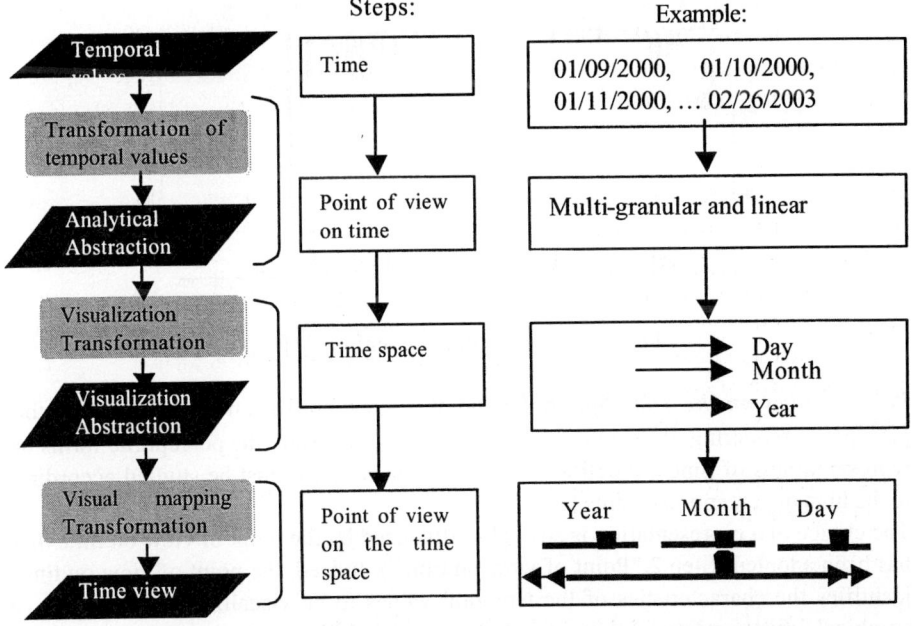

Fig. 4. Visualization process of a temporal dimension

Fig. 4 shows how we apply the Chi's visualization process to the temporal dimension of temporal data: four steps are defined namely time, point of view on time, time space and point of view on the time space.

Time. This step represents the time values to be visualized. Time values are observed according to a time unit as Year, Month, Day, Hour, etc. In the example of Fig. 4, time values are observed according to the Day time unit.

Point of View on Time. This step is defined by the transformation of the time values. This transformation extracts from the time values how time is represented: (i) in which unit system the time values are expressed (ii) are time values linear or periodic? In the example of Fig. 4, time is considered as multi-granular and linear. Multi-granular representation refers to time units composition: a year is composed of twelve months, a month is composed of 28, 29, 30 or 31 days, and so on.

Time Space. At this step, displayable space of the time values are defined. For example, time values observed at the unit Day (the analytical representation of "the point of view on time" step), could be mapped onto a matrix. One dimension of the matrix represents the months (Month is a unit coarser than Day), while the other represents the days. In the example of Fig. 4, each time unit is considered as linear: one time axis is then associated to each of them. Moreover at this step, the number of dimensions of the graphical representation in which the temporal values will be visualized is fixed. In the Cave Plots technique [5] of Fig. 5 the X axis is dedicated to represent time within a two-dimensional space. In this example, two representations of the time axis are used: one at the top and the other at the bottom of the representation. Other visualization techniques such as the Dynamic Timelines technique [14] represent time within a three-dimensional space.

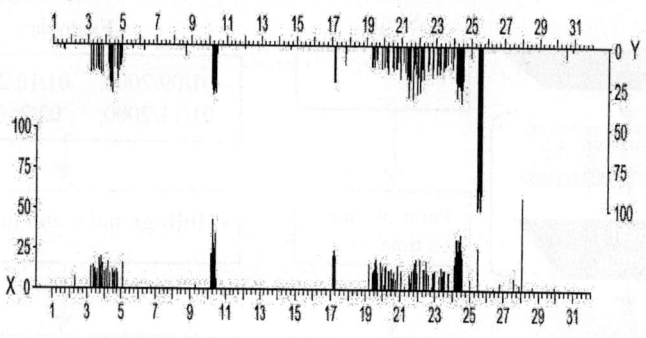

Fig. 5. Cave plots technique [5]

Point of View on the Time Space. The point of view on the time space refers to the perceptible rendering of the temporal dimension. At this step, the perceptible forms or representations of time are defined. These representations must be studied according to the human perception of time [12].

The choice of a representation is strongly influenced by the point of view on time that has been adopted (Step 2 "Point of view on time"). Indeed, the point of view on time identifies the characteristics of the temporal values to be visualized. For example, a graphical representation of time in a cyclic form could be used because the temporal values are periodic: periodicity is a characteristic that has been identified during the step "Point of view on time". Fig. 6 shows a star representation to enhance a cyclic perception of time. Other representations such as the spiral representation in [17] could be used to enhance the cyclic perception of time. A linear representation is another classical way to express time, as depicted in Fig. 4. In the example of Fig. 4, four timelines [11] are used to interact with the time space: one timeline for each time unit (Year, Month and Day) and one timeline to present an overview of the selected time values.

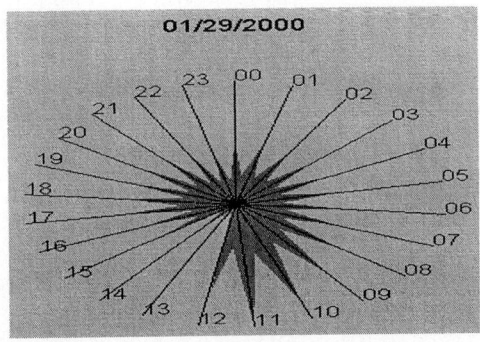

Fig. 6. Star representation [9]

In this section, we focused on the visualization process of the temporal dimension. However a temporal data is an association of two dimensions: a structural dimension and a temporal dimension. In the next section, we illustrate the complete visualization process of temporal data by considering the Star Representation Technique that we have developed. This visualization technique of temporal data relies on several forms of time used simultaneously making its design process challenging.

4 Star Representation Technique

Fig. 7 presents the Star Representation Technique (SRT) while Fig. 8 presents its visualization process. As shown in Fig. 8, we distinguish two visualization processes: one dedicated to the temporal dimension (as described in the previous section) and one dedicated to the structural dimension. The visualization process of the temporal dimension of the SRT (on the left in Fig. 8) is completely achieved independently from that of the structural dimension (on the right in Fig. 8), whereas the opposite is not no true. We note that other linking configurations between the two visualization processes exist: Considering the different linking configurations between the two visualization processes enables us to define classes of visualization techniques in [9].
As shown in Fig. 7, the SRT technique relies on two forms of time used simultaneously. In the visualization process of the temporal dimension of Fig. 8, two time perceptions are consequently considered at the *point of view on time* step: linear and periodic perceptions. The linear perception of time is used in the design of the perspective wall timeline, whereas the periodic perception is used in the design of the structural space, the star representation of Fig. 7.

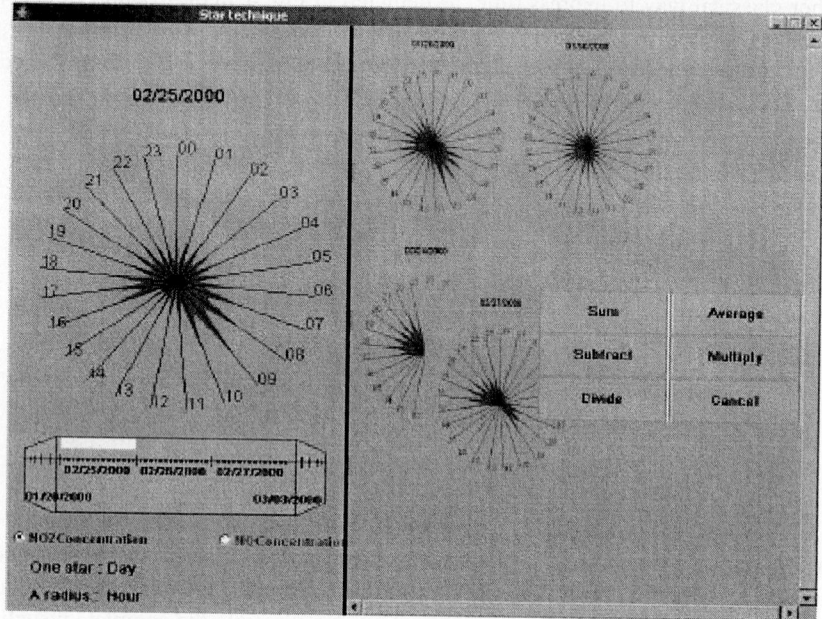

Fig. 7. Star representation technique

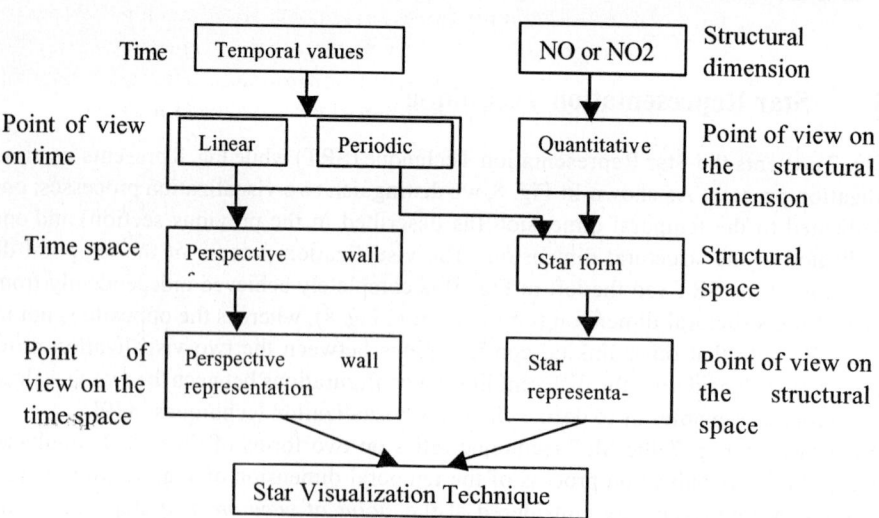

Fig. 8. Visualization process of Star Visualization Technique

Perspective Wall Timeline

We applied the visualization process (as described in the previous paragraph) to visualize the temporal dimension as a perspective wall timeline. As shown in Fig. 9, the perspective wall representation [15] distinguishes three facets: one in the front to represent data in detail, and two facets to represent the perspective effect. The perspective effect enhances the fact that time values are not limited to those visualized in the front of the timeline. The first and last observation instants of the data are visualized in the correspondent perspective facet (1921 and 1999 in Fig. 9). Consequently, the user can deduce the cardinality of the temporal domain.

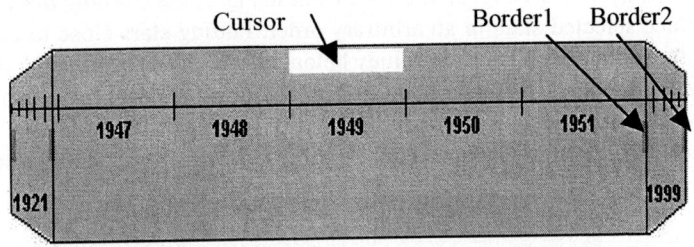

Fig. 9. Perspective wall timeline

The user can customize the timeline: s/he can modify its size and the number of the visualized time values within its front facet. The form of a perspective wall provides two kinds of borders: Border1 of Fig. 9 delimits the facet in the front from the two perspective facets whereas Border2 delimits the timeline itself. By stretching the timeline from Border1, the user can augment or reduce the number of time values represented in the front facet. Similarly, by stretching the timeline from Border2, s/he can change the size of the timeline in order to improve the visibility of the visualized time values.

The perspective wall timeline offers two navigation modes to explore the time space. With the first mode, the user drags the cursor within the front facet of the timeline which leads to quick moving of time values. This mode is used when the user is searching a time value positioned far from the currently selected time value. By opposition, with the second mode, the user explores the time space step-by-step. To do so, s/he clicks in a perspective facet depending on the direction s/he wants.

As the visualization process of the temporal dimension is realized independently from that of the structural dimension, the resulting time representation can be reused to implement several visualization techniques of temporal data. In addition to the SRT technique, we reused the perspective wall timeline in three different visualization techniques [9].

Star Representation

The visualization process of the structural dimension of the SRT is presented on the right in Fig. 8. During the *visualization space* step, a star representation is used to denote the evolution of the visualized history during a fixed-length period of time. The choice of the star representation is strongly influenced by the fact that we considered the periodic perception of time to define the visualization space (the anchoring point between the temporal and structural processes) and by the fact that the data are quantitative. In the example of Fig. 8, two quantitative temporal data are visualized, the NO and NO2 concentrations corresponding to pollution measures. In Fig. 7, a star denotes a day whereas the radii denotes the twenty four hours of a day.

The STR interface provides two visualization areas. The first one, located on the left in Fig. 7 and named the *reference area*, contains stars ordered in time. Within this area, a timeline is used to navigate through time. The displayed star corresponds to the period pointed by the cursor within the timeline. The user can directly observe the evolution of data over a given period (e.g. a year or a month) as well as from one period to the next. The second area located on the right in Fig. 7, the *working area*, enables the user to place selected stars in an arbitrary order. Putting stars close to each other facilitates the comparison of data values belonging to different periods. As shown in Fig. 7, when the user drags a star on top of another one, a palette of data manipulation operators appears. The user can for example compute the average of two temporal data then observe the result over time. The resulting data are represented as a star.

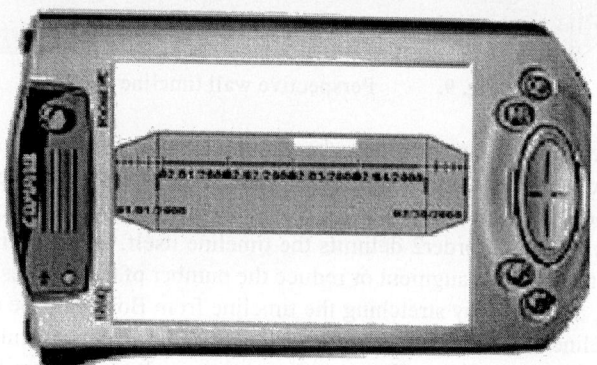

Fig. 10. Physical device to interact with the temporal dimension

5 Conclusion and Future Work

We have presented a visualization process of temporal data. The goal of this work is to gain understanding of the design of visualization techniques of temporal data. The contribution of our visualization process is two-fold:
- First we structure the visualization process of a temporal data as an association of two visualization processes: one of the structural dimension and one of the temporal dimension. Several points of contact between the two processes are possible [9].
- Second we adapt the Ed Chi's visualization process to the case of temporal data.

We illustrated the visualization process by considering the design of the Star Representation Technique (SRT), one technique we have developed for interacting with temporal data. As the temporal dimension is designed independently from the structural dimension, our resulting perspective wall timeline has been reused in three other visualization techniques that are part of the INVEST system [9], a system that allows multiple views of the same temporal data. In a future work, we plan to use a dedicated physical device (as shown in Fig.10) for the perspective wall timeline, making the reusable corresponding software component a reusable physical device. The visualization techniques such as the SRT will consequently be multi-surface, one for the temporal dimension and one for structural dimension.

References

1. Becker R. A., Clark L. A. et Lambert D. Cave Plots: A Graphical Technique for Comparing Time Series. Journal of Computational and Graph. Stat., 3:3 (1994) 277-283.
2. Card S. K. and Mackinlay Jock. The Structure on the Information Visualization Design Space. In Proc. of InfoVis (1997).
3. Card S. K., Robertson G. G., York W. The WebBook and the Web Forager: An Information Workspace for the World-Wide Web (1996). In Proc. of the Conference on Human Factors in Computing Systems CHI'96.
4. Chi E. H. A Taxonomy of Visualization Techniques using the Data State Reference Model. In Proc. of InfoVis (2000).
5. Becker R. A., Clark L. A. et Lambert D. Cave Plots: A Graphical Technique for Comparing Time Series. Journal of Computational and Graph. Stat., 3:3 (1994) 277-283.
6. Card S. K. and Mackinlay Jock. The Structure on the Information Visualization Design Space. In Proc. of InfoVis (1997).
7. Card S. K., Robertson G. G., York W. The WebBook and the Web Forager: An Information Workspace for the World-Wide Web (1996). In Proc. of the Conference on Human Factors in Computing Systems CHI'96.
8. Chi E. H. A Taxonomy of Visualization Techniques using the Data State Reference Model. In Proc. of InfoVis (2000).
9. Daassi C. Techniques d'interaction avec un espace de données temporelles. PhD thesis in Computer Science from Joseph-Fourier University of Grenoble, France, 2003. Available at http://iihm.imag.fr/publs/2003/theseChaoukiDaassi.pdf
10. Dumas M, Tempos: une plate-forme pour le développement d'application temporelles au dessus de SGBD à objets. PhD thesis in Computer Science from Joseph-Fourier University of Grenoble, France, (2000).
11. Dumas M., Daassi C., Fauvet M-C, Nigay N. *"Pointwise Temporal Object Database Browsing". In Proc. Of* ECOOP, France, (2000) 170-184.
12. Freeman W. J. Perception of Time and Causation through the Kinesthesia of intentional action. Cognitive Processing 1, In International Quarterly of Cognitive Science, 18-34.

13. Havre S., Hetzler B. and Nowell L. ThemeRiver: Visualizing Theme changes over Time. In Proc. of the IEEE Symposium on Information Visualization 2000.
14. Kullberg R. L. Dynamic Timelines: Visualizing Historical Information in Three Dimensions. Master Thesis from Media Lab. MIT, (1995).
15. Mackinlay J.D., Robertson G., and Card S.K. The Perspective wall: Detail and Context smoothly integrated, Human factors in computing systems conference proceedings on Reaching through technology, (1991) 173 – 176.
16. Vernier F. La multimodalité en sortie et son application à la visualisation de grandes quantités d'information. PhD thesis in Computer Science from Joseph-Fourier University of Grenoble, France, (2001).
17. Weber M., Alexa M. et Müller W. Visualizing Time-Series on Spirals. In Proc. of InfoVis (2001).

XPQL: A Pictorial Language for Querying Geographic Data

Fernando Ferri[1], Patrizia Grifoni[1], and Maurizio Rafanelli[2]

[1] IRPPS-CNR, via Nizza 128, 00187 Roma, Italy
{f.ferri,p.grifoni}@irpps.cnr.it
[2] IASI-CNR, viale Manzoni 30, 00185 Roma, Italy
{rafanelli}@iasi.cnr.it

Abstract. This paper proposes and discusses an eXtended Pictorial Query Language (XPQL) for geographic data and the possibilities for its use on the Web. This language is mapped on Geographic Markup Language (GML 3.0), which is used for transport on to the Web and storage of geographic information, including spatial and non-spatial properties and temporal and topological properties. The XPQL algebra is described and an example of the language given using the implemented prototype. The method used to solve ambiguities arising when drawing the different features of the pictorial query is also explained. Particular attention is given to queries which include temporal constraints and the way to express these.

1 Introduction

Many researchers have recently focused their attention on the possibility of using a different approach to express queries regarding geographical data. Visual query languages and their evolution have led to the proposal of their pictorial representation, in which both spatial and temporal variables are present. In reality these variables are "always" present in geographical data (where and when), but the query's temporal dimension is often ignored. In addition, computer networks and distributed computing technology have transformed many computer-based applications from the traditional stand-alone mode to the networked mode. This paper, starting from the analysis of query languages for distributed GIS proposes and discusses an eXtended Pictorial Query Language (XPQL) for geographic data, including spatial and temporal relationships, and the possibilities for its use on the Web. This language is mapped on Geographic Markup Language (GML 3.0) [1], which is used for exchanging and storing geographic information via Web.

Various proposals for Visual Query Languages for Geographical Data have recently been made. One regards Cigales [2] and its extension LVIS [3], the first pictorial query languages allowing the user to draw a query. Cigales is based on the idea to express a query by drawing the pattern which corresponds to the result desired by the user. It uses a set of active icons which are able to model the required graphical forms, i.e. the geometrical objects polyline and polygon, as well as the operations carrying out on these objects (intersection, inclusion, adjacency, path and distance). The graphical forms and icons which conceptualize the operators are predefined. Other query languages use the blackboard metaphor, as in Sketch [1] and Spatial-Query-By-Sketch [4]. The user is free to draw shapes or symbols on the screen by hand, to express an operator or object. However, in visual query languages, a query can lead to multiple interpretations and thus ambiguities for the system and user. The eXtended Pictorial Query Language (XPQL) resolves limitations due to such ambiguities, improving and simplifying human-computer interaction.

Some significant example of query languages defined for XML are found in literature [5] [6]. Lorel, developed as a Web query language, has been successively adapted to XML. StruQL is a declarative query language, which (like Lorel) uses the OEM data model. XSL and XQL [7] enable the user to query XML documents one at a time, although they do not solve the problem of querying more than one XML document instance at a time. The need to facilitate human computer interaction resulted in the definition and development of the XML-GL graphical query language [8], which represents XML documents and DTD through a XML graph. Finally, the importance of XQuery [9] is due to the fact that it is a W3C recommendation.

In Section 2 we propose the extension of GeoPQL [10], called XPQL, for its use on the Web. Section 3 describes a representation of the XPQL query by GML, and finally, in section 4 we give conclusions and possible future developments.

2 The eXtended Pictorial Query Language

The XPQL query language is based on an algebra consisting of a set of spatial operators on symbolic geographical objects (sgo). Any geographical object can also be characterized temporally. This section discusses the syntax of XPQL with all the possible topological relationships between two shapes and discusses the proposed solution for the ambiguities arising in particular configurations.

2.1 Base Concepts

An *sgo* is formally defined as a 4-tuple $\psi = <id, objclass, \Sigma, \Lambda >$ where:
- *id* is the *sgo* identifier;
- *objclass* is the set (possibly empty) of classes iconized by ψ;
- Σ (property set) represents the attributes to which the user can assign a set of values; this allows selection among the classes of objects or their instances iconized by ψ. Some properties can be referred to a temporal dimension. In particular, different kinds of temporal dimensions can be considered as represented by temporal intervals or instants.
- Λ is the ordered set of pairs (h, v), which define the *sgo*'s spatial characteristics and position with respect to a reference point in the working area.

We now describethe semantics and properties of the different operators, using the following symbolism:

Let ψ be an *sgo*
$\partial\psi$ is the geometric border of ψ, defined as:
- if ψ is a polygon, $\partial\psi$ is the set of its accumulation points (as defined in the set theory);
- if ψ is an open polyline, $\partial\psi$ is formed by its extreme points;
- if ψ is a point, $\partial\psi$ is the empty set.

$\psi° = \psi - \partial\psi$ is the geometrical interior of ψ.

$\mathrm{Dim}(\psi) = 0$ if ψ contains at least one point but no polylines or polygons
               1   if ψ contains at least one polyline but no polygon
               2   if ψ contains at least one polygon.

These sgo form, together with the null element, the elements of the alphabet **A**. This alphabet and the defined operators form the reference model.

In the following we refer to the hth property of the object ψ_i with $\sigma_{\psi_i}^h$. Properties referred to temporal dimensions can take temporal intervals or instants as values.

2.2 The XPQL Algebra

The XPQL algebra consists of twelve spatial operators, seven temporal operators and other typical operators for alphanumeric values. Spatial operators are: G-union, G-difference, G-disjunction, G-touching, G-inclusion, G-crossing, G-pass-through, G-overlapping, G-equality, G-distance, G-any and G-alias. Temporal operators are: T-before, T-meets, T-overlaps, T-starts, T-during, T-finishes and T-equals.

Below is a brief formal description of these operators.

G-union definition (Uni): The *G-union* of two *sgo* ψ_i and ψ_j is a new *sgo*, defined as the set of all points belonging to ψ_i and/or ψ_j.
Formally: Let $\psi_i, \psi_j \in \mathbf{A}$ be two sgo. Then:
     $\psi_i \, \mathrm{Uni} \, \psi_j \equiv \psi_h = \{ x: x \in \psi_i \lor x \in \psi_j \}$ and $\psi_h \in \mathbf{A}$.

G-touching definition (Tch): G-touching between the *sgo* ψ_i and ψ_j exists if the points common to the two ψ are all contained within the union of their boundaries. If this condition is satisfied, the result of this operation is a new ψ, called ψ_h and defined by the set of points common to ψ_i and ψ_j.

Formally: Let $\psi_i, \psi_j \in \mathbf{A}$ be two sgo. Then:
     $\psi_i \, \mathrm{Tch} \, \psi_j \equiv \psi_h = \{ x: x \in \psi_i \land x \in \psi_j \land x \in (\partial\psi_i \cup \partial\psi_j) \}$ and $\psi_h \in \mathbf{A}$.

G-inclusion definition (Inc): A symbolic feature ψ_i G-includes another symbolic feature ψ_j (and we write $\psi_i \, \mathrm{Inc} \, \psi_j$) if all the points of ψ_j are also points of ψ_i. The result is a symbolic feature ψ_h, which coincides with the second operand ψ_j.

Formally: Let $\psi_i, \psi_j \in \mathbf{A}$ be two sgo, and let $(\psi_i \cap \psi_j = \psi_j) \land (\psi_i \cap \psi_j \neq \psi_i)$. Then:
     $\psi_i \, \mathrm{Inc} \, \psi_j \equiv \psi_h = \{ x: x \in \psi_j \rightarrow x \in \psi_i \}$ and $\psi_h \in \mathbf{A}$.

G-disjunction definition (Dsj): Two sgo ψ_i and ψ_j are G-disjoined between them (formally ψ_i Dsj ψ_j) if the intersection of their borders AND the intersection of their internal points is null.

Formally: Let $\psi_i, \psi_j \in A$ be two sgo and let

$(\partial\psi_i \cap \partial\psi_j = \varnothing) \wedge (\psi°_i \cap \psi°_j = \varnothing) \wedge (\partial\psi_i \cap \psi°_j = \varnothing) \wedge (\psi°_i \cap \partial\psi_j = \varnothing)$ Then:
ψ_i Disj $\psi_j \equiv true$.

G-Pass-through definition (Pth): Let ψ_i be a polyline and let ψ_j be a polygon. Then, the operator G-pass-through is applicable if the polyline is partially within the polygon G-disjoined between them (formally ψ_i Pth ψ_j).

Formally: Let $\psi_i, \psi_j \in A$ be two sgo, where ψ_i is a polyline and ψ_j is a polygon, and let

$(\psi°_i \cap \partial\psi_j \neq \varnothing) \wedge (\psi°_i \cap \psi°_j \neq \varnothing)$ Then:
ψ_i Pth $\psi_j \equiv \psi_h = \{x: x \in \psi_i \cap \psi_j\}$ and $\psi_h \in A$.

G-distance definition (Dst): Let $\psi_i, \psi_j \in A$ be two sgo of any type. Their distance is valuable and ≥ 0 if their intersection is null. The (minimum) distance Dst (ϕ = min) between them is a numeric value representing this distance. This operator can be used to find all the sgo having a distance θ (θ being one of: >, <, =, $\leq$, $\geq$, $\neq$) from the reference sgo. The distance (δ_ϕ) value is given by: $\delta_\phi (\psi_i, \psi_j)_\theta = \psi_h$ where
- ψ_h indicates a bi-oriented segment representing the distance operator between ψ_i, ψ_j
- ϕ is the qualifier which solves the above mentioned ambiguity
- θ is a selection expression which includes conventional operators (>, <, =, $\neq$, etc.) and methods behaving like operators.

G-difference definition (Dif): Let $\psi_i, \psi_j \in A$ be two sgo. The difference between two symbolic objects ψ_i and ψ_j is defined as a new *sgo* (ψ_h) which contains all the points which belong to ψ_i but not to ψ_j.

Formally: Let $\psi_i, \psi_j \in A$ be two sgo,

Dif: ψ_i Dif $\psi_j := \psi_h = \{x : x \in \psi_i \wedge x \notin \psi_j\}$ and $\psi_h \in A$.

G-crossing definition (Crs): Let $\psi_i, \psi_j \in A$ be two polylines, and let $\psi°_i \cap \psi°_j \neq \varnothing$. Then, Cross: ψ_i Crs $\psi_j := \psi_h = \{x: x \in \psi°_i \cap \psi°_j\}$ and $\psi_h \in A$.

G-overlapping Definition (Ovl): Let $\psi_i, \psi_j \in A$ be two sgo of the same type. Between them a not-null overlap exists if their intersection is still not null and has the same dimension as the sgo.

Formally: Let $\psi_i, \psi_j \in A$ be two sgo of the same type (polyline or polygon) and let
$\dim(\psi_h) = \dim(\psi_i) = \dim(\psi_j) \wedge (\psi_h \neq \psi_i) \wedge (\psi_h \neq \psi_j)$. Then

Ovl: ψ_i Ovl $\psi_j := \psi_h = \{x: x \in \psi_i \wedge x \in \psi_j\}$ and $\psi_h \in A$

G-equality definition (Eql): Two symbolic geographical objects ψ_i and ψ_j are topologically equal if they are of the same type and have the same shape.

Formally: Let $\psi_i, \psi_j \in A$ be two sgo of the type and let $(\psi_i \cap \psi_j = \psi_j) \wedge (\psi_i \cap \psi_j = \psi_i)$. Then: ψ_i Eql $\psi_j := \psi_h = \{x: x \in \psi_i \wedge x \in \psi_j\}$ and $\psi_h \in A$.

G-any Definition (Any): Let ψ_i, $\psi_j \in A$ be two sgo. Between them any admissible relationship is valid if the G-any operator is applied between them.
Given a fixed configuration formed by two sgo and leting $\Re$ be the set of all admissible relationships between them, we have: ψ_i Any $\psi_j := \psi_i \Re \psi_j =$ true.

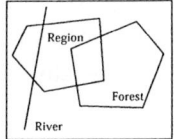 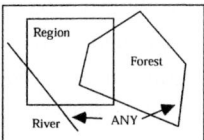

Fig. 1. (a), (b)

To explain the use of the G-any operator, consider the following query: "Find all the regions which are *passed-through* by a river and *overlap* a forest", where the user has no interest in the relationship between the river and forest. If the user draws the configuration of Figure 1-a, the forest and the river are "Disjoined" and the system must interpret the query as "Find all the regions which are *passed-through* by a river and *overlap* a forest, *and the forest is disjoined from the river*". Other query representations imply a spatial relationship between the forest and river.

By the introduction of the G-any operator, the query is correctly drawn as in Figure 1-b. This operator thus allows the query to be interpreted in such a way as to give the answer required by the user..

G-alias Definition (Als): Let ψ_i be a sgo. ψ_j is an *alias* of ψ_i if the only difference between them is their shape.

G-alias allows a query to be implemented with the OR operator (practically, *G-alias* duplicates the *sgo* in order to draw a query in which it is used in the two contrasting "OR" parts).

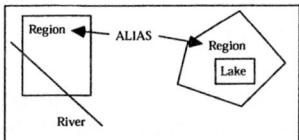

Fig. 2.

For example, Figure 2 gives the pictorial representation of the following query: "Find the regions which are *passed through* by a river OR which *include* a lake".

The temporal operators refer to the temporal attributes of the two sgo. For example, if one sgo represents a province and another represents a road, we can design a query to find all roads built between 1980 and 1990 which passthrough provinces created after 1975, or all roads which passthrough provinces created after 1975 and built after the year in which the province was created.

T-before Definition (Bef): An interval or an instant α of the property $\sigma_{\psi_i}^h$ of the sgo ψ_i is *T-before* another interval or an instant β of the property $\sigma_{\psi_j}^k$ of the sgo ψ_j if α is temporally "before" β. The properties can take both intervals and instants as values.

T-meets Definition (Mts): An interval or an instant α of the property $\sigma_{\psi_i}^{\ h}$ of the sgo ψ_i T-meets another interval or instant β of the property $\sigma_{\psi_j}^{\ k}$ of the sgo ψ_j if α takes the maximum value with "coincidence" with the minimum value of β. The properties can take both intervals and instants as values.

T-overlap Definition (TOv): An interval α of the property $\sigma_{\psi_i}^{\ h}$ of the sgo ψ_i T-overlaps another interval β of the property $\sigma_{\psi_j}^{\ k}$ of the sgo ψ_j if α has its minimum value temporally "before" and its maximum value temporally "after" the minimum value of β. Both properties can take intervals as values.

T-starts Definition (Sts): An interval or instant α of the property $\sigma_{\psi_i}^{\ h}$ of the sgo ψ_i T-starts another interval or instant β of the property $\sigma_{\psi_j}^{\ k}$ of the sgo ψ_j if α takes the minimum value with "coincidence" with the minimum value of β. The properties can take both intervals and instants as values.

T-during Definition (Drg): An interval α of the property $\sigma_{\psi_i}^{\ h}$ of the sgo ψ_i is T-during another interval β of the property $\sigma_{\psi_j}^{\ k}$ of the sgo ψ_j if α has its minimum value temporally "after" the minimum value of β and its maximum value temporally "before" the maximum value of β. Both properties can take intervals as values.

T-finishes Definition (Fns): An interval or instant α of the property $\sigma_{\psi_i}^{\ h}$ of the sgo ψ_i T-finishes another interval or instant β of the property $\sigma_{\psi_j}^{\ k}$ of the sgo ψ_j if α takes the maximum value with "coincidence" with the maximum value of β. The properties can take both intervals and instants as values.

T-equals Definition (Tes): An interval or instant α of the property $\sigma_{\psi_i}^{\ h}$ of the sgo ψ_i T-equals another interval or instant β of the property $\sigma_{\psi_j}^{\ k}$ of the sgo ψ_j if α takes the minimum maximum values with "coincidence" with the minimum maximum values of β. The properties can take both intervals and instants as values.

2.3 The XPQL Query Language

Users interact through the XPQL primitives for querying databases in different Web servers. Each client can access a database's data if the user is logged in and has the correct access rights. The user selects layers of interest available from the different geographical databases and expresses an XPQL querywhich must be translated according to GML syntax. The GML query must be sent to the logged in servers. ArcView accesses the geographical database (for each Web server) to obtain all results for the expressed query. Servers answer the query by sending the GML expression of results to the client, and presenting them to the user by SVG (representing the visualization solution) for the correspondence defined in [11] between GML and SVG.

Figure 3 shows the pictorial representation of the query: <Find all roads built before the year of creation of the province they pass-through or which are included in provinces created after 1975>. The temporal constraint (accessible by means of sub-views) are:

Province.year > 1975
Road.building year < Province.year

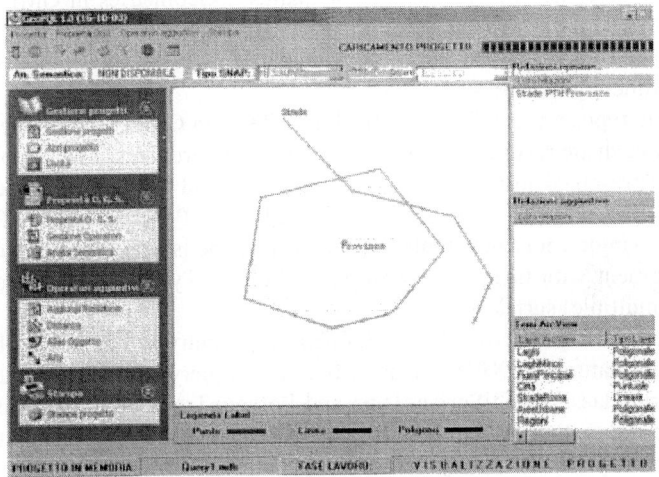

Fig. 3.

3 Query Translation from XPQL to GML

With XPQL the user formulates symbolical queries, formed by graphical objects which symbolically represent types and geographical objects. They have a relevant role due to their feature type and the (topological) relationships existing between them. In query translation from XPQL to GML it is therefore necessary to translate both graphical object feature types and the different relationships existing between pairs of the symbolic objects drawn. GML provides various kinds of objects for describing geography, including features, coordinate reference systems, geometry, topology, time, units of measure and generalized values.

3.1 Coding Data Type

In the geographic domain, the real world can be represented as a set of features. AbstractFeatureType codifies a geographic feature in GML. The state of a feature is defined by a set of properties, each of which is described by a triple {name, type, value}. The number, names and types of properties a feature may have are determined by its type definition. Geographic features with geometry are those with properties that may be geometry-valued. A feature collection can itself be regarded as a feature; as a consequence a feature collection has a feature type.

A query XPQL (represented by a set of symbolic geographical objects) is translated in a GML features collection. Each feature is characterized by a set of properties. Its geometry type is a very important property and its geometry is given in the coordinate reference system. This property is included in the more general property location of the AbstractFeatureType describing the feature's extent, position or relative location. A reference system provides a scale of measurement for assigning values "to a location, time or other descriptive quantity or quality". Geometries in GML indicate the coordinate reference system in which their measurements have been made. This indication is made by the "parent" geometry element of a geometric complex or aggregate for its constituent geometries.

Geometric types are codified on CoordinatesType in GML. CoordinatesType is defined as a text string recording an array of tuples or coorditates. The symbolic features of XPQL represented in GML are Point, Polyline, and Polygon, represented by the GML geometric classes PointType, LineStringType e PolygonType. A PointType is defined by a single coordinate tuple. A LineStringType is a special curve consisting of a single segment with linear interpolation. A PolygonType is a surface defined by a single (not multiple) surface.

The other GML geometric classes defined in geometry.xsd do not explicitly define the symbolic features in XPQL. This is because a query cannot distinguish between the geometric classes MultiSurfaceType and PolygonType, both expressed according to the symbolic feature Polygon. In fact, an XPQL query cannot distinguish between geographical objects formed by one or more than one polygon. Neither can a query expressing the polygon cardinality be formulated. The symbolic geographical object Polygon represents both: i) geographical objects described by one polygon only and ii) geographical objects described by a set of two or more polygons.

The XPQL query can be expressed by a graphical approach, which uses a local coordinate system of the working area (window used for the query). In contrast to the visualization area of geographical data, which is constantly connected to the coordinate reference system of the involved cartography, the working area does not need to be connected to the coordinate reference system because its constraints do not involve geographical coordinates. For example a user can express the following constraints independently of the geographical coordinates: i) a river passes through a region, ii) a road crosses another one. Translating the XPQL query expression into GML constraints is usually independent of the coordinate reference system. These constraints refer explicitly to the geometry typology and the relationships between involved features.

However, the user sometimes needs to express constraints referring explicitly to the geographical coordinates. For this reason XPQL enables users to explicitly express constraints referring to and represented in GML by locations in the coordinate reference system.

XPQL considers Instant and Interval as primitives for temporal information. GML defines them as the geometric primitives in temporal dimension: TimeInstant and TimePeriod. TimePosition can be connected to the temporal reference system, considering *year, year-month, date, or dateTime*.

```
<element    name="TimeInstant"    type="gml:TimeInstantType"    substitutionGroup="gml:_TimePrimitive"/>
<complexType name="TimeInstantType" final="#all">
  <complexContent>
    <extension base="gml:TimePrimitiveType">
```

```
        <sequence>
            <element ref="gml:timePosition"/>
        </sequence>
    </extension>
  </complexContent>
</complexType>

<element name="TimePeriod" type="gml:TimePeriodType" substitution-
Group="gml:_TimePrimitive"/>
<complexType name="TimePeriodType" final="#all">
  <complexContent>
    <extension base="gml:TimePrimitiveType">
        <sequence>
            <element ref="gml:begin"/>
            <element ref="gml:end"/>
            <element ref="gml:_duration" minOccurs="0"/>
        </sequence>
    </extension>
  </complexContent>
</complexType>
```

3.2 Coding Spatial and Temporal Operators

XPQL considers both spatial and temporal operators (see section 2). Operators represent properties existing between the query's symbolic graphical objects. The following schema shows a basic pattern which supports the encoding of property elements in GML3 with a complex content between objects. The XPQL temporal operators are derived from GML: AssociationType For the XPQL spatial operators, FeaturePropertyType is a particular class of properties (using the gml:AssociationType pattern) that defines associations between features.

```
<complexType name="AssociationType">
    <sequence>
        <element ref="gml:_Object" minOccurs="0"/>
    </sequence>
    <attributeGroup ref="gml:AssociationAttributeGroup"/>
</complexType>

<complexType name="FeaturePropertyType">
    <sequence>
        <element ref="gml:_Feature" minOccurs="0"/>
    </sequence>
    <attributeGroup ref="gml:AssociationAttributeGroup"/>
</complexType>
```

In GML3 the type for a property element may thus be derived from GML: FeaturePropertyType. The previous schema is able to support the translation of the different type of XPQL operators, with the exception of G-distance. The representation of the different operators in GML3 considers the restrictions regarding their applicability to the sgo type. Such restrictions are specified in the XPQL operator definitions in Section 5. Finally, XPQL allows the expression of constraints referring to the G-Distance operator between symbolic geographical objects. These are represented by the GML type *MeasureType*. This is an amount encoded as a double, together with a measurement unit indicated by a uom (Unit Of Measure) attribute.

```
<complexType name="MeasureType">
  <simpleContent>
    <extension base="double">
      <attribute name="uom" type="anyURI" use="required"/>
    </extension>
  </simpleContent>
</complexType>
```

4 Conclusions

This paper presents XPQL, a Pictorial Query Language, which enables the user to easily formulate a query. We start from the consideration of geographical information from a spatial point of view, according to a two-dimensional description and taking account of temporal information. Each query can be expressed in GML 3.0 to guarantee exchange of and access to geographical information among the different databases available to each user. We are now focusing our activity on designing and implementing a new prototype with simpler and more effective interaction approaches, in accordance with the growth in multimodal interaction tools.

References

1. S. Cox , P. Daisey, R. Lake, C. Portele, A. Whiteside. "Geography Markup Language (GML) Implementation Specification" OGC 02-023r4, Open GIS Consortium, Inc., 2003.
2. Calcinelli D., Mainguenaud M. "Cigales, a visual language for geographic information system: the user interface" Journal of Visual Languages and Computing, Vol. 5, N. 2, pp. 113-132, June 1994.
3. Aufaures-Portier M.A., Bonhomme C. "A High Level Language for Spatial Data Management" Third Int. Conf. on Visual Information Systems - VISUAL '99, LNCS N. 1614, pp. 325-332, 1999.
4. F. Ferri, F. Massari, M. Rafanelli. "A Pictorial Query Language for Geographic Features in an Object-Oriented Environment". Journal of Visual Languages and Computing, Vol. 10, N. 6, pp. 641-671, Dec. 1999.
5. Bonifati, S. Ceri "Comparative Analysis of Five XML Query Languages", *ACM SIGMOD Record*, 29 (1), 2000
6. D. Lee, W.W. Chu "Comparative Analysis of Six XML Schema Languages", *ACM SIGMOD Record*, 29 (3), 2000.
7. J. Robie, J. Lapp, and D. Schach. "Xml query language (Xql)". In Query Languages 1998.

8. S. Ceri, S. Comai, E. Damiani, P. Fraternali, S. Paraboschi, and L. Tanca. "XML-GL: A graphical language for querying and restructuring XML documents" *Computer Networks*, 31 (11–16), pp. 1171–1187, May 1999.
9. S. Boag, M. F. Fernandez, D. Florescu, J. Robie, J. Siméon "XQuery 1.0: An XML Query Language", W3C Working Draft 02 May 2003, http://www.w3.org/TR/xquery/
10. F.Ferri, P.Grifoni, M.Rafanelli. "GeoPQL: A Geographical Pictorial Query Language" Tech. Rep. (in press)
11. Taladoire Gilles, "Geospatial data integration and visualisation using open standards" 7th EC-GI&GIS Workshop EGII Managing the Mosaic", Postdam, Germany, 13-15 June 2001.

HW-STALKER: A Machine Learning-Based Approach to Transform Hidden Web Data to XML

Vladimir Kovalev[1], Sourav S. Bhowmick[1], and Sanjay Madria[2]

[1] School of Computer Engineering
Nanyang Technological University, Singapore
assourav@ntu.edu.sg

[2] Department of Computer Science
University of Missouri-Rolla, Rolla, MO 65409
madrias@umr.edu

Abstract. In this paper, we propose an algorithm called *HW-Transform* for transforming hidden web data to XML format using machine learning by extending STALKER to handle hyperlinked hidden web pages. One of the key features of our approach is that we identify and transform *key attributes* of query results into XML attributes. These *key attributes* facilitate applications such as change detection and data integration. by efficiently identifying *related* or *identical* results. Based on the proposed algorithm, we have implemented a prototype system called HW-STALKER using Java. Our experiments demonstrate that *HW-Transform* shows acceptable performance for transforming query results to XML.

1 Introduction

Most of the data on the Web is "hidden" in databases and can only be accessed by posing queries over these databases using search forms (lots of databases are available only through HTML forms). This portion of the Web is known as the *hidden Web* or the *deep Web*. Hence, the task of harvesting information from the hidden web can be divided into four parts: (1) Formulate a query or search task description, (2) discover sources that pertain to the task, (3) for each potentially useful source, fill in the source's search form and execute the query, and (4) extract query results from result pages as useful data is embedded into the HTML code. We illustrate these steps with an example.

The AutoTrader.com is one of the largest car Web sites with over 1.5 million used vehicles listed for sale by private owners, dealers, and manufacturers. The search page is available at http://www.autotrader.com/findacar/index.jtmpl?ac_afflt=none. Examples of result pages are shown in Figure 1. The first page containing results of a query contains short descriptions of a set of cars. Each such short description provides a link to a separate page containing more details on the particular car. There is also a link to a page containing the next set of car descriptions that is formatted in a similar way as the first page.

HW-STALKER: A Machine Learning-Based Approach   937

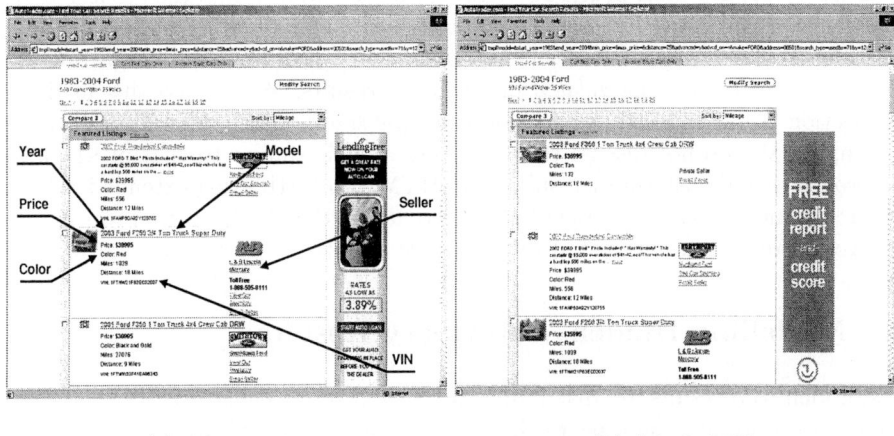

(a) July 1, 2003   (b) July 2, 2003

Fig. 1. AutoTrader.com: Query results for *Ford*

The second page is linked to the third page, and so on. Note that all the pages in this set are generated dynamically. This means that every time a user queries AutoTrader.com with the same query, all the resulting pages and the links that connect them to one another are generated from the hidden web database anew.

In this paper, we will assume that the task is formulated clearly (Step 1). Step 2, *source discovery*, usually begins with a keyword search on one of the search engines or a query to one of the web directory services. The works in [2, 4] address the resource discovery problem and describe the design of topic-specific PIW crawlers. Techniques for automatically querying hidden web search forms (Step 3) has been proposed in [6]. These techniques allow a user to specify complex relational queries to hidden web sites that are executed as combination of real queries. In this paper, we focus on Step 4. We present HW-STALKER, a prototype system for extracting relevant hidden web query results and transforming them to XML using machine learning technique.

We propose an algorithm called *HW-Transform* for transforming hidden web data to XML format. Our approach is based on the STALKER technique [7, 9]. We use STALKER because apart from being easy to use, in most cases it needs only one example to learn extraction rules, even for documents containing lists. Moreover, STALKER models a page as unordered tree and many hidden web query results are unordered. However, STALKER was designed to extract data from a single web page and cannot handle a set of hyperlinked pages. Hence, we need to extend the STALKER technique to extract results from a set of dynamically generated hyperlinked web pages.

We use machine learning-based technique to induce the rules for this transformation. The process of transforming query results from HTML to XML can be divided into three steps: (1) Constructing $\mathcal{EC}$ tree [7, 9] describing the hidden web query results. One of the key features of our approach is that a user maps special *key attributes* (*identifiers* and *peculiarities*) of query results into XML attributes. These *key attributes* facilitate change detection, data integration etc. by efficiently identifying *related* or *identical* results. We discuss this in detail in Section 2. (2) Inducing extraction rules for tree nodes by providing learning examples. We do not discuss this step here as it is similar to that of STALKER approach. (3) Transforming results from HTML to XML using extended $\mathcal{EC}$ tree with assigned rules. We discuss this step in Section 3. Note that we do not address transformation related to client-side scripts in this paper.

2 Modelling Hidden Web Query Results

As hidden web results are distributed between a set of pages, we need a general model to represent these pages. In other words, we should model the links between a collection of hyperlinked hidden web pages. We distinguish these links into two types - *chain links* and *fanout links*. When the pages returned by a query are linked to one another by a set of links, we say that the links between them are the *chain links*. When a result returned by a query contains hyperlinks to pages with additional information, we say that these links are *fanout links*.

2.1 Constructing HW-EC Tree

STALKER uses *Embedded Catalog*($\mathcal{EC}$) formalism to model HTML page. This formalism is used to compose tree-like structure of the page based on *List* and *Element* nodes. $\mathcal{EC}$ tree nodes are unordered. Thus, to be able to apply STALKER to a set of pages we should extend $\mathcal{EC}$ formalism for modelling a set of pages. We add three new types of nodes (*chain*, *fanout*, and *attribute* nodes) to $\mathcal{EC}$ tree formalism. The new formalism is called *Hidden Web Embedded Catalog* ($\mathcal{HW} - \mathcal{EC}$). The *chain* and *fanout* nodes are assigned with descriptions of *chain* and *fanout links* in the results. The *attribute* nodes are used to represent semantic constraints in the query results.

Fanout Node. *Fanout* node models a fanout of pages. The node should be assigned with STALKER extraction rules for extracting the fanout link. This node should be nested at the *List* node, so that the rules for searching a fanout link are applied inside each element of this *List*. Fanout node does not appear in the output XML document. All the nodes that are nested at *fanout* node appear nested at each element of the *List* which is the ancestor of the particular *fanout* node.

Chain Node. *Chain* node models a chain of pages. The node should be assigned with STALKER extraction rules for extracting the chain links. *Chain* node should be nested at the *element* node so that the rules for searching a chain link are applied inside each next page with results. *Chain* node does not appear in output

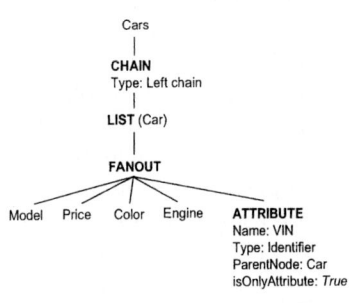

```
<Cars>
    <Car Id="1FTWW33F62EC17133">
        <Model>
            2002 Ford F350 1 Ton Truck 4x4 Crew Cab DRW
        </Model>
        <Price>$36999</Price>
        <Color>Red</Color>
        <Engine>8 Cylinder Diesel</Engine>
    </Car>
    <Car Id="1FTNW21F02EA19799">
        <Model>
            2002 Ford F250 3/4 Ton Truck 4x4 Super Duty Crew Cab
        </Model>
        <Price>$35999</Price>
        <Color>Gray</Color>
        <Engine>8 Cylinder Diesel</Engine>
    </Car>
    <Car Id="1FMPU18L92LA43093">
        <Model>
            2002 Ford Expedition Eddie Bauer 4 Door 4x4
        </Model>
        <Price>$27280</Price>
        <Color>Black</Color>
        <Engine>8 Cylinder Gasoline</Engine>
    </Car>
    ...
</Cars>
```

(a) $\mathcal{HW} - \mathcal{EC}$ description (b) XML representation

Fig. 2. $\mathcal{HW} - \mathcal{EC}$ description and XML representation of result pages in Autotrader

XML document. All the nodes that are nested at *chain* node appear nested at the element that is the ancestor of the particular *chain* node. There is also a parameter *ChainType* that should be specified. This parameter can be assigned with only two possible values: *RightChain* or *LeftChain*. We elaborate on this parameter below.

All the hidden web sites compose chain links in their own way. The main type of chain link that is common for most of the sites is the link to the "next" page containing a set of results. For example, reconsider AutoTrader.com query results. The "next" is followed by different suffix in every page of the results except the last.

STALKER extraction rules are rules for locating the beginning and the end, i.e., prefix and suffix of the piece of data to be extracted. We assign the *chain* node with rules to extract the link to the "next" page of results. Observe that for the "next" link it is common to be followed by (or follow) a block of links to every other page with results. Also a page is the last result page in the chain if no link fits the extraction rule assigned to the particular node. To reduce the number of learning examples for extracting "next" link, we ask a user to specify learning examples for extracting the "next" link along with the block of links to every other page and also to specify if "next" link is followed by or follows the block of links to every other page. We call the first and second choices as *LeftChain* and *RightChain* respectively.

Atrtibute Node. *Attribute* node is a leaf node in the $\mathcal{HW} - \mathcal{EC}$ tree and is used for modelling semantic constraints in the query results. It is transformed to XML attribute in the output XML file. It can be used to identify a result uniquely (*identifier*) or it may provide enough information to determine which results are related and has the potential to be identical (*peculiarity*) in the old and new versions of the query results. There are four parameters that needs to be specified for attribute nodes: *ParentNode*, *Type*, *Name*, and *isOnlyAttribute*.

The *ParentNode* parameter is the link to the particular node in the $\mathcal{HW} - \mathcal{EC}$ description that should be assigned with this attribute in the output XML file. The *Type* parameter is for defining type of attribute (it can be of only two types: *identifier* or *peculiarity*). We discuss these two types in the following subsections. The *Name* denotes the name of this node. The *isOnlyAttribute* contains boolean value. If *isOnlyAttribute* is set to "true" then it denotes that the piece of data extracted for this node should only appear in output XML as a *semantic attribute*. Otherwise, it should appear both as a semantic attribute and as an element. So if this information is needed as a part of XML document then the *isOnlyAttribute* parameter is set to "false" so that the node appears as an element. Following is the example illustrating the $\mathcal{HW} - \mathcal{EC}$ formalism and mapping of set of hidden web pages to XML.

Consider the results from `AutoTrader.com`. Figure 2(a) depicts $\mathcal{HW} - \mathcal{EC}$ tree for these results and Figure 2(b) depicts XML representation of the results according to the tree. For clarity and space, we only show a subset of the attributes in each result of the query. The root `Cars` node is established for uniting all the other nodes. The next node `Chain` models the set of pages connected with "left" *chain* links. `List(Car)` node is assigned with iterative rule for extracting elements of the `Car`. The `fanout` node denotes that each `Car` element contains a link to the page with extra data. `Fanout` is assigned with rules for extracting this link from the piece of HTML document that was extracted for each `Car` element in the previous step. Next level of the tree contains five elements. Four of them are `Element` nodes. The last node is an `Attribute` node containing four parameters. We can see in Figure 2(b) that `VIN` is extracted only once for each `Car` as an attribute. The rest of elements are nested in the output XML the same way they are nested in the tree.

2.2 Identifiers

Some elements in a set of query results can serve as unique identifier for the particular result, distinguishing them from other results. For example, `Flight number` uniquely characterizes every `Flight` information returned as the result of querying an on-line booking site, `VIN` uniquely characterizes every `Car` in the query results from a car database, `Auction Id` is the identifier of `Auction` in the query results from an on-line auctions site, etc. These elements are called *identifiers*. *Identifiers* may be either automatically generated by the hidden web database, like `Auction Id`, or stored in the database along with the data, like `VIN`. In this work we assume that *identifier*, being assigned to a particular query result, does not change for this result through different versions of query results. That is, an *identifier* behaves like an unique identifier or "key" for the result. However, it is possible for *identifier* to be missing in a result. Also, if an *identifier* is specified (not specified) for a node in an initial version of query results or when the node appeared for the first time in the results, then it will remain specified (not specified) throughout all versions, until the node is deleted. This reflects the case for most web sites we have studied. Note that we allow specifying only one *identifier* for each result. As each result is transformed into a subtree in the XML representation of the hidden web query results, we model *identifier* for a particular node in the subtree as XML attribute with name Id and *identifier* information as value. We now illustrate with an example the usefulness of *identifiers* in change detection.

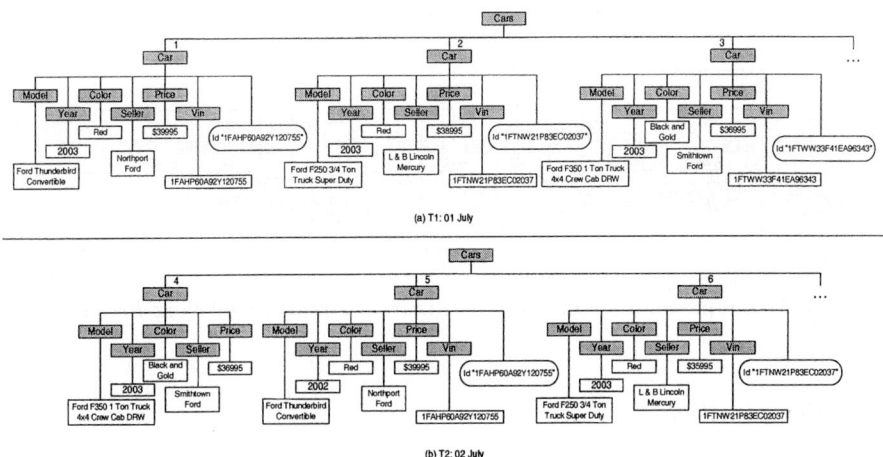

Fig. 3. Tree representation of query results from Figure 1 modelling *Identifiers*

Figure 1 depicts search query results for *Ford* cars in AutoTrader.com, executed on two different days. The results are presented as a list of particular car offerings. Each offering contains details of the car, such as *Model, Year, Price, Color, Seller, VIN*, etc. VIN (Vehicle Identification Number) is the unique identifying number for a specific car assigned by manufacturer. It is obvious that as VIN is the part of information that should be specified by the publisher, it may not be presented in query results for some cars. For instance, the first car in results depicted in Figure 1(b) has no VIN specified. Nevertheless, if we use VINs as *Identifiers* for the cars in the list, then we can distinguish those cars with specified VIN effectively.

A sample of tree representation of the results in Figure 1 is shown in Figure 3. In the tree representation, every offering from the real data is represented by the node Car. The Car nodes in T_1 and T_2 have child attributes with name Id and value equal to VIN. Intuitively, if we wish to detect changes between the two versions of the query results, then we can match Car nodes between two subtrees by comparing Id values. For instance, node 2 in T_1 matches node 6 in T_2 and node 1 in T_1 matches node 5 in T_2. Suppose, there are no more Car nodes in both trees. Then we can say that node 3 is deleted in T_2 as its *identifier* does not match any *identifier* in T_2. Node 3 also does not match node 4 as node 4 does not have any *identifier* attribute. Hence, node 4 is inserted in T_2.

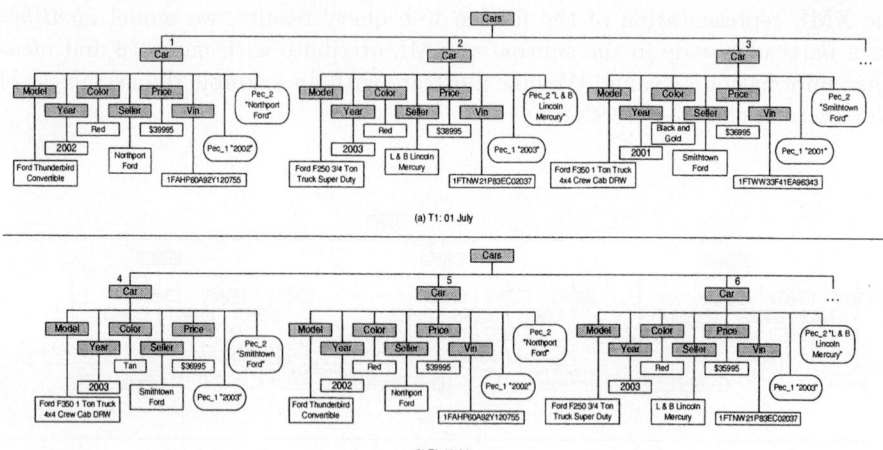

Fig. 4. Tree representation of query results from Figure 1 modelling *Peculiarities*

2.3 Peculiarities

One or more elements in the result of a hidden web query result set can serve as non-unique characteristics for distinguishing the results from other results. Two results that have the same characteristics (same attribute/value pair) can be matched with each other. While results that have different characteristics can not be matched with each other. Examples of types of such characteristics are: `Year` or `Model` of a `Car` node in the query results from car trading site, `Title` or `Year` for a `Movie` node in the query results from movie database, `Title` or `Publisher` for a `Book` node in the query results from on-line book catalog. These non-unique elements are called *peculiarities*. Note that these elements may not identify a result (entity) uniquely. But they may provide enough information to identify results that does not refer to the same entities.

We allow specifying any number of *peculiarities* on a node. *Peculiarities* are denoted by node attributes with names $Pec_1, Pec_2, \ldots, Pec_n$ for all n peculiarity attributes specified for a particular node. If a node does not have a *peculiarity* attribute (the subelement may be missing) then the *peculiarity* value is set to "*". Note that the *peculiarity* attribute for a node can appear in any version of query results, but once it appears we assume that it will not disappear in the future versions. As we never know which *peculiarity* may appear for a node in future, a node with no *peculiarity* attribute should be matched with nodes having *peculiarities*. This statement reflects the case for most hidden web sites we have studied. We illustrate with an example how *peculiarities* can be useful for the change detection problem.

Reconsider Figure 1. We can find several candidates to *Peculiarities* for cars in the list, i.e., *Color*, *Year*, or *Seller*. Figure 4 shows tree representation of the results in Figure 1 highlighting *peculiarities* for various nodes. There are

```
Input: Index, /* index page of query results */
       HW-EC  /* HW-EC description of these results */
Output: Doc   /* XML representation of query results */

1  T. tree    /* for storing tree representation of
                 query results */
2  Ta: tree   /* which is enabled to store attributes
                 for every node */
3  [Te]: set of trees
4  Doc: XML document
5  set T, Ta, [Te], and Doc empty
6  let Root be the root of HW-EC
7  add Root as a root to T
   /* extract information from query results */
8  for all Ch that is a child of Root in HW-EC do
9    add ExtractNode(Index, Ch) to [Te]
10 end for
11 add every Te from [Te] as a child of root node to T
   /* assign attributes */
12 Ta = AssignAttributes(T, HW-EC)
   /* generate XML */
13 Doc = GenerateXML(Ta)
14 Return Doc
```

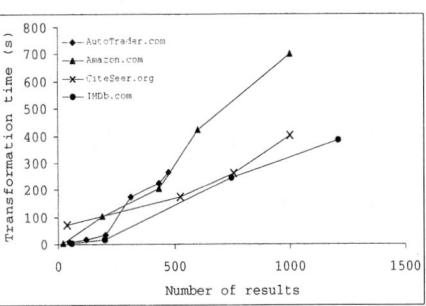

(a) Algorithm HW-Transform (b) Performance study

Fig. 5. Algorithm *HW-Transform*

two *peculiarities* specified, Year as attribute with name Pec_1 and Seller as attribute with name Pec_2 for every Car node.

We can now match Car nodes between the two versions of the tree using *peculiarity* attributes. Using only Pec_1 for matching nodes, we can match exactly node 1 to node 5 as no other nodes have Pec_1 attributes with value "2002". Using only Pec_1 we also observe that node 3 in T_1 does not match any node in T_2 as there are no nodes with Pec_1="2001" in T_2. Thus, we can state that node 3 is deleted in T_2. Using only Pec_1 we can match node 2 to nodes 4 or 6, but we are not able to say which of these two does not match node 2. However, if we use both Pec_1 and Pec_2, then we can answer this question by comparing Pec_2 of nodes 2 with nodes 4 and 6. As we can exactly match node 2 to node 6, we can say that node 4 is inserted in T_2.

3 Algorithm HW-Transform

Figure 5 depicts the *HW-Transform* algorithm for transforming hidden web query results to XML format. This algorithm takes as input the first page of the results and $\mathcal{HW} - \mathcal{EC}$ description of these results, and returns XML representation of the results. There are three main steps in the algorithm. The first step is to extract information from the query results and generate tree T storing extracted information in hierarchical order according to $\mathcal{HW} - \mathcal{EC}$ description of these results. Lines 8-11 in Figure 5 describe this step. The **ExtractNode** function implements a recursive algorithm for extracting pieces of data from the query results corresponding to node N in $\mathcal{HW} - \mathcal{EC}$ description. The next step is to traverse tree T in order to assign attributes to the nodes according to $\mathcal{HW} - \mathcal{EC}$ description of the query results (Line 12). Note that we do not assign attributes to particular nodes while first parsing the tree in the previous step as attributes can be located in different parts of the tree. It is faster to assign all attributes by performing one traversal in a separate step rather than doing a lot of additional traversals in the previous step. In the final step, we generate the XML document from the tree by traversing it starting from the root.

4 Performance Study

In this section, we present performance analysis of our prototype system. All the experiments have been performed on a Pentium 4 CPU 2.4 GHz with 512 MB of RAM. We used Microsoft Windows 2000 Professional as operating system. We have implemented HW-STALKER using Java. We use the data from the following four hidden web sites for our experiments: `AutoTrader.com`, `Amazon.com`, `IMDb.com`, and `CiteSeer.org`.

To evaluate the performance of the extraction of relevant data from hidden web pages to XML format, we have to evaluate the performance of rule induction mechanism and the performance of HTML to XML transformation mechanism. Performance of the rule induction system is determined by the time a user spends on creating $\mathcal{HW} - \mathcal{EC}$ tree. It is also determined by the time a user needs to provide examples of data for each element of $\mathcal{HW} - \mathcal{EC}$ tree. This time dramatically depends on the number of examples a user should provide for each element of results to learn correct extraction rules. The number of training examples for some of the elements of the hidden web data that was used in our experiments are shown in Figure 6(a). Observe that we only need one example to learn extraction rules for one element for 40% of elements in the query results. We need more than five examples for one element for only 5% of the elements. The number of results needed to learn extraction rules for particular element is determined by the number of different HTML-environments which can be found for this element in different results [7].

To evaluate the performance of HTML to XML transformation module using the *HW-Transform* algorithm, we have extracted the results of different queries from the four hidden web sites. The set of queries that we have used in this experiment is shown in Figure 6(b). The summary of this experiment is shown in Figure 5(b).

5 Related Work

WIEN [8] takes as input a set of example pages where data of interest is labelled, and the output is a wrapper that is consistent with each labelled page. **SRV** [5] is an approach for wrapper generation based on the Natural Language Processing (NLP). SRV is a tool for learning extraction rules of text documents, based on a given set of training examples. It is a single-slot tool, like WIEN, thus it supports neither nesting nor semistructured objects. A technique for supervised wrapper generation based on a logic-based declarative language called *Elog* is presented in [1]. This technique is implemented in a system called Lixto which assists the user to semi-automatically create wrapper programs by providing a

(a) Number of samples

Site	Element	Number of samples
AutoTrader.com	AutoTrader	1
	Car	8
	Model	5
	Year	1
	VIN	1
	Price	1
	Color	1
	Miles	2
	CHAIN	3
IMDb.com	IMDB_Comments	2
	Comment	3
	Author	2
	From	2
	Date	1
	Summary	1
	CHAIN	3

Site	Element	Number of samples
Amazon.com	Amazon	1
	Book	6
	ISBN	2
	Title	1
	Price	1
	Year	1
	Authors	3
	Availability	1
	CHAIN	6
	FANOUT	3
CiteSeer.org	CiteSeer	2
	Paper	3
	Title	1
	Year	1
	Conference	1
	Abstract	1
	Authors	1
	CHAIN	4
	FANOUT	3

(b) Different queries to sample sites

Site	Query	Number of results	Number of CHAIN pages	Number of FANOUT pages
AutoTrader.com	2000-2004 Acura of any model within 25 miles from ZIP 00501	48	2	-
	1983-2004 Ford Escort within 25 Miles from ZIP 10001	120	5	-
	1983-2004 Jaguar of any model within 50 Miles from ZIP 00501	202	9	-
	1983-2004 Land Rover Range Rover within 200 Miles from ZIP 00501	310	13	-
	1990-2004 Cadillac with mileage under 75,000 within 50 Miles from ZIP10001	430	18	-
	1991-2004 Toyota with price range from 10,000 to 15,000 within 50 Miles from ZIP 10001	472	19	-
	1983-2004 Ford of any model within 25 Miles from ZIP 10001	500	20	-
Amazon.com	Search for "gardenia"	21	2	21
	Search for "snooker"	190	9	190
	Search for "intranet"	431	44	431
	Search for "dock"	599	60	599
	Search for "dot"	1001	101	1001
IMDb.com	User comments to "Arrival"	58	3	-
	User comments to "Once Upon a Time in Mexico"	201	11	-
	User comments to "Star Wars V"	746	38	-
	User comments to "Harry Potter and the Sorcerer's Stone"	1212	61	-
CiteSeer.org	Search for "hidden web"	38	2	38
	Search for "google"	523	27	523
	Search for "google"	754	38	754
	Search for "web"	1000	50	1000

Fig. 6. Performance study

fully visual and interactive user interface. With Lixto, expressive visual wrapper generation is possible.

Compared to WIEN, which extracts all items at one time, in our approach we use several single slot rules based on STALKER. Also, we support nesting unlike WIEN and SRV. Compared to Lixto, our approach is much more user-friendly as it is based on STALKER. As user should define extraction rules himself in Lixto, it is a complicated task even using GUI. Furthermore, unlike the above approaches, HW-STALKER is developed specifically for hidden web data and hence is able to extract key attributes (identifiers and peculiarities) from the query results. Our system is also focused on extracting data from dynamically generated hyperlinked web pages only.

RoadRunner [3] is the HTML-aware tool for automatic wrapper generation based on the inherent features of HTML documents. The unique feature that distinguishes ROADRUNNER from all other approaches is that the process of wrapper generation is fully automatic and no user intervention is requested. However, such flexibility poses disadvantage as far as extracting hidden web data is concerned as it cannot extract identifiers and peculiarities automatically.

6 Conclusions

In this paper, we present a machine learning-based approach for extracting relevant hidden web query results and transforming them to XML. We propose an algorithm called *HW-Transform* for transforming hidden web data to XML format. In our approach, we extend the STALKER technique to extract results from a set of dynamically generated hyperlinked web pages. The XML representation of query results encapsulates only the data that a user is interested in. One of the key features of our approach is that a user maps special *key attributes* in query results, called *identifiers* and *peculiarities*, into XML attributes. These attributes facilitate change detection, data integration etc. by efficiently identifying related results. As a proof of concept, we have implemented a prototype system called HW-STALKER using Java. Our experiments demonstrate that *HW-Transform* shows acceptable performance for transforming query results to XML.

References

1. R. Baumgartner, S. Flesca, and G. Gottlob. Visual Web Information Extraction with Lixto. In *Proceedings of the 27th VLDB Conference*, Roma, Italy, 2001.
2. S. Chakrabarti, M. van den Berg, and B. Dom. Focused Crawling: A New Approach to Topic-Specific Web Resource Discovery. In *8th World Wide Web Conference*, May 1999.
3. V. Crescenzi, G. Mecca, and P. Merialdo. RoadRunner: Towards Automatic Data Extraction from Large Web Sites. In *Proceedings of the 26th International Conference on Very Large Database Systems*, pages 109–118, Roma, Italy, 2001.
4. M. Diligenti, F. Coetzee, S. Lawrence, C.L. Giles, and M. Gori. Focused Crawling using Context Graphs. In *26th International Conference on Very Large Databases, VLDB 2000*, September 2000.
5. D. Freitag. Machine Learning for Information Extraction in Informal Domains. *Machine Learning*, 39, 2/3:169–202, 2000.
6. H. Davulku, J. Freire, M. Kifer, and I.V. Ramakrishnan. A Layered Architecture for Querying Dynamic Web Content. In *ACM Conference on Management of Data (SIGMOD)*, June 1999.
7. C.A. Knoblock, K. Lerman, S. Minton, and I. Muslea. Accurately and Reliably Extracting Data from the Web: A Machine Learning Approach. *IEEE Data Engineering Bulletin*, 23(4):33–41, 2000.
8. N. Kushmerick. Wrapper Induction: Efficiency and Expressiveness. *Artificial Intelligence Journal*, 118, 1-2:15–68, 2000.
9. I. Muslea, S. Minton, and C.A. Knoblock. Hierarchical Wrapper Induction for Semistructured Information Sources. *Autonomous Agents and Multi-Agent Systems*, 4(1/2):93–114, 2001.

Putting Enhanced Hypermedia Personalization into Practice via Web Mining

Eugenio Cesario, Francesco Folino, and Riccardo Ortale

DEIS, University of Calabria
Via Bucci 41c, 87036 Rende (CS) – Italy
{cesario,ffolino,ortale}@si.deis.unical.it

Abstract. We present a novel personalization engine that provides individualized access to Web contents/services by means of data mining techniques. It associates adaptive content delivery and navigation support with form filling, a functionality that catches the typical interaction of a user with a Web service, in order to automatically fill in its form fields at successive accesses from that visitor. Our proposal was developed within the framework of the ITB@NK system to the purpose of effectively improving users' Web experience in the context of Internet Banking. This study focuses on its software architecture and formally investigates the underlying personalization process.

1 Introduction

We present a novel personalization engine, based on data mining techniques, which automatizes an adaptation process consisting of three main steps: *user categorization*, that aims at grouping users into homogeneous clusters from a behavioral point of view; *behavioral modelling*, that is the act of learning reliable models of the preferences, requirements and browsing behaviour of the users within each cluster; *personalization*, that coincides with the actual delivery of services and contents tailored to the profile of the target user. In particular, personalization is achieved as a combination of three orthogonal functionalities: *adaptive content delivery*, i.e. the recommendation of pages with contents pertaining to visitor interests and requirements; *adaptive navigation support*, i.e. the act of suggesting personalized navigation paths; *adaptive form filling*, i.e. the process of learning the typical input from a user to a Web service in order to fill in its form fields at successive requests from that visitor. Our proposal was developed in the context of the ITB@NK system, a research project targeted at improving users' Web experience with contents and services from traditional bank information-systems. Notwithstanding, its modularity and extensibility features make it an effective solution to the problem of Web individualization across a variety of distinct application environments. Traditional attempts to Web personalization available from the literature divide into four main approaches, namely solutions based on *manual decision rules*, *content-based filtering*, *collaborative filtering*, and *Web usage mining*. Manual decision rule systems [12], apply fixed adaptation rules to static user profiles, typically obtained at registration time.

Their major limitations are the considerable effort required to define and update these rules, the progressive degrade of personalization accuracy due to the aging of static profiles and the involvement of end users in providing their preferences, that typically diminishes the attractiveness of Web sites. Content-based filtering systems [11], first learn a model of user preferences in Web contents, and then try to estimate their interest in unseen Web documents on the basis of some content similarity between these documents and the inferred profiles. A main drawback of such an approach is the inherent difficulty in actually catching a semantic similarity between the contents of two Web pages. Collaborative filtering systems [9] do not rely on any a priori knowledge of Web content. Rather they guess visitor interests in a specific Web item (either a textual content or a service) by detecting a neighborhood of users, whose known preferences in that specific item are then somehow correlated to make suitable interest predictions. However, users with no explicit interests do not benefit from recommendations. Also, the outcome of personalization is affected by the correlation step, that penalizes visitors with few interests. Finally, efficiency and scalability limitations emerge with large numbers of users and items. Systems relying on Web usage mining methods [13, 7, 14] apply machine learning and statistical techniques to visitor clickstream data to automatically reconstruct their browsing activities and, hence, a model of their requirements, preferences and tastes, without any user intervention or a priori knowledge of the specific Web setting. Our approach to personalization conciliates the main benefits of the above studies without suffering from their individual limitations. Specifically, suitable Web usage mining methods permit to infer and regularly update behavioural profiles from raw usage data, without corrective interventions from a human expert being necessary. Cooperation is only required for unknown users when they first access the ITB@NK hyperspace: a concise questionnaire serves to detect visitors' interest in the main content categories. Though potentially disappointing, such a task effectively requires very few clicks and should not be perceived as a deterrent to either ongoing or successive browsing activities. Finally, the adoption of a collaborative approach to refine preference profiles mitigates the effects of poorly answered questionnaires. An overview about methods and techniques for adaptation can be found in [2]. [8] exhaustively surveys recent research efforts in the field of Web usage mining for personalization.

This paper is organized as follows. Section 2 briefly overviews the main functionalities of the ITB@NK system and then provides an insight into the software architecture of its underlying personalization engine. A formal model of the automated adaptation process is proposed in section 3, that also deals with the specific data mining techniques exploited at the different stages of the process. Finally, section 4 draws some conclusions and highlights future developments.

2 A Novel Personalization Engine

ITB@NK is an adaptive front-office that provides personalized access to the contents and services from traditional bank information-systems. Precisely, it provides users with an adaptive Web interface for performing tasks such as online payments and bank transfers, accessing information about their account balances and bank activities, and reading personalized news. ITB@NK exploits a modular and extensible personalization engine, shown in fig. 1. The following analysis focuses on its data sources, main modules and individual components, while section 3 formally deals with the technicalities of its adaptation process.

Data Sources. The *Repository* stores visitors' clickstream and demographic data. It also includes a set of service logs, that keep trace of users' input values to the available Web services. The *Data Warehouse* maintains meaningful information such as visitor browsing sessions, behavioural and interest profiles for disjoint subsets of users, the recent exploitation history of Web services and a suitable index for locating topics scattered on different Web pages. The *CSS/XSL Repository* contains resources detailing the presentation aspects of the hypermedia front-end. XSL shyle sheets contribute to the overall layout of the application front-end, while CSS style sheets specify the presentation properties for front-end elements, such as buttons, scroll bars and hyperlinks.

The Personalization Modules. The adaptation process relies on three functionalities, namely adaptive content delivery, navigation support and form filling, that are entrusted to as many personalization modules. The *Adaptive Content Delivery* module aims at recommending contents presumably of interest to the visitor. The *DataWarehouse Content Manager* accesses information within the *Data Warehouse* on behalf of the whole module. It also interacts with the *User Preferences* and *Preference Clustering* components. The former holds the preferences of the generic user in specific topics. The latter builds partitions of users with homogeneous interests in the *Data Warehouse*. The *Content Indexer* constructs an inverted table representing the relevance of each topic within any available Web page. The *Content Search* exploits information retrieval techniques to efficiently detect pages with contents related to a query topic.

The *Adaptive Navigation Support* module adapts hyperlinks within the application front-end, in such a way to propose personalized navigation paths. The *DataWarehouse Navigation Manager* reconstructs visitor browsing sessions within the *Data Warehouse*, by applying some preprocessing techniques (i.e. data cleaning, user identification, session identification and page-view identification [6]) to the raw usage data within the *Repository*. The *E. M. Clustering* component forms navigational clusters, i.e. groups of users with similar browsing behaviour, and associates a probabilistic characterization to the navigational behaviour of the users within each such cluster. The *Adaptation Algorithm* implements a suitable technique for tailoring links to visitor browsing profile.

The *Form filler* module improves the usability of Web services by automatically filling in their form fields with input values that best describe the typical exploitation pattern of each individual user. The *DataWarehouse Form Manager* builds suitable *Data Warehouse* tables from the service log information within the *Repository*: any such table stores the recent input values from all visitors to a given Web service. The *Service Descriptor* keeps trace of those services that are subjected to form filling. For each such service, it manages details that specify

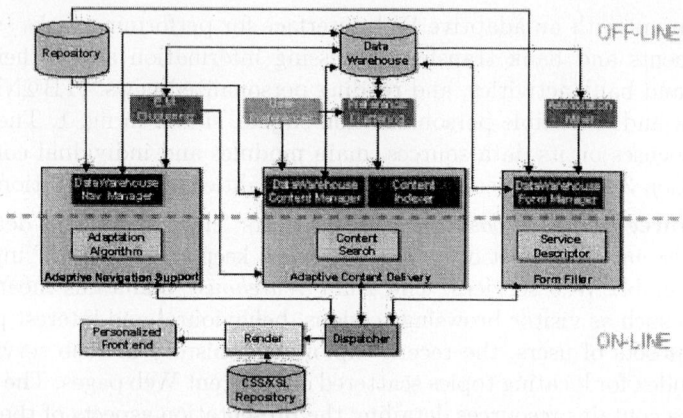

Fig. 1. The software architecture of our personalization engine

what fields are actually manipulated by the *Form Filler*. The *Association Miner* computes the most typical set of input values from any user to a Web service.

Two Main Components. The *Dispatcher* is a core component, since it encodes the control flow of any Web application built on top of the proposed engine. It receives user requests and dynamically associates them with a specific personalization workflow, that depends on a number of characteristics of the request, such as its emitting device and the referred hypermedia resource. The *Dispatcher* coordinates the behaviour of personalization modules and eventually activates the *Render*. This module assembles the contributions from personalization modules into a response, whose mark-up language and presentation are targeted at the access device from which the initial request was originated.

The architecture in fig. 1 is built around the *Model-View-Controller* (MVC) design pattern [4]. This allows to the separate the three essential aspects of an application, i.e. its business, presentation and control logic with the purpose of considerably reducing both time and costs for development and maintenance. Precisely, the *Dispatcher* acts as the Controller in the MVC design pattern, the *Render* pays the role of the View, while the personalization modules and associated components behave as the Model. Finally, it is worth noticing that the exploitation of powerful tools for presenting hypermedia documents supports personalization on a variety of access channels such as the Web, Wap-compliant mobile phones, and the human voice carried out by the telephone system.

3 A Formal Model for the Personalization Process

Let $\mathcal{W} = \{p_1, \ldots, p_n\}$ represent the hyperspace of a Web application, consisting of n Web pages. In the following we assume that $\mathcal{W}$ denotes the ITB@NK hyperspace, though our treatment can be applied to a variety of Web settings. Our formalization addresses the contents, links and services within any page $p \in \mathcal{W}$.

A term vector v_p is associated to each page $p \in \mathcal{W}$ in order to represent it into a multidimensional Euclidean space. Term vector cardinality coincides with that of the so-called Web site dictionary SD, i.e. a collection of all topics within the hyperspace $\mathcal{W}$. Technically, SD is a vector of unique term stems resulting from the application of traditional information retrieval techniques (such as term extraction, term deletion and stemming [5]) to the pages in $\mathcal{W}$. Also, the generic coordinate $v_p[i]$ indicates the relevance of topic $SD[i]$ within p and is computed by means of the *TFIDF* technique.

Notation $\mathcal{L}_p = <(l_1, a_1^x), \ldots, (l_m, a_m^x)>$ indicates the set of m non-contextual links [2] within a page p, i.e. all the available links with the exception of those that are anchored to actual contents. Entities l_j and a_j^x respectively denote the j-th link in $\mathcal{L}_p$ and a corresponding set of annotations, i.e. suitable presentation information concerning l_j. Our model currently focuses on link color (c_j^x), font-type (ft_j^x) and font-size (fs_j^x). Formally, $a_j^x = \{c_j^x, ft_j^x, fs_j^x\}$, where index x represents the relevance of a link to a given user. It takes values in the set $\{n, m, h\}$, whose elements distinguish among three degrees of link reputation, that is navigational (n), moderate (m) and high (h): intuitively, a high link reputation requires brighter colors, more readable font types and larger font sizes. For each x, annotations a_j^x are suitably defined to address particular application requirements. Fig. 2 shows a sample page p. Links within $\mathcal{L}_p = <(l_{news}, a_{news}^h), (l_{markets}, a_{markets}^n), (l_{stockportfolio}, a_{stockportfolio}^m), (l_{yourmoney}, a_{yourmoney}^n)>$ reveal a prominent interest of the current visitor into news and portfolio management. Presentation guidelines provide that *arial* is the font type for anchor text; links with high, moderate and normal reputation are respectively rendered in red, green and blue; correspondingly, a large (14 pt), medium (12 pt), small (10 pt) font-size is exploited. In the specific case of fig. 2, annotations become $a_{news}^h = \{red, arial, 14\}$, $a_{markets}^n = \{blue, arial, 10\}$, $a_{stockportfolio}^m = \{green, arial, 12\}$, $a_{yourmoney}^n = \{blue, arial, 10\}$.

The set of Web services within a page $p \in \mathcal{W}$ is denoted by $\mathcal{S}_p = \{ws_1, \ldots, ws_n\}$. In particular, the form associated to the generic Web service $ws \in \mathcal{S}_p$, namely $\mathcal{F}_{ws}$, is a collection $\mathcal{F}_{ws} = \{f_1, \ldots, f_l\}$ of l form fields. A unique Web service, *search*, appears within the page of fig. 2. In such a case, $\mathcal{S}_p = \{search\}$, and $\mathcal{F}_{search}$ consists of a sole input field.

Finally, pages in $\mathcal{W}$ allow to catch visitor browsing activities. Assume that $\mathcal{U} = \{u_1, \ldots, u_N\}$ corresponds to the overall user population of $\mathcal{W}$. A set of n_u browsing sessions, $D_u = \{s_{u,1}, \ldots, s_{u,j}, \ldots, s_{u,n_u}\}$, is associated with any visitor $u \in \mathcal{U}$, where the generic session $s_{u,j}$ is defined in terms of a sequence of accesses to pages in $\mathcal{W}$. As a consequence, $\mathcal{D} = \{D_{u_1}, \ldots, D_{u_N}\}$ is the data set with all the interactive sessions from the above N users. The following subsections provide an insight into the distinct phases of the devised personalization approach.

3.1 User Clustering and Behavioural Modelling

These are two off-line steps, that respectively address the problem of finding groups of users with similar navigational habits and learning a behavioural profile for the individuals within each such cluster. Both phases rely on a technique

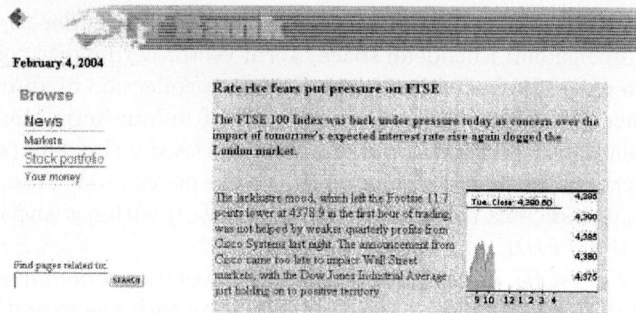

Fig. 2. A sample Web page from ITB@NK hyperspace

introduced in [3] and performed by the *E.M. Clustering* component. We discuss below how the mentioned technique can be seamlessly exploited within our formulation. The main idea is dividing the original set of N users into K sets, in such a way that the generic visitor $u \in \mathcal{U}$ has probability $p(c_u = k)$ of belonging to cluster k, with $1 \leq k \leq K$ and $\sum_{k=1}^{K} p(c_u = k) = 1$. Note that c_u is a random variable that takes into account the cluster membership of u. The behaviour of users within cluster k is characterized by a parameter set Θ_k, that depends on the specific probabilistic approach adopted to model the navigational activities in that cluster. $\Theta = \{\Theta_1, \ldots, \Theta_K\}$ is the set of all cluster parameters. For simplicity, we assume that browsing sessions from individual visitors are independent: though such an hypothesis may not catch some rare behavioural patterns, it works reasonably well in practice. This assumption allows us to adopt a simple, first-order Markov model for the behaviour within individual clusters. Given $p, p_i, p_j \in \mathcal{W}$, for each k between 1 and K, it holds that $\Theta_k = \{\pi_k(p), T_k(p_i, p_j)\}$, where $\pi_k(p)$ is a vector of starting page probabilities and $T_k(p_i, p_j)$ is an $n \times n$ matrix of transition probabilities. From the Markovian definition of a chain of events (i.e. page accesses), the probability of a browsing session $s_{u,j}$ conditioned on cluster membership c_u can be written as follows

$$p(s_{u,j}|c_u = k, \Theta_k) = \pi_k(s_{u,j,1}) \prod_{l=1}^{L_{u,j}-1} T_k(s_{u,j,l+1}, s_{u,j,l}), \quad 1 \leq k \leq K$$

where $s_{u,j,l}$ and $L_{i,j}$ respectively denote the l-th page and the overall number of accesses within $s_{u,j}$. As a consequence, the probability of all navigation sessions D_u, conditioned on u's cluster membership becomes:

$$p(D_u|c_u = k, \Theta_k) = \prod_{j=1}^{n_u} p(s_{u,j}|c_u = k, \Theta_k)$$

Obviously, since there is no a priori knowledge of the cluster to which u belongs, the mixture model below must be exploited:

$$p(D_u|\Theta) = \sum_{k=1}^{K} p(D_u|c_u = k, \Theta_k) \cdot p(c_u = k, \Theta_k)$$

Under the reasonable conjecture that navigation data from distinct users are independent, the likelihood of $\mathcal{D}$ is given by $p(\mathcal{D}|\Theta) = \prod_{j=1}^{N} p(D_{u_j}|\Theta)$. Conceptually, the problem of grouping and profiling Web users reduces to that of computing a suitable estimate of the set Θ, in such a way to maximize clustering quality, here intended as either the maximum likelihood (ML) or the maximum a-posteriori (MAP) likelihood of the data. Formally, it is a question of computing Θ^* such that $\Theta^* = \arg\max_\Theta \{p(\mathcal{D}|\Theta)\}$ or $\Theta_{MAP} = \arg\max_\Theta \{p(\mathcal{D}|\Theta)p(\Theta)\}$ respectively in the ML or MAP case. The Expectation Maximization algorithm in [3] allows to compute Θ^* from an initial estimate Θ by iterating a sequence of two steps, known as Expectation and Maximization, until at least a local maximum of the ML (or MAP) function is reached. Precisely, for each user $u \in \mathcal{U}$ and each cluster index k (with $1 \leq k \leq K$), the Expectation step computes the class probabilities $p(c_u = k|D_u, \Theta)$, on the basis of the current estimate of the parameters Θ. The Maximization step exploits the previous class probabilities for improving the current estimates of $\pi_k(s)$, $T_k(s_i, s_j)$ for each possible value of k. Three main benefits of the technique in [3] are mentioned next. A distinct number of browsing sessions for each user is allowed: individuals with more sessions have a higher impact on the estimation of cluster transition matrices, whereas most of previous studies, such as [7], assume that each historical session comes from a different user, thus affecting profile reliability. Moreover, user sessions are treated as sequences of page accesses, which allows to model navigation paths with variable length: [13] investigates the advantages of exploiting sequences rather than vectors for representing navigation sessions. Finally, no practical distinction between clustering and profiling really exists: both phases are jointly performed. On the contrary, conventional approaches such as [7] exploit distinct methods to find and characterize session clusters.

3.2 Adaptive Content Delivery

This functionality is triggered at the time of a request for a Web page p. Here, the aim is at detecting and suggesting a small subset of Web pages in $\mathcal{W}$, whose contents are presumably of interest to the user. Page recommendation takes into account both visitors' location within the hyperspace $\mathcal{W}$ (topics in p should be of some interest to u, having been required) and their explicit preferences. The generic visitor $u \in \mathcal{U}$ is associated with a preference vector pv_u, obtained from her/his questionnaire, whose entries measure u's interest into the corresponding topics within SD. The *Preference Clustering* component finds a partition $\mathcal{C} = \{C_1, \ldots, C_L\}$ of L sets of homogeneous visitor preferences, according to a technique described in [10], that also synthesizes any such cluster C_l into a representative P_l. For each $l \in [1, L]$, representatives are such that $|P_l| = |SD|$ and

$P_l[i]$ represents the average interest of all users within C_l in topic $SD[i]$. In the following we denote by P_l^u the representative of the interest cluster to which user u belongs. The *DataWarehouse Content Manager* merges the preference vector pv_u with P_l^u. Such a process of *collaborative refining* is conceived to improve the estimates of user tastes, when poor knowledge (i.e. sparse data) about their actual preferences is available. The resulting preference vector pv'_u is defined as:

$$pv'_u = \begin{cases} pv_u[i] & \text{if } pv_u[i] \neq 0 \\ \alpha_u \cdot P_l^u[i] & \text{otherwise} \end{cases} \quad 1 \leq i \leq |SD|, \ 0 < \alpha_u < 1$$

α_u is a damping factor for the relevance of those interests that are likely to be shared by u, being borrowed from other individuals with partly overlapping tastes. Intuitively, for each user $u \in \mathcal{U}$, constant α_u is a degree of correlation between pv_u and P_l^u. So far, u's general preferences have been addressed. Those related to her/his browsing activities are deduced by the term vector v_p, associated to the required page p. Given an interest threshold τ, the *Content Search* component dynamically yields $\mathcal{R} = \{p' \in \mathcal{W} | \alpha_1 \cdot sim(v_{p'}, v_p) + \alpha_2 \cdot sim(v_{p'}, pv'_u) > \tau\}$, a set of recommendations whose top-N pages are added to p (N generally ranges from 2 to 4). Heterogeneity in suggestion topics helps users accomplish distinct tasks within a browsing session. Note that recommendations in $\mathcal{R}$ also refer to new Web pages: indeed, these are processed by the *Content Indexer*, that updates the term-by-document (inverted) table (see sec.2), thus enabling the *Content Search* to retrieve them. Constants α_1 and α_2 determine the degree of recommendation adherence respectively to contents in p and u's general preferences: they are such that $0 \leq \alpha_1, \alpha_2 \leq 1$ and $\alpha_1 + \alpha_2 = 1$. α_1, α_2 and τ are empirically chosen by performing sensitivity analysis on visitors' browsing sessions and preference data. Finally, function sim refers to cosine similarity [5].

3.3 Adaptive Navigation Support

The *Adaptation Algorithm* component performs link annotation [2] to indicate appropriate browsing paths to the user. It dynamically changes some visual cues of links such as their color, font-type and font size to reflect their relevance to the visitor. If k represents the index of the visitor cluster to which the generic user u belongs with highest probability and p denotes the Web page required by u, the annotation of each navigation alternative $l_j \in \mathcal{L}_p$, for each j between 1 and $|\mathcal{L}_p|$, requires detecting a suitable value assignment for the index x of the associated term a_j^x. Let us indicate with p' the page pointed by the generic link $l_j \in \mathcal{L}_p$ and with τ^n and τ^m two probability thresholds. l_j acquires a low relevance to u if $T_k(p, p') < \tau^n$, that is if u has a low probability of accessing p' from p: in such cases, l_j is annotated with a_j^n. Conversely, annotations a_j^m and a_j^h are a consequence of higher transition probabilities: a moderate (resp. high) relevance is attributed to l_j if it holds that $\tau^n < T_k(p, p') \leq \tau^m$ (resp. $T_k(p, p') > \tau^m$). The advantage of link annotation is that it does not alter the layout order of links and avoid the issues arising with incorrect mental maps [2]. The clustering strategy in sec. 3.1 yields behavioural profiles that are one-step transition-probability matrices. Future efforts aim at learning a concept hierarchy from the Web pages in $\mathcal{W}$ so that, at a more abstract domain-level, the underlying reasons behind visitors' browsing paths emerge in terms of interest into particular concepts: clearly, this requires suitably adapting matrices $T_k(p, p')$ to represent the probability of accessing the concept category of page p' from that of p, given the specific trajectory $p \to p'$. Semantic personalization allows more effective recommendations, without suffering from the difficulties inherent in suggesting new Web pages.

3.4 Adaptive Form Filling

This functionality dynamically fills in the form fields of a Web service with the values that the user typically inputs. The *Service Descriptor* keeps trace of the services in $\mathcal{W}$ that are subjected to form filling. In particular, for each such service ws within a Web page $p \in \mathcal{W}$, a sequence of indexes, $i_1, i_2, \ldots, i_h$ (with $1 \leq i_1 < i_2 < \ldots < i_h \leq |\mathcal{F}_{ws}|$), is leveraged to identify a meaningful subset of $\mathcal{F}_{ws}$, namely $\mathcal{F}'_{ws} = \{f_{i_1}, \ldots, f_{i_h}\}$, that contains the form fields of ws to be filled in. Let y_{i_l} represent the input from a user $u \in \mathcal{U}$ to the field $f_{i_l} \in \mathcal{F}'_{ws}$. An interaction of u with ws can be modelled as an itemset $is_{u,ws} = \{y_{i_1}, \ldots, y_{i_h}\}$. The *Association Miner* performs the Apriori algorithm [1] for mining c-itemsets (i.e. itemsets with cardinality c) from the interactions of an individual. Formally, the problem of identifying a set of input values, that closest resembles the typical interaction of u with the Web service ws in a page p, reduces to the computation of a c-itemset $is^*_{u,ws}$ for suitable values of its support and cardinality. Support guarantees a certain degree of input regularity. Cardinality indicates a minimum number of fields in $\mathcal{F}'_{ws}$, that $is^*_{u,ws}$ must cover.

4 Conclusions and Future Developments

The main contribution of our work is the introduction of a novel personalization engine that combines adaptive content delivery and navigation support with adaptive form filling, a feature for enhancing user interaction with Web services. The overall personalization process is parametric w.r.t. the adaptation methods: the above functionalities can be independently implemented by choosing an adhoc suite of data mining techniques, that best suit the peculiarities of a given environment. From this perspective, ITB@NK is a meaningful customization conceived for the context of Internet Banking. Such a customization is formally investigated. Experiments are being performed to measure the effectiveness of the ITB@NK adaptation process in a somehow objective manner, that accounts for subjective perception of personalization. Future developments include three further lines of research, besides that mentioned at the end of sec. 3.3. First, the automatic detection of user interests, achievable by exploiting the term stems within recently accessed Web pages as a model of visitors' current interests and requirements. Second, the enhancement of navigation support, to the purpose of applying annotation and sorting respectively to contextual and non-contextual links [2]. Dynamic link generation may be exploited as a means for shortening navigation paths through the hyperspace. Third, an experimental evaluation of the clustering approach in [13], that employs textual and usage proximity to catch similarities even between pairs of Web pages with heterogeneous contents, such as text and images. This may bring to a more reliable characterization of the browsing behaviour within session clusters w.r.t. to the technique in [3].

Acknowledgments

This work was developed within the framework of the project ITB@NK, which is carried out by Carisiel, in collaboration with ICAR-CNR and DEIS-UNICAL, and is partially funded by a MIUR grant. The authors express their gratitude to Prof. Domenico Saccá, Dr. Giuseppe Manco, Dr. Francesco Natale and to all the members of the ITB@NK project for their precious cooperation.

References

1. R. Agrawal and R. Srikant. Fast algorithms for mining association rules. In *Proc. of Int. Conf. on Very Large Data Bases*, pages 487–499, 1994.
2. P. Brusilovsky. Adaptive hypermedia. *User Modeling and User Adapted Interaction*, 11(1-2):87–100, 2001.
3. I.V. Cadez, S. Gaffney, and P. Smyth. A general probabilistic framework for clustering individuals and objects. In *Proc. of the ACM-SIGKDD Int. Conf. on Knowledge Discovery and Data Mining*, pages 140–149, 2000.
4. S. Ceri, P. Fraternali, A. Bongio, M. Brambilla, S. Comai, and M. Matera. *Designing Data-Intensive Web Applications*. Morgan-Kaufmann, 2002.
5. S. Chakrabarti. *Mining the Web Discovering Knowledge from Hypertext Data*. Morgan-Kaufmann, 2003.
6. R. Cooley, B. Mobasher, and J. Srivastava. Data preparation for mining world wide web browsing patterns. *Knowledge and Information Systems*, 1(1):5–32, 1999.
7. B. Mobasher et al. Discovery and Evaluation of Aggregate Usage Profiles for Web Personalization. *Data Mining and Knowledge Discovery*, 6(1):61–82, January 2002.
8. D. Pierrakos et al. Web usage mining as a tool for personalization: A survey. *User Modeling and User-Adapted Interaction*, 13(4):311 – 372, 2003.
9. J. Herlocker, J. Konstan, A. Borchers, and J. Riedl. An Algorithmic Framework for Performing Collaborative Filtering. In *Proc. of Conf. on Research and Development in Information Retrieval*, 1999.
10. Z. Huang. Extensions to the k-means algorithm for clustering large data sets with categorical values. *Data Mining and Knowledge Discovery*, 2(3):283–304, 1998.
11. H. Lieberman. Letizia: An Agent that Assists Web Browsing. In *Proc. of Int. Joint Conf. on Artificial Intelligence (IJCAI 95)*, pages 924–929, 1995.
12. U. Manber, A. Patel, and J. Robison. Experience with personalization on Yahoo! *Communications of the ACM*, 43(8):35–39, 2000.
13. G. Manco, R. Ortale, and D. Saccà. Similarity-based clustering of web transactions. In *Proc. of ACM Symposium on Applied Computing*, pages 1212–1216, 2003.
14. J. Vlachakis, M. Eirinaki, and S.S. Anand. IKUM: An Integrated Web Personalization Platform Based on Content Structures and User Behaviour. In *Proc. of the IJCAI-03 Workshop on Intelligent Techniques for Web Personalization*, 2003.

Extracting User Behavior by Web Communities Technology on Global Web Logs

Shingo Otsuka[1], Masashi Toyoda[1], Jun Hirai[2], and Masaru Kitsuregawa[1]

[1] Institute of Industrial Science, The University of Tokyo
4-6-1 Komaba, Meguro-ku, Tokyo 153-8505, Japan
{otsuka,toyoda,kitsure}@tkl.iis.u-tokyo.ac.jp
[2] Systems Integration Technology Center, Toshiba Solutions Corporation
3-22, Katamachi, Fuchu-Shi, Tokyo 183-8512, Japan
Hirai.Jun@toshiba-sol.co.jp

Abstract. A lot of work has been done on extracting the model of web user behavior. Most of them target server-side logs that cannot track user behavior outside of the server. Recently, a novel way has been developed to collect web browsing histories, using the same method for determining TV audience ratings; i.e., by collecting data from randomly selected users called panels. The logs collected from panels(called panel logs) cover an extremely broad URL-space, and it is difficult to capture the global behaviors of the users. Here we utilize mining results of web community to group those URLs into easily understandable topics. We also use search keywords in search engine sites because user behavior is deeply related to search keyword according to preliminary experiments on panel logs. We develop a prototype system to extract user access patterns from the panel logs and to capture the global behavior based on web communities.

1 Introduction

Web user behavior analysis is a very important research area, with a wide area of applications such as one-to-one marketing, and user behavior identification. Most research uses access logs on server-side(so called these server logs). On the other hand, a new kind of web business similar to the survey method on TV audience rating has emerged. It collects histories of URLs visited by users(called panels) who are randomly selected without statistical deviation. We call those URLs as *panel logs*.

The panel logs include *panel ID which is assigned to each panel, access time of web pages, reference second of web pages, URLs of accessed web page and so on*. Therefore we know that when or where did each panel access URLs. Moreover panel logs also include search keywords submitted to search engines. However, it is difficult to capture the user behavior based on URL-level analysis because panel logs cover an extremely broad URL-space.

Here we apply web community mining techniques[1] to give a better understanding of user global behavior. A web community is a collection of web pages

---

[1] In this paper, 'community' means 'web community'.

created by individuals or any kind of associations that have a common interest on a specific topic[1]. We use the results of web community mining to map an URL to an easy-to-understand topic. We also statistically analyze the importance of search keywords that appear in the panel sessions and their relation with the pages in the web communities. We propose a system to interactively support the analysis of global user behavior from panel logs and demonstrate the effectiveness of our proposed system.

The rest of the paper is organized as follows. Section 2 will review related work. In section 3 we will explain panel logs and web communities. Our system will be discussed in section 4. Section 5 will show example of using the system and discuss effectiveness of our system, while section 6 will give the conclusion.

2 Related Works

- Extracting user behavior
  This field is a hot topic because it is directly connected to e-commerce business. [2, 3] discussed how to extract user behavior patterns. A method to cluster users with the same behavior patterns is presented in [4]. As for users' grouping, it is discussed in [5].
  These research focus on user behavior on a certain web server because these logs are limited only to web pages in a web server.

- Extracting relevance of web communities
  Most of the works adopt web page link analysis. Recently, some approaches which use access logs have been proposed. [6] proposed web pages clustering using access logs and [7] proposed extracting relevance of web communities from users' access patterns. [8] discussed usability of using OLAP for web access logs analysis.

- Analysis of search keywords
  Search engine vendors are doing analysis of the search keywords. Clustering of search keywords using Lycos's server logs were presented in [9]. [10] showed the result of clustering of Encarta's server logs which is an online encyclopedia provided by Microsoft. The research to improve search precision was discussed in [11]. These works analyze user behavior related to search keywords.

- Visualization of access logs
  To easily understand the results of access logs analysis, [12] proposed a method to visualize access logs. [13] discussed visualization of user behavior at an online yellowpage site.

- Others
  [14] has some similarities with our study. This paper discusses clustering users and web pages, and its purpose is to extract correlation between clustered users and web pages. This research also uses proxy logs which are client side logs. These logs record all URLs which are viewed by users and

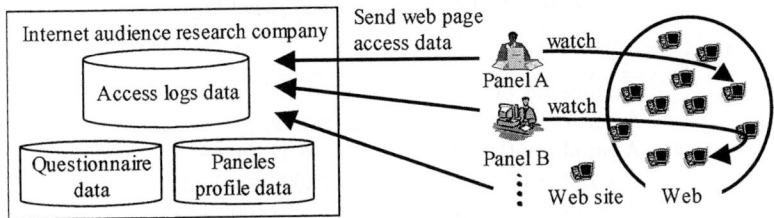

Fig. 1. Collection method of panel logs

are similar to panel logs because it is easy to identify users using their private IP. Recently, they provide the logs in the internet open to the public, but few researches have been done using these logs. Some other works focus on different aspects of web log mining, such as indexing method for large web access logs[15], and analyzing web access logs in mobile environment[16].

As mentioned above, most of the researches focus on the analysis of user behavior in a web site. [14] uses proxy logs which are similar to our study. However, its purpose is to cluster web pages only, while our purpose is extended further to help understanding of the user behavior.

3 Panel Logs and Web Communities

3.1 Panel Logs

In our experiments, we use panel logs built by Video Research Interactive, Inc. that is one of internet rating companies. Panels are randomly selected based on RDD(Random Digit Dialing), and are requested to install a software that automatically reports web access log to the server of Video Research Interactive. Details of the data is shown in Figure 1 and Table 1.

We do not use the questionnaire data and the panels profile data in Figure 1 due to privacy reasons. The panel logs consist of *panel ID, access time of web pages, reference second of web pages, URLs of accessed web page and so on*, and the data size is 10GB and all panels are in Japanese. Panel ID is a unique ID which is assigned to each panel, and it is specific to an individual panel. Notice that panel logs also include search keywords submitted to search engines.

Usually, analysis of access logs uses the concept of *session* which is a sequence of web accesses. A session is defined as a set of URLs visited by a panel during a web browsing activity. We employed a well-known 30 minutes threshold for the maximum interval[17], such that two continuous accesses within 30 minutes interval are regarded as in a same session.

3.2 Web Communities

We use the notion of web community to capture the global behavior of panels. A web community is a set of web pages created by individuals or any kind of

Table 1. The details of the panel logs

An amount of data	about 10(Giga byte)
A term of collecting data	45(weeks)
A number of access	55,415,473(access)
A number of session	1,148,093(session)
A number of panels	about 10,000(persons)
A kind of search keyword	334,232(variety)

associations that have a common interest on a specific topic. By examining how panels navigate through web communities, we can see more abstract behavior of panels than URL-level analysis, such as, what kinds of pages are visited by panels with the same interest.

In this paper, we define a web community as 'a set of relating web page which are combined by hyperlinks'[18]. Most researches on web communities can be loosely classified into two methods. One method is extracting dense subgraphs[19] and the other is extracting complete bipartite graphs[20]. The former method determines the borderline between inside and outside of the web community using the theorem of "Maximum Flow Minimum Cut" based on network theory. The latter method extracts complete bipartite graphs in the web snapshot as the hyperlinks between web pages which include common interest topics represented by complete bipartite graphs.

In our previous work, we created a web community chart[21] which based on the complete bipartite graphs, and extracted communities automatically from a large amount of web pages. We crawled 4.5 million web pages at February 2002 and automatically created 17 hundred thousand communities from one million selected pages. In this paper, we analyze panel logs using web communities extracted by our proposed technique. Moreover, though it is not very accurate, we automatically extract community labels which are word lists expressing the community contents, by analyzing anchor tags of the links to the pages belonging to the communities. Therefore, one can have a summary of communities without actually browsing them.

Since the time of the web page crawling for the web communities is in between the duration of panel logs collection, there are some web pages which are not covered by the crawling due to the change and deletion of pages which were accessed by the panels. Thus we define *matching factor* as follows to examine matching ratio between the URLs belonging to web-communities and the URLs included in panel logs.

$$matching\ factor = \frac{the\ matching\ number\ of\ URLs\ belong\ to\ communities\ and\ included\ in\ panel\ logs}{the\ number\ of\ URLs\ included\ in\ panel\ logs}$$

We measured the *matching factor* and the result was only about 19%. We enhanced the matching factor by softening the matching condition using follow processes.

Table 2. The matching factor between the URLs belonging to web-communities and the URLs included in panel logs

no modification	18.8%
matching when deleting directory(file) part	36.3%
matching when deleting site part	7.7%
no matching	37.2%

- Deleting directory or file part when the URLs included in panel logs do not match the URLs belonging to web-communities[2].
- Deleting site(domain) part when the URLs deleted directory part do not match[3].

The result is shown in Table 2. If we delete directory(file) part in URLs, the matching factor increases about 40% and when we delete 'subdomain part', the matching factor improves further about 8%. By modifying URLs, about 65% of the URLs included in panel logs are covered by the URLs in the web communities.

3.3 Other Results of Preliminary Experiments

According to preliminary experiments on panel logs, user behavior is deeply related to search engine sites and search keywords. We omit the details due to the space limitation. The analysis system also focuses on search keywords as well as the mapping with web communities.

The preliminary experiments also reveal that many panel logs include "Yahoo! shopping", "Yahoo! auctions" and "Rakuten [4] ". We can easily infer the contents of these sites without the labeling from web communities. So we define "Yahoo! shopping" and "Rakuten" as "Shopping sites", "Yahoo! auctions" and "Rakuten auctions" as "Auction sites" and "Search engine or portal sites" as "the search engine group".

4 Panel Logs Analysis System

Our proposed system does not only provide both analysis features based on the community mapping and search keywords, but also supports the synergy between them. Since the search keywords represent the user purposes of web browsing, we can infer the reason behind a user visit to a certain community from the

---

[2] When 'http://xxx.yyy.com/aaa/bbb/ccc.html' does not match, delete 'ccc.html' and check the remaining 'http://xxx.yyy.com/aaa/bbb/'. This process is repeated on the URL includes directory or file part.

[3] When 'http://xxx.yyy.com/' does not match, delete 'xxx' and check the remaining 'http://yyy.com/'. Note we do not check top/second domain name like '.com', 'co.jp' and so on.

[4] Rakuten is the most popular shopping site in Japan.

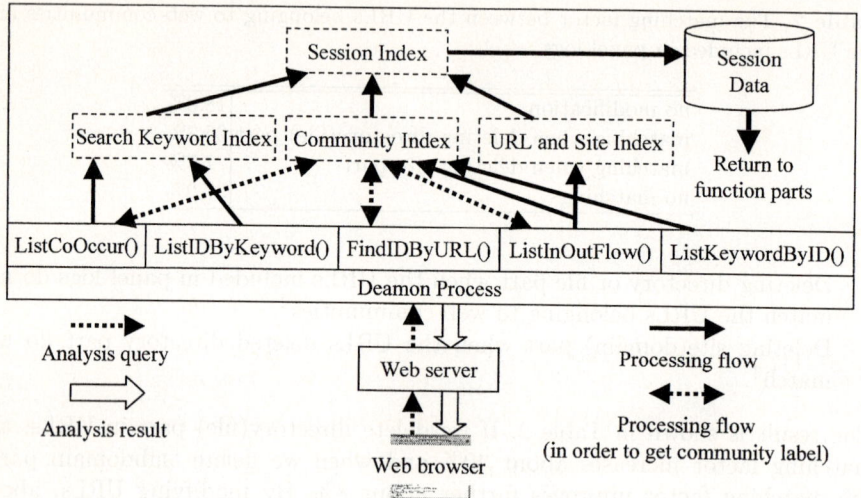

Fig. 2. Architecture of the system

relation between the search keywords and the web community. Even when the search keyword is absent, we can understand some details of the page visit from the relation between pages in the community. Since the results from conventional URL analysis is hard to digest, the relation between web communities will help us to figure out the global user behavior.

The web communities in our system are identified by serial numbers (called *community IDs*). The system has a function FindIDByURL() to find community ID by analyst specified URL, as well as following functions :

- *ListIDByKeyword()* : A function to show a list of web communities visited by users following some search keywords
  If we input some search keywords, we can see the list of communities which are visited using these keywords.

- *ListKeywordByID()* : A function to show lists of search keywords used for visiting the communities
  If any community ID specified, the list of search keywords used for visiting the communities are showed.

- *ListInOutFlow()* : A function to show inflow and outflow communities
  If any community ID, URL or site name specified then the lists of communities visited before and after the specified community are shown.

- *ListCoOccur()* : A function to show co-occurrence of communities
  If we input some search keywords and specify any community ID then the lists of communities in the sessions which include the specified search keywords and community ID.
  This function allows analysts to specify parameters such as co-occurrence number N_{CO} and it can find communities which were visited together with

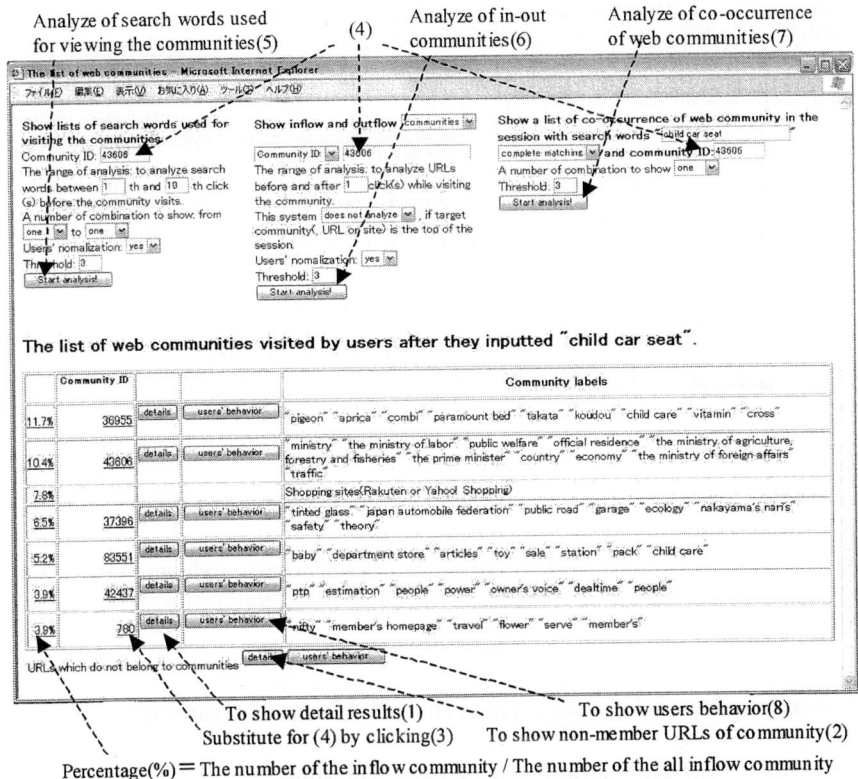

Fig. 3. A list of web communities visited by users following search keyword 'child car seat'

at least other N_{CO} communities in the sessions when users input specified keywords and visit specified community.

Our system also supports *continuous analysis*. We can start new analysis immediately using the current results whenever we find them interesting, Therefore, it is easy to analyze user behavior based on a new perspective of search keywords and visits to the communities.

The architecture of the system is shown in Figure 2. In our system, the panel logs are maintained in session units (labeled as session data) and stored in secondary device. We used a session index to access the session data. The system has indices for communities, search keywords, URLs and site names to find appropriate sessions. Each index holds session IDs, which can be used to access session data through session index. The community index also contains community labels. It is used to search community ID from an URL or to obtain a community label that corresponds to a community ID.

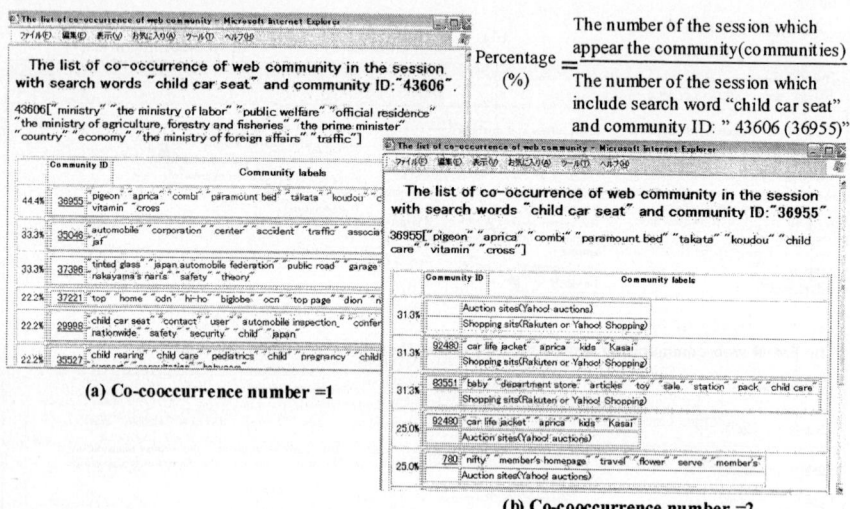

Fig. 4. Lists of co-occurrence of web communities following search keywords 'child car seat' and visiting community 'child car seat vendors' or 'administrative organs'

5 Example of Extracting Global User Behavior

Here we describe some examples of the results obtained by our system to show its effectiveness. In this paper, we used panel logs which are collected from Japanese people. Therefore, all results have been translated from Japanese vocabulary items. We can specify search keywords, community IDs, URLs or site names to begin the analysis. Further queries can be performed based on the previous results.

5.1 Examples of Analysis Results Using Our System

Figure 3 shows a list of web communities visited by users looking for 'child car seat'(by function *ListIDByKeyword()*). The results are sorted according to order of frequency. Using community labels, we infer that community ID of 36957 relates to child car seat vendors. Similarly, we also suppose that community ID of 43606 relates to administrative agencies. We can see a more detailed results on the community by pushing button (1) in Figure 3. As we mentioned in section 3.2, there are 35% of URLs which do not belong to any communities in panel logs. One can also see these URLs by pushing button (2) in Figure 3.

When an analyst is interested in the co-occurrence of web communities in a result, the analyst can analyze further from that point. Figure 4 shows a result of pushing button (7) in Figure 3. Figure 4(a) represents the co-occurrence of web communities in the sessions which include search keywords "child car seat" and administrative agencies' community(community ID is 43606). The

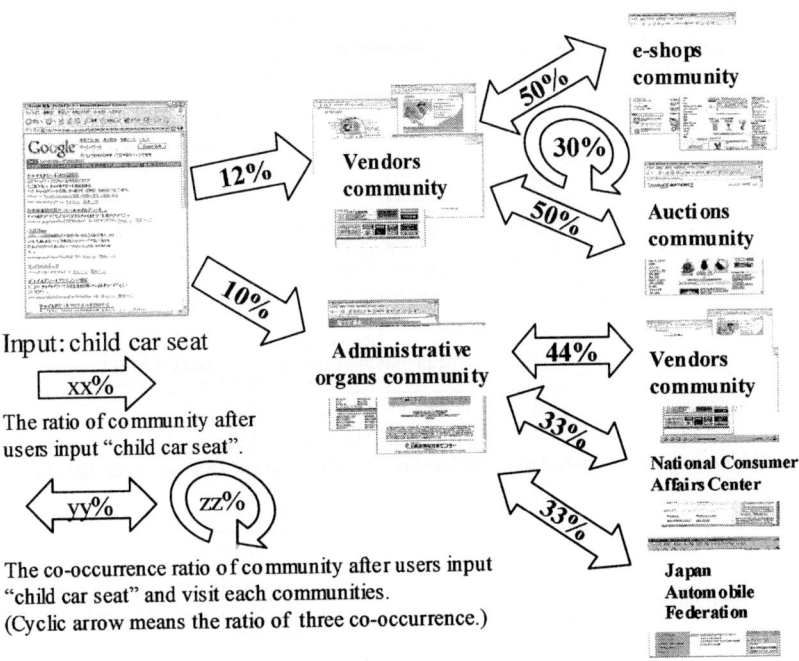

Fig. 5. The user behavior for search keyword 'child car seat'

result indicates that there is a high possibility that users of those sessions also visit child car seat vendors' community or automobile association's community. Further study to each community reveals that community ID "35046" includes only "National Consumer Affairs Center" and community ID "37396" includes only "Japan Automobile federation".

In Figure 4(b), we show the result when the co-occurrence number is two. The result indicates frequent patterns, which represent visits to three communities in the same session because the analyst has already specified community ID 36957(which relates to child car seat vendors). The result shows that those users have a great potential for visiting auction sites *or* shopping sites in the same session. Note that it is easy to understand that community ID "83551" relates to shopping sites and community ID "92480" relates to vendors by using the community labels.

Analysis with the proposed system can clearly depict the global user behavior. For example, the user behavior with search keywords *child car seat* can be classified into user access patterns as shown in Figure 5. Notice that a significant access pattern emerges because the child car seat is used only for a short period. After the child grows up, the child car seat is no longer needed. Thus many owners put the unused seats for sale on the auction sites. The access pattern shows that many users are trying to find secondhand goods at auction sites while simultaneously visiting the child car seat vendors and e-shops to compare the performance and the price. On the other hand, the aim of users which visit

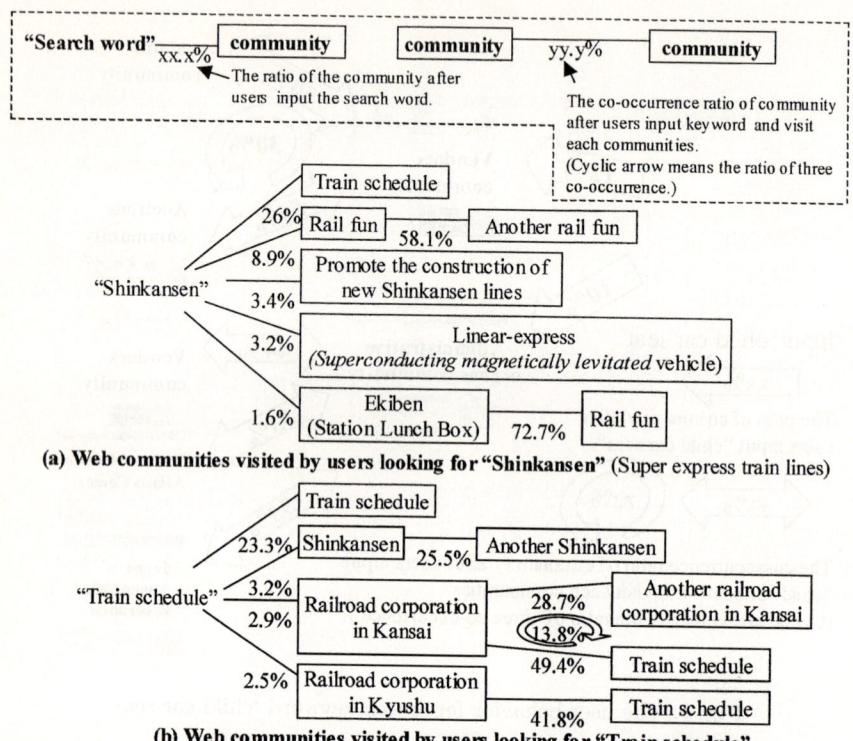

Fig. 6. The other examples of users' behavior

the community concerned with administrative organs is to acquire knowledge of the method of installation, safety standards and so on. These users also tend to visit the communities of child car seat vendors, non-profit organizations and other administrative organs. Most of the these users do not go to the auctions community.

5.2 Users' Behavior on Other Topics

We show users' behavior found using our system in Figure 6. Figure 6(a) indicates users' behavior accompanied search keywords "Shinkansen" (the high speed bullet train). We found interesting transitions between communities such as "Promote the construction of new Shinkansen lines", "Rail fun" and "Ekiben" as well as ordinary results like "Train schedule".

Figure 6(b) shows another example for search keywords "Train schedule". Most of the users visit "Train schedule communities" but we also found some behaviors related to certain regions as the results of co-occurrence community analysis.

6 Conclusion

It is difficult to grasp the user behavior from panel logs because these kind of logs cover an extremely broad URL-space. We proposed some methods to analyze panel logs using web community mapping and also showed the importance of search keywords from panel logs preliminary analysis.

We implemented the methods in a system to analyze user global behavior from panel logs. The system facilitates the mapping with web communities as well as the synergy with the search keyword analysis. We have confirmed the effectiveness of the system. The system can discover the reasons behind some web browsing patterns as well as the relation between them.

Acknowledgment

This research was partially supported by Grant-in-Aid for Scientific Research on Priority Areas(c)(No. 13224014) funded by the Japanese Ministry of Education, Culture, Sports, Science and Technology(MEXT). We also wish to thank Video Research Interactive, Inc. for providing the panel logs.

References

1. Kleinberg, J.: Authoritative sources in a hyperlinked environment. In Proceedings of the ACM-SIAM Symposium on Discrete Algorithms (1998)
2. Shahabi, C., Zarkesh, A., Adibi, J., Shah, V.: Knowledge discovery from users web-page navigation. In Proceedings of the IEEE RIDE97 Workshop (1997)
3. Batista, P., Silva, M.: Mining on-line newspaper web access logs. 12th International Meeting of the Euro Working Group on Decision Support Systems (EWGDSS 2001) (2001)
4. Fu, Y., Sandhu, K., Shih, M.: Clustering of web users based on access patterns. In Proceedings of the 1999 KDD Workshop on Web Mining (WEBKDD'99) (1999)
5. Ungar, L., Foster, D.: Clustering methods for collaborative filtering. AAAI Workshop on Recommendation Systems (1998)
6. Su, Z., Yang, Q., Zhang, H., Xu, X., Hu, Y.: Correlation-based document clustering using web logs. 34th Hawaii International Conference on System Sciences (HICSS-34) (2001)
7. Tan, P., Kumar, V.: Mining association patterns in web usage data. International Conference on Advances in Infrastructure for e-Business, e-Education, e-Science, and e-Medicine on the Internet (2002)
8. Zaiane, O., Xin, M., Han, J.: Discovering web access patterns and trends by applying olap and data mining technology on web logs. in Proc. Advances in Digital Libraries (ADL'98) (1998)
9. Beeferman, D., Berger, A.: Agglomerative clustering of s earch engine query log. The 6th ACM SIGKDD International Conference on Knowledge Discovery and Data Mining (KDD2000) (2000)
10. Wen, J., Nie, J., Zhang, H.: Query clustering using user logs. ACM Transactions on Information Systems (ACM TOIS) 20 (2002) 59-81

11. Ohura, Y., Takahashi, K., Pramudiono, I., Kitsuregawa, M.: Experiments on query expansion for internet yellow page services using web log mining. The 28th International Conference on Very Large Data Bases (VLDB2002) (2002)
12. Koutsoupias, N.: Exploring web access logs with correspondence analysis. Methods and Applications of Artificial Intelligence, Second Hellenic (2002)
13. Prasetyo, B., Pramudiono, I., Takahashi, K., Kitsuregawa, M.: Naviz: Website navigational behavior visualizer. Advances in Knowledge Discovery and Data Mining 6th Pacific-Asia Conference (PAKDD2002) (2002)
14. Zeng, H., Chen, Z., Ma, W.: A unified framework for clustering heterogeneous web objects. The Third International Conference on Web Information Systems Engineering (WISE2002) (2002)
15. Nanopoulos, A., Manolopoulos, Y., Zakrzewicz, M., Morzy, T.: Indexing web access-logs for pattern queries. 4th ACM CIKM Nternational Workshop on Web Information and Data Management (WIDM2002) (2002) 63-68
16. Pramudiono, I., Shintani, T., Takahashi, K., Kitsuregawa, M.: User behavior analysis of location aware search engine. Proceedings of International Conference On Mobile Data Management (MDM'02) (2002) 139-145 [17] Catledge, L., Pitkow, J.: Characterizing browsing behaviors on the world-wide web. Computer Networks and ISDN Systems (1995)
17. Catledge, L., Pitkow, J.: Characterizing browsing behaviors on the world-wide web. Computer Networks and ISDN Systems (1995)
18. Murata, T.: Web community. IPSJ Magazine 44 (2003) 702-706
19. Flake, G., Lawrence, S., Giles, C.L., Coetzee, F.: Self-organization and identification of web communities. IEEE Computer 35 (2002) 66-71
20. Kumar, R., Raghavan, P., Rajagopalan, S., Tomkins, A.: Trawling the web for emerging cyber-communities. Proc. of the 8th WWW conference (1999) 403-416
21. Toyoda, M., Kitsuregawa, M.: Creating a web community chart for navigating related communities. Conference Proceedings of Hypertext 2001 (2001) 103-112

Author Index

Abdolahzadeh Barforush, Ahmad..... 161
Abel, Mara 455
Al-Jadir, Lina 822
Al-Jumaily, Harith T. 652
Alonso, Miguel A. 371
Ameur, Yamine Ait 475
An, Aijun 528
An, Kyounghwan 191
Anutariya, Chutiporn 791
Apers, Peter M.G. 422
Aramburu, María José 318
Ashrafi, Mafruz Zaman 465

Becker, Ludger 854
Belian, Rosalie 171
Bell, David 222
Bellahsène, Zohra 296
Bellatreche, Ladjel 475
Bench-Capon, Trevor 508, 518
Berlanga, Rafael 243, 318
Besqueut, Jean-Yves 151
Bhashyam, Ramesh 730
Bhide, Manish 66
Bhowmick, Sourav S. 285, 580, 936
Bi, Yaxin 222
Blunck, Henrik 854
Bressan, Stephane 684, 694
Bruckner, Robert M. 486, 497
Burgués Illa, Xavier 741

Campbell, John A. 455
Carneiro, Adriana 171
Carvallo, Juan P. 109
Casanova, Marco Antonio 781
Cesario, Eugenio 947
Chan, Chee-Yong 801
Chatvichienchai, Somchai 791
Chen, Ting 801
Cheung, David W. 611
Chorley, Alison 508
Combarro, Elías F. 253
Combi, Carlo 559, 864
Costa, Thiago 171

Crolotte, Alain 730
Csáji, Balázs Csanád 130
Cuadra, Dolores 652
Cuzzocrea, Alfredo 359

Daassi, Chaouki 914
Danger, Roxana 243
De Ros, Luis Fernando 455
de Vries, Denise 663
Debenham, John 181
Devillers, Rodolphe 151
Dharma, T. S. 580
Diab, Khaled 822
Díaz, Irene 253
Ding, Zhiming 411
Dobmeier, Wolfgang 884
Du, Xiaoyong 381
Dubitzky, Werner 222
Dunne, Paul E. 518

Edelweiss, Nina 98
El-Moukaddem, Fatmé 822
Enokido, Tomoya 87, 675

Farré, Carles 77
Fauvet, Marie-Christine 914
Feng, Ling 422, 811
Fernández, Javier 253
Ferri, Fernando 925
Fife, Leslie D. 432
Fisher, Damien K. 569
Folino, Francesco 947
Franch, Xavier 109, 741
Frommholz, Ingo 539

Gao, Hong 339
Gao, Song 622
Garví, Eladio 644
Ghazal, Ahmad 730
Gibson, Simon 1
Greco, Gianluigi 13
Greco, Sergio 44
Grifoni, Patrizia 925

Gruenwald, Le 432
Guo, Gongde 222
Gupta, Ajay 66
Güting, Ralf Hartmut 411
Guzzo, Antonella 13

Haidarian Shahri, Hamid 161
Hammerschmidt, Beda Christoph 273
Han, Peng 141
Hasibuan, Zainal A. 694
Hawarah, Lamis 549
He, Yingjie 381
Helmer, Sven 591
Hidayanto, Achmad Nizar 694
Hinrichs, Klaus 854
Hirait, Jun 957
Ho, Wai Shing 611
Hondjack, Dehainsala 475
Hong, Bonghee 191, 834
Hong, Dong-Kweon 263
Horng, Jorng-Tzong 751
Huang, Hsien-Da 751
Huang, Shir-Ly 751

Imthiyaz, Mohammed Kasim 634
Iwiahara, Mizuho 791

Jonker, Willem 422
Joshi, Mukul 66

Kalnis, Panos 611, 634
Kambayashi, Yahiko 791
Kanne, Carl-Christian 591
Kempa, Martin 273
Kidawara, Yutaka 874, 894
Kim, Kweon-Yang 263
Kim, Myung 349
Kitsuregawa, Masaru 601, 957
Kovalev, Vladimir 936
Kulkarni, Sachin 1
Küng, Josef 130

L'Abbate, Marcello 539
Lagrue, Sylvain 151
Lam, Franky 569
Lemos, Melissa 781
Leonardi, Erwin 580

Li, Jianzhong 339
Li, Yue 201
Liau, Chu Yee 694
Lifu, Yi 601
Lim, Yoonsun 349
Lima Silva, Luís A. 455
Ling, Tok Wang 486, 497, 801
Linnemann, Volker 273
Liu, Chengfei 34
Liu, Han 486, 497
Lo, Eric 611
Lowden, Barry G. T. 391
Luoma, Olli 401

Ma, Liping 232
Macedo, José Antonio Fernandes de 781
Madria, Sanjay 285, 580, 936
Mamoulis, Nikos 611
Martínez, Paloma 652
Mastella, Laura S. 455
Matrangolo, Ugo 359
Milosevic, Zoran 1
Min, Young Soo 212
Minout, Mohammed 904
Miranda, Antonio Basílio de 781
Moerkotte, Guido 591
Mohania, Mukesh 66
Mondal, Anirban 601
Montañés, Elena 253
Mues, Christophe 445
Muschall, Björn 884

Neuhold, Erich 539
Ng, Wee Siong 622
Nguyen Xuan, Dung 475
Nigay, Laurence 914

Oliboni, Barbara 559
Ortale, Riccardo 947
Otoo, Ekow J. 707
Otsuka, Shingo 957

Palkoska, Jürgen 130
Park, Sung Hee 761, 771
Passos, Rômulo 171
Pérez, Juan Manuel 318
Pernul, Günther 884

Pierra, Guy 475
Plaice, John 56
Pontieri, Luigi 13
Pradhan, Sujeet 328
Prakash, Sandeep 285
Priebe, Torsten 884

Qian, Weining 622
Quer, Carme 109
Quintarelli, Elisa 559

Rafanelli, Maurizio 925
Ranilla, José 253
Ray, Indrakshi 24
Ribadas, Francisco J. 306
Rice, Sally 663
Roantree, Mark 296
Robinson, Jerome 391
Roddick, John F. 663
Rodríguez, Nuria 109
Rossato, Rosalba 864
Rotem, Doron 707
Ruíz-Shulcloper, José 243
Ryu, Keun Ho 761, 771

Saccà, Domenico 13
Salgado, Ana Carolina 171
Samos, José 644
Schneider, Markus 844
Seibel, Luiz Fernando Bessa 781
Seo, Youngduk 834
Seshadri, Sridhar 707
Shen, Ruimin 141
Shen, Tao 811
Shen, Yun 811
Shepherd, John 232
Shim, Jeong Min 212
Shoshani, Arie 120
Shu, Yanfeng 381
Shui, William M. 569
Simonet, Ana 549
Simonet, Michel 549
Sirangelo, Cristina 44
Smith, Kate 465
Song, Seok Il 212
Stockinger, Kurt 120
Sugiyama, Yousuke 675

Sun, Yi-Ming 751
Swoboda, Paul 56

Tagg, Roger 1
Takizawa, Makoto 87, 675
Tanaka, Katsumi 328, 874, 894
Taniar, David 465
Tedesco, Patrícia 171
Teniente, Ernest 77
Thiel, Ulrich 539
Thomasian, Alexander 201
Tjoa, A Min 497
Torres, Manuel 644
Toyoda, Masashi 957
Trubitsyna, Irina 44
Tsou, Ann-Ping 751

Uchiyama, Tomoyuki 874
Urpí, Toni 77

Vahrenhold, Jan 854
Vanthienen, Jan 445
Vilares, Jesús 306, 371
Vilares, Manuel 306, 371
Vossough, Ehsan 720

Wagner, Roland 130
Wang, Bing 811
Wang, Hui 222
Wang, Shan 381
Wong, Raymond K. 569
Wu, Kesheng 120
Wuwongse, Vilas 791

Xiaoan, Dong 634
Xie, Bo 141
Xin, Tai 24

Yang, Chang Yong 212
Yang, Fan 141
Yang, Yun 34
Yao, Qingsong 528
Yoo, Jae Soo 212
Yuzhi, Guo 684

Zettsu, Koji 874, 894
Zhang, Ji 486, 497

Zhang, Lijuan 201
Zhao, Xiaohui 34
Zhu, Yajie 24

Zimányi, Esteban............................. 904
Zschornack, Fábio 98
Zumpano, Ester 44

Lecture Notes in Computer Science

For information about Vols. 1–3083

please contact your bookseller or Springer

Vol. 3220: J.C. Lester, R.M. Vicari, F. Paraguá\c cu (Eds.), Intelligent Tutoring Systems. XXI, 920 pages. 2004.

Vol. 3208: H.J. Ohlbach, S. Schaffert (Eds.), Principles and Practice of Semantic Web Reasoning. VII, 165 pages. 2004.

Vol. 3207: L.T. Jang, M. Guo, G.R. Gao, N.K. Jha, Embedded and Ubiquitous Computing. XX, 1116 pages. 2004.

Vol. 3205: N. Davies, E. Mynatt, I. Siio (Eds.), UbiComp 2004: Ubiquitous Computing. XVI, 452 pages. 2004.

Vol. 3198: G.-J. de Vreede, L.A. Guerrero, G. Marín Raventós (Eds.), Groupware: Design, Implementation and Use. XI, 378 pages. 2004.

Vol. 3194: R. Camacho, R. King, A. Srinivasan (Eds.), Inductive Logic Programming. XI, 361 pages. 2004. (Subseries LNAI).

Vol. 3186: Z. Bellahsène, T. Milo, M. Rys, D. Suciu, R. Unland (Eds.), Database and XML Technologies. X, 235 pages. 2004.

Vol. 3184: S. Katsikas, J. Lopez, G. Pernul (Eds.), Trust and Privacy in Digital Business. XI, 299 pages. 2004.

Vol. 3183: R. Traunmüller (Ed.), Electronic Government. XIX, 583 pages. 2004.

Vol. 3182: K. Bauknecht, M. Bichler, B. Pröll (Eds.), E-Commerce and Web Technologies. XI, 370 pages. 2004.

Vol. 3180: F. Galindo, M. Takizawa, R. Traunmüller (Eds.), Database and Expert Systems Applications. XXI, 972 pages. 2004.

Vol. 3178: W. Jonker, M. Petkovic (Eds.), Secure Data Management. VIII, 219 pages. 2004.

Vol. 3177: Z.R. Yang, H. Yin, R. Everson (Eds.), Intelligent Data Engineering and Automated Learning – IDEAL 2004. XVIII, 852 pages. 2004.

Vol. 3175: C.E. Rasmussen, H.H. Bülthoff, B. Schölkopf, M.A. Giese (Eds.), Pattern Recognition. XVIII, 581 pages. 2004.

Vol. 3174: F. Yin, J. Wang, C. Guo (Eds.), Advances in Neural Networks - ISNN 2004. XXXV, 1021 pages. 2004.

Vol. 3172: M. Dorigo, M. Birattari, C. Blum, L. M.Gambardella, F. Mondada, T. Stützle (Eds.), Ant Colony, Optimization and Swarm Intelligence. XII, 434 pages. 2004.

Vol. 3170: P. Gardner, N. Yoshida (Eds.), CONCUR 2004 - Concurrency Theory. XIII, 529 pages. 2004.

Vol. 3166: M. Rauterberg (Ed.), Entertainment Computing – ICEC 2004. XXIII, 617 pages. 2004.

Vol. 3158: I. Nikolaidis, M. Barbeau, E. Kranakis (Eds.), Ad-Hoc, Mobile, and Wireless Networks. IX, 344 pages. 2004.

Vol. 3157: C. Zhang, H. W. Guesgen, W.K. Yeap (Eds.), PRICAI 2004: Trends in Artificial Intelligence. XX, 1023 pages. 2004. (Subseries LNAI).

Vol. 3156: M. Joye, J.-J. Quisquater (Eds.), Cryptographic Hardware and Embedded Systems - CHES 2004. XIII, 455 pages. 2004.

Vol. 3155: P. Funk, P.A. González Calero (Eds.), Advances in Case-Based Reasoning. XIII, 822 pages. 2004. (Subseries LNAI).

Vol. 3154: R.L. Nord (Ed.), Software Product Lines. XIV, 334 pages. 2004.

Vol. 3153: J. Fiala, V. Koubek, J. Kratochvíl (Eds.), Mathematical Foundations of Computer Science 2004. XIV, 902 pages. 2004.

Vol. 3152: M. Franklin (Ed.), Advances in Cryptology – CRYPTO 2004. XI, 579 pages. 2004.

Vol. 3150: G.-Z. Yang, T. Jiang (Eds.), Medical Imaging and Augmented Reality. XII, 378 pages. 2004.

Vol. 3149: M. Danelutto, M. Vanneschi, D. Laforenza (Eds.), Euro-Par 2004 Parallel Processing. XXXIV, 1081 pages. 2004.

Vol. 3148: R. Giacobazzi (Ed.), Static Analysis. XI, 393 pages. 2004.

Vol. 3146: P. Érdi, A. Esposito, M. Marinaro, S. Scarpetta (Eds.), Computational Neuroscience: Cortical Dynamics. XI, 161 pages. 2004.

Vol. 3144: M. Papatriantafilou, P. Hunel (Eds.), Principles of Distributed Systems. XI, 246 pages. 2004.

Vol. 3143: W. Liu, Y. Shi, Q. Li (Eds.), Advances in Web-Based Learning – ICWL 2004. XIV, 459 pages. 2004.

Vol. 3142: J. Diaz, J. Karhumäki, A. Lepistö, D. Sannella (Eds.), Automata, Languages and Programming. XIX, 1253 pages. 2004.

Vol. 3140: N. Koch, P. Fraternali, M. Wirsing (Eds.), Web Engineering. XXI, 623 pages. 2004.

Vol. 3139: F. Iida, R. Pfeifer, L. Steels, Y. Kuniyoshi (Eds.), Embodied Artificial Intelligence. IX, 331 pages. 2004. (Subseries LNAI).

Vol. 3138: A. Fred, T. Caelli, R.P.W. Duin, A. Campilho, D.d. Ridder (Eds.), Structural, Syntactic, and Statistical Pattern Recognition. XXII, 1168 pages. 2004.

Vol. 3137: P. De Bra, W. Nejdl (Eds.), Adaptive Hypermedia and Adaptive Web-Based Systems. XIV, 442 pages. 2004.

Vol. 3136: F. Meziane, E. Métais (Eds.), Natural Language Processing and Information Systems. XII, 436 pages. 2004.

Vol. 3134: C. Zannier, H. Erdogmus, L. Lindstrom (Eds.), Extreme Programming and Agile Methods - XP/Agile Universe 2004. XIV, 233 pages. 2004.

Vol. 3133: A.D. Pimentel, S. Vassiliadis (Eds.), Computer Systems: Architectures, Modeling, and Simulation. XIII, 562 pages. 2004.

Vol. 3132: B. Demoen, V. Lifschitz (Eds.), Logic Programming. XII, 480 pages. 2004.

Vol. 3131: V. Torra, Y. Narukawa (Eds.), Modeling Decisions for Artificial Intelligence. XI, 327 pages. 2004. (Subseries LNAI).

Vol. 3130: A. Syropoulos, K. Berry, Y. Haralambous, B. Hughes, S. Peter, J. Plaice (Eds.), TeX, XML, and Digital Typography. VIII, 265 pages. 2004.

Vol. 3129: Q. Li, G. Wang, L. Feng (Eds.), Advances in Web-Age Information Management. XVII, 753 pages. 2004.

Vol. 3128: D. Asonov (Ed.), Querying Databases Privately. IX, 115 pages. 2004.

Vol. 3127: K.E. Wolff, H.D. Pfeiffer, H.S. Delugach (Eds.), Conceptual Structures at Work. XI, 403 pages. 2004. (Subseries LNAI).

Vol. 3126: P. Dini, P. Lorenz, J.N.d. Souza (Eds.), Service Assurance with Partial and Intermittent Resources. XI, 312 pages. 2004.

Vol. 3125: D. Kozen (Ed.), Mathematics of Program Construction. X, 401 pages. 2004.

Vol. 3124: J.N. de Souza, P. Dini, P. Lorenz (Eds.), Telecommunications and Networking - ICT 2004. XXVI, 1390 pages. 2004.

Vol. 3123: A. Belz, R. Evans, P. Piwek (Eds.), Natural Language Generation. X, 219 pages. 2004. (Subseries LNAI).

Vol. 3122: K. Jansen, S. Khanna, J.D.P. Rolim, D. Ron (Eds.), Approximation, Randomization, and Combinatorial Optimization. IX, 428 pages. 2004.

Vol. 3121: S. Nikoletseas, J.D.P. Rolim (Eds.), Algorithmic Aspects of Wireless Sensor Networks. X, 201 pages. 2004.

Vol. 3120: J. Shawe-Taylor, Y. Singer (Eds.), Learning Theory. X, 648 pages. 2004. (Subseries LNAI).

Vol. 3118: K. Miesenberger, J. Klaus, W. Zagler, D. Burger (Eds.), Computer Helping People with Special Needs. XXIII, 1191 pages. 2004.

Vol. 3116: C. Rattray, S. Maharaj, C. Shankland (Eds.), Algebraic Methodology and Software Technology. XI, 569 pages. 2004.

Vol. 3114: R. Alur, D.A. Peled (Eds.), Computer Aided Verification. XII, 536 pages. 2004.

Vol. 3113: J. Karhumäki, H. Maurer, G. Paun, G. Rozenberg (Eds.), Theory Is Forever. X, 283 pages. 2004.

Vol. 3112: H. Williams, L. MacKinnon (Eds.), Key Technologies for Data Management. XII, 265 pages. 2004.

Vol. 3111: T. Hagerup, J. Katajainen (Eds.), Algorithm Theory - SWAT 2004. XI, 506 pages. 2004.

Vol. 3110: A. Juels (Ed.), Financial Cryptography. XI, 281 pages. 2004.

Vol. 3109: S.C. Sahinalp, S. Muthukrishnan, U. Dogrusoz (Eds.), Combinatorial Pattern Matching. XII, 486 pages. 2004.

Vol. 3108: H. Wang, J. Pieprzyk, V. Varadharajan (Eds.), Information Security and Privacy. XII, 494 pages. 2004.

Vol. 3107: J. Bosch, C. Krueger (Eds.), Software Reuse: Methods, Techniques and Tools. XI, 339 pages. 2004.

Vol. 3106: K.-Y. Chwa, J.I. Munro (Eds.), Computing and Combinatorics. XIII, 474 pages. 2004.

Vol. 3105: S. Göbel, U. Spierling, A. Hoffmann, I. Iurgel, O. Schneider, J. Dechau, A. Feix (Eds.), Technologies for Interactive Digital Storytelling and Entertainment. XVI, 304 pages. 2004.

Vol. 3104: R. Kralovic, O. Sykora (Eds.), Structural Information and Communication Complexity. X, 303 pages. 2004.

Vol. 3103: K. Deb, e. al. (Eds.), Genetic and Evolutionary Computation – GECCO 2004. XLIX, 1439 pages. 2004.

Vol. 3102: K. Deb, e. al. (Eds.), Genetic and Evolutionary Computation – GECCO 2004. L, 1445 pages. 2004.

Vol. 3101: M. Masoodian, S. Jones, B. Rogers (Eds.), Computer Human Interaction. XIV, 694 pages. 2004.

Vol. 3100: J.F. Peters, A. Skowron, J.W. Grzymała-Busse, B. Kostek, R.W. Świniarski, M.S. Szczuka (Eds.), Transactions on Rough Sets I. X, 405 pages. 2004.

Vol. 3099: J. Cortadella, W. Reisig (Eds.), Applications and Theory of Petri Nets 2004. XI, 505 pages. 2004.

Vol. 3098: J. Desel, W. Reisig, G. Rozenberg (Eds.), Lectures on Concurrency and Petri Nets. VIII, 849 pages. 2004.

Vol. 3097: D. Basin, M. Rusinowitch (Eds.), Automated Reasoning. XII, 493 pages. 2004. (Subseries LNAI).

Vol. 3096: G. Melnik, H. Holz (Eds.), Advances in Learning Software Organizations. X, 173 pages. 2004.

Vol. 3095: C. Bussler, D. Fensel, M.E. Orlowska, J. Yang (Eds.), Web Services, E-Business, and the Semantic Web. X, 147 pages. 2004.

Vol. 3094: A. Nürnberger, M. Detyniecki (Eds.), Adaptive Multimedia Retrieval. VIII, 229 pages. 2004.

Vol. 3093: S. Katsikas, S. Gritzalis, J. Lopez (Eds.), Public Key Infrastructure. XIII, 380 pages. 2004.

Vol. 3092: J. Eckstein, H. Baumeister (Eds.), Extreme Programming and Agile Processes in Software Engineering. XVI, 358 pages. 2004.

Vol. 3091: V. van Oostrom (Ed.), Rewriting Techniques and Applications. X, 313 pages. 2004.

Vol. 3089: M. Jakobsson, M. Yung, J. Zhou (Eds.), Applied Cryptography and Network Security. XIV, 510 pages. 2004.

Vol. 3087: D. Maltoni, A.K. Jain (Eds.), Biometric Authentication. XIII, 343 pages. 2004.

Vol. 3086: M. Odersky (Ed.), ECOOP 2004 – Object-Oriented Programming. XIII, 611 pages. 2004.

Vol. 3085: S. Berardi, M. Coppo, F. Damiani (Eds.), Types for Proofs and Programs. X, 409 pages. 2004.

Vol. 3084: A. Persson, J. Stirna (Eds.), Advanced Information Systems Engineering. XIV, 596 pages. 2004.